DATE DUE

JAN 24 2002	

GAYLORD PRINTED IN U.S.A.

Estimation and Inference in Econometrics

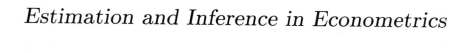

Estimation and Inference in Econometrics

RUSSELL DAVIDSON
JAMES G. MACKINNON

New York Oxford
OXFORD UNIVERSITY PRESS
1993

Oxford University Press

Oxford New York Toronto
Delhi Bombay Calcutta Madras Karachi
Kuala Lumpur Singapore Hong Kong Tokyo
Nairobi Dar es Salaam Cape Town
Melbourne Auckland Madrid

and associated companies in
Berlin Ibadan

Published by Oxford University Press, Inc.,
200 Madison Avenue, New York, New York 10016

Library of Congress Cataloging-in-Publication Data
Davidson, Russell.
Estimation and inference in econometrics /
by Russell Davidson and James G. MacKinnon.
p. cm.
Includes bibliographical references and index.
ISBN 0-19-506011-3
1. Econometrics. I. MacKinnon, James G.
II. Title. HB139.D368 1993
330′.01′5195—dc20 92-12048

4 6 8 9 7 5

Printed in the United States of America
on acid-free paper

To our students

Preface

When we began writing this book, longer ago than we care to admit, our goal was to write a text that could be used for the second and third semesters of a typical graduate sequence in econometrics. We perceived a lack of any textbook that addressed the needs of students trying to acquire a solid understanding of what we think of as the "modern" approach to econometrics. By this we mean an approach that goes beyond the well-known linear regression model, stresses the essential similarities of all the leading estimation methods, and puts as much emphasis on testing and model specification as on estimation.

We soon realized that this plan had a fatal flaw. In order to write a book for the *second* course in econometrics, one must be confident of what will have been covered in the *first* course. Since there was not then, and is not now, a widely accepted standard syllabus for the first course in econometrics, we decided that we would have to start there. We therefore changed our plan, and this book now attempts to develop econometric theory from the ground up. Readers are of course expected to have some acquaintance with elementary econometrics before starting, but no more than would be part of a typical undergraduate curriculum. They are also expected to have the mathematical maturity appropriate to graduate students in economics, although we do provide two appendices that cover the mathematical and statistical prerequisites for understanding the material.

Almost all of the econometric theory we present is *asymptotic*, which means that it is exactly true only in the limit as the sample size tends to infinity, but is thought (or rather hoped) to be approximately true in finite samples. In recent years, researchers have found it increasingly necessary to go beyond the confines of the standard linear regression model, in which restrictive classical assumptions lead to exact results about the distributions of the ordinary least squares estimator and of the familiar t and F statistics. Greater generality in model specification, however, carries the price that exact finite-sample results are very rarely available. Happily, asymptotic econometric theory is now at a mature stage of development, and it provides the main theoretical foundation for the present book.

Our first chapter does not really discuss econometrics at all. Instead, it presents those aspects of the geometry of least squares that are needed in the rest of the book. A key result in this context is the theorem that we have dubbed the Frisch-Waugh-Lovell Theorem. We have found that getting students to understand this theorem, although often a rather challenging task, does a great deal to develop intuition about estimation and testing in econometrics. A particular application of the theorem, which we present in

Chapter 1, is to the question of leverage and influence in regression models. Existing treatments of this important topic have typically been algebraically difficult and unintuitive. Use of the FWL Theorem makes it possible to develop a much simpler treatment. Chapter 1 also briefly discusses the computation of ordinary least squares estimates, a subject about which too many students of econometrics are completely ignorant.

One of our aims in this book is to emphasize nonlinear estimation. In Chapters 2 and 3, we therefore plunge directly into a treatment of the nonlinear regression model. It turns out that it is scarcely any more difficult to develop the essential notions of least-squares estimation, and of statistical inference based on such estimation, in a nonlinear context than it is in the more usual linear one. In fact, the *essential* notions are often easier to come to grips with if one is not distracted by the great wealth of detailed but special results that enrich the linear theory.

After the largely intuitive treatment of Chapters 2 and 3, we provide in Chapters 4 and 5 a fuller and more rigorous account of the asymptotic theory that underlies the nonlinear regression model. Just how far to go in the quest for rigor has been a thorny problem at many points. Much of the recent literature in theoretical econometrics appears to be inaccessible to many students, in large part, we believe, because rigor has taken precedence over the communication of fundamental ideas. We have therefore deliberately not aimed at the same standards of rigor. On the other hand, some rigor is needed in any account that is not merely anecdotal. It is in Chapters 4 and 5, and later in Chapter 8, which lays the foundations of the theory of maximum likelihood, that we have gone as far as we felt we could in the direction of a formal rigorous treatment. At times we even adopt a "theorem-proof" format, something that we have generally avoided in the book. Many instructors will prefer to skim these chapters, especially in a first course, although we hope that most will choose not to omit them entirely.

Although we stress nonlinear models throughout the book, we also emphasize another point that has emerged in the last fifteen years and that has been a central focus of much of our own research over that period. In order to perform statistical inference on the results of a nonlinear estimation procedure, it is almost always possible to make use of artificial *linear* regressions for the purposes of computing test statistics. Chapter 6 is the first chapter in which we discuss an artificial linear regression, and it is a key chapter for understanding much subsequent material. We show how the so-called Gauss-Newton regression can be used for a variety of purposes, most notably the calculation of Lagrange multiplier tests and related test statistics, the computation of nonlinear least squares estimates, and the computation of one-step efficient estimates. The use of artificial regressions for doing diagnostic tests of model specification is emphasized. Other artificial regressions are introduced later in the book for use in contexts more general than that of nonlinear regression models, but the intuition is always the same.

Our treatment of the linear simultaneous equations model begins in Chapter 7, where we discuss single-equation instrumental variables estimation. In line with our emphasis on nonlinear models, we do not stick with linear instrumental variables models only, but also treat the estimation of nonlinear models by instrumental variables and show how the Gauss-Newton regression generalizes to such models. We also introduce the important idea of tests of overidentifying restrictions. However, we do not attempt a full treatment of the linear simultaneous equations model at this point. We have deliberately left this topic, often thought of as the centerpiece of econometric theory, until very late in the book. It is our feeling that modern theory and practice are drifting away from the linear simultaneous equations model, in favor of a more flexible approach in which instrumental variables continue to play a large role but in a much more general context.

The presentation of standard maximum likelihood theory in Chapter 8 relies as much as possible on insights developed earlier for the nonlinear regression model. The basic concepts of consistency and asymptotic normality are already available and can therefore be dealt with quite swiftly. New concepts arise in connection with the information matrix equality and the Cramér-Rao lower bound. In Chapter 9, maximum likelihood methods find their first major application as we develop the methods of generalized least squares. These methods lead naturally to a discussion of multivariate, but not simultaneous, models. We also devote a section of this chapter to problems particular to the analysis of panel data.

Chapter 10 deals with a topic of great concern to all econometricians who work with time series: serial correlation. Few topics in econometrics have been the subject of so vast a literature, much of which is now somewhat outdated. Although we make no attempt to give a complete account of this literature, this chapter is nevertheless one of the longest. It provides a first treatment of time-series methods, since it is here that we describe autoregressive and moving average processes. Methods of testing for the presence of these processes in the error terms of regression equations, and performing estimation in their presence, are discussed. Again, we highlight the possibility of using artificial linear regressions for these purposes. One section is devoted to the important, and in many texts surprisingly neglected, subject of common factor restrictions.

Hypothesis testing and diagnostic testing, always a primary concern, take center stage again in Chapter 11, which discusses tests based on the Gauss-Newton regression. Nonnested hypothesis testing is discussed here, and the principle of Durbin-Wu-Hausman tests, introduced earlier in Chapter 7, is taken up more fully. In addition, a heteroskedasticity-robust version of the Gauss-Newton regression is developed, providing a first look at issues that will be taken up in much more detail in Chapters 16 and 17.

Chapter 12 contains material not found in any other textbook treatment, to our knowledge. Here, in the simple context of the regression model, we discuss the determinants of test power. We show how tests often have power to reject false hypotheses or ill-specified models even when the alternative hypothesis underlying the test is also wrongly specified. The unifying concept is that of a drifting DGP, a generalization of the Pitman drift of standard statistical analysis. This concept makes it possible to develop an asymptotic theory of test power, based on asymptotic noncentrality parameters. The asymptotic power of a test is shown to depend on just two things: its noncentrality parameter and its number of degrees of freedom. We also devote a section to the inverse power function, which has recently been proposed as a useful and powerful tool for the interpretation of test results. We suspect that some instructors will choose to skip this chapter, but we feel strongly that any student who aims to be a specialist in econometrics should be familiar with this material.

In Chapter 13, we turn again to maximum likelihood estimation and develop, rather formally, the theory of the classical hypothesis tests, relying for intuition on some of the material of the preceding two chapters. We treat not only the well-known trio of the likelihood ratio, Lagrange multiplier, and Wald tests, but also the $C(\alpha)$ test of Neyman, which is now emerging from some decades of neglect. The latter test turns out to be particularly easy to implement by means of artificial regressions. It is in this chapter that the well-known OPG regression is introduced.

From Chapter 14 until the end of the book, most chapters constitute relatively self-contained units. In these chapters, we try to discuss many of the topics of importance in modern econometrics. It is here that some readers may well feel that we have been hopelessly misguided in our selection and have left out the one thing that all econometricians must know. In a field as rapidly growing as econometrics is at the moment, they may well be right. We have been guided largely by our own interests and tastes, which are inevitably fallible. Two topics that we could well have discussed if space had permitted are nonparametric and semiparametric techniques and Bayesian methods. We apologize to specialists in these fields, offering only the lame excuse that we are not ourselves specialists in them, and would no doubt have failed to do them justice.

Chapters 14 and 15 deal respectively with models involving transformations of the dependent variable and models involving qualitative and limited dependent variables. Both chapters rely heavily on the theory of estimation and testing for models estimated by maximum likelihood. Courses with an applied orientation might want to emphasize these chapters, and theoretical courses might omit them entirely in favor of more advanced topics.

Chapter 16 deals with a variety of topics, including heteroskedasticity, skewness and kurtosis, conditional moment tests, and information matrix tests. Many relatively recent developments are discussed in this chapter, which leads naturally to Chapter 17, on the generalized method of moments, or GMM. This important estimation technique has not, to our knowledge, been discussed in any detail in previous textbooks. Our treatment depends heavily on earlier results for instrumental variables and generalized least squares. It contains both general results for models estimated by means of any set of moment conditions, and specific results for linear regression models. For the latter, we present estimators that are more efficient than ordinary and two-stage least squares in the presence of heteroskedasticity of unknown form.

A full treatment of the linear simultaneous equations model does not occur until Chapter 18. One advantage of leaving it until late in the book is that previous results on instrumental variables, maximum likelihood, and the generalized method of moments are then available. Thus, in Chapter 18, we are able to provide reasonably advanced discussions of LIML, FIML, and 3SLS estimation as applications of general techniques that students have already learned. The GMM framework also allows us to introduce a variant of 3SLS that is efficient in the presence of heteroskedasticity of unknown form.

Chapters 19 and 20 complete our discussion of time-series issues. The first deals with a number of topics that are important for applied work, including spurious regressions, dynamic models, and seasonality. The second deals with two related topics of substantial current interest that have not to our knowledge been treated in previous textbooks, namely, unit roots and cointegration. These chapters could be covered immediately after Chapter 10 in a course oriented toward applications, although they do make use of results from some intervening chapters.

Finally, Chapter 21 provides a reasonably detailed introduction to Monte Carlo methods in econometrics. These methods are already widely used, and we believe that their use will increase greatly over the next few years as computers become cheaper and more powerful.

One possible way in which this book can be used is to start at the beginning and continue until the end. If three semesters are available, such an approach is not only possible but desirable. If less time is available, however, there are many possible options. One alternative would be to go only as far as Chapter 13 and then, if time remains, select a few chapters or topics from the remainder of the book. Depending on the focus of the course, it is also possible to skip some earlier chapters, such as Chapters 10 and 12, along with parts of Chapters 9, 11, and 13.

In some courses, it may be preferable to skip much of the theoretical material entirely and concentrate on the techniques for estimation and inference, without the underlying theory. In that event, we would recommend that Chapters 4, 5, and 8 be covered lightly, and that Chapter 13 be skipped entirely. For Chapter 4, the notions of consistency and asymptotic normality would need to be treated at some level, but it is possible to be content with simple definitions. A good deal of conceptual material without much mathematical formalism can be found in Section 4.4, in which the key idea of a data-generating process is defined and discussed. For Chapter 5, the results on the consistency and asymptotic normality of the nonlinear least squares estimator should be stated and discussed but need not be proved. The Gauss-Markov Theorem could also be discussed. In Chapter 8, the first two sections contain the material necessary for later chapters and are not at all formal in content. The next six sections could then be skipped. Section 8.9, on testing, could serve as a simpler replacement for the whole of Chapter 13. Finally, Section 8.10 forges the link between maximum likelihood theory and the previously covered material on the nonlinear regression model.

One of us teaches in France, where for several years he has used material from this book as the basis for a series of courses at the upper undergraduate and master's levels. The students have already taken basic courses in mathematics and statistics when they enter the program. In the first year, they are presented with material from the first three chapters and a brief discussion of the main issues of Chapters 4 and 5, followed by Chapters 6 and 7, and accompanied by problem sets to be worked out on the computer. The second year embarks on maximum likelihood theory from Chapters 8 and 9, skips most of Chapter 10 (although the model with AR(1) errors is used as an important example of the uses of the Gauss-Newton regression), and takes up the testing material of Chapters 11, 12, and 13, with relatively little emphasis placed on the last of these. Numerous problem sets accompany the material of these chapters. The third-year course, which is shorter and is joined by students from other programs, varies more in content, although Chapter 13 is always used as a focus for presentation and revision of maximum likelihood methods and testing procedures. Recently, in fact, the first chapter to be discussed was the last, Chapter 21, on Monte Carlo methods.

It is our hope that this book will be useful, not only to students, but also to established researchers in econometrics as a work of reference. Many of the techniques we describe, especially those based on artificial regressions, are difficult to find in the literature or can be found only in exceedingly technical articles. We would especially like to draw attention to Chapter 12, in which we discuss the determinants of test power and the correct interpretation of test statistics; Chapter 17, which is one of very few textbook treatments of the generalized method of moments; and Chapter 21, on Monte Carlo experiments. In these chapters, we think that the book makes a unique contribution. Much of the material in the rest of the book, notably Chapters 6, 11, 16, and 20, is also not to be found in other texts. Even when the material we cover is relatively familiar, we believe that our way of treating it is often novel enough to be enlightening.

One advantage of a book over the research literature is that a coherent approach and, perhaps of even greater importance, a coherent notation can be developed. Thus readers can more readily perceive the relations and similarities between seemingly disparate techniques and arguments. We will not pretend either that our notation is always absolutely consistent or that it was easy to make it even as consistent as it is. For example, the study of time series has for a long time generated a literature distinctly separate from the mainstream of econometrics, and within this literature notational habits have evolved that are incompatible with those that most econometricians are used to. Many people, however, would be taken aback if time series results were presented in a notation too markedly different from that used in the time series literature. We have tried very hard to use notation that is at once consistent and intuitive. The reader will be the judge of the extent to which we have succeeded.

It is inconceivable that a book as long and technical as this one should be free from errors. All the corrections incorporated in this printing and ones discovered later are available in electronic form via the Internet; see page 875. There would have been far more errors if we had not had the help of a great many people in reading preliminary drafts. They pointed out a disconcertingly large number of mistakes, most merely typographical, but some quite serious. We are indebted to our students, in both Canada and France, in this respect. We thank especially Dirk Eddelbüttel, Niels Hansen, Doug Tattrie, Colin Telmer, and John Touchie for the many hours they devoted to going through chapter after chapter with a fine-tooth comb. Many of our colleagues have made extremely valuable suggestions to us. Some suggested topics that we might otherwise have left out, and others were good enough to provide us with detailed comments on our preliminary efforts. Our thanks go to Richard Blundell, Colin Cameron, Gordon Fisher, John Galbraith, Bill Greene, Allan Gregory, Mark Kamstra, Peter Sephton, Gregor Smith, Thanasis Stengos, Timo Teräsvirta, and Diana Whistler. We are also indebted to an anonymous reader, who urged us to refocus the book when our original plan proved infeasible.

It is customary for authors to thank their secretaries for unflagging support, both technical and moral, in the preparation of their manuscript. This custom imposes on us the pleasant duty of thanking each other, since the manuscript was prepared, in TEX, by our own unaided efforts. At times, it seemed that the intricacies of this peerless computer program would take us more time to master than the whole of econometrics itself. We owe a debt of gratitude to Donald Knuth, the original author of TEX, and to the many other people who have contributed to its development.

Finally, we must give thanks where it is due for a great deal of moral support, and for much more besides, during the long period when we talked book, more book, and yet more book. It is with much gratitude that we record our thanks to our wives, Pamela and Susan.

Contents

Estimation and Inference in Econometrics

Chapter 1

The Geometry of Least Squares

1.1 Introduction

The most commonly used, and in many ways the most important, estimation technique in econometrics is **least squares**. It is useful to distinguish between two varieties of least squares, **ordinary least squares**, or **OLS**, and **nonlinear least squares**, or **NLS**. In the case of OLS the regression equation that is to be estimated is linear in all of the parameters, while in the case of NLS it is nonlinear in at least one parameter. OLS estimates can be obtained by direct calculation in several different ways (see Section 1.5), while NLS estimates require iterative procedures (see Chapter 6). In this chapter, we will discuss only ordinary least squares, since understanding linear regression is essential to understanding everything else in this book.

There is an important distinction between the numerical and the statistical properties of estimates obtained using OLS. **Numerical properties** are those that hold as a consequence of the use of ordinary least squares, regardless of how the data were generated. Since these properties are numerical, they can always be verified by direct calculation. An example is the well-known fact that OLS residuals sum to zero when the regressors include a constant term. **Statistical properties**, on the other hand, are those that hold only under certain assumptions about the way the data were generated. These can never be verified exactly, although in some cases they can be tested. An example is the well-known proposition that OLS estimates are, in certain circumstances, unbiased.

The distinction between numerical properties and statistical properties is obviously fundamental. In order to make this distinction as clearly as possible, we will in this chapter discuss only the former. We will study ordinary least squares purely as a computational device, without formally introducing any sort of statistical model (although we will on occasion discuss quantities that are mainly of interest in the context of linear regression models). No statistical models will be introduced until Chapter 2, where we will begin discussing **nonlinear regression models**, of which **linear regression models** are of course a special case.

By saying that we will study OLS as a computational device, we do not mean that we will discuss computer algorithms for calculating OLS estimates (although we will do that to a limited extent in Section 1.5). Instead, we mean that we will discuss the numerical properties of ordinary least squares and, in particular, the geometrical interpretation of those properties. All of the numerical properties of OLS can be interpreted in terms of Euclidean geometry. This geometrical interpretation often turns out to be remarkably simple, involving little more than Pythagoras' Theorem and high-school trigonometry, in the context of finite-dimensional vector spaces. Yet the insight gained from this approach is very great. Once one has a thorough grasp of the geometry involved in ordinary least squares, one can often save oneself many tedious lines of algebra by a simple geometrical argument. Moreover, as we hope the remainder of this book will illustrate, understanding the geometrical properties of OLS is just as fundamental to understanding nonlinear models of all types as it is to understanding linear regression models.

1.2 THE GEOMETRY OF LEAST SQUARES

The essential ingredients of a **linear regression** are a **regressand** $\boldsymbol{y}$ and a matrix of **regressors** $\boldsymbol{X} \equiv [\boldsymbol{x}_1 \dots \boldsymbol{x}_k]$. The regressand $\boldsymbol{y}$ is an n–vector, and the matrix of regressors $\boldsymbol{X}$ is an $n \times k$ matrix, each column $\boldsymbol{x}_i$ of which is an n–vector. The regressand $\boldsymbol{y}$ and each of the regressors $\boldsymbol{x}_1$ through $\boldsymbol{x}_k$ can be thought of as points in **n–dimensional Euclidean space**, E^n. The k regressors, provided they are linearly independent, **span** a k–dimensional **subspace** of E^n. We will denote this subspace by $\mathcal{S}(\boldsymbol{X})$.[1]

The subspace $\mathcal{S}(\boldsymbol{X})$ consists of all points $\boldsymbol{z}$ in E^n such that $\boldsymbol{z} = \boldsymbol{X}\boldsymbol{\gamma}$ for some $\boldsymbol{\gamma}$, where $\boldsymbol{\gamma}$ is a k–vector. Strictly speaking, we should refer to $\mathcal{S}(\boldsymbol{X})$ as the subspace spanned by the columns of $\boldsymbol{X}$, but less formally we will often refer to it simply as the **span** of $\boldsymbol{X}$. The **dimension** of $\mathcal{S}(\boldsymbol{X})$ is always equal to $\rho(\boldsymbol{X})$, the **rank** of $\boldsymbol{X}$ (i.e., the number of columns of $\boldsymbol{X}$ that are linearly independent). We will assume that k is strictly less than n, something which it is reasonable to do in almost all practical cases. If n were less than k, it would be impossible for $\boldsymbol{X}$ to have full column rank k.

A Euclidean space is not defined without defining an **inner product**. In this case, the inner product we are interested in is the so-called **natural inner product**. The natural inner product of any two points in E^n, say $\boldsymbol{z}_i$ and $\boldsymbol{z}_j$, may be denoted $\langle \boldsymbol{z}_i, \boldsymbol{z}_j \rangle$ and is defined by

$$\langle \boldsymbol{z}_i, \boldsymbol{z}_j \rangle \equiv \sum_{t=1}^{n} z_{it} z_{jt} \equiv \boldsymbol{z}_i^{\top} \boldsymbol{z}_j \equiv \boldsymbol{z}_j^{\top} \boldsymbol{z}_i.$$

[1] The notation $\mathcal{S}(\boldsymbol{X})$ is not a standard one, there being no standard notation that we are comfortable with. We believe that this notation has much to recommend it and will therefore use it hereafter.

We remark that the natural inner product is not the only one that could be used; we might, for example, choose to give a different, positive, weight to each element of the sum, as in

$$\sum_{t=1}^{n} w_t z_{it} z_{jt}.$$

As we will see in Chapter 9, performing a linear regression using this inner product would correspond to using a particular form of generalized least squares. For the rest of the book, unless otherwise specified, whenever we speak of an inner product we will mean the natural Euclidean one.

If a point $\boldsymbol{z}$ (which is of course an n–vector) belongs to $\mathcal{S}(\boldsymbol{X})$, we can always write $\boldsymbol{z}$ as a linear combination of the columns of $\boldsymbol{X}$:

$$\boldsymbol{z} = \sum_{i=1}^{k} \gamma_i \boldsymbol{x}_i = \boldsymbol{X}\boldsymbol{\gamma},$$

where γ_1 through γ_k are scalars and $\boldsymbol{\gamma}$ is a k–vector with typical element γ_i. Thus a vector of k coefficients like $\boldsymbol{\gamma}$ identifies *any* point in $\mathcal{S}(\boldsymbol{X})$. Provided that the columns of $\boldsymbol{X}$ are **linearly independent**, it does so uniquely. The vectors $\boldsymbol{x}_1$ through $\boldsymbol{x}_k$ are linearly independent if we cannot write any one of them as a linear combination of the others.

If the k regressors are *not* linearly independent, then they will span a subspace of dimension less than k, say k', where k' is the largest number of columns of $\boldsymbol{X}$ that are linearly independent of each other, that is, $\rho(\boldsymbol{X})$. In this case, $\mathcal{S}(\boldsymbol{X})$ will be identical to $\mathcal{S}(\boldsymbol{X}')$, where $\boldsymbol{X}'$ is an $n \times k'$ matrix consisting of any k' linearly independent columns of $\boldsymbol{X}$. For example, consider the following $\boldsymbol{X}$ matrix, which is 6×3:

$$\begin{bmatrix} 1 & 0 & 1 \\ 1 & 2 & 0 \\ 1 & 0 & 1 \\ 1 & 2 & 0 \\ 1 & 0 & 1 \\ 1 & 0 & 1 \end{bmatrix}.$$

The columns of this matrix are not linearly independent, since

$$\boldsymbol{x}_1 = .5\boldsymbol{x}_2 + \boldsymbol{x}_3.$$

However, any two of the columns are linearly independent, and so

$$\mathcal{S}(\boldsymbol{X}) = \mathcal{S}(\boldsymbol{x}_1, \boldsymbol{x}_2) = \mathcal{S}(\boldsymbol{x}_1, \boldsymbol{x}_3) = \mathcal{S}(\boldsymbol{x}_2, \boldsymbol{x}_3).$$

We have introduced a new notation here: $\mathcal{S}(\boldsymbol{x}_1, \boldsymbol{x}_2)$ denotes the subspace spanned by the two vectors $\boldsymbol{x}_1$ and $\boldsymbol{x}_2$ jointly. More generally, the notation

$\mathcal{S}(\boldsymbol{Z}, \boldsymbol{W})$ will denote the subspace spanned by the columns of the matrices $\boldsymbol{Z}$ and $\boldsymbol{W}$ taken together; thus $\mathcal{S}(\boldsymbol{Z}, \boldsymbol{W})$ means the same thing as $\mathcal{S}([\boldsymbol{Z} \quad \boldsymbol{W}])$. Note that, in many cases, $\mathcal{S}(\boldsymbol{Z}, \boldsymbol{W})$ will be a space of dimension less than the sum of the ranks of $\boldsymbol{Z}$ and $\boldsymbol{W}$, since some of the columns of $\boldsymbol{Z}$ may lie in $\mathcal{S}(\boldsymbol{W})$ and vice versa. For the remainder of this chapter, unless the contrary is explicitly assumed, we will, however, assume that the columns of $\boldsymbol{X}$ are linearly independent.

The first thing to note about $\mathcal{S}(\boldsymbol{X})$ is that we can subject $\boldsymbol{X}$ to any rank-preserving linear transformation without in any way changing the subspace spanned by the transformed $\boldsymbol{X}$ matrix. If $\boldsymbol{z} = \boldsymbol{X}\boldsymbol{\gamma}$ and

$$\boldsymbol{X}^* = \boldsymbol{X}\boldsymbol{A},$$

where $\boldsymbol{A}$ is a nonsingular $k \times k$ matrix, it follows that

$$\boldsymbol{z} = \boldsymbol{X}^*\boldsymbol{A}^{-1}\boldsymbol{\gamma} \equiv \boldsymbol{X}^*\boldsymbol{\gamma}^*.$$

Thus any point $\boldsymbol{z}$ that can be written as a linear combination of the columns of $\boldsymbol{X}$ can just as well be written as a linear combination of any linear transformation of those columns. We conclude that if $\mathcal{S}(\boldsymbol{X})$ is the space spanned by the columns of $\boldsymbol{X}$, it must also be the space spanned by the columns of $\boldsymbol{X}^* = \boldsymbol{X}\boldsymbol{A}$. This means that we could give the same space an infinite number of names, in this case $\mathcal{S}(\boldsymbol{X})$, $\mathcal{S}(\boldsymbol{X}^*)$, or whatever. Some authors (e.g., Seber, 1980; Fisher, 1981) have therefore adopted a notation in which the subspace that we have called $\mathcal{S}(\boldsymbol{X})$ is named without any explicit reference to $\boldsymbol{X}$ at all. We have avoided this **coordinate-free** notation because it tends to obscure the relationship between the results and the regression(s) they concern and because in most cases there is a natural choice for the matrix whose span we are interested in. As we will see, however, many of the principal results about linear regression are coordinate-free in the sense that they depend on $\boldsymbol{X}$ only through $\mathcal{S}(\boldsymbol{X})$.

The **orthogonal complement** of $\mathcal{S}(\boldsymbol{X})$ in E^n, which is denoted $\mathcal{S}^\perp(\boldsymbol{X})$, is the set of all points $\boldsymbol{w}$ in E^n such that, for any $\boldsymbol{z}$ in $\mathcal{S}(\boldsymbol{X}), \boldsymbol{w}^\top\boldsymbol{z} = \boldsymbol{0}$. Thus every point in $\mathcal{S}^\perp(\boldsymbol{X})$ is **orthogonal** to every point in $\mathcal{S}(\boldsymbol{X})$ (two points are said to be orthogonal if their inner product is zero). Since the dimension of $\mathcal{S}(\boldsymbol{X})$ is k, the dimension of $\mathcal{S}^\perp(\boldsymbol{X})$ is $n-k$. It is sometimes convenient to refer not to the dimension of a linear subspace but to its **codimension**. A linear subspace of E^n is said to have codimension j if the dimension of its orthogonal complement is j. Thus, in this case, $\mathcal{S}(\boldsymbol{X})$ has dimension k and codimension $n-k$, and $\mathcal{S}^\perp(\boldsymbol{X})$ has dimension $n-k$ and codimension k.

Before discussing Figure 1.1, which illustrates these concepts, we must say a word about geometrical conventions. The simplest way to represent an n–dimensional vector, say $\boldsymbol{z}$, in a diagram is simply to show it as a point in an n–dimensional space; n of course must be limited to 2 or 3. It is often more intuitive, however, explicitly to show $\boldsymbol{z}$ as a vector, in the geometrical sense.

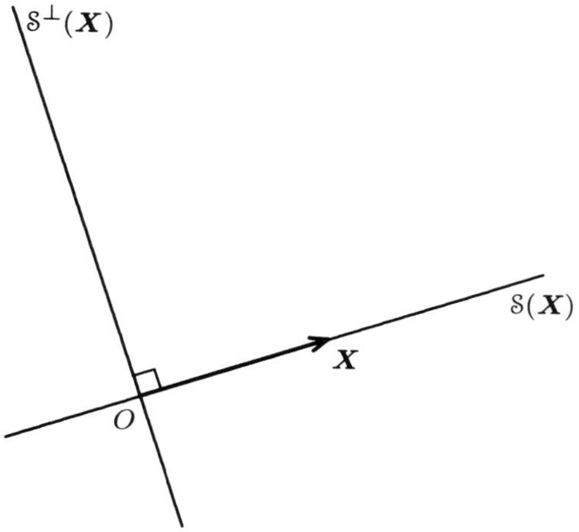

Figure 1.1 The spaces $\mathcal{S}(\boldsymbol{X})$ and $\mathcal{S}^{\perp}(\boldsymbol{X})$

This is done by connecting the point $\boldsymbol{z}$ with the origin and putting an arrowhead at $\boldsymbol{z}$. The resulting arrow then shows graphically the two things about a vector that matter, namely, its **length** and its **direction**. The Euclidean length of a vector $\boldsymbol{z}$ is

$$\|\boldsymbol{z}\| \equiv \left(\sum_{t=1}^{n} z_t^2\right)^{1/2} = \left|(\boldsymbol{z}^{\top}\boldsymbol{z})^{1/2}\right|,$$

where the notation emphasizes that $\|\boldsymbol{z}\|$ is the positive square root of the sum of the squared elements of $\boldsymbol{z}$. The direction is the vector itself normalized to have length unity, that is, $\boldsymbol{z}/\|\boldsymbol{z}\|$. One advantage of this convention is that if we move one of the arrows, being careful to change neither its length nor its direction, the new arrow represents the same vector, even though the arrowhead is now at a different point. It will often be very convenient to do this, and we therefore adopt this convention in most of our diagrams.

Figure 1.1 illustrates the concepts discussed above for the case $n = 2$ and $k = 1$. The matrix of regressors $\boldsymbol{X}$ has only one column in this case, and it is therefore represented by a single vector in the figure. As a consequence, $\mathcal{S}(\boldsymbol{X})$ is one-dimensional, and since $n = 2$, $\mathcal{S}^{\perp}(\boldsymbol{X})$ is also one-dimensional. Notice that $\mathcal{S}(\boldsymbol{X})$ and $\mathcal{S}^{\perp}(\boldsymbol{X})$ would be the same if $\boldsymbol{X}$ were *any* point on the straight line which is $\mathcal{S}(\boldsymbol{X})$, except for the origin. This illustrates the fact that $\mathcal{S}(\boldsymbol{X})$ is invariant to any nonsingular transformation of $\boldsymbol{X}$.

As we have seen, any point in $\mathcal{S}(\boldsymbol{X})$ can be represented by a vector of the form $\boldsymbol{X\beta}$ for some k–vector $\boldsymbol{\beta}$. If one wants to find the point in $\mathcal{S}(\boldsymbol{X})$ that is closest to a given vector $\boldsymbol{y}$, the problem to be solved is that of minimizing, with respect to the choice of $\boldsymbol{\beta}$, the distance between $\boldsymbol{y}$ and $\boldsymbol{X\beta}$. Minimizing this distance is evidently equivalent to minimizing the square of this distance.

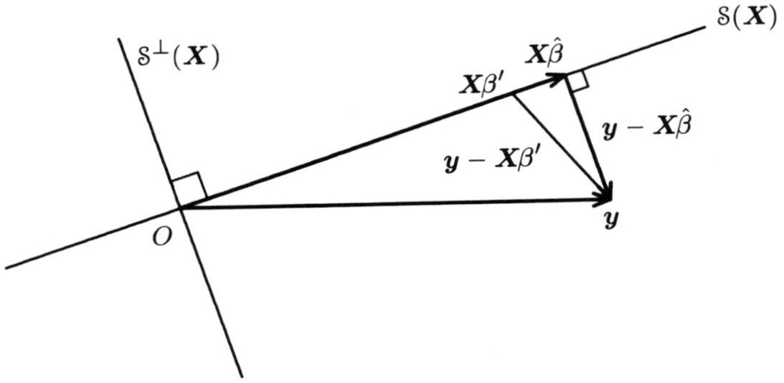

Figure 1.2 The projection of $\boldsymbol{y}$ onto $\mathcal{S}(\boldsymbol{X})$

Thus, solving the problem

$$\min_{\boldsymbol{\beta}} \|\boldsymbol{y} - \boldsymbol{X\beta}\|^2 \tag{1.01}$$

will find the closest point to $\boldsymbol{y}$ in $\mathcal{S}(\boldsymbol{X})$. The value of $\boldsymbol{\beta}$ that solves (1.01), which is the OLS estimate, will be denoted $\hat{\boldsymbol{\beta}}$.

The squared distance between $\boldsymbol{y}$ and $\boldsymbol{X\beta}$ can also be written as

$$\sum_{t=1}^{n}(y_t - \boldsymbol{X}_t\boldsymbol{\beta})^2 = (\boldsymbol{y} - \boldsymbol{X\beta})^{\top}(\boldsymbol{y} - \boldsymbol{X\beta}), \tag{1.02}$$

where y_t and $\boldsymbol{X}_t$ denote, respectively, the tth element of the vector $\boldsymbol{y}$ and the tth row of the matrix $\boldsymbol{X}$.[2] Since the difference between y_t and $\boldsymbol{X}_t\boldsymbol{\beta}$ is commonly referred to as a **residual**, this quantity is generally called the **sum of squared residuals**, or **SSR**. It is also sometimes called the **residual sum of squares**, which more closely parallels the terminology for its counterpart, the **explained sum of squares**. The acronyms would then be RSS and ESS. Unfortunately, some authors use the former to stand for the *regression* sum of squares and the latter for the *error* sum of squares, making it unclear what the acronyms RSS and ESS stand for. When we refer to SSR and ESS, there should be no such ambiguity.

The geometry of ordinary least squares is illustrated in Figure 1.2, which is Figure 1.1 with a few additions. The regressand is now shown as the vector $\boldsymbol{y}$. The vector $\boldsymbol{X}\hat{\beta}$, which is often referred to as the vector of **fitted values**, is the closest point in $\mathcal{S}(\boldsymbol{X})$ to $\boldsymbol{y}$; note that $\hat{\beta}$ is a scalar in this case. It is evident that the line joining $\boldsymbol{y}$ and $\boldsymbol{X}\hat{\beta}$ must form a right angle with $\mathcal{S}(\boldsymbol{X})$ at $\boldsymbol{X}\hat{\beta}$. This line is simply the vector $\boldsymbol{y} - \boldsymbol{X}\hat{\beta}$, translated so that its origin is

[2] We refer to the tth row of $\boldsymbol{X}$ as $\boldsymbol{X}_t$ rather than as $\boldsymbol{x}_t$ to avoid confusion with the columns of $\boldsymbol{X}$, which we have referred to as $\boldsymbol{x}_1$, $\boldsymbol{x}_2$, and so on.

at $X\hat{\beta}$ instead of at zero. The right angle formed by $y - X\hat{\beta}$ and $\mathcal{S}(X)$ is the key feature of least squares. At any other point in $\mathcal{S}(X)$, such as $X\beta'$ in the figure, $y - X\beta'$ does not form a right angle with $\mathcal{S}(X)$ and, as a consequence, $\|y - X\beta'\|$ must necessarily be larger than $\|y - X\hat{\beta}\|$.

The vector of derivatives of the SSR (1.02) with respect to the elements of $\boldsymbol{\beta}$ is

$$-2X^{\top}(y - X\boldsymbol{\beta}),$$

which must equal $\mathbf{0}$ at a minimum. Since we have assumed that the columns of X are linearly independent, the matrix $X^{\top}X$ must have full rank. This, combined with that fact that any matrix of the form $X^{\top}X$ is necessarily nonnegative definite, implies that the sum of squared residuals is a strictly convex function of $\boldsymbol{\beta}$ and must therefore have a unique minimum. Thus $\hat{\boldsymbol{\beta}}$ is uniquely determined by the **normal equations**

$$X^{\top}(y - X\hat{\boldsymbol{\beta}}) = \mathbf{0}. \tag{1.03}$$

These normal equations say that the vector $y - X\hat{\boldsymbol{\beta}}$ must be orthogonal to all of the columns of X and hence to any vector that lies in the space spanned by those columns. The normal equations (1.03) are thus simply a way of stating algebraically what Figure 1.2 showed geometrically, namely, that $y - X\hat{\boldsymbol{\beta}}$ must form a right angle with $\mathcal{S}(X)$.

Since the matrix $X^{\top}X$ has full rank, we can always invert it to solve the normal equations for $\hat{\boldsymbol{\beta}}$. We obtain the standard formula:

$$\hat{\boldsymbol{\beta}} = \left(X^{\top}X\right)^{-1}X^{\top}y. \tag{1.04}$$

Even if X is not of full rank, the fitted values $X\hat{\boldsymbol{\beta}}$ are uniquely defined, because $X\hat{\boldsymbol{\beta}}$ is simply the point in $\mathcal{S}(X)$ that is closest to y. Look again at Figure 1.2 and suppose that X is an $n \times 2$ matrix, but of rank only one. The geometrical point $X\hat{\boldsymbol{\beta}}$ is still uniquely defined. However, since $\boldsymbol{\beta}$ is now a 2–vector and $\mathcal{S}(X)$ is just one-dimensional, the vector $\hat{\boldsymbol{\beta}}$ is not uniquely defined. Thus the requirement that X have full rank is a purely algebraic requirement that is needed to obtain unique estimates $\hat{\boldsymbol{\beta}}$.

If we substitute the right-hand side of (1.04) for $\hat{\boldsymbol{\beta}}$ into $X\hat{\boldsymbol{\beta}}$, we obtain

$$X\hat{\boldsymbol{\beta}} = X\left(X^{\top}X\right)^{-1}X^{\top}y \equiv P_X y. \tag{1.05}$$

This equation defines the $n \times n$ matrix $P_X \equiv X(X^{\top}X)^{-1}X^{\top}$, which **projects** the vector y orthogonally onto $\mathcal{S}(X)$. The matrix P_X is an example of an **orthogonal projection matrix**. Associated with every linear subspace of E^n are two such matrices, one of which projects any point in E^n onto that subspace, and one of which projects any point in E^n onto its orthogonal complement. The matrix that projects onto $\mathcal{S}^{\perp}(X)$ is

$$M_X \equiv \mathbf{I} - P_X \equiv \mathbf{I} - X\left(X^{\top}X\right)^{-1}X^{\top},$$

where $\mathbf{I}$ is the $n \times n$ identity matrix. We say that $\mathcal{S}(\boldsymbol{X})$ is the **range** of the projection $\boldsymbol{P}_X$ while $\mathcal{S}^{\perp}(\boldsymbol{X})$ is the range of $\boldsymbol{M}_X$. Note that both $\boldsymbol{P}_X$ and $\boldsymbol{M}_X$ are symmetric matrices and that

$$\boldsymbol{M}_X + \boldsymbol{P}_X = \mathbf{I}.$$

Any point in E^n, say $\boldsymbol{z}$, is therefore equal to $\boldsymbol{M}_X\boldsymbol{z} + \boldsymbol{P}_X\boldsymbol{z}$. Thus these two projection matrices define an **orthogonal decomposition** of E^n, because the two vectors $\boldsymbol{M}_X\boldsymbol{z}$ and $\boldsymbol{P}_X\boldsymbol{z}$ lie in two orthogonal subspaces.

Throughout this book, we will use $\boldsymbol{P}$ and $\boldsymbol{M}$ subscripted by matrix expressions to denote the matrices that respectively project onto and off the subspaces spanned by the columns of those matrix expressions. Thus $\boldsymbol{P}_Z$ would be the matrix that projects onto $\mathcal{S}(\boldsymbol{Z})$, $\boldsymbol{M}_{X,W}$ would be the matrix that projects off $\mathcal{S}(\boldsymbol{X}, \boldsymbol{W})$, and so on. These projection matrices are of no use whatsoever for computation, because they are of dimension $n \times n$, which makes them much too large to work with on a computer except when the sample size is quite small. But they are nevertheless extremely useful. It is frequently very convenient to express the quantities that arise in econometrics using these matrices, partly because the resulting expressions are relatively compact and partly because the properties of projection matrices often make it easy to understand what those expressions mean.

In the case of any linear regression with regressors $\boldsymbol{X}$, the projection matrices of primary interest are $\boldsymbol{P}_X$ and $\boldsymbol{M}_X$. These matrices have several important properties which can all be seen clearly from Figure 1.2. One property, which is often extremely convenient, is that they are **idempotent**. An idempotent matrix is one that, when multiplied by itself, yields itself again. Thus

$$\boldsymbol{P}_X\boldsymbol{P}_X = \boldsymbol{P}_X \quad \text{and} \quad \boldsymbol{M}_X\boldsymbol{M}_X = \boldsymbol{M}_X.$$

These results are easily proved by a little algebra, but the geometry of the situation makes them obvious. If one takes any point, projects it onto $\mathcal{S}(\boldsymbol{X})$, and then projects it onto $\mathcal{S}(\boldsymbol{X})$ *again*, the second projection can have no effect, because the point is *already* in $\mathcal{S}(\boldsymbol{X})$. This implies that $\boldsymbol{P}_X\boldsymbol{P}_X\boldsymbol{z} = \boldsymbol{P}_X\boldsymbol{z}$ for any vector $\boldsymbol{z}$; therefore, $\boldsymbol{P}_X\boldsymbol{P}_X = \boldsymbol{P}_X$. A similar argument holds for $\boldsymbol{M}_X$.

A second important property of $\boldsymbol{P}_X$ and $\boldsymbol{M}_X$ is that

$$\boldsymbol{P}_X\boldsymbol{M}_X = \mathbf{0}. \tag{1.06}$$

Thus $\boldsymbol{P}_X$ and $\boldsymbol{M}_X$ annihilate each other. Again, this can easily be proved algebraically using the definitions of $\boldsymbol{P}_X$ and $\boldsymbol{M}_X$, but such a proof is quite unnecessary. It should be obvious that (1.06) must hold, because $\boldsymbol{P}_X$ projects onto $\mathcal{S}(\boldsymbol{X})$ and $\boldsymbol{M}_X$ projects onto $\mathcal{S}^{\perp}(\boldsymbol{X})$. The only point that belongs to *both* $\mathcal{S}(\boldsymbol{X})$ and $\mathcal{S}^{\perp}(\boldsymbol{X})$ is the origin, i.e., the zero vector. Thus, if we attempt to project any vector onto both $\mathcal{S}(\boldsymbol{X})$ and its orthogonal complement, we get the zero vector.

In fact, M_X annihilates not just P_X but all points that lie in $\mathcal{S}(X)$, and P_X annihilates not just M_X but all points that lie in $\mathcal{S}^{\perp}(X)$. These properties can again be proved by straightforward algebra, but the geometry of the situation is even simpler. Consider Figure 1.2 again. It is evident that if we project any point in $\mathcal{S}^{\perp}(X)$ orthogonally onto $\mathcal{S}(X)$, we end up at the origin (which is just a vector of zeros), as we do if we project any point in $\mathcal{S}(X)$ orthogonally onto $\mathcal{S}^{\perp}(X)$.

Since the space spanned by the columns of X is invariant to nonsingular linear transformations of the columns of X, so must be the projection matrices P_X and M_X. This can also be seen algebraically. Consider what happens when we postmultiply X by any nonsingular $k \times k$ matrix A. The matrix that projects onto the span of XA is

$$\begin{aligned} P_{XA} &= XA(A^{\top}X^{\top}XA)^{-1}A^{\top}X^{\top} \\ &= XAA^{-1}(X^{\top}X)^{-1}(A^{\top})^{-1}A^{\top}X^{\top} \\ &= X(X^{\top}X)^{-1}X^{\top} = P_X. \end{aligned}$$

This result suggests that perhaps the *best* way to characterize a linear subspace is by the matrix that projects orthogonally onto it, with which it is in a one-to-one correspondence.

If the rank of the matrix X is k, then so is the rank of P_X. This follows from the fact that the range of the projection matrix P_X is just $\mathcal{S}(X)$, the span of X, which has dimension equal to $\rho(X)$. Thus, although P_X is an $n \times n$ matrix, its rank is in general much smaller than n. This crucial fact permits us to make much greater use of simple geometry than might at first seem possible. Since we are working with vectors that lie in an n–dimensional space, with n almost always greater than 3, it might seem that diagrams like Figure 1.2 would almost never be applicable. But most of the time we will be interested only in a small-dimensional subspace of the n–dimensional space in which the regressand and regressors are located. The small-dimensional subspace of interest will generally be either the space spanned by the regressors only or the space spanned by the regressand along with the regressors. These subspaces will have dimensions k and $k+1$, respectively, whatever the sample size n. The former subspace is uniquely characterized by the orthogonal projection P_X, and the latter by the orthogonal projection $P_{X,y}$.

When we look at a figure that is two-dimensional, possibly intended as a two-dimensional projection of a three-dimensional image, the two or three dimensions that we can visualize will therefore be those of $\mathcal{S}(X)$ or $\mathcal{S}(X, y)$. What we lose in collapsing the original n dimensions into just two or three is the possibility of drawing coordinate axes that correspond to the separate observations of a sample. For that to be possible, it would indeed be necessary to restrict ourselves to samples of two or three. But this seems a small price to pay for the possibility of seeing the geometrical interpretation of a great many of the algebraic results in econometrics. That such geometrical interpretations are possible is due to the fact that lengths, angles, inner products, and in fact everything that does not depend explicitly on the individual observations on a set of k linearly independent variables, remain unchanged when we ignore the $n-k$ dimensions orthogonal to the space spanned by the k variables. Thus if, for example, two variables are orthogonal in n dimensions, they are also orthogonal in the two-dimensional space that they span.

Let us now make use of geometrical interpretations to establish some important properties of the linear regression model. We have already seen from (1.05) that $\boldsymbol{P}_X\boldsymbol{y}$ is the vector of fitted values from a regression of $\boldsymbol{y}$ on $\boldsymbol{X}$. This implies that $\boldsymbol{M}_X\boldsymbol{y} = \boldsymbol{y} - \boldsymbol{P}_X\boldsymbol{y}$ is the vector of residuals from the same regression. Property (1.06) tells us that

$$(\boldsymbol{P}_X\boldsymbol{y})^{\top}(\boldsymbol{M}_X\boldsymbol{y}) = \boldsymbol{0};$$

it follows that the residuals must be orthogonal to the fitted values. Indeed, the residuals must be orthogonal to *every* vector that lies in $\mathcal{S}(\boldsymbol{X})$, including all of the regressors and all linear transformations of those regressors. Thus, when $\boldsymbol{X}$ includes a constant term or the equivalent of a constant term, the residuals must sum to zero.

Notice that the fitted values $\boldsymbol{P}_X\boldsymbol{y}$ and residuals $\boldsymbol{M}_X\boldsymbol{y}$ depend on $\boldsymbol{X}$ only through the projection matrices $\boldsymbol{P}_X$ and $\boldsymbol{M}_X$. Thus they depend only on $\mathcal{S}(\boldsymbol{X})$ and not on any characteristics of $\boldsymbol{X}$ that do not affect $\mathcal{S}(\boldsymbol{X})$; in particular, they are invariant to any nonsingular linear transformation of the columns of $\boldsymbol{X}$. Among other things, this implies that for any regression we can multiply any or all of the regressors by any nonzero constant, and in any regression that includes a constant term we can add any constant amount to any or all of the regressors, without affecting the OLS residuals or fitted values at all. As an example, the following two apparently quite dissimilar regressions must yield *exactly* the same fitted values and residuals:[3]

$$\boldsymbol{y} = \beta_1\boldsymbol{x}_1 + \beta_2\boldsymbol{x}_2 + \beta_3\boldsymbol{x}_3 + \text{residuals};$$
$$\boldsymbol{y} = \alpha_1(\boldsymbol{x}_1 + \boldsymbol{x}_2) + \alpha_2(2\boldsymbol{x}_2 - \boldsymbol{x}_3) + \alpha_3(3\boldsymbol{x}_1 - 2\boldsymbol{x}_2 + 5\boldsymbol{x}_3) + \text{residuals}.$$

These two regressions have the same explanatory power (that is, the same fitted values and residuals), because the regressors span exactly the same subspace in each case. Notice that if we let $\boldsymbol{X}^*$ represent the regressor matrix

[3] Here and elsewhere, when we write an equation ending with "+ residuals," we simply mean by residuals whatever the difference between the regressand and the regression function happens to be. These residuals will be OLS residuals only if the parameters of the regression function are evaluated at the OLS estimates. We avoid the more common notation "+ $\boldsymbol{u}$" in this context to avoid any suggestion that the residuals have any statistical properties.

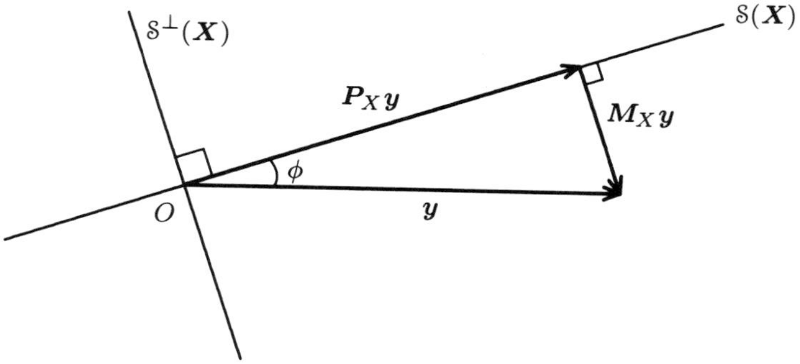

Figure 1.3 The orthogonal decomposition of $\boldsymbol{y}$

from the second equation, then we see that $\boldsymbol{X}^* = \boldsymbol{XA}$ for the matrix

$$\boldsymbol{A} = \begin{bmatrix} 1 & 0 & 3 \\ 1 & 2 & -2 \\ 0 & -1 & 5 \end{bmatrix}.$$

The idempotency of $\boldsymbol{P}_X$ and $\boldsymbol{M}_X$ often makes expressions associated with least squares regression very simple. For example, when evaluated at $\hat{\boldsymbol{\beta}}$, the sum of squared residuals (1.02) is

$$\begin{aligned}(\boldsymbol{y} - \boldsymbol{X}\hat{\boldsymbol{\beta}})^{\top}(\boldsymbol{y} - \boldsymbol{X}\hat{\boldsymbol{\beta}}) &= (\boldsymbol{M}_X\boldsymbol{y})^{\top}(\boldsymbol{M}_X\boldsymbol{y}) \\ &= \boldsymbol{y}^{\top}\boldsymbol{M}_X\boldsymbol{M}_X\boldsymbol{y} = \boldsymbol{y}^{\top}\boldsymbol{M}_X\boldsymbol{y} = \|\boldsymbol{M}_X\boldsymbol{y}\|^2.\end{aligned} \tag{1.07}$$

Similarly, the explained sum of squares is

$$\begin{aligned}(\boldsymbol{X}\hat{\boldsymbol{\beta}})^{\top}(\boldsymbol{X}\hat{\boldsymbol{\beta}}) &= (\boldsymbol{P}_X\boldsymbol{y})^{\top}(\boldsymbol{P}_X\boldsymbol{y}) \\ &= \boldsymbol{y}^{\top}\boldsymbol{P}_X\boldsymbol{P}_X\boldsymbol{y} = \boldsymbol{y}^{\top}\boldsymbol{P}_X\boldsymbol{y} = \|\boldsymbol{P}_X\boldsymbol{y}\|^2.\end{aligned} \tag{1.08}$$

The right-most expression in each of (1.07) and (1.08) makes it clear that the sum of squared residuals and the explained sum of squares are simply the squared lengths of certain vectors, namely, the projections of $\boldsymbol{y}$ onto the ranges of the two projections $\boldsymbol{M}_X$ and $\boldsymbol{P}_X$, which are $\mathcal{S}^{\perp}(\boldsymbol{X})$ and $\mathcal{S}(\boldsymbol{X})$, respectively.

This is shown in Figure 1.3, which is Figure 1.2 redrawn and relabelled. Although the figure is only two-dimensional, it is perfectly general. The two-dimensional space depicted is that spanned by the regressand $\boldsymbol{y}$ and the vector of fitted values $\boldsymbol{P}_X\boldsymbol{y}$. These two vectors form, as shown, two sides of a right-angled triangle. The distance between $\boldsymbol{y}$ and $\boldsymbol{P}_X\boldsymbol{y}$ is $\|\boldsymbol{M}_X\boldsymbol{y}\|$, the distance between the origin and $\boldsymbol{P}_X\boldsymbol{y}$ is $\|\boldsymbol{P}_X\boldsymbol{y}\|$, and the distance between the origin and $\boldsymbol{y}$ is of course $\|\boldsymbol{y}\|$. By applying Pythagoras' Theorem,[4] we immediately conclude that

$$\|\boldsymbol{y}\|^2 = \|\boldsymbol{P}_X\boldsymbol{y}\|^2 + \|\boldsymbol{M}_X\boldsymbol{y}\|^2.$$

Thus the **total sum of squares**, or **TSS**, of the regressand is equal to the explained sum of squares plus the sum of squared residuals. This result depends crucially on the fact that $\boldsymbol{M}_X\boldsymbol{y}$ is orthogonal to $\mathcal{S}(\boldsymbol{X})$, since otherwise we would not have a right-angled triangle and Pythagoras' Theorem would not apply.

The fact that the total variation in the regressand can be divided into two parts, one "explained" by the regressors and one not explained, suggests a natural measure of how well a regression fits. This measure, formally called the **coefficient of determination** but universally referred to as the R^2, actually has several variants. The simplest variant (but not the one most commonly encountered) is the **uncentered** R^2:

$$R_u^2 = \frac{\|\boldsymbol{P}_X\boldsymbol{y}\|^2}{\|\boldsymbol{y}\|^2} = 1 - \frac{\|\boldsymbol{M}_X\boldsymbol{y}\|^2}{\|\boldsymbol{y}\|^2}.$$

It is evident that R_u^2 is unit-free and that it must take on a value between 0 and 1. From Figure 1.3, it is easy to see that R_u^2 has a simple geometrical interpretation. The cosine of the angle between the vectors $\boldsymbol{y}$ and $\boldsymbol{P}_X\boldsymbol{y}$, which is marked ϕ in the figure, is

$$\cos\phi = \frac{\|\boldsymbol{P}_X\boldsymbol{y}\|}{\|\boldsymbol{y}\|}.$$

This is the (uncentered) correlation coefficient between $\boldsymbol{y}$ and $\boldsymbol{P}_X\boldsymbol{y}$. Hence we see that

$$R_u^2 = \cos^2\phi.$$

When $\boldsymbol{y}$ actually lies in $\mathcal{S}(\boldsymbol{X})$, the angle between $\boldsymbol{P}_X\boldsymbol{y}$ and $\boldsymbol{y}$ must be 0, since they will be the same vector, and R_u^2 will thus be 1. In the other extreme, when $\boldsymbol{y}$ lies in $\mathcal{S}^\perp(\boldsymbol{X})$, the angle between $\boldsymbol{P}_X\boldsymbol{y}$ and $\boldsymbol{y}$ will be 90°, and R_u^2 will evidently be 0.

Anything that changes the angle ϕ in Figure 1.3 will change the uncentered R^2. In particular, it is evident that adding a constant to $\boldsymbol{y}$ will normally change that angle, and that this is true even if $\boldsymbol{X}$ includes a constant term. If the R^2 is to be used as a measure of how well a regression fits, it seems undesirable for it to change when we do something as simple as adding a constant to the regressand. It is easy to modify the R^2 to get around this problem.

[4] **Pythagoras' Theorem**, it will be recalled, simply says that for a right-angled triangle the square of the length of the hypotenuse is equal to the sum of the squares of the lengths of the other two sides.

The modified version is known as the **centered** R^2, and we will denote it by R_c^2. It is defined as

$$R_c^2 \equiv 1 - \frac{\|\boldsymbol{M}_X \boldsymbol{y}\|^2}{\|\boldsymbol{M}_\iota \boldsymbol{y}\|^2}, \tag{1.09}$$

where

$$\boldsymbol{M}_\iota \equiv \mathbf{I} - \boldsymbol{\iota}(\boldsymbol{\iota}^\top\boldsymbol{\iota})^{-1}\boldsymbol{\iota}^\top = \mathbf{I} - n^{-1}\boldsymbol{\iota}\boldsymbol{\iota}^\top$$

is the matrix that projects off the space spanned by the constant vector $\boldsymbol{\iota}$, which is simply a vector of n ones. When any vector is multiplied by $\boldsymbol{M}_\iota$, the result is a vector of deviations from the mean. Thus what the centered R^2 measures is the proportion of the total sum of squares of the regressand *around its mean* that is explained by the regressors.

An alternative expression for R_c^2 is

$$\frac{\|\boldsymbol{P}_X \boldsymbol{M}_\iota \boldsymbol{y}\|^2}{\|\boldsymbol{M}_\iota \boldsymbol{y}\|^2}, \tag{1.10}$$

but this is equal to (1.09) only if $\boldsymbol{P}_X \boldsymbol{\iota} = \boldsymbol{\iota}$, which means that $\mathcal{S}(\boldsymbol{X})$ must include the vector $\boldsymbol{\iota}$ (so that either one column of $\boldsymbol{X}$ must be a constant, or some linear combination of the columns of $\boldsymbol{X}$ must equal a constant). In this case, the equality must hold, because

$$\boldsymbol{M}_X \boldsymbol{M}_\iota \boldsymbol{y} = \boldsymbol{M}_X(\mathbf{I} - \boldsymbol{P}_\iota)\boldsymbol{y} = \boldsymbol{M}_X \boldsymbol{y},$$

the second equality here being a consequence of the fact that $\boldsymbol{M}_X$ annihilates $\boldsymbol{P}_\iota$ when $\boldsymbol{\iota}$ belongs to $\mathcal{S}(\boldsymbol{X})$. When this is not the case and (1.10) is not valid, there is no guarantee that R_c^2 will be positive. After all, there will be many cases in which a regressand $\boldsymbol{y}$ is better explained by a constant term than by some set of regressors that does not include a constant term. Clearly, if (1.10) is valid, R_c^2 must lie between 0 and 1, since (1.10) is then simply the uncentered R^2 for a regression of $\boldsymbol{M}_\iota \boldsymbol{y}$ on $\boldsymbol{X}$.

The use of the centered R^2 when $\boldsymbol{X}$ does not include a constant term or the equivalent is thus fraught with difficulties. Some programs for statistics and econometrics refuse to print an R^2 at all in this circumstance; others print R_u^2 (without always warning the user that they are doing so); some print R_c^2, defined as (1.09), which may be either positive or negative; and some print still other quantities, which would be equal to R_c^2 if $\boldsymbol{X}$ included a constant term but are not when it does not. Users of statistical software, be warned!

Notice that R^2 is an interesting number only because we used least squares to estimate $\hat{\boldsymbol{\beta}}$. If we chose an estimate of $\boldsymbol{\beta}$, say $\tilde{\boldsymbol{\beta}}$, in any other way, so that the triangle in Figure 1.3 were no longer a right-angled triangle, we would find that the equivalents of the two definitions of R^2, (1.09) and (1.10), were not the same:

$$1 - \frac{\|\boldsymbol{y} - \boldsymbol{X}\tilde{\boldsymbol{\beta}}\|^2}{\|\boldsymbol{y}\|^2} \neq \frac{\|\boldsymbol{X}\tilde{\boldsymbol{\beta}}\|^2}{\|\boldsymbol{y}\|^2}.$$

If we chose to define R^2 in terms of the residuals, using the first of these expressions, we could not guarantee that it would be positive, and if we chose to define it in terms of the fitted values, using the second, we could not guarantee that it would be less than 1. Thus, when anything other than least squares is used to estimate a regression, one should either ignore what is reported as the R^2 or make sure that one knows exactly how the reported number was computed.

1.3 Restrictions and Reparametrizations

We have stressed the fact that $\mathcal{S}(\boldsymbol{X})$ is invariant to any nonsingular linear transformation of the columns of $\boldsymbol{X}$. This implies that we can always **reparametrize** any regression in whatever way is convenient, without in any way changing the ability of the regressors to explain the regressand. Suppose that we wished to run the regression

$$\boldsymbol{y} = \boldsymbol{X\beta} + \text{residuals} \tag{1.11}$$

and compare the results of this regression with those from another regression in which $\boldsymbol{\beta}$ is subject to the r $(\leq k)$ linearly independent restrictions

$$\boldsymbol{R\beta} = \boldsymbol{r}, \tag{1.12}$$

where $\boldsymbol{R}$ is an $r \times k$ matrix of rank r and $\boldsymbol{r}$ is an r–vector. While it is not difficult to do this by **restricted least squares**, it is often easier to reparametrize the regression so that the restrictions are zero restrictions. The restricted regression can then be estimated in the usual way by OLS. The reparametrization can be done as follows.

First, rearrange the columns of $\boldsymbol{X}$ so that the restrictions (1.12) can be written as

$$\boldsymbol{R}_1\boldsymbol{\beta}_1 + \boldsymbol{R}_2\boldsymbol{\beta}_2 = \boldsymbol{r}, \tag{1.13}$$

where $\boldsymbol{R} \equiv [\boldsymbol{R}_1 \quad \boldsymbol{R}_2]$ and $\boldsymbol{\beta} \equiv [\boldsymbol{\beta}_1 \vdots \boldsymbol{\beta}_2]$,[5] $\boldsymbol{R}_1$ being a nonsingular $r \times r$ matrix and $\boldsymbol{R}_2$ an $r \times (k - r)$ matrix. It must be possible to do this if the restrictions are in fact distinct. Solving equations (1.13) for $\boldsymbol{\beta}_1$ yields

$$\boldsymbol{\beta}_1 = \boldsymbol{R}_1^{-1}\boldsymbol{r} - \boldsymbol{R}_1^{-1}\boldsymbol{R}_2\boldsymbol{\beta}_2.$$

[5] The notation $[\boldsymbol{\beta}_1 \vdots \boldsymbol{\beta}_2]$ means that $\boldsymbol{\beta}_1$ and $\boldsymbol{\beta}_2$ are column vectors that are stacked to form another column vector, in this case $\boldsymbol{\beta}$. A more common notation would be $[\boldsymbol{\beta}_1^\top \quad \boldsymbol{\beta}_2^\top]^\top$, but this is distinctly cumbersome. We are introducing the former notation because one often wants to stack column vectors, and we believe that the new notation is enough of an improvement to be worth introducing.

Thus the original regression (1.11), with the restrictions imposed, can be written as

$$\boldsymbol{y} = \boldsymbol{X}_1(\boldsymbol{R}_1^{-1}\boldsymbol{r} - \boldsymbol{R}_1^{-1}\boldsymbol{R}_2\boldsymbol{\beta}_2) + \boldsymbol{X}_2\boldsymbol{\beta}_2 + \text{residuals}.$$

This is equivalent to

$$\boldsymbol{y} - \boldsymbol{X}_1\boldsymbol{R}_1^{-1}\boldsymbol{r} = (\boldsymbol{X}_2 - \boldsymbol{X}_1\boldsymbol{R}_1^{-1}\boldsymbol{R}_2)\boldsymbol{\beta}_2 + \text{residuals},$$

which, if we define $\boldsymbol{y}^*$ as $\boldsymbol{y} - \boldsymbol{X}_1\boldsymbol{R}_1^{-1}\boldsymbol{r}$ and $\boldsymbol{Z}_2$ as $\boldsymbol{X}_2 - \boldsymbol{X}_1\boldsymbol{R}_1^{-1}\boldsymbol{R}_2$, can be rewritten more compactly as

$$\boldsymbol{y}^* = \boldsymbol{Z}_2\boldsymbol{\beta}_2 + \text{residuals}. \tag{1.14}$$

This is a restricted version of regression (1.11). To obtain a regression equivalent to the original, we have to add back in r regressors that together with $\boldsymbol{Z}_2$ will span the same space as $\boldsymbol{X}$. There is an infinite number of ways to do this. Let the new regression function be written as $\boldsymbol{Z\gamma}$. We have already defined $\boldsymbol{Z}_2$, and $\boldsymbol{Z}_1$ can be any matrix of r columns which along with $\boldsymbol{Z}_2$ span $\mathcal{S}(\boldsymbol{X})$. Further we must have $\gamma_2 = \boldsymbol{\beta}_2$. The new regression is thus

$$\boldsymbol{y}^* = \boldsymbol{Z}_1\gamma_1 + \boldsymbol{Z}_2\gamma_2 + \text{residuals}. \tag{1.15}$$

It should be clear from the way $\boldsymbol{Z}_2$ was constructed that $\mathcal{S}(\boldsymbol{X}_1, \boldsymbol{Z}_2) = \mathcal{S}(\boldsymbol{X})$, and so one possible choice for $\boldsymbol{Z}_1$ is just $\boldsymbol{X}_1$. The fact that the regressand has also been transformed can have no effect on the residuals from the regression, because $\boldsymbol{y}^* = \boldsymbol{y} - \boldsymbol{X}_1\boldsymbol{R}_1^{-1}\boldsymbol{r}$, and the vector $\boldsymbol{X}_1\boldsymbol{R}_1^{-1}\boldsymbol{r}$ lies in $\mathcal{S}(\boldsymbol{X})$.

As a concrete example of the procedure just described, consider the regression

$$\boldsymbol{y} = \beta_1\boldsymbol{x}_1 + \beta_2\boldsymbol{x}_2 + \text{residuals}, \tag{1.16}$$

which is to be estimated subject to the restriction that $\beta_1 + \beta_2 = 1$. The restricted regression, equivalent to (1.14), is thus

$$\boldsymbol{y} - \boldsymbol{x}_1 = \beta_2(\boldsymbol{x}_2 - \boldsymbol{x}_1) + \text{residuals},$$

and the unrestricted regression in the new parametrization, equivalent to (1.15), is

$$\boldsymbol{y}^* = \gamma_1\boldsymbol{z}_1 + \gamma_2\boldsymbol{z}_2 + \text{residuals}, \tag{1.17}$$

in which $\boldsymbol{y}^* \equiv \boldsymbol{y} - \boldsymbol{x}_1$, $\boldsymbol{z}_1 \equiv \boldsymbol{x}_1$, $\boldsymbol{z}_2 \equiv \boldsymbol{x}_2 - \boldsymbol{x}_1$, and $\gamma_2 \equiv \beta_2$. The restriction that $\gamma_1 = 0$ is equivalent to the original restriction that $\beta_1 + \beta_2 = 1$.

This example is illustrated in Figure 1.4, which should be viewed in three dimensions. The figure depicts the span of the two regressors $\boldsymbol{x}_1$ and $\boldsymbol{x}_2$, which span the plane marked $\mathcal{S}(\boldsymbol{X})$ in the figure, and of the regressand $\boldsymbol{y}$, which is here shown as being above the plane $\mathcal{S}(\boldsymbol{X})$. Unrestricted OLS estimation

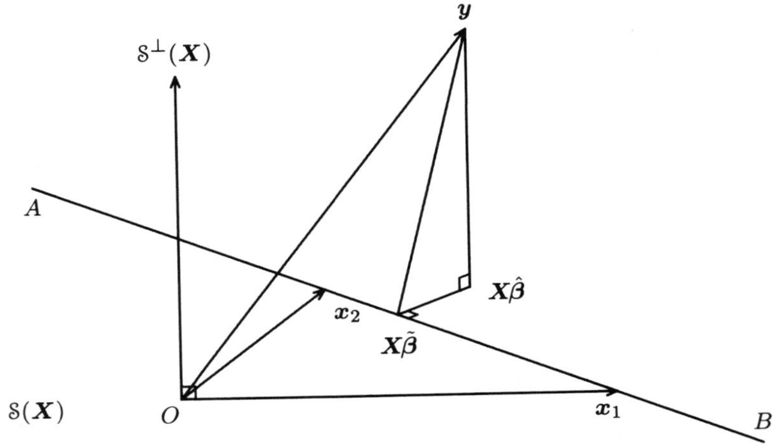

Figure 1.4 Restricted and unrestricted estimation

corresponds to projecting $\boldsymbol{y}$ orthogonally onto the surface of the plane, at the point $\boldsymbol{X}\hat{\boldsymbol{\beta}}$. The restriction that $\beta_1 + \beta_2 = 1$ requires the fitted values to lie on the line AB in the figure, and when we project $\boldsymbol{y}$ orthogonally onto this line, we obtain the point $\boldsymbol{X}\tilde{\boldsymbol{\beta}}$, which corresponds to the vector of fitted values from the restricted estimation.

The reparametrization from (1.16) to (1.17) does not change $\mathcal{S}(\boldsymbol{X})$ at all, but since the regressand is now $\boldsymbol{y} - \boldsymbol{x}_1$ rather than $\boldsymbol{y}$, the location of the regressand has changed relative to the origin. Figure 1.5 is essentially the

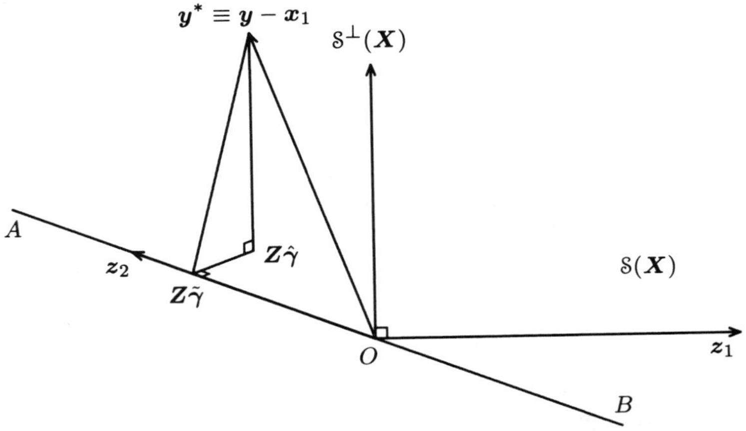

Figure 1.5 Estimation after reparametrization

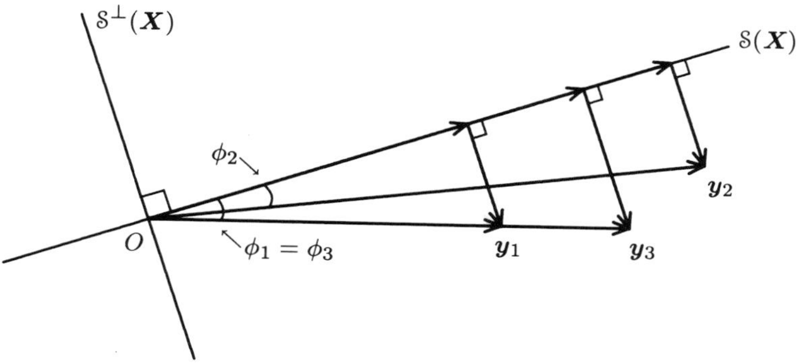

Figure 1.6 Effects on R^2 of different regressands

same as Figure 1.4, except that everything has been labelled in terms of the new parametrization. In fact, Figure 1.5 results from Figure 1.4 by shifting the origin to the tip of the arrow representing the variable $\boldsymbol{x}_1$. The vector $\boldsymbol{z}_1$ is thus the old $\boldsymbol{x}_1$ translated so as to start from the new origin. The second new regressor, $\boldsymbol{z}_2$, lies within the line AB, which in Figure 1.5 passes through the origin. This makes it clear that the restriction means that γ_1 must be zero. Consequently, the vector of fitted values must also lie on the line AB.

We have seen that the residuals from the reparametrized regression (1.15) will be exactly the same as the residuals from (1.11), and this fact is evident from Figures 1.4 and 1.5. This will not be true of either the centered or the uncentered R^2, however, since the total sum of squares depends on how the regressand is expressed. This is another reason to be wary of all variants of the R^2: Equivalent regressions can have very different R^2's. To see this geometrically, consider Figure 1.6, which is similar to Figure 1.3 except that now three different regressands, $\boldsymbol{y}_1$, $\boldsymbol{y}_2$, and $\boldsymbol{y}_3$, are shown. The second of these, $\boldsymbol{y}_2$, was obtained from $\boldsymbol{y}_1$ by shifting the latter to the northeast parallel to $\mathcal{S}(\boldsymbol{X})$ so that $\boldsymbol{M}_X\boldsymbol{y}_2 = \boldsymbol{M}_X\boldsymbol{y}_1$. Notice that ϕ_1 is different from ϕ_2, which implies that the R^2's will be different. On the other hand, $\boldsymbol{y}_3$ was obtained by moving $\boldsymbol{y}_1$ outward while keeping ϕ constant. As a result, $\boldsymbol{M}_X\boldsymbol{y}_3$ will be larger than $\boldsymbol{M}_X\boldsymbol{y}_1$, but the two regressions will have the same (uncentered) R^2. If we interpreted $\mathcal{S}(\boldsymbol{X})$ in the figure as $\mathcal{S}(\boldsymbol{M}_\iota\boldsymbol{X})$ and $\boldsymbol{y}$ as $\boldsymbol{M}_\iota\boldsymbol{y}$, then $\cos^2\phi$ would be the centered R^2 instead of the uncentered one.

1.4 THE FRISCH-WAUGH-LOVELL THEOREM

We now discuss an extremely important and useful property of least squares estimates, which, although widely known, is not as widely appreciated as it should be. We will refer to it as the **Frisch-Waugh-Lovell Theorem**, or **FWL Theorem**, after Frisch and Waugh (1933) and Lovell (1963), since those papers seem to have introduced, and then reintroduced, it to econometricians. The theorem is much more general, and much more generally useful, than a casual reading of those papers might suggest, however. Among other things, it almost totally eliminates the need to invert partitioned matrices when one is deriving many standard results about ordinary (and nonlinear) least squares.

The FWL Theorem applies to any regression where there are two or more regressors, and these can logically be broken up into two groups. The regression can thus be written as

$$\boldsymbol{y} = \boldsymbol{X}_1\boldsymbol{\beta}_1 + \boldsymbol{X}_2\boldsymbol{\beta}_2 + \text{residuals}, \tag{1.18}$$

where $\boldsymbol{X}_1$ is $n \times k_1$ and $\boldsymbol{X}_2$ is $n \times k_2$, with $\boldsymbol{X} \equiv [\boldsymbol{X}_1 \quad \boldsymbol{X}_2]$ and $k = k_1 + k_2$. For example, $\boldsymbol{X}_1$ might be seasonal dummy variables or trend variables and $\boldsymbol{X}_2$ genuine economic variables. This was in fact the type of situation dealt with by Frisch and Waugh (1933) and Lovell (1963). Another possibility is that $\boldsymbol{X}_1$ might be regressors, the joint significance of which we desire to test, and $\boldsymbol{X}_2$ might be other regressors that are not being tested. Or $\boldsymbol{X}_1$ might be regressors that are known to be orthogonal to the regressand, and $\boldsymbol{X}_2$ might be regressors that are not orthogonal to it, a situation which arises very frequently when we wish to test nonlinear regression models; see Chapter 6.

Now consider another regression,

$$\boldsymbol{M}_1\boldsymbol{y} = \boldsymbol{M}_1\boldsymbol{X}_2\boldsymbol{\beta}_2 + \text{residuals}, \tag{1.19}$$

where $\boldsymbol{M}_1$ is the matrix that projects off $\mathcal{S}(\boldsymbol{X}_1)$. In (1.19) we have first regressed $\boldsymbol{y}$ and each of the k_2 columns of $\boldsymbol{X}_2$ on $\boldsymbol{X}_1$ and then regressed the vector of residuals $\boldsymbol{M}_1\boldsymbol{y}$ on the $n \times k_2$ matrix of residuals $\boldsymbol{M}_1\boldsymbol{X}_2$. The FWL Theorem tells us that the residuals from regressions (1.18) and (1.19), and the OLS estimates of $\boldsymbol{\beta}_2$ from those two regressions, will be *numerically identical.* Geometrically, in regression (1.18) we project $\boldsymbol{y}$ directly onto $\mathcal{S}(\boldsymbol{X}) \equiv \mathcal{S}(\boldsymbol{X}_1, \boldsymbol{X}_2)$, while in regression (1.19) we first project $\boldsymbol{y}$ and all of the columns of $\boldsymbol{X}_2$ off $\mathcal{S}(\boldsymbol{X}_1)$ and then project the residuals $\boldsymbol{M}_1\boldsymbol{y}$ onto the span of the matrix of residuals, $\mathcal{S}(\boldsymbol{M}_1\boldsymbol{X}_2)$. The FWL Theorem tells us that these two apparently rather different procedures actually amount to the same thing.

The FWL Theorem can be proved in several different ways. One standard proof is based on the algebra of partitioned matrices. First, observe that the estimate of $\boldsymbol{\beta}_2$ from (1.19) is

$$\left(\boldsymbol{X}_2^{\top}\boldsymbol{M}_1\boldsymbol{X}_2\right)^{-1}\boldsymbol{X}_2^{\top}\boldsymbol{M}_1\boldsymbol{y}. \tag{1.20}$$

This simple expression, which we will make use of many times, follows immediately from substituting $\boldsymbol{M}_1\boldsymbol{X}_2$ for $\boldsymbol{X}$ and $\boldsymbol{M}_1\boldsymbol{y}$ for $\boldsymbol{y}$ in expression (1.04) for the vector of OLS estimates. The algebraic proof would now use results on the inverse of a partitioned matrix (see Appendix A) to demonstrate that the OLS estimate from (1.18), $\hat{\boldsymbol{\beta}}_2$, is identical to (1.20) and would then go on to demonstrate that the two sets of residuals are likewise identical. We leave this as an exercise for the reader and proceed, first with a simple semi-geometric proof and then with a more detailed discussion of the geometry of the situation.

Let $\hat{\boldsymbol{\beta}} \equiv [\hat{\boldsymbol{\beta}}_1 \vdots \hat{\boldsymbol{\beta}}_2]$ denote the OLS estimates from (1.18). Then

$$\boldsymbol{y} = \boldsymbol{P}_X\boldsymbol{y} + \boldsymbol{M}_X\boldsymbol{y} = \boldsymbol{X}_1\hat{\boldsymbol{\beta}}_1 + \boldsymbol{X}_2\hat{\boldsymbol{\beta}}_2 + \boldsymbol{M}_X\boldsymbol{y}. \tag{1.21}$$

Multiplying $\boldsymbol{y}$ and the right-hand expression in (1.21), which is equal to $\boldsymbol{y}$, by $\boldsymbol{X}_2^\top\boldsymbol{M}_1$, where $\boldsymbol{M}_1 \equiv \mathbf{I} - \boldsymbol{X}_1(\boldsymbol{X}_1^\top\boldsymbol{X}_1)^{-1}\boldsymbol{X}_1^\top$, we obtain

$$\boldsymbol{X}_2^\top\boldsymbol{M}_1\boldsymbol{y} = \boldsymbol{X}_2^\top\boldsymbol{M}_1\boldsymbol{X}_2\hat{\boldsymbol{\beta}}_2. \tag{1.22}$$

The first term on the right-hand side of (1.21) has dropped out because $\boldsymbol{M}_1$ annihilates $\boldsymbol{X}_1$. The last term has dropped out because $\boldsymbol{M}_1\boldsymbol{X}_2 = \boldsymbol{X}_2 - \boldsymbol{P}_1\boldsymbol{X}_2$ belongs to $\mathcal{S}(\boldsymbol{X})$, which implies that

$$\boldsymbol{M}_X\boldsymbol{M}_1\boldsymbol{X}_2 = \mathbf{0}. \tag{1.23}$$

Solving (1.22) for $\hat{\boldsymbol{\beta}}_2$, we see immediately that

$$\hat{\boldsymbol{\beta}}_2 = \left(\boldsymbol{X}_2^\top\boldsymbol{M}_1\boldsymbol{X}_2\right)^{-1}\boldsymbol{X}_2^\top\boldsymbol{M}_1\boldsymbol{y},$$

which is expression (1.20). This proves the second part of the theorem.

If we had multiplied (1.21) by $\boldsymbol{M}_1$ instead of by $\boldsymbol{X}_2^\top\boldsymbol{M}_1$, we would have obtained

$$\boldsymbol{M}_1\boldsymbol{y} = \boldsymbol{M}_1\boldsymbol{X}_2\hat{\boldsymbol{\beta}}_2 + \boldsymbol{M}_X\boldsymbol{y}. \tag{1.24}$$

The regressand here is the regressand from regression (1.19). Because $\hat{\boldsymbol{\beta}}_2$ is the estimate of $\boldsymbol{\beta}_2$ from (1.19), the first term on the right-hand side of (1.24) is the vector of fitted values from that regression. Thus the second term must be the vector of residuals from regression (1.19). But $\boldsymbol{M}_X\boldsymbol{y}$ is also the vector of residuals from regression (1.18), and this therefore proves the first part of the theorem.

Let us now consider the geometry of the situation in more detail. Because $\mathcal{S}(\boldsymbol{X}_1)$ and $\mathcal{S}(\boldsymbol{X}_2)$ are not in general mutually orthogonal subspaces, the first two terms in the right-hand expression in (1.21), $\boldsymbol{X}_1\hat{\boldsymbol{\beta}}_1$ and $\boldsymbol{X}_2\hat{\boldsymbol{\beta}}_2$, are not in general mutually orthogonal either. If we decompose $\boldsymbol{X}_2\hat{\boldsymbol{\beta}}_2$ as follows:

$$\boldsymbol{X}_2\hat{\boldsymbol{\beta}}_2 = \boldsymbol{P}_1\boldsymbol{X}_2\hat{\boldsymbol{\beta}}_2 + \boldsymbol{M}_1\boldsymbol{X}_2\hat{\boldsymbol{\beta}}_2 \tag{1.25}$$

and regroup the terms of (1.21), we obtain

$$\begin{aligned}
\boldsymbol{y} &= (\boldsymbol{X}_1\hat{\boldsymbol{\beta}}_1 + \boldsymbol{P}_1\boldsymbol{X}_2\hat{\boldsymbol{\beta}}_2) + \boldsymbol{M}_1\boldsymbol{X}_2\hat{\boldsymbol{\beta}}_2 + \boldsymbol{M}_X\boldsymbol{y} \\
&= \boldsymbol{P}_1(\boldsymbol{X}_1\hat{\boldsymbol{\beta}}_1 + \boldsymbol{X}_2\hat{\boldsymbol{\beta}}_2) + \boldsymbol{M}_1\boldsymbol{X}_2\hat{\boldsymbol{\beta}}_2 + \boldsymbol{M}_X\boldsymbol{y} \\
&= \boldsymbol{P}_1\boldsymbol{y} + \boldsymbol{M}_1\boldsymbol{P}_X\boldsymbol{y} + \boldsymbol{M}_X\boldsymbol{y},
\end{aligned} \tag{1.26}$$

because $\boldsymbol{X}_1\hat{\boldsymbol{\beta}}_1 + \boldsymbol{P}_1\boldsymbol{X}_2\hat{\boldsymbol{\beta}}_2$ is evidently $\boldsymbol{P}_1\boldsymbol{P}_X\boldsymbol{y} = \boldsymbol{P}_1\boldsymbol{y}$, while $\boldsymbol{M}_1\boldsymbol{X}_2\hat{\boldsymbol{\beta}}_2$ is equal to $\boldsymbol{M}_1(\boldsymbol{X}_1\hat{\boldsymbol{\beta}}_1+\boldsymbol{X}_2\hat{\boldsymbol{\beta}}_2)$, which can be rewritten as $\boldsymbol{M}_1\boldsymbol{P}_X\boldsymbol{y}$. The last expression in (1.26) makes it clear that $\boldsymbol{y}$ is the sum of three mutually orthogonal terms. The result (1.26) then implies that

$$\boldsymbol{M}_1\boldsymbol{y} = \boldsymbol{y} - \boldsymbol{P}_1\boldsymbol{y} = \boldsymbol{M}_1\boldsymbol{P}_X\boldsymbol{y} + \boldsymbol{M}_X\boldsymbol{y}. \tag{1.27}$$

Consider now Figure 1.7, in which this is illustrated for the simplest case to which the theorem applies, namely, the case $k_1 = k_2 = 1$. In panel (a) of the figure, which is intended to represent three dimensions, the vector $\boldsymbol{y}$ is shown along with its projection $\boldsymbol{P}_X\boldsymbol{y}$ onto the span of the two regressors $\boldsymbol{X}_1$ and $\boldsymbol{X}_2$, depicted as the horizontal plane, and the complementary (vertical)

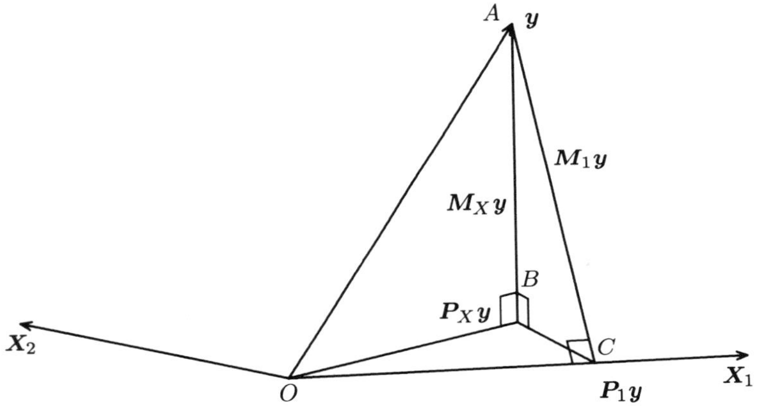

(a) Two projections of $\boldsymbol{y}$

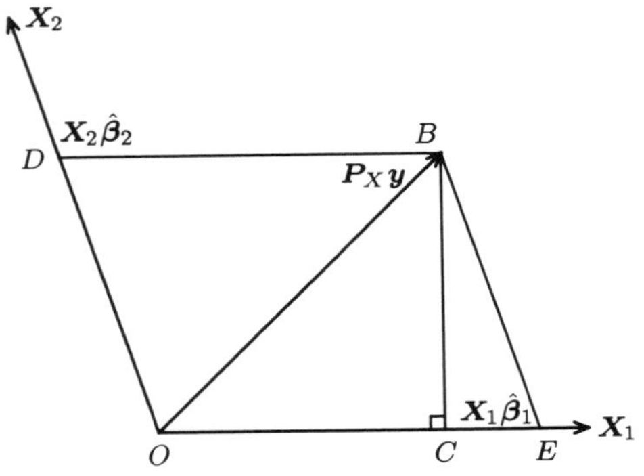

(b) The span $\mathcal{S}(\boldsymbol{X})$ of the regressors

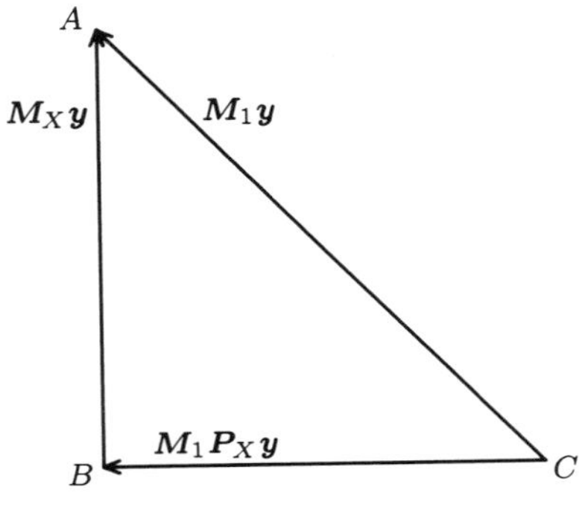

(c) The decomposition of $\boldsymbol{M}_1\boldsymbol{y}$

Figure 1.7 The Frisch-Waugh-Lovell Theorem

projection $\boldsymbol{M}_X\boldsymbol{y}$. Also shown is the projection $\boldsymbol{P}_1\boldsymbol{y}$ of $\boldsymbol{y}$ onto the direction of the first regressor $\boldsymbol{X}_1$ and its complement $\boldsymbol{M}_1\boldsymbol{y}$. Observe that the triangle ABC, formed by the point $\boldsymbol{y}$ itself, the point $\boldsymbol{P}_X\boldsymbol{y}$, and the point $\boldsymbol{P}_1\boldsymbol{y}$, is a right-angled triangle in the vertical plane perpendicular to the direction of $\boldsymbol{X}_1$.

The two-dimensional panel (b) depicts the horizontal plane that is the range $\mathcal{S}(\boldsymbol{X})$ of the projection $\boldsymbol{P}_X$. The oblique decomposition of $\boldsymbol{P}_X\boldsymbol{y}$ as $\boldsymbol{X}_1\hat{\boldsymbol{\beta}}_1 + \boldsymbol{X}_2\hat{\boldsymbol{\beta}}_2$ is shown via the parallelogram $ODBE$, where the sides OE and DB represent $\boldsymbol{X}_1\hat{\boldsymbol{\beta}}_1$, and the sides OD and EB represent $\boldsymbol{X}_2\hat{\boldsymbol{\beta}}_2$. The triangle EBC shows the decomposition (1.25) of $\boldsymbol{X}_2\hat{\boldsymbol{\beta}}_2$ into the sum of $\boldsymbol{P}_1\boldsymbol{X}_2\hat{\boldsymbol{\beta}}_2$, represented by EC, and $\boldsymbol{M}_1\boldsymbol{X}_2\hat{\boldsymbol{\beta}}_2 = \boldsymbol{M}_1\boldsymbol{P}_X\boldsymbol{y}$, represented by CB. Note that both of these vectors lie in $\mathcal{S}(\boldsymbol{X})$. The fact that the second of these does so follows from equation (1.23). Lastly, panel (c) shows in two dimensions the triangle ABC. This represents the decomposition of $\boldsymbol{M}_1\boldsymbol{y}$, given in (1.27), into $\boldsymbol{M}_1\boldsymbol{P}_X\boldsymbol{y}$, corresponding to CB, and $\boldsymbol{M}_X\boldsymbol{y}$, corresponding to BA.

This last panel can now be used to illustrate the FWL Theorem. The point to grasp is that the orthogonal decomposition (1.27) of $\boldsymbol{M}_1\boldsymbol{y}$ into the sum of $\boldsymbol{M}_X\boldsymbol{y}$ and $\boldsymbol{M}_1\boldsymbol{P}_X\boldsymbol{y} = \boldsymbol{M}_1\boldsymbol{X}_2\hat{\boldsymbol{\beta}}_2$ is the orthogonal decomposition that is effected by the regression of $\boldsymbol{M}_1\boldsymbol{y}$, the vector decomposed, on the columns of $\boldsymbol{M}_1\boldsymbol{X}_2$, in short, the regression (1.19). This should be clear geometrically; algebraically, it follows, first, from the fact that the term $\boldsymbol{M}_1\boldsymbol{X}_2\hat{\boldsymbol{\beta}}_2$ is evidently a linear combination of the columns of $\boldsymbol{M}_1\boldsymbol{X}_2$ and, second, from the fact that the other term, $\boldsymbol{M}_X\boldsymbol{y}$, is orthogonal to all these columns. This second fact follows from the relation $\boldsymbol{M}_X\boldsymbol{M}_1 = \boldsymbol{M}_X$, which is true because $\mathcal{S}^\perp(\boldsymbol{X})$ is a subspace of $\mathcal{S}^\perp(\boldsymbol{X}_1)$, for then, as we saw in equation (1.23),

$$\boldsymbol{M}_X\boldsymbol{M}_1\boldsymbol{X}_2 = \boldsymbol{M}_X\boldsymbol{X}_2 = \mathbf{0},$$

which implies that $\boldsymbol{y}^\top\boldsymbol{M}_X\boldsymbol{M}_1\boldsymbol{X}_2 = \mathbf{0}$. Thus we have shown that

$$\boldsymbol{P}_{M_1X_2}\boldsymbol{M}_1\boldsymbol{y} = \boldsymbol{M}_1\boldsymbol{X}_2\hat{\boldsymbol{\beta}}_2 \quad \text{and} \tag{1.28}$$

$$\boldsymbol{M}_{M_1X_2}\boldsymbol{M}_1\boldsymbol{y} = \boldsymbol{M}_X\boldsymbol{y}. \tag{1.29}$$

One part of the FWL Theorem states that regressions (1.18) and (1.19) have the same residuals. These common residuals are constituted by the vector $\boldsymbol{M}_X\boldsymbol{y}$, as is plain from (1.21) for regression (1.18) and from (1.29) for regression (1.19). The other part of the theorem states that the estimates of $\hat{\boldsymbol{\beta}}_2$ are the same from the two regressions. This is now immediate from (1.28), in which the $\hat{\boldsymbol{\beta}}_2$ from regression (1.18) yields the vector of fitted values $\boldsymbol{P}_{M_1X_2}\boldsymbol{M}_1\boldsymbol{y}$ for regression (1.19).

We will encounter many applications of the FWL Theorem throughout this book. A simple example is the use of dummy variables for seasonal adjustment, which was Lovell's (1963) original application. Many economic time series that are collected on a monthly or quarterly basis display systematic seasonal variation. One way to model this is to add a set of **seasonal dummy**

variables to a regression. For example, suppose that the data are quarterly and that seasonal dummy variables $\boldsymbol{D}_1$ through $\boldsymbol{D}_3$ are defined as follows:

$$\boldsymbol{D}_1 = \begin{bmatrix} 1 \\ 0 \\ 0 \\ -1 \\ 1 \\ 0 \\ 0 \\ -1 \\ \vdots \end{bmatrix} \qquad \boldsymbol{D}_2 = \begin{bmatrix} 0 \\ 1 \\ 0 \\ -1 \\ 0 \\ 1 \\ 0 \\ -1 \\ \vdots \end{bmatrix} \qquad \boldsymbol{D}_3 = \begin{bmatrix} 0 \\ 0 \\ 1 \\ -1 \\ 0 \\ 0 \\ 1 \\ -1 \\ \vdots \end{bmatrix}.$$

Notice that these dummy variables have been defined in such a way that they sum to zero over each full year. Consider the regressions

$$\boldsymbol{y} = \boldsymbol{X\beta} + \boldsymbol{D\gamma} + \text{residuals} \quad \text{and} \tag{1.30}$$

$$\boldsymbol{M_D y} = \boldsymbol{M_D X\beta} + \text{residuals}, \tag{1.31}$$

where $\boldsymbol{D} \equiv [\boldsymbol{D}_1 \;\; \boldsymbol{D}_2 \;\; \boldsymbol{D}_3]$ and $\boldsymbol{M_D}$ is the matrix that projects orthogonally onto $\mathcal{S}^{\perp}(\boldsymbol{D})$. In (1.30) we include seasonal dummy variables in a regression in which all the data are unadjusted. In (1.31) we seasonally adjust the data by regressing them on dummy variables and then run a regression on the "seasonally adjusted" data. The FWL Theorem implies that these two procedures will yield identical estimates of $\boldsymbol{\beta}$.

The regressand $\boldsymbol{M_D y}$ and regressors $\boldsymbol{M_D X}$ that appear in (1.31) can be thought of as seasonally adjusted versions of $\boldsymbol{y}$ and $\boldsymbol{X}$, because all of the variation in $\boldsymbol{y}$ and $\boldsymbol{X}$ that can be attributed to systematic differences in the quarterly means has been eliminated from $\boldsymbol{M_D y}$ and $\boldsymbol{M_D X}$. Thus the equivalence of (1.30) and (1.31) is often used to justify the idea that it does not matter whether one uses "raw" or seasonally adjusted data in estimating a regression model with time-series data. Unfortunately, such a conclusion is unwarranted. Official seasonal adjustment procedures are almost never based on regression; using official seasonally adjusted data is therefore *not* equivalent to using residuals from regression on a set of dummy variables. Moreover, if (1.30) is not a sensible specification (and it would not be if, for example, the seasonal pattern were not constant over time), then (1.31) is not a sensible specification either. Seasonality is actually a difficult practical problem in applied work with time series data; see Chapter 19.

In this book, our principal use of the FWL Theorem will be to facilitate the derivation of theoretical results. It is generally much easier to deal with an equation like (1.19), in which there is a single matrix of regressors, rather than one like (1.18), in which the matrix of regressors is partitioned. An example of how the FWL Theorem may be used to derive theoretical results is found in Section 1.6.

1.5 COMPUTING OLS ESTIMATES

In this section, we will briefly discuss how OLS estimates are actually calculated using digital computers. This is a subject that most students of econometrics, and not a few econometricians, are largely unfamiliar with. The vast majority of the time, well-written regression programs will yield reliable results, and applied econometricians therefore do not need to worry about how those results are actually obtained. But not all programs for OLS regression are written well, and even the best programs can run into difficulties if the data are sufficiently ill-conditioned. We therefore believe that every user of software for least squares regression should have some idea of what the software is actually doing. Moreover, the particular method for OLS regression on which we will focus is interesting from a purely theoretical perspective.

Before we discuss algorithms for least squares regression, we must say something about how digital computers represent real numbers and how this affects the accuracy of calculations carried out on such computers. With rare exceptions, the quantities of interest in regression problems — $\boldsymbol{y}$, $\boldsymbol{X}$, $\hat{\boldsymbol{\beta}}$, and so on — are real numbers rather than integers or rational numbers. In general, it requires an infinite number of digits to represent a real number exactly, and this is clearly infeasible. Trying to represent each number by as many digits as are necessary to approximate it with "sufficient" accuracy would mean using a different number of digits to represent different numbers; this would be difficult to do and would greatly slow down calculations. Computers therefore normally deal with real numbers by approximating them using a *fixed* number of digits (or, more accurately, bits, which correspond to digits in base 2). But in order to handle numbers that may be very large or very small, the computer has to represent real numbers as **floating-point numbers**.[6]

The basic idea of floating-point numbers is that any real number x can always be written in the form

$$(b^c)m,$$

where m, the **mantissa** (or fractional part), is a signed number less than 1 in absolute value, b is the **base** of the system of floating-point numbers, and c is the **exponent**, which may be of either sign. Thus 663.725 can be written using base 10 as

$$0.663725 \times 10^3.$$

Storing the mantissa 663725 and the exponent 3 separately provides a convenient way for the computer to store the number 663.725. The advantage of this scheme is that very large and very small numbers can be stored just as easily as numbers of more moderate magnitudes; numbers such as $-0.192382 \times 10^{-23}$ and 0.983443×10^{17} can be handled just as easily as a number like 3.42 $(= 0.342 \times 10^1)$.

[6] Our introduction to this topic is necessarily very superficial. For more details, see Knuth (1981) or Sterbenz (1974).

In practice, modern computers do not use 10 as a base; instead, they always use a base that is a power of 2 (2, 4, 8, and 16 are all employed as bases in computers that are quite widely used), but the principle is the same. The only complication is that numbers which can be represented exactly in base 10 often (indeed, usually) cannot be represented exactly in the base used by the computer. Thus it is quite common to enter a value of, say, 6.8, into a computer program and see it printed out as 6.799999. What has happened is that 6.8 has been converted into the base used by the computer and then converted back again for printing, and a small error was introduced during this process.

Very few real numbers can be represented exactly using any base, and even fewer numbers can be represented exactly using a particular base. Thus most numbers can be stored only as approximations. How accurate such an approximation is depends principally on the number of bits used to store the mantissa. Typically, programmers have two choices: **single precision** and **double precision**. On most computers, the mantissa of a single-precision floating-point number will be able to hold at most 21 or 22 significant bits, while that of a double-precision number will be able to hold between 50 and 54 significant bits. These translate into 6 or maybe 7 and roughly 15 or 16 decimal digits, respectively.[7]

The chief problem with floating-point arithmetic is not that numbers are stored as approximations. Since most economic data are not accurate to as many as six digits anyway, single precision is generally adequate to represent such data. The real difficulty is that when arithmetic operations are carried out on floating-point numbers, errors build up. As we will see below, these errors can easily get so large that the answer may be accurate to no digits at all! The worst type of problem occurs when numbers of different sizes and signs are added together. For example, consider the expression

$$2,393,121 - 1.0235 - 2,393,120, \tag{1.32}$$

which is equal to -0.0235. Suppose we attempt to evaluate this expression using a computer that uses base 10 and stores six digits in the mantissa. If we evaluate it in the order in which it is written, we obtain the answer

$$0.239312 \times 10^7 - 0.102350 \times 10^1 - 0.239312 \times 10^7 \cong 0.000000 \times 10^1,$$

[7] Different computers store floating-point numbers in different ways. Most modern computers use 32-bit single-precision and 64-bit double-precision floating-point numbers. Some of these bits are used to store the exponent and the sign of the mantissa. Depending on the base employed, some of the bits used to store the mantissa may not always contain useful information, hence the numbers in the text for meaningful bits in the mantissa. A few computers use more than 32 bits to represent single-precision numbers: 36, 48, 60, and 64 are all in use. On these machines, both single- and double-precision arithmetic will be correspondingly more accurate than on 32-bit machines.

or zero, since $0.239312 \times 10^7 - 0.102350 \times 10^1 \cong 0.239312 \times 10^7$, where "$\cong$" denotes equality in the arithmetic used by the computer. Alternatively, we could change the order of evaluation so as to obtain

$$0.239312 \times 10^7 - 0.239312 \times 10^7 - 0.102350 \times 10^1 \cong -0.102350 \times 10^1,$$

or -1.0235. Neither of these answers would be acceptable for many purposes.

Obviously, we can make this problem less severe by using double precision instead of single precision. In this case, if we had used floating-point numbers with at least 11 digits in the mantissa, we would have obtained the correct answer. But it is clear that no matter how many digits we use in our calculations, there will always be problems similar to (1.32) but with even larger and smaller numbers involved, where those numbers are such that it is impossible for the computer to obtain an acceptable answer. Such problems may be referred to loosely as **ill-conditioned**.

The fundamental limitation of floating-point arithmetic that we have just discussed is of considerable practical importance to econometricians. Suppose, for example, that we wish to calculate the sample mean and variance of a sequence of numbers y_t, $t = 1, \ldots, n$. Every student of statistics knows that

$$\bar{y} = \frac{1}{n}\sum_{t=1}^{n} y_t$$

and that an unbiased estimate of the variance of the y_t's is

$$\frac{1}{n-1}\sum_{t=1}^{n}(y_t - \bar{y})^2 \tag{1.33}$$

$$= \frac{1}{n-1}\left(\sum_{t=1}^{n} y_t^2 - n\bar{y}^2\right). \tag{1.34}$$

The equality here is true algebraically, but it is *not* true when calculations are done using floating-point arithmetic. The first expression, (1.33), can in general be evaluated reasonably accurately, so long as the y_t's are not greatly different in magnitude from $\bar{y}$. Expression (1.34), however, involves subtracting $n\bar{y}^2$ from $\sum y_t^2$, and when $\bar{y}$ is large relative to the variance of the y_t's, the difference between these two quantities can be very large. Thus, in this situation, expression (1.34) may calculate the variance very inaccurately. Such expressions are often referred to as **numerically unstable**, because they are prone to error when evaluated using floating-point arithmetic.

The magnitude of numerical problems that one can encounter may be illustrated by a simple numerical example. We first generated 1000 pseudo-random numbers from the normal distribution (see Chapter 21) and then

Table 1.1 Absolute Errors in Calculating the Sample Variance

μ	(1.33) single	(1.33) double	(1.34) single	(1.34) double
0	0.880×10^{-4}	0.209×10^{-13}	0.880×10^{-4}	0.209×10^{-13}
10	0.868×10^{-4}	0.207×10^{-13}	0.126×10^{0}	0.281×10^{-11}
10^2	0.553×10^{-4}	0.208×10^{-13}	0.197×10^{1}	0.478×10^{-9}
10^3	0.756×10^{-3}	0.194×10^{-13}	0.410×10^{2}	0.859×10^{-8}
10^4	0.204×10^{0}	0.179×10^{-13}	0.302×10^{4}	0.687×10^{-6}
10^5	0.452×10^{2}	0.180×10^{-14}	0.733×10^{6}	0.201×10^{-3}

normalized them so that the sample mean was exactly μ and the sample variance was exactly unity.[8] We then calculated the sample variance for various values of μ using both single and double precision and using both (1.33) and (1.34).[9] The results, expressed as the absolute value of the *difference* between the calculated variance and the true variance of unity (and presented using floating-point notation, since these differences varied greatly in magnitude), are presented in Table 1.1.

This example illustrates two important points. First of all, except when $\mu = 0$ so that no serious numerical problems arise for either formula, expression (1.33) yields much more accurate results than expression (1.34), as our previous discussion suggested. Secondly, double-precision arithmetic yields very much more accurate results than single-precision arithmetic. One is actually better off to evaluate the numerically unstable expression (1.34) using double precision than to evaluate the numerically stable expression (1.33) using single precision. The best results are of course achieved by evaluating expression (1.33) using double-precision arithmetic. With this approach, accuracy is excellent for all values of μ in the table (it does begin to deteriorate gradually once μ significantly exceeds 10^6). In contrast, when μ is 10^5, both formulas yield nonsense when evaluated using single-precision arithmetic, and

[8] Actually, the normalization was not *exact*, but it was extremely accurate because we used **quadruple precision**, which is about twice as accurate as double precision. Quadruple-precision arithmetic is not available on many computers (especially smaller computers) and is typically much slower than double-precision arithmetic, but it can yield much more accurate results. We are confident that the series we started with does indeed have mean μ and variance 1 to at least 30 decimal digits.

[9] All calculations were performed using FORTRAN VS on an IBM mainframe running VM/CMS. Results on other machines, even if they also use 32 and 64 bits to represent single- and double-precision floating-point numbers, would be somewhat different. In particular, most personal computers would give more accurate results.

(1.34) yields a seriously inaccurate answer even when double precision is employed.

We hope this example makes it clear that attempts to compute estimates by evaluating standard algebraic expressions without regard for issues of machine precision and numerical stability are extremely unwise. The best rule to follow is always to use software written by experts who have taken such considerations into account. If such software is not available, one should probably always use double precision, with higher precision (if available) being used for sensitive calculations.[10] As the example indicates, even numerically stable procedures may give nonsense results with 32-bit single precision if the data are ill-conditioned.

Let us now return to the principal topic of this section, which is the computation of ordinary least squares estimates. Many good references on this subject exist — see, among others, Chambers (1977), Kennedy and Gentle (1980), Maindonald (1984), Farebrother (1988), and Golub and Van Loan (1989) — and we will therefore not go into many details.

The obvious way to obtain $\hat{\boldsymbol{\beta}}$ is first to form a matrix of sums of squares and cross-products of the regressors and the regressand or, equivalently, the matrix $\boldsymbol{X}^\top\boldsymbol{X}$ and the vector $\boldsymbol{X}^\top\boldsymbol{y}$. One would then invert the former by a general matrix inversion routine and postmultiply $(\boldsymbol{X}^\top\boldsymbol{X})^{-1}$ by $\boldsymbol{X}^\top\boldsymbol{y}$. Unfortunately, this procedure has all the disadvantages of expression (1.34). It may work satisfactorily if double precision is used throughout, all the columns of $\boldsymbol{X}$ are similar in magnitude, and the $\boldsymbol{X}^\top\boldsymbol{X}$ matrix is not too close to being singular, but it cannot be recommended for general use.

There are two principal approaches to computing least squares estimates that can be recommended. One approach is essentially a more sophisticated version of the naive one just described. It still involves constructing a matrix of sums of squares and cross-products of the regressors and regressand, but this is done in a way that reduces numerical problems. One good way to avoid such problems is to subtract the means of all variables before the squares and cross-products are taken. Doing this requires two passes through the data, however, which can be undesirable if the data set is too large to fit in the computer's main memory, and an alternative technique that is almost as accurate may be used instead; see Maindonald (1984). With either of these techniques, the original matrix of sums of squares and cross-products is then reconstructed, and the normal equations are subsequently solved using either a variant of the Cholesky decomposition or conventional Gaussian elimination. It is important for numerical accuracy to solve the normal equations, which

[10] A classic example is calculating an inner product. This is normally done in a loop, with the value of the inner product being accumulated in a scalar variable. The numerical properties of such a procedure can be greatly improved by storing this variable in the highest possible precision, even if all the other calculations are done using less precise arithmetic.

can produce the inverse of $\boldsymbol{X}^\top\boldsymbol{X}$ as a by-product, rather than simply to invert $\boldsymbol{X}^\top\boldsymbol{X}$ and then form $\hat{\boldsymbol{\beta}}$ by multiplication. Using the Cholesky decomposition takes advantage of the fact that $\boldsymbol{X}^\top\boldsymbol{X}$ is a positive definite, symmetric matrix and may therefore be somewhat more efficient than Gaussian elimination. For details, see Maindonald (1984).

The second approach to computing least squares estimates involves finding an **orthonormal basis** for the subspace spanned by the columns of $\boldsymbol{X}$. This is another $n \times k$ matrix, say $\boldsymbol{Q}$, with the properties that $\mathcal{S}(\boldsymbol{Q}) = \mathcal{S}(\boldsymbol{X})$ and $\boldsymbol{Q}^\top\boldsymbol{Q} = \mathbf{I}$. This approach is the one we will focus on, partly because it yields the most accurate results (although at a significant penalty in terms of computer time) and partly because it is interesting from a theoretical perspective. It is the only approach that is recommended by Chambers (1977), and it is also the approach that Maindonald (1984) recommends if accuracy is of paramount importance. Readers should consult these references for the many details that our discussion will omit.

For any matrix of regressors $\boldsymbol{X}$ with rank k, it is possible to perform what is called a **QR decomposition**. This means finding an $n \times k$ matrix $\boldsymbol{Q}$ and a $k \times k$ upper-triangular matrix $\boldsymbol{R}$ such that

$$\boldsymbol{X} = \boldsymbol{QR} \quad \text{and} \quad \boldsymbol{Q}^\top\boldsymbol{Q} = \mathbf{I}. \tag{1.35}$$

The second condition here implies that the columns of $\boldsymbol{Q}$ are orthonormal: They each have Euclidean length unity, and they are mutually orthogonal. The fact that $\boldsymbol{R}$ is triangular implies that the columns of $\boldsymbol{Q}$ are related recursively. The first column of $\boldsymbol{Q}$ is just the first column of $\boldsymbol{X}$, rescaled to have length unity; the second column of $\boldsymbol{Q}$ is a linear transformation of the first two columns of $\boldsymbol{X}$ that is orthogonal to the first column of $\boldsymbol{Q}$ and also has length unity; and so on. There are several ways to find $\boldsymbol{Q}$ and $\boldsymbol{R}$, of which the two principal ones are the Gram-Schmidt method and the Householder transformation. These are computationally quite similar, and descriptions may be found in the Chambers and Maindonald references. Both techniques are simple and numerically stable, provided that a method is available for dealing with cases in which $\boldsymbol{X}$ does not have full rank.

Deciding when $\boldsymbol{X}$ does not have full rank is a difficult problem for every least squares algorithm, since because of round-off errors computers cannot reliably distinguish between numbers that are actually zero and numbers that are very close to zero. This is one of the reasons for which it is important that the data be scaled similarly. When m columns of $\boldsymbol{X}$ are linearly dependent on the remaining columns, the algorithm must be modified so that $\boldsymbol{Q}$ has $k-m$ columns and $\boldsymbol{R}$ is $(k-m) \times k$. The estimates $\hat{\boldsymbol{\beta}}$ are then usually made unique by arbitrarily setting the coefficients of the last m of the linearly dependent regressors to zero.

Let us suppose that we have found $\boldsymbol{Q}$ and $\boldsymbol{R}$ which satisfy (1.35). It is then very easy to calculate all the quantities that interest us. The regression function $\boldsymbol{X\beta}$ may be written as $\boldsymbol{QR\beta} = \boldsymbol{Q\gamma}$, and it is easy to see that the

OLS estimate of γ is

$$\hat{\gamma} = (\boldsymbol{Q}^\top\boldsymbol{Q})^{-1}\boldsymbol{Q}^\top\boldsymbol{y} = \boldsymbol{Q}^\top\boldsymbol{y},$$

which is trivial to compute. It is equally easy to compute the fitted values $\boldsymbol{Q}\hat{\gamma}$ and the residuals

$$\hat{\boldsymbol{u}} = \boldsymbol{y} - \boldsymbol{Q}\hat{\gamma} = \boldsymbol{y} - \boldsymbol{Q}\boldsymbol{Q}^\top\boldsymbol{y}. \tag{1.36}$$

Thus, if we are simply interested in residuals and/or fitted values, we do not need to compute $\hat{\boldsymbol{\beta}}$ at all.

Notice from (1.36) that the projection matrices $\boldsymbol{P}_X$ and $\boldsymbol{M}_X$ are equal to $\boldsymbol{Q}\boldsymbol{Q}^\top$ and $\mathbf{I} - \boldsymbol{Q}\boldsymbol{Q}^\top$, respectively. The simplicity of these expressions follows from the fact that $\boldsymbol{Q}$ forms an orthonormal basis for $\mathcal{S}(\boldsymbol{X})$. Geometrically, nothing would change in any of the figures we have drawn if we used $\boldsymbol{Q}$ instead of $\boldsymbol{X}$ as the matrix of regressors, since $\mathcal{S}(\boldsymbol{Q}) = \mathcal{S}(\boldsymbol{X})$. If we were to show the columns of $\boldsymbol{Q}$ in the figures, each column would be a point in $\mathcal{S}(\boldsymbol{X})$ located on the unit sphere (i.e., the sphere with radius one centered at the origin) and at right angles to the points representing the other columns of $\boldsymbol{Q}$.

In order to calculate $\hat{\boldsymbol{\beta}}$ and $(\boldsymbol{X}^\top\boldsymbol{X})^{-1}$, which, along with the residuals and the fitted values, allow us to calculate all the main quantities of interest, we make use of the facts that $\hat{\boldsymbol{\beta}} = \boldsymbol{R}^{-1}\hat{\gamma}$ and

$$(\boldsymbol{X}^\top\boldsymbol{X})^{-1} = (\boldsymbol{R}^\top\boldsymbol{Q}^\top\boldsymbol{Q}\boldsymbol{R})^{-1} = (\boldsymbol{R}^\top\boldsymbol{R})^{-1} = \boldsymbol{R}^{-1}(\boldsymbol{R}^{-1})^\top.$$

Thus, once we have computed $\boldsymbol{R}^{-1}$, we can very easily calculate the least squares estimates $\hat{\boldsymbol{\beta}}$ and their estimated covariance matrix (see Chapter 2). Since $\boldsymbol{R}$ is a triangular matrix, its inverse is very easily and cheaply computed; we do not even have to check for possible singularity, since $\boldsymbol{R}$ will fail to have full rank only if $\boldsymbol{X}$ does not have full rank, and that will already have shown up and been dealt with when we formed $\boldsymbol{Q}$ and $\boldsymbol{R}$.

The most costly part of these procedures is forming the matrices $\boldsymbol{Q}$ and $\boldsymbol{R}$ from $\boldsymbol{X}$. This requires a number of arithmetic operations that is roughly proportional to nk^2. Forming the matrix of sums and cross-products, which is the first step for methods based on solving the normal equations, also requires a number of operations proportional to nk^2, although the factor of proportionality is smaller. Thus linear regression by any method can become expensive when the number of regressors is large and/or the sample size is very large. If one is going to calculate many regressions using the same large data set, it makes sense to economize by doing the expensive calculations only once. Many regression packages allow users first to form the matrix of sums of squares and cross-products for all the variables in a data set and then to calculate estimates for a variety of regressions by retrieving the relevant rows and columns and using normal equation methods. If this approach is used, it is particularly important that the data be scaled so that the various regressors are not too dissimilar in mean and variance.

1.6 Influential Observations and Leverage

Each element of the vector of OLS estimates $\hat{\boldsymbol{\beta}}$ is simply a weighted average of the elements of the vector $\boldsymbol{y}$. To see this, define $\boldsymbol{c}_i$ as the ith row of the matrix $(\boldsymbol{X}^\top\boldsymbol{X})^{-1}\boldsymbol{X}^\top$ and observe from (1.04) that

$$\hat{\beta}_i = \boldsymbol{c}_i\boldsymbol{y}.$$

Since each element of $\hat{\boldsymbol{\beta}}$ is a *weighted* average, some observations may have a much greater influence on $\hat{\boldsymbol{\beta}}$ than others. If one or a few observations are extremely influential, in the sense that deleting them would change some elements of $\hat{\boldsymbol{\beta}}$ substantially, the careful econometrician will normally want to scrutinize the data carefully. It may be that these **influential observations** are erroneous or for some reason untypical of the rest of the sample. As we will see, even a single erroneous observation can have an enormous effect on $\hat{\boldsymbol{\beta}}$ in some cases. Thus it may be extremely important to identify and correct such observations if they are influential. Even if the data are all correct, the interpretation of the results may change substantially if it is known that one or a few observations are primarily responsible for those results, especially if those observations differ systematically in some way from the rest of the data.

The literature on detecting influential observations is relatively recent, and it has not yet been fully assimilated into econometric practice and available software packages. References include Belsley, Kuh, and Welsch (1980), Cook and Weisberg (1982), and Krasker, Kuh, and Welsch (1983). In this section, we merely introduce a few basic concepts and results with which all econometricians should be familiar. Proving those results provides a nice example of how useful the FWL Theorem can be.

The effect of a single observation on $\hat{\boldsymbol{\beta}}$ can be seen by comparing $\hat{\boldsymbol{\beta}}$ with $\hat{\boldsymbol{\beta}}^{(t)}$, the estimate of $\boldsymbol{\beta}$ that would be obtained if OLS were used on a sample from which the tth observation was omitted. The difference between $\hat{\boldsymbol{\beta}}$ and $\hat{\boldsymbol{\beta}}^{(t)}$ will turn out to depend crucially on the quantity

$$h_t \equiv \boldsymbol{X}_t\left(\boldsymbol{X}^\top\boldsymbol{X}\right)^{-1}\boldsymbol{X}_t^\top, \tag{1.37}$$

which is the tth diagonal element of the matrix $\boldsymbol{P}_X$. The notation h_t comes from the fact that $\boldsymbol{P}_X$ is sometimes referred to as the **hat matrix**; because $\hat{\boldsymbol{y}} \equiv \boldsymbol{P}_X\boldsymbol{y}$, $\boldsymbol{P}_X$ "puts a hat on" $\boldsymbol{y}$. Notice that h_t depends solely on the regressor matrix $\boldsymbol{X}$ and not at all on the regressand $\boldsymbol{y}$.

It is illuminating to rewrite h_t as

$$h_t = \boldsymbol{e}_t^\top\boldsymbol{P}_X\boldsymbol{e}_t = \|\boldsymbol{P}_X\boldsymbol{e}_t\|^2, \tag{1.38}$$

where $\boldsymbol{e}_t$ denotes the n–vector with 1 in the tth position and 0 everywhere else. Expression (1.38) follows from (1.37), the definition of $\boldsymbol{P}_X$ and the fact that $\boldsymbol{e}_t^\top\boldsymbol{X} = \boldsymbol{X}_t$. The right-most expression here shows that h_t is the squared length of a certain vector, which ensures that $h_t \geq 0$. Moreover, since $\|e_t\| = 1$, and since the length of the vector $P_X e_t$ can be no greater than the length of e_t itself, it must be the case that $h_t = \|P_X e_t\|^2 \leq 1$. Thus (1.38) makes it clear that

$$0 \leq h_t \leq 1. \tag{1.39}$$

Suppose that $\hat{u}_t$ denotes the tth element of the vector of least squares residuals $M_X y$. We may now state the fundamental result that

$$\hat{\beta}^{(t)} = \hat{\beta} - \left(\frac{1}{1-h_t}\right)(X^\top X)^{-1} X_t^\top \hat{u}_t. \tag{1.40}$$

This expression makes it clear that when $\hat{u}_t$ is large and/or when $1 - h_t$ is small, the effect of the tth observation on at least some elements of $\hat{\beta}$ is likely to be substantial. We will prove this result below.

It is particularly illuminating to see how omitting the tth observation from the regression affects the fitted value for that observation. From (1.40) it is easily derived that

$$X_t \hat{\beta}^{(t)} = X_t \hat{\beta} - \left(\frac{h_t}{1-h_t}\right)\hat{u}_t. \tag{1.41}$$

In practice it can be tedious, using (1.40), to check whether each observation is influential by seeing whether its omission substantially affects any of the $\hat{\beta}_i$'s. But an observation must certainly be influential if omitting it has a large effect on its own fitted value. From (1.41) we see that the change in the tth fitted value resulting from the omission of observation t is $-\hat{u}_t h_t/(1-h_t)$. It follows immediately that the change in the tth residual is

$$\left(\frac{h_t}{1-h_t}\right)\hat{u}_t. \tag{1.42}$$

An easy way to detect observations that are influential in the sense of affecting fitted values and residuals is thus to plot expression (1.42) against t.

These results suggest that we should examine the quantities h_t more closely. We have already established in (1.39) that the h_t's are all between 0 and 1. In fact, they sum to k, a result that is easily shown by using the properties of the trace operator (see Appendix A):

$$\begin{aligned}\sum_{t=1}^{n} h_t &= \operatorname{Tr}(P_X) = \operatorname{Tr}\big(X(X^\top X)^{-1}X^\top\big)\\ &= \operatorname{Tr}\big((X^\top X)^{-1}X^\top X\big) = \operatorname{Tr}(\mathbf{I}_k) = k.\end{aligned}$$

Thus, on average, the h_t's must equal k/n. When there is a constant term, no h_t can be less than $1/n$, a fact that is easily seen from (1.38), because if $\boldsymbol{X}$ simply consisted of a constant vector, $\boldsymbol{e}_t^\top \boldsymbol{P}_X \boldsymbol{e}_t$ would equal $1/n$. Even when there is no constant term, h_t can never be 0 unless every element of $\boldsymbol{X}_t$ is 0. However, it is evidently quite possible for h_t to equal 1. Suppose, for example, that one column of $\boldsymbol{X}$ is the dummy variable $\boldsymbol{e}_t$. In that case, $h_t = \boldsymbol{e}_t^\top \boldsymbol{P}_X \boldsymbol{e}_t = \boldsymbol{e}_t^\top \boldsymbol{e}_t = 1$.

It is interesting to see what happens when we add a dummy variable $\boldsymbol{e}_t$ to a regression. It turns out that $\hat{u}_t$ will equal zero and that the tth observation will have no effect at all on any coefficient except the one corresponding to the dummy variable. The latter simply takes on whatever value is needed to make $\hat{u}_t = 0$, and the remaining coefficients are those that minimize the SSR for the remaining $n-1$ observations. These results are easily established by using the FWL Theorem.

Consider the following two regressions, where for ease of notation the data have been ordered so that observation t is the last observation, and $\boldsymbol{y}_{(t)}$ and $\boldsymbol{X}_{(t)}$ denote the first $n-1$ rows of $\boldsymbol{y}$ and $\boldsymbol{X}$, respectively:

$$\begin{bmatrix} \boldsymbol{y}_{(t)} \\ y_t \end{bmatrix} = \begin{bmatrix} \boldsymbol{X}_{(t)} \\ \boldsymbol{X}_t \end{bmatrix} \boldsymbol{\beta} + \text{residuals}, \tag{1.43}$$

and

$$\begin{bmatrix} \boldsymbol{y}_{(t)} \\ y_t \end{bmatrix} = \begin{bmatrix} \boldsymbol{X}_{(t)} & \mathbf{0} \\ \boldsymbol{X}_t & 1 \end{bmatrix} \begin{bmatrix} \boldsymbol{\beta} \\ \alpha \end{bmatrix} + \text{residuals}. \tag{1.44}$$

Regression (1.43) is simply the regression of $\boldsymbol{y}$ on $\boldsymbol{X}$, which yields parameter estimates $\hat{\boldsymbol{\beta}}$ and least squares residuals $\hat{\boldsymbol{u}}$. Regression (1.44) is regression (1.43) with $\boldsymbol{e}_t$ as an additional regressor. By the FWL Theorem, the estimate of $\boldsymbol{\beta}$ from (1.44) must be identical to the estimate of $\boldsymbol{\beta}$ from the regression

$$\boldsymbol{M}_t \begin{bmatrix} \boldsymbol{y}_{(t)} \\ y_t \end{bmatrix} = \boldsymbol{M}_t \begin{bmatrix} \boldsymbol{X}_{(t)} \\ \boldsymbol{X}_t \end{bmatrix} \boldsymbol{\beta} + \text{residuals}, \tag{1.45}$$

where $\boldsymbol{M}_t$ is the matrix that projects orthogonally onto $\mathcal{S}^\perp(\boldsymbol{e}_t)$. Multiplying any vector by $\boldsymbol{M}_t$ merely annihilates the last element of that vector. Thus regression (1.45) is simply

$$\begin{bmatrix} \boldsymbol{y}_{(t)} \\ 0 \end{bmatrix} = \begin{bmatrix} \boldsymbol{X}_{(t)} \\ \mathbf{0} \end{bmatrix} \boldsymbol{\beta} + \text{residuals}. \tag{1.46}$$

The last observation, in which the regressand and all regressors are zero, obviously has no effect at all on parameter estimates. Regression (1.46) is therefore equivalent to regressing $\boldsymbol{y}_{(t)}$ on $\boldsymbol{X}_{(t)}$ and so must yield OLS estimates $\hat{\boldsymbol{\beta}}^{(t)}$. For regression (1.46), the residual for observation t is clearly zero; the FWL Theorem then implies that the residual for observation t from regression (1.44) must likewise be zero, which implies that $\hat{\alpha}$ must equal $y_t - \boldsymbol{X}_t \hat{\boldsymbol{\beta}}^{(t)}$.

These results make it easy to derive the results (1.40) and (1.41), which were earlier stated without proof. Readers who are not interested in the proofs may wish to skip the next three paragraphs. However, these proofs illustrate the power of simple algebra, combined with the FWL Theorem and an understanding of the geometry involved. It might therefore be instructive to contrast them with conventional proofs such as those in Appendix 2A of Belsley, Kuh, and Welsch (1980).

Using the results we have just proved, we see that the fitted values from regression (1.44) are $\boldsymbol{X}\hat{\boldsymbol{\beta}}^{(t)} + \boldsymbol{e}_t\hat{\alpha}$, while those from regression (1.43) are $\boldsymbol{X}\hat{\boldsymbol{\beta}}$. Minus their difference, which is equal to the difference between the residuals from (1.43) and (1.44), is $\boldsymbol{X}\hat{\boldsymbol{\beta}} - \boldsymbol{X}\hat{\boldsymbol{\beta}}^{(t)} - \boldsymbol{e}_t\hat{\alpha}$. Premultiplying this difference by $\boldsymbol{M}_X$ (where of course $\boldsymbol{X} \equiv [\boldsymbol{X}_{(t)} \vdots \boldsymbol{X}_t]$) yields

$$\begin{aligned} \boldsymbol{M}_X\big(\boldsymbol{X}(\hat{\boldsymbol{\beta}} - \hat{\boldsymbol{\beta}}^{(t)}) - \boldsymbol{e}_t\hat{\alpha}\big) &= \boldsymbol{M}_X\big(\hat{\boldsymbol{u}}^{(t)} - \hat{\boldsymbol{u}}\big) \\ &= \hat{\boldsymbol{u}}^{(t)} - \hat{\boldsymbol{u}} = -\boldsymbol{M}_X\boldsymbol{e}_t\,\hat{\alpha}, \end{aligned} \tag{1.47}$$

where $\hat{\boldsymbol{u}}^{(t)}$ denotes the residuals from (1.44). We now premultiply both sides of the last equality in (1.47) by $-\boldsymbol{e}_t^{\top}$. As we demonstrated above, $\hat{u}_t^{(t)} = 0$, which implies that $\boldsymbol{e}_t^{\top}\hat{\boldsymbol{u}}^{(t)} = 0$. The result of the premultiplication is therefore

$$\boldsymbol{e}_t^{\top}\boldsymbol{M}_X\boldsymbol{e}_t\,\hat{\alpha} = \hat{u}_t. \tag{1.48}$$

By definition, $\boldsymbol{e}_t^{\top}\boldsymbol{M}_X\boldsymbol{e}_t = 1 - h_t$. Thus (1.48) implies that

$$\hat{\alpha} = \frac{\hat{u}_t}{1 - h_t}. \tag{1.49}$$

Since $\hat{\alpha}$ is $y_t - \boldsymbol{X}_t\hat{\boldsymbol{\beta}}^{(t)}$, the result (1.49) gives us almost everything that we need. The change in the tth residual brought about by omitting the tth observation must be

$$\hat{\alpha} - \hat{u}_t = \frac{\hat{u}_t}{1 - h_t} - \hat{u}_t = \left(\frac{h_t}{1 - h_t}\right)\hat{u}_t,$$

which is expression (1.42). The change in the tth fitted value must be minus the change in the tth residual. Hence,

$$\boldsymbol{X}_t\hat{\boldsymbol{\beta}}^{(t)} - \boldsymbol{X}_t\hat{\boldsymbol{\beta}} = -\left(\frac{h_t}{1 - h_t}\right)\hat{u}_t,$$

from which the result (1.41) follows immediately.

We can now derive (1.40). Using (1.47), we see that

$$\hat{\boldsymbol{u}} - \hat{\boldsymbol{u}}^{(t)} = \boldsymbol{X}\hat{\boldsymbol{\beta}}^{(t)} + \boldsymbol{e}_t\hat{\alpha} - \boldsymbol{X}\hat{\boldsymbol{\beta}}.$$

Premultiplying this by $(\boldsymbol{X}^{\top}\boldsymbol{X})^{-1}\boldsymbol{X}^{\top}$ yields

$$\begin{aligned} \mathbf{0} &= \big(\boldsymbol{X}^{\top}\boldsymbol{X}\big)^{-1}\boldsymbol{X}^{\top}\boldsymbol{X}\hat{\boldsymbol{\beta}}^{(t)} - \big(\boldsymbol{X}^{\top}\boldsymbol{X}\big)^{-1}\boldsymbol{X}^{\top}\boldsymbol{X}\hat{\boldsymbol{\beta}} + \big(\boldsymbol{X}^{\top}\boldsymbol{X}\big)^{-1}\boldsymbol{X}^{\top}\boldsymbol{e}_t\hat{\alpha} \\ &= \hat{\boldsymbol{\beta}}^{(t)} - \hat{\boldsymbol{\beta}} + \big(\boldsymbol{X}^{\top}\boldsymbol{X}\big)^{-1}\boldsymbol{X}^{\top}\boldsymbol{e}_t\hat{\alpha}, \end{aligned}$$

where the left-hand side is zero because $\hat{\boldsymbol{u}} - \hat{\boldsymbol{u}}^{(t)}$ lies in $\mathcal{S}^{\perp}(\boldsymbol{X})$. Solving for $\hat{\boldsymbol{\beta}}^{(t)}$ and using (1.49), we obtain the fundamental result (1.40):

$$\begin{aligned}\hat{\boldsymbol{\beta}}^{(t)} &= \hat{\boldsymbol{\beta}} - \left(\boldsymbol{X}^{\top}\boldsymbol{X}\right)^{-1}\boldsymbol{X}^{\top}\boldsymbol{e}_t(1-h_t)^{-1}\hat{u}_t \\ &= \hat{\boldsymbol{\beta}} - \left(\frac{1}{1-h_t}\right)\left(\boldsymbol{X}^{\top}\boldsymbol{X}\right)^{-1}\boldsymbol{X}_t^{\top}\hat{u}_t.\end{aligned}$$

We have seen that the quantities h_t must be no smaller than 0 and no larger than 1 and must on average equal k/n. We have also seen that when h_t is relatively large, dropping observation t will have a relatively large effect on $\hat{\boldsymbol{\beta}}$, unless $\hat{u}_t$ is very close to zero. Thus the quantities h_t may be used to measure the **leverage**, or potential effect on $\hat{\boldsymbol{\beta}}$, of each of the observations. Observations for which h_t is relatively large (say, greater than $2k/n$) may be said to have high leverage, or to be **leverage points**. If all the h_t's were equal to k/n, as they would be for example if the only regressor were a constant term, then every observation would have the same leverage. This situation, which is sometimes referred to as a **balanced design**, is in some ways the most desirable one, but since in econometrics the design of the $\boldsymbol{X}$ matrix is rarely under the control of the investigator, it is rarely encountered. Notice that observation t can have high leverage but not be very influential, if h_t is large but $\hat{u}_t$ is small. A leverage point is *potentially* influential, but whether the potential is actually realized depends on y_t.

One way to think about leverage is to use the fact that $h_t = \boldsymbol{e}_t^{\top}\boldsymbol{P}_X\boldsymbol{e}_t$. From this we see that h_t will be large if the matrix of regressors $\boldsymbol{X}$ has a lot of explanatory power for the dummy variable $\boldsymbol{e}_t$ and small if it does not. Imagine that we were to replace $\boldsymbol{y}$ by $\boldsymbol{y} + \delta\boldsymbol{e}_t$, thereby adding δ to y_t for observation t only. If observation t had little leverage (small h_t), $\hat{\boldsymbol{\beta}}$ would not change by very much and $\hat{u}_t$ would have to change by almost the full change in y_t, that is δ. On the other hand, if observation t had a lot of leverage (large h_t), at least one element of $\hat{\boldsymbol{\beta}}$ would change by a lot and $\hat{u}_t$ would change by much less than δ. Thus the value of y_t will have a much greater impact on $\hat{\boldsymbol{\beta}}$, and a much smaller impact on $\hat{u}_t$, the greater is the leverage of observation t.

Figure 1.8 illustrates a case for which $k = 1$, that is, there is only one regressor, and for which the second observation has much more leverage than the first. Exceptionally, the two axes, horizontal and vertical, drawn in the figure *do* represent the first two observations. Thus, what we are looking at is the projection of the vector representing the regressor $\boldsymbol{X}$ onto the space spanned by the two vectors $\boldsymbol{e}_1$ and $\boldsymbol{e}_2$ that correspond to the first two observations, as indicated by the fact that these two vectors are contained in the two axes. The projection of $\boldsymbol{X}$ is the vector denoted by $\boldsymbol{P}_{1,2}\boldsymbol{X}$ in the figure. When as here there is only one regressor, the quantities h_t become simply $X_t^2/\|X\|^2$, as can be seen from (1.38). Thus the ratio of h_2 to h_1, or the leverage of observation 2 relative to that of observation 1, is just the ratio of the squared lengths of the vectors $X_1\boldsymbol{e}_1$ and $X_2\boldsymbol{e}_2$ in the figure. The

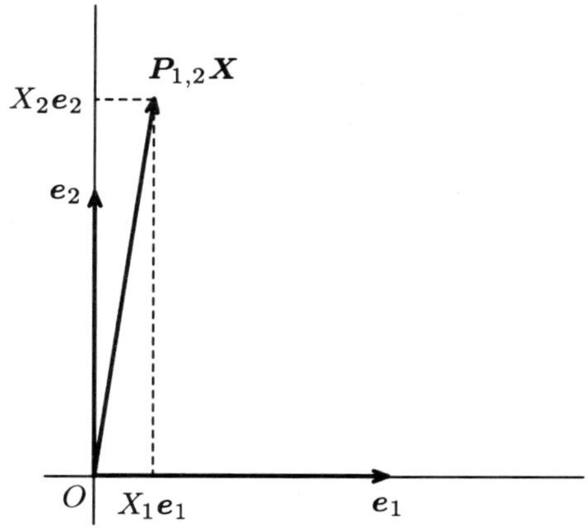

Figure 1.8 Observation 2 has relatively high leverage

greater leverage of observation 2 means that X_2 must be much larger than X_1, as drawn. If on the contrary X_1 and X_2 were roughly equal, so that $P_{1,2}X$ formed approximately the same angle with both axes, then h_1 and h_2 would be roughly equal.

We now use a numerical example to illustrate the enormous influence that a single erroneous observation can have. The example also shows that examining leverage points can be extremely useful in identifying data errors which affect the estimates substantially. The correct data set, including the $\hat{u}_t$'s and h_t's, is shown in Table 1.2. The corresponding OLS estimates are

$$\hat{\beta}_1 = 1.390, \quad \hat{\beta}_2 = 1.223, \quad R^2 = 0.7278. \tag{1.50}$$

Table 1.2 Numerical Example: Correct Data Set

t	X_t		y_t	$\hat{u}_t$	h_t	$\hat{u}_t h_t/(1-h_t)$
1	1	1.51	2.88	−0.357	0.203	−0.091
2	1	2.33	3.62	−0.620	0.105	−0.073
3	1	3.57	5.64	−0.116	0.536	−0.134
4	1	2.12	3.43	−0.553	0.101	−0.062
5	1	1.54	3.21	−0.064	0.194	−0.015
6	1	1.71	4.49	1.008	0.151	0.179
7	1	2.68	4.50	−0.168	0.156	−0.031
8	1	2.25	4.28	−0.138	0.101	0.016
9	1	1.32	2.98	−0.025	0.269	−0.009
10	1	2.80	5.57	0.755	0.186	0.173

Table 1.3 Numerical Example: Incorrect Data Set

t	$\boldsymbol{X}_t$		y_t	$\hat{u}_t$	h_t	$\hat{u}_t h_t/(1-h_t)$
1	1	1.51	2.88	−0.900	0.143	−0.150
2	1	2.33	3.62	−0.356	0.104	−0.041
3	1	3.57	5.64	1.369	0.125	0.195
4	1	2.12	3.43	−0.496	0.110	−0.061
5	1	1.54	3.21	−0.578	0.141	−0.095
6	1	1.71	4.49	0.662	0.130	0.099
7	1	7.68	4.50	−0.751	0.883	−5.674
8	1	2.25	4.28	0.323	0.106	0.038
9	1	1.32	2.98	−0.755	0.158	−0.142
10	1	2.80	5.57	1.482	0.100	0.165

The largest h_t here is 0.536, for observation 3. It is over 5 times as large as the smallest h_t and is greater than $2k/n$ (= 0.40 in this case). Thus observation 3 is a leverage point. This is not surprising, since the value of X_{2t} for observation 3 is by far the largest value of X_{2t}. However, since two other observations also have values of h_t greater than 0.20, observation 3 is certainly not a point of extreme leverage. As the last column of the table shows, it is also not particularly influential.

Now let us see what happens when we deliberately introduce an error into $\boldsymbol{X}$. Suppose that X_{2t} for observation 7 is accidentally changed from 2.68 to 7.68. The resulting data set, together with the $\hat{u}_t$'s and h_t's, is shown in Table 1.3. The corresponding OLS estimates are

$$\hat{\beta}_1 = 3.420, \quad \hat{\beta}_2 = 0.238, \quad R^2 = 0.1996.$$

These estimates differ dramatically from the earlier ones (1.50). The strong relationship between X_{2t} and y_t that was apparent before has all but vanished as a result of the error in observation 7.[11] Examination of the residuals alone would not tell us that there is anything amiss with that observation, since $\hat{u}_7$ is by no means the largest residual. But examination of the h_t's *would* suggest looking at that observation more closely; because h_7 is more than 5 times as large as any of the other h_t's, observation 7 is clearly a point of very

[11] Since we are, in this chapter, discussing only the *numerical* aspects of least squares, we have not presented estimated standard errors or t statistics for this example. We note, however, that the difference between the two sets of estimates using the correct and incorrect data is large relative to conventionally calculated standard errors; for example, the t statistic for the correct $\hat{\beta}_2$ of 1.223 is 4.62, while the t statistic for the $\hat{\beta}_2$ of 0.238 obtained using the incorrect data is only 1.41.

high leverage indeed. It is also highly influential, as the last column of the table shows. Thus, in this case, anyone looking at either h_t or $\hat{u}_t h_t/(1 - h_t)$ would, in all likelihood, be led to discover the harmful data error.

This example suggests that the careful econometrician will routinely want to look at the quantities h_t and $\hat{u}_t h_t/(1 - h_t)$. Unfortunately, not all regression packages make this easy to do. This is surprising, because the h_t's are very easily calculated if the OLS estimates are computed using the QR decomposition. Since $\boldsymbol{P}_X = \boldsymbol{Q}\boldsymbol{Q}^\top$, it is easily seen that

$$h_t = \sum_{i=1}^{k} Q_{ti}^2.$$

Thus the calculation is trivial once $\boldsymbol{Q}$ is known. Once computed, h_t and/or $\hat{u}_t h_t/(1 - h_t)$ may easily be plotted against t. If there are leverage points and/or unduly influential observations, then it would be wise to check the accuracy of the data for those observations and to see whether removing them from the sample affects the results appreciably. Such informal procedures for detecting influential observations, especially those due to data errors, generally work well. More formal procedures are discussed in Belsley, Kuh, and Welsch (1980) and Krasker, Kuh, and Welsch (1983).

1.7 Further Reading and Conclusion

The use of geometry as an aid to the understanding of linear regression has a long history; see Herr (1980). Early and important papers include Fisher (1915), Durbin and Kendall (1951), Kruskal (1961, 1968, 1975), and Seber (1964). One valuable reference on linear models that takes the geometric approach is Seber (1980), although that book may be too terse for many readers. A recent expository paper that is quite accessible is Bryant (1984). The approach has not been used as much in econometrics as it has in statistics, but a number of econometrics texts — notably Malinvaud (1970a) and also Madansky (1976), Pollock (1979), and Wonnacott and Wonnacott (1979) — use it to a greater or lesser degree. Our approach could be termed *semi-geometric*, since we have not emphasized the coordinate-free nature of the analysis quite as much as some authors; see Kruskal's papers, the Seber book or, in econometrics, Fisher (1981, 1983) and Fisher and McAleer (1984).

In this chapter, we have entirely ignored statistical models. Linear regression has been treated purely as a computational device which has a geometrical interpretation, rather than as an estimation procedure for a family of statistical models. All the results discussed have been true numerically, as a consequence of how ordinary least squares estimates are computed, and have not depended in any way on how the data were actually generated. We emphasize this, because conventional treatments of the linear regression model often fail to distinguish between the numerical and statistical properties of least squares.

In the remainder of this book, we will move on to consider a variety of statistical models, some of them regression models and some of them not, which are of practical use to econometricians. For most of the book, we will focus on two classes of models: ones that can be treated as linear and nonlinear regression models and ones that can be estimated by the method of maximum likelihood (the latter being a very broad class of models indeed). As we will see, understanding the geometrical properties of linear regression turns out to be central to understanding both nonlinear regression models and the method of maximum likelihood. We will therefore assume throughout our discussion that readers are familiar with the basic results that were presented in this chapter.

TERMS AND CONCEPTS

balanced design
base, exponent and mantissa (of floating-point numbers)
codimension (of a linear subspace)
coefficient of determination (R^2)
coordinate-free results
dimension (of a linear subspace)
direction (of a vector)
Euclidean n–space, E^n
explained sum of squares, ESS
fitted values
floating-point numbers
Frisch-Waugh-Lovell (FWL) Theorem
hat matrix
h_t (diagonals of hat matrix)
idempotent matrix
ill-conditioned problem
influential observations
inner product
least squares residuals
length (of a vector)
leverage
leverage points
linear independence (of vectors)
linear regression models
natural inner product
nonlinear least squares (NLS)
nonlinear regression models
normal equations
numerical vs. statistical properties
numerically unstable formulas
ordinary least squares (OLS)
orthogonal complement (of a subspace)
orthogonal decomposition
orthogonal projection matrix
orthogonal vectors
orthonormal basis
precision of floating-point numbers (single, double, quadruple)
projection
Pythagoras' Theorem (and least squares)
QR decomposition
R^2, centered and uncentered
range of a projection
rank of a matrix
regressand
regression, linear and nonlinear
regressors
reparametrization (of a regression)
residuals
restricted least squares
seasonal dummy variables
span of, or subspace spanned by the columns of, a matrix
sum of squared residuals, SSR
total sum of squares, TSS

Chapter 2

Nonlinear Regression Models and Nonlinear Least Squares

2.1 Introduction

In Chapter 1, we discussed in some detail the geometry of ordinary least squares and its properties as a computational device. That material is important because many commonly used statistical models are usually estimated by some variant of least squares. Among these is the most commonly encountered class of models in econometrics, the class of **regression models**, of which we now begin our discussion. Instead of restricting ourselves to the familiar territory of **linear regression models**, which can be estimated directly by OLS, we will consider the much broader family of **nonlinear regression models**, which may be estimated by **nonlinear least squares**, or **NLS**. Occasionally we will specifically treat linear regression models if there are results which are true for them that do not generalize to the nonlinear case.

In this and the next few chapters on regression models, we will restrict our attention to **univariate models**, meaning models in which there is a single dependent variable. These are a good deal simpler to deal with than **multivariate models**, in which there are several jointly dependent variables. Univariate models are far more commonly encountered in practice than are multivariate ones, and a good understanding of the former is essential to understanding the latter. Extending results for univariate models to the multivariate case is quite easy to do, as we will demonstrate in Chapter 9.

We begin by writing the univariate nonlinear regression model in its generic form as

$$y_t = x_t(\boldsymbol{\beta}) + u_t, \quad u_t \sim \mathrm{IID}(0, \sigma^2), \quad t = 1, \ldots, n. \tag{2.01}$$

Here y_t is the tth observation on the **dependent variable**, which is a scalar random variable, and $\boldsymbol{\beta}$ is a k-vector of (usually) unknown parameters. The scalar function $x_t(\boldsymbol{\beta})$ is a (generally nonlinear) **regression function** that determines the mean value of y_t conditional on $\boldsymbol{\beta}$ and (usually) on certain **independent variables**. The latter have not been shown explicitly in (2.01), but the t subscript of $x_t(\boldsymbol{\beta})$ does indicate that this function varies from observation to observation. In most cases, the reason for this is that $x_t(\boldsymbol{\beta})$ depends on one or more independent variables that do so. Thus $x_t(\boldsymbol{\beta})$ should be interpreted as the mean of y_t *conditional* on the values of those independent variables. More precisely, as we will see in Section 2.4, it should be interpreted as the mean of y_t conditional on some information set to which those independent variables belong.[1]

In some cases, $x_t(\boldsymbol{\beta})$ may also depend on lagged values of y_t. A model for which that is the case is called a **dynamic model**, and dealing with such models complicates the analysis somewhat. We will assume for the time being that $x_t(\boldsymbol{\beta})$ does not depend on lagged values of y_t, as it would if (2.01) were a dynamic model, but we will relax this assumption in Chapter 5 when we provide a first treatment of the asymptotic theory of nonlinear least squares. As the term is used in this book, **asymptotic** results are ones that are strictly true only in the limit as the sample size n tends to infinity. Most of the standard analytical results for nonlinear regression models, and nonlinear models in general, are asymptotic ones, because finite-sample results that are readily interpreted are often extremely hard to obtain.

The feature that distinguishes **regression models** from all other statistical models is that the only way in which randomness affects the dependent variable is through an additive **error term** or **disturbance**. In the case of (2.01), this error term is called u_t, and the notation "$u_t \sim \text{IID}(0, \sigma^2)$" is a shorthand way of saying that the error terms u_t are assumed to be **independent and identically distributed**, or **i.i.d.**, with mean zero and variance σ^2. By this, we will not necessarily mean that the random variables u_t have distributions identical in all respects but merely that they all have mean zero and the same variance σ^2. In this respect, readers should perhaps be warned that we depart from standard usage. As we will see in Section 2.6, the properties of these error terms are extremely important, for they determine all the statistical properties of a model and, indeed, whether or not a regression model can sensibly be used at all. However, since NLS estimates (like OLS estimates) can be computed regardless of how the data were generated, we will discuss the computation of NLS estimates before we discuss their statistical properties.

The remainder of this chapter treats a number of aspects of nonlinear least squares and nonlinear regression models. In Section 2.2, we discuss nonlinear least squares as a computational procedure that is an extension of ordinary least squares. We demonstrate that minimizing the sum of squared

[1] Readers should be aware that the notation we have used here is slightly nonstandard. Many authors use $f_t(\boldsymbol{\beta})$ where we have used $x_t(\boldsymbol{\beta})$. We prefer our notation for two reasons. First of all, it lets us use the notation $f(\cdot)$ to stand for things other than regression functions without creating ambiguity. Secondly, with our notation it is natural to let $X_{ti}(\boldsymbol{\beta})$ denote $\partial x_t(\boldsymbol{\beta})/\partial \beta_i$ (see Section 2.2 below). The matrix with typical element $X_{ti}(\boldsymbol{\beta})$ is in fact very closely related to the ordinary $\boldsymbol{X}$ matrix used in most treatments of the linear regression model, and we hope the similarity of notation will help to keep this fact in mind.

residuals for a nonlinear regression model like (2.01) is very similar, in terms of the geometry involved, to running a linear regression. A nonlinear regression model must be **identified** if unique parameter estimates are to be obtained. We therefore discuss the important concept of identification in Section 2.3. In the second half of the chapter, we begin to consider the statistical (and economic) aspects of nonlinear regression models. In Section 2.4, we discuss how regression equations like (2.01) can be interpreted and the distinction between models and data-generating processes. Examples of linear and nonlinear regression functions are then discussed in Section 2.5, while error terms are discussed in Section 2.6. Making inferences from models estimated by NLS will be the topic of Chapter 3.

2.2 The Geometry of Nonlinear Least Squares

By far the most common way to estimate nonlinear as well as linear regression models is to minimize the sum of squared residuals, or SSR, as a function of $\boldsymbol{\beta}$. For the model (2.01), the **sum-of-squares function** is

$$SSR(\boldsymbol{\beta}) = \sum_{t=1}^{n} \big(y_t - x_t(\boldsymbol{\beta})\big)^2.$$

It is usually more convenient to write this in matrix notation as

$$SSR(\boldsymbol{\beta}) = \big(\boldsymbol{y} - \boldsymbol{x}(\boldsymbol{\beta})\big)^{\top}\big(\boldsymbol{y} - \boldsymbol{x}(\boldsymbol{\beta})\big), \tag{2.02}$$

where $\boldsymbol{y}$ is an n–vector of observations y_t and $\boldsymbol{x}(\boldsymbol{\beta})$ is an n–vector of regression functions $x_t(\boldsymbol{\beta})$. As we saw in Chapter 1, another notation, which is perhaps not so convenient to work with algebraically but is more compact and emphasizes the geometry involved, is

$$SSR(\boldsymbol{\beta}) = \big\|\boldsymbol{y} - \boldsymbol{x}(\boldsymbol{\beta})\big\|^2, \tag{2.03}$$

where $\|\boldsymbol{y} - \boldsymbol{x}(\boldsymbol{\beta})\|$ is the length of the vector $\boldsymbol{y} - \boldsymbol{x}(\boldsymbol{\beta})$. Expression (2.03) makes it clear that when we minimize $SSR(\boldsymbol{\beta})$, we are in fact minimizing the Euclidean distance between $\boldsymbol{y}$ and $\boldsymbol{x}(\boldsymbol{\beta})$, an interpretation that we will discuss at length below.

The sum-of-squares function (2.02) can be rewritten as

$$SSR(\boldsymbol{\beta}) = \boldsymbol{y}^{\top}\boldsymbol{y} - 2\boldsymbol{y}^{\top}\boldsymbol{x}(\boldsymbol{\beta}) + \boldsymbol{x}^{\top}(\boldsymbol{\beta})\boldsymbol{x}(\boldsymbol{\beta}).$$

Differentiating this expression with respect to the components of the k–vector $\boldsymbol{\beta}$ and setting all the partial derivatives to zero yields first-order conditions that must be satisfied by any NLS estimates $\hat{\boldsymbol{\beta}}$ which correspond to an interior minimum of $SSR(\boldsymbol{\beta})$. These first-order conditions, or normal equations, are

$$-2\boldsymbol{X}^{\top}(\hat{\boldsymbol{\beta}})\boldsymbol{y} + 2\boldsymbol{X}^{\top}(\hat{\boldsymbol{\beta}})\boldsymbol{x}(\hat{\boldsymbol{\beta}}) = \boldsymbol{0}, \tag{2.04}$$

where the $n \times k$ matrix $\boldsymbol{X}(\boldsymbol{\beta})$ has typical element

$$X_{ti}(\boldsymbol{\beta}) \equiv \frac{\partial x_t(\boldsymbol{\beta})}{\partial \beta_i}.$$

Since each of the vectors in (2.04) has k elements, there are k normal equations to determine the k elements of $\boldsymbol{\beta}$.

The matrix $\boldsymbol{X}(\boldsymbol{\beta})$ will reappear many times in our discussion of nonlinear least squares. Each element of this matrix is the partial derivative of an element of $\boldsymbol{x}(\boldsymbol{\beta})$ with respect to an element of $\boldsymbol{\beta}$. As the notation we have used should suggest, the matrix $\boldsymbol{X}(\boldsymbol{\beta})$ corresponds precisely to the $\boldsymbol{X}$ matrix in the linear regression case. Thus when the regression function $\boldsymbol{x}(\boldsymbol{\beta})$ is the linear function $\boldsymbol{X\beta}$, we see immediately that $\boldsymbol{X}(\boldsymbol{\beta}) = \boldsymbol{X}$.

The first-order conditions (2.04) may be simplified slightly by collecting terms, dropping the factor of -2, and making the definitions $\hat{\boldsymbol{x}} \equiv \boldsymbol{x}(\hat{\boldsymbol{\beta}})$ and $\hat{\boldsymbol{X}} \equiv \boldsymbol{X}(\hat{\boldsymbol{\beta}})$.[2] The result is

$$\hat{\boldsymbol{X}}^{\top}(\boldsymbol{y} - \hat{\boldsymbol{x}}) = \boldsymbol{0}. \tag{2.05}$$

These normal equations simply say that the residuals $\boldsymbol{y} - \hat{\boldsymbol{x}}$ must be orthogonal to the matrix of derivatives $\hat{\boldsymbol{X}}$. This is directly analogous to the result for linear regression models that the residuals $\boldsymbol{y} - \boldsymbol{X}\hat{\boldsymbol{\beta}}$ must be orthogonal to the $\boldsymbol{X}$ matrix. The nonlinear case differs from the linear one in that *both* the vector of fitted values $\hat{\boldsymbol{x}}$ *and* the matrix $\hat{\boldsymbol{X}}$ now depend on $\hat{\boldsymbol{\beta}}$. Thus we cannot, in general, hope to solve (2.05) analytically for $\hat{\boldsymbol{\beta}}$, although this may be possible in some special cases, including of course the linear one.

Notice that satisfying the first-order conditions (2.05) is necessary but not sufficient for $\hat{\boldsymbol{\beta}}$ to be an interior global minimum of the sum-of-squares function. There may be many values of $\boldsymbol{\beta}$ that satisfy (2.05) but represent **local minima**, **stationary points**, or even **local maxima**. This is illustrated in Figure 2.1 for a case in which there is only one parameter, and β is therefore a scalar. In the figure the global minimum is at $\hat{\beta}$, but there is another local minimum at β', a local maximum at β'', and a stationary point at β^*.

No decent **minimization algorithm** will be fooled into stopping at a local maximum or a stationary point, because it is easy to check that the second-order conditions for a minimum are not satisfied at such points. But an algorithm may well stop at the wrong local minimum. Based only on local information, no algorithm can tell the difference between a local minimum like β' and a global minimum like $\hat{\beta}$. In order to find the global minimum, it

[2] It is often convenient to indicate in this way the dependence of a vector or matrix on a vector of parameters that may have been estimated. Thus if $\boldsymbol{\alpha}_0$ were a set of true parameters, and $\hat{\boldsymbol{\alpha}}$ and $\tilde{\boldsymbol{\alpha}}$ were two different sets of estimates, we might let $\boldsymbol{Z}_0$ denote $\boldsymbol{Z}(\boldsymbol{\alpha}_0)$, $\hat{\boldsymbol{Z}}$ denote $\boldsymbol{Z}(\hat{\boldsymbol{\alpha}})$, and $\tilde{\boldsymbol{Z}}$ denote $\boldsymbol{Z}(\tilde{\boldsymbol{\alpha}})$.

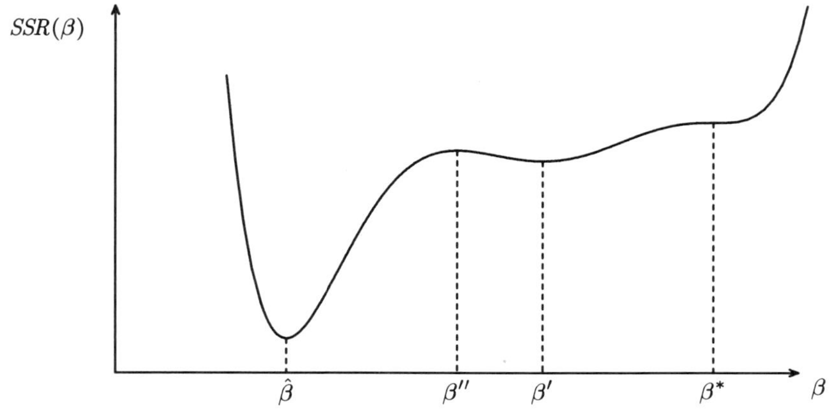

Figure 2.1 A sum-of-squares function

may therefore be necessary to minimize $SSR(\boldsymbol{\beta})$ a number of times, beginning at a variety of different starting points. In the case illustrated here, a good algorithm should be able to find $\hat{\beta}$ if it starts anywhere to the left of β'' but may not be able to find it otherwise. In the one-dimensional case, it is easy to make sure that one finds a global minimum, since a graph like Figure 2.1 will show where it is. In higher-dimensional cases, however, graphical methods are generally not applicable, and even if one starts an algorithm at a number of starting places, there is no guarantee that one will find the global minimum if there are several local minima. Methods of computing NLS estimates will be discussed further in Chapter 6.

It is instructive to consider the analog of Figures 1.1 and 1.3 for the nonlinear regression case. Recall that $\boldsymbol{y}$ can be thought of as a point in the space of observations E^n and that the linear regression function $\boldsymbol{X\beta}$ then defines a k-dimensional linear subspace of that space. In Figure 1.3 we illustrated, for the simplest possible case of $n = 2$ and $k = 1$, how ordinary least squares projects $\boldsymbol{y}$ orthogonally onto $\mathcal{S}(\boldsymbol{X})$, the subspace spanned by the columns of $\boldsymbol{X}$. When the regression function $\boldsymbol{x}(\boldsymbol{\beta})$ is nonlinear, but everywhere differentiable, it defines a k-dimensional **manifold**,[3] or smooth surface, which in general is no longer a *linear* subspace. Every point on this manifold, which we will denote $\mathcal{X}$, corresponds (by assumption) to a different value of $\boldsymbol{\beta}$, and so a particular point that corresponds to $\boldsymbol{\beta}^1$, say, may be referred to as $\mathcal{X}(\boldsymbol{\beta}^1)$. It is essential that every component of the vector $\boldsymbol{x}(\boldsymbol{\beta})$ be differentiable everywhere for $\mathcal{X}$ to be smooth everywhere. At any arbitrary point, say $\bar{\boldsymbol{\beta}}$, the matrix $\bar{\boldsymbol{X}} \equiv \boldsymbol{X}(\bar{\boldsymbol{\beta}})$ defines a **tangent space** $\mathcal{S}^*(\bar{\boldsymbol{X}})$, which is simply the k-dimensional

[3] For formal definitions of a manifold, and thorough discussion of the properties of manifolds, see, among others, Spivak (1965) for an elementary approach and Lang (1972) for a more advanced one.

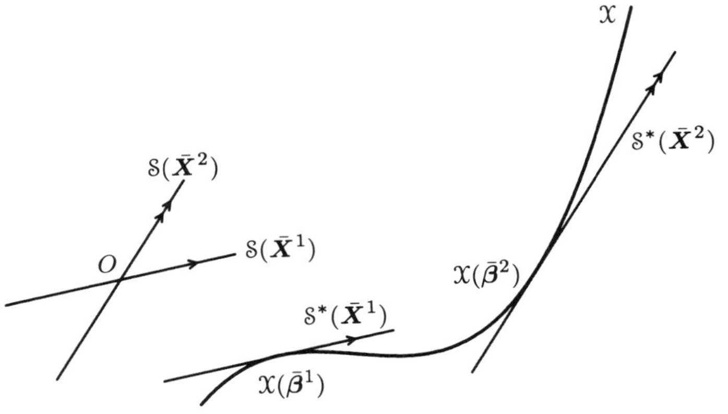

Figure 2.2 Tangent spaces to a curved manifold

linear subspace $\mathcal{S}(\bar{\boldsymbol{X}})$ displaced so that the origin is at the point $\mathcal{X}(\bar{\boldsymbol{\beta}})$. This means that $\mathcal{S}^*(\bar{\boldsymbol{X}})$ is tangent to $\mathcal{X}$ at this point.

Figure 2.2 illustrates these ideas for the case $k = 1$. In order to be able to draw $\boldsymbol{x}(\beta)$ on the page, we suppose that it lies, locally at least, in a two-dimensional subspace of $\mathbb{R}^n$. The figure shows the curved manifold $\mathcal{X}$, the tangent spaces $\mathcal{S}^*(\bar{\boldsymbol{X}}^1)$ and $\mathcal{S}^*(\bar{\boldsymbol{X}}^2)$ at two arbitrary points $\mathcal{X}(\bar{\boldsymbol{\beta}}^1)$ and $\mathcal{X}(\bar{\boldsymbol{\beta}}^2)$, and the corresponding linear subspaces $\mathcal{S}(\bar{\boldsymbol{X}}^1)$ and $\mathcal{S}(\bar{\boldsymbol{X}}^2)$. The latter, as the arrows in the figure indicate, are, respectively, parallel to $\mathcal{S}^*(\bar{\boldsymbol{X}}^1)$ and $\mathcal{S}^*(\bar{\boldsymbol{X}}^2)$ but are not parallel to each other. If $\mathcal{X}$ were straight, as it would be if the regression function were linear, then of course there would be no distinction between $\mathcal{X}$, $\mathcal{S}(\bar{\boldsymbol{X}}^1)$, $\mathcal{S}(\bar{\boldsymbol{X}}^2)$, $\mathcal{S}^*(\bar{\boldsymbol{X}}^1)$, and $\mathcal{S}^*(\bar{\boldsymbol{X}}^2)$. It is the presence of such distinctions that makes nonlinear models harder to deal with than linear ones. Notice also that although the manifold defined by a linear regression function always includes the origin, that is not true in general for a nonlinear one, as can be seen in the figure.

Figure 2.3 shows the same regression manifold $\mathcal{X}$ as Figure 2.2, but $\mathcal{S}(\bar{\boldsymbol{X}}^1)$, $\mathcal{S}(\bar{\boldsymbol{X}}^2)$, $\mathcal{S}^*(\bar{\boldsymbol{X}}^1)$, and $\mathcal{S}^*(\bar{\boldsymbol{X}}^2)$ are no longer shown. A regressand $\boldsymbol{y}$ is now shown, and it is projected orthogonally onto $\mathcal{X}$ at the point $\hat{\mathcal{X}} \equiv \mathcal{X}(\hat{\boldsymbol{\beta}})$. Notice that since $\mathcal{S}^*(\hat{\boldsymbol{X}})$ is tangent to $\mathcal{X}$ at $\hat{\boldsymbol{\beta}}$, $\boldsymbol{y} - \hat{\boldsymbol{x}}$ must be orthogonal to $\mathcal{S}^*(\hat{\boldsymbol{X}})$ as well as to $\mathcal{X}$ at the point $\hat{\mathcal{X}}$, which is precisely what the first-order conditions (2.05) require. Because in this figure the regression function $\boldsymbol{x}(\boldsymbol{\beta})$ is only moderately nonlinear, and hence also the manifold $\mathcal{X}$, there is just one point, $\hat{\mathcal{X}}$, that satisfies the first-order conditions. It is clear from the figure that $\boldsymbol{y}$ can be projected at right angles onto $\mathcal{X}$ at $\hat{\mathcal{X}}$ and at no other point.

In contrast, consider Figure 2.4. In this figure, the manifold $\mathcal{X}$ is highly nonlinear, and there are three points, $\hat{\mathcal{X}}$, $\mathcal{X}'$, and $\mathcal{X}''$ (corresponding to $\hat{\boldsymbol{\beta}}$, $\boldsymbol{\beta}'$, and $\boldsymbol{\beta}''$), at which the first-order conditions are satisfied. At each one of these points, denoted generically by $\bar{\mathcal{X}}$, $\boldsymbol{y} - \bar{\boldsymbol{x}}$ forms a right angle with $\bar{\mathcal{X}}$ and hence

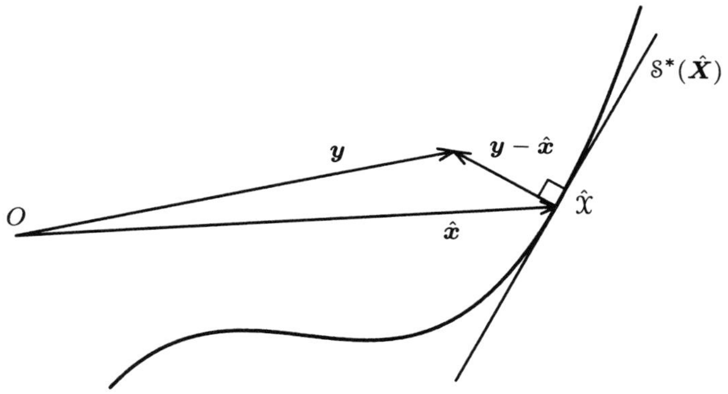

Figure 2.3 A regressand $\boldsymbol{y}$ projected onto a nonlinear manifold

also with $\mathcal{S}^*(\bar{\boldsymbol{X}})$. However, in this case it is evident that $\hat{\mathcal{X}}$ corresponds to a global minimum, $\mathcal{X}''$ to a local minimum, and $\mathcal{X}'$ to a local maximum of $SSR(\boldsymbol{\beta})$. Thus we see once again that a point which satisfies the first-order conditions does not necessarily yield NLS estimates.

It should be clear from these figures that the amount of nonlinearity in the regression function $\boldsymbol{x}(\boldsymbol{\beta})$ is very important. When $\boldsymbol{x}(\boldsymbol{\beta})$ is almost linear, nonlinear least squares is very similar to ordinary least squares. When $\boldsymbol{x}(\boldsymbol{\beta})$ is very nonlinear, however, all sorts of strange things can happen. Figure 2.4 only hints at these, since there are many different ways for multiple values of $\boldsymbol{\beta}$ to satisfy the first-order conditions (2.05) when $\mathcal{X}$ is a high-dimensional manifold.

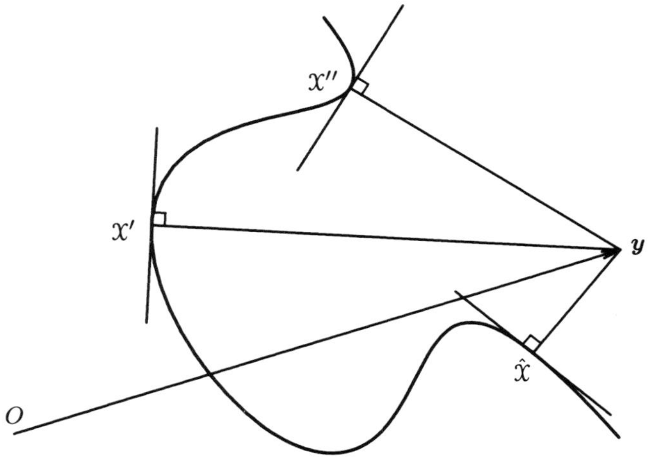

Figure 2.4 A highly nonlinear manifold

2.3 IDENTIFICATION IN NONLINEAR REGRESSION MODELS

If we are to minimize $SSR(\boldsymbol{\beta})$ successfully, it is necessary that the model be identified. **Identification** is a geometrically simple concept that applies to a very wide variety of models and estimation techniques. Unfortunately, the term *identification* has come to be associated in the minds of many students of econometrics with the tedious algebra of the linear simultaneous equations model. Identification is indeed an issue in such models, and there are some special problems that arise for them (see Chapters 7 and 18), but the concept is applicable to *every* econometric model. Essentially, a nonlinear regression model is **identified by a given data set** if, for that data set, we can find a *unique* $\hat{\boldsymbol{\beta}}$ that minimizes $SSR(\boldsymbol{\beta})$. If a model is not identified by the data being used, then there will be more than one $\hat{\boldsymbol{\beta}}$, perhaps even an infinite number of them. Some models may not be identifiable by any conceivable data set, while other models may be identified by some data sets but not by others.

There are two types of identification, **local** and **global**. The least squares estimate $\hat{\boldsymbol{\beta}}$ will be **locally identified** if whenever $\hat{\boldsymbol{\beta}}$ is perturbed slightly, the value of $SSR(\boldsymbol{\beta})$ increases. This may be stated formally as the requirement that the function $SSR(\boldsymbol{\beta})$ be strictly convex at $\hat{\boldsymbol{\beta}}$. Thus

$$SSR(\hat{\boldsymbol{\beta}}) < SSR(\hat{\boldsymbol{\beta}} + \boldsymbol{\delta})$$

for all "small" perturbations $\boldsymbol{\delta}$. Recall that strict convexity is guaranteed if the Hessian matrix $\boldsymbol{H}(\boldsymbol{\beta})$, of which a typical element is

$$H_{ij}(\boldsymbol{\beta}) \equiv \frac{\partial^2 SSR(\boldsymbol{\beta})}{\partial \beta_i \partial \beta_j},$$

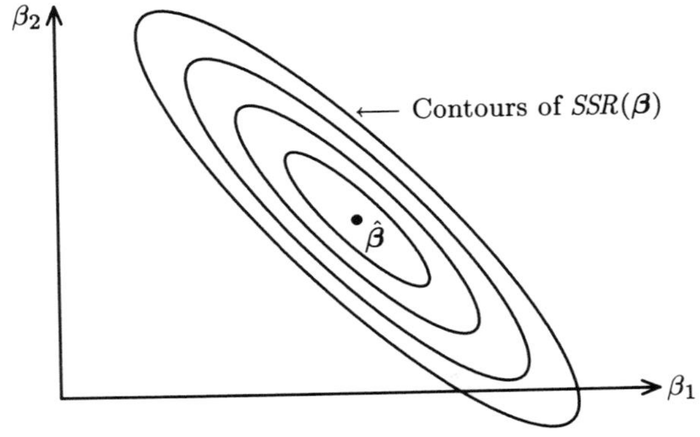

Figure 2.5 Identified minimum of a sum-of-squares function

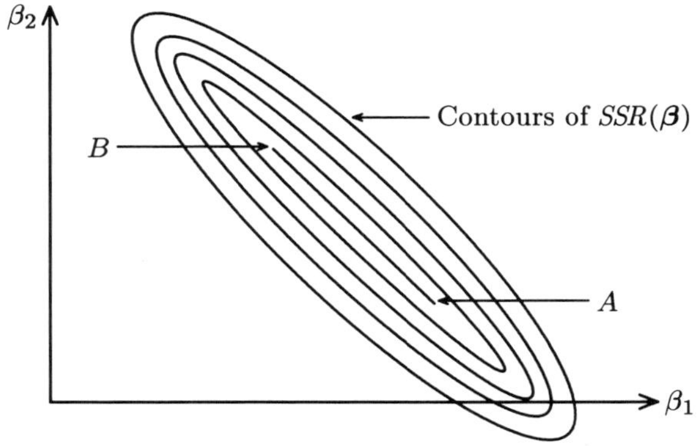

Figure 2.6 Unidentified minimum of a sum-of-squares function

is positive definite at $\hat{\boldsymbol{\beta}}$. Strict convexity implies that $SSR(\boldsymbol{\beta})$ is curved in every direction; no flat directions are allowed. If $SSR(\boldsymbol{\beta})$ were flat in some direction near $\hat{\boldsymbol{\beta}}$, we could move away from $\hat{\boldsymbol{\beta}}$ in that direction without changing the value of the sum of squared residuals at all (remember that the first derivatives of $SSR(\boldsymbol{\beta})$ are zero at $\hat{\boldsymbol{\beta}}$, which implies that $SSR(\boldsymbol{\beta})$ must be equal to $SSR(\hat{\boldsymbol{\beta}})$ everywhere in the flat region). Hence $\hat{\boldsymbol{\beta}}$ would not be the unique NLS estimator but merely one of an infinite number of points that all minimize $SSR(\boldsymbol{\beta})$. Figure 2.5 shows the contours of $SSR(\boldsymbol{\beta})$ for the usual case in which $\hat{\boldsymbol{\beta}}$ is a unique local minimum, while Figure 2.6 shows them for a case in which the model is not identified, because all points along the line AB minimize $SSR(\boldsymbol{\beta})$.

Local identification is necessary but not sufficient for us to obtain unique estimates $\hat{\boldsymbol{\beta}}$. A more general requirement is **global identification**, which may be stated formally as

$$SSR(\hat{\boldsymbol{\beta}}) < SSR(\boldsymbol{\beta}^*) \quad \text{for all } \boldsymbol{\beta}^* \neq \hat{\boldsymbol{\beta}}.$$

This definition of global identification is really just a restatement of the condition that $\hat{\boldsymbol{\beta}}$ be the *unique* minimizer of $SSR(\hat{\boldsymbol{\beta}})$. Notice that even if a model is locally identified, it is quite possible for it to have two (or more) distinct estimates, say $\hat{\boldsymbol{\beta}}^1$ and $\hat{\boldsymbol{\beta}}^2$, with $SSR(\hat{\boldsymbol{\beta}}^1) = SSR(\hat{\boldsymbol{\beta}}^2)$. As an example, consider the model

$$y_t = \beta\gamma + \gamma^2 z_t + u_t. \tag{2.06}$$

It is obvious that if $(\hat{\beta}, \hat{\gamma})$ minimizes the SSR for the model (2.06), then so will $(-\hat{\beta}, -\hat{\gamma})$. Hence this model is globally unidentifiable by *any* data set, even though the first- and second-order conditions are satisfied at both minima. This example may seem silly, but exactly the same phenomenon arises in many models that economists use all the time. One example is any time series model with a moving average error component; see Chapter 10.

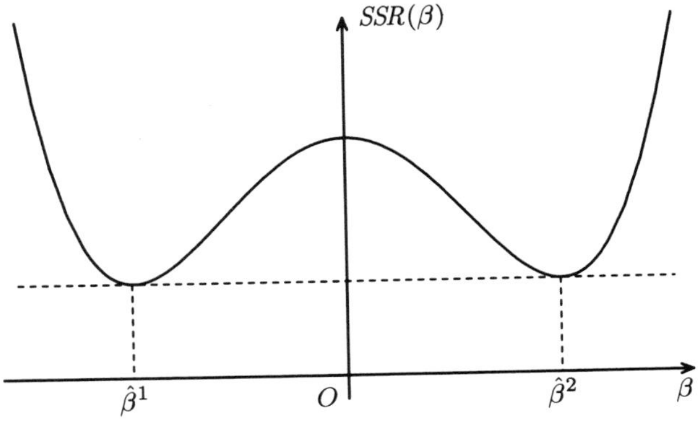

Figure 2.7 A case for which β is locally but not globally identified

Figure 2.7 illustrates what the sum-of-squares function can look like for a model that is locally but not globally identified in the way described above. The sum-of-squares function has only one argument, β, and is symmetric about the origin of β. The minimum of *SSR* is therefore achieved both at β^1 and β^2. Each of these potential estimates is locally identified, but the model is globally unidentified.

It is also quite possible for a model to be globally identified but nevertheless to fail to satisfy, for certain values of $\hat{\boldsymbol{\beta}}$ only, the local identification condition that the Hessian matrix be positive definite. This type of lack of identification causes no difficulties if a realized $\hat{\boldsymbol{\beta}}$ is not near these values, and we succeed in finding it, but it may make estimating the model difficult. As an example, consider the regression function

$$x_t(\boldsymbol{\beta}) = \beta_1 + \beta_2 z_t^{\beta_3}. \tag{2.07}$$

It is obvious that a model incorporating this regression function will be unidentified whenever $\hat{\beta}_2 = 0$, because β_3 will then have no effect on the value of $x_t(\boldsymbol{\beta})$ and hence no effect on $SSR(\boldsymbol{\beta})$. Consequently, any value of β_3 would serve as well as any other for $\hat{\beta}_3$. Similarly, the model will also be unidentified whenever $\hat{\beta}_3 = 0$, because $z_t^{\beta_3}$ will then be indistinguishable from the constant term. Because $\hat{\beta}_2$ or $\hat{\beta}_3$ will be precisely zero only for most unusual data sets, this model will in fact be identified by all but those unusual data sets.

The regression function (2.07) serves as an example of something which is much more common in practice than models that are unidentified, namely, models that are **poorly identified**. A poorly identified model is one for which the Hessian matrix $\boldsymbol{H}(\boldsymbol{\beta})$ is not actually singular but is close to being singular for values of $\boldsymbol{\beta}$ near $\hat{\boldsymbol{\beta}}$. Those are the values of $\boldsymbol{\beta}$ that we care most about, since the minimization algorithm will necessarily encounter them when trying to minimize $SSR(\boldsymbol{\beta})$. Although $SSR(\boldsymbol{\beta})$ is not actually flat for a poorly identified model, it is close to being flat, and as a result the algorithm that is trying to minimize $SSR(\boldsymbol{\beta})$ may have a difficult time doing so. In the context of linear regression models this phenomenon is often referred to as **collinearity** or **multicollinearity** (although the prefix seems redundant), and it shows up as an $\boldsymbol{X}^\top\boldsymbol{X}$ matrix that is close to being singular.

The continuity of the regression function implies that a model incorporating the regression function (2.07) will be poorly identified whenever the true value of either β_2 or β_3 is close, but not actually equal, to zero. In fact, it is likely to be poorly identified even for values of these parameters that are far from zero, because, for most sets of data on z_t, the Hessian for this model will be fairly close to singular. As we will demonstrate in Chapter 5, for nonlinear regression models the Hessian $\boldsymbol{H}(\boldsymbol{\beta})$ is, for values of $\boldsymbol{\beta}$ near $\hat{\boldsymbol{\beta}}$, generally approximated quite well by the matrix

$$2\boldsymbol{X}^\top(\boldsymbol{\beta})\boldsymbol{X}(\boldsymbol{\beta}).$$

For the regression function (2.07), the tth row of the matrix $\boldsymbol{X}(\boldsymbol{\beta})$ is

$$\begin{bmatrix} 1 & z_t^{\beta_3} & \beta_2 z_t^{\beta_3}\log(z_t) \end{bmatrix}.$$

The third column of $\boldsymbol{X}(\boldsymbol{\beta})$ is thus very similar to the second column, each element of the latter being equal to the corresponding element of the former times a constant and $\log(z_t)$. Unless the range of z_t is very great, or there are some values of z_t very close to zero, $z_t^{\beta_3}$ and $\beta_2 z_t^{\beta_3}\log(z_t)$ will tend to be very highly correlated. Thus the matrix $\boldsymbol{X}^\top(\boldsymbol{\beta})\boldsymbol{X}(\boldsymbol{\beta})$, and hence in most cases the Hessian as well, will often be close to singular. This example will be discussed in more detail in Chapter 6.

The concepts of local and global identification discussed above are different from the corresponding concepts of **asymptotic identification**, which we will discuss in Chapter 5. A model is asymptotically identified in either the local or the global sense if, as the sample size n tends to infinity, the model is always identified in the appropriate sense. This is a property of the model and of the way in which the data are generated (see Section 2.4 for a discussion of data-generating processes) rather than a property of the model and a given data set. As we will see in Chapter 5, it is quite possible for a model to be identified in finite samples by almost all data sets and yet to be asymptotically unidentified; and it is likewise possible for a model to be asymptotically identified and yet not be identified by many actual data sets.

2.4 MODELS AND DATA-GENERATING PROCESSES

In economics, it is probably not often the case that a relationship like (2.01) actually represents the way in which a dependent variable is generated, as it might if $x_t(\boldsymbol{\beta})$ were a physical response function and u_t merely represented errors in measuring y_t. Instead, it is usually a way of modeling how y_t varies with the values of certain variables. They may be the only variables about which we have information or the only ones that we are interested in for a particular purpose. If we had more information about potential explanatory variables, we might very well specify $x_t(\boldsymbol{\beta})$ differently so as to make use of that additional information.

It is sometimes desirable to make explicit the fact that $x_t(\boldsymbol{\beta})$ represents the **conditional mean** of y_t, that is, the mean of y_t conditional on the values of a number of other variables. The set of variables on which y_t is conditioned is often referred to as an **information set**. If Ω_t denotes the information set on which the expectation of y_t is to be conditioned, one could define $x_t(\boldsymbol{\beta})$ formally as $E(y_t \,|\, \Omega_t)$. There may be more than one such information set. Thus we might well have both

$$x_{1t}(\boldsymbol{\beta}_1) \equiv E(y_t \,|\, \Omega_{1t}) \quad \text{and} \quad x_{2t}(\boldsymbol{\beta}_2) \equiv E(y_t \,|\, \Omega_{2t}),$$

where Ω_{1t} and Ω_{2t} denote two different information sets. The functions $x_{1t}(\boldsymbol{\beta}_1)$ and $x_{2t}(\boldsymbol{\beta}_1)$ might well be quite different, and we might want to estimate both of them for different purposes. There are many circumstances in which we might not want to condition on all available information. For example, if the ultimate purpose of specifying a regression function is to use it for forecasting, there may be no point in conditioning on information that will not be available at the time the forecast is to be made. Even when we do want to take account of all available information, the fact that a certain variable belongs to Ω_t does not imply that it will appear in $x_t(\boldsymbol{\beta})$, since its value may tell us nothing useful about the conditional mean of y_t, and including it may impair our ability to estimate how other variables affect that conditional mean.

For any given dependent variable y_t and information set Ω_t, one is always at liberty to consider the difference $y_t - E(y_t \,|\, \Omega_t)$ as the error term associated with the tth observation. But for a *regression model* to be applicable, these differences must generally have the i.i.d. property. Actually, it is possible, when the sample size is large, to deal with cases in which the error terms are independent, but identically distributed only as regards their means, and not necessarily as regards their variances. We will discuss techniques for dealing with such cases in Chapters 16 and 17, in the latter of which we will also relax the independence assumption. As we will see in Chapter 3, however, conventional techniques for making inferences from regression models are unreliable when models lack the i.i.d. property, even when the regression function $x_t(\boldsymbol{\beta})$ is "correctly" specified. Thus we are in general not at liberty to choose an arbitrary information set and estimate a properly specified regression function based on it if we want to make inferences using conventional procedures.

There are, however, exceptional cases in which we can choose any information set we like, because models based on different information sets will always be mutually consistent. For example, suppose that the vector consisting of y_t and each of x_{1t} through x_{mt} is independently and identically distributed according to the multivariate normal distribution. Then if $\boldsymbol{x}_t^*$ denotes a vector consisting of *any* subset of x_{1t} through x_{mt}, we can always write

$$y_t = \beta_0^* + \boldsymbol{x}_t^* \boldsymbol{\beta}^* + u_t, \quad u_t \sim \text{NID}(0, \sigma_*^2), \tag{2.08}$$

where the notation "$u_t \sim \text{NID}(0, \sigma_*^2)$" is a shorthand way of saying that the u_t's are **normally and independently distributed**, or **n.i.d.**, with mean zero and variance σ_*^2. This is true for any subset of the x_{it}'s because any linear combination of variables that are jointly distributed as multivariate normal is itself normally distributed. Thus the error term u_t implicitly defined by (2.08) will be normally and independently distributed, regardless of what x_{it}'s we include in $\boldsymbol{x}_t^*$, and can always be made to have mean zero by choosing β_0^* appropriately. This is true even if $\boldsymbol{x}_t^*$ is a null vector, since then (2.08) just says that y_t is equal to its mean plus a random variable u_t which is n.i.d. with mean zero, and y_t is itself normally distributed. For more on this and other special cases, and for a much more extensive treatment of the interpretation of regression models, see Spanos (1986).

A **model** such as (2.01) should be distinguished from a **data-generating process**, or **DGP**, such as

$$y_t = x_t(\boldsymbol{\beta}_0) + u_t, \quad u_t \sim \text{NID}(0, \sigma_0^2), \quad t = 1, \ldots, n. \tag{2.09}$$

A regression model such as (2.01) specifies that the mean of y_t conditional on a *specified* set of variables $\boldsymbol{Z}_t$ is a *given* function of $\boldsymbol{Z}_t$ and the (generally unknown) parameters $\boldsymbol{\beta}$. It also specifies that the y_t's are mutually independent and have the same variance around their conditional means. On the other hand, a DGP is a *complete* characterization of the statistical properties of the dependent variable. If the DGP is known, then both the values of all parameters and the distributions of all random quantities must be specified.

Thus there are two important differences between the model (2.01) and the DGP (2.09). The former involves an *unknown* vector of coefficients $\boldsymbol{\beta}$, while the latter involves a specific coefficient vector $\boldsymbol{\beta}_0$, which would be known if we knew the DGP. The error terms u_t for the model are merely specified to be independent and identically distributed, with mean zero and unknown variance σ^2. In contrast, those for the DGP have been specified to be *normally* and independently distributed with known variance σ_0^2, which implies that we could actually generate a sequence of u_t's if we wanted to. Of course, we could just as well have specified a DGP with errors that follow some distribution other than the normal; what matters is that the distribution be specified completely. On the other hand, we may be interested in what happens under a whole family of DGPs, and in such cases a complete specification would be inappropriate.

A model can thus be viewed as a **set of DGPs**. In the process of estimating a model, what we are doing is to try to obtain some estimated characterization of the DGP that actually did generate the data; in the case of the nonlinear regression model (2.01), the desired characterization is a set of **parameter estimates**, that is, estimates of the unknown parameters $\boldsymbol{\beta}$ of the regression function, plus an estimate of the **error variance**, σ^2. Since in a nonlinear regression only the mean and variance of the errors are specified, the characterization of the DGP obtained by estimating the model is *partial*, or *incomplete*. Later in the book, in Chapter 8, we will discuss another estimation method, that of maximum likelihood, which yields a *complete* characterization of a DGP after estimation. Thus we can say that this method produces a *unique* estimated DGP, whereas any method used to estimate a nonlinear regression model will produce a *set* of DGPs, all satisfying the estimated characterization.

This set of DGPs, or the single estimated DGP when appropriate, belongs of course to the set of DGPs defined by the model itself. Statistical estimation can therefore be regarded as a procedure by which from a given set of DGPs, called the model, a subset is selected. The selection is of course a *random* procedure, since a single DGP belonging to the model can generate different sets of random observations that yield different random estimated characterizations. One can then discuss the *probability*, for a given DGP, that the estimated characterization is *close*, in some sense, to the DGP itself. Different estimation procedures can be ranked by these probabilities, and we will usually prefer **efficient** estimation procedures, that is, those for which the probability is high that the subset selected by the procedure is close to the DGP, always assuming, of course, that the DGP actually does belong to the model.

It is impossible to say anything of interest about the *statistical* properties of estimators and test statistics without specifying *both* the model *and* the process that generated the data. In practice, of course, we almost never know the DGP, unless we are conducting a Monte Carlo experiment and have the privilege of generating the data ourselves (see Chapter 21). Thus, when we actually estimate models, we cannot reasonably expect the process that actually generated the data to be a special case of the model we have estimated, as (2.09) is of (2.01), unless we are exceptionally fortunate. In the course of this book, we will nevertheless frequently assume that this is indeed the case, because it is then easy to obtain definite results. But we will also explicitly deal with many situations in which the DGP is *not* a special case of the model being estimated.

The additive structure of the nonlinear regression model makes it natural to discuss the model's two component parts separately. We first discuss regression functions, which determine the conditional mean of y_t, and then discuss error terms, which determine all of its higher conditional moments. It is important to remember that every time we estimate a model like (2.01), we are, implicitly if not explicitly, making what are usually rather strong assumptions about *both* $x_t(\boldsymbol{\beta})$ and u_t. Since it is typically impossible using standard techniques to make valid inferences if these assumptions are false, it is important to be aware of them and, of course, to test them against the evidence provided by the data.

2.5 LINEAR AND NONLINEAR REGRESSION FUNCTIONS

The general regression function $x_t(\boldsymbol{\beta})$ can be made specific in a very large number of ways. It is worthwhile to consider a number of special cases so as to get some idea of the variety of specific regression functions that are commonly used in practice.

The very simplest regression function is

$$x_t(\boldsymbol{\beta}) = \beta_1 \iota_t = \beta_1, \tag{2.10}$$

where ι_t is the tth element of an n–vector $\boldsymbol{\iota}$, each element of which is 1. In this case, the model (2.01) says that the conditional mean of y_t is simply a constant. While this is a trivial example of a regression function, since $x_t(\boldsymbol{\beta})$ is the same for all t, it is nevertheless a good example to start with and to keep in mind. All regression functions are simply fancier versions of (2.10). And any regression function that cannot fit the data at least as well as (2.10) should be considered a highly unsatisfactory one.

The next-simplest regression function is the **simple linear regression function**

$$x_t(\boldsymbol{\beta}) = \beta_1 + \beta_2 z_t, \tag{2.11}$$

where z_t is a single independent variable. Actually, an even simpler model would be one with a single independent variable and no constant term. However, in most applied problems it does not make sense to omit the constant term. Many linear regression functions are used as approximations to unknown conditional mean functions, and such approximations will rarely be accurate if they are constrained to pass through the origin. Equation (2.11) has two parameters, an **intercept** β_1 and a **slope** β_2. This function is linear in both variables (ι_t and z_t, or just z_t if one chooses not to call ι_t a variable) and parameters (β_1 and β_2). Although this model is often too simple, it does have some advantages. Because it is very easy to graph y_t against z_t, we can use such a graph to see what the regression function looks like, how well the model fits, and whether a linear relationship adequately describes the data. "Eyeballing" the data in this way is harder, and therefore much less often done, when a model involves more than one independent variable.

One obvious generalization of (2.11) is the **multiple linear regression function**

$$x_t(\boldsymbol{\beta}) = \beta_1 z_{t1} + \beta_2 z_{t2} + \beta_3 z_{t3} + \cdots + \beta_k z_{tk}, \tag{2.12}$$

where z_{t1} through z_{tk} are independent variables, and z_{t1} may or may not be a constant term. This regression function could also have been written more compactly as

$$x_t(\boldsymbol{\beta}) = \boldsymbol{Z}_t \boldsymbol{\beta},$$

where $\boldsymbol{Z}_t$ is a $1 \times k$ vector and $\boldsymbol{\beta}$ is a $k \times 1$ vector. Notice that (2.12) embodies what may be a very strong assumption, namely, that the effect of a change in any particular independent variable on y_t is independent of the values of all the other independent variables. When this assumption is inappropriate, multiple linear regression models may be seriously misleading.

Next come a whole array of regression functions like

$$x_t(\boldsymbol{\beta}) = \beta_1 z_{t1} + \beta_2 z_{t2} + \beta_3 z_{t2}^2 + \beta_4 z_{t1} z_{t2},$$

which are linear in the parameters but have some of the independent variables entering in a nonlinear fashion. Models involving this sort of regression function can be handled like any other linear regression model, simply by defining new regressors in an appropriate fashion. Here, for example, one might define z_{t3} as z_{t2}^2 and z_{t4} as $z_{t1}z_{t2}$. Using this type of function allows one to avoid assuming that all effects are additive, as implied by (2.12), but may easily require one to estimate more parameters than is practical with many data sets. Because of this, unless there is some theoretical reason to expect powers or products of independent variables to appear in the regression function, most applied econometricians tend to ignore this type of specification.

A regression function that allows all the independent variables to interact without requiring the estimation of additional parameters is the multiplicative function

$$x_t(\boldsymbol{\beta}) = e^{\beta_1} z_{t2}^{\beta_2} z_{t3}^{\beta_3}. \tag{2.13}$$

Observe that this function can be evaluated only when z_{t2} and z_{t3} are positive for all t. It is the first genuinely nonlinear regression function we have seen, since it is clearly linear neither in parameters nor in variables. However, a nonlinear model like

$$y_t = e^{\beta_1} z_{t2}^{\beta_2} z_{t3}^{\beta_3} + u_t \tag{2.14}$$

is very rarely estimated in practice. The reason is that the assumption of identically distributed, additive error terms is both implausible and inconvenient. It is implausible because the z_{ti}'s enter multiplicatively, which implies that their effects depend on the levels of all the other variables, while the error terms enter additively, which implies that their effect does not depend on the level of any of the independent variables. It is inconvenient because (2.14) has to be estimated by nonlinear rather than ordinary least squares.

It is easy to modify (2.14) so that the error terms enter multiplicatively. The most obvious such model is

$$y_t = \left(e^{\beta_1} z_{t2}^{\beta_2} z_{t3}^{\beta_3}\right)(1 + v_t) \equiv e^{\beta_1} z_{t2}^{\beta_2} z_{t3}^{\beta_3} + u_t, \tag{2.15}$$

where the disturbances $1 + v_t$, which are dimensionless quantities, are multiplicative. Although the underlying errors v_t are i.i.d., the additive errors u_t are now proportional to the regression function. If the model fits reasonably well, the v_t's should be quite small (say, less than about 0.05). Now recall that $e^w \cong 1 + w$ for w close to zero. Hence, for models that fit reasonably well, (2.15) will be very similar to the model

$$y_t = e^{\beta_1} z_{t2}^{\beta_2} z_{t3}^{\beta_3} e^{v_t}. \tag{2.16}$$

Now suppose we take logarithms of both sides of (2.16). The result is

$$\log(y_t) = \beta_1 + \beta_2 \log(z_{t2}) + \beta_3 \log(z_{t3}) + v_t, \tag{2.17}$$

which is a linear regression model. It is obvious that this model, which is linear in the parameters and in the logarithms of all the variables, will be very much easier to estimate than the nonlinear model (2.14). The above arguments suggest that it is, if anything, more plausible. Thus it should come as no surprise to learn that loglinear regression models, like (2.17), are estimated very frequently in practice, while multiplicative models with additive error terms, like (2.14), are very rarely estimated.

A purely multiplicative model like (2.16) can be made linear by taking logarithms. However, a model that mixes additive and multiplicative components cannot be transformed to a linear model. Thus, no matter how one specifies the error terms, models involving regression functions like

$$x_t(\boldsymbol{\beta}) = \beta_1 + \beta_2 z_{t2}^{\beta_3} + \beta_4 z_{t3} \quad \text{and} \tag{2.18}$$

$$x_t(\boldsymbol{\beta}) = \beta_1 + \beta_2 z_{t2}^{\beta_3} z_{t3}^{\beta_4} \tag{2.19}$$

must inevitably be estimated by nonlinear methods. As one might expect, such models are not estimated nearly as frequently as linear or loglinear models, partly out of laziness, no doubt, but mainly because there are often neither theoretical nor empirical reasons to choose this type of specification over more conventional ones. Indeed, regression functions like (2.18) and (2.19) are notoriously difficult to deal with because it is hard to estimate all the parameters jointly with any degree of precision. Recall the discussion of how models based on the regression function (2.07), which is very similar to these, are likely to be poorly identified.

The final example of a nonlinear regression function that we will consider is very different in spirit from ones like (2.18). Consider the regression function

$$x_t(\boldsymbol{\beta}) = \beta_1 + \beta_2(z_{t2} - \beta_3 z_{t3}) + \beta_4(z_{t4} - \beta_3 z_{t5}). \tag{2.20}$$

This function is linear in the independent variables ι_t and z_{t2} through z_{t5}, but it is nonlinear in the parameters β_1 through β_4. It is in fact a linear regression function with a single **nonlinear restriction** on the coefficients. To see this, consider the unrestricted linear regression function

$$x_t(\boldsymbol{\beta}) = \gamma_1 + \gamma_2 z_{t2} + \gamma_3 z_{t3} + \gamma_4 z_{t4} + \gamma_5 z_{t5}.$$

If we impose the nonlinear restriction

$$\frac{\gamma_3}{\gamma_5} = \frac{\gamma_2}{\gamma_4}, \tag{2.21}$$

and then reparametrize so that

$$\beta_1 = \gamma_1, \quad \beta_2 = \gamma_2, \quad \beta_3 = -\frac{\gamma_5}{\gamma_4}, \quad \text{and} \quad \beta_4 = \gamma_4,$$

we obtain (2.20). Note that the restriction (2.21) can be written in many equivalent ways, including

$$\gamma_3 = \frac{\gamma_2\gamma_5}{\gamma_4}, \quad \gamma_2 = \frac{\gamma_3\gamma_4}{\gamma_5}, \quad \text{and} \quad \frac{\gamma_2}{\gamma_3} = \frac{\gamma_4}{\gamma_5}.$$

It is typical of nonlinear restrictions that they can be written in many different but equivalent ways, and in consequence the regression function can be parametrized in many different ways.

Regression functions like (2.20) are very commonly encountered in econometrics. They arise, for example, in many models with rational expectations — see Hoffman and Schmidt (1981) or Gregory and Veall (1985, 1987) — and in models with serial correlation (see Chapter 10). Such models are generally not particularly difficult to estimate, provided that the restrictions are more or less true.

2.6 Error Terms

When we specify a regression model, we must specify two things: the regression function $x_t(\boldsymbol{\beta})$ and at least some of the properties of the error terms u_t. We have already seen how important the second of these can be. When we added errors with constant variance to the multiplicative regression function (2.13), we obtained a genuinely nonlinear regression model. But when we added errors that were proportional to the regression function, as in (2.15), and made use of the approximation $e^w \cong 1 + w$, which is a very good one when w is small, we obtained a loglinear regression model. It should be clear from this example that how we specify the error terms will have a major effect on the model which is actually estimated.

In (2.01) we specified that the error terms were independent with identical means of zero and variances σ^2, but we did not specify how they were actually distributed. Even these assumptions may often be too strong. They rule out any sort of dependence across observations and any type of variation over time or with the values of any of the independent variables. They also rule out distributions where the tails are so thick that the error terms do not have a finite variance. One such distribution is the Cauchy distribution. A random variable that is distributed as Cauchy not only has no finite variance but no finite mean either. See Chapter 4 and Appendix B.

There are several meanings of the word *independence* in the literature on statistics and econometrics. Two random variables z_1 and z_2 are said to be **stochastically independent** if their joint probability distribution function $F(z_1, z_2)$ is equal to the product of their two marginal distribution functions $F(z_1, \infty)$ and $F(\infty, z_2)$. This is sometimes called **independence in probability**, but we will employ the former, more modern, terminology. Some authors say that two random variables z_1 and z_2 are **linearly independent** if $E(z_1 z_2) = E(z_1)E(z_2)$, a weaker condition, which is implied by stochastic independence but does not imply it. This terminology is unfortunate, because this meaning of "linearly independent" is not the same as its usual meaning in linear algebra, and we will therefore not use it. Instead, in this situation we will merely say that z_1 and z_2 are **uncorrelated**, or have zero covariance. If either z_1 or z_2 has mean zero and they are uncorrelated, $E(z_1 z_2) = 0$. There is a sense in which z_1 and z_2 are **orthogonal** in this situation, and we will sometimes use this terminology as well.

When we say that the u_t's are independent, we mean that they are stochastically independent. This implies not only that $E(u_t u_s) = 0$ for all $t \neq s$, but also that $E\big(h_1(u_t)h_2(u_s)\big) = 0$ for all (measurable) functions $h_1(\cdot)$ and $h_2(\cdot)$. Error terms that are independent and have the same means and variances are sometimes said to be **white noise**. This terminology, which is taken from the engineering literature, refers to the fact that, just as white light contains equal amounts of light of all frequencies, white noise errors contain equal amounts of randomness of all frequencies. Numerous different definitions of white noise are in use in econometrics and in other disciplines, and the term is often used in ways that are not in accord with its strict meaning.

Notice the important distinction between error terms and **residuals**. *Any* linear or nonlinear regression generates a vector of residuals, whether it makes sense or not. Residuals will have certain properties simply as a result of how they are obtained, regardless of how the data were actually generated. For example, OLS residuals will always be orthogonal to all the regressors, and NLS residuals will always be orthogonal to the matrix $\hat{\boldsymbol{X}}$. Error terms, on the other hand, are unobservable (but estimable) quantities about which we have to make certain assumptions as part of the specification of the model. We will of course often want to test those assumptions and will often do so by calculating test statistics that depend on the residuals.

A large part of the literature on the specification and testing of regression models is concerned with testing for particular violations of the assumption of i.i.d. errors. When such violations are found, it may then be possible to transform a model with non-i.i.d. errors into one where the transformed errors are i.i.d. Either the independence assumption or the assumption of identical means and variances, or both at once, may be violated. The independence assumption is commonly violated when one uses **time-series data**; successive error terms u_t may appear to be correlated with each other, giving rise to the phenomenon of **serial correlation**. The assumption of identical distributions is commonly violated when one uses **cross-section data**; different u_t's may seem to come from the same family of distributions but to have different variances, giving rise to the phenomenon of **heteroskedasticity**. The opposite of heteroskedasticity, incidentally, is **homoskedasticity**. Whenever error terms have a common variance, they are said to be **homoskedastic**; when they do not, they are said to be **heteroskedastic**. Of course, correlation of error terms across observations is by no means a feature only of time-series data, and heteroskedasticity is by no means a feature only of cross-section data. Both these phenomena can occur with all types of data sets, although *serial* correlation is necessarily associated with time-series data and heteroskedasticity is particularly common with cross-section data.

We will deal with serial correlation and heteroskedasticity at length in subsequent chapters (notably in Chapters 9, 10, 11, and 16). For the moment, as an illustration, consider a simple form of heteroskedasticity:

$$u_t = w_t v_t, \quad v_t \sim \text{IID}(0, \sigma_v^2),$$

where w_t is an independent variable that is always nonzero. This specification implies that u_t has mean zero and variance $\sigma_v^2 w_t^2$. Now suppose that the regression function to which the errors u_t adhere additively is

$$x_t(\boldsymbol{\beta}) = \beta_1 + \beta_2 z_t + \beta_3 w_t.$$

Evidently we can obtain a model with i.i.d. errors by dividing the dependent variable and all the independent variables, including the constant term, by w_t. This transformed model is

$$\frac{y_t}{w_t} = \beta_1 \frac{1}{w_t} + \beta_2 \frac{z_t}{w_t} + \beta_3 + v_t. \tag{2.22}$$

Notice that the regressors are now $1/w_t$, z_t/w_t, and a constant, but the coefficient on the constant in (2.22) is actually the coefficient on w_t in the original model, while the coefficient on $1/w_t$ is the constant in the original model. Thus it is very easy to eliminate heteroskedasticity in a case like this, but one has to be careful in interpreting the coefficients of the transformed model.

As we will discuss in Chapter 8, it is common in econometrics to make the rather strong assumption that

$$u_t \sim \text{NID}(0, \sigma^2), \quad t = 1, \ldots, n,$$

which says that the u_t's are normally and independently distributed with mean zero and variance σ^2. Thus each individual u_t is assumed to follow the **normal distribution** with probability density function

$$f(u_t) = \frac{1}{\sqrt{2\pi}} \frac{1}{\sigma} \exp\left(-\frac{u_t^2}{2\sigma^2}\right).$$

The joint density of the n–vector $\boldsymbol{u}$ (of which a typical element is u_t) is therefore assumed to be

$$f(\boldsymbol{u}) = \prod_{t=1}^{n} f(u_t) = \left(\frac{1}{2\pi}\right)^{n/2} \frac{1}{\sigma^n} \exp\left(-\frac{1}{2\sigma^2}\sum_{t=1}^{n} u_t^2\right).$$

There are three principal reasons for assuming normality. The first reason is that because of its computational convenience and familiar properties we often want to use least squares to estimate regression models, and the justification for doing so is much stronger when the errors are normally distributed than when they are not. As we will see in Chapter 8, least squares applied to a regression model has excellent asymptotic properties when the errors are normal, but when the errors have some other known distribution, its properties are no longer so good. The second reason is that when we assume normality, we can often obtain much stronger results than when we merely make an i.i.d. assumption. In particular, for linear regression models with fixed regressors and normal errors, we can obtain exact finite-sample results (see Chapter 3); such results are not available even for linear models when the errors are merely assumed to be i.i.d. The third reason is that once we leave the realm of regression models and try to deal with more general nonlinear models, it often becomes necessary to make distributional assumptions, and the normal distribution is frequently the most convenient one to work with.

None of these practical reasons for assuming that error terms are normally distributed provides any *justification* for making such an assumption. The usual argument is that error terms represent the combined effects of many omitted variables and many different measurement errors. **Central limit theorems** (which are discussed in Chapter 4) tell us, very roughly, that when we average a large number of random variables, the resulting average is approximately normally distributed, more or less regardless of how the original random variables are distributed. The usual argument is that the normality assumption makes sense because we may think of the error terms in regression models as being such an average.

There are at least two problems with this line of argument. First of all, as we will see in Chapter 4, central limit theorems require moderately strong assumptions. They apply to situations in which many random variables, no one of which is "large" relative to the others, are being averaged. It is easy to think of economic variables that might well be omitted from regression models, and therefore form part of the error terms, but which would often be large relative to those error terms. In the case of time-series models, strikes, elections or other political events, and hurricanes or other extreme weather conditions are a few examples that come to mind. There is certainly no reason *a priori* to expect the effects of such events to be responsible for only a small part of the overall error term for any given observation. In the case of cross-section models, the argument for normality is probably even weaker. Whenever we have a large sample of individuals or firms, we are bound to have some observations included in the sample that really do not belong there. Consider, for example, the effect on a cross-section model of the demand for meat of including a few individuals who are vegetarians! Inevitably, the error terms associated with such observations will be large, making it highly unlikely that the distribution of the error terms for the model as a whole will be normal.

The second problem with the central limit theorem argument is that many central limit theorems do not apply to situations in which the number of random variables being averaged is itself random. But since we do not know what variables were omitted and thrown into the error term, we have no real reason for thinking that the number is the same from one observation to the next. Thus we cannot always legitimately invoke a central limit theorem.

These arguments are not intended to suggest that it is silly to assume normality. But whether we have explicitly assumed normality or not, it makes sense to see whether the error terms are in fact approximately normal. If they are not approximately normal, then the wisdom of using least squares is questionable. There are, of course, an infinite number of nonnormal distributions and hence an infinite number of types of nonnormality to look for. Most tests for nonnormality, however, focus on two properties of the normal distribution. If $\varepsilon \sim N(\mu, \sigma^2)$, then

$$E\big((\varepsilon - \mu)^3\big) = 0 \quad \text{and} \tag{2.23}$$

$$E\big((\varepsilon - \mu)^4\big) = 3\sigma^4. \tag{2.24}$$

Expression (2.23) tells us that for the normal distribution, the third **central moment** (that is, the moment about the mean) is zero. This moment is commonly used to measure **skewness**. If it is positive, the distribution is skewed to the right, and if it is negative, the distribution is skewed to the left. Figure 2.8 shows two skewed distributions and, for comparison, a symmetric distribution. Testing for skewness is quite easy; such tests will be discussed in Chapter 16.

Expression (2.24) tells us that the fourth central moment of a normal random variable is 3 times the square of its variance. A random variable with a fourth moment larger than 3 times the square of the second moment has thicker tails than a normally distributed random variable. It may be said to display **excess kurtosis**, or to be **leptokurtic**. On the other hand, a random variable with a fourth moment less than 3 times the square of the second moment has thinner tails than a normally distributed random variable. Such random variables are sometimes referred to as **platykurtic**. Similarly, random variables that follow the normal distribution are sometimes said to be **mesokurtic**. Readers who are familiar with Greek may think that these definitions are in error, since *lepto* means *slim* and *platy* means *fat*. As explained by Kendall and Stuart (1977, p. 88), these terms were originally used to refer not to the tails but to the central part of the distribution; thus leptokurtic

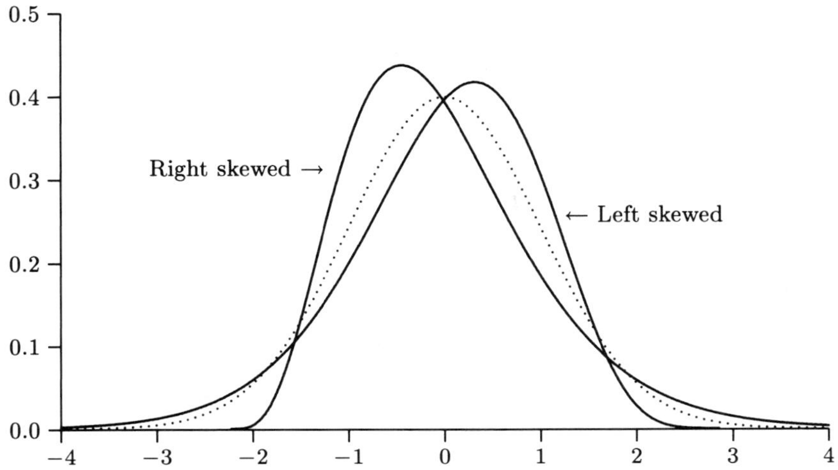

Figure 2.8 Skewed distributions

distributions got their name not because they have thick tails but because they have a (relatively) thin central part, and platykurtic distributions got their name not because they have thin tails but because they have a (relatively) fat central part. However, it is the tails that modern statisticians are referring to when they use these terms. Figure 2.9 illustrates leptokurtic and platykurtic distributions. The standard normal distribution (dotted) is shown for comparison.

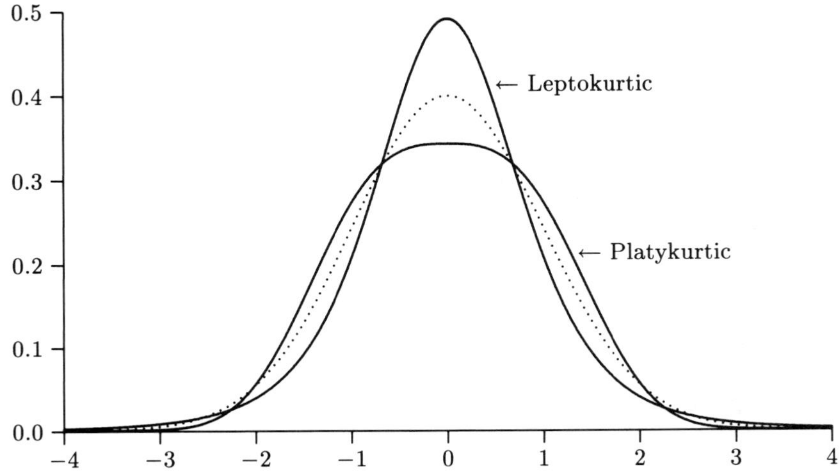

Figure 2.9 Leptokurtic and platykurtic distributions

Thin tails are not much of a problem (and are also not very often encountered), but thick tails can cause serious difficulties for estimation and inference. If the error terms follow a distribution with much thicker tails than the normal distribution, then unusually large error terms will occur by chance relatively often. The least squares procedure weights these large error terms heavily and may therefore yield highly inefficient parameter estimates.

It is quite easy to test for excess kurtosis; see Chapter 16. What one should do if one finds a substantial amount of it is not entirely clear, however. It would certainly be advisable to examine the specification of the model, since heteroskedasticity may lead to the *appearance* of kurtosis, as may an incorrectly specified regression function. If one is confident that the regression function is correctly specified, and that there is no heteroskedasticity, then one should probably consider using estimation methods other than least squares. There is a large literature on what statisticians call "robust" estimation methods, which give less weight to outliers than least squares does; see Krasker, Kuh, and Welsch (1983) for a review of this literature. Alternatively, one could postulate some other distribution than the normal, one with thicker tails, and then apply the method of maximum likelihood, which will be discussed extensively in Chapter 8 and subsequent chapters.

2.7 CONCLUSION

This chapter has provided a nonrigorous introduction to nonlinear regression models, focusing on basic concepts such as the geometry of nonlinear regression. Books that provide more rigorous treatments include Gallant (1987), Bates and Watts (1988), and Seber and Wild (1989). The next chapter deals with how to make inferences from nonlinear regression models and introduces the basic ideas of hypothesis testing in the context of such models. The next step is to provide a treatment of the asymptotic properties of nonlinear least squares, and that is done in Chapters 4 and 5. Then Chapter 6 discusses an "artificial" linear regression called the Gauss-Newton regression, which is associated with every nonlinear regression model. This artificial regression will prove to be very useful for a variety of purposes, including the computation of NLS estimates and the calculation of test statistics.

Terms and Concepts

asymptotic identification
asymptotic results
central limit theorems
central moments
collinearity (multicollinearity)
conditional mean
cross-section data
data-generating process (DGP); relation to models
dynamic models
efficient estimation methods
error terms (disturbances)
error variance
heteroskedasticity
homoskedasticity
identification by a given data set
identification: local and global
independence: stochastic and linear
independent and identically distributed (i.i.d.) random variables
information set
intercept and slope (of a simple linear regression function)
kurtosis: leptokurtosis, mesokurtosis, platykurtosis, excess kurtosis
minima: local and global
minimization algorithm
model: a set of DGPs
nonlinear least squares (NLS)
nonlinear restrictions
normal distribution
normally and independently distributed (n.i.d.) random variables
orthogonal random variables
parameter estimates
poorly identified model
regression functions: linear and nonlinear; simple and multiple
regression manifold
regression models: linear and nonlinear; univariate and multivariate
residuals
serial correlation
skewness
stationary point
sum-of-squares function
tangent space
time-series data
uncorrelated random variables
variables: dependent and independent
white noise

Chapter 3

Inference in Nonlinear Regression Models

3.1 Introduction

Suppose that one is given a vector $\boldsymbol{y}$ of observations on some dependent variable, a vector $\boldsymbol{x}(\boldsymbol{\beta})$ of, in general nonlinear, regression functions, which may and normally will depend on independent variables, and the data needed to evaluate $\boldsymbol{x}(\boldsymbol{\beta})$. Then, assuming that these data allow one to identify all elements of the parameter vector $\boldsymbol{\beta}$ and that one has access to a suitable computer program for nonlinear least squares and enough computer time, one can always obtain NLS estimates $\hat{\boldsymbol{\beta}}$. In order to interpret these estimates, one generally makes the heroic assumption that the model is "correct," which means that $\boldsymbol{y}$ is in fact generated by a DGP from the family

$$\boldsymbol{y} = \boldsymbol{x}(\boldsymbol{\beta}) + \boldsymbol{u}, \quad \boldsymbol{u} \sim \mathrm{IID}(\mathbf{0}, \sigma^2\mathbf{I}). \tag{3.01}$$

Without this assumption, or some less restrictive variant, it would be very difficult to say anything about the properties of $\hat{\boldsymbol{\beta}}$, although in certain special cases one can do so.

It is clear that $\hat{\boldsymbol{\beta}}$ must be a vector of random variables, since it will depend on $\boldsymbol{y}$ and hence on the vector of error terms $\boldsymbol{u}$. Thus, if we are to make inferences about $\boldsymbol{\beta}$, we must recognize that $\hat{\boldsymbol{\beta}}$ is random and quantify its randomness. In Chapter 5, we will demonstrate that it is reasonable, when the sample size is large enough, to treat $\hat{\boldsymbol{\beta}}$ as being normally distributed around the true value of $\boldsymbol{\beta}$, which we may call $\boldsymbol{\beta}_0$. Thus the only thing we need to know if we are to make asymptotically valid inferences about $\boldsymbol{\beta}$ is the **covariance matrix** of $\hat{\boldsymbol{\beta}}$, say $\boldsymbol{V}(\hat{\boldsymbol{\beta}})$. In the next section, we discuss how this covariance matrix may be estimated for linear and nonlinear regression models and. In Section 3.3, we show how the resulting estimates may be used to make inferences about $\boldsymbol{\beta}$. In Section 3.4, we discuss the basic ideas that underlie all types of hypothesis testing. In Section 3.5, we then discuss procedures for testing hypotheses in linear regression models. In Section 3.6, we discuss similar procedures for testing hypotheses in nonlinear regression models. The latter section provides an opportunity to introduce the three fundamental principles on which most hypothesis tests are based: the Wald, Lagrange multiplier, and likelihood ratio principles. Finally, in Section 3.7, we discuss the effects of imposing incorrect restrictions and introduce the notion of preliminary test estimators.

3.2 COVARIANCE MATRIX ESTIMATION

In the case of the linear regression model

$$\boldsymbol{y} = \boldsymbol{X\beta} + \boldsymbol{u}, \quad \boldsymbol{u} \sim \mathrm{IID}(\mathbf{0}, \sigma^2 \mathbf{I}), \tag{3.02}$$

it is well known that when the DGP satisfies (3.02) for specific parameter values $\boldsymbol{\beta}_0$ and σ_0, the covariance matrix of the vector of OLS estimates $\hat{\boldsymbol{\beta}}$ is

$$\boldsymbol{V}(\hat{\boldsymbol{\beta}}) = \sigma_0^2 \big(\boldsymbol{X}^{\top}\boldsymbol{X}\big)^{-1}. \tag{3.03}$$

The proof of this familiar result is quite straightforward. The covariance matrix $\boldsymbol{V}(\hat{\boldsymbol{\beta}})$ is defined as the expectation of the outer product of $\hat{\boldsymbol{\beta}} - \boldsymbol{\beta}_0$ with itself. Starting with this definition, we first replace $\hat{\boldsymbol{\beta}}$ by what it is equal to under the DGP, then take expectations, and finally simplify the algebra to obtain (3.03):

$$\begin{aligned}
\boldsymbol{V}(\hat{\boldsymbol{\beta}}) &\equiv E(\hat{\boldsymbol{\beta}} - \boldsymbol{\beta}_0)(\hat{\boldsymbol{\beta}} - \boldsymbol{\beta}_0)^{\top} \\
&= E\big((\boldsymbol{X}^{\top}\boldsymbol{X})^{-1}\boldsymbol{X}^{\top}\boldsymbol{y} - \boldsymbol{\beta}_0\big)\big((\boldsymbol{X}^{\top}\boldsymbol{X})^{-1}\boldsymbol{X}^{\top}\boldsymbol{y} - \boldsymbol{\beta}_0\big)^{\top} \\
&= E\big((\boldsymbol{X}^{\top}\boldsymbol{X})^{-1}\boldsymbol{X}^{\top}(\boldsymbol{X\beta}_0 + \boldsymbol{u}) - \boldsymbol{\beta}_0\big)\big((\boldsymbol{X}^{\top}\boldsymbol{X})^{-1}\boldsymbol{X}^{\top}(\boldsymbol{X\beta}_0 + \boldsymbol{u}) - \boldsymbol{\beta}_0\big)^{\top} \\
&= E\big(\boldsymbol{\beta}_0 + (\boldsymbol{X}^{\top}\boldsymbol{X})^{-1}\boldsymbol{X}^{\top}\boldsymbol{u} - \boldsymbol{\beta}_0\big)\big(\boldsymbol{\beta}_0 + (\boldsymbol{X}^{\top}\boldsymbol{X})^{-1}\boldsymbol{X}^{\top}\boldsymbol{u} - \boldsymbol{\beta}_0\big)^{\top} \\
&= E\big(\boldsymbol{X}^{\top}\boldsymbol{X}\big)^{-1}\boldsymbol{X}^{\top}\boldsymbol{u}\boldsymbol{u}^{\top}\boldsymbol{X}\big(\boldsymbol{X}^{\top}\boldsymbol{X}\big)^{-1} \\
&= \big(\boldsymbol{X}^{\top}\boldsymbol{X}\big)^{-1}\boldsymbol{X}^{\top}(\sigma_0^2\mathbf{I})\boldsymbol{X}\big(\boldsymbol{X}^{\top}\boldsymbol{X}\big)^{-1} \\
&= \sigma_0^2\big(\boldsymbol{X}^{\top}\boldsymbol{X}\big)^{-1}\boldsymbol{X}^{\top}\boldsymbol{X}\big(\boldsymbol{X}^{\top}\boldsymbol{X}\big)^{-1} \\
&= \sigma_0^2\big(\boldsymbol{X}^{\top}\boldsymbol{X}\big)^{-1}.
\end{aligned}$$

Deriving an analogous result for the nonlinear regression model (3.01) requires a few concepts of asymptotic analysis that we have not yet developed, plus a certain amount of mathematical manipulation. We will therefore postpone this derivation until Chapter 5 and merely state an approximate result here.

For a nonlinear model, we cannot in general obtain an exact expression for $\boldsymbol{V}(\hat{\boldsymbol{\beta}})$ in the finite-sample case. In Chapter 5, on the assumption that the data are generated by a DGP which is a special case of (3.01), we will, however, obtain an asymptotic result which allows us to state that

$$\boldsymbol{V}(\hat{\boldsymbol{\beta}}) \cong \sigma_0^2\big(\boldsymbol{X}^{\top}(\boldsymbol{\beta}_0)\boldsymbol{X}(\boldsymbol{\beta}_0)\big)^{-1}, \tag{3.04}$$

where $\cong$ means "is approximately equal to," and $\boldsymbol{X}(\boldsymbol{\beta}_0)$ is the matrix of partial derivatives of the regression functions introduced in (2.04). How good this approximation is will depend on the model and on the sample size; it will generally be better for models that are closer to linearity and for larger sample sizes.

In practice, of course, we cannot use (3.04) because we do not know σ_0^2 or $\boldsymbol{\beta}_0$; we have to estimate these. The only sensible way to estimate $\boldsymbol{\beta}_0$ in this context is to use $\hat{\boldsymbol{\beta}}$, but there are at least two ways to estimate σ_0^2. As a result, there are two ways to estimate $\boldsymbol{V}(\hat{\boldsymbol{\beta}})$. One is to use

$$\hat{\boldsymbol{V}}(\hat{\boldsymbol{\beta}}) \equiv \hat{\sigma}^2 \big(\hat{\boldsymbol{X}}^\top \hat{\boldsymbol{X}}\big)^{-1}, \tag{3.05}$$

where $\hat{\sigma}^2 \equiv n^{-1} SSR(\hat{\boldsymbol{\beta}})$, and the other is to use

$$\boldsymbol{V}_s(\hat{\boldsymbol{\beta}}) \equiv s^2 \big(\hat{\boldsymbol{X}}^\top \hat{\boldsymbol{X}}\big)^{-1}, \tag{3.06}$$

where $s^2 \equiv (n-k)^{-1} SSR(\hat{\boldsymbol{\beta}})$.

The first of these estimators, expression (3.05), employs the maximum likelihood estimator of σ^2 (see Chapter 8), which is biased downward. To see this, notice that, because $SSR(\hat{\boldsymbol{\beta}})$ minimizes $SSR(\boldsymbol{\beta})$,

$$SSR(\hat{\boldsymbol{\beta}}) \leq SSR(\boldsymbol{\beta}_0).$$

Moreover, under the assumed DGP,

$$E\big(SSR(\boldsymbol{\beta}_0)\big) = n\sigma_0^2,$$

because $SSR(\boldsymbol{\beta}_0)$ is then simply $\sum_{t=1}^{n} u_t^2$, and u_t^2 has expectation σ_0^2. Thus, by using $\hat{\sigma}^2$ in (3.05), we tend to underestimate σ^2 and hence tend to underestimate the variability of the parameter estimates.

This suggests that we should use s^2 rather than $\hat{\sigma}^2$ when estimating covariance matrices for parameter estimates from nonlinear regression models, despite the fact that there is no exact finite-sample justification for doing so. There seems to be an emerging consensus in favor of this approach, although some nonlinear regression packages still use $\hat{\sigma}^2$. The reason for using s^2 is that in the linear regression case it yields an unbiased estimate of σ^2. Common sense, asymptotic theory (to be discussed in Section 5.6), and evidence from Monte Carlo experiments all suggest that it will typically yield a *less* biased estimate in the nonlinear case as well.

The result that s^2 provides an unbiased estimate of σ^2 in the linear regression case is undoubtedly familiar to most readers. However, it is sufficiently important that we now sketch the argument. For the linear regression case in which $\boldsymbol{x}(\boldsymbol{\beta}) = \boldsymbol{X\beta}$,

$$\begin{aligned} SSR(\hat{\boldsymbol{\beta}}) &\equiv (\boldsymbol{y} - \boldsymbol{X}\hat{\boldsymbol{\beta}})^{\top}(\boldsymbol{y} - \boldsymbol{X}\hat{\boldsymbol{\beta}}) \\ &= (\boldsymbol{y} - \boldsymbol{X}(\boldsymbol{X}^{\top}\boldsymbol{X})^{-1}\boldsymbol{X}^{\top}\boldsymbol{y})^{\top}(\boldsymbol{y} - \boldsymbol{X}(\boldsymbol{X}^{\top}\boldsymbol{X})^{-1}\boldsymbol{X}^{\top}\boldsymbol{y}) \\ &= \boldsymbol{y}^{\top}(\mathbf{I} - \boldsymbol{X}(\boldsymbol{X}^{\top}\boldsymbol{X})^{-1}\boldsymbol{X}^{\top})\boldsymbol{y} \\ &= \boldsymbol{y}^{\top}\boldsymbol{M}_X\boldsymbol{y}. \end{aligned} \tag{3.07}$$

Under the DGP we have been using, $\boldsymbol{y}^{\top}\boldsymbol{M}_X\boldsymbol{y}$ becomes

$$(\boldsymbol{X\beta}_0 + \boldsymbol{u})^{\top}\boldsymbol{M}_X(\boldsymbol{X\beta}_0 + \boldsymbol{u}).$$

But recall that $\boldsymbol{M}_X$ annihilates everything that lies in $\mathcal{S}(\boldsymbol{X})$. Since the conditional mean $\boldsymbol{X\beta}_0$ certainly lies in $\mathcal{S}(\boldsymbol{X})$, $SSR(\hat{\boldsymbol{\beta}})$ reduces to

$$\boldsymbol{u}^{\top}\boldsymbol{M}_X\boldsymbol{u}.$$

The expectation of this expression is

$$\begin{aligned} E(\boldsymbol{u}^{\top}\boldsymbol{M}_X\boldsymbol{u}) &= E\big(\mathrm{Tr}(\boldsymbol{u}^{\top}\boldsymbol{M}_X\boldsymbol{u})\big) \\ &= E\big(\mathrm{Tr}(\boldsymbol{M}_X\boldsymbol{u}\boldsymbol{u}^{\top})\big) \\ &= \mathrm{Tr}\big(\boldsymbol{M}_X\sigma_0^2\mathbf{I}\big) \\ &= \sigma_0^2\mathrm{Tr}\big(\boldsymbol{M}_X\big) \\ &= \sigma_0^2(n-k), \end{aligned} \tag{3.08}$$

where the second and last lines of (3.08) both make use of a convenient property of the trace operator that we previously used in Section 1.6. Readers who are not familiar with the result in (3.08) will probably wish to consult Appendix A.

The intuition of expression (3.08) is clear. It tells us that, *on average*, the squared residuals are $(n-k)/n$ times as large as the original squared errors. In effect, then, each one of the k dimensions of the span of $\boldsymbol{X}$ "eats up" one of the original error terms. This "eating up" is depicted in Figure 3.1 for the case of a linear regression model with $k = 1$. Here $\boldsymbol{y}$ is actually equal to $\boldsymbol{X\beta}_0 + \boldsymbol{u}$. The length of the vector $\hat{\boldsymbol{u}} = \boldsymbol{M}_X\boldsymbol{y}$ is less than the length of the true error vector $\boldsymbol{u}$, because the former is orthogonal to $\mathcal{S}(\boldsymbol{X})$ while the latter is not.

This "eating up" of the original error terms gives rise to the errors that least squares makes in estimating the coefficient vector. Components of $\boldsymbol{u}$ that are not orthogonal to $\boldsymbol{X}$ get projected onto $\mathcal{S}(\boldsymbol{X})$ and hence end up in $\hat{\boldsymbol{\beta}}$. This happens to the different elements of $\boldsymbol{u}$ to different degrees. As the discussion of leverage in Section 1.6 should have made clear, some squared residuals will

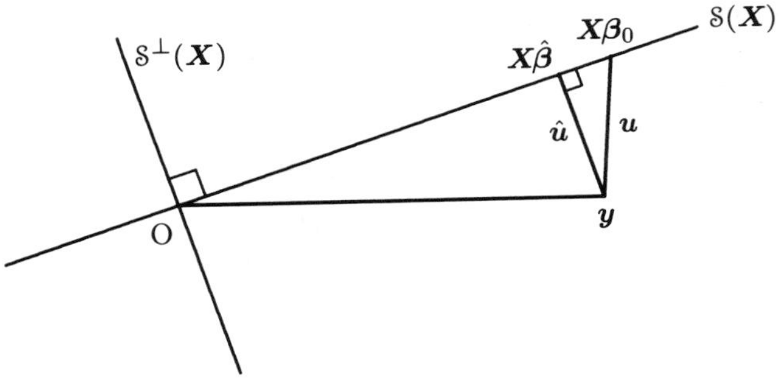

Figure 3.1 Residuals are smaller than error terms

be less than $(n-k)/n$ times as large as the corresponding squared errors, while others will be greater than $(n-k)/n$ times as large. In fact, a little algebra shows that

$$\begin{aligned}
E(\hat{u}_t^2) &= E(y_t - X_t\hat{\beta})^2 \\
&= E(y_t - X_t\beta_0 + X_t\beta_0 - X_t\hat{\beta})^2 \\
&= E\big(u_t - X_t(\hat{\beta} - \beta_0)\big)^2 \\
&= E(u_t^2) - 2E\big(u_t X_t(X^\top X)^{-1}X^\top u\big) \\
&\quad + E\big(X_t(X^\top X)^{-1}X^\top uu^\top X(X^\top X)^{-1}X_t^\top\big) \\
&= \sigma_0^2 - 2\sigma_0^2 X_t(X^\top X)^{-1}X_t^\top + \sigma_0^2 X_t(X^\top X)^{-1}X_t^\top \\
&= \sigma_0^2\big(1 - X_t(X^\top X)^{-1}X_t^\top\big) \\
&= \sigma_0^2 M_{tt},
\end{aligned}$$

where X_t is the tth row of X. Here M_{tt}, the tth diagonal element of M_X, is equal to $1 - h_t$, h_t being the tth diagonal element of P_X. This result uses the fact that $E(u_t u_s) = 0$ for $t \neq s$. For observations that have high leverage (i.e., large h_t) the expectation of the squared residual $\hat{u}_t^2$ will be substantially smaller than $\big((n-k)/n\big)\sigma_0^2$.

From (3.08), it is clear that the estimator

$$s^2 \equiv \frac{y^\top M_X y}{n-k} \tag{3.09}$$

will have expectation σ_0^2 if the data were actually generated by a special case of (3.02). This estimator therefore seems a reasonable one to use in the context of ordinary least squares, and it is what virtually all ordinary least squares regression programs use when calculating the OLS covariance matrix. But notice that although s^2 is unbiased for σ^2, s is *not* unbiased for σ, because taking the square root of s^2 is a nonlinear operation.

These results make it clear that, in the case of *linear* regression models, the standard OLS covariance estimator,

$$\boldsymbol{V}_s(\hat{\boldsymbol{\beta}}) \equiv s^2\big(\boldsymbol{X}^\top\boldsymbol{X}\big)^{-1}, \tag{3.10}$$

provides an unbiased estimate of the true covariance matrix $\sigma_0^2(\boldsymbol{X}^\top\boldsymbol{X})^{-1}$. However, in sharp contrast to the linear case, any attempt to draw inferences from estimates of nonlinear regression models will be hampered by the facts that (3.04) is itself only an approximation and that (3.06) is merely an estimate of (3.04). Despite this fact, most applied workers treat (3.06), or even (3.05), in exactly the same way as they treat the usual OLS covariance matrix (3.10), to form confidence intervals for and test hypotheses about various elements of $\boldsymbol{\beta}$. Because (3.06) is only an estimate, this is a risky thing to do. Nevertheless, in the next two sections, we discuss what is involved in doing so.

3.3 Confidence Intervals and Confidence Regions

A **confidence interval** for a single parameter at some level α (between 0 and 1) is an interval of the real line constructed in such a way that we are confident that the true value of the parameter will lie in that interval $(1-\alpha)\%$ of the time. A **confidence region** is conceptually the same, except that it is a region in an l–dimensional space (usually the l–dimensional analog of an ellipse) which is constructed so that we are confident that the true values of an l–vector of parameters will lie in that region $(1-\alpha)\%$ of the time. Notice that, when we find a confidence interval or region, we are not making a statement about the distribution of the parameter itself but rather about the probability that our *random* interval, because of the way it is constructed in terms of the estimates of the parameters and of their covariance matrix, will include the true value.

In the context of regression models, we normally construct a confidence interval by using an estimate of the single parameter in question, an estimate of its standard error, and, in addition, a certain **critical value** taken from either the normal or the Student's t distribution. The estimated standard error is of course simply the square root of the appropriate diagonal element of the estimated covariance matrix. The critical value depends on $1-\alpha$, the probability that the confidence interval will include the true value; if we want this probability to be very close to one, the critical value must be relatively large, and hence so must be the confidence interval.

Suppose that the parameter we are interested in is β_1, that the NLS estimate of it is $\hat{\beta}_1$, and that the estimated standard error of the estimator is

$$\hat{S}(\hat{\beta}_1) \equiv s\big((\hat{\boldsymbol{X}}^\top\hat{\boldsymbol{X}})_{11}\big)^{-1/2}.$$

We first need to know how long our confidence interval has to be in terms of the estimated standard errors $\hat{S}(\hat{\beta}_1)$. We therefore look up α in a table of two-tail critical values of the normal or Student's t distributions or look up $\alpha/2$ in a table of one-tail critical values.[1] This gives us a critical value c_α. We then find an *approximate* confidence interval

$$\hat{\beta}_1 - c_\alpha \hat{S}(\hat{\beta}_1) \quad \text{to} \quad \hat{\beta}_1 + c_\alpha \hat{S}(\hat{\beta}_1), \tag{3.11}$$

that will include the true value of β_1 roughly $(1-\alpha)\%$ of the time. For example, if α were .05 and we used tables for the normal distribution, we would find that a two-tail critical value was 1.96. This means that for the normal distribution with mean μ and variance ω^2, 95% of the probability mass of this distribution lies between $\mu - 1.96\omega$ and $\mu + 1.96\omega$. Hence, in this case, our approximate confidence interval would be

$$\hat{\beta}_1 - 1.96\hat{S}(\hat{\beta}_1) \quad \text{to} \quad \hat{\beta}_1 + 1.96\hat{S}(\hat{\beta}_1).$$

We are obviously making some very strong assumptions when we create a confidence interval in this way. First, we are assuming that $\hat{\beta}_1$ is normally distributed, something that is strictly justified only if we are dealing with a linear regression model with fixed regressors and normal errors.[2] Second, we are assuming that $\hat{S}(\hat{\beta}_1)$ is the true standard deviation of $\hat{\beta}_1$, which will never actually be the case. Unless the DGP is a special case of the model we have estimated, our estimate of the covariance matrix of $\hat{\boldsymbol{\beta}}$, (3.06), will generally not be valid, even as an approximation. Even if it is valid, s^2 is only an estimate of σ^2 and $\hat{\boldsymbol{X}}^\top\hat{\boldsymbol{X}}$ is only an estimate of $\boldsymbol{X}^\top(\boldsymbol{\beta}_0)\boldsymbol{X}(\boldsymbol{\beta}_0)$. Thus $\hat{S}(\hat{\beta}_1)$ may be quite a poor estimate of $S(\hat{\beta}_1)$.

In the linear case, it is customary to deal with one (but only one) of these problems, namely, the problem that s^2 is only an estimate of σ^2. As we will show in Section 3.5 below, for linear regression models with fixed regressors and normal errors, the quantity

$$\frac{\hat{\beta}_i - \beta_{0i}}{\hat{S}(\hat{\beta}_i)} \tag{3.12}$$

is distributed as Student's t with $n-k$ degrees of freedom when the DGP is a special case of the model being estimated. Thus, by taking the critical values we used in (3.11) from the $t(n-k)$ distribution instead of from the $N(0,1)$ distribution, we can get an exact confidence interval in this very special case.

[1] Actually, nowadays we would probably let a computer do this. Any good statistics program should be able to find the critical value associated with any significance level α, and the significance level associated with any critical value, for the normal, t, F, and χ^2 distributions.

[2] It is justified in this case because $\hat{\boldsymbol{\beta}} - \boldsymbol{\beta}_0 = (\boldsymbol{X}^\top\boldsymbol{X})^{-1}\boldsymbol{X}^\top\boldsymbol{u}$, which implies that $\hat{\boldsymbol{\beta}} - \boldsymbol{\beta}_0$ is simply a linear combination of the normally distributed random variables $\boldsymbol{u}$ and must therefore be normally distributed itself.

Using the t distribution automatically takes into account the fact that s is a biased estimator.

When dealing with a nonlinear model, it is usually more reliable to use the $t(n-k)$ distribution rather than the standard normal distribution. The resulting confidence interval will be a little wider, but in many cases it will still not be wide enough. Most (but not all) of the time, the problems mentioned above result in estimated confidence intervals that are too narrow. Thus it is good practice mentally to reduce the level of confidence attached to any such interval. This is especially important when the model is highly nonlinear, when the error terms may be substantially nonnormal, and when the sample size is small. Unfortunately, there is no easy rule of thumb that can tell us how much to reduce the level of confidence in most given cases. All we can usually do is to rely on experience, evidence from Monte Carlo simulations, and common sense.

When we are interested in two or more parameters, it can be very misleading to look at the confidence intervals for the individual parameters rather than at the confidence region for all the parameters jointly. To see why this is so, we must understand why a joint confidence region for l parameters has the form of the l–dimensional analog of an ellipse. One of the results presented in Appendix B is that if $\boldsymbol{x}$ is an l–vector distributed normally with (vector) mean zero and covariance matrix a nonsingular $l \times l$ matrix $\boldsymbol{V}$, then the scalar random variable given by the quadratic form $\boldsymbol{x}^\top \boldsymbol{V}^{-1}\boldsymbol{x}$ has the χ^2 distribution with l degrees of freedom. We can construct a confidence region for any subset of the components of $\boldsymbol{\beta}$ by using this result.

Suppose that we wish to construct a confidence region for the first l components of the k–vector $\boldsymbol{\beta}$, where $l > 1$. To do this, we will need an estimate of the covariance matrix of the first l elements of $\hat{\boldsymbol{\beta}}$. If $l = k$, we can use either $\hat{\boldsymbol{V}}(\hat{\boldsymbol{\beta}})$ or $\boldsymbol{V}_s(\hat{\boldsymbol{\beta}})$, as given by (3.05) and (3.06). If $l < k$, we must use an $l \times l$ submatrix of one of these estimated covariance matrices. This submatrix can be obtained by the use of a formula for the inverse of a partitioned matrix (see Appendix A) or, more easily, by use of the FWL theorem.[3] If we partition the complete parameter vector $\boldsymbol{\beta}$ as $[\boldsymbol{\beta}_1 \vdots \boldsymbol{\beta}_2]$, with $\boldsymbol{\beta}_1$ denoting the subvector of interest, and let $\hat{\sigma}^2$ be the estimate of σ^2, we obtain

$$\hat{\boldsymbol{V}}(\hat{\boldsymbol{\beta}}_1) = \hat{\sigma}^2 \big(\hat{\boldsymbol{X}}_1^\top \hat{\boldsymbol{M}}_2 \hat{\boldsymbol{X}}_1\big)^{-1},$$

where $\hat{\boldsymbol{M}}_2$ projects off $\mathcal{S}(\hat{\boldsymbol{X}}_2)$. It is thus just as easy to deal with the case $l < k$ as the case $l = k$. To keep the notation simple, however, we will for the remainder of this discussion assume that we are constructing a confidence

[3] While it is clear that the FWL Theorem can be used here if we are interested in a linear regression model, it may not at this point be clear that it is also applicable when the model is nonlinear. In the nonlinear case we must apply the FWL Theorem to the Gauss-Newton regression that will be discussed in Chapter 6.

region for the entire parameter vector $\boldsymbol{\beta}$, implying that $l = k$. For concreteness, we will also assume that the estimated covariance matrix of $\hat{\boldsymbol{\beta}}$ is $\hat{\boldsymbol{V}}(\hat{\boldsymbol{\beta}})$, although it could just as well be $\boldsymbol{V}_s(\hat{\boldsymbol{\beta}})$.

Let us denote the true (but unknown) value of $\boldsymbol{\beta}$ by $\boldsymbol{\beta}_0$. Consider the quadratic form

$$(\hat{\boldsymbol{\beta}} - \boldsymbol{\beta}_0)^{\top}\hat{\boldsymbol{V}}^{-1}(\hat{\boldsymbol{\beta}})(\hat{\boldsymbol{\beta}} - \boldsymbol{\beta}_0). \tag{3.13}$$

This is just a random scalar that depends on the random vector $\hat{\boldsymbol{\beta}}$. For neither a linear nor a nonlinear regression will it actually have the χ^2 distribution with l degrees of freedom in finite samples. But it is reasonable to hope that it will be approximately distributed as $\chi^2(l)$, and in fact such an approximation is valid when the sample is large enough; see Section 5.7. Consequently, with just as much justification (or lack of it) as for the case of a single parameter, the confidence region for $\boldsymbol{\beta}$ is constructed as if (3.13) did indeed have the $\chi^2(l)$ distribution.[4]

For a given set of estimates $\hat{\boldsymbol{\beta}}$, the (approximate) confidence region at level α can be defined as the set of vectors $\boldsymbol{\beta}$ for which the value of (3.13) with $\boldsymbol{\beta}_0$ replaced by $\boldsymbol{\beta}$ is less than some critical value, say $c_\alpha(l)$. This critical value will be such that, if z is a random variable with the $\chi^2(l)$ distribution,

$$\Pr\big(z > c_\alpha(l)\big) = \alpha.$$

The confidence region is therefore the set of all $\boldsymbol{\beta}$ for which

$$(\hat{\boldsymbol{\beta}} - \boldsymbol{\beta})^{\top}\hat{\boldsymbol{V}}^{-1}(\hat{\boldsymbol{\beta}})(\hat{\boldsymbol{\beta}} - \boldsymbol{\beta}) < c_\alpha(l). \tag{3.14}$$

Since the left-hand side of this equation is quadratic in $\boldsymbol{\beta}$, the region is, for $l = 2$, the interior of an ellipse and, for $l > 2$, the interior of an l–dimensional ellipsoid.

Figure 3.2 illustrates what a confidence ellipse can look like in the two-parameter case. In this case, the two parameter estimates are negatively correlated and are centered at the parameter estimates $(\hat{\beta}_1, \hat{\beta}_2)$. Confidence intervals for β_1 and β_2 are also shown, and it should now be clear why it can be misleading to consider only these rather than the confidence ellipse. On the one hand, there are clearly many points, such as (β_1^*, β_2^*), that lie outside the confidence ellipse but inside the two confidence intervals, and on the other hand there are points, like (β_1', β_2'), that are contained in the ellipse but lie outside one or both of the confidence regions.

[4] It is also possible, of course, to construct an approximate confidence region by using the F distribution with l and $n - k$ degrees of freedom, and this might well provide a better approximation in finite samples. Our discussion utilizes the χ^2 distribution primarily because it simplifies the exposition.

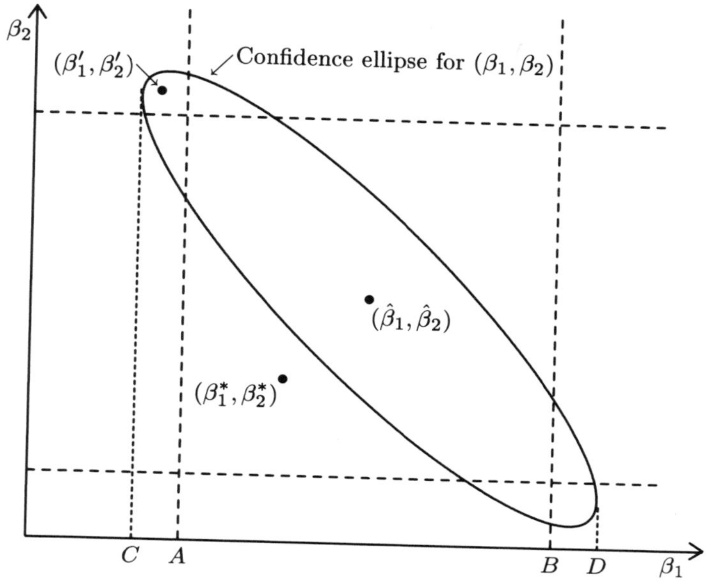

Figure 3.2 Confidence ellipses and confidence intervals

It is worth spending a little more time on Figure 3.2 in order to see more precisely the relation between a confidence ellipse and one-dimensional confidence intervals. It is tempting to think that the latter should be given by the extreme points of the confidence ellipse, which would imply that, for example, the confidence interval for β_1 in the figure would be given by the line segment CD. This is, however, incorrect, a fact that can be seen in two different, and illuminating, ways.

The first argument is as follows. The right-hand side of (3.14) is a critical value for a χ^2 distribution with, in the case of the figure, two degrees of freedom. If one is interested in a confidence interval for one single parameter, the relevant χ^2 distribution would have only one degree of freedom. For a given confidence level α, the critical value is an increasing function of the number of degrees of freedom. In the present case, the 5% critical value for a χ^2 variable with one degree of freedom is 3.84, and for two degrees of freedom it is 5.99. Therefore the ratio of the length of the confidence interval for β_1, AB in the figure, to the length of the extension of the ellipse in the β_1 direction, CD in the figure, is the square root of the ratio of 3.84 to 5.99.

The second argument is more general. Recall that a confidence region is defined so that it contains the true parameter value(s) with probability $1 - \alpha$. But we can reverse the roles of $\boldsymbol{\beta}$ and $\hat{\boldsymbol{\beta}}$. If the true parameter values were given by $\boldsymbol{\beta}$, the region defined by (3.14) would be a region in which the random variable $\hat{\boldsymbol{\beta}}$ would be realized with probability $1 - \alpha$. Thus the

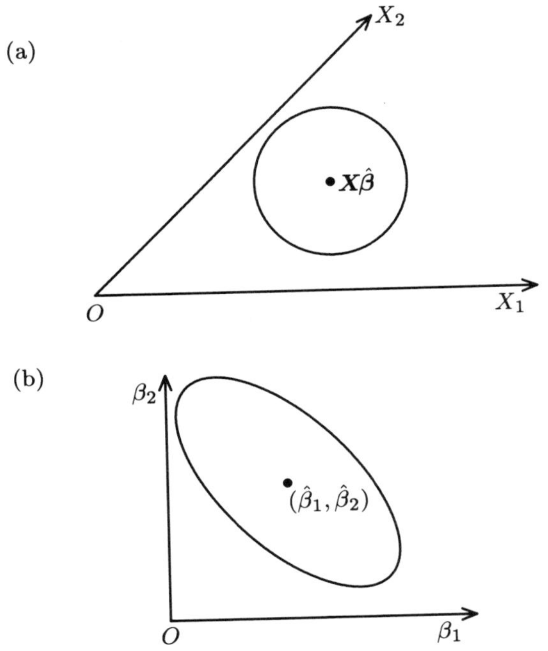

Figure 3.3 Why confidence ellipses are elliptical

confidence ellipse contains a probability mass of $1-\alpha$. So does the confidence interval for β_1: It too must contain a probability mass of $1 - \alpha$. In the *two-dimensional* framework of Figure 3.2, the entire infinitely high rectangle bounded by the vertical lines through the points A and B must have this probability mass, since we are willing to allow β_2 to take on any real value. Because the infinite rectangle and the confidence ellipse must contain the *same* probability mass, neither can contain the other, and we see why the ellipse must protrude outside the region defined by the one-dimensional confidence interval.

It is clear from (3.13) that the orientation of the confidence ellipse and the relative lengths of its axes are determined by the estimated covariance matrix $\hat{V}(\hat{\beta})$. If the latter were diagonal, the axes of the ellipse would be parallel to the coordinate axes. And if all the diagonal elements were equal, the confidence region would be a sphere. There is, however, another way of representing a confidence region geometrically, a way in which it will *always* take the form of the l–dimensional analog of a sphere. This representation is quite illuminating. For simplicity, we will restrict our attention to the case of linear regression models with n observations and two parameters, β_1 and β_2.

Consider the n–dimensional space in which variables are represented as vectors. Now restrict attention to the two-dimensional subset of the original n–dimensional space spanned by the two vectors $\boldsymbol{X}_1$ and $\boldsymbol{X}_2$. This two-dimensional space is shown in panel (a) of Figure 3.3, in which we also see the vector of fitted values, $\boldsymbol{X}\hat{\boldsymbol{\beta}}$. We claim that the circle drawn round $\boldsymbol{X}\hat{\boldsymbol{\beta}}$ with radius $\hat{\sigma}\sqrt{c_\alpha(2)}$ corresponds to the confidence ellipse for β_1 and β_2. In fact, this is easy to see. The equation of the circle is

$$\|\boldsymbol{y} - \boldsymbol{X}\hat{\boldsymbol{\beta}}\| = \hat{\sigma}\sqrt{c_\alpha(2)}. \tag{3.15}$$

Any vector $\boldsymbol{y}$ that belongs to $\mathcal{S}(\boldsymbol{X})$ can be expressed as $\boldsymbol{X\beta}$ for some $\boldsymbol{\beta}$. Thus (3.15) can be written as

$$\|\boldsymbol{X\beta} - \boldsymbol{X}\hat{\boldsymbol{\beta}}\| = \hat{\sigma}\sqrt{c_\alpha(2)}$$

or, on squaring,

$$(\hat{\boldsymbol{\beta}} - \boldsymbol{\beta})^\top \boldsymbol{X}^\top \boldsymbol{X}(\hat{\boldsymbol{\beta}} - \boldsymbol{\beta}) = \hat{\sigma}^2 c_\alpha(2). \tag{3.16}$$

Since the estimate of the covariance matrix of $\hat{\boldsymbol{\beta}}$ is $\hat{\sigma}^2(\boldsymbol{X}^\top\boldsymbol{X})^{-1}$, (3.16) is just the equation of the boundary of the confidence ellipse for $\boldsymbol{\beta}$; compare (3.14).

What this means is that we have *two* possible geometrical representations of the space in which $\boldsymbol{\beta}$ is situated. One of these is the straightforward one shown in Figure 3.2 and in panel (b) of Figure 3.3, in which there are two mutually perpendicular axes for the directions of the two parameters β_1 and β_2, and in which the confidence region has an elliptical shape. The second is the one seen in panel (a) of Figure 3.3, in which a point $\boldsymbol{\beta}$ is represented by the vector $\boldsymbol{X\beta}$. In a sense, it is the second representation that is more natural, for in it the confidence region is perfectly symmetrical in all directions. Of course, this symmetry depends on the assumption that all the error terms have the same variance, σ^2, and would no longer obtain if $E(u_t^2 \mid \boldsymbol{X}_t)$ were a function of $\boldsymbol{X}_t$. The key point is that the circle in panel (a) and the ellipse in panel (b) both contain the same confidence region.

Our discussion of confidence intervals and confidence regions has been brief and geometrically oriented. For a more traditional treatment, interested readers may wish to consult a standard reference such as Kendall and Stuart (1979, Chapter 20). It provides a much more detailed discussion of the meaning of confidence intervals and of how to construct various types of confidence intervals and regions when the sampling distribution of the parameter estimates is known. The problem with nonlinear regression models is that this sampling distribution is never known exactly. As a result, unless the sample is very large, there is often not much point in trying to construct sophisticated forms of confidence intervals and confidence regions.

3.4 Hypothesis Testing: Introduction

Economists frequently wish to test hypotheses about the regression models they estimate. Such hypotheses normally take the form of equality restrictions on some of the parameters. They might involve testing whether a single parameter takes on a certain value (say, $\beta_2 = 1$), whether two parameters are related in a specific way (say, $\beta_3 = 2\beta_4$), whether a nonlinear restriction such as $\beta_1/\beta_3 = \beta_2/\beta_4$ holds, or perhaps whether a whole set of linear and/or nonlinear restrictions holds. The hypothesis that the restriction or set of restrictions to be tested does in fact hold is called the **null hypothesis** and is often denoted H_0. The model in which the restrictions do not hold is usually called the **alternative hypothesis**, or sometimes the **maintained hypothesis**, and may be denoted H_1. The terminology "maintained hypothesis" reflects the fact that in a statistical test only the null hypothesis H_0 is under test. Rejecting H_0 does not in any way oblige us to accept H_1, since it is not H_1 that we are testing. Consider what would happen if the DGP were not a special case of H_1. Clearly both H_0 and H_1 would then be false, and it is quite possible that a test of H_0 would lead to its rejection. Other tests might well succeed in rejecting the false H_1, but only if it then played the role of the null hypothesis and some new maintained hypothesis were found.

All the hypothesis tests discussed in this book involve generating a **test statistic**. A test statistic, say T, is a random variable of which the probability distribution is known, either exactly or approximately, under the null hypothesis. We then see how likely the observed value of T is to have occurred, according to that probability distribution. If T is a number that could easily have occurred by chance, then we have no evidence against the null hypothesis H_0. However, if it is a number that would occur by chance only rarely, we do have evidence against the null, and we may well decide to reject it.

The classical way to perform a test is to divide the set of possible values of T into two regions, the **acceptance region** and the **rejection region** (or **critical region**). If T falls into the acceptance region, the null hypothesis is accepted (or at any rate not rejected), while if it falls into the rejection region, it is rejected.[5] For example, if T were known to have a χ^2 distribution, the acceptance region would consist of all values of T equal to or less than a certain **critical value**, say C, and the rejection region would then consist of all values greater than C. If instead T were known to have a normal distribution, then for a two-tailed test the acceptance region would consist of all *absolute values* of T less than or equal to C. Thus the rejection region would consist of

[5] The terms "acceptance region" and "rejection region" are also used to refer to subsets of the sample space. Any given sample, say $\boldsymbol{y}$, generates a test statistic T. If T falls within its rejection region, then so does $\boldsymbol{y}$, and similarly if T falls within its acceptance region. In this way, the entire sample space can be divided into two regions that correspond to acceptance and rejection of the null hypothesis.

two parts, one part containing values greater than C and one part containing values less than $-C$.

The **size** of a test is the probability that the test statistic will reject the null hypothesis when the latter is true. Let $\boldsymbol{\theta}$ denote the vector of parameters to be tested; Θ_0, the set of values of $\boldsymbol{\theta}$ that satisfy H_0; and R, the rejection region. Then the size of the test T is

$$\alpha \equiv \Pr(T \in R \mid \boldsymbol{\theta} \in \Theta_0).$$

The size of a test is also called its **significance level**. Conventionally it is chosen to be a small number, generally in the range of .001 to .10. It is often chosen more or less arbitrarily, and as we discuss below this feature of classical hypothesis testing is sometimes rather unsatisfactory.

We perform tests in the hope that they will reject the null hypothesis when it is false. Accordingly, the **power** of a test is of great interest. The power of a test statistic T is the probability that T will reject the null hypothesis when the latter is not true. Formally, it may be defined as

$$\Pr(T \in R \mid \boldsymbol{\theta} \notin \Theta_0).$$

Power will obviously depend on how the data were actually generated. If the null hypothesis were only slightly false, we would expect power to be lower than if it were grossly false. We would also expect power to increase with the sample size, n. If for any $\boldsymbol{\theta}$ in a certain region of the parameter space, say Θ_1, the power of a test tends to unity as $n \to \infty$, that test is said to be **consistent** against alternatives in Θ_1. Of course a test may be consistent against some alternatives and not against others. Just what determines the power of test statistics, when the DGP is and is not a special case of the alternative hypothesis, will be discussed in Chapters 12 and 13.

The classical way to perform a test is first to choose its size and then to use that size to determine a critical value by looking at tables of the appropriate distribution. For example, if a test statistic is distributed as $\chi^2(1)$ under the null, a critical value at the .05 (or 5%) level is 3.84, because the probability of obtaining a random drawing from a $\chi^2(1)$ distribution that is greater than 3.84 is .05. Then if the test statistic turned out to be, say, 3.51, we would not reject the null at the .05 level, while if it turned out to be, say, 5.43, we would reject the null at that level.

There are two problems with this procedure. First, the choice of test size is more or less arbitrary. It simply reflects how willing we are to make the mistake of rejecting a null hypothesis when it is true (or committing a **Type I error**) rather than accepting the null when it is false (or committing a **Type II error**). If we want very badly to avoid Type I errors, we will use a very low significance level, certainly no more than .01 and probably .001 or even less. If we are more concerned with Type II errors, we will use a higher level, like .05 or even .10. If one investigator decides to conduct a test at the .05 level and another decides to conduct the same test at the .01 level, they may come up with different results. This creates serious problems for readers who are trying to interpret those results, especially if only the outcomes of the tests (rather than the actual values of the test statistics) have been reported. Reporting only the outcomes of tests is a practice that we abhor and strongly advise against.

This brings up the second problem. If an investigator actually reports the values of test statistics, readers can potentially draw their own conclusions, but it may require some effort on their part to convert reported test statistics into meaningful numbers. It is much easier for readers if authors adopt an alternative way of reporting the results of tests, which is now becoming quite common. This is to report the ***P* value** (or **marginal significance level**) associated with every test statistic, either in addition to or instead of the statistics themselves, since the latter contain no more information than the P values. The P value is the probability, if the test statistic really were distributed as it would be under the null hypothesis, of observing a test statistic no less extreme than the one actually observed. If it is less than α, then we would reject at the α level.

It is not usually possible to calculate P values from tables of distributions, but it is easy to do so if one has appropriate computer software (which should be included in most modern regression packages); the increasingly widespread use of more and more powerful computers probably accounts for the growing popularity of the P value approach. In the example above, instead of reporting test statistics of 3.51 and 5.43, the investigator would use the fact that these are supposed to have come from a $\chi^2(1)$ distribution under the null and report P values of .0610 and .0198, respectively. These P values tell us that for the $\chi^2(1)$ distribution, numbers as large or larger than 3.51 would occur by chance about 6.1% of the time, while numbers as large or larger than 5.43 would occur by chance just under 2% of the time.

The P value approach does not necessarily force us to make a decision about the null hypothesis. If we obtain a P value of, say, .000001, we will almost certainly want to reject the null. But if we obtain a P value of, say, .04 or even .004, we are not *obliged* to reject it. We may simply file the result away as information that casts some doubt on the null hypothesis, but that is not, by itself, conclusive. We believe that this somewhat agnostic attitude toward test statistics, in which they are merely regarded as pieces of information that we may or may not want to act upon, is usually the most sensible one to take. It is perhaps especially appropriate in the case of nonlinear regression models, where P values are generally only approximate (and sometimes rather inaccurate).

It is important to be clear that a P value is *not* the probability that the null hypothesis is correct. By itself, it cannot let us deduce this probability. In the classical framework of hypothesis testing, a hypothesis either is or is not true, and we cannot speak about the *probability* that it is true. In the

Bayesian framework, which we will not employ in this book, one *can* talk about the probability that a hypothesis is true, but one has to make use of **prior information** on this probability, and one has to specify what other hypotheses might be true. Then given the prior probability that a hypothesis is true and the evidence from the test statistic, one can compute a **posterior probability** that the hypothesis holds. The latter may be very much larger than the P value.[6]

As we indicated above, the distribution that a test statistic is supposed to have under the null hypothesis may or may not be known precisely. If it is known, then the test is commonly referred to as an **exact test**; if not, the test will usually be based on a distribution that is known to apply only asymptotically and so may be referred to as an **asymptotic test**. Exact tests are rarely available for nonlinear regression models. However, there is a very special case in which exact tests of linear restrictions are available. The regression function must be linear, it must be possible to treat the regressors as if they were **fixed in repeated samples**, and the error terms must be normally and independently distributed. In the next section, we will define the term "fixed in repeated samples" and discuss this special case. Then, in Section 3.6, we will discuss the three basic principles that underlie the construction of most test statistics and show how they may be applied to nonlinear regression models.

3.5 HYPOTHESIS TESTING IN LINEAR REGRESSION MODELS

All students of econometrics are familiar with ***t* statistics** for testing hypotheses about a single parameter and ***F* statistics** for testing hypotheses about several parameters jointly. If $\hat{\beta}_i$ denotes the least squares estimate of the parameter β_i, the t statistic for testing the hypothesis that β_i is equal to some specified value β_{0i} is simply expression (3.12), that is, $\hat{\beta}_i - \beta_{0i}$ divided by the estimated standard error of $\hat{\beta}_i$. If $\hat{\boldsymbol{\beta}}$ denotes a set of unrestricted least squares estimates and $\tilde{\boldsymbol{\beta}}$ denotes a set of estimates subject to r distinct restrictions, then the F statistic for testing those restrictions may be calculated as

$$\frac{\big(SSR(\tilde{\boldsymbol{\beta}}) - SSR(\hat{\boldsymbol{\beta}})\big)/r}{SSR(\hat{\boldsymbol{\beta}})/(n-k)} = \frac{1}{rs^2}\big(SSR(\tilde{\boldsymbol{\beta}}) - SSR(\hat{\boldsymbol{\beta}})\big). \tag{3.17}$$

Tests based on t and F statistics may be either exact or approximate. In the very special case referred to at the end of the last section, in which the regression model and the restrictions are both linear in the parameters, the regressors are (or can be treated as) fixed in repeated samples, and the error terms are normally and independently distributed, ordinary t and F statistics

[6] For discussion of the relationship between P values and Bayesian inference, see Lindley (1957), Shafer (1982), and Berger and Sellke (1987), among others.

actually are distributed in finite samples under the null hypotheses according to their namesake distributions. Although this case is not encountered nearly as often as one might hope, these results are sufficiently important that they are worth a separate section. Moreover, it is useful to keep the linear case firmly in mind when considering the case of nonlinear regression models.

Consider the restricted model

$$\boldsymbol{y} = \boldsymbol{X}_1\boldsymbol{\beta}_1 + \boldsymbol{u} \tag{3.18}$$

and the unrestricted model

$$\boldsymbol{y} = \boldsymbol{X}_1\boldsymbol{\beta}_1 + \boldsymbol{X}_2\boldsymbol{\beta}_2 + \boldsymbol{u}, \tag{3.19}$$

where the error terms $\boldsymbol{u}$ are assumed to follow the multivariate normal distribution with mean vector zero and covariance matrix $\sigma^2\mathbf{I}$. The parameter vector $\boldsymbol{\beta}$ has been divided into two subvectors, $\boldsymbol{\beta}_1$ and $\boldsymbol{\beta}_2$, with $k-r$ and r components, respectively. We are interested in testing the null hypothesis that $\boldsymbol{\beta}_2 = \mathbf{0}$. The restricted estimates are $\tilde{\boldsymbol{\beta}} = [\tilde{\boldsymbol{\beta}}_1 \vdots \mathbf{0}]$, and the unrestricted ones are $\hat{\boldsymbol{\beta}} = [\hat{\boldsymbol{\beta}}_1 \vdots \hat{\boldsymbol{\beta}}_2]$. By limiting our attention to a test of zero restrictions, we in no way limit the generality of our results, since, as we showed in Section 1.3, any set of *linear* restrictions on a linear model can always, by a suitable reparametrization, be rewritten as a set of zero restrictions.

It follows from expression (3.07) that $SSR(\tilde{\boldsymbol{\beta}}) = \boldsymbol{y}^{\top}\boldsymbol{M}_1\boldsymbol{y}$, where $\boldsymbol{M}_1$ denotes the projection onto $\mathcal{S}^{\perp}(\boldsymbol{X}_1)$, the orthogonal complement of the span of $\boldsymbol{X}_1$. Similarly, $SSR(\hat{\boldsymbol{\beta}}) = \boldsymbol{y}^{\top}\boldsymbol{M}_X\boldsymbol{y}$, where $\boldsymbol{M}_X$ denotes the projection onto $\mathcal{S}^{\perp}(\boldsymbol{X})$, the orthogonal complement of the span of $\boldsymbol{X} \equiv [\boldsymbol{X}_1 \ \ \boldsymbol{X}_2]$. By the FWL Theorem (see Section 1.4), $\boldsymbol{y}^{\top}\boldsymbol{M}_X\boldsymbol{y}$, which is the sum of squared residuals from regression (3.19), is identical to the SSR from the regression

$$\boldsymbol{M}_1\boldsymbol{y} = \boldsymbol{M}_1\boldsymbol{X}_2\boldsymbol{\beta}_2 + \text{residuals}.$$

Thus we see that

$$SSR(\hat{\boldsymbol{\beta}}) \equiv \boldsymbol{y}^{\top}\boldsymbol{M}_X\boldsymbol{y} = \boldsymbol{y}^{\top}\boldsymbol{M}_1\boldsymbol{y} - \boldsymbol{y}^{\top}\boldsymbol{M}_1\boldsymbol{X}_2\big(\boldsymbol{X}_2^{\top}\boldsymbol{M}_1\boldsymbol{X}_2\big)^{-1}\boldsymbol{X}_2^{\top}\boldsymbol{M}_1\boldsymbol{y}. \tag{3.20}$$

From (3.07) and (3.20), it then follows that r times the numerator of the F statistic (3.17) is

$$\boldsymbol{y}^{\top}\boldsymbol{M}_1\boldsymbol{X}_2\big(\boldsymbol{X}_2^{\top}\boldsymbol{M}_1\boldsymbol{X}_2\big)^{-1}\boldsymbol{X}_2^{\top}\boldsymbol{M}_1\boldsymbol{y} = \big\|\boldsymbol{P}_{M_1X_2}\boldsymbol{y}\big\|^2, \tag{3.21}$$

where $\boldsymbol{P}_{M_1X_2} \equiv \boldsymbol{M}_1\boldsymbol{X}_2(\boldsymbol{X}_2^{\top}\boldsymbol{M}_1\boldsymbol{X}_2)^{-1}\boldsymbol{X}_2^{\top}\boldsymbol{M}_1$ is the matrix that projects onto $\mathcal{S}(\boldsymbol{M}_1\boldsymbol{X}_2)$. Under the DGP

$$\boldsymbol{y} = \boldsymbol{X}_1\boldsymbol{\beta}_{10} + \boldsymbol{u}, \quad \boldsymbol{u} \sim N(\mathbf{0}, \sigma_0^2\mathbf{I}), \tag{3.22}$$

the two sides of expression (3.21) become

$$\boldsymbol{u}^{\top}\boldsymbol{M}_1\boldsymbol{X}_2\big(\boldsymbol{X}_2^{\top}\boldsymbol{M}_1\boldsymbol{X}_2\big)^{-1}\boldsymbol{X}_2^{\top}\boldsymbol{M}_1\boldsymbol{u} = \big\|\boldsymbol{P}_{M_1X_2}\boldsymbol{u}\big\|^2, \tag{3.23}$$

because $\boldsymbol{M}_1$ annihilates $\boldsymbol{X}_1\boldsymbol{\beta}_{10}$.

Expression (3.23), which is r times the numerator of the F statistic under the DGP (3.22), can be thought of as a quadratic form in the random r–vector

$$\boldsymbol{v} \equiv \boldsymbol{X}_2^{\top}\boldsymbol{M}_1\boldsymbol{u}, \tag{3.24}$$

which is normally distributed (since it is just a linear combination of the normally distributed random variables that are the elements of $\boldsymbol{u}$) with mean zero and covariance matrix

$$\boldsymbol{\Omega} \equiv E\big(\boldsymbol{X}_2^{\top}\boldsymbol{M}_1\boldsymbol{u}\boldsymbol{u}^{\top}\boldsymbol{M}_1\boldsymbol{X}_2\big) = \sigma_0^2\boldsymbol{X}_2^{\top}\boldsymbol{M}_1\boldsymbol{X}_2. \tag{3.25}$$

Thus, using (3.24) and (3.25), the left-hand side of expression (3.23) becomes

$$\sigma_0^2\boldsymbol{v}^{\top}\boldsymbol{\Omega}^{-1}\boldsymbol{v}. \tag{3.26}$$

This is σ_0^2 times a quadratic form in the r–vector $\boldsymbol{v}$, which is multivariate normal with mean vector zero, and in the inverse of its covariance matrix, $\boldsymbol{\Omega}$. Thus from the familiar result on quadratic forms in normal random vectors that was used previously in Section 3.3, we conclude that $1/\sigma_0^2$ times (3.26) is distributed as $\chi^2(r)$.

If the sample size were infinitely large, we could stop at this point. The estimate s^2 would be indistinguishable from the true value σ_0^2. Therefore, under the null hypothesis, r times the F statistic (3.17) would be equal to

$$\frac{1}{\sigma_0^2}\,\boldsymbol{u}^{\top}\boldsymbol{M}_1\boldsymbol{X}_2\big(\boldsymbol{X}_2^{\top}\boldsymbol{M}_1\boldsymbol{X}_2\big)^{-1}\boldsymbol{X}_2^{\top}\boldsymbol{M}_1\boldsymbol{u},$$

and we have just seen that this quantity is distributed as $\chi^2(r)$ under H_0. In a finite sample, however, s^2 will be a random variable that estimates σ_0^2 with precision that increases with $n-k$. We must therefore consider how the denominator of the F statistic (3.17) is distributed. Under the DGP (3.22), $(n-k)s^2$ is, by equation (3.09), equal to

$$\boldsymbol{u}^{\top}\boldsymbol{M}_X\boldsymbol{u}. \tag{3.27}$$

In Appendix B, we demonstrate that any idempotent quadratic form in independent standard normal random variables has the χ^2 distribution with number of degrees of freedom equal to the rank of the idempotent matrix. Clearly $\boldsymbol{u}^{\top}\boldsymbol{M}_X\boldsymbol{u}/\sigma_0^2$ is such an idempotent quadratic form, and since the rank of $\boldsymbol{M}_X$ is $n-k$, we conclude that $1/\sigma_0^2$ times the denominator of the F statistic is distributed as $\chi^2(n-k)$.

Thus the F statistic (3.17) is $(n-k)/r$ times the ratio of two random variables, the numerator being distributed as $\chi^2(r)$ and the denominator as $\chi^2(n-k)$. Provided that these two random variables are independent of each other, their ratio will be distributed as $F(r, n-k)$ (see Appendix B). A sufficient condition for them to be independent is that

$$\boldsymbol{M}_X \boldsymbol{P}_{M_1 X_2} = \mathbf{0}.$$

This is indeed the case, because $\mathcal{S}(\boldsymbol{M}_1\boldsymbol{X}_2)$, the space spanned by $\boldsymbol{M}_1\boldsymbol{X}_2$, is a subspace of $\mathcal{S}(\boldsymbol{X})$, the space spanned by $\boldsymbol{X}_1$ and $\boldsymbol{X}_2$ jointly; to see this, observe that $\boldsymbol{M}_1\boldsymbol{X}_2 = \boldsymbol{X}_2 - \boldsymbol{P}_1\boldsymbol{X}_2$. Thus $\boldsymbol{M}_X$ annihilates $\boldsymbol{P}_{M_1X_2}$.

A more intuitive explanation of why the quadratic forms (3.23) and (3.27) are independent is the following. The quadratic form that appears in the denominator, (3.27), is the sum of squared residuals from the unrestricted model (3.19). Those residuals are what is left after $\boldsymbol{u}$ is projected off everything that lies in $\mathcal{S}(\boldsymbol{X})$. In contrast, the quadratic form that appears in the numerator, (3.23), is the sum of squared *reductions* in the residuals from the restricted model achieved by adding $\boldsymbol{X}_2$ to the regression. Those reductions must lie in $\mathcal{S}(\boldsymbol{X})$. As a result, the random variables that appear in the numerator lie in a subspace orthogonal to the one in which lie the random variables that appear in the denominator. These two sets of random variables are therefore independent. This can be seen quite clearly in Panel (a) of Figure 1.7, for the case $r = 1$ and $k = 2$.

We have now verified that the F statistic (3.17) does indeed have the F distribution with r and $n-k$ degrees of freedom for the case of linear models subject to linear restrictions and normally distributed error terms. A simple corollary of this result is that for the same case, the ordinary t statistic (3.12) has the Student's t distribution with $n-k$ degrees of freedom. To see this, suppose that $\boldsymbol{X}_2$ consists of a single column, which we will call $\boldsymbol{x}_2$. Then, by the FWL Theorem, the estimate of β_2 from (3.19) is identical to the estimate from the regression

$$\boldsymbol{M}_1\boldsymbol{y} = \boldsymbol{M}_1\boldsymbol{x}_2\beta_2 + \text{residuals},$$

which is equal to

$$\left(\boldsymbol{x}_2^{\top}\boldsymbol{M}_1\boldsymbol{x}_2\right)^{-1}\boldsymbol{x}_2^{\top}\boldsymbol{M}_1\boldsymbol{y}.$$

The estimated standard error of $\hat{\beta}_2$ is $s(\boldsymbol{x}_2^{\top}\boldsymbol{M}_1\boldsymbol{x}_2)^{-1/2}$. Thus the t statistic for $\beta_2 = 0$ is

$$\frac{\boldsymbol{x}_2^{\top}\boldsymbol{M}_1\boldsymbol{y}}{s(\boldsymbol{x}_2^{\top}\boldsymbol{M}_1\boldsymbol{x}_2)^{1/2}}.$$

The square of this t statistic is

$$\frac{1}{s^2}\,\boldsymbol{y}^{\top}\boldsymbol{M}_1\boldsymbol{x}_2\left(\boldsymbol{x}_2^{\top}\boldsymbol{M}_1\boldsymbol{x}_2\right)^{-1}\boldsymbol{x}_2^{\top}\boldsymbol{M}_1\boldsymbol{y}, \tag{3.28}$$

which is evidently just the F statistic (3.17) for the special case $r = 1$. Since the square root of a random variable that has the $F(1, n-k)$ distribution has the $t(n-k)$ distribution (see Appendix B), we have proved the corollary we set out to prove.

The geometry of t and F statistics is interesting. The square of the t statistic we have been looking at is given by (3.28). It depends on s, the OLS estimate of σ, which is given by

$$s \equiv \left(\frac{\boldsymbol{y}^\top \boldsymbol{M}_X \boldsymbol{y}}{n-k}\right)^{1/2}. \tag{3.29}$$

From the FWL Theorem we know that

$$\boldsymbol{y}^\top \boldsymbol{M}_X \boldsymbol{y} = \boldsymbol{y}^\top \boldsymbol{M}_1 \boldsymbol{M}_{M_1 x_2} \boldsymbol{M}_1 \boldsymbol{y}, \tag{3.30}$$

where $\boldsymbol{M}_{M_1 x_2}$ denotes the matrix that projects off $\mathcal{S}(\boldsymbol{M}_1 \boldsymbol{x}_2)$. In words, this result simply says that the sum of squared residuals from regressing $\boldsymbol{y}$ on $\boldsymbol{X}$ is the same as the sum of squared residuals from regressing $\boldsymbol{M}_1 \boldsymbol{y}$ on $\boldsymbol{M}_1 \boldsymbol{x}_2$. Using (3.29) and (3.30), we can rewrite the squared t statistic (3.28) as

$$\begin{aligned} &(n-k)\,\frac{\boldsymbol{y}^\top \boldsymbol{M}_1 \boldsymbol{x}_2 \left(\boldsymbol{x}_2^\top \boldsymbol{M}_1 \boldsymbol{x}_2\right)^{-1} \boldsymbol{x}_2^\top \boldsymbol{M}_1 \boldsymbol{y}}{\boldsymbol{y}^\top \boldsymbol{M}_1 \boldsymbol{M}_{M_1 x_2} \boldsymbol{M}_1 \boldsymbol{y}} \\ &= (n-k)\,\frac{\boldsymbol{y}^\top \boldsymbol{M}_1 \boldsymbol{P}_{M_1 x_2} \boldsymbol{M}_1 \boldsymbol{y}}{\boldsymbol{y}^\top \boldsymbol{M}_1 \boldsymbol{M}_{M_1 x_2} \boldsymbol{M}_1 \boldsymbol{y}}, \end{aligned} \tag{3.31}$$

and the t statistic itself can therefore be written as

$$\operatorname{sign}(\boldsymbol{y}^\top \boldsymbol{M}_1 \boldsymbol{x}_2)\,(n-k)^{1/2}\,\frac{\|\boldsymbol{P}_{M_1 x_2} \boldsymbol{M}_1 \boldsymbol{y}\|}{\|\boldsymbol{M}_{M_1 x_2} \boldsymbol{M}_1 \boldsymbol{y}\|}.$$

We thus see that t statistics have a simple geometric interpretation. If we interpret $\boldsymbol{y}$ in Figure 1.3 as representing $\boldsymbol{M}_1 \boldsymbol{y}$ and $\mathcal{S}(\boldsymbol{X})$ as representing $\mathcal{S}(\boldsymbol{M}_1 \boldsymbol{x}_2)$, then it is evident that the t statistic on β_2 is just $(n-k)^{1/2}$ times the *cotangent* of the angle ϕ (see Appendix A). When that angle is zero, so that $\boldsymbol{M}_1 \boldsymbol{x}_2$ explains $\boldsymbol{M}_1 \boldsymbol{y}$ perfectly, the t statistic is either plus or minus infinity, depending on the sign of $\hat{\beta}_2$. On the other hand, when that angle is $90°$, so that $\boldsymbol{M}_1 \boldsymbol{x}_2$ has no explanatory power at all for $\boldsymbol{M}_1 \boldsymbol{y}$, the t statistic is zero. For any angle ϕ that is neither zero nor $90°$, the magnitude of the t statistic will be proportional to $(n-k)^{1/2}$. Thus, if $\boldsymbol{M}_1 \boldsymbol{x}_2$ does in fact have some ability to explain $\boldsymbol{M}_1 \boldsymbol{y}$, we would expect the t statistic to allow us to reject the null hypothesis with probability one when the sample size is large enough.

The above results evidently apply with slight modification to F statistics as well. If $\boldsymbol{X}_2$ has r columns instead of one, the F statistic for testing $\boldsymbol{\beta}_2 = \mathbf{0}$ can be written in a form equivalent to (3.31) as

$$\begin{aligned} &\frac{n-k}{r} \times \frac{\boldsymbol{y}^\top \boldsymbol{M}_1 \boldsymbol{X}_2 \big(\boldsymbol{X}_2^\top \boldsymbol{M}_1 \boldsymbol{X}_2\big)^{-1} \boldsymbol{X}_2^\top \boldsymbol{M}_1 \boldsymbol{y}}{\boldsymbol{y}^\top \boldsymbol{M}_1 \boldsymbol{M}_{M_1 X_2} \boldsymbol{M}_1 \boldsymbol{y}} \\ &= \frac{n-k}{r} \times \frac{\|\boldsymbol{P}_{M_1 X_2} \boldsymbol{M}_1 \boldsymbol{y}\|^2}{\|\boldsymbol{M}_{M_1 X_2} \boldsymbol{M}_1 \boldsymbol{y}\|^2}. \end{aligned} \tag{3.32}$$

Hence the F statistic is equal to $(n-k)/r$ times the squared cotangent of the angle ϕ between the vectors $\boldsymbol{M}_1\boldsymbol{y}$ and $\boldsymbol{P}_{M_1 X_2}\boldsymbol{M}_1\boldsymbol{y}$; see Figure 1.3 again, keeping in mind that $\boldsymbol{M}_1\boldsymbol{y}$ now plays the role of $\boldsymbol{y}$ and $\mathcal{S}(\boldsymbol{M}_1\boldsymbol{X}_2)$ plays the role of $\mathcal{S}(\boldsymbol{X})$. As we saw in Chapter 1, the squared cosine of ϕ is the R^2 for the regression of, in this case, $\boldsymbol{M}_1\boldsymbol{y}$ on $\boldsymbol{M}_1\boldsymbol{X}_2$. This suggests that there must be a close relationship between F statistics and R^2. That is indeed the case.

A common use of the F test is to test the null hypothesis that all coefficients except the constant term are zero. This is a test for $\boldsymbol{\beta}_2 = \mathbf{0}$ in the regression model

$$\boldsymbol{y} = \beta_1 + \boldsymbol{X}_2\boldsymbol{\beta}_2 + \boldsymbol{u}, \tag{3.33}$$

where $\boldsymbol{X}_2$ is now $n \times (k-1)$. By the FWL Theorem, the SSR from this regression is identical to the SSR from the regression

$$\boldsymbol{M}_\iota \boldsymbol{y} = \boldsymbol{M}_\iota \boldsymbol{X}_2 \boldsymbol{\beta}_2 + \text{residuals},$$

which is

$$\boldsymbol{y}^\top \boldsymbol{M}_\iota \boldsymbol{y} - \boldsymbol{y}^\top \boldsymbol{M}_\iota \boldsymbol{X}_2 \big(\boldsymbol{X}_2^\top \boldsymbol{M}_\iota \boldsymbol{X}_2\big)^{-1} \boldsymbol{X}_2^\top \boldsymbol{M}_\iota \boldsymbol{y}.$$

Thus the difference between the restricted and unrestricted sums of squared residuals is

$$\boldsymbol{y}^\top \boldsymbol{M}_\iota \boldsymbol{X}_2 \big(\boldsymbol{X}_2^\top \boldsymbol{M}_\iota \boldsymbol{X}_2\big)^{-1} \boldsymbol{X}_2^\top \boldsymbol{M}_\iota \boldsymbol{y} = \big\|\boldsymbol{P}_{M_\iota X_2} \boldsymbol{M}_\iota \boldsymbol{y}\big\|^2,$$

and the F statistic for the hypothesis that $\boldsymbol{\beta}_2 = \mathbf{0}$ is

$$\frac{n-k}{k-1} \times \frac{\|\boldsymbol{P}_{M_\iota X_2} \boldsymbol{M}_\iota \boldsymbol{y}\|^2}{\|\boldsymbol{M}_{M_\iota X_2} \boldsymbol{M}_\iota \boldsymbol{y}\|^2}, \tag{3.34}$$

which is a special case of (3.32).

Because (3.33) does contain a constant term, the centered R^2 for that regression is

$$R_c^2 = \frac{\|\boldsymbol{P}_{M_\iota X_2} \boldsymbol{M}_\iota \boldsymbol{y}\|^2}{\|\boldsymbol{M}_\iota \boldsymbol{y}\|^2}.$$

Evidently this is, as usual, the squared cosine of the angle between $\boldsymbol{P}_{M_\iota X_2}\boldsymbol{M}_\iota\boldsymbol{y}$ and $\boldsymbol{M}_\iota\boldsymbol{y}$, while the F statistic (3.34) is equal to $(n-k)/(k-1)$ times the squared cotangent of the same angle. It is thus possible to express this F statistic as

$$\frac{n-k}{k-1} \times \frac{R_c^2}{1-R_c^2}.$$

This result can be shown by using the fact that $\cot^2\phi = \cos^2\phi/(1 - \cos^2\phi)$ or by simple algebra from the definitions of F and R_c^2. Note, however, that one should normally avoid computing an F statistic in this way, unless *both* R_c^2 and $1 - R_c^2$ are known to at least as many digits of accuracy as are desired for the F statistic. Many regression packages report the R^2 as a three or four digit number, and $1 - R^2$ may then be accurate to only one or two digits.

It is possible to express the centered R^2 as

$$R_c^2 = 1 - \frac{\|\boldsymbol{M}_{M_\iota X_2}\boldsymbol{M}_\iota \boldsymbol{y}\|^2}{\|\boldsymbol{M}_\iota \boldsymbol{y}\|^2} = 1 - \frac{\|\boldsymbol{M}_X \boldsymbol{y}\|^2/n}{\|\boldsymbol{M}_\iota \boldsymbol{y}\|^2/n}.$$

The numerator of the second term on the right-hand side here is simply $\hat{\sigma}^2$, which we have seen is a biased estimate of σ^2. The denominator is likewise a biased estimate of the variance of y_t around its unconditional mean. It seems natural to replace these biased estimates by unbiased ones. Doing so yields $\bar{R}^2$, the **adjusted $\boldsymbol{R^2}$**, which is defined by

$$\bar{R}^2 = 1 - \frac{\|\boldsymbol{M}_X \boldsymbol{y}\|^2/(n-k)}{\|\boldsymbol{M}_\iota \boldsymbol{y}\|^2/(n-1)} = 1 - \frac{n-1}{n-k}\frac{\|\boldsymbol{M}_X \boldsymbol{y}\|^2}{\|\boldsymbol{M}_\iota \boldsymbol{y}\|^2}.$$

One almost never sees an uncentered version of $\bar{R}^2$, and so we have omitted the c subscript here.

The quantity $\bar{R}^2$ is reported by virtually all regression packages. In most cases, however, it is not an estimate of any model parameter (since for most models the variance of y_t around its unconditional mean will depend on the distribution of the right-hand side variables), and it is not particularly useful in practice. The widespread use of $\bar{R}^2$ dates from the early days of econometrics, when sample sizes were often small and investigators were often overly impressed with models that fit well in the sense of having a large R_c^2. People quickly found that adding extra regressors to a linear regression *always* increased the ordinary (centered or uncentered) R^2, especially when the sample size was small. This led some investigators to estimate severely overparametrized models. The use of $\bar{R}^2$ rather than R_c^2 was advocated as a way to deal with this problem, because adding an extra regressor will increase $\bar{R}^2$ only if the proportional reduction in the SSR is greater than the proportional reduction in $n - k$.

As we remarked at the beginning of this section, all of the exact results on the distribution of t and F statistics (and on the finite-sample distribution of OLS estimators in general) require that the error terms be normally distributed. They also require that the regressors either be fixed in repeated samples or can be treated as if they were. The latter possibility requires some comment. The reason it is convenient to assume fixed regressors is that we want to be able to treat matrix expressions which depend on the regressors as constants for the purpose of taking expectations. Thus with this assumption we can, for example, assert that

$$E\big((\boldsymbol{X}^\top\boldsymbol{X})^{-1}\boldsymbol{X}^\top\boldsymbol{u}\big) = \big(\boldsymbol{X}^\top\boldsymbol{X}\big)^{-1}\boldsymbol{X}^\top E(\boldsymbol{u}) = \mathbf{0}. \tag{3.35}$$

The fixed regressors assumption certainly allows us to do this, but it is uncomfortably strong in most econometric applications.

A weaker assumption which has the same effect is to assume that all expectations we take are *conditional* on the $\boldsymbol{X}$ matrix; thus, for example, $E(\boldsymbol{u})$ in (3.35) is to be interpreted as $E(\boldsymbol{u}\,|\,\boldsymbol{X})$. Since we are conditioning on $\boldsymbol{X}$, we are in effect treating it as fixed. However, unless the $\boldsymbol{X}$ matrix is genuinely independent of the errors $\boldsymbol{u}$, the t and F statistics will no longer be distributed according to their nominal distributions. This problem arises in the case of a dynamic model, in which $\boldsymbol{u}$ cannot be independent of lagged values of the dependent variable.

3.6 Hypothesis Testing in Nonlinear Regression Models

There are at least three different ways that we can derive test statistics for hypotheses about the parameters of nonlinear regression models. They are to utilize the **Wald principle**, the **Lagrange multiplier principle**, and the **likelihood ratio principle**. These yield what are often collectively referred to as the three "classical" test statistics. In this section, we introduce these three principles and show how they yield test statistics for hypotheses about $\boldsymbol{\beta}$ in nonlinear regression models (and implicitly in linear regression models as well, since linear models are simply a special case of nonlinear ones). The three principles are very widely applicable and will reappear in other contexts throughout the book.[7] A formal treatment of these tests in the context of least squares will be provided in Chapter 5. They will be reintroduced in the context of maximum likelihood estimation in Chapter 8, and a detailed treatment in that context will be provided in Chapter 13. Valuable references include Engle (1984) and Godfrey (1988), and an illuminating introductory discussion may be found in Buse (1982).

[7] We refer to tests based on the "Lagrange multiplier principle," "Wald principle," and "likelihood ratio principle" rather than to "Lagrange multiplier tests," "Wald tests," and "likelihood ratio tests" because many authors use the latter terms in a rather narrow sense to refer only to tests for models estimated by the method of maximum likelihood (see Chapters 8 and 13). We believe this narrow usage of the terms is likely to diminish over time as the general applicability of the three principles becomes more widely recognized.

The Wald principle, which is due to Wald (1943), is to construct a test statistic based on unrestricted parameter estimates and an estimate of the unrestricted covariance matrix. If the hypothesis involves just one restriction, say that $\beta_i = \beta_i^*$, then one can calculate the **pseudo-*t* statistic**

$$\frac{\hat{\beta}_i - \beta_i^*}{\hat{S}(\hat{\beta}_i)}. \tag{3.36}$$

We refer to this as a "pseudo-t" statistic because it will not actually have the Student's t distribution with $n - k$ degrees of freedom in finite samples when $x_t(\boldsymbol{\beta})$ is nonlinear in the parameters, $x_t(\boldsymbol{\beta})$ depends on lagged values of y_t, or the errors u_t are not normally distributed. However, it will be asymptotically distributed as $N(0, 1)$ under quite weak conditions (see Chapter 5), and its finite-sample distribution is frequently approximated quite well by $t(n - k)$.

In the more general case in which there are r restrictions rather than just one to be tested, Wald tests make use of the fact that if $\boldsymbol{v}$ is a random r–vector which is normally distributed with mean vector zero and covariance matrix $\boldsymbol{\Lambda}$, then the quadratic form

$$\boldsymbol{v}^{\top}\boldsymbol{\Lambda}^{-1}\boldsymbol{v} \tag{3.37}$$

must be distributed as $\chi^2(r)$. This result is proved in Appendix B, and we used it in Sections 3.3 and 3.5 above.

To construct an asymptotic Wald test, then, we simply have to find a vector of random variables that should under the null hypothesis be asymptotically normally distributed with mean vector zero and a covariance matrix which we can estimate. For example, suppose that $\boldsymbol{\beta}$ is subject to the r ($\leq k$) linearly independent restrictions

$$\boldsymbol{R\beta} = \boldsymbol{r}, \tag{3.38}$$

where $\boldsymbol{R}$ is an $r \times k$ matrix of rank r and $\boldsymbol{r}$ is an r–vector. We have assumed that the restrictions are linear purely for simplicity, not because Wald tests cannot handle nonlinear restrictions. However, because Wald tests are not invariant to nonlinear reparametrizations of the model or the restrictions, one must exercise caution when testing nonlinear restrictions by means of such tests. This will be discussed in Chapter 13; see Gregory and Veall (1985), Lafontaine and White (1986), and Phillips and Park (1988). Thus it seems appropriate to restrict attention to the linear case for now.

Suppose that we evaluate the vector $\boldsymbol{R\beta} - \boldsymbol{r}$ at the vector of unrestricted estimates $\hat{\boldsymbol{\beta}}$ so as to obtain the random r–vector

$$\boldsymbol{R}\hat{\boldsymbol{\beta}} - \boldsymbol{r}. \tag{3.39}$$

As we will prove in Chapter 5, if the data were actually generated by the model being tested, the vector of estimates $\hat{\boldsymbol{\beta}}$ would tend asymptotically to the true parameter vector $\boldsymbol{\beta}_0$, and the covariance matrix of $\hat{\boldsymbol{\beta}}$ around $\boldsymbol{\beta}_0$ could be validly estimated by $s^2(\hat{\boldsymbol{X}}^\top\hat{\boldsymbol{X}})^{-1}$. If the restriction (3.38) does in fact hold, it must be the case that

$$\boldsymbol{R}\hat{\boldsymbol{\beta}} - \boldsymbol{r} = \boldsymbol{R}(\hat{\boldsymbol{\beta}} - \boldsymbol{\beta}_0) + \boldsymbol{R}\boldsymbol{\beta}_0 - \boldsymbol{r} = \boldsymbol{R}(\hat{\boldsymbol{\beta}} - \boldsymbol{\beta}_0).$$

This shows that each element of $\boldsymbol{R}\hat{\boldsymbol{\beta}} - \boldsymbol{r}$ is just a linear combination of the elements of $\hat{\boldsymbol{\beta}} - \boldsymbol{\beta}_0$. Thus the covariance matrix of (3.39) must be

$$\boldsymbol{V}\big(\boldsymbol{R}(\hat{\boldsymbol{\beta}} - \boldsymbol{\beta}_0)\big) = \boldsymbol{R}\boldsymbol{V}(\hat{\boldsymbol{\beta}})\boldsymbol{R}^\top,$$

which can be estimated by the matrix

$$s^2\boldsymbol{R}\big(\hat{\boldsymbol{X}}^\top\hat{\boldsymbol{X}}\big)^{-1}\boldsymbol{R}^\top. \tag{3.40}$$

Putting together (3.39) and (3.40), we obtain the Wald statistic

$$\begin{aligned}&(\boldsymbol{R}\hat{\boldsymbol{\beta}} - \boldsymbol{r})^\top\big(s^2\boldsymbol{R}(\hat{\boldsymbol{X}}^\top\hat{\boldsymbol{X}})^{-1}\boldsymbol{R}^\top\big)^{-1}(\boldsymbol{R}\hat{\boldsymbol{\beta}} - \boldsymbol{r})\\ &= \frac{1}{s^2}(\boldsymbol{R}\hat{\boldsymbol{\beta}} - \boldsymbol{r})^\top\big(\boldsymbol{R}(\hat{\boldsymbol{X}}^\top\hat{\boldsymbol{X}})^{-1}\boldsymbol{R}^\top\big)^{-1}(\boldsymbol{R}\hat{\boldsymbol{\beta}} - \boldsymbol{r}).\end{aligned} \tag{3.41}$$

Provided that $\hat{\boldsymbol{\beta}}$ is asymptotically normally distributed and that $\boldsymbol{V}(\hat{\boldsymbol{\beta}})$ does indeed converge asymptotically to its true covariance matrix, it should be clear that (3.41) will be asymptotically distributed as $\chi^2(r)$. If we were testing the simple hypothesis that $\beta_i = \beta_i^*$, $\boldsymbol{R}$ would be a row vector with 1 in the ith position and zeros everywhere else, and $\boldsymbol{r}$ would be equal to β_i^*. In this case, the square of the pseudo-t statistic (3.36) is precisely the Wald statistic (3.41).

The second approach to calculating test statistics is to estimate the model subject to the restrictions that are to be tested and then to base a test statistic on those restricted estimates. This is often referred to as the Lagrange multiplier (or LM) principle, because one way to derive restricted least squares estimates is to set up a Lagrangian that is simultaneously minimized with respect to the parameters and maximized with respect to the Lagrange multipliers. If the restrictions were in fact true, one would expect the estimated Lagrange multipliers to have mean zero (at least asymptotically); the idea of LM tests is to see whether this is in fact the case.

To estimate a model like (3.01) subject to the restrictions (3.38), we may set up the Lagrangian

$$\tfrac{1}{2}\big(\boldsymbol{y} - \boldsymbol{x}(\boldsymbol{\beta})\big)^\top\big(\boldsymbol{y} - \boldsymbol{x}(\boldsymbol{\beta})\big) + (\boldsymbol{R}\boldsymbol{\beta} - \boldsymbol{r})^\top\boldsymbol{\lambda}, \tag{3.42}$$

where $\boldsymbol{\lambda}$ is an r–vector of Lagrange multipliers, and the function $SSR(\boldsymbol{\beta})$ has been multiplied by one-half to simplify the algebra. The first-order conditions obtained by differentiating (3.42) with respect to $\boldsymbol{\beta}$ and $\boldsymbol{\lambda}$ and setting the derivatives to zero are

$$-\boldsymbol{X}^{\top}(\tilde{\boldsymbol{\beta}})\big(\boldsymbol{y}-\boldsymbol{x}(\tilde{\boldsymbol{\beta}})\big)+\boldsymbol{R}^{\top}\tilde{\boldsymbol{\lambda}}=\mathbf{0} \tag{3.43}$$

$$\boldsymbol{R}\tilde{\boldsymbol{\beta}}-\boldsymbol{r}=\mathbf{0}, \tag{3.44}$$

where $\tilde{\boldsymbol{\beta}}$ denotes the restricted estimates and $\tilde{\boldsymbol{\lambda}}$ denotes the estimated Lagrange multipliers. From (3.43), we see that

$$\boldsymbol{R}^{\top}\tilde{\boldsymbol{\lambda}}=\tilde{\boldsymbol{X}}^{\top}(\boldsymbol{y}-\tilde{\boldsymbol{x}}), \tag{3.45}$$

where, as usual, $\tilde{\boldsymbol{x}}$ and $\tilde{\boldsymbol{X}}$ denote $\boldsymbol{x}(\tilde{\boldsymbol{\beta}})$ and $\boldsymbol{X}(\tilde{\boldsymbol{\beta}})$. The expression on the right-hand side of (3.45) is minus the k-vector of the derivatives of $\frac{1}{2}SSR(\boldsymbol{\beta})$ with respect to all the elements of $\boldsymbol{\beta}$, evaluated at $\tilde{\boldsymbol{\beta}}$. This vector is often called the **score vector**. Since $\boldsymbol{y}-\tilde{\boldsymbol{x}}$ is simply a vector of residuals, which should converge asymptotically under H_0 to the vector of error terms $\boldsymbol{u}$, it seems plausible that the asymptotic covariance matrix of the vector of scores is

$$\sigma_0^2\boldsymbol{X}^{\top}(\boldsymbol{\beta}_0)\boldsymbol{X}(\boldsymbol{\beta}_0). \tag{3.46}$$

Subject to certain asymptotic niceties, that is indeed the case, and a more rigorous version of this result will be proved in Chapter 5.

The obvious way to estimate (3.46) is to use $\tilde{s}^2\tilde{\boldsymbol{X}}^{\top}\tilde{\boldsymbol{X}}$, where $\tilde{s}^2$ is $SSR(\tilde{\boldsymbol{\beta}})/(n-k+r)$. Putting this estimate together with the expressions on each side of (3.45), we can construct two apparently different, but numerically identical, test statistics. The first of these is

$$\tilde{\boldsymbol{\lambda}}^{\top}\boldsymbol{R}\big(\tilde{s}^2\tilde{\boldsymbol{X}}^{\top}\tilde{\boldsymbol{X}}\big)^{-1}\boldsymbol{R}^{\top}\tilde{\boldsymbol{\lambda}}=\frac{1}{\tilde{s}^2}\tilde{\boldsymbol{\lambda}}^{\top}\boldsymbol{R}\big(\tilde{\boldsymbol{X}}^{\top}\tilde{\boldsymbol{X}}\big)^{-1}\boldsymbol{R}^{\top}\tilde{\boldsymbol{\lambda}}. \tag{3.47}$$

In this form, the test statistic is clearly a Lagrange multiplier statistic. Since $\tilde{\boldsymbol{\lambda}}$ is an r-vector, it should not be surprising that this statistic would be asymptotically distributed as $\chi^2(r)$. A proof that this is the case follows from essentially the same arguments used in the case of the Wald test, since (3.47) is a quadratic form similar to (3.37). Of course, the result depends critically on the vector $\tilde{\boldsymbol{\lambda}}$ being asymptotically normally distributed, something that we will prove in Chapter 5.

The second test statistic, which we stress is numerically identical to the first, is obtained by substituting $\tilde{\boldsymbol{X}}^{\top}(\boldsymbol{y}-\tilde{\boldsymbol{x}})$ for $\tilde{\boldsymbol{\lambda}}^{\top}\boldsymbol{R}$ in (3.47). The result, which is the **score form** of the LM statistic, is

$$\frac{1}{\tilde{s}^2}(\boldsymbol{y}-\tilde{\boldsymbol{x}})^{\top}\tilde{\boldsymbol{X}}\big(\tilde{\boldsymbol{X}}^{\top}\tilde{\boldsymbol{X}}\big)^{-1}\tilde{\boldsymbol{X}}^{\top}(\boldsymbol{y}-\tilde{\boldsymbol{x}})=\frac{1}{\tilde{s}^2}(\boldsymbol{y}-\tilde{\boldsymbol{x}})^{\top}\tilde{\boldsymbol{P}}_X(\boldsymbol{y}-\tilde{\boldsymbol{x}}), \tag{3.48}$$

where $\tilde{\boldsymbol{P}}_X\equiv\tilde{\boldsymbol{X}}(\tilde{\boldsymbol{X}}^{\top}\tilde{\boldsymbol{X}})^{-1}\tilde{\boldsymbol{X}}^{\top}$. It is evident that this expression is simply the explained sum of squares from the **artificial linear regression**

$$\frac{1}{\tilde{s}}(\boldsymbol{y}-\tilde{\boldsymbol{x}})=\tilde{\boldsymbol{X}}\boldsymbol{b}+\text{residuals}, \tag{3.49}$$

where $\boldsymbol{b}$ is a k-vector of artificial parameters. In regression (3.49), the residuals $\boldsymbol{y} - \tilde{\boldsymbol{x}}$ are each divided by $\tilde{s}$, the estimated standard error of the restricted regression, and then regressed on the matrix $\tilde{\boldsymbol{X}}$. This regression is an example of the **Gauss-Newton regression**, or **GNR**, which will be discussed at length in Chapter 6. It is clear that the score form of the LM statistic can easily be calculated once the restricted estimates $\tilde{\boldsymbol{\beta}}$ have been obtained, whether or not the Lagrangian (3.42) was explicitly used to obtain them. LM tests can almost always be calculated by means of artificial linear regressions, as we will see in Chapter 6 for nonlinear regression models and in Chapters 13, 14, and 15 for models estimated by maximum likelihood.

The third and final approach to testing hypotheses about $\boldsymbol{\beta}$ is to estimate the model both subject to the restrictions and unrestrictedly, thus obtaining two values of $SSR(\boldsymbol{\beta})$, which we will denote $SSR(\tilde{\boldsymbol{\beta}})$ and $SSR(\hat{\boldsymbol{\beta}})$. A pseudo-$F$ statistic may then be calculated as

$$\frac{\big(SSR(\tilde{\boldsymbol{\beta}}) - SSR(\hat{\boldsymbol{\beta}})\big)/r}{SSR(\hat{\boldsymbol{\beta}})/(n-k)} = \frac{SSR(\tilde{\boldsymbol{\beta}}) - SSR(\hat{\boldsymbol{\beta}})}{rs^2}. \tag{3.50}$$

We have already seen that this test statistic has exactly the $F(r, n-k)$ distribution when it is used to test linear restrictions on linear models with normal errors. We will prove in Chapter 5 that it has in general the $F(r, n-k)$ distribution (and also that r times it has the $\chi^2(r)$ distribution), asymptotically. As we will see in Chapter 6, asymptotically valid pseudo-F statistics may also be calculated from artificial regressions similar to (3.49) but in which the regressand has not necessarily been divided by $\tilde{s}$. We simply replace $SSR(\hat{\boldsymbol{\beta}})$ in (3.50) by the sum of squared residuals from the artificial regression.

The basic idea of the test statistic (3.50) is to look at the difference between the values of the objective function $SSR(\boldsymbol{\beta})$ at the restricted and unrestricted estimates. The denominator simply serves as a normalizing factor. Later in the book, when we discuss maximum likelihood estimation, we will find that hypothesis tests can also be based on the difference between the restricted and unrestricted values of the log of the likelihood function. Because the difference of two logarithms is the logarithm of a ratio (in this case, the ratio of the unrestricted to the restricted value of the likelihood function), these are known as **likelihood ratio tests**, or **LR tests**. It may be stretching terminology somewhat to call (3.50) an LR test, but it is certainly reasonable to say that (3.50) is based on the likelihood ratio principle if the latter is broadly defined to mean basing a test on the difference between the values of an objective function at the restricted and unrestricted estimates.

One of the remarkable features of the LM, LR, and Wald principles is that tests based on them are **asymptotically equivalent**. Intuitively, what this means is that if the sample size were large enough and the hypothesis being tested were either true or almost true (in a sense to be made precise in Chapters 12 and 13), then test statistics of the same null hypothesis based on any of the three principles would yield exactly the same results. Of course, in finite samples and with models that may not be true, the three principles can sometimes yield tests that give quite different results. As a result, the choice among tests often depends on which test has a finite-sample distribution that is most closely approximated by its large-sample distribution.

A proof of the asymptotic equivalence of LM, LR, and Wald tests in the context of nonlinear regression models is well beyond the scope of this chapter. However, for the special case of linear regression models, such a proof is quite easy. For simplicity, we will assume the situation of Section 3.5, without the normality assumption, since we are no longer trying to derive exact results. The null hypothesis is that $\boldsymbol{\beta}_2 = \mathbf{0}$ in the regression

$$\boldsymbol{y} = \boldsymbol{X\beta} + \boldsymbol{u} = \boldsymbol{X}_1\boldsymbol{\beta}_1 + \boldsymbol{X}_2\boldsymbol{\beta}_2 + \boldsymbol{u}, \quad \boldsymbol{u} \sim \mathrm{IID}(\mathbf{0}, \sigma^2\mathbf{I}).$$

As we saw in Section 3.5, application of the likelihood ratio principle to this testing problem yields the F statistic

$$\frac{\|\boldsymbol{P}_{M_1X_2}\boldsymbol{y}\|^2}{rs^2}, \tag{3.51}$$

r times which would be asymptotically distributed as $\chi^2(r)$. Of course, there is nothing in the LR principle to require us to use an F test rather than a χ^2 test, and nothing in the Wald or LM principles to require us to employ χ^2 tests rather than F tests. The choice between the F and χ^2 forms should normally be based on finite-sample considerations, which generally favor the F form.

Now let us see what happens when we apply the Wald and LM principles. The general formula for the Wald test of a nonlinear regression model is (3.41). In this case, $\boldsymbol{R}\hat{\boldsymbol{\beta}} - \boldsymbol{r}$ is just $\hat{\boldsymbol{\beta}}_2$. We can use the FWL Theorem to derive an expression for the latter, thereby obtaining

$$\boldsymbol{R}\hat{\boldsymbol{\beta}} - \boldsymbol{r} = \hat{\boldsymbol{\beta}}_2 = \left(\boldsymbol{X}_2^\top\boldsymbol{M}_1\boldsymbol{X}_2\right)^{-1}\boldsymbol{X}_2^\top\boldsymbol{M}_1\boldsymbol{y}.$$

In this case, the matrix $\boldsymbol{R}$ is just $[\mathbf{0}_{k-r} \quad \mathbf{I}_r]$. Thus $\boldsymbol{R}(\boldsymbol{X}^\top\boldsymbol{X})^{-1}\boldsymbol{R}^\top$, which we need to calculate the Wald statistic, is just the lower right-hand $r \times r$ block of the matrix $(\boldsymbol{X}^\top\boldsymbol{X})^{-1}$. We can easily find this using the FWL Theorem or the formulas for partitioned inverses in Appendix A; it is simply $(\boldsymbol{X}_2^\top\boldsymbol{M}_1\boldsymbol{X}_2)^{-1}$. Hence the Wald statistic (3.41) is

$$\begin{aligned}
&\frac{1}{s^2}\,\boldsymbol{y}^\top\boldsymbol{M}_1\boldsymbol{X}_2\left(\boldsymbol{X}_2^\top\boldsymbol{M}_1\boldsymbol{X}_2\right)^{-1}\boldsymbol{X}_2^\top\boldsymbol{M}_1\boldsymbol{X}_2\left(\boldsymbol{X}_2^\top\boldsymbol{M}_1\boldsymbol{X}_2\right)^{-1}\boldsymbol{X}_2^\top\boldsymbol{M}_1\boldsymbol{y} \\
&= \frac{1}{s^2}\,\boldsymbol{y}^\top\boldsymbol{M}_1\boldsymbol{X}_2\left(\boldsymbol{X}_2^\top\boldsymbol{M}_1\boldsymbol{X}_2\right)^{-1}\boldsymbol{X}_2^\top\boldsymbol{M}_1\boldsymbol{y} = \frac{1}{s^2}\left\|\boldsymbol{P}_{M_1X_2}\boldsymbol{y}\right\|^2,
\end{aligned} \tag{3.52}$$

which is equal to r times (3.51). Thus, in this case, the Wald and LR principles yield essentially the same test statistics. The only difference is that we chose to write the Wald statistic (3.52) in χ^2 form and the LR statistic (3.51) in F form.

What about the LM principle? We have seen that the LM statistic (3.48) is equal to the explained sum of squares from the artificial regression (3.49), which in this case is

$$\frac{1}{\tilde{s}}\boldsymbol{M}_1\boldsymbol{y} = \boldsymbol{X}_1\boldsymbol{b}_1 + \boldsymbol{X}_2\boldsymbol{b}_2 + \text{residuals}. \tag{3.53}$$

Since the regressand here is orthogonal to $\boldsymbol{X}_1$, the explained sum of squares from (3.53) must, by the FWL Theorem, be equal to the explained sum of squares from the regression

$$\frac{1}{\tilde{s}}\boldsymbol{M}_1\boldsymbol{y} = \boldsymbol{M}_1\boldsymbol{X}_2\boldsymbol{b}_2 + \text{residuals},$$

which is

$$\frac{1}{\tilde{s}^2}\boldsymbol{y}^{\top}\boldsymbol{M}_1\boldsymbol{X}_2\big(\boldsymbol{X}_2^{\top}\boldsymbol{M}_1\boldsymbol{X}_2\big)^{-1}\boldsymbol{X}_2^{\top}\boldsymbol{M}_1\boldsymbol{y} = \frac{1}{\tilde{s}^2}\big\|\boldsymbol{P}_{M_1X_2}\boldsymbol{y}\big\|^2.$$

Thus, for linear restrictions on linear regression models, the only difference between the LM statistic and the Wald and LR statistics is that the former uses $\tilde{s}^2$ to estimate σ^2 while both of the latter use s^2. If σ^2 were known, all three test statistics would be identical. If the null hypothesis holds, both $\tilde{s}^2$ and s^2 should tend to σ^2 as the sample size becomes large. Thus all three test statistics are seen to be asymptotically equivalent. Even in finite samples, one would expect $\tilde{s}^2$ and s^2 to be quite similar when H_0 is true unless the sample is extremely small. If the null were in fact true, substantial differences between the three statistics would therefore be unlikely. Of course, if the null were false, $\tilde{s}^2$ and s^2 could differ substantially, and hence the LM statistic could be quite different from the other two test statistics in that case.

3.7 Restrictions and Pretest Estimators

In the preceding three sections, we have discussed hypothesis testing at some length, but we have not said anything about one of the principal reasons for imposing and testing restrictions. In many cases, restrictions are not implied by any economic theory but are imposed by the investigator in the hope that a restricted model will be easier to estimate and will yield more efficient estimates than an unrestricted model. Tests of this sort of restriction include DWH tests (Chapter 7), tests for serial correlation (Chapter 10), common factor restriction tests (Chapter 10), tests for structural change (Chapter 11), and tests on the length of a distributed lag (Chapter 19). In these and many other cases, restrictions are tested in order to decide which model to use as a basis for inference about the parameters of interest and to weed out models that appear to be incompatible with the data. However, because estimation and testing are based on the same data, the properties of the final estimates may be very difficult to analyze. This is the problem of **pretesting**.

For simplicity, we will in this section consider only the case of linear regression models with fixed regressors, some coefficients of which are subject to zero restrictions. The restricted model will be (3.18), in which $\boldsymbol{y}$ is regressed on an $n \times (k-r)$ matrix $\boldsymbol{X}_1$, and the unrestricted model will be (3.19), in which $\boldsymbol{y}$ is regressed on $\boldsymbol{X}_1$ and an $n \times r$ matrix $\boldsymbol{X}_2$. The OLS estimates of the parameters of the restricted model are

$$\tilde{\boldsymbol{\beta}}_1 = \left(\boldsymbol{X}_1^\top \boldsymbol{X}_1\right)^{-1} \boldsymbol{X}_1^\top \boldsymbol{y}.$$

The OLS estimates of these same parameters in the unrestricted model can easily be found by using the FWL Theorem. They are

$$\hat{\boldsymbol{\beta}}_1 = \left(\boldsymbol{X}_1^\top \boldsymbol{M}_2 \boldsymbol{X}_1\right)^{-1} \boldsymbol{X}_1^\top \boldsymbol{M}_2 \boldsymbol{y},$$

where $\boldsymbol{M}_2$ denotes the matrix that projects orthogonally onto $\mathcal{S}^\perp(\boldsymbol{X}_2)$.

It is natural to ask how well the estimators $\tilde{\boldsymbol{\beta}}_1$ and $\hat{\boldsymbol{\beta}}_1$ perform relative to each other. If the data are actually generated by the DGP (3.22), which is a special case of the restricted model, they are evidently both unbiased. However, as we will demonstrate in a moment, the restricted estimator $\tilde{\boldsymbol{\beta}}_1$ is more **efficient** than the unrestricted estimator $\hat{\boldsymbol{\beta}}_1$. One estimator is said to be more efficient than another if the covariance matrix of the inefficient estimator minus the covariance matrix of the efficient one is a positive semidefinite matrix; see Section 5.5. If $\tilde{\boldsymbol{\beta}}_1$ is more efficient than $\hat{\boldsymbol{\beta}}_1$ in this sense, then any linear combination of the elements of $\tilde{\boldsymbol{\beta}}_1$ must have variance no larger than the corresponding linear combination of the elements of $\hat{\boldsymbol{\beta}}_1$.

The proof that $\tilde{\boldsymbol{\beta}}_1$ is more efficient than $\hat{\boldsymbol{\beta}}_1$ under the DGP (3.22) is very simple. The difference between the covariance matrices of $\hat{\boldsymbol{\beta}}_1$ and $\tilde{\boldsymbol{\beta}}_1$ is

$$\sigma_0^2 \left(\boldsymbol{X}_1^\top \boldsymbol{M}_2 \boldsymbol{X}_1\right)^{-1} - \sigma_0^2 \left(\boldsymbol{X}_1^\top \boldsymbol{X}_1\right)^{-1}. \tag{3.54}$$

It is easy to show that this difference is a positive semidefinite matrix by using a result proved in Appendix A. According to this result, the difference between two symmetric, positive definite matrices is positive semidefinite if and only if the difference of their inverses reversed is positive semidefinite. Therefore, consider the difference

$$\boldsymbol{X}_1^\top \boldsymbol{X}_1 - \boldsymbol{X}_1^\top \boldsymbol{M}_2 \boldsymbol{X}_1 = \boldsymbol{X}_1^\top \boldsymbol{P}_2 \boldsymbol{X}_1, \tag{3.55}$$

where $\boldsymbol{P}_2 = \mathbf{I} - \boldsymbol{M}_2$. Since the right-hand side of (3.55) is clearly a positive semidefinite matrix, so must be (3.54).

We have just established that the restricted estimator $\tilde{\boldsymbol{\beta}}_1$ is more efficient (or, at least, no less efficient) than the unrestricted estimator $\hat{\boldsymbol{\beta}}_1$ when the DGP satisfies the restrictions. But what happens when it does not satisfy them? Suppose the DGP is

$$\boldsymbol{y} = \boldsymbol{X}_1 \boldsymbol{\beta}_{10} + \boldsymbol{X}_2 \boldsymbol{\beta}_{20} + \boldsymbol{u}, \quad \boldsymbol{u} \sim N(\mathbf{0}, \sigma_0^2 \mathbf{I}), \tag{3.56}$$

with $\beta_{20} \neq 0$. Then it is easy to see that the restricted estimator $\tilde{\beta}_1$ will, in general, be biased. Under this DGP,

$$\begin{aligned} E(\tilde{\beta}_1) &= E\Big(\big(X_1^\top X_1\big)^{-1} X_1^\top y\Big) \\ &= E\Big(\big(X_1^\top X_1\big)^{-1} X_1^\top (X_1 \beta_{10} + X_2 \beta_{20} + u)\Big) \\ &= \beta_{10} + \big(X_1^\top X_1\big)^{-1} X_1^\top X_2 \beta_{20}. \end{aligned} \tag{3.57}$$

Unless $X_1^\top X_2$ is a zero matrix or β_{20} is a zero vector, $\tilde{\beta}_1$ will be a biased estimator. The magnitude of the bias will depend on the matrices $X_1^\top X_1$ and $X_1^\top X_2$ and the vector β_{20}.

Results very similar to (3.57) are available for all types of restrictions, not just for linear restrictions, and for all sorts of models in addition to linear regression models. We will not attempt to deal with nonlinear models here because that requires a good deal of technical apparatus, which will be developed in Chapter 12. Results analogous to (3.57) for nonlinear regression models and other types of nonlinear models may be found in Kiefer and Skoog (1984). The important point is that imposition of false restrictions on some of the parameters of a model generally causes all of the parameter estimates to be biased. This bias does not go away as the sample size gets larger.

Even though $\tilde{\beta}_1$ is biased when the DGP is (3.56), it is still of interest to ask how well it performs. The analog of the covariance matrix for a biased estimator is the **mean squared error matrix**, which in this case is

$$\begin{aligned} & E\big(\tilde{\beta}_1 - \beta_{10}\big)\big(\tilde{\beta}_1 - \beta_{10}\big)^\top \\ &= E\big(X_1^\top X_1\big)^{-1} X_1^\top (X_2 \beta_{20} + u)\big)\big(X_1^\top X_1\big)^{-1} X_1^\top (X_2 \beta_{20} + u)\big)^\top \\ &= \sigma_0^2 \big(X_1^\top X_1\big)^{-1} + \big(X_1^\top X_1\big)^{-1} X_1^\top X_2 \beta_{20} \beta_{20}^\top X_2^\top X_1 \big(X_1^\top X_1\big)^{-1}. \end{aligned} \tag{3.58}$$

The third line here is the sum of two matrices: the covariance matrix of $\tilde{\beta}_1$ when the DGP satisfies the restrictions, and the outer product of the second term in the last line of (3.57) with itself. It is possible to compare (3.58) with $V(\hat{\beta}_1)$, the covariance matrix of the unrestricted estimator $\hat{\beta}_1$, only if σ_0 and β_{20} are known. Since the first term of (3.58) is smaller in the matrix sense than $V(\hat{\beta}_1)$, it is clear that if β_{20} is small enough (3.58) will be smaller than $V(\hat{\beta}_1)$. Thus it may be desirable to use the restricted estimator $\tilde{\beta}_1$ when the restrictions are false, provided they are not too false.

Applied workers frequently find themselves in a situation like the one we have been discussing. They want to estimate β_1 and do not know whether or not $\beta_2 = 0$. It then seems natural to define a new estimator,

$$\breve{\beta}_1 = \begin{cases} \tilde{\beta}_1 & \text{if } F_{\beta_2 = 0} < c_\alpha; \\ \hat{\beta}_1 & \text{if } F_{\beta_2 = 0} \geq c_\alpha. \end{cases}$$

Here $F_{\beta_2=0}$ is the usual F test statistic for the null hypothesis that $\beta_2 = \mathbf{0}$, and c_α is the critical value for a test of size α given by the $F(r, n-k)$ distribution. Thus $\check{\beta}_1$ will be the restricted estimator $\tilde{\beta}_1$ when the F test does not reject the hypothesis that the restrictions are satisfied and will be the unrestricted estimator $\hat{\beta}_1$ when the F test does reject that hypothesis. It is an example of what is called a **preliminary test estimator** or **pretest estimator**.

Pretest estimators are used all the time. Whenever we test some aspect of a model's specification and then decide, on the basis of the test results, what version of the model to estimate or what estimation method to use, we are employing a pretest estimator. Unfortunately, the properties of pretest estimators are, in practice, very difficult to know. The problems can be seen from the example we have been studying. Suppose the restrictions hold. Then the estimator we would like to use is the restricted estimator, $\tilde{\beta}_1$. But, $\alpha\%$ of the time, the F test will incorrectly reject the null hypothesis and $\check{\beta}_1$ will be equal to the unrestricted estimator $\hat{\beta}_1$ instead. Thus $\check{\beta}_1$ must be less efficient than $\tilde{\beta}_1$ when the restrictions do in fact hold. Moreover, since the estimated covariance matrix reported by the regression package will not take the pretesting into account, inferences about $\check{\beta}_1$ may be misleading.

On the other hand, when the restrictions do not hold, we may or may not want to use the unrestricted estimator $\hat{\beta}_1$. Depending on how much power the F test has, $\check{\beta}_1$ will sometimes be equal to $\tilde{\beta}_1$ and sometimes be equal to $\hat{\beta}_1$. It will certainly not be unbiased, because $\tilde{\beta}_1$ is not unbiased, and it may be more or less efficient (in the sense of mean squared error) than the unrestricted estimator. Inferences about $\check{\beta}_1$ based on the usual estimated OLS covariance matrix for whichever of $\tilde{\beta}_1$ and $\hat{\beta}_1$ it turns out to be equal to may be misleading, because they fail to take into account the pretesting that occurred previously.

In practice, there is often not very much that we can do about the problems caused by pretesting, except to recognize that pretesting adds an additional element of uncertainly to most problems of statistical inference. Since α, the level of the preliminary test, will affect the properties of $\check{\beta}_1$, it may be worthwhile to try using different values of α. Conventional significance levels such as .05 are certainly not optimal in general, and there is a literature on how to choose better ones in specific cases; see, for example, Toyoda and Wallace (1976). However, real pretesting problems are much more complicated than the one we have discussed as an example or the ones that have been studied in the literature. Every time one subjects a model to any sort of test, the result of that test may affect the form of the final model, and the implied pretest estimator therefore becomes even more complicated. It is hard to see how this can be analyzed formally.

Our discussion of pretesting has been very brief. More detailed treatments may be found in Fomby, Hill, and Johnson (1984, Chapter 7), Judge, Hill, Griffiths, Lütkepohl, and Lee (1985, Chapter 21), and Judge and Bock (1978). In the remainder of this book, we entirely ignore the problems caused by pretesting, not because they are unimportant but because, in practice, they are generally intractable.

3.8 Conclusion

This chapter has provided an introduction to several important topics: estimation of covariance matrices for NLS estimates, the use of such covariance matrix estimates for constructing confidence intervals, basic ideas of hypothesis testing, the justification for testing linear restrictions on linear regression models by means of t and F tests, the three classical principles of hypothesis testing and their application to nonlinear regression models, and pretesting. At a number of points we were forced to be a little vague and to refer to results on the asymptotic properties of nonlinear least squares estimates that we have not yet proved. Proving those results will be the object of the next two chapters. Chapter 4 discusses the basic ideas of asymptotic analysis, including consistency, asymptotic normality, central limit theorems, laws of large numbers, and the use of "big-O" and "little-o" notation. Chapter 5 then uses these concepts to prove the consistency and asymptotic normality of nonlinear least squares estimates of univariate nonlinear regression models and to derive the asymptotic distributions of the test statistics discussed in this chapter. It also proves a number of related asymptotic results that will be useful later on.

Terms and Concepts

acceptance region
adjusted R^2, or $\bar{R}^2$
artificial regressions
asymptotic test
asymptotically equivalent tests
confidence ellipses: relation to confidence intervals
confidence intervals and regions, exact and approximate
consistent test
covariance matrix (of a vector of parameter estimates)
critical region, or rejection region
critical value (for a test statistic)
efficient estimator
exact test
F statistic and F distribution
fixed in repeated samples
Gauss-Newton regression (GNR)
hypotheses: null and alternative
Lagrange multiplier (LM) principle
likelihood ratio (LR) principle
maintained hypothesis
maximum likelihood
mean squared error matrix
P value, or marginal significance level
posterior probability
power (of a test)
preliminary test (pretest) estimator
pretesting
prior information
pseudo-F and pseudo-t statistics
score form (of the LM statistic)
score vector
significance level (of a test)
size (of a test)
t statistic and Student's t distribution
test statistics
Type I and Type II errors
Wald principle

Chapter 4

Introduction to Asymptotic Theory and Methods

4.1 Introduction

Once one leaves the context of ordinary (linear) least squares with fixed regressors and normally distributed errors, it is frequently impossible, or at least impractical, to obtain exact statistical results. It is therefore necessary to resort to **asymptotic theory**, that is, theory which applies to the case in which the sample size is infinitely large. Infinite samples are not available in this finite universe, and only if they were would there be a context in which asymptotic theory was exact. Of course, since statistics itself would be quite unnecessary if samples were infinitely large, asymptotic theory would not be useful if it were exact. In practice, asymptotic theory is used as an approximation — sometimes a good one, sometimes not so good.

Most of the time, it is a pious hope rather than a firmly founded belief that asymptotic results have some relevance to the data with which one actually works. Unfortunately, more accurate approximations are available only in the simplest cases. At this time, it is probably fair to say that the principal means of getting evidence on these matters is to use Monte Carlo experiments, which we will discuss in the last chapter of this book. Since one cannot resort to a Monte Carlo experiment every time one obtains a test statistic or a set of estimates, a thorough knowledge of asymptotic theory is necessary in the present state of the art and science of econometrics. The purpose of this chapter is therefore to embark on the study of the asymptotic theory that will be used throughout the rest of the book. All of this theory is ultimately based on **laws of large numbers** and **central limit theorems**, and we will therefore spend considerable time discussing these fundamental results.

In this chapter, we discuss the basic ideas of, and mathematical prerequisites to, asymptotic theory in econometrics. We begin the next section by treating the fundamental notion of an infinite sequence, either of random or of nonrandom elements. Much of this material should be familiar to those who have studied calculus, but it is worth reviewing because it leads directly to the fundamental notions of limits and convergence, which allow us to state and prove a simple law of large numbers. In Section 4.3, we introduce the "big-O," "little-o" notation and show how the idea of a limit can be used to obtain more precise and detailed results than were obtained in Section 4.2. Data-generating processes capable of generating infinite sequences of data are introduced in Section 4.4, and this necessitates a little discussion of stochastic processes. Section 4.5 then introduces the property of consistency of an estimator and shows how this property can often be established with the help of a law of large numbers. Asymptotic normality is the topic of Section 4.6, and this property is obtained for some simple estimators by use of a central limit theorem. Then, in Section 4.7, we provide, mostly for the sake of later reference, a collection of definitions and theorems, the latter being laws of large numbers and central limit theorems much more sophisticated than those actually discussed in the text. In addition, we present in Section 4.7 two sets of conditions, one centered on a law of large numbers, the other on a central limit theorem, which will be very useful subsequently as a summary of the regularity conditions needed for results proved in later chapters.

4.2 Sequences, Limits, and Convergence

The concept of infinity is one of unending fascination for mathematicians. One noted twentieth-century mathematician, Stanislaw Ulam, wrote that the continuing evolution of various notions of infinity is one of the chief driving forces behind research in mathematics (Ulam, 1976). However that may be, seemingly impractical and certainly unattainable infinities are at the heart of almost all valuable and useful applications of mathematics presently in use, among which we may count econometrics.

The reason for the widespread use of infinity is that it can provide workable approximations in circumstances in which exact results are difficult or impossible to obtain. The crucial mathematical operation which yields these approximations is that of **passage to the limit**, the limit being where the notion of infinity comes in. The limits of interest may be zero, finite, or infinite. Zero or finite limits usually provide the approximations that are sought: Things difficult to calculate in a realistic, finite, context are replaced by their limits as an approximation.

The first and most frequently encountered mathematical construct which may possess a limit is that of a **sequence**. A sequence is a countably infinite collection of things, such as numbers, vectors, matrices, or more general mathematical objects, and thus by its mere definition cannot be represented in the actual physical world. But some sequences are nevertheless very familiar. Consider the most famous sequence of all: the sequence

$$\{1, 2, 3, \ldots\}$$

of the natural numbers. This is a simple-minded example perhaps, but one that exhibits some of the important properties which sequences may possess.

The first of these is that a sequence must embody a **rule** that defines it. In the physical world, we may define a collection by indicating or pointing to all of its members, for these must be finite in number, but that is impossible for an infinite collection. Consequently there must be a method of generating the members of a sequence, and the rule performs this function. For the natural numbers, the rule is simple: One goes from any member of the sequence to its **successor** by adding 1.

This last remark illustrates another property of sequences as opposed to other infinite collections: A sequence is **ordered**. Thus one can speak of the first, second, third, and so forth members of the sequence, and the rule that defines the sequence must be capable of generating the nth member, for any positive integer n.

The natural number sequence is in a certain sense the model for all sequences, because it expresses the notion of the succession of elements, that is, the notion of going from one element to the next, its successor. Formally, a sequence can be defined as a mapping from the set or sequence of natural numbers to some other set, for example, the real numbers or the set of $n \times m$ matrices, from which the members of the sequence are drawn. This mapping embodies the defining rule of the sequence, since it associates to any integer n the nth member of the sequence. If the action of this mapping can be expressed simply, then it provides a very convenient notation for sequences. One simply encloses in braces the nth element of the sequence, and, just as one does with the summation sign, one may optionally indicate the range of the sequence. Thus the natural number sequence can be denoted as $\{n\}$ or as $\{n\}_{n=1}^{\infty}$. Note that the "first" element of a sequence need not have the index 1: We may perfectly well consider the sequence $\{n\}_{n=m}^{\infty}$ of integers greater than or equal to m.

As we indicated above, for asymptotic analysis we will primarily be interested in sequences that have finite limits. The natural number sequence does not possess such a limit, but it is not hard to find sequences that do. For example, $\{1/n\}, \{e^{-n}\}, \{1/\log n\}$, and $\{n^{-2}\}$ all have limits of zero. The following sequences, on the other hand, all have nonzero finite limits:

$$\left\{\frac{n}{n+1}\right\}, \quad \left\{n \sin\left(\tfrac{1}{n}\right)\right\}, \quad \left\{1+\tfrac{1}{n}\right\}, \quad \left\{n\left(y^{1/n}-1\right)\right\}.$$

If the reader cannot calculate the values of these limits, it would be very useful to learn how to do so. The last one is not too easy, but, as we will see in Chapter 14, it is sometimes quite useful in econometric modeling.

The limits of these sequences are the limits **as n tends to infinity**. We may sometimes say instead that n becomes infinitely large, or even, by abuse of language, just large. Another possibility is to talk of the limit for large n. In all cases, the meaning should be clear. The formal definition of the limit of a **real-valued sequence**, that is, a sequence of which the elements are real numbers, is as follows:

Definition 4.1.

> The real-valued sequence $\{a_n\}$ has the real number a for its limit, or converges to a, if for any positive ε, no matter how small, it is possible to find a positive integer N such that for all integers n greater than N, $|a_n - a| < \varepsilon$.

In other words, as n becomes large, we can always reach a point in the sequence beyond which all the members of the sequence are closer to the limit than any prespecified tolerance level.

In Definition 4.1, we used the important word *converge*. If sequences have limits, they are said to **converge** to them. A sequence that converges is in turn said to be **convergent**. Alternatively, a sequence that has no limit may **diverge**, or be **divergent**, if the absolute values of the members of the sequence increase without bound as n gets larger. There are other possibilities, especially if the members of the sequence are more complicated entities than real numbers, such as matrices. The convergence or otherwise of a sequence can be discussed only if the elements of the sequence belong to a set on which the idea of **closeness** is defined, because of the need to speak of the elements becoming arbitrarily close to the limit as n tends to infinity. Thus, for a sequence of vectors or matrices to converge, we need to be able to say whether or not any two vectors or matrices are, to a given tolerance level, close or not. For vectors, this is easy: We can use the nonnegative real number $\|\boldsymbol{v}_1 - \boldsymbol{v}_2\|$, the Euclidean distance, as a measure of the closeness or otherwise of two vectors $\boldsymbol{v}_1$ and $\boldsymbol{v}_2$ in a Euclidean space. For matrices, a comparable measure is the norm of the difference between two matrices; see Appendix A for the definition of the norm of a matrix, and recall also that the notation used for it is usually $\|\cdot\|$, just as for Euclidean distance. This fact will make for conciseness in writing definitions.

The general discussion of closeness is the subject matter of the mathematical discipline of topology. Convergence and limits are defined only on **topological spaces**. The set of real numbers and Euclidean spaces have what are called **natural topologies**. Those are what we used in Definition 4.1 for real numbers and can use in the extension of the definition to vectors and matrices based on the use of the Euclidean norm $\|\cdot\|$. These topologies are in fact so natural that, when speaking of the convergence of real-, vector- or matrix-valued sequences, it is quite unnecessary to be explicit about any topological matters. This is unfortunately not the case when we consider sequences of **random variables**.[1] To make matters worse, there is no single natural topology for random variables; at least three or four are in regular use.

It is not necessary and would be undesirable in a book of this sort to give formal definitions of the different topologies used with random variables, and we will not do so. For readers who are consequently unsatisfied, we

[1] For a discussion of the meaning of the term **random variable**, see Appendix B.

may recommend the two books by Billingsley (1968, 1979). But anything of any importance to us about a topology is known if we can say whether a given sequence converges or not for that topology, and so we will do perfectly well if we provide definitions of the different kinds of convergence for random variables.

Probably the most useful kind of stochastic convergence, that is, convergence for random variables, is **convergence in probability**. We begin with the formal definition:

Definition 4.2.

The sequence $\{\boldsymbol{a}_n\}$ of real- or vector-valued random variables tends in probability to the limiting random variable $\boldsymbol{a}$ if for all ε and $\delta > 0$ there is an N such that for all $n > N$,

$$\Pr\big(\|\boldsymbol{a}_n - \boldsymbol{a}\| > \varepsilon\big) < \delta. \tag{4.01}$$

In this case, $\boldsymbol{a}$ is called the **limit in probability** or the **probability limit** or simply the **plim** of the sequence $\{\boldsymbol{a}_n\}$. One writes

$$\operatorname*{plim}_{n\to\infty} \boldsymbol{a}_n = \boldsymbol{a} \quad \text{or} \quad \boldsymbol{a}_n \xrightarrow{\;p\;} \boldsymbol{a}.$$

Note the absence of the braces in these last expressions. Note also that, for real-valued random variables, the Euclidean norm $\|\cdot\|$ simplifies to the ordinary absolute value $|\cdot|$.

Condition (4.01) says, in effect, that for any given tolerance level ε, one can go to a member far enough down the sequence that, beyond that member, the probability of finding a discrepancy exceeding the tolerance level between an element of the sequence and the limit random variable is below another arbitrarily prespecified tolerance level δ. Note that although the above definition defined the probability limit $\boldsymbol{a}$ to be a random variable (or vector of random variables), it may in fact be an ordinary nonrandom number or vector, in which case it is said to be **nonstochastic**, or constant.

A well-worn example of a nonstochastic probability limit is given by considering the limit of the sequence of proportions of heads in a series of independent tosses of an unbiased coin. It is worth demonstrating formally that the probability limit is indeed one-half, since this will give us the opportunity to see some useful techniques of proof and acquire some intuition about how probability limits differ from ordinary ones.

For each coin toss, then, define a random variable y_t equal to 1 if the outcome is heads and 0 if it is tails. This means that $\{y_t\}$ is a sequence of random variables, provided that we can imagine the coin tossing going on ad infinitum. Then, after n tosses, the proportion of heads is just

$$a_n \equiv \frac{1}{n}\sum_{t=1}^{n} y_t, \tag{4.02}$$

and, of course, a_n is a real (in fact rational) number contained in the unit interval [0,1]. Expression (4.02) defines another sequence of random variables $\{a_n\}$, and it is the limit in probability of this sequence that we wish to calculate.

We first calculate the mean and variance of a_n. The statement that the coin is unbiased means that, for all t, $\Pr(y_t = 1) = \frac{1}{2}$ and $\Pr(y_t = 0) = \frac{1}{2}$. Since the operation of taking expectations is linear, and all the expectations are the same,

$$E(a_n) = \frac{1}{n}\sum_{t=1}^{n} E(y_t) = E(y_t) = \frac{1}{2}.$$

Calculating the variance is a little harder. We see that

$$\mathrm{Var}(a_n) = E\big(a_n - E(a_n)\big)^2 = E\big(a_n - \tfrac{1}{2}\big)^2 = E\bigg(\frac{1}{n}\sum_{t=1}^{n}\Big(y_t - \frac{1}{2}\Big)\bigg)^2.$$

Before proceeding, let us define a new sequence of independent random variables $\{z_t\}$ by the rule $z_t = y_t - \frac{1}{2}$. Because $E(z_t) = 0$, $\{z_t\}$ is a **centered sequence**, by which we mean that every element of the sequence has expectation zero, we then find that

$$a_n - E(a_n) = \frac{1}{n}\sum_{t=1}^{n} y_t - \frac{1}{2} = \frac{1}{n}\sum_{t=1}^{n}\Big(y_t - \frac{1}{2}\Big) = \frac{1}{n}\sum_{t=1}^{n} z_t.$$

We can define another centered sequence $\{b_n\}$ by the rule

$$b_n = a_n - E(a_n) = a_n - \frac{1}{2} \tag{4.03}$$

and see that $\mathrm{Var}(a_n) = \mathrm{Var}(b_n)$. We also see that

$$b_n = \frac{1}{n}\sum_{t=1}^{n} z_t. \tag{4.04}$$

Because the z_t's are mutually independent,

$$\mathrm{Var}(b_n) = \frac{1}{n^2}\sum_{t=1}^{n}\mathrm{Var}(z_t) = n^{-1}\mathrm{Var}(z_t).$$

It is simple to see that

$$\mathrm{Var}(z_t) = \big(\tfrac{1}{2}\big)^2\big(\Pr(z_t = \tfrac{1}{2})\big) + \big(-\tfrac{1}{2}\big)^2\big(\Pr(z_t = -\tfrac{1}{2})\big) = \tfrac{1}{4},$$

from which it follows that

$$\mathrm{Var}(a_n) = \mathrm{Var}(b_n) = \frac{1}{4n}. \tag{4.05}$$

This result is crucial to the result we are seeking, since it implies that

$$\lim_{n\to\infty} \mathrm{Var}(a_n) = 0, \tag{4.06}$$

and it is thus intuitively obvious that the limit of the sequence $\{a_n\}$ is nonrandom. But formally we are still a few steps away from establishing the needed result, which, by application of (4.01) to the present circumstances, is that for any ε and $\delta > 0$, there is an N such that

$$\Pr\big(|a_n - \tfrac{1}{2}| > \varepsilon\big) < \delta \quad \text{for all } n > N. \tag{4.07}$$

The main gap between (4.06) and (4.07) is filled by the use of the **Chebyshev inequality** (see Appendix B). This inequality tells us that if a random variable y of zero mean possesses a variance V, then for any positive number α

$$\Pr\big(|y| > \alpha\big) < \frac{V}{\alpha^2}.$$

If we apply this to the variable b_n, then from (4.05) we get

$$\Pr\big(|b_n| > \varepsilon\big) < \frac{1}{4n\varepsilon^2}.$$

From the definition (4.03) of b_n, this means that

$$\Pr\big(|a_n - \tfrac{1}{2}| > \varepsilon\big) < \frac{1}{4n\varepsilon^2}.$$

Thus (4.07) will be true if we choose, for a given ε, a critical value of N equal to the next integer greater than $(4\varepsilon^2\delta)^{-1}$. The convergence in probability of $\{a_n\}$ to $\frac{1}{2}$,

$$\operatorname*{plim}_{n\to\infty} a_n = \frac{1}{2}, \tag{4.08}$$

is, finally, rigorously proved.

As a by-product of the preceding proof, we see that the Chebyshev inequality shows that any centered sequence of which the variance tends to zero tends in probability to zero. Suppose that the sequence $\{y_n\}$ is centered, that $v_n = \mathrm{Var}(y_n)$, and that $v_n \to 0$ as $n \to \infty$. By Definition 4.1 of the limit of a sequence, this last supposition means that for all $\eta > 0$, an $N(\eta)$ can be found such that $v_n < \eta$ for all $n > N(\eta)$. Then we look at the probability that appears in Definition 4.2 of convergence in probability. For some $\varepsilon > 0$,

$$\Pr\big(|y_n| > \varepsilon\big) < v_n\varepsilon^{-2}, \quad \text{by the Chebyshev inequality.}$$

Now consider for any positive δ the critical index $N(\delta\varepsilon^2)$, which is such that, for all $n > N(\delta\varepsilon^2)$, $v_n < \delta\varepsilon^2$. For such n we find that

$$\Pr\big(|y_n| > \varepsilon\big) < \delta\varepsilon^2\varepsilon^{-2} = \delta,$$

exactly as required by Definition 4.2.

The result (4.08) is a first example of what is called a **law of large numbers**. The idea behind this example is in fact the same as that behind all laws of large numbers, and so it is worthwhile to spend a moment considering it more closely. The members of the sequence $\{a_n\}$ are all *averages*, the proportion of the time that a coin has come up heads in a given run of tosses. As we go to increasing values of n, we expect that the average calculated from any random sample of size n will be a more and more accurate measure of something. Here the something is just the number $\frac{1}{2}$, the reciprocal of the number of sides the coin has. If we threw dice instead of tossing coins, we would expect to get $\frac{1}{6}$ instead of $\frac{1}{2}$.

Evidently, the same sort of result will prevail if we measure something of more interest to economists than the proportion of times that a coin comes up heads. We might, for example, be interested in measuring the proportion who own their own homes, say α, of some group of people. Assuming that we can devise a method of sampling randomly from the relevant population (which is often by no means an easy task), we may ask all the people in the sample whether they own their homes or not. Each response may then be treated just like the toss of a coin; we let the random variable y_t equal 1 for the home-owning respondents and 0 for the others. What the law of large numbers then tells us is that, as the number of responses becomes large, we should expect the proportion of respondents who own their homes, $a_n \equiv n^{-1}\sum_{t=1}^{n} y_t$, to converge to the true value α. Intuitively, the reason for the increasing accuracy is that each successive toss provides another piece of information about α.

We can introduce some standard terminology at this point. The form of law of large numbers that we have just proved for the coin-tossing example, in which we showed that the probability limit of the proportion of heads tends to one-half, is called a **weak law of large numbers**, because the kind of convergence proved is convergence in probability. There exist **strong laws of large numbers**, which use, as the term suggests, a stronger notion of convergence of random variables, called **almost sure convergence**. Here is the definition:

Definition 4.3.

The sequence $\{\boldsymbol{a}_n\}$ of real- or vector-valued random variables $\boldsymbol{a}_n$ is said to converge almost surely (a.s.) to a limiting random variable $\boldsymbol{a}$ if

$$\Pr\Big(\lim_{n\to\infty} \boldsymbol{a}_n = \boldsymbol{a}\Big) = 1. \tag{4.09}$$

One writes

$$\lim_{n\to\infty} \boldsymbol{a}_n = \boldsymbol{a} \text{ a.s.} \quad \text{or} \quad \boldsymbol{a}_n \xrightarrow{\text{a.s.}} \boldsymbol{a} \quad \text{or} \quad \boldsymbol{a}_n \to \boldsymbol{a} \text{ a.s.},$$

and $\boldsymbol{a}$ is called the **almost sure limit** of $\{\boldsymbol{a}_n\}$.

A full understanding of the above definition requires some deeper acquaintance with probability theory than we are willing to require of our readers, and so we will discuss it no further. Similarly, a proof of the strong law of large numbers, even for the simple coin-tossing example, is beyond the scope of this book. A rigorous and imaginative proof can be found in the first chapter of Billingsley (1979), and the classical treatment is given in Feller (1968). In the remainder of the book, we will be content to employ weak laws of large numbers, even if strong ones might be available, since the distinction between the two forms has no practical implications for econometrics.

A third form of stochastic convergence is called **convergence in distribution**, or sometimes **convergence in law**, following the usage by which the distribution of a random variable is termed its **law**. It is convergence in distribution that is usually proved in a central limit theorem, as we will see later in this chapter.

Definition 4.4.

The sequence $\{\boldsymbol{a}_n\}$ of real- or vector-valued random variables $\boldsymbol{a}_n$ is said to converge in distribution to a limiting random variable $\boldsymbol{a}$ if

$$\lim_{n\to\infty} \Pr(\boldsymbol{a}_n \leq \boldsymbol{b}) = \Pr(\boldsymbol{a} \leq \boldsymbol{b}) \qquad (4.10)$$

for all real numbers or vectors $\boldsymbol{b}$ such that the limiting distribution function $\Pr(\boldsymbol{a} \leq \boldsymbol{b}')$ is continuous in $\boldsymbol{b}'$ at $\boldsymbol{b}' = \boldsymbol{b}$. One writes:

$$\boldsymbol{a}_n \xrightarrow{D} \boldsymbol{a}.$$

The inequalities in (4.10) are to be interpreted, in the case of vector-valued random variables, as valid for each component of the vectors separately. This is exactly as in the formal definition in Appendix B of the joint probability distribution of a set of random variables. The requirement in the definition that $\Pr(\boldsymbol{a} \leq \boldsymbol{b}')$ be continuous in $\boldsymbol{b}'$ at $\boldsymbol{b}' = \boldsymbol{b}$ is evidently unnecessary in the case of continuous distributions, for which the definition requires simply that the distribution functions of the $\boldsymbol{a}_n$'s converge pointwise to the distribution function of $\boldsymbol{a}$. But if the limiting random variable is nonstochastic, this requirement is necessary. The reason is that the cumulative distribution function (c.d.f. for short) is necessarily discontinuous in this case. Consider the following example.

Let x_n be normally distributed as $N(0, n^{-1})$. Clearly, $\{x_n\}$ converges to zero in any useful sense, and, in particular, it must do so in distribution. Because the variance of x_n is n^{-1}, its c.d.f. is $\Phi(n^{1/2}x)$, in the sense that

$$\Pr(x_n < x) = \Phi(n^{1/2}x) \quad \text{for all real } x.$$

Here $\Phi(\cdot)$ is the c.d.f. of the standard normal, or $N(0,1)$ distribution; see Appendix B for details. For fixed x we have

$$\lim_{n\to\infty} n^{1/2}x = \begin{cases} \infty & \text{if } x > 0; \\ 0 & \text{if } x = 0; \\ -\infty & \text{if } x < 0. \end{cases}$$

Since

$$\lim_{x \to \infty} \Phi(x) = 1, \quad \lim_{x \to -\infty} \Phi(x) = 0, \quad \text{and} \quad \Phi(0) = \tfrac{1}{2},$$

we obtain

$$\lim_{n \to \infty} \Pr(x_n < x) = \begin{cases} 0 & \text{if } x < 0; \\ \frac{1}{2} & \text{if } x = 0; \\ 1 & \text{if } x > 0. \end{cases}$$

The above limit almost coincides with the c.d.f. for a "random" variable x_0 that is in fact always equal to zero. This c.d.f., which is said to correspond to a **degenerate distribution** concentrated at 0, is

$$\Pr(x_0 < x) = \begin{cases} 0 & \text{if } x \leq 0; \\ 1 & \text{if } x > 0. \end{cases}$$

It is only at $x = 0$ that the limit of the c.d.f.'s of the x_n's is not equal to the c.d.f. of the constant random variable. But it is precisely here that the latter is necessarily discontinuous, hence the exception explicitly made in the definition. A c.d.f. that has discontinuities at certain points is said to have **atoms** at these points. Note that a c.d.f. with atoms may perfectly well be the limit of a sequence of c.d.f.'s that have none and are therefore continuous everywhere.

We will conclude this section by stating without proof the relations among the three kinds of stochastic convergence we have so far introduced. Almost sure convergence is, as the name *strong* law of large numbers suggests, the strongest kind. If $\{\boldsymbol{a}_n\}$ converges almost surely to a limiting variable $\boldsymbol{a}$, then it also converges to $\boldsymbol{a}$ in probability and in distribution. Convergence in probability, while not necessarily implying almost sure convergence, does imply convergence in distribution. Convergence in distribution is the weakest of the three and does not necessarily imply either of the other two.

4.3 Rates of Convergence

We covered a lot of ground in the last section, so much so that we have by now, even if very briefly, touched on all the important purely mathematical topics to be discussed in this chapter. What remains is to flesh out the treatment of some matters and to begin to apply our theory to statistics and econometrics. The subject of this section is **rates of convergence**. In treating it we will introduce some very important notation, called the $\boldsymbol{O}, \boldsymbol{o}$ **notation**, which is read as "big-O, little-o notation." Here O and o stand for order and are often referred to as **order symbols**. Roughly speaking, when we say that some quantity is, say, $O(x)$, we mean that is of the same order, asymptotically, as the quantity x, while when we say that it is $o(x)$, we mean that it is of lower order than the quantity x. Just what this means will be made precise below.

In the last section, we discussed the random variable b_n at some length and saw from (4.05) that its variance converged to zero, because it was proportional to n^{-1}. This implies that the sequence converges in probability to zero, and it can be seen that the higher moments of b_n, the third, fourth, and so on, must also tend to zero as $n \to \infty$. A somewhat tricky calculation, which interested readers are invited to try for themselves, reveals that the fourth moment of b_n is

$$E(b_n^4) = \frac{3}{16}n^{-2} - \frac{1}{8}n^{-3}, \tag{4.11}$$

that is, the sum of two terms, one proportional to n^{-2} and the other to n^{-3}. The third moment of b_n, like the first, is zero, simply because the random variable is **symmetric** about zero, a fact which implies that all its odd-numbered moments vanish. Thus the second, third, and fourth moments of b_n all converge to zero, but at different *rates*. Again, the two terms in the fourth moment (4.11) converge at different rates, and it is the term which is proportional to n^{-2} that has the greatest importance asymptotically.

The word "asymptotically" has here been used in a slightly wider sense than we have used up to now. In Section 4.1, we said that asymptotic theory dealt with limits as some index, usually the sample size in econometrics, tends to infinity. Here we are concerned with rates of convergence rather than limits per se. Limits can be used to determine the rates of convergence of sequences as well as their limits: These rates of convergence can be defined as the limits of other sequences. For example, in the comparison of n^{-2} and n^{-3}, the other sequence that interests us is the sequence of the *ratio* of n^{-3} to n^{-2}, that is, the sequence $\{n^{-1}\}$. This last sequence has a limit of zero, and so, asymptotically, we can treat n^{-3}, or anything proportional to it, as zero in the presence of n^{-2}, or anything proportional to it. All of this can be expressed by the little-o notation, which expresses what is called the **small-order relation**: We write $n^{-3} = o(n^{-2})$, meaning that n^{-3} is of lower order than n^{-2}. In general, we have the following definition:

Definition 4.5.

If $f(\cdot)$ and $g(\cdot)$ are two real-valued functions of the positive integer variable n, then the notation

$$f(n) = o\big(g(n)\big) \quad \text{[optionally, as } n \to \infty\text{]}$$

means that

$$\lim_{n\to\infty}\left(\frac{f(n)}{g(n)}\right) = 0.$$

One may say that $f(n)$ is of smaller order than $g(n)$ asymptotically or as n tends to infinity.

Note that $g(n)$ itself may have any sort of behavior as $n \to \infty$. It may or may not have a limit, and if it has, the limit may be zero, finite and nonzero, or infinite. What is important is the *comparison* performed by the ratio. Most often $g(n)$ is a power of n, which may be positive, negative, or zero. In the last case, since $n^0 = 1$ for all n, we would write $f(n) = o(1)$, and this would mean by the definition that

$$\lim_{n\to\infty}\left(\frac{f(n)}{1}\right) = \lim_{n\to\infty}\big(f(n)\big) = 0;$$

in other words, simply that $f(n)$ tends to zero as n tends to infinity. But if we say that $f(n) = o(n^{-1})$, for instance, or that $f(n)$ *is* $o(n^{-1})$, it means that $f(n)$ goes to zero *faster* than n^{-1}. We could also say that $f(n)$ is $o(n)$, and then we do not know whether $f(n)$ has a limit as $n \to \infty$ or not. But we do know that if it tends to infinity, it does so less rapidly than n.

The big-O notation, which expresses the **same-order relation**, is more precise than the little-o notation, since it tells us the greatest rate at which things may change with n. Here is the definition.

Definition 4.6.

If $f(\cdot)$ and $g(\cdot)$ are two real-valued functions of the positive integer variable n, then the notation

$$f(n) = O\big(g(n)\big)$$

means that there exists a constant $K > 0$, independent of n, and a positive integer N such that $|f(n)/g(n)| < K$ for all $n > N$.

We say that $f(n)$ and $g(n)$ are of the same order asymptotically or as $n \to \infty$. Once again it is the *ratio* of $f(n)$ and $g(n)$ that is in question. The definition does *not* exclude the possibility that the limit of the ratio should be zero, and so the verbal expression "of the same order" can be misleading.

Another relation exists which avoids this uncertainty: We call it **asymptotic equality**.

Definition 4.7.

If $f(\cdot)$ and $g(\cdot)$ are two real-valued functions of the positive integer variable n, then they are asymptotically equal if

$$\lim_{n\to\infty}\left(\frac{f(n)}{g(n)}\right) = 1.$$

We write this as $f(n) \stackrel{a}{=} g(n)$. The standard notation for this relation (outside of econometrics) is not $\stackrel{a}{=}$, but $\sim$. Since the symbol $\sim$ is used to denote the distribution of a random variable, it will be plain why we do not use this notation in this book.

Asymptotic equality avoids the difficulty we have alluded to in connection with the big-O or same-order relation, at the expense of imposing a stronger condition. Unlike asymptotic equality, the big-O relation does not require that the ratio $f(n)/g(n)$ should have any limit. It may have, but it may also oscillate boundedly for ever.

The relations we have defined so far are for nonstochastic real-valued sequences. Of greater interest to econometricians are the so-called **stochastic order relations**. These are perfectly analogous to the relations we have defined but instead use one or other of the forms of stochastic convergence. Formally:

Definition 4.8.

If $\{a_n\}$ is a sequence of random variables, and $g(n)$ is a real-valued function of the positive integer argument n, then the notation $a_n = o_p\big(g(n)\big)$ means that

$$\operatorname*{plim}_{n\to\infty}\left(\frac{a_n}{g(n)}\right) = 0.$$

Similarly, the notation $a_n = O_p\big(g(n)\big)$ means that there is a constant K such that, for all $\varepsilon > 0$, there is a positive integer N such that

$$\Pr\left(\left|\frac{a_n}{g(n)}\right| > K\right) < \varepsilon \quad \text{for all } n > N.$$

If $\{b_n\}$ is another sequence of random variables, the notation $a_n \overset{a}{=} b_n$ means that

$$\operatorname*{plim}_{n\to\infty}\left(\frac{a_n}{b_n}\right) = 1.$$

Comparable definitions may be written down for almost sure convergence and convergence in distribution, but we will not use these. In fact, after this section we will not bother to use the subscript p in the stochastic order symbols, because it will always be plain when random variables are involved. When they are, $O(\cdot)$ and $o(\cdot)$ should be read as $O_p(\cdot)$ and $o_p(\cdot)$.

The order symbols are very easy to manipulate, and we now present a few useful rules for doing so. For simplicity, we restrict ourselves to functions $g(n)$ that are just powers of n, for that is all we use in this book. The rules for addition and subtraction are

$$\begin{aligned}
O(n^p) \pm O(n^q) &= O\big(n^{\max(p,q)}\big);\\
o(n^p) \pm o(n^q) &= o\big(n^{\max(p,q)}\big);\\
O(n^p) \pm o(n^q) &= O(n^p) \quad \text{if } p \geq q;\\
O(n^p) \pm o(n^q) &= o(n^q) \quad \text{if } p < q.
\end{aligned}$$

The rules for multiplication, and by implication for division, are

$$\begin{aligned}
O(n^p)O(n^q) &= O(n^{p+q});\\
o(n^p)o(n^q) &= o(n^{p+q});\\
O(n^p)o(n^q) &= o(n^{p+q}).
\end{aligned}$$

Although these rules cover all simple cases adequately, they do not cover cases in which quantities that are all of a certain order are summed. Such cases arise frequently. Provided the number of terms in the sum is independent of n, the sum has the same order as the highest-order summand, by one of the rules above. But if the number of terms is proportional to a power of n, the order of the sum depends on the number of terms. The simplest case is that in which n terms, each $O(1)$, are summed. The answer is then $O(n)$, *unless* the terms all have zero mean and a central limit theorem can be applied (see Section 4.6). When that is so, the order of the sum is just $O(n^{1/2})$. Thus, if x_t has mean μ and a central limit theorem applies to it,

$$\sum_{t=1}^{n} x_t = O(n) \quad \text{and} \quad \sum_{t=1}^{n} (x_t - \mu) = O(n^{1/2}).$$

Let us now use the coin-tossing example of Section 4.2 to illustrate the use of these order symbols. If we denote the second moment of the random variable b_n by $v(b_n)$, then by (4.05) we see that

$$v(b_n) = \tfrac{1}{4}n^{-1} = O(n^{-1}).$$

Similarly, from (4.11), we see that the fourth moment, $E(b_n^4)$, is the sum of two terms, one of them $O(n^{-2})$ and the second $O(n^{-3})$. Thus we conclude that the fourth moment itself is $O(n^{-2})$.

These results for b_n use the ordinary, not the stochastic, order relations. But now recall that

$$\operatorname*{plim}_{n\to\infty} a_n = \tfrac{1}{2} \quad \text{and} \quad \operatorname*{plim}_{n\to\infty} b_n = 0,$$

which allows us to write

$$a_n = O(1) \quad \text{and} \quad b_n = o(1).$$

Notice the difference here. The sequence a_n is of the *same* order as unity whereas b_n is of smaller order. Yet the only difference between the two is that b_n is centered and a_n is not. Both sequences have nonstochastic plims, and so the limiting variance is zero. But the limiting mean, which is just the plim itself, is zero for b_n and nonzero for a_n. The order of a random variable can thus be seen to depend on (at least) the first and second moments of the variable. It is precisely the subtraction of the first moment, the centering, which takes place in the definition of b_n, that allows us to see that the second moment is of smaller order than unity.

Recall now the example we used in Section 4.2 to illustrate convergence in distribution to a nonstochastic limit. We looked at a sequence of random variables $\{x_n\}$ such that x_n was distributed as $N(0, n^{-1})$. Note that the variance n^{-1} is proportional to the variance of b_n, which is $\frac{1}{4}n^{-1}$; see (4.05). In deriving the c.d.f. of the random variables x_n we saw that $n^{1/2}x_n$ had the standard normal distribution, which was described by its c.d.f. Φ. Clearly, then, the sequence $\{x_n\}$, multiplied by $n^{1/2}$, yields a new sequence of which the limit is a random variable distributed as $N(0,1)$. Thus we have discovered that $n^{1/2}x_n = O(1)$, which of course implies that $x_n = o(1)$ but is not implied by it. This construction has given us the **rate of convergence** of the sequence $\{x_n\}$, since we can now assert that $x_n = O(n^{-1/2})$.

We will now try the same maneuver with the sequence $\{b_n\}$, by considering the new sequence $\{n^{1/2}b_n\}$. From (4.04) we get

$$n^{1/2}b_n = n^{-1/2}\sum_{t=1}^{n} z_t.$$

Evidently, $E(n^{1/2}b_n) = 0$. Moreover, either directly or from (4.05), we see that

$$\operatorname{Var}(n^{1/2}b_n) = \frac{1}{4}. \tag{4.12}$$

Thus we conclude that $n^{1/2}b_n$ is $O(1)$, which implies that b_n itself is $O(n^{-1/2})$. The random variables a_n and b_n are in this respect typical of the many variables which resemble sample averages that arise in econometrics. The former, which is the average of n quantities that have a common nonzero mean, is $O(1)$, while the latter, which is the average of n quantities that have a zero mean, is $O(n^{-1/2})$.

The result (4.12) further indicates that if the sequence $\{n^{1/2}b_n\}$ has a limit, it will be a **nondegenerate** one, that is, it will not be a simple nonrandom number. We will see in Section 4.6 that this sequence does indeed have a limit, at least in distribution, and moreover that this limit is a *normal* random variable. The added fact of normality will be the conclusion of a **central limit theorem**. Such theorems, along with the laws of large numbers, are fundamental to all asymptotic theory in statistics and econometrics.

4.4 DATA-GENERATING PROCESSES AND ASYMPTOTIC THEORY

In this section, we apply the mathematical theory developed in the preceding sections to econometric estimation and testing from an asymptotic point of view. In order to say anything about how estimators and test statistics are distributed, we have to specify how the data of which they are functions are generated. That is why we introduced the idea of a data-generating process, or DGP, in Section 2.4. But what precisely do we mean by a data-generating process in an asymptotic context? When we spoke of DGPs before, it was enough to restrict our attention to a particular given sample size and characterize a DGP by the law of probability that governs the random variables in a sample of that size. But, since when we say "asymptotic" we refer to a limiting process in which the sample size goes to infinity, it is clear that such a restricted characterization will no longer suffice. It is in order to resolve this difficulty that we make use of the notion of a **stochastic process**. Since this notion allows us to consider an infinite sequence of random variables, it is well adapted to our needs.

In full generality, a **stochastic process** is a collection of random variables indexed by some suitable index set. This index set may be finite, in which case we have no more than a vector of random variables, or it may be infinite, with either a discrete or a continuous infinity of elements. We are interested here almost exclusively in the case of a discrete infinity of random variables, in fact with sequences of random variables such as those we have already discussed at length in the preceding sections. To fix ideas, let the index set be $\mathbb{N}$, the set $\{1, 2, \ldots\}$ of the natural numbers. Then a stochastic process is just a mapping from $\mathbb{N}$ to a set of random variables. It is in fact precisely what we previously defined as a sequence of random variables, and so we see that these sequences are special cases of stochastic processes. They are the only kind of stochastic process that we will need in this book; the more general notion of stochastic process is introduced here only so that we may use the numerous available results on stochastic processes for our own purposes.

The first of these results, which we will present in a moment, has to do with existence. Existence is seldom a serious issue when one sticks with finite mathematics, but it almost always is once infinity slips in. It is easy enough to define a finite set by pointing at things and deciding whether they do or do not belong to the set. In the case of an infinite set, such a procedure must be replaced by a *rule*, as we remarked earlier in our discussion of sequences. Rules are all very well; they certainly themselves exist, but it is not at all evident that any given rule necessarily defines anything interesting or indeed anything at all — hence the question of existence.

For stochastic processes in general, the matter of existence is settled by a famous theorem due to the eminent Soviet mathematician, probabilist, and physicist, A. N. Kolmogorov. Because he has put his stamp on many fields of research, readers may well have encountered his name before. The content of his theorem is that a sequence of random variables is well defined by a rule if the rule generates for every *finite* subsequence a joint finite-dimensional probability distribution that is *compatible*, in a certain sense, with those generated for all the other finite subsequences. Thus it is never necessary to consider infinite-dimensional distributions, even supposing that a way could be found to do so. Instead, **Kolmogorov's existence theorem** tells us that if two compatibility conditions are satisfied, a well-defined random sequence exists.

These two compatibility conditions are very clear intuitively. The first requires that if one asks for the distribution of the random variables indexed by a finite set of indices $\{t_1, t_2, \ldots, t_n\}$, say, and then asks again for the distribution of the random variables indexed by a permutation or jumbling-up of the same set, then one must get the appropriate answer. The second condition requires that if one asks for the distribution function of the variables indexed by some finite set $\{t_1, t_2, \ldots, t_n\}$, and then asks again for the distribution of the variables indexed by a *subset* of $\{t_1, t_2, \ldots, t_n\}$, then one must get the marginal distribution that would be calculated in the standard way from the first answer for the variables in the subset.

These two simple and easily checked conditions are sufficient to take care of the matter of existence. We consider, then, a sequence of possibly vector random variables that we can denote in the usual way by $\{\boldsymbol{y}_t\}_{t=1}^{\infty}$. For this sequence to be a well-defined stochastic process, by Kolmogorov's existence theorem it is enough that one should be able to define the joint probability distribution of any finite subset of the elements $\boldsymbol{y}_t$ of the sequence in a way compatible with all other joint probability distributions of finite subsets of the $\boldsymbol{y}_t$'s. It turns out that this is equivalent to two simple requirements. First, we must be able to define the joint probability distribution of the random variables contained in any finite-sized **sample**, by which we mean a subset of the form $\boldsymbol{y}^n \equiv \{\boldsymbol{y}_t\}_{t=1}^{n}$, for some finite **sample size** n.[2] Second, the distribution of the sample of size n should be the distribution obtained from the distribution of the sample of size $n+1$ by integrating out the last variable. Since we should in any conceivable set of circumstances wish to impose these requirements, we have the good fortune that the mathematical idea of a stochastic process or random sequence corresponds exactly to what is needed if we are to construct an asymptotic theory in econometrics.

In order to be able to do asymptotic theory, we must be able to define a DGP. In order to do that, we must be able to specify the joint distribution of the set of random variables corresponding to the observations contained in a sample of arbitrarily large size. This is plainly a very strong requirement. In econometrics, or any other empirical discipline for that matter, we deal exclusively with finite samples. How then can we, even theoretically, treat infinite samples? The answer is the same one that allowed us to deal with infinite sequences in general: We must in some way create a *rule* that allows one to generalize from finite samples to an infinite stochastic process. Unfortunately, for any observational framework, there is an infinite number of ways in which such a rule can be constructed, and different rules can lead to widely different asymptotic conclusions.

The following simple example illustrates the points at issue. It is frequent practice to include a **time trend** $\boldsymbol{\tau} \equiv [1 \,\vdots\, 2 \,\vdots\, 3 \cdots n]$ among the regressors of a linear regression model. The time trend can also be defined by the definition of each of its components:

$$\tau_t = t, \quad t = 1, 2, 3 \cdots. \tag{4.13}$$

[2] We will use this sort of notation rather generally. A subscript index will refer to a particular observation, while a superscript index will refer to the sample size.

The example is a model in which this time trend is the only regressor:

$$\boldsymbol{y} = \alpha\boldsymbol{\tau} + \boldsymbol{u}, \quad E(\boldsymbol{u}\boldsymbol{u}^\top) = \sigma^2\mathbf{I}. \tag{4.14}$$

The estimate of the parameter α is then

$$\hat{\alpha} = \left(\boldsymbol{\tau}^\top\boldsymbol{\tau}\right)^{-1}\boldsymbol{\tau}^\top\boldsymbol{y}. \tag{4.15}$$

Assuming that the DGP is indeed (4.14) with $\alpha = \alpha_0$ and $\sigma^2 = \sigma_0^2$, it is easy to see that this estimate becomes

$$\hat{\alpha} = \alpha_0 + \left(\boldsymbol{\tau}^\top\boldsymbol{\tau}\right)^{-1}\boldsymbol{\tau}^\top\boldsymbol{u}. \tag{4.16}$$

Evidently, the properties of the estimate (4.15) will depend on the properties of the random term $(\boldsymbol{\tau}^\top\boldsymbol{\tau})^{-1}\boldsymbol{\tau}^\top\boldsymbol{u}$. If the sample size is n, then

$$\boldsymbol{\tau}^\top\boldsymbol{\tau} = \sum_{t=1}^{n} t^2 = \tfrac{1}{6}n(2n+1)(n+1) = O(n^3).$$

The expression used here for the sum $\sum_{t=1}^{n} t^2$ is easily shown to be correct by induction. The second factor in expression (4.16), $\boldsymbol{\tau}^\top\boldsymbol{u}$, will have mean zero as usual (implying that $\hat{\alpha}$ must certainly be unbiased) and variance $\sigma_0^2\boldsymbol{\tau}^\top\boldsymbol{\tau}$. Thus the variance of $\hat{\alpha}$ itself is

$$\operatorname{Var}(\hat{\alpha}) = \sigma_0^2\left(\boldsymbol{\tau}^\top\boldsymbol{\tau}\right)^{-1} = O(n^{-3}). \tag{4.17}$$

In this example, it is natural to extend the trend $\boldsymbol{\tau}$ to arbitrarily large sample sizes by means of the rule (4.13), and it was by so doing that we obtained the result that the variance of $\hat{\alpha}$ is $O(n^{-3})$. But this is *not* the sort of rule always employed in asymptotic analysis. Rather, the assumption is frequently made, as we did in Section 3.5 in connection with exact properties of test statistics, that the regressors are fixed in repeated samples. In the present context this means that the rule used to extend a finite sample to an arbitrarily large one is the following: For observed sample size m one considers *only* samples of size $n \equiv Nm$, for positive integers N. Clearly, as $N \to \infty$ the sample size n tends to infinity as well. Then in each *repetition* of the sample (hence the terminology "repeated samples") the regressors are assumed to be the *same* as they were in the observed sample, and only the random disturbances are supposed to be different. In fact, for any sample size n, one typically assumes that u is an n-vector such that $\boldsymbol{u} \sim \text{IID}(\mathbf{0}, \sigma_0^2\mathbf{I}_n)$ where $\mathbf{I}_n$ is the identity matrix of order n and σ_0^2 is some constant variance.

This fixed-in-repeated-samples idea is of course excellent for **cross-section data**, that is, data sets in which the separate observations are all recorded at one time. These observations will typically be on members of a population assumed to be characterized by certain statistical regularities that one wishes to estimate, or the existence of which one wishes to test. In that case, the fixed-in-repeated-samples idea corresponds to assuming that, as one gathers more data, they will be "more of the same." To put it somewhat differently, it amounts to assuming that the sample one already has is sufficiently *representative* of the population under study. Many of the data sets used in microeconometrics are cross sections. They will often consist of data on individual economic agents such as firms or households, as in the home-ownership example of Section 4.2.

The difficulties discussed in this section about how to extend DGPs to arbitrarily large samples generally do not concern cross-section data.[3] They do, however, concern **time-series data**. For such data sets, the separate observations are temporally ordered; to each observation there corresponds a *date*, perhaps just a year, but perhaps a quarter, month, day, or even, as in the case of some data sets on financial markets, an hour or a minute. The difficulties of sample extension arise with even more force in the case of what are called **panel data**; see Section 9.10. Such data are obtained when a cross section is observed at several different times. Thus the same member of the population being studied, usually either a household or a firm, can be traced through time. To perform asymptotic analysis for such data, it is necessary to define a rule for extending the sample size to infinity in two different ways, one corresponding to the cross-section dimension and the other to the time-series dimension of the data. In our subsequent discussion of the difficulties of extending DGPs to large samples, we will always, explicitly or implicitly, be discussing time-series data or the time-series dimension of panel data.

Suppose that we now make the fixed-in-repeated-samples assumption for the model (4.14). Then, if the observed sample size were m, for a sample of size $n = Nm$ we should have

$$\hat{\alpha} = \alpha_0 + \Big(N(\boldsymbol{\tau}^m)^\top \boldsymbol{\tau}^m\Big)^{-1} \sum_{k=1}^{N} (\boldsymbol{\tau}^m)^\top \boldsymbol{u}_k,$$

where $\boldsymbol{\tau}^m$ denotes a trend with just m elements, and the $\boldsymbol{u}_k$, $k = 1, 2, \ldots, N$, are independent random m-vectors with the usual properties. Then

$$N(\boldsymbol{\tau}^m)^\top \boldsymbol{\tau}^m = \tfrac{1}{6} n(2m+1)(m+1) = O(n) \quad \text{and}$$

$$\operatorname{Var}\Big(\sum_{k=1}^{N} (\boldsymbol{\tau}^m)^\top \boldsymbol{u}_k\Big) = \tfrac{1}{6}\sigma_0^2 n(2m+1)(m+1) = O(n),$$

which imply that

$$\operatorname{Var}(\hat{\alpha}) = \sigma_0^2 \Big(\tfrac{1}{6} n(2m+1)(m+1)\Big)^{-1} = O(n^{-1}). \tag{4.18}$$

[3] This statement may be too sanguine. Consider, for example, a cross section of countries. If we have a data set with information on all of the OECD countries, it is hard to imagine any rule at all for extending the sample!

A comparison of (4.17) and (4.18) reveals that the behavior of the estimator $\hat{\alpha}$ is quite different under the two different rules for sample-size extension.

There is not always a simple resolution to the sort of problem posed in the above example. It is *usually* unrealistic to assume that linear time trends of the form of $\boldsymbol{\tau}$ will continue to increase forever, but it suffices to look at price series in the twentieth century (and many other centuries) to realize that some economic variables do not seem to have natural upper bounds. Even quantity series such as real GNP or personal consumption are sometimes fruitfully considered as being unbounded. Nevertheless, although the asymptotic theories resulting from different kinds of rules for extending DGPs to arbitrarily large samples can be very different, it is important to be clear that deciding among competing asymptotic theories of this sort is *not* an empirical issue. For any given empirical investigation, the sample size is what it is, even if the *possibility* of collecting further relevant data exists. The issue is always one of selecting a suitable *model*, not only for the data that exist, but for a set of economic *phenomena*, of which the data are supposed to be a manifestation. There is always an infinity of models (not all plausible of course) that are compatible with any finite data set. As a consequence, the issue of model selection among a set of such models can be decided only on the basis of such criteria as the explanatory power of the concepts used in the model, simplicity of expression, or ease of interpretation, but not on the basis of the information contained in the data themselves.

Although, in the model (4.14), the assumption that the time trend variable goes to infinity with the sample size may seem more plausible than the fixed-in-repeated-samples assumption, we will throughout most of this book assume that the DGP is of the latter rather than the former type. The problem with allowing t_t to go to infinity with the sample size is that each additional observation gives us more information about the value of α than any of the preceding observations. That is why $\text{Var}(\hat{\alpha})$ turned out to be $O(n^{-3})$ when we made that assumption about the DGP. It seems much more plausible in most cases that each additional observation should, on average, give us the same amount of information as the preceding observations. This implies that the variance of parameter estimates will be $O(n^{-1})$, as was $\text{Var}(\hat{\alpha})$ when we assumed that the DGP was of the fixed-in-repeated-samples type. Our general assumptions about DGPs will likewise lead to the conclusion that the variance of parameter estimates is $O(n^{-1})$, although we will consider DGPs that do not lead to this conclusion in Chapter 20, which deals with dynamic models.

4.5 Consistency and Laws of Large Numbers

We begin this section by introducing the notion of **consistency**, one of the most basic ideas of asymptotic theory. When one is interested in estimating parameters from data, it is desirable that the parameter estimates should have certain properties. In Chapters 2 and 3, we saw that, under certain regularity conditions, the OLS estimator is unbiased and follows a normal distribution with a covariance matrix that is known up to a factor of the error variance, which factor can itself be estimated in an unbiased manner. We were not able in those chapters to prove any corresponding results for the NLS estimator, and it was remarked that asymptotic theory would be necessary in order to do so. Consistency is the first of the desirable **asymptotic properties** that an estimator may possess. In Chapter 5 we will provide conditions under which the NLS estimator is consistent. Here we will content ourselves with introducing the notion itself and illustrating the close link that exists between laws of large numbers and proofs of consistency.

An estimator $\hat{\boldsymbol{\beta}}$ of a vector of parameters $\boldsymbol{\beta}$ is said to be **consistent** if it converges to its true value as the sample size tends to infinity. That statement is not false or even seriously misleading, but it implicitly makes a number of assumptions and uses undefined terms. Let us try to rectify this and, in so doing, gain a better understanding of what consistency means.

First, how can an *estimator* converge? It can do so if we convert it to a sequence. To this end, we write $\hat{\boldsymbol{\beta}}^n$ for the estimator that results from a sample of size n and then define the estimator $\hat{\boldsymbol{\beta}}$ itself as the sequence $\{\hat{\boldsymbol{\beta}}^n\}_{n=m}^{\infty}$. The lower limit m of the sequence will usually be assumed to be the smallest sample size that allows $\hat{\boldsymbol{\beta}}^n$ to be computed. For example, if we denote the regressand and regressor matrix for a linear regression done on a sample of size n by $\boldsymbol{y}^n$ and $\boldsymbol{X}^n$, respectively, and if $\boldsymbol{X}^n$ is an $n \times k$ matrix, then m cannot be any smaller than k, the number of regressors. For $n > k$ we have as usual that $\hat{\boldsymbol{\beta}}^n = \big((\boldsymbol{X}^n)^\top \boldsymbol{X}^n\big)^{-1}(\boldsymbol{X}^n)^\top \boldsymbol{y}^n$, and this formula embodies the rule which generates the sequence $\hat{\boldsymbol{\beta}}$.

An element of a sequence $\hat{\boldsymbol{\beta}}$ is a random variable. If it is to converge to a true value, we must say what kind of convergence we have in mind, since we have seen that more than one kind is available. If we use almost sure convergence, we will say that we have **strong consistency** or that the estimator is **strongly consistent**. Sometimes such a claim is possible. More frequently we use convergence in probability and so obtain only **weak consistency**. Here "strong" and "weak" are used in the same sense as in the definitions of strong and weak laws of large numbers.

Next, what is meant by the "true value"? We answer this question in detail in the next chapter, but here we must at least note that convergence of a sequence of random variables to any kind of limit depends on the rule, or DGP, which generated the sequence. For example, if the rule ensures that, for any sample size n, the regressand and regressor matrix of a linear regression are in fact related by the equation

$$\boldsymbol{y}^n = \boldsymbol{X}^n \boldsymbol{\beta}_0 + \boldsymbol{u}^n, \tag{4.19}$$

for some fixed vector $\boldsymbol{\beta}_0$, with $\boldsymbol{u}^n$ an n-vector of white noise errors, then the true value for this DGP will be $\boldsymbol{\beta}_0$. The estimator $\hat{\boldsymbol{\beta}}$, to be consistent, should converge, under the DGP (4.19), to $\boldsymbol{\beta}_0$ *whatever* the fixed value $\boldsymbol{\beta}_0$ happens to be. However, if the DGP is such that (4.19) does not hold for any $\boldsymbol{\beta}_0$ at all, then we cannot give any meaning to the term "consistency" as we are using it at present.

After this preamble, we can finally investigate consistency in a particular case. We could take as an example the linear regression (4.19), but that would lead us into consideration of too many side issues that will be dealt with in the next chapter. Instead, we will consider the very instructive example that is afforded by the **Fundamental Theorem of Statistics**, a simple version of which we will now prove. This theorem, which is indeed fundamental to all statistical inference, states that if we sample randomly with replacement from a population, the empirical distribution function is consistent for the population distribution function.

Let us formalize this statement and then prove it. The term **population** is used in its statistical sense of a set, finite or infinite, from which independent **random draws** can be made. Each such draw is a member of the population. By **random sampling with replacement** is meant a procedure which ensures that in each draw the probability that any given member of the population is drawn is unchanging. A **random sample** will be a finite set of draws. Formally, the population is represented by a c.d.f. $F(x)$ for a scalar random variable x. The draws from the population are identified with different, independent, realizations of x.

A random sample of size n can be denoted by $\{Y_t\}_{t=1}^n$, where the Y_t's are independent realizations. Then, by the **empirical distribution function** generated by the sample, we mean the following cumulative distribution function

$$\hat{F}^n(x) \equiv \frac{1}{n}\sum_{t=1}^{n} I_{(-\infty,x)}(Y_t). \tag{4.20}$$

The **indicator function** I associated with the interval $(-\infty, x)$ takes the value 1 if its argument is contained in the interval and 0 otherwise. (Indicator functions can be defined similarly for any subset of the real line or of any other space in which random variables can take their values.) We leave it as an exercise to show that expression (4.20) does indeed define the cumulative distribution function for the discrete distribution which allocates a probability mass of n^{-1} to each realization contained in the sample $\{Y_t\}_{t=1}^n$.

Next, we pass from the empirical distribution function (4.20), associated with a given sample, to a *random* distribution function. To this end, the realizations Y_t are replaced by random variables y_t. As we supposed that the different draws in an actual sample were independent, so we now suppose that the different random variables y_t are independent. In effect, we are dealing with a DGP that can generate random sequences $\{y_t\}_{t=1}^n$ of arbitrary length n. For any given n, then, we have a random c.d.f. as follows:

$$\hat{F}^n(x) = \frac{1}{n}\sum_{t=1}^{n} I_{(-\infty,x)}(y_t). \tag{4.21}$$

The empirical distribution function of a random sample $\{Y_t\}_{t=1}^n$ is thus a realization of (4.21). To prove the Fundamental Theorem of Statistics, we must show that, for all real x, $\hat{F}^n(x)$ tends in probability to $F(x)$ as $n \to \infty$.

First, let us fix some real value of x. Then we may observe that each term in the sum on the right-hand side of (4.21) depends only on the single variable y_t. Since the y_t's are mutually independent, so then are these terms. Each term uses the *same* fixed value of x, and so in each term we have the *same* function. Since the y_t's all follow the same distribution, so then must the terms of the sum. Thus (4.21) is the mean of n random terms, all mutually independent and all with the same distribution. This distribution is not difficult to describe. An indicator function, by construction, can take on one of only two values, 0 and 1. We will have described the distribution completely, then, if we give the probability of each of these two values. By the definition of I,

$$\begin{aligned} \Pr\big(I_{(-\infty,x)}(y_t) = 1\big) &= \Pr\big(y_t \in (-\infty, x)\big) \\ &= \Pr\big(y_t < x\big) \\ &= F(x), \end{aligned} \tag{4.22}$$

where the last line follows from the definition of the c.d.f. $F(\cdot)$. The complementary probability, $\Pr\big(I_{(-\infty,x)}(y_t) = 0\big)$, is then of course just $1 - F(x)$.

In Section 4.2, we proved a weak law of large numbers for a coin-tossing example. We looked at the mean of a sequence of independent and identically distributed random variables with a distribution similar to that of the indicator functions here, such that only two values, 0 and 1, were possible. Because of the assumption that the coin was unbiased, there was the added restriction that each of those values had probability one-half. The problem here, then, is plainly identical to the problem of the limiting proportion of heads in a sequence of tosses of a *biased* coin. It would be simple to modify the proof of Section 4.2 in order to make it apply to this case. Instead, we prefer to prove now a more general (weak) law of large numbers, which will encompass this case but also many others.

Theorem 4.1. Simple Weak Law of Large Numbers. (Chebyshev)

Suppose that for each positive integer n we have a set of independent scalar random variables $\{y_1^n, y_2^n, \ldots, y_n^n\}$. Let

$$S_n \equiv \sum_{i=1}^{n} y_i^n,$$

and suppose further that $E(y_i^n) = m_i^n$ and that $\mathrm{Var}(y_i^n) = v_i^n$. Then the limit in probability as $n \to \infty$ of the sequence

$$\left\{N_n^{-1}\Big(S_n - \sum_{i=1}^{n} m_i^n\Big)\right\}$$

is zero for all nonrandom sequences of positive real numbers N_n that tend to infinity with n and are such that

$$V_n \equiv \sum_{i=1}^{n} v_i^n = o(N_n^2).$$

Proof: The technique of proof is the same as that for the weak law proved in Section 4.2 for the coin-tossing example: We make use of the Chebyshev inequality. Note first that

$$\mathrm{Var}\Bigl(N_n^{-1}\Bigl(S_n - \sum_{i=1}^{n} m_i^n\Bigr)\Bigr) = N_n^{-2} V_n \equiv w_n.$$

It is clear that as $n \to \infty$, $w_n \to 0$, because $V_n = o(N_n^2)$, and as n tends to infinity, so does N_n. But we observed in Section 4.2 that any centered sequence of random variables for which the variances tend to zero as n tends to infinity, tends in probability to zero. Thus the proof is complete.

Note that this theorem requires the existence of both the first and second moments of the variables y_i^n. In Section 4.7, we will list, but not prove, theorems with weaker regularity conditions. On the other hand, we have introduced a fair degree of generality. Our random variables y_i^n must still be independent (that requirement too will be relaxed in Section 4.7), but they may have their own means and variances, and of course their own higher moments, to the extent that these exist at all. Moreover, the explicit n-dependence in y_i^n means that, as a sample size grows, the random variables indexed by low values of n are not inexorably the same as they were in the earlier, smaller samples.

Plainly Theorem 4.1 gives more than we need to conclude that

$$\Bigl\{\frac{1}{n}\sum_{t=1}^{n} I_{(-\infty,x)}(y_t) - F(x)\Bigr\}$$

tends in probability to zero as $n \to \infty$. From (4.22) we find that

$$E\bigl(I_{(-\infty,x)}(y_t)\bigr) = F(x) \quad \text{and}$$
$$\mathrm{Var}\bigl(I_{(-\infty,x)}(y_t)\bigr) = F(x)\bigl(1 - F(x)\bigr).$$

Thus the variance V_n in this case is $nF(x)\bigl(1 - F(x)\bigr)$. This last quantity is $O(n)$, and hence also $o(n^2)$, as required by the theorem with $N_n = n$. We have therefore completed the proof of our version of the Fundamental Theorem of Statistics.

This proof can serve as a model for proofs of consistency of a great many simple estimators. For example, one often wishes to estimate the **moments** of a given distribution. If x is a random variable that follows this distribution, then by definition the kth moment of the distribution is $\mu_k \equiv E(x^k)$. The most intuitive estimator for μ_k is the corresponding **sample moment**. The kth sample moment M_k from a realized sample $\{Y_t\}_{t=1}^n$ is defined as the kth moment of the empirical distribution of the sample, which is easily seen to be

$$M_k = \frac{1}{n}\sum_{t=1}^{n} Y_t^k.$$

If as before we replace the realizations Y_t in the above summation by random variables y_t, and the realized moment M_k by a random variable m_k, we can see that m_k consistently estimates μ_k by considering $m_k - \mu_k$, which is

$$m_k - \mu_k = \frac{1}{n}\sum_{t=1}^{n}\big(y_t^k - E(y_t^k)\big).$$

The random variables $y_t^k - E(y_t^k)$ are centered, and so we see that the right-hand side of this equation will satisfy the conditions of Theorem 4.1 if the $(2k)^{\text{th}}$ population moment exists. Thus, under this fairly weak condition, we conclude that sample moments consistently estimate population moments.

Just as it is almost mandatory in finite-sample analysis to prove that an estimator is unbiased, it is almost mandatory in asymptotic analysis to prove that an estimator is consistent. Although one may be tempted to infer from this that consistency is the asymptotic equivalent of **unbiasedness**, that is not the case. Consistency neither implies nor is implied by unbiasedness. An estimator may be unbiased and consistent, biased but consistent, unbiased but inconsistent, or biased and inconsistent! Consider the following examples, which all deal with estimating the mean of a population characterized by a mean μ and a variance σ^2, based on a sample of n observations y_t. The sample mean m_1 has already been seen to be consistent and unbiased. But now consider the estimators

$$\tilde{\mu} = \frac{1}{n-3}\sum_{t=1}^{n} y_t, \tag{4.23}$$

$$\ddot{\mu} = \frac{1}{2}y_1 + \frac{1}{2(n-1)}\sum_{t=2}^{n} y_t, \quad \text{and} \tag{4.24}$$

$$\breve{\mu} = \frac{2}{n}\sum_{t=1}^{n} y_t. \tag{4.25}$$

The first of these, (4.23), is clearly *biased*, because

$$E(\tilde{\mu}) = \frac{1}{n-3}\sum_{t=1}^{n}\mu = \frac{n}{n-3}\mu,$$

but it is nevertheless *consistent*, because $\tilde{\mu} = \big(n/(n-3)\big)m_1$ and $n/(n-3) \to 1$ as $n \to \infty$. On the other hand, the second estimator, (4.24), is *unbiased*, because

$$E(\ddot{\mu}) = \frac{1}{2}\mu + \frac{1}{2(n-1)} \sum_{t=2}^{n} \mu = \mu.$$

However, $\ddot{\mu}$ is *inconsistent*, because it has a variance that does not tend to 0 as $n \to \infty$, since y_1 always gets a finite weight no matter how large the sample size. This means that $\ddot{\mu}$ cannot possibly have a nonstochastic plim, which any consistent estimator must have. Finally, the third estimator, (4.25), is clearly biased, and it is inconsistent since it will converge to 2μ instead of to μ.

The relationship between consistency and **asymptotic unbiasedness** is rather more subtle, because at first sight there are two possible definitions for the latter concept. The first is that an estimator is asymptotically unbiased if the mean of its asymptotic distribution is the true value of the parameter. The second is that an estimator is asymptotically unbiased if the limit of the means of the random variables constituting the estimator (a sequence, remember) is the true value of the parameter. These two definitions are not equivalent. The technical reason for this inequivalence is that in none of the topologies induced on sets of random variables by the different kinds of stochastic convergence we have considered does the operation of taking a moment of a random variable induce a continuous mapping from the set of random variables to $\mathbb{R}$.

To see how the problem arises, consider the following "pathological" example. Here is a distinctly odd estimator of a scalar parameter θ:

$$\hat{\theta}^n \equiv \begin{cases} \theta & \text{with probability } 1 - n^{-1} \\ 2n\theta & \text{with probability } n^{-1}. \end{cases}$$

This estimator is clearly consistent: For any $\varepsilon > 0$ whatsoever,

$$\Pr\big(|\hat{\theta}^n - \theta| > \varepsilon\big) \leq \Pr\big(\hat{\theta}^n = 2n\theta\big) = n^{-1},$$

which is less than δ for all $n > \delta^{-1}$. The mean of the estimator exists:

$$E\big(\hat{\theta}^n\big) = 3\theta - n^{-1}\theta,$$

and this mean tends to a well-defined limit of 3θ as $n \to \infty$. The limit of the mean is therefore not the true value of the parameter. However, the asymptotic distribution of the estimator, by which we mean the distribution of the limiting random variable to which the sequence $\{\hat{\theta}^n\}$ tends, has a quite different, and correct, mean of θ. It is a useful exercise to write out the c.d.f. of $\hat{\theta}^n$ and show that it converges pointwise to a degenerate distribution concentrated at θ.

It is clear from this example that the definition which we will want for asymptotic unbiasedness is the one using the limit of the means, not the limiting mean, since the latter is a property of a random variable never actually realized in the finite world. Asymptotics does not provide useful approximations when there are discontinuities at infinity! With this definition, however, consistency does not imply asymptotic unbiasedness, unless one can rule out pathological examples like this one. Such examples often can be ruled out, of course. In this particular example, the *variance* of $\hat{\theta}^n$ is $O(n)$ as $n \to \infty$ and thus does not tend to a finite limit. This pathology cannot arise with a consistent estimator, like m_k for μ_k above, that satisfies a law of large numbers like Theorem 4.1. In such a case, the centering of the sequence carried out for *finite* sample sizes guarantees that the mean of the limiting distribution and the limit of the means are the same. An exactly similar issue will arise in the next section in the context of central limit theorems and limiting variances.

4.6 Asymptotic Normality and Central Limit Theorems

There is the same sort of close connection between the property of **asymptotic normality** and central limit theorems as there is between consistency and laws of large numbers. The easiest way to demonstrate this close connection is by means of an example. Suppose that samples are generated by random drawings from distributions with an unknown mean μ and unknown and variable variances. For example, it might be that the variance of the distribution from which the tth observation is drawn is

$$\sigma_t^2 \equiv \omega^2\Big(1 + \tfrac{1}{2}\big(t(\text{mod } 3)\big)\Big). \tag{4.26}$$

Then σ_t^2 will take on the values ω^2, $1.5\omega^2$, and $2\omega^2$ with equal probability. Thus σ_t^2 varies systematically with t but always remains within certain limits, in this case ω^2 and $2\omega^2$.

We will suppose that the investigator does not know the exact relation (4.26) and is prepared to assume only that the variances σ_t^2 vary between two positive bounds and average out asymptotically to some value σ_0^2, which may or not be known, defined as

$$\sigma_0^2 \equiv \lim_{n\to\infty}\bigg(\frac{1}{n}\sum_{t=1}^{n}\sigma_t^2\bigg).$$

The sample mean may still be used as an estimator of the population mean, since our law of large numbers, Theorem 4.1, is applicable. The investigator is also prepared to assume that the distributions from which the observations are drawn have absolute third moments that are bounded, and so we too will assume that this is so. The investigator wishes to perform asymptotic statistical inference on the estimate derived from a realized sample and is therefore interested in the nondegenerate asymptotic distribution of the sample mean as an estimator. We saw in Section 4.3 that for this purpose we should look at the distribution of $n^{1/2}(m_1 - \mu)$, where m_1 is the sample mean. Specifically, we wish to study

$$n^{1/2}(m_1 - \mu) = n^{-1/2} \sum_{t=1}^{n} (y_t - \mu),$$

where $y_t - \mu$ has variance σ_t^2.

In order to proceed, we will state the following simple **central limit theorem**.

Theorem 4.2. Simple Central Limit Theorem. (Lyapunov)

Let $\{y_t\}$ be a sequence of centered random variables with variances σ_t^2 such that $\underline{\sigma}^2 \le \sigma_t^2 \le \overline{\sigma}^2$ for two finite positive constants, $\underline{\sigma}^2$ and $\overline{\sigma}^2$, and absolute third moments μ_3 such that $\mu_3 \le \bar{\mu}_3$ for a finite constant $\bar{\mu}_3$. Further let

$$\sigma_0^2 \equiv \lim_{n \to \infty} \left(\frac{1}{n} \sum_{t=1}^{n} \sigma_t^2 \right)$$

exist. Then the sequence

$$\left\{ n^{-1/2} \sum_{t=1}^{n} y_t \right\}$$

tends in distribution to a limit characterized by the normal distribution with mean zero and variance σ_0^2.

Theorem 4.2 applies directly to the example (4.26). Thus our hypothetical investigator may, within the limits of asymptotic theory, use the $N(0, \sigma_0^2)$ distribution for statistical inference on the estimate m_1 via the random variable $n^{1/2}(m_1 - \mu)$. Knowledge of σ_0^2 is not necessary, provided that it can be estimated consistently.

Although we do not intend to offer a formal proof of even this simple central limit theorem, in view of the technicalities that such a proof would entail, it is not difficult to give a general idea of why the result is true. For simplicity, let us consider the case in which all the variables y_t of the sequence $\{y_t\}$ have the same distribution with variance σ^2. Then clearly the variable

$$S_n \equiv n^{-1/2} \sum_{t=1}^{n} y_t$$

has mean zero and variance σ^2 for each n. But what of the higher moments of S_n? By way of an example, consider the fourth moment. It is

$$E(S_n^4) = \frac{1}{n^2} \sum_{r=1}^{n} \sum_{s=1}^{n} \sum_{t=1}^{n} \sum_{u=1}^{n} E(y_r y_s y_t y_u). \tag{4.27}$$

Since all the y_t's are mutually independent and have mean zero, no term in the quadruple sum of (4.27) can be nonzero unless the indices either are all the same or fall into pairs (with, for instance, $r = t$ and $s = u$ with $r \neq s$). If all the indices are the same, then the value of the corresponding term is just the fourth moment of the distribution of the y_t's. But there can only be n such terms. With the factor of n^{-2} in (4.27), we see that these terms contribute to (4.27) only to order n^{-1}. On the other hand, the number of terms for which the indices fall in pairs is $3n(n-1)$,[4] which is $O(n^2)$. Thus the latter terms contribute to (4.27) to the order of unity. But, and this is the crux of the argument, the *value* of each of these terms is just the square of the variance of each y_t, or σ^4. Thus, to leading order, the fourth moment of S_n depends only on the variance of the y_t's; it does *not* depend on the fourth moment of the distribution of the y_t's.[5]

A similar argument applies to all the moments of S_n of order higher than 2. Thus, to leading order, all these moments depend only on the variance σ^2 and not on any other property of the distribution of the y_t's. This being so, if it is legitimate to characterize a distribution by its moments, then the limiting distribution of the sequence $\{S_n\}_{n=1}^{\infty}$ depends only on σ^2. Consequently, the limiting distribution must be *the same* for all possible distributions with the variance of y_t equal to σ^2, regardless of other properties of that distribution. This means that we may calculate the limiting distribution making use of whatever distribution we choose, provided it has mean 0 and variance σ^2, and the answer will be independent of our choice.

The simplest choice is the **normal distribution**, $N(0, \sigma^2)$. The calculation of the limiting distribution is very easy for this choice: S_n is just a sum of n independent normal variables, namely, the $n^{-1/2}y_t$'s, all of which have mean 0 and variance $n^{-1}\sigma^2$. Consequently, S_n itself is distributed as $N(0, \sigma^2)$ for all n. If the distribution is $N(0, \sigma^2)$ for all n independent of n, then the limiting distribution is just the $N(0, \sigma^2)$ distribution as well. But if this is so for normal summands, we may conclude by our earlier argument that the limiting distribution of *any* sequence S_n made up from independent mean-zero summands, all with variance σ^2, will be $N(0, \sigma^2)$.

The above discussion has ignored many vital technical details, but it captures the essential fact that drives all proofs of central limit theorems. We may reiterate here that the most important aspect of the central limit result is that the limiting distribution is *normal.*

In practice, we typically wish to estimate a vector of random variables, say $\boldsymbol{\beta}$. Let $\hat{\boldsymbol{\beta}}^n$ denote the estimate for a sample of size n and $\boldsymbol{\beta}_0$ denote

[4] There are three ways of pairing up the four indices, n ways of choosing the index of the first pair, and $n-1$ ways of choosing a different index for the second pair.

[5] The value of this fourth moment is n^{-2} times $3n(n-1)$ times σ^4, which to highest order is just $3\sigma^4$. This is the fourth moment of the normal distribution.

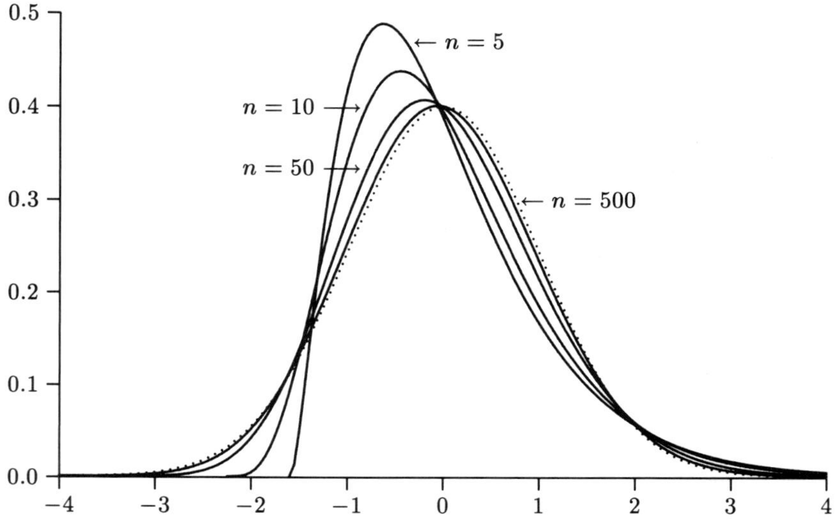

Figure 4.1 The normal approximation for different values of n

the true value. Then, as we will demonstrate in the next chapter, application of a suitable central limit theorem will generally allow us to conclude that $n^{1/2}(\hat{\boldsymbol{\beta}}^n - \boldsymbol{\beta}_0)$ is asymptotically distributed as multivariate normal with mean vector zero and some specified covariance matrix that can be estimated consistently.

Central limit theorems are useful in practice because, in many cases, they provide good approximations even when n is not very large. This is illustrated in Figure 4.1, which deliberately deals with a case in which the underlying random variables are highly nonnormal, and a central limit theorem can therefore be expected to work relatively badly. Each of the underlying random variables y_t is distributed as $\chi^2(1)$, a distribution that exhibits extreme right skewness: The mode of the distribution is zero, there are no values less than zero, and there is a very long right-hand tail. The figure shows the density of

$$n^{-1/2}\sum_{t=1}^{n}\frac{y_t-\mu}{\sigma},$$

where, in this case, $\mu = 1$ and $\sigma = \sqrt{2}$, for $n = 5$, $n = 10$, $n = 50$, and $n = 500$. For comparison, the density of the standard normal distribution is also shown as a dotted line. It is clear that the central limit theorem works very well for $n = 500$ and reasonably well for $n = 50$, despite the highly nonnormal distribution of the y_t's. In many other cases, for example when the y_t's are uniformly distributed, convergence to asymptotic normality is very much faster.

Of course, not every estimator is consistent and asymptotically normal. Sometimes no central limit theorem applies, and, less often, no law of large numbers applies either. In particular, neither is applicable when the summand random variables in the random sequence fail to possess even a first moment. We now illustrate such a case. We let the random variables be distributed according to the **Cauchy distribution**, which can be characterized by its density function,

$$f(x) = \frac{1}{\pi(1+x^2)}.$$

The Cauchy distribution is related to the normal distribution by the fact that the ratio of two independent standard normal variates is distributed as Cauchy; see Appendix B. The distribution has no moments of order 1 or greater, as can be seen from the fact that the integral

$$\int_{-\infty}^{\infty} \frac{x}{\pi(1+x^2)}\,dx \tag{4.28}$$

diverges at both of its limits. An indefinite integral of the integrand in (4.28) is

$$\frac{1}{2\pi}\log(1+x^2),$$

which tends to infinity as $x \to \pm\infty$.

Another property of the Cauchy distribution is the one that gives point to our present example. It is that if one takes the average of any finite number of independent Cauchy random variables, the average itself follows the same Cauchy distribution. We will not take the time to prove this fact but simply take note of some of its consequences.

Suppose that we have a random sample of observations that are drawings from a **translated Cauchy distribution**. That is, there is a **translation parameter** μ, which can no longer be called the mean of the distribution, such that for each observation y_t, the quantity $y_t - \mu$ follows the Cauchy distribution. Now let us look at the properties of the sample mean m_1, which of course always exists, as an estimator of the parameter μ. We have

$$m_1 = \frac{1}{n}\sum_{t=1}^{n} y_t = \frac{1}{n}\sum_{t=1}^{n}(\mu + u_t),$$

where, by definition, $u_t \equiv y_t - \mu$ is a Cauchy random variable. Thus

$$m_1 = \mu + \frac{1}{n}\sum_{t=1}^{n} u_t.$$

The second term on the right-hand side of the above equation is just an average of independent Cauchy variables, and so it follows the Cauchy distribution by the result cited above. Clearly, then, m_1 is not consistent for μ, since, for *any* n, m_1 has a translated Cauchy distribution. It is as if the factor $1/n$ were the proper one, not for the law of large numbers, but for a form of the central limit theorem, since it is the sum of the u_t's divided by n rather than by $n^{1/2}$ that has a nondegenerate asymptotic distribution. Of course, this asymptotic distribution is Cauchy rather than normal. Although m_1 is not a satisfactory estimator of the parameter μ, since μ is both the median and the mode of the distribution, there are other ways that we can estimate it, and in fact the sample median, for example, does provide a consistent estimator.

4.7 Some Useful Results

This section is intended to serve as a reference for much of the rest of the book. We will essentially make a list (with occasional commentary but without proofs) of useful definitions and theorems. At the end of this we will present two sets of regularity conditions that will each have a set of desirable implications. Later, we will be able to make assumptions by which one or other of these whole sets of regularity conditions is satisfied and thereby be able to draw without further ado a wide variety of useful conclusions.

To begin with, we will concentrate on laws of large numbers and the properties that allow them to be satisfied. In all of these theorems, we consider a sequence of sums $\{S_n\}$ where

$$S_n \equiv \frac{1}{n}\sum_{t=1}^{n} y_t.$$

The random variables y_t will be referred to as the (random) **summands**. First, we present a theorem with very little in the way of moment restrictions on the random summands but very strong restrictions on their homogeneity.

Theorem 4.3. (Khinchin)

If the random variables y_t of the sequence $\{y_t\}$ are mutually independent and all distributed according to the same distribution, which possesses a mean of μ, then

$$\Pr\Big(\lim_{n\to\infty} S_n = \mu\Big) = 1.$$

Only the existence of the first moment is required, but all the summands must be identically distributed. Notice that the identical mean of the summands means that we need not bother to center the variables y_t.

Next, we present a theorem due to Kolmogorov, which still requires independence of the summands, and now existence of their second moments, but very little else in the way of homogeneity.

Theorem 4.4. (Kolmogorov)

Let the sequence of mutually independent centered random variables $\{y_t\}$ have the property that

$$\lim_{n\to\infty}\left(n^{-2}\sum_{t=1}^{n}\operatorname{Var}(y_t)\right) < \infty.$$

Then $S_n \to 0$ almost surely.

This is a very strong result, since because of the factor n^{-2} it is not hard to satisfy the specified condition. Bounded variances easily satisfy it, for example.

In the following theorems, the assumption of the independence of the summands is relaxed. Some regularity is of course still needed, and for this reason we need a few definitions. Recall at this point the definition of an indicator function, which will now be used for a vector of random variables: If the random variable $\boldsymbol{y}$ is realized in $\mathbb{R}^k$ and G is any subset of $\mathbb{R}^k$ for which $\Pr(\boldsymbol{y} \in G)$ is well defined, then

$$I_G(\boldsymbol{y}) = \begin{cases} 1 & \text{if } \boldsymbol{y} \in G \\ 0 & \text{otherwise.} \end{cases}$$

Next, we define the important notion of a **conditional expectation**. We will make use of this concept extensively throughout the book.

Definition 4.9.

The expectation of the random variable y conditional on the vector of random variables $\boldsymbol{z}$ is a random variable w which is a deterministic function of the conditioning variables $\boldsymbol{z}$ and which possesses the following defining property. For all $G \subseteq \mathbb{R}^k$ such that $\Pr(\boldsymbol{z} \in G)$ is well defined,

$$E\big(wI_G(\boldsymbol{z})\big) = E\big(yI_G(\boldsymbol{z})\big). \tag{4.29}$$

The conditional expectation w is denoted by $E(y \mid \boldsymbol{z})$.

Observe that a conditional expectation is a *random variable*, being a function of the conditioning variables $\boldsymbol{z}$. The ordinary unconditional expectation, which of course is not random, can be considered as the expectation conditional on a nonstochastic variable. On the other hand, the expectation of a variable conditional on itself is just the variable itself.

An expectation taken conditional on a set of conditioning variables $\boldsymbol{z}$ will be the same as the expectation taken conditional on another set $\boldsymbol{z}'$ if there is one-to-one correspondence associating the set $\boldsymbol{z}$ to the set $\boldsymbol{z}'$, for then any function of $\boldsymbol{z}$ can be transformed into a function of $\boldsymbol{z}'$. A simple consequence is that the expectation of a function $h(y)$ of a random variable y, conditional on y, is just $h(y)$.

Another important consequence of the definition of a conditional expectation is the so-called **law of iterated expectations**, which can be stated as follows:

$$E\big(E(y \mid z)\big) = E(y).$$

The proof of this is an immediate consequence of using the whole of $\mathbb{R}^k$ as the set G in (4.29).

The definitions which follow are rather technical, as are the statements of the laws of large numbers that make use of them. Some readers may therefore wish to skip over them and the discussion of central limit theorems to the definitions of the two sets of regularity conditions, which we call WULLN and CLT, presented at the end of this section. Such readers may return to this point when some reference to it is made later in the book.

Definition 4.10.

The sequence $\{y_t\}$ is said to be **stationary** if for all finite k the joint distribution of the linked set $\{y_t, y_{t+1}, \ldots, y_{t+k}\}$ is independent of the index t.

Definition 4.11.

The stationary sequence $\{y_t\}$ is said to be **ergodic** if, for any two bounded mappings $Y\colon \mathbb{R}^k \to \mathbb{R}$ and $Z\colon \mathbb{R}^l \to \mathbb{R}$,

$$\begin{aligned}\lim_{n\to\infty}&\big|E\big(Y(y_i,\ldots,y_{i+k})Z(y_{i+n},\ldots,y_{i+n+l})\big)\big| \\ &= \big|E\big(Y(y_i,\ldots,y_{i+k})\big)\big|\,\big|E\big(Z(y_i,\ldots,y_{i+l})\big)\big|.\end{aligned}$$

Definition 4.12.

The sequence $\{y_t\}$ is said to be **uniformly mixing**, or **ϕ-mixing**, if there is a sequence of positive numbers $\{\phi_n\}$, convergent to zero, such that, for any two bounded mappings $Y\colon \mathbb{R}^k \to \mathbb{R}$ and $Z\colon \mathbb{R}^l \to \mathbb{R}$,

$$\big|E\big(Y(y_t,\ldots,y_{t+k}) \mid Z(y_{t+n},\ldots,y_{t+n+l})\big) - E\big(Y(y_t,\ldots,y_{t+k})\big)\big| < \phi_n.$$

The symbol $E(\cdot \mid \cdot)$ denotes a conditional expectation, as defined above.

Definition 4.13.

The sequence $\{y_t\}$ is said to be **α-mixing** if there is a sequence of positive numbers $\{\alpha_n\}$, convergent to zero, such that, if Y and Z are as in the preceding definition, then

$$\big|E\big(Y(y_t,\ldots,y_{t+k})Z(y_{t+n},\ldots,y_{t+n+l})\big) - E\big(Y(\cdot)\big)E\big(Z(\cdot)\big)\big| < \alpha_n.$$

The last three definitions can be thought of as defining various forms of **asymptotic independence**. According to them, random variables y_t and y_s are more nearly independent (in some sense) the farther apart are the indices t

and s. For more on these concepts and their implications, see White (1984) and Spanos (1986, Chapter 8). A useful aspect of the mixing and ergodic properties is that if the sequence $\{y_t\}$ has one of the properties, so do sequences of functions of the y_t's, $\{Y(y_t)\}$, in the same way that functions of two independent random variables are themselves independent. A stronger result is also true. A sequence of the form $\{Y(y_t, \ldots, y_{t+i})\}$ also preserves the mixing or ergodic property and, in the case of the ergodic property, the range of dependence i may be infinite. The property of ϕ-mixing is the strongest: It implies α-mixing, which in turn implies ergodicity for stationary sequences.

The mixing properties are important if one wishes to deal with nonstationary sequences. In this book, we will have little to say about the latter (except in Chapter 20), and therefore we prefer to present the next theorem, which is for *stationary* sequences and has the weakest regularity condition, namely, ergodicity. This theorem, due to the celebrated American mathematician G. D. Birkhoff, is in fact famous in the mathematical literature and many other literatures besides that of econometrics.

Theorem 4.5. Ergodic Theorem.

If the stationary sequence $\{y_t\}$ is ergodic in the sense of Definition 4.11 and if the expectation μ of y_t exists and is finite, then S_n tends to μ almost surely as $n \to \infty$.

Again in this theorem no centering is necessary, since the stationarity property ensures that all the y_t's have the *same* mean.

Some more definitions are needed before the next theorem can be stated.

Definition 4.14.

A sequence $\{y_t\}$ of random variables is called a **martingale** if, for all t, $E(|y_t|)$ exists and is finite and if, for all t,

$$E\big(y_{t+1} \,|\, y_t, \ldots, y_1\big) = y_t.$$

Martingales are very important types of sequences. A simple example is provided by a sequence $\{Z_n\}$ of sums of independent centered random variables y_t:

$$E\big(Z_{n+1} \,|\, Z_n, \ldots, Z_1\big) = E\bigg(\sum_{t=1}^{n+1} y_t \,|\, Z_n, \ldots, Z_1\bigg) = E\bigg(\sum_{t=1}^{n+1} y_t \,|\, y_n, \ldots, y_1\bigg),$$

since each of the sets $\{Z_n, \ldots, Z_1\}$ and $\{y_n, \ldots, y_1\}$ determines the other uniquely. Then, as required,

$$\begin{aligned} E\bigg(\sum_{t=1}^{n+1} y_t \,|\, y_n, \ldots, y_1\bigg) &= E\big(y_{n+1} \,|\, y_n, \ldots, y_1\big) + \sum_{t=1}^{n} y_t \\ &= E(y_{n+1}) + \sum_{t=1}^{n} y_t = Z_n. \end{aligned}$$

Martingales do crop up as such from time to time in econometrics, but a more immediately applicable notion is that of a martingale difference sequence.

Definition 4.15.

A sequence $\{y_t\}$ is said to be a **martingale difference sequence** if

$$E\big(y_{t+1}\,|\,y_t,\ldots,y_1\big)=0.$$

This definition is very short because the condition implies not only the existence of the unconditional expectations $E(y_t)$ but also that these are zero, and the sequence is therefore centered. See Spanos (1986, Chapter 8).

Theorem 4.6. (Chow)

If $\{y_t\}$ is a martingale difference sequence and there is an $r \geq 1$ such that the series

$$\sum_{t=1}^{\infty} t^{-(1+r)}E\big(|y_t|^{2r}\big)$$

converges, then $S_n \rightarrow 0$ almost surely.

The regularity condition is quite weak, because of the factor of $t^{-(1+r)}$. Note that

$$\sum_{t=1}^{\infty} t^{-(1+r)}$$

converges for all $r > 0$. In particular the condition is satisfied if the $(2k)^{\text{th}}$ absolute moments of the y_t's, $E(|y_t|^{2r})$, are uniformly bounded, by which we mean that there is a constant K, independent of t, such that $E(|y_t|^{2r}) < K$ for all t. See Stout (1974) and Y. S. Chow (1960, 1967).

We are now ready to move on to a selection of central limit theorems. A useful procedure, analogous to the centering we used so often in our discussion of laws of large numbers, is that of **standardizing** a sequence. For this to be possible, each variable of the sequence $\{y_t\}$ must have both a first and second moment. Then if μ_t and v_t denote, respectively, the mean and the variance of y_t, the sequence with typical element $z_t \equiv (y_t - \mu_t)/\sqrt{v_t}$ is said to be standardized. Thus every variable in such a sequence has zero mean and unit variance. For the purposes of our collection of central limit theorems, the variable S_n associated with a sequence $\{y_t\}$ will be redefined as follows, where μ_t and v_t are, respectively, the mean and variance of y_t:

$$S_n \equiv \frac{\sum_{t=1}^{n}(y_t - \mu_t)}{\big(\sum_{t=1}^{n} v_t\big)^{1/2}}.$$

It is clear that $\{S_n\}$ is standardized if the y_t's are independent.

Theorem 4.7. (Lindeberg-Lévy)

If the variables of the random sequence $\{y_t\}$ are independent and have the same distribution with mean μ and variance v, then S_n converges in distribution to the standard normal distribution $N(0, 1)$.

This theorem has minimal requirements for the moments of the variables but maximal requirements for their homogeneity. Note that, in this case,

$$S_n = (nv)^{-1/2} \sum_{t=1}^{n} y_t.$$

The next theorem allows for much heterogeneity but still requires independence.

Theorem 4.8. (Lyapunov)

For each positive integer n let the finite sequence $\{y_t^n\}_{t=1}^n$ consist of independent centered random variables possessing variances v_t^n. Let $s_n^2 \equiv \sum_{t=1}^n v_t^n$ and let the **Lindeberg condition** be satisfied, namely, that for all $\varepsilon > 0$

$$\lim_{n\to\infty} \left(\sum_{t=1}^{n} s_n^{-2} E\big((y_t^n)^2 I_G(y_t^n)\big) \right) = 0,$$

where the set G used in the indicator function is $\{y : |y| \geq \varepsilon s_n\}$. Then $s_n^{-1} \sum_{t=1}^n y_t^n$ converges in distribution to $N(0, 1)$.

Our last central limit theorem allows for dependent sequences.

Theorem 4.9. (McLeish)

For each positive integer n let the finite sequences $\{y_t^n\}_{t=1}^n$ be martingale difference sequences with $v_t^n \equiv \mathrm{Var}(y_t^n) < \infty$, and $s_n^2 \equiv \sum_{t=1}^n v_t^n$. If for all $\varepsilon > 0$

$$\lim_{n\to\infty} \left(s_n^{-2} \sum_{t=1}^{n} E\big((y_t^n)^2 I_G(y_t^n)\big) \right) = 0,$$

where again the set $G \equiv \{y : |y| \geq \varepsilon s_n\}$, and if the sequence

$$\left\{ \sum_{t=1}^{n} \frac{(y_t^n)^2}{n^{-1} s_n^2} \right\}$$

obeys a law of large numbers and thus converges to 1, then $s_n^{-1} \sum_{t=1}^n y_t^n$ converges in distribution to $N(0, 1)$.

See McLeish (1974). Observe the extra condition needed in this theorem, which ensures that the variance of the limiting distribution is the same as the limit of the variances of the variables in $s_n^{-1} \sum_{t=1}^n y_t^n$.

We are now ready to assemble our collection of suitable regularity conditions for use in the next chapter and elsewhere. It is convenient to begin with the collection we call CLT, because it includes a central limit theorem.

Definition 4.16.

A sequence $\{y_t\}$ of centered random variables is said to satisfy **condition CLT** if it satisfies a central limit theorem as follows: Let $\mathrm{Var}(y_t) = \sigma_t^2$ and $s_n^2 \equiv \sum_{t=1}^{n} \sigma_t^2$, with

$$\operatorname*{plim}_{n\to\infty}\left(s_n^{-2}\sum_{t=1}^{n} y_t^2\right) = 1.$$

Then $s_n^{-1}\sum_{t=1}^{n} y_t$ tends in distribution to $N(0,1)$.

We do not specify which central limit theorem justifies the conclusion; we require only that some such theorem does. The extra condition is imposed so that it is possible to obtain consistent estimates of the variances of asymptotically normal random variables. More precisely, it requires that the variance of $n^{-1/2}\sum_{t=1}^{n} y_t$ be consistently estimated by $n^{-1}\sum_{t=1}^{n} y_t^2$.

In practice, we will frequently wish to apply condition CLT to a **vector-valued sequence**. For example, if we have a scalar-valued function of several parameters, it may be interesting to apply CLT to the vector of its partial derivatives. In this context, the following theorem is extremely useful:

Theorem 4.10. (Multivariate Normality)

If a collection $\{z_1, \ldots, z_m\}$ of normally distributed random variables has the property that any linear combination of the set is also normally distributed, then $\{z_1, \ldots, z_m\}$ are jointly distributed according to a multivariate normal distribution.

See Rao (1973), among others, for references and a proof. The arguments that lead to a conclusion of asymptotic normality for a collection of limiting random variables taken separately will almost always apply to linear combinations of the summands, and so the step to the **multivariate normality** of a collection of limiting variables is usually short. We will sometimes not bother even to mention the issue later in the book and will speak of condition CLT applying directly to a vector-valued sequence.

The second of our two collections of conditions introduces a new idea, that of **uniform convergence** of a sequence, which can be used if the members of the sequence are *functions* of (nonrandom) variables or parameters. This situation will crop up repeatedly when we look in the next chapter at estimation procedures. We will treat sequences of random variables that depend on unknown model parameters and that are required in consequence to satisfy a law of large numbers for any set of values of these parameters in some neighborhood. Uniform convergence is a strengthening of the notion of convergence that allows one to draw conclusions like the continuity or integrability with respect to the parameters of limiting functions if the functions in the sequence are themselves continuous or integrable.

We will give the formal definition next for the purposes of later reference. The details of the definition are not important for present purposes: The point that should be grasped now is that *some* strengthening of the property of convergence is necessary if functions that are limits of sequences of functions are to inherit from the elements of these sequences useful properties like continuity or integrability.

Definition 4.17.

A sequence of random functions $\{y_t(\boldsymbol{\beta})\}$ of a vector of arguments $\boldsymbol{\beta} \in \mathbb{R}^k$ is said to satisfy **condition WULLN** (weak uniform law of large numbers) in some neighborhood R contained in $\mathbb{R}^k$ if the expectations $E\big(y_t(\boldsymbol{\beta})\big)$ exist for all t and $\boldsymbol{\beta} \in R$, if

$$\bar{y}(\boldsymbol{\beta}) \equiv \lim_{n\to\infty}\left(\frac{1}{n}\sum_{t=1}^{n} E\big(y_t(\boldsymbol{\beta})\big)\right) \tag{4.30}$$

exists and is finite for all $\boldsymbol{\beta} \in R$, and if the convergence in (4.30) is uniform in the following sense: For all $\varepsilon > 0$ there exists an N such that, for all $\boldsymbol{\beta} \in R$,

$$\left|\frac{1}{n}\sum_{t=1}^{n} E\big(y_t(\boldsymbol{\beta})\big) - \bar{y}(\boldsymbol{\beta})\right| < \varepsilon \quad \text{for all } n > N, \ \text{ and} \tag{4.31}$$

$$\Pr\left(\max_{\boldsymbol{\beta}\in R}\left|\frac{1}{n}\sum_{t=1}^{n} y_t(\boldsymbol{\beta}) - \bar{y}(\boldsymbol{\beta})\right| > \varepsilon\right) < \varepsilon \quad \text{for all } n > N.$$

We explicitly include in this condition the possibility that the distributions of the y_t's used to calculate the expectations in (4.31) and (4.30) may themselves depend on $\boldsymbol{\beta}$.

4.8 CONCLUSION

We have tried in this chapter to provide an intuitive approach to the tools, mathematical and probabilistic, used in asymptotic theory. Some of the material, especially that of Section 4.7, need not at this stage be perfectly grasped. It is there in order that we may refer to it later in the book, when its purpose will be more evident. The absolutely essential concepts of this chapter are those of laws of large numbers and central limit theorems. It *is* necessary that these be understood intuitively before the next chapter can safely be embarked on. The ideas of consistency and asymptotic normality are probably more familiar, and in any case they will be discussed at some length in the next chapter.

In selecting the theorems presented in this chapter, we have leaned heavily on the books by Billingsley (1979) and White (1984). See also Stout (1974) and Lukacs (1975). These are, however, not exactly elementary texts and are recommended for further reading rather than for clarification of anything which, despite our best efforts, is unclear here. Spanos (1986) provides a treatment of much of this material at a less technically demanding level.

TERMS AND CONCEPTS

almost sure convergence
almost sure limit
as n tends to infinity
asymptotic equality
asymptotic independence
asymptotic normality
asymptotic theory
asymptotic unbiasedness
atoms, for a c.d.f.
Cauchy distribution, ordinary and translated
centered sequence
central limit theorem
Chebyshev inequality
closeness
condition CLT
condition WULLN
conditional expectation
consistency, strong and weak
convergence in distribution (or in law)
convergence in probability
cross-section data
degenerate distribution
empirical distribution function
ergodic (of a sequence)
Fundamental Theorem of Statistics
indicator function
Kolmogorov's existence theorem
law (of a random variable)
law of iterated expectations
law of large numbers, weak and strong
limit in probability, or probability limit (plim)
limits, finite and infinite
Lindeberg condition
martingale
martingale difference sequence
mixing (of a sequence)
moments (of a distribution)
multivariate normality
natural topology
nondegenerate plim
nonstochastic plim
normal distribution
order symbols, ordinary and stochastic
ordered (a sequence is)
O, o notation
panel data
passage to the limit
population
random draw
random sample
random variable
rates of convergence
real-valued sequence
rule (for defining a stochastic process or DGP)
same-order relation
sample moments
sample size
sequences, convergent and divergent
small-order relation
standardizing a sequence
stationary sequence
stochastic order relations
stochastic process
successor (in a sequence)
symmetric distribution
time-series data
time trend
topological space
translation parameter
unbiasedness (and consistency)
uniform convergence (of a sequence)
uniform mixing
vector-valued sequence

Chapter 5

Asymptotic Methods and Nonlinear Least Squares

5.1 Introduction

In the preceding chapter, we introduced some of the fundamental ideas of asymptotic analysis and stated some essential results from probability theory. In this chapter, we use those ideas and results to prove a number of important properties of the nonlinear least squares estimator.

In the next section, we discuss the concept of **asymptotic identifiability** of **parametrized models** and, in particular, of models to be estimated by NLS. In Section 5.3, we move on to treat the **consistency** of the NLS estimator for asymptotically identified models. In Section 5.4, we discuss its **asymptotic normality** and also derive the asymptotic covariance matrix of the NLS estimator. This leads, in Section 5.5, to the **asymptotic efficiency** of NLS, which we prove by extending the well-known Gauss-Markov Theorem for linear regression models to the nonlinear case. In Section 5.6, we deal with various useful properties of NLS residuals. Finally, in Section 5.7, we consider the asymptotic distributions of the test statistics introduced in Section 3.6 for testing restrictions on model parameters.

5.2 Asymptotic Identifiability

When we speak in econometrics of models to be estimated or tested, we refer to sets of DGPs. When we indulge in asymptotic theory, the DGPs in question must be stochastic processes, for the reasons laid out in Chapter 4. Without further ado then, let us denote a model that is to be estimated, tested, or both, as $\mathbb{M}$ and a typical DGP belonging to $\mathbb{M}$ as μ. Precisely what we mean by this notation should become clear shortly.

The simplest model in econometrics is the linear regression model, but even for it there are several different ways in which it can be specified. One possibility is to write

$$\boldsymbol{y} = \boldsymbol{X\beta} + \boldsymbol{u}, \quad \boldsymbol{u} \sim N(\mathbf{0}, \sigma^2 \mathbf{I}_n), \tag{5.01}$$

where $\boldsymbol{y}$ and $\boldsymbol{u}$ are n-vectors and $\boldsymbol{X}$ is a nonrandom $n \times k$ matrix. Then the (possibly implicit) assumptions are made that $\boldsymbol{X}$ can be defined by some rule (see Section 4.2) for all positive integers n larger than some suitable value and that, for all such n, $\boldsymbol{y}$ follows the $N(\boldsymbol{X\beta}, \sigma^2\mathbf{I}_n)$ distribution. This distribution is unique if the parameters $\boldsymbol{\beta}$ and σ^2 are specified. We may therefore say that the DGP is **completely characterized** by the model parameters. In other words, knowledge of the model parameters $\boldsymbol{\beta}$ and σ^2 uniquely identify an element μ of $\mathbb{M}$.

On the other hand, the linear regression model can also be written as

$$\boldsymbol{y} = \boldsymbol{X\beta} + \boldsymbol{u}, \quad \boldsymbol{u} \sim \mathrm{IID}(\mathbf{0}, \sigma^2\mathbf{I}_n), \tag{5.02}$$

with no assumption of normality. Many aspects of the theory of linear regressions are just as applicable to (5.02) as to (5.01); for instance, the OLS estimator is unbiased, and its covariance matrix is $\sigma^2(\boldsymbol{X}^\top\boldsymbol{X})^{-1}$. But the distribution of the vector $\boldsymbol{u}$, and hence also that of $\boldsymbol{y}$, is now only **partially characterized** even when $\boldsymbol{\beta}$ and σ^2 are known. For example, the errors u_t could be skewed to the left or to the right, could have fourth moments larger or smaller than $3\sigma^4$, or might even possess no moments of order higher than, say, the sixth. DGPs with all sorts of properties, some of them very strange, are special cases of the linear regression model if it is defined by (5.02) rather than (5.01).

We may call the sets of DGPs associated with (5.01) and (5.02) $\mathbb{M}_1$ and $\mathbb{M}_2$, respectively. These sets of DGPs are different, $\mathbb{M}_1$ being in fact a proper subset of $\mathbb{M}_2$. Although for any DGP $\mu \in \mathbb{M}_2$ there is a $\boldsymbol{\beta}$ and a σ^2 that correspond to, and partially characterize, μ, the inverse relation does not exist. For a given $\boldsymbol{\beta}$ and σ^2 there is an infinite number of DGPs in $\mathbb{M}_2$ (only one of which is in $\mathbb{M}_1$) that all correspond to the same $\boldsymbol{\beta}$ and σ^2. Thus we must for our present purposes consider (5.01) and (5.02) as different models even though the parameters used in them are the same.

The vast majority of statistical and econometric procedures for estimating models make use, as does the linear regression model, of **model parameters**. Typically, it is these parameters that we will be interested in estimating. As with the linear regression model, the parameters may or may not fully characterize a DGP in the model. In either case, it must be possible to associate a parameter vector in a unique way to any DGP μ in the model $\mathbb{M}$, even if the same parameter vector is associated with many DGPs.

It will be convenient if our notation makes clear the association between the DGPs of a model and the model parameters. Accordingly, we define the **parameter-defining mapping $\boldsymbol{\theta}$** of the model $\mathbb{M}$. By $\boldsymbol{\theta}(\mu)$ we will mean the parameter vector associated with the DGP μ. For example, if $\mathbb{M}$ is a linear regression model, of either type, and μ is a DGP contained in the model, then $\boldsymbol{\theta}(\mu) = (\boldsymbol{\beta}, \sigma^2)$ for the appropriate values of the regression function parameters $\boldsymbol{\beta}$ and the error variance σ^2. The reader may wonder why we have used the complicated term "parameter-defining mapping" instead of the simple word "parametrization." The reason is that, in formal mathematical theory, a parametrization is a mapping that goes in the other direction; therefore, in this case, it would associate a DGP to a given parameter vector. Since we specifically wish to allow a single parameter vector to refer to a *set* of DGPs, we have preferred the clumsier term.

In general, the mapping $\boldsymbol{\theta}$ acts from the model $\mathbb{M}$ to a **parameter space** Θ, which will usually be either $\mathbb{R}^k$ or a subset of $\mathbb{R}^k$. Here k is a positive integer: It gives the **dimensionality**, or just the **dimension**, of the parameter space Θ. The relation among the mapping $\boldsymbol{\theta}$, its **domain** $\mathbb{M}$, and its **range** Θ is denoted as $\boldsymbol{\theta}\colon \mathbb{M} \rightarrow \Theta$. We may write $\boldsymbol{\theta}_0 \equiv \boldsymbol{\theta}(\mu_0)$ if the parameter vector associated with the DGP μ_0 is $\boldsymbol{\theta}_0$. If we refer to a particular DGP as, say, μ_0 or μ_1, then we can follow our usual practice and write simply $\boldsymbol{\theta}_0$ for $\boldsymbol{\theta}(\mu_0)$ or $\boldsymbol{\theta}_1$ for $\boldsymbol{\theta}(\mu_1)$. We will use the notation $(\mathbb{M}, \boldsymbol{\theta})$ for a model along with its associated parameter-defining mapping and call the pair $(\mathbb{M}, \boldsymbol{\theta})$ a **parametrized model**.

The introduction of the mapping $\boldsymbol{\theta}$ allows us to treat, in the asymptotic context, the question of the **identification** of the parametrized model $(\mathbb{M}, \boldsymbol{\theta})$ or, more precisely here, of the model parameters $\boldsymbol{\theta}$. Before we present the formal definition of asymptotic identification, a preliminary remark. The mere fact that $\boldsymbol{\theta}$ is to be defined as a mapping from $\mathbb{M}$ to Θ means that only one parameter vector can ever be associated with a given DGP μ. Thus we have ruled out from the very beginning the possibility of regression models with a regression function like (2.07). An example of such a model is

$$y_t = \beta_1 + \beta_2 X_{t2}^{\beta_3} + u_t, \quad u_t \sim \text{IID}(0, \sigma^2). \tag{5.03}$$

In this case, if $\beta_2 = 0$, one and the same DGP is associated with a whole set of parameter vectors, since the choice of the value of β_3 is then irrelevant. Similarly, if $\beta_3 = 0$, there will be no way to identify β_1 and β_2 separately, and an infinite number of parameter vectors may again be associated with the same DGP. Since models like (5.03) crop up rather frequently in applied work, it is important to remember that the results we are about to derive in this chapter do not apply to them, at least not without the imposition of some further conditions. In the case of (5.03), a simple solution is to define the parameter space Θ of the model so as to exclude the values $\beta_2 = 0$ and $\beta_3 = 0$, and a well-behaved parameter-defining mapping would then exist for the model restricted in this way. On other occasions it may be possible to find a reparametrization of the model for which a parameter-defining mapping exists.

In Section 2.3, for models that were to be estimated by nonlinear least squares, a model was said to be identified by a given data set if the model sum-of-squares function for the data set had a unique global minimum achieved at a unique parameter vector. We now wish to extend the concept of identification by a data set to the notion of **asymptotic identification**. First, observe that in Chapter 2 identification was defined in terms of the sum-of-squares function, which is used to define the NLS estimator. Since we do not wish to restrict ourselves permanently to the nonlinear regression model, we will for the moment simply speak of an estimator $\hat{\boldsymbol{\theta}}$, without discussing where it came from. Of course, by "estimator" we mean a *sequence* of random variables, $\{\hat{\boldsymbol{\theta}}^n\}_{n=m}^{\infty}$, as discussed in Chapter 4, for which the elements of the sequence take their values in the parameter space Θ. The nth element of the sequence is a function of a sample of size n. Formally, we may write

$$\hat{\boldsymbol{\theta}}^n(\boldsymbol{y}^n) \in \Theta,$$

where the superscript n denotes an entire sample of n observations. For ease of notation, however, we will generally drop the n superscripts unless it is important to make explicit the dependence on the sample size.

A distinction that is not always made clearly in econometrics but that can sometimes be valuable is the distinction between an **estimator** and an **estimate**. The distinction is identical to that made between a random variable (the *estimator*) and a realization of that random variable (the *estimate*). Thus the estimator $\hat{\boldsymbol{\theta}}^n(\boldsymbol{y}^n)$ is a *function* of the random sample $\boldsymbol{y}^n$, while the estimate $\hat{\boldsymbol{\theta}}$ *for a given sample* $\boldsymbol{y}$ is the *value* of the estimator when it is evaluated at $\boldsymbol{y}$. The notation $\hat{\boldsymbol{\theta}}$ does not distinguish between an estimator and an estimate. This may in some ways be unfortunate, but any disadvantages are usually outweighed by the simplicity and generality of the "hat" notation. We will simply make the distinction, when it is important, in words.

The issue of identification of a parameter vector $\boldsymbol{\theta}$ by an estimator $\hat{\boldsymbol{\theta}}$ has to do with whether or not $\hat{\boldsymbol{\theta}}(\boldsymbol{y})$ is *uniquely* determined for any arbitrary sample $\boldsymbol{y}$, or indeed whether it even exists as an element of the parameter space Θ. As we saw in Section 2.3, for a given sample $\boldsymbol{y}$, the sum-of-squares function $SSR(\boldsymbol{\beta})$ may not attain a global minimum for any finite parameter vector $\boldsymbol{\beta}$ at all, may attain it at a forbidden value such as $\beta_2 = 0$ for model (5.03), or may take on a global minimum value at more than one parameter vector. In any of these cases, the sample $\boldsymbol{y}$ does not identify the parameter vector $\boldsymbol{\beta}$. Ruling out this sort of thing more generally can be achieved by a slight extension of the definition of identification used in Chapter 2. We have:

Definition 5.1.

> The parametrized model $(\mathbb{M}, \boldsymbol{\theta})$ is identified by the sample $\boldsymbol{y}$ and by the estimator $\hat{\boldsymbol{\theta}}^n$ if $\hat{\boldsymbol{\theta}}^n(\boldsymbol{y})$ exists and is unique.

Note that this definition applies separately to each possible realized sample $\boldsymbol{y}$, and so it defines a property of that sample rather than of the estimator $\hat{\boldsymbol{\theta}}^n(\boldsymbol{y}^n)$. This is not the case for the concept of **asymptotic identifiability**, which is a property only of the parametrized model $(\mathbb{M}, \boldsymbol{\theta})$.

Definition 5.2.

> A parametrized model $(\mathbb{M}, \boldsymbol{\theta})$ is said to be asymptotically identified if for any $\boldsymbol{\theta}^1, \boldsymbol{\theta}^2 \in \Theta$ with $\boldsymbol{\theta}^1 \neq \boldsymbol{\theta}^2$ there exists some sequence of

functions $\{Q_n\}$ such that

$$\operatorname*{plim_1}_{n\to\infty} Q_n(\boldsymbol{y}^n) \neq \operatorname*{plim_2}_{n\to\infty} Q_n(\boldsymbol{y}^n), \tag{5.04}$$

where at least one of the plims exists and is a finite constant.

The notation

$$\operatorname*{plim_j}_{n\to\infty} \quad \text{for } j = 1, 2$$

means of course that the plim is calculated by means of DGPs characterized by parameter vectors $\boldsymbol{\theta}^j$. The definition extends the idea that only one parameter vector can be associated to a given DGP and requires that any two DGPs characterized by different parameters should be different not only for finite samples but asymptotically. By this is meant that one can always find a sequence Q which can distinguish between the two asymptotically. If no Q satisfying (5.04) existed, the limiting properties of any statistics, be they estimators or test statistics, would be identical under the two DGPs, and in that case we would wish to consider the DGPs as asymptotically equivalent. Definition 5.2 specifically excludes the possibility that DGPs associated with different parameter vectors should be asymptotically equivalent in this sense.

The most obvious choice for the sequence of functions Q in (5.04) is simply the ith component of a "well-behaved" estimator $\hat{\boldsymbol{\theta}}$ of the model parameters, (assuming that such exists), where of course i has to be chosen so that $\theta_i^1 \neq \theta_i^2$. If the estimator is indeed well-behaved, we would certainly expect that

$$\operatorname*{plim_1}_{n\to\infty}(\hat{\theta}_i) \neq \operatorname*{plim_2}_{n\to\infty}(\hat{\theta}_i),$$

and the estimator $\hat{\theta}_i$ therefore distinguishes asymptotically between $\boldsymbol{\theta}^1$ and $\boldsymbol{\theta}^2$. Thus the idea of the asymptotic identifiability of a model is clearly linked to the *possibility* of finding a well-behaved estimator for the model parameters. If a model is not asymptotically identified, then there exist at least two DGPs of the model, characterized by different parameters, which are such that *no* estimator exists capable of distinguishing asymptotically between them.

The following example provides a case of a model which in finite samples is identified by any data set, but is nevertheless unidentified asymptotically. It is in effect the time-trend example (4.14) stood on its head:

$$y_t = \alpha\frac{1}{t} + u_t, \tag{5.05}$$

with the error terms u_t distributed $\text{NID}(0, \sigma^2)$ for a sample of size n. The NLS estimator of α for sample size n is

$$\hat{\alpha}^n = \left(\sum_{t=1}^{n} t^{-2}\right)^{-1}\left(\sum_{t=1}^{n} t^{-1} y_t\right).$$

This is of course just the OLS estimator, since (5.05) is a linear regression, and so we can be sure that $\hat{\alpha}^n$ is the unique global minimizer of the sum-of-squares function. That is, the parameter α is identified by *any* data set $\boldsymbol{y}^n$. If the true DGP is given by (5.05) with $\alpha = \alpha_0$, then we find in the usual way that

$$\hat{\alpha}^n = \alpha_0 + \left(\sum_{t=1}^{n} t^{-2}\right)^{-1}\left(\sum_{t=1}^{n} t^{-1}u_t\right). \tag{5.06}$$

In an ordinary regression model, the $\boldsymbol{X}^\top\boldsymbol{X}$ matrix is $O(n)$. But here the $\boldsymbol{X}^\top\boldsymbol{X}$ matrix is the scalar quantity $\sum_{t=1}^{n} t^{-2}$, and the series $\sum_{t=1}^{n} t^{-2}$ converges to the limit $\pi^2/6$ as $n \to \infty$.[1] The random factor $\sum_{t=1}^{n} t^{-1}u_t$ is normally distributed with mean zero, since all the u_t's are, and has variance equal to $\sigma^2\sum_{t=1}^{n} t^{-2}$, a quantity that tends to $\sigma^2\pi^2/6$. Thus $\hat{\alpha}^n$ equals α_0 plus a mean-zero normal random variable with a variance that tends to $6\sigma^2/\pi^2$ as $n \to \infty$. This limiting variance is *not* zero, and the plim of the estimator $\hat{\alpha}$ is therefore nondegenerate: It is not a nonstochastic constant. To be sure, the plim is different for different values of α_0, but Definition 5.2 requires functions Q that have *nonstochastic* plims.

It would be quite tedious to show that there can exist *no* Q satisfying the conditions of definition 5.2 and capable of distinguishing different values of the parameter α of (5.05). More important than such a formal proof is an intuitive understanding of why (5.05) is asymptotically unidentified, since readers may very well feel that the business of requiring a nonstochastic plim is just a quibble. The point is simply that for a linear regression model of the form (5.01) in which $\boldsymbol{X}^\top\boldsymbol{X} = O(n)$ as $n \to \infty$, the covariance matrix of the estimated parameters tends to zero as $n \to \infty$. This means that, as the sample size grows, the **precision**[2] of the OLS estimator becomes arbitrarily large. This is the case also for the NLS estimator, as the rest of this chapter will show. In contrast, as we saw from (5.06), the precision of $\hat{\alpha}$ in the model (5.05) tends to a finite limit, no matter how large the sample becomes. It is in order to rule out models such as (5.05) that Definition 5.2 contains the conditions it does.

A parametrized model may be asymptotically identified but not asymptotically identified by a particular estimator. Any satisfactory estimator should be able, like the Q of Definition 5.2, to distinguish between DGPs characterized by different parameter vectors if it is expected to estimate the parameter vector. Of course, this is not possible if the model is not itself

[1] See, for instance, Abramowitz and Stegun (1965), equation 23.2.24, page 807, or any discussion of the Riemann zeta function.

[2] The **precision** of a random variable is simply the reciprocal of its variance, and the **precision matrix** of a vector-valued random variable is the inverse of its covariance matrix. Despite the simplicity of the relation between the two concepts, it is sometimes more intuitive to think in terms of precision than in terms of variance.

asymptotically identified, but if it is, a satisfactory estimator must be able to identify the model parameters asymptotically. The property required of the estimator is that of **consistency**, which we discussed in Section 4.5. Formally:

Definition 5.3.

An estimator $\hat{\boldsymbol{\theta}} \equiv \{\hat{\boldsymbol{\theta}}^n\}$ consistently estimates the parameters of the parametrized model $(\mathbb{M}, \boldsymbol{\theta})$, or is consistent for those parameters, if for any $\mu_0 \in \mathbb{M}$,

$$\operatorname*{plim}_{n\to\infty}{}_0 \big(\hat{\boldsymbol{\theta}}^n\big) = \boldsymbol{\theta}_0. \tag{5.07}$$

The notation "plim_0" simply means that we are taking the probability limit under the DGP μ_0, characterized by $\boldsymbol{\theta}_0$.

A consistent estimator clearly provides a Q for Definition 5.2, since for μ_1 and $\mu_2 \in \mathbb{M}$ such that $\boldsymbol{\theta}_1 \equiv \boldsymbol{\theta}(\mu_1) \neq \boldsymbol{\theta}(\mu_2) \equiv \boldsymbol{\theta}_2$, we immediately have from (5.07) that

$$\operatorname*{plim}_{n\to\infty}{}_1 \big(\hat{\boldsymbol{\theta}}\big) = \boldsymbol{\theta}_1 \neq \boldsymbol{\theta}_2 = \operatorname*{plim}_{n\to\infty}{}_2 \big(\hat{\boldsymbol{\theta}}\big),$$

as required by the definition. Thus any parametrized model for which a consistent estimator exists is, a fortiori, asymptotically identified. On the other hand, not all conceivable estimators of an asymptotically identified model succeed in asymptotically identifying it. In practice, this is seldom an important issue. Rarely is one faced with two serious estimation procedures, one of which asymptotically identifies the parameters of a parametrized model while the other does not. But one curious and important exception to this remark is that the NLS estimator does not identify the error variance σ^2, since the sum-of-squares function, which defines the NLS estimator, does not even depend on σ^2. This does not matter a great deal, since we can estimate σ^2 anyway, but it does distinguish NLS estimation from other methods, such as maximum likelihood, which do identify the error variance.

In the next section, we will turn our attention to the NLS estimator and demonstrate that when a model is asymptotically identified by this estimator, the estimator is consistent.

5.3 CONSISTENCY OF THE NLS ESTIMATOR

A univariate "nonlinear regression model" has up to now been expressed in the form

$$\boldsymbol{y} = \boldsymbol{x}(\boldsymbol{\beta}) + \boldsymbol{u}, \quad \boldsymbol{u} \sim \text{IID}(\boldsymbol{0}, \sigma^2\mathbf{I}_n), \tag{5.08}$$

where $\boldsymbol{y}$, $\boldsymbol{x}(\boldsymbol{\beta})$, and $\boldsymbol{u}$ are n–vectors for some sample size n. The model parameters are therefore $\boldsymbol{\beta}$ and either σ or σ^2. The regression function $x_t(\boldsymbol{\beta})$, which is the tth element of $\boldsymbol{x}(\boldsymbol{\beta})$, will in general depend on a row vector of variables $\boldsymbol{Z}_t$. The specification of the vector of error terms $\boldsymbol{u}$ is not complete, since the distribution of the u_t's has not been specified. Thus, for a sample of size n, the model $\mathbb{M}$ described by (5.08) is the set of all DGPs generating samples $\boldsymbol{y}$ of size n such that the expectation of y_t conditional on some information set Ω_t that includes $\boldsymbol{Z}_t$ is $x_t(\boldsymbol{\beta})$ for some parameter vector $\boldsymbol{\beta} \in \mathbb{R}^k$, and such that the differences $y_t - x_t(\boldsymbol{\beta})$ are independently distributed error terms with common variance σ^2, usually unknown.

It will be convenient to generalize this specification of the DGPs in $\mathbb{M}$ a little, in order to be able to treat **dynamic models**, that is, models in which there are **lagged dependent variables**. Therefore, we explicitly recognize the possibility that the regression function $x_t(\boldsymbol{\beta})$ may include among its (until now implicit) dependences an arbitrary but bounded number of lags of the dependent variable itself. Thus x_t may depend on $y_{t-1}, y_{t-2}, \ldots, y_{t-l}$, where l is a fixed positive integer that does not depend on the sample size. When the model uses time-series data, we will therefore take $x_t(\boldsymbol{\beta})$ to mean the expectation of y_t conditional on an information set that includes the entire past of the dependent variable, which we can denote by $\{y_s\}_{s=1}^{t-1}$, and also the entire history of the exogenous variables up to and including the period t, that is, $\{\boldsymbol{Z}_t\}_{s=1}^{t}$. The requirements on the disturbance vector $\boldsymbol{u}$ are unchanged.

For asymptotic theory to be applicable, we must next provide a rule for extending (5.08) to samples of arbitrarily large size. For models which are not dynamic (including models estimated with cross-section data, of course), so that there are no time trends or lagged dependent variables in the regression functions x_t, there is nothing to prevent the simple use of the fixed-in-repeated-samples notion that we discussed in Section 4.4. Specifically, we consider only sample sizes that are integer multiples of the actual sample size m and then assume that $x_{Nm+t}(\boldsymbol{\beta}) = x_t(\boldsymbol{\beta})$ for $N > 1$. This assumption makes the asymptotics of nondynamic models very simple compared with those for dynamic models.[3]

Some econometricians would argue that the above solution is too simple-minded when one is working with time-series data and would prefer a rule like the following. The variables $\boldsymbol{Z}_t$ appearing in the regression functions will usually themselves display regularities as time series and may be susceptible to modeling as one of the standard stochastic processes used in time-series analysis; we will discuss these standard processes at somewhat greater length in Chapter 10. In order to extend the DGP (5.08), the out-of-sample values for the $\boldsymbol{Z}_t$'s should themselves be regarded as random, being generated by appropriate processes. The introduction of this additional randomness complicates the asymptotic analysis a little, but not really a lot, since one would always assume that the stochastic processes generating the $\boldsymbol{Z}_t$'s were independent of the stochastic process generating the disturbance vector $\boldsymbol{u}$.

[3] Indeed, even for *linear* dynamic models it is by no means trivial to show that least squares yields consistent, asymptotically normal estimates. The classic reference on this subject is Mann and Wald (1943).

In the case of dynamic models, there is little doubt that the second method of extending DGPs, based on finding standard time-series representations for all the variables that enter in the regression functions, is more intuitively satisfying than the fixed-in-repeated-samples notion. The regression equation (5.08) is then to be interpreted as a stochastic difference equation, defining the stochastic process that generates the vector of observations on the dependent variable, $\boldsymbol{y}$, in terms of the realizations of $\boldsymbol{Z}$ and the **innovations** $\boldsymbol{u}$. The latter will always be assumed to be white noise, that is, to have the property $\boldsymbol{u} \sim \text{IID}(\mathbf{0}, \sigma^2 \mathbf{I}_n)$ for any sample size n. Further, we will assume that the stochastic process generating the innovations is independent of the stochastic processes generating the $\boldsymbol{Z}_t$'s and that the latter processes are the *same* for all DGPs in the model. Thus the actual values of the model parameters have no effect on the processes generating any variables other than the dependent variable.

The issue of how the variables on which regression functions depend are related to the dependent variable(s) has been a major subject of research in econometrics. The assumptions we have made about the $\boldsymbol{Z}_t$'s imply that they are **exogenous** or, to use the terminology of Engle, Hendry, and Richard (1983), **strictly exogenous**. Numerous definitions of exogeneity are available, as will be clear from a perusal of that paper. We will consider the matter at greater length when we come to discuss simultaneous equations models in Chapter 18.

With the above preamble, we are now ready to discuss the consistency of the NLS estimator. For this purpose, as well as for the treatment of asymptotic identification, we study the properties of the sum-of-squares function as the sample size n tends to infinity. Since this function does not depend on σ^2, we will simplify by assuming that, although any DGP μ in the model $\mathbb{M}$ under consideration must be such that all the observations are characterized by a single (unknown) error variance σ^2, this parameter is not defined by the parameter-defining mapping, which for obvious reasons we will now call $\boldsymbol{\beta}$ rather than $\boldsymbol{\theta}$. By thus excluding σ^2 from the list of model parameters we may concentrate on the question of whether the NLS estimator identifies the other model parameters, namely, those in the regression function.

We will make explicit the dependence of the sum-of-squares function on the sample size n and sample $\boldsymbol{y}$:

$$SSR^n(\boldsymbol{y}, \boldsymbol{\beta}) \equiv \sum_{t=1}^{n} \big(y_t - x_t(\boldsymbol{\beta})\big)^2. \tag{5.09}$$

This function is the sum of n nonnegative terms which will not usually tend to zero as $n \to \infty$, and so in general it tends to infinity with n. Since infinity is not usually an interesting limit, we prefer to work with the average of these terms rather than with their sum. Thus we define

$$ssr^n(\boldsymbol{y}, \boldsymbol{\beta}) \equiv n^{-1} SSR^n(\boldsymbol{y}, \boldsymbol{\beta}). \tag{5.10}$$

Since the function ssr^n is defined as an average, we may expect to be able to apply a law of large numbers to it. If we can, then we can make the following definition:

$$\overline{ssr}(\boldsymbol{\beta}, \mu) \equiv \operatorname*{plim}_{n\to\infty}{}_{\mu}\, ssr^n(\boldsymbol{y}, \boldsymbol{\beta}) = \lim_{n\to\infty} E_\mu\big(ssr^n(\boldsymbol{y}, \boldsymbol{\beta})\big), \tag{5.11}$$

where plim_μ and E_μ indicate that we are taking plims or expectations under the DGP μ.

The question of asymptotic identifiability of a nonlinear regression model can be expressed in terms of the limiting function $\overline{ssr}$, if it exists, just as the question of ordinary identifiability is expressed in terms of SSR^n or, equivalently, ssr^n. Does $\overline{ssr}$ exist in general? At the level of generality we have assumed so far, that is, of general dynamic models, the answer is no. We will discuss this point in more detail below. Unless $\overline{ssr}$ does exist, however, the discussion of this chapter is inapplicable. There are models for which $\overline{ssr}$ does not exist but which are, nevertheless, asymptotically identified by the NLS estimator; Chapter 20 provides some examples. For such models, however, the NLS estimator will not have the standard properties of asymptotic normality and root-n consistency that we demonstrate in the next section.

The property of $\overline{ssr}$ that gives us the consistency of the NLS estimator is the following. Let $\boldsymbol{\beta}_0$ and σ_0 denote the values of $\boldsymbol{\beta}$ and σ under the DGP μ_0 that actually generated the data. Then, under suitable regularity conditions, it can be shown that

$$\overline{ssr}(\boldsymbol{\beta}_0, \mu_0) < \overline{ssr}(\boldsymbol{\beta}, \mu_0) \quad \text{for all } \boldsymbol{\beta} \neq \boldsymbol{\beta}_0. \tag{5.12}$$

In words, the limit of the average of the squared residuals is minimized when the residuals are calculated using the true parameter vector $\boldsymbol{\beta}_0$. Why does this imply consistency? Without going into technical detail, we can see why if we accept that the limit of the finite-sample NLS estimators $\hat{\boldsymbol{\beta}}^n$, defined so as to minimize ssr^n, is the value of $\boldsymbol{\beta}$ which minimizes the limiting function $\overline{ssr}$. For then this value, by (5.12), is just the true value $\boldsymbol{\beta}_0$.

For all its plausibility, this argument is deceptively simple. When we make a very similar argument in Chapter 8, in the context of maximum likelihood estimation, we will be a little more careful about things, without, however, being fully rigorous. For now, we will content ourselves with presenting a theorem in which we assume enough regularity for the passage from (5.12) to the consistency of the NLS estimator to be justified. We will then discuss for some important practical cases when and why $\overline{ssr}$ exists, and when and why, if it does, (5.12) is true or not true.

Theorem 5.1. Consistency Theorem for Nonlinear Least Squares.

Suppose that

(i) the nonlinear regression model (5.08), considered as a parametrized model $(\mathbb{M}, \boldsymbol{\beta})$, with parameter space Θ, is asymptotically identified by the function $\overline{ssr}$. Thus, for all $\mu_0 \in \mathbb{M}$,

$$\overline{ssr}(\boldsymbol{\beta}_0, \mu_0) \neq \overline{ssr}(\boldsymbol{\beta}, \mu_0) \tag{5.13}$$

for all $\boldsymbol{\beta} \in \Theta$ such that $\boldsymbol{\beta} \neq \boldsymbol{\beta}_0$;

(ii) the sequence $\{n^{-1}\sum_{t=1}^{n} x_t(\boldsymbol{\beta})u_t\}$ satisfies condition WULLN of Definition 4.17 with probability limit of zero, for each $\mu_0 \in \mathbb{M}$ and for all $\boldsymbol{\beta} \in \Theta$; and

(iii) the probability limit of the sequence $\{n^{-1}\sum_{t=1}^{n} x_t(\boldsymbol{\beta})x_t(\boldsymbol{\beta}')\}$, for any $\boldsymbol{\beta}' \in \Theta$, is finite, continuous in $\boldsymbol{\beta}$ and $\boldsymbol{\beta}'$, nonstochastic, and uniform with respect to $\boldsymbol{\beta}$ and $\boldsymbol{\beta}'$,

then the NLS estimator $\hat{\boldsymbol{\beta}}$ is consistent for the parameters $\boldsymbol{\beta}_0$.

We will not prove this theorem but will now present a discussion in which we try to make clear intuitively what function is served by the various regularity conditions of the theorem. First, observe that in condition (i) of the theorem, we require that the model should be asymptotically identified by $\overline{ssr}$. This function is not an estimator, as the other functions playing the role of Q in Definition 5.2 have been up to now, but it is the function that defines the NLS estimator asymptotically, and so it is convenient to express the asymptotic identifiability condition in terms of it. Condition (5.13) is a little more complicated than (5.04). The reason is that $\overline{ssr}(\boldsymbol{\beta}, \mu_0)$, as a scalar function, will take on the same value at many different values of $\boldsymbol{\beta} \neq \boldsymbol{\beta}_0$. But we need only that these values all be different from $\overline{ssr}(\boldsymbol{\beta}_0, \mu_0)$.

Now let us look a little more closely at $\overline{ssr}$ and at the inequality (5.12). From (5.08), (5.09), and (5.10) we have

$$\begin{aligned} ssr^n(\boldsymbol{y}, \boldsymbol{\beta}) &= \frac{1}{n}\sum_{t=1}^{n}\big(x_t(\boldsymbol{\beta}_0) - x_t(\boldsymbol{\beta}) + u_t\big)^2 \qquad (5.14)\\ &= \frac{1}{n}\sum_{t=1}^{n}\big(x_t(\boldsymbol{\beta}_0) - x_t(\boldsymbol{\beta})\big)^2 + \frac{2}{n}\sum_{t=1}^{n}\big(x_t(\boldsymbol{\beta}_0) - x_t(\boldsymbol{\beta})\big)u_t + \frac{1}{n}\sum_{t=1}^{n}u_t^2. \end{aligned}$$

The last term of the last expression here is the easiest to treat. Since the random variables u_t are i.i.d. under μ_0, Theorem 4.3, the simplest of all of the laws of large numbers, can immediately be applied to yield

$$\operatorname*{plim}_{n\to\infty}{}_0\left(\frac{1}{n}\sum_{t=1}^{n}u_t^2\right) = E(u_t^2) = \sigma_0^2.$$

We turn next to the second term in the last expression of (5.14). Any randomness in the regression functions x_t must be due either to the presence of lagged dependent variables or to randomness of the $\boldsymbol{Z}_t$'s, the other variables on which the regression functions may depend, which would then be independent of the disturbances u_t. Lagged dependent variables at period t can depend only on the disturbances contained in the sequence $\{u_s\}_{s=1}^{t-1}$, and these are of course independent of u_t itself. Thus in all circumstances the two factors in each term of the sum

$$\frac{2}{n}\sum_{t=1}^{n}\big(x_t(\boldsymbol{\beta}_0) - x_t(\boldsymbol{\beta})\big)u_t = \frac{2}{n}\sum_{t=1}^{n} x_t(\boldsymbol{\beta}_0)u_t - \frac{2}{n}\sum_{t=1}^{n} x_t(\boldsymbol{\beta})u_t \tag{5.15}$$

are independent, and so each term of this sum has zero expectation, since u_t has. The successive terms are, however, not necessarily mutually independent, since the presence of lagged dependent variables in $x_t(\boldsymbol{\beta}_0)-x_t(\boldsymbol{\beta})$ would lead to possible correlation of this expression with the terms indexed by $t-1,\ldots,t-i$ of the sum (5.15), and most representations of the $\boldsymbol{Z}_t$'s as time-series will lead to such correlations as well. Thus, if we are to use a law of large numbers in order to conclude that the probability limit of (5.15) is zero, we must explicitly make assumptions sufficient to ensure that such a law of large numbers applies. What is required is that we should be able to apply a uniform law of large numbers to

$$\frac{1}{n}\sum_{t=1}^{n} x_t(\boldsymbol{\beta})u_t \tag{5.16}$$

for all $\boldsymbol{\beta} \in \Theta$. That is why condition (ii) of Theorem 5.1 was imposed.

For the first term in the last expression in (5.14) we wish to be able to apply a uniform law of large numbers to

$$\frac{1}{n}\sum_{t=1}^{n} x_t(\boldsymbol{\beta})x_t(\boldsymbol{\beta}') \tag{5.17}$$

for arbitrary $\boldsymbol{\beta}, \boldsymbol{\beta}' \in \Theta$, and this accounts for condition (iii) of the theorem.

Under the conditions of the theorem, then, we obtain the result

$$\overline{ssr}(\boldsymbol{\beta}, \mu_0) = \sigma_0^2 + \operatorname*{plim}_{n\to\infty}{}_0\left(\frac{1}{n}\sum_{t=1}^{n}\big(x_t(\boldsymbol{\beta}_0) - x_t(\boldsymbol{\beta})\big)^2\right). \tag{5.18}$$

It is immediately evident from (5.18) that $\overline{ssr}(\boldsymbol{\beta}, \mu_0)$ is minimized by $\boldsymbol{\beta} = \boldsymbol{\beta}_0$, and so we have established that (5.12) holds with weak inequality. The strong inequality required for the consistency of the NLS estimator is provided by condition (i) of the theorem, the asymptotic identification condition.

Can we find easily understood sufficient conditions for the conditions of Theorem 5.1? Yes, but unfortunately conditions that are easily understood tend to be quite restrictive. One of the simplest assumptions is just that the regression functions $x_t(\boldsymbol{\beta})$ are independent and uniformly bounded. This permits the use of the law of large numbers of Theorem 4.4, from which we can conclude that

$$\operatorname*{plim}_{n\to\infty}{}_0\left(\frac{1}{n}\sum_{t=1}^{n}\big(x_t(\boldsymbol{\beta}_0) - x_t(\boldsymbol{\beta})\big)u_t\right) = 0$$

and also that

$$\operatorname*{plim_0}_{n\to\infty}\left(\frac{1}{n}\sum_{t=1}^{n}\big(x_t(\boldsymbol{\beta}_0)-x_t(\boldsymbol{\beta})\big)^2\right) \tag{5.19}$$

exists and is a nonnegative, nonstochastic quantity. If the model is asymptotically identified, this quantity will be strictly positive for all $\boldsymbol{\beta} \neq \boldsymbol{\beta}_0$.

The assumption of independence is of course often much too strong. More generally, we would like to consider the case of a regression function $x_t(\boldsymbol{\beta})$ that depends only on nonrandom variables and on a finite number of lagged dependent variables:

$$x_t(\boldsymbol{\beta}) = x_t(\boldsymbol{Z}_t, y_{t-1}, \ldots, y_{t-i}; \boldsymbol{\beta}). \tag{5.20}$$

Unfortunately, the form (5.20) is *not* in general such that a law of large numbers can be applied to (5.16) and (5.17). The most clear-cut case is provided by an **explosive process**, of which a particularly simple example is provided by the DGP

$$y_t = \alpha y_{t-1} + u_t, \quad u_t \sim \mathrm{IID}(0, \sigma^2) \tag{5.21}$$

for any α with $|\alpha| > 1$. That this specification gives rise to an explosive process is easy to see: Suppose that the variance of y_1 is σ_1^2, and calculate the variance of y_t. We find that

$$\begin{aligned}
\mathrm{Var}(y_t) &= \mathrm{Var}(\alpha y_{t-1} + u_t)\\
&= \alpha^2 \mathrm{Var}(y_{t-1}) + \sigma^2\\
&= \alpha^4 \mathrm{Var}(y_{t-2}) + \sigma^2(1+\alpha^2)\\
&= \alpha^{2(t-1)}\sigma_1^2 + \sigma^2(\alpha^2-1)^{-1}(\alpha^{2(t-1)}-1),
\end{aligned} \tag{5.22}$$

where the last line in (5.22) is obtained by repeated substitution of the result contained in the first line. One sees immediately that, since $|\alpha| > 1$, the variance of y_t tends to infinity with t. The term which corresponds to $x_t(\boldsymbol{\beta})u_t$ for the regression function αy_{t-1} of (5.21) is $\alpha y_{t-1}u_t$, and we see that the variance of this term likewise tends to infinity with t. Thus no law of large numbers can in general apply to (5.16).

Econometricians usually take good care that the regression functions they use do not give rise to explosive processes like the one just considered. If we require that $|\alpha| < 1$ in (5.21), we find that the process is not explosive.[4] In order to deal with this case, and more generally with the regression function (5.20) when it does not lead to an explosive process, the most useful law of

[4] Such processes will be discussed in Chapter 10 in connection with our discussion of serial correlation.

large numbers is the martingale one, Theorem 4.6. Note first that this theorem can be applied directly to the terms $x_t(\boldsymbol{\beta})u_t$, since the expectation of $x_t(\boldsymbol{\beta})u_t$, conditional on $\{x_s(\boldsymbol{\beta})u_s\}_{s=1}^{t-1}$, is zero, because u_t is independent of both u_s and $x_s(\boldsymbol{\beta})$ for all $s \leq t$. Thus the only further requirement of the theorem is very weak and can be guaranteed by requiring that the expectations of the $x_t(\boldsymbol{\beta})$'s be uniformly bounded.

There remains the question of whether we can be sure that expression (5.19) exists and is nonstochastic. This is a question that can only be answered once the regression function and the DGP have been specified in detail. We will therefore adopt the attitude that (5.19) must exist and be nonstochastic if the process defined by the regression function (5.20) is not to be explosive. Thus when we say that a process is not explosive, we will mean that (5.19) exists and is finite and nonstochastic. By this means one can consider nonlinear regression models with regression functions like (5.20) as they occur one by one and determine whether or not they are explosive.

As an example, consider the simple model of (5.21), but now with $|\alpha| < 1$. For this specification, (5.19) becomes

$$(\alpha_0 - \alpha)^2 \operatorname*{plim}_0_{n\to\infty} \left(\frac{1}{n}\sum_{t=1}^{n} y_{t-1}^2\right). \tag{5.23}$$

For our purposes the factor $(\alpha_0 - \alpha)^2$ is irrelevant, and we have to investigate the actual probability limit. Unfortunately, this is not particularly easy without more general asymptotic theory of stochastic processes than we have given up to now, or indeed intend to give in this book.[5] But we will see in Chapter 10 that the sequence $\{y_t\}$ generated by (5.21) is what is called an autoregressive process of order 1, or an AR(1) process for short, and that for $|\alpha| < 1$ it is stationary and ergodic. The same properties hold therefore for the sequence $\{y_t^2\}$. Consequently, we may apply the ergodic theorem, Theorem 4.5, in order to obtain the desired result that the process (5.21) with $|\alpha| < 1$ is not explosive. The nonlinear least squares estimator of the parameter α in (5.21), which here is simply the OLS estimator, of course, is therefore consistent. This follows from Theorem 5.1, since the required uniformity of convergence can be shown to be a consequence of the structure of (5.23) as a product of a factor dependent only on the parameter α and a factor dependent only on the random process $\{y_t\}$.

If the above discussion seems a little cavalier about whether or not processes are explosive, it is unfortunately necessary in the present state of knowledge that it be so. It is often extremely difficult to tell, sometimes even if one has unlimited computer time to try a variety of simulations, whether or not the stochastic process generated by some given regression function of the form (5.20) is explosive. Interested readers are urged to consult White (1984)

[5] See Lamperti (1977) for a general discussion of stochastic processes at an advanced level.

to get an idea of the mathematical complexity involved. Outside the context of the standard time-series processes (which do not contain variables other than the dependent variable itself; see Chapter 10) not very much can be said in general. Practicing econometricians may be forgiven for feeling that the mathematical complexity is not worth it, since the issue is not an empirical one but only one of how best to model data. We will discuss a number of issues relating to nonstationary processes in Chapter 20.

5.4 Asymptotic Normality of the NLS Estimator

In this section, we discuss the asymptotic normality of the nonlinear least squares estimator. For this, we will require a bit more regularity than was needed for consistency, as we will see. First, a formal definition of asymptotic normality:

Definition 5.4.

> A consistent estimator $\hat{\boldsymbol{\beta}} \equiv \{\hat{\boldsymbol{\beta}}^n\}$ of the parameters of the asymptotically identified parametrized model $(\mathbb{M}, \boldsymbol{\beta})$ is asymptotically normal if for every DGP $\mu_0 \in \mathbb{M}$, the sequence of random variables $\{n^{1/2}(\hat{\boldsymbol{\beta}}^n - \boldsymbol{\beta}_0)\}$ tends in distribution to a (multivariate) normal distribution, with mean zero and finite covariance matrix.

The crucial difference between the property of asymptotic normality and that of consistency discussed in the preceding section is the factor of $n^{1/2}$. This factor "blows up" $\hat{\boldsymbol{\beta}} - \boldsymbol{\beta}_0$, which, if $\hat{\boldsymbol{\beta}}$ is consistent for $\boldsymbol{\beta}_0$, tends to zero as n tends to infinity. Thus the product $n^{1/2}(\hat{\boldsymbol{\beta}} - \boldsymbol{\beta}_0)$ tends to a vector of nonzero random variables. Asymptotic normality, when it holds, will of course imply consistency, since if $n^{1/2}(\hat{\boldsymbol{\beta}} - \boldsymbol{\beta}_0)$ is $O(1)$, it follows that $\hat{\boldsymbol{\beta}} - \boldsymbol{\beta}_0$ must be $O(n^{-1/2})$. If the estimator $\hat{\boldsymbol{\beta}}$ satisfies the latter property, it is said to be **root-*n* consistent**, meaning that the difference between the estimator and the true value is proportional to one over $\sqrt{n}$. An estimator that is root-n consistent must also be weakly consistent, since $\operatorname{plim}(\hat{\boldsymbol{\beta}} - \boldsymbol{\beta}_0) = \mathbf{0}$. Not all consistent estimators are root-n consistent, however.

As in the last section, we will first state a theorem which gives conditions sufficient for the asymptotic normality of the NLS estimator and then discuss the circumstances in which we may hope that the conditions are satisfied. First, some notation. As usual we let $\boldsymbol{X}_t(\boldsymbol{\beta}) \equiv D_\beta\, x_t(\boldsymbol{\beta})$ denote the row vector of partial derivatives of the regression function $x_t(\boldsymbol{\beta})$; then $\boldsymbol{A}_t(\boldsymbol{\beta}) \equiv D_{\beta\beta}\, x_t(\boldsymbol{\beta})$ will denote the Hessian of $x_t(\boldsymbol{\beta})$, and $\boldsymbol{H}_t(y_t, \boldsymbol{\beta}) \equiv D_{\beta\beta}(y_t - x_t(\boldsymbol{\beta}))^2$ will denote the Hessian of the contribution to the sum-of-squares function from observation t. This last is readily seen to be

$$\boldsymbol{H}_t(y_t, \boldsymbol{\beta}) = 2\Big(\boldsymbol{X}_t^{\top}(\boldsymbol{\beta})\boldsymbol{X}_t(\boldsymbol{\beta}) - \boldsymbol{A}_t(\boldsymbol{\beta})\big(y_t - x_t(\boldsymbol{\beta})\big)\Big). \tag{5.24}$$

Evidently, the Hessian $\boldsymbol{A}_t$ of the regression function will be a zero matrix if the regression function x_t is linear, and $\boldsymbol{X}_t(\boldsymbol{\beta})$ will just be $\boldsymbol{X}_t$. In that case, $\boldsymbol{H}_t(y_t, \boldsymbol{\beta})$ will simplify to $2(\boldsymbol{X}_t^\top \boldsymbol{X}_t)$, which is necessarily positive semidefinite.

Theorem 5.2. Asymptotic Normality Theorem for Nonlinear Least Squares.

If the nonlinear regression model (5.08) is asymptotically identified and satisfies the regularity conditions of Theorem 5.1, so that the NLS estimator for the model is consistent, and if in addition, for all $\mu_0 \in \mathbb{M}$,

(i) the sequence $\{n^{-1}\sum_{t=1}^{n} \boldsymbol{H}_t(y_t, \boldsymbol{\beta})\}$ satisfies condition WULLN of Definition 4.17 for $\boldsymbol{\beta}$ in the neighborhood of $\boldsymbol{\beta}_0$, and

(ii) the sequence $\{n^{-1/2}\sum_{t=1}^{n} \boldsymbol{X}_t^\top(\boldsymbol{\beta})u_t\}$ satisfies condition CLT of Definition 4.16, and

(iii) the Hessian of the limiting sum-of-squares function evaluated at the true parameters, $D_{\beta\beta}\,\overline{ssr}(\boldsymbol{\beta}_0, \mu_0)$, is a positive definite matrix, which ensures that the second-order sufficient condition for the minimum in (5.12) is satisfied,

then, under all DGPs μ_0 such that $\boldsymbol{\beta}_0$ is contained in the interior of the parameter space Θ, the NLS estimator $\hat{\boldsymbol{\beta}}$ is asymptotically normal as in Definition 5.4. Further, if σ_0^2 is the error variance associated with μ_0, the **asymptotic covariance matrix** of $n^{1/2}(\hat{\boldsymbol{\beta}} - \boldsymbol{\beta}_0)$ is

$$\sigma_0^2 \operatorname*{plim}_{n\to\infty}{}_0 \left(n^{-1}\boldsymbol{X}_0^\top \boldsymbol{X}_0\right)^{-1}. \tag{5.25}$$

Here $\boldsymbol{X}_0 \equiv \boldsymbol{X}(\boldsymbol{\beta}_0)$ denotes the $n \times k$ matrix with typical row $\boldsymbol{X}_t(\boldsymbol{\beta}_0)$.

We start our discussion of this theorem from the requirement that the DGP, which we will denote μ_0, must be such that $\boldsymbol{\beta}_0$ is in the interior of the parameter space Θ. If that is the case, then with probability arbitrarily close to unity, so will be the estimator $\hat{\boldsymbol{\beta}}$ for large enough n, since we have supposed that $\hat{\boldsymbol{\beta}}$ is consistent. This means that $\hat{\boldsymbol{\beta}}$ must satisfy the first-order necessary condition for an interior minimum:

$$D_\beta\, ssr^n(\boldsymbol{y}, \hat{\boldsymbol{\beta}}) = \boldsymbol{0}. \tag{5.26}$$

The consistency of $\hat{\boldsymbol{\beta}}$ means that it must be *close* to $\boldsymbol{\beta}_0$ if n is large. Accordingly we will expand (5.26) in a short Taylor series about $\boldsymbol{\beta}_0$, as follows:

$$\boldsymbol{0} = D_\beta\, ssr^n(\boldsymbol{y}, \boldsymbol{\beta}_0) + (\hat{\boldsymbol{\beta}} - \boldsymbol{\beta}_0)^\top D_{\beta\beta}\, ssr^n(\boldsymbol{y}, \boldsymbol{\beta}^*). \tag{5.27}$$

Here $\boldsymbol{\beta}^*$ is a convex combination of $\hat{\boldsymbol{\beta}}$ and $\boldsymbol{\beta}_0$, which may be different for each row of the equation, as required by Taylor's Theorem.

Our next step is to consider the limit of the right-hand side of (5.27) as $n \to \infty$. The Hessian $D_{\beta\beta}\, ssr^n(\boldsymbol{y}, \boldsymbol{\beta})$, evaluated at arbitrary $\boldsymbol{\beta} \in \Theta$, can be written as

$$D_{\beta\beta}\, ssr^n(\boldsymbol{y}, \boldsymbol{\beta}) = \frac{1}{n}\sum_{t=1}^{n} D_{\beta\beta}\big(y_t - x_t(\boldsymbol{\beta})\big)^2 = \frac{1}{n}\sum_{t=1}^{n} \boldsymbol{H}_t(y_t, \boldsymbol{\beta}). \tag{5.28}$$

This has the form required for the application of a law of large numbers, whence condition (i) of Theorem 5.2. We may also conclude that

$$\operatorname*{plim}_{n\to\infty}{}_0\big(D_{\beta\beta}\, ssr^n(\boldsymbol{y},\boldsymbol{\beta})\big) = D_{\beta\beta}\, \overline{ssr}(\boldsymbol{\beta},\mu_0). \tag{5.29}$$

To see this, recall that WULLN permits integrability to be preserved when one passes to the limit as $n \to \infty$. The sequence $\{D_{\beta\beta}\, ssr^n(\boldsymbol{y},\boldsymbol{\beta})\}$ can be integrated to $\{ssr^n(\boldsymbol{y},\boldsymbol{\beta})\}$, which converges to $\overline{ssr}(\boldsymbol{\beta},\mu_0)$ under μ_0. Thus the limit of $\{D_{\beta\beta}\, ssr^n(\boldsymbol{y},\boldsymbol{\beta})\}$ under μ_0 must integrate up to $\overline{ssr}(\boldsymbol{\beta},\mu_0)$, and since $\overline{ssr}(\boldsymbol{\beta},\mu_0)$ can have only one Hessian, we obtain (5.29).

Since $\boldsymbol{\beta}^*$ is a convex combination of $\hat{\boldsymbol{\beta}}$ and $\boldsymbol{\beta}_0$, and $\hat{\boldsymbol{\beta}}$ is consistent for $\boldsymbol{\beta}_0$, then so must be $\boldsymbol{\beta}^*$. Thus we have, on account of the uniformity of convergence guaranteed by WULLN,

$$\operatorname*{plim}_{n\to\infty}{}_0\big(D_{\beta\beta}\, ssr^n(\boldsymbol{y},\boldsymbol{\beta}^*)\big) = D_{\beta\beta}\, \overline{ssr}(\boldsymbol{\beta}_0,\mu_0).$$

If condition (iii) of Theorem 5.2 is satisfied, this last matrix is positive definite and therefore also nonsingular and invertible. This condition can be referred to as a condition for **strong asymptotic identifiability**, since it requires not only that (5.12) be satisfied but also that the sufficient second-order condition be satisfied at the minimum. The result is that under condition (iii) we can rewrite (5.27) as

$$\hat{\boldsymbol{\beta}} - \boldsymbol{\beta}_0 = -\big(D_{\beta\beta}\, ssr^n(\boldsymbol{y},\boldsymbol{\beta}^*)\big)^{-1} D_\beta^\top ssr^n(\boldsymbol{y},\boldsymbol{\beta}_0), \tag{5.30}$$

where the inverse matrix on the right-hand side will exist with probability arbitrarily close to one, for n large enough, and satisfies

$$\operatorname*{plim}_{n\to\infty}{}_0\big(D_{\beta\beta}\, ssr^n(\boldsymbol{y},\boldsymbol{\beta}^*)\big)^{-1} = \big(D_{\beta\beta}\, \overline{ssr}(\boldsymbol{\beta}_0,\mu_0)\big)^{-1}. \tag{5.31}$$

The argument of the preceding paragraph used a law of large numbers. If we multiply (5.30) by $n^{1/2}$, we can also use a central limit theorem. The result of the multiplication is

$$n^{1/2}(\hat{\boldsymbol{\beta}} - \boldsymbol{\beta}_0) = -\big(D_{\beta\beta}\, ssr^n(\boldsymbol{y},\boldsymbol{\beta}^*)\big)^{-1}\big(n^{1/2} D_\beta^\top ssr^n(\boldsymbol{y},\boldsymbol{\beta}_0)\big). \tag{5.32}$$

The second factor on the right-hand side of this equation is

$$\begin{aligned} n^{1/2} D_\beta^\top ssr^n(\boldsymbol{y},\boldsymbol{\beta}_0) &= n^{-1/2}\sum_{t=1}^{n} D_\beta^\top\big(y_t - x_t(\boldsymbol{\beta}_0)\big)^2 \\ &= -2n^{-1/2}\sum_{t=1}^{n} \boldsymbol{X}_t^\top(\boldsymbol{\beta}_0)u_t. \end{aligned} \tag{5.33}$$

The reason for condition (ii) of Theorem 5.2 is now clear: Under that condition (5.33) has a normal, zero-mean **asymptotic distribution**. Further, its limiting covariance matrix will be

$$\lim_{n\to\infty}\left(\frac{4}{n}\sum_{t=1}^{n} E_0\big(u_t^2 \boldsymbol{X}_t^\top(\boldsymbol{\beta}_0)\boldsymbol{X}_t(\boldsymbol{\beta}_0)\big)\right).$$

But since, for any $\boldsymbol{\beta}$, u_t is independent of $x_t(\boldsymbol{\beta})$ and hence also of $\boldsymbol{X}_t(\boldsymbol{\beta})$, this covariance matrix becomes just

$$4\sigma_0^2 \operatorname*{plim}_{n\to\infty}{}_0\big(n^{-1}\boldsymbol{X}_0^\top\boldsymbol{X}_0\big). \tag{5.34}$$

Condition (i) of Theorem 5.2 allows us to assume that WULLN holds for $\{n^{-1}\sum_{t=1}^{n}\boldsymbol{H}_t(\boldsymbol{y}_t,\boldsymbol{\beta})\}$. From (5.24) we see that $\{n^{-1}\sum_{t=1}^{n}\boldsymbol{X}_t^\top(\boldsymbol{\beta})\boldsymbol{X}(\boldsymbol{\beta})\}$ is part of $\{n^{-1}\sum_{t=1}^{n}\boldsymbol{H}_t(\boldsymbol{y}_t,\boldsymbol{\beta})\}$, and so we can assume that WULLN applies to it as well.

We now have enough to compute the limiting distribution of the left-hand side of (5.32), that is, of $n^{1/2}(\hat{\boldsymbol{\beta}}-\boldsymbol{\beta}_0)$. From (5.31) and (5.34) we see that this distribution is normal, with expectation zero and covariance matrix

$$4\sigma_0^2\big(D_{\beta\beta}\,\overline{ssr}(\boldsymbol{\beta}_0,\mu_0)\big)^{-1}\operatorname*{plim}_{n\to\infty}{}_0\big(n^{-1}\boldsymbol{X}_0^\top\boldsymbol{X}_0\big)\big(D_{\beta\beta}\,\overline{ssr}(\boldsymbol{\beta}_0,\mu_0)\big)^{-1}. \tag{5.35}$$

This expression can be simplified. From (5.24) and (5.28),

$$\begin{aligned} D_{\beta\beta}\,ssr^n(\boldsymbol{y},\boldsymbol{\beta}_0) &= \frac{1}{n}\sum_{t=1}^{n}\boldsymbol{H}_t(y_t,\boldsymbol{\beta}_0)\\ &= \frac{1}{n}\sum_{t=1}^{n}2\big(\boldsymbol{X}_t^\top(\boldsymbol{\beta}_0)\boldsymbol{X}_t(\boldsymbol{\beta}_0)-\boldsymbol{A}_t(\boldsymbol{\beta}_0)u_t\big). \end{aligned} \tag{5.36}$$

Because u_t and $\boldsymbol{A}_t(\boldsymbol{\beta}_0)$ are independent, as are u_t and $\boldsymbol{X}_t(\boldsymbol{\beta}_0)$,

$$E_0\big(\boldsymbol{A}_t(\boldsymbol{\beta}_0)u_t\big)=\mathbf{0}. \tag{5.37}$$

Since condition (i) of Theorem 5.2 allows us to use a law of large numbers on (5.36), it follows from (5.37) that

$$\begin{aligned} D_{\beta\beta}\,\overline{ssr}(\boldsymbol{\beta}_0,\mu_0) &= \operatorname*{plim}_{n\to\infty}{}_0\big(D_{\beta\beta}\,ssr^n(\boldsymbol{y},\boldsymbol{\beta}_0)\big)\\ &= \operatorname*{plim}_{n\to\infty}{}_0\left(\frac{1}{n}\sum_{t=1}^{n}2\big(\boldsymbol{X}_t^\top(\boldsymbol{\beta}_0)\boldsymbol{X}_t(\boldsymbol{\beta}_0)-\boldsymbol{A}_t(\boldsymbol{\beta}_0)u_t\big)\right)\\ &= 2\operatorname*{plim}_{n\to\infty}{}_0\big(n^{-1}\boldsymbol{X}_0^\top\boldsymbol{X}_0\big). \end{aligned} \tag{5.38}$$

Consequently, the limiting covariance matrix of $n^{1/2}(\hat{\boldsymbol{\beta}} - \boldsymbol{\beta}_0)$ is, from (5.35) and (5.38),

$$\sigma_0^2 \operatorname*{plim}_{n\to\infty}{}_0 \left(n^{-1}\boldsymbol{X}_0^\top\boldsymbol{X}_0\right)^{-1}.$$

Since this is expression (5.25), we have now demonstrated the last part of Theorem 5.2.

It will be useful to rewrite (5.32) in the light of (5.33) and (5.38). It becomes

$$n^{1/2}(\hat{\boldsymbol{\beta}} - \boldsymbol{\beta}_0) = \left(n^{-1}\boldsymbol{X}_0^\top\boldsymbol{X}_0\right)^{-1} n^{-1/2}\boldsymbol{X}_0^\top\boldsymbol{u} + o(1). \tag{5.39}$$

For the case of a linear regression model with $\boldsymbol{x}(\boldsymbol{\beta}) = \boldsymbol{X\beta}$, the equality would be exact without the $o(1)$ term. All the factors of powers of n are unnecessary in that case, and we obtain the familiar result

$$\hat{\boldsymbol{\beta}} - \boldsymbol{\beta}_0 = \left(\boldsymbol{X}^\top\boldsymbol{X}\right)^{-1}\boldsymbol{X}^\top\boldsymbol{u}. \tag{5.40}$$

The result (5.39) is thus seen to be the asymptotic counterpart of (5.40) for nonlinear regression models. We will make use of (5.39) and other results of this section in Section 5.6 in order to establish the properties of NLS residuals. Meanwhile, in the next section, we study another important property of the NLS estimator, **asymptotic efficiency**.

5.5 ASYMPTOTIC EFFICIENCY OF NONLINEAR LEAST SQUARES

Up to this point, we have said nothing at all about how well either the OLS or the NLS estimator compares with other estimators. One estimator is said to be more **efficient** than another if, on average, the first estimator yields more accurate estimates than the second. The reason for the terminology is that an estimator which yields more accurate estimates can be said to utilize the information available in the sample more efficiently. We could define efficiency in as many different ways as we could think of to evaluate the relative accuracy of two estimators, and there are thus many definitions of efficiency in the literature. We will deal with only two of the most widely used ones here.

Suppose that $\hat{\boldsymbol{\theta}}$ and $\check{\boldsymbol{\theta}}$ are two unbiased estimators of a k-vector of parameters $\boldsymbol{\theta}$, with true value $\boldsymbol{\theta}_0$, and that these two estimators have covariance matrices

$$\boldsymbol{V}(\hat{\boldsymbol{\theta}}) \equiv E(\hat{\boldsymbol{\theta}} - \boldsymbol{\theta}_0)(\hat{\boldsymbol{\theta}} - \boldsymbol{\theta}_0)^\top \quad \text{and}$$
$$\boldsymbol{V}(\check{\boldsymbol{\theta}}) \equiv E(\check{\boldsymbol{\theta}} - \boldsymbol{\theta}_0)(\check{\boldsymbol{\theta}} - \boldsymbol{\theta}_0)^\top,$$

respectively. Then we have:

Definition 5.5.

The unbiased estimator $\hat{\boldsymbol{\theta}}$, with covariance matrix $\boldsymbol{V}(\hat{\boldsymbol{\theta}})$, is said to be more efficient than the unbiased estimator $\check{\boldsymbol{\theta}}$, with covariance matrix

$\boldsymbol{V}(\hat{\boldsymbol{\theta}})$, if and only if $\boldsymbol{V}(\check{\boldsymbol{\theta}}) - \boldsymbol{V}(\hat{\boldsymbol{\theta}})$, the difference of the two covariance matrices, is a positive semidefinite matrix.

If $\hat{\boldsymbol{\theta}}$ is more efficient than $\check{\boldsymbol{\theta}}$ in the sense of this definition, then every individual parameter in the vector $\boldsymbol{\theta}$, and every linear combination of those parameters, is estimated at least as efficiently by $\hat{\boldsymbol{\theta}}$ as by $\check{\boldsymbol{\theta}}$, by which we mean that the variance of the estimator based on $\hat{\boldsymbol{\theta}}$ is never greater than that of the estimator based on $\check{\boldsymbol{\theta}}$. To see this, consider an arbitrary linear combination of the parameters in $\boldsymbol{\theta}$, say $\boldsymbol{w}^\top\boldsymbol{\theta}$, where $\boldsymbol{w}$ is a k–vector. Then the variances of the two estimates of this quantity are $\boldsymbol{w}^\top\boldsymbol{V}(\check{\boldsymbol{\theta}})\boldsymbol{w}$ and $\boldsymbol{w}^\top\boldsymbol{V}(\hat{\boldsymbol{\theta}})\boldsymbol{w}$, and so the difference between them is

$$\boldsymbol{w}^\top\boldsymbol{V}(\check{\boldsymbol{\theta}})\boldsymbol{w} - \boldsymbol{w}^\top\boldsymbol{V}(\hat{\boldsymbol{\theta}})\boldsymbol{w} = \boldsymbol{w}^\top\big(\boldsymbol{V}(\check{\boldsymbol{\theta}}) - \boldsymbol{V}(\hat{\boldsymbol{\theta}})\big)\boldsymbol{w}.$$

Since $\boldsymbol{V}(\check{\boldsymbol{\theta}}) - \boldsymbol{V}(\hat{\boldsymbol{\theta}})$ is a positive semidefinite matrix, this quantity must be either positive or zero. Thus whatever parameter or linear combination of parameters we are trying to estimate, we can be sure that $\hat{\boldsymbol{\theta}}$ will yield an estimator at least as good as $\check{\boldsymbol{\theta}}$ if the difference between their covariance matrices is positive semidefinite. In practice, when one estimator is more efficient than another, this difference is very often positive definite. When that is the case, *every* parameter or linear combination of parameters will in fact be estimated more efficiently using $\hat{\boldsymbol{\theta}}$.

When estimating nonlinear regression models and other types of nonlinear models, we rarely encounter unbiased estimates, and we are rarely able to work out the finite-sample covariance matrices of estimators. It is therefore natural to seek an asymptotic concept comparable to efficiency in the finite-sample case. The appropriate concept is **asymptotic efficiency**, which is defined as follows:

Definition 5.6.

Suppose that $\hat{\boldsymbol{\theta}}$ and $\check{\boldsymbol{\theta}}$ are two consistent estimators of the same parameter vector $\boldsymbol{\theta}$. Let the asymptotic covariance matrices of these two estimators be

$$\begin{aligned}\boldsymbol{V}^\infty\big(n^{1/2}(\hat{\boldsymbol{\theta}} - \boldsymbol{\theta}_0)\big) &\equiv \lim_{n\to\infty} E_0\big(n(\hat{\boldsymbol{\theta}} - \boldsymbol{\theta}_0)(\hat{\boldsymbol{\theta}} - \boldsymbol{\theta}_0)^\top\big) \quad \text{and}\\ \boldsymbol{V}^\infty\big(n^{1/2}(\check{\boldsymbol{\theta}} - \boldsymbol{\theta}_0)\big) &\equiv \lim_{n\to\infty} E_0\big(n(\check{\boldsymbol{\theta}} - \boldsymbol{\theta}_0)(\check{\boldsymbol{\theta}} - \boldsymbol{\theta}_0)^\top\big).\end{aligned}$$

Then the estimator $\hat{\boldsymbol{\theta}}$ is asymptotically more efficient than the estimator $\check{\boldsymbol{\theta}}$ if

$$\boldsymbol{V}^\infty\big(n^{1/2}(\check{\boldsymbol{\theta}} - \boldsymbol{\theta}_0)\big) - \boldsymbol{V}^\infty\big(n^{1/2}(\hat{\boldsymbol{\theta}} - \boldsymbol{\theta}_0)\big)$$

is a positive semidefinite matrix.

A famous result on efficiency is the **Gauss-Markov Theorem**. This theorem applies to the linear regression model

$$\boldsymbol{y} = \boldsymbol{X\beta} + \boldsymbol{u}, \quad E(\boldsymbol{uu}^\top) = \sigma^2\mathbf{I}, \tag{5.41}$$

where the regressors $\boldsymbol{X}$ are fixed or can be treated as fixed because we are conditioning on them (see Section 3.5). It is as follows:

Theorem 5.3. Gauss-Markov Theorem.

> The OLS estimator $\hat{\boldsymbol{\beta}} \equiv (\boldsymbol{X}^\top\boldsymbol{X})^{-1}\boldsymbol{X}^\top\boldsymbol{y}$ of the parameters $\boldsymbol{\beta}$ of the linear regression model (5.41) is the **best linear unbiased estimator**, or **BLUE** for short. This means that if $\boldsymbol{V}(\hat{\boldsymbol{\beta}})$ is the covariance matrix of $\hat{\boldsymbol{\beta}}$ under a DGP belonging to the model (5.41), and if $\boldsymbol{V}(\check{\boldsymbol{\beta}})$ is the covariance matrix of any other unbiased estimator $\check{\boldsymbol{\beta}}$, linear in the vector $\boldsymbol{y}$, then $\boldsymbol{V}(\check{\boldsymbol{\beta}}) - \boldsymbol{V}(\hat{\boldsymbol{\beta}})$ is a positive semidefinite matrix.

The proof of this theorem is both easy and illuminating. Since $\check{\boldsymbol{\beta}}$ is a linear function of $\boldsymbol{y}$, we can write it as

$$\check{\boldsymbol{\beta}} = \boldsymbol{Ay} = (\boldsymbol{X}^\top\boldsymbol{X})^{-1}\boldsymbol{X}^\top\boldsymbol{y} + \boldsymbol{Cy}, \tag{5.42}$$

where $\boldsymbol{C}$ is *defined* as $\boldsymbol{A} - (\boldsymbol{X}^\top\boldsymbol{X})^{-1}\boldsymbol{X}^\top$. We assume that the data are generated by a DGP that is a special case of (5.41), with $\boldsymbol{\beta} = \boldsymbol{\beta}_0$ and $\sigma^2 = \sigma_0^2$. We can thus substitute $\boldsymbol{X\beta}_0 + \boldsymbol{u}$ for $\boldsymbol{y}$ in (5.42) to obtain

$$\begin{aligned} \check{\boldsymbol{\beta}} &= \big((\boldsymbol{X}^\top\boldsymbol{X})^{-1}\boldsymbol{X}^\top + \boldsymbol{C}\big)(\boldsymbol{X\beta}_0 + \boldsymbol{u}) \\ &= \boldsymbol{\beta}_0 + \boldsymbol{CX\beta}_0 + (\boldsymbol{X}^\top\boldsymbol{X})^{-1}\boldsymbol{X}^\top\boldsymbol{u} + \boldsymbol{Cu}. \end{aligned} \tag{5.43}$$

It is clear from (5.43) that $E(\check{\boldsymbol{\beta}})$ can equal $\boldsymbol{\beta}_0$ only if $\boldsymbol{CX\beta}_0$ is equal to a zero vector. That can be guaranteed for all values of $\boldsymbol{\beta}_0$ only if $\boldsymbol{CX} = \mathbf{0}$. Thus the requirement that $\check{\boldsymbol{\beta}}$ be a linear *unbiased* estimator implies, first, that the second term on the right-hand side of (5.42), $\boldsymbol{Cy}$, has mean zero because $\boldsymbol{CX\beta}_0 = \mathbf{0}$, and second, that the two terms on the right-hand side of (5.42) have zero covariance. To see this second point, observe that

$$\begin{aligned} E\big((\boldsymbol{X}^\top\boldsymbol{X})^{-1}\boldsymbol{X}^\top\boldsymbol{yy}^\top\boldsymbol{C}^\top\big) &= E\Big(\big(\boldsymbol{\beta}_0 + (\boldsymbol{X}^\top\boldsymbol{X})^{-1}\boldsymbol{X}^\top\boldsymbol{u}\big)\boldsymbol{u}^\top\boldsymbol{C}^\top\Big) \\ &= \sigma_0^2(\boldsymbol{X}^\top\boldsymbol{X})^{-1}\boldsymbol{X}^\top\boldsymbol{C}^\top \\ &= \mathbf{0}. \end{aligned} \tag{5.44}$$

Consequently, equation (5.42) says that the unbiased linear estimator $\check{\boldsymbol{\beta}}$ is equal to the least squares estimator $\hat{\boldsymbol{\beta}}$ plus a random component $\boldsymbol{Cy}$ which is uncorrelated with $\hat{\boldsymbol{\beta}}$. As we will see below and in Chapter 8, something very like this is true in general: Asymptotically, an inefficient estimator is always equal to an efficient estimator plus an independent random noise term.

The result (5.44) essentially proves the Gauss-Markov Theorem, since it implies that

$$\begin{aligned} &E(\check{\boldsymbol{\beta}} - \boldsymbol{\beta}_0)(\check{\boldsymbol{\beta}} - \boldsymbol{\beta}_0)^{\top} \\ &= E\Big(\big((\boldsymbol{X}^{\top}\boldsymbol{X})^{-1}\boldsymbol{X}^{\top}\boldsymbol{u} + \boldsymbol{C}\boldsymbol{u}\big)\big((\boldsymbol{X}^{\top}\boldsymbol{X})^{-1}\boldsymbol{X}^{\top}\boldsymbol{u} + \boldsymbol{C}\boldsymbol{u}\big)^{\top}\Big) \\ &= \sigma_0^2(\boldsymbol{X}^{\top}\boldsymbol{X})^{-1} + \sigma_0^2\boldsymbol{C}\boldsymbol{C}^{\top}. \end{aligned} \tag{5.45}$$

Thus the difference between the covariance matrices of $\check{\boldsymbol{\beta}}$ and $\hat{\boldsymbol{\beta}}$ is $\sigma_0^2\boldsymbol{C}\boldsymbol{C}^{\top}$, which is a positive semidefinite matrix. Notice that the assumption that $E(\boldsymbol{u}\boldsymbol{u}^{\top}) = \sigma_0^2\mathbf{I}$ is crucial here. If instead we had $E(\boldsymbol{u}\boldsymbol{u}^{\top}) = \boldsymbol{\Omega}$, with $\boldsymbol{\Omega}$ an arbitrary $n \times n$ positive definite matrix, the last line of (5.45) would be

$$\begin{aligned} &(\boldsymbol{X}^{\top}\boldsymbol{X})^{-1}\boldsymbol{X}^{\top}\boldsymbol{\Omega}\boldsymbol{X}(\boldsymbol{X}^{\top}\boldsymbol{X})^{-1} \\ &\qquad + \boldsymbol{C}\boldsymbol{\Omega}\boldsymbol{C}^{\top} + (\boldsymbol{X}^{\top}\boldsymbol{X})^{-1}\boldsymbol{X}^{\top}\boldsymbol{\Omega}\boldsymbol{C}^{\top} + \boldsymbol{C}\boldsymbol{\Omega}\boldsymbol{X}(\boldsymbol{X}^{\top}\boldsymbol{X})^{-1}, \end{aligned}$$

and we could draw no conclusion about the relative efficiency of $\hat{\boldsymbol{\beta}}$ and $\check{\boldsymbol{\beta}}$.

As a simple example of the Gauss-Markov Theorem in action, suppose that $\check{\boldsymbol{\beta}}$ is the OLS estimator obtained by regressing $\boldsymbol{y}$ on $\boldsymbol{X}$ and $\boldsymbol{Z}$ jointly, where $\boldsymbol{Z}$ is a matrix of regressors such that $E(\boldsymbol{y} \,|\, \boldsymbol{X}, \boldsymbol{Z}) = E(\boldsymbol{y} \,|\, \boldsymbol{X}) = \boldsymbol{X}\boldsymbol{\beta}$. Since the information that $\boldsymbol{Z}$ does not belong in the regression is being ignored when we construct $\check{\boldsymbol{\beta}}$, the latter must in general be inefficient. Using the FWL Theorem, we find that

$$\check{\boldsymbol{\beta}} = (\boldsymbol{X}^{\top}\boldsymbol{M}_Z\boldsymbol{X})^{-1}\boldsymbol{X}^{\top}\boldsymbol{M}_Z\boldsymbol{y}, \tag{5.46}$$

where, as usual, $\boldsymbol{M}_Z$ is the matrix that projects orthogonally onto $\mathcal{S}^{\perp}(\boldsymbol{Z})$. If we write $\check{\boldsymbol{\beta}}$ as in (5.42), we obtain

$$\begin{aligned} \check{\boldsymbol{\beta}} &= (\boldsymbol{X}^{\top}\boldsymbol{X})^{-1}\boldsymbol{X}^{\top}\boldsymbol{y} + \big((\boldsymbol{X}^{\top}\boldsymbol{M}_Z\boldsymbol{X})^{-1}\boldsymbol{X}^{\top}\boldsymbol{M}_Z - (\boldsymbol{X}^{\top}\boldsymbol{X})^{-1}\boldsymbol{X}^{\top}\big)\boldsymbol{y} \\ &= (\boldsymbol{X}^{\top}\boldsymbol{X})^{-1}\boldsymbol{X}^{\top}\boldsymbol{y} + (\boldsymbol{X}^{\top}\boldsymbol{M}_Z\boldsymbol{X})^{-1}(\boldsymbol{X}^{\top}\boldsymbol{M}_Z - \boldsymbol{X}^{\top}\boldsymbol{M}_Z\boldsymbol{X}(\boldsymbol{X}^{\top}\boldsymbol{X})^{-1}\boldsymbol{X}^{\top})\boldsymbol{y} \\ &= (\boldsymbol{X}^{\top}\boldsymbol{X})^{-1}\boldsymbol{X}^{\top}\boldsymbol{y} + (\boldsymbol{X}^{\top}\boldsymbol{M}_Z\boldsymbol{X})^{-1}\Big(\boldsymbol{X}^{\top}\boldsymbol{M}_Z\big(\mathbf{I} - \boldsymbol{X}(\boldsymbol{X}^{\top}\boldsymbol{X})^{-1}\boldsymbol{X}^{\top}\big)\Big)\boldsymbol{y} \\ &= (\boldsymbol{X}^{\top}\boldsymbol{X})^{-1}\boldsymbol{X}^{\top}\boldsymbol{y} + (\boldsymbol{X}^{\top}\boldsymbol{M}_Z\boldsymbol{X})^{-1}\boldsymbol{X}^{\top}\boldsymbol{M}_Z\boldsymbol{M}_X\boldsymbol{y} \\ &= \hat{\boldsymbol{\beta}} + \boldsymbol{C}\boldsymbol{y}. \end{aligned} \tag{5.47}$$

Thus, in this case, the matrix $\boldsymbol{C}$ is the matrix $(\boldsymbol{X}^{\top}\boldsymbol{M}_Z\boldsymbol{X})^{-1}\boldsymbol{X}^{\top}\boldsymbol{M}_Z\boldsymbol{M}_X$. We see that the inefficient estimator $\check{\boldsymbol{\beta}}$ is equal to the efficient estimator $\hat{\boldsymbol{\beta}}$ plus a random component which is uncorrelated with it. That $\hat{\boldsymbol{\beta}}$ and $\boldsymbol{C}\boldsymbol{y}$ are uncorrelated follows from the fact (required for $\boldsymbol{C}\boldsymbol{y}$ to have mean zero) that $\boldsymbol{C}\boldsymbol{X} = \mathbf{0}$, which is true because $\boldsymbol{M}_X$ annihilates $\boldsymbol{X}$. Further, we see that

$$\begin{aligned} E(\check{\boldsymbol{\beta}} - \boldsymbol{\beta}_0)(\check{\boldsymbol{\beta}} - \boldsymbol{\beta}_0)^{\top} &= \sigma_0^2(\boldsymbol{X}^{\top}\boldsymbol{X})^{-1} \\ &+ \sigma_0^2(\boldsymbol{X}^{\top}\boldsymbol{M}_Z\boldsymbol{X})^{-1}\boldsymbol{X}^{\top}\boldsymbol{M}_Z\boldsymbol{M}_X\boldsymbol{M}_Z\boldsymbol{X}(\boldsymbol{X}^{\top}\boldsymbol{M}_Z\boldsymbol{X})^{-1}. \end{aligned} \tag{5.48}$$

The second term on the right-hand side of (5.48) will in general be a positive semidefinite matrix, as expected. It will be a zero matrix if $\boldsymbol{Z}$ is orthogonal to $\boldsymbol{X}$, in which case $\boldsymbol{M}_Z\boldsymbol{X} = \boldsymbol{X}$ and $\boldsymbol{M}_X\boldsymbol{M}_Z\boldsymbol{X} = \mathbf{0}$. Thus we obtain the familiar result that adding explanatory variables which do not belong in a regression will reduce efficiency except in the rare case in which the extra variables are orthogonal to those that do belong.

It is important to keep in mind the limitations of the Gauss-Markov Theorem. It does *not* say that the OLS estimator $\hat{\boldsymbol{\beta}}$ is better than every conceivable estimator. Estimators which are nonlinear and/or biased may well perform better than OLS in certain circumstances. In particular, as we will see in Chapter 8, only with the assumption of normally distributed error terms will OLS generally coincide with the maximum likelihood estimator, which will be asymptotically "best" under fairly general conditions when the distribution of the error terms is known. Moreover, the theorem applies only to a correctly specified model with homoskedastic errors.

To see the importance of correct specification, let us reconsider the linear regression example in which $E(\boldsymbol{y}\,|\,\boldsymbol{X}, \boldsymbol{Z}) = \boldsymbol{X\beta}$. If one does not know that the expectation of $\boldsymbol{y}$ conditional on $\boldsymbol{X}$ and $\boldsymbol{Z}$ is independent of $\boldsymbol{Z}$, it is reasonable to estimate the regression model

$$\boldsymbol{y} = \boldsymbol{X\beta} + \boldsymbol{Z\gamma} + \boldsymbol{u}. \tag{5.49}$$

The OLS estimator of $\boldsymbol{\beta}$, (5.46), is, by the Gauss-Markov Theorem, asymptotically efficient for the complete model (5.49), which admits DGPs for which the value of $\boldsymbol{\gamma}$ is nonzero. But it is inefficient relative to the estimator $(\boldsymbol{X}^\top\boldsymbol{X})^{-1}\boldsymbol{X}^\top\boldsymbol{y}$ for the class of DGPs for which $\boldsymbol{\gamma} = \mathbf{0}$. This is, however, a *restricted* class of DGPs, and the estimator $(\boldsymbol{X}^\top\boldsymbol{X})^{-1}\boldsymbol{X}^\top\boldsymbol{y}$ is in general *inconsistent* for DGPs satisfying (5.49) with $\boldsymbol{\gamma} \neq \mathbf{0}$. Its greater efficiency has been bought at the cost of supposing that $\boldsymbol{\gamma} = \mathbf{0}$ and risking inconsistency if this supposition is false.

It is plain that the Gauss-Markov Theorem cannot be applied to the NLS estimator, since that estimator is in general neither linear nor unbiased. Nevertheless, it is asymptotically efficient (Definition 5.6) in a certain sense. Recall the result (5.39) from Section 5.4, which we can rewrite slightly as

$$n^{1/2}(\hat{\boldsymbol{\beta}} - \boldsymbol{\beta}_0) \overset{a}{=} \operatorname*{plim}_{n\to\infty}\left(n^{-1}\boldsymbol{X}_0^\top\boldsymbol{X}_0\right)^{-1} n^{-1/2}\boldsymbol{X}_0^\top\boldsymbol{u}.$$

It is possible to consider a class of estimators, which we may again denote by $\check{\boldsymbol{\beta}}$, with the property that

$$n^{1/2}(\check{\boldsymbol{\beta}} - \boldsymbol{\beta}_0) \overset{a}{=} \Big(\operatorname*{plim}_{n\to\infty}\left(n^{-1}\boldsymbol{X}_0^\top\boldsymbol{X}_0\right)^{-1}\left(n^{-1/2}\boldsymbol{X}_0^\top\right) + n^{-1/2}\boldsymbol{C}\Big)\boldsymbol{u}, \tag{5.50}$$

where each element of the $k \times n$ matrix $\boldsymbol{C}$ (which may depend on $\boldsymbol{\beta}$) is $O(1)$, and it is assumed that

$$\operatorname*{plim}_{n\to\infty}\left(n^{-1}\boldsymbol{Cu}\right) = \mathbf{0} \quad \text{and} \quad \operatorname*{plim}_{n\to\infty}\left(n^{-1}\boldsymbol{CX}_0\right) = \mathbf{0}.$$

Notice that, according to (5.50), $n^{1/2}(\check{\boldsymbol{\beta}}-\boldsymbol{\beta}_0)$ is asymptotically a linear function of the vector of error terms $\boldsymbol{u}$. These assumptions are sufficient to ensure that $\check{\boldsymbol{\beta}}$ is consistent if $\hat{\boldsymbol{\beta}}$ is. Demonstrating that

$$\boldsymbol{V}^{\infty}\big(n^{1/2}(\check{\boldsymbol{\beta}}-\boldsymbol{\beta}_0)\big)-\boldsymbol{V}^{\infty}\big(n^{1/2}(\hat{\boldsymbol{\beta}}-\boldsymbol{\beta}_0)\big)$$

is a positive semidefinite matrix is then an exercise extremely similar to proving the Gauss-Markov Theorem. Hence we conclude that NLS is asymptotically more efficient than any estimator of the form (5.50). We will refer to such estimators as **consistent and asymptotically linear**, with NLS seen to be the best consistent and asymptotically linear estimator.

This result may not seem very meaningful because, up to this point, we have not seen any other estimators that are consistent and asymptotically linear. However, it should be clear from the similarity of NLS and OLS that if we were to estimate the model

$$\boldsymbol{y}=\boldsymbol{x}(\boldsymbol{\beta},\boldsymbol{\gamma})+\boldsymbol{u},\quad E(\boldsymbol{u}\boldsymbol{u}^{\top})=\sigma^2\mathbf{I},$$

where $\boldsymbol{x}(\boldsymbol{\beta},\mathbf{0})=\boldsymbol{x}(\boldsymbol{\beta})$, we would obtain an estimator that satisfies (5.50) asymptotically. The particular form of (5.50) would be similar to expression (5.47) for the linear case. Other consistent and asymptotically linear estimators include the generalized nonlinear least squares estimator to be considered in Chapter 9 and the nonlinear instrumental variables estimator to be considered in Chapter 7.

A stronger result on the efficiency of NLS is available if we assume that the error terms are normally distributed. In that case the NLS estimator of the parameter vector $\boldsymbol{\beta}$ is also the maximum-likelihood estimator. As we will see in Chapter 8, the ML estimator is asymptotically efficient in a very strong sense, provided that the entire stochastic structure of the model is correctly specified. What this implies is that the NLS estimator is asymptotically efficient relative to a very wide class of estimating techniques for the class of nonlinear regression models with disturbances which are homoskedastic, independent, and normally distributed.

5.6 PROPERTIES OF NONLINEAR LEAST SQUARES RESIDUALS

We have by now discussed most of the points of interest concerning the asymptotic properties of the nonlinear least squares estimator. In this section, we wish to discuss the properties of the **NLS residuals**, that is, the sequence $\{y_t-\hat{x}_t\}$. These properties are important for a variety of reasons, not least because the residuals will be used to estimate the error variance σ^2.

In order to obtain the asymptotic properties of the NLS residuals, we begin by making a Taylor expansion of a typical residual around $\boldsymbol{\beta}=\boldsymbol{\beta}_0$.

This expansion is

$$\begin{aligned}\hat{u}_t \equiv y_t - x_t(\hat{\boldsymbol{\beta}}) &= y_t - x_{0t} - \boldsymbol{X}_t^*(\hat{\boldsymbol{\beta}} - \boldsymbol{\beta}_0) \\ &= u_t - \boldsymbol{X}_t^*(\hat{\boldsymbol{\beta}} - \boldsymbol{\beta}_0),\end{aligned} \tag{5.51}$$

where, as usual, $\boldsymbol{X}_t^* \equiv \boldsymbol{X}_t(\boldsymbol{\beta}^*)$ for some convex combination $\boldsymbol{\beta}^*$ of $\hat{\boldsymbol{\beta}}$ and $\boldsymbol{\beta}_0$. Under the conditions of Theorem 5.2, $\hat{\boldsymbol{\beta}} - \boldsymbol{\beta}_0 = O(n^{-1/2})$. Thus we can conclude immediately that

$$\hat{u}_t = u_t + O(n^{-1/2}), \tag{5.52}$$

which implies that the residuals consistently estimate the actual disturbances.

The simple result (5.52) is immensely valuable, but it is not detailed enough for all purposes. To see why not, consider the expression

$$n^{-1/2}\boldsymbol{a}^\top \hat{\boldsymbol{u}} = n^{-1/2}\sum_{t=1}^{n} a_t \hat{u}_t \tag{5.53}$$

for some vector $\boldsymbol{a}$ with elements forming a nonstochastic sequence $\{a_t\}$. If each a_t is of order unity, then substituting (5.52) into (5.53) shows that the latter is equal to

$$n^{-1/2}\sum_{t=1}^{n} a_t u_t + n^{-1/2}\sum_{t=1}^{n} O(n^{-1/2}). \tag{5.54}$$

If a central limit theorem applies to the first term of (5.54), then this term is of order unity. But the second term is also of order unity, on account of the summation over t of n terms, and therefore cannot be ignored if we wish to elucidate the properties of (5.53). This is an extremely important result, for we will very often in asymptotic analysis be interested in quantities like (5.53). The result tells us that for such purposes we cannot ignore the distinction between the error terms u_t and the residuals $\hat{u}_t$.

For this reason, we will now obtain a refinement of the result (5.52). In order to do this, we use the main asymptotic normality result (5.39). It can be rewritten as

$$\hat{\boldsymbol{\beta}} - \boldsymbol{\beta}_0 = n^{-1/2}\Big(\big(n^{-1}\boldsymbol{X}_0^\top\boldsymbol{X}_0\big)^{-1} n^{-1/2}\boldsymbol{X}_0^\top\boldsymbol{u} + o(1)\Big). \tag{5.55}$$

Substituting (5.55) into the second line of (5.51) gives

$$\hat{u}_t = u_t - n^{-1/2}\boldsymbol{X}_t^*\big(n^{-1}\boldsymbol{X}_0^\top\boldsymbol{X}_0\big)^{-1} n^{-1/2}\boldsymbol{X}_0^\top\boldsymbol{u} + o(n^{-1/2}). \tag{5.56}$$

It should be clear that the first term is $O(1)$ and the second is $O(n^{-1/2})$. Thus (5.56) gives the first two terms in what is called the **stochastic expansion** of the residual $\hat{u}_t$. But this expansion is still unnecessarily complicated, because we have

$$\boldsymbol{X}_t^* = \boldsymbol{X}_{0t} + \boldsymbol{A}_t^*(\hat{\boldsymbol{\beta}} - \boldsymbol{\beta}_0) = \boldsymbol{X}_{0t} + O(n^{-1/2})$$

by Taylor's Theorem and the fact that $\hat{\boldsymbol{\beta}} - \boldsymbol{\beta}_0 = O(n^{-1/2})$; recall that $\boldsymbol{A}_t$ is the Hessian of the regression function $x_t(\boldsymbol{\beta})$. Thus (5.56) can be written more simply as

$$\hat{u}_t = u_t - n^{-1/2}\boldsymbol{X}_{0t}\big(n^{-1}\boldsymbol{X}_0^\top\boldsymbol{X}_0\big)^{-1}n^{-1/2}\boldsymbol{X}_0^\top\boldsymbol{u} + o(n^{-1/2}).$$

Since this is true for all t, we have the vector equation

$$\hat{\boldsymbol{u}} = \boldsymbol{u} - \boldsymbol{X}_0\big(\boldsymbol{X}_0^\top\boldsymbol{X}_0\big)^{-1}\boldsymbol{X}_0^\top\boldsymbol{u} + o(n^{-1/2}),$$

where the small-order symbol is now to be interpreted as an n–vector, each component of which is $o(n^{-1/2})$. This equation can be rewritten in terms of the projection $\boldsymbol{P}_0 \equiv \boldsymbol{X}_0(\boldsymbol{X}_0^\top\boldsymbol{X}_0)^{-1}\boldsymbol{X}_0^\top$ and its complementary projection $\boldsymbol{M}_0 \equiv \mathbf{I} - \boldsymbol{P}_0$:

$$\hat{\boldsymbol{u}} = \boldsymbol{u} - \boldsymbol{P}_0\boldsymbol{u} + o(n^{-1/2}) = \boldsymbol{M}_0\boldsymbol{u} + o(n^{-1/2}). \tag{5.57}$$

This is the asymptotic equivalent of the exact result that, for linear models, the OLS residuals are the orthogonal projection of the disturbances off the regressors. Recall that if one runs the regression $\boldsymbol{y} = \boldsymbol{X\beta} + \boldsymbol{u}$, and the DGP is indeed a special case of this model, then we have exactly that

$$\hat{\boldsymbol{u}} = \boldsymbol{M}_X\boldsymbol{u}. \tag{5.58}$$

The result (5.57) reduces to this when the model is linear. The projection matrix $\boldsymbol{M}_0$ is now equal to $\boldsymbol{M}_X$, and the $o(n^{-1/2})$ term, which was due only to the nonlinearity of $\boldsymbol{x}(\boldsymbol{\beta})$, no longer appears.

Now let us substitute the right-most expression of (5.57) into (5.53). The latter becomes

$$n^{-1/2}\boldsymbol{a}^\top\hat{\boldsymbol{u}} = n^{-1/2}\boldsymbol{a}^\top\boldsymbol{M}_0\boldsymbol{u} + n^{-1/2}\sum_{t=1}^{n} o(n^{-1/2}). \tag{5.59}$$

The first term on the right-hand side here is clearly $O(1)$, while the second is $o(1)$. Thus, in contrast to what happened when we simply replaced $\hat{u}_t$ by u_t, we can ignore the second term on the right-hand side of (5.59). So the result (5.57) provides what we need if we are to undertake asymptotic analysis of expressions like (5.53).

We should pause for a moment here in order to make clear the relation between the asymptotic result (5.57), the exact linear result (5.58), and two other results. These other results are (1.03), which states that the OLS residuals are orthogonal to the regressors, and (2.05), which we may express as $\hat{\boldsymbol{X}}^\top\hat{\boldsymbol{u}} = \mathbf{0}$, and which states that the NLS residuals are orthogonal to $\boldsymbol{X}(\hat{\boldsymbol{\beta}})$. This second pair of results yields *numerical* properties of OLS and NLS that must hold regardless of how the data were generated. In contrast, (5.57) and (5.58) are *statistical* results that hold only if the DGP actually does belong to the appropriate regression model. Both OLS and NLS perform, perfectly mechanically, what may be called an orthogonal projection; that is what the results (1.03) and (2.05) tell us. If in addition the DGP belongs to the linear or nonlinear model under consideration, this projection corresponds to the projection of the actual disturbance vector $\boldsymbol{u}$ off the subspace $\mathcal{S}(\boldsymbol{X}_0)$. It is because this projection annihilates only a fixed, finite number of directions (k in the notation we have been using) that we obtain the simple result (5.52).

The annihilated directions of $\boldsymbol{u}$, $\boldsymbol{P}_0\boldsymbol{u}$, correspond asymptotically (in the linear case, exactly) to the errors committed in estimating the parameters. To see this, we may rewrite (5.55) as

$$\hat{\boldsymbol{\beta}} - \boldsymbol{\beta}_0 \overset{a}{=} \left(\boldsymbol{X}_0^\top\boldsymbol{X}_0\right)^{-1}\boldsymbol{X}_0^\top\boldsymbol{u}, \tag{5.60}$$

whence

$$\boldsymbol{X}_0(\hat{\boldsymbol{\beta}} - \boldsymbol{\beta}_0) \overset{a}{=} \boldsymbol{P}_0\boldsymbol{u}. \tag{5.61}$$

Rewriting (5.57) using the same simplified notation, we see that

$$\hat{\boldsymbol{u}} \overset{a}{=} \boldsymbol{u} - \boldsymbol{P}_0\boldsymbol{u} = \boldsymbol{M}_0\boldsymbol{u}. \tag{5.62}$$

It is thus quite intuitive that, since the variance of the estimator $\hat{\boldsymbol{\beta}}$ tends to zero as the sample size tends to infinity, the disturbances are better and better estimated by the residuals as the sample size increases.

The asymptotic results (5.60), (5.61), and (5.62) are the essential *statistical* results on which the asymptotic study of NLS is based, if the DGP is assumed to belong to the nonlinear regression model that is estimated. Of course, if it does not, these results no longer hold. We will for the most part make this assumption, however implausible it may be. However, when we discuss what determines the power of tests in Chapter 12, we will consider what happens when the DGP *almost* belongs to the model that is estimated. And in Chapter 11, in the context of what is called nonnested hypothesis testing, we will encounter a case in which the analysis depends on the properties of least squares fitted values when the DGP does not belong to the model that is estimated at all.

One important use of the residuals $\hat{u}_t$ is to estimate the error variance σ^2. The two principal estimators that were suggested in Chapter 2 are

$$\hat{\sigma}^2 \equiv \frac{1}{n}\sum_{t=1}^{n}\big(y_t - x_t(\hat{\boldsymbol{\beta}})\big)^2 \quad \text{and}$$

$$s^2 \equiv \frac{1}{n-k}\sum_{t=1}^{n}\big(y_t - x_t(\hat{\boldsymbol{\beta}})\big)^2.$$

We will now demonstrate that both these estimators are consistent but that s^2 is preferable to $\hat{\sigma}^2$.

The fundamental asymptotic result for NLS residuals, equation (5.57), can be rewritten as

$$\hat{\boldsymbol{u}} = \boldsymbol{M}_0\boldsymbol{u} + o(n^{-1/2})\boldsymbol{a} \tag{5.63}$$

for some random n–vector $\boldsymbol{a}$, each element of which is $O(1)$. The notation here means that each element of $\boldsymbol{a}$ is multiplied by a scalar which is $o(n^{-1/2})$. Using (5.63), we see that

$$\begin{aligned}\hat{\sigma}^2 &\equiv n^{-1}\hat{\boldsymbol{u}}^\top\hat{\boldsymbol{u}} \\ &= n^{-1}\boldsymbol{u}^\top\boldsymbol{M}_0\boldsymbol{u} + 2n^{-1}o(n^{-1/2})\boldsymbol{a}^\top\boldsymbol{M}_0\boldsymbol{u} + n^{-1}o(n^{-1})\boldsymbol{a}^\top\boldsymbol{a} \\ &= n^{-1}\boldsymbol{u}^\top\boldsymbol{u} - n^{-1}\boldsymbol{u}^\top\boldsymbol{P}_0\boldsymbol{u} + 2o(n^{-3/2})\boldsymbol{a}^\top\boldsymbol{M}_0\boldsymbol{u} + o(n^{-2})\boldsymbol{a}^\top\boldsymbol{a}.\end{aligned} \tag{5.64}$$

The last line here can be used to provide several interesting results.

The first term in the last line of (5.64) is evidently $O(1)$. Moreover, since this term is just n^{-1} times the sum of n independent squared error terms, a law of large numbers will apply to it under mild regularity conditions. Thus the plim of this first term is just σ_0^2. We will show in a moment that the other three terms in the last line of (5.64) are either $O(n^{-1})$ or $o(n^{-1})$. Thus the plim of $\hat{\sigma}^2$ is simply the plim of the first term, and so we conclude that $\hat{\sigma}^2$ is consistent for σ_0^2. Because $s^2 = \big(n/(n-k)\big)\hat{\sigma}^2$ and the plim of $n/(n-k)$ is unity, s^2 is evidently also a consistent estimator.

The second term in the last line of (5.64) can be rewritten as

$$n^{-1}\big(n^{-1/2}\boldsymbol{u}^\top\boldsymbol{X}_0\big)\big(n^{-1}\boldsymbol{X}_0^\top\boldsymbol{X}_0\big)^{-1}\big(n^{-1/2}\boldsymbol{X}_0^\top\boldsymbol{u}\big).$$

This is n^{-1} times the product of three factors, each of which is $O(1)$, which implies that the second term as a whole must be $O(n^{-1})$.

The third and fourth terms are of even lower order. The fourth term is easy to deal with. The quantity $\boldsymbol{a}^\top\boldsymbol{a}$ must be $O(n)$, because it is simply the sum of n squares, each of which is $O(1)$. Thus the fourth term is evidently $o(n^{-1})$. If the components of the vector $\boldsymbol{a}$ were nonstochastic, it would be equally easy to deal with the third term. By arguments similar to the ones used in connection with (5.59), one could show that $2n^{-1}\boldsymbol{a}^\top\boldsymbol{M}_0\boldsymbol{u}$ was $O(n^{-1/2})$. It would then follow immediately that the third term was $o(n^{-1})$. The problem is that the vector $\boldsymbol{a}$ is not in fact nonstochastic, since it will depend on $\hat{\boldsymbol{\beta}}$. It is nevertheless possible to prove that the third term in the last line of (5.64) is indeed of order less than n^{-1}. The proof requires a second-order Taylor expansion of $\hat{u}_t \equiv y_t - x_t(\hat{\boldsymbol{\beta}})$ around $\boldsymbol{\beta}_0$ and makes use of the fundamental result (5.39). We leave it as an exercise for the interested reader.

Using the above results on the orders of the four terms in the last line of (5.64), we can now compare the properties of $\hat{\sigma}^2$ and s^2 to order n^{-1}.

We have already seen that both these estimators are consistent. Using familiar techniques, similar to those used in (3.08), it is easy to show that $E(n^{-1}\boldsymbol{u}^{\top}\boldsymbol{P}_0\boldsymbol{u}) = (k/n)\sigma_0^2$. Therefore, to order n^{-1},

$$E(\hat{\sigma}^2) = \frac{n-k}{n}\,\sigma_0^2.$$

Thus, as we already knew, $\hat{\sigma}^2$ is biased downward. In contrast, it is easy to see that, to the same order, s^2 is unbiased. This result strongly suggests that one should employ s^2 rather than $\hat{\sigma}^2$ when estimating the variance of the error terms of a nonlinear regression model, just as one would do in the case of a linear model. Of course, the fact that s^2 is unbiased to order n^{-1} does not imply that it will have no bias at all. It will, in general, be biased to lower order than n^{-1}.

The proof of the consistency of s^2 (or $\hat{\sigma}^2$) was very different from the proof for $\hat{\boldsymbol{\beta}}$, because although σ^2 is a parameter of the nonlinear regression model, it is not an argument of the sum-of-squares function. As we mentioned earlier, the parameter σ^2 is not *identified*, asymptotically or otherwise, by the NLS procedure. Consequently, a quite different estimation strategy, in fact a thoroughly ad hoc one, has to be used. One unfortunate consequence of this ad hoc method is that no estimate of the variance of s^2 is automatically provided, and so statistical inference on σ^2 is as yet impossible. In fact, in order for it to be possible, it would be necessary to know or be able to estimate the fourth moment of the disturbances u_t, as can be seen from the following argument. We construct, by analogy with results for the estimator $\hat{\boldsymbol{\beta}}$, the random variable $n^{1/2}(s^2-\sigma_0^2)$. From (5.64) and the arguments that follow it, we conclude that $\hat{\boldsymbol{u}}^{\top}\hat{\boldsymbol{u}} = \boldsymbol{u}^{\top}\boldsymbol{u} + O(1)$. Thus we can write

$$n^{1/2}(s^2-\sigma_0^2) = n^{-1/2}\sum_{t=1}^{n}(u_t^2-\sigma_0^2) + O(n^{-1/2}).$$

Since one can immediately apply a central limit theorem to the first term on the right-hand side of this relation, we can in fact conclude that s^2 is asymptotically normal. But the asymptotic variance is just $\mathrm{Var}(u_t^2)$, and in order to calculate that we would need to know the fourth moment of u_t.

The fourth moment of u_t could of course be estimated, but we will not pursue this possibility here. The important point for now is that σ^2 is not a parameter of the nonlinear regression model in the usual sense, and one must therefore leave the nonlinear regression context if one wishes to perform statistical inference on σ^2. As there are other estimation methods than NLS, for which σ^2 does not have this special status, this point should be kept in mind when working with NLS. One of these other methods is of course that of maximum likelihood, and when we come in Chapters 8 and 9 to look at regression models from the perspective of that method, we will see that assumptions about the distribution of the disturbances, of a sort not made in the purely NLS context, are indeed necessary.

5.7 Test Statistics Based on NLS Estimates

In this section, we provide proofs of some of the results in Section 3.6 about the asymptotic distributions of test statistics based on NLS estimates. Most of the results turn out to be immediate consequences of the asymptotic normality of the NLS estimator, the form (5.25) of its limiting covariance matrix, and the consistency of $\hat{\sigma}^2$.

We will generalize slightly over the treatment given in Section 3.6 by considering a set of *nonlinear* restrictions on the parameters $\boldsymbol{\beta}$ of a nonlinear regression model. We may write these restrictions as

$$\boldsymbol{r}(\boldsymbol{\beta}) = \mathbf{0}, \tag{5.65}$$

where the number of restrictions is r $(< k)$, and the (at least) twice continuously differentiable mapping $\boldsymbol{r}$ acts from the parameter space Θ to $\mathbb{R}^r$. We will denote the $r \times k$ Jacobian of $\boldsymbol{r}(\boldsymbol{\beta})$ by the matrix $\boldsymbol{R}(\boldsymbol{\beta})$ and assume that this matrix has full rank r. If it did not, either some of the restrictions would be redundant or the set of restrictions would be impossible to satisfy. If $\boldsymbol{R}(\boldsymbol{\beta})$ is evaluated at $\boldsymbol{\beta}_0$, the parameter vector corresponding to the DGP, we will as usual write $\boldsymbol{R}_0$ for $\boldsymbol{R}(\boldsymbol{\beta}_0)$. Since we assume that the DGP satisfies the restrictions, $\boldsymbol{r}_0 \equiv \boldsymbol{r}(\boldsymbol{\beta}_0) = \mathbf{0}$.

The easiest test statistic to deal with is the Wald statistic, expression (3.41). For the nonlinear restrictions (5.65), it may be written as

$$\frac{1}{\hat{\sigma}^2}\hat{\boldsymbol{r}}^{\top}\big(\hat{\boldsymbol{R}}(\hat{\boldsymbol{X}}^{\top}\hat{\boldsymbol{X}})^{-1}\hat{\boldsymbol{R}}^{\top}\big)^{-1}\hat{\boldsymbol{r}}, \tag{5.66}$$

where, as usual, $\hat{\boldsymbol{r}} \equiv \boldsymbol{r}(\hat{\boldsymbol{\beta}})$, $\hat{\boldsymbol{X}} \equiv \boldsymbol{X}(\hat{\boldsymbol{\beta}})$, and $\hat{\boldsymbol{R}} \equiv \boldsymbol{R}(\hat{\boldsymbol{\beta}})$. We now need to make a Taylor expansion around $\boldsymbol{\beta}_0$ of the quantities appearing in (5.66). We will first treat a single component of the vector-valued function $\boldsymbol{r}(\boldsymbol{\beta})$, as follows:

$$r_i(\hat{\boldsymbol{\beta}}) = r_i(\boldsymbol{\beta}_0) + \boldsymbol{R}_{i.}(\boldsymbol{\beta}_0)(\hat{\boldsymbol{\beta}} - \boldsymbol{\beta}_0) + \tfrac{1}{2}(\hat{\boldsymbol{\beta}} - \boldsymbol{\beta}_0)^{\top}\big(D^2 r_i(\boldsymbol{\beta}^*)\big)(\hat{\boldsymbol{\beta}} - \boldsymbol{\beta}_0), \tag{5.67}$$

where $\boldsymbol{R}_{i.}$ denotes the ith row of the Jacobian $\boldsymbol{R}$, and $D^2 r_i$ denotes the $k \times k$ Hessian of r_i. As usual in a short Taylor expansion, $\boldsymbol{\beta}^*$ is some convex combination of $\hat{\boldsymbol{\beta}}$ and $\boldsymbol{\beta}_0$. Because $\hat{\boldsymbol{\beta}} - \boldsymbol{\beta}_0 = O(n^{-1/2})$, the second and third terms on the right-hand side of (5.67) are $O(n^{-1/2})$ and $O(n^{-1})$, respectively. Since $r_i(\boldsymbol{\beta}_0)$ is zero by (5.65), we may multiply (5.67) by $n^{1/2}$ to obtain an equation in which the terms of leading order are $O(1)$. If we work only to leading order, we can treat the whole vector $\boldsymbol{r}$ at once and obtain

$$n^{1/2}\boldsymbol{r}(\hat{\boldsymbol{\beta}}) = \boldsymbol{R}_0 n^{1/2}(\hat{\boldsymbol{\beta}} - \boldsymbol{\beta}_0) + O(n^{-1/2}). \tag{5.68}$$

The first term on the right-hand side of (5.68) is just a linearization of $\boldsymbol{r}(\hat{\boldsymbol{\beta}})$. If the restrictions were linear, (5.68) would be true without the $O(n^{-1/2})$

term. The sort of result displayed in (5.68) occurs very frequently. The *twice* continuous differentiability of $\boldsymbol{r}(\boldsymbol{\beta})$ means that Taylor's Theorem can be applied to order two, and then it is possible to discover from the last term in that expansion exactly the order of the error, in this case $O(n^{-1})$, committed by neglecting it. In future we will not be explicit about this reasoning and will simply mention that twice continuous differentiability gives a result similar to (5.68).

The quantities in (5.66) other than $\hat{\boldsymbol{r}}$ are **asymptotically nonstochastic**. By this we mean that

$$\hat{\boldsymbol{R}} = \boldsymbol{R}_0 + O(n^{-1/2}) \quad \text{and} \quad \hat{\boldsymbol{X}} = \boldsymbol{X}_0 + O(n^{-1/2}). \tag{5.69}$$

Again, a short Taylor-series argument, this time only to first order, produces these results. They are to be interpreted component by component for the matrices $\boldsymbol{R}$ and $\boldsymbol{X}$. This is not a matter of consequence for the $r \times k$ matrix $\boldsymbol{R}$, but it is for the $n \times k$ matrix $\boldsymbol{X}$. We have to be careful because in matrix products like $\hat{\boldsymbol{X}}^\top\hat{\boldsymbol{X}}$ we run across sums of n terms, which will of course have different orders in general from the terms of the sums. However, if we explicitly use the fact that $\hat{\boldsymbol{r}} = O(n^{-1/2})$ to rewrite (5.66) as

$$\left(n^{1/2}\hat{\boldsymbol{r}}\right)^\top\left(\hat{\sigma}^2\hat{\boldsymbol{R}}(n^{-1}\hat{\boldsymbol{X}}^\top\hat{\boldsymbol{X}})^{-1}\hat{\boldsymbol{R}}^\top\right)^{-1}\left(n^{1/2}\hat{\boldsymbol{r}}\right), \tag{5.70}$$

we see that we are concerned, not with $\hat{\boldsymbol{X}}^\top\hat{\boldsymbol{X}}$ itself, but rather with $n^{-1}\hat{\boldsymbol{X}}^\top\hat{\boldsymbol{X}}$, and the latter *is* asymptotically nonstochastic:

$$\begin{aligned}
n^{-1}(\hat{\boldsymbol{X}}^\top\hat{\boldsymbol{X}})_{ij} &= n^{-1}\sum_{t=1}^{n}\hat{X}_{ti}\hat{X}_{tj} \\
&= n^{-1}\sum_{t=1}^{n}\left(X_{ti}^0 + O(n^{-1/2})\right)\left(X_{tj}^0 + O(n^{-1/2})\right) \\
&= n^{-1}\sum_{t=1}^{n}\left(X_{ti}^0X_{tj}^0 + O(n^{-1/2})\right) \\
&= n^{-1}(\boldsymbol{X}_0^\top\boldsymbol{X}_0)_{ij} + O(n^{-1/2}),
\end{aligned}$$

where X_{ti}^0 denotes the ti^{th} element of $\boldsymbol{X}_0$. The second line uses (5.69). The third line follows because the sum of n terms of order $n^{-1/2}$ can be at most of order $n^{1/2}$; when divided by n, it becomes of order $n^{-1/2}$. Note that $n^{-1}\boldsymbol{X}_0^\top\boldsymbol{X}_0$ itself is $O(1)$.

Next, we use the asymptotic normality result (5.39) to obtain a more convenient expression for $n^{1/2}\hat{\boldsymbol{r}}$. We have

$$n^{-1/2}\hat{\boldsymbol{r}} = \boldsymbol{R}_0\left(n^{-1}\boldsymbol{X}_0^\top\boldsymbol{X}_0\right)^{-1}n^{-1/2}\boldsymbol{X}_0^\top\boldsymbol{u} + o(1). \tag{5.71}$$

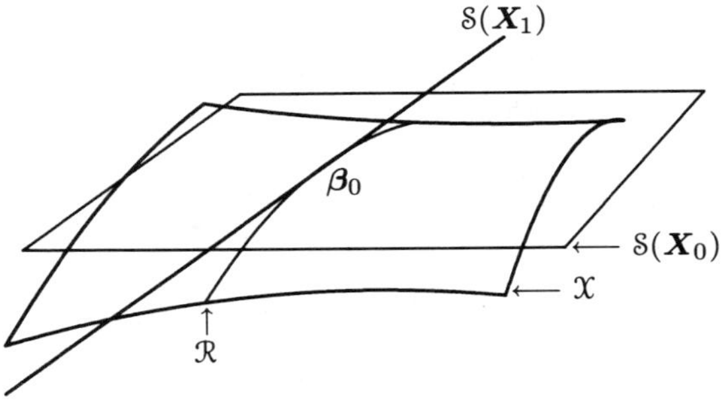

Figure 5.1 The linear subspace $\mathcal{S}(\boldsymbol{X}_1)$ of $\mathcal{S}(\boldsymbol{X}_0)$

If we substitute (5.71) into (5.70) and use the facts that $\hat{\boldsymbol{R}}$ and $n^{-1}\hat{\boldsymbol{X}}^\top\hat{\boldsymbol{X}}$ are asymptotically nonstochastic, and that $\hat{\sigma}^2$ tends in probability to σ_0^2, the Wald statistic is seen to be asymptotically equivalent to

$$\sigma_0^{-2}\boldsymbol{u}^\top\boldsymbol{X}_0(\boldsymbol{X}_0^\top\boldsymbol{X}_0)^{-1}\boldsymbol{R}_0^\top\big(\boldsymbol{R}_0(\boldsymbol{X}_0^\top\boldsymbol{X}_0)^{-1}\boldsymbol{R}_0^\top\big)^{-1}\boldsymbol{R}_0(\boldsymbol{X}_0^\top\boldsymbol{X}_0)^{-1}\boldsymbol{X}_0^\top\boldsymbol{u}.$$

It is easy to see that this is just

$$\sigma_0^{-2}\boldsymbol{u}^\top\boldsymbol{P}_2\boldsymbol{u}, \tag{5.72}$$

where $\boldsymbol{P}_2$ is the orthogonal projection onto the span of the r columns of the matrix $\boldsymbol{X}_0(\boldsymbol{X}_0^\top\boldsymbol{X}_0)^{-1}\boldsymbol{R}_0^\top$. This orthogonal projection has a very interesting geometrical and statistical interpretation, which we now present. It will account for the seemingly odd choice of the index 2 in $\boldsymbol{P}_2$.

Consider first the linear subspace $\mathcal{S}(\boldsymbol{X}_0)$, which is the range of the projection $\boldsymbol{P}_0$. This subspace has dimension k, the dimensionality of the entire unrestricted parameter space Θ, since it is the tangent space to the curved k–dimensional manifold $\mathcal{X}$ generated by the variation of the k-dimensional parameter vector $\boldsymbol{\beta}$ at the point $\mathcal{X}(\boldsymbol{\beta}_0)$. (See the discussion of Figure 2.2 for a reminder of this notation.)

We may define a submanifold $\mathcal{R}$ of $\mathcal{X}$, of dimension $k-r$, by restricting the variation of $\boldsymbol{\beta}$ to values that satisfy the restrictions (5.65). In particular, the point $\mathcal{X}(\boldsymbol{\beta}_0)$ belongs to $\mathcal{R}$ because we have supposed that $\boldsymbol{\beta}_0$ satisfies the restrictions. This submanifold, like $\mathcal{X}$ itself, has a tangent space at $\mathcal{X}(\boldsymbol{\beta}_0)$, which is a (linear) subspace of the full tangent space $\mathcal{S}(\boldsymbol{X}_0)$. We will let $\mathcal{S}(\boldsymbol{X}_1)$ denote this restricted tangent space and $\boldsymbol{P}_1$ denote the orthogonal projection onto it.[6] The manifolds $\mathcal{X}$ and $\mathcal{R}$, with the tangent spaces $\mathcal{S}(\boldsymbol{X}_0)$ and $\mathcal{S}(\boldsymbol{X}_1)$, are depicted in Figure 5.1.

[6] Our notation here differs from that which is often used in connection with tests of hypotheses. It is not uncommon to let H_0 denote the null hypothesis and H_1 denote the alternative hypothesis. If that convention were adopted, all of the 0 and 1 subscripts would be interchanged.

Algebraically, the tangent space $\mathcal{S}(\boldsymbol{X}_0)$ can be characterized as the set of all linear combinations of the columns of the matrix $\boldsymbol{X}_0$. All vectors in the subspace $\mathcal{S}(\boldsymbol{X}_1)$ are necessarily such linear combinations. Suppose then that for some $k \times 1$ vector $\boldsymbol{b}$ the vector $\boldsymbol{X}_0\boldsymbol{b}$ lies in $\mathcal{S}(\boldsymbol{X}_1)$. We now show this can be so if and only if $\boldsymbol{b}$ satisfies the relation $\boldsymbol{R}_0\boldsymbol{b} = \mathbf{0}$.

Suppose that $\boldsymbol{\beta}_1$ obeys the restrictions (5.65) and is close to $\boldsymbol{\beta}_0$. Then, by a short Taylor expansion,

$$\boldsymbol{x}(\boldsymbol{\beta}_1) = \boldsymbol{x}(\boldsymbol{\beta}_0) + \boldsymbol{X}^*(\boldsymbol{\beta}_1 - \boldsymbol{\beta}_0), \tag{5.73}$$

where $\boldsymbol{X}^* \equiv \boldsymbol{X}(\boldsymbol{\beta}^*)$ and, as usual, $\boldsymbol{\beta}^*$ is a convex combination of $\boldsymbol{\beta}_0$ and $\boldsymbol{\beta}_1$. If we let $\boldsymbol{\beta}_1$ approach $\boldsymbol{\beta}_0$ through values that always satisfy (5.65), then the tangent at $\mathcal{X}(\boldsymbol{\beta}_0)$ to the curve along which $\boldsymbol{\beta}_1$ moves toward $\boldsymbol{\beta}_0$ is the limit, as $\|\boldsymbol{\beta}_1 - \boldsymbol{\beta}_0\| \to \mathbf{0}$, of the n-vector

$$\frac{\boldsymbol{x}(\boldsymbol{\beta}_1) - \boldsymbol{x}(\boldsymbol{\beta}_0)}{\|\boldsymbol{\beta}_1 - \boldsymbol{\beta}_0\|}.$$

By (5.73), this limit is just $\boldsymbol{X}_0\boldsymbol{b}$, where we define $\boldsymbol{b}$ as the k-vector that is the limit of $(\boldsymbol{\beta}_1 - \boldsymbol{\beta}_0)/\|\boldsymbol{\beta}_1 - \boldsymbol{\beta}_0\|$ as $\boldsymbol{\beta}_1$ tends to $\boldsymbol{\beta}_0$. Thus $\boldsymbol{b}$ is just the limit of a unit vector in the direction of the line segment joining $\boldsymbol{\beta}_0$ and $\boldsymbol{\beta}_1$.

Since $\boldsymbol{r}(\boldsymbol{\beta}_1) = \mathbf{0}$, another short Taylor expansion gives

$$\mathbf{0} = \boldsymbol{R}(\boldsymbol{\beta}^*)(\boldsymbol{\beta}_1 - \boldsymbol{\beta}_0).$$

If we again let $\boldsymbol{\beta}_1$ tend to $\boldsymbol{\beta}_0$ as above, a calculation exactly similar to the one above shows that $\boldsymbol{R}_0\boldsymbol{b} = \mathbf{0}$. Thus tangents to all curves that lie in $\mathcal{R}$ and that pass through $\mathcal{X}(\boldsymbol{\beta}_0)$ can be expressed as $\boldsymbol{X}_0\boldsymbol{b}$ for a k-vector $\boldsymbol{b}$ that satisfies $\boldsymbol{R}_0\boldsymbol{b} = \mathbf{0}$. One can easily check that the argument just given runs equally well in the opposite direction, and it follows that the condition $\boldsymbol{R}_0\boldsymbol{b} = \mathbf{0}$ is necessary and sufficient for $\boldsymbol{X}_0\boldsymbol{b}$ to lie in $\mathcal{S}(\boldsymbol{X}_1)$. Notice that $\mathcal{S}(\boldsymbol{X}_1)$ can also be expressed in terms of the projection $\boldsymbol{P}_1$, as $\mathcal{S}(\boldsymbol{P}_1)$.

If $\boldsymbol{R}_0\boldsymbol{b} = \mathbf{0}$, the vector $\boldsymbol{X}_0\boldsymbol{b}$ is orthogonal to all the columns of the matrix

$$\boldsymbol{X}_0\big(\boldsymbol{X}_0^{\top}\boldsymbol{X}_0\big)^{-1}\boldsymbol{R}_0^{\top}$$

and thus to every vector in $\mathcal{S}(\boldsymbol{P}_2)$. This is straightforward to show, since

$$\boldsymbol{R}_0\big(\boldsymbol{X}_0^{\top}\boldsymbol{X}_0\big)^{-1}\boldsymbol{X}_0^{\top}\boldsymbol{X}_0\boldsymbol{b} = \boldsymbol{R}_0\boldsymbol{b} = \mathbf{0}.$$

Thus the two subspaces $\mathcal{S}(\boldsymbol{P}_1)$ and $\mathcal{S}(\boldsymbol{P}_2)$ are orthogonal to each other. These are both subspaces of $\mathcal{S}(\boldsymbol{X}_0)$, of dimensions $k - r$ and r, respectively. Since $\mathcal{S}(\boldsymbol{X}_0)$ itself is of dimension k, it follows that the orthogonal projection onto it is the sum of the other two:

$$\boldsymbol{P}_0 = \boldsymbol{P}_1 + \boldsymbol{P}_2.$$

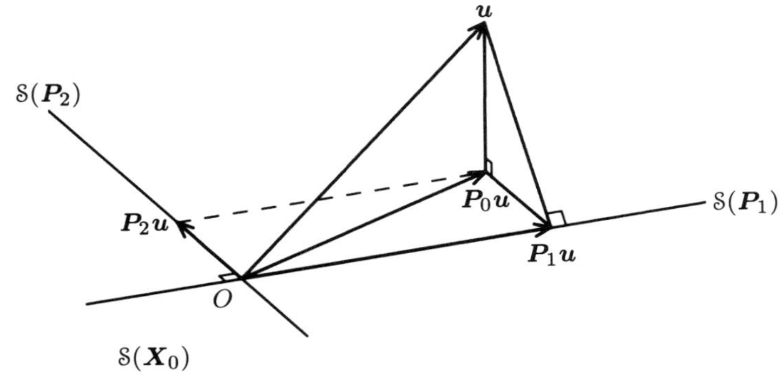

Figure 5.2 The projections leading to the Wald test

Using this result and (5.72), we can obtain another expression for the random variable that the Wald test statistic tends to asymptotically:

$$\begin{aligned} \sigma_0^{-2}\boldsymbol{u}^\top\boldsymbol{P}_2\boldsymbol{u} &= \sigma_0^{-2}\boldsymbol{u}^\top(\boldsymbol{P}_0-\boldsymbol{P}_1)\boldsymbol{u} \\ &= \sigma_0^{-2}\big\|(\boldsymbol{P}_0-\boldsymbol{P}_1)\boldsymbol{u}\big\|^2 = \sigma_0^{-2}\big\|\boldsymbol{P}_0\boldsymbol{u}-\boldsymbol{P}_1\boldsymbol{u}\big\|^2. \end{aligned} \tag{5.74}$$

This result, which is illustrated in Figure 5.2, is quite illuminating. The vector $\boldsymbol{P}_0\boldsymbol{u}$ is the projection of the error vector $\boldsymbol{u}$ onto $\mathcal{S}(\boldsymbol{X}_0)$. It is $\boldsymbol{P}_0\boldsymbol{u}$ that gives rise to the estimation error in the NLS estimates $\hat{\boldsymbol{\beta}}$: If $\boldsymbol{P}_0\boldsymbol{u} = \boldsymbol{0}$, we would have $\hat{\boldsymbol{\beta}} = \boldsymbol{\beta}_0$ and consequently no estimation error. The vector $\boldsymbol{P}_1\boldsymbol{u}$ is the projection of $\boldsymbol{u}$, and also of $\boldsymbol{P}_0\boldsymbol{u}$, onto $\mathcal{S}(\boldsymbol{P}_1)$, the $(k-r)$-dimensional subspace of $\mathcal{S}(\boldsymbol{X}_0)$ that corresponds to the restrictions. This vector is responsible for the part of the estimation error that does not violate the restrictions (5.65). The other part of $\boldsymbol{P}_0\boldsymbol{u}$ is the difference $(\boldsymbol{P}_0 - \boldsymbol{P}_1)\boldsymbol{u} = \boldsymbol{P}_2\boldsymbol{u}$, which is orthogonal to the subspace $\mathcal{S}(\boldsymbol{X}_0)$. This part of the estimation error leads to an unrestricted estimate that in general fails to satisfy (5.65). The random variable (5.74) is seen to be just the squared length of this component of the estimation error, normalized by the variance of the u_t's. Provided the true value $\boldsymbol{\beta}_0$ satisfies the restrictions (5.65), the variable (5.74) should therefore be distributed as chi-squared with r degrees of freedom. However, if $\boldsymbol{x}(\boldsymbol{\beta}_0)$ does not belong to the restricted manifold $\mathcal{R}$, the variable will contain a nonrandom term corresponding to the squared distance between $\boldsymbol{x}(\boldsymbol{\beta}_0)$ and $\mathcal{R}$ and will consequently be larger.

The second test statistic is the Lagrange multiplier, or LM, statistic, which is expression (3.47) in its LM form and (3.48) in its score form. Since these two forms of the LM statistic are numerically identical, we will concern ourselves only with the latter.

Note first that, by analogy with (5.62), the residuals $\tilde{\boldsymbol{u}} \equiv \boldsymbol{y} - \boldsymbol{x}(\tilde{\boldsymbol{\beta}})$ from the restricted estimation satisfy

$$\tilde{\boldsymbol{u}} \overset{a}{=} \boldsymbol{M}_1\boldsymbol{u}, \tag{5.75}$$

since $\boldsymbol{P}_1$ plays the same role for the manifold $\mathcal{R}$ as does $\boldsymbol{P}_0$ for $\mathcal{X}$. The LM statistic (3.48) is

$$\frac{1}{\tilde{\sigma}^2}(\boldsymbol{y}-\tilde{\boldsymbol{x}})^\top \tilde{\boldsymbol{P}}_X(\boldsymbol{y}-\tilde{\boldsymbol{x}}). \tag{5.76}$$

If we express the statistic in terms of quantities that are $O(1)$, we obtain

$$\frac{1}{\tilde{\sigma}^2} n^{-1/2}(\boldsymbol{y}-\tilde{\boldsymbol{x}})^\top \tilde{\boldsymbol{X}}\big(n^{-1}\tilde{\boldsymbol{X}}^\top\tilde{\boldsymbol{X}}\big)^{-1} n^{-1/2}\tilde{\boldsymbol{X}}^\top(\boldsymbol{y}-\tilde{\boldsymbol{x}}). \tag{5.77}$$

Like $\hat{\boldsymbol{X}}_t$, $\tilde{\boldsymbol{X}}_t$ is asymptotically nonstochastic. Therefore, from (5.75),

$$\begin{aligned}
n^{-1/2}\tilde{\boldsymbol{X}}^\top(\boldsymbol{y}-\tilde{\boldsymbol{x}}) &= n^{-1/2}\sum_{t=1}^{n}\tilde{\boldsymbol{X}}_t^\top \tilde{u}_t \\
&= n^{-1/2}\sum_{t=1}^{n}\boldsymbol{X}_{0t}^\top(\boldsymbol{M}_1\boldsymbol{u})_t + o(1) \\
&= n^{-1/2}\sum_{t=1}^{n}(\boldsymbol{M}_1\boldsymbol{X}_0)_t u_t + o(1) \\
&= n^{-1/2}\boldsymbol{X}_0^\top\boldsymbol{M}_1\boldsymbol{u} + o(1).
\end{aligned}$$

The matrix $n^{-1}\tilde{\boldsymbol{X}}^\top\tilde{\boldsymbol{X}}$ is asymptotically nonstochastic, just as $n^{-1}\hat{\boldsymbol{X}}^\top\hat{\boldsymbol{X}}$ is, and so the LM statistic (5.77) is asymptotically equivalent to

$$\boldsymbol{u}^\top\boldsymbol{M}_1\boldsymbol{X}_0\big(\sigma_0^2\boldsymbol{X}_0^\top\boldsymbol{X}_0\big)^{-1}\boldsymbol{X}_0\boldsymbol{M}_1\boldsymbol{u} = \sigma_0^{-2}\boldsymbol{u}^\top\boldsymbol{M}_1\boldsymbol{P}_0\boldsymbol{M}_1\boldsymbol{u}. \tag{5.78}$$

Since $\mathcal{S}(\boldsymbol{X}_1)$ is a subspace of $\mathcal{S}(\boldsymbol{X}_0)$, we have $\boldsymbol{P}_1\boldsymbol{P}_0 = \boldsymbol{P}_0\boldsymbol{P}_1 = \boldsymbol{P}_1$, from which it follows that $\boldsymbol{M}_1\boldsymbol{P}_0\boldsymbol{M}_1 = \boldsymbol{P}_0 - \boldsymbol{P}_1$. Expression (5.78) thus becomes

$$\sigma_0^{-2}\boldsymbol{u}^\top(\boldsymbol{P}_0-\boldsymbol{P}_1)\boldsymbol{u} = \sigma_0^{-2}\boldsymbol{u}^\top\boldsymbol{P}_2\boldsymbol{u}. \tag{5.79}$$

Comparison of (5.79) with (5.72) shows that the LM statistic is asymptotically equal to the Wald statistic. Thus it too is asymptotically $\chi^2(r)$ under the null hypothesis.

The third of the three test statistics discussed in Section 3.6 was the one based on the likelihood ratio principle, the pseudo-F statistic (3.50). Since we are interested in asymptotic results only, we rewrite it here in a form in which it should be asymptotically distributed as $\chi^2(r)$:

$$\frac{1}{s^2}\big(SSR(\tilde{\boldsymbol{\beta}}) - SSR(\hat{\boldsymbol{\beta}})\big) \tag{5.80}$$

and will (somewhat loosely) refer to it as the LR statistic. We have already seen that $s^2 \to \sigma_0^2$ as $n\to\infty$. It remains to show that $SSR(\tilde{\boldsymbol{\beta}}) - SSR(\hat{\boldsymbol{\beta}})$, when divided by σ_0^2, is asymptotically $\chi^2(r)$. From (5.64), we have

$$\hat{\sigma}^2 = \frac{1}{n}\boldsymbol{u}^\top\boldsymbol{M}_0\boldsymbol{u} + o(n^{-1}),$$

from which we obtain, after multiplying by n,

$$SSR(\hat{\boldsymbol{\beta}}) = \boldsymbol{u}^{\top}\boldsymbol{M}_0\boldsymbol{u} + o(1).$$

The analogous result for the restricted sum of squares is

$$SSR(\tilde{\boldsymbol{\beta}}) = \boldsymbol{u}^{\top}\boldsymbol{M}_1\boldsymbol{u} + o(1),$$

and so, to leading order asymptotically, expression (5.80) becomes

$$\sigma_0^{-2}\boldsymbol{u}^{\top}(\boldsymbol{M}_1 - \boldsymbol{M}_0)\boldsymbol{u} = \sigma_0^{-2}\boldsymbol{u}^{\top}(\boldsymbol{P}_0 - \boldsymbol{P}_1)\boldsymbol{u} = \sigma_0^{-2}\boldsymbol{u}^{\top}\boldsymbol{P}_2\boldsymbol{u}. \tag{5.81}$$

The right-most expression in (5.81) is precisely the random variable on the right-hand side of (5.79) and the first expression in (5.74), which we previously showed were asymptotically equivalent to the LM statistic and the Wald statistic, respectively. Thus we conclude not only that the statistic (5.80) is asymptotically distributed as $\chi^2(r)$ but also that it is asymptotically the same random variable as the other two test statistics.

We may now collect the results of this section into a theorem:

Theorem 5.4.

For a nonlinear regression model (5.08) subject to nonlinear restrictions (5.65), where both the restricted estimates $\tilde{\boldsymbol{\beta}}$ and the unrestricted estimates $\hat{\boldsymbol{\beta}}$ are consistent and asymptotically normal, the Wald test statistic (5.66), the LM test statistic (5.76), and the LR test statistic (5.80) are under the null hypothesis asymptotically equal to the random variable

$$\sigma_0^{-2}\boldsymbol{u}^{\top}\boldsymbol{P}_2\boldsymbol{u},$$

which is asymptotically distributed as $\chi^2(r)$. Here $\boldsymbol{P}_2 \equiv \boldsymbol{P}_0 - \boldsymbol{P}_1$, where $\boldsymbol{P}_0$ denotes the projection onto the k-dimensional subspace $\mathcal{S}(\boldsymbol{X}_0)$, and $\boldsymbol{P}_1$ denotes the projection onto the $(k-r)$-dimensional subspace of $\mathcal{S}(\boldsymbol{X}_0)$ that corresponds to parameter variations which satisfy the restrictions.

5.8 Further Reading and Conclusion

We have in this chapter provided a reasonably full asymptotic treatment of the estimation of nonlinear regression models by nonlinear least squares. Readers seeking a treatment that is fuller, more rigorous, or based on weaker assumptions, should consult Jennrich (1969), which is a classic article on the asymptotic properties of the NLS estimator, Malinvaud (1970b), Wu (1981), or the books by White (1984), Gallant (1987), and Gallant and White (1988). The latter provide the asymptotic theory for a wide range of models of interest to econometricians. Somewhat less technical references include Amemiya

(1983), Bates and Watts (1988), and Seber and Wild (1989, Chapter 12). The analysis of this chapter depends in large measure on the fact that the NLS estimator is defined by the minimization of the sum-of-squares function. It turns out that the analysis carries over in many of its aspects to other estimators defined by the minimization or maximization of other criterion functions; see Chapter 17. Treatments that deal abstractly with estimators defined in this way may be found in Amemiya (1985, Chapter 4) and Huber (1981). When we deal with maximum likelihood estimation in Chapter 8, the results of this chapter will provide models for the derivation of similar results in another context.

TERMS AND CONCEPTS

asymptotic covariance matrix
asymptotic distribution
asymptotic efficiency
asymptotic identifiability
asymptotic normality
asymptotically nonstochastic
best linear unbiased estimator (BLUE)
characterization of DGPs, complete or partial
consistency of estimators
consistent and asymptotically linear estimator
dimension, or dimensionality
domain (of a mapping)
dynamic models
efficiency (of an estimator)
estimate (of model parameters)
estimator (of model parameters)
estimator vs. estimate
exogenous variables
explosive process
extension of a DGP to arbitrarily large samples
Gauss-Markov Theorem
identification (of parametrized model)
innovations
lagged dependent variables
model parameters
NLS residuals
parameter space
parameter-defining mapping
parametrized model
precision of estimators
range (of a mapping)
root-n consistency
rules for generating infinite stochastic processes
stochastic expansion
strictly exogenous variables
strong asymptotic identifiability

Chapter 6

The Gauss-Newton Regression

6.1 Introduction

Associated with the nonlinear regression model is an **artificial regression** called the **Gauss-Newton regression**, or **GNR**. We have already encountered a version of the Gauss-Newton regression; we used it in Section 3.6 to compute Lagrange multiplier tests for nonlinear regression models. Artificial regressions are simply linear regressions that are used as calculating devices. As we will see, many types of nonlinear models in econometrics have artificial regressions associated with them. The regressand and regressors are deliberately constructed so that when the artificial regression is run, certain of the numbers printed by the regression program are quantities which we want to compute. Much of the output from artificial regressions may be of no interest whatsoever. For example, we often run artificial regressions in which all the coefficient estimates will be equal to zero!

Artificial regressions can be used for at least five different purposes:

(i) to verify that the first-order conditions for a minimum or maximum are satisfied sufficiently accurately;

(ii) to calculate estimated covariance matrices;

(iii) to calculate test statistics after a model has been estimated subject to restrictions, without ever estimating the unrestricted model;

(iv) to calculate one-step efficient estimates;

(v) as a key part of procedures for numerical optimization that are used to find nonlinear least squares and other types of estimates.

In this chapter, we will discuss how the Gauss-Newton regression can be used in all these different ways. Later, when we encounter other artificial regressions, we will see that they may often be used in exactly the same ways as the GNR. Indeed, many of the results we obtain in this chapter will reappear several times in later chapters with different vectors and matrices substituting for those that appear here. The algebra (and the geometrical interpretation of it) will be identical in every case; only the underlying statistical model, and thus the definitions of the regressand and regressors, will change.

As in previous chapters, we will be dealing with the univariate nonlinear regression model

$$\boldsymbol{y} = \boldsymbol{x}(\boldsymbol{\beta}) + \boldsymbol{u}, \quad \boldsymbol{u} \sim \text{IID}(\mathbf{0}, \sigma^2\mathbf{I}), \tag{6.01}$$

where $\boldsymbol{X}(\boldsymbol{\beta}) \equiv \boldsymbol{D}\boldsymbol{x}(\boldsymbol{\beta})$ is an $n \times k$ matrix of which the ti^{th} element is the derivative of $x_t(\boldsymbol{\beta})$ with respect to β_i. The vector of functions $\boldsymbol{x}(\boldsymbol{\beta})$ and its matrix of derivatives $\boldsymbol{X}(\boldsymbol{\beta})$ are assumed to satisfy the conditions for consistency and asymptotic normality detailed in Theorems 5.1 and 5.2.

The easiest way to derive the Gauss-Newton regression is to take a first-order Taylor-series approximation to (6.01) around some parameter vector $\boldsymbol{\beta}^*$. This yields

$$\boldsymbol{y} = \boldsymbol{x}(\boldsymbol{\beta}^*) + \boldsymbol{X}(\boldsymbol{\beta}^*)(\boldsymbol{\beta} - \boldsymbol{\beta}^*) + \text{higher-order terms} + \boldsymbol{u}.$$

Taking $\boldsymbol{x}(\boldsymbol{\beta}^*)$ over to the left-hand side, combining the higher-order terms and the error terms $\boldsymbol{u}$ into something we will simply call "residuals," and replacing $\boldsymbol{\beta} - \boldsymbol{\beta}^*$ by an unspecified k-vector $\boldsymbol{b}$, we obtain

$$\boldsymbol{y} - \boldsymbol{x}(\boldsymbol{\beta}^*) = \boldsymbol{X}(\boldsymbol{\beta}^*)\boldsymbol{b} + \text{residuals}. \tag{6.02}$$

This is the simplest version of the Gauss-Newton regression in its generic form. The regressand looks like a vector of residuals, because it is the difference between the vector of actual values of the dependent variable and the vector of values "predicted" by the model $\boldsymbol{x}(\boldsymbol{\beta}^*)$. There are k regressors, each of which is a vector of derivatives of $\boldsymbol{x}(\boldsymbol{\beta})$ with respect to one of the elements of $\boldsymbol{\beta}$. It therefore makes sense to think of the ith regressor as being associated with β_i. As we have seen, when $\boldsymbol{x}(\boldsymbol{\beta})$ is a linear regression model with $\boldsymbol{X}$ being the matrix of independent variables, $\boldsymbol{X}(\boldsymbol{\beta})$ is simply equal to $\boldsymbol{X}$. Thus, for linear models, the GNR will have exactly the same regressors as the original model.

The properties of regression (6.02) will depend on how the parameter vector $\boldsymbol{\beta}^*$ is chosen. Let us first see what happens when $\boldsymbol{\beta}^* = \hat{\boldsymbol{\beta}}$, the unrestricted NLS estimates of $\boldsymbol{\beta}$. The Gauss-Newton regression becomes

$$\boldsymbol{y} - \hat{\boldsymbol{x}} = \hat{\boldsymbol{X}}\boldsymbol{b} + \text{residuals}, \tag{6.03}$$

where $\hat{\boldsymbol{x}} \equiv \boldsymbol{x}(\hat{\boldsymbol{\beta}})$ and $\hat{\boldsymbol{X}} \equiv \boldsymbol{X}(\hat{\boldsymbol{\beta}})$. Now recall that the first-order conditions for a minimum of the sum of squares function are

$$(\boldsymbol{y} - \hat{\boldsymbol{x}})^{\top}\hat{\boldsymbol{X}} = \mathbf{0}. \tag{6.04}$$

The OLS estimate of $\boldsymbol{b}$ from (6.03) is

$$\hat{\boldsymbol{b}} = \big(\hat{\boldsymbol{X}}^{\top}\hat{\boldsymbol{X}}\big)^{-1}\hat{\boldsymbol{X}}^{\top}(\boldsymbol{y} - \hat{\boldsymbol{x}}),$$

which, by (6.04), must equal zero. Thus, in this case, the GNR will have no explanatory power whatsoever. This may seem an uninteresting result. After all, why would anyone want to run an artificial regression all the coefficients of which are known in advance to be zero? There are in fact two very good reasons for doing so.

First of all, the GNR (6.03) provides a very easy way to check that the first-order conditions (6.04) are in fact satisfied sufficiently accurately. Given the limitations of floating-point arithmetic on digital computers, the *approximation* to $\hat{\boldsymbol{\beta}}$ that a nonlinear least squares program prints out will never satisfy the first-order conditions exactly. If the program is a good one and the data are sufficiently informative to allow $\boldsymbol{\beta}$ to be estimated with some degree of precision, then the approximate $\hat{\boldsymbol{\beta}}$ will be very close to the true $\hat{\boldsymbol{\beta}}$ and (6.04) will be almost true. As a consequence, the estimates $\hat{\boldsymbol{b}}$ from the GNR should be very close to zero, and the explanatory power of the GNR should be essentially zero. In these circumstances, one would expect the printed t statistics on $\hat{\boldsymbol{b}}$ all to be less than roughly 10^{-3} or 10^{-4} in magnitude, and the R^2 to be zero to several decimal places. It is better to look at the t statistics rather than at $\hat{\boldsymbol{b}}$ itself because the former are dimensionless quantities; some elements of $\hat{\boldsymbol{b}}$ could be quite large if the corresponding columns of $\hat{\boldsymbol{X}}$ were very small, even if the estimate of $\hat{\boldsymbol{\beta}}$ were very accurate.

If one were to run the GNR (6.03) and find that some of the t statistics on $\hat{\boldsymbol{b}}$ were greater than, say, 10^{-2}, one would have reason to doubt the validity of the reported $\hat{\boldsymbol{\beta}}$. Possibly the estimation should be done again using a tighter convergence criterion or a different algorithm (see Section 6.8 below). Or perhaps the data and model are such that an accurate estimate of $\hat{\boldsymbol{\beta}}$ is difficult or impossible to obtain, in which case one may want to estimate another, simpler model or acquire more data.

The GNR (6.03) is especially useful when an estimate of $\hat{\boldsymbol{\beta}}$ has been obtained using a nonlinear least squares program that cannot be trusted (such programs are not unknown!) or using an ad hoc procedure. Ad hoc procedures are often used when a model is only slightly nonlinear. In particular, there are a great many nonlinear models that are linear conditional on one parameter. An example is the model

$$y_t = \beta_1 + \beta_2 z_{t1} + \beta_3 z_{t2}^{\beta_4} + u_t, \tag{6.05}$$

in which z_{t1} and z_{t2} are exogenous regressors. This model is linear conditional on β_4. It is often convenient to estimate such models by searching over the single parameter that causes the nonlinearity, in this case β_4, and estimating the other parameters using ordinary least squares conditional on each value of β_4. Whether the resulting approximation to $\hat{\boldsymbol{\beta}}$ is sufficiently accurate can easily be answered by running the GNR, which in the case of (6.05) is

$$\begin{aligned} &y_t - \hat{\beta}_1 - \hat{\beta}_2 z_{t1} - \hat{\beta}_3 z_{t2}^{\hat{\beta}_4} \\ &\quad = b_1 + b_2 z_{t1} + b_3 z_{t2}^{\hat{\beta}_4} + b_4 \hat{\beta}_3 (\log z_{t2}) z_{t2}^{\hat{\beta}_4} + \text{residual}. \end{aligned} \tag{6.06}$$

If the t statistics on $\hat{b}_1$ through $\hat{b}_4$ are all sufficiently small, one can confidently accept the calculated $\hat{\boldsymbol{\beta}}$ as being sufficiently close to the NLS estimates.

In Section 1.6, we discussed techniques for detecting leverage points and influential observations in the context of OLS. In the case of a nonlinear regression model, one can apply these techniques to the GNR (6.03). The tth diagonal element of the hat matrix for the GNR is

$$\hat{h}_t \equiv \hat{\boldsymbol{X}}_t\big(\hat{\boldsymbol{X}}^\top\hat{\boldsymbol{X}}\big)^{-1}\hat{\boldsymbol{X}}_t^\top,$$

which many regression packages can compute very easily as a by-product of computing OLS estimates. Using $\hat{h}_t$, one can easily calculate

$$\left(\frac{\hat{h}_t}{1-\hat{h}_t}\right)\hat{u}_t$$

for all t. This expression is the analog of expression (1.42), and plotting it against t provides an effective way to detect influential observations. Of course, in the nonlinear case it will not be exactly equal to the change in the residual for observation t brought about by omitting that observation from the regression, as it would be if $\boldsymbol{x}(\boldsymbol{\beta})$ were linear in $\boldsymbol{\beta}$, but it will usually provide a good approximation. Thus, by applying standard techniques for detecting influential observations in linear regression models to the GNR (6.03), one can detect data problems for nonlinear regression models just as easily as for linear ones.

6.2 Computing Covariance Matrices

The second major reason to use the GNR (6.03) is to calculate the estimated covariance matrix of $\hat{\boldsymbol{\beta}}$. Recall the asymptotic result, Theorem 5.2, that for a correctly specified nonlinear regression model

$$n^{1/2}(\hat{\boldsymbol{\beta}}-\boldsymbol{\beta}_0) \overset{a}{\sim} N\big(\mathbf{0},\, \sigma_0^2(n^{-1}\boldsymbol{X}_0^\top\boldsymbol{X}_0)^{-1}\big), \tag{6.07}$$

where $\boldsymbol{X}_0 \equiv \boldsymbol{X}(\boldsymbol{\beta}_0)$. In practice, we are interested in the distribution of $\hat{\boldsymbol{\beta}}-\boldsymbol{\beta}_0$ rather than that of $n^{1/2}(\hat{\boldsymbol{\beta}}-\boldsymbol{\beta}_0)$, and so to obtain an *estimated* covariance matrix we first want to replace σ_0^2 and $(n^{-1}\boldsymbol{X}_0^\top\boldsymbol{X}_0)^{-1}$ in (6.07) by quantities that estimate them consistently, and then divide by n.

Now consider the GNR (6.03) again. The covariance matrix estimate that the regression program will print is

$$s^2\big(\hat{\boldsymbol{X}}^\top\hat{\boldsymbol{X}}\big)^{-1}, \tag{6.08}$$

where

$$s^2 \equiv \frac{(\boldsymbol{y}-\hat{\boldsymbol{x}})^\top(\boldsymbol{y}-\hat{\boldsymbol{x}})}{n-k}$$

is the OLS estimate of the regression variance from both the artificial regression (6.03) and the original nonlinear regression (6.01). Because the GNR has no explanatory power, both these regressions have exactly the same residuals.

It is obvious that s^2 consistently estimates σ_0^2 and, since $\hat{\boldsymbol{\beta}}$ consistently estimates $\boldsymbol{\beta}_0$, $n^{-1}\hat{\boldsymbol{X}}^\top\hat{\boldsymbol{X}}$ must consistently estimate $n^{-1}\boldsymbol{X}_0^\top\boldsymbol{X}_0$; see Section 5.7. Thus it is clearly reasonable to use (6.08) to estimate the covariance matrix of $\hat{\boldsymbol{\beta}} - \boldsymbol{\beta}_0$. The ordinary covariance matrix for $\hat{\boldsymbol{b}}$ printed by the least squares program will provide a perfectly valid, and very easily calculated, estimate of the covariance matrix of the NLS estimates. Especially when $\hat{\boldsymbol{\beta}}$ has been obtained by some method other than nonlinear least squares, the GNR (6.03) provides an extremely easy way to calculate an estimate of the covariance matrix of $\hat{\boldsymbol{\beta}}$; recall the model (6.05) and the associated GNR (6.06).

There is of course more than one way to estimate σ^2 consistently. One estimator that is frequently employed is

$$\hat{\sigma}^2 = \frac{1}{n}(\boldsymbol{y} - \hat{\boldsymbol{x}})^\top(\boldsymbol{y} - \hat{\boldsymbol{x}}).$$

As we will see in Chapter 8, this is the maximum likelihood estimator of σ^2. However, as was shown in Section 3.2, $\hat{\sigma}^2$ will tend to underestimate σ^2 on average. In fact, as was shown in Section 5.6, the bias of $\hat{\sigma}^2$ for nonlinear regression models is, to order $O(n^{-1})$, the same as its exact bias for linear regression models. This result essentially followed from the asymptotic result (5.57), which can be rewritten as

$$\boldsymbol{y} - \hat{\boldsymbol{x}} \stackrel{a}{=} \boldsymbol{M}_0\boldsymbol{u}, \tag{6.09}$$

where $\boldsymbol{M}_0 \equiv \mathbf{I} - \boldsymbol{X}_0(\boldsymbol{X}_0^\top\boldsymbol{X}_0)^{-1}\boldsymbol{X}_0^\top$ is the matrix that projects orthogonally onto $\mathcal{S}^\perp(\boldsymbol{X}_0)$. The result (6.09) is analogous to the finite-sample result, for linear regression models, that

$$\boldsymbol{y} - \boldsymbol{X}\hat{\boldsymbol{\beta}} = \boldsymbol{M}_X\boldsymbol{u}.$$

Thus the fact that s^2 is an unbiased estimator of σ^2 for linear regression models suggests that, in large samples, s^2 should be approximately unbiased for nonlinear models as well and should certainly be preferable to $\hat{\sigma}^2$.

Unfortunately, not all nonlinear least squares programs use s^2. One reason for running the GNR (6.03) is to see whether the estimated covariance matrix for $\hat{\boldsymbol{\beta}}$ produced by the program is actually the same as the one produced by the GNR. The two may simply differ by the factor of proportionality $(n - k)/n$, in which case one should probably use the larger of the two estimates (i.e., the one produced by the GNR). If they differ in any other way, one should regard the nonlinear least squares program with great suspicion and should certainly rely on the covariance matrix estimate from the GNR rather than the one printed by the program. There is one possible exception to this advice. Some modern packages may print a **heteroskedasticity-consistent covariance matrix estimate**, or **HCCME**, instead of the usual estimate (which assumes homoskedasticity) that we have dealt with here; see Section 16.3. In such cases, it may be quite illuminating to run the GNR and compare the two covariance matrix estimates.

6.3 Collinearity in Nonlinear Regression Models

We remarked in Section 2.3 that linear regression models which are poorly identified are often said to display **collinearity** or **multicollinearity**. The two words mean the same thing, and we therefore prefer the shorter one, even though "multicollinearity" is probably more widely used in the econometric literature. The relationship between collinearity and identification is apparent if one studies the Gauss-Newton regression. As we will now show, if a nonlinear regression model is poorly identified in the neighborhood of some parameter vector $\boldsymbol{\beta}^*$ that is not too far from $\boldsymbol{\beta}_0$ (recall that for nonlinear models, identification will generally depend on the values of the parameters), then the GNR evaluated at $\boldsymbol{\beta}^*$ will display collinearity. We will also provide an intuitive explanation of what collinearity involves in linear and nonlinear regression models.

In Section 2.3, we somewhat loosely defined a **poorly identified model** as one for which the Hessian matrix $\boldsymbol{H}(\boldsymbol{\beta})$ of the sum-of-squares function is close to being singular for interesting values of $\boldsymbol{\beta}$. We deliberately avoided any attempt to be more specific, because whether a model is poorly identified or not inevitably depends on why we care about its identifiability. A model may, for example, be badly enough identified that some nonlinear least squares programs are unable to estimate it but not so badly identified that the best such programs cannot handle it. Or a model may be well-enough identified that there is no difficulty estimating it but not well-enough identified for us to obtain parameter estimates as precise as we need.

Normally, how close a matrix is to being singular is determined by looking at its **condition number**, which is the ratio of its largest to its smallest eigenvalue. However, the condition number of $\boldsymbol{H}(\boldsymbol{\beta})$ can be changed drastically by reparametrizing the model, even when the reparametrization simply involves rescaling some of the regressors. For example, in the linear regression case, in which $\boldsymbol{x}(\boldsymbol{\beta}) = \boldsymbol{X}\boldsymbol{\beta}$, the Hessian $\boldsymbol{H}(\boldsymbol{\beta})$ is equal to $2\boldsymbol{X}^{\top}\boldsymbol{X}$. If we multiply one column of $\boldsymbol{X}$ by, say, 10^6, we will drastically change the condition number of $\boldsymbol{X}^{\top}\boldsymbol{X}$, almost certainly making it much larger unless the elements of that column of $\boldsymbol{X}$ were very small to begin with. Since this sort of simple rescaling will certainly not let us learn anything more from the data (although it may well affect the performance of nonlinear least squares algorithms), we cannot sensibly classify models as well or poorly identified on the basis of something as simple as a condition number alone.[1] In fact, there does not seem to be any purely mechanical way to decide when a model is "poorly" identified. However, as we will now see, the Gauss-Newton regression can be used to tell us when identification is likely to be a problem.

In Section 5.4, we saw that

$$n^{-1}\boldsymbol{H}(\boldsymbol{\beta}_0) \overset{a}{=} 2n^{-1}\boldsymbol{X}^{\top}(\boldsymbol{\beta}_0)\boldsymbol{X}(\boldsymbol{\beta}_0). \tag{6.10}$$

Thus, if the Hessian matrix is close to singular, we can expect the matrix $\boldsymbol{X}^{\top}(\boldsymbol{\beta})\boldsymbol{X}(\boldsymbol{\beta})$ to be close to singular as well, provided that both are evaluated at a point reasonably close to $\boldsymbol{\beta}_0$. This requirement arises because (6.10) holds only at $\boldsymbol{\beta}_0$, since that result depends on the fact that $\boldsymbol{y} - \boldsymbol{x}(\boldsymbol{\beta}_0) = \boldsymbol{u}_0$; see the discussion leading to (5.38). The continuity of $\boldsymbol{x}(\boldsymbol{\beta})$ suggests that (6.10) should be approximately true for $\boldsymbol{\beta}$ reasonably close to $\boldsymbol{\beta}_0$, however. Hence it would be most surprising if the Gauss-Newton regression failed to display collinearity when the Hessian was in fact close to singular.

As an example, consider the nonlinear regression model

$$y_t = \beta_1 + \beta_2 z_t^{\beta_3} + u_t, \tag{6.11}$$

which we previously encountered in Section 2.3. For this model, the tth row of $\boldsymbol{X}(\boldsymbol{\beta})$ is

$$\begin{bmatrix} 1 & z_t^{\beta_3} & \beta_2 z_t^{\beta_3}\log(z_t) \end{bmatrix}. \tag{6.12}$$

From this we see immediately that the matrix $\boldsymbol{X}^{\top}(\boldsymbol{\beta})\boldsymbol{X}(\boldsymbol{\beta})$ will be singular whenever either β_2 or β_3 equals zero. In the former case the third column of $\boldsymbol{X}(\boldsymbol{\beta})$ will be a column of zeros, while in the latter the second column will be indistinguishable from the column corresponding to the constant term. Thus this model is asymptotically unidentified at points where $\beta_2 = 0$ or $\beta_3 = 0$, even though it will be identified by almost all data sets.

If a model is not identified asymptotically, it is likely to be of limited interest, even if it is identified by a particular set of data, since without asymptotic identification valid inference is impossible. Moreover, if a model is not asymptotically identified at $\boldsymbol{\beta}_0$, nonlinear least squares will not yield consistent estimates. On the other hand, a model that is asymptotically identified may not be identified by a particular set of data. One would have to obtain more data in order to estimate such a model.

Even at parameter values where it is identified, that is, values other than $\beta_2 = 0$ and $\beta_3 = 0$, the model (6.11) is likely to be poorly identified. That this will usually be the case, depending on the data and parameter values, should

[1] If the matrix $\boldsymbol{X}$ were scaled in such a way that all columns had the same length—for example, unit length—it would then make sense to use the condition number of $\boldsymbol{X}^{\top}\boldsymbol{X}$ as a measure of collinearity. See Belsley, Kuh, and Welsch (1980, Chapter 3).

be clear from (6.12). The second column of $\boldsymbol{X}(\boldsymbol{\beta})$ is very similar to the third column, each element of the latter being equal to the corresponding element of the former times a constant and $\log(z_t)$. Unless the range of z_t is very great, or there are some values of z_t very close to zero, $z_t^{\beta_3}$ and $\beta_2 \log(z_t) z_t^{\beta_3}$ will tend to be very highly correlated. For example, if $\boldsymbol{z}^\top$ consists of the five observations $[1 \quad 2 \quad 3 \quad 4 \quad 5]$, which are more spread out than most regressors would be in econometric applications, and β_3 is equal to 1, the correlation between the two vectors is 0.9942; if $\boldsymbol{z}^\top$ consists of the five observations $[5 \quad 6 \quad 7 \quad 8 \quad 9]$, the correlation is a whopping 0.9996. Notice that how poorly the model is identified depends on the data as well as on the values of the parameters and the structure of the model.

We have already seen that the Gauss-Newton regression

$$\boldsymbol{y} - \hat{\boldsymbol{x}} = \hat{\boldsymbol{X}}\boldsymbol{b} + \text{residuals},$$

where $\boldsymbol{x}(\boldsymbol{\beta})$ and $\boldsymbol{X}(\boldsymbol{\beta})$ are evaluated at the NLS estimates $\hat{\boldsymbol{\beta}}$, yields a valid estimate of the covariance matrix of $\hat{\boldsymbol{\beta}}$ when the DGP is a special case of the model that was estimated. It is clear that the GNR

$$\boldsymbol{y} - \boldsymbol{x}_0 = \boldsymbol{X}_0\boldsymbol{b} + \text{residuals}, \tag{6.13}$$

where $\boldsymbol{x}(\boldsymbol{\beta})$ and $\boldsymbol{X}(\boldsymbol{\beta})$ are evaluated at $\boldsymbol{\beta}_0$, would also yield a valid estimate of $\boldsymbol{V}(\hat{\boldsymbol{\beta}})$, although of course in practice this regression is not feasible because it requires knowledge of the DGP. Nevertheless, it is useful to think of $\boldsymbol{V}(\hat{\boldsymbol{\beta}})$ as having been generated by this equation. If we ignore the asymptotic niceties, so as to avoid carrying around various factors of n, we can easily use equation (6.13) to shed light on the problem of collinearity in both linear and nonlinear regression models.

Suppose we are interested in the variance of the NLS estimate of a single element of $\boldsymbol{\beta}$, which we may without loss of generality call β_1. We can always partition $\boldsymbol{X}(\boldsymbol{\beta})$ as $[\boldsymbol{x}_1(\boldsymbol{\beta}) \quad \boldsymbol{X}_2(\boldsymbol{\beta})]$, where $\boldsymbol{x}_1(\boldsymbol{\beta})$ denotes the single column of $\boldsymbol{X}(\boldsymbol{\beta})$ that corresponds to β_1, and $\boldsymbol{X}_2(\boldsymbol{\beta})$ denotes the remaining $k-1$ columns. If we drop the 0 subscripts for clarity, the GNR (6.13) thus becomes

$$\boldsymbol{u} = \boldsymbol{x}_1 b_1 + \boldsymbol{X}_2\boldsymbol{b}_2 + \text{residuals}.$$

By the FWL Theorem, the estimate of b_1 from this artificial regression will be numerically identical to that from the regression

$$\boldsymbol{M}_2\boldsymbol{u} = \boldsymbol{M}_2\boldsymbol{x}_1 b_1 + \text{residuals}, \tag{6.14}$$

where $\boldsymbol{M}_2 \equiv \mathbf{I} - \boldsymbol{X}_2(\boldsymbol{X}_2^\top\boldsymbol{X}_2)^{-1}\boldsymbol{X}_2^\top$ is the matrix that projects orthogonally off $\mathcal{S}(\boldsymbol{X}_2)$, the span of $\boldsymbol{X}_2$.

Regression (6.14) has only one regressor, $\boldsymbol{M}_2\boldsymbol{x}_1$. It is easy to see that

$$V(\hat{b}_1) = \sigma_0^2\left(\boldsymbol{x}_1^\top\boldsymbol{M}_2\boldsymbol{x}_1\right)^{-1} = \frac{\sigma_0^2}{\boldsymbol{x}_1^\top\boldsymbol{M}_2\boldsymbol{x}_1}.$$

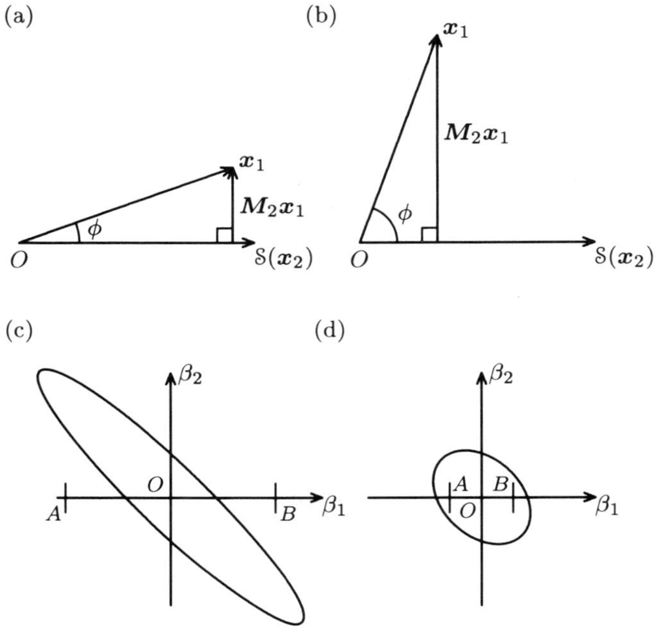

Figure 6.1 Collinearity and precision of estimation

This is asymptotically the same as the variance of $\hat{\beta}_1$. Notice that $\boldsymbol{x}_1^{\top}\boldsymbol{M}_2\boldsymbol{x}_1$ is simply the sum of squared residuals from the regression

$$\boldsymbol{x}_1 = \boldsymbol{X}_2\boldsymbol{c}_2 + \text{residuals}. \tag{6.15}$$

Thus we conclude that the variance of $\hat{\beta}_1$ is proportional to the inverse of the sum of squared residuals from regression (6.15). When $\boldsymbol{x}_1$ is well explained by the other columns of $\boldsymbol{X}$, this SSR will be small, and the variance of $\hat{\beta}_1$ will consequently be large. When $\boldsymbol{x}_1$ is not well explained by the other columns of $\boldsymbol{X}$, this SSR will be large, and the variance of $\hat{\beta}_1$ will be small. These two cases are illustrated in Figure 6.1, for the case in which there are just two regressors. This figure should be compared with Figure 3.3. Essentially the same issues arise in both figures, since the length of a confidence interval for a given parameter is proportional to the square root of the estimated variance of that parameter.

The regressor $\boldsymbol{x}_2$, which represents in the figure all the regressors other than $\boldsymbol{x}_1$, the regressor of interest, is the same on both sides of the figure. On the other hand, the regressor $\boldsymbol{x}_1$ is oriented differently with respect to $\boldsymbol{x}_2$ on the two sides. For simplicity, both regressors have the same length, and the only variable is the angle, ϕ, between them. In the top left panel, panel (a), $\boldsymbol{x}_2$ explains $\boldsymbol{x}_1$ very well; consequently, the angle ϕ and the sum of squared residuals from (6.15) are relatively small. The latter is the squared length of the vector of residuals $\boldsymbol{M}_2\boldsymbol{x}_1$. In panel (b), $\boldsymbol{x}_2$ explains $\boldsymbol{x}_1$ much less well; consequently, the angle ϕ and the SSR from (6.15) are relatively large. Clearly the degree of collinearity between $\boldsymbol{x}_1$ and $\boldsymbol{x}_2$ is greater when ϕ is small or, equivalently, when $\boldsymbol{x}_2$ explains $\boldsymbol{x}_1$ well.

In the bottom panels, (c) and (d), confidence ellipses and confidence intervals for $\hat{\beta}_1$ are shown, corresponding to the regressors depicted in the panels above them. For simplicity, these have been drawn for the case in which $\hat{\boldsymbol{\beta}} = \mathbf{0}$: In any real instance, the only aspect of the figures that would be different is that the origin would move elsewhere, leaving sizes and relative positions of things unchanged. Notice that the two bottom panels are drawn to the same scale. The confidence intervals, which are the segments AB in the figure, are therefore of very different lengths. As explained in Section 3.3, a higher degree of collinearity gives rise to an elliptical confidence region of greater eccentricity, and this can be seen clearly in the figure. For the situation shown, in which only the angle ϕ varies, it can be shown that both the area of the confidence ellipse and the length of the confidence interval for $\hat{\beta}_1$ are inversely proportional to $\sin\phi$. Consequently, as ϕ tends to zero and the two regressors become more nearly collinear, the length of the confidence interval tends to infinity. This is of course a reflection of the fact that the variance of $\hat{\beta}_1$ tends to infinity as ϕ tends to zero.

Collinearity arises when one or more of the columns of $\boldsymbol{X}$ are extremely well explained by the remaining columns, and estimates of the parameters associated with those columns are very imprecise. One simple way to characterize the presence or absence of collinearity, as it affects the estimation of the single parameter β_1, is to consider the ratio of $\boldsymbol{x}_1^{\top}\boldsymbol{M}_2\boldsymbol{x}_1$ to $\boldsymbol{x}_1^{\top}\boldsymbol{M}_\iota\boldsymbol{x}_1$, where $\boldsymbol{M}_\iota \equiv \mathbf{I} - \boldsymbol{\iota}(\boldsymbol{\iota}^{\top}\boldsymbol{\iota})^{-1}\boldsymbol{\iota}^{\top}$ is the matrix that takes deviations from the mean (as usual, $\boldsymbol{\iota}$ denotes a vector of n ones). The numerator of this ratio measures variation in $\boldsymbol{x}_1$ that is not explained by variation in $\boldsymbol{X}_2$, while the denominator measures variation in $\boldsymbol{x}_1$ around its mean. If the ratio is very small, collinearity may well be a problem.

When a model is poorly identified for some value of $\boldsymbol{\beta}$, say $\boldsymbol{\beta}^*$, the Gauss-Newton regression will typically display a great deal of collinearity when it is evaluated at $\boldsymbol{\beta}^*$. If one is having difficulty obtaining NLS estimates, or if one has not yet begun to estimate the model and suspects that there may be difficulties doing so, it may be very useful to see whether the Gauss-Newton regression does in fact suffer from substantial collinearity for plausible parameter values. If it does, then the model is probably poorly identified by the data. It may well be impossible to obtain reasonably precise estimates of the model with that data set, or perhaps even to locate the minimum of $SSR(\boldsymbol{\beta})$ at all (see Section 6.8).

What does one do when confronted with a nonlinear regression model that is poorly identified? There are basically two options: Get more data, or estimate a less demanding model, perhaps the original one after some restrictions have been imposed on it. If it is not feasible to obtain more data, then one must accept the fact that the data one has contain a limited amount of information and must simplify the model accordingly. Trying to estimate models that are too complicated is one of the most common mistakes among inexperienced applied econometricians. A model like (6.11), for example, is asking a great deal of the data and will likely be very difficult to estimate with many data sets. Only if the number of observations is very large, and/or the range of z_t is very great, will it be feasible to obtain precise estimates of β_2 and β_3 for this type of model.

6.4 Testing Restrictions

The best-known of the uses to which the Gauss-Newton regression can be put is to provide a very simple way of computing test statistics. Once restricted estimates have been obtained, a variant of the GNR can be used to test any type of equality restriction on $\boldsymbol{\beta}$ without having to estimate the unrestricted model. These tests are based on the Lagrange multiplier principle, which was discussed in Sections 3.6 and 5.7. Several numerically different, but asymptotically equivalent, test statistics can be calculated based on the GNR. In this section, we deal only with test statistics that are based on restricted NLS estimates. As we will see in Section 6.7, the GNR can also be used to compute tests based on any root-n consistent estimates.

We will write the null and alternative hypotheses as

$$\left.\begin{aligned} H_0 :\ & \boldsymbol{y} = \boldsymbol{x}(\boldsymbol{\beta}_1, \mathbf{0}) + \boldsymbol{u} \\ H_1 :\ & \boldsymbol{y} = \boldsymbol{x}(\boldsymbol{\beta}_1, \boldsymbol{\beta}_2) + \boldsymbol{u} \end{aligned}\right\} \quad \boldsymbol{u} \sim \mathrm{IID}(\mathbf{0}, \sigma^2\mathbf{I}),$$

where $\boldsymbol{\beta}_1$ is $(k-r)\times 1$ and $\boldsymbol{\beta}_2$ is $r \times 1$. We consider zero restrictions for the sake of clarity, but this in no way limits the generality of the results, because, as we discuss below, any set of r equality restrictions can be converted to a set of r zero restrictions by an appropriate reparametrization. We assume that the unrestricted model is asymptotically identified in the neighborhood of the DGP, which is assumed to belong to the family of DGPs

$$\boldsymbol{y} = \boldsymbol{x}(\boldsymbol{\beta}_{01}, \mathbf{0}) + \boldsymbol{u}, \quad \boldsymbol{u} \sim \mathrm{IID}(\mathbf{0}, \sigma_0^2\mathbf{I}).$$

Thus we are assuming that H_0 did in fact generate the data. The matrix $\boldsymbol{X}(\boldsymbol{\beta})$ can be partitioned into two parts, $\boldsymbol{X}_1(\boldsymbol{\beta})$ and $\boldsymbol{X}_2(\boldsymbol{\beta})$, which correspond to $\boldsymbol{\beta}_1$ and $\boldsymbol{\beta}_2$ and are $n \times (k-r)$ and $n \times r$, respectively.

It is not obvious that all equality restrictions can be converted to zero restrictions by means of appropriate reparametrizations. In Section 3.6, for example, we considered linear restrictions of the form $\boldsymbol{R}\gamma = \boldsymbol{r}$, where $\boldsymbol{R}$ is an $r \times k$ matrix and $\boldsymbol{r}$ is an $r \times 1$ vector. Here γ denotes the k-vector of parameters on which restrictions are imposed. We will use $\boldsymbol{\beta}$ to denote an alternative parametrization in which all restrictions are zero restrictions. For the latter, the matrix $\boldsymbol{R}$ has the form $[\mathbf{0} \;\; \mathbf{I}_r]$, and the vector $\boldsymbol{r}$ is a zero vector. Thus we see that

$$\boldsymbol{R\gamma} - \boldsymbol{r} = \mathbf{0} = [\mathbf{0} \;\; \mathbf{I}_r]\boldsymbol{\beta}, \tag{6.16}$$

where $\boldsymbol{\gamma}$ and $\boldsymbol{\beta}$ denote the parameter vectors in the two different parametrizations. Evidently, we can identify β_i with γ_i for $i = 1, \ldots, k - r$, while from equation (6.16) we see that

$$\beta_i = \sum_{j=1}^{k} R_{ij}\gamma_j - r_i$$

for $i = k - r + 1, \ldots, k$. Thus it is straightforward to convert the linear restrictions $\boldsymbol{R\gamma} = \boldsymbol{r}$ in the $\boldsymbol{\gamma}$ parametrization into zero restrictions in the $\boldsymbol{\beta}$ parametrization. It is also possible to convert nonlinear restrictions, such as those discussed in Section 5.7, into zero restrictions. One simply has to define the new parameters in terms of the restrictions on the old parameters. For example, if one of the restrictions were $\gamma_1^{\gamma_2} - 5 = 0$, one might define a new parameter β_1 so that it equaled $\gamma_1^{\gamma_2} - 5$. Of course, this sort of nonlinear reparametrization is not always easy to do in practice if there are several complicated nonlinear restrictions. As we saw in Sections 3.6 and 5.7, however, it is not actually necessary to perform a reparametrization in order to use a GNR to test restrictions.

Asymptotic identification implies that the matrix $n^{-1}\boldsymbol{X}_0^{\top}\boldsymbol{X}_0$ must tend to a matrix which is positive definite. This assumption rules out certain types of models and restrictions. For example, we could not deal with a model like

$$y_t = \beta_1 + \beta_2 \exp(\beta_3 z_t) + u_t$$

subject to either the restriction that $\beta_2 = 0$ or the restriction that $\beta_3 = 0$, since the model would then be asymptotically unidentified. We will denote the estimates of $\boldsymbol{\beta}$ under H_0 by $\tilde{\boldsymbol{\beta}}$ to distinguish them from the unrestricted estimates $\hat{\boldsymbol{\beta}}$; any quantities marked with a $\sim$ are evaluated at the restricted estimates. In this case, $\tilde{\boldsymbol{\beta}} \equiv [\tilde{\boldsymbol{\beta}}_1 \,\vdots\, \mathbf{0}]$.

We now discuss the distribution of several closely related test statistics, all of which may be obtained by running the Gauss-Newton regression with $\boldsymbol{\beta}$ evaluated at $\tilde{\boldsymbol{\beta}}$. All of these test statistics are asymptotically equivalent to the LM test statistic (3.47), or its score form variant (3.48), which was shown in Section 5.7 to be asymptotically distributed as $\chi^2(r)$ under the null hypothesis. The Gauss-Newton regression evaluated at $\boldsymbol{\beta} = \tilde{\boldsymbol{\beta}}$ is

$$\boldsymbol{y} - \tilde{\boldsymbol{x}} = \tilde{\boldsymbol{X}}_1\boldsymbol{b}_1 + \tilde{\boldsymbol{X}}_2\boldsymbol{b}_2 + \text{residuals}. \tag{6.17}$$

This is extremely similar to regression (3.49), which we introduced in Section 3.6 as a way to calculate Lagrange multiplier statistics. In fact, the only difference is that the regressand has not been divided by an estimate of σ. As we will see below, the test statistic is no more difficult to calculate by running (6.17) than by running (3.49).

Limiting our attention to zero restrictions makes it possible for us to gain a little more insight into the connection between the GNR and LM tests. Using the FWL Theorem, we see that regression (6.17) will yield exactly the same estimates of $\boldsymbol{b}_2$, namely $\tilde{\boldsymbol{b}}_2$, and exactly the same sum of squared residuals as the regression

$$\boldsymbol{y} - \tilde{\boldsymbol{x}} = \tilde{\boldsymbol{M}}_1 \tilde{\boldsymbol{X}}_2 \boldsymbol{b}_2 + \text{residuals}, \tag{6.18}$$

where $\tilde{\boldsymbol{M}}_1$ is the matrix that projects onto $\mathcal{S}^\perp(\tilde{\boldsymbol{X}}_1)$. The regressand here is not multiplied by $\tilde{\boldsymbol{M}}_1$ because the first-order conditions imply that $\boldsymbol{y} - \tilde{\boldsymbol{x}}$ already lies in $\mathcal{S}^\perp(\tilde{\boldsymbol{X}}_1)$, which in turn implies that $\tilde{\boldsymbol{M}}_1(\boldsymbol{y} - \tilde{\boldsymbol{x}}) = (\boldsymbol{y} - \tilde{\boldsymbol{x}})$. The sum of squared residuals from regression (6.18) is

$$(\boldsymbol{y} - \tilde{\boldsymbol{x}})^\top(\boldsymbol{y} - \tilde{\boldsymbol{x}}) - (\boldsymbol{y} - \tilde{\boldsymbol{x}})^\top \tilde{\boldsymbol{X}}_2 \big(\tilde{\boldsymbol{X}}_2^\top \tilde{\boldsymbol{M}}_1 \tilde{\boldsymbol{X}}_2\big)^{-1} \tilde{\boldsymbol{X}}_2^\top (\boldsymbol{y} - \tilde{\boldsymbol{x}}).$$

Since $\boldsymbol{y} - \tilde{\boldsymbol{x}}$ lies in $\mathcal{S}^\perp(\tilde{\boldsymbol{X}}_1)$, it is orthogonal to $\tilde{\boldsymbol{X}}_1$. Thus, if we had not included $\tilde{\boldsymbol{X}}_2$ in the regression, the SSR would have been $(\boldsymbol{y} - \tilde{\boldsymbol{x}})^\top(\boldsymbol{y} - \tilde{\boldsymbol{x}})$. Hence the reduction in the SSR of regression (6.17) brought about by the inclusion of $\tilde{\boldsymbol{X}}_2$ is

$$(\boldsymbol{y} - \tilde{\boldsymbol{x}})^\top \tilde{\boldsymbol{X}}_2 \big(\tilde{\boldsymbol{X}}_2^\top \tilde{\boldsymbol{M}}_1 \tilde{\boldsymbol{X}}_2\big)^{-1} \tilde{\boldsymbol{X}}_2^\top (\boldsymbol{y} - \tilde{\boldsymbol{x}}). \tag{6.19}$$

This quantity is also the explained sum of squares (around zero) from regression (6.17), again because $\tilde{\boldsymbol{X}}_1$ has no explanatory power. We can now show directly that this quantity, divided by any consistent estimate of σ^2, is asymptotically distributed as $\chi^2(r)$ under the null hypothesis. We already showed this in Section 5.7, but the argument that the number of degrees of freedom is r was an indirect one.

First, observe that

$$n^{-1/2}(\boldsymbol{y} - \tilde{\boldsymbol{x}})^\top \tilde{\boldsymbol{X}}_2 \stackrel{a}{=} n^{-1/2} \boldsymbol{u}^\top \boldsymbol{M}_1 \boldsymbol{X}_2 \equiv \boldsymbol{\nu}^\top,$$

where $\boldsymbol{M}_1 \equiv \boldsymbol{M}_1(\boldsymbol{\beta}_0)$ and $\boldsymbol{X}_2 \equiv \boldsymbol{X}_2(\boldsymbol{\beta}_0)$. The asymptotic equality here follows from the fact that $\tilde{\boldsymbol{u}} \stackrel{a}{=} \boldsymbol{M}_1 \boldsymbol{u}$, which is the result (6.09) for the case in which the model is estimated subject to the restrictions that $\boldsymbol{\beta}_2 = \mathbf{0}$. The covariance matrix of the $r \times 1$ random vector $\boldsymbol{\nu}$ is

$$\begin{aligned} E(\boldsymbol{\nu}\boldsymbol{\nu}^\top) &= E\big(n^{-1}\boldsymbol{X}_2^\top \boldsymbol{M}_1 \boldsymbol{u}\boldsymbol{u}^\top \boldsymbol{M}_1 \boldsymbol{X}_2\big) = n^{-1}\boldsymbol{X}_2^\top \boldsymbol{M}_1 (\sigma_0^2 \mathbf{I}) \boldsymbol{M}_1 \boldsymbol{X}_2 \\ &= n^{-1}\sigma_0^2 (\boldsymbol{X}_2^\top \boldsymbol{M}_1 \boldsymbol{X}_2) \equiv \sigma_0^2 \boldsymbol{V}. \end{aligned}$$

The consistency of $\tilde{\boldsymbol{\beta}}$ and the regularity conditions for Theorem 5.1 imply that

$$n^{-1}\tilde{\boldsymbol{X}}_2^\top \tilde{\boldsymbol{M}}_1 \tilde{\boldsymbol{X}}_2 \stackrel{a}{=} n^{-1}\boldsymbol{X}_2^\top \boldsymbol{M}_1 \boldsymbol{X}_2 = \boldsymbol{V}.$$

Under the regularity conditions for Theorem 5.2, we can apply a central limit theorem and conclude that $\boldsymbol{\nu}$ is asymptotically normally distributed with mean vector zero and covariance matrix $\sigma_0^2\boldsymbol{V}$. Thus any test statistic that is constructed by dividing (6.19) by a consistent estimate of σ^2 is asymptotically equal to

$$\frac{1}{\sigma_0^2}\boldsymbol{\nu}^{\top}\boldsymbol{V}^{-1}\boldsymbol{\nu}.$$

We see immediately that this quantity is asymptotically distributed as $\chi^2(r)$, since it is a quadratic form in random r-vectors which asymptotically have mean zero and covariance matrix $\sigma_0^2\boldsymbol{V}$; see Appendix B.

Because we may use any consistent estimate of σ^2, this result justifies the use of a number of different test statistics. One possibility is to use the explained sum of squares from regression (3.49), in which we have divided the regressand of (6.17) by a consistent estimate of σ. However, the two most common test statistics are n times the *uncentered* R^2 from regression (6.17) and the ordinary F statistic for $\boldsymbol{b}_2 = \mathbf{0}$ from that regression. To see that the nR^2 form of the test is valid, observe that since R_u^2, the uncentered R^2, is equal to the explained sum of squares divided by the total sum of squares,

$$\begin{aligned} nR_u^2 &= \frac{n(\boldsymbol{y}-\tilde{\boldsymbol{x}})^{\top}\tilde{\boldsymbol{X}}_2\big(\tilde{\boldsymbol{X}}_2^{\top}\tilde{\boldsymbol{M}}_1\tilde{\boldsymbol{X}}_2\big)^{-1}\tilde{\boldsymbol{X}}_2^{\top}(\boldsymbol{y}-\tilde{\boldsymbol{x}})}{(\boldsymbol{y}-\tilde{\boldsymbol{x}})^{\top}(\boldsymbol{y}-\tilde{\boldsymbol{x}})} \\ &= \frac{\|\boldsymbol{P}_{\tilde{M}_1\tilde{X}_2}(\boldsymbol{y}-\tilde{\boldsymbol{x}})\|^2}{\|\boldsymbol{y}-\tilde{\boldsymbol{x}}\|^2/n}. \end{aligned}$$

This variant of the test implicitly uses $\tilde{\sigma}^2$, the restricted maximum likelihood estimate, to estimate σ^2. As we have seen, this estimate will tend to be too small, at least when the null hypothesis is true. It would probably be safer to use $(n-k+r)R_u^2$ as the test statistic, since this would implicitly use $\tilde{s}^2$, the OLS estimate of σ^2 from the restricted model, instead of $\tilde{\sigma}^2$; the resulting test statistic would be equal to the ESS from (3.49).

One practical problem with tests based on R_u^2 from an artificial regression is that many regression packages do not print the uncentered R^2. In most cases, this will create no difficulty, because R_u^2 will be identical to the ordinary centered R^2. This will be so whenever the restricted model $\boldsymbol{x}(\boldsymbol{\beta}_1, \mathbf{0})$ contains the equivalent of a constant term and $\boldsymbol{y}-\tilde{\boldsymbol{x}}$ will therefore have mean zero. In cases for which $\boldsymbol{y}-\tilde{\boldsymbol{x}}$ does not have mean zero, however, the centered and uncentered R^2's will differ, and the former will not yield a valid test statistic. It is important that users of the nR^2 and $(n-k+r)R^2$ test statistics be aware of this possibility and check to make sure that the regressand for the test regression (6.17) does in fact have mean zero. A simple way to avoid having to compute R_u^2 is to run the GNR in the form (3.49), that is, with the regressand divided by $\tilde{s}$. The explained sum of squares from (3.49) is just $(n-k+r)R_u^2$. If the regression program does not print this quantity directly, it may be computed as $n-k+r$ minus the sum of squared residuals.

It is also possible, and may well be preferable, to use the ordinary F statistic for $\boldsymbol{b}_2 = \mathbf{0}$ from the Gauss-Newton regression. If RSSR and USSR denote the restricted and unrestricted sums of squared residuals from regression (6.17), this F statistic is

$$\frac{(\mathrm{RSSR} - \mathrm{USSR})/r}{\mathrm{USSR}/(n-k)} \tag{6.20}$$

$$= \frac{(\boldsymbol{y} - \tilde{\boldsymbol{x}})^{\top}\tilde{\boldsymbol{X}}_2\big(\tilde{\boldsymbol{X}}_2^{\top}\tilde{\boldsymbol{M}}_1\tilde{\boldsymbol{X}}_2\big)^{-1}\tilde{\boldsymbol{X}}_2^{\top}(\boldsymbol{y} - \tilde{\boldsymbol{x}})/r}{\big((\boldsymbol{y} - \tilde{\boldsymbol{x}})^{\top}(\boldsymbol{y} - \tilde{\boldsymbol{x}}) - (\boldsymbol{y} - \tilde{\boldsymbol{x}})^{\top}\tilde{\boldsymbol{X}}_2\big(\tilde{\boldsymbol{X}}_2^{\top}\tilde{\boldsymbol{M}}_1\tilde{\boldsymbol{X}}_2\big)^{-1}\tilde{\boldsymbol{X}}_2^{\top}(\boldsymbol{y} - \tilde{\boldsymbol{x}})\big)/(n-k)}.$$

The denominator here is the OLS estimate of σ^2 from (6.17), which under H_0 tends to σ_0^2 as $n \to \infty$. The numerator is $1/r$ times expression (6.19). Thus it is clear that r times (6.20) will be asymptotically distributed as $\chi^2(r)$.

In finite samples, comparing (6.20) to the $F(r, n-k)$ distribution is just as valid as comparing r times it to the $\chi^2(r)$ distribution. Indeed, there is evidence that the F statistic (6.20) has better finite-sample properties than the nR^2 statistic based on the same Gauss-Newton regression; see Kiviet (1986). This evidence is entirely in accord with theory, because, as we have seen, $\hat{\boldsymbol{u}} \overset{a}{=} \boldsymbol{M}_0\boldsymbol{u}$. Thus using the F distribution, which treats the estimate s^2 based on NLS residuals as if it were based on OLS residuals, makes more sense than using the χ^2 distribution, which treats $\hat{\sigma}^2$ as if it were based not on residuals but on error terms. Based partly on theory and evidence, then, and partly on the convenience of using the same form of test for Gauss-Newton regressions as would normally be used with genuine regressions, we therefore recommend using the F test rather than the nR^2 test or the numerically identical test based on regression (3.49).

Expression (6.20) can be simplified somewhat by noting that it is simply $(n-k)/r$ times the ratio of the squared lengths of two vectors:

$$\frac{n-k}{r} \times \frac{\|\boldsymbol{P}_{\tilde{M}_1\tilde{X}_2}(\boldsymbol{y} - \tilde{\boldsymbol{x}})\|^2}{\|\boldsymbol{M}_{\tilde{X}}(\boldsymbol{y} - \tilde{\boldsymbol{x}})\|^2}. \tag{6.21}$$

The numerator is the squared length of the vector $\boldsymbol{P}_{\tilde{M}_1\tilde{X}_2}(\boldsymbol{y} - \tilde{\boldsymbol{x}})$, which is the residual vector $\boldsymbol{y} - \tilde{\boldsymbol{x}}$ projected onto $\mathcal{S}(\tilde{\boldsymbol{M}}_1\tilde{\boldsymbol{X}}_2)$. The denominator is the squared length of the vector $\boldsymbol{M}_{\tilde{X}}(\boldsymbol{y} - \tilde{\boldsymbol{x}}) = \boldsymbol{M}_{\tilde{M}_1\tilde{X}_2}(\boldsymbol{y} - \tilde{\boldsymbol{x}})$, which is the residual vector projected off $\mathcal{S}(\tilde{\boldsymbol{X}}) = \mathcal{S}(\tilde{\boldsymbol{X}}_1, \tilde{\boldsymbol{X}}_2)$. The geometry of the F test in this case is identical to the geometry of the F test in the linear regression case, which was discussed in Section 3.5. The only difference is that $\tilde{\boldsymbol{X}}_1$ and $\tilde{\boldsymbol{X}}_2$ are functions of the restricted estimates $\tilde{\boldsymbol{\beta}}$.

In Section 3.5, we proved that, for linear regression models, the t statistic for the hypothesis that a single parameter value is zero is numerically equal to the square root of an F statistic for the same null hypothesis. Since this is a numerical result, it is as true for artificial regressions as for genuine ones.

Thus, when b_2 is a scalar, the t statistic on $\tilde{b}_2$ from the GNR (6.17) is just as valid as any of the test statistics we have been discussing.

Why does regressing residuals from the restricted model on the derivatives of $\boldsymbol{x}(\boldsymbol{\beta})$ allow us to compute valid test statistics? Why do we need to include all the derivatives and not merely those that correspond to the parameters which were restricted? The above discussion has provided formal answers to these questions, but perhaps not ones that are intuitively appealing. Let us therefore consider the matter from a slightly different point of view. In Section 5.7, we showed that Wald, LR, and LM statistics for testing the same set of restrictions are all asymptotically equal to the same random variable under the null hypothesis and that this random variable is asymptotically distributed as $\chi^2(r)$. For the nonlinear regression models we have been discussing, the LR statistic is simply the difference between $SSR(\hat{\boldsymbol{\beta}})$ and $SSR(\tilde{\boldsymbol{\beta}})$, divided by any consistent estimate of σ^2. To see why the LM statistic is valid and why the GNR must include the derivatives with respect to all parameters, we will view the LM statistic based on the GNR as a quadratic approximation to this LR statistic. That this should be the case makes sense, since the GNR itself is a linear approximation to the nonlinear regression model.

One way to view the Gauss-Newton regression is to think of it as a way of approximating the function $SSR(\boldsymbol{\beta})$ by a quadratic function that has the same first derivatives and, asymptotically, the same second derivatives at the point $\tilde{\boldsymbol{\beta}}$. This quadratic approximating function, which we will call $SSR^*(\tilde{\boldsymbol{\beta}}, \boldsymbol{b})$, is simply the sum-of-squares function for the artificial regression. It is defined as

$$SSR^*(\tilde{\boldsymbol{\beta}}, \boldsymbol{b}) = (\boldsymbol{y} - \tilde{\boldsymbol{x}} - \tilde{\boldsymbol{X}}\boldsymbol{b})^{\top}(\boldsymbol{y} - \tilde{\boldsymbol{x}} - \tilde{\boldsymbol{X}}\boldsymbol{b}).$$

The explained sum of squares from the GNR is precisely the difference between $SSR(\tilde{\boldsymbol{\beta}})$ and $SSR^*(\tilde{\boldsymbol{\beta}}, \tilde{\boldsymbol{b}})$. If $\tilde{\boldsymbol{\beta}}$ is reasonably close to $\hat{\boldsymbol{\beta}}$, $SSR^*(\cdot)$ should provide a good approximation to $SSR(\cdot)$ in the neighborhood of $\hat{\boldsymbol{\beta}}$. Indeed, provided that the restrictions are true and that the sample size is sufficiently large, $\tilde{\boldsymbol{\beta}}$ and $\hat{\boldsymbol{\beta}}$ must be close to each other because they are both consistent for $\boldsymbol{\beta}_0$. Therefore, $SSR^*(\cdot)$ *must* provide a good approximation to $SSR(\cdot)$. This implies that $SSR^*(\tilde{\boldsymbol{\beta}}, \tilde{\boldsymbol{b}})$ will be close to $SSR(\hat{\boldsymbol{\beta}})$ and that the explained sum of squares from the GNR will provide a good approximation to $SSR(\tilde{\boldsymbol{\beta}}) - SSR(\hat{\boldsymbol{\beta}})$. When we divide the explained sum of squares by a consistent estimate of σ^2, the resulting LM test statistic should therefore be similar to the LR test statistic.

It should now be clear why the GNR has to include $\tilde{\boldsymbol{X}}_1$ as well as $\tilde{\boldsymbol{X}}_2$. If it did not, the GNR would not be minimizing $SSR^*(\tilde{\boldsymbol{\beta}}, \boldsymbol{b})$, but rather *another* approximation to $SSR(\boldsymbol{\beta})$,

$$SSR^{**}(\tilde{\boldsymbol{\beta}}, \boldsymbol{b}_2) = (\boldsymbol{y} - \tilde{\boldsymbol{x}} - \tilde{\boldsymbol{X}}_2\boldsymbol{b}_2)^{\top}(\boldsymbol{y} - \tilde{\boldsymbol{x}} - \tilde{\boldsymbol{X}}_2\boldsymbol{b}_2).$$

Although $SSR^*(\cdot)$ should normally provide a reasonably good approximation to $SSR(\cdot)$, $SSR^{**}(\cdot)$ normally will not, because it does not have enough free

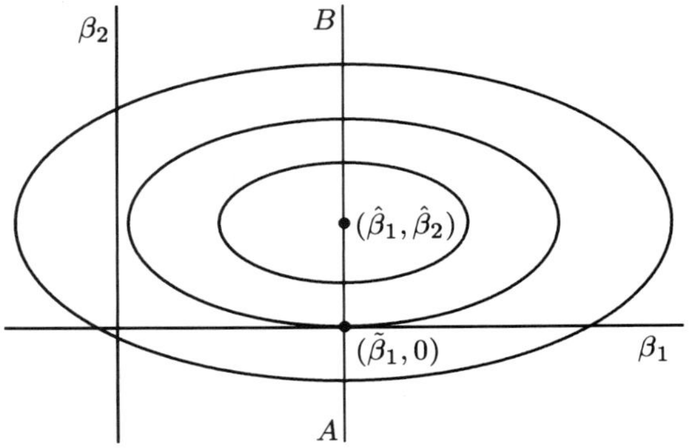

Figure 6.2 A case for which minimizing SSR^{**} will work well

parameters. When we minimize $SSR^{**}(\cdot)$, we can do so only in the directions that correspond to $\boldsymbol{\beta}_2$ but not in the directions that correspond to $\boldsymbol{\beta}_1$. Only if the contours of $SSR(\cdot)$ form an approximate ellipse of which the axes are approximately parallel to the axes of $\boldsymbol{\beta}_1$ and $\boldsymbol{\beta}_2$, so that $\hat{\boldsymbol{\beta}}_1$ and $\tilde{\boldsymbol{\beta}}_1$ are very similar, will $SSR^{**}(\cdot)$ work reasonably well. In other cases, the minimum of $SSR^{*}(\cdot)$ can be very different from the minimum of $SSR^{**}(\cdot)$, and the minimizing values can be correspondingly different.

This is illustrated in Figures 6.2 and 6.3 for the case in which $k = 2$ and $r = 1$. In the former figure, the vectors $\tilde{\boldsymbol{x}}_1$ and $\tilde{\boldsymbol{x}}_2$ are orthogonal, which implies that the axes of the ellipse formed by the contours of $SSR(\cdot)$ are exactly parallel to the axes. In this case, the minimum of $SSR^{**}(\tilde\beta_1, b_2)$, which must lie on the line AB, coincides with the minimum of $SSR(\beta_1, \beta_2)$ at the point $(\hat\beta_1, \hat\beta_2)$. In the latter figure, on the other hand, $\tilde{\boldsymbol{x}}_1$ and $\tilde{\boldsymbol{x}}_2$ are negatively correlated, which implies that the axes of the ellipse formed by the contours of $SSR(\cdot)$ slope upward to the right. In this case, the minimum of $SSR^{**}(\tilde\beta_1, b_2)$, which again must lie on the line AB, is evidently very different from the minimum of $SSR(\beta_1, \beta_2)$.

Obviously, the minimum of $SSR^{**}(\cdot)$ will normally be larger, and certainly cannot be smaller, than the minimum of $SSR^{*}(\cdot)$. Thus, if we were inadvertently to omit $\tilde{\boldsymbol{X}}_1$ from the GNR and calculate nR_u^2 or one of the other equivalent test statistics, we would obtain a numerically smaller test statistic than the correct one. This can be a useful fact to bear in mind. In some cases, it may be easy to construct $\tilde{\boldsymbol{X}}_2$ but hard to construct $\tilde{\boldsymbol{X}}_1$. In such a case it may be useful, in the first instance, to regress $\tilde{\boldsymbol{u}}$ on $\tilde{\boldsymbol{X}}_2$ alone. If that artificial regression yields convincing evidence against the null hypothesis, then we may safely decide to reject H_0 without running the correct GNR. However, if a regression of $\tilde{\boldsymbol{u}}$ on $\tilde{\boldsymbol{X}}_2$ alone fails to reject the null, we cannot safely draw any conclusions from that fact and must run the correct GNR before we can do so.

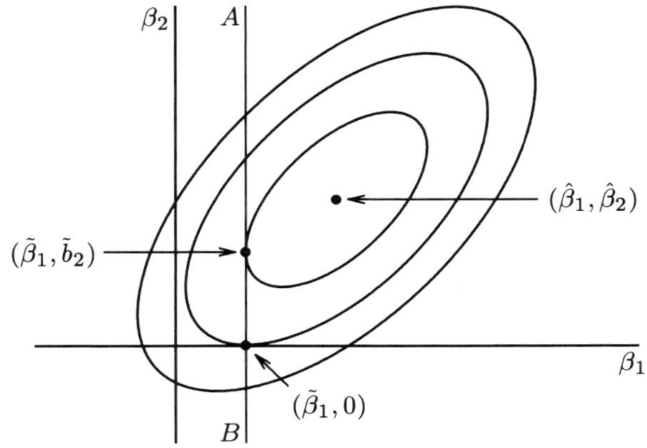

Figure 6.3 A case for which minimizing *SSR*** will work badly

The GNR (6.17) would remain valid if we replaced $\tilde{\boldsymbol{X}}_2$ by *any* $n \times r$ matrix, say $\boldsymbol{Z}(\boldsymbol{\beta})$, evaluated at $\tilde{\boldsymbol{\beta}}$, which was asymptotically uncorrelated with $\boldsymbol{u}$ under the null hypothesis, satisfied the same regularity conditions as $\boldsymbol{X}(\boldsymbol{\beta})$, and might or might not actually depend on $\boldsymbol{\beta}$. Thus, if the model to be tested were

$$\boldsymbol{y} = \boldsymbol{x}(\boldsymbol{\beta}) + \boldsymbol{u}, \quad \boldsymbol{u} \sim \mathrm{IID}(\boldsymbol{0}, \sigma^2\mathbf{I}), \tag{6.22}$$

and $\boldsymbol{Z}(\boldsymbol{\beta})$ were a matrix constructed so that, if the model were correct, $n^{-1}\boldsymbol{Z}_0^\top\boldsymbol{u}$ would tend to a zero vector, we could always run the GNR

$$\tilde{\boldsymbol{u}} = \tilde{\boldsymbol{X}}\boldsymbol{b} + \tilde{\boldsymbol{Z}}\boldsymbol{c} + \text{residuals} \tag{6.23}$$

and calculate an F test for $\mathbf{c} = \mathbf{0}$ or one of the equivalent test statistics. Implicitly, of course, $\tilde{\boldsymbol{Z}}$ must correspond to the matrix $\tilde{\boldsymbol{X}}_2$ for *some* unrestricted model that includes (6.22) as a special case. But there are cases in which it is natural to derive the GNR (6.23) without explicitly specifying such a model, so as to calculate a **diagnostic test**. Such tests are widely used when one has estimated a model and wishes to see if there is any evidence that it is incorrectly specified. We will encounter such tests in the next section and throughout the book.

6.5 Diagnostic Tests for Linear Regression Models

The above results on how the GNR may be used to test restrictions on the parameters of nonlinear regression models are of course equally applicable to linear regression models. It is worthwhile briefly to consider the special case of the latter, partly because so much of the literature is concerned with it, partly because it provides an opportunity to discuss diagnostic tests (which are often, incorrectly, thought of as being somehow different from other tests of restrictions), and partly because there is always merit in considering the simplest possible case.

Suppose that we have estimated a linear regression model

$$\boldsymbol{y} = \boldsymbol{X\beta} + \boldsymbol{u}, \quad \boldsymbol{u} \sim N(\mathbf{0}, \sigma^2\mathbf{I}), \tag{6.24}$$

where $\boldsymbol{X}$ is an $n \times k$ matrix and $\boldsymbol{\beta}$ is a k–vector, and that we wish to test it for possible misspecification of the regression function. Normality is assumed for the moment in order that we may discuss exact tests. Recall that the regression function is supposed to specify $E(\boldsymbol{y}\,|\,\Omega)$, the mean of $\boldsymbol{y}$ conditional on some information set Ω. Let $\boldsymbol{Z}$ denote an $n \times l$ matrix of observations on any set of regressors that belong to Ω but do not lie in $\mathcal{S}(\boldsymbol{X})$. Then, if the null hypothesis that $E(\boldsymbol{y}\,|\,\Omega) = \boldsymbol{X\beta}$ is correct, the estimate of the vector $\boldsymbol{\gamma}$ in the regression

$$\boldsymbol{y} = \boldsymbol{X\beta} + \boldsymbol{Z\gamma} + \boldsymbol{u} \tag{6.25}$$

should be insignificantly different from zero. This hypothesis may of course be tested by computing an ordinary F statistic for $\boldsymbol{\gamma} = \mathbf{0}$ as

$$\frac{(\text{RSSR} - \text{USSR})/l}{\text{USSR}/(n-k-l)}, \tag{6.26}$$

where RSSR and USSR are the sums of squared residuals from (6.24) and (6.25), respectively. If the resulting test statistic is large (so that the associated P value is small), we will want to reject the null hypothesis and thus conclude that the model (6.24) is misspecified. This is an example of what some authors, notably Pagan (1984a) and Pagan and Hall (1983), call **variable addition tests**.

What would happen if we used a Gauss-Newton regression here in place of the more obvious regression (6.25)? The GNR (6.17) becomes

$$\boldsymbol{M_X y} = \boldsymbol{Xb} + \boldsymbol{Zc} + \text{residuals}, \tag{6.27}$$

which by the FWL Theorem yields the same SSR as the regression

$$\boldsymbol{M_X y} = \boldsymbol{M_X Z c} + \text{residuals}. \tag{6.28}$$

But if we apply the FWL Theorem to regression (6.25), we see that the SSR from that regression is identical to the SSR from regression (6.28). Thus, in this case, the F statistic based on the Gauss-Newton regression (6.27) will be identical to (6.26), the F statistic based on the ordinary regression (6.25). We see that tests based on the GNR are equivalent to variable addition tests when the latter are applicable.

It often seems attractive to base tests for model misspecification on the residuals $\hat{\boldsymbol{u}}$ because they provide estimates of the error terms $\boldsymbol{u}$. Pagan and Hall (1983) show how to construct a large number of tests using this approach.

Thus it might seem natural to test whether a model is misspecified by simply regressing the residuals $\hat{\boldsymbol{u}} = \boldsymbol{M}_X \boldsymbol{y}$ on the test regressors $\boldsymbol{Z}$. As we saw in the preceding section, however, this procedure, which is equivalent to using a GNR without the regressors corresponding to the model parameters, yields test statistics that are too small. It is worthy of note that the well-known Durbin-Watson statistic is asymptotically equivalent to a statistic computed in this way, and that the DW statistic fails to reject the null hypothesis often enough when there are lagged dependent variables for precisely the reason just discussed. All of this is discussed further in Chapter 10.

The hypothesis that $E(\boldsymbol{y} \,|\, \Omega) = \boldsymbol{X\beta}$ can be tested against any alternative specification of the conditional mean by testing the significance of some matrix of test regressors $\boldsymbol{Z}$ in regressions (6.25) or (6.27). All that is required is that the elements of $\boldsymbol{Z}$ be asymptotically uncorrelated with the elements of $\boldsymbol{u}$ and not depend on anything which is not in the information set Ω. A great many such specification tests have been proposed, and we will encounter many of them in the course of this book. One well-known example is the **Regression Specification Error Test**, or **RESET** for short, proposed by Ramsey (1969); a precursor is Anscombe (1961). This test was recast in the form of an F test for omitted variables by Ramsey and Schmidt (1976). Each column of $\boldsymbol{Z}$ then consists of some power of the fitted values $\boldsymbol{X}\hat{\boldsymbol{\beta}}$, such as squared fitted values, cubed fitted values, and so on. In the simplest case, there is only one test regressor, which is the vector of squared fitted values, and this simplest version of the RESET test is often the most useful. It is interesting to observe that it can be derived directly as an application of the Gauss-Newton regression.

Suppose that the model under test is once again (6.24) and that we wish to test it against the explicit alternative

$$y_t = \boldsymbol{X}_t\boldsymbol{\beta}(1 + \theta\boldsymbol{X}_t\boldsymbol{\beta}) + u_t, \tag{6.29}$$

where θ is an unknown parameter to be estimated. When $\theta = 0$, this model reduces to (6.24) but, when θ is nonzero, it allows for a nonlinear relationship between $\boldsymbol{X}_t$ and y_t. Since many other nonlinear models would be well approximated by (6.29) in the neighborhood of $\theta = 0$, this seems like a sensible alternative. It is easy to see that the GNR corresponding to (6.29) is

$$y_t - \boldsymbol{X}_t\boldsymbol{\beta}(1 + \theta\boldsymbol{X}_t\boldsymbol{\beta}) = \big(2\theta(\boldsymbol{X}_t\boldsymbol{\beta})\boldsymbol{X}_t + \boldsymbol{X}_t\big)\boldsymbol{b} + (\boldsymbol{X}_t\boldsymbol{\beta})^2 c + \text{residual}.$$

When this is evaluated at $\hat{\boldsymbol{\beta}}$, the OLS estimates under the null hypothesis that $\theta = 0$, it reduces to

$$y_t - \boldsymbol{X}_t\hat{\boldsymbol{\beta}} = \boldsymbol{X}_t\boldsymbol{b} + (\boldsymbol{X}_t\hat{\boldsymbol{\beta}})^2 c + \text{residual}, \tag{6.30}$$

and, as we have seen, the t statistic on $\hat{c}$ from this GNR will be identical to the t statistic on the estimate of c from the regression

$$y_t = \boldsymbol{X}_t\boldsymbol{\beta} + (\boldsymbol{X}_t\hat{\boldsymbol{\beta}})^2 c + \text{residual},$$

which is the regression for performing the simplest version of the RESET test. Thus the RESET test provides a simple way of testing for nonlinearity in the relationship between $\boldsymbol{X}$ and $\boldsymbol{y}$; for more on this, see MacKinnon and Magee (1990). This test is clearly applicable to nonlinear as well as to linear regression models. If the model under test were $y_t = x_t(\boldsymbol{\beta}) + u_t$, we would simply have to replace $\boldsymbol{X}_t\hat{\boldsymbol{\beta}}$ by $\hat{x}_t$ twice, where it occurs in regression (6.30), to obtain an appropriate GNR.

6.6 One-Step Efficient Estimation

It is sometimes easy to obtain consistent but inefficient estimates but relatively difficult to obtain NLS estimates. This may, for example, be the case when the nonlinear model to be estimated is really a linear model subject to nonlinear restrictions, as many rational expectations models are. In these circumstances, a useful result is that taking just *one* step from these initial consistent estimates, using the Gauss-Newton regression, yields estimates that are asymptotically equivalent to NLS estimates.

Let $\acute{\boldsymbol{\beta}}$ denote the initial estimates, which are assumed to be root-n consistent. The GNR is then

$$\boldsymbol{y} - \acute{\boldsymbol{x}} = \acute{\boldsymbol{X}}\boldsymbol{b} + \text{residuals},$$

and the estimate of $\boldsymbol{b}$ from this regression is

$$\acute{\boldsymbol{b}} = \big(\acute{\boldsymbol{X}}^\top\acute{\boldsymbol{X}}\big)^{-1}\acute{\boldsymbol{X}}^\top(\boldsymbol{y} - \acute{\boldsymbol{x}}). \tag{6.31}$$

Thus the **one-step efficient estimator** is

$$\grave{\boldsymbol{\beta}} = \acute{\boldsymbol{\beta}} + \acute{\boldsymbol{b}}.$$

Taylor expanding $\boldsymbol{x}(\acute{\boldsymbol{\beta}})$ around $\boldsymbol{\beta} = \boldsymbol{\beta}_0$ yields

$$\acute{\boldsymbol{x}} \cong \boldsymbol{x}_0 + \boldsymbol{X}_0(\acute{\boldsymbol{\beta}} - \boldsymbol{\beta}_0),$$

where $\boldsymbol{x}_0 \equiv \boldsymbol{x}(\boldsymbol{\beta}_0)$ and $\boldsymbol{X}_0 \equiv \boldsymbol{X}(\boldsymbol{\beta}_0)$. Substituting this into (6.31), replacing $\boldsymbol{y}$ by its value under the DGP, $\boldsymbol{x}_0 + \boldsymbol{u}$, and inserting appropriate powers of n so that all quantities are $O(1)$, leads to the result that

$$\begin{aligned} n^{1/2}\acute{\boldsymbol{b}} &\cong n^{-1/2}\big(n^{-1}\acute{\boldsymbol{X}}^\top\acute{\boldsymbol{X}}\big)^{-1}\acute{\boldsymbol{X}}^\top\big(\boldsymbol{x}_0 + \boldsymbol{u} - \boldsymbol{x}_0 - \boldsymbol{X}_0(\acute{\boldsymbol{\beta}} - \boldsymbol{\beta}_0)\big) \\ &= \big(n^{-1}\acute{\boldsymbol{X}}^\top\acute{\boldsymbol{X}}\big)^{-1}\big(n^{-1/2}\acute{\boldsymbol{X}}^\top\boldsymbol{u} - (n^{-1}\acute{\boldsymbol{X}}^\top\boldsymbol{X}_0)n^{1/2}(\acute{\boldsymbol{\beta}} - \boldsymbol{\beta}_0)\big). \end{aligned}$$

But notice that

$$n^{-1}\acute{\boldsymbol{X}}^\top\acute{\boldsymbol{X}} \overset{a}{=} n^{-1}\boldsymbol{X}_0^\top\boldsymbol{X}_0 \overset{a}{=} n^{-1}\acute{\boldsymbol{X}}^\top\boldsymbol{X}_0,$$

which is a consequence of the consistency of $\acute{\boldsymbol{\beta}}$. Thus

$$n^{1/2}\acute{\boldsymbol{b}} \overset{a}{=} \big(n^{-1}\boldsymbol{X}_0^{\top}\boldsymbol{X}_0\big)^{-1}\big(n^{-1/2}\boldsymbol{X}_0^{\top}\boldsymbol{u}\big) - n^{1/2}(\acute{\boldsymbol{\beta}} - \boldsymbol{\beta}_0).$$

Adding this expression to $n^{1/2}\acute{\boldsymbol{\beta}}$ to obtain $n^{1/2}$ times the one-step efficient estimator $\grave{\boldsymbol{\beta}}$, we see that

$$n^{1/2}(\grave{\boldsymbol{\beta}} - \boldsymbol{\beta}_0) \cong \big(n^{-1}\boldsymbol{X}_0^{\top}\boldsymbol{X}_0\big)^{-1}\big(n^{-1/2}\boldsymbol{X}_0^{\top}\boldsymbol{u}\big).$$

After we take the probability limit of $n^{-1}\boldsymbol{X}_0^{\top}\boldsymbol{X}_0$, this becomes

$$n^{1/2}(\grave{\boldsymbol{\beta}} - \boldsymbol{\beta}_0) \overset{a}{=} \operatorname*{plim}_{n\to\infty}\big(n^{-1}\boldsymbol{X}_0^{\top}\boldsymbol{X}_0\big)^{-1}\big(n^{-1/2}\boldsymbol{X}_0^{\top}\boldsymbol{u}\big). \tag{6.32}$$

The right-hand side of this expression should look familiar. In fact, the result (5.39) from Chapter 5 shows that $n^{1/2}(\hat{\boldsymbol{\beta}} - \boldsymbol{\beta}_0)$ is asymptotically equal to the right-hand side of (6.32). Thus we have proved that the one-step estimator $\grave{\boldsymbol{\beta}}$ is asymptotically equivalent to the NLS estimator $\hat{\boldsymbol{\beta}}$. It must therefore have the same asymptotic distribution, and so we conclude that

$$n^{1/2}(\grave{\boldsymbol{\beta}} - \boldsymbol{\beta}_0) \overset{a}{\sim} N\big(\boldsymbol{0}, \sigma^2(n^{-1}\boldsymbol{X}_0^{\top}\boldsymbol{X}_0)^{-1}\big).$$

One-step estimation can be particularly useful for imposing nonlinear restrictions on a model that is easy to estimate unrestrictedly but difficult to estimate subject to the restrictions. In particular, suppose that the unrestricted regression function is $\boldsymbol{X\beta}$ and that the restricted regression function can be written as $\boldsymbol{X\beta}(\boldsymbol{\gamma})$, where $\boldsymbol{\beta}(\boldsymbol{\gamma})$ is a k-vector of smooth functions of the l-vector $\boldsymbol{\gamma}$, l being smaller than k. Thus the restricted model is nonlinear only in the parameters. Some elements of $\boldsymbol{\beta}(\boldsymbol{\gamma})$ may of course be zero. In this case, the restricted model is

$$\boldsymbol{y} = \boldsymbol{X\beta}(\boldsymbol{\gamma}) + \boldsymbol{u}, \tag{6.33}$$

and the unrestricted model is

$$\boldsymbol{y} = \boldsymbol{X\beta} + \boldsymbol{u}. \tag{6.34}$$

The OLS estimates of (6.34), $\hat{\boldsymbol{\beta}}$, provide initial consistent estimates $\hat{\boldsymbol{\gamma}}$. These may or may not be easy to compute and will certainly not be unique, since there are fewer elements of $\boldsymbol{\gamma}$ than of $\boldsymbol{\beta}$. The regression for obtaining one-step estimates is the GNR corresponding to (6.33), with the parameter vector $\boldsymbol{\gamma}$ evaluated at $\hat{\boldsymbol{\gamma}}$:

$$\boldsymbol{y} - \boldsymbol{X\beta}(\hat{\boldsymbol{\gamma}}) = \hat{\boldsymbol{X}}^{*}\boldsymbol{c} + \text{residuals},$$

where the $n \times l$ matrix $\hat{\boldsymbol{X}}^{*}$ is defined by

$$\hat{\boldsymbol{X}}^{*} \equiv \boldsymbol{X}\,\frac{\partial\boldsymbol{\beta}(\boldsymbol{\gamma})}{\partial\boldsymbol{\gamma}}\bigg|_{\boldsymbol{\gamma}=\hat{\boldsymbol{\gamma}}}.$$

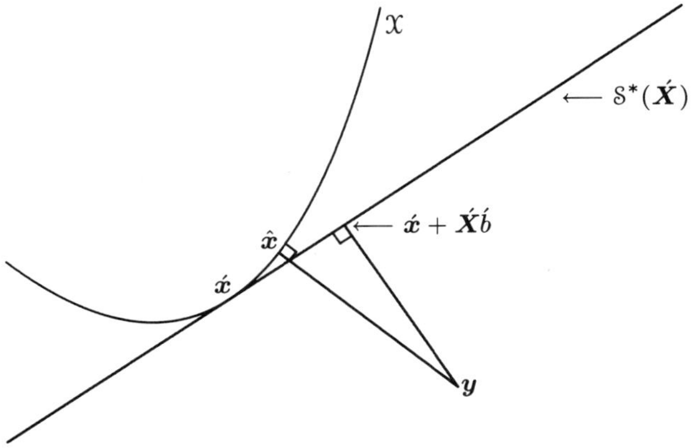

Figure 6.4 One-step efficient estimation

As usual, the one-step estimates are $\grave{\gamma} = \hat{\gamma} + \hat{\boldsymbol{c}}$, and these will be asymptotically equivalent to the restricted estimates $\tilde{\gamma}$, which may be a good deal more expensive to obtain.

Intuitively, one-step efficient estimators based on the GNR are asymptotically equivalent to NLS estimators for a reason very similar to the one we gave in the last section for the validity of tests based on the Gauss-Newton regression. What the GNR does is to minimize $SSR^*(\acute{\boldsymbol{\beta}}+\boldsymbol{b})$, which is a quadratic approximation to $SSR(\boldsymbol{\beta})$ around $\acute{\boldsymbol{\beta}}$. Asymptotically, the function $SSR(\boldsymbol{\beta})$ is quadratic in the neighborhood of $\boldsymbol{\beta}_0$. When the sample size is large enough, the consistency of $\acute{\boldsymbol{\beta}}$ implies that we will be taking the quadratic approximation at a point very near $\boldsymbol{\beta}_0$, and so the approximation will coincide with $SSR(\boldsymbol{\beta})$ itself asymptotically.

We can see what is happening by considering Figure 6.4. As in previous figures of this type (e.g., Figure 2.2), $k = 1$ and we suppose that $\boldsymbol{x}(\beta)$ lies, locally at least, in a two-dimensional subspace of $\mathbb{R}^n$. Otherwise, we could not draw it on the page. It is deliberately made highly nonlinear within that space so as to make the issues easier to grasp. The manifold $\mathcal{X}$ thus forms a sharply curved line in $\mathbb{R}^n$. At the point $\acute{\boldsymbol{x}} \equiv \boldsymbol{x}(\acute{\beta})$ we take a linear approximation, $\acute{\boldsymbol{x}} + \acute{\boldsymbol{X}}b$. The subspace spanned by the columns of $\acute{\boldsymbol{X}}$, translated so that it is tangent to the manifold $\mathcal{X}$ at $\acute{\boldsymbol{x}}$, is denoted by $\mathcal{S}^*(\acute{\boldsymbol{X}})$. One-step estimation involves projecting $\boldsymbol{y}$ orthogonally onto this subspace so as to yield a coefficient estimate $\acute{b}$. From this we then obtain the one-step estimate $\grave{\beta} = \acute{\beta} + \acute{b}$. Nonlinear least squares, in contrast, involves projecting $\boldsymbol{y}$ orthogonally onto $\mathcal{X}$ itself, at the point $\hat{\boldsymbol{x}}$. Evidently, $\hat{\beta}$ and $\grave{\beta}$ will in general differ unless $\mathcal{S}^*(\acute{\boldsymbol{X}})$ coincides with $\mathcal{X}$ in a neighborhood of $\acute{\beta}$. But the NLS and one-step estimates are nevertheless asymptotically equivalent because the consistency of $\acute{\boldsymbol{x}}$ implies that, asymptotically, it is so close to $\hat{\boldsymbol{x}}$ that $\mathcal{X}$ can have no appreciable curvature between those two points.

Unfortunately, the fact that one-step estimators based on the GNR are asymptotically equivalent to NLS estimators does *not* imply that the former will have finite-sample properties similar to those of the latter. Remember that the equivalence requires that the DGP be $\boldsymbol{y} = \boldsymbol{x}(\boldsymbol{\beta}_0) + \boldsymbol{u}$. If the DGP is not a special case of the model, the equivalence breaks down. Even if it is, a great deal depends on the quality of the initial consistent estimator $\acute{\boldsymbol{\beta}}$. When $\acute{\boldsymbol{\beta}}$ is close to $\boldsymbol{\beta}_0$ and the sample is large enough, $SSR^*(\acute{\boldsymbol{\beta}} + \boldsymbol{b})$ should be a very good approximation to $SSR(\boldsymbol{\beta})$, and so $\grave{\boldsymbol{\beta}}$ should be close to the NLS estimate $\hat{\boldsymbol{\beta}}$. On the other hand, when the initial consistent estimate is far from $\boldsymbol{\beta}_0$ (and the fact that an estimator is consistent does not prevent it from being extremely inefficient), the one-step estimates may differ greatly from the NLS estimates. When the two differ significantly, we would recommend using the NLS estimates, although without doing a detailed study of the particular model involved, one cannot categorically recommend one estimator over another when the two are asymptotically equivalent. One-step estimation makes most sense when the sample size is large, which implies that the initial consistent estimator is likely to be good and also that nonlinear least squares may be expensive.

6.7 Hypothesis Tests Using Any Consistent Estimates

The procedures for testing that we discussed in Sections 6.4 and 6.5 all involve evaluating the artificial regression at restricted NLS estimates and thus yield test statistics based on the LM principle. But when the restricted regression function is nonlinear, it is not always convenient to obtain NLS estimates. Luckily, one can perform tests by means of a GNR whenever any root-n consistent estimates that satisfy the null hypothesis are available. We briefly discuss how to do so in this section.

Suppose we are dealing with the situation discussed in Section 6.4, in which the parameter vector $\boldsymbol{\beta}$ is partitioned as $[\boldsymbol{\beta}_1 \,\vdots\, \boldsymbol{\beta}_2]$, and the null hypothesis is that $\boldsymbol{\beta}_2 = \mathbf{0}$. Assume that we have available a vector of root-n consistent estimates $\acute{\boldsymbol{\beta}} \equiv [\acute{\boldsymbol{\beta}}_1 \,\vdots\, \mathbf{0}]$. Then the GNR, in obvious notation, is

$$\boldsymbol{y} - \acute{\boldsymbol{x}} = \acute{\boldsymbol{X}}_1 \boldsymbol{b}_1 + \acute{\boldsymbol{X}}_2 \boldsymbol{b}_2 + \text{residuals}. \tag{6.35}$$

The explained sum of squares from this regression is

$$(\boldsymbol{y} - \acute{\boldsymbol{x}})^\top \acute{\boldsymbol{P}}_1 (\boldsymbol{y} - \acute{\boldsymbol{x}}) + (\boldsymbol{y} - \acute{\boldsymbol{x}})^\top \acute{\boldsymbol{M}}_1 \acute{\boldsymbol{X}}_2 \big(\acute{\boldsymbol{X}}_2^\top \acute{\boldsymbol{M}}_1 \acute{\boldsymbol{X}}_2\big)^{-1} \acute{\boldsymbol{X}}_2^\top \acute{\boldsymbol{M}}_1 (\boldsymbol{y} - \acute{\boldsymbol{x}}). \tag{6.36}$$

The first term here is the explained sum of squares from a regression of $\boldsymbol{y} - \acute{\boldsymbol{x}}$ on $\acute{\boldsymbol{X}}_1$ alone, and the second term is the increase in the explained sum of squares brought about by the inclusion of $\acute{\boldsymbol{X}}_2$. Note that the first term is in general not zero, because $\acute{\boldsymbol{\beta}}_1$ will not in general satisfy the first-order conditions for NLS estimates of the restricted model.

The difference between the explained sum of squares from (6.35) and the explained sum of squares from a regression of $\boldsymbol{y} - \acute{\boldsymbol{x}}$ on $\acute{\boldsymbol{X}}_1$ alone is

$$(\boldsymbol{y} - \acute{\boldsymbol{x}})^\top \acute{\boldsymbol{M}}_1 \acute{\boldsymbol{X}}_2 \big(\acute{\boldsymbol{X}}_2^\top \acute{\boldsymbol{M}}_1 \acute{\boldsymbol{X}}_2\big)^{-1} \acute{\boldsymbol{X}}_2^\top \acute{\boldsymbol{M}}_1 (\boldsymbol{y} - \acute{\boldsymbol{x}}) = \big\|\boldsymbol{P}_{\acute{M}_1 \acute{X}_2}(\boldsymbol{y} - \acute{\boldsymbol{x}})\big\|^2.$$

This looks just like the numerator of the F statistic (6.21). In fact, the sole difference is that everything is evaluated at the root-n consistent estimates $\acute{\boldsymbol{\beta}}$ rather than at the restricted NLS estimates $\tilde{\boldsymbol{\beta}}$. It should therefore come as no surprise to learn that the F statistic for $\boldsymbol{b}_2 = \boldsymbol{0}$ in (6.35) is asymptotically the same (under the null hypothesis) as the F statistic for $\boldsymbol{b}_2 = \boldsymbol{0}$ in the more familiar LM test GNR (6.17).

We will not bother to prove this result formally. The intuition is so simple that a proof is hardly necessary. From the results of the preceding section, we know that

$$n^{1/2}(\acute{\boldsymbol{\beta}} + \acute{\boldsymbol{b}} - \boldsymbol{\beta}_0) \overset{a}{=} n^{1/2}(\hat{\boldsymbol{\beta}} - \boldsymbol{\beta}_0),$$

where $\acute{\boldsymbol{b}}$ is the OLS estimate of $\boldsymbol{b}$ from (6.35) and $\hat{\boldsymbol{\beta}}$ is the unrestricted NLS estimate. Evidently, $\acute{\boldsymbol{\beta}} + \acute{\boldsymbol{b}}$ is a vector of one-step consistent estimates. Since $\acute{\boldsymbol{\beta}}_2 = \boldsymbol{0}$, we have that

$$n^{1/2}(\acute{\boldsymbol{b}}_2 - \boldsymbol{\beta}_2^0) \overset{a}{=} n^{1/2}(\hat{\boldsymbol{\beta}}_2 - \boldsymbol{\beta}_2^0),$$

where $\boldsymbol{\beta}_2^0$ is the value of $\boldsymbol{\beta}_2$ under the DGP. Thus the OLS estimate of $\boldsymbol{b}_2$ from (6.35) is asymptotically equivalent to the unrestricted NLS estimate $\hat{\boldsymbol{\beta}}_2$. This should make it intuitively obvious that an F test for $\boldsymbol{b}_2 = \boldsymbol{0}$ in (6.35) is equivalent to a test for $\boldsymbol{\beta}_2 = \boldsymbol{0}$.

We can compute tests for $\boldsymbol{\beta}_2 = \boldsymbol{0}$ using regression (6.35) in the same way that we can using (6.17), with one exception. The quantity nR^2 from (6.17) is a valid test statistic, but the same quantity from (6.35) is not. The reason is that $\acute{\boldsymbol{X}}_1$ will generally have some ability to explain the variation in $\boldsymbol{y} - \acute{\boldsymbol{x}}$, which implies that the first term in (6.36) will not be zero. We could construct a valid test statistic as nR^2 from (6.35) minus nR^2 from a regression of $\boldsymbol{y} - \acute{\boldsymbol{x}}$ on $\acute{\boldsymbol{X}}_1$ alone. However, it is preferable simply to use F or t tests, which are computed just as if (6.35) were a genuine regression rather than an artificial one.

In the literature on maximum likelihood estimation, tests based on arbitrary root-n consistent estimators are called **$C(\alpha)$ tests**. Such tests were originally proposed by Neyman (1959); for more references, and discussion, see Section 13.7. As we will see there, it is possible to interpret the tests we have discussed in this section as $C(\alpha)$ tests. But these tests could also be interpreted as Wald tests in some cases. Suppose that $\acute{\boldsymbol{\beta}} = [\hat{\boldsymbol{\beta}}_1 \vdots \boldsymbol{0}]$, where $\hat{\boldsymbol{\beta}}_1$ is the unrestricted NLS estimate of $\boldsymbol{\beta}_1$. This choice for $\acute{\boldsymbol{\beta}}$ is certainly root-n consistent and satisfies the null hypothesis; thus it will clearly yield valid test statistics. Since the GNR depends only on the unrestricted estimates $\acute{\boldsymbol{\beta}}$, we will refer to tests computed in this way as **Wald-like**, although they are not strictly based on the Wald principle. Such Wald-like tests may well be easier to compute than conventional Wald tests in some cases.

6.8 Nonlinear Estimation Using the GNR

In this section, we discuss how the Gauss-Newton regression can be used as part of an effective algorithm for minimizing sum-of-squares functions. This was actually the original motivation for the GNR. The term "Gauss-Newton" is in fact taken from the literature on numerical optimization as applied to nonlinear least squares problems, and most of the other uses of this artificial regression in econometrics are relatively recent, as we discuss in Section 6.9.

Most effective algorithms that attempt to maximize or minimize a smooth function of two or more variables, say $Q(\boldsymbol{\theta})$, operate in basically the same way. Such an algorithm goes through a series of major iterations, at each of which it starts with a particular value of $\boldsymbol{\theta}$, say $\boldsymbol{\theta}^{(j)}$, and tries to find a better one. The algorithm first chooses a direction in which to search for a better value of $\boldsymbol{\theta}$ and then decides how far to move in that direction. The main differences among unconstrained optimization algorithms are in the way in which the direction to search is chosen and in the way in which the size of the ultimate step in that direction is determined. Numerous choices are available.

Note that any algorithm for minimization can just as easily be used for maximization, since minimizing $Q(\boldsymbol{\theta})$ is equivalent to maximizing $-Q(\boldsymbol{\theta})$. Following the convention used in most of the literature, we will deal with the case of minimization, which is what we wish to do with sum-of-squares functions anyway.[2] In this section, we will attempt to give an overview of how numerical minimization algorithms work and how the Gauss-Newton regression may be used as part of them, but we will not discuss many of the important computer-related issues that substantially affect the performance of computer algorithms. An excellent reference on the art and science of numerical optimization is Gill, Murray, and Wright (1981); see also Bard (1974), Quandt (1983), Press, Flannery, Teukolsky, and Vetterling (1986, Chapter 10), and Seber and Wild (1989, Chapter 14).

One of the most fundamental techniques of numerical optimization is **Newton's method.** Suppose that we wish to minimize a nonlinear function $Q(\boldsymbol{\theta})$, where $\boldsymbol{\theta}$ is a k–vector. Given any initial value, say $\boldsymbol{\theta}^{(1)}$, we can obtain a second-order Taylor-series approximation of $Q(\boldsymbol{\theta})$ around $\boldsymbol{\theta}^{(1)}$:

$$\begin{aligned} Q^*(\boldsymbol{\theta}) &= Q(\boldsymbol{\theta}^{(1)}) + (\boldsymbol{g}^{(1)})^{\top}(\boldsymbol{\theta} - \boldsymbol{\theta}^{(1)}) + \tfrac{1}{2}(\boldsymbol{\theta} - \boldsymbol{\theta}^{(1)})^{\top}\boldsymbol{H}^{(1)}(\boldsymbol{\theta} - \boldsymbol{\theta}^{(1)}) \\ &\cong Q(\boldsymbol{\theta}), \end{aligned}$$

where $\boldsymbol{g}(\boldsymbol{\theta})$, the gradient of $Q(\boldsymbol{\theta})$, is a column vector of length k with typical element $\partial Q(\boldsymbol{\theta})/\partial\theta_i$, and $\boldsymbol{H}(\boldsymbol{\theta})$, the Hessian of $Q(\boldsymbol{\theta})$, is a $k \times k$ matrix with typical element $\partial^2 Q(\boldsymbol{\theta})/\partial\theta_i\partial\theta_l$; $\boldsymbol{g}^{(1)}$ and $\boldsymbol{H}^{(1)}$ denote, respectively, $\boldsymbol{g}(\boldsymbol{\theta}^{(1)})$

[2] When we deal with likelihood functions, however, we will wish to maximize them (see Chapter 8). Most of the following discussion is applicable with minor changes to that case.

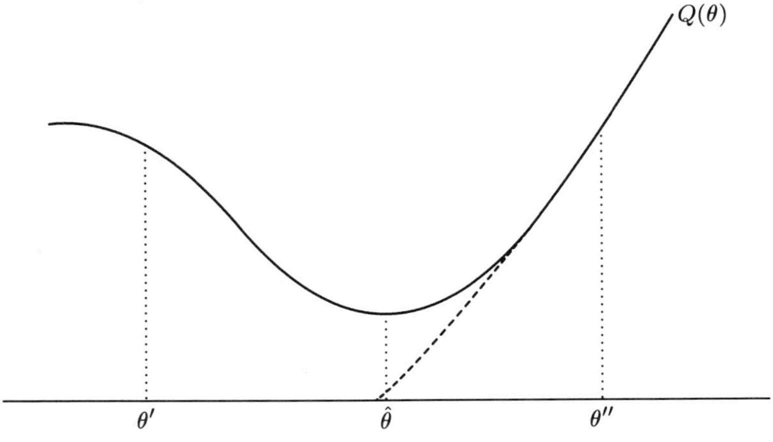

Figure 6.5 Cases for which Newton's method will not work

and $\boldsymbol{H}(\boldsymbol{\theta}^{(1)})$. Solving the first-order conditions for a minimum of $Q^*(\boldsymbol{\theta})$ with respect to $\boldsymbol{\theta}$ yields a new value of $\boldsymbol{\theta}$, which we will call $\boldsymbol{\theta}^{(2)}$. It depends on $\boldsymbol{\theta}^{(1)}$, and on the gradient and the Hessian evaluated at $\boldsymbol{\theta}^{(1)}$, in a very simple way:

$$\boldsymbol{\theta}^{(2)} = \boldsymbol{\theta}^{(1)} - \left(\boldsymbol{H}^{(1)}\right)^{-1}\boldsymbol{g}^{(1)}. \tag{6.37}$$

Equation (6.37) is the heart of Newton's method. If the quadratic approximation $Q^*(\boldsymbol{\theta})$ is a strictly convex function, which it will be if and only if the Hessian $\boldsymbol{H}(\boldsymbol{\theta}^{(1)})$ is positive definite, $\boldsymbol{\theta}^{(2)}$ will be the global minimum of $Q^*(\boldsymbol{\theta})$. If, in addition, $Q^*(\boldsymbol{\theta})$ is a good approximation to $Q(\boldsymbol{\theta})$, $\boldsymbol{\theta}^{(2)}$ should be close to $\hat{\boldsymbol{\theta}}$, the minimum of $Q(\boldsymbol{\theta})$. Newton's method involves using equation (6.37) repeatedly to find a succession of values $\boldsymbol{\theta}^{(2)}$, $\boldsymbol{\theta}^{(3)}, \ldots$. When the original function $Q(\boldsymbol{\theta})$ is quadratic and has a global minimum at $\hat{\boldsymbol{\theta}}$, Newton's method obviously finds $\hat{\boldsymbol{\theta}}$ in a single step, since the quadratic approximation is then exact. When $Q(\boldsymbol{\theta})$ is approximately quadratic, as all sum-of-squares functions are when sufficiently close to their minima, Newton's method generally converges very quickly.

In many other cases, however, Newton's method fails to work at all, especially if $Q(\boldsymbol{\theta})$ is not convex in the neighborhood of $\boldsymbol{\theta}^{(j)}$ for some j in the sequence. To see why, consider Figure 6.5. The one-dimensional function shown there has a global minimum at $\hat{\theta}$, but when Newton's method is started at points such as θ' or θ'', it may never find $\hat{\theta}$. In the former case, $Q(\theta)$ is concave at θ' instead of convex, and that causes Newton's method to head off in the wrong direction. In the latter case, the quadratic approximation at θ'' is extremely poor for values away from θ'', because $Q(\theta)$ is very flat near θ''. The quadratic approximation $Q^*(\theta)$ to $Q(\theta)$ taken at θ'' is shown by the dashed curve. It will evidently have a minimum far to the left of $\hat{\theta}$. Nevertheless, most effective nonlinear optimization techniques for smooth problems are modified versions of Newton's method, which attempt to retain its good qualities while enabling it to surmount problems like those illustrated in Figure 6.5.

Numerical minimization techniques that are based on Newton's method replace (6.37) with the slightly more complicated formula

$$\boldsymbol{\theta}^{(j+1)} = \boldsymbol{\theta}^{(j)} - \alpha^{(j)}\big(\boldsymbol{D}^{(j)}\big)^{-1}\boldsymbol{g}^{(j)}, \tag{6.38}$$

which determines $\boldsymbol{\theta}^{(j+1)}$, the value of $\boldsymbol{\theta}$ at step $j+1$, as a function of $\boldsymbol{\theta}^{(j)}$. Here $\alpha^{(j)}$ is a scalar that is usually determined endogenously, as the algorithm proceeds, and $\boldsymbol{D}^{(j)} \equiv \boldsymbol{D}(\boldsymbol{\theta}^{(j)})$ is a matrix that approximates $\boldsymbol{H}(\boldsymbol{\theta}^{(j)})$ near the minimum but is constructed so that it is always positive definite. Most of these algorithms consist of a series of two alternating steps. Starting from $\boldsymbol{\theta}^{(j)}$ they first compute $\boldsymbol{g}^{(j)}$ and $\boldsymbol{D}^{(j)}$ and thus determine in what direction to search. They then solve a one-dimensional minimization problem to find $\alpha^{(j)}$, which determines how far to go in that direction. These two steps together yield $\boldsymbol{\theta}^{(j+1)}$. The algorithms then return to the first step and continue alternating between the two steps until they decide that they have found a sufficiently accurate approximation to $\hat{\boldsymbol{\theta}}$.

Because they construct $\boldsymbol{D}(\boldsymbol{\theta})$ so that it is always positive definite, these modified Newton algorithms can handle problems where the function to be minimized is not globally convex. Different algorithms choose $\boldsymbol{D}(\boldsymbol{\theta})$ in different ways, some of which are quite ingenious and may be tricky to implement on a digital computer. As we will see, however, for sum-of-squares functions there is a very easy and natural way to choose $\boldsymbol{D}(\boldsymbol{\theta})$, based on the Gauss-Newton regression.

In many cases, $\alpha^{(j)}$ is chosen to minimize $Q\big(\boldsymbol{\theta}^{(j)} - \alpha^{(j)}(\boldsymbol{D}^{(j)})^{-1}\boldsymbol{g}^{(j)}\big)$, regarded as a one-dimensional function of $\alpha^{(j)}$. This means that points like θ'' in Figure 6.5 do not cause difficulties. Some algorithms do not actually minimize $Q\big(\boldsymbol{\theta}^{(j)} - \alpha^{(j)}(\boldsymbol{D}^{(j)})^{-1}\boldsymbol{g}^{(j)}\big)$ with respect to $\alpha^{(j)}$ but merely choose $\alpha^{(j)}$ so as to ensure that $Q(\boldsymbol{\theta}^{(j+1)})$ is less than $Q(\boldsymbol{\theta}^{(j)})$. It is essential that this be the case if we are to be sure that the algorithm will always make progress at each step. The best algorithms, which are designed to economize on computing time, may choose α quite crudely when they are far from $\hat{\boldsymbol{\theta}}$ but usually perform an accurate one-dimensional minimization when they are close to $\hat{\boldsymbol{\theta}}$.

When one is trying to minimize a sum-of-squares function $SSR(\boldsymbol{\beta})$, the Gauss-Newton regression provides a very convenient way to approximate $\boldsymbol{H}(\boldsymbol{\beta})$. Algorithms that do so are said to employ the **Gauss-Newton method**. In Section 5.4, we saw that $\boldsymbol{H}(\boldsymbol{\beta})$ has typical element

$$H_{il}(\boldsymbol{\beta}) = -2\sum_{t=1}^{n}\Big(\big(y_t - x_t(\boldsymbol{\beta})\big)\frac{\partial X_{ti}}{\partial \beta_l} - X_{ti}(\boldsymbol{\beta})X_{tl}(\boldsymbol{\beta})\Big). \tag{6.39}$$

This is equation (5.24) rewritten in scalar notation. We also saw that when the model is correct and the Hessian is evaluated at the true value of $\boldsymbol{\beta}$, this is asymptotically equivalent to

$$2\sum_{t=1}^{n} X_{ti}(\boldsymbol{\beta})X_{tl}(\boldsymbol{\beta});$$

the result is (5.38). Hence a natural choice for $\boldsymbol{D}(\boldsymbol{\beta})$ in a minimization algorithm of the class described by (6.38) is

$$\boldsymbol{D}(\boldsymbol{\beta}) = 2\boldsymbol{X}^{\top}(\boldsymbol{\beta})\boldsymbol{X}(\boldsymbol{\beta}). \tag{6.40}$$

The gradient of $SSR(\boldsymbol{\beta})$ is

$$\boldsymbol{g}(\boldsymbol{\beta}) = -2\boldsymbol{X}^{\top}(\boldsymbol{\beta})\big(\boldsymbol{y} - \boldsymbol{x}(\boldsymbol{\beta})\big). \tag{6.41}$$

Substituting (6.40) and (6.41) into (6.38) yields

$$\begin{aligned}\boldsymbol{\beta}^{(j+1)} &= \boldsymbol{\beta}^{(j)} + \alpha^{(j)}\big(2(\boldsymbol{X}^{(j)})^{\top}\boldsymbol{X}^{(j)}\big)^{-1}\big(2(\boldsymbol{X}^{(j)})^{\top}(\boldsymbol{y} - \boldsymbol{x}^{(j)})\big)\\ &= \boldsymbol{\beta}^{(j)} + \alpha^{(j)}\big((\boldsymbol{X}^{(j)})^{\top}\boldsymbol{X}^{(j)}\big)^{-1}(\boldsymbol{X}^{(j)})^{\top}(\boldsymbol{y} - \boldsymbol{x}^{(j)})\\ &= \boldsymbol{\beta}^{(j)} + \alpha^{(j)}\boldsymbol{b}^{(j)},\end{aligned}$$

where $\boldsymbol{b}^{(j)}$ is the estimate of $\boldsymbol{b}$ from the Gauss-Newton regression with $\boldsymbol{x}(\boldsymbol{\beta})$ and $\boldsymbol{X}(\boldsymbol{\beta})$ both evaluated at $\boldsymbol{\beta}^{(j)}$, and $\boldsymbol{X}^{(j)} \equiv \boldsymbol{X}(\boldsymbol{\beta}^{(j)})$.

The connection between minimization algorithms and the Gauss-Newton regression is now clear. The GNR provides a cheap and convenient way to obtain a matrix that approximates the Hessian of $SSR(\boldsymbol{\beta})$ and is always positive definite (provided, of course, that the model is identified at all points where the GNR is run). It does even more than this, since the vector of coefficients from the GNR is actually equal to $-(\boldsymbol{D}^{(j)})^{-1}\boldsymbol{g}^{(j)}$, which is the direction in which the algorithm will look at each step. By combining the GNR with a good one-dimensional search routine (to find α at each step), we obtain a reasonably effective algorithm for finding nonlinear least squares estimates. Such an algorithm is a major improvement over the original Gauss-Newton method which, like Newton's method in its original form, simply sets α to 1 at each step.

We say "reasonably effective" because further improvements are certainly possible. A major difficulty with the Gauss-Newton method is that the matrix $\boldsymbol{X}^{\top}(\boldsymbol{\beta})\boldsymbol{X}(\boldsymbol{\beta})$ may sometimes be very close to singular, even though the model is reasonably well identified by the data when evaluated near $\boldsymbol{\beta}_0$. When $\boldsymbol{X}^{\top}(\boldsymbol{\beta})\boldsymbol{X}(\boldsymbol{\beta})$ is nearly singular, the algorithm gets into trouble, because $\boldsymbol{b}$ no longer lies in the same k–dimensional space as $\boldsymbol{\beta}$, but rather in a subspace of dimension equal to the effective rank of $\boldsymbol{X}^{\top}(\boldsymbol{\beta})\boldsymbol{X}(\boldsymbol{\beta})$. Since one cannot expect to find $\hat{\boldsymbol{\beta}}$ if one looks for it in a space of too low dimension, an unmodified

Gauss-Newton algorithm can cycle indefinitely without making any progress when this happens. The best algorithms for least squares problems check whether this is happening and replace $\boldsymbol{X}^\top(\boldsymbol{\beta})\boldsymbol{X}(\boldsymbol{\beta})$ with a better-behaved choice for $\boldsymbol{D}$ whenever it does. See the references cited above.

The Gauss-Newton method may also work badly if $2\boldsymbol{X}^\top(\boldsymbol{\beta})\boldsymbol{X}(\boldsymbol{\beta})$ provides a poor approximation to $\boldsymbol{H}(\boldsymbol{\beta})$, that is, if the first term inside the summation in (6.39) is large. This may happen for a correctly specified model when the sample size is small and for an incorrectly specified model no matter what the sample size. Of course, inference based on asymptotic theory will be unreliable in the first of these cases and hopeless in the second. Thus poor performance of the Gauss-Newton method may provide a useful warning.

No numerical minimization procedure ever finds $\hat{\boldsymbol{\theta}}$ *exactly* and, given the limitations of floating-point arithmetic on digital computers, it is often unrealistic to expect to obtain more than six or perhaps eight digits of accuracy. Unless one explicitly tells them to stop, these iterative algorithms will keep searching forever, even though changes in $\boldsymbol{\beta}$ and $SSR(\boldsymbol{\beta})$ are due only to round-off errors in the computer. The choice of **stopping rules** is thus an important part of the art of nonlinear minimization. Several authors — see Quandt (1983) — have suggested that the most natural rule for a Gauss-Newton algorithm is to stop when

$$\frac{\big(\boldsymbol{y} - \boldsymbol{x}(\boldsymbol{\beta}^{(j)})\big)^\top \boldsymbol{X}^{(j)} \big(\boldsymbol{X}^{(j)\top}\boldsymbol{X}^{(j)}\big)^{-1} \boldsymbol{X}^{(j)\top}\big(\boldsymbol{y} - \boldsymbol{x}(\boldsymbol{\beta}^{(j)})\big)}{\big(\boldsymbol{y} - \boldsymbol{x}(\boldsymbol{\beta}^{(j)})\big)^\top\big(\boldsymbol{y} - \boldsymbol{x}(\boldsymbol{\beta}^{(j)})\big)/n} < \varepsilon, \tag{6.42}$$

where ε is a preset convergence criterion that can be adjusted by the user. The left-hand side of (6.42) is just n times the uncentered R^2 from the Gauss-Newton regression of $\boldsymbol{y} - \boldsymbol{x}(\boldsymbol{\beta}^{(j)})$ on $\boldsymbol{X}^{(j)}$, which has exactly the same form as the test statistics we discussed in Section 6.4. Notice that, provided $\boldsymbol{\beta}^{(j)}$ is close to $\boldsymbol{\beta}_0$, expression (6.42) is approximately equal to $\big(SSR(\boldsymbol{\beta}^{(j)}) - SSR(\hat{\boldsymbol{\beta}})\big)/\sigma_0^2$. Hence this stopping rule tells the algorithm to stop when an approximation to $SSR(\boldsymbol{\beta})$ at $\boldsymbol{\beta}^{(j)}$ indicates that the distance between $SSR(\boldsymbol{\beta}^{(j)})$ and $SSR(\hat{\boldsymbol{\beta}})$ is sufficiently small relative to the variance of the error terms.

A geometrical interpretation of this stopping rule is shown in Figure 6.6. The denominator of the left-hand side of (6.42) is

$$\frac{1}{n}\big\|\boldsymbol{y} - \boldsymbol{x}(\boldsymbol{\beta}^{(j)})\big\|^2, \tag{6.43}$$

which is $1/n$ times the squared length of the distance between $\boldsymbol{y}$ and $\boldsymbol{x}(\boldsymbol{\beta}^{(j)})$. The numerator is

$$\big\|\boldsymbol{P}_{X^{(j)}}\big(\boldsymbol{y} - \boldsymbol{x}(\boldsymbol{\beta}^{(j)})\big)\big\|^2, \tag{6.44}$$

which is the squared length of the projection of $\boldsymbol{y} - \boldsymbol{x}(\boldsymbol{\beta}^{(j)})$ onto $\mathcal{S}(\boldsymbol{X}^{(j)})$. The ratio of (6.44) to (6.43), like all quantities that can be interpreted as R^2's, is

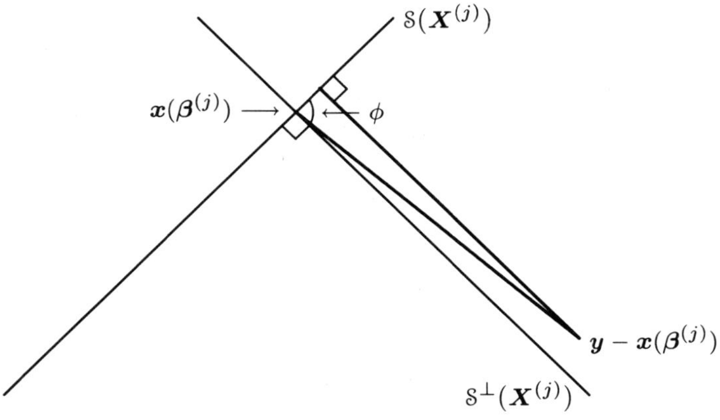

Figure 6.6 Stopping rule is not quite satisfied

the squared cosine of a certain angle. In this case, the angle in question is the one between $\boldsymbol{y} - \boldsymbol{x}(\boldsymbol{\beta}^{(j)})$ and its projection onto $\mathcal{S}(\boldsymbol{X}^{(j)})$, which is labeled ϕ in the figure. When this ratio is small enough, $\boldsymbol{y} - \boldsymbol{x}(\boldsymbol{\beta}^{(j)})$ must be almost orthogonal to $\boldsymbol{X}^{(j)}$, and the first-order conditions must therefore be almost satisfied. The stopping rule (6.42) is actually n times $\cos^2\phi$. Although the factor of n could be omitted, it gives the stopping rule some desirable properties. It makes the criterion that we compare with ε have the same form as the nR^2 test statistics of Section 6.4, and it ensures that the *numerical* accuracy of the estimates will be proportional to $n^{-1/2}$, just like their statistical accuracy. If the sample size were extremely large, however, one might have to be careful not to use too small a value of ε, since otherwise the stopping rule could conceivably call for a level of numerical accuracy not achievable by the computer.

This discussion suggests that the stopping rule (6.42) has a great deal of intuitive appeal. Gill, Murray, and Wright (1981) discusses a number of other stopping rules, all of which suffer from various deficiencies (such as being sensitive to how the parameters are scaled) that are not shared by (6.42).[3] Because it does not suffer from these deficiencies, and because the left-hand side is very easily calculated as a by-product of the Gauss-Newton regression for each $\boldsymbol{\beta}^{(j)}$, (6.42) appears to be a very attractive stopping rule.

Of course, any form of stopping rule may work badly if ε is chosen incorrectly. If ε is too large, the algorithm may stop too soon, when $\boldsymbol{\beta}$ is still far

[3] Oddly enough, Gill, Murray, and Wright (1981) does not discuss this particular rule or any generalizations of it. This may be because (6.42) is an obvious rule to use with the Gauss-Newton regression, but not so obvious if one is dealing with more general minimization problems.

away from $\hat{\boldsymbol{\beta}}$. If it is too small, the algorithm may keep going long after $\boldsymbol{\beta}$ is so close to $\hat{\boldsymbol{\beta}}$ that any differences are due solely to round-off error and may in fact continue forever. It is therefore frequently a good idea to experiment with the value of ε to see how sensitive to it the results are. If the reported $\hat{\boldsymbol{\beta}}$ changes noticeably when ε is reduced, then either the first value of ε was too large, or the algorithm is having trouble finding an accurate minimum. Reasonable values of ε, for this stopping rule, might be somewhere between 10^{-4} and 10^{-12}.

6.9 Further Reading

As noted above, the Gauss-Newton regression has been used for many years as the key part of the Gauss-Newton method, which is actually several related algorithms for nonlinear least squares estimation. Bard (1974) discusses many of these. Newton's method, as its name implies, is very old, and the idea of approximating the Hessian by a matrix that depends only on first derivatives dates back to Gauss (1809). However, because nonlinear estimation was generally not practical until digital computers became widely available, most work in this area has been relatively recent. Important papers in the post-computer development of the Gauss-Newton method include Hartley (1961) and Marquardt (1963). The survey article by Quandt (1983) provides numerous other references, as does Seber and Wild (1989, Chapter 14).

In contrast to its long history in estimation, the use of the GNR for specification testing is quite recent. The first paper in the econometric literature appears to be Durbin (1970), which proposed what amounts to a special case of the GNR as a way of testing linear regression models for serial correlation when there are lagged dependent variables. This procedure was treated in a rather cursory fashion, however, since it was in the same paper that Durbin proposed his well-known h test. What came to be known as Durbin's "alternative procedure," which is really a special case of the GNR, was for some years largely ignored by theoretical econometricians and entirely ignored by practitioners. All this will be discussed further in Chapter 10.

Interest in the Gauss-Newton regression as a way of generating test statistics dates principally from the late 1970s. Godfrey (1978a, 1978b) and Breusch (1978) greatly generalized Durbin's alternative procedure and showed how to calculate LM tests for serial correlation using the GNR. Numerous other authors dealt with other special cases, contributed to the increased understanding of the general case we have discussed in this chapter, and developed related tests. Notable articles include Breusch and Pagan (1980) and Engle (1982a). Much of this literature explicitly assumes normal errors and develops the tests as LM tests within the framework of maximum likelihood estimation. This may be slightly misleading because, as we have seen, no assumption of normality is in fact needed for either nonlinear least squares estimation or tests based on the GNR to be asymptotically valid. More recent papers, such as

Pagan (1984a), Davidson and MacKinnon (1985a), and MacKinnon (1992), have focused on the case of regression models and have tried to unify and clarify the previous literature. We will be seeing a great deal of the Gauss-Newton regression, and also of related artificial regressions that have similar properties, throughout the remainder of the book.

TERMS AND CONCEPTS

algorithms for nonlinear least squares
artificial regression
$C(\alpha)$ tests
collinearity (for artificial regressions) and identifiability
condition number (of a matrix)
diagnostic test
Gauss-Newton method
Gauss-Newton regression (GNR)
heteroskedasticity-consistent covariance matrix estimate (HCCME)
identification and collinearity
Newton's method
nR^2 tests and F tests based on the GNR
numerical optimization algorithms
one-step efficient estimators
poorly identified model
Regression Specification Error Test (RESET)
stopping rules
variable addition tests
Wald-like tests

Chapter 7

Instrumental Variables

7.1 Introduction

Up to this point, the only estimation technique we have considered is least squares, both ordinary and nonlinear. While least squares has many merits, it also has some drawbacks. One major drawback is that least squares yields consistent estimates only if the error terms are asymptotically orthogonal to the regressors or, in the nonlinear case, to the derivatives of the regression function. Consider, for simplicity, the linear regression model

$$\boldsymbol{y} = \boldsymbol{X\beta} + \boldsymbol{u}, \quad \boldsymbol{u} \sim \mathrm{IID}(\boldsymbol{0}, \sigma^2 \mathbf{I}), \tag{7.01}$$

where $\boldsymbol{X}$ is an $n \times k$ matrix of explanatory variables. The issues are the same whether the regression function is linear or nonlinear, and so we will deal with the linear case for simplicity. When the data are generated by the DGP

$$\boldsymbol{y} = \boldsymbol{X\beta}_0 + \boldsymbol{u}, \quad \boldsymbol{u} \sim \mathrm{IID}(\boldsymbol{0}, \sigma_0^2 \mathbf{I}), \tag{7.02}$$

we have seen that the OLS estimate is

$$\hat{\boldsymbol{\beta}} \equiv \big(\boldsymbol{X}^{\top}\boldsymbol{X}\big)^{-1}\boldsymbol{X}^{\top}\boldsymbol{y} = \boldsymbol{\beta}_0 + \big(\boldsymbol{X}^{\top}\boldsymbol{X}\big)^{-1}\boldsymbol{X}^{\top}\boldsymbol{u}. \tag{7.03}$$

It is obvious that if $\hat{\boldsymbol{\beta}}$ is to be consistent for $\boldsymbol{\beta}_0$, the condition

$$\operatorname*{plim}_{n\to\infty}\big(n^{-1}\boldsymbol{X}^{\top}\boldsymbol{u}\big) = \boldsymbol{0}$$

must hold. If $\hat{\boldsymbol{\beta}}$ is to be unbiased, the stronger condition that $E(\boldsymbol{X}^{\top}\boldsymbol{u}) = \boldsymbol{0}$ must hold. These necessary conditions are not directly verifiable, since the orthogonality property of least squares ensures that regardless of whether $\boldsymbol{u}$ is correlated with $\boldsymbol{X}$ or not, the residuals $\hat{\boldsymbol{u}}$ are orthogonal to $\boldsymbol{X}$. This means that, no matter how biased and inconsistent least squares estimates may be, the least squares residuals will provide no evidence that there is a problem.

Suppose that $\mathrm{plim}(n^{-1}\boldsymbol{X}^{\top}\boldsymbol{u}) = \boldsymbol{w}$, a nonzero vector. Then from (7.03) it is clear that $\mathrm{plim}(\hat{\boldsymbol{\beta}}) \neq \boldsymbol{\beta}_0$. Moreover, the probability limit of n^{-1} times the sum of squared residuals will be

$$\operatorname*{plim}_{n\to\infty}\big(n^{-1}\boldsymbol{u}^{\top}\boldsymbol{M}_X\boldsymbol{u}\big) = \sigma_0^2 - \boldsymbol{w}^{\top}\operatorname*{plim}_{n\to\infty}\big(n^{-1}\boldsymbol{X}^{\top}\boldsymbol{X}\big)^{-1}\boldsymbol{w}.$$

If $\boldsymbol{u}$ were asymptotically uncorrelated with $\boldsymbol{X}$, this quantity would just be σ_0^2. Instead, it is *smaller* than σ_0^2. Thus using least squares makes the model fit too well. Because least squares minimizes the distance between $\boldsymbol{y}$ and $\mathcal{S}(\boldsymbol{X})$, part of the variation in $\boldsymbol{y}$ that is really due to variation in the error terms $\boldsymbol{u}$ has incorrectly been attributed to variation in the regressors.

Unfortunately, there are many situations in econometrics in which the error terms cannot be expected to be orthogonal to the $\boldsymbol{X}$ matrix. We will discuss two of them, the cases of errors in variables and simultaneous equations bias, in Sections 7.2 and 7.3. The most general technique for handling such situations is the method of **instrumental variables**, or **IV** for short. This technique, proposed originally by Reiersøl (1941) and further developed by Durbin (1954) and Sargan (1958), among many others, is very powerful and very general. Numerous variants of it appear in many branches of econometrics. These include **two-stage least squares** (Section 7.5), **three-stage least squares** (Chapter 18), and the **generalized method of moments** (Chapter 17).

The plan of the chapter is as follows. In the next section, we discuss the very common problem of errors in variables, for which the method of instrumental variables was originally proposed as a solution. Then, in Section 7.3, we provide an introduction to the linear simultaneous equations model and show that OLS is biased when applied to one equation of such a model. In Section 7.4, we introduce the method of instrumental variables in the context of a linear regression equation and discuss many of its properties. In the following section, we discuss two-stage least squares, which is really just another name for the IV estimator of the parameters of a linear regression model. In Section 7.6, we show how the IV method may be used to estimate nonlinear regression models. In Section 7.7, we generalize the Gauss-Newton regression to the IV case and discuss how to test hypotheses about the coefficients of regression models when they have been estimated by IV. In Section 7.8, we discuss the issue of identification in regression models estimated by IV. Finally, in Section 7.9, we consider a class of tests called Durbin-Wu-Hausman tests, which may be used to decide whether or not it is necessary to employ instrumental variables.

7.2 ERRORS IN VARIABLES

Almost all economic variables are measured with error. This is true to a greater or lesser extent of all macroeconomic time series and is especially true of survey data and many other cross-section data sets. Unfortunately, the statistical consequences of errors in explanatory variables are severe, since explanatory variables that are measured with error are necessarily correlated with the error terms. When this occurs, the problem is said to be one of **errors in variables**. We will illustrate the problem of errors in variables with a simple example.

Suppose, for simplicity, that the DGP is

$$\boldsymbol{y} = \alpha_0 + \beta_0 \boldsymbol{x} + \boldsymbol{u}, \quad \boldsymbol{u} \sim \mathrm{IID}(\mathbf{0}, \sigma_0^2 \mathbf{I}), \tag{7.04}$$

where $\boldsymbol{x}$ is a vector that is observed with error. We actually observe $\boldsymbol{x}^*$, which is related to $\boldsymbol{x}$ by

$$\boldsymbol{x}^* = \boldsymbol{x} + \boldsymbol{v}, \quad \boldsymbol{v} \sim \mathrm{IID}(\mathbf{0}, \omega^2 \mathbf{I}).$$

The vector $\boldsymbol{v}$ is a vector of measurement errors, which are assumed (possibly unrealistically) to have the i.i.d. property and to be independent of $\boldsymbol{x}$ and $\boldsymbol{u}$. Substituting $\boldsymbol{x}^* - \boldsymbol{v}$ for $\boldsymbol{x}$ in (7.04), the DGP becomes

$$\boldsymbol{y} = \alpha_0 + \beta_0 \boldsymbol{x}^* - \beta_0 \boldsymbol{v} + \boldsymbol{u}.$$

Thus the equation we can actually estimate is

$$\boldsymbol{y} = \alpha + \beta \boldsymbol{x}^* + \boldsymbol{u}^*, \tag{7.05}$$

where $\boldsymbol{u}^* \equiv \boldsymbol{u} - \beta_0 \boldsymbol{v}$. It is clear that $\boldsymbol{u}^*$ is not independent of $\boldsymbol{x}^*$. In fact

$$E\big(\boldsymbol{x}^{*\top}\boldsymbol{u}^*\big) = E\big((\boldsymbol{x} + \boldsymbol{v})^\top(\boldsymbol{u} - \beta_0 \boldsymbol{v})\big) = -\beta_0 E\big(\boldsymbol{v}^\top \boldsymbol{v}\big) = -n\beta_0\omega^2,$$

where, as usual, n is the sample size. If we assume for concreteness that $\beta_0 > 0$, the error term $\boldsymbol{u}^*$ is negatively correlated with the regressor $\boldsymbol{x}^*$. This negative correlation means that least squares estimates of β will be biased and inconsistent, as will least squares estimates of α unless $\boldsymbol{x}^*$ happens to have mean zero. Note that the inconsistency of $\hat{\beta}$ is a problem only if we care about the parameter β. If, on the contrary, we were simply interested in finding the mean of $\boldsymbol{y}$ conditional on $\boldsymbol{x}^*$, estimating equation (7.05) by least squares is precisely what we would want to do.

There are many ways to deal with the problem of errors in variables, the method of instrumental variables being only one of them. In the above example, it is clear that if we knew ω^2, we could say something about the bias of $\hat{\beta}$ and hence derive a better estimate. This observation has led to various alternative approaches to the errors in variables problem: See Frisch (1934), Klepper and Leamer (1984), Hausman and Watson (1985), and Leamer (1987), among others.

7.3 SIMULTANEOUS EQUATIONS

The reason most commonly cited in applied econometric work for explanatory variables to be correlated with error terms is that the former are determined endogenously, rather than being exogenous or predetermined. A variable that is **predetermined** at time t is one that was determined, possibly endogenously, at some earlier time period. The simplest example is a lagged dependent variable. A detailed discussion of exogeneity and predeterminedness may be found in Section 18.2. Models in which two or more endogenous variables are determined simultaneously are called **simultaneous equations models**. Indeed, for many years, the linear simultaneous equations model was the centerpiece of econometric theory, and the literature on how to estimate such models is consequently vast. We will devote Chapter 18 to a discussion of this topic. In this section, we will merely discuss a very simple example, a two-equation linear model of price and quantity determination in a competitive market. This example illustrates many of the basic issues and concepts in the analysis of simultaneous equations models. In particular, it makes it clear that there will generally be correlation between error terms and endogenous right-hand side variables. Moreover, the demand-supply model was responsible for much of the early interest in methods for dealing with simultaneous equations models; see Goldberger (1972).

The model we will discuss is

$$Q_t^d = \alpha P_t + \boldsymbol{Z}_t^d \boldsymbol{\beta} + u_t^d \tag{7.06}$$

$$Q_t^s = \gamma P_t + \boldsymbol{Z}_t^s \boldsymbol{\delta} + u_t^s, \tag{7.07}$$

where Q_t^d is the quantity demanded at observation t, Q_t^s is the quantity supplied, P_t is the price, $\boldsymbol{Z}_t^d$ is a vector of exogenous and/or predetermined variables in the demand function, and $\boldsymbol{Z}_t^s$ is a vector of exogenous and/or predetermined variables in the supply function. Price and quantity might well be in logarithms rather than in levels, since a loglinear specification would often be plausible for both demand and supply functions. If our data pertain to a competitive market which is always in equilibrium (something that would not be a plausible assumption in every case), we know that

$$Q_t^d = Q_t^s = Q_t,$$

where Q_t is the quantity actually sold. Thus the price P_t is assumed to be determined endogenously by the equality of (7.06) and (7.07). It is evident that price and quantity are determined simultaneously in this model.

We now want to write the **structural form** of this model. To do so we must replace Q_t^d and Q_t^s by Q_t and rewrite the demand and supply functions (7.06) and (7.07) in terms of the observable variables P_t and Q_t. There are several different ways to do this, all equally valid. The demand function, equation (7.06), can be rewritten in either of two forms:

$$Q_t = \alpha P_t + \boldsymbol{Z}_t^d \boldsymbol{\beta} + u_t^d, \text{ or} \tag{7.08a}$$

$$P_t = \alpha^* Q_t + \boldsymbol{Z}_t^d \boldsymbol{\beta}^* + u_t^{d*}. \tag{7.08b}$$

Similarly, the supply function, equation (7.07), can be rewritten in either of two forms:

$$Q_t = \gamma P_t + \boldsymbol{Z}_t^s \boldsymbol{\delta} + u_t^s, \text{ or} \tag{7.09a}$$

$$P_t = \gamma^* Q_t + \boldsymbol{Z}_t^s \boldsymbol{\delta}^* + u_t^{s*}. \tag{7.09b}$$

The starred quantities in the b equations are related to the unstarred ones in the a equations in an obvious way. For example, the parameters and error terms of (7.08b) are related to those of (7.08a) as follows:

$$\alpha^* = \alpha^{-1}; \quad \boldsymbol{\beta}^* = -\alpha^{-1}\boldsymbol{\beta}; \quad u_t^{d*} = -\alpha^{-1}u_t^d.$$

We can combine either (7.08a) or (7.08b) with either (7.09a) or (7.09b) when writing the entire model. There are thus *four* different ways that we could write this system of equations, each of them just as valid as any of the others. It is conventional to write simultaneous equations models so that each endogenous variable appears on the left-hand side of one and only one equation, but there is nothing sacrosanct about this convention. Indeed, from the point of view of economic theory, it is probably most natural to combine (7.08a) with (7.09a), putting quantity on the left-hand side of both the demand and supply equations.

We have just seen that **normalization** (i.e., determining which endogenous variable should be given a coefficient of unity and put on the left-hand side of each equation) is necessary whenever we deal with a system of simultaneous equations. Because there are two or more endogenous variables, there is no unique way to write the system. Thus, contrary to what some treatments of the subject may seem to imply, there is no such thing as a single structural form for a linear simultaneous equations model. There are as many structural forms as there are ways in which the equation system can be normalized.

The structural form(s) of a simultaneous equations model are to be contrasted with the **reduced forms**, of which there are two varieties. The **restricted reduced form**, or **RRF**, involves rewriting the model so that each endogenous variable appears once and only once. To derive it in this case, we begin by writing the structural form consisting of (7.08a) and (7.09a):

$$\begin{aligned} Q_t - \alpha P_t &= \boldsymbol{Z}_t^d\boldsymbol{\beta} + u_t^d \\ Q_t - \gamma P_t &= \boldsymbol{Z}_t^s\boldsymbol{\delta} + u_t^s. \end{aligned}$$

These two equations can be rewritten using matrix notation as

$$\begin{bmatrix} 1 & -\alpha \\ 1 & -\gamma \end{bmatrix} \begin{bmatrix} Q_t \\ P_t \end{bmatrix} = \begin{bmatrix} \boldsymbol{Z}_t^d\boldsymbol{\beta} \\ \boldsymbol{Z}_t^s\boldsymbol{\delta} \end{bmatrix} + \begin{bmatrix} u_t^d \\ u_t^s \end{bmatrix}.$$

Solving this system for Q_t and P_t, we obtain the restricted reduced form:

$$\begin{bmatrix} Q_t \\ P_t \end{bmatrix} = \begin{bmatrix} 1 & -\alpha \\ 1 & -\gamma \end{bmatrix}^{-1} \begin{bmatrix} \boldsymbol{Z}_t^d\boldsymbol{\beta} \\ \boldsymbol{Z}_t^s\boldsymbol{\delta} \end{bmatrix} + \begin{bmatrix} 1 & -\alpha \\ 1 & -\gamma \end{bmatrix}^{-1} \begin{bmatrix} u_t^d \\ u_t^s \end{bmatrix},$$

which can be written more explicitly as

$$Q_t = \frac{1}{\alpha - \gamma}\big(\alpha\boldsymbol{Z}_t^s\boldsymbol{\delta} - \gamma\boldsymbol{Z}_t^d\boldsymbol{\beta}\big) + v_t^1 \tag{7.10}$$

$$P_t = \frac{1}{\alpha - \gamma}\big(\boldsymbol{Z}_t^s\boldsymbol{\delta} - \boldsymbol{Z}_t^d\boldsymbol{\beta}\big) + v_t^2, \tag{7.11}$$

where the error terms v_t^1 and v_t^2 are linear combinations of the original error terms u_t^d and u_t^s.

Observe that the equations of the RRF, (7.10) and (7.11), are nonlinear in the parameters but linear in the variables $\boldsymbol{Z}_t^d$ and $\boldsymbol{Z}_t^s$. In fact, they are simply restricted versions of the **unrestricted reduced form**, or **URF**,

$$Q_t = \boldsymbol{Z}_t\boldsymbol{\pi}_1 + v_t^1 \tag{7.12}$$

$$P_t = \boldsymbol{Z}_t\boldsymbol{\pi}_2 + v_t^2, \tag{7.13}$$

where $\boldsymbol{Z}_t$ is a vector consisting of all variables that appear in either $\boldsymbol{Z}_t^d$ or $\boldsymbol{Z}_t^s$, and $\boldsymbol{\pi}_1$ and $\boldsymbol{\pi}_2$ are parameter vectors. The two equations of the URF can evidently be estimated consistently by OLS, since only exogenous or predetermined variables appear on the right-hand side. The RRF would be harder to estimate, however, since it involves nonlinear cross-equation restrictions. In fact, estimating the RRF is equivalent to estimating the structural form on which it is based, as we will see in Chapter 18.

If we were content simply to estimate the URF, we could stop at this point, since OLS estimates of (7.12) and (7.13) will clearly be consistent.[1] However, economists often want to estimate a structural form of a simultaneous equations model, either because the parameters of that structural form are of interest or because imposing the cross-equation restrictions implicit in the structural form may lead to substantially increased efficiency. Thus it is of interest to ask what happens if we apply OLS to any one of the equations of one of the structural forms. Consider equation (7.08a). The OLS estimates of α and $\boldsymbol{\beta}$ are

$$\begin{bmatrix}\hat{\alpha}\\ \hat{\boldsymbol{\beta}}\end{bmatrix} = \begin{bmatrix}\boldsymbol{P}^{\top}\boldsymbol{P} & \boldsymbol{P}^{\top}\boldsymbol{Z}_d\\ \boldsymbol{Z}_d^{\top}\boldsymbol{P} & \boldsymbol{Z}_d^{\top}\boldsymbol{Z}_d\end{bmatrix}^{-1}\begin{bmatrix}\boldsymbol{P}^{\top}\boldsymbol{Q}\\ \boldsymbol{Z}_d^{\top}\boldsymbol{Q}\end{bmatrix},$$

where $\boldsymbol{P}$ and $\boldsymbol{Q}$ denote the vectors of observations on P_t and Q_t, and $\boldsymbol{Z}_d$ denotes the matrix of observations on $\boldsymbol{Z}_t^d$. If we assume that the model is correctly specified and replace $\boldsymbol{Q}$ by $\alpha_0\boldsymbol{P} + \boldsymbol{Z}_d\boldsymbol{\beta}_0 + \boldsymbol{u}_d$, we find that

$$\begin{bmatrix}\hat{\alpha}\\ \hat{\boldsymbol{\beta}}\end{bmatrix} = \begin{bmatrix}\alpha_0\\ \boldsymbol{\beta}_0\end{bmatrix} + \begin{bmatrix}\boldsymbol{P}^{\top}\boldsymbol{P} & \boldsymbol{P}^{\top}\boldsymbol{Z}_d\\ \boldsymbol{Z}_d^{\top}\boldsymbol{P} & \boldsymbol{Z}_d^{\top}\boldsymbol{Z}_d\end{bmatrix}^{-1}\begin{bmatrix}\boldsymbol{P}^{\top}\boldsymbol{u}_d\\ \boldsymbol{Z}_d^{\top}\boldsymbol{u}_d\end{bmatrix}. \tag{7.14}$$

It is obvious that these estimates will be biased and inconsistent. They cannot possibly be unbiased, since the endogenous variable P_t appears on the right-hand side of the equation. They will be inconsistent because

$$\operatorname*{plim}_{n\to\infty}\left(n^{-1}\boldsymbol{P}^{\top}\boldsymbol{u}_d\right) \neq 0,$$

[1] It may seem that OLS estimation of the URF would be inefficient, because the error terms of (7.12) and (7.13) will clearly be correlated. However, as we will see in Chapter 9, this correlation cannot be exploited to yield more efficient estimates, because the regressors in the two equations are the same.

since the equilibrium price depends, in part, on the error term in the demand equation. Hence the standard assumption that error terms and regressors are independent is violated in this (and every) system of simultaneous equations. Thus, if we attempt to take the plim of the right-hand side of (7.14), we will find that the second term is not zero. It follows that $\hat{\alpha}$ and $\hat{\boldsymbol{\beta}}$ will be inconsistent.

The results of this simple example are true in general. Since they are determined simultaneously, all the endogenous variables in a simultaneous equation system generally depend on the error terms in all the equations. Thus, except perhaps in a few very special cases, the right-hand side endogenous variables in a structural equation from such a system will always be correlated with the error terms. As a consequence, application of OLS to such an equation will always yield biased and inconsistent estimates.

We have now seen two important situations in which explanatory variables will be correlated with the error terms of regression equations, and are ready to take up the main topic of this chapter, namely, the method of instrumental variables. This method can be used whenever the error terms are correlated with one or more explanatory variables, regardless of how that correlation many have arisen. It is remarkably simple, general, and powerful.

7.4 INSTRUMENTAL VARIABLES: THE LINEAR CASE

The fundamental ingredient of any IV procedure is a matrix of **instrumental variables** (or simply **instruments**, for short). We will call this matrix $\boldsymbol{W}$ and specify that it is $n \times l$. The columns of $\boldsymbol{W}$ are simply exogenous and/or predetermined variables that are known (or at least assumed) to be independent of the error terms $\boldsymbol{u}$. In the context of the simultaneous equations model, a natural choice for $\boldsymbol{W}$ is the matrix of all the exogenous and predetermined variables in the model. There must be at least as many instruments as there are explanatory variables in the equation to be estimated. Thus, if the equation to be estimated is the linear regression model (7.01), with $\boldsymbol{X}$ having k columns, we require that $l \geq k$. This is an identification condition; see Section 7.8 for further discussion of conditions for identification in models estimated by IV. Some of the explanatory variables may appear among the instruments. Indeed, as we will see below, any column of $\boldsymbol{X}$ that is known to be exogenous or predetermined should be included in $\boldsymbol{W}$ if we want to obtain asymptotically efficient estimates.

The intuition behind IV procedures is the following. Least squares minimizes the distance between $\boldsymbol{y}$ and $\mathcal{S}(\boldsymbol{X})$, which leads to inconsistent estimates because $\boldsymbol{u}$ is correlated with $\boldsymbol{X}$. The n–dimensional space in which $\boldsymbol{y}$ is a point can be divided into two orthogonal subspaces, $\mathcal{S}(\boldsymbol{W})$ and $\mathcal{S}^{\perp}(\boldsymbol{W})$. Instrumental variables minimizes only the portion of the distance between $\boldsymbol{y}$ and $\mathcal{S}(\boldsymbol{X})$ that lies in $\mathcal{S}(\boldsymbol{W})$. Provided that $\boldsymbol{u}$ is independent of $\boldsymbol{W}$, as assumed, any correlation between $\boldsymbol{u}$ and $\boldsymbol{X}$ must lie in $\mathcal{S}^{\perp}(\boldsymbol{W})$, asymptotically. In large samples, restricting the minimization to $\mathcal{S}(\boldsymbol{W})$ therefore avoids the effects of correlation between $\boldsymbol{u}$ and $\boldsymbol{X}$.

More formally, when we apply OLS to the model (7.01), we minimize the sum of squared residuals

$$\left\|\boldsymbol{y} - \boldsymbol{X\beta}\right\|^2 \equiv (\boldsymbol{y} - \boldsymbol{X\beta})^{\top}(\boldsymbol{y} - \boldsymbol{X\beta})$$

with respect to $\boldsymbol{\beta}$. In contrast, when we apply IV to the same model, we minimize the **criterion function**

$$\left\|\boldsymbol{P}_W(\boldsymbol{y} - \boldsymbol{X\beta})\right\|^2 \equiv (\boldsymbol{y} - \boldsymbol{X\beta})^{\top}\boldsymbol{P}_W(\boldsymbol{y} - \boldsymbol{X\beta}), \tag{7.15}$$

where $\boldsymbol{P}_W$ is the matrix that projects orthogonally onto $\mathcal{S}(\boldsymbol{W})$. The first-order conditions that characterize a solution to this minimization problem are

$$\boldsymbol{X}^{\top}\boldsymbol{P}_W(\boldsymbol{y} - \boldsymbol{X}\tilde{\boldsymbol{\beta}}) = \boldsymbol{0}, \tag{7.16}$$

where $\tilde{\boldsymbol{\beta}}$ denotes the vector of IV estimates. Thus we see that the IV residuals $\tilde{\boldsymbol{u}}$ must be orthogonal to the projection of the columns of $\boldsymbol{X}$ onto $\mathcal{S}(\boldsymbol{W})$. This contrasts with the situation for OLS, where the residuals are simply orthogonal to $\mathcal{S}(\boldsymbol{X})$. Solving (7.16) for $\tilde{\boldsymbol{\beta}}$, we find that

$$\tilde{\boldsymbol{\beta}} = \left(\boldsymbol{X}^{\top}\boldsymbol{P}_W\boldsymbol{X}\right)^{-1}\boldsymbol{X}^{\top}\boldsymbol{P}_W\boldsymbol{y}. \tag{7.17}$$

Here we have assumed that the matrix $\boldsymbol{X}^{\top}\boldsymbol{P}_W\boldsymbol{X}$ has full rank, which is a necessary condition for $\tilde{\boldsymbol{\beta}}$ to be identified.

It is easy to show that the IV estimator $\tilde{\boldsymbol{\beta}}$ is consistent if the data are actually generated by the DGP (7.02) and certain assumptions are satisfied. These assumptions are

$$\operatorname*{plim}_{n\to\infty}\left(n^{-1}\boldsymbol{W}^{\top}\boldsymbol{u}\right) = \lim_{n\to\infty}\left(n^{-1}E(\boldsymbol{W}^{\top}\boldsymbol{u})\right) = \boldsymbol{0}, \tag{7.18a}$$

$$\operatorname*{plim}_{n\to\infty}\left(n^{-1}\boldsymbol{W}^{\top}\boldsymbol{W}\right) = \lim_{n\to\infty}\left(n^{-1}E(\boldsymbol{W}^{\top}\boldsymbol{W})\right) \text{ exists, is finite,} \tag{7.18b}$$

and is positive definite, and

$$\operatorname*{plim}_{n\to\infty}\left(n^{-1}\boldsymbol{X}^{\top}\boldsymbol{W}\right) \text{ exists, is finite, and has full rank } k. \tag{7.18c}$$

The most critical assumption is (7.18a), which is unfortunately not fully verifiable, although it can be tested to some extent; see Section 7.9.

Substituting (7.02) into (7.17), we see that

$$\begin{aligned}\tilde{\boldsymbol{\beta}} &= \left(\boldsymbol{X}^{\top}\boldsymbol{P}_W\boldsymbol{X}\right)^{-1}\boldsymbol{X}^{\top}\boldsymbol{P}_W(\boldsymbol{X}\boldsymbol{\beta}_0 + \boldsymbol{u}) \\ &= \boldsymbol{\beta}_0 + \left(\boldsymbol{X}^{\top}\boldsymbol{P}_W\boldsymbol{X}\right)^{-1}\boldsymbol{X}^{\top}\boldsymbol{P}_W\boldsymbol{u}.\end{aligned} \tag{7.19}$$

First, we observe that $\text{plim}(n^{-1}\boldsymbol{X}^\top \boldsymbol{P}_W \boldsymbol{X})$ is equal to

$$\operatorname*{plim}_{n\to\infty}\big(n^{-1}\boldsymbol{X}^\top\boldsymbol{W}\big)\operatorname*{plim}_{n\to\infty}\big(n^{-1}\boldsymbol{W}^\top\boldsymbol{W}\big)^{-1}\operatorname*{plim}_{n\to\infty}\big(n^{-1}\boldsymbol{W}^\top\boldsymbol{X}\big).$$

Thus it follows immediately from (7.18) that $\text{plim}(n^{-1}\boldsymbol{X}^\top \boldsymbol{P}_W \boldsymbol{X})$ exists, is finite, and is positive definite. Hence

$$\begin{aligned}\operatorname*{plim}_{n\to\infty}(\tilde{\boldsymbol{\beta}}) = \boldsymbol{\beta}_0 &+ \operatorname*{plim}_{n\to\infty}\big(n^{-1}\boldsymbol{X}^\top\boldsymbol{P}_W\boldsymbol{X}\big)^{-1} \\ &\times \operatorname*{plim}_{n\to\infty}\big(n^{-1}\boldsymbol{X}^\top\boldsymbol{W}\big)\operatorname*{plim}_{n\to\infty}\big(n^{-1}\boldsymbol{W}^\top\boldsymbol{W}\big)^{-1}\operatorname*{plim}_{n\to\infty}\big(n^{-1}\boldsymbol{W}^\top\boldsymbol{u}\big).\end{aligned}$$

Assumptions (7.18) now imply that the second term here is zero, the critical assumption being (7.18a). Thus we conclude that $\tilde{\boldsymbol{\beta}}$ is consistent for $\boldsymbol{\beta}_0$.

Note that although the IV estimator is consistent, it is not unbiased. Because some columns of $\boldsymbol{X}$, and possibly also some columns of $\boldsymbol{W}$, are stochastic, it is clear that

$$E\Big(\big(\boldsymbol{X}^\top\boldsymbol{P}_W\boldsymbol{X}\big)^{-1}\boldsymbol{X}^\top\boldsymbol{P}_W\boldsymbol{u}\Big) \neq \mathbf{0} \tag{7.20}$$

even if we assume that $E(\boldsymbol{W}^\top\boldsymbol{u}) = \mathbf{0}$. We will see later that the expectation in (7.20) may not even exist in some cases. When the expectations of IV estimators do exist, they will generally be biased. We will have more to say about this in the next section.

The IV estimator will be asymptotically normally distributed with a certain covariance matrix if we make the additional assumption that $n^{-1/2}\boldsymbol{W}^\top\boldsymbol{u}$ obeys a central limit theorem. In the case of nonstochastic instruments $\boldsymbol{W}$, this assumption follows immediately from the assumption in (7.02) about the distribution of $\boldsymbol{u}$. From the right-hand expression in (7.19) we can derive that

$$n^{1/2}(\tilde{\boldsymbol{\beta}} - \boldsymbol{\beta}_0) = \big(n^{-1}\boldsymbol{X}^\top\boldsymbol{P}_W\boldsymbol{X}\big)^{-1} n^{-1/2}\boldsymbol{X}^\top\boldsymbol{P}_W\boldsymbol{u}. \tag{7.21}$$

The factor $n^{-1/2}\boldsymbol{X}^\top\boldsymbol{P}_W\boldsymbol{u}$ can be broken up as

$$n^{-1/2}\boldsymbol{X}^\top\boldsymbol{P}_W\boldsymbol{u} = \big(n^{-1}\boldsymbol{X}^\top\boldsymbol{W}\big)\big(n^{-1}\boldsymbol{W}^\top\boldsymbol{W}\big)^{-1} n^{-1/2}\boldsymbol{W}^\top\boldsymbol{u}, \tag{7.22}$$

and, since the factors on the right-hand side of this equation other than $n^{-1/2}\boldsymbol{W}^\top\boldsymbol{u}$ have by assumptions (7.18) well-defined probability limits, it follows that (7.22) is asymptotically normal with limiting covariance matrix

$$\sigma_0^2 \operatorname*{plim}_{n\to\infty}\big(n^{-1}\boldsymbol{X}^\top\boldsymbol{P}_W\boldsymbol{X}\big).$$

Thus we conclude from (7.21) that

$$n^{1/2}(\tilde{\boldsymbol{\beta}} - \boldsymbol{\beta}_0) \overset{a}{\sim} N\Big(\mathbf{0}, \sigma_0^2 \operatorname*{plim}_{n\to\infty}\big(n^{-1}\boldsymbol{X}^\top\boldsymbol{P}_W\boldsymbol{X}\big)^{-1}\Big), \tag{7.23}$$

where, as usual, $\overset{a}{\sim}$ means "is asymptotically distributed as."

In practice, we are interested in the covariance matrix of $\tilde{\boldsymbol{\beta}} - \boldsymbol{\beta}_0$ rather than that of $n^{1/2}(\tilde{\boldsymbol{\beta}} - \boldsymbol{\beta}_0)$, and we will not know σ_0. We may estimate σ^2 by

$$\tilde{\sigma}^2 = \frac{1}{n}(\boldsymbol{y} - \boldsymbol{X}\tilde{\boldsymbol{\beta}})^\top(\boldsymbol{y} - \boldsymbol{X}\tilde{\boldsymbol{\beta}}).$$

It would of course be possible to divide by $n - k$ rather than n here, but that is not necessarily a good idea. Since the SSR is *not* the value of the objective function for IV estimation (in contrast to the situation for least squares), its expectation is not necessarily smaller than $n\sigma_0^2$ and certainly is not equal to $(n-k)\sigma_0^2$. Asymptotically, of course, it makes no difference whether we divide by n or $n - k$. However we define $\tilde{\sigma}$, we will estimate the covariance matrix of $\tilde{\boldsymbol{\beta}} - \boldsymbol{\beta}_0$ by

$$\tilde{\boldsymbol{V}}(\tilde{\boldsymbol{\beta}}) = \tilde{\sigma}^2\big(\boldsymbol{X}^\top\boldsymbol{P}_W\boldsymbol{X}\big)^{-1}. \tag{7.24}$$

The IV estimator $\tilde{\boldsymbol{\beta}}$ that we have been discussing is actually a **generalized IV estimator**. It may be contrasted with the **simple IV estimator** that is discussed in many elementary statistics and econometrics texts and that was developed first. For the simple IV estimator, each explanatory variable has associated with it a single instrument, which may be the variable itself if it is assumed uncorrelated with $\boldsymbol{u}$. Thus the matrix $\boldsymbol{W}$ has the same dimensions, $n \times k$, as the matrix $\boldsymbol{X}$. In this special case, the generalized IV estimator (7.17) simplifies substantially:

$$\begin{aligned}
\tilde{\boldsymbol{\beta}} &= \big(\boldsymbol{X}^\top\boldsymbol{P}_W\boldsymbol{X}\big)^{-1}\boldsymbol{X}^\top\boldsymbol{P}_W\boldsymbol{y} \\
&= \big(\boldsymbol{X}^\top\boldsymbol{W}(\boldsymbol{W}^\top\boldsymbol{W})^{-1}\boldsymbol{W}^\top\boldsymbol{X}\big)^{-1}\boldsymbol{X}^\top\boldsymbol{W}(\boldsymbol{W}^\top\boldsymbol{W})^{-1}\boldsymbol{W}^\top\boldsymbol{y} \\
&= \big(\boldsymbol{W}^\top\boldsymbol{X}\big)^{-1}\boldsymbol{W}^\top\boldsymbol{W}\big(\boldsymbol{X}^\top\boldsymbol{W}\big)^{-1}\boldsymbol{X}^\top\boldsymbol{W}\big(\boldsymbol{W}^\top\boldsymbol{W}\big)^{-1}\boldsymbol{W}^\top\boldsymbol{y} \\
&= \big(\boldsymbol{W}^\top\boldsymbol{X}\big)^{-1}\boldsymbol{W}^\top\boldsymbol{W}\big(\boldsymbol{W}^\top\boldsymbol{W}\big)^{-1}\boldsymbol{W}^\top\boldsymbol{y} \\
&= \big(\boldsymbol{W}^\top\boldsymbol{X}\big)^{-1}\boldsymbol{W}^\top\boldsymbol{y}.
\end{aligned} \tag{7.25}$$

The key result here is that

$$\big(\boldsymbol{X}^\top\boldsymbol{W}(\boldsymbol{W}^\top\boldsymbol{W})^{-1}\boldsymbol{W}^\top\boldsymbol{X}\big)^{-1} = \big(\boldsymbol{W}^\top\boldsymbol{X}\big)^{-1}\boldsymbol{W}^\top\boldsymbol{W}\big(\boldsymbol{X}^\top\boldsymbol{W}\big)^{-1},$$

which depends on the facts that the matrix $\boldsymbol{W}^\top\boldsymbol{X}$ is square and has full rank. The last line of (7.25) is the formula for the simple IV estimator that appears in many textbooks. We will not discuss this estimator further in this chapter but will encounter it again when we discuss the generalized method of moments in Chapter 17.

The biggest problem with using IV procedures in practice is choosing the matrix of instruments $\boldsymbol{W}$. Even though every valid set of instruments will yield consistent estimates, different choices will yield different estimates in any finite sample. When using time-series data, it is natural to use lagged variables, including lagged values of the dependent variable, as instruments. But it is not at all clear how many lags to use. When estimating an equation from a simultaneous equations model, one natural set of instruments is the set of all the exogenous and predetermined variables in the model. However, this can be a very large number if the model has many equations and, for reasons explained in the next section, one may not want to use such a large number of instruments. Thus, in practice, there are usually many reasonable ways to choose $\boldsymbol{W}$.

There are two conflicting objectives in the choice of $\boldsymbol{W}$. On the one hand, we would like to obtain estimates that are as efficient as possible asymptotically. On the other, we would like to obtain estimates that have as small a finite-sample bias as possible. Unfortunately, these objectives turn out to conflict with each other. We will discuss the issue of asymptotic efficiency here and the issue of finite-sample properties in the next section.

Suppose that there are two possible choices of instrument matrix, $\boldsymbol{W}_1$ and $\boldsymbol{W}_2$, where $\boldsymbol{W}_2$ consists of $\boldsymbol{W}_1$ plus at least one more column, which implies that $\mathcal{S}(\boldsymbol{W}_1)$ is a subspace of $\mathcal{S}(\boldsymbol{W}_2)$. The resulting IV estimators are

$$\tilde{\boldsymbol{\beta}}^1 = \left(\boldsymbol{X}^\top \boldsymbol{P}_1 \boldsymbol{X}\right)^{-1} \boldsymbol{X}^\top \boldsymbol{P}_1 \boldsymbol{y} \quad \text{and}$$
$$\tilde{\boldsymbol{\beta}}^2 = \left(\boldsymbol{X}^\top \boldsymbol{P}_2 \boldsymbol{X}\right)^{-1} \boldsymbol{X}^\top \boldsymbol{P}_2 \boldsymbol{y},$$

where $\boldsymbol{P}_1$ and $\boldsymbol{P}_2$ denote the matrices that project orthogonally onto the spans of $\boldsymbol{W}_1$ and $\boldsymbol{W}_2$, respectively. The asymptotic covariance matrices of these two estimators are as follows:

$$\boldsymbol{V}^\infty\left(n^{1/2}(\tilde{\boldsymbol{\beta}}^i - \boldsymbol{\beta}_0)\right) = \sigma_0^2 \operatorname*{plim}_{n\to\infty} \left(n^{-1}\boldsymbol{X}^\top \boldsymbol{P}_i \boldsymbol{X}\right)^{-1} \tag{7.26}$$

for $i = 1, 2$. We will be able to conclude that $\tilde{\boldsymbol{\beta}}^2$ is at least as efficient as $\tilde{\boldsymbol{\beta}}^1$ if the difference between their asymptotic covariance matrices is positive semidefinite. That is indeed the case, as we now demonstrate.

Consider the difference

$$\boldsymbol{X}^\top \boldsymbol{P}_2 \boldsymbol{X} - \boldsymbol{X}^\top \boldsymbol{P}_1 \boldsymbol{X} = \boldsymbol{X}^\top (\boldsymbol{P}_2 - \boldsymbol{P}_1)\, \boldsymbol{X}. \tag{7.27}$$

Since $\mathcal{S}(\boldsymbol{W}_1)$ is a subspace of $\mathcal{S}(\boldsymbol{W}_2)$, $\boldsymbol{P}_1\boldsymbol{P}_2 = \boldsymbol{P}_2\boldsymbol{P}_1 = \boldsymbol{P}_1$, and consequently $\boldsymbol{P}_2 - \boldsymbol{P}_1$ is an orthogonal projection. It follows that (7.27) is positive semidefinite. In Appendix A, we show that the difference between two symmetric, positive definite matrices is positive semidefinite if and only if the difference of their inverses reversed is positive semidefinite. Consequently,

$$\left(\boldsymbol{X}^\top \boldsymbol{P}_1 \boldsymbol{X}\right)^{-1} - \left(\boldsymbol{X}^\top \boldsymbol{P}_2 \boldsymbol{X}\right)^{-1}$$

is also positive semidefinite. Hence, from (7.26), the difference between the asymptotic covariance matrices of $\tilde{\boldsymbol{\beta}}^1$ and $\tilde{\boldsymbol{\beta}}^2$ is positive semidefinite. Thus we conclude that $\tilde{\beta}^2$ is asymptotically at least as efficient as $\tilde{\beta}^1$. This makes sense, since W_2 explains X at least as well as W_1 does.

There is a special case in which $\tilde{\beta}^2$ and $\tilde{\beta}^1$ are equally efficient asymptotically and indeed tend to the same random vector as $n \rightarrow \infty$. This special case arises when W_2 has exactly the same explanatory power for X, asymptotically, as W_1. This will happen if, for example, W_1 consists of all the exogenous and predetermined variables in a linear simultaneous equations model, because the extra variables in W_2 should have no additional explanatory power for X. But this is a very special case. In every other case, $\tilde{\beta}^2$ is asymptotically more efficient than $\tilde{\beta}^1$.

This result seems to suggest that we should always use as many instruments as possible. That is true if n is very large, when asymptotic properties are the only thing we care about. But it is often a bad thing to do with samples of moderate size. The problem is that increasing the number of instruments tends to make the finite-sample bias of IV estimators worse, a subject which we will discuss in the next section.

7.5 Two-Stage Least Squares

What we have referred to as the IV estimator of β in the linear regression model (7.01), $\tilde{\beta}$, is also widely known as the **two-stage least squares**, or **2SLS**, estimator. It was originally proposed by Theil (1953) and, independently, Basmann (1957), in the context of the simultaneous equations model. The name "two-stage least squares" emphasizes a particular method by which this particular IV estimator may be computed, and this terminology is so widely used in econometrics that some discussion is in order. However, the basic idea behind IV estimation is much more general than the idea of 2SLS estimation. As we will show in the next section, for example, IV generalizes naturally to the case of nonlinear regression models, while 2SLS does not. Thus we prefer to emphasize the IV rather than the 2SLS interpretation of the estimator $\tilde{\beta}$.

Two-stage least squares works as follows. In the first stage, all of the current endogenous explanatory variables of a system of simultaneous equations are regressed on the matrix of instruments W. In the second stage, each equation is estimated by OLS after all of the endogenous variables that appear on the right-hand side have been replaced by the fitted values from the corresponding first-stage regressions. Thus, for each structural equation of the system, the left-hand side endogenous variable is regressed on a set of regressors that consists of the exogenous and predetermined variables that appear on the right-hand side of the equation, plus the fitted values from the first-stage regressions for the endogenous explanatory variables in that equation.

Let y denote one of the endogenous variables of the system, X the set of explanatory variables, endogenous or exogenous, that appear in the equation associated with y, and W the set of all the exogenous and predetermined variables in the entire system. Then the second-stage regression for $\boldsymbol{y}$ can simply be written as

$$\boldsymbol{y} = \boldsymbol{P}_W \boldsymbol{X}\boldsymbol{\beta} + \text{residuals}. \tag{7.28}$$

The OLS estimator of $\boldsymbol{\beta}$ from this regression is just the IV estimator (7.17):

$$\tilde{\boldsymbol{\beta}} = \left(\boldsymbol{X}^\top \boldsymbol{P}_W \boldsymbol{X}\right)^{-1} \boldsymbol{X}^\top \boldsymbol{P}_W \boldsymbol{y}.$$

Notice, however, that the OLS covariance matrix estimate from (7.28) is not the estimate we want. This estimate will be

$$\frac{\|\boldsymbol{y} - \boldsymbol{P}_W \boldsymbol{X}\tilde{\boldsymbol{\beta}}\|^2}{n-k} \left(\boldsymbol{X}^\top \boldsymbol{P}_W \boldsymbol{X}\right)^{-1}, \tag{7.29}$$

while the estimate (7.24) that was derived earlier can be written as

$$\frac{\|\boldsymbol{y} - \boldsymbol{X}\tilde{\boldsymbol{\beta}}\|^2}{n} \left(\boldsymbol{X}^\top \boldsymbol{P}_W \boldsymbol{X}\right)^{-1}. \tag{7.30}$$

These two estimates are not the same. They would be the same only if IV and OLS were identical, that is, if $\boldsymbol{X} = \boldsymbol{P}_W \boldsymbol{X}$. In addition, n would have to be replaced by $n - k$ in (7.30). The problem is that the second-stage OLS regression provides an incorrect estimate of σ^2; it uses $\boldsymbol{y} - \boldsymbol{P}_W \boldsymbol{X}\tilde{\boldsymbol{\beta}}$ rather than $\boldsymbol{y} - \boldsymbol{X}\tilde{\boldsymbol{\beta}}$ as the vector of residuals. The second-stage residuals $\boldsymbol{y} - \boldsymbol{P}_W \boldsymbol{X}\tilde{\boldsymbol{\beta}}$ will tend to be too large, asymptotically, since $\boldsymbol{P}_W \boldsymbol{X}$ will have less explanatory power than $\boldsymbol{X}$ itself if the model is correctly specified. This may not be true in finite samples, of course, or if the model is incorrectly specified. If one actually performs 2SLS in two stages, rather than relying on a preprogrammed 2SLS or IV procedure, one must be careful to use (7.30) rather than (7.29) for the estimated covariance matrix.[2] Programs for 2SLS estimation normally replace $\boldsymbol{P}_W \boldsymbol{X}\tilde{\boldsymbol{\beta}}$ by $\boldsymbol{X}\tilde{\boldsymbol{\beta}}$ before calculating the explained sum of squares, the sum of squared residuals, the R^2, and other statistics that depend on these quantities.

There has been an enormous amount of work on the finite-sample properties of 2SLS, that is, the IV estimator $\tilde{\boldsymbol{\beta}}$. A few of the many papers in this area are Anderson (1982), Anderson and Sawa (1979), Mariano (1982), Phillips (1983), and Taylor (1983). Unfortunately, many of the results of this literature are very model-specific. One important result (Kinal, 1980) is that the mth moment of the 2SLS estimator exists if and only if

$$m < l - k + 1.$$

[2] 2SLS is a special case of a regression with what Pagan (1984b, 1986) calls "generated regressors." Even when such regressions provide consistent parameter estimates, they usually provide inconsistent estimates of the covariance matrix of the parameter estimates. The inconsistency of (7.29) provides a simple example of this phenomenon.

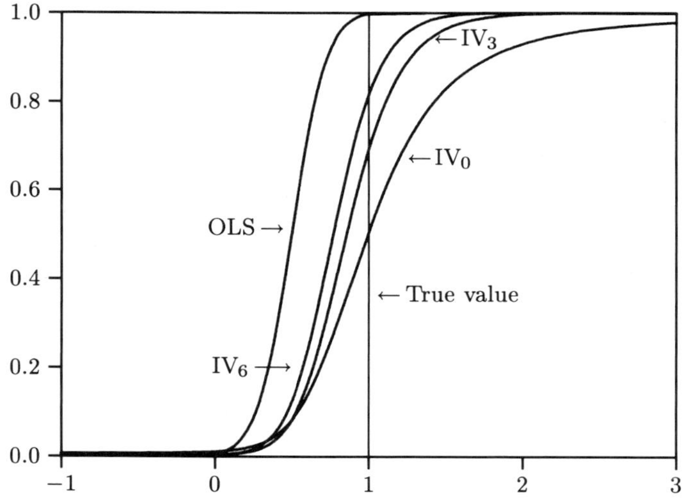

Figure 7.1 Distributions of OLS and IV estimates, $n = 25$

The right-hand side here is the difference between the number of instruments and the number of regressors, plus 1. It is also the degree of overidentification of the equation plus 1; see Section 7.8. According to this result, the 2SLS estimator will not even have a mean if $l = k$ (in which case 2SLS reduces to the simple IV estimator discussed in the previous section). This suggests that its finite-sample properties will be rather poor in this case, and indeed they often are; see Nelson and Startz (1990a, 1990b). Since we would generally like estimators to have at least a mean and a variance, the moral seems to be that, if possible, l should always exceed k by at least 2.

In fact, the asymptotic efficiency result of the previous section suggests that l should be as large as possible. However, finite-sample theory and Monte Carlo results suggest that this is not always a good idea. The fundamental problem is that as more and more columns are added to $\boldsymbol{W}$, the latter does a better and better job of explaining those columns of $\boldsymbol{X}$ that do not actually lie in $\mathcal{S}(\boldsymbol{W})$, and the more $\boldsymbol{P}_W\boldsymbol{X}$ comes to resemble $\boldsymbol{X}$. This is an inevitable consequence of the tendency of OLS to fit too well. As a result, the IV estimator tends to become more and more biased as l increases, eventually approaching the OLS estimator as l approaches n.

Figure 7.1 provides an illustration of this. It shows the distribution functions of the OLS estimator and three different IV estimators in a simple case. The three IV estimators, which we will refer to as IV_0, IV_3, and IV_6, have $l-k$ equal to 0, 3, and 6, respectively. The quantity being estimated is the slope parameter from an equation with one endogenous regressor and a constant term; its true value is unity. The sample size is only 25 so as to make finite-sample biases very apparent. These distribution functions were estimated by

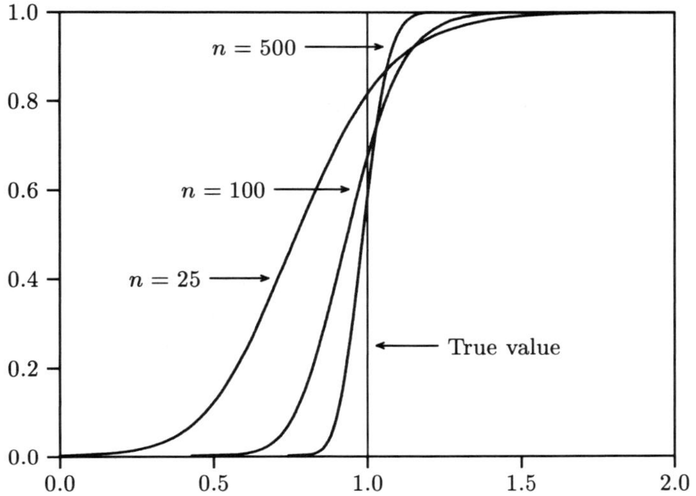

Figure 7.2 Distributions of IV_6 estimates for several sample sizes

means of a Monte Carlo experiment (see Chapter 21), the details of which are unimportant since the figure is purely illustrative.

The left-most curve in Figure 7.1 is the distribution function for OLS, which is severely biased downward in this case. The right-most curve is the one for IV_0, which has approximately the right median but also has much more dispersion (we cannot say variance since it does not have a second moment) and much thicker tails than the OLS estimator. Indeed, among the 50,000 replications we performed, we obtained several IV_0 estimates larger than 1000 in absolute value! The distribution functions for IV_3 and IV_6 mostly lie between those for OLS and IV_0 and have much thinner tails than the latter, with IV_6 being closer to OLS than IV_3, as the above argument predicts. Both these estimators are quite severely biased (remember that $n = 25$ here), although not nearly as much so as OLS, and both evidently have more variance than OLS, as evidenced by the less steep slopes of their distribution functions.

Which estimator is best depends on what criterion is used to choose among them. If one looks only at the median, IV_0 is clearly the best. On the other hand, if one uses mean squared error as a criterion, IV_0 is clearly the worst, since because it has no first or higher moments, its mean squared error is infinite. Based on most criteria, the choice would be between IV_3 and IV_6. For a large enough n, the latter would of course be preferable, since its greater bias will vanish as n increases, while its smaller variance will persist. The effect of increasing sample size is shown in Figure 7.2, which shows the distribution of IV_6 for $n = 25$, $n = 100$, and $n = 500$. As n increases, both the variance and the bias of the estimator decrease, as expected, although even for $n = 500$ the bias is noticeable.

It should be stressed that Figures 7.1 and 7.2 apply only to a particular example, in which the instruments happen to be quite good ones. In other cases, and especially when the instruments have little ability to explain the endogenous regressors, IV estimators may be extremely inefficient, and their finite-sample distributions may be very different from their asymptotic ones.

7.6 Instrumental Variables: The Nonlinear Case

It is easy to generalize the linear IV procedure discussed above to the case of nonlinear regression models. Suppose the model is

$$y_t = x_t(\boldsymbol{\beta}) + u_t, \quad u_t \sim \mathrm{IID}(0, \sigma^2), \tag{7.31}$$

where the regression function $x_t(\boldsymbol{\beta})$ implicitly depends on current endogenous as well as exogenous and predetermined variables, and $\boldsymbol{\beta}$ is a k–vector as usual. Assuming that one has a matrix of valid instruments $\boldsymbol{W}$, with $l \geq k$ as before, the objective is to minimize only the portion of the distance between $\boldsymbol{y}$ and $\boldsymbol{x}(\boldsymbol{\beta})$ that lies in $\mathcal{S}(\boldsymbol{W})$. This can be done by minimizing the criterion function

$$\left\| \boldsymbol{P}_W \big(\boldsymbol{y} - \boldsymbol{x}(\boldsymbol{\beta})\big) \right\|^2 = \big(\boldsymbol{y} - \boldsymbol{x}(\boldsymbol{\beta})\big)^{\top} \boldsymbol{P}_W \big(\boldsymbol{y} - \boldsymbol{x}(\boldsymbol{\beta})\big). \tag{7.32}$$

This criterion function is the nonlinear equivalent of (7.15). The first-order conditions that characterize the IV estimates $\tilde{\boldsymbol{\beta}}$ are

$$\boldsymbol{X}^{\top}(\tilde{\boldsymbol{\beta}}) \boldsymbol{P}_W \big(\boldsymbol{y} - \boldsymbol{x}(\tilde{\boldsymbol{\beta}})\big) = \mathbf{0}, \tag{7.33}$$

where, as usual, the $n \times k$ matrix $\boldsymbol{X}(\boldsymbol{\beta})$ has typical element

$$X_{ti}(\boldsymbol{\beta}) = \frac{\partial x_t(\boldsymbol{\beta})}{\partial \beta_i}.$$

Conditions (7.33) are evidently the nonlinear analogs of the first-order conditions (7.16) for the linear case. They say that the residuals $\boldsymbol{y} - \boldsymbol{x}(\tilde{\boldsymbol{\beta}})$ must be orthogonal to the matrix of derivatives $\boldsymbol{X}(\tilde{\boldsymbol{\beta}})$, after the latter have been projected onto $\mathcal{S}(\boldsymbol{W})$. As in the case of NLS, we cannot hope to solve for $\tilde{\boldsymbol{\beta}}$ analytically, although this may be possible in some special cases.

It is reasonably straightforward to prove, under suitable regularity conditions, that the nonlinear IV estimates $\tilde{\boldsymbol{\beta}}$ are consistent and asymptotically normal. The principal regularity conditions that are needed are those required for NLS to be consistent and asymptotically normal (see Sections 5.3 and 5.4), with the assumption that the error terms are independent of the regression function and its derivatives being dropped and replaced by modified versions of assumptions (7.18a), (7.18b), and (7.18c). In the last of these, the matrix $\boldsymbol{X}_0 \equiv \boldsymbol{X}(\boldsymbol{\beta}_0)$ replaces the matrix $\boldsymbol{X}$, where $\boldsymbol{\beta}_0$ as usual is the value of $\boldsymbol{\beta}$ under the DGP, which is assumed to be a special case of the model being estimated.

The ultimate result is

$$n^{1/2}(\tilde{\boldsymbol{\beta}} - \boldsymbol{\beta}_0) \overset{a}{\sim} N\Big(\mathbf{0}, \sigma_0^2 \operatorname*{plim}_{n\to\infty} \big(n^{-1}\boldsymbol{X}_0^{\top}\boldsymbol{P}_W\boldsymbol{X}_0\big)^{-1}\Big), \tag{7.34}$$

which closely resembles (7.23) for the linear case.

The **nonlinear IV estimator** based on minimizing the criterion function (7.32) was proposed by Amemiya (1974), who very misleadingly called it the **nonlinear two-stage least squares estimator**, or **NL2SLS**. In fact, it is *not* computed in two stages at all. Attempting to compute an estimator analogous to linear 2SLS would in general result in an inconsistent estimator very different from nonlinear IV.

It is illuminating to see why this is so. We must make explicit the dependence of $\boldsymbol{x}(\boldsymbol{\beta})$ on explanatory variables. Thus the model (7.31) may be rewritten as

$$\boldsymbol{y} = \boldsymbol{x}(\boldsymbol{Z}, \boldsymbol{\beta}) + \boldsymbol{u}, \quad \boldsymbol{u} \sim \text{IID}(\mathbf{0}, \sigma^2\mathbf{I}_n),$$

where $\boldsymbol{x}(\boldsymbol{Z}, \boldsymbol{\beta})$ is a vector with typical element $x_t(\boldsymbol{Z}_t, \boldsymbol{\beta})$, $\boldsymbol{Z}$ being a matrix of observations on explanatory variables, with t^{th} row $\boldsymbol{Z}_t$, some columns of which may be correlated with $\boldsymbol{u}$. The $\boldsymbol{Z}$ matrix is not necessarily $n \times k$, because there may be more or fewer parameters than explanatory variables. A 2SLS procedure would regress those columns of $\boldsymbol{Z}$ that are potentially correlated with $\boldsymbol{u}$ on the matrix of instruments $\boldsymbol{W}$ so as to obtain $\boldsymbol{P}_W\boldsymbol{Z}$. It would then minimize the objective function

$$\big(\boldsymbol{y} - \boldsymbol{x}(\boldsymbol{P}_W\boldsymbol{Z}, \boldsymbol{\beta})\big)^{\top}\big(\boldsymbol{y} - \boldsymbol{x}(\boldsymbol{P}_W\boldsymbol{Z}, \boldsymbol{\beta})\big). \tag{7.35}$$

This procedure would yield consistent estimates if the regression functions $x_t(\boldsymbol{Z}_t, \boldsymbol{\beta})$ were linear in all the endogenous elements of $\boldsymbol{Z}_t$. But if the regression functions were nonlinear in any of the endogenous elements of $\boldsymbol{Z}_t$, minimizing (7.35) would not yield consistent estimates, because even though $\boldsymbol{P}_W\boldsymbol{Z}$ would be asymptotically orthogonal to $\boldsymbol{u}$, $\boldsymbol{x}(\boldsymbol{P}_W\boldsymbol{Z}, \boldsymbol{\beta})$ would not be.

As a very simple example, suppose that the regression function $x_t(\boldsymbol{Z}_t, \boldsymbol{\beta})$ were βz_t^2. Thus there would be just one independent variable, which is correlated with u_t, and one parameter. The theory for linear regressions is applicable to this example, since the regression function is linear with respect to the parameter β. What is needed to obtain a consistent estimate of β is to minimize $\|\boldsymbol{P}_W(\boldsymbol{y} - \beta\boldsymbol{z}^2)\|^2$ with respect to β, where $\boldsymbol{z}^2$ means the vector with typical element z_t^2. In contrast, if one first projected $\boldsymbol{z}$ onto $\boldsymbol{W}$ in a 2SLS procedure, one would be minimizing $\|\boldsymbol{y} - \beta(\boldsymbol{P}_W\boldsymbol{z})^2\|^2$, where $(\boldsymbol{P}_W\boldsymbol{z})^2$ means the vector with typical element $(\boldsymbol{P}_W\boldsymbol{z})_t^2$. The latter minimization is evidently not restricted to the subspace $\mathcal{S}(\boldsymbol{W})$ and so will not in general lead to consistent estimates of β.

In many cases, the biggest problem with nonlinear IV procedures is how to choose $\boldsymbol{W}$. With a linear model, it is relatively easy to do so. If the equation to be estimated comes from a system of linear simultaneous equations, we know from the reduced form that all the endogenous variables depend linearly on the exogenous and predetermined ones. Thus one natural thing to do is to make $\boldsymbol{W}$ consist of all the exogenous and predetermined variables in the model, unless there are too many of them. When a model is nonlinear in the endogenous variables, this approach no longer works. There is no unrestricted reduced form comparable to the one for linear models. The endogenous variables may depend on the exogenous and predetermined ones in very nonlinear ways. This suggests using powers and even cross-products of the latter as instruments. But it is not obvious how many powers or cross-products to use, and the problem of having too many instruments is likely to be severe, even when the number of exogenous and predetermined variables is small. For more on this, see Amemiya (1974), Kelejian (1971), and Bowden and Turkington (1984, Chapter 5).

7.7 Hypothesis Tests Based on the GNR

As we saw in Chapter 6, every nonlinear regression model estimated by least squares has associated with it a version of the **Gauss-Newton regression**. So does every nonlinear regression model estimated by instrumental variables. For the latter, the general form of the GNR is

$$\boldsymbol{y} - \boldsymbol{x}(\boldsymbol{\beta}^*) = \boldsymbol{P}_W \boldsymbol{X}(\boldsymbol{\beta}^*)\boldsymbol{b} + \text{residuals}, \tag{7.36}$$

where $\boldsymbol{\beta}^*$ may be any specified value of $\boldsymbol{\beta}$. Thus the only difference between this GNR and the original one is that the regressors are multiplied by $\boldsymbol{P}_W$. This variant of the GNR has almost all the same properties as the original GNR studied in Chapter 6. Like the latter, it may be used for a variety of purposes depending upon where it is evaluated.

If the GNR (7.36) is evaluated at the IV estimates $\tilde{\boldsymbol{\beta}}$, the OLS estimate $\tilde{\boldsymbol{b}}$ will be identically zero. As usual, this can provide a convenient way to check the accuracy of the nonlinear optimization routine employed. Moreover, the OLS covariance matrix estimate from the artificial regression will provide a valid estimate of the covariance matrix of $\tilde{\boldsymbol{\beta}}$. Because $\boldsymbol{P}_W \boldsymbol{X}(\tilde{\boldsymbol{\beta}})$ can have no explanatory power for $\boldsymbol{y} - \boldsymbol{x}(\tilde{\boldsymbol{\beta}})$, the sum of squared residuals must simply be $\|\boldsymbol{y} - \boldsymbol{x}(\tilde{\boldsymbol{\beta}})\|^2$, and the OLS covariance matrix estimate will thus be

$$\frac{\|\boldsymbol{y} - \boldsymbol{x}(\tilde{\boldsymbol{\beta}})\|^2}{n-k} \big(\boldsymbol{X}^\top(\tilde{\boldsymbol{\beta}}) \boldsymbol{P}_W \boldsymbol{X}(\tilde{\boldsymbol{\beta}})\big)^{-1}. \tag{7.37}$$

This expression is the nonlinear analog of expression (7.30), except that $n-k$ rather than n appears in the denominator of the estimate of σ^2. It clearly provides a valid way to estimate the finite-sample analog of the asymptotic covariance matrix which appears in (7.34). There is some doubt about the appropriateness of the degrees-of-freedom adjustment, as we remarked prior to (7.24) above, but expression (7.37) is otherwise just what we want to use to estimate the covariance matrix of $\tilde{\boldsymbol{\beta}}$.

The GNR (7.36) may be used for other purposes, of course. If it is evaluated at consistent but inefficient estimates, it may be used to calculate one-step efficient estimates that are asymptotically equivalent to $\tilde{\boldsymbol{\beta}}$; see Section 6.6. It may also be used as part of a numerical optimization procedure to minimize the criterion function (7.32); see Section 6.8. In both cases, there is essentially no difference between results for the NLS and IV versions of the GNR. The most important application of Gauss-Newton regressions, however, is probably for calculating test statistics based on the Lagrange multiplier and $C(\alpha)$ principles, that is, for testing restrictions on $\boldsymbol{\beta}$ without requiring estimation of the unrestricted model. Since the IV case is slightly different from the NLS case, this topic merits some discussion.

Suppose that $\check{\boldsymbol{\beta}}$ denotes a vector of IV estimates subject to a set of r possibly nonlinear restrictions. To simplify some of the exposition, we assume that the model is parametrized so that $\boldsymbol{x}(\boldsymbol{\beta}) \equiv \boldsymbol{x}(\boldsymbol{\beta}_1, \boldsymbol{\beta}_2)$, where $\boldsymbol{\beta}_1$ is $(k-r)\times 1$ and $\boldsymbol{\beta}_2$ is $r \times 1$, and that the restrictions are $\boldsymbol{\beta}_2 = \mathbf{0}$. However, since the way we write the restrictions is purely a matter of parametrization, the results would be the same if we allowed for general nonlinear restrictions of the form $\boldsymbol{r}(\boldsymbol{\beta}) = \mathbf{0}$.

When we evaluate the GNR (7.36) at the restricted estimates $\check{\boldsymbol{\beta}}$, it becomes

$$\boldsymbol{y} - \check{\boldsymbol{x}} = \boldsymbol{P}_W \check{\boldsymbol{X}} \boldsymbol{b} + \text{residuals}, \tag{7.38}$$

where $\check{\boldsymbol{x}} \equiv \boldsymbol{x}(\check{\boldsymbol{\beta}})$ and $\check{\boldsymbol{X}} \equiv \boldsymbol{X}(\check{\boldsymbol{\beta}})$. This artificial regression generates test statistics in exactly the same way as the ordinary GNR did for the case of nonlinear least squares. The explained sum of squares from (7.38) is

$$(\boldsymbol{y} - \check{\boldsymbol{x}})^{\top} \boldsymbol{P}_W \check{\boldsymbol{X}} \left(\check{\boldsymbol{X}}^{\top} \boldsymbol{P}_W \check{\boldsymbol{X}}\right)^{-1} \check{\boldsymbol{X}}^{\top} \boldsymbol{P}_W (\boldsymbol{y} - \check{\boldsymbol{x}}). \tag{7.39}$$

When this explained sum of squares is divided by any consistent estimate of σ^2, the result is asymptotically distributed under the null hypothesis as $\chi^2(r)$. One valid test statistic can be obtained by calculating n times the uncentered R^2 from the GNR (7.38), and others will be discussed below. Note that this is the OLS R^2, not the R^2 that an IV procedure would print if one regressed $\boldsymbol{y} - \check{\boldsymbol{x}}$ on $\check{\boldsymbol{X}}$ using $\boldsymbol{W}$ as a matrix of instruments.

To see why test statistics based on the GNR are valid, it is convenient to rewrite (7.38) making use of the distinction between $\boldsymbol{\beta}_1$ and $\boldsymbol{\beta}_2$:

$$\boldsymbol{y} - \check{\boldsymbol{x}} = \boldsymbol{P}_W \check{\boldsymbol{X}}_1 \boldsymbol{b}_1 + \boldsymbol{P}_W \check{\boldsymbol{X}}_2 \boldsymbol{b}_2 + \text{residuals}, \tag{7.40}$$

where $\check{\boldsymbol{X}}_i$ consists of those columns of $\check{\boldsymbol{X}}$ that correspond to $\boldsymbol{\beta}_i$ for $i = 1, 2$. Since $\check{\boldsymbol{X}}_1$ can have no explanatory power for $\boldsymbol{y} - \check{\boldsymbol{x}}$ by the first-order conditions for the restricted estimates, the FWL Theorem implies that equation (7.40) must have the same explained sum of squares as

$$\check{\boldsymbol{M}}_1 (\boldsymbol{y} - \check{\boldsymbol{x}}) = \check{\boldsymbol{M}}_1 \boldsymbol{P}_W \check{\boldsymbol{X}}_2 \boldsymbol{b}_2 + \text{residuals},$$

where

$$\check{M}_1 \equiv \mathbf{I} - P_W\check{X}_1\big(\check{X}_1^\top P_W\check{X}_1\big)^{-1}\check{X}_1^\top P_W$$

is the matrix that projects orthogonally onto $\mathcal{S}^\perp(P_W\check{X}_1)$. Thus we see that the explained sum of squares (7.39) can be rewritten as

$$(\boldsymbol{y} - \check{\boldsymbol{x}})^\top\check{M}_1 P_W\check{X}_2\big(\check{X}_2^\top P_W\check{M}_1 P_W\check{X}_2\big)^{-1}\check{X}_2^\top P_W\check{M}_1(\boldsymbol{y} - \check{\boldsymbol{x}}). \tag{7.41}$$

We will not prove that expression (7.41), when divided by anything that estimates σ^2 consistently, is asymptotically distributed as $\chi^2(r)$. The proof closely follows the proof for the nonlinear least squares case that was sketched in Section 6.4. The result evidently follows immediately if we can show that the r–vector

$$n^{-1/2}\check{X}_2^\top P_W\check{M}_1(\boldsymbol{y} - \check{\boldsymbol{x}})$$

is asymptotically normally distributed with covariance matrix

$$\sigma_0^2 \operatorname*{plim}_{n\to\infty}\big(n^{-1}\check{X}_2^\top P_W\check{M}_1 P_W\check{X}_2\big).$$

Readers may find it a good exercise to prove this result. For a more detailed discussion, see Engle (1982a).

The tests just described are based on the LM principle. It is of course also valid to use tests based on the $C(\alpha)$ principle discussed in Section 6.7. The test regressions would look like (7.40), except that the regressand and regressors would be evaluated at estimates $\acute{\boldsymbol{\beta}}$ that are consistent under the null hypothesis but for which the first-order conditions are not satisfied:

$$(\boldsymbol{y} - \acute{\boldsymbol{x}})^\top P_W\acute{X}_1 \neq \mathbf{0}.$$

As a result, the regressand of the GNR would no longer be orthogonal to the regressors that correspond to $\boldsymbol{\beta}_1$, and tests based on the explained sum of squares would not be valid. But any test based on the reduction in the SSR brought about by adding the regressors that correspond to $\boldsymbol{\beta}_2$, such as a pseudo-F test, would still be valid. The easiest approach is simply to run the GNR twice, once with and once without the regressors that correspond to $\boldsymbol{\beta}_2$, and then to compute an F test in the usual way.

This type of test may be particularly useful when the matrix of instruments that would have to be used to estimate the alternative hypothesis has more columns than the one actually used to estimate the null. This can easily happen if the regression function for the alternative model depends on one or more exogenous or predetermined variables that do not appear in the instrument matrix for the null model. To compute a test based on the LM principle, one would have to go back and estimate the null model again, using the same matrix of instruments used to estimate the alternative. This step is unnecessary if one uses a test based on the $C(\alpha)$ principle. One still uses the larger instrument matrix to construct the regressors of the GNR, of course, and as a result the regressand will not be orthogonal to the regressors which correspond to $\boldsymbol{\beta}_1$, but that does not affect the validity of the test statistic.

All of the above discussion assumes that the GNR (7.38) is run by OLS. In practice, however, it might seem easier to regress $\boldsymbol{y} - \check{\boldsymbol{x}}$ on $\check{\boldsymbol{X}}$ by an IV procedure, using $\boldsymbol{W}$ as a matrix of instruments. Although this would avoid the initial step of regressing the columns of $\check{\boldsymbol{X}}$ on $\boldsymbol{W}$, it is not a very good idea; one could not use the explained sum of squares reported by the package to calculate test statistics with more than just one degree of freedom, since it would not actually be the explained sum of squares from regression (7.38) (see Section 7.5). For the same reason, one cannot construct pseudo-F tests using the sums of squared residuals obtained from IV estimation of a restricted and an unrestricted model.

We have seen that if the Gauss-Newton regression is run using an OLS package, it can be used to test restrictions on $\boldsymbol{\beta}$ in precisely the same way as in the context of nonlinear least squares. However, using other methods to do so can be somewhat different. The reason for this is that σ^2 has to be estimated and, as we saw in Section 7.5, it can be tricky to estimate σ^2 when using IV. In the case of the GNR it is clearly valid to estimate σ^2 by

$$\frac{1}{n}(\boldsymbol{y} - \check{\boldsymbol{x}})^{\top}(\boldsymbol{y} - \check{\boldsymbol{x}}),$$

where n might be replaced by $(n - k + r)$. This estimate of σ^2 is based on the restricted estimates. It is also valid to use n^{-1} or $(n - k)^{-1}$ times the sum of squared residuals from the GNR (7.40) itself, despite the fact that the regressors have been multiplied by $\boldsymbol{P}_W$, because under the null hypothesis the GNR should have no explanatory power asymptotically. Hence whether we use the total or residual sum of squares makes no difference asymptotically if we simply wish to test the null hypothesis that $\boldsymbol{\beta}_2 = \mathbf{0}$. This implies that an ordinary F test for $\boldsymbol{b}_2 = \mathbf{0}$ based on OLS estimation of (7.40) would be asymptotically valid.

In the case of linear and nonlinear regression models estimated by least squares, it is possible to test hypotheses about $\boldsymbol{\beta}$ by using exact or asymptotic F tests of the form

$$\frac{(\text{RSSR} - \text{USSR})/r}{\text{USSR}/(n-k)} \overset{a}{\sim} F(r, n-k), \tag{7.42}$$

where RSSR and USSR denote the restricted and unrestricted sums of squared residuals. Tests of this type are also available for models estimated by IV, but they are not quite the same as (7.42) unless, as above, RSSR and USSR are obtained from a GNR. We now discuss these tests in some detail.

For simplicity, we begin by considering the linear case. Suppose the restricted and unrestricted models are

$$\boldsymbol{y} = \boldsymbol{X}_1\boldsymbol{\beta}_1 + \boldsymbol{u}, \quad \boldsymbol{u} \sim \text{IID}(\mathbf{0}, \sigma^2\mathbf{I}), \quad \text{and} \tag{7.43}$$

$$\boldsymbol{y} = \boldsymbol{X}_1\boldsymbol{\beta}_1 + \boldsymbol{X}_2\boldsymbol{\beta}_2 + \boldsymbol{u}, \quad \boldsymbol{u} \sim \text{IID}(\mathbf{0}, \sigma^2\mathbf{I}), \tag{7.44}$$

and that these are estimated by IV using the instrument matrix $\boldsymbol{W}$. Now suppose that the estimates are actually obtained by two-stage least squares. It is easy to see that the sum of squared residuals from the second-stage regression for (7.43), in which $\boldsymbol{X}_1$ is replaced by $\boldsymbol{P}_W\boldsymbol{X}_1$, will be

$$\mathrm{RSSR}^* \equiv \boldsymbol{y}^\top \boldsymbol{M}_1 \boldsymbol{y}, \tag{7.45}$$

where $\boldsymbol{M}_1$ denotes the matrix that projects orthogonally onto $\mathcal{S}^\perp(\boldsymbol{P}_W\boldsymbol{X}_1)$. Similarly, it can be shown (doing so is a good exercise) that the sum of squared residuals from the second-stage regression for (7.44) will be

$$\mathrm{USSR}^* \equiv \boldsymbol{y}^\top \boldsymbol{M}_1 \boldsymbol{y} - \boldsymbol{y}^\top \boldsymbol{M}_1 \boldsymbol{P}_W \boldsymbol{X}_2 \big(\boldsymbol{X}_2^\top \boldsymbol{P}_W \boldsymbol{M}_1 \boldsymbol{P}_W \boldsymbol{X}_2\big)^{-1} \boldsymbol{X}_2^\top \boldsymbol{P}_W \boldsymbol{M}_1 \boldsymbol{y}. \tag{7.46}$$

The difference between (7.45) and (7.46) is

$$\boldsymbol{y}^\top \boldsymbol{M}_1 \boldsymbol{P}_W \boldsymbol{X}_2 \big(\boldsymbol{X}_2^\top \boldsymbol{P}_W \boldsymbol{M}_1 \boldsymbol{P}_W \boldsymbol{X}_2\big)^{-1} \boldsymbol{X}_2^\top \boldsymbol{P}_W \boldsymbol{M}_1 \boldsymbol{y}, \tag{7.47}$$

which bears a striking and by no means coincidental resemblance to expression (7.41). Under the null hypothesis (7.43), $\boldsymbol{y}$ is equal to $\boldsymbol{X}_1\boldsymbol{\beta}_1 + \boldsymbol{u}$. Since $\boldsymbol{P}_W\boldsymbol{M}_1$ annihilates $\boldsymbol{X}_1$, (7.47) reduces to

$$\boldsymbol{u}^\top \boldsymbol{M}_1 \boldsymbol{P}_W \boldsymbol{X}_2 \big(\boldsymbol{X}_2^\top \boldsymbol{P}_W \boldsymbol{M}_1 \boldsymbol{P}_W \boldsymbol{X}_2\big)^{-1} \boldsymbol{X}_2^\top \boldsymbol{P}_W \boldsymbol{M}_1 \boldsymbol{u}$$

under the null. It should be easy to see that, under reasonable assumptions, this quantity, divided by anything which estimates σ^2 consistently, will be asymptotically distributed as $\chi^2(r)$. The needed assumptions are essentially (7.18a)–(7.18c), plus assumptions sufficient for a central limit theorem to apply to $n^{-1/2}\boldsymbol{W}^\top\boldsymbol{u}$.

The problem, then, is to estimate σ^2. Notice that $\mathrm{USSR}^*/(n-k)$ does *not* estimate σ^2 consistently, for the reasons discussed in Section 7.5. As we saw there, the residuals from the second-stage regression will be too large, at least asymptotically. Thus estimates of σ^2 must be based on the set of residuals $\boldsymbol{y} - \boldsymbol{X}\tilde{\boldsymbol{\beta}}$ rather than the set $\boldsymbol{y} - \boldsymbol{P}_W\boldsymbol{X}\tilde{\boldsymbol{\beta}}$. One valid estimate is $\mathrm{USSR}/(n-k)$, where

$$\mathrm{USSR} \equiv \big\|\boldsymbol{y} - \boldsymbol{X}_1\tilde{\boldsymbol{\beta}}_1 - \boldsymbol{X}_2\tilde{\boldsymbol{\beta}}_2\big\|^2.$$

The analog of (7.42) would then be

$$\frac{(\mathrm{RSSR}^* - \mathrm{USSR}^*)/r}{\mathrm{USSR}/(n-k)} \overset{a}{\sim} F(r, n-k). \tag{7.48}$$

Notice that the numerator and denominator of this test statistic are based on different sets of residuals. The numerator is $1/r$ times the difference between the sums of squared residuals from the second-stage regressions, while the denominator is $1/(n-k)$ times the sum of squared residuals that would be printed by a program for IV estimation.

Unfortunately, very few regression packages make it easy to obtain both the starred and unstarred variants of the sum of squared residuals. This means that calculating a test statistic like (7.48) is frequently harder than it should be. If one uses a procedure for IV (or 2SLS) estimation, the package will normally print only the unstarred variant of the sum of squared residuals. To obtain the starred variant one then has to go back and perform the second-stage regression by OLS. Recall that one must use RSSR* − USSR* in the numerator of the test statistic rather than RSSR − USSR, since only the former is equal to (7.41). For more detailed discussions, see Startz (1983) and Wooldridge (1990c).

We now turn to the nonlinear case. Whether or not the model is linear, one can always use tests based on the value of the criterion function (7.15). For nonlinear models, it is natural to base a test on the difference

$$\left\|\boldsymbol{P}_W\big(\boldsymbol{y}-\boldsymbol{x}(\check{\boldsymbol{\beta}})\big)\right\|^2-\left\|\boldsymbol{P}_W\big(\boldsymbol{y}-\boldsymbol{x}(\tilde{\boldsymbol{\beta}})\big)\right\|^2. \tag{7.49}$$

This difference turns out to be asymptotically the same as the explained sum of squares from the GNR (7.38), expression (7.39). Thus (7.49) divided by anything that estimates σ^2 consistently will be asymptotically distributed as $\chi^2(r)$ under the null hypothesis that $\boldsymbol{\beta}_2=\boldsymbol{0}$. This important result will be proved in a moment. Notice that the difference between *any* two values of the criterion function (7.15) is not asymptotically the same as the explained sum of squares from a Gauss-Newton regression. The result is true in this special case because the two values of the criterion function correspond to restricted and unrestricted values of $\boldsymbol{\beta}$, and the GNR corresponding to the unrestricted regression is evaluated at the restricted values.

We will now prove this result. From (7.40) and the fact that $\boldsymbol{P}_W$ is a projection matrix, we see that the explained sum of squares and the parameter estimates $\check{\boldsymbol{b}}$ from the GNR (7.38) are identical to those from the regression

$$\boldsymbol{P}_W(\boldsymbol{y}-\check{\boldsymbol{x}})=\boldsymbol{P}_W\check{\boldsymbol{X}}_1\boldsymbol{b}_1+\boldsymbol{P}_W\check{\boldsymbol{X}}_2\boldsymbol{b}_2+\text{residuals}. \tag{7.50}$$

Suppose now that in the above regression the restriction $\boldsymbol{b}_2=\boldsymbol{0}$ is imposed. The result is

$$\boldsymbol{P}_W(\boldsymbol{y}-\check{\boldsymbol{x}})=\boldsymbol{P}_W\check{\boldsymbol{X}}_1\boldsymbol{b}_1+\text{residuals}. \tag{7.51}$$

The difference between the explained sums of squares from regressions (7.50) and (7.51) is the numerator of all the test statistics for $\boldsymbol{\beta}_2=\boldsymbol{0}$ that are based on the GNR (7.38). This difference is equal to the absolute value of the difference between the two sums of squared residuals. The ESS from regression (7.51) is zero, by the first-order conditions for the minimization of the restricted sum-of-squares function. Thus the SSR is just the total sum of squares, namely,

$$\left\|\boldsymbol{P}_W\big(\boldsymbol{y}-\boldsymbol{x}(\check{\boldsymbol{\beta}})\big)\right\|^2,$$

which is the first term of expression (7.49).

We must now show that the SSR from regression (7.50) is asymptotically equal to minus the second term in expression (7.49). This SSR is

$$\left\|\boldsymbol{P}_W\big(\boldsymbol{y}-\boldsymbol{x}(\check{\boldsymbol{\beta}})-\check{\boldsymbol{X}}\check{\boldsymbol{b}}\big)\right\|^2,$$

where $\check{\boldsymbol{b}}$ is the vector of parameter estimates from OLS estimation of (7.50). Recall from the results of Section 6.6 on one-step estimation that $(\tilde{\boldsymbol{\beta}}-\check{\boldsymbol{\beta}})$ is asymptotically equal to the estimate $\check{\boldsymbol{b}}$ from the GNR (7.38). Thus

$$\boldsymbol{P}_W\big(\boldsymbol{y}-\boldsymbol{x}(\check{\boldsymbol{\beta}})-\check{\boldsymbol{X}}\check{\boldsymbol{b}}\big) \overset{a}{=} \boldsymbol{P}_W\boldsymbol{y}-\boldsymbol{P}_W\boldsymbol{x}(\check{\boldsymbol{\beta}})-\boldsymbol{P}_W\check{\boldsymbol{X}}(\tilde{\boldsymbol{\beta}}-\check{\boldsymbol{\beta}}). \tag{7.52}$$

But a first-order Taylor expansion of $\boldsymbol{x}(\tilde{\boldsymbol{\beta}})$ about $\boldsymbol{\beta}=\check{\boldsymbol{\beta}}$ gives

$$\boldsymbol{x}(\tilde{\boldsymbol{\beta}}) \cong \boldsymbol{x}(\check{\boldsymbol{\beta}})+\boldsymbol{X}(\check{\boldsymbol{\beta}})(\tilde{\boldsymbol{\beta}}-\check{\boldsymbol{\beta}}).$$

Subtracting the right-hand side of this expression from $\boldsymbol{y}$ and multiplying by $\boldsymbol{P}_W$ yields the right-hand side of (7.52). Thus we see that the SSR from regression (7.50) is asymptotically equal to

$$\left\|\boldsymbol{P}_W\big(\boldsymbol{y}-\boldsymbol{x}(\tilde{\boldsymbol{\beta}})\big)\right\|^2,$$

which is the second term of (7.49). We have therefore proved that the difference between the restricted and unrestricted values of the criterion function, expression (7.49), is asymptotically equivalent to the explained sum of squares from the GNR (7.38). Since the latter can be used to construct a valid test statistic, so can the former.

This result is important. It tells us that we can always construct a test of a hypothesis about $\boldsymbol{\beta}$ by taking the difference between the restricted and unrestricted values of the criterion function for IV estimation and dividing it by anything that estimates σ^2 consistently. Moreover, such a test will be asymptotically equivalent to taking the explained sum of squares from the GNR evaluated at $\check{\boldsymbol{\beta}}$ and treating it in the same way. Either of these tests can be turned into an asymptotic F test by dividing numerator and denominator by their respective degrees of freedom, r and $n-k+r$. Whether this is actually a good thing to do in finite samples is unclear, however.

7.8 Identification and Overidentifying Restrictions

Identification is a somewhat more complicated matter in models estimated by IV than in models estimated by least squares, because the choice of instruments affects whether the model is identified or not. A model that would not be identified if it were estimated by least squares will also not be identified if it is estimated by IV. However, a model that would be identified if it were estimated by least squares may not be identified if it is estimated by IV using a particular matrix of instruments. This will inevitably happen if there are fewer instruments than parameters. It may happen in other circumstances as well.

The conditions for a model estimated by IV to be identified by a certain data set are very similar to the ones previously discussed for NLS estimation. For the sake of generality, suppose that we are dealing with the nonlinear model (7.31). The criterion function to be minimized is then expression (7.32). As we saw in Chapters 2 and 5, there are at least three concepts of identification that may be of interest. For a model to be **locally identified** at a local minimum $\tilde{\boldsymbol{\beta}}$ of the criterion function, the matrix of second derivatives of the latter must be positive definite in the neighborhood of $\tilde{\boldsymbol{\beta}}$. For a model to be **globally identified**, the local minimum $\tilde{\boldsymbol{\beta}}$ must be the unique global minimum of the criterion function. For a linear model, local identification implies global identification, but for nonlinear models this is not the case. The third concept of identification is **asymptotic identification**. For a model to be asymptotically identified in the neighborhood of $\boldsymbol{\beta}_0$,

$$\operatorname*{plim}_{n\to\infty}\left(n^{-1}\boldsymbol{X}^{\top}(\boldsymbol{\beta}_0)\boldsymbol{P}_W\boldsymbol{X}(\boldsymbol{\beta}_0)\right)$$

must exist and be a positive definite matrix when the probability limit is calculated under any DGP characterized by the parameter vector $\boldsymbol{\beta}_0$. None of these conditions differs in any substantial way from the corresponding conditions for regression models estimated by NLS. The only differences follow in an obvious way from the presence of $\boldsymbol{P}_W$ in the criterion function.

The issues raised for identification by the use of instruments are the same whether the model is linear or nonlinear. Since linear models are easier to deal with, we will assume for the remainder of this section that the model is linear. Thus we will take the model to be (7.01). It may be estimated consistently either by minimizing the criterion function (7.15) or by a two-stage least squares procedure, provided that the matrix of instruments $\boldsymbol{W}$ is chosen appropriately. These two procedures will yield identical estimates $\tilde{\boldsymbol{\beta}}$.

It should be obvious that the model (7.01) will be neither locally nor globally identified if the matrix $\boldsymbol{X}^{\top}\boldsymbol{P}_W\boldsymbol{X}$ is not positive definite. A necessary condition for this is that $\rho(\boldsymbol{W}) \geq k$. Normally $\rho(\boldsymbol{W})$ will equal l, the number of instruments, and we will assume that this is the case. Thus the necessary condition becomes that there be at least as many instruments as there are regressors. This is still not a sufficient condition, however. If any linear combination of the columns of $\boldsymbol{X}$ happened to lie in $\mathcal{S}^{\perp}(\boldsymbol{W})$, $\boldsymbol{P}_W\boldsymbol{X}$ would have rank less than k and $\boldsymbol{X}^{\top}\boldsymbol{P}_W\boldsymbol{X}$ would then be singular, and so this case must be ruled out. When $\boldsymbol{X}^{\top}\boldsymbol{P}_W\boldsymbol{X}$ is nonsingular, the model (7.01) will be locally identified and, because it is linear, globally identified as well. It is often useful to distinguish between two types of local identification. If there are just as many instruments as regressors, and the model is identified, it is said to be **just identified** or **exactly identified**, because dropping any column of $\boldsymbol{W}$ would cause it to be unidentified. If on the contrary there are more instruments than regressors, so that the model would still be identified if one (or perhaps more than one) column of $\boldsymbol{W}$ were dropped, the model is said to be **overidentified**.

Linear models that are exactly identified have several interesting properties. We have already seen that, for an exactly identified model, the generalized IV estimator (7.17) is equal to the simple IV estimator (7.25). We have also seen that for such models the IV estimator will have no moments of order greater than or equal to 1. A third interesting property is that the minimized value of the criterion function (7.15) is exactly zero. As we will see shortly, this property is a convenient one for certain purposes.

The result that the minimized value of the criterion function (7.15) is zero when $l = k$ is important and illuminating. This value is

$$(\boldsymbol{y} - \boldsymbol{X}\tilde{\boldsymbol{\beta}})^{\top}\boldsymbol{P}_W(\boldsymbol{y} - \boldsymbol{X}\tilde{\boldsymbol{\beta}}) = (\boldsymbol{y} - \boldsymbol{X}\tilde{\boldsymbol{\beta}})^{\top}\boldsymbol{P}_W\boldsymbol{y}.$$

The equality here follows from the first-order conditions for $\tilde{\boldsymbol{\beta}}$, which require that $(\boldsymbol{y} - \boldsymbol{X}\tilde{\boldsymbol{\beta}})^{\top}\boldsymbol{P}_W\boldsymbol{X} = \mathbf{0}$. Using expression (7.17), the minimized value of the criterion function can then be rewritten as

$$\boldsymbol{y}^{\top}\boldsymbol{P}_W\boldsymbol{y} - \boldsymbol{y}^{\top}\boldsymbol{P}_W\boldsymbol{X}\big(\boldsymbol{X}^{\top}\boldsymbol{P}_W\boldsymbol{X}\big)^{-1}\boldsymbol{X}^{\top}\boldsymbol{P}_W\boldsymbol{y} = \boldsymbol{y}^{\top}\big(\boldsymbol{P}_W - \boldsymbol{P}_{P_W X}\big)\boldsymbol{y}. \qquad (7.53)$$

The matrix in the middle of the right-hand expression is in fact an orthogonal projection, since $\mathcal{S}(\boldsymbol{P}_W\boldsymbol{X}) \subseteq \mathcal{S}(\boldsymbol{W})$. Further, it is easy to see that if $\boldsymbol{W}^{\top}\boldsymbol{X}$ is a square nonsingular matrix, $\mathcal{S}(\boldsymbol{P}_W\boldsymbol{X}) = \mathcal{S}(\boldsymbol{W})$, and so the minimized criterion function is zero. The intuition behind this result is very simple. We have seen that IV estimation minimizes only the portion of the distance between $\boldsymbol{y}$ and $\mathcal{S}(\boldsymbol{X})$ that lies in $\mathcal{S}(\boldsymbol{W})$. Since $\mathcal{S}(\boldsymbol{W})$ is a k-dimensional space in this case and we are minimizing with respect to k parameters, the minimization procedure is able to set this distance to zero, thus entirely eliminating any discrepancy between $\boldsymbol{P}_W\boldsymbol{y}$ and $\mathcal{S}(\boldsymbol{P}_W\boldsymbol{X})$.

When there are more instruments than regressors (again we assume that $\rho(\boldsymbol{W})$ is equal to l), the model is said to be overidentified, because there are more instruments than are absolutely needed to ensure identification. The terminology comes from the literature on simultaneous equations models, in which identification has been studied in great detail; see Chapter 18. We saw in Section 7.5 that it is generally desirable for a model to be somewhat overidentified in order to ensure good finite-sample properties for the IV estimator. A second desirable feature of overidentified models is that the validity of the choice of instruments may be tested, at least to a limited extent. This is remarkably easy to do and can be very informative in some cases.

When we specify a model like (7.01), we are assuming that $\boldsymbol{y}$ depends linearly on $\boldsymbol{X}$ and does not depend on any other observable variables. In particular, we are assuming that it does not depend on any columns of $\boldsymbol{W}$ that do not lie in $\mathcal{S}(\boldsymbol{X})$. Otherwise, the assumption that the error terms $\boldsymbol{u}$ in (7.01) are independent of the instruments would be false. In some cases, perhaps in many cases, we may not be entirely sure which columns of $\boldsymbol{W}$ can legitimately be excluded from $\boldsymbol{X}$. Nevertheless, to identify the model at all we have to exclude as many columns of $\boldsymbol{W}$ as there are endogenous variables in $\boldsymbol{X}$. If the model is overidentified, we have excluded more columns of $\boldsymbol{W}$ than we needed to. These extra restrictions, which are called **overidentifying restrictions**, may be tested. This can be done in several different ways. Basmann (1960) is a classic paper, and other references include Byron (1974), Wegge (1978), Hwang (1980), and Fisher (1981). Our approach is simpler than the ones taken in these papers, however.

The easiest way to think about tests of overidentifying restrictions is as special cases of the hypothesis tests discussed in the preceding section. The null hypothesis is the model (7.01). The alternative is the model

$$\boldsymbol{y} = \boldsymbol{X\beta} + \boldsymbol{W}^*\boldsymbol{\gamma} + \boldsymbol{u}, \quad \boldsymbol{u} \sim \mathrm{IID}(\mathbf{0}, \sigma^2\mathbf{I}), \tag{7.54}$$

where $\boldsymbol{W}^*$ is a matrix consisting of $l - k$ columns of $\boldsymbol{W}$ that do not lie in $\mathcal{S}(\boldsymbol{P_W X})$. Thus the $n \times l$ matrix $[\boldsymbol{P_W X} \;\; \boldsymbol{W}^*]$ will have full rank l. Further, $\mathcal{S}(\boldsymbol{P_W X}, \boldsymbol{W}^*) = \mathcal{S}(\boldsymbol{W})$. As we will see in a moment, it is not actually necessary to construct $\boldsymbol{W}^*$ in order to compute the test statistic.

The model (7.54) is constructed so that it is just identified. There are precisely as many regressors as there are instruments. If (7.01) is specified correctly, $\boldsymbol{W}^*$ should have no ability to explain any variation in $\boldsymbol{y}$ not explained by $\boldsymbol{X}$ in an IV regression using $\boldsymbol{W}$ as the matrix of instruments; $\boldsymbol{\gamma}$ should therefore be equal to zero. If this is not the case, that is, if any of the columns of $\boldsymbol{W}^*$ are correlated with $\boldsymbol{u}$, $\boldsymbol{\gamma}$ will be nonzero. This could happen either if some columns of $\boldsymbol{W}^*$ should have been included in $\boldsymbol{X}$ and were not or if some columns of $\boldsymbol{W}^*$ were correlated with $\boldsymbol{u}$ and hence were not valid to use as instruments. Thus by testing the hypothesis that $\boldsymbol{\gamma} = \mathbf{0}$ we can test the *joint* null hypothesis that (7.01) is correctly specified and that $\boldsymbol{W}$ is a valid matrix of instruments. Unfortunately, it is not possible to test the latter hypothesis by itself.

Once the problem has been formulated in this way, it should be clear that we could test the hypothesis that $\boldsymbol{\gamma} = \mathbf{0}$ simply by using any of the tests discussed in Section 7.7. One would begin by obtaining IV estimates of the null hypothesis (7.01) and the alternative (7.54). An asymptotic F test could then be computed as

$$\frac{(\mathrm{RSSR}^* - \mathrm{USSR}^*)/(l-k)}{\mathrm{USSR}/(n-l)} \overset{a}{\sim} F(l-k, n-l), \tag{7.55}$$

where RSSR^* and USSR^* are the sums of squares of the second-stage OLS residuals from 2SLS estimation of (7.01) and (7.54), respectively, and USSR is the sum of squares of the IV residuals from estimation of the latter.

An even simpler procedure is available, however. We have seen that the value of the criterion function (7.15) for the unrestricted model (7.54) must be equal to zero at the optimum. Hence the difference between the restricted and unrestricted values of the criterion function must be equal to the value for the restricted model. From (7.53), the value of the criterion function for the restricted model is

$$\left\|\boldsymbol{P}_W(\boldsymbol{y}-\boldsymbol{X}\tilde{\boldsymbol{\beta}})\right\|^2=\boldsymbol{y}^{\top}\boldsymbol{P}_W\boldsymbol{y}-\boldsymbol{y}^{\top}\boldsymbol{P}_W\boldsymbol{X}\left(\boldsymbol{X}^{\top}\boldsymbol{P}_W\boldsymbol{X}\right)^{-1}\boldsymbol{X}^{\top}\boldsymbol{P}_W\boldsymbol{y}, \qquad (7.56)$$

and it is easy to see that (7.56) is equal to the difference $\text{RSSR}^* - \text{USSR}^*$ which appears in (7.55). This may be divided by anything that estimates σ^2 consistently. Thus one alternative test statistic is

$$\frac{\left\|\boldsymbol{P}_W(\boldsymbol{y}-\boldsymbol{X}\tilde{\boldsymbol{\beta}})\right\|^2}{\left\|(\boldsymbol{y}-\boldsymbol{X}\tilde{\boldsymbol{\beta}})\right\|^2/n}\overset{a}{\sim}\chi^2(l-k). \qquad (7.57)$$

This is just n times the uncentered R^2 from a regression of the IV residuals $\boldsymbol{y}-\boldsymbol{X}\tilde{\boldsymbol{\beta}}$ on the instruments $\boldsymbol{W}$. It is easy to see that this regression is equivalent to the GNR associated with the unrestricted model (7.54). Thus we see that it is not necessary to specify $\boldsymbol{W}^*$ or estimate (7.54) at all.

From (7.57), we see that if the value of the criterion function is small, relative to our estimate of σ^2, we cannot reject the joint hypothesis that (7.01) is correctly specified and that the instruments which appear in $\boldsymbol{W}$ are valid. If, on the other hand, it is large, we will want to reject that hypothesis. This makes sense, since the criterion function (7.15) is the squared length of the vector $\boldsymbol{P}_W(\boldsymbol{y}-\boldsymbol{X}\tilde{\boldsymbol{\beta}})$, which is the observable counterpart of $\|\boldsymbol{P}_W\boldsymbol{u}\|^2$. If $\boldsymbol{W}$ is a valid matrix of instruments, the error terms $\boldsymbol{u}$ should be uncorrelated with $\boldsymbol{W}$, and $\|\boldsymbol{P}_W\boldsymbol{u}\|^2$ should therefore be small. Thus it makes sense that a test should be based on $\|\boldsymbol{P}_W(\boldsymbol{y}-\boldsymbol{X}\tilde{\boldsymbol{\beta}})\|^2$. It also makes sense that the test should have $l-k$ degrees of freedom, since it is only when $l>k$ that the numerator of (7.57) is nonzero.

The test statistic (7.57) has an obvious analog for nonlinear models like (7.31). It is

$$\frac{\left\|\boldsymbol{P}_W\big(\boldsymbol{y}-\boldsymbol{x}(\tilde{\boldsymbol{\beta}})\big)\right\|^2}{\left\|\big(\boldsymbol{y}-\boldsymbol{x}(\tilde{\boldsymbol{\beta}})\big)\right\|^2/n}\overset{a}{\sim}\chi^2(l-k), \qquad (7.58)$$

and it may be computed as n times the uncentered R^2 from a regression of the IV residuals $\boldsymbol{y}-\boldsymbol{x}(\tilde{\boldsymbol{\beta}})$ on the matrix of instruments $\boldsymbol{W}$. Readers may wish to verify, based on the arguments immediately above and those in Section 7.7, that this test statistic is indeed asymptotically distributed as $\chi^2(l-k)$ under standard regularity conditions.

Tests of overidentifying restrictions should be calculated routinely whenever one computes IV estimates. If the test statistic is significantly larger than it should be by chance under the null, one should be extremely cautious in interpreting the estimates, since it is likely either that the model is specified incorrectly or that some of the instruments are invalid. It would be easy for every program for IV estimation of linear and nonlinear regression models to calculate the test statistics (7.57) or (7.58) automatically along with every set of parameter estimates for overidentified models. Unfortunately, at the time of writing, most programs do not do so.

7.9 Durbin-Wu-Hausman Tests

So far, we have assumed that the investigator always knows when it is necessary to use IV rather than least squares. That may not always be the case. Sometimes economic theory suggests that certain explanatory variables could be endogenous, but does not unambiguously indicate that they are, and does not say whether their correlation with the error terms is likely to be great enough that using least squares will result in serious bias. Since least squares is somewhat easier to use than IV and yields more efficient estimates, one would prefer to use it if possible. To decide whether it is necessary to use IV, one has to ask whether a set of estimates obtained by least squares is consistent or not. In this section, we discuss tests that may be used to answer this question.

The question of whether a set of estimates is consistent is rather different from the question that the hypothesis tests we have looked at so far try to answer. These tests simply ask whether certain restrictions on the parameters of a model do in fact hold. In contrast, we now want to ask whether the parameters of interest in a model have been estimated consistently. In a very influential paper, Hausman (1978) proposed a family of tests designed to answer this second question. His basic idea is that one may base a test on a **vector of contrasts**, that is, the vector of differences between two vectors of estimates, one of which will be consistent under weaker conditions than the other. This idea dates back to a famous paper by Durbin (1954). One of the tests proposed by Hausman for testing the consistency of least squares estimates was also proposed by Wu (1973). We will therefore refer to all tests of this general type as **Durbin-Wu-Hausman tests**, or **DWH tests**. There has been a good deal of work on DWH tests in recent years; see in particular Holly (1982), Ruud (1984), and Davidson and MacKinnon (1989). In this section, we merely introduce the basic ideas and show how procedures of this type may be used to test the consistency of least squares estimates when some explanatory variables may be endogenous. Further applications of DWH tests will be discussed in Chapter 11.

Suppose initially that the model of interest is (7.01). The DWH testing principle suggests that we should compare the OLS estimator

$$\hat{\boldsymbol{\beta}} = \left(\boldsymbol{X}^{\top}\boldsymbol{X}\right)^{-1}\boldsymbol{X}^{\top}\boldsymbol{y}$$

with the IV estimator

$$\tilde{\boldsymbol{\beta}} = \left(\boldsymbol{X}^\top \boldsymbol{P}_W \boldsymbol{X}\right)^{-1} \boldsymbol{X}^\top \boldsymbol{P}_W \boldsymbol{y}.$$

If the data were actually generated by a special case of the model (7.01), with $\boldsymbol{\beta} = \boldsymbol{\beta}_0$, and $\boldsymbol{u}$ were asymptotically independent of $\boldsymbol{X}$, the OLS estimator $\hat{\boldsymbol{\beta}}$ would be consistent for $\boldsymbol{\beta}_0$. So would be the IV estimator $\tilde{\boldsymbol{\beta}}$, provided the matrix of instruments $\boldsymbol{W}$ satisfied conditions (7.18). Thus both estimators would have the same probability limit, $\boldsymbol{\beta}_0$. On the other hand, if $\boldsymbol{u}$ were not asymptotically independent of $\boldsymbol{X}$, $\tilde{\boldsymbol{\beta}}$ would still be consistent but $\hat{\boldsymbol{\beta}}$ would not be.

The DWH test is based on the vector of contrasts

$$\begin{aligned}
\tilde{\boldsymbol{\beta}} - \hat{\boldsymbol{\beta}} &= \left(\boldsymbol{X}^\top \boldsymbol{P}_W \boldsymbol{X}\right)^{-1} \boldsymbol{X}^\top \boldsymbol{P}_W \boldsymbol{y} - \left(\boldsymbol{X}^\top \boldsymbol{X}\right)^{-1} \boldsymbol{X}^\top \boldsymbol{y} \\
&= \left(\boldsymbol{X}^\top \boldsymbol{P}_W \boldsymbol{X}\right)^{-1} \Big(\boldsymbol{X}^\top \boldsymbol{P}_W \boldsymbol{y} - \left(\boldsymbol{X}^\top \boldsymbol{P}_W \boldsymbol{X}\right)\left(\boldsymbol{X}^\top \boldsymbol{X}\right)^{-1} \boldsymbol{X}^\top \boldsymbol{y}\Big) \\
&= \left(\boldsymbol{X}^\top \boldsymbol{P}_W \boldsymbol{X}\right)^{-1} \Big(\boldsymbol{X}^\top \boldsymbol{P}_W \big(\mathbf{I} - \boldsymbol{X}(\boldsymbol{X}^\top \boldsymbol{X})^{-1} \boldsymbol{X}^\top\big) \boldsymbol{y}\Big) \\
&= \left(\boldsymbol{X}^\top \boldsymbol{P}_W \boldsymbol{X}\right)^{-1} \boldsymbol{X}^\top \boldsymbol{P}_W \boldsymbol{M}_X \boldsymbol{y}.
\end{aligned} \tag{7.59}$$

We could construct a χ^2 test statistic based directly on this vector in a fairly obvious way. The test statistic would be a quadratic form in the vector (7.59), with the (generalized) inverse[3] of an estimate of its covariance matrix in the middle. But as we will now see, we do not actually have to construct a vector of contrasts to compute this DWH test statistic. In fact, as Davidson and MacKinnon (1989) discuss, one never needs to construct a vector of contrasts to compute a DWH statistic. These statistics can always be computed by means of artificial regressions.

The first factor in (7.59), $(\boldsymbol{X}^\top \boldsymbol{P}_W \boldsymbol{X})^{-1}$, is simply a $k \times k$ matrix with full rank. Its presence will obviously have no effect on any test statistic that we might compute. Hence what we really want to do is test whether the vector

$$\boldsymbol{X}^\top \boldsymbol{P}_W \boldsymbol{M}_X \boldsymbol{y} \tag{7.60}$$

has mean zero asymptotically. It should, because under any DGP belonging to (7.01) it is equal to

$$\boldsymbol{X}^\top \boldsymbol{P}_W \boldsymbol{M}_X \boldsymbol{u}.$$

This vector has k elements, but even if $\boldsymbol{P}_W \boldsymbol{X}$ has full rank, not all of those elements may be random variables, because $\boldsymbol{M}_X$ may annihilate some columns of $\boldsymbol{P}_W \boldsymbol{X}$. It will in fact annihilate all those columns that correspond to explanatory variables which are also instruments. Suppose that k^* is the number of linearly independent columns of $\boldsymbol{P}_W \boldsymbol{X}$ that are not annihilated by $\boldsymbol{M}_X$. Then if we let the corresponding k^* columns of $\boldsymbol{X}$ be denoted by $\boldsymbol{X}^*$, we are really

[3] One has to use a generalized inverse in the many cases in which the covariance matrix of the vector of contrasts does not have full rank. See Hausman and Taylor (1982).

interested in testing whether the vector

$$X^{*\top} P_W M_X y \tag{7.61}$$

has mean zero asymptotically.

Now consider the artificial regression

$$y = X\beta' + P_W X^* \delta + \text{residuals}. \tag{7.62}$$

The regressors $P_W X^*$ are the fitted values from regressing X^*, the columns of X that do not lie in $\mathcal{S}(W)$, on the instrument matrix W. Since

$$\mathcal{S}(X, P_W X^*) = \mathcal{S}(X, P_W X) = \mathcal{S}(X, M_W X) = \mathcal{S}(X, M_W X^*),$$

regression (7.62) must have exactly the same SSR as the regression

$$y = X\beta + M_W X^* \eta + \text{residuals}, \tag{7.63}$$

in which the regressors $M_W X^*$ are the residuals from regressing X^* on W. The DWH test may be based on either of these regressions. It is simply the F test for $\delta = 0$ in (7.62) or the F test for $\eta = 0$ in (7.63). Because (7.62) and (7.63) have the same sums of squared residuals, it is clear that these two tests will be numerically identical.

By the FWL Theorem, the OLS estimate of δ in (7.62) is

$$\tilde{\delta} = \left(X^{*\top} P_W M_X P_W X^*\right)^{-1} X^{*\top} P_W M_X y.$$

It is evident that, in general, $\text{plim}(\tilde{\delta}) = 0$ if and only if (7.61) has mean zero asymptotically. The ordinary F statistic for $\delta = 0$ in (7.62) is

$$\frac{y^\top P_{M_X P_W X^*} y / k^*}{y^\top M_{X,\, M_X P_W X^*} y / (n - k - k^*)} \overset{a}{\sim} F(k^*, n - k - k^*), \tag{7.64}$$

where $P_{M_X P_W X^*}$ is the matrix that projects orthogonally onto $\mathcal{S}(M_X P_W X^*)$, and $M_{X,\, M_X P_W X^*}$ is the matrix that projects onto $\mathcal{S}^\perp(X, M_X P_W X^*)$. If (7.01) actually generated the data and X is independent of u, the statistic (7.64) will clearly be valid asymptotically, since the denominator will then consistently estimate σ^2. It will be exactly distributed as $F(k^*, n - k - k^*)$ in finite samples if the u_t's in (7.01) are normally distributed and X and P_W can be treated as fixed.

This version of the DWH test is often *interpreted* as a test for the exogeneity of those components of X not in the space spanned by W; see Wu (1973), Hausman (1978), and Nakamura and Nakamura (1981). This interpretation is somewhat misleading, since what is being tested is not the exogeneity or endogeneity of some components of X, but rather the effect on the estimates of β of any endogeneity that may be present. The null hypothesis is that the OLS estimates $\hat{\beta}$ are consistent, not that every column of X is asymptotically independent of u. Nevertheless, this version of the DWH test can be quite useful when it is not clear whether it is safe to use least squares rather than instrumental variables.

Regression (7.63) deserves further comment. It has the remarkable feature that the OLS estimates of $\boldsymbol{\beta}$ are numerically identical to the IV estimates of $\boldsymbol{\beta}$ in the original model (7.01). Moreover, the estimated covariance matrices are also the same, except that the OLS estimate from (7.63) uses an inconsistent estimator for σ^2. These results are easy to obtain. Denote by $\boldsymbol{M}^*$ the orthogonal projection onto the space $\mathcal{S}^{\perp}(\boldsymbol{M}_W\boldsymbol{X}^*)$. Then, by the FWL Theorem, the OLS estimates from (7.63) must be identical to those from the regression

$$\boldsymbol{M}^*\boldsymbol{y} = \boldsymbol{M}^*\boldsymbol{X}\boldsymbol{\beta} + \text{residuals}. \tag{7.65}$$

Now

$$\boldsymbol{M}^*\boldsymbol{X} = \boldsymbol{X} - \boldsymbol{M}_W\boldsymbol{X}^*\big(\boldsymbol{X}^{*\top}\boldsymbol{M}_W\boldsymbol{X}^*\big)^{-1}\boldsymbol{X}^{*\top}\boldsymbol{M}_W\boldsymbol{X}.$$

From the fact that $\boldsymbol{M}_W\boldsymbol{X} = [\boldsymbol{M}_W\boldsymbol{X}^* \quad \mathbf{0}]$, it follows that

$$\boldsymbol{X}^{*\top}\boldsymbol{M}_W\boldsymbol{X} = \boldsymbol{X}^{*\top}\boldsymbol{M}_W\big[\boldsymbol{X}^* \quad \mathbf{0}\big].$$

Consequently, we obtain

$$\boldsymbol{M}^*\boldsymbol{X} = \boldsymbol{X} - \big[\boldsymbol{M}_W\boldsymbol{X}^* \quad \mathbf{0}\big] = \boldsymbol{X} - \boldsymbol{M}_W\boldsymbol{X} = \boldsymbol{P}_W\boldsymbol{X}.$$

Then the OLS estimate of $\boldsymbol{\beta}$ from (7.65) is seen to be

$$\big(\boldsymbol{X}^\top\boldsymbol{M}^*\boldsymbol{X}\big)^{-1}\boldsymbol{X}^\top\boldsymbol{M}^*\boldsymbol{y} = \big(\boldsymbol{X}^\top\boldsymbol{P}_W\boldsymbol{X}\big)^{-1}\boldsymbol{X}^\top\boldsymbol{P}_W\boldsymbol{y}. \tag{7.66}$$

The right-hand side of (7.66) is of course the expression for the IV or 2SLS estimate of $\boldsymbol{\beta}$, expression (7.17).

By an extension of this argument, it is easy to see that the estimated OLS covariance matrix of $\hat{\boldsymbol{\beta}}$ from (7.63) will be

$$\tilde{s}^2\big(\boldsymbol{X}^\top\boldsymbol{P}_W\boldsymbol{X}\big)^{-1}, \tag{7.67}$$

where $\tilde{s}^2$ denotes the OLS estimate of the error variance in (7.63). Expression (7.67) looks just like the IV covariance matrix (7.24), except that $\tilde{s}^2$ appears instead of $\tilde{\sigma}^2$. When $\boldsymbol{\eta}$ is nonzero (so that IV estimation is necessary), the variance of the errors in (7.63) will be less than σ^2. As a consequence, $\tilde{s}^2$ will be biased downward as an estimator of σ^2. Of course, it would be easy to obtain a valid estimated covariance matrix by multiplying (7.67) by $\tilde{\sigma}^2/\tilde{s}^2$.

We now return to the DWH test. A variant of this test is applicable to nonlinear models like (7.31) as well as to linear ones. The test would then be based on a variant of the Gauss-Newton regression. If the null were that the NLS estimates $\hat{\boldsymbol{\beta}}$ were consistent, an appropriate test statistic would be an asymptotic F test for $\boldsymbol{c} = \mathbf{0}$ in the GNR

$$\boldsymbol{y} - \hat{\boldsymbol{x}} = \hat{\boldsymbol{X}}\boldsymbol{b} + \boldsymbol{M}_W\hat{\boldsymbol{X}}^*\boldsymbol{c} + \text{residuals}, \tag{7.68}$$

where, as usual, $\hat{\boldsymbol{x}} \equiv \boldsymbol{x}(\hat{\boldsymbol{\beta}})$ and $\hat{\boldsymbol{X}} \equiv \boldsymbol{X}(\hat{\boldsymbol{\beta}})$. It is a good exercise to verify that this procedure does indeed yield a test statistic which is asymptotically equivalent to the test statistic one would obtain if one started with the vector of contrasts $\hat{\boldsymbol{\beta}} - \tilde{\boldsymbol{\beta}}$.

There is one problem with DWH tests for nonlinear models. In the case of such a model, it may be unclear which columns of $\hat{\boldsymbol{X}} \equiv \boldsymbol{X}(\hat{\boldsymbol{\beta}})$ should be included in $\hat{\boldsymbol{X}}^*$ and thus how many degrees of freedom the test should have. Asymptotically, we want $\boldsymbol{X}^*$ to include all the columns of $\boldsymbol{X}$ that do not lie in $\mathcal{S}(\boldsymbol{W})$. The number of degrees of freedom for the test will therefore be

$$\rho\big([\boldsymbol{X}(\boldsymbol{\beta}_0) \quad \boldsymbol{M}_W\boldsymbol{X}(\boldsymbol{\beta}_0)]\big) - k.$$

The problem is that $\boldsymbol{X}(\boldsymbol{\beta}_0)$ depends on $\boldsymbol{\beta}_0$, which of course the investigator does not know. In practice, it is necessary to use $\hat{\boldsymbol{X}}$ instead of $\boldsymbol{X}(\boldsymbol{\beta}_0)$. Unfortunately, it is possible that the rank of $[\hat{\boldsymbol{X}} \quad \boldsymbol{M}_W\hat{\boldsymbol{X}}]$ will not be the same as the rank of $[\boldsymbol{X}(\boldsymbol{\beta}_0) \quad \boldsymbol{M}_W\boldsymbol{X}(\boldsymbol{\beta}_0)]$. When that happens, the test statistic calculated from (7.68) will have the wrong number of degrees of freedom.

It can sometimes be difficult to decide which explanatory variables may validly be used as instruments and which must be treated as endogenous. In such cases, it may be useful to test whether an IV estimator is consistent by using a DWH test. This is easily done: Suppose it is known that some of the explanatory variables should be treated as endogenous, but it is not clear whether q others should be. When the smaller number is to be treated as endogenous, the matrix of instrumental variables should be $\boldsymbol{W}_1$, and when the larger number is to be treated as endogenous, it should be $\boldsymbol{W}_2$, where $\boldsymbol{W}_1$ includes everything that is in $\boldsymbol{W}_2$ plus q additional columns of $\boldsymbol{X}$. Consider the linear case. The two estimators are

$$\tilde{\boldsymbol{\beta}}_1 = \big(\boldsymbol{X}^\top\boldsymbol{P}_1\boldsymbol{X}\big)^{-1}\boldsymbol{X}^\top\boldsymbol{P}_1\boldsymbol{y} \quad \text{and}$$

$$\tilde{\boldsymbol{\beta}}_2 = \big(\boldsymbol{X}^\top\boldsymbol{P}_2\boldsymbol{X}\big)^{-1}\boldsymbol{X}^\top\boldsymbol{P}_2\boldsymbol{y},$$

where $\boldsymbol{P}_1$ and $\boldsymbol{P}_2$ are the matrices that project orthogonally onto $\mathcal{S}(\boldsymbol{W}_1)$ and $\mathcal{S}(\boldsymbol{W}_2)$, respectively. The vector of contrasts is

$$\begin{aligned}\tilde{\boldsymbol{\beta}}_2 - \tilde{\boldsymbol{\beta}}_1 &= \big(\boldsymbol{X}^\top\boldsymbol{P}_2\boldsymbol{X}\big)^{-1}\boldsymbol{X}^\top\boldsymbol{P}_2\boldsymbol{y} - \big(\boldsymbol{X}^\top\boldsymbol{P}_1\boldsymbol{X}\big)^{-1}\boldsymbol{X}^\top\boldsymbol{P}_1\boldsymbol{y} \\ &= \big(\boldsymbol{X}^\top\boldsymbol{P}_2\boldsymbol{X}\big)^{-1}\Big(\boldsymbol{X}^\top\boldsymbol{P}_2\boldsymbol{y} - \big(\boldsymbol{X}^\top\boldsymbol{P}_2\boldsymbol{X}\big)\big(\boldsymbol{X}^\top\boldsymbol{P}_1\boldsymbol{X}\big)^{-1}\boldsymbol{X}^\top\boldsymbol{P}_1\boldsymbol{y}\Big) \\ &= \big(\boldsymbol{X}^\top\boldsymbol{P}_2\boldsymbol{X}\big)^{-1}\Big(\boldsymbol{X}^\top\boldsymbol{P}_2\big(\mathbf{I} - \boldsymbol{P}_1\boldsymbol{X}(\boldsymbol{X}^\top\boldsymbol{P}_1\boldsymbol{X})^{-1}\boldsymbol{X}^\top\boldsymbol{P}_1\big)\boldsymbol{y}\Big) \\ &= \big(\boldsymbol{X}^\top\boldsymbol{P}_2\boldsymbol{X}\big)^{-1}\boldsymbol{X}^\top\boldsymbol{P}_2\boldsymbol{M}_{P_1X}\boldsymbol{y},\end{aligned} \tag{7.69}$$

where $\boldsymbol{M}_{P_1X}$ is the matrix that projects onto $\mathcal{S}^\perp(\boldsymbol{P}_1\boldsymbol{X})$. The third line here makes use of the equality $\boldsymbol{P}_2\boldsymbol{P}_1 = \boldsymbol{P}_2$, which is a consequence of the fact that $\mathcal{S}(\boldsymbol{W}_2)$ is a subspace of $\mathcal{S}(\boldsymbol{W}_1)$.

We leave it as an exercise to prove that a test of whether the vector (7.69) has mean zero asymptotically may be accomplished by testing whether the q-vector $\boldsymbol{\delta}$ is equal to zero in the regression

$$\boldsymbol{y} = \boldsymbol{X\beta} + \boldsymbol{P}_2\boldsymbol{X}^*\boldsymbol{\delta} + \text{residuals}. \tag{7.70}$$

Here $\boldsymbol{P}_2\boldsymbol{X}^*$ consists of the q columns of $\boldsymbol{P}_2\boldsymbol{X}$ that are not annihilated by $\boldsymbol{M}_{P_1X}$. Regression (7.70) must be estimated by IV using $\boldsymbol{W}_1$ as the matrix of instruments, and any of the tests discussed in Section 7.7 may then be used to test whether $\boldsymbol{\delta} = \boldsymbol{0}$.

7.10 Conclusion

This chapter has introduced all of the important concepts associated with the technique of instrumental variables estimation. For a more detailed treatment, see Bowden and Turkington (1984). Another useful reference is Godfrey (1988, Chapter 5), which discusses a large number of specification tests for both linear and nonlinear models that have been estimated by IV.

In this chapter, we applied the method of instrumental variables only to univariate linear and nonlinear regression models with i.i.d. errors. We will encounter numerous other applications later in the book, notably in Chapters 17 and 18, in which we discuss GMM estimation and simultaneous equations models, respectively. In many other cases, we will state a result in the context of OLS or NLS estimation and point out that it goes through with minor modification in the context of IV estimation as well.

Terms and Concepts

criterion function
Durbin-Wu-Hausman (DWH) tests
errors in variables
exactly identified (just identified) model
Gauss-Newton regression (GNR)
generalized IV estimator
identification: local, global, and asymptotic
instrumental variables (IV) estimator
instruments (instrumental variables)
nonlinear IV estimator
nonlinear two-stage least squares (NL2SLS) estimator
normalization (of a simultaneous equations model)
overidentified model
overidentifying restrictions
predetermined variable
reduced form (of a simultaneous equations model)
restricted reduced form (RRF)
simple IV estimator
simultaneous equations bias
simultaneous equations model
structural form (of a simultaneous equations model)
two-stage least squares (2SLS) estimator
unrestricted reduced form (URF)
vector of contrasts

Chapter 8

The Method of Maximum Likelihood

8.1 Introduction

The estimation techniques we have discussed so far — least squares and instrumental variables — are applicable only to regression models. But not every model can be written so that the dependent variable is equal to a regression function plus an additive error term or so that a set of dependent variables, arranged as a vector, is equal to a vector of regression functions plus a vector of errors (see Chapter 9). If not, then least squares and instrumental variables are simply not appropriate. In this chapter, we therefore introduce a third estimation method, which is much more widely applicable than the techniques we have discussed so far, but also requires fairly strong assumptions. This is the method of **maximum likelihood**, or **ML**, estimation.

As an extreme example of how inappropriate least squares can be, consider the model

$$y_t^\gamma = \beta_0 + \beta_1 x_t + u_t, \quad u_t \sim \mathrm{IID}(0, \sigma^2), \tag{8.01}$$

which looks almost like a regression model. This model makes sense so long as the right-hand side of (8.01) is always positive, and it may even be an attractive model in certain cases.[1] For example, suppose that the observations on y_t are skewed to the right but those on x_t are not. Then a conventional regression model could reconcile these two facts only if the error terms u_t were right-skewed, which one would probably not want to assume and which would make the use of least squares dubious. On the other hand, the model (8.01) with $\gamma < 1$ might well be able to reconcile these facts while allowing the error terms to be symmetrically distributed.

If γ were known, (8.01) would be a regression model. But if γ is to be estimated, (8.01) is *not* a regression model. As a result, it cannot sensibly be estimated by least squares. The sum-of-squares function is

$$SSR(\boldsymbol{\beta}, \gamma) = \sum_{t=1}^{n} \left(y_t^\gamma - \beta_0 - \beta_1 x_t\right)^2,$$

[1] Strictly speaking, of course, it is impossible to guarantee that the right-hand side of (8.01) will always be positive, but this model may be regarded as a very good approximation if $\beta_0 + \beta_1 x_t$ is always much larger than σ.

and if, for example, all the y_t's were greater than unity, it is clear that this function could be made arbitrarily close to zero simply by letting γ tend to minus infinity and setting β_0 and β_1 to zero. Hence one could *never* obtain sensible estimates of (8.01) by using least squares. This model can, however, be estimated quite easily using the method of maximum likelihood; just how will be explained in Section 8.10.

The basic idea of maximum likelihood estimation is, as the name implies, to find a set of parameter estimates, say $\hat{\boldsymbol{\theta}}$, such that the **likelihood** of having obtained the actual sample that we are using is maximized. By this we mean that the joint probability density for the model being estimated is evaluated at the observed values of the dependent variable(s) and treated as a function of the model parameters. The vector of ML estimates $\hat{\boldsymbol{\theta}}$ then yields the maximum of this function. This principle of estimation is very widely applicable: If we can write down the joint density of the sample, we can in principle use maximum likelihood, subject of course to certain regularity conditions. Moreover, it has a number of extremely convenient properties, which we will discuss briefly below and in much more detail in the remainder of this chapter. It also has a few properties that are not so convenient and that the applied econometrician must sometimes be wary of.

The easiest way to grasp the fundamental idea of ML estimation is to consider a simple example. Suppose that each observation y_t is generated by the density

$$f(y_t,\theta) = \theta e^{-\theta y_t}, \quad y_t > 0, \ \theta > 0, \tag{8.02}$$

and is independent of all the other y_t's. This is the density of what is called the **exponential distribution.**[2] There is a single unknown parameter θ that we wish to estimate, and we have available n observations with which to do so. The joint density of the y_t's will be referred to as the **likelihood function** and denoted $L(\boldsymbol{y},\theta)$; for any given θ this function tells us how likely in some sense we were to have observed the sample $\boldsymbol{y} \equiv [y_1 \vdots \cdots \vdots y_n]$.

Because the y_t's are independent, their joint density is simply the product of their individual densities. Thus the likelihood function is

$$L(\boldsymbol{y},\theta) = \prod_{t=1}^{n} \theta e^{-\theta y_t}. \tag{8.03}$$

Especially when the sample size is large, (8.03) can easily be an extremely large or extremely small number, well beyond the range of floating-point numbers

[2] The exponential distribution is useful for analyzing events such as waiting times or the duration of unemployment. See any advanced undergraduate- or graduate-level statistics text, such as Cox and Hinkley (1974) or Hogg and Craig (1978). More detailed treatments may be found in, among others, Cox and Oakes (1984), Lawless (1982), and Miller (1981). For applications in economics, see Kiefer (1988) and Lancaster (1990).

that digital computers can handle. For that reason, among others, it is customary to maximize the *logarithm* of the likelihood function rather than the likelihood function itself. We will obviously obtain the same answer by doing so, since the **loglikelihood function** $\ell(\boldsymbol{y},\theta) \equiv \log\bigl(L(\boldsymbol{y},\theta)\bigr)$ is a monotonically increasing function of $L(\boldsymbol{y},\theta)$; if $\hat{\theta}$ maximizes $\ell(\boldsymbol{y},\theta)$, it must also maximize $L(\boldsymbol{y},\theta)$. In the case of (8.03), the loglikelihood function is

$$\ell(\boldsymbol{y},\theta) = \sum_{t=1}^{n}\bigl(\log(\theta) - \theta y_t\bigr) = n\log(\theta) - \theta\sum_{t=1}^{n} y_t. \tag{8.04}$$

Maximizing this loglikelihood function with respect to the single unknown parameter θ is straightforward. Differentiating the right-most expression of (8.04) with respect to θ and setting the derivative to zero yields the first-order condition

$$\frac{n}{\theta} - \sum_{t=1}^{n} y_t = 0, \tag{8.05}$$

and solving this for the ML estimator $\hat{\theta}$ we find that

$$\hat{\theta} = \frac{n}{\sum_{t=1}^{n} y_t}. \tag{8.06}$$

In this case, we do not need to worry about multiple solutions to (8.05). The second derivative of (8.04) is always negative, which allows us to conclude that $\hat{\theta}$ defined by (8.06) is the *unique* ML estimator. Note that this will not always be the case; for many problems the first-order conditions may have multiple solutions.

At this point, we might reasonably ask a number of questions about the properties of $\hat{\theta}$. Is it in any sense a good estimator to use? Is it unbiased? Is it consistent? How is it distributed? And so on. We could certainly study these questions for this particular case. But much of this investigation would be unnecessary, because the fact that $\hat{\theta}$ is an ML estimator immediately tells us a great deal about its properties. That is indeed one of the most attractive features of ML estimation: Because much is known about the properties of ML estimators in general, we often do not need to study particular cases in much detail.

Two major desirable properties of ML estimators are **consistency** and **asymptotic normality**. These are properties that we have already studied extensively in the context of least squares, and no further introduction to them is required at this point. A third desirable property is **asymptotic efficiency**. This turns out to be true in a much stronger sense for ML estimators than it is for least squares ones; since we did not make strong distributional assumptions when discussing least squares, we could assert only that nonlinear least squares estimates were asymptotically efficient within a fairly restricted class of estimators. Partly because the method of maximum likelihood forces us to make explicit distributional assumptions, we will be able to prove much stronger results.

Closely related to these properties is the fact that the covariance matrix of the parameter estimates resulting from ML estimation can be estimated quite easily in several different ways. Further, as we will see in Section 8.9, the ML procedure leads naturally to several asymptotically equivalent test statistics, at least one of which can usually be computed without difficulty. ML estimates themselves are straightforward to compute, because maximization, even nonlinear maximization, is a procedure that is well understood and, at least conceptually, easy to do. Thus one of the most desirable features of ML is **computability**: The ML estimates themselves, as well as estimated standard errors and test statistics, can generally be computed in a straightforward, although not always inexpensive, fashion.

A fifth desirable property of ML estimators is **invariance**, by which we mean invariance to reparametrization of the model. This is easy to illustrate in terms of the example we have been considering. Suppose that we had parametrized the density of y_t not as (8.02) but as

$$f'(y_t, \phi) = (1/\phi)e^{-y_t/\phi}, \tag{8.07}$$

where $\phi \equiv 1/\theta$. We can easily find out how the ML estimate $\hat{\phi}$ is related to $\hat{\theta}$. The loglikelihood in the ϕ parametrization is

$$\ell'(\boldsymbol{y}, \phi) = \sum_{t=1}^{n}\Big(-\log(\phi) - \frac{y_t}{\phi}\Big) = -n\log(\phi) - \frac{1}{\phi}\sum_{t=1}^{n} y_t.$$

The first-order condition for a maximum of ℓ' is thus

$$-\frac{n}{\phi} + \frac{1}{\phi^2}\sum_{t=1}^{n} y_t = 0,$$

and the ML estimate $\hat{\phi}$ is therefore seen to be

$$\hat{\phi} = \frac{1}{n}\sum_{t=1}^{n} y_t = \frac{1}{\hat{\theta}}.$$

We find that $\hat{\phi}$ bears exactly the same relationship to $\hat{\theta}$ as ϕ bears to θ. Thus, in this case, the ML estimate is **invariant to reparametrization**. This is in fact a general property of maximum likelihood. Especially in cases for which parametrization is more or less arbitrary, it can be one of its most attractive features.

Not all of the properties of ML are desirable ones. One major undesirable feature is dependence on explicit distributional assumptions, which the investigator may often feel are too strong. This is not always as serious a problem as it might appear. Although *in general* the asymptotic properties of ML estimators hold only when the model is correctly specified in all respects, there are many special cases in which some or all of these properties hold despite certain misspecifications. For example, nonlinear least squares turns out to be the ML estimator for a nonlinear regression model with independent and identically distributed normal errors (see Section 8.10) and, as we have seen, the consistency and asymptotic normality of NLS do not require the assumption of normality. Nonlinear least squares when the errors are nonnormal is thus an example of a **quasi-ML estimator**, or **QML estimator**, that is, an ML estimator applied to a situation in which it is not strictly valid; see White (1982) and Gouriéroux, Monfort, and Trognon (1984). QML estimators are also sometimes called **pseudo-ML estimators**.

The other major undesirable feature of ML is that its finite-sample properties can be quite different from its asymptotic ones. Even though they are consistent, ML parameter estimates are typically biased, and ML covariance matrix estimates can be seriously misleading. Because finite-sample properties are often unknowable in practice, the investigator has to decide (often without much information) how much reliance to place on known asymptotic properties. This introduces an element of imprecision into many efforts to draw inferences by ML when the sample size is not extremely large.

In the remainder of this chapter, we will discuss most of the important properties of maximum likelihood. The relationship between least squares and maximum likelihood will be introduced in Section 8.10 and will then form part of the subject matter of Chapter 9, which is primarily concerned with generalized least squares and its relationship to ML. Examples of maximum likelihood estimation in econometrics will be provided throughout the remainder of the book. Further examples may be found in Cramer (1986).

8.2 Fundamental Concepts and Notation

Maximum likelihood estimation depends on the notion of the **likelihood** of a given set of observations relative to a model, or set of DGPs. A DGP, being a stochastic process, can be characterized in a number of ways. We now develop notation in which we can readily express one such characterization that is particularly useful for present purposes. We assume that each observation in any sample of size n is a realization of a random variable y_t, $t = 1, \ldots, n$, taking values in $\mathbb{R}^m$. Although the notation y_t ignores the possibility that the observation is in general a vector, it is more convenient to let the vector notation $\boldsymbol{y}$ (or $\boldsymbol{y}^n$ if we wish to make the sample size explicit) denote the entire sample. Thus

$$\boldsymbol{y}^n = [y_1 \;\vdots\; y_2 \;\vdots\; \cdots \;\vdots\; y_n].$$

If each observation is a scalar, $\boldsymbol{y}$ is an n-vector, while if each observation is an m-vector, $\boldsymbol{y}$ is an $n \times m$ matrix. The vector or matrix $\boldsymbol{y}$ may possess a probability density, namely, the joint density of its elements under the DGP. This density, if it exists, is a map to the real line from the set of possible realizations of $\boldsymbol{y}$, a set that we will denote by $\mathcal{Y}^n$ and that is in general an arbitrary subset of $\mathbb{R}^{nm}$. It will be necessary to exercise some care over the definition of the density in certain cases, but for the present it is enough to suppose that it is the ordinary density with respect to Lebesgue measure on $\mathbb{R}^{nm}$.[3] When other possibilities exist, it will turn out that the choice among them is irrelevant for our purposes.

We may now define formally the likelihood function associated with a given model for a given sample $\boldsymbol{y}$. This function is a function of both the parameters of the model and the given data set $\boldsymbol{y}$; its value is just the density associated with the DGP characterized by the parameter vector $\boldsymbol{\theta} \in \Theta$, evaluated at the sample point $\boldsymbol{y}$. Here Θ denotes the **parameter space** in which the parameter vector $\boldsymbol{\theta}$ lies; we will assume that it is a subset of $\mathbb{R}^k$. We will denote the likelihood function by $L : \mathcal{Y}^n \times \Theta \to \mathbb{R}$ and its value for $\boldsymbol{\theta}$ and $\boldsymbol{y}$ by $L(\boldsymbol{y}, \boldsymbol{\theta})$. In many practical cases, such as the one examined in the preceding section, the y_t's are independent and each y_t has probability density $L_t(y_t, \boldsymbol{\theta})$. The likelihood function for this special case is then

$$L(\boldsymbol{y}, \boldsymbol{\theta}) = \prod_{t=1}^{n} L_t(y_t, \boldsymbol{\theta}). \tag{8.08}$$

The likelihood function (8.03) of the preceding section is evidently a special case of this special case. When each of the y_t's is identically distributed with density $f(y_t, \boldsymbol{\theta})$, as in that example, $L_t(y_t, \boldsymbol{\theta})$ is equal to $f(y_t, \boldsymbol{\theta})$ for all t.

Even when the likelihood function cannot be written in the form of (8.08), it is always possible (at least in theory) to factor $L(\boldsymbol{y}, \boldsymbol{\theta})$ into a set of **contributions**, each coming from a single observation. Suppose that the individual observations y_t, $t = 1, \ldots, n$, are *ordered* in some way, as for example by date in a time series. Then this factorization may be accomplished as follows. One starts from the marginal or unconditional[4] density of the first observation y_1, which we may call $L_1(y_1)$, the dependence on $\boldsymbol{\theta}$ being suppressed for the moment for clarity. Then the marginal density of the first two observations jointly can be written as the product of $L_1(y_1)$ and the density of y_2

[3] Thus we have excluded models with qualitative dependent variables and models in which the distribution of the dependent variable has atoms, for in these cases a density with respect to Lebesgue measure does not exist. See Chapter 15.

[4] We use the term "unconditional" for convenience. Some statisticians regard *all* distributions or densities as conditional on something or other, and we do not mean to exclude this view. Distributions, densities, or expectations which we refer to as unconditional should be understood as being conditioned *only* on genuinely exogenous variables, that is, variables of which the DGP is quite independent of the DGP of $\boldsymbol{y}$. Bayesians may also wish to regard the parameters of the DGP as conditioning variables, and this view is not excluded by our treatment either.

conditional on y_1, say $L_2(y_2 \,|\, y_1)$. If we now take the first three observations together, their joint density is the product of the unconditional density of the first two together and the density of the third conditional on the first two, and so on. The result for the entire sample of observations is

$$\begin{aligned} L(\boldsymbol{y}) &= L_1(y_1)L_2(y_2 \,|\, y_1)L_3(y_3 \,|\, y_2, y_1)\cdots L_n(y_n \,|\, y_{n-1}, \ldots, y_1) \\ &= \prod_{t=1}^{n} L_t(y_t \,|\, y_{t-1}, \ldots, y_1). \end{aligned} \tag{8.09}$$

Note that this result is perfectly general and can be applied to *any* density or likelihood function. The ordering of the observations is usually a natural one, as with time series, but even if no natural ordering exists, (8.09) is true for an arbitrary ordering.

As we indicated in the last section, in practice one normally works with the loglikelihood function $\ell(\boldsymbol{y}, \boldsymbol{\theta})$ rather than with the likelihood function $L(\boldsymbol{y}, \boldsymbol{\theta})$. The decomposition of $\ell(\boldsymbol{y}, \boldsymbol{\theta})$ into contributions from individual observations follows from (8.09). It may be written as follows, with the dependence on $\boldsymbol{\theta}$ suppressed for clarity:

$$\ell(\boldsymbol{y}) = \sum_{t=1}^{n} \ell_t(y_t \,|\, y_{t-1}, \ldots, y_1), \tag{8.10}$$

where $\ell_t(y_t \,|\, y_{t-1}, \ldots, y_1) \equiv \log L_t(y_t \,|\, y_{t-1}, \ldots, y_1)$.

We are now in a position to give the definition of the **maximum likelihood estimate**. We say that $\hat{\boldsymbol{\theta}} \in \Theta$ is a maximum likelihood estimate, **ML estimate**, or **MLE**, for the data $\boldsymbol{y}$ if

$$\ell(\boldsymbol{y}, \hat{\boldsymbol{\theta}}) \geq \ell(\boldsymbol{y}, \boldsymbol{\theta}) \quad \text{for all } \boldsymbol{\theta} \in \Theta. \tag{8.11}$$

If the inequality is strict, then $\hat{\boldsymbol{\theta}}$ is the *unique* MLE. An MLE need not exist in general, unless the loglikelihood function ℓ is continuous with respect to the parameters $\boldsymbol{\theta}$, and the set Θ is *compact* (i.e., closed and bounded). For this reason, it is usual in formal treatments of maximum likelihood estimation to assume that Θ is indeed compact. We do not wish to make this assumption, because it accords very ill indeed with standard practice, in which an estimate is accepted from anywhere in $\mathbb{R}^k$. But this means that we must live with the possible nonexistence of the MLE.

It is often convenient to use another, not in general equivalent, definition of the MLE. If the likelihood function does attain an *interior* maximum in the parameter space, then it or, equivalently, the loglikelihood function, must satisfy the first-order conditions for a maximum at the MLE. Thus an MLE can be *defined* as a solution to the **likelihood equations**, which are just the following first-order conditions:

$$\boldsymbol{g}(\boldsymbol{y}, \hat{\boldsymbol{\theta}}) \equiv \boldsymbol{0}, \tag{8.12}$$

where the **gradient vector**, or **score vector**, $\boldsymbol{g} \in \mathbb{R}^k$ is defined by

$$\boldsymbol{g}^\top(\boldsymbol{y}, \boldsymbol{\theta}) \equiv D_\theta \ell(\boldsymbol{y}, \boldsymbol{\theta}) = \sum_{t=1}^{n} D_\theta \ell_t(\boldsymbol{y}, \boldsymbol{\theta}). \tag{8.13}$$

Since $D_\theta \ell$ is a row vector, $\boldsymbol{g}$ is the *column* vector of partial derivatives of the loglikelihood function ℓ with respect to the parameters $\boldsymbol{\theta}$. We have written $\ell_t(\boldsymbol{y}, \boldsymbol{\theta})$, and not $\ell_t(y_t, \boldsymbol{\theta})$, because in general ℓ_t can depend on "past" values of the dependent variable, $y_{t-1}, y_{t-2}, \ldots$. It does not depend on "future" values of course, but the use of the vector notation is still the easiest way to remind ourselves of dependence on more than just y_t.

Because there may be more than one value of $\boldsymbol{\theta}$ that satisfies the likelihood equations (8.12), the definition further requires that $\hat{\boldsymbol{\theta}}$ be associated with a local *maximum* of ℓ and that

$$\operatorname*{plim}_{n\to\infty} \big(n^{-1}\ell(\boldsymbol{y}, \hat{\boldsymbol{\theta}})\big) \geq \operatorname*{plim}_{n\to\infty} \big(n^{-1}\ell(\boldsymbol{y}, \boldsymbol{\theta}^*)\big),$$

where $\boldsymbol{\theta}^*$ is any other root of the likelihood equations. This second definition of the MLE is often associated with Cramér, since it is used in his famous proof of consistency (Cramér, 1946). The requirement that $\text{plim}\big(n^{-1}\ell(\boldsymbol{y}, \hat{\boldsymbol{\theta}})\big) \geq \text{plim}\big(n^{-1}\ell(\boldsymbol{y}, \boldsymbol{\theta}^*)\big)$ is of course in general impossible to verify in practice. The problem is that one does not know the DGP and so cannot calculate the plims analytically. If for a given sample there are two or more roots of the likelihood equations, the one that is associated with the highest value of $\ell(\boldsymbol{y}, \boldsymbol{\theta})$ for that sample may not converge to the one that is associated with the highest value asymptotically. In practice what one does if there is more than one solution to the likelihood equations is to select the one that is associated with the highest value of the loglikelihood function. However, if there are two or more roots for which $\ell(\boldsymbol{y}, \boldsymbol{\theta})$ is quite close, one may very well pick the wrong one.

We repeat that these two definitions of the MLE are not equivalent. Consequently, it is sometimes necessary to speak of **MLEs of Type 1** when we mean those obtained by the maximization over Θ of $\ell(\boldsymbol{y}, \boldsymbol{\theta})$ and **MLEs of Type 2** when we mean those obtained as solutions to the likelihood equations. Although in most practical cases either could be used and in many cases the two will coincide, there are situations in which one does not exist while the other does. In particular, there are models where $\ell(\boldsymbol{\theta})$ is unbounded in some directions, and the Type 1 definition therefore cannot be used, but nevertheless there does exist a $\hat{\boldsymbol{\theta}}$ that is a consistent root of the likelihood equations; see Kiefer (1978) for a model of this kind. On the other hand, the Type 2 definition does not apply to the standard problem of estimating one or both end-points of a uniform distribution, because the likelihood equations are never satisfied.

The problem of estimating the end-point of a uniform distribution is worth looking at. Suppose that for all t the density of y_t is

$$f(y_t) = \begin{cases} 1/\alpha & \text{if } 0 \leq y_t \leq \alpha \\ 0 & \text{otherwise.} \end{cases}$$

Here one end-point of the uniform distribution is known to be zero, and the other end-point, α, is to be estimated. The likelihood and loglikelihood functions are, respectively,

$$L(\boldsymbol{y}, \alpha) = \begin{cases} \alpha^{-n} & \text{if } 0 \le y_t \le \alpha \text{ for all } y_t \\ 0 & \text{otherwise} \end{cases}$$

and

$$\ell(\boldsymbol{y}, \alpha) = \begin{cases} -n \log(\alpha) & \text{if } 0 \le y_t \le \alpha \text{ for all } y_t \\ -\infty & \text{otherwise.} \end{cases} \tag{8.14}$$

The likelihood equation obtained by differentiating $\ell(\boldsymbol{y}, \alpha)$ with respect to α and equating the derivative to zero is

$$-\frac{n}{\alpha} = 0.$$

Since this equation has no finite solution, no Type 2 ML estimate exists. It is clear that we can find a Type 1 ML estimate, however. It is evident from (8.14) that to maximize $\ell(\boldsymbol{y}, \alpha)$ we must make $\hat{\alpha}$ as small as possible. Since $\hat{\alpha}$ cannot be smaller than the largest observed y_t, the Type 1 ML estimate must simply be

$$\hat{\alpha} = \max_t(y_t).$$

By the term **maximum likelihood estimator** we will mean the random variable that associates with each possible random outcome $\boldsymbol{y}$ the corresponding MLE.[5] The distinction between an **estimate** and an **estimator** was made in Section 5.2: We may recall that an estimator, a random variable, is represented as a function (implicit or explicit) of possible sets of observations, while an estimate is the value taken by that function for a specific data set.

Just as there are two possible definitions of ML estimates, so are there two possible definitions of the ML estimator. The following definitions make it clear that the estimator is a random variable, dependent on the realized sample $\boldsymbol{y}$. The **Type 1 estimator**, corresponding to the standard definition (8.11) of the MLE, is $\hat{\boldsymbol{\theta}}(\boldsymbol{y})$ defined by:

$$L\big(\boldsymbol{y}, \hat{\boldsymbol{\theta}}(\boldsymbol{y})\big) > L(\boldsymbol{y}, \boldsymbol{\theta}) \quad \text{for all } \boldsymbol{\theta} \in \Theta \text{ such that } \boldsymbol{\theta} \neq \hat{\boldsymbol{\theta}}(\boldsymbol{y}). \tag{8.15}$$

The **Type 2 estimator**, corresponding to the Cramér definition (8.12), is $\hat{\boldsymbol{\theta}}(\boldsymbol{y})$ defined by:

$$\boldsymbol{g}\big(\boldsymbol{y}, \hat{\boldsymbol{\theta}}(\boldsymbol{y})\big) = \boldsymbol{0}, \tag{8.16}$$

[5] In cases of nonexistence of the MLE for some samples, the estimator can be defined as a proper random variable by assigning to it an arbitrary value, such as $-\infty$, for those samples for which the MLE does not exist.

where $\hat{\boldsymbol{\theta}}(\boldsymbol{y})$ yields a local maximum of ℓ, and

$$\operatorname*{plim}_{n\to\infty}\Big(n^{-1}\ell\big(\boldsymbol{y},\hat{\boldsymbol{\theta}}(\boldsymbol{y})\big)\Big) \geq \operatorname*{plim}_{n\to\infty}\Big(n^{-1}\ell\big(\boldsymbol{y},\boldsymbol{\theta}^*(\boldsymbol{y})\big)\Big) \tag{8.17}$$

for any other solution $\boldsymbol{\theta}^*(\boldsymbol{y})$ of the likelihood equations.

We conclude this section with a variety of definitions to be used in the rest of the chapter and more generally for the rest of the book. By use of the decomposition (8.10) of the loglikelihood function $\ell(\boldsymbol{y},\boldsymbol{\theta})$, we may define an $n \times k$ matrix $\boldsymbol{G}(\boldsymbol{y},\boldsymbol{\theta})$ with typical element

$$G_{ti}(\boldsymbol{y},\boldsymbol{\theta}) \equiv \frac{\partial \ell_t(\boldsymbol{y},\boldsymbol{\theta})}{\partial \theta_i}. \tag{8.18}$$

We will call $\boldsymbol{G}(\boldsymbol{y},\boldsymbol{\theta})$ the **matrix of contributions to the gradient**, or the **CG matrix** for short. This matrix is intimately related to the gradient vector $\boldsymbol{g}$, which is just $\boldsymbol{G}^\top\boldsymbol{\iota}$, where as usual $\boldsymbol{\iota}$ denotes an n–vector, each element of which is 1. The tth row of $\boldsymbol{G}$, which measures the contribution to the gradient from the tth observation, will be denoted $\boldsymbol{G}_t$.

The **Hessian matrix** associated with the loglikelihood function $\ell(\boldsymbol{y},\boldsymbol{\theta})$ is the $k \times k$ matrix $\boldsymbol{H}(\boldsymbol{y},\boldsymbol{\theta})$ with typical element

$$H_{ij}(\boldsymbol{y},\boldsymbol{\theta}) \equiv \frac{\partial^2 \ell(\boldsymbol{y},\boldsymbol{\theta})}{\partial \theta_i \partial \theta_j}. \tag{8.19}$$

We define the **expected average Hessian** for a sample of size n as

$$\mathcal{H}^n(\boldsymbol{\theta}) \equiv E_\theta\big(n^{-1}\boldsymbol{H}(\boldsymbol{y},\boldsymbol{\theta})\big).$$

The notation E_θ means that the expectation is calculated using the DGP characterized by the parameter vector $\boldsymbol{\theta}$ rather than the DGP that might actually have generated any particular given sample. Thus a different DGP is implicitly used to calculate the expectation for each different $\boldsymbol{\theta}$. The **limiting Hessian** or **asymptotic Hessian**, if it exists, is defined as

$$\mathcal{H}(\boldsymbol{\theta}) \equiv \lim_{n\to\infty} \mathcal{H}^n(\boldsymbol{\theta}).$$

This quantity, which is a symmetric, negative semidefinite matrix in general, will appear many times in the asymptotic theory of ML estimation.

We define the **information in observation** $\boldsymbol{t}$ as $\boldsymbol{I}_t(\boldsymbol{\theta})$, the $k \times k$ matrix with typical element

$$\big(\boldsymbol{I}_t(\boldsymbol{\theta})\big)_{ij} \equiv E_\theta\big(G_{ti}(\boldsymbol{\theta})G_{tj}(\boldsymbol{\theta})\big). \tag{8.20}$$

It is an immediate consequence of this definition that $\boldsymbol{I}_t(\boldsymbol{\theta})$ is a symmetric, positive semidefinite matrix in general and that it is positive definite unless a linear relation exists among the components of the random vector $\boldsymbol{G}_t$. The **average information matrix** for a sample of size n is defined as

$$\mathfrak{I}^n(\boldsymbol{\theta}) \equiv \frac{1}{n}\sum_{t=1}^{n} \boldsymbol{I}_t(\boldsymbol{\theta}) = n^{-1}\boldsymbol{I}^n, \tag{8.21}$$

and the **limiting information matrix** or **asymptotic information matrix**, if it exists, is defined as

$$\mathfrak{I}(\boldsymbol{\theta}) \equiv \lim_{n\to\infty} \mathfrak{I}^n(\boldsymbol{\theta}). \tag{8.22}$$

The matrix $\boldsymbol{I}_t(\boldsymbol{\theta})$ measures the *expected* amount of information contained in the tth observation and $\boldsymbol{I}^n \equiv n\mathfrak{I}^n$ measures the expected amount of information contained in the complete sample. The information matrices $\mathfrak{I}^n$ and $\mathfrak{I}$ are, like $\boldsymbol{I}_t$, symmetric, positive semidefinite matrices in general. The average information matrix $\mathfrak{I}^n$ and the expected average Hessian $\mathcal{H}^n$ have been defined so that they are $O(1)$ as $n \to \infty$. This makes them convenient to use in asymptotic analysis. The terminology in this area is not entirely standard. Some authors simply use the term "information matrix" to refer to $\mathfrak{I}^n$, while others use it to refer to n times $\mathfrak{I}^n$, which we have called $\boldsymbol{I}^n$.

8.3 TRANSFORMATIONS AND REPARAMETRIZATIONS

In this and the subsequent sections of this chapter, we develop the classical theory of maximum likelihood estimation and, in particular, demonstrate the properties that make it a desirable estimation method. We will also point out that in some circumstances these properties fail. As we discussed in Section 8.1, the major desirable features of ML estimators are **invariance**, **consistency**, **asymptotic normality**, **asymptotic efficiency**, and **computability**. In this section, we will discuss the first of these, the invariance of ML estimators to reparametrization of the model.

The idea of invariance is an important one in econometric analysis. Let us denote by $\mathbb{M}$ the model in which we are interested. A **parametrization** of the model $\mathbb{M}$ is a mapping, say λ, from a parameter space Θ to $\mathbb{M}$. For any given model $\mathbb{M}$ there may in general exist an infinite number of parametrizations. There are, after all, few constraints on the parameter space Θ, other than its dimensionality. A subset of $\mathbb{R}^k$ of full dimension can be mapped in a one-to-one and differentiable manner onto virtually any other subset of $\mathbb{R}^k$ of full dimension by such devices as translation, rotation, dilation, and so on, and subsequently any of these other subsets can perfectly well serve as the parameter space for the model $\mathbb{M}$. It is because of this fact that one appeals to invariance as a desirable property of estimators. "Invariance" is understood in this context as invariance under the sort of transformation we have been discussing, which we call formally **reparametrization**.

As an illustration of the fact that any model may be parametrized in an infinite number of ways, consider the case of the exponential distribution, which was discussed in Section 8.1. The likelihood function for a sample of independent drawings from this distribution was seen to be (8.03). If we make the definition $\theta \equiv \delta^\alpha$, we can define a whole family of parametrizations indexed by α. We may choose α to be any finite, nonzero number. The likelihood function corresponding to this family of parametrizations is

$$L(\boldsymbol{y}, \delta) = \prod_{t=1}^{n} \delta^\alpha e^{-\delta^\alpha y_t}.$$

Evidently, $\alpha = 1$ corresponds to the θ parametrization of (8.02) and $\alpha = -1$ corresponds to the ϕ parametrization of (8.07).

It is easy to see that ML estimators are invariant to reparametrizations of the model. Let $\boldsymbol{\eta} : \Theta \to \Phi \subseteq \mathbb{R}^k$ denote a smooth mapping that transforms the vector $\boldsymbol{\theta}$ uniquely into another vector $\boldsymbol{\phi} \equiv \boldsymbol{\eta}(\boldsymbol{\theta})$. The likelihood function for the model $\mathbb{M}$ in terms of the new parameters $\boldsymbol{\phi}$, say L', is defined by the relation

$$L'(\boldsymbol{y}, \boldsymbol{\phi}) = L(\boldsymbol{y}, \boldsymbol{\theta}) \quad \text{for } \boldsymbol{\phi} = \boldsymbol{\eta}(\boldsymbol{\theta}). \tag{8.23}$$

Equation (8.23) follows at once from the facts that a likelihood function is the density of a stochastic process and that $\boldsymbol{\theta}$ and $\boldsymbol{\phi} = \boldsymbol{\eta}(\boldsymbol{\theta})$ describe the same stochastic process. Let us define $\hat{\boldsymbol{\phi}}$ as $\boldsymbol{\eta}(\hat{\boldsymbol{\theta}})$ and $\boldsymbol{\phi}^*$ as $\boldsymbol{\eta}(\boldsymbol{\theta}^*)$. Then if

$$L(\boldsymbol{y}, \hat{\boldsymbol{\theta}}) > L(\boldsymbol{y}, \boldsymbol{\theta}^*) \text{ for all } \boldsymbol{\theta}^* \neq \hat{\boldsymbol{\theta}},$$

it follows that

$$L'(\boldsymbol{y}, \hat{\boldsymbol{\phi}}) = L'\big(\boldsymbol{y}, \boldsymbol{\eta}(\hat{\boldsymbol{\theta}})\big) = L(\boldsymbol{y}, \hat{\boldsymbol{\theta}}) > L(\boldsymbol{y}, \boldsymbol{\theta}^*) = L'(\boldsymbol{y}, \boldsymbol{\phi}^*) \text{ for all } \boldsymbol{\phi}^* \neq \hat{\boldsymbol{\phi}}.$$

Thus we will obtain ML estimates $\hat{\boldsymbol{\theta}}$ if we maximize $L(\boldsymbol{\theta})$ and ML estimates $\hat{\boldsymbol{\phi}}$ if we maximize $L'(\boldsymbol{\phi})$. But these two sets of estimates are equivalent, in the sense that they characterize the same DGP, since $L(\hat{\boldsymbol{\theta}}) = L'(\hat{\boldsymbol{\phi}})$.

Once we have chosen one parametrization of a model, say $\lambda : \Theta \to \mathbb{M}$, and have a smooth one-to-one mapping $\boldsymbol{\eta} : \Theta \to \Phi$ that takes the first parameter vector $\boldsymbol{\theta}$ into a second one $\boldsymbol{\phi}$, we may reparametrize the model by mapping from the second parameter space Φ to the first one Θ by $\boldsymbol{\eta}^{-1}$ (which must exist because $\boldsymbol{\eta}$ is one-to-one) and then back to $\mathbb{M}$ by λ. Thus, formally, the new parametrization is the mapping $\mu \equiv \lambda \circ \boldsymbol{\eta}^{-1}$, which maps Φ onto $\mathbb{M}$ in a smooth one-to-one manner. It may be useful for intuition to keep the following commutative diagram in mind:

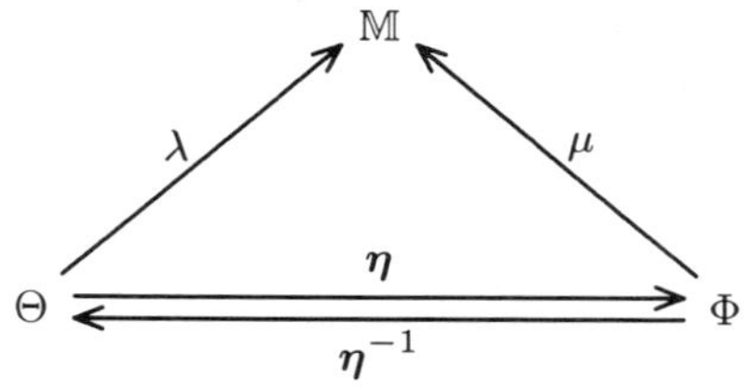

Invariance is in general a desirable property, since it ensures that (possibly arbitrary) changes in the way we write down the model will have no effect on the estimates we obtain. But this property nevertheless implies that ML *parameter* estimators cannot, in general, be unbiased. Suppose that there does exist a parametrization in which the ML estimator of $\boldsymbol{\theta}$ is unbiased. We can write this as

$$E_0(\hat{\boldsymbol{\theta}}) = \boldsymbol{\theta}_0,$$

where E_0 indicates that we are taking expectations with respect to the DGP characterized by the parameter vector $\boldsymbol{\theta}_0$. Then if the function $\boldsymbol{\eta}(\boldsymbol{\theta})$ which yields a new parametrization is nonlinear, as it will be in general, it must be the case that

$$E_0(\hat{\boldsymbol{\phi}}) = E_0\big(\boldsymbol{\eta}(\hat{\boldsymbol{\theta}})\big) \neq \boldsymbol{\phi}_0$$

because, for a nonlinear function $\boldsymbol{\eta}(\boldsymbol{\theta})$,

$$E_0\big(\boldsymbol{\eta}(\hat{\boldsymbol{\theta}})\big) \neq \boldsymbol{\eta}\big(E_0(\hat{\boldsymbol{\theta}})\big) = \boldsymbol{\eta}(\boldsymbol{\theta}_0) = \boldsymbol{\phi}_0.$$

This suggests that, although the parametrization we choose does not matter for estimation of the DGP, it may have a substantial effect on the finite-sample properties of our parameter estimates. By choosing the appropriate parametrization, we can in some cases ensure that our estimates are unbiased or close to unbiased and have distributions close to their asymptotic ones. In contrast, if we choose an inappropriate parametrization, we may inadvertently ensure that our estimates are severely biased and have distributions far from their asymptotic ones.

8.4 CONSISTENCY

One of the reasons that maximum likelihood estimation is widely used is that ML estimators are, under quite general conditions, consistent. In this section, we explain why this is the case. We concern ourselves primarily with the Type 1 ML estimator, although we provide some discussion of the Type 2 estimator as well. We begin by making the definition:

$$\bar{\ell}(\boldsymbol{\theta};\boldsymbol{\theta}_0) \equiv \operatorname*{plim}_{n\to\infty}{}_0\big(n^{-1}\ell^n(\boldsymbol{y}^n,\boldsymbol{\theta})\big), \tag{8.24}$$

where the notation "plim_0" means as usual that the plim is calculated under the DGP characterized by $\boldsymbol{\theta}_0$. The function $\bar{\ell}(\boldsymbol{\theta};\boldsymbol{\theta}_0)$ is the limiting value of n^{-1} times the loglikelihood function, when the data are generated by a special case of the model with $\boldsymbol{\theta} = \boldsymbol{\theta}_0$. An important regularity condition that must be satisfied in order for an ML estimator to be consistent is that the model must be asymptotically identified. By definition, this will be the case if the problem

$$\max_{\boldsymbol{\theta}\in\Theta} \bar{\ell}(\boldsymbol{\theta};\boldsymbol{\theta}_0) \tag{8.25}$$

has a unique solution. This definition implies that any DGP in the model will generate samples which, if they are large enough, identify the model. The interpretation is the same as in the regression model context.

We now wish to demonstrate that $\bar{\ell}(\boldsymbol{\theta};\boldsymbol{\theta}_0)$ is maximized at $\boldsymbol{\theta}_0$, the value of $\boldsymbol{\theta}$ that characterizes the DGP. Let $\hat{\boldsymbol{\theta}} \equiv \hat{\boldsymbol{\theta}}(\boldsymbol{y})$ denote the global maximum of the likelihood function $L(\boldsymbol{y},\boldsymbol{\theta})$, which we will require to be a *continuous* function of $\boldsymbol{\theta}$, and let $\boldsymbol{\theta}^*$ denote any other (nonstochastic) parameter vector in Θ, which is required to be compact. These two requirements mean that there is no problem of possible nonexistence of the MLE. We will denote expectations taken with respect to the DGP by $E_0(\cdot)$. Then

$$E_0\left(\log\left(\frac{L(\boldsymbol{\theta}^*)}{L(\boldsymbol{\theta}_0)}\right)\right) \leq \log\left(E_0\left(\frac{L(\boldsymbol{\theta}^*)}{L(\boldsymbol{\theta}_0)}\right)\right), \tag{8.26}$$

by Jensen's Inequality (see Appendix B), since the logarithm is a concave function. Further, (8.26) will hold with strict inequality whenever $L(\boldsymbol{\theta}^*)/L(\boldsymbol{\theta}_0)$ is a nondegenerate random variable. Degeneracy will occur only if there exists $\boldsymbol{\theta}' \neq \boldsymbol{\theta}_0$ such that $L(\boldsymbol{\theta}')/L(\boldsymbol{\theta}_0)$ is identically unity; $\ell(\boldsymbol{\theta}') - \ell(\boldsymbol{\theta}_0)$ would then be identically zero. But the asymptotic identification condition (8.25) rules out this possibility for large enough sample sizes, since, if it holds, $\boldsymbol{\theta}' \neq \boldsymbol{\theta}_0$ implies that $L(\boldsymbol{\theta}') \neq L(\boldsymbol{\theta}_0)$.

Using the fact that $L(\boldsymbol{\theta}_0)$ is the joint density of $\boldsymbol{y}$, we see that the expectation inside the logarithm on the right-hand side of (8.26) is

$$E_0\left(\frac{L(\boldsymbol{\theta}^*)}{L(\boldsymbol{\theta}_0)}\right) = \int_{\mathcal{Y}^n} \frac{L(\boldsymbol{\theta}^*)}{L(\boldsymbol{\theta}_0)} L(\boldsymbol{\theta}_0)\,d\boldsymbol{y} = \int_{\mathcal{Y}^n} L(\boldsymbol{\theta}^*)\,d\boldsymbol{y} = 1.$$

If it is possible for $L(\boldsymbol{\theta}_0)$ to be zero, we may define the integrand in the second expression here to be zero when that occurs. Since the logarithm of 1 is 0, it follows from (8.26) that

$$E_0\left(\log\left(\frac{L(\boldsymbol{\theta}^*)}{L(\boldsymbol{\theta}_0)}\right)\right) < 0,$$

which can be rewritten as

$$E_0\big(\ell(\boldsymbol{\theta}^*)\big) - E_0\big(\ell(\boldsymbol{\theta}_0)\big) < 0. \tag{8.27}$$

Thus the expectation of the loglikelihood function when evaluated at the true parameter vector, $\boldsymbol{\theta}_0$, is strictly greater than its expectation when evaluated at any other parameter vector, $\boldsymbol{\theta}^*$.

The next step is to show that what is true of the mathematical expectations in (8.27) is also true, in the limit as $n \to \infty$, of the sample analog. This sample analog is

$$\tfrac{1}{n}\big(\ell(\boldsymbol{\theta}^*) - \ell(\boldsymbol{\theta}_0)\big) = \tfrac{1}{n}\sum_{t=1}^{n} \ell_t(\boldsymbol{y},\boldsymbol{\theta}^*) - \tfrac{1}{n}\sum_{t=1}^{n} \ell_t(\boldsymbol{y},\boldsymbol{\theta}_0). \tag{8.28}$$

It is now necessary to assume that the sums in (8.28) satisfy some regularity conditions sufficient for a law of large numbers to be applied to them. As we have seen in Chapter 4, these will require that the ℓ_t's be independent or, at least, not exhibit too much dependence; have some sort of mean (although they do not have to have a common mean); and have variances that are bounded from above; for details, see Section 4.7. Thus we may conveniently require that, for all $\boldsymbol{\theta} \in \Theta$, $\{\ell_t(\boldsymbol{\theta})\}_{t=1}^{\infty}$ satisfies condition WULLN of Section 4.7 for the DGP characterized by $\boldsymbol{\theta}_0$. We can then use (8.27) to assert that

$$\operatorname*{plim}_{n\to\infty}{}_0\big(n^{-1}\ell(\boldsymbol{\theta}^*)\big) - \operatorname*{plim}_{n\to\infty}{}_0\big(n^{-1}\ell(\boldsymbol{\theta}_0)\big) < 0, \tag{8.29}$$

where both plims exist. In fact, by definition (8.24),

$$\operatorname*{plim}_{n\to\infty}{}_0\big(n^{-1}\ell(\boldsymbol{\theta}^*)\big) = \bar{\ell}(\boldsymbol{\theta}^*;\boldsymbol{\theta}_0),$$

which latter function is thereby shown to exist. The inequality in (8.29) has not yet been shown to be strict, since the *limit* of the strict inequalities (8.27) is not necessarily a strict inequality. However, the asymptotic identification condition (8.25) can again be invoked to reinstate strictness.

Given the assumption of asymptotic identification and the result (8.29), it is now easy to see why $\hat{\boldsymbol{\theta}}$ must be consistent. We know that

$$n^{-1}\ell(\hat{\boldsymbol{\theta}}) \geq n^{-1}\ell(\boldsymbol{\theta}_0), \tag{8.30}$$

for all n, because $\hat{\boldsymbol{\theta}}$ maximizes the loglikelihood function. Clearly (8.29) and (8.30) cannot both be true unless

$$\operatorname*{plim}_{n\to\infty}{}_0\big(n^{-1}\ell(\hat{\boldsymbol{\theta}})\big) = \operatorname*{plim}_{n\to\infty}{}_0\big(n^{-1}\ell(\boldsymbol{\theta}_0)\big). \tag{8.31}$$

But if the model is asymptotically identified, the value $\hat{\boldsymbol{\theta}}$ which maximizes (8.24) must be unique. Therefore, (8.31) cannot hold unless $\operatorname{plim}_0(\hat{\boldsymbol{\theta}}) = \boldsymbol{\theta}_0$.[6]

We may now state the following theorem, which is due to Wald (1949):

Theorem 8.1. Wald's Consistency Theorem.

> The ML estimator (8.15) for a model represented by the parametric family of loglikelihood functions $\ell(\boldsymbol{\theta})$ in which $\boldsymbol{\theta}$ is restricted to lie in a compact parameter space is consistent if the contributions $\{\ell_t(\boldsymbol{\theta})\}_{t=1}^{\infty}$ satisfy the regularity conditions WULLN and if, in addition, the model is asymptotically identified.

Note that the result has been proved only for *compact* parameter spaces, since otherwise we could not be sure that $\hat{\boldsymbol{\theta}}$ exists for all n. There are models, for example certain so-called endogenous-regime models, in which the fact that a

[6] Because $\hat{\boldsymbol{\theta}}$ is stochastic, this argument is not rigorous.

variance cannot tend to zero for a well-behaved probability density leads to a failure of compactness of the parameter space (since excluding zero variance leaves a partially open boundary to this space). As a consequence, there may exist no Type 1 MLE with a finite plim; see Kiefer (1978).

There are two main sets of circumstances in which ML estimates may fail to be consistent. The first arises when the number of parameters is not fixed but instead increases with n. This possibility is not even considered in the above theorem, where $\boldsymbol{\theta}$ is independent of n. But it is not surprising that it causes problems, since if the number of parameters is not fixed, it is far from clear that the amount of information the sample gives us about each one will increase sufficiently fast as $n \to \infty$. It is in fact possible to let the number of parameters increase, but the rate of increase must be slow (for example, like $n^{1/4}$). Such cases are beyond the scope of this book; see, among others, Neyman and Scott (1948), Kiefer and Wolfowitz (1956), and Kalbfleisch and Sprott (1970).

The most frequently encountered cases of failure of consistency are those in which the model is not identified asymptotically. This may happen even when it *is* identified in any finite sample. For example, consider the regression model

$$y_t = \alpha\frac{1}{t} + u_t, \quad u_t \sim \text{NID}(0,1),$$

originally considered in Section 5.2. We have already seen that models of this type cannot be estimated consistently by least squares, and it is a simple exercise to show that such models cannot be estimated consistently by maximum likelihood either. One way to think about this type of problem is to observe that, as n increases, each new observation adds less and less information about α. Therefore, even though the finite-sample information matrix $\boldsymbol{I}^n$ always has full rank (of one, in this case), the asymptotic information matrix $\mathfrak{I}$ does not (it converges to zero in this case). In the usual case in which the ML estimator is consistent, each new observation adds roughly the same amount of information and $\mathfrak{I}$, being the limit of the average of the $\boldsymbol{I}_t$'s, will therefore have full rank.

For most purposes, the consistency of the Type 1 ML estimator is all that we need to be concerned with. However, there are cases in which the Type 2 estimator exists and the Type 1 estimator does not. In the remainder of this section, we therefore outline a proof of consistency for the Type 2 ML estimator, as given by (8.16) and (8.17). For this estimator to exist, it is of course necessary that the contributions ℓ_t to the loglikelihood function $\ell(\boldsymbol{y}, \boldsymbol{\theta})$ be differentiable with respect to the parameters $\boldsymbol{\theta}$, and so we will assume that they are at least once continuously differentiable. With this assumption further argument is in many sets of circumstances unnecessary: If the parameter space Θ is compact and the parameter vector $\boldsymbol{\theta}_0$ associated with the DGP is in the interior of Θ, then for large enough samples the probability becomes arbitrarily close to unity that the maximum of ℓ will be achieved at an interior point of Θ. When that happens, the Type 1 and Type 2 estimators will coincide asymptotically. On the other hand, if $\boldsymbol{\theta}_0$ is on the boundary of Θ, there will be a positive probability for arbitrarily large samples that the estimator of Type 2 will not exist. In such a case, the question of its consistency or otherwise does not arise.

The situation is more delicate in the case of a noncompact parameter space. We first remark that if $\boldsymbol{\theta}_0$ lies on the boundary of Θ, then noncompactness is not the issue, and again the Type 2 estimator will have a positive probability of nonexistence. Thus we suppose that $\boldsymbol{\theta}_0$ is in the interior of Θ. We further assume that the condition of the following definition is satisfied:

Definition 8.1.

The model characterized by the loglikelihood function ℓ is **asymptotically identified on a noncompact parameter space** Θ if the model is asymptotically identified and if, in addition, there are no sequences $\{\boldsymbol{\theta}^n\}$ with no limit point that satisfy

$$\bar{\ell}(\boldsymbol{\theta}^n;\boldsymbol{\theta}_0) \longrightarrow \bar{\ell}(\boldsymbol{\theta}_0;\boldsymbol{\theta}_0); \quad \bar{\ell}(\boldsymbol{\theta}^n;\boldsymbol{\theta}_0) < \bar{\ell}(\boldsymbol{\theta}_0;\boldsymbol{\theta}_0). \tag{8.32}$$

The existence of such sequences may appear to be ruled out by asymptotic identifiability, but this is not so. For the sequence to have no limit point, it must diverge to infinity in some direction or else converge to a point which is not a member of the noncompact parameter space, such as a point of zero variance. Thus the fact that $\bar{\ell}(\boldsymbol{\theta}^n;\boldsymbol{\theta}_0)$ tends to the limit $\bar{\ell}(\boldsymbol{\theta}_0;\boldsymbol{\theta}_0)$ does not imply the existence of a point in Θ, say $\boldsymbol{\theta}^\infty$, at which $\bar{\ell}(\boldsymbol{\theta}^\infty;\boldsymbol{\theta}_0) = \bar{\ell}(\boldsymbol{\theta}_0;\boldsymbol{\theta}_0)$. The existence of $\boldsymbol{\theta}^\infty$ would indeed contradict asymptotic identifiability in the usual sense. But for asymptotic identifiability to have its usual interpretation in a noncompact parameter space, the existence of sequences satisfying (8.32) must be ruled out, even if they have no limit point.

We now return to the consideration of Type 2 estimators. Consider a *compact* neighborhood Θ_0 of $\boldsymbol{\theta}_0$. We could define another ML estimator as the point yielding the maximum of ℓ in Θ_0. By Wald's consistency theorem (Theorem 8.1) this new estimator would be consistent. Two possible cases then seem to exist. The first is that in which there is a positive asymptotic probability that this estimator is on the *boundary* of the neighborhood Θ_0 and the second is that in which this probability is zero. In the second case the new estimator and the Type 2 estimator coincide asymptotically, given the condition of asymptotic identifiability for a noncompact Θ, and so the latter is consistent. But the first case cannot in fact arise. For a fixed Θ_0, $\boldsymbol{\theta}_0$ is at a positive distance from the boundary of Θ_0, and the consistency of the new estimator excludes any positive asymptotic probability concentrated on a region bounded away from $\boldsymbol{\theta}_0$. Thus we conclude that when the parameter space is noncompact, provided the DGP lies in the *interior* of this space and the model is asymptotically identified on its noncompact parameter space, the Type 2 estimator is consistent. These results are summarized in the following theorem:

Theorem 8.2. Second Consistency Theorem.

Let a model be represented by a parametric family of at least once continuously differentiable loglikelihood functions $\ell(\boldsymbol{\theta})$ in which $\boldsymbol{\theta}$ is restricted to lie in a not necessarily compact parameter space. Then, for DGPs that lie in the interior of that parameter space, the ML estimator defined by (8.16) and (8.17) is consistent if the contributions $\{\ell_t(\boldsymbol{\theta})\}_{t=1}^{\infty}$ satisfy the regularity conditions WULLN and in addition the parameter space is compact and the model is asymptotically identified, or if the parameter space is noncompact and the model is asymptotically identified in the sense of Definition 8.1.

8.5 The Asymptotic Distribution of the ML Estimator

We begin our analysis by proving a simple but fundamental result about the gradient $\boldsymbol{g}$ and the CG matrix $\boldsymbol{G}$:

$$E_\theta\big(G_{ti}(\boldsymbol{\theta})\big) \equiv E_\theta\left(\frac{\partial \ell_t(\boldsymbol{\theta})}{\partial \theta_i}\right) = 0. \tag{8.33}$$

This result says that, under the DGP characterized by $\boldsymbol{\theta}$, the expectation of every element of the CG matrix, when evaluated at $\boldsymbol{\theta}$, is zero. It implies that

$$E_\theta\big(\boldsymbol{g}(\boldsymbol{\theta})\big) = \mathbf{0} \quad \text{and} \quad E_\theta\big(\boldsymbol{G}(\boldsymbol{\theta})\big) = \mathbf{0}.$$

This is a very important result for several reasons. In particular, it will allow us to apply a central limit theorem to the quantity $n^{-1/2}\boldsymbol{g}(\boldsymbol{\theta}_0)$. The proof is as follows:

$$\begin{aligned}
E_\theta\big(G_{ti}(y_t,\boldsymbol{\theta})\big) &= \int \frac{\partial \log L_t(y_t,\boldsymbol{\theta})}{\partial \theta_i} L_t(y_t,\boldsymbol{\theta})\,dy_t \\
&= \int \frac{1}{L_t(y_t,\boldsymbol{\theta})}\frac{\partial L_t(y_t,\boldsymbol{\theta})}{\partial \theta_i} L_t(y_t,\boldsymbol{\theta})\,dy_t \\
&= \int \frac{\partial L_t(y_t,\boldsymbol{\theta})}{\partial \theta_i}\,dy_t \\
&= \frac{\partial}{\partial \theta_i}\int L_t(y_t,\boldsymbol{\theta})\,dy_t \\
&= \frac{\partial}{\partial \theta_i}(1) = 0.
\end{aligned} \tag{8.34}$$

The second last step is just a consequence of the normalization of the density $L_t(y_t,\boldsymbol{\theta})$. The previous step, in which the orders of differentiation and integration are interchanged, is valid under a variety of regularity conditions, of which the simplest is that the domain of integration, say $\mathcal{Y}_t$, is independent of $\boldsymbol{\theta}$. Alternatively, if that assumption is not true, then it is sufficient that $L_t(y_t, \boldsymbol{\theta})$ vanishes on the boundary of the domain $\mathcal{Y}_t$ and that $\partial \ell_t(y_t, \boldsymbol{\theta})/\partial \boldsymbol{\theta}$ be uniformly bounded; see Appendix B.

Simple results about the asymptotic distribution of ML estimates are most readily found in the context of the Type 2 estimator, as defined by (8.16) and (8.17). Consequently, we will restrict our attention to that case and assume that $\hat{\boldsymbol{\theta}}$ is a root of the likelihood equations (8.12). It is then relatively straightforward to show that $\hat{\boldsymbol{\theta}}$ has the property of **asymptotic normality**, which was discussed in Chapter 5. For a DGP characterized by $\boldsymbol{\theta}_0$, the vector of parameter estimates $\hat{\boldsymbol{\theta}}$ tends to the nonstochastic limit $\boldsymbol{\theta}_0$. However, if we multiply the difference $\hat{\boldsymbol{\theta}} - \boldsymbol{\theta}_0$ by $n^{1/2}$, the resulting quantity $n^{1/2}(\hat{\boldsymbol{\theta}} - \boldsymbol{\theta}_0)$ will have a limit in probability that is a random variable with a multivariate normal distribution. As in the NLS case, we will refer to this distribution as the **asymptotic distribution** of $n^{1/2}(\hat{\boldsymbol{\theta}} - \boldsymbol{\theta}_0)$; we may on occasion also refer to it informally as the asymptotic distribution of $\hat{\boldsymbol{\theta}}$, although this is not technically correct.

We now sketch a proof of the asymptotic normality of the Type 2 MLE. We begin by Taylor expanding the likelihood equations (8.12) around $\boldsymbol{\theta}_0$, obtaining

$$\mathbf{0} = \boldsymbol{g}(\hat{\boldsymbol{\theta}}) = \boldsymbol{g}(\boldsymbol{\theta}_0) + \boldsymbol{H}(\bar{\boldsymbol{\theta}})(\hat{\boldsymbol{\theta}} - \boldsymbol{\theta}_0), \tag{8.35}$$

where $\bar{\boldsymbol{\theta}}$ is a convex combination of $\boldsymbol{\theta}_0$ and $\hat{\boldsymbol{\theta}}$, which may be different for each row of the equation. Solving (8.35) for $\hat{\boldsymbol{\theta}} - \boldsymbol{\theta}_0$ and rewriting so that every factor is $O(1)$ yields

$$n^{1/2}(\hat{\boldsymbol{\theta}} - \boldsymbol{\theta}_0) = -\big(n^{-1}\boldsymbol{H}(\bar{\boldsymbol{\theta}})\big)^{-1}\big(n^{-1/2}\boldsymbol{g}(\boldsymbol{\theta}_0)\big), \tag{8.36}$$

in which we see that $n^{1/2}(\hat{\boldsymbol{\theta}} - \boldsymbol{\theta}_0)$ is equal to a $k \times k$ matrix times a k–vector. The former will turn out to be asymptotically nonstochastic, and the latter will turn out to be asymptotically normal, from which it follows that $n^{1/2}(\hat{\boldsymbol{\theta}} - \boldsymbol{\theta}_0)$ must be asymptotically normal.

We first wish to show that $n^{-1}\boldsymbol{H}(\bar{\boldsymbol{\theta}})$ tends to a certain nonstochastic limiting matrix as $n \to \infty$. Recall that the ij^{th} element of $n^{-1}\boldsymbol{H}(\bar{\boldsymbol{\theta}})$ is

$$\frac{1}{n}\sum_{t=1}^{n} \frac{\partial^2 \ell_t(\boldsymbol{\theta})}{\partial \theta_i \partial \theta_j}, \tag{8.37}$$

evaluated at $\boldsymbol{\theta} = \bar{\boldsymbol{\theta}}$. We will require that condition WULLN apply to the sequence with typical element (8.37). That being so, $n^{-1}\boldsymbol{H}(\bar{\boldsymbol{\theta}})$ must tend to $\mathcal{H}(\bar{\boldsymbol{\theta}})$ as $n \to \infty$. But since $\hat{\boldsymbol{\theta}}$ is consistent for $\boldsymbol{\theta}_0$ and $\bar{\boldsymbol{\theta}}$ lies between $\hat{\boldsymbol{\theta}}$ and $\boldsymbol{\theta}_0$, it is clear that $n^{-1}\boldsymbol{H}(\bar{\boldsymbol{\theta}})$ must also tend to $\mathcal{H}(\boldsymbol{\theta}_0)$. Moreover, if the model is strongly asymptotically identified, the matrix $\mathcal{H}(\boldsymbol{\theta}_0)$ must be negative definite, and we will assume that this is the case.

Using this argument and (8.36), we see that

$$n^{1/2}(\hat{\boldsymbol{\theta}} - \boldsymbol{\theta}_0) \overset{a}{=} -\mathcal{H}^{-1}(\boldsymbol{\theta}_0)\big(n^{-1/2}\boldsymbol{g}(\boldsymbol{\theta}_0)\big). \tag{8.38}$$

The only stochastic thing on the right-hand side of (8.38) is

$$n^{-1/2}\boldsymbol{g}(\boldsymbol{\theta}_0), \tag{8.39}$$

of which a typical element is

$$n^{-1/2}\sum_{t=1}^{n}\frac{\partial \log L_t(y_t, \boldsymbol{\theta})}{\partial \theta_i}\bigg|_{\boldsymbol{\theta}=\boldsymbol{\theta}_0} = n^{-1/2}\sum_{t=1}^{n} G_{ti}(\boldsymbol{\theta}_0).$$

Thus (8.39) is $n^{-1/2}$ times a sum of n quantities. From the result (8.33), we know that each of these quantities has expectation zero. It therefore seems plausible that a central limit theorem applies to it. In a formal proof, one would have to start with appropriate regularity conditions and use them to prove that a particular CLT does indeed apply to (8.39), but we will omit this step. Once we assume that (8.39) is asymptotically normal, it follows immediately from (8.38) that $n^{1/2}(\hat{\boldsymbol{\theta}} - \boldsymbol{\theta}_0)$ must be as well.

The **asymptotic covariance matrix** of $n^{1/2}(\hat{\boldsymbol{\theta}} - \boldsymbol{\theta}_0)$ is simply the asymptotic expectation of $n(\hat{\boldsymbol{\theta}} - \boldsymbol{\theta}_0)(\hat{\boldsymbol{\theta}} - \boldsymbol{\theta}_0)^{\top}$. Using (8.38), this is equal to

$$\big(-\mathcal{H}^{-1}(\boldsymbol{\theta}_0)\big)\Big(\tfrac{1}{n}E_0\big(\boldsymbol{g}(\boldsymbol{\theta}_0)\boldsymbol{g}^{\top}(\boldsymbol{\theta}_0)\big)\Big)\big(-\mathcal{H}^{-1}(\boldsymbol{\theta}_0)\big).$$

A typical element of the expectation in the middle here is

$$\frac{1}{n}E_0\Bigg(\bigg(\sum_{t=1}^{n} G_{ti}(\boldsymbol{\theta}_0)\bigg)\bigg(\sum_{s=1}^{n} G_{sj}(\boldsymbol{\theta}_0)\bigg)\Bigg). \tag{8.40}$$

This is n^{-1} times the expectation of the product of two summations. If we were to write the product out explicitly, we would see that each of the terms in the n^2-fold summation in (8.40) was of the form

$$G_{ti}(\boldsymbol{\theta}_0)G_{sj}(\boldsymbol{\theta}_0) = \frac{\partial \log(L_t)}{\partial \theta_i}\frac{\partial \log(L_s)}{\partial \theta_j}.$$

Except when $t = s$, all these terms must have expectation zero. Assume without loss of generality that $t > s$. Then

$$\begin{aligned} E_0\big(G_{ti}(\boldsymbol{\theta}_0)G_{sj}(\boldsymbol{\theta}_0)\big) &= E_0\Big(E\big(G_{ti}(\boldsymbol{\theta}_0)G_{sj}(\boldsymbol{\theta}_0) \,|\, \boldsymbol{y}^s\big)\Big) \\ &= E_0\Big(G_{sj}(\boldsymbol{\theta}_0)E\big(G_{ti}(\boldsymbol{\theta}_0) \,|\, \boldsymbol{y}^s\big)\Big) = 0. \end{aligned}$$

The last equality here follows from the fact that $E_0\big(G_{ti}(\boldsymbol{\theta}_0) \,|\, \boldsymbol{y}^s\big) = 0$, which is itself true because the proof of the general result (8.33) applies equally well to the conditional as to the unconditional expectation.

Because $E_0\big(G_{ti}(\boldsymbol{\theta}_0)G_{sj}(\boldsymbol{\theta}_0)\big) = 0$ for all $t \neq s$,

$$\frac{1}{n}E_0\left(\left(\sum_{t=1}^{n} G_{ti}(\boldsymbol{\theta}_0)\right)\left(\sum_{s=1}^{n} G_{sj}(\boldsymbol{\theta}_0)\right)\right) = \frac{1}{n}E_0\left(\sum_{t=1}^{n} G_{ti}(\boldsymbol{\theta}_0)G_{tj}(\boldsymbol{\theta}_0)\right). \tag{8.41}$$

From (8.20) and (8.21) we see that the right-hand side of (8.41) is simply $\mathfrak{I}^n(\boldsymbol{\theta}_0)$, the average information matrix for a sample of size n. Using the fact that $\mathfrak{I}(\boldsymbol{\theta}_0)$ is the limit of $\mathfrak{I}^n(\boldsymbol{\theta}_0)$ as $n \to \infty$, we conclude that the asymptotic covariance matrix of $n^{1/2}(\hat{\boldsymbol{\theta}} - \boldsymbol{\theta}_0)$ is

$$\boldsymbol{V}^\infty\big(n^{1/2}(\hat{\boldsymbol{\theta}} - \boldsymbol{\theta}_0)\big) = \mathcal{H}^{-1}(\boldsymbol{\theta}_0)\mathfrak{I}(\boldsymbol{\theta}_0)\mathcal{H}^{-1}(\boldsymbol{\theta}_0). \tag{8.42}$$

In the next section, we will see that this expression can be simplified further.

We may now state the above results formally as follows:

Theorem 8.3. Asymptotic Normality Theorem.

> The Type 2 ML estimator, $\hat{\boldsymbol{\theta}}$, for a strongly asymptotically identified model represented by the parametric family of loglikelihood functions $\ell(\boldsymbol{\theta})$, $\boldsymbol{\theta} \in \Theta$, when it exists and is consistent for the parameter vector $\boldsymbol{\theta}_0$ that characterizes the DGP, is asymptotically normal if
>
> (i) the contributions $\ell_t(\boldsymbol{y}, \boldsymbol{\theta})$ to ℓ are at least twice continuously differentiable in $\boldsymbol{\theta}$ for almost all $\boldsymbol{y}$ and all $\boldsymbol{\theta} \in \Theta$,
>
> (ii) the component sequences of $\{D^2_{\theta\theta}\ell_t(\boldsymbol{y}, \boldsymbol{\theta})\}_{t=1}^{\infty}$ satisfy condition WULLN on Θ, and
>
> (iii) the component sequences of $\{D_\theta \ell_t(\boldsymbol{y}, \boldsymbol{\theta})\}_{t=1}^{\infty}$ satisfy condition CLT.
>
> By asymptotic normality, it is meant that the sequence of random variables $n^{1/2}(\hat{\boldsymbol{\theta}} - \boldsymbol{\theta}_0)$ has a limit in probability which is a random variable of order unity, normally distributed with mean zero and covariance matrix (8.42).

8.6 THE INFORMATION MATRIX EQUALITY

In this section, we will establish an important result that allows a substantial simplification of expression (8.42) for the asymptotic covariance matrix of the ML estimator. This result, which, as the title of the section announces, is called the **information matrix equality**, is

$$\mathcal{H}(\boldsymbol{\theta}_0) = -\mathfrak{I}(\boldsymbol{\theta}_0). \tag{8.43}$$

In words, the limiting Hessian matrix is the negative of the limiting information matrix. An analogous result is true for individual observations:

$$E_0\big(D^2_{\theta\theta}\ell_t(\boldsymbol{y},\boldsymbol{\theta}_0)\big) = -E_0\big(D_\theta^\top\ell_t(\boldsymbol{y},\boldsymbol{\theta}_0)D_\theta\ell_t(\boldsymbol{y},\boldsymbol{\theta}_0)\big). \tag{8.44}$$

The latter result clearly implies the former, given the assumptions that permit the application of a law of large numbers to the sequences $\{D^2_{\theta\theta}\ell_t(\boldsymbol{y},\boldsymbol{\theta}_0)\}_{t=1}^\infty$ and $\{D_\theta^\top\ell_t(\boldsymbol{y},\boldsymbol{\theta}_0)D_\theta\ell_t(\boldsymbol{y},\boldsymbol{\theta}_0)\}_{t=1}^\infty$.

The result (8.44) is proved by an argument very similar to that used at the beginning of the last section in order to show that the expectation of the CG matrix is zero. From the fact that

$$\frac{\partial\ell_t}{\partial\theta_i} = \frac{1}{L_t}\frac{\partial L_t}{\partial\theta_i},$$

we obtain after a further differentiation that

$$\frac{\partial^2\ell_t}{\partial\theta_i\partial\theta_j} = \frac{1}{L_t}\frac{\partial^2 L_t}{\partial\theta_i\partial\theta_j} - \frac{1}{L_t^2}\frac{\partial L_t}{\partial\theta_i}\frac{\partial L_t}{\partial\theta_j}.$$

Consequently,

$$\frac{\partial^2\ell_t}{\partial\theta_i\partial\theta_j} + \frac{\partial\ell_t}{\partial\theta_i}\frac{\partial\ell_t}{\partial\theta_j} = \frac{1}{L_t}\frac{\partial^2 L_t}{\partial\theta_i\partial\theta_j}. \tag{8.45}$$

If now we take the expectation of (8.45) for the DGP characterized by the same value of the parameter vector $\boldsymbol{\theta}$ as that at which the functions ℓ_t and L_t are evaluated (which as usual we denote by E_θ), we find that

$$\begin{aligned} E_\theta\left(\frac{\partial^2\ell_t}{\partial\theta_i\partial\theta_j} + \frac{\partial\ell_t}{\partial\theta_i}\frac{\partial\ell_t}{\partial\theta_j}\right) &= \int L_t\frac{1}{L_t}\frac{\partial^2 L_t}{\partial\theta_i\partial\theta_j}\,dy_t \\ &= \frac{\partial^2}{\partial\theta_i\partial\theta_j}\int L_t\,dy_t = 0, \end{aligned} \tag{8.46}$$

provided that, as for (8.34), the interchange of the order of differentiation and integration can be justified. The result (8.46) now establishes (8.44), since it implies that

$$E_\theta\left(\frac{\partial^2\ell_t}{\partial\theta_i\partial\theta_j}\right) = 0 - E_\theta\left(\frac{\partial\ell_t}{\partial\theta_i}\frac{\partial\ell_t}{\partial\theta_j}\right) = -E_\theta\left(\frac{\partial\ell_t}{\partial\theta_i}\frac{\partial\ell_t}{\partial\theta_j}\right).$$

In order to establish (8.43), recall that, from (8.19) and the law of large numbers,

$$\begin{aligned} \mathcal{H}(\boldsymbol{\theta}) &= \lim_{n\to\infty}\left(\frac{1}{n}\sum_{t=1}^n E_\theta\left(\frac{\partial^2\ell_t(\boldsymbol{\theta})}{\partial\theta_i\partial\theta_j}\right)\right) \\ &= -\lim_{n\to\infty}\left(\frac{1}{n}\sum_{t=1}^n E_\theta\left(\frac{\partial\ell_t(\boldsymbol{\theta})}{\partial\theta_i}\frac{\partial\ell_t(\boldsymbol{\theta})}{\partial\theta_j}\right)\right) \\ &= -\mathfrak{I}(\boldsymbol{\theta}), \end{aligned}$$

where the last line follows immediately from the definition of the limiting information matrix, (8.22). This then establishes (8.43).

By substituting either $-\mathcal{H}(\boldsymbol{\theta}_0)$ for $\mathcal{I}(\boldsymbol{\theta}_0)$ or $\mathcal{I}(\boldsymbol{\theta}_0)$ for $-\mathcal{H}(\boldsymbol{\theta}_0)$ in (8.42), it is now easy to conclude that the asymptotic covariance matrix of the ML estimator is given by either of the two equivalent expressions $-\mathcal{H}(\boldsymbol{\theta}_0)^{-1}$ and $\mathcal{I}(\boldsymbol{\theta}_0)^{-1}$. Formally, we may write

$$\boldsymbol{V}^{\infty}\big(n^{1/2}(\hat{\boldsymbol{\theta}}-\boldsymbol{\theta}_0)\big) = \mathcal{I}^{-1}(\boldsymbol{\theta}_0) = -\mathcal{H}^{-1}(\boldsymbol{\theta}_0).$$

In order to perform any statistical inference, it is necessary to be able to *estimate* $\mathcal{I}^{-1}(\boldsymbol{\theta}_0)$ or $-\mathcal{H}^{-1}(\boldsymbol{\theta}_0)$. One estimator which suggests itself at once is $\mathcal{I}^{-1}(\hat{\boldsymbol{\theta}})$, that is, the inverse of the limiting information matrix evaluated at the MLE, $\hat{\boldsymbol{\theta}}$. Notice that the matrix function $\mathcal{I}(\boldsymbol{\theta})$ is *not* a sample-dependent object. It can, in principle, be computed theoretically as a matrix function of the model parameters from the (sequence of) loglikelihood functions ℓ^n. For some models, this is an entirely feasible computation, and then it yields what is often the preferred estimator of the asymptotic covariance matrix. But for many models the computation, even if feasible, would be excessively laborious, and in these cases it is convenient to have available other consistent estimators of $\mathcal{I}(\boldsymbol{\theta}_0)$ and consequently of the asymptotic covariance matrix.

One common estimator is the negative of the so-called **empirical Hessian**. This matrix is defined as

$$\hat{\mathcal{H}} \equiv \mathcal{H}^n(\boldsymbol{y},\hat{\boldsymbol{\theta}}) = \frac{1}{n}\sum_{t=1}^{n} D^2_{\theta\theta}\ell_t(\boldsymbol{y},\hat{\boldsymbol{\theta}}); \tag{8.47}$$

it is just $\mathcal{H}^n(\boldsymbol{y},\boldsymbol{\theta})$ evaluated at $\hat{\boldsymbol{\theta}}$. The law of large numbers and the consistency of $\hat{\boldsymbol{\theta}}$ itself immediately guarantee the consistency of (8.47) for $\mathcal{H}(\boldsymbol{\theta}_0)$. When the empirical Hessian is readily available, as it will be if maximization routines that use second derivatives are employed, minus its inverse can provide a very convenient way to estimate the covariance matrix of $\hat{\boldsymbol{\theta}}$. However, the Hessian is often difficult to compute, and if it is not already being calculated for other purposes, it probably does not make sense to compute it just to estimate a covariance matrix.

Another commonly used estimator of the information matrix is known as the **outer-product-of-the-gradient estimator**, or **OPG estimator**. It is based on the definition

$$\mathcal{I}(\boldsymbol{\theta}) \equiv \lim_{n\to\infty}\left(\frac{1}{n}\sum_{t=1}^{n} E_\theta\big(D_\theta^{\top}\ell_t(\boldsymbol{\theta})D_\theta\ell_t(\boldsymbol{\theta})\big)\right).$$

The OPG estimator is

$$\hat{\mathcal{I}}_{\mathrm{OPG}} \equiv \frac{1}{n}\sum_{t=1}^{n} D_\theta^{\top}\ell_t(\boldsymbol{y},\hat{\boldsymbol{\theta}})D_\theta\ell_t(\boldsymbol{y},\hat{\boldsymbol{\theta}}) = \frac{1}{n}\boldsymbol{G}^{\top}(\hat{\boldsymbol{\theta}})\boldsymbol{G}(\hat{\boldsymbol{\theta}}), \tag{8.48}$$

and its consistency is again guaranteed by condition CLT, which includes a law of large numbers for the sum in (8.48).

The OPG estimator of the information matrix was advocated by Berndt, Hall, Hall, and Hausman (1974) in a very well-known paper and is therefore sometimes referred to as the BHHH estimator. They also suggested its use as part of a general scheme for maximizing loglikelihood functions, analogous to the schemes based on the Gauss-Newton regression that we discussed in Section 6.8. Unfortunately, the estimator (8.48) turns out in practice to be rather noisy, which limits its usefulness for both estimating covariance matrices and numerical maximization.[7] Whereas in $\mathcal{I}(\hat{\boldsymbol{\theta}})$ the only stochastic element is the MLE $\hat{\boldsymbol{\theta}}$ itself, both the empirical Hessian and the OPG estimator depend explicitly on the realized sample $\boldsymbol{y}$, and this imparts to them additional noise that makes inferences based on them less reliable than one would often like. The OPG estimator often seems to be particularly poor, as we discuss in Chapter 13.

In certain cases, it is possible to find estimators somewhere between the (usually) preferred estimator $\mathcal{I}(\hat{\boldsymbol{\theta}})$ and the OPG estimator, in which one can take the expectations of some of the terms appearing in (8.48) but not of all. This generally appears to be a good thing to do, in terms of the quality of statistical inference that one can draw based on the asymptotic distributions of estimators or test statistics. The Gauss-Newton covariance matrix estimator is of this type whenever the model contains lagged dependent variables, since the matrix $n^{-1}\boldsymbol{X}^{\top}(\hat{\boldsymbol{\beta}})\boldsymbol{X}(\hat{\boldsymbol{\beta}})$ will then depend on lagged values of $\boldsymbol{y}$ as well as on $\hat{\boldsymbol{\beta}}$. Several more examples of this type of estimator will appear later in the book, most notably in Chapters 14 and 15.

The above discussion has perhaps not made clear a point that is of the highest practical importance when one is trying to make inferences about a set of ML estimates $\hat{\boldsymbol{\theta}}$. All of the asymptotic distribution theory is in terms of $n^{1/2}(\hat{\boldsymbol{\theta}} - \boldsymbol{\theta}_0)$, but in practice we actually want to use $\hat{\boldsymbol{\theta}}$ to make inferences about $\boldsymbol{\theta}$. This means that we must base our inferences *not* on quantities which estimate $\mathcal{I}(\boldsymbol{\theta}_0)$ but rather on quantities which estimate $n\mathcal{I}(\boldsymbol{\theta}_0)$. Thus three estimators that may be used in practice to estimate $\boldsymbol{V}(\hat{\boldsymbol{\theta}})$ are the inverse of the negative of the numerical Hessian,

$$\big(-\boldsymbol{H}(\hat{\boldsymbol{\theta}})\big)^{-1}, \tag{8.49}$$

the inverse of the OPG estimator of the $O(n)$ information matrix,

$$\big(\boldsymbol{G}^{\top}(\hat{\boldsymbol{\theta}})\boldsymbol{G}(\hat{\boldsymbol{\theta}})\big)^{-1}, \tag{8.50}$$

and the inverse of the $O(n)$ information matrix itself,

$$\big(n\mathcal{I}(\hat{\boldsymbol{\theta}})\big)^{-1} \equiv \big(\boldsymbol{I}^{n}(\hat{\boldsymbol{\theta}})\big)^{-1}. \tag{8.51}$$

[7] There will be some further discussion of alternative ways to estimate the covariance matrix of ML estimates in Chapter 13. For evidence on the performance of the OPG estimator in the BHHH estimation scheme, see Belsley (1980).

In addition to (8.49), (8.50), and (8.51), which are very widely applicable, there are various hybrid estimators for certain classes of models, such as estimators based on the Gauss-Newton and other artificial regressions. Note that all these covariance matrix estimators will be n times smaller than the estimators of the covariance matrix of $n^{1/2}(\hat{\boldsymbol{\theta}} - \boldsymbol{\theta}_0)$, such as (8.47) and (8.48), which we have been discussing up to this point.

Although it is common to take as many expectations as possible when estimating the covariance matrix of $\hat{\boldsymbol{\theta}}$, it is not obvious that doing so is always a good thing. Consider the following example. Suppose that $y_t = \beta x_t + u_t$, where x_t is a binary variable that is known to take the value 1 with probability p and the value 0 with probability $1 - p$. Suppose further (for simplicity) that the variance of u_t is known and equal to unity. Then the information matrix, which is just a scalar in this case, is $E\left(n^{-1}\sum_{t=1}^{n} x_t^2\right) = p$. Thus the usual estimate of the variance of $\hat{\beta}$ based on the information matrix is simply $(np)^{-1}$.

It should be obvious that, when np is small, $(np)^{-1}$ could be a very misleading estimate of the actual variance of $\hat{\beta}$ conditional on the particular sample that was observed. Suppose, for example, that n were 100 and p were .02. The usual variance estimate would be $\frac{1}{2}$. But it could well be the case that none of the x_t's in the sample happened to be equal to 1; this would happen with probability .133. Then that particular sample would not identify β at all, and the variance of $\hat{\beta}$ would be infinite. Alternatively, it might be that just one of the x_t's in the sample was equal to 1. Then β would be identified, but $\frac{1}{2}$ would clearly be an underestimate of the actual variance of $\hat{\beta}$. On the other hand, if more than two of the x_t's were equal to 1, $\hat{\beta}$ would have variance smaller than $(np)^{-1}$. Only if np happened to equal its expected value of 2 would the asymptotic variance estimate correspond to the actual variance of $\hat{\beta}$ conditional on the observed sample.

This example is very special, but the phenomenon it deals with is quite general. Whenever we calculate the covariance matrix of some vector of parameter estimates, we presumably care about the accuracy of that particular set of estimates. That depends on the amount of information that has been provided by the sample at hand rather than the amount of information that would be provided by a typical sample of the same size. Hence, in a very real sense, it is the *observed* information matrix rather than the *expected* information matrix that we should be interested in. For a much more extensive discussion of this point, see Efron and Hinkley (1978).

8.7 CONCENTRATING THE LOGLIKELIHOOD FUNCTION

It often happens that the parameters on which a loglikelihood function depends can be partitioned into two sets in a way which makes it easy to write down the ML estimator of one set of parameters as a function of the values of the other set. We will encounter an example of this, in connection with

ML estimation of regression models, in Section 8.10, and further examples in Chapter 9. In this situation, it can be very convenient to **concentrate** the loglikelihood function by writing it as a function of only one of the two sets of parameters. Suppose that we can write the loglikelihood function $\ell(\boldsymbol{y}, \boldsymbol{\theta})$ as $\ell(\boldsymbol{y}, \boldsymbol{\theta}_1, \boldsymbol{\theta}_2)$. The first-order conditions which define the (Type 2) ML estimators $\hat{\boldsymbol{\theta}}_1$ and $\hat{\boldsymbol{\theta}}_2$ are

$$D_1\ell(\boldsymbol{y}, \boldsymbol{\theta}_1, \boldsymbol{\theta}_2) = \mathbf{0} \quad \text{and} \quad D_2\ell(\boldsymbol{y}, \boldsymbol{\theta}_1, \boldsymbol{\theta}_2) = \mathbf{0},$$

where, as usual, $D_i\ell$ denotes the row vector of partial derivatives $\partial\ell/\partial\boldsymbol{\theta}_i$ for $i = 1, 2$. Assume that it is possible to solve the second of these first-order conditions, so as to be able to write

$$\boldsymbol{\theta}_2 = \boldsymbol{\tau}(\boldsymbol{y}, \boldsymbol{\theta}_1).$$

Then this implies that, identically in $\boldsymbol{\theta}_1$,

$$D_2\ell\big(\boldsymbol{y}, \boldsymbol{\theta}_1, \boldsymbol{\tau}(\boldsymbol{y}, \boldsymbol{\theta}_1)\big) = \mathbf{0}. \tag{8.52}$$

Substituting $\boldsymbol{\tau}(\boldsymbol{y}, \boldsymbol{\theta}_1)$ for $\boldsymbol{\theta}_2$ in $\ell(\boldsymbol{y}, \boldsymbol{\theta}_1, \boldsymbol{\theta}_2)$, we obtain the **concentrated loglikelihood function**

$$\ell^c(\boldsymbol{y}, \boldsymbol{\theta}_1) \equiv \ell\big(\boldsymbol{y}, \boldsymbol{\theta}_1, \boldsymbol{\tau}(\boldsymbol{y}, \boldsymbol{\theta}_1)\big).$$

If $\hat{\boldsymbol{\theta}}_1$ maximizes this, we can then obtain $\hat{\boldsymbol{\theta}}_2$ as $\boldsymbol{\tau}(\boldsymbol{y}, \hat{\boldsymbol{\theta}}_1)$, and it is evident that $[\hat{\boldsymbol{\theta}}_1 \,\vdots\, \hat{\boldsymbol{\theta}}_2]$ will maximize $\ell(\boldsymbol{y}, \boldsymbol{\theta})$. In some cases, this strategy can substantially reduce the amount of effort required to obtain ML estimates.

It is obvious that $\ell^c(\boldsymbol{y}, \hat{\boldsymbol{\theta}}_1)$ will be identical to $\ell(\boldsymbol{y}, \hat{\boldsymbol{\theta}})$. However, it is not obvious that we can calculate an estimated covariance matrix for $\hat{\boldsymbol{\theta}}_1$ based on $\ell^c(\boldsymbol{y}, \boldsymbol{\theta}_1)$ in the same way that we can based on $\ell(\boldsymbol{y}, \boldsymbol{\theta})$. In fact, provided we use as the estimator the inverse of the negative of the empirical Hessian, it is possible to do just that. The reason is that, by virtue of the way in which ℓ^c is constructed, the inverse of its Hessian with respect to $\boldsymbol{\theta}_1$ is equal to the $(\boldsymbol{\theta}_1, \boldsymbol{\theta}_1)$ block of the inverse of the Hessian of $\ell(\boldsymbol{y}, \boldsymbol{\theta})$ with respect to the full parameter vector $\boldsymbol{\theta}$. This follows from the envelope theorem and standard results on partitioned matrices, as we now demonstrate.

By the first-order condition (8.52), the gradient of ℓ^c with respect to $\boldsymbol{\theta}_1$ is

$$\begin{aligned} D_1\ell^c(\boldsymbol{\theta}_1) &= D_1\ell\big(\boldsymbol{\theta}_1, \boldsymbol{\tau}(\boldsymbol{\theta}_1)\big) + D_2\ell\big(\boldsymbol{\theta}_1, \boldsymbol{\tau}(\boldsymbol{\theta}_1)\big)D\boldsymbol{\tau}(\boldsymbol{\theta}_1) \\ &= D_1\ell\big(\boldsymbol{\theta}_1, \boldsymbol{\tau}(\boldsymbol{\theta}_1)\big), \end{aligned}$$

where the explicit dependence on $\boldsymbol{y}$ has been suppressed. This result is just the envelope theorem applied to ℓ^c. Thus the Hessian of $\ell^c(\boldsymbol{\theta}_1)$ is

$$D_{11}\ell^c(\boldsymbol{\theta}_1) = D_{11}\ell\big(\boldsymbol{\theta}_1, \boldsymbol{\tau}(\boldsymbol{\theta}_1)\big) + D_{12}\ell\big(\boldsymbol{\theta}_1, \boldsymbol{\tau}(\boldsymbol{\theta}_1)\big)D\boldsymbol{\tau}(\boldsymbol{\theta}_1). \tag{8.53}$$

In order to express the right-hand side of (8.53) in terms of blocks of the Hessian of ℓ only, we differentiate (8.52) with respect to $\boldsymbol{\theta}_1$, obtaining

$$D_{21}\ell(\boldsymbol{\theta}_1, \boldsymbol{\tau}(\boldsymbol{\theta}_1)) + D_{22}\ell(\boldsymbol{\theta}_1, \boldsymbol{\tau}(\boldsymbol{\theta}_1))D\boldsymbol{\tau}(\boldsymbol{\theta}_1) = \mathbf{0}.$$

Solving this equation for $D\boldsymbol{\tau}(\boldsymbol{\theta}_1)$ and substituting the result into (8.53), the expression for the Hessian of ℓ^c, gives

$$D_{11}\ell^c = D_{11}\ell - D_{12}\ell(D_{22}\ell)^{-1}D_{21}\ell, \tag{8.54}$$

in which the arguments of ℓ and ℓ^c have been dropped for simplicity. The Hessian of ℓ can be written in partitioned form as

$$D_{\theta\theta}\,\ell = \begin{bmatrix} D_{11}\ell & D_{12}\ell \\ D_{21}\ell & D_{22}\ell \end{bmatrix}.$$

Standard results on partitioned matrices (see Appendix A) tell us that the $(\boldsymbol{\theta}_1, \boldsymbol{\theta}_1)$ block of the inverse of this Hessian is

$$\big(D_{11}\ell - D_{12}\ell(D_{22}\ell)^{-1}D_{21}\ell\big)^{-1},$$

the inverse of which is just the expression for $D_{11}\ell^c$ in (8.54).

Using concentrated loglikelihood functions has some disadvantages. The original loglikelihood function can in most cases be conveniently written as

$$\ell(\boldsymbol{y}, \boldsymbol{\theta}) = \sum_{t=1}^{n} \ell_t(y_t, \boldsymbol{\theta}). \tag{8.55}$$

This is generally not true for the concentrated loglikelihood function, however. The equivalent of (8.55) is

$$\ell^c(\boldsymbol{y}, \boldsymbol{\theta}_1) = \sum_{t=1}^{n} \ell_t\big(y_t, \boldsymbol{\theta}_1, \boldsymbol{\tau}(\boldsymbol{y}, \boldsymbol{\theta}_1)\big),$$

and it is evident that, because of the dependence of $\boldsymbol{\tau}(\cdot)$ on the entire vector $\boldsymbol{y}$, there is in general no simple way to write $\ell^c(\boldsymbol{y}, \boldsymbol{\theta}_1)$ as a sum of contributions from each of the observations. This means that the OPG estimator of the information matrix is generally not available for concentrated loglikelihood functions. One can of course use $\ell^c(\boldsymbol{y}, \boldsymbol{\theta}_1)$ for estimation and then turn to $\ell(\boldsymbol{y}, \boldsymbol{\theta})$ when it comes time to estimate the covariance matrix of the estimates.

8.8 Asymptotic Efficiency of the ML Estimator

In this section, we will demonstrate the **asymptotic efficiency** of the ML estimator or, strictly speaking, of the Type 2 ML estimator. Asymptotic efficiency means that the variance of the asymptotic distribution of any consistent estimator of the model parameters differs from that of an asymptotically efficient estimator by a positive semidefinite matrix; see Definition 5.6. One says *an* asymptotically efficient estimator rather than *the* asymptotically efficient estimator because, since the property of asymptotic efficiency is a property only of the asymptotic distribution, there can (and do) exist many estimators that differ in finite samples but have the same, efficient, asymptotic distribution. An example can be taken from the nonlinear regression model, in which, as we will see in Section 8.10, NLS is equivalent to ML estimation if we assume normality of the error terms. As we saw in Section 6.6, there are nonlinear models that are just linear models with some nonlinear restrictions imposed on them. In such cases, one-step estimation starting from the estimates of the linear model was seen to be asymptotically equivalent to NLS, and hence asymptotically efficient. One-step estimation is possible in the general maximum likelihood context as well and can often provide an efficient estimator that is easier to compute than the ML estimator itself.

We will begin our proof of the asymptotic efficiency of the ML estimator by a discussion applicable to any root-n consistent and asymptotically unbiased estimator of the parameters of the model represented by the loglikelihood function $\ell(\boldsymbol{y}, \boldsymbol{\theta})$. Note that consistency by itself does not imply asymptotic unbiasedness without the imposition of various regularity conditions. Since every econometrically interesting consistent estimator that we are aware of is in fact asymptotically unbiased, we will deal only with such estimators here. Let such an estimator be denoted by $\hat{\boldsymbol{\theta}}(\boldsymbol{y})$, where the notation emphasizes the fact that the estimator is a random variable, dependent on the realized sample $\boldsymbol{y}$. Note that we have changed notation here, since $\hat{\boldsymbol{\theta}}(\boldsymbol{y})$ is in general not the ML estimator. Instead, the latter will be denoted $\tilde{\boldsymbol{\theta}}(\boldsymbol{y})$; the new notation is designed to be consistent with our treatment throughout the book of restricted and unrestricted estimators, since in an important sense the ML estimator corresponds to the former and the arbitrary consistent estimator $\hat{\boldsymbol{\theta}}(\boldsymbol{y})$ corresponds to the latter.

Because $\hat{\boldsymbol{\theta}}(\boldsymbol{y})$ is assumed to be asymptotically unbiased, we have that

$$\lim_{n\to\infty} E_\theta\big(\hat{\boldsymbol{\theta}}(\boldsymbol{y}) - \boldsymbol{\theta}\big) = \mathbf{0}.$$

In more explicit notation, this becomes:

$$\lim_{n\to\infty}\left(\int_{\mathcal{Y}^n} L^n(\boldsymbol{y}^n, \boldsymbol{\theta})\hat{\boldsymbol{\theta}}^n(\boldsymbol{y}^n)\,d\boldsymbol{y}^n - \boldsymbol{\theta}\right) = \mathbf{0}, \tag{8.56}$$

where, as before, $\mathcal{Y}^n$ denotes the subspace of $\mathbb{R}^{nm}$ over which the sample vector $\boldsymbol{y}^n$ may vary in a sample of size n. The next steps involve differentiating the relation (8.56) with respect to the elements of $\boldsymbol{\theta}$, interchanging the order of the operations of differentiation and integration, and taking the limit as $n \to \infty$. We omit discussion of the regularity conditions necessary for this to be admissible and proceed directly to write down the result of differentiating the jth component of (8.56) with respect to the ith component of $\boldsymbol{\theta}$:

$$\lim_{n\to\infty} \int_{y^n} L^n(\boldsymbol{y}^n, \boldsymbol{\theta}) \frac{\partial \ell^n(\boldsymbol{y}^n, \boldsymbol{\theta})}{\partial \theta_i} \hat{\theta}_j(\boldsymbol{y}^n) d\boldsymbol{y}^n = \delta^i_j. \tag{8.57}$$

The right-hand side of this equation is the Kronecker delta, equal to 1 when $i = j$ and equal to 0 otherwise. Equation (8.57) can be rewritten as

$$\lim_{n\to\infty} E_\theta \left(n^{-1/2} \frac{\partial \ell^n(\boldsymbol{y}^n, \boldsymbol{\theta})}{\partial \theta_i} n^{1/2} (\hat{\theta}_j - \theta_j) \right) = \delta^i_j, \tag{8.58}$$

where we have put in some powers of n to ensure that the quantities which appear in the expression have probability limits of order unity. We have also subtracted θ_j from $\hat{\theta}_j$; this was possible because $E_\theta\big(D_\theta \ell(\boldsymbol{\theta})\big) = \mathbf{0}$, and hence θ_j times $E_\theta\big(D_\theta \ell(\boldsymbol{\theta})\big)$ is also equal to zero.

Expression (8.58) can be written without any limiting operation if we use the limiting distributions of the gradient $D_\theta \ell$ and the vector $n^{1/2}(\hat{\boldsymbol{\theta}} - \boldsymbol{\theta})$. Let us introduce a little more notation for the purposes of discussing limiting random variables. We make the definitions

$$\boldsymbol{s}^n(\boldsymbol{\theta}) \equiv n^{-1/2} \boldsymbol{g}(\boldsymbol{y}^n, \boldsymbol{\theta}), \quad \boldsymbol{s}(\boldsymbol{\theta}) \equiv \operatorname*{plim}_{n\to\infty}{}_\theta\, \boldsymbol{s}^n(\boldsymbol{\theta}), \tag{8.59}$$

$$\hat{\boldsymbol{t}}^n(\boldsymbol{\theta}) \equiv n^{1/2} (\hat{\boldsymbol{\theta}} - \boldsymbol{\theta}), \text{ and } \hat{\boldsymbol{t}}(\boldsymbol{\theta}) \equiv \operatorname*{plim}_{n\to\infty}{}_\theta\, \hat{\boldsymbol{t}}^n(\boldsymbol{\theta}). \tag{8.60}$$

Thus $\boldsymbol{s}(\boldsymbol{\theta})$ and $\hat{\boldsymbol{t}}(\boldsymbol{\theta})$ are k–vectors with typical elements $s_i(\boldsymbol{\theta})$ and $\hat{t}_j(\boldsymbol{\theta})$, respectively. The former is the limiting value of $n^{-1/2}$ times a typical element of the gradient of $\ell(\boldsymbol{y}, \boldsymbol{\theta})$, while the latter is the limiting value of $n^{1/2}$ times a typical element of the difference between $\hat{\boldsymbol{\theta}}$ and $\boldsymbol{\theta}$. The notation is intended to be mnemonic, $\boldsymbol{s}(\boldsymbol{\theta})$ corresponding to the *score* vector and $\hat{\boldsymbol{t}}(\boldsymbol{\theta})$ corresponding to *theta hat.* In this convenient new notation, expression (8.58) becomes

$$E_\theta\big(\hat{\boldsymbol{t}}(\boldsymbol{\theta}) \boldsymbol{s}^\top(\boldsymbol{\theta})\big) = \mathbf{I}_k, \tag{8.61}$$

where $\mathbf{I}_k$ is simply the $k \times k$ identity matrix.

It is not generally true for *any* consistent estimator that the plim in (8.60) exists or, if it does, is not zero. The class of estimators for which it exists and is nonzero is called the class of **root-n consistent estimators**. As we discussed in Chapter 5, this means that the rate of convergence, as $n \to \infty$, of the estimator $\hat{\boldsymbol{\theta}}$ to the true value $\boldsymbol{\theta}$ is the same as the rate of convergence of $n^{-1/2}$ to zero. The existence of a nonzero plim in (8.60) clearly implies just that, and we have already shown that the ML estimator is root-n consistent.

The consistency of $\hat{\boldsymbol{\theta}}$ also implies that the expectation of the limiting random variable $\hat{\boldsymbol{t}}(\boldsymbol{\theta})$ is zero.

For the next part of the argument, we first consider the simple case in which $k = 1$. Then instead of (8.61) we have the scalar relation

$$E_\theta\big(\hat{t}(\theta)s(\theta)\big) = \mathrm{Cov}_\theta\big(\hat{t}(\theta), s(\theta)\big) = 1. \tag{8.62}$$

We have here used the fact that the expectations of both $\hat{t}(\theta)$ and $s(\theta)$ are zero. The result (8.62) implies the well-known Cauchy-Schwartz inequality:

$$1 = \Big(\mathrm{Cov}_\theta\big(\hat{t}(\theta), s(\theta)\big)\Big)^2 \le \mathrm{Var}_\theta\big(\hat{t}(\theta)\big)\mathrm{Var}_\theta\big(s(\theta)\big) = \mathrm{Var}_\theta\big(\hat{t}(\theta)\big)\mathfrak{I}(\theta), \tag{8.63}$$

where the last equality follows from the definition (8.59) of $s(\theta)$ and the definition of the limiting information matrix $\mathfrak{I}(\theta)$, which is in this case a scalar. The inequality (8.63) implies that

$$\mathrm{Var}_\theta\big(\hat{t}(\theta)\big) \ge \frac{1}{\mathfrak{I}(\theta)}. \tag{8.64}$$

This result establishes, in this one-dimensional case, that the asymptotic variance of any root-n consistent estimator cannot be less than the reciprocal of what it seems logical to call the information scalar. Since the right-hand side of (8.64) is precisely the asymptotic variance of the ML estimator, the asymptotic efficiency of the latter is also established by this result. Note that (8.64) rules out any estimator for which the plim of $n^{1/2}(\hat{\boldsymbol{\theta}} - \boldsymbol{\theta}_0)$ is zero. Such an estimator would of course be *more* efficient asymptotically than the ML estimator, since it would converge more rapidly to the true value of $\boldsymbol{\theta}$.

The general result analogous to (8.64) for the case $k \ge 1$ can now be established by just a little more work. Consider the full covariance matrix of all of the components of $\hat{\boldsymbol{t}}$ and $\boldsymbol{s}$, that is, the covariance matrix of $[\hat{\boldsymbol{t}}(\boldsymbol{\theta}) \vdots \boldsymbol{s}(\boldsymbol{\theta})]$. Let the covariance matrix of $\hat{\boldsymbol{t}}$ be denoted by $\boldsymbol{V}$. Then (8.61) and the fact that $\mathrm{Var}_\theta\big(\boldsymbol{s}^\top(\boldsymbol{\theta})\big) = \mathfrak{I}(\boldsymbol{\theta})$ mean that the covariance matrix of $[\hat{\boldsymbol{t}}(\boldsymbol{\theta}) \vdots \boldsymbol{s}(\boldsymbol{\theta})]$ can be written as

$$\mathrm{Var}(\hat{\boldsymbol{t}}, \boldsymbol{s}) = \begin{bmatrix} \boldsymbol{V} & \mathbf{I}_k \\ \mathbf{I}_k & \mathfrak{I} \end{bmatrix}.$$

Since it is a covariance matrix, this must be positive semidefinite. Thus, for any k–vector $\boldsymbol{a}$, the following expression is nonnegative:

$$\begin{bmatrix} \boldsymbol{a}^\top & -\boldsymbol{a}^\top\mathfrak{I}^{-1} \end{bmatrix} \begin{bmatrix} \boldsymbol{V} & \mathbf{I}_k \\ \mathbf{I}_k & \mathfrak{I} \end{bmatrix} \begin{bmatrix} \boldsymbol{a} \\ -\mathfrak{I}^{-1}\boldsymbol{a} \end{bmatrix} = \boldsymbol{a}^\top(\boldsymbol{V} - \mathfrak{I}^{-1})\boldsymbol{a}.$$

But this implies, since $\boldsymbol{a}$ is arbitrary, that the matrix $\big(\boldsymbol{V} - \mathfrak{I}^{-1}\big)$ is positive semidefinite, which is what we wanted to prove.

This result is a special case of the **Cramér-Rao lower bound**, originally suggested by Fisher (1925) in one of the classic early papers on ML estimation and enunciated in its modern form by Cramér (1946) and Rao (1945). It is special because it is an asymptotic version of the original result. The Cramér-Rao lower bound actually applies to *any* unbiased estimator regardless of sample size. However, since ML estimators are not in general unbiased, it is only the asymptotic version of the result that is of interest in the context of ML estimation, and so we have restricted our attention to the asymptotic case.

The fact that the ML estimator asymptotically achieves the Cramér-Rao lower bound implies that any root-n consistent estimator can be written as the sum of the ML estimator and another random vector which is asymptotically independent of it. This result provides an illuminating way to think about the relationship between efficient and inefficient estimators. To derive it, we begin by making the definitions

$$\begin{aligned}&\tilde{\boldsymbol{t}}^n(\boldsymbol{\theta}) \equiv n^{1/2}(\tilde{\boldsymbol{\theta}} - \boldsymbol{\theta}), \quad \tilde{\boldsymbol{t}}(\boldsymbol{\theta}) \equiv \operatorname*{plim}_{n\to\infty}{}_{\theta}\big(\tilde{\boldsymbol{t}}^n(\boldsymbol{\theta})\big),\\ &\boldsymbol{v}^n \equiv \hat{\boldsymbol{t}}^n(\boldsymbol{\theta}) - \tilde{\boldsymbol{t}}^n(\boldsymbol{\theta}), \text{ and } \boldsymbol{v} \equiv \hat{\boldsymbol{t}}(\boldsymbol{\theta}) - \tilde{\boldsymbol{t}}(\boldsymbol{\theta}).\end{aligned} \tag{8.65}$$

As may be seen from the definitions (8.60) and (8.65), $\boldsymbol{v}^n$ and $\boldsymbol{v}$ do not depend directly on $\boldsymbol{\theta}$.

We wish to show that the covariance matrix of $\boldsymbol{v}$ and $\tilde{\boldsymbol{t}}$ is a zero matrix. This covariance matrix is

$$\begin{aligned}\operatorname{Cov}_\theta\big(\boldsymbol{v}, \tilde{\boldsymbol{t}}(\boldsymbol{\theta})\big) &= E_\theta\big(\boldsymbol{v}\tilde{\boldsymbol{t}}^\top(\boldsymbol{\theta})\big)\\ &= E_\theta\Big(\big(\hat{\boldsymbol{t}}(\boldsymbol{\theta}) - \tilde{\boldsymbol{t}}(\boldsymbol{\theta})\big)\tilde{\boldsymbol{t}}^\top(\boldsymbol{\theta})\Big)\\ &= E_\theta\big(\hat{\boldsymbol{t}}(\boldsymbol{\theta})\tilde{\boldsymbol{t}}^\top(\boldsymbol{\theta})\big) - \mathfrak{I}^{-1}(\boldsymbol{\theta}).\end{aligned} \tag{8.66}$$

Using the information matrix equality, the result (8.38) can be written as

$$n^{1/2}(\tilde{\boldsymbol{\theta}} - \boldsymbol{\theta}_0) \overset{a}{=} \big(\mathfrak{I}(\boldsymbol{\theta})\big)^{-1}\big(n^{-1/2}\boldsymbol{g}(\boldsymbol{\theta})\big).$$

In the notation of (8.59) and (8.60), this becomes

$$\tilde{\boldsymbol{t}}(\boldsymbol{\theta}) = \mathfrak{I}^{-1}(\boldsymbol{\theta})\boldsymbol{s}(\boldsymbol{\theta}).$$

Thus, continuing from the last line of (8.66), we have

$$\begin{aligned}\operatorname{Cov}_\theta\big(\boldsymbol{v}, \tilde{\boldsymbol{t}}(\boldsymbol{\theta})\big) &= E_\theta\big(\hat{\boldsymbol{t}}(\boldsymbol{\theta})\boldsymbol{s}^\top(\boldsymbol{\theta})\mathfrak{I}^{-1}(\boldsymbol{\theta})\big) - \mathfrak{I}^{-1}(\boldsymbol{\theta})\\ &= E_\theta\big(\hat{\boldsymbol{t}}(\boldsymbol{\theta})\boldsymbol{s}^\top(\boldsymbol{\theta})\big)\mathfrak{I}^{-1}(\boldsymbol{\theta}) - \mathfrak{I}^{-1}(\boldsymbol{\theta})\\ &= \mathfrak{I}^{-1}(\boldsymbol{\theta}) - \mathfrak{I}^{-1}(\boldsymbol{\theta}) = \mathbf{0}.\end{aligned}$$

The fundamental result (8.61) has been used to obtain the last line here.

Thus we conclude that

$$\hat{\boldsymbol{t}}(\boldsymbol{\theta}) = \tilde{\boldsymbol{t}}(\boldsymbol{\theta}) + \boldsymbol{v}, \tag{8.67}$$

with $\boldsymbol{v}$ being asymptotically uncorrelated with $\tilde{\boldsymbol{t}}$. If $\hat{\boldsymbol{t}}$ is asymptotically normal along with $\tilde{\boldsymbol{t}}$, this asymptotic zero correlation further implies asymptotic independence. Another way to write the result (8.67) is

$$\hat{\boldsymbol{\theta}} \stackrel{a}{=} \tilde{\boldsymbol{\theta}} + n^{-1/2}\boldsymbol{v}^n.$$

This makes it clear that an inefficient but consistent estimator $\hat{\boldsymbol{\theta}}$ can always be decomposed, asymptotically, into the sum of the asymptotically efficient ML estimator $\tilde{\boldsymbol{\theta}}$ and another random variable, which tends to zero as $n \to \infty$ and is asymptotically uncorrelated with the efficient estimator. Evidently, the full range of asymptotically normal consistent estimators can be generated from the ML estimator $\tilde{\boldsymbol{\theta}}$ by adding to it multivariate normal zero-mean random variables independent of $\tilde{\boldsymbol{\theta}}$. These can be thought of as noise contaminating the efficient signal given by $\tilde{\boldsymbol{\theta}}$. The interpretation of the Cramér-Rao result is quite obvious now: Since the variance of the sum of two independent random variables is the sum of their respective variances, the positive semidefinite matrix which is the difference between the covariance matrices of $\hat{\boldsymbol{\theta}}$ and $\tilde{\boldsymbol{\theta}}$ is just the (possibly degenerate) covariance matrix of the vector of noise variables $n^{-1/2}\boldsymbol{v}$.

These results for ML estimators are similar to, but much stronger than, the results we obtained for nonlinear least squares in Section 5.5. There we saw that any consistent but inefficient estimator which is asymptotically linear in the error terms can be written as the sum of the efficient estimator plus a random variable (or vector) which is asymptotically uncorrelated with the efficient estimator. The proof of the Gauss-Markov Theorem also involved a similar result.

8.9 The Three Classical Test Statistics

One of the attractive features of ML estimation is that test statistics based on the three principles we first discussed in Chapter 3 — the likelihood ratio, Lagrange multiplier, and Wald principles — are always available and are often easy to compute. These three principles of hypothesis testing were first enunciated in the context of ML estimation, and many authors still use the terms "likelihood ratio," "Lagrange multiplier," and "Wald" only in the context of tests based on ML estimates. In this section, we provide an introduction to what are often referred to as the **three classical tests**. All three of these test statistics have the same distribution asymptotically under the null hypothesis; if there are r equality restrictions, they are distributed as $\chi^2(r)$. In fact, they actually tend to the same random variable asymptotically, both under the null and under all sequences of DGPs that are close to the null in a certain sense. An adequate treatment of these important results requires more space than we have available in this section. We will therefore defer it until Chapter 13, which provides a much more detailed discussion of the three classical test statistics.

Conceptually the simplest of the three classical tests is the **likelihood ratio**, or **LR**, test. The test statistic is simply twice the difference between the restricted and unrestricted values of the loglikelihood function,

$$2\big(\ell(\hat{\boldsymbol{\theta}}) - \ell(\tilde{\boldsymbol{\theta}})\big), \tag{8.68}$$

where $\hat{\boldsymbol{\theta}}$ denotes the unrestricted ML estimate of $\boldsymbol{\theta}$, $\tilde{\boldsymbol{\theta}}$ denotes the ML estimate subject to r distinct restrictions, and the dependence of ℓ on $\boldsymbol{y}$ has been suppressed for notational simplicity. The LR statistic gets its name from the fact that (8.68) is equal to

$$2\log\left(\frac{L(\hat{\boldsymbol{\theta}})}{L(\tilde{\boldsymbol{\theta}})}\right),$$

or twice the logarithm of the ratio of the likelihood functions. It is trivially easy to compute when both restricted and unrestricted estimates are available, and that is one of its attractive features.

To derive the asymptotic distribution of the LR statistic one begins by taking a second-order Taylor-series approximation to $\ell(\tilde{\boldsymbol{\theta}})$ around $\hat{\boldsymbol{\theta}}$. Although we will not complete the derivation in this section, it is illuminating to go through the first few steps. The result of the Taylor-series approximation is

$$\ell(\tilde{\boldsymbol{\theta}}) \cong \ell(\hat{\boldsymbol{\theta}}) + \tfrac{1}{2}(\tilde{\boldsymbol{\theta}} - \hat{\boldsymbol{\theta}})^{\top}\boldsymbol{H}(\hat{\boldsymbol{\theta}})(\tilde{\boldsymbol{\theta}} - \hat{\boldsymbol{\theta}}). \tag{8.69}$$

There is no first-order term here because $\boldsymbol{g}(\hat{\boldsymbol{\theta}}) = \mathbf{0}$ by the first-order conditions (8.12). Rearranging (8.69) yields

$$\begin{aligned} 2\big(\ell(\hat{\boldsymbol{\theta}}) - \ell(\tilde{\boldsymbol{\theta}})\big) &\cong -(\tilde{\boldsymbol{\theta}} - \hat{\boldsymbol{\theta}})^{\top}\boldsymbol{H}(\hat{\boldsymbol{\theta}})(\tilde{\boldsymbol{\theta}} - \hat{\boldsymbol{\theta}}) \\ &\overset{a}{=} \big(n^{1/2}(\tilde{\boldsymbol{\theta}} - \hat{\boldsymbol{\theta}})\big)^{\top}\mathfrak{I}(\hat{\boldsymbol{\theta}})\big(n^{1/2}(\tilde{\boldsymbol{\theta}} - \hat{\boldsymbol{\theta}})\big). \end{aligned} \tag{8.70}$$

This exercise makes it clear where the factor of 2 in the definition of the LR statistic comes from. The next step would be to replace $n^{1/2}(\tilde{\boldsymbol{\theta}} - \hat{\boldsymbol{\theta}})$ in (8.70) by

$$n^{1/2}(\tilde{\boldsymbol{\theta}} - \boldsymbol{\theta}_0) - n^{1/2}(\hat{\boldsymbol{\theta}} - \boldsymbol{\theta}_0)$$

and then to use the result (8.38), together with an analogous result for restricted estimates that we will obtain shortly, to obtain the asymptotic distribution of the LR statistic. We will do this in Chapter 13.

We now turn our attention to the **Lagrange multiplier**, or **LM**, test. This test statistic actually has two names and two different forms, which turn out to be numerically identical if the same estimate of the information matrix is used to calculate them. One form, originally proposed by Rao (1948), is called the **score form of the LM test**, or simply the **score test**, and is calculated using the gradient or score vector of the unrestricted model evaluated at the restricted estimates. The other form, which gives the test its name, was proposed by Aitchison and Silvey (1958, 1960) and Silvey (1959). This latter form is calculated using the vector of Lagrange multipliers which emerge if one maximizes the likelihood function subject to constraints by means of a Lagrangian. Econometricians generally use the LM test in its score form but nevertheless insist on calling it an LM test, perhaps because Lagrange multipliers are so widely used in economics. References on LM tests in econometrics include Breusch and Pagan (1980) and Engle (1982a, 1984). Buse (1982) provides an intuitive discussion of the relationships among the LR, LM, and Wald tests.

One way to maximize $\ell(\boldsymbol{\theta})$ subject to the exact restrictions

$$\boldsymbol{r}(\boldsymbol{\theta}) = \mathbf{0}, \tag{8.71}$$

where $\boldsymbol{r}(\boldsymbol{\theta})$ is an r-vector with $r \leq k$, is simultaneously to maximize the Lagrangian

$$\ell(\boldsymbol{\theta}) - \boldsymbol{r}^{\top}(\boldsymbol{\theta})\boldsymbol{\lambda}$$

with respect to $\boldsymbol{\theta}$ and minimize it with respect to the r-vector of Lagrange multipliers $\boldsymbol{\lambda}$. The first-order conditions that characterize the solution to this problem are

$$\begin{aligned} \boldsymbol{g}(\tilde{\boldsymbol{\theta}}) - \boldsymbol{R}^{\top}(\tilde{\boldsymbol{\theta}})\tilde{\boldsymbol{\lambda}} &= \mathbf{0} \\ \boldsymbol{r}(\tilde{\boldsymbol{\theta}}) &= \mathbf{0}, \end{aligned} \tag{8.72}$$

where $\boldsymbol{R}(\boldsymbol{\theta})$ is a $r \times k$ matrix with typical element $\partial r_i(\boldsymbol{\theta})/\partial \theta_j$.

We are interested in the distribution of $\tilde{\boldsymbol{\lambda}}$ under the null hypothesis, so we will suppose that the DGP satisfies (8.71) with parameter vector $\boldsymbol{\theta}_0$. The value of the vector of Lagrange multipliers $\boldsymbol{\lambda}$ if $\tilde{\boldsymbol{\theta}}$ were equal to $\boldsymbol{\theta}_0$ would be zero. Thus it seems natural to take a first-order Taylor expansion of the first-order conditions (8.72) around the point $(\boldsymbol{\theta}_0, \mathbf{0})$. This yields

$$\begin{aligned} \boldsymbol{g}(\boldsymbol{\theta}_0) + \boldsymbol{H}(\bar{\boldsymbol{\theta}})(\tilde{\boldsymbol{\theta}} - \boldsymbol{\theta}_0) - \boldsymbol{R}^{\top}(\tilde{\boldsymbol{\theta}})\tilde{\boldsymbol{\lambda}} &= \mathbf{0} \\ -\boldsymbol{R}(\ddot{\boldsymbol{\theta}})(\tilde{\boldsymbol{\theta}} - \boldsymbol{\theta}_0) &= \mathbf{0}, \end{aligned}$$

where $\bar{\boldsymbol{\theta}}$ and $\ddot{\boldsymbol{\theta}}$ denote values of $\boldsymbol{\theta}$ that lie between $\tilde{\boldsymbol{\theta}}$ and $\boldsymbol{\theta}_0$. These equations may be rewritten as

$$\begin{bmatrix} -\boldsymbol{H}(\bar{\boldsymbol{\theta}}) & \boldsymbol{R}^{\top}(\tilde{\boldsymbol{\theta}}) \\ \boldsymbol{R}(\ddot{\boldsymbol{\theta}}) & \mathbf{0} \end{bmatrix} \begin{bmatrix} \tilde{\boldsymbol{\theta}} - \boldsymbol{\theta}_0 \\ \tilde{\boldsymbol{\lambda}} \end{bmatrix} = \begin{bmatrix} \boldsymbol{g}(\boldsymbol{\theta}_0) \\ \mathbf{0} \end{bmatrix}. \tag{8.73}$$

If we multiply $\boldsymbol{H}(\bar{\boldsymbol{\theta}})$ by n^{-1}, $\tilde{\boldsymbol{\theta}} - \boldsymbol{\theta}_0$ by $n^{1/2}$, $\boldsymbol{g}(\boldsymbol{\theta}_0)$ by $n^{-1/2}$, and $\tilde{\boldsymbol{\lambda}}$ by $n^{-1/2}$, we do not change the equality in (8.73), and we render all quantities that appear in it $O(1)$. Readers may wish to verify that these factors of n are indeed the appropriate ones and, in particular, that $\tilde{\boldsymbol{\lambda}}$ must be multiplied by $n^{-1/2}$. Using the fact that $\tilde{\boldsymbol{\theta}}$ and hence $\bar{\boldsymbol{\theta}}$ and $\ddot{\boldsymbol{\theta}}$ are consistent, applying a suitable law of large numbers to $n^{-1}\boldsymbol{H}(\bar{\boldsymbol{\theta}})$, and solving the resulting system of equations, yields

$$\begin{bmatrix} n^{1/2}(\tilde{\boldsymbol{\theta}} - \boldsymbol{\theta}_0) \\ n^{-1/2}\tilde{\boldsymbol{\lambda}} \end{bmatrix} \stackrel{a}{=} \begin{bmatrix} -\mathcal{H}_0 & \boldsymbol{R}_0^{\top} \\ \boldsymbol{R}_0 & \mathbf{0} \end{bmatrix}^{-1} \begin{bmatrix} n^{-1/2}\boldsymbol{g}(\boldsymbol{\theta}_0) \\ \mathbf{0} \end{bmatrix}, \tag{8.74}$$

where $\mathcal{H}_0$ denotes $\mathcal{H}(\boldsymbol{\theta}_0)$ and $\boldsymbol{R}_0$ denotes $\boldsymbol{R}(\boldsymbol{\theta}_0)$.

The system of equations (8.74) is, for the restricted case, the equivalent of equation (8.38) for the unrestricted case. The first thing to notice about it is that the k elements of $n^{1/2}(\tilde{\boldsymbol{\theta}} - \boldsymbol{\theta}_0)$ and the r elements of $n^{-1/2}\tilde{\boldsymbol{\lambda}}$ all depend on the random k–vector $n^{-1/2}\boldsymbol{g}(\boldsymbol{\theta}_0)$. We have already seen that, under standard regularity conditions, the latter is asymptotically normally distributed with mean vector zero and covariance matrix $\mathcal{I}(\boldsymbol{\theta}_0)$. Thus from (8.74) we see that both $n^{1/2}(\tilde{\boldsymbol{\theta}} - \boldsymbol{\theta}_0)$ and $n^{-1/2}\tilde{\boldsymbol{\lambda}}$ must be asymptotically normally distributed. Observe that the $(k + r)$–vector on the left-hand side of (8.74) must have a singular covariance matrix, since its rank cannot exceed k, which is the rank of $\mathcal{I}(\boldsymbol{\theta}_0)$.

By analytically inverting the partitioned matrix and then multiplying the two factors on the right-hand side of (8.74), one readily if somewhat tediously obtains expressions for $n^{1/2}(\tilde{\boldsymbol{\theta}} - \boldsymbol{\theta}_0)$ and $n^{-1/2}\tilde{\boldsymbol{\lambda}}$. These are

$$n^{1/2}(\tilde{\boldsymbol{\theta}} - \boldsymbol{\theta}_0) \stackrel{a}{=} -\mathcal{H}_0^{-1}\big(\mathbf{I} - \boldsymbol{R}_0^{\top}(\boldsymbol{R}_0\mathcal{H}_0^{-1}\boldsymbol{R}_0^{\top})^{-1}\boldsymbol{R}_0\mathcal{H}_0^{-1}\big)\big(n^{-1/2}\boldsymbol{g}(\boldsymbol{\theta}_0)\big)$$

and

$$n^{-1/2}\tilde{\boldsymbol{\lambda}} \stackrel{a}{=} \big(\boldsymbol{R}_0\mathcal{H}_0^{-1}\boldsymbol{R}_0^{\top}\big)^{-1}\boldsymbol{R}_0\mathcal{H}_0^{-1}\big(n^{-1/2}\boldsymbol{g}(\boldsymbol{\theta}_0)\big).$$

From the second of these, the asymptotic normality of $n^{-1/2}\boldsymbol{g}(\boldsymbol{\theta}_0)$, and the information equality, it is easy to see that

$$n^{-1/2}\tilde{\boldsymbol{\lambda}} \stackrel{a}{\sim} N\big(\mathbf{0}, (\boldsymbol{R}_0\mathcal{I}_0^{-1}\boldsymbol{R}_0^{\top})^{-1}\big). \tag{8.75}$$

It is now straightforward to derive the Lagrange multiplier test in its LM form. The test statistic is simply a quadratic form in the r–vector $n^{-1/2}\tilde{\boldsymbol{\lambda}}$:

$$\big(n^{-1/2}\tilde{\boldsymbol{\lambda}}\big)^{\top}\big(\tilde{\boldsymbol{R}}\tilde{\mathcal{I}}^{-1}\tilde{\boldsymbol{R}}^{\top}\big)\big(n^{-1/2}\tilde{\boldsymbol{\lambda}}\big) = \frac{1}{n}\tilde{\boldsymbol{\lambda}}^{\top}\tilde{\boldsymbol{R}}\tilde{\mathcal{I}}^{-1}\tilde{\boldsymbol{R}}^{\top}\tilde{\boldsymbol{\lambda}}. \tag{8.76}$$

Here $\tilde{\mathcal{I}}$ may be any matrix that uses the restricted estimates $\tilde{\boldsymbol{\theta}}$ to estimate $\mathcal{I}(\boldsymbol{\theta}_0)$ consistently. Different variants of the LM statistic will use different estimates of $\mathcal{I}(\boldsymbol{\theta}_0)$. It is obvious from (8.75) that under standard regularity conditions this test statistic will be asymptotically distributed as $\chi^2(r)$ under the null hypothesis.

The LM statistic (8.76) is numerically equal to a test based on the score vector $\boldsymbol{g}(\tilde{\boldsymbol{\theta}})$. By the first set of first-order conditions (8.72), $\boldsymbol{g}(\tilde{\boldsymbol{\theta}}) = \boldsymbol{R}^\top\tilde{\boldsymbol{\lambda}}$. Substituting $\boldsymbol{g}(\tilde{\boldsymbol{\theta}})$ for $\boldsymbol{R}^\top\tilde{\boldsymbol{\lambda}}$ in (8.76) yields the score form of the LM test,

$$\frac{1}{n}\tilde{\boldsymbol{g}}^\top\tilde{\mathfrak{I}}^{-1}\tilde{\boldsymbol{g}}. \tag{8.77}$$

In practice, this score form is often more useful than the LM form because, since restricted estimates are rarely obtained via a Lagrangian, $\tilde{\boldsymbol{g}}$ is generally readily available while $\tilde{\boldsymbol{\lambda}}$ typically is not. However, deriving the test via the Lagrange multipliers is illuminating, because this derivation makes it quite clear why the test has r degrees of freedom.

The third of the three classical tests is the **Wald test**. This test is very easy to derive. It asks whether the vector of restrictions, evaluated at the unrestricted estimates, is close enough to a zero vector for the restrictions to be plausible. In the case of the restrictions (8.71), the Wald test is based on the vector $\boldsymbol{r}(\hat{\boldsymbol{\theta}})$, which should tend to a zero vector asymptotically if the restrictions hold. As we have seen in Sections 8.5 and 8.6,

$$n^{1/2}(\hat{\boldsymbol{\theta}} - \boldsymbol{\theta}_0) \overset{a}{\sim} N\big(\mathbf{0},\, \mathfrak{I}^{-1}(\boldsymbol{\theta}_0)\big).$$

A Taylor-series approximation of $\boldsymbol{r}(\hat{\boldsymbol{\theta}})$ around $\boldsymbol{\theta}_0$ yields $\boldsymbol{r}(\hat{\boldsymbol{\theta}}) \cong \boldsymbol{R}_0(\hat{\boldsymbol{\theta}} - \boldsymbol{\theta}_0)$. Therefore,

$$\boldsymbol{V}\big(n^{1/2}\boldsymbol{r}(\hat{\boldsymbol{\theta}})\big) \overset{a}{=} \boldsymbol{R}_0\,\mathfrak{I}_0^{-1}\boldsymbol{R}_0^\top.$$

It follows that an appropriate test statistic is

$$n\boldsymbol{r}^\top(\hat{\boldsymbol{\theta}})\big(\hat{\boldsymbol{R}}\hat{\mathfrak{I}}^{-1}\hat{\boldsymbol{R}}^\top\big)^{-1}\boldsymbol{r}(\hat{\boldsymbol{\theta}}), \tag{8.78}$$

where $\hat{\mathfrak{I}}$ denotes any consistent estimate of $\mathfrak{I}(\boldsymbol{\theta}_0)$ based on the unrestricted estimates $\hat{\boldsymbol{\theta}}$. Different variants of the Wald test will use different estimates of $\mathfrak{I}(\boldsymbol{\theta}_0)$. It is easy to see that given suitable regularity the test statistic (8.78) will be asymptotically distributed as $\chi^2(r)$ under the null.

The fundamental property of the three classical test statistics is that under the null hypothesis, as $n \to \infty$, they all tend to the same random variable, which is distributed as $\chi^2(r)$. We will prove this result in Chapter 13. The implication is that, in large samples, it does not really matter which of the three tests we use. If both $\hat{\boldsymbol{\theta}}$ and $\tilde{\boldsymbol{\theta}}$ are easy to compute, it is attractive to use the LR test. If $\tilde{\boldsymbol{\theta}}$ is easy to compute but $\hat{\boldsymbol{\theta}}$ is not, as is often the case for tests of model specification, then the LM test becomes attractive. If on the other hand $\hat{\boldsymbol{\theta}}$ is easy to compute but $\tilde{\boldsymbol{\theta}}$ is not, as may be the case when we are interested in nonlinear restrictions on a linear model, then the Wald test becomes attractive. When the sample size is not large, choice among the three tests is complicated by the fact that they may have very different finite-sample properties, which may further differ greatly among the alternative variants of the LM and Wald tests. This makes the choice of tests rather more complicated in practice than asymptotic theory would suggest.

8.10 Nonlinear Regression Models

In this section, we discuss how the method of maximum likelihood may be used to estimate univariate nonlinear regression models. When the error terms are assumed to be normally and independently distributed with constant variance, ML estimation of these models is, at least as regards the estimation of the parameters of the regression function, numerically identical to NLS estimation. The exercise is nevertheless a useful one. First of all, it provides a concrete illustration of how to use the method of maximum likelihood. Secondly, it provides an asymptotic covariance matrix for the estimates of $\boldsymbol{\beta}$ and σ jointly, whereas NLS provides one for the estimates of $\boldsymbol{\beta}$ alone. Finally, by considering some extensions of the normal regression model, we are able to demonstrate the power of ML estimation.

The class of models that we will consider is

$$\boldsymbol{y} = \boldsymbol{x}(\boldsymbol{\beta}) + \boldsymbol{u}, \quad \boldsymbol{u} \sim N(\mathbf{0}, \sigma^2\mathbf{I}), \tag{8.79}$$

where the regression function $\boldsymbol{x}(\boldsymbol{\beta})$ satisfies the conditions for Theorems 5.1 and 5.2, and the data are assumed to have been generated by a special case of (8.79). The parameter vector $\boldsymbol{\beta}$ is assumed to be of length k, which implies that there are $k+1$ parameters to be estimated. The notation "$\boldsymbol{u} \sim N(\mathbf{0}, \sigma^2\mathbf{I})$" means that the vector of error terms $\boldsymbol{u}$ is assumed to be distributed as multivariate normal with mean vector zero and covariance matrix $\sigma^2\mathbf{I}$. Thus the individual error terms u_t are independent, each distributed as $N(0, \sigma^2)$. The density of u_t is

$$f(u_t) = \frac{1}{\sqrt{2\pi}}\frac{1}{\sigma}\exp\left(-\frac{u_t^2}{2\sigma^2}\right).$$

In order to construct the likelihood function, we need the density of y_t rather than the density of u_t. This requires us to use a standard result in statistics which is discussed in Appendix B.

The result in question says that if a random variable x_1 has density $f_1(x_1)$ and another random variable x_2 is related to it by

$$x_1 = h(x_2),$$

where the function $h(\cdot)$ is continuously differentiable and monotonic, then the density of x_2 is given by

$$f_2(x_2) = f_1\big(h(x_2)\big)\left|\frac{\partial h(x_2)}{\partial x_2}\right|.$$

The second factor here is the absolute value of the Jacobian of the transformation. In many cases, as we discuss below, its presence gives rise to **Jacobian terms** in loglikelihood functions. In this case, however, the function that relates u_t to y_t is

$$u_t = y_t - x_t(\boldsymbol{\beta}).$$

The Jacobian factor $|\partial u_t/\partial y_t|$ is therefore equal to unity. Thus we conclude that the density of y_t is

$$\frac{1}{\sqrt{2\pi}}\frac{1}{\sigma}\exp\biggl(-\frac{\bigl(y_t - x_t(\boldsymbol{\beta})\bigr)^2}{2\sigma^2}\biggr). \tag{8.80}$$

The contribution to the loglikelihood function made by the tth observation is the logarithm of (8.80),

$$\ell_t(y_t, \boldsymbol{\beta}, \sigma) = -\tfrac{1}{2}\log(2\pi) - \log(\sigma) - \frac{1}{2\sigma^2}\bigl(y_t - x_t(\boldsymbol{\beta})\bigr)^2.$$

Since all the observations are independent, the loglikelihood function itself is just the sum of the contributions $\ell_t(y_t, \boldsymbol{\beta}, \sigma)$ over all t, or

$$\begin{aligned}\ell(\boldsymbol{y}, \boldsymbol{\beta}, \sigma) &= -\tfrac{n}{2}\log(2\pi) - n\log(\sigma) - \frac{1}{2\sigma^2}\sum_{t=1}^{n}\bigl(y_t - x_t(\boldsymbol{\beta})\bigr)^2 \\ &= -\tfrac{n}{2}\log(2\pi) - n\log(\sigma) - \frac{1}{2\sigma^2}\bigl(\boldsymbol{y} - \boldsymbol{x}(\boldsymbol{\beta})\bigr)^{\top}\bigl(\boldsymbol{y} - \boldsymbol{x}(\boldsymbol{\beta})\bigr).\end{aligned} \tag{8.81}$$

The first step in maximizing $\ell(\boldsymbol{y}, \boldsymbol{\beta}, \sigma)$ is to concentrate it with respect to σ, as discussed in Section 8.7. Differentiating the second line of (8.81) with respect to σ and equating the derivative to zero yields

$$\frac{\partial \ell(\boldsymbol{y}, \boldsymbol{\beta}, \sigma)}{\partial \sigma} = -\frac{n}{\sigma} + \frac{1}{\sigma^3}\bigl(\boldsymbol{y} - \boldsymbol{x}(\boldsymbol{\beta})\bigr)^{\top}\bigl(\boldsymbol{y} - \boldsymbol{x}(\boldsymbol{\beta})\bigr) = 0,$$

and solving this yields the result that

$$\hat{\sigma}(\boldsymbol{\beta}) = \Bigl(\tfrac{1}{n}\bigl(\boldsymbol{y} - \boldsymbol{x}(\boldsymbol{\beta})\bigr)^{\top}\bigl(\boldsymbol{y} - \boldsymbol{x}(\boldsymbol{\beta})\bigr)\Bigr)^{1/2}.$$

Here the notation $\hat{\sigma}(\boldsymbol{\beta})$ signifies that the ML estimate of σ is now a function of $\boldsymbol{\beta}$. Notice that we have divided by n rather than by $n - k$. If we could evaluate $\hat{\sigma}^2(\boldsymbol{\beta})$ at the true value $\boldsymbol{\beta}_0$, we would obtain an unbiased estimate of σ^2. However, we will actually evaluate it at the ML estimate $\hat{\boldsymbol{\beta}}$, which, as we are about to see, is equal to the NLS estimate. Thus, as we saw in Section 3.2, $\hat{\sigma}^2$ must be biased downward as an estimator of σ^2.

Substituting $\hat{\sigma}(\boldsymbol{\beta})$ into the second line of (8.81) yields the concentrated loglikelihood function

$$\begin{aligned}\ell^c(\boldsymbol{y}, \boldsymbol{\beta}) &= -\tfrac{n}{2}\log(2\pi) - \tfrac{n}{2}\log\Bigl(\tfrac{1}{n}\bigl(\boldsymbol{y} - \boldsymbol{x}(\boldsymbol{\beta})\bigr)^{\top}\bigl(\boldsymbol{y} - \boldsymbol{x}(\boldsymbol{\beta})\bigr)\Bigr) - \tfrac{n}{2} \\ &= C - \tfrac{n}{2}\log\Bigl(\bigl(\boldsymbol{y} - \boldsymbol{x}(\boldsymbol{\beta})\bigr)^{\top}\bigl(\boldsymbol{y} - \boldsymbol{x}(\boldsymbol{\beta})\bigr)\Bigr),\end{aligned} \tag{8.82}$$

where C is a constant term. The second term in (8.82) is minus $n/2$ times the logarithm of the sum of squared residuals. Thus we see that *maximizing* the concentrated loglikelihood function is equivalent to *minimizing* $SSR(\boldsymbol{\beta})$. The ML estimates $\hat{\boldsymbol{\beta}}$ will simply be the NLS estimates with which we are already familiar.

The constant term in (8.82) is actually

$$\frac{n}{2}\big(\log(n) - 1 - \log(2\pi)\big).$$

Since this expression does not depend on $\boldsymbol{\beta}$, it can be ignored for every purpose except actually computing the value of $\ell(\boldsymbol{y}, \boldsymbol{\beta}, \sigma)$. Such constants are often ignored completely in theoretical work and are sometimes ignored even by computer programs, as a result of which the values of loglikelihood functions for the same model and data set reported by different computer programs may sometimes differ.

The fact that the ML estimator $\hat{\boldsymbol{\beta}}$ for the class of models (8.79) is simply the NLS estimator has an important implication. As we saw in Section 8.8, ML estimators are asymptotically efficient. NLS will therefore be asymptotically efficient whenever the error terms are normally and independently distributed with constant variance. If the error terms have some other known distribution, however, the ML estimator will in general differ from the NLS one and will be more efficient than it (see below for an extreme example). Thus, although NLS is consistent under quite weak conditions on the distribution of the error terms, as we saw in Section 5.3, and is efficient within the class of asymptotically linear estimators that are applicable under these weak conditions, it coincides with the efficient ML estimator only if the error terms are assumed to be normally distributed. What this means is the following. If the only assumption about the error terms that one is willing to make is that they satisfy the regularity conditions for NLS, then the NLS estimator is asymptotically efficient within the class of consistent and asymptotically linear estimators of the parameters of the regression function. However, if one is prepared to specify the actual distribution of the error terms, then in general the ML estimator will be more efficient, *provided the presumed error specification is correct.* The ML estimator will fail to be more efficient only if the errors are presumed to be normal, since in that case ML and NLS are equivalent.

In Section 8.6, we saw that if $\hat{\boldsymbol{\theta}}$ is a vector of ML estimates, then the vector $n^{1/2}(\hat{\boldsymbol{\theta}} - \boldsymbol{\theta}_0)$ is asymptotically normally distributed with mean vector zero and covariance matrix equal to the inverse of the limiting information matrix $\mathfrak{I}(\boldsymbol{\theta}_0)$. This result means that it is almost always of interest to calculate $\mathfrak{I}(\boldsymbol{\theta})$ for any model which is estimated by maximum likelihood. We have seen that there are in general two ways to do this. One is to find minus the plim of n^{-1} times the Hessian matrix, and the other is to find the plim of n^{-1} times $\boldsymbol{G}^\top(\boldsymbol{\theta})\boldsymbol{G}(\boldsymbol{\theta})$, where $\boldsymbol{G}(\boldsymbol{\theta})$ is the CG matrix. Both these methods will yield the same answer, if it is feasible to calculate $\mathcal{I}(\boldsymbol{\theta})$ at all, although one approach may be easier than the other in any given situation.

For the nonlinear regression model (8.79), the parameter vector $\boldsymbol{\theta}$ is the vector $[\boldsymbol{\beta} \vdots \sigma]$. We now calculate the limiting information matrix $\mathcal{I}(\boldsymbol{\beta}, \sigma)$ for this model using the second method, based on the CG matrix, which requires only first derivatives. It is a good exercise to repeat the derivation using the Hessian, which requires second derivatives, and verify that it yields the same results. The first derivative of $\ell_t(y_t, \boldsymbol{\beta}, \sigma)$ with respect to β_i is

$$\frac{\partial \ell_t}{\partial \beta_i} = \frac{1}{\sigma^2}\big(y_t - x_t(\boldsymbol{\beta})\big)X_{ti}(\boldsymbol{\beta}) = \frac{1}{\sigma^2}e_t(\boldsymbol{\beta})X_{ti}(\boldsymbol{\beta}), \tag{8.83}$$

where $e_t(\boldsymbol{\beta}) \equiv y_t - x_t(\boldsymbol{\beta})$ and, as usual, $X_{ti}(\boldsymbol{\beta}) \equiv \partial x_t(\boldsymbol{\beta})/\partial \beta_i$. The first derivative of $\ell_t(y_t, \boldsymbol{\beta}, \sigma)$ with respect to σ is

$$\frac{\partial \ell_t}{\partial \sigma} = -\frac{1}{\sigma} + \frac{\big(y_t - x_t(\boldsymbol{\beta})\big)^2}{\sigma^3} = -\frac{1}{\sigma} + \frac{e_t^2(\boldsymbol{\beta})}{\sigma^3}. \tag{8.84}$$

Expressions (8.83) and (8.84) are all that we need to calculate the information matrix using the CG matrix. The column of that matrix which corresponds to σ will have typical element (8.84), while the remaining k columns, which correspond to the $\boldsymbol{\beta}_i$'s, will have typical element (8.83).

The element of $\mathcal{I}(\boldsymbol{\beta}, \sigma)$ corresponding to β_i and β_j is

$$\mathcal{I}(\beta_i, \beta_j) = \operatorname*{plim}_{n\to\infty}\left(\frac{1}{n}\sum_{t=1}^{n}\frac{e_t^2(\boldsymbol{\beta})}{\sigma^4}X_{ti}(\boldsymbol{\beta})X_{tj}(\boldsymbol{\beta})\right).$$

Since $e_t^2(\boldsymbol{\beta})$ has expectation σ^2 under the DGP characterized by $(\boldsymbol{\beta}, \sigma)$ and is independent of $\boldsymbol{X}(\boldsymbol{\beta})$, we can replace it by σ^2 here to yield

$$\mathcal{I}(\beta_i, \beta_j) = \operatorname*{plim}_{n\to\infty}\left(\frac{1}{n}\sum_{t=1}^{n}\frac{1}{\sigma^2}X_{ti}(\boldsymbol{\beta})X_{tj}(\boldsymbol{\beta})\right).$$

Thus we see that the whole $(\boldsymbol{\beta}, \boldsymbol{\beta})$ block of the limiting information matrix is

$$\frac{1}{\sigma^2}\operatorname*{plim}_{n\to\infty}\left(\frac{1}{n}\boldsymbol{X}^{\top}(\boldsymbol{\beta})\boldsymbol{X}(\boldsymbol{\beta})\right). \tag{8.85}$$

The element of $\mathcal{I}(\boldsymbol{\beta}, \sigma)$ corresponding to σ is

$$\begin{aligned}\mathcal{I}(\sigma, \sigma) &= \operatorname*{plim}_{n\to\infty}\left(\frac{1}{n}\sum_{t=1}^{n}\left(\frac{1}{\sigma^2} + \frac{e_t^4(\boldsymbol{\beta})}{\sigma^6} - \frac{2e_t^2(\boldsymbol{\beta})}{\sigma^4}\right)\right)\\ &= \frac{1}{n}\left(\frac{n}{\sigma^2} + \frac{3n\sigma^4}{\sigma^6} - \frac{2n\sigma^2}{\sigma^4}\right)\\ &= \frac{2}{\sigma^2}.\end{aligned} \tag{8.86}$$

Here we have used the facts that, under the DGP characterized by $(\boldsymbol{\beta}, \sigma)$, $E\big(e_t^2(\boldsymbol{\beta})\big) = \sigma^2$ and $E\big(e_t^4(\boldsymbol{\beta})\big) = 3\sigma^4$, the latter being a well-known property of the normal distribution (see Section 2.6 and Appendix B).

Finally, the element of $\mathcal{I}(\boldsymbol{\beta}, \sigma)$ corresponding to β_i and σ is

$$\begin{aligned}\mathcal{I}(\beta_i, \sigma) &= \operatorname*{plim}_{n\to\infty}\left(\frac{1}{n}\sum_{t=1}^{n}\left(-\frac{e_t(\boldsymbol{\beta})X_{ti}(\boldsymbol{\beta})}{\sigma^3} + \frac{e_t^3(\boldsymbol{\beta})X_{ti}(\boldsymbol{\beta})}{\sigma^5}\right)\right) \\ &= 0.\end{aligned} \tag{8.87}$$

This equals zero because, under the DGP characterized by $(\boldsymbol{\beta}, \sigma)$, $e_t(\boldsymbol{\beta})$ is independent of $\boldsymbol{X}(\boldsymbol{\beta})$, and the fact that the error terms are normally distributed implies that $E\big(e_t(\boldsymbol{\beta})\big) = E\big(e_t^3(\boldsymbol{\beta})\big) = 0$.

Collecting the results (8.85), (8.86), and (8.87), we conclude that

$$\mathcal{I}(\boldsymbol{\beta}, \sigma) = \frac{1}{\sigma^2}\begin{bmatrix}\operatorname{plim}\big(n^{-1}\boldsymbol{X}^{\top}(\boldsymbol{\beta})\boldsymbol{X}(\boldsymbol{\beta})\big) & \mathbf{0} \\ \mathbf{0}^{\top} & 2\end{bmatrix}. \tag{8.88}$$

Our results on the asymptotic distribution of ML estimators (Sections 8.5 and 8.6) then allow us to conclude that

$$\begin{bmatrix} n^{1/2}(\hat{\boldsymbol{\beta}} - \boldsymbol{\beta}_0) \\ n^{1/2}(\hat{\sigma} - \sigma_0)\end{bmatrix} \overset{a}{\sim} N\left(\mathbf{0}, \begin{bmatrix}\sigma_0^2 \operatorname{plim}\big(n^{-1}\boldsymbol{X}_0^{\top}\boldsymbol{X}_0\big)^{-1} & \mathbf{0} \\ \mathbf{0}^{\top} & \sigma_0^2/2\end{bmatrix}\right), \tag{8.89}$$

where $\boldsymbol{\beta}_0$ and σ_0 denote the values of $\boldsymbol{\beta}$ and σ under the DGP, and $\boldsymbol{X}_0$ denotes $\boldsymbol{X}(\boldsymbol{\beta}_0)$. Because the information matrix (8.88) is block-diagonal between the $(\boldsymbol{\beta}, \boldsymbol{\beta})$ block and the (σ, σ) block (which is a scalar), its inverse is simply the matrix that consists of each block inverted separately. As we will see in Chapter 9, this type of block-diagonality is a very important property of regression models with normal errors.

From (8.89), we see that the asymptotic covariance matrix of $n^{1/2}(\hat{\boldsymbol{\beta}} - \boldsymbol{\beta}_0)$ is the same asymptotic covariance matrix previously derived for the NLS estimates of the parameters of a regression function, which is not surprising since $\hat{\boldsymbol{\beta}}$ is simply a vector of NLS estimates. But here we have derived it as a special case of the general results of Section 8.6 on the asymptotic distribution of ML estimators. The result that the asymptotic variance of $n^{1/2}(\hat{\sigma} - \sigma_0)$ is $\sigma_0^2/2$ is new. As we saw in Chapter 5, the method of nonlinear least squares does not directly yield an estimate of σ, although it is easy to construct several estimates once $\hat{\boldsymbol{\beta}}$ has been obtained. The method of maximum likelihood, when coupled with the assumption of normality, does directly yield an estimate of σ and also a measure of the variability of that estimate. However, the latter is in general valid only under the assumption of normality. Moreover, as we discussed above, the ML estimate $\hat{\sigma}^2 = n^{-1}SSR(\hat{\boldsymbol{\beta}})$ is biased downward, and in practice it may therefore be preferable to use $s^2 = (n-k)^{-1}SSR(\hat{\boldsymbol{\beta}})$.

In the derivation of (8.88) and (8.89), we chose to write the information matrix in terms of $\boldsymbol{\beta}$ and σ. Many authors choose to write it in terms of $\boldsymbol{\beta}$ and σ^2. The result equivalent to (8.89) in this alternative parametrization is

$$\begin{bmatrix} n^{1/2}(\hat{\boldsymbol{\beta}} - \boldsymbol{\beta}_0) \\ n^{1/2}(\hat{\sigma}^2 - \sigma_0^2) \end{bmatrix} \overset{a}{\sim} N\left(\mathbf{0}, \begin{bmatrix} \sigma_0^2 \operatorname{plim}\bigl(n^{-1}\boldsymbol{X}_0^{\top}\boldsymbol{X}_0\bigr)^{-1} & \mathbf{0} \\ \mathbf{0}^{\top} & 2\sigma_0^4 \end{bmatrix}\right). \tag{8.90}$$

This result and (8.89) are both correct. However, in any finite sample, the confidence interval for σ based on (8.89) will be different from the confidence interval based on (8.90). As we will discuss in Chapter 13, the former confidence interval will generally be more accurate, because the distribution of $n^{1/2}(\hat{\sigma} - \sigma_0)$ will be closer to the normal distribution in finite samples than that of $n^{1/2}(\hat{\sigma}^2 - \sigma_0^2)$. It is therefore preferable to parametrize the model in terms of σ rather than σ^2.

In practice, of course, we are interested in $\hat{\boldsymbol{\beta}}$ and $\hat{\sigma}$ rather than in $n^{1/2}(\hat{\boldsymbol{\beta}} - \boldsymbol{\beta}_0)$ and $n^{1/2}(\hat{\sigma} - \sigma_0)$. Thus, instead of using (8.88), we would actually make inferences based on the estimated covariance matrix

$$\hat{\boldsymbol{V}}(\hat{\boldsymbol{\beta}}, \hat{\sigma}) = \begin{bmatrix} \hat{\sigma}^2(\hat{\boldsymbol{X}}^{\top}\hat{\boldsymbol{X}})^{-1} & \mathbf{0} \\ \mathbf{0}^{\top} & \hat{\sigma}^2/2n \end{bmatrix},$$

the upper left $k \times k$ block of which is the usual NLS covariance matrix estimator for $\hat{\boldsymbol{\beta}}$.

In Section 8.1, we considered a simple model, (8.01), that could not be estimated by least squares. If we make the additional assumption that the error terms are normally distributed, this model becomes

$$y_t^{\gamma} = \beta_0 + \beta_1 x_t + u_t, \quad u_t \sim \mathrm{NID}(0, \sigma^2), \tag{8.91}$$

which looks almost like a regression model, except that the dependent variable is subject to a nonlinear transformation.

The loglikelihood function corresponding to (8.91) is

$$\begin{aligned} \ell(\boldsymbol{\beta}, \gamma, \sigma) = &-\tfrac{n}{2}\log(2\pi) - n\log(\sigma) - \frac{1}{2\sigma^2}\sum_{t=1}^{n}\bigl(y_t^{\gamma} - \beta_0 - \beta_1 x_t\bigr)^2 \\ &+ n\log|\gamma| + (\gamma - 1)\sum_{t=1}^{n}\log(y_t). \end{aligned} \tag{8.92}$$

The first three terms are just the loglikelihood function we would get if we treated y_t^{γ} as the dependent variable. The fourth and fifth terms are actually one term, a Jacobian term. This term arises because $\partial u_t/\partial y_t = \gamma y_t^{\gamma-1}$. Hence the contribution to the likelihood function made by observation t must include the Jacobian factor $|\gamma y_t^{\gamma-1}|$, which is the absolute value of $\partial u_t/\partial y_t$. Summing over all t and then taking the logarithm yields the Jacobian term that appears in (8.92).

Concentrating the loglikelihood function with respect to σ yields

$$\begin{aligned}\ell^c(\boldsymbol{\beta}, \gamma) = C - n \log\biggl(\sum_{t=1}^{n}\bigl(y_t^{\gamma} - \beta_0 - \beta_1 x_t\bigr)^2\biggr) \\ + n \log|\gamma| + (\gamma - 1)\sum_{t=1}^{n}\log(y_t).\end{aligned} \tag{8.93}$$

Maximizing this with respect to γ and $\boldsymbol{\beta}$ is straightforward. If a suitable nonlinear optimization program is not available, one can simply do a one-dimensional search over γ, calculating β_0 and β_1 conditional on γ by means of least squares, so as to find the value $\hat{\gamma}$ that maximizes (8.93). Of course, one cannot use the OLS covariance matrix obtained in this way, since it treats $\hat{\gamma}$ as fixed. The information matrix is *not* block-diagonal between $\boldsymbol{\beta}$ and the other parameters of (8.91), so one must calculate and invert the full information matrix to obtain an estimated covariance matrix.

ML estimation works in this case because of the Jacobian term that appears in (8.92) and (8.93). It vanishes when $\gamma = 1$ but plays an extremely important role for all other values of γ. We saw in Section 8.1 that if one applied NLS to (8.01) and all the y_t's were greater than unity, one would end up with an infinitely large and negative estimate of γ. That will not happen if one uses maximum likelihood, because the term $(\gamma - 1)\sum_{t=1}^{n}\log(y_t)$ will tend to minus infinity as $\gamma \rightarrow \infty$ much faster than the logarithm of the sum-of-squares term tends to plus infinity. This example illustrates how useful ML estimation can be for dealing with modified regression models in which the dependent variable is subject to a transformation. We will encounter other problems of this type in Chapter 14.

ML estimation can also be very useful when it is believed that the error terms are nonnormal. As an extreme example, consider the following model:

$$y_t = \boldsymbol{X}_t\boldsymbol{\beta} + \alpha\varepsilon_t, \quad f(\varepsilon_t) = \frac{1}{\pi(1 + \varepsilon_t^2)}, \tag{8.94}$$

where $\boldsymbol{\beta}$ is a k–vector and $\boldsymbol{X}_t$ is the tth row of an $n \times k$ matrix. The density of ε_t here is the Cauchy density (see Section 4.6) and ε_t therefore has no finite moments. The parameter α is simply a scale parameter, *not* the standard error of the error terms; since the Cauchy distribution has no moments, the error terms do not have a standard error.

If we write ε_t as a function of y_t, we find that

$$\varepsilon_t = \frac{y_t - \boldsymbol{X}_t\boldsymbol{\beta}}{\alpha}.$$

Thus the density of y_t is

$$f(y_t) = \frac{1}{\pi\alpha}\left(1 + \frac{(y_t - \boldsymbol{X}_t\boldsymbol{\beta})^2}{\alpha^2}\right)^{-1},$$

the factor $1/\alpha$ being a Jacobian factor. The contribution to the loglikelihood function from the tth observation is thus

$$-\log(\pi) - \log(\alpha) - \log\left(1 + \frac{(y_t - \boldsymbol{X}_t\boldsymbol{\beta})^2}{\alpha^2}\right),$$

and the loglikelihood function itself is

$$\ell(\boldsymbol{\beta}, \alpha) = -n\log(\pi) - n\log(\alpha) - \sum_{t=1}^{n}\log\left(1 + \frac{(y_t - \boldsymbol{X}_t\boldsymbol{\beta})^2}{\alpha^2}\right). \tag{8.95}$$

The first-order conditions for $\hat{\beta}_i$ can be written as

$$-2\hat{\alpha}^{-2}\sum_{t=1}^{n}\left(1 + \frac{(y_t - \boldsymbol{X}_t\hat{\boldsymbol{\beta}})^2}{\hat{\alpha}^2}\right)^{-1}(y_t - \boldsymbol{X}_t\hat{\boldsymbol{\beta}})X_{ti} = 0. \tag{8.96}$$

The equivalent expression for ML estimation with normal errors (i.e., OLS) is

$$-\hat{\sigma}^{-2}\sum_{t=1}^{n}(y_t - \boldsymbol{X}_t\hat{\boldsymbol{\beta}})X_{ti} = 0. \tag{8.97}$$

The difference between the likelihood equations (8.96) and (8.97) is striking. The latter says that an unweighted sum of the residuals times each of the regressors must equal zero. The former says that a *weighted* sum of the same quantities must equal zero, with the weights being inversely related to the size of the residuals. The reason for this is that the Cauchy distribution generates many extreme values. There will thus generally be quite a few very large error terms, and to avoid having them influence the estimates too much, the ML procedure for estimating $\hat{\boldsymbol{\beta}}$ puts much less weight on outliers than OLS does. These ML estimates have all the usual properties of consistency, asymptotic normality, and so on. In contrast, if one simply applied OLS to the model (8.94), the extremely large error terms frequently generated by the Cauchy distribution would ensure that the estimates were not even consistent. The usual consistency theorem for least squares does not apply here because the ε_t's have no finite moments.

Because the likelihood equations (8.96) depend on the residuals, the value of $\hat{\alpha}$ affects the value of $\hat{\boldsymbol{\beta}}$ that solves them. It is thus necessary to solve for $\hat{\boldsymbol{\beta}}$ and $\hat{\alpha}$ jointly. Unfortunately, there are in general multiple solutions to these equations; see Reeds (1985). Thus it may take a great deal of effort to locate the global maximum of the loglikelihood function (8.95).

8.11 CONCLUSION

This chapter has provided an introduction to all the major features of maximum likelihood estimation and specification testing, which we will make use of throughout the remainder of the book. Chapter 9 of Cox and Hinkley (1974) provides a more detailed treatment of many of the topics we have covered. Another useful reference is Rothenberg (1973). In the next two chapters, we will use some of the results of this chapter, along with previous results for NLS and IV estimators, to deal with various topics of interest to econometricians. Chapter 9 deals with the method of generalized nonlinear least squares, which is treated both as an example of ML estimation and as an extension of least squares. Chapter 10 then deals with the very important topic of serial correlation. Chapter 13 will provide a much more detailed treatment of the three classical test statistics than did Section 8.9 and will introduce an artificial regression, comparable to the Gauss-Newton regression, for use with models estimated by ML.

TERMS AND CONCEPTS

asymptotic covariance matrix
asymptotic distribution (of an estimator)
asymptotic efficiency
asymptotic normality
CG matrix
classical test statistics
computability (of an estimator)
concentrated loglikelihood function
consistency of Type 1 and Type 2 estimators
contributions to likelihood function and loglikelihood function
Cramér-Rao bound
estimate vs. estimator
exponential distribution
gradient vector of loglikelihood function (score vector)
Hessian matrix (of loglikelihood function): asymptotic, empirical, and expected average
identification: asymptotic and strongly asymptotic, asymptotic on a noncompact parameter space, global, local
information in observation t
information matrix: asymptotic, empirical and expected average
information matrix equality
invariance (to reparametrization)
Jacobian term
Lagrange multiplier (LM) test
likelihood equations
likelihood function
likelihood ratio test
loglikelihood function
maximum likelihood (ML)
maximum likelihood estimate (MLE): Type 1 and Type 2
maximum likelihood estimator: Type 1 and Type 2
maximum likelihood estimator, properties of: asymptotic efficiency, asymptotic normality, computability, consistency, invariance
outer-product-of-the-gradient (OPG) information matrix estimator
parameter space
parametrization (of a model)
reparametrization
quasi-ML (QML) or pseudo-ML estimator
root-n consistent estimator
score test (score form of LM test)
Wald test

Chapter 9

Maximum Likelihood and Generalized Least Squares

9.1 Introduction

Up to this point, we have assumed that the errors adhering to regression models are independently distributed with constant variance. This is a strong assumption, which is often untenable in practice. In this chapter, we consider estimation techniques that allow it to be relaxed. These are **generalized least squares**, or **GLS**, and **generalized nonlinear least squares**, or **GNLS**, on the one hand, and various applications of the method of maximum likelihood on the other. We treat GLS and ML together because, when ML is applied to regression models with normal errors, the estimators that result are very closely related to GLS estimators.

The plan of the chapter is as follows. First of all, in Section 9.2, we relax the assumption that the error terms are independently distributed with constant variance. ML estimation of regression models without those assumptions turns out to be conceptually straightforward and to be closely related to the method of GNLS. In Section 9.3, we discuss the geometry of GLS and consider an important special case in which OLS and GLS estimates are identical. In Section 9.4, we show how a version of the Gauss-Newton regression may be used with models estimated by GNLS. In Section 9.5, we show how GNLS is related to **feasible GNLS** and discuss a number of fundamental results about both GNLS and feasible GNLS. The relationship between GNLS and ML is then treated in Section 9.6. In Sections 9.7 through 9.9, we consider **multivariate nonlinear regression models**. Although such models may often seem very complicated, primarily because of the notational complexities of allowing for several jointly dependent variables, we show that they are actually quite straightforward to estimate by means of GNLS or ML. Finally, in Section 9.10, we discuss models for dealing with panel data and other data sets that combine time series and cross sections. In this chapter, we do not discuss what is probably the most commonly encountered application of GLS in applied work, namely, the estimation of regression models with serial correlation. The enormous literature on this subject will be the topic of Chapter 10.

9.2 GENERALIZED LEAST SQUARES

In this section, we will consider the class of models

$$\boldsymbol{y} = \boldsymbol{x}(\boldsymbol{\beta}) + \boldsymbol{u}, \quad \boldsymbol{u} \sim N(\boldsymbol{0}, \boldsymbol{\Omega}), \tag{9.01}$$

where $\boldsymbol{\Omega}$, an $n \times n$ positive definite matrix, is the covariance matrix of the vector of error terms $\boldsymbol{u}$. The normality assumption can of course be relaxed, but we retain it for now since we want to use the method of maximum likelihood. In some applications the matrix $\boldsymbol{\Omega}$ may be known. In others it may be known only up to a multiplicative constant, which implies that we can write $\boldsymbol{\Omega} = \sigma^2\boldsymbol{\Delta}$, with $\boldsymbol{\Delta}$ a known $n \times n$ matrix and σ^2 an unknown positive scalar. In most applications, only the structure of $\boldsymbol{\Omega}$ will be known; one might know for example that it arises from a particular pattern of heteroskedasticity or serial correlation and hence depends on a certain number of parameters in a certain way. We will consider all three cases.

The density of the vector $\boldsymbol{u}$ is the multivariate normal density

$$f(\boldsymbol{u}) = (2\pi)^{-n/2}|\boldsymbol{\Omega}|^{-1/2}\exp\Big(-\frac{1}{2}\boldsymbol{u}^{\top}\boldsymbol{\Omega}^{-1}\boldsymbol{u}\Big). \tag{9.02}$$

In order to pass from the density of the vector of error terms $\boldsymbol{u}$ to that of the vector of dependent variables $\boldsymbol{y}$, we must first replace $\boldsymbol{u}$ by $\boldsymbol{y} - \boldsymbol{x}(\boldsymbol{\beta})$ in (9.02) and then multiply by the absolute value of the determinant of the Jacobian matrix associated with the transformation that expresses $\boldsymbol{u}$ in terms of $\boldsymbol{y}$. This use of a Jacobian factor is analogous to what we did in Section 8.10 with scalar random variables: For details, see Appendix B. In this case, the Jacobian matrix is the identity matrix, and so the determinant is unity. Hence the likelihood function is

$$L^n(\boldsymbol{y}, \boldsymbol{\beta}, \boldsymbol{\Omega}) = (2\pi)^{-n/2}|\boldsymbol{\Omega}|^{-1/2}\exp\Big(-\frac{1}{2}\big(\boldsymbol{y} - \boldsymbol{x}(\boldsymbol{\beta})\big)^{\top}\boldsymbol{\Omega}^{-1}\big(\boldsymbol{y} - \boldsymbol{x}(\boldsymbol{\beta})\big)\Big),$$

and the loglikelihood function is

$$\ell^n(\boldsymbol{y}, \boldsymbol{\beta}, \boldsymbol{\Omega}) = -\frac{n}{2}\log(2\pi) - \frac{1}{2}\log|\boldsymbol{\Omega}| - \frac{1}{2}\big(\boldsymbol{y} - \boldsymbol{x}(\boldsymbol{\beta})\big)^{\top}\boldsymbol{\Omega}^{-1}\big(\boldsymbol{y} - \boldsymbol{x}(\boldsymbol{\beta})\big). \tag{9.03}$$

If the matrix $\boldsymbol{\Omega}$ is known, it is clear that this function can be maximized by minimizing the **generalized sum of squared residuals**

$$SSR(\boldsymbol{\beta} \,|\, \boldsymbol{\Omega}) = \big(\boldsymbol{y} - \boldsymbol{x}(\boldsymbol{\beta})\big)^{\top}\boldsymbol{\Omega}^{-1}\big(\boldsymbol{y} - \boldsymbol{x}(\boldsymbol{\beta})\big). \tag{9.04}$$

This minimization problem is the one solved by **generalized nonlinear least squares**, or **GNLS**. Differentiating (9.04) with respect to $\boldsymbol{\beta}$ and setting the result to zero yields k first-order conditions comparable to conditions (2.04):

$$-2\boldsymbol{X}^{\top}(\tilde{\boldsymbol{\beta}})\boldsymbol{\Omega}^{-1}\big(\boldsymbol{y} - \boldsymbol{x}(\tilde{\boldsymbol{\beta}})\big) = \boldsymbol{0}. \tag{9.05}$$

Solving these equations yields $\tilde{\boldsymbol{\beta}}$, which is the vector of both ML and GNLS estimates for this problem. It is straightforward to extend the asymptotic theory of Chapter 5 to show that

$$n^{1/2}(\tilde{\boldsymbol{\beta}} - \boldsymbol{\beta}_0) \overset{a}{\sim} N\Big(\mathbf{0}, \operatorname*{plim}_{n\to\infty}\big(n^{-1}\boldsymbol{X}^{\top}(\boldsymbol{\beta}_0)\boldsymbol{\Omega}^{-1}\boldsymbol{X}(\boldsymbol{\beta}_0)\big)^{-1}\Big), \tag{9.06}$$

where $\boldsymbol{\beta}_0$ is the value of $\boldsymbol{\beta}$ under the DGP. This result implies that we can make inferences about GNLS estimates in essentially the same way that we make inferences about NLS ones.

In the linear case, in which $\boldsymbol{x}(\boldsymbol{\beta}) = \boldsymbol{X\beta}$, the first-order conditions (9.05) become

$$-2\boldsymbol{X}^{\top}\boldsymbol{\Omega}^{-1}\boldsymbol{y} + 2\boldsymbol{X}^{\top}\boldsymbol{\Omega}^{-1}\boldsymbol{X}\tilde{\boldsymbol{\beta}} = \mathbf{0}.$$

These can be solved analytically to yield the standard formula for the **generalized least squares**, or **GLS**, estimator[1]

$$\tilde{\boldsymbol{\beta}} = \big(\boldsymbol{X}^{\top}\boldsymbol{\Omega}^{-1}\boldsymbol{X}\big)^{-1}\boldsymbol{X}^{\top}\boldsymbol{\Omega}^{-1}\boldsymbol{y}. \tag{9.07}$$

In practice, one rarely computes GLS estimates using this formula, however. Suppose that $\boldsymbol{\eta}$ is an $n \times n$ matrix which has the property that

$$\boldsymbol{\eta}^{\top}\boldsymbol{\eta} = \boldsymbol{\Omega}^{-1}. \tag{9.08}$$

There are many different ways to obtain a matrix $\boldsymbol{\eta}$ that satisfies (9.08) (see Appendix A); it is usually but not necessarily chosen to be triangular. Given $\boldsymbol{\eta}$, it is possible to compute GLS estimates by means of the OLS regression

$$\boldsymbol{\eta y} = \boldsymbol{\eta X\beta} + \boldsymbol{\eta u}. \tag{9.09}$$

This regression has errors that are independent and have constant variance of unity, since

$$E\big(\boldsymbol{\eta u u}^{\top}\boldsymbol{\eta}^{\top}\big) = \boldsymbol{\eta\Omega\eta}^{\top} = \boldsymbol{\eta}\big(\boldsymbol{\eta}^{\top}\boldsymbol{\eta}\big)^{-1}\boldsymbol{\eta}^{\top} = \boldsymbol{\eta\eta}^{-1}\big(\boldsymbol{\eta}^{\top}\big)^{-1}\boldsymbol{\eta}^{\top} = \mathbf{I}_n,$$

where $\mathbf{I}_n$ is the identity matrix of order n. The OLS estimate of $\boldsymbol{\beta}$ from regression (9.09) is

$$\tilde{\boldsymbol{\beta}} = \big(\boldsymbol{X}^{\top}\boldsymbol{\eta}^{\top}\boldsymbol{\eta X}\big)^{-1}\boldsymbol{X}^{\top}\boldsymbol{\eta}^{\top}\boldsymbol{\eta y} = \big(\boldsymbol{X}^{\top}\boldsymbol{\Omega}^{-1}\boldsymbol{X}\big)^{-1}\boldsymbol{X}^{\top}\boldsymbol{\Omega}^{-1}\boldsymbol{y},$$

which is the GLS estimate (9.07).

[1] The GLS estimator is occasionally referred to as the **Aitken estimator**, because it was proposed by Aitken (1935).

The case in which $\boldsymbol{\Omega} = \sigma^2 \boldsymbol{\Delta}$, with σ^2 unknown but $\boldsymbol{\Delta}$ known, is almost the same as that in which $\boldsymbol{\Omega}$ is known. The loglikelihood function (9.03) becomes

$$\begin{aligned}\ell^n(\boldsymbol{y}, \boldsymbol{\beta}, \boldsymbol{\Delta}, \sigma) = &- \frac{n}{2}\log(2\pi) - n\log(\sigma) - \frac{1}{2}\log|\boldsymbol{\Delta}| \\ &- \frac{1}{2\sigma^2}\big(\boldsymbol{y} - \boldsymbol{x}(\boldsymbol{\beta})\big)^{\top}\boldsymbol{\Delta}^{-1}\big(\boldsymbol{y} - \boldsymbol{x}(\boldsymbol{\beta})\big).\end{aligned}$$

Concentrating this with respect to σ^2 yields the concentrated loglikelihood function

$$\ell^c(\boldsymbol{y}, \boldsymbol{\beta}, \boldsymbol{\Delta}) = C - \frac{1}{2}\log|\boldsymbol{\Delta}| - \frac{n}{2}\log\Big(\big(\boldsymbol{y} - \boldsymbol{x}(\boldsymbol{\beta})\big)^{\top}\boldsymbol{\Delta}^{-1}\big(\boldsymbol{y} - \boldsymbol{x}(\boldsymbol{\beta})\big)\Big).$$

Evidently, this can be maximized by minimizing the generalized sum of squared residuals

$$SSR(\boldsymbol{\beta} \,|\, \boldsymbol{\Delta}) = \big(\boldsymbol{y} - \boldsymbol{x}(\boldsymbol{\beta})\big)^{\top}\boldsymbol{\Delta}^{-1}\big(\boldsymbol{y} - \boldsymbol{x}(\boldsymbol{\beta})\big),$$

which looks exactly like (9.04) except that $\boldsymbol{\Delta}$ now plays the role of $\boldsymbol{\Omega}$. Thus, for purposes of estimation, it makes no difference whether we know $\boldsymbol{\Omega}$ completely or merely know it up to a multiplicative constant.

We have seen that if the covariance matrix $\boldsymbol{\Omega}$ is known, at least up to a multiplicative constant, it is conceptually straightforward to find GLS or GNLS estimates. However, doing so may not be easy in practice if n is large and $\boldsymbol{\Omega}^{-1}$ or $\boldsymbol{\eta}$ have to be computed numerically. Luckily, when $\boldsymbol{\Omega}$ is known, or the form of $\boldsymbol{\Omega}$ is known, it usually depends on a relatively small number of parameters, and once these have been specified it is often possible to find $\boldsymbol{\Omega}^{-1}$ and $\boldsymbol{\eta}$ analytically. In many such cases, the form of $\boldsymbol{\eta}$ is such that it is very easy to premultiply $\boldsymbol{y}$ and $\boldsymbol{X}$ by it. We will encounter several examples of this when we discuss serial correlation in Chapter 10.

Consider the following simple example, in which the error terms are heteroskedastic but not correlated with one another:

$$E(u_t^2) = \sigma^2 w_t^{\alpha}, \quad E(u_t u_s) = 0 \text{ for } t \neq s, \tag{9.10}$$

where w_t is an observation on an exogenous variable and α is a parameter. This type of specification might well make sense if w_t were a variable related to the scale of the dependent variable, such as firm size if the dependent variable were profits. In this case the matrix $\boldsymbol{\Omega}$ is diagonal, with $\sigma^2 w_t^{\alpha}$ as its tth diagonal element. Thus the matrix $\boldsymbol{\Omega}^{-1}$ is also a diagonal matrix with $\sigma^{-2} w_t^{-\alpha}$ as its tth diagonal element, and $\boldsymbol{\eta}$ is a diagonal matrix with $\sigma^{-1} w_t^{-\alpha/2}$ as its tth diagonal element. The function $\sigma^2 w_t^{\alpha}$ is what is sometimes called a **skedastic function**. In the same way that a regression function determines the conditional mean of a random variable, a skedastic function determines its conditional variance.

In this case, it is particularly easy to see that we do not have to know σ in order to obtain GLS estimates, since the subspace spanned by the columns of $\boldsymbol{\eta X}$ does not change if we multiply $\boldsymbol{\eta}$ by any constant. As long as α is known, we can run the regression

$$\frac{y_t}{w_t^{\alpha/2}} = \sum_{i=1}^{k} \beta_i \frac{X_{ti}}{w_t^{\alpha/2}} + \text{residual.} \tag{9.11}$$

It will yield exactly the same GLS estimates $\tilde{\boldsymbol{\beta}}$ as regression (9.09), which in this case is

$$\frac{y_t}{\sigma w_t^{\alpha/2}} = \sum_{i=1}^{k} \beta_i \frac{X_{ti}}{\sigma w_t^{\alpha/2}} + \text{residual.}$$

We can easily estimate σ from (9.11); the estimate is simply the OLS estimate of the standard error of the regression. This type of GLS procedure, in which the regressand and regressors are simply multiplied by weights that vary across observations, is often called **weighted least squares**. It is appropriate whenever the error terms are heteroskedastic with variances known up to a multiplicative constant and not correlated with one another.

Evidently, there is no conceptual difficulty in estimating models like (9.01) when the covariance matrix $\boldsymbol{\Omega}$ is known and likewise no difficulty proving that those estimates have the same properties as NLS estimates on a correctly specified model. However, estimating $\boldsymbol{\beta}$ becomes a good deal more difficult when $\boldsymbol{\Omega}$ is not known. There are two ways to proceed in this case: feasible GNLS, in which the unknown $\boldsymbol{\Omega}$ is replaced by something that estimates it consistently, and maximum likelihood. We consider these techniques in Sections 9.5 and 9.6, respectively.

9.3 The Geometry of GLS

In this section, we briefly discuss the geometry of generalized least squares. The fitted values from the GLS regression of $\boldsymbol{y}$ on $\boldsymbol{X}$ are

$$\boldsymbol{X}\big(\boldsymbol{X}^{\top}\boldsymbol{\Omega}^{-1}\boldsymbol{X}\big)^{-1}\boldsymbol{X}^{\top}\boldsymbol{\Omega}^{-1}\boldsymbol{y}.$$

Hence the matrix that projects $\boldsymbol{y}$ onto $\mathcal{S}(\boldsymbol{X})$ is in this case

$$\boldsymbol{P}_X^{\Omega} \equiv \boldsymbol{X}\big(\boldsymbol{X}^{\top}\boldsymbol{\Omega}^{-1}\boldsymbol{X}\big)^{-1}\boldsymbol{X}^{\top}\boldsymbol{\Omega}^{-1}. \tag{9.12}$$

The complementary projection matrix is

$$\boldsymbol{M}_X^{\Omega} \equiv \mathbf{I} - \boldsymbol{X}\big(\boldsymbol{X}^{\top}\boldsymbol{\Omega}^{-1}\boldsymbol{X}\big)^{-1}\boldsymbol{X}^{\top}\boldsymbol{\Omega}^{-1}. \tag{9.13}$$

As can easily be verified, these projection matrices are idempotent, just like the more familiar projection matrices $\boldsymbol{P}_X$ and $\boldsymbol{M}_X$ associated with ordinary

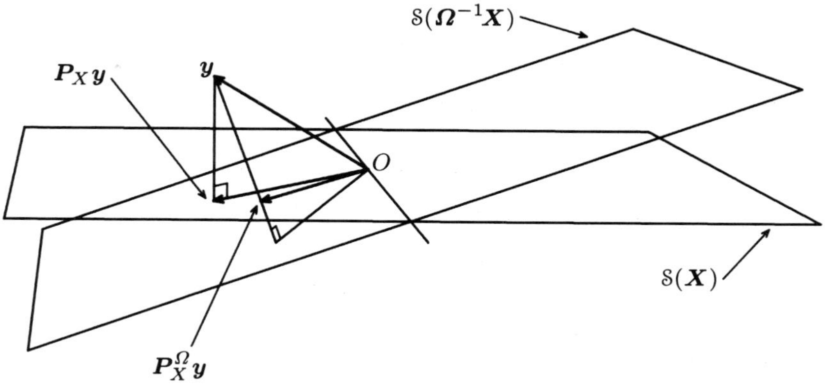

Figure 9.1 Relation between OLS and GLS estimates

least squares. However, as they are not symmetric, $\boldsymbol{P}_X^{\Omega}$ does not project *orthogonally* onto $\mathcal{S}(\boldsymbol{X})$, and $\boldsymbol{M}_X^{\Omega}$ projects onto $\mathcal{S}^{\perp}(\boldsymbol{\Omega}^{-1}\boldsymbol{X})$ rather than $\mathcal{S}^{\perp}(\boldsymbol{X})$. They are examples of what are called **oblique projection matrices**, because the angle between the residuals $\boldsymbol{M}_X^{\Omega}\boldsymbol{y}$ and the fitted values $\boldsymbol{P}_X^{\Omega}\boldsymbol{y}$ is in general not 90°. To see this, observe that

$$\begin{aligned}\boldsymbol{y}^{\top}\boldsymbol{P}_X^{\Omega\top}\boldsymbol{M}_X^{\Omega}\boldsymbol{y} &= \boldsymbol{y}^{\top}\boldsymbol{\Omega}^{-1}\boldsymbol{X}\big(\boldsymbol{X}^{\top}\boldsymbol{\Omega}^{-1}\boldsymbol{X}\big)^{-1}\boldsymbol{X}^{\top}\Big(\mathbf{I}-\boldsymbol{X}\big(\boldsymbol{X}^{\top}\boldsymbol{\Omega}^{-1}\boldsymbol{X}\big)^{-1}\boldsymbol{X}^{\top}\boldsymbol{\Omega}^{-1}\Big)\boldsymbol{y}\\ &= \boldsymbol{y}^{\top}\boldsymbol{\Omega}^{-1}\boldsymbol{X}\big(\boldsymbol{X}^{\top}\boldsymbol{\Omega}^{-1}\boldsymbol{X}\big)^{-1}\boldsymbol{X}^{\top}\boldsymbol{y}\\ &\quad-\boldsymbol{y}^{\top}\boldsymbol{\Omega}^{-1}\boldsymbol{X}\big(\boldsymbol{X}^{\top}\boldsymbol{\Omega}^{-1}\boldsymbol{X}\big)^{-1}\boldsymbol{X}^{\top}\boldsymbol{X}\big(\boldsymbol{X}^{\top}\boldsymbol{\Omega}^{-1}\boldsymbol{X}\big)^{-1}\boldsymbol{X}^{\top}\boldsymbol{\Omega}^{-1}\boldsymbol{y},\end{aligned}$$

which is equal to zero only in certain very special circumstances, such as when $\boldsymbol{\Omega}$ is proportional to $\mathbf{I}_n$. Thus GLS residuals are in general not orthogonal to GLS fitted values.

Figure 9.1 illustrates the distinction between OLS and GLS estimates. For the purposes of having at most a three-dimensional representation, some simplifying assumptions have been made. First, $\boldsymbol{X}$ and $\boldsymbol{\Omega}^{-1}\boldsymbol{X}$ each have only two columns, in order that $\mathcal{S}(\boldsymbol{X})$ and $\mathcal{S}(\boldsymbol{\Omega}^{-1}\boldsymbol{X})$ may be two-dimensional. They are shown in the figure as two intersecting planes, but in general they will intersect only at the origin. Next, $\boldsymbol{y}$ is (of necessity) shown as belonging to the same three-dimensional space as the two planes. In general, this will not be so: Normally, five dimensions would be needed for Figure 9.1 to be a proper representation. Nevertheless, the figure suffices for present purposes.

The OLS fitted values correspond to the vector $\boldsymbol{P}_X\boldsymbol{y}$, the orthogonal projection of $\boldsymbol{y}$ onto the plane $\mathcal{S}(\boldsymbol{X})$. In order to see how the GLS residuals and fitted values can be constructed geometrically, recall from (9.13) that the range of $\boldsymbol{M}_X^{\Omega}$ is the orthogonal complement of $\mathcal{S}(\boldsymbol{\Omega}^{-1}\boldsymbol{X})$. The GLS residuals must therefore lie in $\mathcal{S}^{\perp}(\boldsymbol{\Omega}^{-1}\boldsymbol{X})$. On the other hand, the GLS fitted values must lie in $\mathcal{S}(\boldsymbol{X})$, and so $\boldsymbol{y}$ must be expressed as the sum of two vectors, not mutually orthogonal, one in $\mathcal{S}(\boldsymbol{X})$ and one in $\mathcal{S}^{\perp}(\boldsymbol{\Omega}^{-1}\boldsymbol{X})$. This decomposition of $\boldsymbol{y}$ is shown in the figure, in which we can see directly that the GLS residuals are indeed perpendicular to $\mathcal{S}(\boldsymbol{\Omega}^{-1}\boldsymbol{X})$.

Another point that should be clear from the figure is that the GLS residual vector, being the result of an oblique projection, must necessarily be longer than the OLS residual vector, which is constructed to be as short as possible. On the other hand, the vector $\boldsymbol{P}_X^{\Omega}\boldsymbol{y}$ of GLS fitted values can be either longer or shorter than the vector $\boldsymbol{P}_X\boldsymbol{y}$ of OLS fitted values. In fact, unlike $\boldsymbol{P}_X\boldsymbol{y}$, which is always shorter than $\boldsymbol{y}$, $\boldsymbol{P}_X^{\Omega}\boldsymbol{y}$ may in some circumstances be longer than $\boldsymbol{y}$ itself. Which of these possibilities is realized depends on the covariance matrix $\boldsymbol{\Omega}$. For any given data set there are many different sets of GLS estimates, one for each possible choice of $\boldsymbol{\Omega}$.

We could say a good deal more about the geometry of GLS and the properties of oblique projection matrices; a classic reference is Seber (1980). However, as we saw above, GLS is always equivalent to OLS on a regression in which the regressand and regressors have been suitably transformed. Thus everything that we have already learned about OLS is directly applicable to GLS, once the original model has been transformed as in (9.09). In particular, the Gauss-Markov Theorem applies to models estimated by GLS. If the data are generated by a special case of

$$\boldsymbol{y} = \boldsymbol{X\beta} + \boldsymbol{u}, \quad E(\boldsymbol{u}\boldsymbol{u}^{\top}) = \boldsymbol{\Omega},$$

(note that the normality assumption is not needed here), then the GLS estimator (9.07) is the best linear unbiased estimator. This result follows from the application of the ordinary Gauss-Markov Theorem proved in Section 5.5 to regression (9.09). Similarly, if the DGP is a special case of (9.01) (possibly with $\boldsymbol{\Omega} = \sigma^2\boldsymbol{\Delta}$ where only $\boldsymbol{\Delta}$ is known), then the GNLS estimator will be the best consistent and asymptotically linear estimator.

Before leaving this section, we must discuss the important possibility that GLS and OLS may in certain cases yield identical estimates. Our discussion follows Kruskal (1968), and we will therefore refer to the result as **Kruskal's Theorem**. The result is simple to state: OLS and GLS estimates are the same if and only if the two subspaces $\mathcal{S}(\boldsymbol{X})$ and $\mathcal{S}(\boldsymbol{\Omega}^{-1}\boldsymbol{X})$ are the same. The result is evident from Figure 9.1; just imagine $\mathcal{S}(\boldsymbol{\Omega}^{-1}\boldsymbol{X})$ swiveling into coincidence with $\mathcal{S}(\boldsymbol{X})$. Formally, in order to see that the OLS and GLS estimates must coincide if $\mathcal{S}(\boldsymbol{\Omega}^{-1}\boldsymbol{X})$ and $\mathcal{S}(\boldsymbol{X})$ are the same, it is enough to observe that the OLS decomposition of $\boldsymbol{y}$ into a vector of fitted values and a vector of residuals satisfies the requirements for the (unique) GLS decomposition: $\boldsymbol{P}_X\boldsymbol{y}$ lies in $\mathcal{S}(\boldsymbol{X})$, and $\boldsymbol{M}_X\boldsymbol{y}$ is orthogonal to $\mathcal{S}(\boldsymbol{X})$ and hence also to $\mathcal{S}(\boldsymbol{\Omega}^{-1}\boldsymbol{X})$. If the OLS fitted values $\boldsymbol{X}\hat{\boldsymbol{\beta}}$ and the GLS fitted values $\boldsymbol{X}\tilde{\boldsymbol{\beta}}$ are identical, then if the parameter estimates $\hat{\boldsymbol{\beta}}$ and $\tilde{\boldsymbol{\beta}}$ are unique, they too must be identical.

The converse result, namely, that if OLS and GLS yield the same estimates for any realization of the vector $\boldsymbol{y}$, then $\mathcal{S}(\boldsymbol{X})$ and $\mathcal{S}(\boldsymbol{\Omega}^{-1}\boldsymbol{X})$ must be the same, is also easily seen. Note that one and the same vector of residuals must be orthogonal to both $\mathcal{S}(\boldsymbol{X})$ and $\mathcal{S}(\boldsymbol{\Omega}^{-1}\boldsymbol{X})$ and hence to $\mathcal{S}(\boldsymbol{X}, \boldsymbol{\Omega}^{-1}\boldsymbol{X})$. Since only the k elements of $\boldsymbol{\beta}$ are estimated, the residuals can be orthogonal to a space of at most k dimensions, and so $\mathcal{S}(\boldsymbol{X}, \boldsymbol{\Omega}^{-1}\boldsymbol{X})$ can be at most k-dimensional. But since $\mathcal{S}(\boldsymbol{X})$ and $\mathcal{S}(\boldsymbol{\Omega}^{-1}\boldsymbol{X})$ are both themselves k-dimensional, they must coincide.

Since in some applications it is $\boldsymbol{\Omega}$ and in others $\boldsymbol{\Omega}^{-1}$ that has the simpler form to work with, it can be useful to note that $\mathcal{S}(\boldsymbol{X}) = \mathcal{S}(\boldsymbol{\Omega}^{-1}\boldsymbol{X})$ if and only if $\mathcal{S}(\boldsymbol{X}) = \mathcal{S}(\boldsymbol{\Omega}\boldsymbol{X})$. The reasoning is as follows: $\mathcal{S}(\boldsymbol{X}) \subseteq \mathcal{S}(\boldsymbol{\Omega}^{-1}\boldsymbol{X})$ if and only if for all $\boldsymbol{\beta} \in \mathbb{R}^k$ there exists $\boldsymbol{\lambda} \in \mathbb{R}^k$ such that $\boldsymbol{X\beta} = \boldsymbol{\Omega}^{-1}\boldsymbol{X\lambda}$. But this is equivalent to saying that $\boldsymbol{\Omega X\beta} = \boldsymbol{X\lambda}$, which implies that $\mathcal{S}(\boldsymbol{\Omega X}) \subseteq \mathcal{S}(\boldsymbol{X})$. Running the argument again with $\boldsymbol{X}$ and $\boldsymbol{\Omega}^{-1}\boldsymbol{X}$ interchanged gives the result in full. The situation in which OLS and GLS estimates are identical does not come up very frequently, but we will encounter one important application of Kruskal's Theorem in Section 9.8.

Another way to see why Kruskal's Theorem holds is to notice that the GLS estimator (9.07) can be interpreted as a simple IV estimator with instrument matrix $\boldsymbol{\Omega}^{-1}\boldsymbol{X}$. We know from Section 7.4 that the simple IV estimator is identical to the generalized IV estimator. This implies that

$$\tilde{\boldsymbol{\beta}} = \left(\boldsymbol{X}^\top\boldsymbol{\Omega}^{-1}\boldsymbol{X}\right)^{-1}\boldsymbol{X}^\top\boldsymbol{\Omega}^{-1}\boldsymbol{y} = \left(\boldsymbol{X}^\top\boldsymbol{P}_{\Omega^{-1}X}\boldsymbol{X}\right)^{-1}\boldsymbol{X}^\top\boldsymbol{P}_{\Omega^{-1}X}\boldsymbol{y},$$

where, as usual, $\boldsymbol{P}_{\Omega^{-1}X}$ denotes the projection onto $\mathcal{S}(\boldsymbol{\Omega}^{-1}\boldsymbol{X})$. When $\mathcal{S}(\boldsymbol{\Omega}^{-1}\boldsymbol{X}) = \mathcal{S}(\boldsymbol{X})$, $\boldsymbol{P}_{\Omega^{-1}X} = \boldsymbol{P}_X$. Thus the second expression for $\tilde{\boldsymbol{\beta}}$ here simplifies to the OLS estimator $\hat{\boldsymbol{\beta}}$.

The fact that the GLS estimator looks like an IV estimator is of more theoretical than practical interest, because one would not want to obtain GLS estimates by using an IV package. The parameter estimates would be correct, but the covariance matrix estimate would not be. The correct GLS covariance matrix is proportional to $(\boldsymbol{X}^\top\boldsymbol{\Omega}^{-1}\boldsymbol{X})^{-1}$, but the IV estimate is proportional to $(\boldsymbol{X}^\top\boldsymbol{P}_{\Omega^{-1}X}\boldsymbol{X})^{-1}$.

9.4 THE GAUSS-NEWTON REGRESSION

Associated with the method of GNLS is a version of the Gauss-Newton regression which may be used in all the ways that the original Gauss-Newton regression can be used (see Chapter 6). This GNR is

$$\boldsymbol{\eta}\big(\boldsymbol{y} - \boldsymbol{x}(\boldsymbol{\beta})\big) = \boldsymbol{\eta}\boldsymbol{X}(\boldsymbol{\beta})\boldsymbol{b} + \text{residuals}, \qquad (9.14)$$

where $\boldsymbol{b}$ is a k-vector of coefficients to be estimated and $\boldsymbol{\eta}$ is any $n \times n$ matrix that satisfies equation (9.08). It is not coincidental that regression (9.14) resembles regression (9.09), which was used to compute GLS estimates in the linear case. The GNR is in fact a linearization of the original nonlinear model, with both regressand and regressors transformed so as to make the covariance matrix of the error terms proportional to an identity matrix.

If we evaluate both $\boldsymbol{x}(\boldsymbol{\beta})$ and $\boldsymbol{X}(\boldsymbol{\beta})$ at $\tilde{\boldsymbol{\beta}}$, running regression (9.14) yields $\tilde{\boldsymbol{b}} = \mathbf{0}$ and the estimated covariance matrix

$$\frac{(\boldsymbol{y}-\tilde{\boldsymbol{x}})^{\top}\boldsymbol{\eta}^{\top}\boldsymbol{\eta}(\boldsymbol{y}-\tilde{\boldsymbol{x}})}{n-k}\left(\tilde{\boldsymbol{X}}^{\top}\boldsymbol{\eta}^{\top}\boldsymbol{\eta}\tilde{\boldsymbol{X}}\right)^{-1} = \frac{SSR(\tilde{\boldsymbol{\beta}}\,|\,\boldsymbol{\Omega})}{n-k}\left(\tilde{\boldsymbol{X}}^{\top}\boldsymbol{\Omega}^{-1}\tilde{\boldsymbol{X}}\right)^{-1}. \tag{9.15}$$

The first factor on the right-hand side of (9.15) is just the OLS estimate of the variance of the GNR; as we explain in a moment, it should tend to 1 as $n \to \infty$ if the covariance matrix of $\boldsymbol{u}$ is actually $\boldsymbol{\Omega}$. This first factor would normally be omitted in practice.[2] Comparing the second factor on the right-hand side of (9.15) with the covariance matrix that appears in (9.06), it is evident that the former provides a sensible estimate of the covariance matrix of $\tilde{\boldsymbol{\beta}}$.

In the preceding discussion, we asserted that $(n-k)^{-1}SSR(\tilde{\boldsymbol{\beta}}\,|\,\boldsymbol{\Omega})$ should tend to 1 as $n \to \infty$. In doing so we implicitly made use of the result that

$$\operatorname*{plim}_{n\to\infty}\left(\frac{1}{n}\tilde{\boldsymbol{u}}^{\top}\boldsymbol{\Omega}^{-1}\tilde{\boldsymbol{u}}\right) = 1. \tag{9.16}$$

This result requires justification. First of all, we must assume that the eigenvalues of $\boldsymbol{\Omega}$, which are all strictly positive since $\boldsymbol{\Omega}$ is assumed to be positive definite, are bounded from above and below as $n \to \infty$. These assumptions imply that the eigenvalues of $\boldsymbol{\eta}$ have the same properties. Next, we use the result that

$$\tilde{\boldsymbol{u}} = \boldsymbol{M}_0^{\Omega}\boldsymbol{u} + o(n^{-1/2}). \tag{9.17}$$

Here $\boldsymbol{M}_0^{\Omega}$ is an oblique projection matrix essentially the same as (9.13) but depending on the matrix of derivatives $\boldsymbol{X}_0 \equiv \boldsymbol{X}(\boldsymbol{\beta}_0)$ rather than on a regressor matrix $\boldsymbol{X}$. The result (9.17) is clearly the GNLS analog of the result (5.57) for ordinary NLS, and we will therefore not bother to derive it.

Since the bounded eigenvalue assumption allows us to conclude that

$$\boldsymbol{\eta}\tilde{\boldsymbol{u}} = \boldsymbol{\eta}\boldsymbol{M}_0^{\Omega}\boldsymbol{u} + o(n^{-1/2}),$$

the quantity of which we wish to take the probability limit in (9.16) is

$$\begin{aligned}\frac{1}{n}\tilde{\boldsymbol{u}}^{\top}\boldsymbol{\Omega}^{-1}\tilde{\boldsymbol{u}} &= \frac{1}{n}\Big(\boldsymbol{u}^{\top}(\boldsymbol{M}_0^{\Omega})^{\top}\boldsymbol{\Omega}^{-1}\boldsymbol{M}_0^{\Omega}\boldsymbol{u} + o(n^{1/2})\Big)\\ &= \frac{1}{n}\boldsymbol{u}^{\top}(\boldsymbol{M}_0^{\Omega})^{\top}\boldsymbol{\Omega}^{-1}\boldsymbol{M}_0^{\Omega}\boldsymbol{u} + o(n^{-1/2}).\end{aligned} \tag{9.18}$$

[2] This statement is true only if $\boldsymbol{\Omega}$ is completely known. As we will see below, the GNLS estimator is unchanged if $\boldsymbol{\Omega}$ is known only up to a multiplicative constant, and this is a situation that is commonly encountered in practice. In this case, the first factor in (9.15) would be used to estimate that constant.

The first term in the second line is

$$\begin{aligned}
&\frac{1}{n}\boldsymbol{u}^{\top}(\boldsymbol{M}_0^{\Omega})^{\top}\boldsymbol{\Omega}^{-1}\boldsymbol{M}_0^{\Omega}\boldsymbol{u} \\
&= \frac{1}{n}\boldsymbol{u}^{\top}\boldsymbol{\Omega}^{-1}\boldsymbol{u} - \frac{2}{n}\boldsymbol{u}^{\top}(\boldsymbol{P}_0^{\Omega})^{\top}\boldsymbol{\Omega}^{-1}\boldsymbol{u} + \frac{1}{n}\boldsymbol{u}^{\top}(\boldsymbol{P}_0^{\Omega})^{\top}\boldsymbol{\Omega}^{-1}\boldsymbol{P}_0^{\Omega}\boldsymbol{u} \\
&= \frac{1}{n}\boldsymbol{u}^{\top}\boldsymbol{\Omega}^{-1}\boldsymbol{u} - \frac{1}{n}\boldsymbol{u}^{\top}\boldsymbol{\Omega}^{-1}\boldsymbol{P}_0^{\Omega}\boldsymbol{u},
\end{aligned} \tag{9.19}$$

where

$$\boldsymbol{P}_0^{\Omega} \equiv \mathbf{I} - \boldsymbol{M}_0^{\Omega} \equiv \boldsymbol{X}_0\big(\boldsymbol{X}_0^{\top}\boldsymbol{\Omega}^{-1}\boldsymbol{X}_0\big)^{-1}\boldsymbol{X}_0^{\top}\boldsymbol{\Omega}^{-1}$$

is essentially the same as $\boldsymbol{P}_X^{\Omega}$ defined in (9.12). Only the first term of (9.19) is $O(1)$. Intuitively, the reason for this is that when $\boldsymbol{u}$ is projected onto $\mathcal{S}(\boldsymbol{X}_0)$, the result lies in a k–dimensional space. Thus an expression like the second term of (9.19), which can be written as

$$n^{-1}\big(n^{-1/2}\boldsymbol{u}^{\top}\boldsymbol{\Omega}^{-1}\boldsymbol{X}_0\big)\big(n^{-1}\boldsymbol{X}_0^{\top}\boldsymbol{\Omega}^{-1}\boldsymbol{X}_0\big)^{-1}\big(n^{-1/2}\boldsymbol{X}_0^{\top}\boldsymbol{\Omega}^{-1}\boldsymbol{u}\big),$$

is $O(n^{-1})$, since every factor except the first is $O(1)$.

From (9.18) and (9.19) we conclude that

$$\frac{1}{n}\tilde{\boldsymbol{u}}^{\top}\boldsymbol{\Omega}^{-1}\tilde{\boldsymbol{u}} \overset{a}{=} \frac{1}{n}\boldsymbol{u}^{\top}\boldsymbol{\Omega}^{-1}\boldsymbol{u}. \tag{9.20}$$

The quadratic form on the right-hand side of (9.20) can be expressed very simply by using a matrix $\boldsymbol{\eta}$ that satisfies (9.08). We obtain

$$\frac{1}{n}\boldsymbol{u}^{\top}\boldsymbol{\Omega}^{-1}\boldsymbol{u} = \frac{1}{n}\sum_{t=1}^{n}(\boldsymbol{\eta}\boldsymbol{u})_t^2.$$

The vector $\boldsymbol{\eta}\boldsymbol{u}$ has mean zero and variance matrix equal to $\mathbf{I}_n$. The terms of the sum of the right-hand side of this expression are therefore uncorrelated and asymptotically independent. Thus we may apply a law of large numbers and assert that the probability limit of the sum is unity. It follows that

$$\operatorname*{plim}_{n\to\infty}\Big(\frac{1}{n}\boldsymbol{u}^{\top}\boldsymbol{\Omega}^{-1}\boldsymbol{u}\Big) = 1.$$

From (9.20), we then conclude that this is still true if $\boldsymbol{u}$ is replaced by $\tilde{\boldsymbol{u}}$, which was what we originally set out to show.

This result can be used to test whether $\boldsymbol{\Omega}$ really is the covariance matrix of the error terms. An appropriate test statistic is $\tilde{\boldsymbol{u}}^{\top}\boldsymbol{\Omega}^{-1}\tilde{\boldsymbol{u}}$, which is simply the SSR from the original GNLS regression after transformation. It should be asymptotically distributed as $\chi^2(n-k)$ under the null hypothesis.

9.5 Feasible Generalized Least Squares

In practice, the covariance matrix $\boldsymbol{\Omega}$ is rarely known, but it is often assumed to depend in a particular way on a vector of unknown parameters $\boldsymbol{\alpha}$. In such a case, there are two ways to proceed. One is to obtain a consistent estimate of $\boldsymbol{\alpha}$, say $\check{\boldsymbol{\alpha}}$, by some auxiliary procedure. This then yields an estimate of $\boldsymbol{\Omega}$, $\boldsymbol{\Omega}(\check{\boldsymbol{\alpha}})$, that is used in place of the true covariance matrix $\boldsymbol{\Omega}_0 \equiv \boldsymbol{\Omega}(\boldsymbol{\alpha}_0)$ in what is otherwise a standard GLS procedure. This approach, which will be the topic of this section, is called **feasible GLS** because it is feasible in many cases when ordinary GLS is not. The other approach is to use maximum likelihood to estimate $\boldsymbol{\alpha}$ and $\boldsymbol{\beta}$ jointly, generally under the assumption of normality; it will be discussed in Section 9.6.[3]

Under reasonable conditions, feasible GLS yields estimates that are not only consistent but also asymptotically equivalent to genuine GLS estimates, and therefore share their efficiency properties. However, even when this is the case, the performance in finite samples of feasible GLS may be much inferior to that of genuine GLS if $\check{\boldsymbol{\alpha}}$ is a poor estimator of $\boldsymbol{\alpha}$.

In most cases, the estimates of $\boldsymbol{\alpha}$ that are used by feasible GLS are based on OLS or NLS residuals, of which a typical one is $\hat{u}_t \equiv y_t - x_t(\hat{\boldsymbol{\beta}})$. It is possible to use these residuals for the purposes of estimating $\boldsymbol{\alpha}$ because, in many circumstances, they consistently estimate the error terms u_t, despite being based on an estimation procedure that uses the wrong covariance matrix. It is obvious that *if* the OLS or NLS estimates $\hat{\boldsymbol{\beta}}$ consistently estimate $\boldsymbol{\beta}$, the residuals will consistently estimate the error terms. What is not so obvious (and is not always true) is that $\hat{\boldsymbol{\beta}}$ will consistently estimate $\boldsymbol{\beta}$.

A rigorous treatment of the conditions under which NLS estimates are consistent when the error terms u_t do not satisfy the i.i.d. assumption is beyond the scope of this book. See Gallant (1987) for such a treatment. However, it is worth seeing how the consistency proof of Section 5.3 would be affected if we relaxed that assumption. Recall that the consistency of $\hat{\boldsymbol{\beta}}$ depends entirely on the properties of n^{-1} times the sum-of-squares function:

$$ssr(\boldsymbol{y}, \boldsymbol{\beta}) \equiv \frac{1}{n}\sum_{t=1}^{n}\big(y_t - x_t(\boldsymbol{\beta})\big)^2 = \frac{1}{n}\sum_{t=1}^{n}\big(x_t(\boldsymbol{\beta}_0) - x_t(\boldsymbol{\beta}) + u_t\big)^2. \tag{9.21}$$

The right-most expression here can be rewritten as

$$\frac{1}{n}\sum_{t=1}^{n}\big(x_t(\boldsymbol{\beta}_0) - x_t(\boldsymbol{\beta})\big)^2 + \frac{2}{n}\sum_{t=1}^{n}\big(x_t(\boldsymbol{\beta}_0) - x_t(\boldsymbol{\beta})\big)u_t + \frac{1}{n}\sum_{t=1}^{n}u_t^2. \tag{9.22}$$

[3] All of this assumes that the structure of $\boldsymbol{\Omega}$ is known. When that is not the case, one generally cannot use GNLS or ML. However, as we will see in Chapter 17, it may still be possible to obtain estimates that are more efficient than NLS estimates by using the generalized method of moments.

As we saw in Section 5.3, the three terms in (9.22) must each satisfy a crucial property. The first term must satisfy

$$\underset{n\to\infty}{\text{plim}}\left(\frac{1}{n}\sum_{t=1}^{n}\big(x_t(\boldsymbol{\beta}_0)-x_t(\boldsymbol{\beta})\big)^2\right)>0 \tag{9.23}$$

for all $\boldsymbol{\beta} \neq \boldsymbol{\beta}_0$. This property must hold if the model is to be asymptotically identified, and we will assume that it is. Condition (9.23) evidently depends only on the specification of the regression function and not on whether or not the u_t's are i.i.d., and so it need not concern us further.

The second crucial property is that the second term in (9.22) must tend asymptotically to zero. This property clearly does depend on the properties of the error terms u_t. If they are independent, even if not identically distributed, then the argument of Section 5.3 applies unchanged and shows that this second term has expectation zero. Provided the variances of the u_t's and of the regression functions $x_t(\boldsymbol{\beta})$ are suitably bounded, the martingale law of large numbers, Theorem 4.6, can be applied, and we obtain the desired result. If the u_t's are not independent, however, and if $x_t(\boldsymbol{\beta})$ depends on lagged dependent variables, it is quite likely that the second term in (9.22) will not have mean zero. We evidently have to rule out the dangerous combination of a regression function that depends on lagged dependent variables and error terms that are serially dependent. As a general rule, we also have to rule out u_t's with potentially unbounded variances if we wish to use laws of large numbers.

The third crucial property is that the final term in (9.22) should have a deterministic probability limit. In the i.i.d. case, it simply tends to σ_0^2. If the u_t's are independent but not necessarily identically distributed, this property will hold if the limit of the *average* of the error variances exists. Again, we must in general rule out potentially unbounded variances. But the property may also fail to hold if the u_t's have too much correlation with each other. As an example of this possibility, suppose that the u_t's are identically distributed but **equicorrelated**, which means that the correlation between u_t and u_s is the same for all $t \neq s$. This implies that we can write

$$u_t = \delta v + e_t, \tag{9.24}$$

for some δ, where v and e_t are independent random variables each with variance ω^2. Hence

$$E(u_t^2) = (\delta^2 + 1)\omega^2 \equiv \sigma^2$$

and, for $t \neq s$,

$$E(u_t u_s) = \delta^2\omega^2.$$

It follows that the correlation between u_t and u_s is $\delta^2/(\delta^2+1)$. By varying δ, we can evidently make this correlation any number between 0 and 1 that we choose.

The key feature of this example is property (9.24). Substituting this into the third term of (9.22), we obtain

$$\begin{aligned}\frac{1}{n}\sum_{t=1}^{n} u_t^2 &= \frac{1}{n}\sum_{t=1}^{n}(\delta v + e_t)^2 \\ &= \frac{1}{n}\sum_{t=1}^{n}(\delta^2 v^2 + 2\delta e_t v + e_t^2) \\ &= \delta^2 v^2 + \frac{1}{n}\sum_{t=1}^{n}(2\delta e_t v + e_t^2).\end{aligned}$$

If we work conditionally on v, the second term of the last expression above satisfies the simplest law of large numbers and tends to the deterministic probability limit of ω^2. But the first term, which is independent of the sample size, is a nondegenerate random variable. As a result, n^{-1} times the sum-of-squares function, expression (9.21), will not be asymptotically nonstochastic, and the NLS estimates $\hat{\boldsymbol{\beta}}$ will not be consistent.

We now return to the topic of feasible GLS. If we can rule out the possibility of unbounded variances, too much serial dependence (as in the pathological case just discussed), and the combination of serial correlation and lagged dependent variables, the NLS estimates $\hat{\boldsymbol{\beta}}$ will be consistent and so will be the residuals $\hat{u}_t$. We can then use those residuals to obtain root-n consistent estimates of the parameters $\boldsymbol{\alpha}$. Feasible GLS works whenever we can do so.

As an example, consider (9.10). According to this model, the variance of u_t is $\sigma^2 w_t^{\alpha}$, which depends on the unknown parameters α and σ^2. One way to estimate α is to run the nonlinear regression

$$\hat{u}_t^2 = \sigma^2 w_t^{\alpha} + \text{residual}. \tag{9.25}$$

Provided that $\hat{u}_t^2$ does indeed estimate u_t^2 consistently, it seems highly plausible that the NLS estimate $\check{\alpha}$ from (9.25) will provide a root-n consistent estimate of α. This case is actually an unusually difficult one, since the auxiliary regression to estimate the parameter of the covariance matrix, α, is nonlinear. Another way of estimating α will be discussed in the next section. We will encounter some simpler cases, in which the parameters of the covariance matrix may be estimated by ordinary least squares, in Chapter 10.

We now provide a nonrigorous explanation of why feasible GNLS is asymptotically equivalent to GNLS itself. The first-order conditions for GNLS are

$$-2\boldsymbol{X}^{\top}(\tilde{\boldsymbol{\beta}})\boldsymbol{\Omega}_0^{-1}\big(\boldsymbol{y} - \boldsymbol{x}(\tilde{\boldsymbol{\beta}})\big) = \mathbf{0}. \tag{9.26}$$

The first-order conditions for feasible GNLS are

$$-2\boldsymbol{X}^{\top}(\check{\boldsymbol{\beta}})\check{\boldsymbol{\Omega}}^{-1}\big(\boldsymbol{y} - \boldsymbol{x}(\check{\boldsymbol{\beta}})\big) = \mathbf{0}, \tag{9.27}$$

where $\check{\boldsymbol{\beta}}$ denotes the feasible GNLS estimator and $\check{\boldsymbol{\Omega}} \equiv \boldsymbol{\Omega}(\check{\boldsymbol{\alpha}})$. Evidently, these two sets of first-order conditions look very similar indeed, the only difference being that $\boldsymbol{\Omega}^{-1}$ appears in (9.26) and $\check{\boldsymbol{\Omega}}^{-1}$ appears in (9.27). But since $\check{\boldsymbol{\alpha}}$ is assumed to be root-n consistent, and $\boldsymbol{\Omega}$ is assumed to depend differentiably on $\boldsymbol{\alpha}$, we can write

$$\check{\boldsymbol{\Omega}}^{-1} = \boldsymbol{\Omega}_0^{-1} + \boldsymbol{A}, \quad \boldsymbol{A} = O(n^{-1/2}). \tag{9.28}$$

By this notation, we mean that every element of the matrix $\boldsymbol{A}$ is $O(n^{-1/2})$, which implies that every element of $\check{\boldsymbol{\Omega}}^{-1}$ differs from the corresponding element of $\boldsymbol{\Omega}_0^{-1}$ by an amount that is asymptotically negligible. Hence (9.27) becomes

$$-2\boldsymbol{X}^{\top}(\check{\boldsymbol{\beta}})\boldsymbol{\Omega}_0^{-1}\big(\boldsymbol{y} - \boldsymbol{x}(\check{\boldsymbol{\beta}})\big) - 2\boldsymbol{X}^{\top}(\check{\boldsymbol{\beta}})\boldsymbol{A}\big(\boldsymbol{y} - \boldsymbol{x}(\check{\boldsymbol{\beta}})\big) = \boldsymbol{0}. \tag{9.29}$$

Since $\boldsymbol{\Omega}_0$ is $O(1)$ while $\boldsymbol{A}$ is $O(n^{-1/2})$, the second term here becomes negligible relative to the first term as $n \to \infty$. But the first term is simply the left-hand side of (9.26). Thus, asymptotically, the equations that define the feasible GNLS estimator $\check{\boldsymbol{\beta}}$ are the same as those that define the GNLS estimator $\tilde{\boldsymbol{\beta}}$. Hence the two estimators are asymptotically equivalent.

We stress that the above discussion is not rigorous. We have not shown formally that it is valid to write (9.28) or that the second term on the left-hand side of (9.29) is asymptotically negligible relative to the first. A fully rigorous proof of the asymptotic equivalence of GLS and feasible GLS estimates is quite technical, however, and not very intuitive. See Amemiya (1973a, 1973b) and Carroll and Ruppert (1982), among others.

In practice, the desirability of using feasible GLS as an estimation method depends on how good an estimate of $\boldsymbol{\Omega}$ one can obtain. If $\boldsymbol{\Omega}(\check{\boldsymbol{\alpha}})$ is a very good estimate of $\boldsymbol{\Omega}_0$, then feasible GLS will indeed have essentially the same properties as GLS, and inferences based on the usual GLS covariance matrix

$$\big(\check{\boldsymbol{X}}^{\top}\check{\boldsymbol{\Omega}}^{-1}\check{\boldsymbol{X}}\big)^{-1} \tag{9.30}$$

will be reasonably reliable. However, if $\boldsymbol{\Omega}(\check{\boldsymbol{\alpha}})$ is a poor estimate of $\boldsymbol{\Omega}_0$, feasible GLS estimates may have quite different properties from real GLS estimates and (9.30) may yield very misleading inferences.

9.6 MAXIMUM LIKELIHOOD AND GNLS

A second approach that is widely used in place of feasible GLS when $\boldsymbol{\Omega}$ is assumed to equal $\boldsymbol{\Omega}(\boldsymbol{\alpha})$ with $\boldsymbol{\alpha}$ unknown is the method of maximum likelihood. To use it we must make some assumption about the distribution of the error terms (in practice, almost always an assumption of normality). This allows us to write down the appropriate loglikelihood function as a function of the q-vector $\boldsymbol{\alpha}$ and the k-vector $\boldsymbol{\beta}$.

Consider the class of models

$$\boldsymbol{y} = \boldsymbol{x}(\boldsymbol{\beta}) + \boldsymbol{u}, \quad \boldsymbol{u} \sim N\big(\boldsymbol{0}, \boldsymbol{\Omega}(\boldsymbol{\alpha})\big). \tag{9.31}$$

By modifying the loglikelihood function (9.03) slightly, we find that the loglikelihood function corresponding to (9.31) is

$$\begin{aligned} \ell^n(\boldsymbol{y}, \boldsymbol{\beta}, \boldsymbol{\alpha}) = & -\tfrac{n}{2}\log(2\pi) - \tfrac{1}{2}\log|\boldsymbol{\Omega}(\boldsymbol{\alpha})| \\ & -\tfrac{1}{2}\big(\boldsymbol{y} - \boldsymbol{x}(\boldsymbol{\beta})\big)^{\top}\boldsymbol{\Omega}^{-1}(\boldsymbol{\alpha})\big(\boldsymbol{y} - \boldsymbol{x}(\boldsymbol{\beta})\big). \end{aligned} \tag{9.32}$$

There will be two sets of first-order conditions, one for $\boldsymbol{\alpha}$ and one for $\boldsymbol{\beta}$. The latter will be similar to the first-order conditions (9.05) for GNLS:

$$-2\boldsymbol{X}^{\top}(\hat{\boldsymbol{\beta}})\,\boldsymbol{\Omega}^{-1}(\hat{\boldsymbol{\alpha}})\big(\boldsymbol{y} - \boldsymbol{x}(\hat{\boldsymbol{\beta}})\big) = \boldsymbol{0}.$$

The former will be rather complicated and will depend on precisely how $\boldsymbol{\Omega}$ is related to $\boldsymbol{\alpha}$. For a more detailed treatment, see Magnus (1978).

In Section 8.10, we saw that the information matrix for $\boldsymbol{\beta}$ and σ in a nonlinear regression model with covariance matrix $\sigma^2\mathbf{I}$ is block-diagonal between $\boldsymbol{\beta}$ and σ. An analogous result turns out to be true for the model (9.31) as well: The information matrix is block-diagonal between $\boldsymbol{\beta}$ and $\boldsymbol{\alpha}$. This means that, asymptotically, the vectors $n^{1/2}(\hat{\boldsymbol{\beta}} - \boldsymbol{\beta}_0)$ and $n^{1/2}(\hat{\boldsymbol{\alpha}} - \boldsymbol{\alpha}_0)$ are independent. Thus the fact that $\hat{\boldsymbol{\alpha}}$ is estimated jointly with $\hat{\boldsymbol{\beta}}$ can be ignored, and $\hat{\boldsymbol{\beta}}$ will have the same properties asymptotically as the GNLS estimator $\tilde{\boldsymbol{\beta}}$ and the feasible GNLS estimator $\check{\boldsymbol{\beta}}$.

The above argument does not require that the error terms u_t actually be normally distributed. All that we require is that the vectors $n^{1/2}(\hat{\boldsymbol{\beta}} - \boldsymbol{\beta}_0)$ and $n^{1/2}(\hat{\boldsymbol{\alpha}} - \boldsymbol{\alpha}_0)$ be asymptotically independent and $O(1)$ under whatever DGP actually generated the data. It can be shown that this is in fact the case under fairly general conditions, similar to the conditions detailed in Chapter 5 for least squares to be consistent and asymptotically normal; see White (1982) and Gouriéroux, Monfort, and Trognon (1984) for fundamental results in this area. As we saw in Section 8.1, when the method of maximum likelihood is applied to a data set for which the DGP was not in fact a special case of the model being estimated, the resulting estimator is called a quasi-ML, or QML, estimator. In practice, of course, almost all the ML estimators we use are actually QML estimators, since some of the assumptions of our models are almost always wrong. It is therefore comforting that in certain common situations, including this one, the properties of QML estimators are very similar to those of genuine ML estimators, although asymptotic efficiency is of course lost.

As a concrete example of GLS, feasible GLS, and ML estimation, consider the model

$$\boldsymbol{y} = \boldsymbol{x}(\boldsymbol{\beta}) + \boldsymbol{u}, \;\; \boldsymbol{u} \sim N(\boldsymbol{0}, \boldsymbol{\Omega}), \;\; \Omega_{tt} = \sigma^2 w_t^{\alpha}, \;\; \Omega_{ts} = 0 \text{ for all } t \neq s. \tag{9.33}$$

This model has heteroskedasticity of the form (9.10). Since the determinant of $\boldsymbol{\Omega}$ is

$$\sigma^{2n}\prod_{t=1}^{n} w_t^{\alpha},$$

we see from (9.32) that the loglikelihood function is

$$\begin{aligned}\ell^n(\boldsymbol{y},\boldsymbol{\beta},\alpha,\sigma) = &-\tfrac{n}{2}\log(2\pi) - n\log\sigma - \tfrac{\alpha}{2}\sum_{t=1}^{n}\log(w_t)\\ &-\sum_{t=1}^{n}\frac{\big(y_t - x_t(\boldsymbol{\beta})\big)^2}{2\sigma^2 w_t^{\alpha}}.\end{aligned} \tag{9.34}$$

If α were known, we could obtain GNLS estimates by estimating the weighted nonlinear regression

$$\frac{y_t}{w_t^{\alpha/2}} = \frac{x_t(\boldsymbol{\beta})}{w_t^{\alpha/2}} + \frac{u_t}{w_t^{\alpha/2}}, \tag{9.35}$$

whether or not we knew σ. The weighted NLS estimates from (9.35) would be the GNLS estimates $\tilde{\boldsymbol{\beta}}$. The Gauss-Newton regression corresponding to (9.35) would be

$$\frac{1}{w_t^{\alpha/2}}\big(y_t - x_t(\boldsymbol{\beta})\big) = \frac{1}{w_t^{\alpha/2}}\boldsymbol{X}_t(\boldsymbol{\beta})\boldsymbol{b} + \text{residual},$$

which is a special case of (9.14).

If α were not known, we would have to use either feasible GNLS or ML. The difficulty with the former is obtaining a consistent estimate of α without too much effort. The first step is to perform a nonlinear regression of $\boldsymbol{y}$ on $\boldsymbol{x}(\boldsymbol{\beta})$, ignoring the heteroskedasticity of the error terms, so as to obtain a set of least squares residuals $\check{\boldsymbol{u}}$ (we use $\check{\boldsymbol{u}}$ rather than the more natural $\hat{\boldsymbol{u}}$ because, in this section, the latter would denote an ML estimate). We can then use those residuals to estimate α. In the previous section we suggested using nonlinear least squares on equation (9.25) to do this. That is one approach, but not necessarily the best one. The model (9.33) implies that

$$u_t^2 = \sigma^2 w_t^{\alpha}\varepsilon_t^2, \tag{9.36}$$

where ε_t is $N(0,1)$. This specification of the skedastic function does not lend itself naturally to the use of least squares. In fact, the most attractive way to estimate α is to pretend that $\check{u}_t$ is actually u_t and to estimate α from (9.36) by maximum likelihood. If we replace $y_t - x_t(\boldsymbol{\beta})$ in (9.34) by $\check{u}_t$, we obtain

$$\ell^n(\boldsymbol{y},\alpha,\sigma) = -\tfrac{n}{2}\log(2\pi) - n\log(\sigma) - \tfrac{\alpha}{2}\sum_{t=1}^{n}\log(w_t) - \sum_{t=1}^{n}\frac{\check{u}_t^2}{2\sigma^2 w_t^{\alpha}}. \tag{9.37}$$

This is the loglikelihood function for α and σ conditional on $\boldsymbol{\beta}$ being equal to the vector of NLS estimates $\check{\boldsymbol{\beta}}$. The first-order condition for σ^2 is

$$-\frac{n}{2\sigma^2} + \sum_{t=1}^{n} \frac{2w_t^{\alpha}\check{u}_t^2}{4\sigma^4 w_t^{2\alpha}} = 0,$$

and solving it yields

$$\check{\sigma}^2 = \frac{1}{n}\sum_{t=1}^{n} \frac{\check{u}_t^2}{w_t^{\alpha}}.$$

Substituting $\check{\sigma}^2$ into (9.37) then yields the concentrated loglikelihood function

$$\ell^c(\boldsymbol{y}, \alpha) = C - \frac{n}{2}\log\left(\frac{1}{n}\sum_{t=1}^{n}\frac{\check{u}_t^2}{w_t^{\alpha}}\right) - \frac{\alpha}{2}\sum_{t=1}^{n}\log(w_t). \qquad (9.38)$$

This can be maximized by a one-dimensional search over α.

Notice that as α becomes larger, the second and third terms in $\ell^c(\boldsymbol{y}, \alpha)$ will change in opposite directions. The second term is a sum-of-squares term, while the third term is a Jacobian term. For concreteness, suppose that $w_t > 1$ for all t. Then as α becomes larger, the second term will become larger (since each $\check{u}_t^2$ will be divided by a larger number, and the sum of squared weighted residuals will consequently decline), but the third term will become smaller (since $\sum\log(w_t)$, which will be positive, will be multiplied by a larger negative number). Moreover, one can show that when α is sufficiently close to zero, the rise in the second term must be greater than the decline in the third term and that when α is sufficiently large, the opposite must be true. Thus there must be a finite, positive value $\check{\alpha}$ that maximizes (9.38). This value would then be used in the nonlinear regression (9.35) to obtain feasible GNLS estimates $\check{\boldsymbol{\beta}}$.

To obtain ML estimates $(\hat{\alpha}, \hat{\boldsymbol{\beta}})$ we must maximize (9.34). Concentrating it with respect to σ^2 yields the concentrated loglikelihood function

$$\ell^c(\boldsymbol{y}, \boldsymbol{\beta}, \alpha) = C - \frac{n}{2}\log\left(\frac{1}{n}\sum_{t=1}^{n}\frac{\big(y_t - x_t(\boldsymbol{\beta})\big)^2}{w_t^{\alpha}}\right) - \frac{\alpha}{2}\sum_{t=1}^{n}\log(w_t). \qquad (9.39)$$

This can be maximized with respect to α and $\boldsymbol{\beta}$ jointly, using a general algorithm for numerical optimization.[4] It can also be maximized by using a combination of one-dimensional search over α and k-dimensional search over $\boldsymbol{\beta}$

[4] Most general numerical optimization algorithms work in essentially the same way as the algorithms for nonlinear least squares discussed in Section 6.8. The major difference is that the Gauss-Newton regression cannot be used to determine the direction in which to search at each major iteration. For maximizing loglikelihood functions, other artificial regressions, to be discussed in Chapters 13, 14, and 15, may be used instead, although by no means all effective algorithms use artificial regressions for this purpose. See Cramer (1986).

conditional on α. The former approach is probably the most attractive one if $\boldsymbol{x}(\boldsymbol{\beta})$ is nonlinear, but the latter may be attractive if $\boldsymbol{x}(\boldsymbol{\beta}) = \boldsymbol{X\beta}$, since estimating $\boldsymbol{\beta}$ conditional on α will then require only a single OLS regression. In the latter case, we can effectively concentrate out $\boldsymbol{\beta}$ and reduce (9.39) to a function of α alone.

All of the above discussion has assumed that there is no functional relationship between the parameters $\boldsymbol{\beta}$ of the regression function and the parameters $\boldsymbol{\alpha}$ which determine $\boldsymbol{\Omega}(\boldsymbol{\alpha})$, and this is usually a reasonable assumption. One can certainly write down models in which there is such a relationship, however. One example is the model

$$y_t = \beta_0 + \beta_1\big(x_t^{\beta_2} z_t^{\beta_3}\big) + u_t, \quad u_t \sim N\big(0, \sigma^2 x_t^{\beta_2} z_t^{\beta_3}\big).$$

Here the parameters β_2 and β_3 appear both in the regression function and in the skedastic function. Thus it is impossible for the information matrix to be block-diagonal between the parameters of the former and those of the latter. In a case like this, maximum likelihood can easily be used to estimate all parameters efficiently, while techniques like feasible GNLS that attempt to estimate the parameters of the regression function conditional on those of the skedastic function cannot do so.

9.7 INTRODUCTION TO MULTIVARIATE REGRESSION MODELS

Up to this point in the book, although we have sometimes formally allowed for the possibility that the dependent variable in the models we have dealt with may be a vector rather than a scalar, we have not actually discussed any models in which this is the case. Now that we are familiar with generalized least squares and with the use of maximum likelihood to estimate regression models, we are ready to discuss the **multivariate nonlinear regression model**

$$y_{ti} = \xi_{ti}(\boldsymbol{\beta}) + u_{ti}, \quad t = 1, \ldots, n; \; i = 1, \ldots, m. \tag{9.40}$$

Here y_{ti} is the tth observation on the ith dependent variable, $\xi_{ti}(\boldsymbol{\beta})$ is the tth observation on the regression function which determines the conditional mean of that dependent variable, $\boldsymbol{\beta}$ is a k–vector of parameters to be estimated, and u_{ti} is an error term with mean zero and other properties that we will discuss shortly.

Multivariate regression models arise in many circumstances. As a simple example, suppose that there are observations on a dependent variable for, say, five countries over 120 quarters (which implies that $m = 5$ and $n = 120$). Each country might have a different regression function determining the conditional mean of the dependent variable. If the same parameters appeared in more than one of the regression functions, the system would be said to be subject to **cross-equation restrictions**. In the presence of such restrictions, it is obvious that one would want to estimate all five equations as a system rather than individually, in order to obtain efficient estimates. Even in the absence of cross-equation restrictions, it seems very likely that the unobserved features of the economic environments of the different countries would be related at each point in time. Therefore, in all likelihood, u_{ti} would be correlated with u_{tj} for $i \neq j$. In this situation, the system of equations forms what Zellner (1962) dubbed a set of **seemingly unrelated regressions**, or an **SUR system** for short. Actually, it might seem more logical to refer to them as "seemingly related regressions," but it is too late to change the terminology at this point. As Zellner showed, estimating a set of seemingly unrelated regressions jointly as a system will, except in certain special cases to be discussed below, yield more efficient estimates than estimating each of them separately, even when there are no cross-equation restrictions. Thus we would normally want to treat an SUR system as a multivariate model.

There are many situations in which economic theory suggests the use of a multivariate regression model. One very widely used class of models is the class of **demand systems**, in which the shares of consumer expenditure on various classes of goods and services are related to total expenditure and to relative prices. The literature on demand systems is vast; see, among many others, Barten (1964, 1969, 1977), Brown and Heien (1972), Christensen, Jorgenson, and Lau (1975), Deaton (1974, 1978), Deaton and Muellbauer (1980), Parks (1969), Pollak and Wales (1969, 1978, 1981, 1987), Prais and Houthakker (1955), and Stone (1954). Demand systems may be estimated using either aggregate time-series data (generally annual but sometimes quarterly) or, less frequently, cross-section data or mixed time-series/cross-section data on households.

In many cases (although this is less true of the more recent literature), the functional forms for demand systems are obtained simply by maximizing a utility function of some known form subject to a budget constraint. As an example, suppose that the utility function is

$$\sum_{i=1}^{m+1} \alpha_i \log(q_i - \gamma_i), \tag{9.41}$$

where there are $m + 1$ commodities, q_i is the quantity of commodity i consumed, and α_i and γ_i are parameters. Why we have assumed that there are $m + 1$ commodities will be apparent shortly. The α_i's are subject to the normalization restriction that $\sum_{i=1}^{m+1} \alpha_i = 1$.

The utility function (9.41) is known as the **Stone-Geary utility function**. Maximizing it subject to the budget constraint

$$\sum_{i=1}^{m+1} q_i p_i = E,$$

where p_i is the price of commodity i and E is total expenditure on all the commodities, yields the demand system:

$$s_i(E, \boldsymbol{p}, \boldsymbol{\alpha}, \boldsymbol{\gamma}) = \frac{\gamma_i p_i}{E} + \alpha_i \left(\frac{E - \sum_{j=1}^{m+1}(p_j \gamma_j)}{E} \right),$$

where $s_i(E, \boldsymbol{p}, \boldsymbol{\alpha}, \boldsymbol{\gamma})$ denotes the share of expenditure that is predicted to be spent on commodity i, conditional on total expenditure E, the price vector $\boldsymbol{p}$ and the parameter vectors $\boldsymbol{\alpha}$ and $\boldsymbol{\gamma}$. This particular demand system is known as the **linear expenditure system**; it has a long history dating back to Stone (1954). Notice that although α_i appears only in the ith share equation, γ_i appears in all $m+1$ share equations, and there are consequently a great many cross-equation restrictions.

By definition, the shares spent on all the commodities must add to one. This has an important implication for the error terms, which we have not yet specified. Suppose we make the assumption that

$$s_{ti} = s_i(E_t, \boldsymbol{p}_t, \boldsymbol{\alpha}, \boldsymbol{\gamma}) + u_{ti},$$

where s_{ti} is the observed share of expenditure on commodity i for observation t, and u_{ti} is an error term. Then

$$\sum_{i=1}^{m+1} s_{ti} = \sum_{i=1}^{m+1} s_i(E_t, \boldsymbol{p}_t, \boldsymbol{\alpha}, \boldsymbol{\gamma}) + \sum_{i=1}^{m+1} u_{ti}.$$

Summing both sides of this equation over i, we find that $1 = 1 + \sum_{i=1}^{m+1} u_{ti}$, which implies that

$$\sum_{i=1}^{m+1} u_{ti} = 0. \tag{9.42}$$

Thus the error terms for every observation must sum to zero over all the expenditure shares. As Barten (1968) showed, this does not create a problem for estimation; we simply have to drop any one share equation and estimate the system for the remaining m shares. Moreover, if we use maximum likelihood, it does not matter which equation we drop; the estimates of $\boldsymbol{\alpha}$ and $\boldsymbol{\gamma}$ that we obtain will be identical (recall that the α_i's are normalized to sum to unity; that is why we can get away with not estimating one of them).

Although (9.42) does not raise serious problems for estimation, it does make it absolutely clear that the error terms u_{ti} and u_{tj} must in general be correlated with each other. Strictly speaking, we should not assume that the u_{ti}'s are normally distributed, because $0 \le s_{ti} \le 1$, which implies that the u_{ti}'s must be bounded from above and below; see Wales and Woodland (1983). However, provided that the sample does not contain observations which are, relative to the standard errors of the u_{ti}'s, near 0 or 1, it is probably not unreasonable, as an approximation, to assume normality, and that is what almost all authors have done. Thus, if $\boldsymbol{U}_t$ denotes a row vector with typical element u_{ti}, we might specify the distribution of the $\boldsymbol{U}_t$'s to be $N(\mathbf{0}, \boldsymbol{\Sigma})$, where $\boldsymbol{\Sigma}$ is an $(m+1) \times (m+1)$ singular covariance matrix. Then

$$\boldsymbol{U}_t^* \sim N(\mathbf{0}, \boldsymbol{\Sigma}^*),$$

where $\boldsymbol{U}_t^*$ is $\boldsymbol{U}_t$ minus one element, say the last, and $\boldsymbol{\Sigma}^*$ is then an $m \times m$ submatrix of $\boldsymbol{\Sigma}$. Because $\boldsymbol{\Sigma}$ is a singular matrix, equation systems for which the error terms sum to zero over all equations are frequently referred to as **singular equation systems**; see Berndt and Savin (1975). There are many examples of singular equation systems in addition to demand systems. These include systems of factor shares, as in Berndt and Christensen (1974) and Fuss (1977), and systems of asset-allocation equations, as in Aigner (1973).

We now return to multivariate models in general. The biggest difficulty with such models is notation. Since $\xi_{ti}(\boldsymbol{\beta})$ already has two indices, its first and second derivatives with respect to the elements of $\boldsymbol{\beta}$ must have three and four indices, respectively. This makes it difficult to deal with multivariate models using conventional matrix notation, which is not really designed to handle quantities with more than two indices. Different authors handle this problem in different ways. At one extreme, following the practice in modern physics, Davidson and MacKinnon (1983b) advocate using the "Einstein summation convention," a notation that largely avoids the use of matrices by treating everything as scalar expressions involving (typically) several summations over indices. This approach has many advantages. Unfortunately, although it has been used by some influential econometricians, for example Sargan (1980b) and Phillips (1982), its use is not widespread in econometrics, and it would probably look strange to most readers of this book. At the other extreme, some authors make extensive use of Kronecker products ($\otimes$), vec operators, vech operators, and so on, so as to use matrix notation exclusively; see Magnus and Neudecker (1988). Like Malinvaud (1970a), we will attempt to steer a middle course, using primarily a mixture of scalar and matrix notation which, we hope, will be both easy to understand and reasonably easy to manipulate.

While we are on the subject of notation, note that the model (9.40) could be rewritten in either of the following ways:

$$\boldsymbol{Y}_t = \boldsymbol{\xi}_t(\boldsymbol{\beta}) + \boldsymbol{U}_t, \tag{9.43}$$

where $\boldsymbol{Y}_t$, $\boldsymbol{\xi}_t(\boldsymbol{\beta})$, and $\boldsymbol{U}_t$ are $1 \times m$ vectors with typical elements y_{ti}, $\xi_{ti}(\boldsymbol{\beta})$, and u_{ti}, respectively, or

$$\boldsymbol{Y} = \boldsymbol{\xi}(\boldsymbol{\beta}) + \boldsymbol{U}, \tag{9.44}$$

where $\boldsymbol{Y}$, $\boldsymbol{\xi}(\boldsymbol{\beta})$, and $\boldsymbol{U}$ are $n \times m$ matrices with $\boldsymbol{Y}_t$, $\boldsymbol{\xi}_t(\boldsymbol{\beta})$, and $\boldsymbol{U}_t$ as typical rows. The approach based on summation conventions would start from (9.40), while the approach based on Kronecker products would start from (9.44), using the vec operator to stack the columns of $\boldsymbol{Y}$, $\boldsymbol{\xi}(\boldsymbol{\beta})$, and $\boldsymbol{U}$. Our approach will start from (9.43).

9.8 GLS ESTIMATION OF MULTIVARIATE REGRESSION MODELS

In practice, multivariate regression models are usually estimated either by feasible GLS or by maximum likelihood, assuming normality. Except in very rare circumstances, it makes no sense to assume that u_{ti} is independent of u_{tj} for $i \neq j$, as we have already seen in the case of both seemingly unrelated regressions and demand systems. Depending on whether we intend to use ML or feasible GNLS, we may or may not want to assume that the vector of error terms $\boldsymbol{U}_t$ is normally distributed. We will in either case make the assumption that

$$\boldsymbol{U}_t \sim \mathrm{IID}(\mathbf{0}, \boldsymbol{\Sigma}),$$

where $\boldsymbol{\Sigma}$ is a (usually unknown) $m \times m$ covariance matrix, sometimes referred to as the **contemporaneous covariance matrix**. Thus we are assuming that u_{ti} is correlated with u_{tj} but not with u_{sj} for $s \neq t$. This is of course a strong assumption, which should be tested; we will discuss one test that may sometimes be appropriate below. Under these assumptions, the generalized sum of squared residuals for the model (9.43) is

$$\sum_{t=1}^{n} \big(\boldsymbol{Y}_t - \boldsymbol{\xi}_t(\boldsymbol{\beta})\big)\boldsymbol{\Sigma}^{-1}\big(\boldsymbol{Y}_t - \boldsymbol{\xi}_t(\boldsymbol{\beta})\big)^{\top}. \tag{9.45}$$

Let us suppose initially that $\boldsymbol{\Sigma}$ is known. Then $\boldsymbol{\Sigma}$ may be used to transform the multivariate model (9.40) into a univariate one. Suppose that $\boldsymbol{\psi}$ is an $m \times m$ matrix (usually triangular) such that

$$\boldsymbol{\psi}\boldsymbol{\psi}^{\top} = \boldsymbol{\Sigma}^{-1}. \tag{9.46}$$

If we postmultiply each term in (9.43) by $\boldsymbol{\psi}$, we obtain the regression

$$\boldsymbol{Y}_t\boldsymbol{\psi} = \boldsymbol{\xi}_t(\boldsymbol{\beta})\boldsymbol{\psi} + \boldsymbol{U}_t\boldsymbol{\psi}. \tag{9.47}$$

The $1 \times m$ error vector $\boldsymbol{U}_t\boldsymbol{\psi}$ has covariance matrix

$$E\big(\boldsymbol{\psi}^{\top}\boldsymbol{U}_t^{\top}\boldsymbol{U}_t\boldsymbol{\psi}\big) = \boldsymbol{\psi}^{\top}\boldsymbol{\Sigma}\boldsymbol{\psi} = \mathbf{I}_m. \tag{9.48}$$

As written, (9.47) has only one observation, and all terms are $1 \times m$ vectors. In order to run this regression, we must somehow convert these $1 \times m$ vectors into $nm \times 1$ vectors for all observations together. There is more than one way to do this.

One approach is simply to transpose each $1 \times m$ vector of (9.47) and then stack the m–vectors so created. However, that is not the easiest way to proceed. An easier approach is first to form m sets of n–vectors, as follows. For the dependent variable, the tth component of the ith vector would be $\boldsymbol{Y}_t\boldsymbol{\psi}_i$, where $\boldsymbol{\psi}_i$ is the ith column of $\boldsymbol{\psi}$, and for the regression functions the corresponding component would be $\boldsymbol{\xi}_t(\boldsymbol{\beta})\boldsymbol{\psi}_i$. Then nm–vectors would be obtained by stacking these n–vectors. The *univariate* nonlinear regression so defined can be expressed in terms of partitioned matrices as

$$\begin{bmatrix} \boldsymbol{Y\psi}_1 \\ \vdots \\ \boldsymbol{Y\psi}_m \end{bmatrix} = \begin{bmatrix} \boldsymbol{\xi}(\boldsymbol{\beta})\boldsymbol{\psi}_1 \\ \vdots \\ \boldsymbol{\xi}(\boldsymbol{\beta})\boldsymbol{\psi}_m \end{bmatrix} + \begin{bmatrix} \boldsymbol{U\psi}_1 \\ \vdots \\ \boldsymbol{U\psi}_m \end{bmatrix}. \tag{9.49}$$

Recall from (9.44) that $\boldsymbol{Y}$, $\boldsymbol{\xi}(\boldsymbol{\beta})$, and $\boldsymbol{U}$ are all $n \times m$ matrices. This stacked univariate regression will have covariance matrix $\mathbf{I}_{mn}$, from (9.48) and because we have assumed that there is no noncontemporaneous correlation of the error terms. Even if $\boldsymbol{\psi}$ were known only up to a multiplicative constant, this univariate regression could be estimated by nonlinear least squares, just like any univariate nonlinear regression. Using the notation of (9.47), its sum of squared residuals would be

$$\begin{aligned} &\sum_{t=1}^{n} \big(\boldsymbol{Y}_t\boldsymbol{\psi} - \boldsymbol{\xi}_t(\boldsymbol{\beta})\boldsymbol{\psi}\big)\big(\boldsymbol{Y}_t\boldsymbol{\psi} - \boldsymbol{\xi}_t(\boldsymbol{\beta})\boldsymbol{\psi}\big)^{\top} \\ &= \sum_{t=1}^{n} \big(\boldsymbol{Y}_t - \boldsymbol{\xi}_t(\boldsymbol{\beta})\big)\boldsymbol{\psi}\boldsymbol{\psi}^{\top}\big(\boldsymbol{Y}_t - \boldsymbol{\xi}_t(\boldsymbol{\beta})\big)^{\top} \\ &= \sum_{t=1}^{n} \big(\boldsymbol{Y}_t - \boldsymbol{\xi}_t(\boldsymbol{\beta})\big)\boldsymbol{\Sigma}^{-1}\big(\boldsymbol{Y}_t - \boldsymbol{\xi}_t(\boldsymbol{\beta})\big)^{\top}. \end{aligned}$$

Thus we see that running the univariate nonlinear regression (9.47) or (9.49) will yield exactly the same GNLS estimates as minimizing the generalized sum of squared residuals (9.45).

Normally, the contemporaneous covariance matrix $\boldsymbol{\Sigma}$ will not be known and hence neither will be $\boldsymbol{\psi}$. However, it is often not hard to obtain a consistent estimate of $\boldsymbol{\Sigma}$, say $\check{\boldsymbol{\Sigma}}$. Provided that each individual equation, for $i = 1, \ldots, m$, is identified (possibly an unrealistic assumption in the case of some nonlinear multivariate models such as demand systems), one can estimate each equation by OLS or NLS so as to obtain the $n \times m$ matrix of residuals $\check{\boldsymbol{U}}$. Then it is easy to see that, under reasonably weak conditions,

$$\check{\boldsymbol{\Sigma}} \equiv n^{-1}\check{\boldsymbol{U}}^{\top}\check{\boldsymbol{U}} \tag{9.50}$$

will provide a consistent estimate of $\boldsymbol{\Sigma}$. Given $\check{\boldsymbol{\Sigma}}$, one can easily compute $\check{\boldsymbol{\psi}}$ using (9.46). Then NLS estimation of (9.47), with $\check{\boldsymbol{\psi}}$ replacing $\boldsymbol{\psi}$, will yield feasible GNLS estimates which, as usual, are asymptotically equivalent to ordinary GNLS estimates. This is the procedure advocated by Zellner (1962) in the SUR case.

The first-order conditions for the minimization of the generalized sum of squared residuals (9.45) can be written in several different ways. The basic reason for this is that the derivative of $\xi_{ti}(\boldsymbol{\beta})$ with respect to β_j, the jth

element of $\boldsymbol{\beta}$, necessarily involves three subscripts. One approach is to define $\boldsymbol{\Xi}_t(\boldsymbol{\beta})$ as a $k \times m$ matrix with typical element

$$\Xi_{t,ji}(\boldsymbol{\beta}) \equiv \frac{\partial \xi_{ti}(\boldsymbol{\beta})}{\partial \beta_j}.$$

The first-order conditions can then be written as

$$\sum_{t=1}^{n} \boldsymbol{\Xi}_t(\tilde{\boldsymbol{\beta}})\boldsymbol{\Sigma}^{-1}\big(\boldsymbol{Y}_t - \boldsymbol{\xi}_t(\tilde{\boldsymbol{\beta}})\big)^{\top} = \mathbf{0}. \tag{9.51}$$

A second approach is to define $\boldsymbol{y}_i$ as the ith column of $\boldsymbol{Y}$ and $\boldsymbol{x}_i(\boldsymbol{\beta})$ as the vector of regression functions for the ith equation of the system, that is, an n–vector with typical component $\xi_{ti}(\boldsymbol{\beta})$. Then if one arranges the derivatives of $\boldsymbol{x}_i(\boldsymbol{\beta})$ with respect to $\boldsymbol{\beta}$ into an $n \times k$ matrix $\boldsymbol{Z}_i(\boldsymbol{\beta})$ with typical element

$$(\boldsymbol{Z}_i)_{tj}(\boldsymbol{\beta}) \equiv \frac{\partial \xi_{ti}(\boldsymbol{\beta})}{\partial \beta_j} \tag{9.52}$$

and lets the ij^{th} element of $\boldsymbol{\Sigma}^{-1}$ be denoted by σ^{ij}, a little algebra shows that (9.51) becomes

$$\sum_{i=1}^{m}\sum_{j=1}^{m} \sigma^{ij}\boldsymbol{Z}_i^{\top}(\boldsymbol{\beta})\big(\boldsymbol{y}_j - \boldsymbol{x}_j(\boldsymbol{\beta})\big) = \mathbf{0}. \tag{9.53}$$

A case of special interest arises when there are no cross-equation restrictions in the system. The full parameter vector can then be partitioned as $\boldsymbol{\beta} = [\boldsymbol{\beta}_1 \vdots \ldots \vdots \boldsymbol{\beta}_m]$, where the components of the k_i–vector $\boldsymbol{\beta}_i$ are the parameters that appear only in the ith equation. We require, of course, that $\sum_{i=1}^{m} k_i = k$. The matrices $\boldsymbol{Z}_i$ can be seen to contain many zero elements in this case, because ξ_{ti} depends only on the components of $\boldsymbol{\beta}_i$. It is convenient to define $n \times k_i$ matrices $\bar{\boldsymbol{Z}}_i$ without the zero elements; the typical element will be $(\bar{\boldsymbol{Z}}_i)_{tj} \equiv \partial \xi_{ti}/\partial(\boldsymbol{\beta}_i)_j$ for $j = 1, \ldots, k_i$. This makes it possible to break up the first-order conditions (9.53) equation by equation, so as to obtain

$$\sum_{j=1}^{m} \sigma^{ij}\bar{\boldsymbol{Z}}_i^{\top}(\boldsymbol{\beta}_i)\big(\boldsymbol{y}_j - \boldsymbol{x}_j(\boldsymbol{\beta}_j)\big) = \mathbf{0}, \quad i = 1, \ldots, m. \tag{9.54}$$

It is clear from (9.54) that if $\boldsymbol{\Sigma}$ is proportional to an identity matrix, the first-order conditions collapse to those of equation-by-equation NLS when there are no cross-equation restrictions. This implies that there can be no gain from performing a system estimation unless the contemporaneous correlations of the error terms are different from zero. In the context of feasible GNLS, it is extremely improbable that the estimated error covariance matrix $\check{\boldsymbol{\Sigma}}$ of

(9.50) will be proportional to an identity matrix even if the true $\boldsymbol{\Sigma}$ is. In that case, the system estimates and the equation-by-equation estimates will be numerically, but not asymptotically, different. If $\boldsymbol{\Sigma}$ is proportional to an identity matrix, so also will be $\boldsymbol{\psi}$. Then the stacked system (9.49) becomes

$$\begin{bmatrix} \boldsymbol{y}_1 \\ \vdots \\ \boldsymbol{y}_m \end{bmatrix} = \begin{bmatrix} \boldsymbol{x}_1(\boldsymbol{\beta}_1) \\ \vdots \\ \boldsymbol{x}_m(\boldsymbol{\beta}_m) \end{bmatrix} + \begin{bmatrix} \boldsymbol{u}_1 \\ \vdots \\ \boldsymbol{u}_m \end{bmatrix}, \tag{9.55}$$

where the n–vector $\boldsymbol{u}_i$ is the vector of error terms associated with the ith equation. If the stacked system (9.55) were estimated by NLS, the sum of squared residuals would be just

$$\sum_{i=1}^{m} \big(\boldsymbol{y}_i - \boldsymbol{x}_i(\boldsymbol{\beta}_i)\big)^{\top}\big(\boldsymbol{y}_i - \boldsymbol{x}_i(\boldsymbol{\beta}_i)\big).$$

Since the components of each $\boldsymbol{\beta}_i$ appear in only one term of the sum over i, this sum is minimized by minimizing each term separately with respect to the parameters on which it depends. Thus NLS estimation of (9.55) is just equation-by-equation NLS.

In the special case of a linear system with no cross-equation restrictions, the first-order conditions (9.53) can be used directly in order to obtain GLS or feasible GLS estimates of the parameter vector $\boldsymbol{\beta}$. This uses the fact that, as we saw in Section 9.3, any GLS estimator can be interpreted as a simple IV estimator for a suitable choice of instruments. In this case, the stacked regression functions for the system can be written as

$$\boldsymbol{X\beta} \equiv \begin{bmatrix} \boldsymbol{X}_1 & \cdots & \mathbf{0} \\ \vdots & \ddots & \vdots \\ \mathbf{0} & \cdots & \boldsymbol{X}_m \end{bmatrix} \begin{bmatrix} \boldsymbol{\beta}_1 \\ \vdots \\ \boldsymbol{\beta}_m \end{bmatrix}.$$

Here $\boldsymbol{X}_i$ denotes the $n \times k_i$ matrix of regressors appearing in the ith equation of the system. In terms of the notation of (9.54), we have $\boldsymbol{X}_i = \bar{\boldsymbol{Z}}_i(\boldsymbol{\beta}_i)$, where $\boldsymbol{X}_i$ does not depend on $\boldsymbol{\beta}_i$ because the system is linear. If we suppose that the contemporaneous covariance matrix $\boldsymbol{\Sigma}$ is known, we can form the $nm \times k$ matrix $\boldsymbol{W}$ as

$$\boldsymbol{W} = \begin{bmatrix} \sigma^{11}\boldsymbol{X}_1 & \cdots & \sigma^{1m}\boldsymbol{X}_m \\ \vdots & \ddots & \vdots \\ \sigma^{m1}\boldsymbol{X}_1 & \cdots & \sigma^{mm}\boldsymbol{X}_m \end{bmatrix}. \tag{9.56}$$

Thus $\boldsymbol{W}$ is a partitioned matrix with typical block the $n \times k_j$ matrix $\sigma^{ij}\boldsymbol{X}_j$. If $\boldsymbol{\Sigma}$ is not known, but can be estimated, then $\boldsymbol{\Sigma}$ should be replaced in (9.56) by $\check{\boldsymbol{\Sigma}}$.

It is easy to see that the GLS estimator is the same as the simple IV estimator

$$\tilde{\boldsymbol{\beta}} \equiv \begin{bmatrix} \tilde{\boldsymbol{\beta}}_1 \\ \vdots \\ \tilde{\boldsymbol{\beta}}_m \end{bmatrix} = \left(\boldsymbol{W}^\top \boldsymbol{X}\right)^{-1} \boldsymbol{W}^\top \boldsymbol{y},$$

where $\boldsymbol{y} \equiv [\boldsymbol{y}_1 \vdots \dots \vdots \boldsymbol{y}_m]$. This estimator, although given explicitly by the above formula, can be defined by means of the first-order conditions

$$\boldsymbol{W}^\top \boldsymbol{X} \tilde{\boldsymbol{\beta}} = \boldsymbol{W}^\top \boldsymbol{y}.$$

If one writes these conditions out in detail, using the definitions of $\boldsymbol{X}$ and $\boldsymbol{W}$, it can be seen that they are identical to (9.54). Thus, for linear SURs with no cross-equation restrictions, the GLS parameter estimates can be obtained by employing an IV procedure to estimate the stacked univariate regression $\boldsymbol{y} = \boldsymbol{X\beta} + \boldsymbol{u}$, in which the matrix $\boldsymbol{W}$ defined in (9.56) is used as the instrument matrix. Of course, as we remarked earlier, the estimated covariance matrix will be incorrect.

We saw above that there is no asymptotic gain in efficiency obtainable from the estimation of a set of SURs as a system over equation-by-equation estimation if there is no contemporaneous correlation of the error terms associated with the different equations of the system. There is another case in which system estimation also produces no efficiency gain, this time because the two estimation methods lead to *numerically* identical parameter estimates. It arises in the context of a linear SUR when all the regressor matrices $\boldsymbol{X}_i$ in (9.56) are the same. The parameter estimates are identical because Kruskal's Theorem (see section 9.3) applies.

We show this by demonstrating that the span of the instruments $\boldsymbol{W}$ is the same as that of the regressors $\boldsymbol{X}$ whenever $\boldsymbol{X}_i = \boldsymbol{X}^*$, say, for all $i = 1, \dots, m$. Thus, as is made clear by the interpretation of a GLS estimator as an IV estimator, $\boldsymbol{W}$ plays the role of $\boldsymbol{\Omega}^{-1}\boldsymbol{X}$ in the general statement of Kruskal's Theorem. The span of the columns of $\boldsymbol{W}$ is the set of all nm-vectors of the form $[\boldsymbol{X}^*\boldsymbol{\gamma}_1 \vdots \dots \vdots \boldsymbol{X}^*\boldsymbol{\gamma}_m]$, for arbitrary vectors $\boldsymbol{\gamma}_i$ with as many components as $\boldsymbol{X}^*$ has columns. All such nm-vectors can also be generated as linear combinations of the columns of $\boldsymbol{X}$, which is just a block-diagonal matrix with identical blocks $\boldsymbol{X}^*$ along the main diagonal. It follows that $\mathcal{S}(\boldsymbol{W}) = \mathcal{S}(\boldsymbol{X})$, and the result is proved.

Associated with every multivariate nonlinear regression model is a particular version of the Gauss-Newton regression. For the tth observation, this regression may be written as

$$\big(\boldsymbol{Y}_t - \boldsymbol{\xi}_t(\boldsymbol{\beta})\big)\boldsymbol{\psi} = \boldsymbol{b}^\top \boldsymbol{\Xi}_t(\boldsymbol{\beta})\boldsymbol{\psi} + \text{residuals}. \tag{9.57}$$

In practice, this regression will be run in stacked form. Define a set of m matrices $\boldsymbol{X}_i(\boldsymbol{\beta})$, all with dimensions $n \times k$, in terms of the matrices $\boldsymbol{Z}_i(\boldsymbol{\beta})$

introduced in (9.52), as follows:

$$\boldsymbol{X}_i(\boldsymbol{\beta}) = \sum_{j=1}^{m} \boldsymbol{Z}_j(\boldsymbol{\beta})\psi_{ji}.$$

Then the stacked GNR is

$$\begin{bmatrix} (\boldsymbol{Y} - \boldsymbol{\xi}(\boldsymbol{\beta}))\boldsymbol{\psi}_1 \\ \vdots \\ (\boldsymbol{Y} - \boldsymbol{\xi}(\boldsymbol{\beta}))\boldsymbol{\psi}_m \end{bmatrix} = \begin{bmatrix} \boldsymbol{X}_1(\boldsymbol{\beta}) \\ \vdots \\ \boldsymbol{X}_m(\boldsymbol{\beta}) \end{bmatrix} \boldsymbol{b} + \text{residuals}. \tag{9.58}$$

The OLS estimates from the GNR (9.58) will be defined by the first-order conditions

$$\Big(\sum_{i=1}^{m} \boldsymbol{X}_i^{\top}(\boldsymbol{\beta})\boldsymbol{X}_i(\boldsymbol{\beta})\Big)\grave{\boldsymbol{b}} = \sum_{i=1}^{m} \boldsymbol{X}_i^{\top}(\boldsymbol{\beta})\big(\boldsymbol{Y} - \boldsymbol{\xi}(\boldsymbol{\beta})\big)\boldsymbol{\psi}_i. \tag{9.59}$$

Some manipulation of (9.59) based on the definition of the $\boldsymbol{X}_i$'s and of $\boldsymbol{\psi}$ shows that this is equivalent to

$$\sum_{i=1}^{m}\sum_{j=1}^{m} \sigma^{ij}\boldsymbol{Z}_i^{\top}(\boldsymbol{\beta})\big(\boldsymbol{y}_j - \boldsymbol{x}_j(\boldsymbol{\beta}) - \boldsymbol{Z}_j(\boldsymbol{\beta})\boldsymbol{b}\big) = \boldsymbol{0}. \tag{9.60}$$

Thus we see that regression (9.58) has all the properties we have come to expect from the Gauss-Newton regression. If we evaluate it at $\boldsymbol{\beta} = \tilde{\boldsymbol{\beta}}$, the regression will have no explanatory power at all, because (9.60) is satisfied with $\boldsymbol{b} = \boldsymbol{0}$ by the first-order conditions (9.53). The estimated covariance matrix from regression (9.58) with $\boldsymbol{\beta} = \tilde{\boldsymbol{\beta}}$ will be

$$\tilde{s}^2\Big(\sum_{i=1}^{m}\sum_{j=1}^{m} \sigma^{ij}\tilde{\boldsymbol{Z}}_i^{\top}\tilde{\boldsymbol{Z}}_j^{\top}\Big)^{-1}, \tag{9.61}$$

where $\tilde{s}^2$ is the estimate of the variance that the regression package will generate, which will evidently tend to 1 asymptotically if $\boldsymbol{\Sigma}$ is in fact the contemporaneous covariance matrix of $\boldsymbol{U}_t$. If (9.61) is rewritten as a sum of contributions from the successive observations, the result is

$$\tilde{s}^2\Big(\sum_{t=1}^{n} \tilde{\boldsymbol{\Xi}}_t\boldsymbol{\Sigma}^{-1}\tilde{\boldsymbol{\Xi}}_t^{\top}\Big)^{-1},$$

from which it is clear that (9.61) is indeed the proper GNLS covariance matrix estimator.

We could also run the GNR (9.58) with all quantities evaluated at a set of restricted ML estimates $\acute{\boldsymbol{\beta}}$, where the restrictions are on $\boldsymbol{\beta}$ only and not on the elements of $\boldsymbol{\Sigma}$. The explained sum of squares from this regression would be

$$\left(\sum_{t=1}^{n}(\boldsymbol{Y}_t - \acute{\boldsymbol{\xi}}_t)\boldsymbol{\Sigma}^{-1}\acute{\boldsymbol{\Xi}}_t^{\top}\right)\left(\sum_{t=1}^{n}\acute{\boldsymbol{\Xi}}_t\boldsymbol{\Sigma}^{-1}\acute{\boldsymbol{\Xi}}_t^{\top}\right)^{-1}\left(\sum_{t=1}^{n}(\boldsymbol{Y}_t - \acute{\boldsymbol{\xi}}_t)\boldsymbol{\Sigma}^{-1}\acute{\boldsymbol{\Xi}}_t^{\top}\right)^{\top}.$$

This is clearly an LM statistic. It can be used to test any sort of restriction on $\boldsymbol{\beta}$, including the hypothesis that the error terms are serially uncorrelated. For more on LM statistics in multivariate regression models, see Engle (1982a) and Godfrey (1988).

The foregoing results could all have been expected in view of the fact that a multivariate regression model can always be rewritten as a univariate regression model. Nevertheless, it is useful to have specific results for multivariate models. In particular, the ability to compute Gauss-Newton regressions provides a convenient way to obtain GNLS estimates, to verify that those estimates are accurate, to compute covariance matrix estimates, and to calculate LM test statistics for restrictions on $\boldsymbol{\beta}$. Evidently, all these results also hold for feasible GNLS, where $\boldsymbol{\Sigma}$ is not available but the consistent estimate $\check{\boldsymbol{\Sigma}}$ is.

9.9 ML Estimation of Multivariate Regression Models

The principal competitor to feasible GLS is maximum likelihood estimation based on the assumption of normally distributed error terms. As we saw in Section 9.6, ML estimates will be consistent even if that assumption is false, and so it seems a safe assumption to make. Thus the model is now

$$\boldsymbol{Y}_t = \boldsymbol{\xi}_t(\boldsymbol{\beta}) + \boldsymbol{U}_t, \quad \boldsymbol{U}_t \sim \mathrm{NID}(\boldsymbol{0}, \boldsymbol{\Sigma}).$$

The density of $\boldsymbol{U}_t$ is

$$(2\pi)^{-m/2}|\boldsymbol{\Sigma}|^{-1/2}\exp\Big(-\tfrac{1}{2}\boldsymbol{U}_t\boldsymbol{\Sigma}^{-1}\boldsymbol{U}_t^{\top}\Big).$$

Therefore, the density of $\boldsymbol{Y}_t$ is

$$(2\pi)^{-m/2}|\boldsymbol{\Sigma}|^{-1/2}\exp\Big(-\tfrac{1}{2}\big(\boldsymbol{Y}_t - \boldsymbol{\xi}_t(\boldsymbol{\beta})\big)\boldsymbol{\Sigma}^{-1}\big(\boldsymbol{Y}_t - \boldsymbol{\xi}_t(\boldsymbol{\beta})\big)^{\top}\Big).$$

Hence the loglikelihood function $\ell(\boldsymbol{Y}, \boldsymbol{\beta}, \boldsymbol{\Sigma})$ is

$$-\frac{mn}{2}\log(2\pi) - \frac{n}{2}\log|\boldsymbol{\Sigma}| - \frac{1}{2}\sum_{t=1}^{n}\big(\boldsymbol{Y}_t - \boldsymbol{\xi}_t(\boldsymbol{\beta})\big)\boldsymbol{\Sigma}^{-1}\big(\boldsymbol{Y}_t - \boldsymbol{\xi}_t(\boldsymbol{\beta})\big)^{\top}. \tag{9.62}$$

Notice that the last term here is just minus one-half the generalized sum of squared residuals (9.45). Thus, if $\boldsymbol{\Sigma}$ were known, the ML estimates of $\boldsymbol{\beta}$ would be identical to the GLS estimates.

The first step in maximizing $\ell(\boldsymbol{Y}, \boldsymbol{\beta}, \boldsymbol{\Sigma})$ is to concentrate it with respect to $\boldsymbol{\Sigma}$. Since $|\boldsymbol{\Sigma}| = |\boldsymbol{\Sigma}^{-1}|^{-1}$, (9.62) can be expressed purely in terms of the inverse matrix $\boldsymbol{\Sigma}^{-1}$. It turns out to be easier to concentrate the loglikelihood by using the first-order conditions given by differentiating it with respect to the elements of $\boldsymbol{\Sigma}^{-1}$. The matrix of partial derivatives thus obtained is (see Appendix A for details of the differentiation)

$$\frac{\partial \ell}{\partial \boldsymbol{\Sigma}^{-1}} = \frac{n}{2}\boldsymbol{\Sigma} - \frac{1}{2}\sum_{t=1}^{n}\big(\boldsymbol{Y}_t - \boldsymbol{\xi}_t(\boldsymbol{\beta})\big)^{\top}\big(\boldsymbol{Y}_t - \boldsymbol{\xi}_t(\boldsymbol{\beta})\big). \tag{9.63}$$

Setting the right-hand side of (9.63) equal to zero yields

$$-\frac{n}{2}\boldsymbol{\Sigma} = -\frac{1}{2}\sum_{t=1}^{n}\big(\boldsymbol{Y}_t - \boldsymbol{\xi}_t(\boldsymbol{\beta})\big)^{\top}\big(\boldsymbol{Y}_t - \boldsymbol{\xi}_t(\boldsymbol{\beta})\big),$$

from which we see that

$$\boldsymbol{\Sigma}(\boldsymbol{\beta}) = \frac{1}{n}\sum_{t=1}^{n}\big(\boldsymbol{Y}_t - \boldsymbol{\xi}_t(\boldsymbol{\beta})\big)^{\top}\big(\boldsymbol{Y}_t - \boldsymbol{\xi}_t(\boldsymbol{\beta})\big). \tag{9.64}$$

Thus the ML estimator of $\boldsymbol{\Sigma}$ is exactly what one might expect it to be, namely, the matrix of sums of squares and cross-products of the residuals, divided by the sample size.

We can easily substitute (9.64) into the last term of (9.62) if we observe that the trace of a scalar is just the scalar itself and that the trace of a matrix product is invariant under a cyclic permutation of the factors of the product. We obtain

$$\begin{aligned}
\big(\boldsymbol{Y}_t - \boldsymbol{\xi}_t(\boldsymbol{\beta})\big)\boldsymbol{\Sigma}^{-1}\big(\boldsymbol{Y}_t - \boldsymbol{\xi}_t(\boldsymbol{\beta})\big)^{\top} &= \operatorname{Tr}\Big(\big(\boldsymbol{Y}_t - \boldsymbol{\xi}_t(\boldsymbol{\beta})\big)\boldsymbol{\Sigma}^{-1}\big(\boldsymbol{Y}_t - \boldsymbol{\xi}_t(\boldsymbol{\beta})\big)^{\top}\Big) \\
&= \operatorname{Tr}\Big(\boldsymbol{\Sigma}^{-1}\big(\boldsymbol{Y}_t - \boldsymbol{\xi}_t(\boldsymbol{\beta})\big)^{\top}\big(\boldsymbol{Y}_t - \boldsymbol{\xi}_t(\boldsymbol{\beta})\big)\Big).
\end{aligned}$$

Summing over t yields

$$\begin{aligned}
\sum_{t=1}^{n}\big(\boldsymbol{Y}_t - \boldsymbol{\xi}_t(\boldsymbol{\beta})\big)\boldsymbol{\Sigma}^{-1}\big(\boldsymbol{Y}_t - \boldsymbol{\xi}_t(\boldsymbol{\beta})\big)^{\top} &= \sum_{t=1}^{n}\operatorname{Tr}\Big(\boldsymbol{\Sigma}^{-1}\big(\boldsymbol{Y}_t - \boldsymbol{\xi}_t(\boldsymbol{\beta})\big)^{\top}\big(\boldsymbol{Y}_t - \boldsymbol{\xi}_t(\boldsymbol{\beta})\big)\Big) \\
&= \operatorname{Tr}\Big(\boldsymbol{\Sigma}^{-1}\sum_{t=1}^{n}\big(\boldsymbol{Y}_t - \boldsymbol{\xi}_t(\boldsymbol{\beta})\big)^{\top}\big(\boldsymbol{Y}_t - \boldsymbol{\xi}_t(\boldsymbol{\beta})\big)\Big) \\
&= \operatorname{Tr}\big(\boldsymbol{\Sigma}^{-1}n\boldsymbol{\Sigma}\big) = mn.
\end{aligned}$$

Thus the concentrated loglikelihood function that corresponds to (9.62) is

$$\begin{aligned}
\ell^{c}(\boldsymbol{Y}, \boldsymbol{\beta}) &= C - \frac{n}{2}\log\Big|\frac{1}{n}\sum_{t=1}^{n}\big(\boldsymbol{Y}_t - \boldsymbol{\xi}_t(\boldsymbol{\beta})\big)^{\top}\big(\boldsymbol{Y}_t - \boldsymbol{\xi}_t(\boldsymbol{\beta})\big)\Big| \\
&= C - \frac{n}{2}\log|\boldsymbol{\Sigma}(\boldsymbol{\beta})|,
\end{aligned} \tag{9.65}$$

where $\boldsymbol{\Sigma}(\boldsymbol{\beta})$ has been defined implicitly, and C, a constant that does not depend on $\boldsymbol{\beta}$, is equal to

$$-\frac{mn}{2}\big(\log(2\pi)+1\big).$$

Expression (9.65) is the multivariate analog of the concentrated loglikelihood function (8.82) for univariate nonlinear regression models.

From (9.65), we see that to obtain ML estimates $\hat{\boldsymbol{\beta}}$ we will have to minimize the logarithm of the determinant of the contemporaneous covariance matrix, $|\boldsymbol{\Sigma}(\boldsymbol{\beta})|$. This can be done quite easily by using the rule for computing derivatives of logarithms of determinants given in Appendix A. This rule states that if $\boldsymbol{A}$ is a nonsingular $m \times m$ matrix, then the derivative of $\log|\boldsymbol{A}|$ with respect to the ij^{th} element of $\boldsymbol{A}$ is the ji^{th} element of $\boldsymbol{A}^{-1}$. By the chain rule, the derivative of $\log|\boldsymbol{\Sigma}(\boldsymbol{\beta})|$ with respect to β_i is

$$\begin{aligned}
\frac{\partial \log|\boldsymbol{\Sigma}(\boldsymbol{\beta})|}{\partial \beta_i} &= \sum_{j=1}^{m}\sum_{l=1}^{m} \frac{\partial \log|\boldsymbol{\Sigma}(\boldsymbol{\beta})|}{\partial \sigma_{jl}} \frac{\partial \sigma_{jl}(\boldsymbol{\beta})}{\partial \beta_i} \\
&= \sum_{j=1}^{m}\sum_{l=1}^{m} \big(\boldsymbol{\Sigma}^{-1}(\boldsymbol{\beta})\big)_{lj} \frac{\partial \sigma_{jl}(\boldsymbol{\beta})}{\partial \beta_i} \\
&= \operatorname{Tr}\left(\boldsymbol{\Sigma}^{-1}(\boldsymbol{\beta}) \frac{\partial \boldsymbol{\Sigma}(\boldsymbol{\beta})}{\partial \beta_i}\right).
\end{aligned}$$

It is easy to see that

$$\frac{\partial \boldsymbol{\Sigma}(\boldsymbol{\beta})}{\partial \beta_i} = -\frac{2}{n}\sum_{t=1}^{n} \boldsymbol{U}_t^{\top}(\boldsymbol{\beta})\, \frac{\partial \boldsymbol{\xi}_t(\boldsymbol{\beta})}{\partial \beta_i},$$

from which the gradient of (9.65) can be seen to be

$$\sum_{t=1}^{n} \boldsymbol{\Xi}_t(\boldsymbol{\beta})\boldsymbol{\Sigma}(\boldsymbol{\beta})^{-1}\big(\boldsymbol{Y}_t - \boldsymbol{\xi}_t(\boldsymbol{\beta})\big)^{\top}. \tag{9.66}$$

By setting this gradient to zero, we recover the first-order conditions (9.51) obtained from the GNLS method, but with $\boldsymbol{\Sigma}(\boldsymbol{\beta})$ for covariance matrix.

In the case of univariate regression models, the fact that least squares estimates are chosen so as to minimize the sum of squared residuals ensures that, on average, the residuals will be smaller than the true error terms. For the same reason, the fact that ML estimates minimize the determinant of the contemporaneous covariance matrix of the model ensures that, on average, the residuals associated with these estimates will be both too small and too highly correlated with each other. We observe both effects, because the determinant of the covariance matrix can be made smaller either by reducing the sums of squared residuals associated with the individual equations or by increasing the correlation among different equations. This is likely to be most noticeable when m and/or k are large relative to n.

It is of interest to consider the information matrix for the model (9.43). As with all regression models, this information matrix will turn out to be block-diagonal between the part that corresponds to $\boldsymbol{\beta}$ and the part that corresponds to $\boldsymbol{\Sigma}$ or, equivalently, to $\boldsymbol{\Sigma}^{-1}$. To see this, observe from (9.63) that

$$\frac{\partial \ell_t}{\partial \boldsymbol{\Sigma}^{-1}} = \frac{1}{2}\boldsymbol{\Sigma} - \frac{1}{2}\big(\boldsymbol{Y}_t - \boldsymbol{\xi}_t(\boldsymbol{\beta})\big)^{\top}\big(\boldsymbol{Y}_t - \boldsymbol{\xi}_t(\boldsymbol{\beta})\big).$$

This is an $m \times m$ symmetric matrix with $m(m+1)/2$ independent elements. A typical element of it is

$$\frac{\partial \ell_t}{\partial \sigma^{ij}} = \frac{1}{2}\sigma_{ij} - \frac{1}{2}\big(y_{ti} - \xi_{ti}(\boldsymbol{\beta})\big)^{\top}\big(y_{tj} - \xi_{tj}(\boldsymbol{\beta})\big). \tag{9.67}$$

From (9.66), we also find that the gradient of ℓ_t with respect to $\boldsymbol{\beta}$ is

$$\boldsymbol{\Xi}_t(\boldsymbol{\beta})\boldsymbol{\Sigma}^{-1}\big(\boldsymbol{Y}_t - \boldsymbol{\xi}_t(\boldsymbol{\beta})\big)^{\top}. \tag{9.68}$$

If we multiply (9.67) by (9.68), the product will involve either one or three occurrences of a component of $\boldsymbol{Y}_t - \boldsymbol{\xi}_t(\boldsymbol{\beta}) = \boldsymbol{U}_t$. Because the first and third moments of the error terms are zero (a consequence of normality), such a product must have expectation zero. Thus the information matrix must be block-diagonal between $\boldsymbol{\beta}$ and $\boldsymbol{\Sigma}$.

Now consider the $(\boldsymbol{\beta}, \boldsymbol{\beta})$ block of the information matrix. By definition, it is the limit of the expectation of $1/n$ times the outer product of the gradient, namely,

$$\begin{aligned}
\mathfrak{I}_{\beta\beta} &= \lim_{n\to\infty} E\bigg(\frac{1}{n}\sum_{t=1}^{n} \boldsymbol{\Xi}_t(\boldsymbol{\beta})\boldsymbol{\Sigma}^{-1}\big(\boldsymbol{Y}_t - \boldsymbol{\xi}_t(\boldsymbol{\beta})\big)^{\top}\big(\boldsymbol{Y}_t - \boldsymbol{\xi}_t(\boldsymbol{\beta})\big)\boldsymbol{\Sigma}^{-1}\boldsymbol{\Xi}_t^{\top}(\boldsymbol{\beta})\bigg) \\
&= \lim_{n\to\infty}\bigg(\frac{1}{n}\sum_{t=1}^{n} \boldsymbol{\Xi}_t(\boldsymbol{\beta})\boldsymbol{\Sigma}^{-1}\boldsymbol{\Sigma}\boldsymbol{\Sigma}^{-1}\boldsymbol{\Xi}_t^{\top}(\boldsymbol{\beta})\bigg) \\
&= \lim_{n\to\infty}\bigg(\frac{1}{n}\sum_{t=1}^{n} \boldsymbol{\Xi}_t(\boldsymbol{\beta})\boldsymbol{\Sigma}^{-1}\boldsymbol{\Xi}_t^{\top}(\boldsymbol{\beta})\bigg).
\end{aligned}$$

Thus we conclude that

$$n^{1/2}(\hat{\boldsymbol{\beta}} - \boldsymbol{\beta}_0) \overset{a}{\sim} N\bigg(\boldsymbol{0},\ \operatorname*{plim}_{n\to\infty}\bigg(\frac{1}{n}\sum_{t=1}^{n} \boldsymbol{\Xi}_t(\boldsymbol{\beta})\boldsymbol{\Sigma}^{-1}\boldsymbol{\Xi}_t^{\top}(\boldsymbol{\beta})\bigg)^{-1}\bigg). \tag{9.69}$$

Notice that, except for the factor of $\tilde{s}^2$, the covariance matrix estimate (9.61) obtained by running the Gauss-Newton regression is precisely the estimate that the result (9.69) would suggest using. If the GNR is computed at the ML estimates $\hat{\boldsymbol{\beta}}$, the estimated error variance for it, $\hat{s}^2$, will be equal to

$$\begin{aligned}&\frac{1}{mn-k}\sum_{t=1}^{n}(\boldsymbol{Y}_t-\hat{\boldsymbol{\xi}}_t)\hat{\boldsymbol{\psi}}\hat{\boldsymbol{\psi}}^{\top}(\boldsymbol{Y}_t-\hat{\boldsymbol{\xi}}_t)^{\top}\\ &=\frac{1}{mn-k}\sum_{t=1}^{n}(\boldsymbol{Y}_t-\hat{\boldsymbol{\xi}}_t)\hat{\boldsymbol{\Sigma}}^{-1}(\boldsymbol{Y}_t-\hat{\boldsymbol{\xi}}_t)^{\top}=\frac{mn}{mn-k}.\end{aligned} \tag{9.70}$$

The last equality here follows from an argument almost identical to the one used to establish (9.65). Since it is evident that (9.70) tends asymptotically to 1, expression (9.61), which is in this case

$$\frac{mn}{mn-k}\left(\sum_{t=1}^{n}\hat{\boldsymbol{\Xi}}_t\hat{\boldsymbol{\Sigma}}^{-1}\hat{\boldsymbol{\Xi}}_t^{\top}\right)^{-1},$$

provides a natural and very convenient way to estimate the covariance matrix of $\hat{\boldsymbol{\beta}}$.

We have now established all the principal results of interest concerning the estimation of multivariate nonlinear regression models. Since those results have been in terms of a rather general and abstract model, it may help to make them more concrete if we indicate precisely how our general notation relates to the case of the linear expenditure system that we discussed earlier. For concreteness, we will assume that $m = 2$, which means that there is a total of three commodities. Then we see that

$$\boldsymbol{Y}_t = [s_{t1} \quad s_{t2}];$$

$$\boldsymbol{\beta} = [\alpha_1 \;\vdots\; \alpha_2 \;\vdots\; \gamma_1 \;\vdots\; \gamma_2 \;\vdots\; \gamma_3];$$

$$\boldsymbol{\xi}_t(\boldsymbol{\beta}) = \left[\frac{\gamma_1 p_{1t}}{E_t}+\frac{\alpha_1}{E_t}\left(E_t-\sum_{j=1}^{3}p_{jt}\gamma_j\right) \quad \frac{\gamma_2 p_{2t}}{E_t}+\frac{\alpha_2}{E_t}\left(E_t-\sum_{j=1}^{3}p_{jt}\gamma_j\right)\right];$$

$$\boldsymbol{\Xi}_t(\boldsymbol{\beta}) = \begin{bmatrix}\left(E_t-\sum_{j=1}^{3}p_{jt}\gamma_j\right)/E_t & 0\\ 0 & E_t-\sum_{j=1}^{3}p_{jt}\gamma_j\\ (1-\alpha_1)p_{1t}/E_t & -\alpha_2 p_{1t}/E_t\\ -\alpha_1 p_{2t}/E_t & (1-\alpha_2)p_{2t}/E_t\\ -\alpha_1 p_{3t}/E_t & -\alpha_2 p_{3t}/E_t\end{bmatrix}.$$

It may be a useful exercise to set up the GNR for testing the hypothesis that $\gamma_1 = \gamma_2 = \gamma_3 = 0$, where estimates subject to that restriction have been obtained.

Our treatment of multivariate models has been relatively brief. A much fuller treatment, but only for linear SUR models, may be found in Srivastava and Giles (1987), which is also an excellent source for references to the econometric and statistical literature on the subject.

9.10 MODELING TIME-SERIES/CROSS-SECTION DATA

Many data sets have both a time-series and a cross-section dimension. For example, they might contain 40 years of data on 20 countries, or 132 quarters of data on 50 states. The advantage of such data sets is that the sample size is usually quite large (for the above examples, $40 \times 20 = 800$ and $132 \times 50 = 6600$), which means that they should potentially be very informative about the parameters to be estimated. The disadvantage is that it is necessary to take the two-dimensional nature of the data into account. A particular type of time-series/cross-section data arises when the same sample of individuals, households, or firms is observed at two or more points in time. Data of this type are often referred to as **panel data**. A panel data set generally consists of a fairly small number of temporal observations on a large number of cross-section units. The imbalance between the two dimensions of the sample may make it necessary to use special techniques and can make reliance on standard asymptotic theory inappropriate.

If we let t index the time dimension of the data and i index the cross-section dimension, we can write a univariate nonlinear regression model for time-series/cross-section data as

$$y_{ti} = x_{ti}(\boldsymbol{\beta}) + u_{ti}, \quad t = 1, \ldots, T, \; i = 1, \ldots, n. \tag{9.71}$$

There are T time periods and n cross-sectional units, for a total of nT observations. If we were willing to assume that the u_{ti}'s are homoskedastic and independent, we could simply estimate (9.71) by NLS. But often this will not be a realistic assumption. The variance of u_{ti} might well vary systematically with t or i or both of them. Moreover, it seems plausible that the error terms u_{ti} and u_{tj} will be correlated for some $i \neq j$ if certain shocks affect several cross-sectional units at the same point in time. Similarly, it seems plausible that the error terms u_{ti} and u_{si} will be correlated for some $t \neq s$ if certain shocks affect the same cross-section unit at more than one point in time. Whether any of these failures of the i.i.d. assumption will occur for any given data set is difficult to say a priori. But if they do occur, and we simply use NLS, we will obtain an estimated covariance matrix that is inconsistent and may lead to serious errors of inference. In some circumstances, we may even obtain inconsistent parameter estimates.

In principle, it is straightforward to deal with failures of the i.i.d. assumption of the types just discussed. One simply writes down the assumed covariance matrix of the u_{ti}'s as a function of one or more unknown parameters, uses least squares to obtain residuals from which to estimate those parameters consistently, and then applies feasible GLS. Alternatively, one can use maximum likelihood to estimate the parameters of the regression function and the parameters of the covariance matrix simultaneously. In practice, of course, it is not always easy to apply this prescription, and there is an enormous literature on particular techniques for doing so. Chamberlain (1984),

Hsiao (1986), Judge, Hill, Griffiths, Lütkepohl, and Lee (1985, Chapter 13), and Greene (1990a, Chapter 16) are useful references. In this section, we will discuss only a few of the simplest and most widely applicable techniques for dealing with time-series/cross-section data.

When one of T and n is quite small and the other is reasonably large, it is natural to recast the univariate model (9.71) as a multivariate one. Suppose, for concreteness, that there are only a few cross-sectional units and numerous time periods. Then it seems natural to group observations $t1$ through tn into a vector $\boldsymbol{u}_t$ and assume that

$$\boldsymbol{u}_t \sim \text{IID}(\mathbf{0}, \boldsymbol{\Sigma}).$$

Thus we are assuming that u_{ti} is in general correlated with u_{tj} for $i \neq j$ and that $\boldsymbol{u}_t$ is not correlated with $\boldsymbol{u}_s$ for $t \neq s$. With this error specification, the univariate model (9.71) becomes a special case of the multivariate non-linear regression model (9.40) and can be estimated by either feasible GLS (Section 9.8) or maximum likelihood (Section 9.9). Of course, there will be a great many cross-equation restrictions, since the parameters in all equations are assumed to be the same, but either of these techniques should be able to handle them with no difficulty.

Treating a model like (9.71) as a multivariate model is attractive because one can employ standard software for the estimation of such models. Moreover, it becomes natural to test the (not always plausible) assumption that the same regression function $x_{ti}(\boldsymbol{\beta})$ applies to all cross-sectional units. At the very least, one would always want to check the possibility that each cross-sectional unit might have a different intercept. This can be done in several ways. Two possibilities are to estimate the unrestricted model as well and then compute an LR or equivalent test and to calculate an LM test based on a GNR like (9.58). In addition, one would surely want to test for correlation of the error terms across time periods. This can be done by using standard tests for serial correlation in multivariate models, which can also be based on the GNR (9.58). This topic will be discussed very briefly in Section 10.11; see also Engle (1984) and Godfrey (1988). One might also wish to test for heteroskedasticity across time periods, which can be done by straightforward extensions of the techniques to be discussed in Chapters 11 and 16.

Although there is much to recommend the approach of treating a univariate model estimated using time-series/cross-section data as a multivariate model, it is not attractive when neither n nor T is particularly small. For example, suppose that $n = 30$ and $T = 40$. Then a multivariate model that treats each cross-sectional unit separately will have 30 equations, and the matrix $\boldsymbol{\Sigma}$ will have $\frac{1}{2}(30 \times 31) = 465$ distinct elements, which must each be estimated using only 40 observations. Estimating a 30-equation model is by no means infeasible. However, with only 40 observations, it will be difficult to obtain good estimates of $\boldsymbol{\Sigma}$, and thus one might expect the finite-sample properties of feasible GLS and ML estimates to be poor.

A second approach, which is very popular, is to use what is called an **error-components model**. The idea is to model u_{ti} as consisting of three individual shocks, each assumed to be independent of the others:

$$u_{ti} = e_t + v_i + \varepsilon_{ti}. \tag{9.72}$$

Here e_t affects all observations for time period t, v_i affects all observations for cross-section unit i, and ε_{ti} affects only observation ti. In the most common versions of error-components models, the e_t's are assumed to be independent across t, the v_i's are assumed to be independent across i, and the ε_{ti}'s are assumed to be independent across all i and t. These assumptions can of course be relaxed, as in Revankar (1979) and Baltagi and Li (1991), but we will not discuss how to do so here.

There are two ways to estimate a regression model with error terms that are assumed to consist of several error components, as in (9.72). The first is to estimate what is called a **fixed-effects model**, and the second is to estimate what is called a **random-effects model**. These two approaches are conceptually quite different. In the first of them we estimate the model conditionally on the errors e_t and v_i, and in the second we estimate the model unconditionally. A fixed-effects model can be estimated by ordinary (or nonlinear) least squares, while a random-effects model requires GLS or ML. One advantage of the fixed-effects model is that, since we are conditioning on e_t and v_i, we do not need to assume that they are independent of the regressors. However, as we will see, the random-effects model will yield more efficient estimates when it is appropriate. Mundlak (1978) is a classic reference on the relationship between the fixed-effects and random-effects models.

For simplicity and concreteness, we will in the remainder of this section assume that there are no time-specific shocks, which implies that $e_t = 0$ for all t. This simplifies the algebra without changing the nature of the results. We will also assume that the regression function for observation ti is $\boldsymbol{X}_{ti}\boldsymbol{\beta}$. Under these assumptions, the error-components model can be written as

$$y_{ti} = \boldsymbol{X}_{ti}\boldsymbol{\beta} + v_i + \varepsilon_{ti}. \tag{9.73}$$

The idea of the fixed-effects model is simply to treat the v_i's as unknown parameters and estimate them jointly with $\boldsymbol{\beta}$. This may be done by adding n dummy variables D^j_{ti} to regression (9.73), each equal to unity when $i = j$ and equal to zero otherwise. Of course, if $\boldsymbol{X}_{ti}$ includes a constant term or the equivalent, one of the dummy variables will have to be omitted.

In matrix notation, the fixed-effects version of (9.73) can be written as

$$\boldsymbol{y} = \boldsymbol{X}\boldsymbol{\beta} + \boldsymbol{D}\boldsymbol{v} + \boldsymbol{\varepsilon}, \tag{9.74}$$

where $\boldsymbol{v}$ is an n–vector with typical element v_i. Provided the ε_{ti}'s are i.i.d., the model (9.74) may be estimated by OLS. Using the FWL Theorem, we see that the fixed-effects estimator of $\boldsymbol{\beta}$ is

$$\acute{\boldsymbol{\beta}} = \big(\boldsymbol{X}^\top\boldsymbol{M}_D\boldsymbol{X}\big)^{-1}\boldsymbol{X}^\top\boldsymbol{M}_D\boldsymbol{y}, \tag{9.75}$$

where the matrix $\boldsymbol{M}_D$ is simply the matrix that takes deviations from the group means $\bar{\boldsymbol{X}}_{.i}$ for $i = 1, \ldots, n$. Thus a typical element of $\boldsymbol{M}_D\boldsymbol{X}$ is

$$(\boldsymbol{M}_D\boldsymbol{X})_{ti} = \boldsymbol{X}_{ti} - \bar{\boldsymbol{X}}_{.i}.$$

This makes it easy to compute $\acute{\boldsymbol{\beta}}$ even when n is so large that it would be infeasible to run regression (9.74). One simply has to compute the group means $y_{.i}$ and $\boldsymbol{X}_{.i}$ for all i and then regress $y_{ti} - \bar{y}_{.i}$ on $\boldsymbol{X}_{ti} - \bar{\boldsymbol{X}}_{.i}$ for all t and i. The estimated covariance matrix should then be adjusted to reflect the fact that the number of degrees of freedom used in estimation is actually $n + k$ rather than k.

Because the fixed-effects estimator (9.75) depends only on the deviations of the regressand and regressors from their respective group means, it is sometimes called the **within-groups estimator**. As this name implies, it makes no use of the fact that the group means are in general different for different groups. This property of the estimator can be an advantage or a disadvantage, depending on circumstances. As we mentioned above, it may well be the case that the cross-sectional effects v_i are correlated with the regressors $\boldsymbol{X}_{ti}$ and consequently also with the respective group means of the regressors. In that event the OLS estimator (without fixed effects) based on the full sample would be inconsistent, but the within-groups estimator would remain consistent. However, if on the contrary the fixed effects *are* independent of the regressors, the within-groups estimator is not fully efficient. In the extreme case in which any one of the independent variables does not vary at all within groups, but only between groups, then the coefficient corresponding to that variable will not even be identifiable by the within-groups estimator.

An alternative inefficient estimator that uses only the variation among the group means is called the **between-groups estimator**. It may be written as

$$\grave{\boldsymbol{\beta}} = \left(\boldsymbol{X}^\top\boldsymbol{P}_D\boldsymbol{X}\right)^{-1}\boldsymbol{X}^\top\boldsymbol{P}_D\boldsymbol{y}. \tag{9.76}$$

Since $\boldsymbol{P}_D\boldsymbol{X}_{ti} = \bar{\boldsymbol{X}}_{.i}$, this estimator really involves only n distinct observations rather than nT. It will clearly be inconsistent if the cross-sectional effects, the v_i's, are correlated with the group means of the regressors, the $\bar{\boldsymbol{X}}_{.i}$'s. The OLS estimator can be written as a matrix-weighted average of the within-groups and between-groups estimators:

$$\begin{aligned}
\hat{\boldsymbol{\beta}} &= \left(\boldsymbol{X}^\top\boldsymbol{X}\right)^{-1}\boldsymbol{X}^\top\boldsymbol{y} \\
&= \left(\boldsymbol{X}^\top\boldsymbol{X}\right)^{-1}\left(\boldsymbol{X}^\top\boldsymbol{M}_D\boldsymbol{y} + \boldsymbol{X}^\top\boldsymbol{P}_D\boldsymbol{y}\right) \\
&= \left(\boldsymbol{X}^\top\boldsymbol{X}\right)^{-1}\boldsymbol{X}^\top\boldsymbol{M}_D\boldsymbol{X}\acute{\boldsymbol{\beta}} + \left(\boldsymbol{X}^\top\boldsymbol{X}\right)^{-1}\boldsymbol{X}^\top\boldsymbol{P}_D\boldsymbol{X}\grave{\boldsymbol{\beta}}.
\end{aligned}$$

Thus we see immediately that OLS will be inconsistent whenever the between-groups estimator (9.76) is inconsistent.

Even when it is consistent, OLS will usually be inefficient. If the cross-sectional effects are uncorrelated with the group means of the regressors, then we want to use a random-effects model, in which the v_i's are not treated as fixed but as components of the error terms. OLS weights all observations equally, but that is not the optimal thing to do for the error-components model (9.73). The variance of u_{ti} is, using an obvious notation, $\sigma_v^2 + \sigma_\varepsilon^2$. The covariance of u_{ti} with u_{tj} is, by assumption, zero for $i \neq j$. But the covariance of u_{ti} with u_{si} for $s \neq t$ is σ_v^2. Thus, if the data are ordered first by i and then by t, the covariance matrix of the u_{ti}'s can be written as

$$\begin{bmatrix} \boldsymbol{\Sigma} & \mathbf{0} & \cdots & \mathbf{0} \\ \mathbf{0} & \boldsymbol{\Sigma} & \cdots & \mathbf{0} \\ \vdots & \vdots & & \vdots \\ \mathbf{0} & \mathbf{0} & \cdots & \boldsymbol{\Sigma} \end{bmatrix},$$

where $\boldsymbol{\Sigma}$ is the $T \times T$ matrix

$$\begin{bmatrix} \sigma_v^2 + \sigma_\varepsilon^2 & \sigma_v^2 & \cdots & \sigma_v^2 \\ \sigma_v^2 & \sigma_v^2 + \sigma_\varepsilon^2 & \cdots & \sigma_v^2 \\ \vdots & \vdots & & \vdots \\ \sigma_v^2 & \sigma_v^2 & \cdots & \sigma_v^2 + \sigma_\varepsilon^2 \end{bmatrix} = \sigma_\varepsilon^2 \mathbf{I} + \sigma_v^2 \boldsymbol{\iota}\boldsymbol{\iota}^\top.$$

This covariance matrix reflects the fact that for fixed i the errors are equicorrelated; compare (9.24).

In order to compute GLS estimates, we need to find $\boldsymbol{\Sigma}^{-1/2}$. It can easily be verified that

$$\boldsymbol{\Sigma}^{-1/2} = \frac{1}{\sigma_\varepsilon}(\mathbf{I} - \alpha \boldsymbol{P}_{\iota}),$$

where $\boldsymbol{P}_{\iota} = T^{-1}\boldsymbol{\iota}\boldsymbol{\iota}^\top$ and α, which must be between 0 and 1, is defined by

$$\alpha = 1 - \frac{\sigma_\varepsilon}{(T\sigma_v^2 + \sigma_\varepsilon^2)^{1/2}}. \tag{9.77}$$

This implies that a typical element of $\boldsymbol{\Sigma}^{-1/2}\boldsymbol{y}_{.i}$ is $\sigma_\varepsilon^{-1}(y_{ti} - \alpha\bar{y}_{.i})$, and a typical element of $\boldsymbol{\Sigma}^{-1/2}\boldsymbol{X}_{.i}$ is $\sigma_\varepsilon^{-1}(\boldsymbol{X}_{ti} - \alpha\bar{\boldsymbol{X}}_{.i})$. GLS estimates may then be found by running the OLS regression

$$y_{ti} - \alpha\bar{y}_{.i} = (\boldsymbol{X}_{ti} - \alpha\bar{\boldsymbol{X}}_{.i})\boldsymbol{\beta} + \text{residual},$$

which may be written in matrix terms as

$$(\mathbf{I} - \alpha\boldsymbol{P}_D)\boldsymbol{y} = (\mathbf{I} - \alpha\boldsymbol{P}_D)\boldsymbol{X}\boldsymbol{\beta} + (\mathbf{I} - \alpha\boldsymbol{P}_D)\boldsymbol{u}. \tag{9.78}$$

In practice, of course, α will be unknown, and we will have to use feasible GLS or maximum likelihood. The former is very easy to implement, since we can obtain estimates of the quantities we need by estimating the fixed-effects model. The error terms for that model are simply the ε_{ti}'s, and so by estimating it we immediately obtain a consistent estimate of σ_ε^2. We can then estimate σ_v^2 in various ways, the simplest estimator being the average of the squared estimates of the v_i's. This estimator will also be consistent, provided that T (and not merely nT) is allowed to tend to infinity. Using these estimates of σ_ε^2 and σ_v^2, we can easily obtain a consistent estimate of α from (9.77). We will not discuss ML estimation, which is conceptually straightforward but computationally more difficult than feasible GLS; the classic reference is Balestra and Nerlove (1966).

It is interesting to see how the GLS estimator defined by regression (9.78) is related to the OLS estimator and the within-groups estimator (9.75). When $\alpha = 0$, the GLS estimator evidently reduces to the OLS estimator. This makes sense because, from (9.77), we see that α will be 0 only when $\sigma_v = 0$, in which case the error term has only one component. When $\alpha = 1$, the GLS estimator reduces to the within-groups estimator. This also makes sense, because α will be 1 only when $\sigma_\varepsilon = 0$, in which case the error terms associated with within-group variation will all be zero. This implies that we can obtain perfectly accurate estimates of $\boldsymbol{\beta}$ by using the within-groups estimator. In every other case, α will be between 0 and 1, and the GLS estimator will make use of both within-groups and between-groups variation.

The problem with panel data is that n is usually very large and T is frequently very small. Thus parameters that are identified by variation across the cross-sectional units will tend to be estimated very well, while parameters that are identified only by variation across time may be estimated quite poorly. One could not expect to estimate σ_v at all precisely in a random-effects model, for example. If one were not concerned with variation across time, one would simply use a fixed-effects model. Instead of explicitly removing the group means, one could take first differences of all the data with respect to the time dimension, causing the individual effects to vanish. In practice, however, we are often interested in parameters that are not identified solely by within-groups variation. Econometricians have therefore proposed a wide range of procedures for dealing with panel data. See, among many others, Hausman and Taylor (1981), Chamberlain (1984), Hsiao (1986), and Holtz-Eakin, Newey, and Rosen (1988).

9.11 CONCLUSION

GLS and GNLS are very important estimation techniques that are widely used in applied econometrics. We will encounter variants of them throughout the remainder of this book, most notably in Chapter 10, where we deal with serial correlation, and in Chapter 18, where we deal with full-system techniques for estimating simultaneous equations models. Nevertheless, it is important to remember that GLS and GNLS are really just fancy variants of least squares. Any mistake that one can make in specifying a model estimated by OLS (such as incorrectly specifying the regression function or failing to account for serial correlation or heteroskedasticity) can equally well be made in specifying models estimated by GLS, GNLS, and the various maximum likelihood methods related to them. It is therefore just as important to test such models for misspecification as it is to test the simplest linear regression model. The Gauss-Newton regressions (9.14) and (9.58) often provide convenient ways to do this. However, it is our experience that the amount of misspecification testing to which a model is subjected is inversely related to the difficulty of estimating the model in the first place. Since it generally requires a good deal more effort to estimate models, especially multivariate models, by GLS or GNLS than univariate regression models by OLS, the former are often subjected to much less misspecification testing than we would consider appropriate.

TERMS AND CONCEPTS

asymptotic equivalence of GNLS, feasible GNLS, and ML
between-groups estimator
contemporaneous covariance matrix
cross-equation restrictions
demand systems
equicorrelated errors
error-components models
feasible GLS and GNLS
fixed-effects models
generalized least squares (GLS)
generalized nonlinear least squares (GNLS)
generalized sum of squared residuals
GLS (Aitken) estimator
Kruskal's Theorem
linear expenditure system
multivariate nonlinear regression model
oblique projection matrix
panel data
random-effects models
seemingly unrelated regressions (SUR system)
singular equation system
skedastic function
Stone-Geary utility function
time-series/cross-section data
weighted least squares
within-groups estimator

Chapter 10

Serial Correlation

10.1 Introduction

The phenomenon of **serial correlation**, in which successive residuals appear to be correlated with each other, is very often encountered in models estimated with time-series data. As a result, testing for serial correlation and estimating models that take account of it are both topics which have been studied for a very long time by econometricians, and the literature is consequently vast. Happily, the results we have already obtained about NLS, GNLS, and ML allow us to handle most of the problems associated with serial correlation in a straightforward way.

Although error terms may fail to be independent in any sort of model, lack of independence is most often observed in models estimated with time-series data. In particular, observations that are close in time often have error terms which appear to be correlated, while observations that are far apart in time rarely do. We say *appear* to be correlated because misspecification of the regression function may lead residuals to be correlated across observations, even when the actual error terms are not. In any case, whether the appearance of serial correlation in time-series models is genuine or not, one particularly simple model of serial correlation has become very popular. In this model, the error terms u_t are assumed to follow the **first-order autoregressive**, or **AR(1)**, process

$$u_t = \rho u_{t-1} + \varepsilon_t, \quad \varepsilon_t \sim \mathrm{IID}(0, \omega^2), \quad |\rho| < 1. \tag{10.01}$$

This stochastic process says that the error at time t, u_t, is equal to some fraction ρ of the error at time $t-1$ (with the sign changed if $\rho < 0$), plus a new error term or **innovation** ε_t that is homoskedastic and independent of all past and future innovations. Thus in each period part of the error term is the last period's error term, shrunk somewhat toward zero and possibly changed in sign, and part is the innovation ε_t.

The condition that $|\rho| < 1$ is called a **stationarity condition**. It ensures that the variance of u_t tends to a limiting value, σ^2, rather than increasing without limit as t gets large. By substituting successively for u_{t-1}, u_{t-2}, u_{t-3}, and so on in (10.01), we see that

$$u_t = \varepsilon_t + \rho\varepsilon_{t-1} + \rho^2\varepsilon_{t-2} + \rho^3\varepsilon_{t-3} + \cdots.$$

Thus, using the fact that the innovations ε_t, $\varepsilon_{t-1}\cdots$ are independent, the variance of u_t is seen to be

$$\sigma^2 \equiv V(u_t) = \omega^2 + \rho^2\omega^2 + \rho^4\omega^2 + \rho^6\omega^2 + \cdots = \frac{\omega^2}{1-\rho^2}. \qquad (10.02)$$

The right-most expression in (10.02) is true only if the stationarity condition $|\rho| < 1$ holds, since that condition is necessary for the infinite series $1 + \rho^2 + \rho^4 + \rho^6 + \cdots$ to converge. In conventional econometric applications, where u_t is the error term appended to a regression model, this is a very reasonable condition to impose, since we certainly would not want the variance of the error terms to blow up as the sample size was increased.

We have seen that, for a stationary AR(1) process which has been going on for a reasonable length of time, the error terms u_t will each have variance $\sigma^2 = \omega^2/(1-\rho^2)$. We can write

$$u_t = \varepsilon_t + \rho\varepsilon_{t-1} + \cdots + \rho^{j-1}\varepsilon_{t-j+1} + \rho^j u_{t-j}, \qquad (10.03)$$

expressing u_t as a function of u_{t-j} and of all the innovations between periods $t-j+1$ and t. Hence the covariance of u_t and u_{t-j} may be calculated as

$$E\big((\varepsilon_t + \rho\varepsilon_{t-1}\cdots\rho^{j-1}\varepsilon_{t-j+1} + \rho^j u_{t-j})u_{t-j}\big). \qquad (10.04)$$

Since the innovations between periods $t-j+1$ and t are independent of u_{t-j}, the covariance (10.04) is simply

$$E\big(\rho^j u_{t-j}^2\big) = \rho^j E(u_t^2) = \frac{\rho^j\omega^2}{1-\rho^2} = \rho^j\sigma^2.$$

Thus we conclude that the covariance matrix of $\boldsymbol{u}$ is

$$\boldsymbol{\Omega} = \frac{\omega^2}{1-\rho^2}\begin{bmatrix} 1 & \rho & \rho^2 & \cdots & \rho^{n-1} \\ \rho & 1 & \rho & \cdots & \rho^{n-2} \\ \vdots & \vdots & \vdots & & \vdots \\ \rho^{n-1} & \rho^{n-2} & \rho^{n-3} & \cdots & 1 \end{bmatrix}, \qquad (10.05)$$

the matrix in brackets being the correlation matrix of $\boldsymbol{u}$. It is evident from (10.05) that every element of $\boldsymbol{u}$ is correlated with every other element of $\boldsymbol{u}$, but except when $|\rho|$ is very close to 1, this correlation will tend to die out quite quickly as the time periods become further apart. This accords well both with intuition and with the actual behavior of the residuals from many regression models estimated with time-series data. Thus it is not surprising that the AR(1) process is very frequently used in applied econometric work.

The AR(1) process is of course a very special case. There are numerous other stochastic processes that error terms could reasonably follow. We will discuss some of these in Sections 10.5 and 10.7, below. However, because most of the issues involved in estimating models with, and testing for, serial correlation arise in the AR(1) case, and because it is by far the most commonly encountered error process in applied work, we will restrict our attention to the AR(1) case for the moment.

The chapter proceeds as follows. In the next section, we discuss the effects on least squares estimates of serial correlation that is not accounted for. In the following two sections, we discuss methods for estimating regression models that allow for AR(1) errors but ignore the first observation. Then, in Section 10.5, we discuss higher-order AR processes. Section 10.6 deals with methods for taking account of the initial observations, and Section 10.7 deals with moving average errors. In Section 10.8, we discuss tests for serial correlation and, in the following section, tests of common factor restrictions. Section 10.10 deals with serial correlation in models estimated by instrumental variables. Finally, in Section 10.11, we briefly discuss serial correlation in multivariate models.

10.2 SERIAL CORRELATION AND LEAST SQUARES ESTIMATION

What are the consequences if we use least squares to estimate a model in which the error terms are in fact serially correlated? For simplicity, we will consider the linear case, because all the results carry over to the nonlinear case in an obvious fashion. Thus suppose that we estimate the model

$$\boldsymbol{y} = \boldsymbol{X\beta} + \boldsymbol{u}, \quad E(\boldsymbol{u}\boldsymbol{u}^{\top}) = \sigma^2\mathbf{I},$$

when the data-generating process is actually

$$y_t = \boldsymbol{X}_t\boldsymbol{\beta}_0 + u_t, \quad u_t = \rho_0 u_{t-1} + \varepsilon_t, \quad \varepsilon_t \sim \mathrm{IID}(0, \omega_0^2). \tag{10.06}$$

The OLS estimator is

$$\hat{\boldsymbol{\beta}} = (\boldsymbol{X}^{\top}\boldsymbol{X})^{-1}\boldsymbol{X}^{\top}\boldsymbol{y},$$

which under the DGP (10.06) is equal to

$$(\boldsymbol{X}^{\top}\boldsymbol{X})^{-1}\boldsymbol{X}^{\top}(\boldsymbol{X}\boldsymbol{\beta}_0 + \boldsymbol{u}) = \boldsymbol{\beta}_0 + (\boldsymbol{X}^{\top}\boldsymbol{X})^{-1}\boldsymbol{X}^{\top}\boldsymbol{u}.$$

Provided that $\boldsymbol{X}$ is exogenous, $\hat{\boldsymbol{\beta}}$ will still be unbiased, because the fact that the u_t's are serially correlated does not prevent $E(\boldsymbol{X}^{\top}\boldsymbol{u})$ from being zero. If $\boldsymbol{X}$ is not exogenous, $\hat{\boldsymbol{\beta}}$ will be consistent as long as $\mathrm{plim}(n^{-1}\boldsymbol{X}^{\top}\boldsymbol{u})$ is equal to zero.

Inferences about $\boldsymbol{\beta}$ will not be correct, however. Assuming that $\boldsymbol{X}$ is exogenous, we see that

$$\begin{aligned} E(\hat{\boldsymbol{\beta}} - \boldsymbol{\beta}_0)(\hat{\boldsymbol{\beta}} - \boldsymbol{\beta}_0)^{\top} &= E\big((\boldsymbol{X}^{\top}\boldsymbol{X})^{-1}\boldsymbol{X}^{\top}\boldsymbol{u}\boldsymbol{u}^{\top}\boldsymbol{X}(\boldsymbol{X}^{\top}\boldsymbol{X})^{-1}\big) \\ &= (\boldsymbol{X}^{\top}\boldsymbol{X})^{-1}\boldsymbol{X}^{\top}\boldsymbol{\Omega}_0\boldsymbol{X}(\boldsymbol{X}^{\top}\boldsymbol{X})^{-1}, \end{aligned} \tag{10.07}$$

where $\boldsymbol{\Omega}_0$ is the matrix $\boldsymbol{\Omega}(\rho)$ defined in (10.05), evaluated at ρ_0. Evidently, (10.07) will in general not be consistently estimated by the OLS covariance matrix estimator $s^2(\boldsymbol{X}^\top\boldsymbol{X})^{-1}$. Except in special cases, it is not possible to say whether the incorrect standard error estimates obtained using OLS will be larger or smaller than the correct ones obtained by taking the square roots of the diagonal elements of (10.07). However, analysis of special cases suggests that for values of ρ greater than 0 (the most commonly encountered case) the incorrect OLS standard errors are usually too small; see, among others, Nicholls and Pagan (1977), Sathe and Vinod (1974), and Vinod (1976).

Expression (10.07) applies to any situation in which OLS is incorrectly used in place of GLS and not merely to situations in which the errors follow an AR(1) process. So does the previous result that $\hat{\boldsymbol{\beta}}$ is unbiased if $\boldsymbol{X}$ is fixed and $E(\boldsymbol{X}^\top\boldsymbol{u}) = \mathbf{0}$. But recall from Section 9.5 that, even when these conditions are satisfied, $\hat{\boldsymbol{\beta}}$ may fail to be consistent if the errors are correlated enough among themselves. We may conclude that, when the regressors are fixed and the covariance matrix of the error terms is such that there is not too much correlation of the error terms, the OLS estimates will be consistent, but the OLS covariance matrix estimate will not be. A consistent estimate of the covariance matrix of the OLS estimator can usually be found. However, since the proof of the Gauss-Markov Theorem depended on the assumption that $E(\boldsymbol{u}\boldsymbol{u}^\top) = \sigma^2\mathbf{I}$, OLS is not the best linear unbiased estimator when this assumption does not hold.

The preceding discussion assumed that there were no lagged dependent variables among the columns of $\boldsymbol{X}$. When this assumption is dropped, the results change drastically, and OLS is seen to be both biased and inconsistent. The simplest way to see this is to think about an element of $\boldsymbol{X}^\top\boldsymbol{u}$ corresponding to the lagged dependent variable (or to one of the lagged dependent variables if there is more than one). If the dependent variable is lagged j periods, this element is

$$\sum_{t=1}^{n} y_{t-j}u_t. \tag{10.08}$$

Now recall expression (10.03), in which we expressed u_t as a function of u_{t-j} and of all the innovations between periods $t-j+1$ and t. Since y_{t-j} is equal to $\boldsymbol{X}_{t-j}\boldsymbol{\beta} + u_{t-j}$, it is clear from (10.03) that (10.08) cannot possibly have expectation zero. Thus we conclude that when $\boldsymbol{X}$ includes lagged dependent variables and u_t is serially correlated,

$$\operatorname*{plim}_{n\to\infty}\left(\frac{1}{n}\boldsymbol{X}^\top\boldsymbol{u}\right) \neq \mathbf{0}, \tag{10.09}$$

which implies that

$$\operatorname*{plim}_{n\to\infty}(\hat{\boldsymbol{\beta}} - \boldsymbol{\beta}_0) = \operatorname*{plim}_{n\to\infty}\left(\frac{1}{n}\boldsymbol{X}^\top\boldsymbol{X}\right)^{-1}\operatorname*{plim}_{n\to\infty}\left(\frac{1}{n}\boldsymbol{X}^\top\boldsymbol{u}\right) \neq \mathbf{0}. \tag{10.10}$$

Because $X^\top y$ is premultiplied by $(X^\top X)^{-1}$, every element of $X^\top u$ generally affects $\hat{\beta}$, unless the matrix $X^\top X$ has very special features. Thus it is evident from (10.10) that every element of β will generally be estimated inconsistently, even if there is only one lagged dependent variable and, in consequence, only one element of (10.09) is nonzero.

The foregoing discussion makes it clear why econometricians have worried so much about serial correlation. Even when there are no lagged dependent variables, it causes least squares estimates to be inefficient and makes inference based on them invalid. When there are lagged dependent variables, serial correlation causes least squares to be biased and inconsistent. Nevertheless, it is important to remember that many types of misspecification can bring about the *appearance* of serial correlation. Thus the situation we have just analyzed, in which the model was correctly specified except for the failure to take serial correlation into account, probably does not account for a very high proportion of the cases in which the residuals from a regression model appear to be serially correlated.

10.3 Estimating Regression Models with AR(1) Errors

Suppose that we want to estimate a nonlinear regression model with error terms that follow an AR(1) process:

$$y_t = x_t(\beta) + u_t, \quad u_t = \rho u_{t-1} + \varepsilon_t, \quad \varepsilon_t \sim \mathrm{IID}(0, \omega^2). \tag{10.11}$$

Because $u_{t-1} = y_{t-1} - x_{t-1}(\beta)$, this model can be rewritten as

$$y_t = x_t(\beta) + \rho\big(y_{t-1} - x_{t-1}(\beta)\big) + \varepsilon_t, \quad \varepsilon_t \sim \mathrm{IID}(0, \omega^2), \tag{10.12}$$

which is also a nonlinear regression model, but one with error terms that are (by assumption) serially uncorrelated. Since (10.12) is a nonlinear regression model with well-behaved error terms, it seems natural to estimate it by nonlinear least squares and to make inferences about it by using the Gauss-Newton regression. The regression function is simply

$$x'_t(\beta, \rho) = x_t(\beta) + \rho\big(y_{t-1} - x_{t-1}(\beta)\big), \tag{10.13}$$

which depends on ρ as well as on β.

There are two potential problems with (10.12). First of all, the regression function $x'_t(\beta, \rho)$ necessarily depends on y_{t-1}, whether or not $x_t(\beta)$ depends on any lagged values of the dependent variable. As we saw in Chapter 5, this dependence does not prevent nonlinear least squares from having desirable asymptotic properties provided that certain regularity conditions are satisfied. It can be shown that, as long as $x_t(\beta)$ satisfies the regularity conditions of Theorems 5.1 and 5.2 and the stationarity condition that $|\rho| < 1$ holds, this will indeed be the case for (10.12). However, if the stationarity condition did not hold, standard results about nonlinear least squares, in particular Theorem 5.2, the asymptotic normality theorem, would no longer apply to (10.12).

The second problem with (10.12) is what to do about the first observation. Presumably we do not have data for y_0 and for all the exogenous and predetermined variables needed to evaluate $x_0(\boldsymbol{\beta})$, since if we did the sample would not have started with the observation corresponding to $t = 1$. Thus we cannot evaluate $x'_1(\boldsymbol{\beta}, \rho)$, which depends on y_0 and $x_0(\boldsymbol{\beta})$. The easiest solution to this problem is simply to drop the first observation, requiring that (10.12) hold only for observations 2 through n. Dropping one observation makes no difference asymptotically, and so we can safely do so whenever the sample size is reasonably large.

Another solution to the problem of what to do about the first observation would be to treat it differently from all the subsequent observations, by defining $x'_1(\boldsymbol{\beta}, \rho)$ as $x_1(\boldsymbol{\beta})$ instead of as $x_1(\boldsymbol{\beta}) + \rho\big(y_0 - x_0(\boldsymbol{\beta})\big)$. In that case, the error term for observation 1 would be u_1 rather than ε_1. We have already seen that, provided the AR(1) process is stationary, u_t has unconditional variance $\omega^2/(1-\rho^2)$ for all t, including $t = 1$. By including the first observation in this way, we would be creating heteroskedasticity: Observation 1 would have variance $\omega^2/(1-\rho^2)$, while the remaining observations all have variance ω^2. Moreover, the parameter ρ would now affect not only the regression function $\boldsymbol{x}'(\boldsymbol{\beta}, \rho)$ but also the variance of the first observation. This suggests that if we want to include the first observation, it will no longer be appropriate simply to use nonlinear least squares. In fact, taking account of the first observation will complicate matters substantially, and we will therefore discuss this issue at some length in Section 10.6.

When $x_t(\boldsymbol{\beta})$ is nonlinear, NLS estimation of (10.12) evidently requires a nonlinear maximization algorithm, such as the ones based on the Gauss-Newton regression that were discussed in Section 6.8. In most cases, this estimation should not be too much harder than estimation of the corresponding model with errors assumed to be independent. This approach is also a very reasonable one to use when the original model is linear, i.e., when $x_t(\boldsymbol{\beta}) = \boldsymbol{X}_t\boldsymbol{\beta}$. In practice, however, most regression packages provide special procedures for estimating linear regression models with AR(1) errors. These procedures may or may not work better than nonlinear least squares applied to (10.12) and, as implemented by some packages, may yield incorrect covariance matrix estimates in some cases (see Section 10.4).

All of the specialized estimation procedures for linear regression models with AR(1) errors make use of the fact that, conditional on the value of ρ, estimates of $\boldsymbol{\beta}$ can easily be obtained by ordinary least squares. For the linear regression case, (10.12) can be rewritten as

$$y_t - \rho y_{t-1} = (\boldsymbol{X}_t - \rho\boldsymbol{X}_{t-1})\boldsymbol{\beta} + \varepsilon_t, \quad \varepsilon_t \sim \mathrm{IID}(0, \omega^2). \tag{10.14}$$

Thus, if we make the definitions

$$y_t^*(\rho) \equiv y_t - \rho y_{t-1} \quad \text{and} \quad \boldsymbol{X}_t^*(\rho) \equiv \boldsymbol{X}_t - \rho \boldsymbol{X}_{t-1},$$

we simply have to regress $\boldsymbol{y}^*(\rho)$ on $\boldsymbol{X}^*(\rho)$ in order to estimate $\boldsymbol{\beta}$ conditional on ρ.

It is evident that any consistent estimate of ρ, say $\acute{\rho}$, will yield a consistent estimate of $\boldsymbol{\beta}$ when $\boldsymbol{y}^*(\acute{\rho})$ is regressed on $\boldsymbol{X}^*(\acute{\rho})$. There are numerous techniques in the literature for obtaining such estimates. However, it is probably desirable on grounds of efficiency actually to find the NLS estimate $\hat{\rho}$, and with present-day computing facilities it is hard to justify not doing so. The two widely used techniques for finding $\hat{\rho}$ are **grid search** and **back-and-forth search**. The former can be used in many other situations in which a nonlinear model is easily estimated conditional on a single parameter, and the latter can be used in a wide variety of situations in which a nonlinear model is easily estimated conditional on each of two nonintersecting subsets of parameters. These two techniques are thus of some general interest.

The use of grid search to find estimates $(\hat{\boldsymbol{\beta}}, \hat{\rho})$ that minimize the sum of squared residuals from (10.14), and hence from (10.12) as well, was advocated by Hildreth and Lu (1960), and the procedure is therefore often referred to in the literature as the **Hildreth-Lu procedure**. The basic idea is simplicity itself. For any value of ρ, say $\rho^{(j)}$, we can run a linear regression of $\boldsymbol{y}^*(\rho^{(j)})$ on $\boldsymbol{X}^*(\rho^{(j)})$ to find OLS estimates

$$\boldsymbol{\beta}^{(j)} = \left(\boldsymbol{X}^{*\top}(\rho^{(j)})\boldsymbol{X}^*(\rho^{(j)})\right)^{-1}\boldsymbol{X}^{*\top}(\rho^{(j)})\boldsymbol{y}^*(\rho^{(j)}) \qquad (10.15)$$

and an associated sum of squared residuals, $SSR(\boldsymbol{\beta}^{(j)}, \rho^{(j)})$. We do this for values of ρ that fall on some predetermined grid, say all values between -0.999 and 0.999 at intervals of 0.1 (i.e., $-0.999, -0.9, -0.8, \ldots, 0.8, 0.9, 0.999$). The end points here are ± 0.999 rather than ± 1 so as to avoid violating the stationarity condition.

One of the values $\rho^{(j)}$ on the grid, say $\rho^{(J)}$, must yield the lowest value of $SSR(\boldsymbol{\beta}^{(j)}, \rho^{(j)})$.[1] Then provided that the grid is sufficiently fine, and assuming that $\rho^{(J)}$ is not one of the end points, it is reasonable to expect that $\hat{\rho}$ will lie somewhere between $\rho^{(J-1)}$ and $\rho^{(J+1)}$. If $\rho^{(J)}$ is one of the end points, then $\hat{\rho}$ presumably lies between $\rho^{(J)}$ and the nearest point on the grid. In either case, one can next either establish a new grid over that shorter interval and repeat the grid search or else use $\rho^{(J)}$ as a starting value for some other search procedure, such as the back-and-forth search to be described below.

[1] In rare cases, there might be two or conceivably more $\rho^{(j)}$'s that yielded identical minimal values of $SSR(\boldsymbol{\beta}^{(j)}, \rho^{(j)})$. If these $\rho^{(j)}$'s are adjacent, there is no real problem. If not, the possibility of multiple minima should be investigated by doing a finer grid search in the neighborhood of both minimizing $\rho^{(j)}$'s.

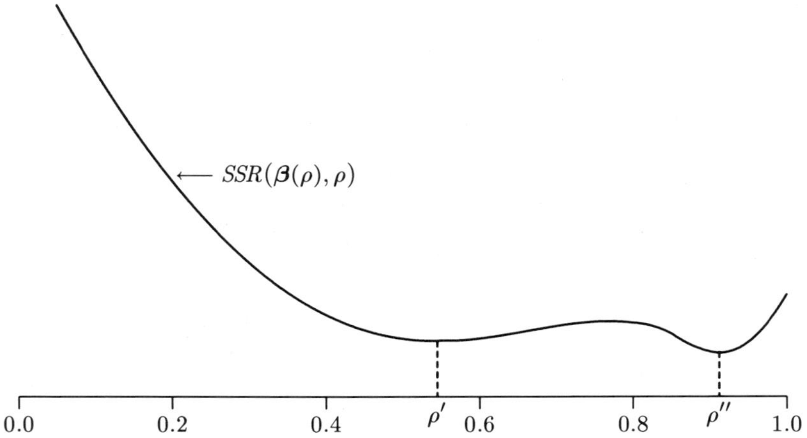

Figure 10.1 A case for which $SSR(\boldsymbol{\beta}(\rho), \rho)$ has two minima

The advantage of grid search is that it can handle problems where there is more than one local minimum. Consider Figure 10.1. Here $SSR(\boldsymbol{\beta}(\rho), \rho)$ has two local minima, one at ρ' and another, which is the global minimum, at ρ''. Provided the grid is fine enough, the first-stage grid search will correctly conclude that $\hat{\rho}$ is near 0.9. Many estimation techniques, in contrast, would incorrectly conclude that it lies near the local minimum at ρ', especially if they were initially started at $\rho = 0$. This is not merely a theoretical advantage for grid search. As several authors have shown — see Dufour, Gaudry, and Liem (1980) and Betancourt and Kelejian (1981) — $SSR(\boldsymbol{\beta}(\rho), \rho)$ will often have multiple minima. This is especially likely if $\boldsymbol{X}$ includes a lagged dependent variable. In that case, there are often two minima: one with a small value of ρ and a large value of the coefficient on the lagged dependent variable, and one with a large value of ρ and a small value of that coefficient. Either may be the global minimum.

The second specialized procedure for linear regression models with AR(1) errors that we will discuss is back-and-forth search. This procedure, which was originally proposed for this problem by Cochrane and Orcutt (1949) and is generally referred to as the (iterated) **Cochrane-Orcutt procedure**, is much more widely used than grid search. It is based on the facts that $\boldsymbol{\beta}$ is very easy to calculate conditional on ρ and that ρ is equally easy to calculate conditional on $\boldsymbol{\beta}$. The Cochrane-Orcutt algorithm starts with an initial value of ρ, $\rho^{(1)}$, which may be equal to zero or may be set to some other value if prior information is available. It then uses that value of ρ to find a new value of $\boldsymbol{\beta}$, $\boldsymbol{\beta}^{(1)} \equiv \boldsymbol{\beta}(\rho^{(1)})$, which is in turn used to find a new value of ρ, $\rho^{(2)}$, and so on until convergence is achieved. At each step, the new value of ρ or $\boldsymbol{\beta}$ is the one that minimizes the sum of squared residuals *conditional* on the given value of $\boldsymbol{\beta}$ or ρ.

For any value of ρ, say $\rho^{(j)}$, an OLS regression of $\boldsymbol{y}^*(\rho^{(j)})$ on $\boldsymbol{X}^*(\rho^{(j)})$ yields $\boldsymbol{\beta}^{(j)} \equiv \boldsymbol{\beta}(\rho^{(j)})$, which minimizes $SSR(\boldsymbol{\beta}\,|\,\rho^{(j)})$, that is, the SSR conditional on $\rho^{(j)}$; the formula for $\boldsymbol{\beta}^{(j)}$ is given in (10.15). Given $\boldsymbol{\beta}^{(j)}$, one can then compute residuals

$$u_t^{(j)} \equiv y_t - \boldsymbol{X}_t\boldsymbol{\beta}^{(j)}.$$

The sum of squared residuals as a function of ρ, conditional on $\boldsymbol{\beta}^{(j)}$, is

$$SSR\big(\rho\,|\,\boldsymbol{\beta}^{(j)}\big) = \sum_{t=2}^{n}\Big(u_t^{(j)} - \rho u_{t-1}^{(j)}\Big)^2. \tag{10.16}$$

This is simply the sum of squared residuals for a linear regression of $u_t^{(j)}$ on $u_{t-1}^{(j)}$ for observations 2 to n, and so the value of ρ that minimizes (10.16) is just the OLS estimate of ρ from that linear regression, which is

$$\rho^{(j+1)} = \frac{\sum_{t=2}^{n} u_t^{(j)} u_{t-1}^{(j)}}{\sum_{t=2}^{n}\big(u_{t-1}^{(j)}\big)^2}. \tag{10.17}$$

The Cochrane-Orcutt procedure thus consists of a sequence of least squares regressions. The first one involves regressing $\boldsymbol{y}^*(\rho^{(1)})$ on $\boldsymbol{X}^*(\rho^{(1)})$, the second, $u_t^{(1)}$ on $u_{t-1}^{(1)}$, the third, $\boldsymbol{y}^*(\rho^{(2)})$ on $\boldsymbol{X}^*(\rho^{(2)})$, and so on. At each step, $SSR(\boldsymbol{\beta}, \rho)$ is minimized with respect to either ρ or $\boldsymbol{\beta}$, and the algorithm is allowed to proceed until some convergence criterion is satisfied (usually that $\rho^{(j)}$ and $\rho^{(j+1)}$ are sufficiently close). Such a procedure must eventually converge to a local minimum of the sum-of-squares function; see Sargan (1964, Appendix A) and Oberhofer and Kmenta (1974). Unfortunately, there is no guarantee that this local minimum will also be a global minimum. It is therefore advisable to employ the Cochrane-Orcutt procedure only after a preliminary grid search has either established that there is only one local minimum or determined approximately where the global minimum is located. Note that although iterated Cochrane-Orcutt works well in many cases, it can sometimes be much slower than using a general NLS algorithm based on the Gauss-Newton regression.

We have seen that the stationarity condition $|\rho| < 1$ is essential if the AR(1) process is to make sense and conventional estimation techniques are to be valid. In practice, however, the NLS estimate $\hat{\rho}$ may be greater than 1 in absolute value. If this happens, or even if $|\hat{\rho}|$ is very close to 1, the investigator should probably treat this as evidence of model inadequacy. Perhaps the model should be respecified in first differences rather than levels (Harvey, 1980), or perhaps the specification of the regression function, the specification of the AR(1) error process, or both, is inconsistent with the data. We will discuss one method of detecting misspecification in models that appear to have AR(1) errors in Section 10.9, below.

Most of the foregoing discussion has been concerned with methods for obtaining NLS estimates of linear regression models with AR(1) errors. When the sample size is very large, it may not be worth the time to obtain NLS estimates, because **one-step estimates** that are asymptotically equivalent to NLS may be quite adequate. Recall from Section 6.6 that, if $\acute{\boldsymbol{\beta}}$ denotes any vector of consistent estimates for the model $\boldsymbol{y} = \boldsymbol{x}(\boldsymbol{\beta}) + \boldsymbol{u}$, the estimator

$$\grave{\boldsymbol{\beta}} \equiv \acute{\boldsymbol{\beta}} + \big(\acute{\boldsymbol{X}}^{\top}\acute{\boldsymbol{X}}\big)^{-1}\acute{\boldsymbol{X}}^{\top}(\boldsymbol{y} - \acute{\boldsymbol{x}}),$$

where $\acute{\boldsymbol{X}} \equiv \boldsymbol{X}(\acute{\boldsymbol{\beta}})$ and $\acute{\boldsymbol{x}} \equiv \boldsymbol{x}(\acute{\boldsymbol{\beta}})$, is asymptotically equivalent to the NLS estimator $\hat{\boldsymbol{\beta}}$. The term that is added to $\acute{\boldsymbol{\beta}}$ here is simply the OLS estimate of $\boldsymbol{b}$ from the Gauss-Newton regression

$$\boldsymbol{y} - \acute{\boldsymbol{x}} = \acute{\boldsymbol{X}}\boldsymbol{b} + \text{residuals},$$

and the OLS covariance matrix from this regression provides a valid estimate of the covariance matrix of $\grave{\boldsymbol{\beta}}$.

With the first observation dropped, as usual, a linear regression model with AR(1) errors can be written as

$$\boldsymbol{y} = \boldsymbol{X\beta} + \rho\boldsymbol{y}_{-1} - \rho\boldsymbol{X}_{-1}\boldsymbol{\beta} + \boldsymbol{\varepsilon}, \tag{10.18}$$

where $\boldsymbol{y}_{-1}$ has typical element y_{t-1} and $\boldsymbol{X}_{-1}$ has typical row $\boldsymbol{X}_{t-1}$. The GNR for calculating the one-step estimates will be

$$\boldsymbol{y} - \acute{\rho}\boldsymbol{y}_{-1} - \big(\boldsymbol{X}\acute{\boldsymbol{\beta}} - \acute{\rho}\boldsymbol{X}_{-1}\acute{\boldsymbol{\beta}}\big) = \big(\boldsymbol{X} - \acute{\rho}\boldsymbol{X}_{-1}\big)\boldsymbol{b} + r\acute{\boldsymbol{u}}_{-1} + \text{residuals}, \tag{10.19}$$

where $\acute{\boldsymbol{u}}_{-1} \equiv \boldsymbol{y}_{-1} - \boldsymbol{X}_{-1}\acute{\boldsymbol{\beta}}$. This GNR is straightforward to calculate once $\acute{\rho}$ and $\acute{\boldsymbol{\beta}}$, the initial consistent estimates of ρ and $\boldsymbol{\beta}$, are known. The problem is to obtain these estimates. If $\boldsymbol{X}$ does not contain any lagged dependent variables, this is very easy. The OLS estimates $\tilde{\boldsymbol{\beta}}$ obtained by regressing $\boldsymbol{y}$ on $\boldsymbol{X}$ will be consistent for $\boldsymbol{\beta}$, and a consistent estimate of ρ may then be obtained by regressing $\tilde{u}_t$ on $\tilde{u}_{t-1}$ for $t = 2$ to n. If $\boldsymbol{X}$ does include one or more lagged values of $\boldsymbol{y}$, however, this simple approach will not work, because the OLS estimates $\tilde{\boldsymbol{\beta}}$ will not be consistent. We now discuss how to deal with this problem.

The nonlinear regression model (10.18) is a special case of the linear regression model

$$\boldsymbol{y} = \boldsymbol{X\beta} + \rho\boldsymbol{y}_{-1} + \boldsymbol{X}_{-1}\boldsymbol{\gamma} + \boldsymbol{\varepsilon}, \tag{10.20}$$

where the former imposes the restriction that $\boldsymbol{\gamma} = -\rho\boldsymbol{\beta}$. Later, in Section 10.9, we will make use of this fact to test the adequacy of the AR(1) specification. For the moment, following Durbin (1960), we will merely use it to obtain a consistent estimate of ρ. It might seem that we could obtain consistent estimates of both $\boldsymbol{\beta}$ and ρ by using OLS to estimate (10.20). That will rarely be the case, however, because many of the coefficients in (10.20) will not be identifiable. For example, if $\boldsymbol{X}$ includes a constant term, one of the elements of $\boldsymbol{\beta}$ will be the coefficient on the constant and one of the elements of $\boldsymbol{\gamma}$ will be the coefficient on the constant lagged; obviously, these two parameters cannot be separately identified.

It is easy to obtain a consistent estimate of ρ from (10.20) if all the lags of the dependent variable included in $\boldsymbol{X}$ are greater than 1; the estimated coefficient on $\boldsymbol{y}_{-1}$ provides it. Unfortunately, the case in which $\boldsymbol{y}_{-1}$ is included in $\boldsymbol{X}$ is likely to be the most common one. To explain the difficulties that arise in this case, we will for simplicity suppose that the original model is

$$y_t = \beta_0 + \beta_1 y_{t-1} + \beta_2 z_t + u_t, \quad u_t = \rho u_{t-1} + \varepsilon_t. \tag{10.21}$$

Then the model that we really want to estimate, (10.18), is

$$y_t = \beta_0(1-\rho) + (\rho + \beta_1)y_{t-1} - \rho\beta_1 y_{t-2} + \beta_2 z_t - \rho\beta_2 z_{t-1} + \varepsilon_t, \tag{10.22}$$

and the unrestricted model (10.20) can be written as

$$y_t = \delta_0 + \delta_1 y_{t-1} + \delta_2 y_{t-2} + \delta_3 z_t + \delta_4 z_{t-1} + \varepsilon_t. \tag{10.23}$$

Note that this unrestricted model has five regression coefficients, compared with four for the restricted model (10.22). Estimating (10.23) by OLS yields $\acute{\delta}_0$ through $\acute{\delta}_4$, which are consistent estimates of the parameters δ_0 through δ_4. The latter are related to ρ and the β_i's by the equations

$$\delta_0 = \beta_0(1-\rho);\ \ \delta_1 = \rho + \beta_1;\ \ \delta_2 = -\rho\beta_1;\ \ \delta_3 = \beta_2;\ \ \delta_4 = -\rho\beta_2. \tag{10.24}$$

There are several ways to obtain a consistent estimate of ρ using these equations. The easiest is to substitute the second-last equation of (10.24) into the last, yielding the result that

$$\acute{\rho} = -\acute{\delta}_4/\acute{\delta}_3. \tag{10.25}$$

Provided that $|\acute{\rho}| < 1$, this consistent estimate of ρ can be used to obtain a consistent estimate of $\boldsymbol{\beta}$ by calculating $\boldsymbol{y}^*(\acute{\rho})$ and $\boldsymbol{X}^*(\acute{\rho})$ and regressing the former on the latter to obtain $\acute{\boldsymbol{\beta}}$. One can then calculate the one-step estimates using the Gauss-Newton regression (10.19). Of course, since in many cases the original model will have more than one regressor like z_t, there will often be several ways to obtain consistent estimates of ρ. This introduces an element of arbitrariness into any one-step estimation procedure, which may explain why such procedures are not widely used.

A different approach is to estimate the original model by instrumental variables to obtain consistent estimates of $\boldsymbol{\beta}$, using instruments for the lagged dependent variables. One can then use those estimates to obtain a consistent estimate of ρ by regressing residuals on lagged residuals in the usual way and, subsequently, estimate (10.19) to obtain one-step estimates asymptotically equivalent to NLS estimates. This is the approach taken by Hatanaka (1974), who also simplifies (10.19) slightly by not subtracting $\boldsymbol{X}\acute{\boldsymbol{\beta}} - \acute{\rho}\boldsymbol{X}_{-1}\acute{\boldsymbol{\beta}}$ from the regressand. As a result of this simplification, the one-step estimates of $\boldsymbol{\beta}$ are now just $\grave{\boldsymbol{b}}$ rather than $\grave{\boldsymbol{b}} + \acute{\boldsymbol{\beta}}$. Like the other procedures we have discussed, Hatanaka's procedure involves an element of arbitrariness, because the initial consistent estimates will depend on the instruments used.

10.4 Standard Errors and Covariance Matrices

It can require a certain amount of care to obtain valid estimates of the covariance matrix of the parameter estimates for a model with serial correlation. If one uses nonlinear least squares to estimate the nonlinear regression model (10.12) that results when the original model $\boldsymbol{y} = \boldsymbol{x}(\boldsymbol{\beta}) + \boldsymbol{u}$ is transformed to allow for AR(1) errors, the obvious way to estimate the covariance matrix of $\hat{\rho}$ and $\hat{\boldsymbol{\beta}}$ is to use the Gauss-Newton regression. In this case, the GNR will be

$$\boldsymbol{y} - \hat{\boldsymbol{x}} - \hat{\rho}(\boldsymbol{y}_{-1} - \hat{\boldsymbol{x}}_{-1}) = (\hat{\boldsymbol{X}} - \hat{\rho}\hat{\boldsymbol{X}}_{-1})\boldsymbol{b} + r(\boldsymbol{y}_{-1} - \hat{\boldsymbol{x}}_{-1}) + \text{residuals} \tag{10.26}$$

for observations 2 through n. The regressand is the vector of residuals from nonlinear least squares estimation of (10.12). There are $k+1$ regressors, one corresponding to each of the k elements of $\boldsymbol{\beta}$ and one corresponding to ρ. In the linear case, the regressor corresponding to $\boldsymbol{\beta}_i$ is simply the ith column of $\boldsymbol{X}^*(\hat{\rho})$, and the regressor corresponding to ρ is the vector $\boldsymbol{y} - \boldsymbol{X}\hat{\boldsymbol{\beta}}$ lagged once. Note that this last regressor is *not* just the lagged vector of residuals from OLS estimation of the original model without serial correlation, because $\hat{\boldsymbol{\beta}}$ is the vector of estimates from the model (10.12) which has been corrected for AR(1) errors.

The results of Chapters 5 and 6 make it clear that the GNR (10.26) will yield an asymptotically valid covariance matrix estimate, and this is what most nonlinear least squares packages would produce. Thus, if the original model (10.11) is nonlinear, or if one uses NLS when the original model is linear, there is no problem generating a valid covariance matrix estimate. However, the estimate generated by (10.26) is *not* the estimate that many implementations of the Cochrane-Orcutt and Hildreth-Lu procedures would produce. As they are often implemented, those procedures typically report an estimated covariance matrix for $\hat{\boldsymbol{\beta}}$ from the final regression of $\boldsymbol{y}^*(\hat{\rho})$ on $\boldsymbol{X}^*(\hat{\rho})$, that is, the regression

$$\boldsymbol{y} - \hat{\rho}\boldsymbol{y}_{-1} = (\boldsymbol{X} - \hat{\rho}\boldsymbol{X}_{-1})\boldsymbol{\beta} + \text{residuals}, \tag{10.27}$$

which yields the NLS coefficient vector $\hat{\boldsymbol{\beta}}$. The resulting estimated covariance matrix, computed from just $n-1$ observations, will be

$$\frac{SSR(\hat{\boldsymbol{\beta}}, \hat{\rho})}{n-k-1}\big(\boldsymbol{X}^{*\top}(\hat{\rho})\boldsymbol{X}^*(\hat{\rho})\big)^{-1}, \tag{10.28}$$

which is, in general, valid only *conditional* on $\hat{\rho}$. Since ρ has in fact been estimated, we want an estimated covariance matrix that is valid unconditionally. As we now demonstrate, (10.28) may or may not provide such an estimated covariance matrix.

For the case of a linear model, the GNR (10.26) will be

$$\boldsymbol{y} - \hat{\rho}\boldsymbol{y}_{-1} - (\boldsymbol{X} - \hat{\rho}\boldsymbol{X}_{-1})\hat{\boldsymbol{\beta}} = (\boldsymbol{X} - \hat{\rho}\boldsymbol{X}_{-1})\boldsymbol{b} + r\hat{\boldsymbol{u}}_{-1} + \text{residuals}, \tag{10.29}$$

where $\hat{\boldsymbol{u}}_{-1} \equiv \boldsymbol{y}_{-1} - \boldsymbol{X}_{-1}\hat{\boldsymbol{\beta}}$. Notice that (10.27) and (10.29) have exactly the same residuals. In (10.29), the regressand is orthogonal to all the regressors, and so the vector of residuals is just the regressand. The residuals from (10.27) have the same algebraic form as the regressand of (10.29) and coincide with it because the value of $\boldsymbol{\beta}$ that is used in (10.27) is precisely $\hat{\boldsymbol{\beta}}$.

The estimated covariance matrix for $\hat{\boldsymbol{\beta}}$ from the GNR (10.29) will be the upper left-hand $k \times k$ block of the matrix

$$\frac{SSR(\hat{\boldsymbol{\beta}}, \hat{\rho})}{n-k-2} \begin{bmatrix} \boldsymbol{X}^{*\top}(\hat{\rho})\boldsymbol{X}^{*}(\hat{\rho}) & \boldsymbol{X}^{*\top}(\hat{\rho})\hat{\boldsymbol{u}}_{-1} \\ \hat{\boldsymbol{u}}_{-1}^{\top}\boldsymbol{X}^{*}(\hat{\rho}) & \hat{\boldsymbol{u}}_{-1}^{\top}\hat{\boldsymbol{u}}_{-1} \end{bmatrix}^{-1}. \tag{10.30}$$

The first factors in (10.28) and (10.30) differ only in the number of degrees of freedom in the denominator of the estimate of ω^2; the numerators are the same because both (10.27) and (10.29) have the same sum of squared residuals.[2] The difference between the second factors is what matters. The second factor in (10.28) is the inverse of the matrix $\boldsymbol{X}^{*\top}(\hat{\rho})\boldsymbol{X}^{*}(\hat{\rho})$, while the second factor in the covariance matrix estimate from the GNR is the upper left-hand $k \times k$ block of the inverse of a $(k+1) \times (k+1)$ matrix. Provided that $\boldsymbol{X}$ does not contain lagged dependent variables, $\boldsymbol{u}_{-1}$ will be independent of $\boldsymbol{X}$, which implies that

$$\operatorname*{plim}_{n\to\infty} \left(\frac{\boldsymbol{X}^{*\top}(\hat{\rho})\hat{\boldsymbol{u}}_{-1}}{n-1} \right) = \mathbf{0}.$$

Thus $(n-1)^{-1}$ times the matrix in (10.30) will be asymptotically block-diagonal, and its inverse will therefore be asymptotically equal to

$$\begin{aligned} &\begin{bmatrix} (n-1)^{-1}\boldsymbol{X}^{*\top}(\hat{\rho})\boldsymbol{X}^{*}(\hat{\rho}) & \mathbf{0} \\ \mathbf{0}^{\top} & (n-1)^{-1}\hat{\boldsymbol{u}}_{-1}^{\top}\hat{\boldsymbol{u}}_{-1} \end{bmatrix}^{-1} \\ &= (n-1) \begin{bmatrix} \left(\boldsymbol{X}^{*\top}(\hat{\rho})\boldsymbol{X}^{*}(\hat{\rho})\right)^{-1} & \mathbf{0} \\ \mathbf{0}^{\top} & \left(\hat{\boldsymbol{u}}_{-1}^{\top}\hat{\boldsymbol{u}}_{-1}\right)^{-1} \end{bmatrix}. \end{aligned} \tag{10.31}$$

This makes it clear that (10.28) will provide a valid estimate of the upper left-hand $k \times k$ block of the inverse in (10.30).

Provided that $\boldsymbol{X}$ does not include any lagged dependent variables (or any other variables that may be correlated with $\boldsymbol{u}_{-1}$), regression (10.27) will yield an asymptotically valid estimate of the covariance matrix of $\hat{\boldsymbol{\beta}}$. On the other hand, if $\boldsymbol{X}$ *does* include lagged dependent variables, or if it is not independent of the lagged error terms $\boldsymbol{u}_{-1}$ for any other reason, the conditional covariance matrix estimate (10.28) will *not* be valid. With many regression packages,

[2] Recall that ω^2 is the variance of the error terms ε_t which appear in the nonlinear regression (10.12).

the reported covariance matrix from the Cochrane-Orcutt and Hildreth-Lu procedures will thus be invalid in many cases. One either has to calculate the GNR (10.29) oneself or use nonlinear least squares from the beginning so that the regression package will do so.

When the conditional covariance matrix estimate is invalid, reported standard errors are always too small (asymptotically). In fact, the covariance matrix estimate produced by the GNR (10.29) for the estimates of $\boldsymbol{\beta}$ differs from that produced by (10.27) by a positive definite matrix, if we ignore the fact that the degrees of freedom are different. To see this, notice that the Gauss-Newton regression (10.29) has the same regressors as (10.27), plus one additional regressor, $\hat{\boldsymbol{u}}_{-1}$. If we apply the FWL Theorem to (10.29), we see that the covariance matrix estimate from it is the same as that from a regression in which all the variables are projected onto the orthogonal complement of $\hat{\boldsymbol{u}}_{-1}$. The residuals are unchanged by the projection and so are identical to those of (10.27), as we saw above. The difference between the covariance matrix estimates for $\hat{\boldsymbol{\beta}}$ from (10.29) and (10.27) is therefore proportional to

$$\big(\boldsymbol{X}^{*\top}(\hat{\rho})\boldsymbol{M}_{\hat{u}_{-1}}\boldsymbol{X}^*(\hat{\rho})\big)^{-1} - \big(\boldsymbol{X}^{*\top}(\hat{\rho})\boldsymbol{X}^*(\hat{\rho})\big)^{-1}, \tag{10.32}$$

except for an asymptotically negligible effect due to the different degrees-of-freedom factors. If we subtract the inverses of the two matrices in (10.32) in the opposite order, we obtain

$$\boldsymbol{X}^{*\top}(\hat{\rho})\boldsymbol{P}_{\hat{u}_{-1}}\boldsymbol{X}^*(\hat{\rho}),$$

which is evidently positive semidefinite. It then follows from a result proved in Appendix A that (10.32) is itself positive semidefinite. If $\hat{\boldsymbol{u}}_{-1}$ is substantially correlated with the columns of $\boldsymbol{X}^*(\hat{\rho})$, the incorrect variance estimate from regression (10.27) may be much smaller than the correct variance estimate from the GNR (10.29).

The Gauss-Newton regressions (10.26) and (10.29) yield estimated standard errors for $\hat{\rho}$ as well as for $\hat{\boldsymbol{\beta}}$. If the covariance matrix is asymptotically block-diagonal between ρ and $\boldsymbol{\beta}$, we see from (10.31) that the asymptotic variance of $n^{1/2}(\hat{\rho} - \rho_0)$ will be equal to

$$\omega^2 \operatorname*{plim}_{n\to\infty}\left(\frac{\hat{\boldsymbol{u}}_{-1}^{\top}\hat{\boldsymbol{u}}_{-1}}{n-1}\right)^{-1} = \omega^2\left(\frac{1-\rho_0^2}{\omega^2}\right) = 1 - \rho_0^2. \tag{10.33}$$

Thus, in this special case, the variance of $\hat{\rho}$ can be estimated by

$$\frac{1-\hat{\rho}^2}{n-1}. \tag{10.34}$$

It may seem puzzling that neither the asymptotic variance $1-\rho_0^2$ nor the estimate (10.34) depends on ω^2. After all, we normally expect the variance of an estimator of a coefficient in a regression function to be proportional to the variance of the error terms. The reason that the variance of $\hat{\rho}$ does not depend on ω^2 is that ω^2 actually affects it in two different ways, which exactly cancel out. This can be seen from the middle expression in (10.33). The variance of u_{t-1} is directly proportional to ω^2. Thus, as ω^2 increases, the *ratio* of the variability of ε_t to the variability of the regressor $\hat{u}_{t-1}$ in the GNR (10.29) stays constant. Since it is this ratio that matters for the variance of the coefficient estimate, the latter does not depend on ω^2 at all.

The use of the GNR to calculate the covariance matrix of $(\hat{\boldsymbol{\beta}}, \hat{\rho})$ from a linear regression with AR(1) errors was advocated by Davidson and MacKinnon (1980). A very different approach, which is both more difficult and less general, was earlier suggested by Cooper (1972a). The advantages of an analysis based on the Gauss-Newton regression are evident if one contrasts the approach of the latter paper with the above treatment.

10.5 Higher-Order AR Processes

Although the AR(1) process (10.01) is by far the most popular one in applied econometric work, there are many other stochastic processes that could reasonably be used to describe the evolution of error terms over time. Anything resembling a complete treatment of this topic would lead us far afield, into the vast literature on **time-series methods**. This literature, which evolved quite independently of econometrics and has influenced it substantially in recent years, deals with many aspects of the modeling of time series but especially with models in which variables depend *only* (or at least primarily) on their own past values. Such models are obviously appropriate for describing the evolution of many physical systems and may be appropriate for some economic systems as well. However, much of the use of time-series methods in econometrics has been to model the evolution of the error terms that adhere to more conventional regression models, and we will treat only that aspect of time-series methods here. A classic reference on times-series techniques is Box and Jenkins (1976), some books that may be more accessible to economists are Harvey (1981, 1989) and Granger and Newbold (1986), and a review of time-series methods for econometricians is Granger and Watson (1984).

The AR(1) process (10.01) is actually a special case of the $\boldsymbol{p}^{\text{th}}$**-order autoregressive**, or **AR(*p*)**, process

$$u_t = \rho_1 u_{t-1} + \rho_2 u_{t-2} + \cdots + \rho_p u_{t-p} + \varepsilon_t, \quad \varepsilon_t \sim \text{IID}(0, \omega^2), \tag{10.35}$$

in which u_t depends on up to p lagged values of itself, as well as on ε_t. The AR(p) process (10.35) can be expressed more compactly as

$$(1 - \rho_1 L - \rho_2 L^2 - \cdots - \rho_p L^p)u_t = \varepsilon_t, \quad \varepsilon_t \sim \text{IID}(0, \omega^2), \tag{10.36}$$

where L denotes the **lag operator**. The lag operator L has the property that when L multiplies anything with a time subscript, this subscript is lagged one period. Thus

$$Lu_t = u_{t-1}, \quad L^2 u_t = u_{t-2}, \quad L^p u_t = u_{t-p},$$

and so on. The expression in parentheses in (10.36) is a polynomial in the lag operator L, with coefficients 1 and $-\rho_1, \ldots, -\rho_p$. If we define $A(L, \boldsymbol{\rho})$ as being equal to this polynomial, $\boldsymbol{\rho}$ representing the vector $[\rho_1 \vdots \rho_2 \vdots \cdots \vdots \rho_p]$, we can write (10.36) even more compactly as

$$A(L, \boldsymbol{\rho})u_t = \varepsilon_t, \quad \varepsilon_t \sim \mathrm{IID}(0, \omega^2). \tag{10.37}$$

For the same reasons that we wish to impose the condition $|\rho_1| < 1$ on AR(1) processes so as to ensure that they are stationary, we would like to impose stationarity conditions on general AR(p) processes. The stationarity condition for such processes may be expressed in several ways; one of them is that all the roots of the polynomial equation in z,

$$A(z, \boldsymbol{\rho}) \equiv 1 - \rho_1 z - \rho_2 z^2 - \cdots - \rho_p z^p = 0 \tag{10.38}$$

must lie **outside the unit circle**, which simply means that all of the roots of (10.38) must be greater than 1 in absolute value. This condition can lead to quite complicated restrictions on $\boldsymbol{\rho}$ for general AR(p) processes.

It rarely makes sense to specify a high-order AR(p) process (i.e., one with p a large number) when trying to model the error terms associated with a regression model. The AR(2) process is much more flexible, but also much more complicated, than the AR(1) process; it is often all that is needed when the latter is too restrictive. The additional complexity of the AR(2) process is easily seen. For example, the variance of u_t, assuming stationarity, is

$$\sigma^2 = \frac{1 - \rho_2}{1 + \rho_2} \times \frac{\omega^2}{(1 - \rho_2)^2 - \rho_1^2},$$

which is substantially more complicated than the corresponding expression (10.02) for the AR(1) case, and stationarity now requires that three conditions hold:

$$\rho_1 + \rho_2 < 1; \quad \rho_2 - \rho_1 < 1; \quad \rho_2 > -1. \tag{10.39}$$

Conditions (10.39) define a **stationarity triangle**. This triangle has vertices at $(-2, -1)$, $(2, -1)$, and $(0, 1)$. Provided that the point (ρ_1, ρ_2) lies within the triangle, the AR(2) process will be stationary.

Autoregressive processes of order higher than 2 arise quite frequently with time-series data that exhibit seasonal variation. It is not uncommon, for example, for error terms in models estimated using quarterly data apparently to follow the **simple AR(4) process**

$$u_t = \rho_4 u_{t-4} + \varepsilon_t, \quad \varepsilon_t \sim \mathrm{IID}(0, \omega^2), \tag{10.40}$$

in which the error term in period t depends on the error in the same quarter of the previous year, but not on any intervening error terms. Another possibility is that the error terms may appear to follow a combined first- and fourth-order AR process

$$(1-\rho_1 L)(1-\rho_4 L^4)u_t = \varepsilon_t, \quad \varepsilon_t \sim \text{IID}(0,\omega^2) \tag{10.41}$$

or, multiplying out the polynomial on the left-hand side,

$$(1-\rho_1 L - \rho_4 L^4 + \rho_1\rho_4 L^5)u_t = \varepsilon_t, \quad \varepsilon_t \sim \text{IID}(0,\omega^2).$$

This is a restricted special case of an AR(5) process, but with only two parameters instead of five to estimate. Various ways of modeling seasonality, including **seasonal AR processes** such as (10.40) and (10.41), will be discussed in Chapter 19.

It is clear that estimating a regression model with errors that follow an AR(p) process is not fundamentally different from estimating the same model with errors that follow an AR(1) process. Thus if, for example, we wish to estimate the model

$$y_t = x_t(\boldsymbol{\beta}) + u_t, \;\; (1-\rho_1 L)(1-\rho_4 L^4)u_t = \varepsilon_t, \;\; \varepsilon_t \sim \text{IID}(0,\omega^2),$$

we simply have to transform it into the model

$$\begin{aligned} y_t = x_t(\boldsymbol{\beta}) &+ \rho_1\big(y_{t-1} - x_{t-1}(\boldsymbol{\beta})\big) + \rho_4\big(y_{t-4} - x_{t-4}(\boldsymbol{\beta})\big) \\ &- \rho_1\rho_4\big(y_{t-5} - x_{t-5}(\boldsymbol{\beta})\big) + \varepsilon_t, \quad \varepsilon_t \sim \text{IID}(0,\omega^2), \end{aligned}$$

drop the first *five* observations, and use nonlinear least squares. As in the AR(1) case, the covariance matrix of $(\hat{\boldsymbol{\rho}}, \hat{\boldsymbol{\beta}})$ may then be estimated using the Gauss-Newton regression. Having to drop five observations may make us uncomfortable, especially if the sample size is modest, but it is certainly valid asymptotically, and since all our results on nonlinear least squares are asymptotic, there is no compelling reason not to do so. We will discuss alternative approaches in the next section.

10.6 Initial Observations in Models with AR Errors

So far, when we have transformed regression models with autoregressive errors so as to make their error terms white noise, we have simply dropped as many observations at the beginning of the sample as necessary to make the transformed model a nonlinear regression model. Although this is clearly valid asymptotically and is certainly the simplest way to proceed, investigators may well be reluctant to throw away the information contained in the initial observation(s). There is good reason for this reluctance. As we will see, these initial observations can sometimes contain much more information about parameter values than their number in relation to the sample size would suggest. Therefore, dropping them may result in a serious loss of efficiency.

We begin by discussing the nonlinear regression model with AR(1) errors. As we have seen, the AR(1) process is the simplest AR process to analyze and the one most commonly encountered in empirical work. Moreover, it allows us to introduce all the important conceptual issues associated with the treatment of initial observations. The model is

$$y_t = x_t(\boldsymbol{\beta}) + u_t, \quad u_t = \rho u_{t-1} + \varepsilon_t, \quad \varepsilon_t \sim \mathrm{IID}(0, \omega^2), \quad |\rho| < 1. \tag{10.42}$$

The covariance matrix of the u_t's is given by expression (10.05). It can be verified by multiplication that the inverse of this matrix is

$$\boldsymbol{\Omega}^{-1} = \frac{1}{\omega^2}\begin{bmatrix} 1 & -\rho & 0 & \cdots & 0 & 0 \\ -\rho & 1+\rho^2 & -\rho & \cdots & 0 & 0 \\ 0 & -\rho & 1+\rho^2 & \cdots & 0 & 0 \\ \vdots & \vdots & \vdots & & \vdots & \vdots \\ 0 & 0 & 0 & \cdots & 1+\rho^2 & -\rho \\ 0 & 0 & 0 & \cdots & -\rho & 1 \end{bmatrix} \equiv \frac{\boldsymbol{\Delta}^{-1}(\rho)}{\omega^2}. \tag{10.43}$$

It can similarly be verified that for the matrix $\boldsymbol{\eta}(\rho)$, which must satisfy

$$\boldsymbol{\eta}^{\top}(\rho)\boldsymbol{\eta}(\rho) \equiv \boldsymbol{\Delta}^{-1}(\rho),$$

one can use

$$\boldsymbol{\eta}(\rho) = \begin{bmatrix} (1-\rho^2)^{1/2} & 0 & 0 & \cdots & 0 & 0 \\ -\rho & 1 & 0 & \cdots & 0 & 0 \\ 0 & -\rho & 1 & \cdots & 0 & 0 \\ \vdots & \vdots & \vdots & & \vdots & \vdots \\ 0 & 0 & 0 & \cdots & -\rho & 1 \end{bmatrix}. \tag{10.44}$$

This transformation matrix was derived by Prais and Winsten (1954), and is sometimes referred to as the **Prais-Winsten transformation**. Thus, if ρ were known, we could obtain GNLS estimates by running the nonlinear regression

$$\boldsymbol{\eta}(\rho)\boldsymbol{y} = \boldsymbol{\eta}(\rho)\boldsymbol{x}(\boldsymbol{\beta}) + \boldsymbol{\eta}(\rho)\boldsymbol{u}$$

or, changing notation in an obvious way,

$$\boldsymbol{y}^*(\rho) = \boldsymbol{x}^*(\boldsymbol{\beta}, \rho) + \boldsymbol{u}^*. \tag{10.45}$$

Postmultiplying $\boldsymbol{\eta}(\rho)$ by $\boldsymbol{y}$ and $\boldsymbol{x}(\boldsymbol{\beta})$, we see that the regressand $\boldsymbol{y}^*(\rho)$ and the vector of regression functions $\boldsymbol{x}^*(\rho)$ are, respectively,

$$\begin{aligned} y_1^*(\rho) &= (1-\rho^2)^{1/2}y_1; \\ y_t^*(\rho) &= y_t - \rho y_{t-1} \text{ for all } t \geq 2; \\ x_1^*(\boldsymbol{\beta},\rho) &= (1-\rho^2)^{1/2}x_1(\boldsymbol{\beta}); \\ x_t^*(\boldsymbol{\beta},\rho) &= x_t(\boldsymbol{\beta}) - \rho x_{t-1}(\boldsymbol{\beta}) \text{ for all } t \geq 2. \end{aligned} \tag{10.46}$$

Thus, for observations 2 through n, the transformed model (10.45) is identical to the nonlinear regression model (10.12) in which we dropped the first observation. What is new is that (10.45) has n observations instead of only $n-1$.

Regression (10.45) makes it possible to compute estimates of $\boldsymbol{\beta}$ by GNLS and, by extension, by feasible GNLS, taking account of all n observations. Feasible GNLS will be available whenever it is possible to obtain an initial consistent estimate of ρ. As we saw in Section 10.3, that will be easy if $x_t(\boldsymbol{\beta})$ does not depend on lagged values of y_t, since we just need to estimate the model by NLS and regress the residuals from that estimation on themselves lagged once. But if $x_t(\boldsymbol{\beta})$ does depend on lagged values of y_t, regression (10.45) does not provide an appropriate way to deal with the first observation. The first observation of (10.45) can be written as

$$(1-\rho^2)^{1/2}y_1 = (1-\rho^2)^{1/2}x_1(\boldsymbol{\beta}) + (1-\rho^2)^{1/2}u_1, \tag{10.47}$$

which shows that the only effect of the transformation (10.44) is to multiply everything by $(1-\rho^2)^{1/2}$. We saw in Section 10.2 that a regression function which depends on lags of the dependent variable is correlated with its corresponding error term if the error terms are serially correlated. If this is the case for $x_1(\boldsymbol{\beta})$ and u_1, we see from (10.47) that it must also be the case for $x_1^*(\boldsymbol{\beta},\rho)$ and $u_1^*(\rho)$. Of course, since the correlation between $x_1^*(\boldsymbol{\beta},\rho)$ and $u_1^*(\rho)$ affects one observation only, it is perfectly valid asymptotically to treat the first observation in this way, just as it is perfectly valid to drop it entirely. It is possible, but by no means easy, to take proper account of the first observation in a linear regression model with a single lagged dependent variable and AR(1) errors; see Pesaran (1981). However, it is very much more common simply to drop the first observation in this case. For the remainder of this section, we will therefore assume that $x_t(\boldsymbol{\beta})$ does not depend on lagged values of y_t.

We have now seen how to obtain GNLS and feasible GNLS estimates of the model (10.42) which use all n observations. If we further assume that the ε_t's are normally distributed, we can obtain ML estimates. Because these are asymptotically equivalent to GNLS, they will be consistent even if the normality assumption is false. Techniques that estimate this model by maximum likelihood and take all observations into account are often called **full ML estimation** or **exact ML estimation**.

There are several ways to derive the loglikelihood function. The easiest approach is probably the following. For observations 2 through n, we have seen that

$$y_t = \rho y_{t-1} + x_t(\boldsymbol{\beta}) - \rho x_{t-1}(\boldsymbol{\beta}) + \varepsilon_t.$$

This can be turned around so that ε_t is written as a function of y_t. The density of ε_t is

$$\frac{1}{\sqrt{2\pi}}\frac{1}{\omega}\exp\left(-\frac{\varepsilon_t^2}{2\omega^2}\right).$$

Since $\partial\varepsilon_t/\partial y_t = 1$, the Jacobian factor is unity, and so the partial loglikelihood function for observations 2 through n only is

$$\begin{aligned}\ell^{2,n}(\boldsymbol{y},\boldsymbol{\beta},\rho,\omega) = &-\frac{n-1}{2}\log(2\pi) - (n-1)\log(\omega) \\ &-\frac{1}{2\omega^2}\sum_{t=2}^{n}\big(y_t - \rho y_{t-1} - x_t(\boldsymbol{\beta}) + \rho x_{t-1}(\boldsymbol{\beta})\big)^2.\end{aligned} \tag{10.48}$$

The density of $u_1 = y_1 - x_1(\boldsymbol{\beta})$ is

$$\frac{1}{\sqrt{2\pi}}\frac{1}{\sigma}\exp\left(-\frac{u_1^2}{2\sigma^2}\right) = \frac{1}{\sqrt{2\pi}}\frac{1}{\omega}(1-\rho^2)^{1/2}\exp\left(-\frac{1-\rho^2}{2\omega^2}u_1^2\right), \tag{10.49}$$

where the first expression writes this density in terms of σ, and the second expression writes it in terms of $\omega = \sigma(1-\rho^2)^{1/2}$. Thus the contribution to the loglikelihood function made by observation 1 is

$$\begin{aligned}\ell^{1}(\boldsymbol{y},\boldsymbol{\beta},\rho,\omega) = &-\tfrac{1}{2}\log(2\pi) - \log(\omega) + \tfrac{1}{2}\log(1-\rho^2) \\ &-\frac{1-\rho^2}{2\omega^2}\big(y_1 - x_1(\boldsymbol{\beta})\big)^2.\end{aligned} \tag{10.50}$$

Combining (10.48) and (10.50) yields the full loglikelihood function

$$\begin{aligned}\ell^{n}(\boldsymbol{y},\boldsymbol{\beta},\rho,\omega) = &-\tfrac{n}{2}\log(2\pi) - n\log(\omega) + \tfrac{1}{2}\log(1-\rho^2) \\ -\frac{1}{2\omega^2}&\left(\sum_{t=2}^{n}\big(y_t - \rho y_{t-1} - x_t(\boldsymbol{\beta}) + \rho x_{t-1}(\boldsymbol{\beta})\big)^2 + (1-\rho^2)\big(y_1 - x_1(\boldsymbol{\beta})\big)^2\right).\end{aligned} \tag{10.51}$$

Concentrating $\ell^n(\boldsymbol{y},\boldsymbol{\beta},\rho,\omega)$ with respect to ω yields the full concentrated loglikelihood function $\ell^c(\boldsymbol{y},\boldsymbol{\beta},\rho)$:

$$C + \tfrac{1}{2}\log(1-\rho^2) - \tfrac{n}{2}\log\Big(\big(\boldsymbol{y} - \boldsymbol{x}(\boldsymbol{\beta})\big)^{\top}\boldsymbol{\Delta}^{-1}(\rho)\big(\boldsymbol{y} - \boldsymbol{x}(\boldsymbol{\beta})\big)\Big), \tag{10.52}$$

where the $n \times n$ matrix $\boldsymbol{\Delta}^{-1}(\rho)$ was implicitly defined by (10.43).

The function (10.52) can be maximized in various ways. In particular, for the case in which $\boldsymbol{x}(\boldsymbol{\beta}) = \boldsymbol{X\beta}$, Beach and MacKinnon (1978a) proposed an algorithm similar to the iterated Cochrane-Orcutt procedure discussed in Section 10.3. They showed that to maximize $\ell^c(\boldsymbol{y}, \boldsymbol{\beta}, \rho)$ conditional on $\boldsymbol{\beta}$ one simply has to find the middle root of a certain cubic equation in ρ. The formula for doing so, together with the linear version of regression (10.45), allow one to compute a succession of values $\boldsymbol{\beta}^{(0)}$, $\rho^{(1)}$, $\boldsymbol{\beta}^{(1)}$, $\rho^{(2)}$, and so on, which by the same arguments used in the case of iterated Cochrane-Orcutt must eventually converge to a local maximum of (10.52).

The term $\frac{1}{2}\log(1-\rho^2)$ that appears in both (10.51) and (10.52) is a Jacobian term. This may not be obvious from the way we have derived the loglikelihood function. One can think of the first observation as being

$$(1-\rho^2)^{1/2}y_1 = (1-\rho^2)^{1/2}x_1(\boldsymbol{\beta}) + \varepsilon_1, \tag{10.53}$$

where ε_1 is $N(0, \omega^2)$.[3] Thus the density (10.49) is derived by transforming from ε_1 to y_1, and the Jacobian factor $(1-\rho^2)^{1/2}$ arises from this transformation. The resulting Jacobian term $\frac{1}{2}\log(1-\rho^2)$ plays a very important role in estimation. Since it tends to minus infinity as ρ tends to ± 1, its presence in the loglikelihood function ensures that there must be a maximum within the **stationarity region** $-1 < \rho < 1$. Thus full maximum likelihood estimation is *guaranteed* to yield an estimate of ρ for which the AR(1) process for the error terms is stationary. This is not the case for other estimation techniques. Techniques that drop the first observation can and sometimes do yield estimates of ρ greater than 1 in absolute value. Iterated Cochrane-Orcutt (if it converges to the global maximum) is equivalent to maximizing the loglikelihood function (10.48) for the last $n-1$ observations only, and there is nothing to prevent the maximum occurring at a value of ρ outside the stationarity region. Even iterated Prais-Winsten, a procedure similar to iterated Cochrane-Orcutt but that uses the transformation (10.44) to find $\boldsymbol{\beta}$ conditional on ρ, so as to minimize $\big(\boldsymbol{y}-\boldsymbol{x}(\boldsymbol{\beta})\big)^{\top}\boldsymbol{\Delta}^{-1}(\rho)\big(\boldsymbol{y}-\boldsymbol{x}(\boldsymbol{\beta})\big)$, can run into this problem. Of course, since the transformation (10.44) makes no sense if $|\rho| > 1$, such estimates should be discarded.

The covariance matrix of the vector of ML estimates $[\hat{\boldsymbol{\beta}} \,\vdots\, \hat{\rho} \,\vdots\, \hat{\omega}]$ can be estimated by finding the inverse of the information matrix and evaluating it at $[\hat{\boldsymbol{\beta}} \,\vdots\, \hat{\rho} \,\vdots\, \hat{\omega}]$. The result is

$$\hat{\boldsymbol{V}}(\hat{\boldsymbol{\beta}}, \hat{\rho}, \hat{\omega}) = \begin{bmatrix} \hat{\omega}^2\big(\hat{\boldsymbol{X}}^{*\top}\hat{\boldsymbol{X}}^{*}\big)^{-1} & \mathbf{0} \\ \mathbf{0} & \hat{\boldsymbol{V}}(\hat{\rho}, \hat{\omega}) \end{bmatrix}, \tag{10.54}$$

[3] Notice, however, that ε_1 in (10.53) is not simply the innovation in the first period but rather another random variable, with the same distribution, which actually depends on all the innovations up to and including that of period 1. In fact, as can be seen from (10.47), $\varepsilon_1 = (1-\rho^2)^{1/2}u_1$.

where $\hat{\boldsymbol{X}}^*$ denotes the $n \times k$ matrix of the derivatives of the vector of nonlinear functions $\boldsymbol{x}^*(\boldsymbol{\beta}, \rho)$, defined in (10.46), with respect to the elements of $\boldsymbol{\beta}$, evaluated at $(\hat{\boldsymbol{\beta}}, \hat{\rho})$, and

$$\hat{\boldsymbol{V}}(\hat{\rho}, \hat{\omega}) = \begin{bmatrix} \dfrac{n}{1-\hat{\rho}^2} + \dfrac{3\hat{\rho}^2 - 1}{(1-\hat{\rho}^2)^2} & \dfrac{2\hat{\rho}}{\hat{\omega}(1-\hat{\rho}^2)} \\ \dfrac{2\hat{\rho}}{\hat{\omega}(1-\hat{\rho}^2)} & \dfrac{2n}{\hat{\omega}^2} \end{bmatrix}^{-1}.$$

The estimated covariance matrix (10.54) is block-diagonal between $\boldsymbol{\beta}$ and ρ and between $\boldsymbol{\beta}$ and ω (recall that we have ruled out lagged dependent variables). However, unlike the situation with regression models, it is not block-diagonal between ρ and ω. The off-diagonal terms in the (ρ, ω) block of the information matrix are $O(1)$, while the diagonal terms are $O(n)$. Thus $\boldsymbol{V}(\hat{\boldsymbol{\beta}}, \hat{\rho}, \hat{\omega})$ will be asymptotically block-diagonal between $\boldsymbol{\beta}$, ρ, and ω. This is what we would expect, since it is only the first observation, which is asymptotically negligible, that prevents (10.54) from being block-diagonal in the first place.

It is an excellent exercise to derive the estimated covariance matrix (10.54). One starts by taking the second derivatives of (10.51) with respect to all of the parameters of the model to find the Hessian, then takes expectations of minus it to obtain the information matrix. One then replaces parameters by their ML estimates and inverts the information matrix to obtain (10.54). Although this exercise is straightforward, there are plenty of opportunities to make mistakes. For example, Beach and MacKinnon (1978a) fail to take all possible expectations and, as a result, end up with an excessively complicated estimated covariance matrix.

The preceding discussion makes it clear that taking the first observation into account is significantly harder than ignoring it. Even if an appropriate computer program is available, so that estimation is straightforward, one runs into trouble when one wants to test the model. Since the transformed model is no longer a regression model, the Gauss-Newton regression no longer applies and cannot be used to do model specification tests; see Sections 10.8 and 10.9. One could of course estimate the model twice, once taking account of the first observation, in order to obtain the most efficient possible estimates, and once dropping it, in order to be able to test the specification, but this clearly involves some extra work. The obvious question that arises, then, is whether the additional trouble of taking the first observation into account is worth it.

There is a large literature on this subject, including Kadiyala (1968), Rao and Griliches (1969), Maeshiro (1976, 1979), Beach and MacKinnon (1978a), Chipman (1979), Spitzer (1979), Park and Mitchell (1980), Ansley and Newbold (1980), Poirier (1981), Magee (1987), and Thornton (1987). In many cases, retaining the first observation yields more efficient estimates but not by very much. However, when the sample size is modest and there is one or

Table 10.1 Original and Transformed Data

C_t	T_t	$C_t^*(.5)$	$T_t^*(.5)$	$C_t^*(.9)$	$T_t^*(.9)$
1.0	1.0	0.866	0.866	0.436	0.436
1.0	2.0	0.5	1.5	0.1	1.1
1.0	3.0	0.5	2.0	0.1	1.2
1.0	4.0	0.5	2.5	0.1	1.3
1.0	5.0	0.5	3.0	0.1	1.4
1.0	6.0	0.5	3.5	0.1	1.5
1.0	7.0	0.5	4.0	0.1	1.6
1.0	8.0	0.5	4.5	0.1	1.7
1.0	9.0	0.5	5.0	0.1	1.8
1.0	10.0	0.5	5.5	0.1	1.9

more trending regressors, it can be very important to retain the first observation. In such cases, ML or GLS using the transformation that drops the first observation may be substantially less efficient than ML or GLS using the full sample and may even be less efficient than OLS.

To see why the first observation can be very important in some cases, consider the following simple example. The model is

$$y_t = \beta_0 C_t + \beta_1 T_t + u_t,$$

where C_t is a constant and T_t is a linear time trend. In Table 10.1, 10 observations on C_t and T_t are shown before and after the transformation (10.46) for $\rho = 0.5$ and $\rho = 0.9$.

We see from Table 10.1 that the transformed data for the first observation look very different from those for all subsequent observations. As a result, that observation contributes a great deal of information about the parameters. That this is so can be seen by examining the diagonal elements of the "hat matrix" $\boldsymbol{P}_{C,T}$ which projects onto $\mathcal{S}(\boldsymbol{C}^*, \boldsymbol{T}^*)$, for various values of ρ. These are shown in Table 10.2.

As we saw in Section 1.6, the diagonal elements of the hat matrix measure the *leverage* of the various observations, that is, their potential effect on the parameter estimates. Thus from Table 10.2 we see that, as ρ increases, the first observation becomes more and more influential relative to the rest of the sample. For $\rho = 0.9$, it is a point of very high leverage indeed (remember that the diagonal elements of an orthogonal projection matrix can never exceed 1). On the other hand, when we drop the first observation, as in the final column of the table, no observation has nearly as much leverage as the first observation previously did. Thus it is not surprising to find that the standard errors of the parameter estimates rise sharply when the first observation is omitted. For example, when $\rho = 0.5$, the standard errors of $\hat{\beta}_0$ and $\hat{\beta}_1$ increase by factors

Table 10.2 Diagonals of $\boldsymbol{P}_{C,T}$

$\rho = 0$	$\rho = 0.5$	$\rho = 0.9$	$\rho = 0.5$ and $\rho = 0.9$, $t = 2, 10$
0.3455	0.6808	0.9847	
0.2485	0.1277	0.0598	0.3778
0.1758	0.0993	0.0693	0.2611
0.1273	0.0851	0.0805	0.1778
0.1030	0.0851	0.0932	0.1278
0.1030	0.0993	0.1075	0.1111
0.1273	0.1277	0.1234	0.1278
0.1758	0.1702	0.1409	0.1778
0.2485	0.2270	0.1600	0.2611
0.3455	0.2979	0.1807	0.3778

of 1.765 and 1.533, respectively, when the first observation is dropped. When $\rho = 0.9$, they increase by factors of 8.039 and 4.578.

This example is of course an extreme case. We rarely use samples as small as 10 observations, and we would rarely want to regress anything on a constant and a time trend (or on a regressor that looks like a time trend; when data are strongly trending, we would often want to transform them to remove the trend before estimating a model). Nevertheless, it makes it clear that how the first observation is treated can be important.

The issue of how to treat the initial observations arises in regression models with higher-order AR errors just as in models with AR(1) errors. For the general AR(p) case, the model (assuming normality) is

$$y_t = x_t(\boldsymbol{\beta}) + u_t, \quad u_t = \sum_{j=1}^{p} \rho_j u_{t-j} + \varepsilon_t, \quad \varepsilon_t \sim \text{NID}(0, \omega^2),$$

where the ρ_j's are assumed to satisfy the stationarity condition that the roots of the polynomial equation (10.38) must lie outside the unit circle. As in the AR(1) case, the easiest way to derive the loglikelihood function for this model is to treat it as the sum of two loglikelihood functions, one for the first p observations and the other for observations $p+1$ through n conditional on the first p observations. The second of these is

$$\begin{aligned} \ell^{p+1,n}(\boldsymbol{y}, \boldsymbol{\beta}, \boldsymbol{\rho}, \omega) = &-\frac{n-p}{2}\log(2\pi) - (n-p)\log(\omega) \\ &- \frac{1}{2\omega^2}\sum_{t=p+1}^{n}\left(y_t - x_t(\boldsymbol{\beta}) - \sum_{j=1}^{p}\rho_j\big(y_{t-j} - x_{t-j}(\boldsymbol{\beta})\big)\right)^2. \end{aligned} \tag{10.55}$$

This is evidently very similar to (10.48) for the AR(1) case.

The loglikelihood function for the first p observations is the logarithm of the joint density of the vector $\boldsymbol{y}^p$, which consists of the first p observations on y_t. If we let $\omega^2\boldsymbol{\Delta}_p$ denote the $p \times p$ covariance matrix of the first p u_t's and let $\boldsymbol{x}^p(\boldsymbol{\beta})$ denote the first p observations on $x_t(\boldsymbol{\beta})$, it will be

$$\begin{aligned} \ell^p(\boldsymbol{y}, \boldsymbol{\beta}, \boldsymbol{\rho}, \omega) = &-\tfrac{p}{2}\log(2\pi) - p\log(\omega) + \tfrac{1}{2}\log|\boldsymbol{\Delta}_p^{-1}| \\ &- \frac{1}{2\omega^2}\big(\boldsymbol{y}^p - \boldsymbol{x}^p(\boldsymbol{\beta})\big)^{\top}\boldsymbol{\Delta}_p^{-1}\big(\boldsymbol{y}^p - \boldsymbol{x}^p(\boldsymbol{\beta})\big). \end{aligned} \tag{10.56}$$

If $p = 1$, $|\boldsymbol{\Delta}_p^{-1}| = \boldsymbol{\Delta}_p^{-1} = 1 - \rho^2$. Thus (10.50) is seen to be a special case of (10.56).

The full loglikelihood function is the sum of (10.55) and (10.56). As in the AR(1) case, the presence of the Jacobian term $\frac{1}{2}\log|\boldsymbol{\Delta}_p^{-1}|$ ensures that this function will have at least one maximum within the stationarity region. However, it also makes evaluating and maximizing the function a good deal more difficult. Some authors (e.g., Box and Jenkins (1976)) have therefore suggested ignoring it and maximizing the rest of the loglikelihood function. Other references on the estimation of models with AR(p) errors include Ansley (1979), Kendall, Stuart, and Ord (1983), and Granger and Newbold (1986). Beach and MacKinnon (1978b) discuss the AR(2) case in some detail.

10.7 Moving Average and ARMA Processes

Autoregressive processes are not the only way to model stationary time series. The other basic type of stochastic process is the **moving average**, or **MA**, process. The simplest moving average process is the **first-order moving average**, or **MA(1)**, process

$$u_t = \varepsilon_t + \alpha_1\varepsilon_{t-1}, \quad \varepsilon_t \sim \mathrm{IID}(0, \omega^2), \tag{10.57}$$

in which the error u_t is literally a moving average of two successive innovations, ε_t and ε_{t-1}. Thus ε_t affects both u_t and u_{t+1} but does not affect u_{t+j} for $j > 1$. The more general MA(q) process may be written either as

$$u_t = \varepsilon_t + \alpha_1\varepsilon_{t-1} + \alpha_2\varepsilon_{t-2} + \cdots + \alpha_q\varepsilon_{t-q}, \quad \varepsilon_t \sim \mathrm{IID}(0, \omega^2)$$

or, using lag-operator notation, as

$$u_t = \big(1 + \alpha_1 L + \cdots + \alpha_q L^q\big)\varepsilon_t \equiv B(L, \boldsymbol{\alpha})\varepsilon_t, \quad \varepsilon_t \sim \mathrm{IID}(0, \omega^2), \tag{10.58}$$

where $\boldsymbol{\alpha} \equiv [\alpha_1 \,\vdots\, \alpha_2 \,\vdots\, \cdots \,\vdots\, \alpha_q]$.

Finite-order MA processes are necessarily stationary, since each u_t is a weighted sum of a finite number of innovations ε_t, $\varepsilon_{t-1} \cdots$. Thus we do not have to impose stationarity conditions. We do, however, have to impose an

invertibility condition if we want $\boldsymbol{\alpha}$ to be identifiable from data. In the MA(1) case, this condition is that $|\alpha_1| \leq 1$. The reason we need an invertibility condition is that otherwise there will, in general, be more than one value of $\boldsymbol{\alpha}$ that will yield any observed behavior pattern of the u_t's. For example, the MA(1) process (10.57) with $\alpha_1 = \gamma$, $-1 < \gamma < 1$, can be shown to be indistinguishable from an MA(1) process with $\alpha_1 = 1/\gamma$. This will be discussed further below, when we discuss ML estimation of models with MA(1) errors. The invertibility condition for an MA(q) process is that the roots of the polynomial

$$B(z, \boldsymbol{\alpha}) \equiv 1 + \alpha_1 z + \alpha_2 z^2 + \cdots + \alpha_q z^q = 0 \tag{10.59}$$

must lie outside the unit circle. This condition on (10.59) is formally identical to the condition on (10.38) which ensures that an AR(p) process is stationary.

It is straightforward to calculate the covariance matrix for a moving average process. For example, in the MA(1) case the variance of u_t is evidently

$$\sigma^2 \equiv E\big(\varepsilon_t + \alpha_1 \varepsilon_{t-1}\big)^2 = \omega^2 + \alpha_1^2 \omega^2 = \big(1 + \alpha_1^2\big)\omega^2,$$

the covariance of u_t and u_{t-1} is

$$E\big(\varepsilon_t + \alpha_1 \varepsilon_{t-1}\big)\big(\varepsilon_{t-1} + \alpha_1 \varepsilon_{t-2}\big) = \alpha_1 \omega^2,$$

and the covariance of u_t and u_{t-j} for $j > 1$ is zero. Thus the covariance matrix of $\boldsymbol{u}$ is

$$\omega^2 \begin{bmatrix} 1+\alpha_1^2 & \alpha_1 & 0 & \cdots & 0 & 0 & 0 \\ \alpha_1 & 1+\alpha_1^2 & \alpha_1 & \cdots & 0 & 0 & 0 \\ \vdots & \vdots & \vdots & & \vdots & \vdots & \vdots \\ 0 & 0 & 0 & \cdots & \alpha_1 & 1+\alpha_1^2 & \alpha_1 \\ 0 & 0 & 0 & \cdots & 0 & \alpha_1 & 1+\alpha_1^2 \end{bmatrix}. \tag{10.60}$$

The structure of this covariance matrix is very simple. Notice that the correlation between successive error terms varies only between -0.5 and 0.5, since those are the smallest and largest possible values of $\alpha_1/(1 + \alpha_1^2)$, achieved when $\alpha_1 = -1$ and $\alpha_1 = 1$, respectively. It is thus evident from inspection of (10.60) that an MA(1) process cannot be appropriate when the observed correlation between successive residuals is large in absolute value.

Although moving average processes are not as widely employed in econometrics as autoregressive ones, probably because the former are harder to estimate, there are circumstances in which MA processes can arise naturally. Consider the problem of estimating an equation to explain the value of some financial instrument such as 90-day treasury bills or 3-month forward contracts on foreign exchange. If one used monthly data, then any innovation occurring in month t would affect the value of instruments maturing in months t, $t+1$, and $t+2$ but would not directly affect the value of instruments maturing later, because the latter would not yet have been issued. This suggests that the error term should be modeled by an MA(2) process; see Frankel (1980) and Hansen and Hodrick (1980). Moving average errors also arise when data are gathered using a survey that includes some of the same respondents in consecutive periods, such as the labor force surveys in both the United States and Canada, which are used to estimate unemployment rates; see Hausman and Watson (1985).

It is generally somewhat harder to estimate regression models with moving average errors than to estimate models with autoregressive errors. To see why, suppose that we want to estimate the model

$$y_t = x_t(\boldsymbol{\beta}) + u_t, \quad u_t = \varepsilon_t - \alpha\varepsilon_{t-1}, \quad \varepsilon_t \sim \mathrm{IID}(0, \omega^2). \tag{10.61}$$

Compared with (10.57), we have dropped the subscript from α and changed its sign for convenience; the sign change is of course purely a normalization. Let us make the asymptotically innocuous assumption that the unobserved innovation ε_0 is equal to zero (techniques that do not make this assumption will be discussed below). Then we see that

$$\begin{aligned} y_1 &= x_1(\boldsymbol{\beta}) + \varepsilon_1 \\ y_2 &= x_2(\boldsymbol{\beta}) - \alpha\big(y_1 - x_1(\boldsymbol{\beta})\big) + \varepsilon_2 \\ y_3 &= x_3(\boldsymbol{\beta}) - \alpha\big(y_2 - x_2(\boldsymbol{\beta})\big) - \alpha^2\big(y_1 - x_1(\boldsymbol{\beta})\big) + \varepsilon_3, \end{aligned} \tag{10.62}$$

and so on. By making the definitions

$$\begin{aligned} &y_0^* = 0; \quad y_t^* = y_t + \alpha y_{t-1}^*, \ \ t = 1, \ldots, n; \\ &x_0^* = 0; \quad x_t^*(\boldsymbol{\beta}, \alpha) = x_t(\boldsymbol{\beta}) + \alpha x_{t-1}^*(\boldsymbol{\beta}, \alpha), \ \ t = 1, \ldots, n, \end{aligned} \tag{10.63}$$

we can write equations (10.62) in the form

$$y_t = -\alpha y_{t-1}^* + x_t^*(\boldsymbol{\beta}, \alpha) + \varepsilon_t, \tag{10.64}$$

which makes it clear that we have a nonlinear regression model. But the regression function depends on the entire sample up to period t, since y_{t-1}^* depends on all previous values of y_t and x_t^* depends on $x_{t-i}(\boldsymbol{\beta})$ for all $i \geq 0$. In the by no means unlikely case in which $\alpha = 1$, the dependence of y_t on past values does not even tend to diminish as those values recede into the distant past. If we have a specialized program for estimation with MA(1) errors, or a smart nonlinear least squares program that allows us to define the regression function recursively, as in (10.63), estimating (10.64) need not be any more difficult than estimating other nonlinear regression models. But if appropriate software is lacking, this estimation can be quite difficult.

If we assume that the error terms are normally distributed, the model (10.61) becomes

$$y_t = x_t(\boldsymbol{\beta}) + u_t, \quad u_t = \varepsilon_t - \alpha\varepsilon_{t-1}, \quad \varepsilon_t \sim \text{NID}(0, \omega^2). \tag{10.65}$$

We previously made the asymptotically innocuous assumption that the unobserved innovation ε_0 is equal to zero. Although asymptotically innocuous, that assumption is clearly false, since according to (10.65) ε_0 must be distributed as $N(0, \omega^2)$. The simplest way to take proper account of this fact was suggested by MacDonald and MacKinnon (1985); our treatment follows theirs.

The concentrated loglikelihood function for the model (10.65) is

$$C - \frac{n}{2}\log\Big(\big(\boldsymbol{y} - \boldsymbol{x}(\boldsymbol{\beta})\big)^{\top}\boldsymbol{\Delta}^{-1}(\alpha)\big(\boldsymbol{y} - \boldsymbol{x}(\boldsymbol{\beta})\big)\Big) - \frac{1}{2}\log|\boldsymbol{\Delta}(\alpha)|, \tag{10.66}$$

where $\omega^2\boldsymbol{\Delta}(\alpha)$ is the covariance matrix of the vector of error terms $\boldsymbol{u}$, expression (10.60).[4] As discussed by Box and Jenkins (1976) and others, the Jacobian term $\frac{1}{2}\log|\boldsymbol{\Delta}(\alpha)|$ is

$$\frac{1}{2}\log\big(1 - \alpha^2\big) - \frac{1}{2}\log\big(1 - \alpha^{2n+2}\big). \tag{10.67}$$

When $|\alpha| = 1$, both terms in (10.67) are undefined. In that case, by using l'Hôpital's Rule, one can show that

$$\lim_{|\alpha|\to 1}\Big(\frac{1}{2}\log\big(1 - \alpha^2\big) - \frac{1}{2}\log\big(1 - \alpha^{2n+2}\big)\Big) = -\frac{1}{2}\log(n + 1).$$

This result allows the loglikelihood function (10.66) to be evaluated for any value of α in the invertibility region $-1 \leq \alpha \leq 1$.

It is important to be able to deal with the case in which $|\alpha| = 1$, since in practice one not infrequently obtains ML estimates with $|\hat{\alpha}| = 1$, especially when the sample size is small; see, for example, Osborn (1976) and Davidson (1981). The reason for this is that if we concentrate the loglikelihood function with respect to $\boldsymbol{\beta}$ and ω to obtain $\ell^c(\alpha)$, we will find that $\ell^c(\alpha)$ has the same value for α and $1/\alpha$. That, of course, is the reason for imposing the invertibility condition that $|\alpha| \leq 1$. Thus, if $\ell^c(\alpha)$ is rising as $\alpha \to 1$ or as $\alpha \to -1$, it must have a maximum precisely at $\alpha = 1$ or $\alpha = -1$. This is a distinctly undesirable feature of the model (10.65). When $|\hat{\alpha}| = 1$, one cannot make inferences about α in the usual way, since $\hat{\alpha}$ is then on the boundary of the parameter space. Since $\hat{\alpha}$ can equal ± 1 with finite probability,

[4] In fact, expression (10.66) could be the concentrated loglikelihood function for a nonlinear regression model with error terms that follow any sort of **autoregressive moving average**, or **ARMA**, process, provided that $\boldsymbol{\Delta}(\alpha)$ were replaced by the covariance matrix for $\boldsymbol{u}$ implied by that ARMA process.

using the normal distribution to approximate its finite-sample distribution is a somewhat dubious procedure. Thus, if $\hat{\alpha}$ is equal to or even close to 1 in absolute value, the investigator should exercise care in making inferences about α. Of course, as $n \rightarrow \infty$ the fact that $\hat{\alpha}$ is consistent means that the number of times that $|\hat{\alpha}| = 1$ tends to zero, unless $|\alpha_0| = 1$.

It is not easy to evaluate (10.66) directly; see Pesaran (1973), Osborn (1976), and Balestra (1980), among others.[5] We therefore use a trick that provides an alternative way to do so. Recall equations (10.62), in which we explicitly wrote $y_1, \ldots, y_n$ as functions of current and lagged values of $x_t(\boldsymbol{\beta})$ and lagged values of y_t. We may rewrite these equations, taking account of observation zero, as

$$\begin{aligned} 0 &= -v + \varepsilon_0 \\ y_1 &= x_1(\boldsymbol{\beta}) - \alpha v + \varepsilon_1 \\ y_2 &= x_2(\boldsymbol{\beta}) - \alpha\big(y_1 - x_1(\boldsymbol{\beta})\big) - \alpha^2 v + \varepsilon_2 \\ y_3 &= x_3(\boldsymbol{\beta}) - \alpha\big(y_2 - x_2(\boldsymbol{\beta})\big) - \alpha^2\big(y_1 - x_1(\boldsymbol{\beta})\big) - \alpha^3 v + \varepsilon_3, \end{aligned} \tag{10.68}$$

and so on. Here we have added both one observation and one parameter to equations (10.62). The extra observation is observation zero, which as written here simply says that the unknown parameter v is *defined* to equal the error term ε_0. This unknown parameter also appears in all subsequent observations, multiplied by larger and larger powers of α, to reflect the dependence of y_t for all observations on ε_0. Notice that because we have added both an extra parameter and an extra observation, we have not changed the number of degrees of freedom (i.e., the number of observations minus the number of parameters estimated) at all.

If we make the definitions

$$\begin{aligned} y_0^* &= 0; \quad y_t^* = y_t + \alpha y_{t-1}^*, \ \ t = 1, \ldots, n; \\ x_0^* &= 0; \quad x_t^*(\boldsymbol{\beta}, \alpha) = x_t(\boldsymbol{\beta}) + \alpha x_{t-1}^*(\boldsymbol{\beta}, \alpha), \ \ t = 1, \ldots, n; \\ z_0^* &= -1; \quad z_t^* = \alpha z_{t-1}^*, \end{aligned}$$

we can write equations (10.68) in the form

$$y_t^*(\alpha) = x_t^*(\boldsymbol{\beta}, \alpha) + v z_t^* + \varepsilon_t, \tag{10.69}$$

making them look like very much like a nonlinear regression model. The sum of squared residuals would then be

$$\sum_{t=1}^{n} \big(y_t^*(\alpha) - x_t^*(\boldsymbol{\beta}, \alpha) - v z_t^*\big)^2. \tag{10.70}$$

[5] Another approach to the estimation of models with moving average errors has been proposed by Harvey and Phillips (1979) and by Gardner, Harvey, and Phillips (1980). It requires specialized software.

When evaluated at the value of v that minimizes it, the sum of squared residuals (10.70) is equal to the generalized sum of squares

$$\big(\boldsymbol{y} - \boldsymbol{x}(\boldsymbol{\beta})\big)^{\top}\boldsymbol{\Delta}^{-1}(\alpha)\big(\boldsymbol{y} - \boldsymbol{x}(\boldsymbol{\beta})\big), \tag{10.71}$$

which appears in the loglikelihood function (10.66); this result was proved by Pagan and Nicholls (1976). Thus we can replace (10.71) by (10.70) in (10.66), which makes it very much simpler to evaluate the latter. When $x_t(\boldsymbol{\beta})$ is linear, the simplest approach is probably to search over α in the interval from -1 to $+1$, since we can then minimize the SSR (10.70) by OLS and plug the result into (10.66) to evaluate the loglikelihood function. When $x_t(\boldsymbol{\beta})$ is nonlinear, we can directly maximize (10.66) with respect to α and $\boldsymbol{\beta}$ jointly. If $x_t(\boldsymbol{\beta})$ is linear and there are no lagged dependent variables among the regressors, inferences about $\boldsymbol{\beta}$ can be made by using the ordinary OLS covariance matrix for $\hat{\boldsymbol{\beta}}$ conditional on $\hat{\alpha}$ from regression (10.69). Otherwise, we can use the Gauss-Newton regression corresponding to (10.69).

We may specify a model that combines both autoregressive and moving average components. The result is the so-called **ARMA(p, q)** model,

$$A(L, \boldsymbol{\rho})u_t = B(L, \boldsymbol{\alpha})\varepsilon_t, \quad \varepsilon_t \sim \text{IID}(0, \omega^2). \tag{10.72}$$

The left-hand side of (10.72) looks like the AR(p) model (10.37), and the right-hand side looks like the MA(q) model (10.58). The advantage of ARMA models is that a relatively parsimonious model, such as ARMA(1, 1) or ARMA(2, 1), can often provide a representation of a time series which is as good as that obtained from a much less parsimonious AR or MA model.

Finally, we must mention the class of **ARIMA models**. These are simply ARMA models applied to data that have been differenced some integer number of times, say d. Thus the **ARIMA(p, d, q)** model is

$$A(L, \boldsymbol{\rho})(1 - L)^d u_t = B(L, \boldsymbol{\alpha})\varepsilon_t, \quad \varepsilon_t \sim \text{IID}(0, \omega^2). \tag{10.73}$$

When $d = 0$, this collapses to a standard ARMA(p, q) model. The I in ARIMA means **integrated**, since an integrated series has to be differenced to achieve stationarity. Differencing is often used to induce stationarity in time series that would otherwise be nonstationary. Although we obviously do not expect the error terms that adhere to a regression model to be nonstationary, many economic time series are themselves (apparently) nonstationary and should normally be differenced before they can be used in an econometric model. Nonstationary time series will be discussed in Chapters 19 and 20.

Our treatment of regression models with MA errors has been brief and confined to the MA(1) case. Those who need to estimate such models, or models with ARMA errors, are normally advised to use specialized software, which will typically employ estimation techniques such as those discussed in Newbold (1974), Box and Jenkins (1976), Dent (1977), Ansley (1979), Zinde-Walsh and Galbraith (1991), and Galbraith and Zinde-Walsh (1992).

10.8 Testing for Serial Correlation

A very substantial fraction of all the literature in econometrics has been devoted to the problem of testing for serial correlation in the error terms of regression models. The largest part of that fraction has dealt with testing the null hypothesis that the errors for a linear regression model are serially independent against the alternative that they follow an AR(1) process. Although serial correlation is certainly a widespread phenomenon with time-series data, so that testing for it is clearly important, the amount of effort devoted to this problem seems somewhat disproportionate. As we will see, asymptotic tests for serial correlation can readily be derived as applications of the Gauss-Newton regression. Only when it is possible to make inferences that are exact in finite samples is there any reason to make use of more specialized and difficult procedures.

Suppose we wish to test the null hypothesis that the errors u_t in the model

$$y_t = x_t(\boldsymbol{\beta}) + u_t \tag{10.74}$$

are serially independent against the alternative that they follow an AR(1) process. As we have already seen, for observations $t = 2, \ldots, n$, this alternative model can be written as

$$y_t = x'_t(\boldsymbol{\beta}, \rho) + \varepsilon_t \equiv x_t(\boldsymbol{\beta}) + \rho\big(y_{t-1} - x_{t-1}(\boldsymbol{\beta})\big) + \varepsilon_t, \tag{10.75}$$

where ε_t is assumed to be $\mathrm{IID}(0, \omega^2)$. As we saw in Chapter 6, any restrictions on the parameters of a nonlinear regression function can be tested by running a Gauss-Newton regression evaluated at estimates that are root-n consistent under the null hypothesis. These would typically, but not necessarily, be restricted NLS estimates. Thus, in this case, the restriction that $\rho = 0$ can be tested by regressing $y_t - x'_t$ on the derivatives of the regression function $x'_t(\boldsymbol{\beta}, \rho)$ with respect to all of the parameters, where both x'_t and its derivatives are evaluated at the estimates of the parameter vector $[\boldsymbol{\beta} \,\vdots\, \rho]$ under the null. Assuming that (10.74) has been estimated by least squares, these estimates are simply $[\tilde{\boldsymbol{\beta}} \,\vdots\, 0]$, where $\tilde{\boldsymbol{\beta}}$ denotes the least squares estimates of $\boldsymbol{\beta}$ conditional on $\rho = 0$.[6] Since the derivatives are

$$\frac{\partial x'_t}{\partial \beta_i} = \boldsymbol{X}_t(\boldsymbol{\beta}) - \rho \boldsymbol{X}_{t-1}(\boldsymbol{\beta}); \qquad \frac{\partial x'_t}{\partial \rho} = y_{t-1} - x_{t-1}(\boldsymbol{\beta}),$$

the required GNR is

$$y_t - x_t(\tilde{\boldsymbol{\beta}}) = \boldsymbol{X}_t(\tilde{\boldsymbol{\beta}})\boldsymbol{b} + r\big(y_{t-1} - x_{t-1}(\tilde{\boldsymbol{\beta}})\big) + \text{residual}.$$

[6] There is an issue as to which sample, $t = 1$ to n or $t = 2$ to n, to use to estimate $\tilde{\boldsymbol{\beta}}$; we will discuss this below.

This can be rewritten more compactly as

$$\tilde{\boldsymbol{u}} = \tilde{\boldsymbol{X}}\boldsymbol{b} + r\tilde{\boldsymbol{u}}_{-1} + \text{residuals}, \tag{10.76}$$

where $\tilde{\boldsymbol{u}}$ denotes the vector of least squares residuals with typical element $y_t - x_t(\tilde{\boldsymbol{\beta}})$, $\tilde{\boldsymbol{X}}$ denotes the matrix of derivatives of the regression function $x_t(\boldsymbol{\beta})$ with typical element $X_{ti}(\tilde{\boldsymbol{\beta}})$, and $\tilde{\boldsymbol{u}}_{-1}$ denotes the vector with typical element $\tilde{u}_{t-1}$. This is an extremely simple regression to set up, especially when the original model (10.74) is linear. In that case, since $\tilde{\boldsymbol{X}}$ is simply the matrix of regressors, we just have to regress the residuals on the original regressors and on the lagged residuals. The test statistic may be either n times the uncentered R^2 or the ordinary t statistic for $r = 0$. The former will be asymptotically distributed as $\chi^2(1)$ under the null, the latter as $N(0,1)$. In practice, it is generally preferable to use the t statistic and to compare it to the Student's t distribution with appropriate degrees of freedom; see Kiviet (1986).

The preceding discussion has ignored the practical problem of how to treat the initial observation. The alternative model (10.75) is defined only for observations 2 through n, which suggests that $\tilde{\boldsymbol{\beta}}$ should also be obtained by estimation using that shorter sample period. Happily, this is quite unnecessary. One approach is simply to estimate $\tilde{\boldsymbol{\beta}}$ using the full sample and run the GNR using observations 2 through n only. The only problem with this approach is that $\tilde{\boldsymbol{u}}$ will no longer be orthogonal to $\tilde{\boldsymbol{X}}$. As a result, the R^2 for the GNR will not be zero even if $\tilde{\boldsymbol{u}}_{-1}$ is left out, as a consequence of which the nR^2 version of tests based on this regression may tend to reject somewhat too often in finite samples. This will not be a problem if the test statistic is the t statistic for $r = 0$. Another approach is to obtain $\tilde{\boldsymbol{\beta}}$ from full-sample estimation and run the GNR over the whole sample period as well, setting the unobserved $\tilde{u}_0$ equal to zero.

When the original model is linear, a slight variation on this procedure is possible. Because $\boldsymbol{X}\tilde{\boldsymbol{\beta}}$ lies in $\mathcal{S}(\boldsymbol{X})$, the regression

$$\boldsymbol{y} = \boldsymbol{X}\boldsymbol{c} + r\tilde{\boldsymbol{u}}_{-1} + \text{residuals} \tag{10.77}$$

will in this case have exactly the same sum of squared residuals, and exactly the same t statistic for $r = 0$, as the original test regression (10.76). Thus, for linear models, the easiest way to test for AR(1) errors is simply to rerun the original regression with one additional regressor, equal to 0 for observation 1 and equal to $\tilde{u}_{t-1}$ for all subsequent observations. One must then use the ordinary t statistic on that additional regressor as the test statistic, since it is obviously *not* valid to use nR^2 from (10.77).

Extending these procedures to test for higher-order AR errors is straightforward. Suppose the alternative is that the u_t's in (10.74) follow a general AR(p) error process. The alternative model can be written as

$$y_t = x_t(\boldsymbol{\beta}) + \sum_{j=1}^{p} \rho_j\bigl(y_{t-j} - x_{t-j}(\boldsymbol{\beta})\bigr) + \varepsilon_t, \quad \varepsilon_t \sim \text{IID}(0, \omega^2),$$

which implies that the test regression analogous to (10.76) is

$$\tilde{\boldsymbol{u}} = \tilde{\boldsymbol{X}}\boldsymbol{b} + \sum_{j=1}^{p} r_j \tilde{\boldsymbol{u}}_{-j} + \text{residuals}. \tag{10.78}$$

One possible test statistic is n times the uncentered R^2 from this regression, which will be asymptotically distributed as $\chi^2(p)$ under the null. Another, which probably has better finite-sample properties, is an asymptotic F test for $r_1 = r_2 = \cdots = r_p = 0$. This will have p and $n-k-p$ degrees of freedom, assuming that (10.78) is run over the entire sample period, with zeros used to pad out the initial elements of $\tilde{\boldsymbol{u}}_{-j}$ as necessary. When the original model is linear, it is always valid to replace the regressand $\tilde{\boldsymbol{u}}$ by the original dependent variable $\boldsymbol{y}$, as in (10.77). When that is done, of course, the nR^2 variant of the test cannot be used.

Suppose that we wished to test against MA(1) rather than AR(1) errors. The alternative model would then be the rather complicated one given by equations (10.62) or (10.64). The derivatives of this model with respect to $\boldsymbol{\beta}$ and α are also rather complicated, but they simplify enormously when evaluated under the null hypothesis that $\alpha = 0$. In fact, when we evaluate them at $[\tilde{\boldsymbol{\beta}} \,\vdots\, 0]$, we find that, for all observations, the derivative with respect to β_i is $X_{ti}(\tilde{\boldsymbol{\beta}})$ and, for observations 2 through n, the derivative with respect to α is $y_{t-1} - x_{t-1}(\tilde{\boldsymbol{\beta}})$.[7] Thus the GNR for testing against the alternative of MA(1) errors is *identical* to the GNR for testing against AR(1) errors. This is a consequence of the fact that, under the null hypothesis of no serial correlation, regression models with AR(1) and MA(1) errors are what Godfrey and Wickens (1982) call **locally equivalent alternatives**, that is, models which have identical derivatives when evaluated under the null hypothesis. Since tests based on the GNR use only information about the first derivatives of the alternative model, it is not surprising that if two models are locally equivalent in this sense under a certain null, the resulting GNRs are identical; see Godfrey (1981).

To see that an AR(1) process is locally equivalent to an MA(1) process, recall that the former can be rewritten as

$$u_t = \varepsilon_t + \rho\varepsilon_{t-1} + \rho^2\varepsilon_{t-2} + \rho^3\varepsilon_{t-3} + \cdots.$$

If we differentiate the right-hand side with respect to ρ and evaluate the derivatives at $\rho = 0$, the result will simply be ε_{t-1}. But that is also the derivative of the MA(1) process (10.57) with respect to its single parameter. So we see that AR(1) and MA(1) processes are indeed locally equivalent alternatives.

In view of the result that exactly the same Gauss-Newton regression may be used to test against MA(1) as against AR(1) errors, it should come as no surprise to find that the GNR for testing against MA(q) errors is identical

[7] Since for observation 1 this derivative is zero, our earlier suggestion to use zero in place of the unknown $\tilde{u}_0$ is precisely appropriate here.

to the one for testing against AR(q) errors. Perhaps more surprisingly, the same artificial regression also turns out to be appropriate for testing against ARMA(p,q) errors, with $p+q$ lags of $\tilde{\boldsymbol{u}}$ now being included in the regression. For more details, see Godfrey (1978b, 1988).

Using something very like the Gauss-Newton regression to test for serial correlation was first suggested by Durbin (1970) in a paper that also introduced what has become known as **Durbin's *h* test**. The latter procedure, which we will not discuss in detail, is an asymptotic test for AR(1) errors that can be used when the null hypothesis is a linear regression model which includes the dependent variable lagged once, and possibly more than once as well, among the regressors. The h test can be calculated with a hand calculator from the output for the original regression printed by most regression packages, although in some cases it cannot be calculated at all because it would be necessary to compute the square root of a negative number. For reasons that today seem hard to understand (but are presumably related to the primitive state of computer hardware and econometric software in the early 1970s), Durbin's h test became widely used, while his so-called **alternative procedure**, a t test based on the modified GNR (10.77), was all but ignored for quite some time.[7] It was finally rediscovered and extended by Breusch (1978) and Godfrey (1978a, 1978b). All of these papers assumed that the error terms ε_t were normally distributed, and they developed tests based on the GNR as Lagrange multiplier tests based on maximum likelihood estimation. The normality assumption is of course completely unnecessary.

Equally unnecessary is any assumption about the presence or absence of lagged dependent variables in the regression function $x_t(\boldsymbol{\beta})$. All we require is that this function satisfy the regularity conditions of Chapter 5, in order that nonlinear least squares estimates will be consistent and asymptotically normal under both the null and alternative hypotheses. As the above history implies, and as we will discuss below, many tests for serial correlation require that $x_t(\boldsymbol{\beta})$ not depend on lagged dependent variables, and all of the literature cited in the previous paragraph was written with the specific aim of handling the case in which $x_t(\boldsymbol{\beta})$ is linear and depends on one or more lagged values of the dependent variable.

The problem with tests based on the GNR is that they are valid only asymptotically. This is true whether or not $x_t(\boldsymbol{\beta})$ is linear, because $\tilde{\boldsymbol{u}}_{-1}$ is only an estimate of $\boldsymbol{u}_{-1}$. Indeed, as we saw in Section 5.6, $\tilde{\boldsymbol{u}} \overset{a}{=} \boldsymbol{M}_0\boldsymbol{u}$, where $\boldsymbol{M}_0 \equiv \mathbf{I} - \boldsymbol{X}_0(\boldsymbol{X}_0^{\top}\boldsymbol{X}_0)^{-1}\boldsymbol{X}_0^{\top}$ and $\boldsymbol{X}_0 \equiv \boldsymbol{X}(\boldsymbol{\beta}_0)$. This is just the asymptotic equality (5.57). The asymptotic equality is replaced by an exact equality if $\boldsymbol{x}(\boldsymbol{\beta}) = \boldsymbol{X\beta}$.

[7] Maddala and Rao (1973), Spencer (1975), and Inder (1984), among others, have provided Monte Carlo evidence on Durbin's h test as compared with the test based on the GNR. This evidence does not suggest any strong reason to prefer one test over the other. Thus the greater convenience and more general applicability of the test based on the GNR are probably the main factors in its favor.

This relationship makes it clear that even if the u_t's are serially independent, the $\tilde{u}_t$'s typically will not be, and the test may therefore incorrectly reject the null hypothesis. The problem disappears when the sample size is large enough, since $\tilde{\boldsymbol{u}}$ tends to $\boldsymbol{u}$ as the sample size tends to infinity, provided of course that the model being estimated includes the DGP as a special case. In practice, it does not seem to be a serious problem even when the sample size is moderate (say, 50 or more), provided the right form of the test is used. The results of Kiviet (1986) suggest that F tests based on the GNR generally perform quite well even with samples as small as 20 (provided that the number of regressors is also small), but that tests computed as nR^2 are less reliable and may tend to reject the null hypothesis substantially too often when there is actually no serial correlation.

The most popular test for serial correlation in econometrics is designed to handle the problems which result from the fact that $\tilde{\boldsymbol{u}}$ does not have quite the same properties as $\boldsymbol{u}$, but only for linear models without lagged dependent variables and with error terms that are assumed to be normally distributed. This is the ***d* statistic** proposed by Durbin and Watson (1950, 1951) and commonly referred to as the **DW statistic**. It is defined as

$$d = \frac{\sum_{t=2}^{n}(\tilde{u}_t - \tilde{u}_{t-1})^2}{\sum_{t=1}^{n}\tilde{u}_t^2}, \tag{10.79}$$

where, as usual, $\tilde{u}_t$ is the tth residual from OLS estimation of the regression that is being tested for possible first-order serial correlation. This regression may be linear or nonlinear, although finite-sample results depend on linearity.

It is easy to see that the numerator of the d statistic is approximately equal to

$$2\left(\sum_{t=2}^{n}\tilde{u}_t^2 - \sum_{t=2}^{n}\tilde{u}_t\tilde{u}_{t-1}\right). \tag{10.80}$$

Thus the d statistic itself is approximately equal to $2 - 2\tilde{\rho}$, where $\tilde{\rho}$ is the estimate of ρ obtained by regressing $\tilde{u}_t$ on $\tilde{u}_{t-1}$:

$$\tilde{\rho} = \frac{\sum_{t=2}^{n}\tilde{u}_t\tilde{u}_{t-1}}{\sum_{t=2}^{n}\tilde{u}_{t-1}^2}. \tag{10.81}$$

These results are true only as approximations because (10.79), (10.80), and (10.81) treat the first and last observations differently. Any effects of those observations must, however, vanish asymptotically. Thus it is clear that in samples of reasonable size the d statistic must vary between 0 and 4, and that a value of 2 corresponds to the complete absence of serial correlation. Values of the d statistic less than 2 correspond to $\tilde{\rho} > 0$, while values greater than 2 correspond to $\tilde{\rho} < 0$.

It is possible, but computationally demanding, to calculate the exact distribution of the d statistic when the u_t's are normally distributed, the underlying regression model is linear, and $\boldsymbol{X}$ contains only fixed regressors. This distribution necessarily depends on $\boldsymbol{X}$. The calculation uses the fact that the d statistic can be written as

$$\frac{\boldsymbol{u}^\top \boldsymbol{M}_X \boldsymbol{A} \boldsymbol{M}_X \boldsymbol{u}}{\boldsymbol{u}^\top \boldsymbol{M}_X \boldsymbol{u}}, \tag{10.82}$$

where $\boldsymbol{A}$ is the $n \times n$ matrix

$$\begin{bmatrix} 1 & -1 & 0 & 0 & \cdots & 0 & 0 & 0 \\ -1 & 2 & -1 & 0 & \cdots & 0 & 0 & 0 \\ 0 & -1 & 2 & -1 & \cdots & 0 & 0 & 0 \\ \vdots & \vdots & \vdots & \vdots & & \vdots & \vdots & \vdots \\ 0 & 0 & 0 & 0 & \cdots & -1 & 2 & -1 \\ 0 & 0 & 0 & 0 & \cdots & 0 & -1 & 1 \end{bmatrix}.$$

From (10.82), the d statistic is seen to be a ratio of quadratic forms in normally distributed random variables, and the distributions of such ratios can be evaluated using several numerical techniques; see Durbin and Watson (1971) and Savin and White (1977) for references.

Most applied workers never attempt to calculate the exact distribution of the d statistic corresponding to their particular $\boldsymbol{X}$ matrix. Instead, they use the fact that the critical values for its distribution are known to fall between two bounding values, d_L and d_U, which depend on the sample size, n, the number of regressors, k, and whether or not there is a constant term. Tables of d_L and d_U may be found in some econometrics textbooks and in papers such as Durbin and Watson (1951) and Savin and White (1977). As an example, when $n = 50$ and $k = 6$ (counting the constant term as one of the regressors), for a test against $\rho > 0$ at the .05 level, $d_L = 1.335$ and $d_U = 1.771$. Thus, if one calculated a d statistic for this sample size and number of regressors and it was less than 1.335, one could confidently decide to reject the null hypothesis of no serial correlation at the .05 level. If the statistic was greater than 1.771, one could confidently decide not to reject. However, if the statistic was in the "inconclusive region" between 1.335 and 1.771, one would be unsure of whether to reject or not. When the sample size is small, and especially when it is small relative to the number of regressors, the inconclusive region can be very large. This means that the d statistic may not be very informative when used in conjunction with the tables of d_L and d_U.[8] In such cases, one may have no choice but to calculate the exact distribution of the statistic, if one wants to make inferences from the d statistic in a small sample. A few software packages, such as SHAZAM, allow one to do this. Of course,

[8] There is reason to believe that when the regressors are slowly changing, a situation which may often be the case with time-series data, d_U provides a better approximation than d_L. See Hannan and Terrell (1966).

because the assumptions of normally distributed errors and fixed regressors are uncomfortably strong, even "exact" finite-sample inferences are really only approximate.

As we have already mentioned, the d statistic is not valid, even asymptotically, when $\boldsymbol{X}$ includes lagged values of the dependent variable. The easiest way to see why this is so is to use the fact that the d statistic is asymptotically equivalent to the t statistic on the estimate of ρ in the regression

$$\tilde{\boldsymbol{u}} = \rho\tilde{\boldsymbol{u}}_{-1} + \text{residuals}; \tag{10.83}$$

see the discussion leading up to (10.81). The only difference between regression (10.83) and the Gauss-Newton regression (10.76), which generates an asymptotically valid t statistic on the coefficient of $\tilde{\boldsymbol{u}}_{-1}$, is that (10.83) does not include the matrix $\tilde{\boldsymbol{X}}$ among the regressors. We discussed this point in Section 6.4, where we saw that the correct t statistic, from (10.76), must be larger (or at least no smaller) asymptotically than the generally incorrect one from (10.83).

If $\boldsymbol{x}(\boldsymbol{\beta})$ does not depend on lagged dependent variables, $x_t(\boldsymbol{\beta})$ and hence $\boldsymbol{X}_t(\boldsymbol{\beta})$ must be uncorrelated with all lagged values of u_t. Consequently, $\tilde{\boldsymbol{X}}$ will have no explanatory power for $\tilde{\boldsymbol{u}}_{-1}$, asymptotically, and the t statistics from (10.76) and (10.83) will be asymptotically the same. But if $\boldsymbol{x}(\boldsymbol{\beta})$ does depend on lagged dependent variables, $\boldsymbol{X}_t(\boldsymbol{\beta})$ will be correlated with some lagged values of u_t, since lagged values of the dependent variable are certainly correlated with lagged values of the error term. Thus the t statistic from (10.83) will be smaller, asymptotically, than the one from (10.76), and the d statistic will consequently be biased toward 2. The d statistic may still be informative, however. If its value is such that we could reject the null hypothesis of no serial correlation if $\boldsymbol{x}(\boldsymbol{\beta})$ did not depend on lagged dependent variables, then a correct statistic based on the GNR would certainly allow us to do so.

We conclude this section with a very brief discussion of some other tests for serial correlation. Kobayashi (1991) proposed a test that is exact to order $n^{-1/2}$ for nonlinear regression models without lagged dependent variables. It is based on the estimate of ρ under the alternative hypothesis, which is then corrected to reduce bias. Wallis (1972) proposed an analog of the d statistic to test against a simple AR(4) process. His $\boldsymbol{d_4}$ **statistic** is

$$d_4 = \frac{\sum_{t=5}^{n}(\tilde{u}_t - \tilde{u}_{t-4})^2}{\sum_{t=1}^{n}\tilde{u}_t^2}, \tag{10.84}$$

and its properties are very similar to those of the original d statistic. When the model is linear, there are no lagged dependent variables, and the sample size is small, d_4 can be used instead of the standard GNR-based test that involves regressing $\tilde{\boldsymbol{u}}$ on $\tilde{\boldsymbol{X}}$ and $\tilde{\boldsymbol{u}}_{-4}$.

A very different type of test, which he calls "point-optimal" because it is designed to test against a *simple* alternative, was proposed by King (1985a). It is based on the ratio of the sum of squared residuals for a regression with a fixed value of ρ, say $\rho = 0.5$ or $\rho = 0.75$, to the SSR for a regression with no serial correlation. Critical values can be calculated by methods similar to those used to calculate the exact distribution of the d statistic. There is evidence that this test may, as its name implies, have more power than conventional tests when the actual value of ρ is both some distance from zero and not too far from the hypothesized value used in computing the test statistic. Other references on point-optimal tests include King (1985b), King and McAleer (1987), Dastoor and Fisher (1988), and Dufour and King (1991).

In the time-series literature, numerous tests for residual autocorrelation have been proposed. Two that are widely used are the tests proposed by Box and Pierce (1970) and Ljung and Box (1978), which are both based on the **residual autocorrelations**, i.e., the correlations between $\tilde{u}_t$ and $\tilde{u}_{t-1}$, $\tilde{u}_t$ and $\tilde{u}_{t-2}$, and so on, often up to quite long lags. These tests are valid when used for their original purpose, namely, testing ARIMA models for residual autocorrelation, but they are not generally valid when used with the residuals from linear or nonlinear regression models that include both exogenous variables and lagged dependent variables in the regression functions. The reason they are invalid in such cases is essentially the same reason that the d statistic is invalid when there are lagged dependent variables among the regressors; see Poskitt and Tremayne (1981).

10.9 COMMON FACTOR RESTRICTIONS

If the regression function is misspecified, the residuals may display serial correlation even when the error terms are in fact serially independent. This might happen if a variable that was itself serially correlated, or a lagged dependent variable, were incorrectly omitted from the regression function. In such a case, we can in general make valid inferences only by eliminating the misspecification rather than by "correcting" the model for AR(1) errors or some other simple error process. If we simply do the latter, as used to be done all too frequently in applied work, we may well end up with a seriously misspecified model.

There is no universally effective way to avoid misinterpreting misspecification of the regression function as the presence of serially correlated errors. Model specification is an art as much as a science, and with the short samples typical of time-series data we can never expect to detect all forms of misspecification. Nevertheless, there is one family of tests that has been shown to be very effective in detecting misspecification in models which appear to have errors that follow a low-order AR process. These are tests of what are, for reasons that will be apparent shortly, generally called **common factor restrictions**. The basic idea of testing common factor restrictions, although not the terminology, may be found in Sargan (1964). More recent references include Hendry and Mizon (1978), Mizon and Hendry (1980), and Sargan (1980a). An illuminating example is provided by Hendry (1980), who presents a grossly misspecified model that yields apparently sensible results after "correction" for AR(1) errors and then shows that a test for common factor restrictions would detect the misspecification.

In order to fix ideas, we will assume for the moment that the model to be tested is a linear regression model that apparently has AR(1) errors. It is natural to think of there being *three* nested models in this case. The first of these is the original linear regression model with error terms assumed to be serially independent,

$$H_0: \ y_t = \boldsymbol{X}_t\boldsymbol{\beta} + u_t, \quad u_t \sim \mathrm{IID}(0, \sigma^2). \tag{10.85}$$

The second is the nonlinear model that results when the errors u_t of (10.85) are assumed to follow the AR(1) process $u_t = \rho u_{t-1} + \varepsilon_t$,

$$H_1: \ y_t = \boldsymbol{X}_t\boldsymbol{\beta} + \rho(y_{t-1} - \boldsymbol{X}_{t-1}\boldsymbol{\beta}) + \varepsilon_t, \quad \varepsilon_t \sim \mathrm{IID}(0, \omega^2). \tag{10.86}$$

The third is the linear model that results when the nonlinear restrictions on (10.86) are relaxed:

$$H_2: \ y_t = \boldsymbol{X}_t\boldsymbol{\beta} + \rho y_{t-1} + \boldsymbol{X}_{t-1}\boldsymbol{\gamma} + \varepsilon_t, \quad \varepsilon_t \sim \mathrm{IID}(0, \omega^2), \tag{10.87}$$

where $\boldsymbol{\beta}$ and $\boldsymbol{\gamma}$ are both k–vectors. We encountered H_2 previously, in Section 10.3, where it was used to obtain an initial consistent estimate of ρ.

Provided that all of these models are estimated over the same sample period (probably observations 2 through n, since H_1 and H_2 cannot be estimated for observation 1), the original model, H_0, is a special case of the model incorporating a correction for AR(1) errors, H_1, which in turn is a special case of the unrestricted linear model, H_2. Tests for serial correlation, such as those we discussed in Section 10.8, are designed to test H_0 against H_1. If such a test rejects the null hypothesis, it may be because H_1 in fact generated the data, but it may also be because the model is misspecified in some other way. Testing H_1 against H_2 is one way to see if the former is a reasonable model. This is an example of testing common factor restrictions.

It is natural to ask why the restrictions that (10.86) imposes on (10.87) are called *common factor* restrictions. Using lag operator notation, we can rewrite the former as

$$(1 - \rho L)y_t = (1 - \rho L)\boldsymbol{X}_t\boldsymbol{\beta} + \varepsilon_t \tag{10.88}$$

and the latter as

$$(1 - \rho L)y_t = \boldsymbol{X}_t\boldsymbol{\beta} + L\boldsymbol{X}_t\boldsymbol{\gamma} + \varepsilon_t. \tag{10.89}$$

It is evident that in (10.88), but not in (10.89), the common factor $1 - \rho L$ appears on both sides of the equation. This explains the name given to the restrictions.

Although our discussion will focus on the AR(1) case, common factor restrictions are implicit in linear regression models with autoregressive errors of any order. For example, a linear regression model with AR(2) errors can be written as

$$(1 - \rho_1 L - \rho_2 L^2) y_t = (1 - \rho_1 L - \rho_2 L^2) \boldsymbol{X}_t \boldsymbol{\beta} + \varepsilon_t, \tag{10.90}$$

while the unrestricted version corresponding to (10.89) can be written as

$$(1 - \rho_1 L - \rho_2 L^2) y_t = \boldsymbol{X}_t \boldsymbol{\beta} + L \boldsymbol{X}_t \boldsymbol{\gamma}_1 + L^2 \boldsymbol{X}_t \boldsymbol{\gamma}_2 + \varepsilon_t, \tag{10.91}$$

where $\boldsymbol{\gamma}_1$ and $\boldsymbol{\gamma}_2$ are two k–vectors of coefficients. Again, we see that the factor $1 - \rho_1 L - \rho_2 L^2$ appears on both sides of equation (10.90) but only on the left-hand side of equation (10.91). Tests of common factor restrictions in models with higher-order AR errors are essentially the same as tests in models with AR(1) errors; for simplicity, our discussion of these tests will deal only with the AR(1) case.

In most cases, the easiest, and probably also the most reliable, way to test common factor restrictions is to use an asymptotic F test. Thus the statistic for testing H_1 above against H_2, that is (10.86) against (10.87), would be

$$\frac{(\mathrm{SSR}_1 - \mathrm{SSR}_2)/l}{\mathrm{SSR}_2/(n - k - l - 2)}, \tag{10.92}$$

where SSR_1 is the sum of squared residuals from least squares estimation of H_1, SSR_2 is the sum of squared residuals from least squares estimation of H_2, and $l \leq k$ is the number of degrees of freedom for the test, about which more below. The denominator degrees of freedom is $n - k - l - 2$ because H_2 is estimated over $n - 1$ observations and has $k + 1 + l$ parameters, corresponding to k β_i's, ρ, and l additional parameters. Note that although this test is perfectly valid asymptotically, it will not be exact in finite samples, regardless of how the ε_t's are distributed, because both H_1 and H_2 include lagged dependent variables on the right-hand side and also because H_1 is nonlinear in the parameters.

We now come to the one aspect of common factor testing that is slightly tricky: determining the number of restrictions, l. In the case of testing H_1 against H_2 above, it might *seem* that there are k restrictions. After all, H_1 has $k + 1$ parameters (k β_i's and ρ) and H_2 seems to have $2k + 1$ parameters (k β_i's, k γ_i's, and ρ). The difference is $(2k + 1) - (k + 1)$, which equals k. In fact, however, the number of restrictions will almost always be *less* than k, because, except in rare cases, the number of *identifiable* parameters in H_2 will be less than $2k+1$. The easiest way to see why this will almost always be the case is to consider an example.

Suppose that the regression function $x_t(\boldsymbol{\beta})$ for the original H_0 model is

$$\beta_0 + \beta_1 z_t + \beta_2 t + \beta_3 z_{t-1} + \beta_4 y_{t-1}, \tag{10.93}$$

where z_t is the tth observation on an economic time series, and t is the tth observation on a linear time trend. The regression function for the unrestricted H_2 model which corresponds to (10.93) is

$$\begin{aligned} &\beta_0 + \beta_1 z_t + \beta_2 t + \beta_3 z_{t-1} + \beta_4 y_{t-1} + \rho y_{t-1} \\ &\quad + \gamma_0 + \gamma_1 z_{t-1} + \gamma_2 (t-1) + \gamma_3 z_{t-2} + \gamma_4 y_{t-2}. \end{aligned} \tag{10.94}$$

This regression function appears to have 11 parameters, but 4 of them are in fact unidentifiable. It is obvious that we cannot estimate both β_0 and γ_0, since there cannot be two constant terms. Similarly, we cannot estimate both β_3 and γ_1, since there cannot be two coefficients on z_{t-1}, and we cannot estimate both β_4 and ρ, since there cannot be two coefficients on y_{t-1}. We also cannot estimate γ_2 along with β_2 and the constant, because t, $t-1$ and the constant term are perfectly collinear, since $t-(t-1)=1$. Thus the version of H_2 that can actually be estimated has the regression function

$$\delta_0 + \beta_1 z_t + \delta_1 t + \delta_2 z_{t-1} + \delta_3 y_{t-1} + \gamma_3 z_{t-2} + \gamma_4 y_{t-2}, \tag{10.95}$$

where

$$\delta_0 = \beta_0 + \gamma_0 - \gamma_2; \quad \delta_1 = \beta_2 + \gamma_2; \quad \delta_2 = \beta_3 + \gamma_1; \text{ and } \delta_3 = \rho + \beta_4.$$

We see that (10.95) has seven identifiable parameters: β_1, γ_3, γ_4, and δ_0 through δ_3, instead of the eleven parameters, many of them not identifiable, of (10.94). The regression function for the restricted model, H_1, is

$$\begin{aligned} &\beta_0 + \beta_1 z_t + \beta_2 t + \beta_3 z_{t-1} + \beta_4 y_{t-1} + \rho y_{t-1} \\ &\quad - \rho\beta_0 - \rho\beta_1 z_{t-1} - \rho\beta_2 (t-1) - \rho\beta_3 z_{t-2} - \rho\beta_4 y_{t-2}, \end{aligned}$$

and it has six parameters, ρ and β_0 through β_4. Thus, in this case, l, the number of restrictions that H_1 imposes on H_2, is just 1.

While this is a slightly extreme example, similar problems arise in almost every attempt to test common factor restrictions. Constant terms, many types of dummy variables (notably seasonal dummies and time trends), lagged dependent variables, and independent variables that appear with more than one time subscript almost always result in an unrestricted model H_2 of which not all parameters will be identifiable. Luckily, it is very easy to deal with these problems when one does an F test; one simply has to omit the redundant regressors when estimating H_2. One can then calculate l as the number of parameters in H_2 minus the number in H_1, which is $k + 1$. Since many regression packages automatically drop redundant regressors, one naive but often effective approach is simply to attempt to estimate H_2 in something close to its original form and then to count the number of parameters that the regression package is actually able to estimate.

The F test (10.92) is not the only way to test common factor restrictions. Since the regression function for H_2 is linear in all parameters, while the one for H_1 is nonlinear, it is natural to try to base tests on the OLS estimates of H_2 alone. One approach to this problem is discussed by Sargan (1980a), but it is quite complicated and requires specialized computer software. A simpler approach is to use a one-step estimator of H_1. Consistent estimates of the parameters of H_1 may be obtained from the estimates of H_2, as discussed in Section 10.3, and the GNR (10.19) is then used to obtain one-step estimates. These estimates themselves are not necessarily of interest. All that is needed is the sum of squared residuals from the GNR, which may be used in place of SSR_1 in the formula (10.92) for the F test. However, since it is generally neither difficult nor expensive to estimate H_1 with modern computers and software packages, situations in which there is a significant advantage from the use of this one-step procedure are likely to be rare.

Something very like a test of common factor restrictions can be employed even when the original (H_0) model is nonlinear. In this case, the H_1 model can be written as

$$(1 - \rho L)y_t = (1 - \rho L)x_t(\boldsymbol{\beta}) + \varepsilon_t. \tag{10.96}$$

A version of (10.96) in which the common factor restriction does not hold is

$$(1 - \rho L)y_t = (1 - \delta L)x_t(\boldsymbol{\beta}) + \varepsilon_t. \tag{10.97}$$

Evidently, (10.96) is just (10.97) subject to the restriction that $\delta = \rho$. This restriction can be tested by a Gauss-Newton regression in the usual way. This GNR is

$$\begin{aligned} \boldsymbol{y} - \hat{\boldsymbol{x}} - \hat{\rho}(\boldsymbol{y}_{-1} - \hat{\boldsymbol{x}}_{-1}) = (\hat{\boldsymbol{X}} - \hat{\rho}\hat{\boldsymbol{X}}_{-1})\boldsymbol{b} \\ + r(\boldsymbol{y}_{-1} - \hat{\boldsymbol{x}}_{-1}) + d\hat{\boldsymbol{x}}_{-1} + \text{residuals}, \end{aligned} \tag{10.98}$$

where $\hat{\rho}$ and $\hat{\boldsymbol{\beta}}$ are the NLS estimates of H_1, and $\hat{\boldsymbol{x}} \equiv \boldsymbol{x}(\hat{\boldsymbol{\beta}})$. Regression (10.98) looks exactly like the GNR (10.26), which we used to calculate the covariance matrix of $\hat{\boldsymbol{\beta}}$ and $\hat{\rho}$, with the addition of the extra regressor $\hat{\boldsymbol{x}}_{-1}$, the coefficient of which is d. The t statistic for $d = 0$ will be an asymptotically valid test statistic.

Notice that this GNR could be used even if $x_t(\boldsymbol{\beta})$ were a linear function. Since this variant of the common factor restrictions test necessarily has only one degree of freedom, it would not be the same as the usual form of the test, discussed above, for any model with $l > 1$. The difference arises because the test based on (10.98) is testing against a less general alternative than the usual form of the test. When $x_t(\boldsymbol{\beta})$ is linear, (10.97) can be written as

$$(1-\rho L)y_t = \boldsymbol{X}_t\boldsymbol{\beta} - \delta\boldsymbol{X}_{t-1}\boldsymbol{\beta} + \varepsilon_t, \tag{10.99}$$

which is in general (but not when $l = 1$) more restrictive than equation (10.89). Thus consideration of the nonlinear regression case reveals that there are really two different tests of common factor restrictions when the original model is linear. The first, which tests (10.88) against (10.89), is the F test (10.92). It will have l degrees of freedom, where $1 \leq l \leq k$. The second, which tests (10.88) against (10.99), is the t test of $d = 0$ in the Gauss-Newton regression (10.98). It will always have one degree of freedom. Either test might perform better than the other, depending on how the data were actually generated; see Chapter 12. When $l = 1$, the two tests will coincide, a fact that it may be a good exercise to demonstrate.

10.10 Instrumental Variables and Serial Correlation

So far in this chapter, we have assumed that the regression function $\boldsymbol{x}(\boldsymbol{\beta})$ depends only on exogenous and predetermined variables. However, there is no reason for serially correlated errors not to occur in models for which current endogenous variables appear in the regression function. As we discussed in Chapter 7, the technique of instrumental variables (IV) estimation is commonly used to obtain consistent estimates for such models. In this section, we briefly discuss how IV methods can be used to estimate univariate regression models with errors that are serially correlated and to test for serial correlation in such models.

Suppose that we wish to estimate the model (10.12) by instrumental variables. Then, as we saw in Section 7.6, the IV estimates may be obtained by minimizing, with respect to $\boldsymbol{\beta}$, the criterion function

$$\big(\boldsymbol{y} - \boldsymbol{x}'(\boldsymbol{\beta},\rho)\big)^{\top}\boldsymbol{P}_W\big(\boldsymbol{y} - \boldsymbol{x}'(\boldsymbol{\beta},\rho)\big), \tag{10.100}$$

where the regression function $\boldsymbol{x}'(\boldsymbol{\beta},\rho)$ is defined by (10.13), and $\boldsymbol{P}_W$ is the matrix that projects orthogonally onto $\boldsymbol{W}$, a suitable matrix of instruments. The IV form of the Gauss-Newton regression can be used as the basis for an algorithm to minimize (10.100). Given suitable regularity conditions on $x_t(\boldsymbol{\beta})$, and assuming that $|\rho| < 1$, these estimates will be consistent and asymptotically normal. See Sargan (1959) for a full treatment of the case in which $\boldsymbol{x}(\boldsymbol{\beta})$ is linear.

The only potential difficulty with this IV procedure is that one has to find a "suitable" matrix of instruments $\boldsymbol{W}$. For asymptotic efficiency, one always wants the instruments to include all the exogenous and predetermined variables that appear in the regression function. From (10.13), we see that more such variables appear in the regression function $x'_t(\boldsymbol{\beta}, \rho)$ for the transformed model than in the original regression function $x_t(\boldsymbol{\beta})$. Thus the optimal choice of instruments may differ according to whether one takes account of serial correlation or assumes that it is absent.

To make this point more clearly, let us assume that the original model is linear, with regression function

$$x_t(\boldsymbol{\beta}) = \boldsymbol{Z}_t\boldsymbol{\beta}_1 + \boldsymbol{Y}_t\boldsymbol{\beta}_2, \tag{10.101}$$

where $\boldsymbol{Z}_t$ is a row vector of explanatory variables that are exogenous or predetermined, and $\boldsymbol{Y}_t$ is a row vector of current endogenous variables; the dimension of $\boldsymbol{\beta} \equiv [\boldsymbol{\beta}_1 \,\vdots\, \boldsymbol{\beta}_2]$ is k. The regression function for the transformed model is then

$$x'_t(\boldsymbol{\beta}, \rho) = \rho y_{t-1} + \boldsymbol{Z}_t\boldsymbol{\beta}_1 + \boldsymbol{Y}_t\boldsymbol{\beta}_2 - \rho\boldsymbol{Z}_{t-1}\boldsymbol{\beta}_1 - \rho\boldsymbol{Y}_{t-1}\boldsymbol{\beta}_2. \tag{10.102}$$

In (10.101), the only exogenous or predetermined variables were the variables in $\boldsymbol{Z}_t$. In (10.102), however, they are y_{t-1} and the variables in $\boldsymbol{Z}_t$, $\boldsymbol{Z}_{t-1}$, and $\boldsymbol{Y}_{t-1}$ (the same variables may occur in more than one of these, of course; see the discussion of common factor restrictions in the previous section). All these variables would normally be included in the matrix of instruments $\boldsymbol{W}$. Since the number of these variables is almost certain to be greater than $k+1$, it would not normally be necessary to include any additional instruments to ensure that all parameters are identified.

For more discussion of the estimation of single linear equations with serially correlated errors and current endogenous regressors, see Sargan (1959, 1961), Amemiya (1966), Fair (1970), Dhrymes, Berner, and Cummins (1974), Hatanaka (1976), and Bowden and Turkington (1984).

Testing for serial correlation in models estimated by IV is straightforward if one uses a variant of the Gauss-Newton regression. In Section 7.7, we discussed the GNR (7.37), in which the regressand and regressors are evaluated at the restricted estimates, and showed how it can be used to calculate test statistics. Testing for serial correlation is simply an application of this procedure. Suppose we want to test a nonlinear regression model for AR(1) errors. The alternative model is given by (10.12), for observations 2 through n, with the null hypothesis being that $\rho = 0$. In this case, the GNR (7.38) is

$$\tilde{\boldsymbol{u}} = \boldsymbol{P}_W\tilde{\boldsymbol{X}}\boldsymbol{b} + r\boldsymbol{P}_W\tilde{\boldsymbol{u}}_{-1} + \text{residuals}, \tag{10.103}$$

where $\tilde{\boldsymbol{\beta}}$ denotes the IV estimates under the null hypothesis of no serial correlation, $\tilde{\boldsymbol{u}}$ denotes $\boldsymbol{y} - \boldsymbol{x}(\tilde{\boldsymbol{\beta}})$, and $\tilde{\boldsymbol{X}}$ denotes $\boldsymbol{X}(\tilde{\boldsymbol{\beta}})$. This is clearly the IV analog of regression (10.76); if the two occurrences of $\boldsymbol{P}_W$ were removed, (10.76) and (10.103) would be identical. The t statistic on the estimate of r from this regression will be a valid test statistic. This will be true both when (10.103) is estimated explicitly by OLS and when $\tilde{\boldsymbol{u}}$ is regressed on $\tilde{\boldsymbol{X}}$ and $\tilde{\boldsymbol{u}}_{-1}$ using an IV procedure with $\boldsymbol{W}$ as the matrix of instruments. However, when an artificial regression like (10.103) is used to test for higher-order serial correlation, the regression must be estimated explicitly by OLS if an ordinary F test is to be valid. All of this was discussed in Section 7.7.

As usual, there are two minor issues that must be settled before this procedure can be implemented. First of all, there is the question of what to do about the first observation. The simplest approach is probably to retain it and to set the unobserved residual $\tilde{u}_0$ to zero for the purposes of the GNR (10.103), but there are other possibilities that will yield different results in finite samples; see Section 10.8.

Secondly, there is the question of what instruments to use when running the GNR (10.103). If we were minimizing the criterion function (10.100) to obtain estimates of both $\boldsymbol{\beta}$ and ρ, then, as we discussed above, it would usually be desirable to use more instruments than were used to obtain $\tilde{\boldsymbol{\beta}}$. Similarly, it will usually be desirable when testing the hypothesis that $\rho = 0$ for $\boldsymbol{W}$ to include both $\boldsymbol{y}_{-1}$ and the regressors that appear in $\boldsymbol{x}_{-1}(\tilde{\boldsymbol{\beta}})$. In that case, as we saw in Section 7.7, the test statistic must be computed as a pseudo-t or pseudo-F test based on the $C(\alpha)$ principle.

For more on testing for serial correlation in models estimated by IV, see Godfrey (1976, 1988), Harvey and Phillips (1980, 1981), and Sargan and Mehta (1983).

10.11 Serial Correlation and Multivariate Models

We discussed multivariate regression models in Section 9.7. When such models are estimated using time-series data, one might well expect them to display serial correlation. Methods for estimation and testing of multivariate models with serial correlation are for the most part obvious combinations of the techniques previously discussed in this chapter and those discussed in Section 9.7. There are a few new aspects to the problem, however, and those are what we will concentrate on in this short section.

Consider the class of models

$$\boldsymbol{y}_t = \boldsymbol{\xi}_t(\boldsymbol{\beta}) + \boldsymbol{u}_t, \quad \boldsymbol{u}_t = \boldsymbol{u}_{t-1}\boldsymbol{R} + \boldsymbol{\varepsilon}_t, \quad \boldsymbol{\varepsilon}_t \sim \mathrm{IID}(\boldsymbol{0}, \boldsymbol{\Omega}), \tag{10.104}$$

where $\boldsymbol{y}_t$, $\boldsymbol{\xi}_t(\boldsymbol{\beta})$, $\boldsymbol{u}_t$, and $\boldsymbol{\varepsilon}_t$ are $1 \times m$ vectors, and $\boldsymbol{R}$ and $\boldsymbol{\Omega}$ are $m \times m$ matrices. This defines the general class of multivariate regression models with AR(1) errors. It is conceptually straightforward to transform (10.104) into

$$\boldsymbol{y}_t = \boldsymbol{\xi}_t(\boldsymbol{\beta}) + \boldsymbol{y}_{t-1}\boldsymbol{R} - \boldsymbol{\xi}_{t-1}(\boldsymbol{\beta})\boldsymbol{R} + \boldsymbol{\varepsilon}_t, \quad \boldsymbol{\varepsilon}_t \sim \mathrm{IID}(\boldsymbol{0}, \boldsymbol{\Omega}), \tag{10.105}$$

and then treat (10.105) like any other multivariate regression model. But note that instead of a scalar parameter ρ we now have an $m \times m$ matrix $\boldsymbol{R}$, which allows each element of $\boldsymbol{u}_t$ to depend on each element of $\boldsymbol{u}_{t-1}$. Thus, if m is large, allowing for even first-order serial correlation evidently introduces a large number of additional parameters, which may make it difficult to obtain reliable estimates of the parameters $\boldsymbol{\beta}$ and $\boldsymbol{R}$. In order to reduce the number of parameters to be estimated, investigators may wish to impose some restrictions on $\boldsymbol{R}$. A natural restriction is that it be a diagonal matrix, which implies that u_{ti} depends only on $u_{t-1,i}$ and not on $u_{t-1,j}$ for $j \neq i$.

In Section 9.7, we discussed and gave examples of singular equation systems, in which the error terms are constrained to sum to zero across the equations. We saw that such systems arise very frequently in practice. Berndt and Savin (1975) demonstrated that if an equation system is singular, this places severe restrictions on the form that the matrix $\boldsymbol{R}$ can take. In particular, if $\boldsymbol{R}$ is assumed to be diagonal, all the diagonal elements must be the same. To see why this is so, let us assume for simplicity that $m = 2$ and write the AR process $\boldsymbol{u}_t = \boldsymbol{u}_{t-1}\boldsymbol{R} + \boldsymbol{\varepsilon}_t$ as

$$\begin{aligned} u_{t1} &= r_{11}u_{t-1,1} + \varepsilon_{t1} \\ u_{t2} &= r_{22}u_{t-1,2} + \varepsilon_{t2}. \end{aligned}$$

Summing over all equations, we see that

$$u_{t1} + u_{t2} = r_{11}u_{t-1,1} + r_{22}u_{t-1,2} + \varepsilon_{t1} + \varepsilon_{t2}. \tag{10.106}$$

By assumption, $u_{t-1,1} + u_{t-1,2} = 0$ and $\varepsilon_{t1} + \varepsilon_{t2} = 0$. But these two conditions will imply that $u_{t1} + u_{t2} = 0$ only if $r_{11} = r_{22} = \rho$. If so, (10.106) can be rewritten as

$$u_{t1} + u_{t2} = \rho(u_{t-1,1} + u_{t-1,2}) + \varepsilon_{t1} + \varepsilon_{t2} = \rho \cdot 0 + 0 = 0.$$

Thus, when $r_{11} = r_{22} = \rho$, it is easy to see that if the ε_{ti}'s sum to zero, so will the u_{ti}'s; just imagine starting with $u_{0i} = 0$ and then solving recursively.

The Berndt-Savin result, which of course generalizes to nondiagonal $\boldsymbol{R}$ matrices and higher-order AR processes, means that one must be careful when specifying time-series processes for the error terms of singular equation systems. If one accidentally specifies an $\boldsymbol{R}$ matrix that does not satisfy the Berndt-Savin restrictions, the transformed system (10.105) will no longer be singular, and as a result one will obtain different parameter estimates by dropping different equations. On the other hand, the fact that if $\boldsymbol{R}$ is diagonal all the diagonal elements must be the same allows for considerable simplification in some cases. Beach and MacKinnon (1979) use this result to develop an ML estimator that retains the first observation for singular equation systems with AR(1) errors and a diagonal $\boldsymbol{R}$ matrix.

This section has been rather short. A much more detailed discussion of serial correlation in multivariate models, and various references, may be found in Srivastava and Giles (1987, Chapter 7).

10.12 CONCLUSION

Despite the length of this chapter, we have by no means covered all the important aspects of serial correlation. Our discussion of time-series issues has been deliberately brief; readers who are not familiar with this literature will likely want to consult Harvey (1981, 1989), Granger and Newbold (1986), or one of the more advanced books cited by Granger and Watson (1984). A number of topics closely related to those dealt with in this chapter will be discussed in Chapters 19 and 20.

In this chapter, we have tried to emphasize specification tests, principally tests based on the Gauss-Newton regression. A number of other specification tests based on the GNR, some of which may be viewed as alternatives to testing for serial correlation, and most of which are applicable to models that incorporate a transformation for serial correlation, will be discussed in Chapter 11. How the results of specification tests such as these should be interpreted will be the topic of Chapter 12. All of the tests for serial correlation and common factor restrictions that have been presented in this chapter can best be understood in the context of the results to be presented there.

TERMS AND CONCEPTS

AR(1), AR(2), AR(4), and AR(p) processes
ARIMA(p, d, q) process
ARMA(p, q) process
autoregressive error process
autoregressive moving average process
back-and-forth search
Cochrane-Orcutt procedure
common factor restrictions
d statistic (DW statistic)
d_4 statistic
Durbin's alternative procedure
Durbin's h test
full ML estimation
grid search
Hildreth-Lu procedure
independence (of error terms)
innovation
integrated time series
invertibility condition
lag operator
locally equivalent alternative
MA(1) and MA(q) processes
moving average error process
one-step estimates
Prais-Winsten transformation
residual autocorrelations
roots outside the unit circle
seasonal AR process
serial correlation
simple AR(4) process
stationarity condition
stationarity region
stationarity triangle for AR(2) process
time-series methods

Chapter 11

Tests Based on the Gauss-Newton Regression

11.1 Introduction

In Section 6.4, we showed that the Gauss-Newton regression provides a simple way to test restrictions on the parameters of a regression function whenever root-n consistent parameter estimates that satisfy the restrictions are available. In most cases, these will be least squares estimates of the restricted model. In Section 10.8, we showed that tests for virtually any type of serial correlation may be performed by using appropriate variants of the GNR. In this chapter, we discuss several additional tests based on the GNR that can be highly useful in applied econometric work. These are:

(i) tests for the equality of two (or more) sets of regression parameters;

(ii) nonnested hypothesis tests, in which a regression model is tested against the evidence provided by one or more nonnested alternative models;

(iii) tests based on comparing two sets of estimates, where generally one set is consistent under weaker conditions than the other; and

(iv) tests for heteroskedasticity of known form.

In the final section of the chapter, we preview some very important material that will be covered in more depth in Chapter 16. The Gauss-Newton regression is valid only under the assumption that the error terms are homoskedastic, an assumption that is sometimes uncomfortably strong. In this final section, we discuss an artificial regression which may be used for computing test statistics in any circumstances in which the GNR may be so used, and which has the remarkable property that the resulting test statistics are asymptotically valid even when the error terms display heteroskedasticity of unknown form. We introduce this artificial regression here because it is a logical extension of the Gauss-Newton regression and because it can be extremely useful in practice.

11.2 TESTS FOR EQUALITY OF TWO PARAMETER VECTORS

A classic problem in econometrics is determining whether the coefficients of a regression model (usually a linear one) are the same in two (or sometimes more than two) separate subsamples. In the case of time-series data, the subsamples would normally correspond to different time periods, and these tests are then often referred to as tests for **structural change**. Sometimes we may be interested in testing whether the coefficients are the same in two or more different time periods simply as a way of testing whether the model is specified correctly. In such cases, time-series data sets may be divided into earlier and later periods in a fairly arbitrary way for purposes of testing. This is legitimate, but such tests are more interesting when there is reason to believe that the subsamples correspond to different economic environments, such as different exchange-rate or policy regimes.[1] In the case of cross-section data, arbitrary division almost never makes sense; instead, the subsamples might correspond to such potentially different groups of observations as large firms and small firms, rich countries and poor countries, or men and women. In these cases, the results of the test are often of interest for their own sake. For example, a labor economist might be interested in testing whether the earnings functions of men and women or of two different ethnic groups are the same.[2]

The classic treatment of this problem has deep roots in the statistical literature on the analysis of variance (Scheffé, 1959). An early and very influential paper in econometrics is G. C. Chow (1960), and as a result the standard F test for the equality of two sets of coefficients in linear regression models is commonly referred to by economists as the **Chow test**. Fisher (1970) provides a neater exposition of the classic Chow test procedure. Dufour (1982) provides a more geometrical exposition and generalizes the test to handle any number of subsamples, some of which may have fewer observations than there are regressors.

The standard way of posing the problem is to partition the data into two parts, the n–vector $\boldsymbol{y}$ of observations on the dependent variable being divided into two vectors $\boldsymbol{y}_1$ and $\boldsymbol{y}_2$, of lengths n_1 and n_2, respectively, and the $n \times k$ matrix $\boldsymbol{X}$ of observations on the regressors being divided into two matrices $\boldsymbol{X}_1$ and $\boldsymbol{X}_2$, of dimensions $n_1 \times k$ and $n_2 \times k$, respectively. This partitioning may of course require that the data be reordered. Thus the maintained hypothesis

[1] When there is no reason to expect parameters to have changed at any particular point in time, it may make sense to use a procedure that does not specify such a point. Examples include the CUSUM and CUSUM of squares procedures of Brown, Durbin, and Evans (1975).

[2] An earnings function relates earnings to a number of right-hand side variables, such as age, education, and experience. As examples of the use of F tests for the equality of two sets of coefficients in this context, see Oaxaca (1973, 1974).

may be written as

$$\begin{bmatrix} \boldsymbol{y}_1 \\ \boldsymbol{y}_2 \end{bmatrix} = \begin{bmatrix} \boldsymbol{X}_1 & \mathbf{0} \\ \mathbf{0} & \boldsymbol{X}_2 \end{bmatrix} \begin{bmatrix} \boldsymbol{\beta}_1 \\ \boldsymbol{\beta}_2 \end{bmatrix} + \begin{bmatrix} \boldsymbol{u}_1 \\ \boldsymbol{u}_2 \end{bmatrix}, \quad E(\boldsymbol{u}\boldsymbol{u}^\top) = \sigma^2 \mathbf{I}, \tag{11.01}$$

where $\boldsymbol{\beta}_1$ and $\boldsymbol{\beta}_2$ are each k–vectors of parameters to be estimated. The null hypothesis to be tested is that $\boldsymbol{\beta}_1 = \boldsymbol{\beta}_2 = \boldsymbol{\beta}$. Under that null hypothesis, equation (11.01) reduces to

$$\boldsymbol{y} \equiv \begin{bmatrix} \boldsymbol{y}_1 \\ \boldsymbol{y}_2 \end{bmatrix} = \begin{bmatrix} \boldsymbol{X}_1 \\ \boldsymbol{X}_2 \end{bmatrix} \boldsymbol{\beta} + \begin{bmatrix} \boldsymbol{u}_1 \\ \boldsymbol{u}_2 \end{bmatrix} \equiv \boldsymbol{X}\boldsymbol{\beta} + \boldsymbol{u}, \quad E(\boldsymbol{u}\boldsymbol{u}^\top) = \sigma^2 \mathbf{I}. \tag{11.02}$$

When both n_1 and n_2 are greater than k, which is the usual case, it is easy to construct a test of (11.01) against (11.02) by using the ordinary F test that we first discussed in Section 3.5. The unrestricted sum of squared residuals from estimation of (11.01) is

$$\text{USSR} = \boldsymbol{y}_1^\top \boldsymbol{M}_1 \boldsymbol{y}_1 + \boldsymbol{y}_2^\top \boldsymbol{M}_2 \boldsymbol{y}_2 = \text{SSR}_1 + \text{SSR}_2,$$

where $\boldsymbol{M}_i \equiv \mathbf{I} - \boldsymbol{X}_i \left(\boldsymbol{X}_i^\top \boldsymbol{X}_i\right)^{-1} \boldsymbol{X}_i^\top$ for $i = 1, 2$. Thus USSR is simply the sum of the two sums of squared residuals from the regressions of $\boldsymbol{y}_1$ on $\boldsymbol{X}_1$ and $\boldsymbol{y}_2$ on $\boldsymbol{X}_2$, respectively. The restricted sum of squared residuals, from estimation of (11.02), is

$$\text{RSSR} = \boldsymbol{y}^\top \boldsymbol{M}_X \boldsymbol{y},$$

where $\boldsymbol{M}_X \equiv \mathbf{I} - \boldsymbol{X}(\boldsymbol{X}^\top \boldsymbol{X})^{-1} \boldsymbol{X}^\top$. Thus the ordinary F statistic is

$$\frac{(\boldsymbol{y}^\top \boldsymbol{M}_X \boldsymbol{y} - \boldsymbol{y}_1^\top \boldsymbol{M}_1 \boldsymbol{y}_1 - \boldsymbol{y}_2^\top \boldsymbol{M}_2 \boldsymbol{y}_2)/k}{(\boldsymbol{y}_1^\top \boldsymbol{M}_1 \boldsymbol{y}_1 + \boldsymbol{y}_2^\top \boldsymbol{M}_2 \boldsymbol{y}_2)/(n - 2k)} = \frac{(\text{RSSR} - \text{SSR}_1 - \text{SSR}_2)/k}{(\text{SSR}_1 + \text{SSR}_2)/(n - 2k)}. \tag{11.03}$$

This test has k and $n - 2k$ degrees of freedom. There are k restrictions because the restricted model has k parameters while the unrestricted model has $2k$.

The test statistic (11.03) is what many applied econometricians think of as the Chow test. There are three obvious limitations of this test. The first limitation is that it is not applicable if $\min(n_1, n_2) < k$, since then at least one of the two subsample regressions cannot be computed. The original Chow (1960) paper recognized this problem and derived an alternative test for this case. Our treatment based on the GNR will make clear the relationship between the ordinary test (11.03) and the alternative test. The second limitation is that (11.03) applies only to linear regression models. An obvious nonlinear analog, which requires two additional nonlinear estimations (one for each of the two subsamples), can of course be constructed. But our treatment based on the GNR will provide a simpler way to handle the nonlinear case.

The third limitation of (11.03) is that, like all conventional F tests, it is generally valid only under the rather strong assumption that $E(\boldsymbol{u}\boldsymbol{u}^\top) = \sigma^2\mathbf{I}$. This assumption may be particularly implausible when one is testing the equality of two sets of regression parameters, since if the parameter vector $\boldsymbol{\beta}$ differs between two regimes, the variance σ^2 may well be different as well. A number of papers have addressed this issue, including Toyoda (1974), Jayatissa (1977), Schmidt and Sickles (1977), Watt (1979), Honda (1982), Phillips and McCabe (1983), Ali and Silver (1985), Ohtani and Toyoda (1985), Toyoda and Ohtani (1986), Weerahandi (1987), Buse and Dastoor (1989), and Thursby (1992). All of these papers are concerned with the case in which the variance of the error terms is σ_1^2 for the first regime and σ_2^2 for the second regime. An approach which is often simpler and is valid much more generally is to use a test statistic that is robust to heteroskedasticity of unknown form (MacKinnon, 1989). We will discuss an artificial regression that yields such heteroskedasticity-robust test statistics for any case to which the GNR is applicable in Section 11.6, below. It may often be wise to calculate these heteroskedasticity-robust tests in addition to ordinary Chow tests or tests based on the GNR, unless there is evidence that the assumption of homoskedasticity is a reasonable one.

Let us now consider testing for structural change in a nonlinear regression model. For simplicity, we will assume that the sample is to be divided into only two groups of observations; extensions to the many-group case are obvious. We first define a vector $\boldsymbol{\delta} \equiv [\delta_1 \cdots \delta_n]^\top$, letting $\delta_t = 0$ if observation t belongs to group 1 and $\delta_t = 1$ if observation t belongs to group 2. Suppose that the null hypothesis is

$$H_0\colon\ y_t = x_t(\boldsymbol{\beta}) + u_t, \quad E(\boldsymbol{u}\boldsymbol{u}^\top) = \sigma^2\mathbf{I},$$

where, as usual, the functions $x_t(\boldsymbol{\beta})$ are assumed to satisfy the regularity conditions given in Chapter 5. The alternative hypothesis may be written as

$$H_1\colon\ y_t = x_t\big(\boldsymbol{\beta}_1(1-\delta_t) + \boldsymbol{\beta}_2\delta_t\big) + u_t, \quad E(\boldsymbol{u}\boldsymbol{u}^\top) = \sigma^2\mathbf{I}.$$

Thus, when observation t belongs to group 1, so that $\delta_t = 0$, the regression function is $x_t(\boldsymbol{\beta}_1)$, while when observation t belongs to group 2, so that $\delta_t = 1$, the regression function is $x_t(\boldsymbol{\beta}_2)$.

The alternative hypothesis H_1 can be rewritten as

$$y_t = x_t\big(\boldsymbol{\beta}_1 + (\boldsymbol{\beta}_2 - \boldsymbol{\beta}_1)\delta_t\big) + u_t = x_t(\boldsymbol{\beta}_1 + \boldsymbol{\gamma}\delta_t) + u_t,$$

where $\boldsymbol{\gamma} \equiv \boldsymbol{\beta}_2 - \boldsymbol{\beta}_1$. This makes it clear that H_0 is equivalent to the null hypothesis that $\boldsymbol{\gamma} = \mathbf{0}$. Since the latter null hypothesis is simply a set of zero restrictions on the parameters of a nonlinear regression function, we can clearly use a Gauss-Newton regression to test it. This GNR is

$$y_t - x_t(\hat{\boldsymbol{\beta}}) = \boldsymbol{X}_t(\hat{\boldsymbol{\beta}})\boldsymbol{b} + \delta_t\boldsymbol{X}_t(\hat{\boldsymbol{\beta}})\boldsymbol{c} + \text{residual}, \qquad (11.04)$$

where $\hat{\boldsymbol{\beta}}$ denotes the NLS estimates of $\boldsymbol{\beta}$ for the whole sample. The GNR (11.04) may be written more compactly as

$$\hat{\boldsymbol{u}} = \hat{\boldsymbol{X}}\boldsymbol{b} + \boldsymbol{\delta}{*}\hat{\boldsymbol{X}}\boldsymbol{c} + \text{ residuals,} \tag{11.05}$$

where $\hat{\boldsymbol{u}}$ has typical element $y_t - x_t(\hat{\boldsymbol{\beta}})$, and $\hat{\boldsymbol{X}}$ has typical element $\boldsymbol{X}_t(\hat{\boldsymbol{\beta}})$. Here $*$ denotes the **direct product** of two matrices. Since $\delta_t X_{ti}(\hat{\boldsymbol{\beta}})$ is a typical element of $\boldsymbol{\delta}{*}\hat{\boldsymbol{X}}$, $\delta_t{*}\hat{\boldsymbol{X}}_t = \hat{\boldsymbol{X}}_t$ when $\delta_t = 1$ and $\delta_t{*}\hat{\boldsymbol{X}}_t = \boldsymbol{0}$ when $\delta_t = 0$. To perform the test, we simply have to estimate the model using the entire sample and regress the residuals from that estimation on the matrix of derivatives $\hat{\boldsymbol{X}}$ and on that matrix with the rows which correspond to group 1 observations set to zero. We do not have to reorder the data. As usual, there are several asymptotically valid test statistics, the best probably being the ordinary F statistic for the null hypothesis that $\boldsymbol{c} = \boldsymbol{0}$. In the usual case with k less than $\min(n_1, n_2)$, that test statistic will have k degrees of freedom in the numerator and $n - 2k$ degrees of freedom in the denominator.

Notice that the sum of squared residuals from regression (11.05) is equal to the SSR from the GNR

$$\hat{\boldsymbol{u}} = \hat{\boldsymbol{X}}\boldsymbol{b} + \text{ residuals} \tag{11.06}$$

run over observations 1 to n_1 plus the SSR from the same GNR run over observations $n_1 + 1$ to n. This is the unrestricted sum of squared residuals for the F test of $\boldsymbol{c} = \boldsymbol{0}$ in (11.05). The restricted sum of squared residuals for that test is simply the SSR from (11.06) run over all n observations, which is the same as the SSR from nonlinear estimation of the null hypothesis H_0. Thus the ordinary Chow test for the GNR (11.06) will be numerically identical to the F test of $\boldsymbol{c} = \boldsymbol{0}$ in (11.05). This provides the easiest way to calculate the test statistic.

As we mentioned above, the ordinary Chow test (11.03) is not applicable if $\min(n_1, n_2) < k$. Using the GNR framework, it is easy to see why this is so. Suppose that $n_2 < k$ and $n_1 > k$, without loss of generality, since the numbering of the two groups of observations is arbitrary. Then the matrix $\boldsymbol{\delta}{*}\hat{\boldsymbol{X}}$, which has k columns, will have $n_2 < k$ rows that are not just rows of zeros and hence will have rank at most n_2. Thus, when equation (11.05) is estimated, at most n_2 elements of $\boldsymbol{c}$ will be identifiable, and the residuals corresponding to all observations that belong to group 2 will be zero. The number of degrees of freedom for the numerator of the F statistic must therefore be at most n_2. In fact, it will be equal to the rank of $[\hat{\boldsymbol{X}} \quad \boldsymbol{\delta}{*}\hat{\boldsymbol{X}}]$ minus the rank of $\hat{\boldsymbol{X}}$, which might be less than n_2 in some cases. The number of degrees of freedom for the denominator will be the number of observations for which (11.05) has nonzero residuals, which will normally be n_1, minus the number of regressors that affect those observations, which will be k, for a total of $n_1 - k$. Thus we can use the GNR whether or not $\min(n_1, n_2) < k$, provided that we use the appropriate numbers of degrees of freedom for the numerator and denominator of the F test.

It should be clear that when $x_t(\boldsymbol{\beta}) = \boldsymbol{X}_t\boldsymbol{\beta}$ and $\min(n_1, n_2) > k$, the F test based on the GNR (11.05) is *numerically identical* to the Chow test (11.03). This follows from the fact that the sum of squared residuals from (11.05) will then be equal to $\mathrm{SSR}_1 + \mathrm{SSR}_2$, the sum of the SSRs from estimating the regression separately over the two groups of observations. It may be a good exercise to demonstrate that when $x_t(\boldsymbol{\beta}) = \boldsymbol{X}_t\boldsymbol{\beta}$ and $\min(n_1, n_2) < k$, Chow's (1960) "alternative" test is also numerically identical to the corresponding test based on the GNR (which will in regular cases have n_2 and $n_1 - k$ degrees of freedom).

In some cases, it may be of interest to test whether a subset of the parameters of a model, rather than all of the parameters, are the same over two subsamples. It is very easy to modify the tests already discussed to deal with this case. The null and alternative hypotheses can now be written as

$$H_0\colon\ y_t = x_t(\boldsymbol{\alpha}, \boldsymbol{\beta}) + u_t, \quad E(\boldsymbol{u}\boldsymbol{u}^\top) = \sigma^2\mathbf{I}, \text{ and} \tag{11.07}$$

$$H_1\colon\ y_t = x_t\big(\boldsymbol{\alpha},\ \boldsymbol{\beta}_1(1-\delta_t) + \boldsymbol{\beta}_2\delta_t\big) + u_t, \quad E(\boldsymbol{u}\boldsymbol{u}^\top) = \sigma^2\mathbf{I},$$

where $\boldsymbol{\alpha}$ is an l–vector of parameters that are assumed to be the same over the two subsamples, and $\boldsymbol{\beta}$ is an m–vector of parameters the constancy of which is to be tested. The GNR is easily seen to be

$$\hat{\boldsymbol{u}} = \hat{\boldsymbol{X}}_{\boldsymbol{\alpha}}\boldsymbol{a} + \hat{\boldsymbol{X}}_{\boldsymbol{\beta}}\boldsymbol{b} + \boldsymbol{\delta}{*}\hat{\boldsymbol{X}}_{\boldsymbol{\beta}}\boldsymbol{c} + \text{residuals},$$

where $\hat{\boldsymbol{X}}_{\boldsymbol{\alpha}}$ is an $n \times l$ matrix with typical element $\partial x_t(\boldsymbol{\alpha}, \boldsymbol{\beta})/\partial\alpha_i$, evaluated at the estimates from (11.07), $(\hat{\boldsymbol{\alpha}}, \hat{\boldsymbol{\beta}})$, and $\hat{\boldsymbol{X}}_{\boldsymbol{\beta}}$ is an $n \times m$ matrix with typical element $\partial x_t(\boldsymbol{\alpha}, \boldsymbol{\beta})/\partial\beta_j$, also evaluated at $(\hat{\boldsymbol{\alpha}}, \hat{\boldsymbol{\beta}})$. Provided that m is less than $\min(n_1, n_2)$, the test statistic will have m and $n - l - 2m$ degrees of freedom. Even when $x_t(\boldsymbol{\alpha}, \boldsymbol{\beta})$ is linear, it is not now possible to compute a test in quite the same way as the classic Chow test (11.03). Because the parameter vector $\boldsymbol{\alpha}$ is assumed to be the same for both subsamples, one cannot obtain the unrestricted SSR by estimation over the two subsamples separately.

The preceding discussion has been entirely in the context of least squares estimation. When instrumental variables estimation is used, there is a slight complication concerning the choice of instruments to be used in estimating the null and alternative models. From the results of Section 7.7, the IV equivalent of (11.05) is seen to be

$$\tilde{\boldsymbol{u}} = \boldsymbol{P}_W\tilde{\boldsymbol{X}}\boldsymbol{b} + \boldsymbol{P}_W\boldsymbol{\delta}{*}\tilde{\boldsymbol{X}}\boldsymbol{c} + \text{residuals}, \tag{11.08}$$

where $\tilde{\boldsymbol{u}}$ and $\tilde{\boldsymbol{X}}$ are evaluated at (generalized) IV estimates $\tilde{\boldsymbol{\beta}}$ under the null hypothesis. As usual, there are several available test statistics.

Regression (11.08) seems straightforward enough, but there is a problem. If we simply use the same matrix of instruments $\boldsymbol{W}$ that was used to estimate the model originally, it is quite possible that the matrix $[\boldsymbol{P}_W\tilde{\boldsymbol{X}} \quad \boldsymbol{P}_W\boldsymbol{\delta} * \tilde{\boldsymbol{X}}]$

will fail to have full rank. For estimation of the restricted model, $\boldsymbol{W}$ must have at least k columns, while for running regression (11.08) it must have at least $2k$. If $\boldsymbol{W}$ has fewer than $2k$ columns, the test statistic will have fewer than k degrees of freedom and will actually be testing against a less general alternative than H_1. The obvious solution is effectively to double the number of instruments by using the matrix

$$\boldsymbol{W}^* \equiv \begin{bmatrix} \boldsymbol{W}_1 & \mathbf{0} \\ \mathbf{0} & \boldsymbol{W}_2 \end{bmatrix} \tag{11.09}$$

in place of $\boldsymbol{W}$ in the GNR (11.08). This allows the relationships between the endogenous regressors and the instruments to differ in the two parts of the sample, which seems quite reasonable. If one wants to use an LM test, that is, a test based on the explained sum of squares from regression (11.08), one must be careful to use $\boldsymbol{W}^*$ when one estimates the *restricted* model as well. However, as we discussed in Section 7.7, that is not necessary if one uses a $C(\alpha)$ test, that is, a pseudo-F test for $\boldsymbol{c} = \mathbf{0}$ in regression (11.08).

It is perhaps worth spelling out just how one should proceed if one wishes to test H_0 against H_1 when using IV estimation:

(i) Estimate the model H_0 using a suitable matrix $\boldsymbol{W}$ consisting of at least k, and preferably more than k, instruments, including all exogenous and predetermined variables in the regression function.

(ii) Create a new instrument matrix $\boldsymbol{W}^*$ as in (11.09). Then, to obtain the restricted SSR, run the GNR

$$\tilde{\boldsymbol{u}} = \boldsymbol{P}_{W^*}\tilde{\boldsymbol{X}}\boldsymbol{b} + \text{residuals}$$

over the entire sample, where $\tilde{\boldsymbol{u}}$ and $\tilde{\boldsymbol{X}}$ are evaluated at the IV estimates found in stage (i).

(iii) To obtain the unrestricted SSR, run the GNR

$$\tilde{\boldsymbol{u}}_j = \boldsymbol{P}_{W_j}\tilde{\boldsymbol{X}}_j\boldsymbol{b} + \text{residuals}$$

over each of the two subsamples separately and sum the two sums of squared residuals. Here $\tilde{\boldsymbol{u}}_j$, $\boldsymbol{W}_j$, and $\tilde{\boldsymbol{X}}_j$ denote the subvectors or submatrices of $\tilde{\boldsymbol{u}}$, $\boldsymbol{W}$, and $\tilde{\boldsymbol{X}}$ corresponding to the two subsamples.

(iv) Compute a $C(\alpha)$, or pseudo-F, test statistic based on the regression results obtained in (ii) and (iii), as described in Section 7.7.

An alternative procedure, which would be considerably more difficult in the nonlinear case, would be to estimate both the restricted and unrestricted models, using $\boldsymbol{W}^*$ for the instruments in both cases. For the unrestricted model, this would mean doing IV estimation for each part of the sample separately, using $\boldsymbol{W}_j$ as instruments for subsample j. Then one could calculate any of the test statistics based on restricted and unrestricted estimates that were discussed in Section 7.7.

The literature on tests for structural change is very large, much larger than we can possibly deal with in this section. A number of recent contributions to the area, along with a useful bibliography, may be found in Krämer (1989).

11.3 TESTING NONNESTED REGRESSION MODELS

All the tests that we have considered so far involve **nested models**. This simply means that the model being tested, the null hypothesis, is a special case of the alternative model against which it is being tested. For example, a regression model with serially independent errors is a special case of an alternative model with AR(1) errors, and a model with coefficients that are constant over the entire sample is a special case of an alternative model with coefficients that differ in two subsamples. Although nested alternatives like these occur very frequently, there are also many situations in which two or more competing models are not nested. The literature on **nonnested hypothesis testing** has made it possible to handle such cases within the framework of the Gauss-Newton regression.

Although our treatment is in terms of artificial regressions, much of the earlier literature on nonnested hypothesis testing is not. The classic references are two papers by Cox (1961, 1962) and two papers by Atkinson (1969, 1970). Cox's basic ideas were adapted to linear regression models by Pesaran (1974) and to nonlinear regression models by Pesaran and Deaton (1978). The artificial regression approach is due to Davidson and MacKinnon (1981a).

Suppose that two different economic theories (or two different implementations of what is basically the same theoretical model), both of which purport to explain the same dependent variable, yield the two nonlinear regression models:

$$H_1:\ \ \boldsymbol{y} = \boldsymbol{x}(\boldsymbol{\beta}) + \boldsymbol{u}_1, \quad E(\boldsymbol{u}_1\boldsymbol{u}_1^{\top}) = \sigma_1^2\mathbf{I}, \text{ and}$$

$$H_2:\ \ \boldsymbol{y} = \boldsymbol{z}(\boldsymbol{\gamma}) + \boldsymbol{u}_2, \quad E(\boldsymbol{u}_2\boldsymbol{u}_2^{\top}) = \sigma_2^2\mathbf{I},$$

where $\boldsymbol{\beta}$ and $\boldsymbol{\gamma}$ are vectors of lengths k_1 and k_2, respectively. These models are said to be **nonnested** if it is in general impossible to find restrictions on $\boldsymbol{\beta}$ such that, for arbitrary $\boldsymbol{\gamma}$, $\boldsymbol{x}(\boldsymbol{\beta})$ equals $\boldsymbol{z}(\boldsymbol{\gamma})$, and impossible to find restrictions on $\boldsymbol{\gamma}$ such that, for arbitrary $\boldsymbol{\beta}$, $\boldsymbol{z}(\boldsymbol{\gamma})$ equals $\boldsymbol{x}(\boldsymbol{\beta})$. Thus there must not exist a mapping, say $\boldsymbol{g}$, defined on the whole parameter space on which $\boldsymbol{\gamma}$ is defined, such that $\boldsymbol{z}(\boldsymbol{\gamma}) = \boldsymbol{x}\big(\boldsymbol{g}(\boldsymbol{\gamma})\big)$ identically in $\boldsymbol{\gamma}$. Similarly, there must be no mapping $\boldsymbol{h}$ such that $\boldsymbol{x}(\boldsymbol{\beta}) = \boldsymbol{z}\big(\boldsymbol{h}(\boldsymbol{\beta})\big)$ identically in $\boldsymbol{\beta}$.

In the case of linear regression models, what is required is that each of the two regression functions contain at least one regressor that is not in the other. For example, the following two regression functions are nonnested:

$$x_t(\boldsymbol{\beta}) = \beta_0 + \beta_1 X_{t1} + \beta_2 X_{t2} \quad \text{and} \tag{11.10}$$

$$z_t(\boldsymbol{\gamma}) = \gamma_0 + \gamma_1 X_{t1} + \gamma_3 X_{t3}. \tag{11.11}$$

However, if X_{t2} were added to (11.11) to yield the new regression function

$$z_t^*(\gamma) = \gamma_0 + \gamma_1 X_{t1} + \gamma_2 X_{t2} + \gamma_3 X_{t3}, \tag{11.12}$$

(11.10) would then be nested within (11.12), since by setting γ_3 to zero we could make (11.12) equivalent to (11.10).

The easiest nonnested tests to perform are those based on **artificial nesting**. The basic idea is to embed both of the two competing regression functions in a more general one and then to test one or both of the original models against it. Consider the artificial compound model

$$H_C: \;\; \boldsymbol{y} = (1-\alpha)\boldsymbol{x}(\boldsymbol{\beta}) + \alpha \boldsymbol{z}(\boldsymbol{\gamma}) + \boldsymbol{u}, \tag{11.13}$$

where α is a parameter that has been introduced so as to nest H_1 and H_2 within H_C; when $\alpha = 0$, H_C collapses to H_1, and when $\alpha = 1$, H_C collapses to H_2. The problem is that, in most cases, the artificial model (11.13) will not be estimable, because the parameters α, $\boldsymbol{\beta}$, and $\boldsymbol{\gamma}$ will not all be separately identifiable. For example, in the case of (11.10) and (11.11), H_C will have seven parameters in total (3 β_i's, 3 γ_i's, and α) but only four parameters that can actually be identified and estimated (a constant term and the three coefficients on X_1, X_2, and X_3).

One solution to this problem, originally suggested in Davidson and MacKinnon (1981a), is to replace H_C by a model in which the unknown parameters of the model that is *not* being tested are replaced by estimates of those parameters that would be consistent if the DGP actually belonged to the model for which they are defined. Suppose it is H_1 that we wish to test. Then the idea is to replace $\boldsymbol{\gamma}$ in (11.13) by something that estimates it consistently under H_2. There are many ways to do so, since there are many ways to estimate $\boldsymbol{\gamma}$ consistently, but the simplest and asymptotically most attractive solution is to replace $\boldsymbol{\gamma}$ by $\hat{\boldsymbol{\gamma}}$, the NLS estimate of $\boldsymbol{\gamma}$. Thus H_C becomes

$$H_C': \;\; \boldsymbol{y} = (1-\alpha)\boldsymbol{x}(\boldsymbol{\beta}) + \alpha \hat{\boldsymbol{z}} + \boldsymbol{u}, \tag{11.14}$$

where $\hat{\boldsymbol{z}} \equiv \boldsymbol{z}(\hat{\boldsymbol{\gamma}})$. The new compound model H_C' has only $k_1 + 1$ parameters to estimate, one more than H_1. Provided that H_1 and H_2 really are nonnested and H_1 is asymptotically identified, both α and $\boldsymbol{\beta}$ must be asymptotically identifiable. One can then test H_1 by testing the null hypothesis that $\alpha = 0$, using any standard test. Two possibilities for such a test were suggested in Davidson and MacKinnon (1981a). The ***J* test** uses the t statistic for $\alpha = 0$ from nonlinear estimation of (11.14). It was called the J test because α and $\boldsymbol{\beta}$ are estimated *jointly*. Since that may be hard to do when $\boldsymbol{x}(\boldsymbol{\beta})$ is nonlinear, an alternative procedure was suggested, called the ***P* test**. It uses the t statistic for $a = 0$ from the Gauss-Newton regression

$$\boldsymbol{y} - \hat{\boldsymbol{x}} = \hat{\boldsymbol{X}}\boldsymbol{b} + a(\hat{\boldsymbol{z}} - \hat{\boldsymbol{x}}) + \text{residuals}, \tag{11.15}$$

where $\hat{\boldsymbol{x}} \equiv \boldsymbol{x}(\hat{\boldsymbol{\beta}})$ and $\hat{\boldsymbol{X}} \equiv \boldsymbol{X}(\hat{\boldsymbol{\beta}})$, $\boldsymbol{X}(\boldsymbol{\beta})$ denoting the $n \times k_1$ matrix of derivatives of $\boldsymbol{x}(\boldsymbol{\beta})$ with respect to $\boldsymbol{\beta}$ and $\hat{\boldsymbol{\beta}}$ denoting the NLS estimate of $\boldsymbol{\beta}$ under H_1. The test regressor $\hat{\boldsymbol{z}} - \hat{\boldsymbol{x}}$ is obtained, as usual, by partially differentiating the regression function for model H_C' with respect to α and evaluating it at $\alpha = 0$, $\boldsymbol{\beta} = \hat{\boldsymbol{\beta}}$.[3]

In view of the general results on Gauss-Newton regressions of Chapter 6, it is obvious that the J and P tests are asymptotically equivalent under H_1. Thus, if one of these tests is asymptotically valid, both of them must be. However, it is not immediately obvious that either test is in fact valid, since $\hat{\boldsymbol{z}}$, which depends on $\boldsymbol{y}$, appears on the right-hand side of (11.14). The intuition behind this result is nevertheless very simple. Provided that, under H_1, the vector $\hat{\boldsymbol{\gamma}}$ converges asymptotically to some constant vector, say $\boldsymbol{\gamma}_1$, then the vector $\hat{\boldsymbol{z}} \equiv \boldsymbol{z}(\hat{\boldsymbol{\gamma}})$ must likewise converge to a vector $\boldsymbol{z}(\boldsymbol{\gamma}_1)$. It is therefore asymptotically valid to treat the vector $\hat{\boldsymbol{z}}$ as if it were a vector of observations on a predetermined variable.

When $\boldsymbol{x}(\boldsymbol{\beta}) = \boldsymbol{X}\boldsymbol{\beta}$, the model under test is linear. In this case, the J-test regression (11.14) must yield exactly the same result as the P-test regression (11.15). Because $\hat{\boldsymbol{x}} = \boldsymbol{X}\hat{\boldsymbol{\beta}}$, it is clear that $\mathcal{S}(\boldsymbol{X}, \hat{\boldsymbol{z}})$ is exactly the same as $\mathcal{S}(\boldsymbol{X}, \hat{\boldsymbol{z}} - \hat{\boldsymbol{x}})$. Thus both regressions must have the same explanatory power and hence must yield identical test statistics.

It is just as valid to test H_2 against H_C as to test H_1 against H_C, and the artificial regression for doing so is essentially the same as before, but with the roles of H_1 and H_2 reversed. Thus the J-test regression equivalent to (11.14) is

$$\boldsymbol{y} = (1 - \phi)\boldsymbol{z}(\boldsymbol{\gamma}) + \phi\hat{\boldsymbol{x}} + \boldsymbol{u},$$

and the P-test regression equivalent to (11.15) is

$$\boldsymbol{y} - \hat{\boldsymbol{z}} = \hat{\boldsymbol{Z}}\boldsymbol{c} + p(\hat{\boldsymbol{x}} - \hat{\boldsymbol{z}}) + \text{residuals}.$$

Note that it would *not* be valid to use either (11.14) or (11.15) to test H_2.

When one does a pair of nonnested tests, there are four possible outcomes, since each of H_1 and H_2 may or may not be rejected. If, say, H_1 is rejected and H_2 is not, then it seems reasonable to pick H_2 as the preferred model. But it is quite possible that both models, or neither model, may be rejected. When both are rejected, we must conclude that neither model is satisfactory, a result that may not be welcome but that will perhaps spur us to develop better models. When neither is rejected, we must conclude that both models apparently fit the data about equally well and that neither provides evidence that the other is misspecified. Presumably, either the two models are very similar, or the data set is not very informative. The fact that a pair of nonnested tests often does not in general allow us to choose one model rather

[3] Note that the P test could also be used in cases in which root-n consistent estimates of $\boldsymbol{\beta}$ and $\boldsymbol{\gamma}$ were available but least squares estimates were not. This is a simple application of the results in Section 6.7.

than the other may be seen as a deficiency of these tests. That is so only if one misinterprets their nature. Nonnested hypothesis tests are specification tests, and since there is almost never any reason a priori to believe that either of the models actually generated the data, it is appropriate that nonnested tests, like other model specification tests, may well tell us that neither model seems to be compatible with the data.

It is important to stress that the purpose of nonnested tests is *not* to choose one out of a fixed set of models as the "best" one. That is the subject of an entirely different strand of the econometric literature, which deals with criteria for **model selection**. We will not discuss the rather large literature on model selection in this book. Two useful surveys are Amemiya (1980) and Leamer (1983), and an interesting recent paper is Pollak and Wales (1991).

It is of interest to examine more closely the case in which both models are linear, that is, $\boldsymbol{x}(\boldsymbol{\beta}) = \boldsymbol{X\beta}$ and $\boldsymbol{z}(\boldsymbol{\gamma}) = \boldsymbol{Z\gamma}$. This will allow us to see why the J and P tests (which in this case are identical) are asymptotically valid and also to see why these tests may not always perform well in finite samples. The J-test regression for testing H_1 against H_2 is

$$\boldsymbol{y} = \boldsymbol{Xb} + \alpha \boldsymbol{P}_Z \boldsymbol{y} + \text{residuals}, \tag{11.16}$$

where $\boldsymbol{P}_Z = \boldsymbol{Z}(\boldsymbol{Z}^\top \boldsymbol{Z})^{-1}\boldsymbol{Z}^\top$ and $\boldsymbol{b} = (1-\alpha)\boldsymbol{\beta}$. Using the FWL Theorem, we see that the estimate of α from (11.16) will be the same as the estimate from the regression

$$\boldsymbol{M}_X \boldsymbol{y} = \alpha \boldsymbol{M}_X \boldsymbol{P}_Z \boldsymbol{y} + \text{residuals}. \tag{11.17}$$

Thus, if $\acute{s}$ denotes the OLS estimate of σ from (11.17), the t statistic for $\alpha = 0$ will be

$$\frac{\boldsymbol{y}^\top \boldsymbol{P}_Z \boldsymbol{M}_X \boldsymbol{y}}{\acute{s}(\boldsymbol{y}^\top \boldsymbol{P}_Z \boldsymbol{M}_X \boldsymbol{P}_Z \boldsymbol{y})^{1/2}}. \tag{11.18}$$

First of all, notice that when only one column of $\boldsymbol{Z}$, say $\boldsymbol{Z}_1$, does not belong to $\mathcal{S}(\boldsymbol{X})$, it must be the case that

$$\mathcal{S}(\boldsymbol{X}, \boldsymbol{P}_Z \boldsymbol{y}) = \mathcal{S}(\boldsymbol{X}, \boldsymbol{Z}) = \mathcal{S}(\boldsymbol{X}, \boldsymbol{Z}_1).$$

Therefore, the J-test regression (11.16) must yield exactly the same SSR as the regression

$$\boldsymbol{y} = \boldsymbol{Xb} + \delta \boldsymbol{Z}_1 + \text{residuals}. \tag{11.19}$$

Thus, in this special case, the J test is numerically equal to the t statistic on the estimate of δ from (11.19).

When two or more columns of $\boldsymbol{Z}$ do not belong to $\mathcal{S}(\boldsymbol{X})$, this special result is no longer available. If the data were actually generated by H_1, we can replace $\boldsymbol{y}$ in the numerator of (11.18) by $\boldsymbol{X\beta} + \boldsymbol{u}$. Since $\boldsymbol{M}_X \boldsymbol{X\beta} = \boldsymbol{0}$, that numerator becomes

$$\boldsymbol{\beta}^\top \boldsymbol{X}^\top \boldsymbol{P}_Z \boldsymbol{M}_X \boldsymbol{u} + \boldsymbol{u}^\top \boldsymbol{P}_Z \boldsymbol{M}_X \boldsymbol{u}. \tag{11.20}$$

The two terms of (11.20) are of different orders. The first term is a weighted sum of the elements of the vector $\boldsymbol{u}$, each of which has mean zero. Thus, under suitable regularity conditions, it is easy to see that

$$n^{-1/2}\boldsymbol{\beta}^{\top}\boldsymbol{X}^{\top}\boldsymbol{P}_Z\boldsymbol{M}_X\boldsymbol{u} \overset{a}{\sim} N\Big(\mathbf{0},\ \operatorname*{plim}_{n\to\infty}\big(n^{-1}\sigma_1^2\boldsymbol{\beta}^{\top}\boldsymbol{X}^{\top}\boldsymbol{P}_Z\boldsymbol{M}_X\boldsymbol{P}_Z\boldsymbol{X}\boldsymbol{\beta}\big)\Big).$$

This first term is thus $O(n^{1/2})$. The second term, in contrast, is $O(1)$, since

$$\begin{aligned}\operatorname*{plim}_{n\to\infty}\big(\boldsymbol{u}^{\top}\boldsymbol{P}_Z\boldsymbol{M}_X\boldsymbol{u}\big) &= \operatorname*{plim}_{n\to\infty}\big(\boldsymbol{u}^{\top}\boldsymbol{P}_Z\boldsymbol{u} - \boldsymbol{u}^{\top}\boldsymbol{P}_Z\boldsymbol{P}_X\boldsymbol{u}\big)\\ &= \sigma_1^2 k_2 - \sigma_1^2\operatorname{Tr}\Big(\lim_{n\to\infty}\boldsymbol{P}_Z\boldsymbol{P}_X\Big),\end{aligned}$$

and the trace of $\boldsymbol{P}_Z\boldsymbol{P}_X$ is $O(1)$. Thus, asymptotically, it is only the first term in (11.20) that matters.

Similarly, under H_1 the factor in parentheses in the denominator of (11.18) is equal to

$$\boldsymbol{\beta}^{\top}\boldsymbol{X}^{\top}\boldsymbol{P}_Z\boldsymbol{M}_X\boldsymbol{P}_Z\boldsymbol{X}\boldsymbol{\beta} + 2\boldsymbol{\beta}^{\top}\boldsymbol{X}^{\top}\boldsymbol{P}_Z\boldsymbol{M}_X\boldsymbol{P}_Z\boldsymbol{u} + \boldsymbol{u}^{\top}\boldsymbol{P}_Z\boldsymbol{M}_X\boldsymbol{P}_Z\boldsymbol{u}. \tag{11.21}$$

By arguments similar to those used in connection with the numerator, the first of the three terms in (11.21) may be shown to be $O(n)$, the second $O(n^{1/2})$, and the third $O(1)$. Moreover, it is clear that $\acute{s} \to \sigma_1$ under H_1. Thus, asymptotically under H_1, the test statistic (11.18) tends to the random variable

$$\frac{\boldsymbol{\beta}^{\top}\boldsymbol{X}^{\top}\boldsymbol{P}_Z\boldsymbol{M}_X\boldsymbol{u}}{\sigma_1\big(\boldsymbol{\beta}^{\top}\boldsymbol{X}^{\top}\boldsymbol{P}_Z\boldsymbol{M}_X\boldsymbol{P}_Z\boldsymbol{X}\boldsymbol{\beta}\big)^{1/2}},$$

which can be shown to be distributed asymptotically as $N(0,1)$.

This analysis not only makes it clear why the J and P tests are valid asymptotically but also indicates why they may not be well behaved in finite samples. When the sample size is small or $\boldsymbol{Z}$ contains many regressors that are not in $\mathcal{S}(\boldsymbol{X})$, the quantity $\boldsymbol{u}^{\top}\boldsymbol{P}_Z\boldsymbol{M}_X\boldsymbol{u}$, which is asymptotically negligible, may actually be large and positive. Hence, in such circumstances, the J-test statistic (11.18) may have a mean that is substantially greater than zero.

Several ways of reducing or eliminating this bias have been suggested. The simplest, which was first proposed by Fisher and McAleer (1981) and further studied by Godfrey (1983), is to replace $\hat{\gamma}$ in the J-test and P-test regressions by $\tilde{\gamma}$, which is the estimate of γ obtained by minimizing

$$\big(\hat{\boldsymbol{x}} - \boldsymbol{z}(\boldsymbol{\gamma})\big)^{\top}\big(\hat{\boldsymbol{x}} - \boldsymbol{z}(\boldsymbol{\gamma})\big).$$

Thus $\tilde{\gamma}$ is the NLS estimate of γ obtained when one uses the fitted values $\hat{\boldsymbol{x}}$ instead of the dependent variable $\boldsymbol{y}$. In the linear case, this means that the J-test regression (11.16) is replaced by the regression

$$\boldsymbol{y} = \boldsymbol{X}\boldsymbol{b} + \alpha\boldsymbol{P}_Z\boldsymbol{P}_X\boldsymbol{y} + \text{residuals}. \tag{11.22}$$

This regression yields what is called the $\boldsymbol{J_A}$ **test** because Fisher and McAleer attributed the basic idea to Atkinson (1970). Godfrey (1983) showed, using a result of Milliken and Graybill (1970), that the t statistic on the estimate of α from regression (11.22) actually has the t distribution in finite samples under the usual conditions for t statistics to have this distribution ($\boldsymbol{u}$ normally distributed, $\boldsymbol{X}$ and $\boldsymbol{Z}$ independent of $\boldsymbol{y}$). The intuition for this result is quite simple. The vector of fitted values $\boldsymbol{P_X y}$ contains only the part of $\boldsymbol{y}$ that lies in $\mathcal{S}(\boldsymbol{X})$. It must therefore be independent of $\boldsymbol{M_X y}$, which is what the residuals from (11.22) would be if $\alpha = 0$. Therefore, we can treat $\boldsymbol{P_Z P_X y}$ (or any other regressor that depends on $\boldsymbol{y}$ only through $\boldsymbol{P_X y}$) as if it were a fixed regressor.[4] The $\boldsymbol{P_A}$ **test** is to the P test as the J_A test is to the J test.

Unfortunately, the J_A and P_A tests are in many circumstances much less powerful than the ordinary J and P tests; see Davidson and MacKinnon (1982) and Godfrey and Pesaran (1983). Thus if, for example, the J test rejects the null hypothesis and the J_A test does not, it is hard to know whether this is because the former is excessively prone to commit a Type I error or because the latter is excessively prone to commit a Type II error.

A second approach is to estimate the expectation of $\boldsymbol{u}^\top \boldsymbol{M_X P_Z u}$, subtract it from $\boldsymbol{y}^\top \boldsymbol{M_X P_Z y}$, and then divide it by an estimate of the square root of the variance of the resulting quantity so as to obtain a test statistic that would be asymptotically $N(0,1)$. This approach was originally proposed in a somewhat more complicated form by Godfrey and Pesaran (1983); a simpler version may be found in the "Reply" of MacKinnon (1983). This second approach is a good deal harder to use than the J_A test, since it involves matrix calculations that cannot be performed by a sequence of regressions, and it does not yield an exact test. It also requires the assumption of normality. However, it does seem to yield a test with much better finite-sample properties under the null than the J test and, at least in some circumstances, much better power than the J_A test.

The vector $\tilde{\gamma}$ is of interest in its own right. The original Cox test used the fact that, under H_1,

$$\operatorname*{plim}_{n\to\infty}(\tilde{\gamma}) = \operatorname*{plim}_{n\to\infty}(\hat{\gamma}).$$

It is possible to construct a test based directly on the difference between $\hat{\gamma}$ and $\tilde{\gamma}$. Such a test, originally proposed by Dastoor (1983) and developed further by Mizon and Richard (1986), looks at whether the value of $\boldsymbol{\gamma}$ predicted by the H_1 model (i.e., $\tilde{\gamma}$) is the same as the value obtained by direct estimation of H_2 (i.e., $\hat{\gamma}$). These tests are called **encompassing tests**, because if H_1 does explain the performance of H_2, it may be said to "encompass" it; see Mizon (1984). The principle on which they are based is sometimes called the **encompassing principle**.

[4] By the same argument, the RESET test discussed in Section 6.5 is exact in finite samples whenever an ordinary t test would be exact.

There are some practical difficulties with encompassing tests for nonlinear regression models, and we will therefore not discuss such tests in this book. In the linear case, however, the encompassing test is both simple and attractive. When both models are linear, the two estimates of $\boldsymbol{\gamma}$ are

$$\hat{\gamma} = (\boldsymbol{Z}^\top\boldsymbol{Z})^{-1}\boldsymbol{Z}^\top\boldsymbol{y} \quad \text{and}$$
$$\tilde{\gamma} = (\boldsymbol{Z}^\top\boldsymbol{Z})^{-1}\boldsymbol{Z}^\top\boldsymbol{P}_X\boldsymbol{y}.$$

The difference between them is therefore

$$(\boldsymbol{Z}^\top\boldsymbol{Z})^{-1}\boldsymbol{Z}^\top\boldsymbol{y} - (\boldsymbol{Z}^\top\boldsymbol{Z})^{-1}\boldsymbol{Z}^\top\boldsymbol{P}_X\boldsymbol{y} = (\boldsymbol{Z}^\top\boldsymbol{Z})^{-1}\boldsymbol{Z}^\top\boldsymbol{M}_X\boldsymbol{y}. \tag{11.23}$$

The factor $(\boldsymbol{Z}^\top\boldsymbol{Z})^{-1}$ is clearly irrelevant to any test statistic we may construct. The vector $\boldsymbol{Z}^\top\boldsymbol{M}_X\boldsymbol{y}$ will in general contain some elements that are identically zero, one for every column of $\boldsymbol{Z}$ that lies in $\mathcal{S}(\boldsymbol{X})$. Let $\boldsymbol{Z}^*$ denote the matrix made up of the remaining columns of $\boldsymbol{Z}$. Then it should be clear from (11.23) that what we really want to test is whether the vector $\boldsymbol{Z}^{*\top}\boldsymbol{M}_X\boldsymbol{y}$, which under H_1 must equal $\boldsymbol{Z}^{*\top}\boldsymbol{M}_X\boldsymbol{u}$ and should therefore have mean zero, does in fact do so.[5] Constructing a χ^2 test statistic as a quadratic form in this vector, we find that any statistic asymptotically equivalent to

$$\frac{1}{\sigma_1^2}\,\boldsymbol{u}^\top\boldsymbol{M}_X\boldsymbol{Z}^*\big(\boldsymbol{Z}^{*\top}\boldsymbol{M}_X\boldsymbol{Z}^*\big)^{-1}\boldsymbol{Z}^{*\top}\boldsymbol{M}_X\boldsymbol{u}$$

will do the job. But this test statistic is evidently equivalent to an ordinary F test for $\boldsymbol{\gamma}^* = \boldsymbol{0}$ in the linear regression

$$\boldsymbol{y} = \boldsymbol{X\beta} + \boldsymbol{Z}^*\boldsymbol{\gamma}^* + \boldsymbol{u}. \tag{11.24}$$

Thus it turns out that, in this case, the encompassing test is no more than an ordinary F test of H_1 against the alternative hypothesis (11.24). Such a test is easy to perform and will be exact under the usual conditions.

The relative merits of one-degree-of-freedom tests like the J test and many-degree-of-freedom tests like the encompassing test have been much discussed in the literature; see Pesaran (1982) and the survey paper by MacKinnon (1983), especially the comments of several discussants. The J test and tests equivalent to it will be more powerful than many-degree-of-freedom tests when the data were actually generated by H_2 but may be less powerful when the data were generated in some other way. Why this is so should become clear when, in Chapter 12, we discuss what determines the power of a test.

In the remainder of this section, we briefly discuss two special cases. The first is regression models with serially correlated errors. Even if a regression model is initially linear, transforming it to take into account an AR(1) or some other error process turns it into a nonlinear model, as we saw in Chapter 10.

[5] If $\boldsymbol{X}$ or $\boldsymbol{Z}$ includes lagged dependent variables, then we are interested in the asymptotic mean of $n^{-1/2}\boldsymbol{Z}^{*\top}\boldsymbol{M}_X\boldsymbol{y}$ rather than the actual mean of $\boldsymbol{Z}^{*\top}\boldsymbol{M}_X\boldsymbol{y}$.

Suppose then that the two competing models are

$$H_1: \quad y_t = \boldsymbol{X}_t\boldsymbol{\beta} + u_{1t}, \quad u_{1t} = \rho_1 u_{1,t-1} + \varepsilon_{1t}, \text{ and}$$

$$H_2: \quad y_t = \boldsymbol{Z}_t\boldsymbol{\gamma} + u_{2t}, \quad u_{2t} = \rho_2 u_{2,t-1} + \varepsilon_{2t}.$$

The simplest approach is to transform these into the two nonlinear regression models

$$H_1: \quad y_t = \rho_1 y_{t-1} + \big(\boldsymbol{X}_t - \rho_1\boldsymbol{X}_{t-1}\big)\boldsymbol{\beta} + \varepsilon_{1t} \quad \text{and}$$

$$H_2: \quad y_t = \rho_2 y_{t-1} + \big(\boldsymbol{Z}_t - \rho_2\boldsymbol{Z}_{t-1}\big)\boldsymbol{\gamma} + \varepsilon_{2t},$$

for observations 2 through n. One can then use the P or P_A tests to test H_1 against H_2, or vice versa, in the usual way.

Note that to obtain the estimates $(\tilde{\boldsymbol{\gamma}}, \tilde{\rho}_2)$ needed to test H_1 against H_2 using the P_A test, one must run the nonlinear regression

$$\hat{\rho}_1 y_{t-1} + \big(\boldsymbol{X}_t - \hat{\rho}_1\boldsymbol{X}_{t-1}\big)\hat{\boldsymbol{\beta}} = \rho_2 y_{t-1} + \big(\boldsymbol{Z}_t - \rho_2\boldsymbol{Z}_{t-1}\big)\boldsymbol{\gamma} + \varepsilon_{2t}. \tag{11.25}$$

This would have to be done using a general routine for NLS estimation, since routines that implement the Cochrane-Orcutt or Hildreth-Lu procedures would use $\hat{\rho}_1 y_{t-1} + \big(\boldsymbol{X}_t - \hat{\rho}_1\boldsymbol{X}_{t-1}\big)\hat{\boldsymbol{\beta}}$ lagged once rather than y_{t-1} on the right-hand side of (11.25). Several procedures for nonnested testing of models with serial correlation are discussed and compared using Monte Carlo experiments in Bernanke, Bohn, and Reiss (1988) and McAleer, Pesaran, and Bera (1990).

A second special case of interest is regression models estimated by instrumental variables. Ericsson (1983) and Godfrey (1983) discuss various ways to handle this case. The easiest approach, suggested by MacKinnon, White, and Davidson (1983), is simply to modify the J and P tests so that they are valid in this case. The P-test regression (11.15) becomes

$$\boldsymbol{y} - \hat{\boldsymbol{x}} = \boldsymbol{P}_W\hat{\boldsymbol{X}}\boldsymbol{b} + a\boldsymbol{P}_W(\hat{\boldsymbol{z}} - \hat{\boldsymbol{x}}) + \text{residuals}, \tag{11.26}$$

where now $\hat{\boldsymbol{x}}$, $\hat{\boldsymbol{X}}$, and $\hat{\boldsymbol{z}}$ are evaluated at IV estimates $\hat{\boldsymbol{\beta}}$ and $\hat{\boldsymbol{\gamma}}$. The easiest way to obtain a test statistic is simply to regress $\boldsymbol{y} - \hat{\boldsymbol{x}}$ on $\hat{\boldsymbol{X}}$ and $\hat{\boldsymbol{z}} - \hat{\boldsymbol{x}}$ using an IV procedure with $\boldsymbol{W}$ as the matrix of instruments. The pseudo-t statistic on the estimate of a will then be an asymptotically valid test statistic, provided that $\boldsymbol{W}$ is the set of instruments used to obtain IV estimates of H_1 and that the usual regularity conditions for nonlinear IV estimation are satisfied (see Section 7.6).

This completes our discussion of nonnested hypothesis tests for regression models. Obviously, we have not discussed by any means every aspect of this problem. Two papers that deal with aspects we have not discussed are MacKinnon, White, and Davidson (1983), who adapt the J and P tests to models involving different transformations of the dependent variable, and Davidson and MacKinnon (1983b), who adapt them to multivariate nonlinear regression models (see Chapter 9). The surveys by MacKinnon (1983) and McAleer (1987) provide many additional references.

11.4 TESTS BASED ON COMPARING TWO SETS OF ESTIMATES

In Section 7.9, we introduced a class of tests, which we called Durbin-Wu-Hausman, or DWH, tests, that can be used to see whether least squares estimates are consistent when some of the regressors may be correlated with the error terms. These tests were developed by Durbin (1954), Wu (1973), and Hausman (1978). There has been a good deal of work on DWH tests in recent years; see the survey paper by Ruud (1984). In this section, we show that DWH tests can be useful in a variety of circumstances unrelated to IV estimation, although still in the context of regression models.

The basic idea of DWH tests is to base a test on a **vector of contrasts**, that is, the difference between two sets of estimates, one of which will be consistent under weaker conditions than the other. Suppose, for simplicity, that the model to be tested is

$$\boldsymbol{y} = \boldsymbol{X\beta} + \boldsymbol{u}, \quad \boldsymbol{u} \sim \mathrm{IID}(\mathbf{0}, \sigma^2\mathbf{I}), \tag{11.27}$$

where there are n observations and k regressors. In this context, the DWH principle of testing suggests that we should compare the OLS estimator

$$\hat{\boldsymbol{\beta}} = \left(\boldsymbol{X}^{\top}\boldsymbol{X}\right)^{-1}\boldsymbol{X}^{\top}\boldsymbol{y} \tag{11.28}$$

with some other linear estimator

$$\check{\boldsymbol{\beta}} = \left(\boldsymbol{X}^{\top}\boldsymbol{A}\boldsymbol{X}\right)^{-1}\boldsymbol{X}^{\top}\boldsymbol{A}\boldsymbol{y}, \tag{11.29}$$

where $\boldsymbol{A}$ is a symmetric $n \times n$ matrix assumed for simplicity to have rank no less than k (otherwise, not all elements of $\check{\boldsymbol{\beta}}$ could be estimated, and we would be able to compare only the estimable part of $\check{\boldsymbol{\beta}}$ with the corresponding subvector of $\hat{\boldsymbol{\beta}}$; see the discussion of differencing specification tests below). In the case we studied in Section 7.9, $\check{\boldsymbol{\beta}}$ is the IV estimator

$$\tilde{\boldsymbol{\beta}} \equiv \left(\boldsymbol{X}^{\top}\boldsymbol{P}_W\boldsymbol{X}\right)^{-1}\boldsymbol{X}^{\top}\boldsymbol{P}_W\boldsymbol{y}.$$

Thus, in this case, the matrix $\boldsymbol{A}$ is $\boldsymbol{P}_W$, the matrix that projects orthogonally onto $\mathcal{S}(\boldsymbol{W})$, where $\boldsymbol{W}$ is a matrix of instruments.

If the data were actually generated by the model (11.27), with $\boldsymbol{\beta} = \boldsymbol{\beta}_0$, the two estimates (11.28) and (11.29) would have the same probability limit. To see this, observe that

$$\operatorname*{plim}_{n\to\infty} \check{\boldsymbol{\beta}} = \operatorname*{plim}_{n\to\infty}\left(\frac{1}{n}\boldsymbol{X}^{\top}\boldsymbol{A}\boldsymbol{X}\right)^{-1}\left(\operatorname*{plim}_{n\to\infty}\left(\frac{1}{n}\boldsymbol{X}^{\top}\boldsymbol{A}\boldsymbol{X}\right)\boldsymbol{\beta}_0 + \operatorname*{plim}_{n\to\infty}\left(\frac{1}{n}\boldsymbol{X}^{\top}\boldsymbol{A}\boldsymbol{u}\right)\right),$$

which equals $\boldsymbol{\beta}_0$ provided that $\mathrm{plim}\left(n^{-1}\boldsymbol{X}^{\top}\boldsymbol{A}\boldsymbol{u}\right) = \mathbf{0}$. Thus, if $\check{\boldsymbol{\beta}}$ and $\hat{\boldsymbol{\beta}}$ differ by more than can reasonably be attributed to random variation, we may conclude that the data were *not* generated by the model (11.27).

For a regression model like (11.27), it is easy to compute a DWH test by means of an artificial regression. We saw some examples of this in Section 7.9 and will discuss further examples below. However, there is another way to compute DWH tests, and it can be more convenient in some cases. For some model that need not necessarily be a regression model, let $\hat{\boldsymbol{\theta}}$ denote an efficient estimator of the model parameters and $\check{\boldsymbol{\theta}}$ an estimator that is less efficient but consistent under weaker conditions than those of the model. Let us denote the vector of contrasts between $\check{\boldsymbol{\theta}}$ and $\hat{\boldsymbol{\theta}}$ by $\boldsymbol{e}$. Then we have seen that

$$n^{1/2}(\check{\boldsymbol{\theta}} - \boldsymbol{\theta}_0) \overset{a}{=} n^{1/2}(\hat{\boldsymbol{\theta}} - \boldsymbol{\theta}_0) + n^{1/2}\boldsymbol{e}, \tag{11.30}$$

where $n^{1/2}\boldsymbol{e}$ is asymptotically uncorrelated with $n^{1/2}(\hat{\boldsymbol{\theta}} - \boldsymbol{\theta}_0)$. This result was proved for models estimated by maximum likelihood in Section 8.8; its finite-sample equivalent for linear regression models was proved as part of the proof of the Gauss-Markov Theorem in Section 5.5. Because the two terms on the right-hand side of (11.30) are asymptotically uncorrelated, the asymptotic covariance matrix of the left-hand side is just the sum of the asymptotic covariance matrices of those two terms. Therefore, we obtain

$$\lim_{n\to\infty} \boldsymbol{V}\big(n^{1/2}(\check{\boldsymbol{\theta}} - \boldsymbol{\theta}_0)\big) = \lim_{n\to\infty} \boldsymbol{V}\big(n^{1/2}(\hat{\boldsymbol{\theta}} - \boldsymbol{\theta}_0)\big) + \lim_{n\to\infty} \boldsymbol{V}(n^{1/2}\boldsymbol{e}),$$

from which, in simplified notation, we may deduce the asymptotic covariance matrix of the vector of contrasts:

$$\boldsymbol{V}^{\infty}(\check{\boldsymbol{\theta}} - \hat{\boldsymbol{\theta}}) = \boldsymbol{V}^{\infty}(\check{\boldsymbol{\theta}}) - \boldsymbol{V}^{\infty}(\hat{\boldsymbol{\theta}}). \tag{11.31}$$

In words, the asymptotic covariance matrix of the difference between $\check{\boldsymbol{\theta}}$ and $\hat{\boldsymbol{\theta}}$ is equal to the difference of their respective asymptotic covariance matrices. This important result is due to Hausman (1978).

The result (11.31) can be used to construct DWH tests of the form

$$(\check{\boldsymbol{\theta}} - \hat{\boldsymbol{\theta}})^{\top}\big(\check{\boldsymbol{V}}(\check{\boldsymbol{\theta}}) - \hat{\boldsymbol{V}}(\hat{\boldsymbol{\theta}})\big)^{-1}(\check{\boldsymbol{\theta}} - \hat{\boldsymbol{\theta}}), \tag{11.32}$$

where $\check{\boldsymbol{V}}(\check{\boldsymbol{\theta}})$ and $\hat{\boldsymbol{V}}(\hat{\boldsymbol{\theta}})$ denote estimates of the covariance matrices of $\check{\boldsymbol{\theta}}$ and $\hat{\boldsymbol{\theta}}$, respectively. The test statistic (11.32) will be asymptotically distributed as chi-squared with as many degrees of freedom as the rank of $\boldsymbol{V}^{\infty}(\check{\boldsymbol{\theta}}) - \boldsymbol{V}^{\infty}(\hat{\boldsymbol{\theta}})$. Note that the inverse in (11.32) will have to be replaced by a generalized inverse if, as is often the case, the rank of $\boldsymbol{V}^{\infty}(\check{\boldsymbol{\theta}}) - \boldsymbol{V}^{\infty}(\hat{\boldsymbol{\theta}})$ is less than the number of parameters in $\boldsymbol{\theta}$; see Hausman and Taylor (1982). There can be practical difficulties with (11.32) if $\check{\boldsymbol{V}}(\check{\boldsymbol{\theta}}) - \hat{\boldsymbol{V}}(\hat{\boldsymbol{\theta}})$ is not positive semidefinite or if the rank of $\check{\boldsymbol{V}}(\check{\boldsymbol{\theta}}) - \hat{\boldsymbol{V}}(\hat{\boldsymbol{\theta}})$ differs from the rank of $\boldsymbol{V}^{\infty}(\check{\boldsymbol{\theta}}) - \boldsymbol{V}^{\infty}(\hat{\boldsymbol{\theta}})$. That is why we emphasize the approach based on artificial regressions.

In the case of the linear regression (11.27), where the two estimators are (11.28) and (11.29), the DWH test is based on the vector of contrasts

$$\check{\boldsymbol{\beta}} - \hat{\boldsymbol{\beta}} = \big(\boldsymbol{X}^{\top}\boldsymbol{A}\boldsymbol{X}\big)^{-1}\boldsymbol{X}^{\top}\boldsymbol{A}\boldsymbol{M}_X\boldsymbol{y}. \tag{11.33}$$

This looks just like expression (7.59), with $\boldsymbol{A}$ replacing $\boldsymbol{P}_W$, and may be derived in exactly the same way. The first factor in (11.33), $(\boldsymbol{X}^\top\boldsymbol{A}\boldsymbol{X})^{-1}$, is simply a $k \times k$ matrix with full rank, which will have no effect on any test statistic that we might compute. Therefore, what we really want to do is test whether the vector

$$n^{-1/2}\boldsymbol{X}^\top\boldsymbol{A}\boldsymbol{M}_X\boldsymbol{y} \tag{11.34}$$

has mean zero asymptotically. This vector has k elements, but even if $\boldsymbol{AX}$ has full rank, not all those elements may be random variables, because $\boldsymbol{M}_X$ may annihilate some columns of $\boldsymbol{AX}$. Suppose that k^* is the number of linearly independent columns of $\boldsymbol{AX}$ that are not annihilated by $\boldsymbol{M}_X$. Then testing (11.34) is equivalent to testing whether the vector

$$n^{-1/2}\boldsymbol{X}^{*\top}\boldsymbol{A}\boldsymbol{M}_X\boldsymbol{y} \tag{11.35}$$

has mean zero asymptotically, where $\boldsymbol{X}^*$ denotes k^* columns of $\boldsymbol{X}$ with the property that none of the columns of $\boldsymbol{AX}^*$ is annihilated by $\boldsymbol{M}_X$.

Now consider the artificial regression

$$\boldsymbol{y} = \boldsymbol{X\beta} + \boldsymbol{AX}^*\boldsymbol{\delta} + \text{residuals}. \tag{11.36}$$

It is easily shown by using the FWL Theorem that the OLS estimate of $\boldsymbol{\delta}$ is

$$\acute{\boldsymbol{\delta}} = \left(\boldsymbol{X}^{*\top}\boldsymbol{A}\boldsymbol{M}_X\boldsymbol{A}\boldsymbol{X}^*\right)^{-1}\boldsymbol{X}^{*\top}\boldsymbol{A}\boldsymbol{M}_X\boldsymbol{y},$$

and it is evident that, in general, $\operatorname{plim}(\acute{\boldsymbol{\delta}}) = \mathbf{0}$ if and only if (11.35) holds. The ordinary F statistic for $\boldsymbol{\delta} = \mathbf{0}$ in (11.36) is

$$\frac{\boldsymbol{y}^\top\boldsymbol{P}_{M_XAX^*}\boldsymbol{y}/k^*}{\boldsymbol{y}^\top\boldsymbol{M}_{X,\,M_XAX^*}\boldsymbol{y}/(n-k-k^*)}, \tag{11.37}$$

where $\boldsymbol{P}_{M_XAX^*}$ is the matrix that projects onto $\mathcal{S}(\boldsymbol{M}_X\boldsymbol{A}\boldsymbol{X}^*)$, and $\boldsymbol{M}_{X,\,M_XAX^*}$ is the matrix that projects onto $\mathcal{S}^\perp(\boldsymbol{X}, \boldsymbol{M}_X\boldsymbol{A}\boldsymbol{X}^*)$. If (11.27) actually generated the data, the statistic (11.37) will certainly be valid asymptotically, since the denominator will then consistently estimate σ^2. It will be exactly distributed as $F(k^*, n-k-k^*)$ in finite samples if the u_t's in (11.27) are normally distributed and $\boldsymbol{X}$ and $\boldsymbol{A}$ can be treated as fixed. Regression (11.36) and expression (11.37) are essentially the same as regression (7.62) and expression (7.64), respectively; the latter are special cases of the former.

The most common type of DWH test is the one we dealt with in Section 7.9, which asks whether least squares estimates are consistent when some of the regressors may be correlated with the error terms. However, there are numerous other possibilities. For example, $\check{\boldsymbol{\beta}}$ might be the OLS estimator for $\boldsymbol{\beta}$ in the model

$$\boldsymbol{y} = \boldsymbol{X\beta} + \boldsymbol{Z\gamma} + \boldsymbol{u}, \tag{11.38}$$

where $\boldsymbol{Z}$ is an $n \times l$ matrix of regressors not in the span of the columns of $\boldsymbol{X}$. Using the FWL Theorem, we see that

$$\check{\boldsymbol{\beta}} = \left(\boldsymbol{X}^{\top}\boldsymbol{M}_Z\boldsymbol{X}\right)^{-1}\boldsymbol{X}^{\top}\boldsymbol{M}_Z\boldsymbol{y},$$

from which it is clear that $\boldsymbol{M}_Z$ is playing the role of $\boldsymbol{A}$. This form of the DWH test is thus asking whether the estimates $\check{\boldsymbol{\beta}}$ when $\boldsymbol{Z}$ is included in the model are significantly different from the estimates $\hat{\boldsymbol{\beta}}$ when $\boldsymbol{Z}$ is excluded from the model. This is a simple example of the case examined, in a much more general context, by Holly (1982). It turns out that this version of the DWH test is equivalent to an ordinary F test for $\boldsymbol{\gamma} = \boldsymbol{0}$, provided that $k \geq l$ and a certain matrix has full rank, and not equivalent otherwise. This may be seen from regression (11.36), which in this case is

$$\boldsymbol{y} = \boldsymbol{X}\boldsymbol{\beta} + \boldsymbol{M}_Z\boldsymbol{X}\boldsymbol{\delta} + \text{residuals} \tag{11.39}$$

$$= \boldsymbol{X}(\boldsymbol{\beta} + \boldsymbol{\delta}) - \boldsymbol{P}_Z\boldsymbol{X}\boldsymbol{\delta} + \text{residuals}. \tag{11.40}$$

It is evident from (11.40) that whenever the matrix $\boldsymbol{Z}^{\top}\boldsymbol{X}$ has rank l, regression (11.39) will have exactly the same explanatory power as regression (11.38), since $\boldsymbol{X}$ and $\boldsymbol{P}_Z\boldsymbol{X} = \boldsymbol{Z}(\boldsymbol{Z}^{\top}\boldsymbol{Z})^{-1}\boldsymbol{Z}^{\top}\boldsymbol{X}$ will jointly span the same subspace as $\boldsymbol{X}$ and $\boldsymbol{Z}$. The F test for $\boldsymbol{\delta} = \boldsymbol{0}$ in (11.39) will thus be identical to the F test for $\boldsymbol{\gamma} = \boldsymbol{0}$ in (11.38), which is Holly's result specialized to the linear regression case. A necessary but not sufficient condition for $\boldsymbol{Z}^{\top}\boldsymbol{X}$ to have rank l is that $k \geq l$. For more on the relationship between DWH tests and classical hypothesis tests, see Holly and Monfort (1986) and Davidson and MacKinnon (1989).

There is an interesting relationship between the "exogeneity" variant of the DWH test and the "omitted-variables" variant. In the former, $\boldsymbol{A} = \boldsymbol{P}_W$ and $\boldsymbol{P}_W\boldsymbol{X}^*$ consists of all the columns of $\boldsymbol{P}_W\boldsymbol{X}$ that do not lie in the span of $\boldsymbol{X}$. Thus the test regression is

$$\boldsymbol{y} = \boldsymbol{X}\boldsymbol{\beta} + \boldsymbol{P}_W\boldsymbol{X}^*\boldsymbol{\delta} + \text{residuals}. \tag{11.41}$$

In the latter, $\boldsymbol{M}_Z\boldsymbol{X}^* = \boldsymbol{M}_Z\boldsymbol{X}$, provided the matrix $[\boldsymbol{X} \;\; \boldsymbol{Z}]$ has full rank. Now suppose that we expand $\boldsymbol{Z}$ so that it equals $\boldsymbol{W}$, which means that it includes at least as many variables as $\boldsymbol{X}$, including some variables that are in the span of $\boldsymbol{X}$. Evidently, $\boldsymbol{X}^*$ will then consist of those columns of $\boldsymbol{X}$ that are not in the span of $\boldsymbol{W}$, and the test regression will be

$$\boldsymbol{y} = \boldsymbol{X}\boldsymbol{\beta} + \boldsymbol{M}_W\boldsymbol{X}^*\boldsymbol{\delta} + \text{residuals}. \tag{11.42}$$

Because the matrices $[\boldsymbol{X} \;\; \boldsymbol{P}_W\boldsymbol{X}]$ and $[\boldsymbol{X} \;\; \boldsymbol{M}_W\boldsymbol{X}]$ span the same subspace, regressions (11.41) and (11.42) will have exactly the same explanatory power. This means that the test which is *interpreted* as a test for consistency despite possible endogeneity and the test which is *interpreted* as a test for the consistency of parameter estimates when certain variables have been omitted are in fact exactly the same test. Ruud (1984) provides a fuller discussion.

The final example of DWH tests that we will discuss is the **differencing specification test**, which was proposed in Plosser, Schwert, and White (1982). The basic idea of this test is to compare estimates in levels and estimates in first differences as a test of specification. Our treatment follows that of Davidson, Godfrey, and MacKinnon (1985), which shows how to calculate the test by means of an artificial regression.

As usual, the OLS levels estimate is $\hat{\boldsymbol{\beta}} = (\boldsymbol{X}^\top\boldsymbol{X})^{-1}\boldsymbol{X}^\top\boldsymbol{y}$. The OLS estimate using first-differenced data is

$$\check{\boldsymbol{\beta}} = \big(\dot{\boldsymbol{X}}^\top\dot{\boldsymbol{X}}\big)^{-1}\dot{\boldsymbol{X}}^\top\dot{\boldsymbol{y}},$$

where $\dot{\boldsymbol{y}}$ and $\dot{\boldsymbol{X}}$ denote the vector and matrix with typical rows $\dot{y}_t = y_t - y_{t-1}$ and $\dot{\boldsymbol{X}}_t = \boldsymbol{X}_t - \boldsymbol{X}_{t-1}$, respectively. For the moment, we will ignore the fact that if $\boldsymbol{X}$ includes a constant term, $\dot{\boldsymbol{X}}$ will include a column of zeros. We will also ignore the fact that $\dot{\boldsymbol{X}}_1$ and $\dot{\boldsymbol{y}}_1$ may not be computable without making arbitrary assumptions if $\boldsymbol{X}_0$ and $\boldsymbol{y}_0$ are not available.

The crucial result that makes it possible to calculate the differencing test by means of an artificial regression is that, if $\ddot{\boldsymbol{X}}$ denotes the matrix with typical row $\boldsymbol{X}_{t+1} - 2\boldsymbol{X}_t + \boldsymbol{X}_{t-1}$ (i.e., the matrix of second differences of $\boldsymbol{X}$, led one period), then

$$\check{\boldsymbol{\beta}} \overset{a}{=} \big(-\ddot{\boldsymbol{X}}^\top\boldsymbol{X}\big)^{-1}\big(-\ddot{\boldsymbol{X}}^\top\boldsymbol{y}\big) = \big(\ddot{\boldsymbol{X}}^\top\boldsymbol{X}\big)^{-1}\ddot{\boldsymbol{X}}^\top\boldsymbol{y}. \tag{11.43}$$

To prove this, consider typical elements of the matrices that appear in (11.43). Let $\boldsymbol{r}$ denote any column of $\boldsymbol{X}$ and $\boldsymbol{s}$ denote the same or another column of $\boldsymbol{X}$, or possibly $\boldsymbol{y}$. Hence any element of $\dot{\boldsymbol{X}}^\top\dot{\boldsymbol{X}}$, or any element of $\dot{\boldsymbol{X}}^\top\dot{\boldsymbol{y}}$, can be written as $\dot{\boldsymbol{r}}^\top\dot{\boldsymbol{s}}$, while any element of $\ddot{\boldsymbol{X}}^\top\boldsymbol{X}$, or any element of $\ddot{\boldsymbol{X}}^\top\boldsymbol{y}$, can be written as $\ddot{\boldsymbol{r}}^\top\boldsymbol{s}$. We wish to show that $\dot{\boldsymbol{r}}^\top\dot{\boldsymbol{s}} \overset{a}{=} -\ddot{\boldsymbol{r}}^\top\boldsymbol{s}$. By definition,

$$\begin{aligned}\dot{\boldsymbol{r}}^\top\dot{\boldsymbol{s}} &= \sum_{t=1}^{n}\big(r_t - r_{t-1}\big)\big(s_t - s_{t-1}\big)\\ &= \sum_{t=1}^{n}\big(r_t s_t + r_{t-1}s_{t-1} - r_t s_{t-1} - r_{t-1}s_t\big).\end{aligned} \tag{11.44}$$

Similarly,

$$\begin{aligned}-\ddot{\boldsymbol{r}}^\top\boldsymbol{s} &= -\sum_{t=1}^{n}\big(r_{t+1} - 2r_t + r_{t-1}\big)s_t\\ &= \sum_{t=1}^{n}\big(2r_t s_t - r_{t+1}s_t - r_{t-1}s_t\big).\end{aligned} \tag{11.45}$$

Subtracting (11.45) from (11.44), we obtain

$$r_0 s_0 - r_n s_n - r_1 s_0 + r_{n+1} s_n.$$

This expression is evidently $O(1)$, while quantities like $\dot{\boldsymbol{X}}^\top \dot{\boldsymbol{X}}$ and $\ddot{\boldsymbol{X}}^\top \boldsymbol{X}$ are $O(n)$. Any difference between $\dot{\boldsymbol{r}}^\top \dot{\boldsymbol{s}}$ and $-\ddot{\boldsymbol{r}}^\top \boldsymbol{s}$ must therefore be asymptotically negligible, which proves the result (11.43).[6]

Using this result and the fact that $\boldsymbol{y} = \boldsymbol{P}_X \boldsymbol{y} + \boldsymbol{M}_X \boldsymbol{y} = \boldsymbol{X}\hat{\boldsymbol{\beta}} + \boldsymbol{M}_X \boldsymbol{y}$, we see that

$$\begin{aligned}
\check{\boldsymbol{\beta}} - \hat{\boldsymbol{\beta}} &\overset{a}{=} \left(\ddot{\boldsymbol{X}}^\top \boldsymbol{X}\right)^{-1} \ddot{\boldsymbol{X}}^\top \boldsymbol{y} - \left(\boldsymbol{X}^\top \boldsymbol{X}\right)^{-1} \boldsymbol{X}^\top \boldsymbol{y} \\
&= \left(\ddot{\boldsymbol{X}}^\top \boldsymbol{X}\right)^{-1} \ddot{\boldsymbol{X}}^\top (\boldsymbol{X}\hat{\boldsymbol{\beta}} + \boldsymbol{M}_X \boldsymbol{y}) - \hat{\boldsymbol{\beta}} \\
&= \left(\ddot{\boldsymbol{X}}^\top \boldsymbol{X}\right)^{-1} \ddot{\boldsymbol{X}}^\top \boldsymbol{M}_X \boldsymbol{y}.
\end{aligned}$$

Thus the differencing specification test is really a test of the hypothesis that the vector $n^{-1/2} \ddot{\boldsymbol{X}}^\top \boldsymbol{M}_X \boldsymbol{y}$ has mean zero asymptotically. By an argument similar to the one that led to the artificial regression (11.36), it is easy to show that this hypothesis can be tested using an asymptotic F test for $\boldsymbol{\delta} = \boldsymbol{0}$ in the artificial regression

$$\boldsymbol{y} = \boldsymbol{X}\boldsymbol{\beta} + \ddot{\boldsymbol{X}}\boldsymbol{\delta} + \text{residuals}. \tag{11.46}$$

Moreover, from the definition of $\ddot{\boldsymbol{X}}$ we see that $\mathcal{S}(\boldsymbol{X}, \ddot{\boldsymbol{X}}) = \mathcal{S}(\boldsymbol{X}, \boldsymbol{C})$, where $\boldsymbol{C}$ is a matrix with typical row $\boldsymbol{X}_{t-1} + \boldsymbol{X}_{t+1}$. Thus the test for $\boldsymbol{\delta} = \boldsymbol{0}$ in (11.46) will be numerically identical to the test for $\boldsymbol{\eta} = \boldsymbol{0}$ in

$$\boldsymbol{y} = \boldsymbol{X}\boldsymbol{\beta} + \boldsymbol{C}\boldsymbol{\eta} + \text{residuals}. \tag{11.47}$$

Regression (11.47) makes it clear what to do about the constant term and any other regressor(s) belonging to $\boldsymbol{X}$ that, after first-differencing, cause the matrix $\dot{\boldsymbol{X}}$ not to have full rank. If any such regressors are included, the matrix $[\boldsymbol{X} \;\; \boldsymbol{C}]$ will not have full rank. One must therefore drop from $\boldsymbol{C}$ any columns that prevent $[\boldsymbol{X} \;\; \boldsymbol{C}]$ from having full rank. The number of degrees of freedom for the test statistic will then be the number of columns left in $\boldsymbol{C}$.

Regression (11.47) also makes it clear that the differencing specification test is a curious test indeed. The additional regressors $\boldsymbol{C}$ are the sums of the leading and lagging values of the original regressors. While it is easy to justify testing whether lagged values of $\boldsymbol{X}$ should have been included in a regression model, it is harder to justify testing whether leading values of $\boldsymbol{X}$ should have been included. In many cases, one would not expect the information set on which $\boldsymbol{y}$ is conditioned to include leading values of $\boldsymbol{X}$. Certainly the test will

[6] This result can also be proved by using a **differencing matrix**, say $\boldsymbol{D}$, with the properties that $\dot{\boldsymbol{X}} = \boldsymbol{D}\boldsymbol{X}$ and $\ddot{\boldsymbol{X}}_{-1} = \boldsymbol{D}^2\boldsymbol{X}$. Such a proof would be more compact but perhaps less readily grasped.

not make sense if $\boldsymbol{X}$ may depend on lagged values of $\boldsymbol{u}$, since in that case u_t might well be correlated with $\boldsymbol{X}_{t+1}$.

There are numerous other applications of the DWH test to linear and nonlinear regression models. See Boothe and MacKinnon (1986), Breusch and Godfrey (1986), Godfrey (1988), and Ruud (1984). We discussed tests of the difference between IV and least squares estimates of nonlinear regression models in Section 7.9, and most of that discussion applies equally well to other applications of the DWH test to nonlinear regression models.

It is often argued that DWH tests may fruitfully be used when the null hypothesis is *not* that the data were generated by (11.27) but simply that the OLS estimates $\hat{\boldsymbol{\beta}}$ from (11.27) are consistent. While this is true up to a point, there is a serious difficulty with trying to use these tests in this way. As we have seen, DWH tests do not directly test the hypothesis that parameters are estimated consistently. Instead, they test whether certain linear combinations of the parameters on omitted variables are zero, because if this were so, it would imply that the parameters of the null are consistently estimated. As a consequence, there are situations in which all parameters will be estimated consistently and yet DWH tests will almost invariably reject the null.

To see how this can happen, consider the following very simple case. Suppose that the restricted model is

$$\boldsymbol{y} = \boldsymbol{X\beta} + \boldsymbol{u} \tag{11.48}$$

and the unrestricted one is

$$\boldsymbol{y} = \boldsymbol{X\beta} + \gamma\boldsymbol{z} + \boldsymbol{u}, \tag{11.49}$$

with the $n \times k$ random matrix $\boldsymbol{X}$ and the $n \times 1$ random vectors $\boldsymbol{z}$ and $\boldsymbol{u}$ being distributed in such a way that $\operatorname{plim}\bigl(n^{-1}\boldsymbol{X}^{\top}\boldsymbol{z}\bigr) = \boldsymbol{0}$ and $\operatorname{plim}\bigl(n^{-1}\boldsymbol{X}^{\top}\boldsymbol{u}\bigr) = \boldsymbol{0}$. It is clear that OLS estimation of (11.48) will yield consistent estimates of $\boldsymbol{\beta}$ even if the DGP is (11.49) with $\gamma \neq 0$. Now consider the DWH test, which may be based on the regression

$$\boldsymbol{y} = \boldsymbol{X\beta} + \boldsymbol{z}\bigl(\boldsymbol{z}^{\top}\boldsymbol{z}\bigr)^{-1}\boldsymbol{z}^{\top}\boldsymbol{x}^{*}\delta + \text{residuals}, \tag{11.50}$$

where $\boldsymbol{x}^{*}$ is one of the columns of $\boldsymbol{X}$. Unless $\boldsymbol{z}^{\top}\boldsymbol{x}^{*}$ happens to be numerically equal to zero, in which case the test cannot be computed, a t test for $\delta = 0$ in (11.50) will be numerically identical to a t test for $\gamma = 0$ in (11.49). Thus, if $\gamma \neq 0$ and the sample is large enough, the DWH test will reject the null hypothesis with probability one, even though $\hat{\boldsymbol{\beta}}$ is in fact consistent. The reason for this apparently puzzling result is that in a finite sample we have computed a DWH test which it would have been impossible to compute asymptotically, because the regressor $\boldsymbol{z}(\boldsymbol{z}^{\top}\boldsymbol{z})^{-1}\boldsymbol{z}^{\top}\boldsymbol{x}^{*}$ would then be a column of zeros. Unfortunately, it is often possible to do this. In such circumstances, it is clear that finite-sample results from DWH tests may easily be misinterpreted.

11.5 TESTING FOR HETEROSKEDASTICITY

The tests based on the Gauss-Newton regression that we have discussed so far are all designed to test various aspects of the specification of the regression function. However, variants of the GNR can also be used to test some aspects of the specification of the error terms, in particular the assumption that they have constant variance. In this section, we show how some popular tests for heteroskedasticity can be derived as applications of the GNR. Additional tests for heteroskedasticity will be discussed in Chapter 16.

A plausible model of heteroskedasticity is

$$E(u_t^2) = h(\alpha + \boldsymbol{Z}_t\boldsymbol{\gamma}), \tag{11.51}$$

where $h(\cdot)$ is a possibly nonlinear function that may only take on positive values, $\boldsymbol{Z}_t$ is a $1 \times q$ vector of observations on exogenous or predetermined variables, α is a scalar parameter, and $\boldsymbol{\gamma}$ is a q–vector of parameters. Equation (11.51) says that the expectation of the squared error term u_t is $h(\alpha + \boldsymbol{Z}_t\boldsymbol{\gamma})$. As we saw in Section 9.2, the function $h(\cdot)$ is called a **skedastic function**. If all elements of the vector $\boldsymbol{\gamma}$ are equal to zero, $h(\alpha + \boldsymbol{Z}_t\boldsymbol{\gamma})$ collapses to $h(\alpha)$, which is simply a constant. We can think of this constant as being σ^2. Thus we may test the null hypothesis of homoskedasticity against the heteroskedastic alternative (11.51) by testing the restriction that $\boldsymbol{\gamma} = \mathbf{0}$.

Now let us define e_t as the difference between u_t^2 and its expectation. This allows us to write an equation for u_t^2:

$$u_t^2 = h(\alpha + \boldsymbol{Z}_t\boldsymbol{\gamma}) + e_t. \tag{11.52}$$

Equation (11.52) is a regression model. While we would not expect the error term e_t to be as well behaved as the error terms in most regression models, since the distribution of u_t^2 will generally be skewed to the right, it does have mean zero by definition, and we will assume that it has a finite, and constant, variance. This assumption would probably be an excessively strong one if $\boldsymbol{\gamma}$ were nonzero (it can be relaxed by use of the techniques discussed in the next section). Under the null hypothesis that $\boldsymbol{\gamma} = \mathbf{0}$, however, it does not seem unreasonable to assume that the variance of e_t is constant.

Let us suppose to begin with that we actually observe u_t. Then we can certainly estimate (11.52) in the usual way by NLS. Under the null hypothesis that $\boldsymbol{\gamma} = \mathbf{0}$, the NLS estimate of α is whatever value $\tilde{\alpha}$ solves the equation

$$h(\tilde{\alpha}) = \frac{1}{n}\sum_{t=1}^{n} u_t^2 \equiv \tilde{\sigma}^2.$$

Thus we simply have to estimate the sample mean of the u_t^2's, $\tilde{\sigma}^2$. We could then test the hypothesis that $\boldsymbol{\gamma} = \mathbf{0}$ by means of the Gauss-Newton regression. This GNR would be

$$u_t^2 - \tilde{\sigma}^2 = h'(\tilde{\alpha})a + h'(\tilde{\alpha})\boldsymbol{Z}_t\boldsymbol{c} + \text{residual}, \tag{11.53}$$

where $h'(\tilde{\alpha})$ is the derivative of $h(\cdot)$ with respect to its one argument, evaluated at $\alpha = \tilde{\alpha}$ and $\boldsymbol{\gamma} = \mathbf{0}$. Since $h'(\tilde{\alpha})$ is a constant, (11.53) simplifies to

$$\boldsymbol{v} - \boldsymbol{\iota}\tilde{\sigma}^2 = \boldsymbol{\iota}a + \boldsymbol{Z}\boldsymbol{c} + \text{residuals}, \tag{11.54}$$

where $\boldsymbol{v}$ is an n–vector of which the tth element is u_t^2, $\boldsymbol{\iota}$ is an n–vector of ones, and $\boldsymbol{Z}$ is an $n \times q$ matrix of which the tth row is $\boldsymbol{Z}_t$. Since neither the function $h(\cdot)$ nor its derivatives appear in (11.54) at all, a test based on this artificial regression will not depend on the functional form of $h(\cdot)$. This is because all models of the form (11.52) are locally equivalent alternatives. We saw an earlier example of this in Section 10.8; see Godfrey (1981) and Godfrey and Wickens (1982).

As usual, the GNR test statistic for $\boldsymbol{\gamma} = \mathbf{0}$ is either an F test for $\boldsymbol{c} = \mathbf{0}$ in (11.54) or nR^2 from that regression. Since $\boldsymbol{\iota}$ appears on both sides of (11.54), the regression can be further simplified to

$$\boldsymbol{v} = \boldsymbol{\iota}a^* + \boldsymbol{Z}\boldsymbol{c} + \text{residuals}. \tag{11.55}$$

The centered R^2 from (11.55) will be identical to both the centered and uncentered R^2's from (11.54), which are the same because the regressand of the latter has mean zero by construction. The F statistic for $\boldsymbol{c} = \mathbf{0}$, which is printed by almost all regression packages, will evidently be identical for the two regressions.

In practice, of course, the error terms u_t appear in a regression model like $\boldsymbol{y} = \boldsymbol{x}(\boldsymbol{\beta}) + \boldsymbol{u}$, and we do not actually observe them. However, since we do observe $\boldsymbol{y}$ and whatever regressors it is supposed to depend on, we can easily obtain least squares residuals $\hat{\boldsymbol{u}}$. The model that is estimated may be linear or nonlinear; its exact form is irrelevant. As we saw in Section 5.6, consistency of the parameter estimates from NLS estimation implies that $\hat{\boldsymbol{u}} \overset{a}{=} \boldsymbol{u}$. Therefore, the regression

$$\hat{\boldsymbol{v}} = \boldsymbol{\iota}a^* + \boldsymbol{Z}\boldsymbol{c} + \text{residuals}, \tag{11.56}$$

where $\hat{\boldsymbol{v}}$ has typical element $\hat{u}_t^2$, will generate test statistics that have the same asymptotic properties as test statistics generated by (11.55). As before, an ordinary F test for $\boldsymbol{c} = \mathbf{0}$ will be asymptotically valid, as will n times the centered R^2.

It may seem remarkable that we can replace $\boldsymbol{v}$ by $\hat{\boldsymbol{v}}$ without doing anything to allow for the fact that $\boldsymbol{\beta}$ had to be estimated to obtain $\hat{\boldsymbol{u}}$, since when we use a GNR to test the specification of a regression function, we do have to allow for it. The reason for the difference should be clear from the following two examples. First of all, consider the regression models

$$\boldsymbol{y} = \boldsymbol{X}\boldsymbol{\beta} + \boldsymbol{u} \quad \text{and} \tag{11.57}$$

$$\boldsymbol{y} = \boldsymbol{X}\boldsymbol{\beta} + \gamma\boldsymbol{z} + \boldsymbol{u}. \tag{11.58}$$

To test (11.57) against (11.58), we would normally use a t statistic, the numerator of which would be

$$\boldsymbol{z}^\top\hat{\boldsymbol{u}} = \boldsymbol{z}^\top\boldsymbol{M}_X\boldsymbol{u} = \boldsymbol{z}^\top\boldsymbol{u} - \boldsymbol{z}^\top\boldsymbol{P}_X\boldsymbol{u}.$$

Since both $\boldsymbol{z}^\top\boldsymbol{u}$ and $\boldsymbol{z}^\top\boldsymbol{P}_X\boldsymbol{u}$ are $O(n^{1/2})$, it would clearly be wrong to treat $\boldsymbol{z}^\top\hat{\boldsymbol{u}}$ as if it were asymptotically equivalent to $\boldsymbol{z}^\top\boldsymbol{u}$. That is why we can calculate an asymptotically valid test statistic by regressing $\hat{\boldsymbol{u}}$ on $\boldsymbol{X}$ and $\boldsymbol{z}$ but not by regressing $\hat{\boldsymbol{u}}$ on $\boldsymbol{z}$ alone.

Now suppose that we wish to see whether the squared error terms from (11.57) are correlated with $\boldsymbol{z}$. Recall that $\boldsymbol{v}$ is the vector of squared error terms and $\hat{\boldsymbol{v}}$ is the vector of squared residuals. If we use $\hat{\boldsymbol{v}}$ as a proxy for $\boldsymbol{v}$ and regress it on a constant term and $\boldsymbol{z}$, as in (11.56), the numerator of the t statistic is

$$\begin{aligned}\boldsymbol{z}^\top\boldsymbol{M}_\iota\hat{\boldsymbol{v}} &= \boldsymbol{z}^\top\boldsymbol{M}_\iota\boldsymbol{v} - 2\boldsymbol{z}^\top\boldsymbol{M}_\iota\big((\boldsymbol{P}_X\boldsymbol{u})*\boldsymbol{u}\big) + \boldsymbol{z}^\top\boldsymbol{M}_\iota\big((\boldsymbol{P}_X\boldsymbol{u})*(\boldsymbol{P}_X\boldsymbol{u})\big)\\ &= \boldsymbol{z}^\top\boldsymbol{M}_\iota\boldsymbol{v} + \boldsymbol{z}^\top\boldsymbol{M}_\iota\big((\boldsymbol{P}_X\boldsymbol{u})*(\boldsymbol{P}_X\boldsymbol{u} - 2\boldsymbol{u})\big),\end{aligned} \tag{11.59}$$

where $\boldsymbol{M}_\iota$ is the matrix that takes deviations from the mean, and $*$ denotes the direct product of two vectors. It is easy to see that the first term in the second line of (11.59) is $O(n^{1/2})$; it is simply the sum of n terms, each of which has mean zero because of the presence of $\boldsymbol{M}_\iota$. The second term, however, can be shown to be $O(1)$, which means that it is asymptotically negligible relative to the first term. Thus $\boldsymbol{z}^\top\boldsymbol{M}_\iota\hat{\boldsymbol{v}}$ is asymptotically equivalent to $\boldsymbol{z}^\top\boldsymbol{M}_\iota\boldsymbol{v}$, and we can ignore the distinction between $\boldsymbol{v}$ and $\hat{\boldsymbol{v}}$ when calculating test statistics for heteroskedasticity.

Another way of looking at the problem is to recall that, as we saw in Section 8.10 when we discussed the nonlinear regression model in the framework of maximum likelihood estimation, the covariance matrix of the parameter estimates from such a model is block-diagonal between the parameters of the regression function (in this case $\boldsymbol{\beta}$) and the parameters of the skedastic function (in this case α and $\boldsymbol{\gamma}$). This block-diagonality property implies that we can treat the former parameters as known for the purpose of tests on the latter parameters, and vice versa, even though they are actually estimated.

Although the family of tests just outlined seems to be a very natural application of the Gauss-Newton regression, that is not how it was developed in the econometric literature. Godfrey (1978c) and Breusch and Pagan (1979) proposed test statistics that, although based on a slight modification of the artificial regression (11.56), were not the same as those suggested here. These authors explicitly assumed that the error terms u_t were normally distributed. This allowed them to derive their tests as Lagrange multiplier tests using maximum likelihood theory, and they therefore obtained somewhat different test statistics which are valid, even asymptotically, only under the assumption of normality. Koenker (1981) pointed out this weakness of the Godfrey/Breusch-Pagan tests and suggested as an alternative the nR^2 test based on regression

(11.56). The F test for $\boldsymbol{c} = \mathbf{0}$ based on the same regression is just as valid asymptotically and may well be more attractive in finite samples. Unfortunately, nR^2 and F tests may often have less power than LM tests based on the normality assumption. Honda (1988) has recently shown how to obtain modified versions of the latter that have better finite-sample properties. See Section 16.5 and Godfrey (1988, Section 4.5) for a fuller discussion of all these tests.

In place of (11.51), one could start with the more general model

$$E|u_t|^p = h(\alpha + \boldsymbol{Z}_t\boldsymbol{\gamma}).$$

Glejser (1969) considered the case $p = 1$ and proposed a test based on an artificial regression similar to (11.56) but with the regressand equal to the absolute values of the residuals. In Newey and Powell (1987), it is shown that Glejser's test can be considerably more powerful than the usual test, based on squared residuals, in cases in which the error terms have thicker tails than the normal distribution. This suggests that it may often be wise to employ both types of test.

11.6 A HETEROSKEDASTICITY-ROBUST VERSION OF THE GNR

In many cases we know, or at least suspect, that the error terms which adhere to a regression model display heteroskedasticity, but are not at all sure what form it takes. Especially when using cross-section data, the presumption should probably be that the errors are heteroskedastic. This should make us uneasy about using tests based on the Gauss-Newton regression, or indeed any of the tests we have discussed so far, since they are valid only under the assumption of homoskedasticity. In fact, it turns out to be quite simple to derive an artificial regression that can be used whenever the GNR can be used and that yields asymptotically valid inferences even in the presence of heteroskedasticity of unknown form. In this section, we discuss this procedure briefly. A much fuller treatment of this and related topics will be provided in Chapter 16.

As we have seen, a typical Gauss-Newton regression for testing restrictions can be written as

$$\acute{\boldsymbol{u}} = \acute{\boldsymbol{X}}\boldsymbol{b} + \acute{\boldsymbol{Z}}\boldsymbol{c} + \text{residuals}, \tag{11.60}$$

where $\acute{\boldsymbol{X}}$ is an $n \times k$ matrix made up of derivatives of the regression function $\boldsymbol{x}(\boldsymbol{\beta})$ evaluated at estimates $\acute{\boldsymbol{\beta}}$ that satisfy the restrictions and are root-n consistent, and $\acute{\boldsymbol{Z}}$ is an $n \times r$ matrix of test regressors. In most of the cases we have dealt with, $\acute{\boldsymbol{\beta}}$ is equal to $\tilde{\boldsymbol{\beta}}$, the vector of restricted NLS estimates, in which case $\acute{\boldsymbol{u}}^\top\acute{\boldsymbol{X}} = \tilde{\boldsymbol{u}}^\top\tilde{\boldsymbol{X}} = \mathbf{0}$. However, since there is no advantage for the purposes of this section in making the stronger assumption, we will not do so.

The numerator of the F statistic for $\boldsymbol{c} = \mathbf{0}$ is equal to the explained sum of squares from the regression

$$\acute{\boldsymbol{M}}_X \acute{\boldsymbol{u}} = \acute{\boldsymbol{M}}_X \acute{\boldsymbol{Z}} \boldsymbol{c} + \text{residuals}. \tag{11.61}$$

If $\acute{s}^2$ is the OLS estimate of the variance from (11.60), the test statistic is $1/r$ times

$$\frac{1}{\acute{s}^2} \acute{\boldsymbol{u}}^\top \acute{\boldsymbol{M}}_X \acute{\boldsymbol{Z}} \big(\acute{\boldsymbol{Z}}^\top \acute{\boldsymbol{M}}_X \acute{\boldsymbol{Z}} \big)^{-1} \acute{\boldsymbol{Z}}^\top \acute{\boldsymbol{M}}_X \acute{\boldsymbol{u}}. \tag{11.62}$$

The second factor here is the explained sum of squares from (11.61). Expression (11.62) makes it clear that what we are really testing is whether the r–vector

$$n^{-1/2} \acute{\boldsymbol{Z}}^\top \acute{\boldsymbol{M}}_X \acute{\boldsymbol{u}} \tag{11.63}$$

has mean zero asymptotically. If $E(\boldsymbol{u}\boldsymbol{u}^\top) = \sigma^2 \mathbf{I}$, the asymptotic covariance matrix of this vector is

$$\sigma^2 \operatorname*{plim}_{n\to\infty} \Big(\frac{1}{n} \acute{\boldsymbol{Z}}^\top \acute{\boldsymbol{M}}_X \acute{\boldsymbol{Z}} \Big). \tag{11.64}$$

Since (11.62) is a quadratic form in the vector (11.63) and something that estimates its covariance matrix consistently, it is easy to see that it will be asymptotically distributed as $\chi^2(r)$ under the null.

We now consider what happens when there is heteroskedasticity. In particular, suppose that

$$E(\boldsymbol{u}\boldsymbol{u}^\top) = \boldsymbol{\Omega}, \tag{11.65}$$

where $\boldsymbol{\Omega}$ is a diagonal matrix with diagonal elements ω_t^2 which satisfy the condition

$$\omega_{\min}^2 < \omega_t^2 < \omega_{\max}^2 \quad \text{for all } t,$$

$\omega_{\min}^2$ and $\omega_{\max}^2$ being finite positive lower and upper bounds. This condition rules out the possibility that ω_t^2 may grow or shrink without limit as $t \to \infty$. It is obvious that if we do not know anything about the ω_t^2's, we will not be able to estimate them consistently, since there will be one ω_t^2 to estimate for every observation. Nevertheless, it is possible to obtain consistent estimates of quantities like

$$\operatorname*{plim}_{n\to\infty} \Big(\frac{1}{n} \boldsymbol{W}^\top \boldsymbol{\Omega} \boldsymbol{W} \Big), \tag{11.66}$$

where $\boldsymbol{W}$ is a matrix with n rows that satisfies the conditions necessary for (11.66) to exist. The simplest way to do this is to use the estimator

$$\frac{1}{n} \boldsymbol{W}^\top \acute{\boldsymbol{\Omega}} \boldsymbol{W},$$

where $\acute{\boldsymbol{\Omega}}$ is a diagonal matrix with $\acute{u}_t^2$ as its tth diagonal element. This extremely important result is due to Eicker (1963, 1967) and White (1980). It makes it possible to obtain estimated covariance matrices and test statistics that are valid despite heteroskedasticity of unknown form. We will prove this result and discuss **heteroskedasticity-consistent covariance matrix estimators**, or **HCCMEs**, in Chapter 16. For now, we will use it only to construct test statistics based on an artificial regression.

If the covariance matrix of $\boldsymbol{u}$ is given by (11.65), the asymptotic covariance matrix of the vector (11.63) will be

$$\operatorname*{plim}_{n\to\infty}\Big(\frac{1}{n}\acute{\boldsymbol{Z}}^\top\acute{\boldsymbol{M}}_X\boldsymbol{\Omega}\acute{\boldsymbol{M}}_X\acute{\boldsymbol{Z}}\Big). \tag{11.67}$$

Using the Eicker-White result, this can be estimated consistently by

$$\frac{1}{n}\acute{\boldsymbol{Z}}^\top\acute{\boldsymbol{M}}_X\acute{\boldsymbol{\Omega}}\acute{\boldsymbol{M}}_X\acute{\boldsymbol{Z}} = \frac{1}{n}\acute{\boldsymbol{Z}}^\top\acute{\boldsymbol{M}}_X\acute{\boldsymbol{U}}\acute{\boldsymbol{U}}\acute{\boldsymbol{M}}_X\acute{\boldsymbol{Z}},$$

where $\acute{\boldsymbol{U}}$ is an $n\times n$ diagonal matrix with $\acute{u}_t$ as its tth diagonal element. Hence the test statistic

$$\begin{aligned}&\acute{\boldsymbol{u}}^\top\acute{\boldsymbol{M}}_X\acute{\boldsymbol{Z}}\big(\acute{\boldsymbol{Z}}^\top\acute{\boldsymbol{M}}_X\acute{\boldsymbol{U}}\acute{\boldsymbol{U}}\acute{\boldsymbol{M}}_X\acute{\boldsymbol{Z}}\big)^{-1}\acute{\boldsymbol{Z}}^\top\acute{\boldsymbol{M}}_X\acute{\boldsymbol{u}}\\ &=\boldsymbol{\iota}^\top\acute{\boldsymbol{U}}\acute{\boldsymbol{M}}_X\acute{\boldsymbol{Z}}\big(\acute{\boldsymbol{Z}}^\top\acute{\boldsymbol{M}}_X\acute{\boldsymbol{U}}\acute{\boldsymbol{U}}\acute{\boldsymbol{M}}_X\acute{\boldsymbol{Z}}\big)^{-1}\acute{\boldsymbol{Z}}^\top\acute{\boldsymbol{M}}_X\acute{\boldsymbol{U}}^\top\boldsymbol{\iota},\end{aligned} \tag{11.68}$$

where, as usual, $\boldsymbol{\iota}$ is an n–vector each element of which is 1, must be asymptotically distributed as $\chi^2(r)$ under the null hypothesis. This test statistic may be calculated as the explained sum of squares, which is equal to n minus the sum of squared residuals, from the artificial regression

$$\boldsymbol{\iota} = \acute{\boldsymbol{U}}\acute{\boldsymbol{M}}_X\acute{\boldsymbol{Z}}\boldsymbol{c} + \text{residuals}. \tag{11.69}$$

We will refer to this as the **heteroskedasticity-robust Gauss-Newton regression**, or **HRGNR**, since the test statistic (11.68) is a **heteroskedasticity-robust** test statistic.

Of course, in practice one would never actually construct the $n\times n$ matrix $\acute{\boldsymbol{U}}$ in order to run the HRGNR. Instead, one simply has to do the following:

(i) Regress each column of $\acute{\boldsymbol{Z}}$ on $\acute{\boldsymbol{X}}$ and store the residuals $\acute{\boldsymbol{M}}_X\acute{\boldsymbol{Z}}$.

(ii) Multiply the tth element of each vector of residuals by $\acute{u}_t$.

(iii) Regress a vector of 1s on the r regressors created in step (ii). This is regression (11.69).

(iv) Calculate the test statistic, $n-\text{SSR}$. It will be asymptotically distributed as $\chi^2(r)$ under H_0.

It thus turns out to be remarkably simple to calculate a heteroskedasticity-robust test that can be used in any situation in which test statistics based on the GNR can be used. For more details, see Davidson and MacKinnon (1985b), Wooldridge (1990a, 1990b, 1991a), and MacKinnon (1992). We will discuss the HRGNR further in Chapter 16.

It should, of course, be stressed that the theoretical results on which the heteroskedasticity-robust test statistic (11.68) are based are purely asymptotic ones. While this is also true for test statistics based on the GNR, it is almost certainly more difficult to estimate the covariance matrix (11.67) than the covariance matrix (11.64). Thus one may expect heteroskedasticity-robust tests to be less well behaved in finite samples than ordinary tests. However, there is some evidence that, if anything, tests based on the HRGNR tend to reject the null hypothesis too infrequently, especially at the .01 level; see Davidson and MacKinnon (1985b).

In practice, it is usually wise to use tests based on both the GNR and the HRGNR. If tests against the same alternative based on both artificial regressions yield similar results, those results should probably be believed. If not, one may well want to test for, and perhaps transform the model to take account of, plausible patterns of heteroskedasticity. One would never want to rely on tests based on the GNR if the HRGNR yields very different results.

11.7 CONCLUSION

In this chapter and in Chapters 6 and 10, we have seen that the Gauss-Newton regression and its heteroskedasticity-robust variant provide very simple ways to test a great many aspects of model specification for regression models. However, we have not said anything about how the results of these and other specification tests should be interpreted. That is the subject of the next chapter.

TERMS AND CONCEPTS

artificial nesting
Chow test
DWH tests
differencing matrix
differencing specification test
direct product
encompassing principle
encompassing tests
heteroskedasticity-consistent covariance matrix estimator (HCCME)
heteroskedasticity-robust Gauss-Newton regression (HRGNR)
heteroskedasticity-robust test
instrumental variables (IV) (tests of models estimated by)
J test
J_A test
model selection
nested models
nonnested hypothesis tests
nonnested models
P test
P_A test
skedastic function
structural change
tests for heteroskedasticity
vector of contrasts

Chapter 12

Interpreting Tests in Regression Directions

12.1 Introduction

In previous chapters, we have discussed a large number of different test statistics for linear and nonlinear regression models. Most of these were tests in **regression directions**, that is, tests of the specification of the regression function. The use of the word "directions" in this context may at first seem a little odd, but it should become much less so as the chapter proceeds. Essentially, tests in regression directions are tests of the specification of the regression function, while tests in **nonregression directions** are tests of other aspects of the model, such as tests for heteroskedasticity.

It is now time to discuss what the results of hypothesis tests mean and how they should be interpreted. This discussion requires a certain amount of technical apparatus, in particular the concept of a **drifting DGP**, which will be introduced in Section 12.3. What comes out of this apparatus, however, is an extremely simple and intuitive set of results, which can be of great utility in interpreting the test statistics that one actually obtains when doing applied work. In this chapter, we discuss only tests in regression directions of regression models estimated by NLS. Although this is quite restrictive, it simplifies the exposition considerably. In the next chapter, we will discuss both tests of nonregression models and tests of regression models in nonregression directions, in the context of the three classical tests based on ML estimation, namely, the Wald, LR, and LM tests. As we will see there, the principal results of this chapter carry over almost unchanged to the more general case. They also carry over, with obvious modifications, to models estimated by IV and GLS.

In Section 3.4, we introduced the ideas of the size and power of a test. The size of a test, it will be recalled, is the probability of its rejecting the null hypothesis when the null is true, while the power of a test is the probability that it will reject the null hypothesis when the null is false. Obviously, power will depend on how the data were in fact generated. Thus we cannot speak of power without specifying a data-generating process (or possibly a family of DGPs). In general, the power of a test will depend on the null hypothesis, H_0, the alternative against which it is being tested, H_1, and the DGP that is assumed to have generated the data. We will discuss some concepts related to the size and power of tests more fully in Section 12.2.

The power of a test may depend on the details of how the test is constructed, but generally this will not matter if we are concerned only with asymptotic analysis. Many tests are **asymptotically equivalent** under the null and under all drifting DGPs, even though they may differ substantially in finite samples. Two tests are said to be asymptotically equivalent if they tend to the same random variable. For example, F tests and χ^2 tests based on the same Gauss-Newton regression will be asymptotically equivalent to each other, provided of course that the F test is multiplied by its numerator degrees of freedom. These tests will also be equivalent to asymptotic F or χ^2 tests against the same alternative hypothesis based on comparing the sums of squared residuals from restricted and unrestricted models.[1] We will not attempt to prove this result here; it is a consequence of more general results that are proved in Davidson and MacKinnon (1987). However, it is an important result, because it allows us to study only tests based on the GNR and to assert that our results are much more generally applicable. In this chapter, then, we will explicitly discuss what determines the asymptotic power of tests in regression directions based on the GNR and implicitly discuss what determines the asymptotic power of all tests in regression directions.

The null hypothesis can be written as

$$H_0: \ \boldsymbol{y} = \boldsymbol{x}(\boldsymbol{\beta}) + \boldsymbol{u}, \quad E(\boldsymbol{u}\boldsymbol{u}^{\top}) = \sigma^2\mathbf{I}. \tag{12.01}$$

Let the k–vector $\tilde{\boldsymbol{\beta}}$ denote the NLS estimates of $\boldsymbol{\beta}$. Then several equivalent test statistics may be calculated using the GNR

$$\boldsymbol{y} - \tilde{\boldsymbol{x}} = \tilde{\boldsymbol{X}}\boldsymbol{b} + \tilde{\boldsymbol{Z}}\boldsymbol{c} + \text{residuals}, \tag{12.02}$$

where, as usual, $\tilde{\boldsymbol{x}}$ denotes $\boldsymbol{x}(\tilde{\boldsymbol{\beta}})$, and the $n \times k$ matrix $\tilde{\boldsymbol{X}} \equiv \boldsymbol{X}(\tilde{\boldsymbol{\beta}})$ has typical element $\partial x_t(\boldsymbol{\beta})/\partial\beta_i$, evaluated at $\tilde{\boldsymbol{\beta}}$. As we have seen, the $n \times r$ matrix $\tilde{\boldsymbol{Z}} \equiv \boldsymbol{Z}(\tilde{\boldsymbol{\beta}})$ can be specified in many different ways, depending on what alternative we wish to test against. The simplest possibility is that $\boldsymbol{x}(\boldsymbol{\beta})$ is a special case of $\boldsymbol{x}(\boldsymbol{\beta}, \boldsymbol{\gamma})$ with $\boldsymbol{\gamma} = \mathbf{0}$, which allows us to write

$$H_1: \ \boldsymbol{y} = \boldsymbol{x}(\boldsymbol{\beta}, \boldsymbol{\gamma}) + \boldsymbol{u}, \quad E(\boldsymbol{u}\boldsymbol{u}^{\top}) = \sigma^2\mathbf{I}. \tag{12.03}$$

In this case, $\tilde{\boldsymbol{Z}} = \tilde{\boldsymbol{X}}_{\gamma}$, where $\tilde{\boldsymbol{X}}_{\gamma}$ has typical element $\partial x_t(\boldsymbol{\beta}, \boldsymbol{\gamma})/\partial\gamma_j$, evaluated at $(\tilde{\boldsymbol{\beta}}, \mathbf{0})$. As we saw in Chapter 11, however, constructing a test against an explicit alternative such as (12.03) is only one of several ways of generating a test based on the GNR (12.02).

[1] All these tests are also asymptotically equivalent to tests based on the heteroskedasticity-robust Gauss-Newton regression discussed in Section 11.6, but only if there is in fact no heteroskedasticity. See Davidson and MacKinnon (1985b).

The simplest test statistic based on (12.02) is

$$\frac{1}{\tilde{s}^2}(\boldsymbol{y} - \tilde{\boldsymbol{x}})^\top \tilde{\boldsymbol{Z}}\big(\tilde{\boldsymbol{Z}}^\top \tilde{\boldsymbol{M}}_X \tilde{\boldsymbol{Z}}\big)^{-1} \tilde{\boldsymbol{Z}}^\top (\boldsymbol{y} - \tilde{\boldsymbol{x}}), \tag{12.04}$$

where $\tilde{\boldsymbol{M}}_X \equiv \mathbf{I} - \tilde{\boldsymbol{X}}(\tilde{\boldsymbol{X}}^\top \tilde{\boldsymbol{X}})^{-1}\tilde{\boldsymbol{X}}^\top$ and $\tilde{s}^2 \equiv (\boldsymbol{y} - \tilde{\boldsymbol{x}})^\top (\boldsymbol{y} - \tilde{\boldsymbol{x}})/(n-k)$. The test statistic (12.04) is $1/\tilde{s}^2$ times the explained sum of squares from (12.02). For simplicity, we will consider only this test statistic in this chapter. Because (12.04) is asymptotically equivalent to other tests based on (12.02) and also to tests against the same alternative based on the LR and Wald principles, our results are nevertheless quite general.

In addition to specifying the null hypothesis (12.01) and the test statistic (12.04), we must specify how the data are assumed to have been generated if we are to discuss test power. This turns out to involve the important new concept of a drifting DGP, which we have already mentioned. Without this concept, it would be very difficult to analyze the asymptotic properties of test statistics when the null hypothesis did not generate the data, and we therefore discuss drifting DGPs at length in Section 12.3. In the two sections following that, we analyze the asymptotic properties of the test statistic (12.04) under certain drifting DGPs and provide a geometrical interpretation of the results. In Section 12.6, we explain how one may compare the power of tests of which the distributions are known only asymptotically. In Section 12.7, we use the results obtained previously to discuss how one should interpret the results of tests in regression directions that reject the null hypothesis. Finally, in Section 12.8, we discuss how one should interpret the results of tests that do not reject the null hypothesis.

12.2 SIZE AND POWER

We introduced the concepts of the size and the power of hypothesis tests in Section 3.4. One way to see how these concepts are related is to study the **size-power tradeoff curve** for any given test. For simplicity, let us consider a test statistic that is always a positive number (test statistics which are asymptotically distributed as F or χ^2 under the null hypothesis should have this property). If we choose a critical value of zero, the test will always reject the null, whether or not the DGP is actually a special case of the null. As we choose larger and larger critical values, the probability that the test will reject the null will decrease. If the test is a useful one, this probability will initially decrease much less rapidly when the null is false than when it is true. The size-power tradeoff curve shows, for some given sample size, these two probabilities graphed against each other. The horizontal axis shows the size, computed for a DGP that satisfies the null hypothesis, and the vertical axis shows the power, for some other given DGP that will not in general satisfy it. Thus the tradeoff curve shows what the power of the test against the given DGP is for every size of test that we may choose.

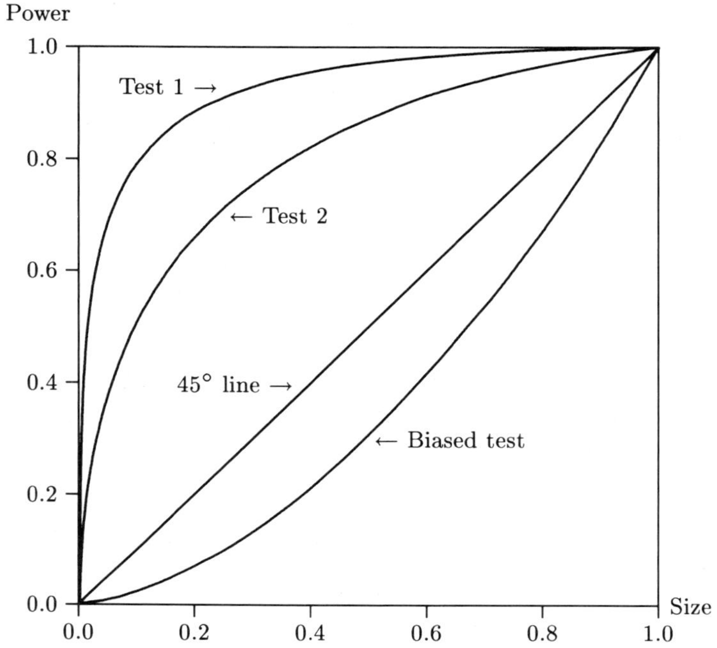

Figure 12.1 Size-power tradeoff curves

Now consider Figure 12.1, which shows several size-power tradeoff curves for different hypothetical test statistics. The horizontal axis measures size. The vertical axis measures power, when the data are generated by a given DGP. The size-power tradeoff curve is generated by varying the critical value for the test. The upper right-hand corner of the graph corresponds to a critical value of zero. Both size and power are 1 at this point. The lower left-hand corner corresponds to a very large critical value, so large that the test statistic will never exceed it. Both size and power are 0 at this point. For many test statistics, such as those that have χ^2 distributions under the null, this latter critical value is in principle plus infinity. However, we could easily pick a finite critical value such that the test statistic would exceed it with probability as close to zero as we chose.

A test for which size always equals power has a size-power tradeoff curve given by the 45° line. This will be so by definition if the DGP for which the tradeoff is constructed actually satisfies the null hypothesis. Except in that circumstance, a test which gave this result would evidently not be very useful. Normally, we would expect the power of a test to exceed its size for any given critical value, except when size and power are both equal to 0 or 1. The curves labelled "Test 1" and "Test 2" in the figure are examples of tests for which this is the case. However, there are some tests for which size exceeds power for certain DGPs. They are called **biased tests**, and the curve labelled "Biased Test" in the figure illustrates this. For further discussion of biased tests, which are evidently not of very much use, see Kendall and Stuart (1979, Chapter 23).

It is clear from Figure 12.1 that Test 1 is more useful than Test 2. Except at the two ends, the size-power tradeoff curve for the former is everywhere outside the size-power tradeoff curve for the latter. Thus, for any given size, the power of Test 1 exceeds that of Test 2. As the sample size increases, we would expect the size-power tradeoff curve for any well-behaved test to improve (that is, to become further from the 45° line). In the limit, as $n \to \infty$, the size-power tradeoff curve would look like a Γ, joining the points $(0,0)$, $(0,1)$, and $(1,1)$.

Size-power tradeoff curves can be generated by what is called the **power function** of a test. This function gives the power of a test as a function of its size (or, equivalently, the critical value used), the sample size, and the DGP. Usually, the DGP is restricted so as to belong to some particular alternative hypothesis characterized by a finite set of parameters. Spanos (1986, Chapter 14) provides a formal definition of power functions in this context. Suppose, for concreteness, that we are concerned with a single parameter θ and that the null hypothesis is $\theta = 0$. When $\theta = 0$, the power of the test will evidently be equal to its size. For any other value of θ, power will be greater than size if the test is unbiased. For a well-behaved test, we expect that, for any reasonable fixed sample size, power will increase monotonically with $|\theta|$ and approach unity as $|\theta| \to \infty$. Similarly, for any fixed $\theta \neq 0$, we expect that power will tend to unity as the sample size tends to infinity. Figure 12.2 shows two illustrative power functions, for the same test but different sample sizes. The data are generated from the $N(\theta, 1)$ distribution, and the null hypothesis is that $\theta = 0$. Power functions are shown for tests at the 5% level with sample sizes of 25 and 100. These power functions are symmetric around zero. As we would expect, the power function for $n = 100$ is everywhere above the power function for $n = 25$, except at $\theta = 0$.

If a test rejects a false null hypothesis with probability one asymptotically, it is said to be **consistent**. The concept of test consistency was introduced by Wald and Wolfowitz (1940). It is a simple and intuitive concept and is evidently a most desirable property for a test to have. The test in the example of Figure 12.2 is consistent. Therefore, as $n \to \infty$, the power function tends to the shape of a $\top$, with power equal to 1 for every value of θ except $\theta = 0$. We may define **consistency** of a hypothesis test formally as follows.

Definition 12.1.

> A test is consistent against a certain class of DGPs none of which satisfies the null hypothesis if, whenever the data were generated by a fixed member of that class, the probability of rejecting the null hypothesis tends to unity as the sample size n tends to infinity, for any critical value associated with nonzero size.

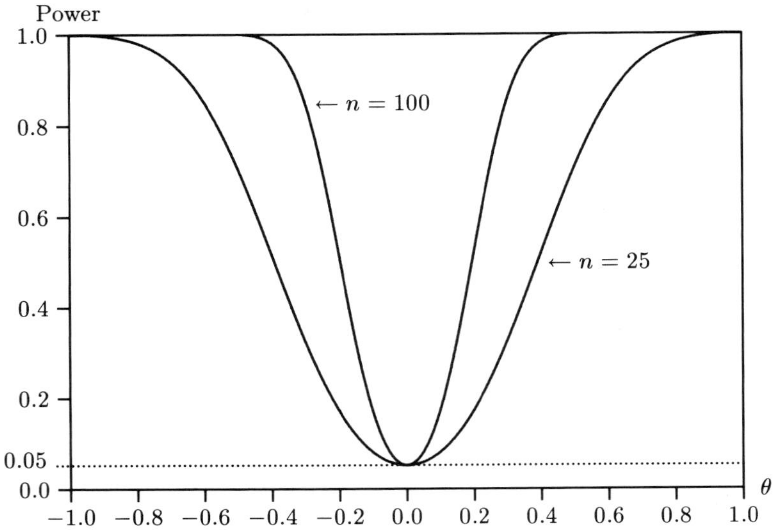

Figure 12.2 Power functions for tests of $\theta = 0$ at .05 level

Notice that whether or not a test is consistent will depend on how the data were actually generated. A test that is consistent against certain DGPs may not be consistent against others. Intuitively, the reason tests are often consistent is that as $n \to \infty$ the amount of information that the sample conveys about the validity of the null hypothesis increases without limit. As this happens, this information overwhelms the noise in the data and eventually allows us to conclude with probability one that the test statistic is *not* a drawing from whatever its distribution under the null is supposed to be.

With these preliminaries out of the way, we are ready to consider what determines the power of tests in regression directions. Since we are dealing with nonlinear regression models, we must resort to asymptotic analysis. This raises a serious technical problem, however. All of the tests we have considered so far are consistent when the data are generated by a fixed DGP within the set of the alternatives for which they were designed, and indeed they are consistent much more widely than that. If a test is consistent, the value of the test statistic will tend to plus or minus infinity as $n \to \infty$. This makes it impossible to speak of the **asymptotic distribution** of such a test statistic and hence impossible to compare the asymptotic distributions of competing test statistics when both are consistent, if the DGP is fixed. The solution is to allow the DGP to drift toward the null at a certain rate. We discuss the concept of drifting DGPs in the next section.

12.3 DRIFTING DGPs

In order to determine any of the statistical properties of a test, one must specify how the data are actually generated. Since, in this chapter, we are concerned solely with tests in regression directions, we will restrict our attention to DGPs that differ from the null hypothesis only in such directions. This restriction is by no means innocuous. It means that we cannot say anything about the power of tests in regression directions when the model is false in a nonregression direction (e.g., when the error terms suffer from unmodeled heteroskedasticity). Some aspects of this topic will be discussed in Chapter 16.

The natural way to specify a DGP for the purpose of analyzing the power of a test is to assume that it is a particular member of the set of DGPs which together form the alternative hypothesis. There are two problems with this simple approach, however. The first problem is that one may well be interested in the power of certain tests when the data are generated by a DGP which is not a special case of the alternative hypothesis. It does not make sense to rule out this interesting case.

The second problem, which we alluded to in the previous section, is that most test statistics that are of interest to us will have no nondegenerate asymptotic distribution under a fixed DGP that is not a special case of the null hypothesis. If they did, then they would not be consistent. One long-standing solution to this problem is to consider the distribution of the test statistic of interest under what is called a **sequence of local alternatives**. When $\boldsymbol{\theta}$ is the parameter vector of interest, such a sequence may be written as

$$\boldsymbol{\theta}^n = \boldsymbol{\theta}_0 + n^{-1/2}\boldsymbol{\delta}. \tag{12.05}$$

Here $\boldsymbol{\theta}^n$ is the parameter vector for a sample of size n, $\boldsymbol{\theta}_0$ is a parameter vector that satisfies the null hypothesis, and $\boldsymbol{\delta}$ is some nonzero vector. Evidently, $\boldsymbol{\theta}^n$ approaches $\boldsymbol{\theta}_0$ at a rate proportional to $n^{-1/2}$. The originator of this device was Neyman (1937). However, it is often attributed to Pitman (1949) and is therefore sometimes referred to as a "Pitman sequence" or "Pitman drift"; see McManus (1991). This technique has been widely used in econometric theory; see, for example, Gallant and Holly (1980) and Engle (1984).

In order to avoid ruling out the interesting case in which the data are generated by a DGP that is not a special case of the alternative hypothesis, Davidson and MacKinnon (1985a, 1987) generalized the idea of sequences of local alternatives to the idea of drifting DGPs. This chapter is largely based on the approach of those two papers.[2]

A class of drifting DGPs that is suitable for studying the power of the test statistic (12.04) is

$$\boldsymbol{y} = \boldsymbol{x}(\boldsymbol{\beta}_0) + \alpha n^{-1/2}\boldsymbol{a} + \boldsymbol{u}, \quad E(\boldsymbol{u}) = \mathbf{0}, \;\; E(\boldsymbol{u}\boldsymbol{u}^\top) = \sigma_0^2\mathbf{I}. \tag{12.06}$$

[2] Actually, the term we used in Davidson and MacKinnon (1985a, 1987) was "sequence of local DGPs." We now prefer the term "drifting DGP," however.

Here $\boldsymbol{\beta}_0$ and σ_0^2 denote particular values of $\boldsymbol{\beta}$ and σ^2, $\boldsymbol{a}$ is an n–vector that may depend on exogenous variables, on the parameter vector $\boldsymbol{\beta}_0$, and possibly on past values of y_t, and α is a parameter which determines how far the DGP is from the **simple null hypothesis**

$$\boldsymbol{y} = \boldsymbol{x}(\boldsymbol{\beta}_0) + \boldsymbol{u}, \quad E(\boldsymbol{u}) = \boldsymbol{0}, \;\; E(\boldsymbol{u}\boldsymbol{u}^{\top}) = \sigma_0^2 \mathbf{I}. \tag{12.07}$$

The drifting DGP (12.06) tends to this simple null hypothesis as $n \rightarrow \infty$. Exactly what the vector $\boldsymbol{a}$ corresponds to will be discussed shortly. Notice that, as n becomes larger, the entire vector $\boldsymbol{y}$ approaches what it would be under the simple null (12.07) at a rate proportional to $n^{-1/2}$.

It is no accident that the drifting DGP (12.06) approaches the simple null (12.07) at a rate of $n^{-1/2}$. This rate is carefully chosen so that the test statistic (12.04), and all asymptotically equivalent test statistics, will have an asymptotic distribution in the limit as $n \rightarrow \infty$. Similarly, for a fixed size of test, as $n \rightarrow \infty$ with a DGP drifting toward the null at rate $n^{-1/2}$, the value of the power function tends to a limit that in general is neither zero nor unity. This limiting function is called the **asymptotic power function** of the test statistic.

The drifting DGP (12.06) provides a perfectly general *local* representation of any regression model that is sufficiently close to the simple null (12.07). For example, suppose that we wanted to see how a certain test performed when the data were generated by an alternative like (12.03), with $\boldsymbol{\gamma} \neq \boldsymbol{0}$. We could simply specify a sequence of local alternatives as

$$\boldsymbol{y} = \boldsymbol{x}(\boldsymbol{\beta}_0, \, \alpha n^{-1/2}\boldsymbol{\gamma}_0) + \boldsymbol{u}, \tag{12.08}$$

where $\boldsymbol{\gamma}_0$ is fixed and may be normalized to have any arbitrary length, and α determines how far (12.08) is from the simple null (12.07). Because (12.08) approaches (12.07) as $n^{-1/2} \rightarrow 0$, a first-order Taylor approximation to (12.08) around $\alpha = 0$ must yield exactly the same results, in an asymptotic analysis, as (12.08) itself. This approximation is

$$\boldsymbol{y} = \boldsymbol{x}(\boldsymbol{\beta}_0, \mathbf{0}) + \alpha n^{-1/2}\boldsymbol{X}_{\gamma}(\boldsymbol{\beta}_0, \mathbf{0})\boldsymbol{\gamma}_0 + \boldsymbol{u}, \tag{12.09}$$

where $\boldsymbol{X}_{\gamma}(\boldsymbol{\beta}_0, \mathbf{0})$ has typical element $\partial x_t(\boldsymbol{\beta}, \boldsymbol{\gamma})/\partial \gamma_j$ evaluated at $[\boldsymbol{\beta}_0 \,\vdots\, \mathbf{0}]$. If we define $\boldsymbol{x}(\boldsymbol{\beta}_0)$ as $\boldsymbol{x}(\boldsymbol{\beta}_0, \mathbf{0})$ and $\boldsymbol{a}$ as $\boldsymbol{X}_{\gamma}(\boldsymbol{\beta}_0, \mathbf{0})\boldsymbol{\gamma}_0$, we see immediately that (12.09) is simply a particular case of the drifting DGP (12.06).

The above argument should make it clear that (12.06) is a perfectly general way to specify a drifting DGP corresponding to *any* alternative regression model that includes the null hypothesis (12.01). Every specific alternative simply yields a different vector $\boldsymbol{a}$. If $\boldsymbol{a}$ is a zero vector, then the DGP is a special case of the null, and the test will have power equal to its size and hence will have size-power tradeoff curve the 45° line (see Figure 12.1). If $\boldsymbol{a}$ is derived from the alternative against which the test is constructed, then the drifting DGP (12.06) is actually a sequence of local alternatives like (12.05). In general, however, neither of these special cases will hold.

12.4 The Asymptotic Distribution of Test Statistics

We are now ready to find the asymptotic distribution of the test statistic (12.04) under the family of drifting DGPs (12.06). In order for our asymptotic analysis to be valid, we must assume that various regularity conditions hold. Thus we will assume that $n^{-1}\boldsymbol{X}_0^{\top}\boldsymbol{X}_0$, $n^{-1}\boldsymbol{Z}_0^{\top}\boldsymbol{Z}_0$, and $n^{-1}\boldsymbol{Z}_0^{\top}\boldsymbol{X}_0$ all tend to finite limiting matrices with ranks k, r and $\min(k,r)$, respectively, as $n \to \infty$. We will further assume that there exists an N such that, for all $n > N$, the rank of the matrix $[\boldsymbol{X}_0 \quad \boldsymbol{Z}_0]$ is $k+r$, that $n^{-1}\boldsymbol{a}^{\top}\boldsymbol{a}$ tends to a finite limiting scalar, and that $n^{-1}\boldsymbol{a}^{\top}\boldsymbol{X}_0$ and $n^{-1}\boldsymbol{a}^{\top}\boldsymbol{Z}_0$ both tend to finite limiting vectors of dimensions $1 \times k$ and $1 \times r$, respectively. Here $\boldsymbol{X}_0$ denotes $\boldsymbol{X}(\boldsymbol{\beta}_0)$ and $\boldsymbol{Z}_0$ denotes $\boldsymbol{Z}(\boldsymbol{\beta}_0)$. Whether these regularity conditions will in fact hold depends on the vector $\boldsymbol{a}$, the null hypothesis (12.01), the alternative hypothesis (whether or not it is explicit), and the simple null (12.07).

We begin by rewriting the test statistic (12.04) so that it is a product of four factors, each of which is $O(1)$:

$$\frac{1}{\tilde{s}^2}\big(n^{-1/2}(\boldsymbol{y}-\tilde{\boldsymbol{x}})^{\top}\tilde{\boldsymbol{Z}}\big)\big(n^{-1}\tilde{\boldsymbol{Z}}^{\top}\tilde{\boldsymbol{M}}_X\tilde{\boldsymbol{Z}}\big)^{-1}\big(n^{-1/2}\tilde{\boldsymbol{Z}}^{\top}(\boldsymbol{y}-\tilde{\boldsymbol{x}})\big). \tag{12.10}$$

What we must do now is to replace the quantities $\tilde{s}$, $n^{-1/2}(\boldsymbol{y}-\tilde{\boldsymbol{x}})^{\top}\tilde{\boldsymbol{Z}}$, and $n^{-1}\tilde{\boldsymbol{Z}}^{\top}\tilde{\boldsymbol{M}}_X\tilde{\boldsymbol{Z}}$ by what they tend to asymptotically under (12.06). We state the following results without proof. They can all be derived by suitable modification of arguments used in Chapter 5:

$$\tilde{s}^2 \xrightarrow{\;p\;} \sigma_0^2, \tag{12.11}$$

$$n^{-1}\tilde{\boldsymbol{Z}}^{\top}\tilde{\boldsymbol{M}}_X\tilde{\boldsymbol{Z}} \xrightarrow{\;p\;} \operatorname*{plim}_{n\to\infty}\big(n^{-1}\boldsymbol{Z}_0^{\top}\boldsymbol{M}_X\boldsymbol{Z}_0\big), \tag{12.12}$$

and

$$n^{-1/2}(\boldsymbol{y}-\tilde{\boldsymbol{x}})^{\top}\tilde{\boldsymbol{Z}} \overset{a}{=} n^{-1/2}\big(\boldsymbol{u}+\alpha n^{-1/2}\boldsymbol{a}\big)^{\top}\boldsymbol{M}_X\boldsymbol{Z}_0, \tag{12.13}$$

where $\boldsymbol{M}_X \equiv \mathbf{I} - \boldsymbol{X}_0(\boldsymbol{X}_0^{\top}\boldsymbol{X}_0)^{-1}\boldsymbol{X}_0^{\top}$.

The intuition behind the results (12.11) and (12.12) is straightforward. The drifting DGP (12.06) approaches the simple null (12.07) fast enough that the limits of $\tilde{s}^2$ and $n^{-1}\tilde{\boldsymbol{Z}}^{\top}\tilde{\boldsymbol{M}}_X\tilde{\boldsymbol{Z}}$ are exactly the same as they would be under (12.07). These limits, σ_0^2 and $\operatorname{plim}\big(n^{-1}\boldsymbol{Z}_0^{\top}\boldsymbol{M}_X\boldsymbol{Z}_0\big)$, are nonstochastic because the difference between $\tilde{\boldsymbol{\beta}}$ and $\boldsymbol{\beta}_0$, which is $O(n^{-1/2})$, has no effect on either $\tilde{s}^2$ or $n^{-1}\tilde{\boldsymbol{Z}}^{\top}\tilde{\boldsymbol{M}}_X\tilde{\boldsymbol{Z}}$ asymptotically. It is thus not surprising that the difference between the drifting DGP (12.06) and the simple null (12.07), which is likewise $O(n^{-1/2})$, also has no effect on $\tilde{s}^2$ and $n^{-1}\tilde{\boldsymbol{Z}}^{\top}\tilde{\boldsymbol{M}}_X\tilde{\boldsymbol{Z}}$ asymptotically.

In contrast, $n^{-1/2}(\boldsymbol{y}-\tilde{\boldsymbol{x}})^{\top}\tilde{\boldsymbol{Z}}$ tends to a stochastic probability limit. The result (12.13) follows from the fact that

$$\boldsymbol{y}-\tilde{\boldsymbol{x}} = \boldsymbol{M}_X\big(\boldsymbol{u}+\alpha n^{-1/2}\boldsymbol{a}\big) + o(n^{-1/2}),$$

which is analogous to the familiar result (5.57) for the case in which $\alpha = 0$. The reason $\alpha n^{-1/2}\boldsymbol{a}$ plays a role here is that $\tilde{\boldsymbol{Z}}^\top\tilde{\boldsymbol{M}}_X\boldsymbol{u}$ and $\alpha n^{-1/2}\tilde{\boldsymbol{Z}}^\top\tilde{\boldsymbol{M}}_X\boldsymbol{a}$ are of the same order, $O(n^{1/2})$. Thus, by specifying the drifting DGP (12.06) as we did, we ensure that quantities which are asymptotically nonstochastic under the simple null (12.07) are unchanged under (12.06), while quantities which are asymptotically stochastic do change.

Substituting (12.11), (12.12), and (12.13) into (12.10), we find that the test statistic (12.04) is asymptotically equal to

$$\frac{1}{n\sigma_0^2}(\alpha n^{-1/2}\boldsymbol{a}+\boldsymbol{u})^\top\boldsymbol{M}_X\boldsymbol{Z}\operatorname*{plim}_{n\to\infty}\Big(\frac{1}{n}\boldsymbol{Z}^\top\boldsymbol{M}_X\boldsymbol{Z}\Big)^{-1}\boldsymbol{Z}^\top\boldsymbol{M}_X(\alpha n^{-1/2}\boldsymbol{a}+\boldsymbol{u}), \tag{12.14}$$

where, for ease of notation, we let $\boldsymbol{Z}$ denote $\boldsymbol{Z}_0$. It remains to determine the asymptotic distribution of this quantity. First, define $\boldsymbol{\psi}$ as an $r\times r$ triangular matrix such that

$$\boldsymbol{\psi}\boldsymbol{\psi}^\top \equiv \operatorname*{plim}_{n\to\infty}\Big(\frac{1}{n}\boldsymbol{Z}^\top\boldsymbol{M}_X\boldsymbol{Z}\Big)^{-1}. \tag{12.15}$$

Then define the r–vector $\boldsymbol{\eta}$ as

$$\boldsymbol{\eta} \equiv \frac{1}{\sigma_0}\boldsymbol{\psi}^\top\boldsymbol{Z}^\top\boldsymbol{M}_X(\alpha n^{-1}\boldsymbol{a} + n^{-1/2}\boldsymbol{u}).$$

The quantity (12.14) now takes the very simple form $\boldsymbol{\eta}^\top\boldsymbol{\eta}$; it is simply the sum of r squared random variables, the elements of the vector $\boldsymbol{\eta}$.

It is easy to see that, asymptotically, the mean of $\boldsymbol{\eta}$ is the vector

$$\operatorname*{plim}_{n\to\infty}\Big(\frac{1}{n}\alpha\sigma_0^{-1}\boldsymbol{\psi}^\top\boldsymbol{Z}^\top\boldsymbol{M}_X\boldsymbol{a}\Big) \tag{12.16}$$

and that its covariance matrix is

$$\operatorname*{plim}_{n\to\infty}\Big(\frac{1}{n}\sigma_0^{-2}\boldsymbol{\psi}^\top\boldsymbol{Z}^\top\boldsymbol{M}_X E(\boldsymbol{u}\boldsymbol{u}^\top)\boldsymbol{M}_X\boldsymbol{Z}\boldsymbol{\psi}\Big) = \boldsymbol{\psi}^\top\operatorname*{plim}_{n\to\infty}\Big(\frac{1}{n}\boldsymbol{Z}^\top\boldsymbol{M}_X\boldsymbol{Z}\Big)\boldsymbol{\psi} = \mathbf{I}_r.$$

The last equality here follows from the definition of $\boldsymbol{\psi}$ in (12.15). Since $\boldsymbol{\eta}$ is equal to the sum of a term that tends to the nonstochastic limit (12.16) and $n^{-1/2}$ times a weighted sum of random variables with finite variance, and since our assumptions keep those weights bounded from above and below, a central limit theorem can be applied to it. The test statistic (12.04) is thus asymptotically equal to a sum of r independent squared normal random variates, each with variance unity and mean given by an element of the vector (12.16). Such a sum has the **noncentral chi-squared distribution** with r degrees of freedom and **noncentrality parameter**, or **NCP**, given by the squared norm of the mean vector (12.16).

The noncentral χ^2 distribution plays a central role in the analysis of the asymptotic power of most econometric tests. This distribution is discussed briefly in Appendix B; for a more detailed discussion, readers should consult Johnson and Kotz (1970b, Chapter 28). The shape of this distribution depends on two things: the number of degrees of freedom and the noncentrality parameter or NCP. The NCP is always a positive number; if it were zero, we would have the ordinary central χ^2 distribution.

To develop intuition, it is illuminating to consider the two-degree-of-freedom case. Suppose that ε_1 and ε_2 are independent random variables, each distributed as $N(0,1)$, and that $\xi_1 = \mu_1 + \varepsilon_1$ and $\xi_2 = \mu_2 + \varepsilon_2$, where μ_1 and μ_2 are fixed numbers. Then the statistic

$$\zeta^C \equiv \varepsilon_1^2 + \varepsilon_2^2$$

will be distributed as $\chi^2(2)$, while the statistic

$$\zeta^N \equiv \xi_1^2 + \xi_2^2 = \left(\varepsilon_1^2 + \varepsilon_2^2\right) + \left(\mu_1^2 + \mu_2^2\right) + \left(2\mu_1\varepsilon_1 + 2\mu_2\varepsilon_2\right) \tag{12.17}$$

will be distributed as noncentral chi-squared with two degrees of freedom and NCP $\mu_1^2+\mu_2^2$. A standard notation for the noncentral chi-squared distribution is $\chi^2(r, \Lambda)$, where r is the degrees of freedom and Λ is the NCP. Thus, in this case, we may say that ζ^N is distributed as $\chi^2(2, \mu_1^2 + \mu_2^2)$.[3]

The mean of ζ^N is larger than that of ζ^C. The latter mean is 2, while the former is $2 + \mu_1^2 + \mu_2^2$. Thus, on average, ζ^N will be larger than ζ^C. Hence if we were to test the (false) hypothesis that ζ^N came from the *central* $\chi^2(2)$ distribution using a test of size δ, we would reject that hypothesis more than $100\delta\%$ of the time. The power of this test, since we are holding degrees of freedom constant, will depend solely on the NCP, $\mu_1^2 + \mu_2^2$. In view of (12.17), this may seem surprising. It may seem that the distribution of ζ^N should depend on μ_1 and μ_2 individually rather than on the sum of their squares. In fact, changes in μ_1 and μ_2 that do not change $\mu_1^2 + \mu_2^2$ have no effect on the distribution of ζ^N. It may be a good exercise to prove this.

Associated with the noncentral χ^2 are two more distributions, called the noncentral F and the doubly noncentral F. They are defined analogously to the ordinary (central) F distribution, as a ratio of independent χ^2 random variables, each divided by its degrees of freedom. For the noncentral F, the random variable in the numerator has a noncentral χ^2 distribution, while the one in the denominator has a central χ^2. For the doubly noncentral F, both

[3] Note that some authors, and some computer software, use the square root of Λ, rather than Λ itself, as the noncentrality parameter and then refer to this square root as the NCP. It makes no difference which way the noncentral χ^2 distribution is parametrized. However, the parametrization we use is more natural as well as more standard: If $x_1 \sim \chi^2(r_1, \Lambda_1)$ and $x_2 \sim \chi^2(r_2, \Lambda_2)$ are independent, then $z = x_1 + x_2$ is distributed as $\chi^2(r_1 + r_2, \Lambda_1 + \Lambda_2)$. This should make it clear that Λ, rather than its square root, is the natural choice for the NCP.

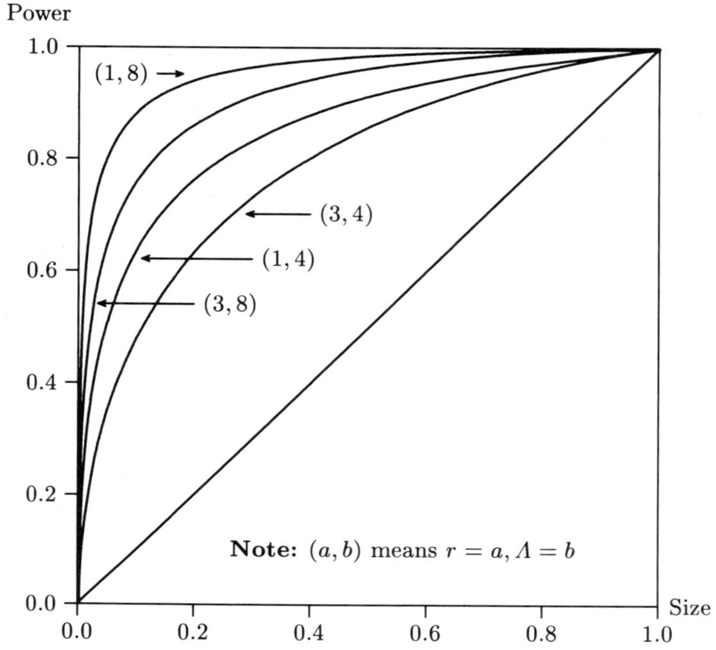

Figure 12.3 Size-power tradeoff curves depend on r and Λ

numerator and denominator random variables have noncentral χ^2 distributions. If one studies the power of the ordinary F test in the linear regression model with normal errors, using a fixed rather than a drifting DGP, one finds that the test statistic is distributed as either noncentral F (if the DGP is a special case of the alternative) or doubly noncentral F (if the DGP is not a special case of the alternative). The additional complexity of the doubly noncentral F arises in the latter case because there is no drifting DGP involved. The estimate of σ^2 under the alternative thus does not have expectation σ_0^2, and we cannot take a limit as $n \to \infty$. In many ways, then, the asymptotic analysis of nonlinear models is simpler than the finite-sample analysis of linear models. For a discussion of the linear case, see Thursby and Schmidt (1977).

If a test statistic has the $\chi^2(r)$ distribution under the null and the $\chi^2(r, \Lambda)$ distribution under some drifting DGP, the power of the test will depend solely on r and Λ. In fact, it will be strictly increasing in Λ and strictly decreasing in r; see Das Gupta and Perlman (1974). The mean of the test statistic will be $r + \Lambda$. Thus, as Λ increases, the chance of obtaining a test statistic that exceeds whatever critical value is being used must increase. In the limit, as $\Lambda \to \infty$, the power of the test tends to unity for any fixed critical value. The dependence of power on r and Λ is illustrated in Figure 12.3, which shows size-power tradeoff curves for four specific cases. These four cases, listed in order of decreasing power for a given size of test, are (1,8), (3,8), (1,4), and (3,4), where the first element in each pair is r and the second is Λ.

Let us now return to the test statistic (12.04). We have seen that it is asymptotically distributed as $\chi^2(r,\Lambda)$ with noncentrality parameter Λ equal to the squared norm of (12.16). Specifically,

$$\Lambda = \frac{\alpha^2}{\sigma_0^2} \operatorname*{plim}_{n\to\infty}\Big(\frac{1}{n}\boldsymbol{a}^{\top}\boldsymbol{M}_X\boldsymbol{Z}\Big) \operatorname*{plim}_{n\to\infty}\Big(\frac{1}{n}\boldsymbol{Z}^{\top}\boldsymbol{M}_X\boldsymbol{Z}\Big)^{-1} \operatorname*{plim}_{n\to\infty}\Big(\frac{1}{n}\boldsymbol{Z}^{\top}\boldsymbol{M}_X\boldsymbol{a}\Big). \quad (12.18)$$

For a given test of a given model, $\boldsymbol{M}_X$, $\boldsymbol{Z}$, and r are fixed. The only thing that can change is the drifting DGP which is assumed to have generated the data. By studying (12.18), we can see how the scalar α and the vector $\boldsymbol{a}$ affect Λ and hence how they affect the power of the test. We see immediately that Λ is proportional to α^2. Thus α is simply a parameter that measures how far the drifting DGP (12.06) is from the simple null (12.07). In contrast, $\boldsymbol{a}$ measures the *direction* in which the DGP differs from the simple null (12.07).

In order to understand expression (12.18) and its implications for test power properly, it is extremely illuminating to consider the geometry of the situation. This is done in the next section.

12.5 THE GEOMETRY OF TEST POWER

The NCP (12.18) is not very illuminating as it stands. It can, however, be rewritten in a much more illuminating way. Consider, first of all, the vector $\alpha n^{-1/2}\boldsymbol{M}_X\boldsymbol{a}$, the squared length of which, asymptotically, is

$$\alpha^2 \operatorname*{plim}_{n\to\infty}\Big(\frac{1}{n}\boldsymbol{a}^{\top}\boldsymbol{M}_X\boldsymbol{a}\Big). \quad (12.19)$$

This quantity is α^2 times the plim of the sum of squared residuals from a regression of $n^{-1/2}\boldsymbol{a}$ on $\boldsymbol{X}_0$. Suppose that for fixed n the DGP corresponding to that sample size is represented by the vector $\boldsymbol{x}(\boldsymbol{\beta}_0)+\alpha n^{-1/2}\boldsymbol{a}$ in E^n. If the null hypothesis is represented as in Section 2.2 by the manifold $\mathcal{X}$ generated by the vectors $\boldsymbol{x}(\boldsymbol{\beta})$ as $\boldsymbol{\beta}$ varies, then the above sum of squared residuals is the square of the Euclidean distance from the point representing the DGP to the linear approximation $\mathcal{S}(\boldsymbol{X}_0)$ to the manifold $\mathcal{X}$ at the point $\boldsymbol{\beta}_0$. It thus provides a measure of the discrepancy, for given n, between the model being tested and the data-generating process.

Now consider the artificial regression

$$(\alpha/\sigma_0)n^{-1/2}\boldsymbol{M}_X\boldsymbol{a} = \boldsymbol{M}_X\boldsymbol{Z}\boldsymbol{d} + \text{residuals}, \quad (12.20)$$

where $\boldsymbol{d}$ is simply an r-vector of coefficients that will be chosen by least squares to make this regression fit as well as possible. The plim of the total

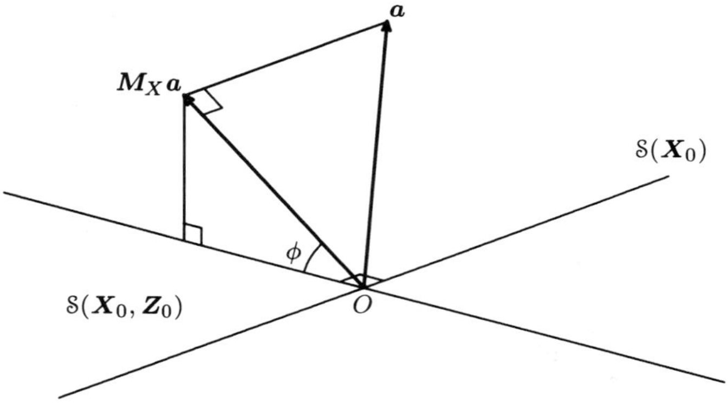

Figure 12.4 The null and alternative hypotheses, the DGP, and the angle ϕ

sum of squares for this regression is expression (12.19) divided by σ_0^2. The plim of the explained sum of squares is the NCP (12.18). Thus the asymptotic uncentered R^2 from regression (12.20) is

$$\frac{\operatorname{plim}\bigl(n^{-1}\boldsymbol{a}^{\top}\boldsymbol{M}_X\boldsymbol{Z}\bigr)\operatorname{plim}\bigl(n^{-1}\boldsymbol{Z}^{\top}\boldsymbol{M}_X\boldsymbol{Z}\bigr)^{-1}\operatorname{plim}\bigl(n^{-1}\boldsymbol{Z}^{\top}\boldsymbol{M}_X\boldsymbol{a}\bigr)}{\operatorname{plim}\bigl(n^{-1}\boldsymbol{a}^{\top}\boldsymbol{M}_X\boldsymbol{a}\bigr)}. \tag{12.21}$$

Like all R^2's, this one can be interpreted as the squared cosine of a certain angle. In this case, it is the squared cosine of the plim of the angle between the vector $\alpha n^{-1/2}\boldsymbol{M}_X\boldsymbol{a}$ and the projection of that vector onto the subspace $\mathcal{S}(\boldsymbol{X}_0, \boldsymbol{Z}_0)$. The plim of that projection is

$$\operatorname*{plim}_{n\to\infty}\Bigl(\alpha n^{-1/2}\boldsymbol{M}_X\boldsymbol{Z}\bigl(n^{-1}\boldsymbol{Z}^{\top}\boldsymbol{M}_X\boldsymbol{Z}\bigr)^{-1}\bigl(n^{-1}\boldsymbol{Z}^{\top}\boldsymbol{M}_X\boldsymbol{a}\bigr)\Bigr). \tag{12.22}$$

If we let ϕ denote the plim of the angle between $\alpha n^{-1/2}\boldsymbol{M}_X\boldsymbol{a}$ and the projection (12.22), then it is easily seen by the definition of a cosine that $\cos^2\phi$ is equal to the R^2 (12.21).[4]

All of this is shown in Figure 12.4, for the case in which the null hypothesis has one parameter and a single restriction is being tested. The one-dimensional linear subspace $\mathcal{S}(\boldsymbol{X}_0)$ corresponds to the null hypothesis, and the two-dimensional linear subspace $\mathcal{S}(\boldsymbol{X}_0, \boldsymbol{Z}_0)$ corresponds to the alternative hypothesis. If the null hypothesis were nonlinear, it could be shown on the figure as a curved one-dimensional manifold tangent to $\mathcal{S}(\boldsymbol{X}_0)$ at the point $(\boldsymbol{\beta}_0, \boldsymbol{0})$. If the alternative hypothesis were nonlinear, it could be shown on the figure as a two-dimensional curved manifold tangent to $\mathcal{S}(\boldsymbol{X}_0, \boldsymbol{Z}_0)$ at the point $(\boldsymbol{\beta}_0, \boldsymbol{0})$, with the one-dimensional manifold corresponding to the null

[4] Recall that if $\boldsymbol{a}$ and $\boldsymbol{b}$ are arbitrary vectors, the cosine of the angle between them is $(\boldsymbol{a}^{\top}\boldsymbol{b})/(\|\boldsymbol{a}\|\|\boldsymbol{b}\|)$. In the special case for which $\boldsymbol{a} = \boldsymbol{P}\boldsymbol{b}$, $\boldsymbol{P}$ being a projection matrix, this simplifies to $\|\boldsymbol{P}\boldsymbol{b}\|/\|\boldsymbol{b}\|$.

hypothesis embedded in it. To avoid complicating the figure, we have not shown either of these manifolds. Thus the figure as drawn implicitly assumes that both the null and alternative hypotheses are linear regression models. This assumption, however, has no effect at all on the geometry of the situation, because everything depends on linear approximations anyway.

The DGP is simply denoted $\boldsymbol{a}$ in the figure. Of course, the DGP is really $\boldsymbol{x}(\boldsymbol{\beta}_0) + \alpha n^{-1/2}\boldsymbol{a}$, but we can treat $\boldsymbol{x}(\boldsymbol{\beta}_0)$ as the origin, and since the factor of $\alpha n^{-1/2}$ is irrelevant to the geometry, it is arbitrarily set to 1 for the time being. The important point about the DGP in the figure is that it does not belong to the alternative $\mathcal{S}(\boldsymbol{X}_0, \boldsymbol{Z}_0)$. It could belong to it, of course, but as the figure makes clear, that would be a very special case. In the figure, we first project $\boldsymbol{a}$ onto $\mathcal{S}^{\perp}(\boldsymbol{X}_0)$, yielding the point $\boldsymbol{M}_X\boldsymbol{a}$. Although $\boldsymbol{a}$ is the discrepancy between the simple null $\boldsymbol{x}(\boldsymbol{\beta}_0)$ and the DGP, what matters for testing is $\boldsymbol{M}_X\boldsymbol{a}$, because it is the discrepancy between $\boldsymbol{a}$ and the closest point in $\mathcal{S}(\boldsymbol{X}_0)$ (which is of course $\boldsymbol{P}_X\boldsymbol{a}$). In the figure, we next project $\boldsymbol{M}_X\boldsymbol{a}$ onto $\mathcal{S}(\boldsymbol{X}_0, \boldsymbol{Z}_0)$. This is equivalent to running regression (12.20). The squared cosine of the angle ϕ between $\boldsymbol{M}_X\boldsymbol{a}$ and its projection onto $\mathcal{S}(\boldsymbol{X}_0, \boldsymbol{Z}_0)$ is then the finite-sample equivalent of expression (12.21).

The reason we talk about tests in regression *directions* should now be clear. Taking $\boldsymbol{x}(\boldsymbol{\beta}_0)$ as the origin, any model at all corresponds to some direction or set of directions. The null hypothesis corresponds to all the directions in which one can move away from $\boldsymbol{x}(\boldsymbol{\beta}_0)$ while still staying in $\mathcal{S}(\boldsymbol{X}_0)$. In Figure 12.4 there are only two such directions, because $\mathcal{S}(\boldsymbol{X}_0)$ is one-dimensional, but this is a very special case. Similarly, the alternative hypothesis corresponds to all the directions in which one can move away from $\boldsymbol{x}(\boldsymbol{\beta}_0)$ while still staying in the subspace $\mathcal{S}(\boldsymbol{X}_0, \boldsymbol{Z}_0)$. Finally, the DGP corresponds to the single direction given by the vector $\boldsymbol{a}$. The set of all possible regression directions consists of all directions in E^n. This is, locally, the set of all possible DGPs that retain the regression structure of the model.

Let us now return to the algebra of the situation. The above results allow us to rewrite the NCP (12.18) as

$$\sigma_0^{-2}\alpha^2 \operatorname*{plim}_{n\to\infty}\big(n^{-1}\boldsymbol{a}^{\top}\boldsymbol{M}_X\boldsymbol{a}\big)\cos^2\phi. \tag{12.23}$$

We have already seen that, for a given number of degrees of freedom r, the asymptotic power of the test statistic (12.04) will depend solely on this NCP. Thus expression (12.23) tells us everything we need to know about what determines the asymptotic power of tests in regression directions.

The NCP (12.23) is the product of two factors. The first factor may be written as

$$\frac{\alpha^2 \operatorname{plim}\big(n^{-1}\boldsymbol{a}^{\top}\boldsymbol{M}_X\boldsymbol{a}\big)}{\sigma_0^2}. \tag{12.24}$$

The numerator of (12.24) is expression (12.19). It is the square of the plim of the distance between the DGP (12.06) and the closest point on a linear approximation to the null hypothesis around the simple null hypothesis (12.07). The denominator is the variance of the innovations $\boldsymbol{u}$ in the DGP (12.06), indicating that as the DGP becomes noisier it will become harder to reject any null hypothesis. If we double the squared distance between the DGP and the null, and also double σ_0^2, the ratio (12.24) remains constant, indicating that our ability to detect the fact that the null is false will remain unchanged. The important point about this ratio is that it does not depend in any way on $\boldsymbol{Z}$. It will be the same for all tests in regression directions of any given null hypothesis with any given data set.

The most interesting factor in expression (12.23) is the second one, $\cos^2\phi$. It is solely through this factor that the choice of $\boldsymbol{Z}$ affects the NCP. A test will have maximal power, for a given number of degrees of freedom, when $\cos^2\phi$ is 1, that is, when the artificial regression (12.20) has an asymptotic R^2 of 1. This will be the case whenever the vector $\boldsymbol{a}$ lies in the subspace $\mathcal{S}(\boldsymbol{X}_0, \boldsymbol{Z}_0)$ but not in the space $\mathcal{S}(\boldsymbol{X}_0)$. In other words, it will be the case whenever the DGP is a special case of the alternative hypothesis against which the test is constructed, but does not satisfy the null hypothesis.

On the other hand, a test will have power equal to its size (and hence no **useful power** at all) when $\cos^2\phi$ is zero. This will evidently occur when $\boldsymbol{a}$ lies in $\mathcal{S}(\boldsymbol{X}_0)$, which means that the null hypothesis (or at least a linear approximation to it) is true. It will also occur when $\boldsymbol{M}_X\boldsymbol{a}$ is asymptotically orthogonal to $\boldsymbol{M}_X\boldsymbol{Z}$, something which in general might seem to be highly unlikely. However, special features of a model, or of the sample design, may make such a situation less uncommon than one might think. Nevertheless, it is probably not very misleading to assert that, when a null hypothesis is false in a regression direction, most tests in regression directions can be expected to have *some* power, although perhaps not very much.

When $\cos^2\phi$ is 1, the NCP (12.23) is just

$$\frac{\alpha^2}{\sigma_0^2}\operatorname*{plim}_{n\to\infty}\Big(\frac{1}{n}\boldsymbol{a}^\top\boldsymbol{M}_X\boldsymbol{a}\Big). \tag{12.25}$$

Since $\cos^2\phi = 1$ implies that $\boldsymbol{M}_X\boldsymbol{a}$ belongs to $\mathcal{S}(\boldsymbol{M}_X\boldsymbol{Z})$, this expression can also be written as

$$\frac{\alpha^2}{\sigma_0^2}\operatorname*{plim}_{n\to\infty}\Big(\frac{1}{n}\boldsymbol{d}^\top\boldsymbol{Z}^\top\boldsymbol{M}_X\boldsymbol{Z}\boldsymbol{d}\Big) \tag{12.26}$$

for some vector $\boldsymbol{d}$. In a conventional analysis of power based on sequences of local alternatives — for example Engle (1984) — the null hypothesis would be $\boldsymbol{y} = \boldsymbol{x}(\boldsymbol{\beta}, \boldsymbol{0}) + \boldsymbol{u}$, the alternative would be $\boldsymbol{y} = \boldsymbol{x}(\boldsymbol{\beta}, \boldsymbol{\gamma}) + \boldsymbol{u}$, and the DGP would be $\boldsymbol{y} = \boldsymbol{x}(\boldsymbol{\beta}_0, \alpha n^{-1/2}\boldsymbol{\gamma}_0) + \boldsymbol{u}$. Then $\boldsymbol{Z}$ would be the matrix $\boldsymbol{X}_\gamma$ with typical element $\partial x_t(\boldsymbol{\beta}, \boldsymbol{\gamma})/\partial\gamma_j$, evaluated at $(\boldsymbol{\beta}_0, \boldsymbol{0})$, and $\boldsymbol{d}$ would be the vector $\boldsymbol{\gamma}_0$. The NCP (12.26) would then be

$$\frac{\alpha^2}{\sigma_0^2}\operatorname*{plim}_{n\to\infty}\Big(\frac{1}{n}\boldsymbol{\gamma}_0^\top\boldsymbol{X}_\gamma^\top\boldsymbol{M}_X\boldsymbol{X}_\gamma\boldsymbol{\gamma}_0\Big).$$

The conventional analysis is thus a special case of the analysis based on drifting DGPs.

The foregoing results allow us to define two new concepts, which are sometimes very useful in thinking about tests. The **implicit alternative hypothesis** of a test is the set of DGPs (that is, the model or set of models) for which the test will have $\cos^2\phi$ of unity. Locally, this set must have dimension $k+r$, that is, the dimension of the null hypothesis plus the number of degrees of freedom of the test statistic. Note that this may include more than just the **explicit alternative** against which the test was constructed, because there may be many models that are locally equivalent in the neighborhood of the null hypothesis; see Godfrey (1981) and Godfrey and Wickens (1982). As an example of this, we saw in Section 10.8 that a GNR for which the test column is a vector of residuals lagged once may be used to test against the hypotheses that a regression model has either AR(1) or MA(1) errors. Since treating either of these hypotheses as the explicit alternative yields exactly the same test, they must both belong to the implicit alternative of this test.

In contrast, the **implicit null hypothesis** of a test is the set of DGPs against which that test will have $\cos^2\phi$ of zero and will thus asymptotically have no useful power at all. The implicit null hypothesis must include the actual null hypothesis but may well include other DGPs as well, since $\cos^2\phi$ will be zero whenever $\boldsymbol{a}^\top \boldsymbol{M}_X \boldsymbol{Z} = \boldsymbol{0}$. In some cases, it is a desirable feature of a test if its implicit null is large, because then the test will have power only in certain directions. In other cases, however, we want tests to have power in many directions and would like the implicit null to be as small as possible.

These results make it clear that there is always a tradeoff when we choose what regression directions to test against. At one extreme, we may choose to test against a very restricted alternative, using a test that has only one degree of freedom. At the other extreme, we may choose to test against a very general alternative, using a test with a great many degrees of freedom. By increasing the number of columns in $\boldsymbol{Z}$, we can always increase $\cos^2\phi$, or at worst leave it unchanged, which by itself will increase the power of the test. But doing so also increases r, the number of degrees of freedom, which by itself reduces the power of the test. Thus power may either rise or fall as we increase the number of directions in which we test. This tradeoff is at the heart of a number of controversies in the literature on hypothesis testing.

Consider the relative power of a test for AR(1) errors and a test for AR(p) errors. The former has one degree of freedom, while the latter has p degrees of freedom. The test against AR(1) errors thus has a smaller (i.e., lower-dimensional) implicit alternative and a larger implicit null than the test against AR(p) errors. If the error terms actually followed an AR(1) process, it would clearly be optimal to test against AR(1) errors, because such a test would have $r = 1$ and $\cos^2\phi = 1$. The test against AR(p) errors would also have $\cos^2\phi = 1$ in this case, but it would be less powerful than the test against AR(1) errors because $p > 1$. If the errors were generated by an AR process of order greater than 1 but no greater than p, the situation would be quite different. Now $\cos^2\phi$ would be less than 1 for the test against AR(1) errors, and equal to 1 for the test against AR(p) errors. The difference in degrees of freedom could still make the former test more powerful than the latter in certain cases. In certain other cases, however, the DGP would actually belong to the implicit null of the test against AR(1) errors, and the latter would therefore have power equal to its size, asymptotically.

The discussion of the previous paragraph applies almost without change to many different situations. For example, there has been some controversy in the literature on the relative merits of one-degree-of-freedom nonnested hypothesis tests and many-degree-of-freedom encompassing tests, both of which were discussed in Section 11.3; see Dastoor (1983) and Mizon and Richard (1986). The nonnested tests are analogous to testing against AR(1) errors, the encompassing tests to testing against AR(p) errors. We see immediately that nonnested tests must have a smaller implicit alternative and a larger implicit null than encompassing tests. The former will be more powerful than the latter if the data were actually generated by the nonnested alternative against which the test was constructed but may be more or less powerful otherwise.

If we temporarily drop our assumption of drifting DGPs and assume that the above results still hold, we see that the tradeoff between $\cos^2\phi$ and degrees of freedom is affected by the sample size. If n increases because more information becomes available to an investigator, the NCP can be expected to increase, since in those circumstances the DGP is not drifting toward the null as the sample size grows. Thus a given change in $\cos^2\phi$ may be expected to have a larger effect on power the larger is n. On the other hand, the effect of r on the critical value for the test is independent of sample size. Thus, when n is small, it is particularly important to use tests with few degrees of freedom, while when n is large, it becomes feasible to look in many directions at once so as to maximize $\cos^2\phi$.

Strictly speaking, the preceding analysis is invalid, since by abandoning the device of drifting DGPs we have invalidated the results on which it is based. However, Monte Carlo work generally suggests that those results work well as approximations for a fixed DGP and a fixed sample size, provided that the DGP is sufficiently close to the null hypothesis and n is sufficiently large.[5] If we treat them as approximations, then it does make sense to ask what happens as we change n while keeping the DGP fixed.

If we were confident that the null could be false in a single direction only (that is, if we knew exactly what the vector $\boldsymbol{a}$ might be), the optimal procedure

[5] See, for example, Davidson and MacKinnon (1985c). The case examined there was not actually a test in regression directions, but as we will see in Chapter 13, the theory for the power of tests in general is very similar to the theory for the power of tests in regression directions.

would be to have only one column in $\boldsymbol{Z}$, that column being proportional to $\boldsymbol{a}$. In practice, we are rarely in that happy position. There are normally a number of things that we suspect might be wrong with our model and hence a large number of regression directions in which to test. Faced with this situation, there are at least two ways to proceed.

One approach is to test against each type of potential misspecification separately, with each test having only one or a few degrees of freedom. If the model is in fact wrong in one or a few of the regression directions in which these tests are carried out, such a procedure is as likely as any to inform us of that fact. However, the investigator must be careful to control the overall size of the test, since when one does, say, 10 different tests each at the .05 level, the overall size could be as high as .40; see Savin (1980). Moreover, one should avoid jumping to the conclusion that the model is wrong in a particular way just because a certain test statistic is significant. One must remember that $\cos^2\phi$ will often be well above zero for *many* tests, even if only one thing is wrong with the model.

Alternatively, it is possible to test for a great many types of misspecification at once by putting all the regression directions we want to test against into one big $\boldsymbol{Z}$ matrix. This maximizes $\cos^2\phi$ and hence maximizes the chance that the test is consistent, and it also makes it easy to control the size of the test. But because such a test will have many degrees of freedom, power may be poor except when the sample size is large. Moreover, if such a test rejects the null, that rejection gives us very little information as to what may be wrong with the model. Of course, the coefficients on the individual columns of $\boldsymbol{Z}$ in the test regression may well be informative.

This raises the question of what to do when one or more tests reject the null hypothesis. That is a very difficult question, and we will discuss it in Section 12.7.

12.6 Asymptotic Relative Efficiency

Since all consistent tests reject with probability one as the sample size tends to infinity, it is not obvious how to compare the power of tests of which the distributions are known only asymptotically. Various approaches have been proposed in the statistical literature, of which the best known is probably the concept of **asymptotic relative efficiency**, or **ARE**. This concept, which is closely related to the idea of local alternatives, is due to Pitman (1949), and has since been developed by many other authors; see Kendall and Stuart (1979, Chapter 25). Suppose that we have two test statistics, say τ_1 and τ_2, both of which have the same asymptotic distribution under the null and both of which, like all the test statistics we have discussed in this chapter, are root-n consistent. This means that, for the test to have a nondegenerate asymptotic distribution, the drifting DGP must approach the simple null hypothesis at a rate proportional to $n^{-1/2}$. In this case, the asymptotic efficiency of τ_2 relative to τ_1 is defined as

$$\text{ARE}_{21} = \lim_{n\to\infty}\left(\frac{n_1}{n_2}\right),$$

where n_1 and n_2 are sample sizes such that τ_1 and τ_2 have the same power, and the limit is taken as both n_1 and n_2 tend to infinity. If, for example, ARE_{21} were 0.25, τ_2 would asymptotically require 4 times as large a sample as τ_1 to achieve the same power.

For tests with the same number of degrees of freedom, it is easy to see that

$$\text{ARE}_{21} = \frac{\cos^2\phi_2}{\cos^2\phi_1}.$$

Recall from expression (12.23) that the NCP is proportional to $\cos^2\phi$. If the DGP did not drift, it would also be proportional to the sample size. If τ_1 and τ_2 are to be equally powerful in this case, they must have the same NCP. This means that n_1/n_2 must be equal to $\cos^2\phi_2/\cos^2\phi_1$. Suppose, for example, that $\cos^2\phi_1 = 1$ and $\cos^2\phi_2 = 0.5$. Then the implicit alternative hypothesis for τ_1 must include the DGP, while the implicit alternative for τ_2 does not. Thus the directions in which τ_1 is testing explain all of the divergence between the null hypothesis and the DGP, while the directions in which τ_2 is testing explain only half of it. But we can compensate for this reduced explanatory power by making n_2 twice as large as n_1, so as to make both tests equally powerful asymptotically. Hence ARE_{21} must be 0.5. See Davidson and MacKinnon (1987) for more on this special case.

In the more general case in which τ_1 and τ_2 have different numbers of degrees of freedom, calculating the ARE becomes more complicated. The optimal test will be one for which the implicit alternative hypothesis includes the drifting DGP (so that $\cos^2\phi = 1$) and that involves only one degree of freedom. There may of course be many asymptotically equivalent tests that satisfy these criteria, or there may in practice be none at all. Tests that involve more than one degree of freedom, or have $\cos^2\phi < 1$, will be asymptotically less efficient than the optimal test and hence will have AREs less than 1.

The consequences of using tests with $r > 1$ and/or $\cos^2\phi < 1$ are illustrated in Table 12.1. The effect of changing $\cos^2\phi$ does not depend on either the size or power of the test, but the effect of changing r depends on both of these; see Rothe (1981) and Saikkonen (1989). The table was calculated for a size of .05 and powers of .90 (the first entry in each cell) and .50 (the second entry). Each entry in the table is the ARE for the specified test relative to that for the optimal one. Thus each entry may be interpreted as the factor by which the sample size for the optimal test may be smaller than the sample size for the nonoptimal test if both are to have equal asymptotic power.

From Table 12.1, we see that the cost of using a test with a needlessly large number of degrees of freedom, or with a value of $\cos^2\phi$ less than 1,

Table 12.1 ARE of Other Tests Versus Optimal Test

r	$\cos^2\phi$: 1.0	0.8	0.5	0.2
1	1.000	0.800	0.500	0.200
	1.000	0.800	0.500	0.200
2	0.830	0.664	0.415	0.166
	0.775	0.620	0.388	0.155
5	0.638	0.510	0.319	0.128
	0.549	0.440	0.275	0.110
10	0.512	0.409	0.256	0.102
	0.418	0.334	0.209	0.084
20	0.402	0.322	0.201	0.080
	0.313	0.251	0.157	0.063
50	0.283	0.227	0.142	0.057
	0.210	0.168	0.105	0.042

can be modest in some cases but very substantial in others. In the worst case tabulated, where the nonoptimal test has $r = 50$ and $\cos^2\phi = 0.2$, the optimal test is so much more powerful than the nonoptimal one that it is like having a sample size more than 20 times larger.

12.7 INTERPRETING TEST STATISTICS THAT REJECT THE NULL

Suppose that we test a regression model in one or more regression directions and obtain a test statistic that is inconsistent with the null hypothesis at whatever significance level we have chosen. How are we to interpret it? We have decided that the DGP does not belong to the implicit null hypothesis of the test, since we have rejected the null and hence rejected the proposition that $\cos^2\phi$ is zero. Does the DGP belong to the implicit alternative, then? Possibly it does, but by no means necessarily. The NCP is the product of expression (12.24), which does not depend in any way on the alternative we are testing against, and $\cos^2\phi$, which does. For a given value of (12.24), the NCP will be maximized when $\cos^2\phi = 1$. But the fact that the NCP is nonzero (which is all that a single significant test statistic tells us) merely implies that neither $\cos^2\phi$ nor expression (12.24) is zero. Thus all we can conclude from a single significant test statistic is that the DGP is not a special case of the model under test and that the directions represented by $\boldsymbol{Z}$ have some explanatory power for the direction $\boldsymbol{a}$ in which the model is actually false.

If we are going to make any inferences at all about the directions in which a model under test is wrong, we will evidently have to calculate more than one test statistic. Since expression (12.24) is the same for all tests in regression directions, any differences between the values of the various test statistics must be due to differences in numbers of degrees of freedom, differences in

$\cos^2\phi$, or simple randomness (including of course differences between finite-sample and asymptotic behavior of the tests). Suppose that we test a model against several sets of regression directions, represented by regressor matrices $\boldsymbol{Z}_1$, $\boldsymbol{Z}_2$, and so on. Suppose further that the jth regressor matrix, $\boldsymbol{Z}_j$, has r_j columns and generates a test statistic T_j, which is distributed as $\chi^2(r_j)$ asymptotically under the null. Each of the test statistics T_j can be used to estimate the corresponding NCP, say Λ_j. Since the mean of a noncentral chi-squared random variable with r degrees of freedom is r plus the NCP, the obvious estimate of Λ_j is $T_j - r_j$. Of course, this estimator is necessarily inconsistent, since under a drifting DGP the test statistic is a random variable no matter how large the sample size. Nevertheless, it seems reasonable that if $T_l - r_l$ is substantially larger than $T_j - r_j$ for all $j \neq l$, the logical place to look for a better model is in the directions tested by $\boldsymbol{Z}_l$.

It is far from certain that $\boldsymbol{Z}_l$, the regressor matrix with the highest estimated NCP, actually represents truly omitted directions. After all, it is quite possible that we have not tested in the right direction at all, in which case $\boldsymbol{M}_X\boldsymbol{a}$ may not lie in the subspace $\mathcal{S}(\boldsymbol{X}_0, \boldsymbol{Z}_j)$ for any j. Nevertheless, modifying the model in the directions represented by $\boldsymbol{Z}_l$ will surely be a reasonable thing to do in many cases, especially when the number of columns in $\boldsymbol{Z}_l$ is small and $T_l - r_l$ is substantially larger than any of the other estimated NCPs. One possible strategy is to construct a matrix of test regressors $\boldsymbol{Z}_J$ so that it spans the subspace spanned by all of the $\boldsymbol{Z}_j$'s jointly. That is, pick $\boldsymbol{Z}_J$ so that its columns are all of the columns which appear in any of the other $\boldsymbol{Z}_j$'s, less any columns which are redundant. Thus the test statistic T_J corresponding to $\boldsymbol{Z}_J$ must be larger than any of the other test statistics. In this case, if T_J were not much larger than T_l, and in particular did not exceed it by much more than the difference in degrees of freedom, one might feel reasonably confident that the directions represented by $\boldsymbol{Z}_l$ adequately captured the discrepancy between the null and the DGP.

It may help to fix the ideas of this chapter if we consider a simple and commonly encountered example. Suppose that the null hypothesis is

$$H_0\colon\ y_t = \boldsymbol{X}_t\boldsymbol{\beta} + u_t, \quad u_t \sim \text{IID}(0, \sigma^2),$$

where $\boldsymbol{X}_t$ is a row vector, and that we are interested in testing it against two different alternative hypotheses,

$$H_1\colon\ y_t = \boldsymbol{X}_t\boldsymbol{\beta} + \rho(y_{t-1} - \boldsymbol{X}_{t-1}\boldsymbol{\beta}) + u_t, \ \ u_t \sim \text{IID}(0, \sigma^2), \text{ and} \quad (12.27)$$

$$H_2\colon\ y_t = \boldsymbol{X}_t\boldsymbol{\beta} + \delta y_{t-1} + u_t, \ \ u_t \sim \text{IID}(0, \sigma^2). \quad (12.28)$$

Thus the null hypothesis H_0 is nested within both H_1 and H_2. The former alternative modifies it by having error terms that follow an AR(1) process, while the latter modifies it by adding a lagged dependent variable.

Our objective is to calculate the NCPs and corresponding values of $\cos^2\phi$ for tests of H_0 against both H_1 and H_2 when the data are generated by (12.28). Thus we will suppose that the data are generated by a drifting DGP that is a special case of H_2. This drifting DGP can be written as

$$y_t = \boldsymbol{X}_t\boldsymbol{\beta}_0 + \alpha_0 n^{-1/2}(\boldsymbol{X}_{t-1}\boldsymbol{\beta}_0 + u_{t-1}) + u_t, \quad u_t \sim \mathrm{IID}(0, \sigma_0^2). \tag{12.29}$$

Note that this DGP does not involve the recursive calculation of y_t, as (12.28) seems to require, because (12.29) is locally equivalent to (12.28) in the neighborhood of $\delta = 0$ and $\alpha_0 = 0$.

When we test H_0 against H_2, we will be testing in the direction of the DGP and $\cos^2\phi$ will evidently be unity. Using expression (12.25), we see that the NCP for this test is

$$\Lambda_{22} \equiv \frac{\alpha_0^2}{\sigma_0^2} \operatorname*{plim}_{n\to\infty}\Big(\tfrac{1}{n}(\boldsymbol{X}_{-1}\boldsymbol{\beta}_0 + \boldsymbol{u}_{-1})^{\top}\boldsymbol{M}_X(\boldsymbol{X}_{-1}\boldsymbol{\beta}_0 + \boldsymbol{u}_{-1})\Big), \tag{12.30}$$

where $\boldsymbol{u}_{-1}$ and $\boldsymbol{X}_{-1}$ denote, respectively, the vector with typical element u_{t-1} and the matrix with typical row $\boldsymbol{X}_{t-1}$. Here $\boldsymbol{X}_{-1}\boldsymbol{\beta}_0 + \boldsymbol{u}_{-1}$ is playing the role of the vector $\boldsymbol{a}$ in expression (12.25). The notation Λ_{22} means that H_2 is the alternative against which we are testing and that the DGP belongs to H_2. Taking the probability limit, (12.30) becomes

$$\begin{aligned}\Lambda_{22} &= \frac{\alpha_0^2}{\sigma_0^2}\Big(\sigma_0^2 + \operatorname*{plim}_{n\to\infty}\tfrac{1}{n}\big\|\boldsymbol{M}_X\boldsymbol{X}_{-1}\boldsymbol{\beta}_0\big\|^2\Big)\\ &= \alpha_0^2\Big(1 + \sigma_0^{-2}\operatorname*{plim}_{n\to\infty}\tfrac{1}{n}\big\|\boldsymbol{M}_X\boldsymbol{X}_{-1}\boldsymbol{\beta}_0\big\|^2\Big).\end{aligned}$$

Now let us see what happens when we test H_0 against H_1. In the neighborhood of H_0, the latter is locally equivalent to

$$\boldsymbol{y} = \boldsymbol{X\beta} + \rho\boldsymbol{u}_{-1} + \boldsymbol{u}, \quad \boldsymbol{u} \sim \mathrm{IID}(\boldsymbol{0}, \sigma^2\mathbf{I}), \tag{12.31}$$

which avoids the recursive calculation that (12.27) seems to require. Because AR(1) and MA(1) processes are locally equivalent near the point where their respective parameters are zero, this looks like a model with an MA(1) error process. We see from (12.31) that $\boldsymbol{u}_{-1}$ plays the role of $\boldsymbol{Z}$. Once again, $\boldsymbol{X}_{-1}\boldsymbol{\beta}_0 + \boldsymbol{u}_{-1}$ plays the role of $\boldsymbol{a}$. Thus, from (12.18), the NCP is given by

$$\begin{aligned}\Lambda_{12} = \frac{\alpha_0^2}{\sigma_0^2} &\operatorname*{plim}_{n\to\infty}\Big(\tfrac{1}{n}(\boldsymbol{X}_{-1}\boldsymbol{\beta}_0 + \boldsymbol{u}_{-1})^{\top}\boldsymbol{M}_X\boldsymbol{u}_{-1}\Big)\operatorname*{plim}_{n\to\infty}\Big(\tfrac{1}{n}\boldsymbol{u}_{-1}{}^{\top}\boldsymbol{M}_X\boldsymbol{u}_{-1}\Big)^{-1}\\ &\times \operatorname*{plim}_{n\to\infty}\Big(\tfrac{1}{n}\boldsymbol{u}_{-1}{}^{\top}\boldsymbol{M}_X(\boldsymbol{X}_{-1}\boldsymbol{\beta}_0 + \boldsymbol{u}_{-1})\Big).\end{aligned} \tag{12.32}$$

Because

$$\begin{aligned}&\operatorname*{plim}_{n\to\infty}\Big(\frac{1}{n}(\boldsymbol{X}_{-1}\boldsymbol{\beta}_0+\boldsymbol{u}_{-1})^{\top}\boldsymbol{M}_X\boldsymbol{u}_{-1}\Big)\\&=\operatorname*{plim}_{n\to\infty}\Big(\frac{1}{n}\big(\boldsymbol{\beta}_0^{\top}\boldsymbol{X}_{-1}^{\top}\boldsymbol{M}_X\boldsymbol{u}_{-1}+\boldsymbol{u}_{-1}^{\top}\boldsymbol{M}_X\boldsymbol{u}_{-1}\big)\Big)=\sigma_0^2,\end{aligned}$$

expression (12.32) simplifies to

$$\frac{\alpha_0^2}{\sigma_0^2}\sigma_0^2(\sigma_0^{-2})\sigma_0^2=\alpha_0^2.$$

Since the data were generated by a special case of H_2, $\cos^2\phi$ for the test against H_1 is simply the ratio of the NCP Λ_{12} to the NCP Λ_{22}. Thus

$$\begin{aligned}\cos^2\phi&=\alpha_0^2\Big(\alpha_0^2\Big(1+\sigma_0^{-2}\operatorname{plim}\frac{1}{n}\big\|\boldsymbol{M}_X\boldsymbol{X}_{-1}\boldsymbol{\beta}_0\big\|^2\Big)\Big)^{-1}\\&=\Big(1+\frac{\operatorname{plim}n^{-1}\|\boldsymbol{M}_X\boldsymbol{X}_{-1}\boldsymbol{\beta}_0\|^2}{\sigma_0^2}\Big)^{-1}.\end{aligned}\tag{12.33}$$

The second line of (12.33) provides a remarkably simple expression for $\cos^2\phi$ for this special case. It depends only on the ratio of the probability limit of n^{-1} times the squared length of the vector $\boldsymbol{M}_X\boldsymbol{X}_{-1}\boldsymbol{\beta}_0$ to the variance of the error terms in the DGP (12.29). As this ratio tends to zero, $\cos^2\phi$ tends to unity. Conversely, as this ratio tends to infinity, $\cos^2\phi$ tends to zero. The intuition is very simple. As the ratio of $\operatorname{plim}n^{-1}\|\boldsymbol{M}_X\boldsymbol{X}_{-1}\boldsymbol{\beta}_0\|^2$ to σ_0^2 tends to zero, because for instance $\boldsymbol{\beta}_0$ tends to zero, $\boldsymbol{M}_X\boldsymbol{y}_{-1}$ (where $\boldsymbol{y}_{-1}$ has typical element y_{t-1}) becomes indistinguishable from $\boldsymbol{M}_X\boldsymbol{u}_{-1}$. When that happens, a test against H_1 becomes indistinguishable from a test against H_2. On the other hand, as the ratio tends in the other direction toward infinity, the correlation between y_{t-1} and u_{t-1} tends to zero, and the directions in which H_1 and H_2 differ from H_0 tend to become mutually orthogonal.

The foregoing analysis could just as easily have been performed under the assumption that the data were generated by a special case of H_1. The drifting DGP would then be

$$y_t=\boldsymbol{X}_t\boldsymbol{\beta}_0+\rho_0n^{-1/2}u_{t-1}+u_t,\quad u_t\sim\text{IID}(0,\sigma_0^2).$$

When we test H_0 against H_1, $\cos^2\phi$ is now unity, and by an even simpler argument than the one that led to (12.32) we see that the NCP is

$$\Lambda_{11}=\frac{\rho_0^2}{\sigma_0^2}\operatorname*{plim}_{n\to\infty}\Big(\frac{1}{n}\boldsymbol{u}_{-1}^{\top}\boldsymbol{M}_X\boldsymbol{u}_{-1}\Big)=\rho_0^2.$$

Similarly, when we test H_0 against H_2, the NCP is

$$\begin{aligned}\Lambda_{21} = \frac{\rho_0^2}{\sigma_0^2} \operatorname*{plim}_{n\to\infty} \Big(\tfrac{1}{n} \boldsymbol{u}_{-1}{}^{\top} \boldsymbol{M}_X (\boldsymbol{X}_{-1}\boldsymbol{\beta}_0 + \boldsymbol{u}_{-1}\Big) \\ \times \operatorname*{plim}_{n\to\infty} \Big(\tfrac{1}{n} (\boldsymbol{X}_{-1}\boldsymbol{\beta}_0 + \boldsymbol{u}_{-1})^{\top} \boldsymbol{M}_X (\boldsymbol{X}_{-1}\boldsymbol{\beta}_0 + \boldsymbol{u}_{-1})\Big)^{-1} \\ \times \operatorname*{plim}_{n\to\infty} \Big(\tfrac{1}{n} (\boldsymbol{X}_{-1}\boldsymbol{\beta}_0 + \boldsymbol{u}_{-1})^{\top} \boldsymbol{M}_X \boldsymbol{u}_{-1}\Big).\end{aligned}$$

This simplifies to

$$\begin{aligned}&\frac{\rho_0^2}{\sigma_0^2} \sigma_0^2 \Big(\sigma_0^2 + \operatorname{plim} \tfrac{1}{n} \big\| \boldsymbol{M}_X \boldsymbol{X}_{-1}\boldsymbol{\beta}_0 \big\|^2\Big)^{-1} \sigma_0^2 \\ &= \rho_0^2 \Big(1 + \sigma_0^{-2} \operatorname{plim} \tfrac{1}{n} \big\| \boldsymbol{M}_X \boldsymbol{X}_{-1}\boldsymbol{\beta}_0 \big\|^2\Big)^{-1}.\end{aligned}$$

Evidently, $\cos^2\phi$ for the test of H_0 against H_2 is the right-hand expression here divided by ρ_0^2, which is

$$\left(1 + \frac{\operatorname{plim} n^{-1} \|\boldsymbol{M}_X \boldsymbol{X}_{-1}\boldsymbol{\beta}_0\|^2}{\sigma_0^2}\right)^{-1}. \tag{12.34}$$

This last result is worth comment. We have found that $\cos^2\phi$ for the test against H_2 when the data were generated by H_1, expression (12.34), is identical to $\cos^2\phi$ for the test against H_1 when the data were generated by H_2, expression (12.33). This result is true not just for this example, but for every case in which both alternatives involve one-degree-of-freedom tests. Geometrically, this equivalence simply reflects the fact that when $\boldsymbol{z}$ is a vector, the angle between $\alpha n^{-1/2} \boldsymbol{M}_X \boldsymbol{a}$ and the projection of $\alpha n^{-1/2} \boldsymbol{M}_X \boldsymbol{a}$ onto $\mathcal{S}(\boldsymbol{X}, \boldsymbol{z})$, which is

$$\alpha n^{-1/2} \boldsymbol{M}_X \boldsymbol{z} \big(\boldsymbol{z}^{\top} \boldsymbol{M}_X \boldsymbol{z}\big)^{-1} \boldsymbol{z}^{\top} \boldsymbol{M}_X \boldsymbol{a},$$

is the same as the angle between $\alpha n^{-1/2} \boldsymbol{M}_X \boldsymbol{a}$ and $\alpha n^{-1/2} \boldsymbol{M}_X \boldsymbol{z}$. The reason for this is that $(\boldsymbol{z}^{\top} \boldsymbol{M}_X \boldsymbol{z})^{-1} \boldsymbol{z}^{\top} \boldsymbol{M}_X \boldsymbol{a}$ is a scalar when $\boldsymbol{z}$ is a vector. Hence, if we reverse the roles of $\boldsymbol{a}$ and $\boldsymbol{z}$, the angle is unchanged. This geometrical fact also results in two numerical facts. First, in the regressions

$$\begin{aligned}\boldsymbol{y} &= \boldsymbol{X}\boldsymbol{\alpha} + \gamma \boldsymbol{z} + \text{residuals} \quad \text{and} \\ \boldsymbol{z} &= \boldsymbol{X}\boldsymbol{\beta} + \delta \boldsymbol{y} + \text{residuals},\end{aligned}$$

the t statistic on $\boldsymbol{z}$ in the first is equal to that on $\boldsymbol{y}$ in the second. Second, in the regressions

$$\begin{aligned}\boldsymbol{M}_X \boldsymbol{y} &= \gamma \boldsymbol{M}_X \boldsymbol{z} + \text{residuals} \quad \text{and} \\ \boldsymbol{M}_X \boldsymbol{z} &= \delta \boldsymbol{M}_X \boldsymbol{y} + \text{residuals},\end{aligned}$$

the t statistics on γ and δ are numerically identical and so are the uncentered R^2's.

The analysis of power for this example illustrates the simplicity and generality of the idea of drifting DGPs. Although the case considered is rather simple, it is very commonly encountered in applied work. Regression models with time-series data frequently display evidence of serial correlation in the form of low Durbin-Watson statistics or other significant test statistics for AR(1) errors. We have seen that (except when $\operatorname{plim} n^{-1}\|\boldsymbol{M}_X\boldsymbol{X}_{-1}\boldsymbol{\beta}_0\|^2$ is large relative to σ_0^2) this evidence is almost as consistent with the hypothesis that the model should have included a lagged dependent variable as with the hypothesis that the error terms actually follow an AR(1) process. Thus one should be very cautious indeed when one has to interpret the results of a test against AR(1) errors that rejects the null. One would certainly want to consider several possible alternative models in addition to the alternative that the errors actually follow an AR(1) process. At the very least, before even tentatively accepting that alternative, one would want to subject it to the tests for common factor restrictions that we discussed in Section 10.9.

In the foregoing example, it was easy to evaluate analytically the values of Λ and $\cos^2\phi$ in which we were interested. This will of course not always be the case. However, it is always possible to calculate approximations to these quantities numerically. To do this one simply has to run regression (12.20), evaluating $\boldsymbol{X}(\boldsymbol{\beta})$, $\boldsymbol{a}$, and $\boldsymbol{Z}$ at assumed (or estimated) parameter values. If $\boldsymbol{a}$ and/or $\boldsymbol{Z}$ were stochastic, one would have to generate them randomly and use a very large number of generated observations (which can be obtained by repeating the actual observations as many times as necessary) so as to approximate the desired probability limits. The uncentered R^2 from the regression approximates $\cos^2\phi$ and the explained sum of squares approximates Λ.

12.8 TEST STATISTICS THAT DO NOT REJECT THE NULL

For most of this chapter, we have been concerned with how to interpret test statistics that reject the null hypothesis. In many instances, of course, test statistics fail to reject. Thus it is just as important to know how to interpret a failure to reject as it is to know how to interpret a rejection. Even though we may sometimes speak about "accepting" a null hypothesis when one or more tests fail to reject it, any such acceptance should obviously be provisional and tempered with caution. Just how cautious we should be depends on the power of the test or tests that did not reject the null. We can be most confident about the validity of the null hypothesis if tests that are known to have high power against the alternatives of interest fail to reject it.

As we have seen, the power of a test depends on the way the data are actually generated. In a recent paper, Andrews (1989) has suggested that, as an aid to interpreting nonrejection of a null hypothesis by a particular test, one might consider the power the test would have under the DGPs associated with alternative hypotheses of interest. It seems reasonable that such alternatives should not be ruled out in favor of the null on the basis of tests that would, under those alternatives, have had low probability of rejecting the null. In other words, a test cannot be held to have *discriminated* against an alternative in favor of the null if it would have little chance of rejecting the null even if the alternative were true.

The analytical tool used by Andrews is the **inverse power function**, which, as its name implies, is related to the power function we discussed in Section 12.3. For present purposes, we assume that the alternative hypotheses of interest can be expressed in terms of a set of parameters and that the null corresponds to a set of restrictions on these parameters. Then, for given test size α and for given desired power π, the inverse power function for a given test statistic specifies parameter values characterizing DGPs that have power π to reject the null hypothesis on a test of size α. If the parameter values given by the inverse power function are close to parameter values that obey the restrictions of the null hypothesis, a failure to reject the null can be interpreted to mean that the null is not seriously false in any direction corresponding to the specified alternatives. If, on the other hand, the inverse power function yields parameter values far from the null, a failure to reject tells us little about whether the null is true, since this failure is compatible with many possible alternatives.

Andrews shows how to calculate inverse power functions for a wide class of asymptotic tests for both single and multiple restrictions. We will discuss only the single-restriction case, because it is a good deal easier to deal with than the multiple-restriction one. Suppose the hypothesis of interest is that a certain parameter, say θ, has a given value, say θ_0. For concreteness, we may suppose that θ is one of the parameters of a nonlinear regression function. There are numerous asymptotically equivalent test statistics, of which the simplest is just

$$\frac{\hat{\theta} - \theta_0}{\hat{\sigma}_\theta}. \tag{12.35}$$

Since the denominator here is an estimate of the standard error of $\hat{\theta}$, (12.35) is just an asymptotic t statistic. This test statistic is asymptotically equivalent to the signed square root of (12.04).

By considering (12.35), we are breaking our rule of considering only asymptotically χ^2 statistics. We do so in the interests of simplicity. Consider the drifting DGP for which $\theta = \theta_0 + n^{-1/2}\delta$, and suppose that under this DGP $\hat{\sigma}_\theta \overset{a}{=} n^{-1/2}\tau$, for some $\tau = O(1)$ as $n \to \infty$, since $\hat{\theta}$ is root-n consistent. Then the asymptotic distribution of (12.35) is $N(\lambda, 1)$, with $\lambda = \delta/\tau$. This simple fact enables us to compute the asymptotic power function of the statistic (12.35). If the critical value for a two-tailed test of size α based on the $N(0,1)$ distribution is denoted by c_α, the probability of rejecting the null under our drifting DGP is the probability that a variable distributed as $N(\lambda, 1)$ has absolute value greater than c_α. Letting $\Phi(\cdot)$ denote the c.d.f. of the standard normal distribution, this probability is

$$P(\alpha, \lambda) \equiv 1 - \Phi(c_\alpha - \lambda) + \Phi(-c_\alpha - \lambda). \tag{12.36}$$

In order to find the inverse power function corresponding to (12.36), we let $P(\alpha, \lambda) = \pi$ for some desired level of power π. This equation implicitly defines the inverse power function. It is easy to check from (12.36) that $P(\alpha, -\lambda) = P(\alpha, \lambda)$. Thus, if $P(\alpha, \lambda) = \pi$, then $P(\alpha, -\lambda) = \pi$ also. However, the nonuniqueness of λ would not arise if we were to square the test statistic to obtain a χ^2 form. No closed-form expression exists giving the (absolute) value of λ as a function of α and π in the present example, but for any given arguments λ is not hard to calculate numerically.

What interpretation should we give to the resulting function $\lambda(\alpha, \pi)$? If we square the asymptotically normal statistic (12.36) in order to obtain a χ^2 form, the result will have a limiting distribution of $\chi^2(1, \Lambda)$ with $\Lambda = \lambda^2$. Then it appears that $\Lambda = (\lambda(\alpha, \pi))^2$ is asymptotically the smallest NCP needed in order that a test of size α based on the square of (12.36) should have probability at least π of rejecting the null.

Let the nonlinear regression model be written, as usual, as

$$\boldsymbol{y} = \boldsymbol{x}(\boldsymbol{\beta}) + \boldsymbol{u}, \tag{12.37}$$

where the parameter of interest θ is a component of the parameter vector $\boldsymbol{\beta}$. If we denote by $\boldsymbol{X}_\theta$ the derivative of the vector $\boldsymbol{x}(\boldsymbol{\beta})$ with respect to θ, evaluated at the parameters $\boldsymbol{\beta}_0$, and by $\boldsymbol{M}_X$ the projection off all the columns of $\boldsymbol{X}(\boldsymbol{\beta})$ other than $\boldsymbol{X}_\theta$, then the asymptotic variance of the least squares estimator $\hat{\theta}$ is $\sigma_0^2(\boldsymbol{X}_\theta^\top \boldsymbol{M}_X \boldsymbol{X}_\theta)^{-1}$, where σ_0^2 is the variance of the components of $\boldsymbol{u}$. If we consider a DGP with a parameter $\theta \neq \theta_0$, then for a given sample size n, the parameter δ of the drifting DGP becomes $n^{1/2}(\theta - \theta_0)$, and $\Lambda = \lambda^2$ becomes

$$\Lambda = \frac{1}{\sigma_0^2}(\theta - \theta_0)^2 \boldsymbol{X}_\theta^\top \boldsymbol{M}_X \boldsymbol{X}_\theta. \tag{12.38}$$

This may be compared with the general expression (12.26). Now let $\theta(\alpha, \pi)$ be the value of θ that makes Λ in (12.38) equal to $(\lambda(\alpha, \pi))^2$ as given above by the inverse power function. We see that, within an asymptotic approximation, DGPs with values of θ closer to the θ_0 of the null hypothesis than $\theta(\alpha, \pi)$ will have probability less than π of rejecting the null on a test of size α.

We should be unwilling to regard a failure to reject the null as evidence against some other DGP or set of DGPs if, under the latter, there is not a fair probability of rejecting the null. What do we mean by a "fair probability" here? Some intuition on this matter can be obtained by considering what we would learn in the present context by using a standard tool of conventional statistical inference, namely, a confidence interval. Armed with the estimate $\hat{\theta}$ and an estimate of its standard error, $\hat{\sigma}_\theta$, we can form a confidence interval

$[\hat{\theta} - c_\alpha \hat{\sigma}_\theta,\, \hat{\theta} + c_\alpha \hat{\sigma}_\theta]$. Under the conventional assumption that the DGP is obtained by giving specific values to the parameters of the nonlinear regression (12.37), this confidence interval has probability close to $1-\alpha$, in large samples, of bracketing the true parameter. Any null hypothesis characterized by a θ_0 inside the confidence interval will not be rejected on a test of size α. A confidence interval is *random*: It depends on the actual estimate $\hat{\theta}$. The inverse power function, on the other hand, is nonrandom, and so we must be careful not to draw false analogies. Nevertheless, it seems reasonable that, when we wish to abstract away from actual data sets, we should refuse to regard the event of nonrejection of a given null hypothesis as evidence against any DGPs the parameters of which are contained in a region similar in size to a confidence interval.

What does this mean for our choice of desired power, π? An approximate answer to that question is very simple to find. Suppose that in (12.38) we require that $\theta - \theta_0$ divided by the standard error of $\hat{\theta}$ be equal to c_α. This means precisely that the difference between θ and θ_0 is half the length of a confidence interval associated with size α for the given value of the standard error. For given α and π, the value of the inverse power function $\lambda(\alpha, \pi)$ implies a value of θ, by (12.38). We may therefore ask what value of π will yield our desired condition on the difference $\theta - \theta_0$. This value of π is evidently given as the solution of the equation $\lambda(\alpha, \pi) = c_\alpha$, or, in terms of the power function P itself, $P(\alpha, c_\alpha) = \pi$. If we now replace P above by its explicit expression from (12.36), we require that

$$\pi = 1 - \Phi(0) + \Phi(-2c_\alpha) = \tfrac{1}{2} + \Phi(-2c_\alpha).$$

For reasonable choices of α, the last term here will be very small. For instance, if $\alpha = .05$, so that $c_\alpha \cong 1.96$, we find that $\Phi(-3.92) = .0000443$. Therefore, to a very good order of approximation, we find that $\pi = \frac{1}{2}$, independent of α.

This result is satisfying to the intuition. Moving away from the parameter value θ_0 associated with some null hypothesis by an amount that corresponds to half the length of a confidence interval for any reasonable test size brings us to parameter values associated with DGPs that have probability .5 of rejecting the null on a test of the same size.

Other choices of π are of course possible. One choice that seems very natural in some contexts is $\pi = 1 - \alpha$, for this makes the probability of Type I error equal to the probability of Type II error in a certain sense. When we choose a size α, we accept the fact that, with probability α, we will reject a true null hypothesis. When we refuse to treat a failure to reject a null by a test of size α as evidence against parameter values that generate NCPs smaller than the inverse power function evaluated at α and $1 - \alpha$, we accept the fact that those parameter values that we do reject, based on a failure to reject the null, would have failed to do so with probability α.

A word of caution must be uttered at this point. All of the above analysis is based on the supposition that the true DGP belongs to the class of DGPs

Table 12.2 Some Values of $\Lambda(1, \alpha, \pi)$

α	π: .50	.90	.95	.99
0.10	2.701	8.564	10.822	15.770
0.05	3.841	10.507	12.995	18.372
0.01	6.635	14.879	17.814	24.031

that can be described by the nonlinear regression model (12.37). There exist in general many DGPs not satisfying (12.37) for which the probability of rejecting a given null hypothesis satisfying (12.37) is small. Typically, such DGPs would involve more or better explanatory variables than (12.37). Unfortunately, a rejection of or a failure to reject a hypothesis based on the formulation (12.37) can tell us nothing about the possibility that better models exist. It is the task of the human econometrician, rather than of statistical test procedures, to construct potentially better models that can subsequently be subjected to formal testing procedures.

Although our theoretical exposition was facilitated by the use of the power function (12.36) based on the normal distribution, in practice, when one wishes to compute inverse power functions, it is easier to use the properties of the noncentral χ^2 distribution. Let $c_\alpha(r)$ denote the critical value for a test of size α based on the central χ^2 distribution with r degrees of freedom. Then the probability that a random variable distributed as $\chi^2(r, \Lambda)$ exceeds $c_\alpha(r)$ can be expressed in terms of the c.d.f. $F_{(r,\Lambda)}(\cdot)$ of that distribution. The required probability is just $1 - F_{(r,\Lambda)}(c_\alpha(r))$. Therefore, the inverse power function is obtained by solving the following equation for Λ in terms of r, α, and π:

$$\pi = 1 - F_{(r,\Lambda)}\big(c_\alpha(r)\big).$$

The value of Λ so obtained may be used in a formula like (12.38) in order to determine the actual parameter values that generate NCPs equal to Λ.

Andrews (1989) provides tables of the values of the inverse power function, which we may denote as $\Lambda(r, \alpha, \pi)$, for a variety of values of the arguments r, α, and π, but in fact modern computer software obviates the need to use such tables. Any program that can compute the c.d.f. of the noncentral χ^2 distribution can be used to compute the inverse power function as well. For the benefit of readers whose computers are not at hand as they read this, we display some typical values in Table 12.2.

Now let us consider a simple example of how the inverse power function may be used in practice. Suppose that θ_0 is unity and the standard error of $\hat{\theta}$ is 0.60. Then for a test at the .05 level, the values of θ given by the inverse power function for $\pi = .5$ are -0.176 and 2.176. Thus, for any θ between these two values, the probability that the test will reject the null hypothesis is less than .5. If instead we chose $\pi = 1 - \alpha = .95$, the values of θ given by the inverse power function would be -0.974 and 2.974, a wider interval in which the probability that the test will reject is less than .95.

This example illustrates the way the inverse power function is intended to be used. It provides a simple way to see for which values of θ the test is likely to have low or high power. The inverse power function is extremely easy to calculate, at least for tests of single restrictions. Thus it would seem to be worth calculating whenever a test of a single restriction fails to reject the null hypothesis. Inverse power functions can also be computed for tests of multiple restrictions, but the calculations are harder and interpretation is more difficult. Readers should consult the original Andrews paper for details.

12.9 Conclusion

Asymptotic analysis is inevitably an approximation, since it ignores everything that is not of the highest order in the sample size. The analysis of power based on drifting DGPs involves an additional approximation, since it assumes that the DGP is "close" to the null hypothesis. Thus, although the results of this chapter have the merits of simplicity and very wide applicability, we cannot expect them to provide good approximations in all circumstances. In particular, if the DGP were a long way from the null hypothesis, one would not expect the theory to perform very well.[6] In that case, of course, one would expect many tests to reject the null emphatically. Most investigators would then start again with a less restrictive model corresponding to one of the alternatives against which the original null hypothesis was rejected, which would presumably be closer to the DGP.

The objective of this chapter is not to provide a foolproof technique for choosing a correctly specified model. Such a technique does not exist. Rather, it is to provide a framework within which to interpret the results of hypothesis tests. The temptation to interpret a significant test statistic as lending support to the alternative hypothesis is often very strong. Think of how often one observes a t statistic of, say, 10 and concludes that the parameter to which it corresponds is *definitely* nonzero. As we have seen, such a conclusion is quite unjustified. We may certainly conclude that the model with that parameter set to zero is seriously misspecified, and, in the linear case, we may reasonably suspect that the variable to which the parameter corresponds is highly correlated with whatever is really missing from the rest of the model. But a single significant t statistic, by itself, can never tell us *why* the model with that parameter set to zero is misspecified. On the other hand, as we saw in Section 12.8, an insignificant test statistic is of interest

[6] Nelson and Savin (1990) analyze a simple example in which the asymptotic local power of a test statistic provides a very poor guide to its actual power when the DGP is some distance from the null hypothesis.

only if the test would have had good power against economically interesting alternatives.

In the next chapter, we will take up the topic of hypothesis testing again, this time in the context of maximum likelihood estimation. Maximum likelihood theory provides a convenient framework for developing many procedures which test in nonregression directions, that is, in directions which do not simply correspond to different specifications of the regression function. The tests for heteroskedasticity that we discussed in Section 11.5 are examples of such tests; they test in **skedastic directions** instead of regression directions (see Section 16.5). Most of the results of this chapter are true, in slightly modified form, for tests in nonregression as well as regression directions; we will discuss this to some extent in the next chapter. They are also true for models estimated by GLS and/or IV procedures.

TERMS AND CONCEPTS

asymptotic distribution (of a test statistic)
asymptotic power function
asymptotic relative efficiency (ARE)
asymptotically equivalent tests
biased test
consistency (of a test)
drifting DGP
explicit alternative hypothesis
implicit alternative hypothesis
implicit null hypothesis
inverse power function
noncentral χ^2 distribution
noncentrality parameter (NCP)
nonregression directions
power function
regression directions
sequence of local alternatives
simple null hypothesis
size-power tradeoff curve
skedastic directions
useful power

Chapter 13

The Classical Hypothesis Tests

13.1 Introduction

We first encountered hypothesis tests based on the LM, Wald, and LR principles in Chapter 3. However, the **three classical test statistics** themselves, often irreverently referred to as the "Holy Trinity," were not introduced until Section 8.9 because, if the tests are to be called *classical*, they must be carried out in the context of maximum likelihood (ML) estimation. As we emphasized in Chapter 8, ML estimation imposes a more restrictive setting on us than NLS or IV estimation does, because the DGPs of an estimated model must be completely characterized by the model parameters. This implies that we must make strong distributional assumptions if we wish to use ML estimation. In return for this, ML allows us to estimate a much wider variety of models than does NLS. Moreover, as we will see in this chapter, *tests* based on ML estimates are much more widely applicable than those used in an NLS context. This means that we will be able to construct tests in directions other than the regression directions studied in detail in the last chapter.

Fortunately, using ML does not oblige us to abandon the use of artificial regressions. Although the Gauss-Newton regression, which we have used so much in the context of least squares and IV estimation, is not in general applicable to models estimated by ML, we introduce in Section 13.7 another artificial regression that is. It is the **outer-product-of-the-gradient regression**, or **OPG regression**. The OPG regression can be used for covariance matrix estimation, hypothesis testing, one-step efficient estimation, and so on, in the ML context, in exactly the same way that the GNR can be used in the NLS and IV context. Later in the book, we will encounter other artificial regressions, which are usually better behaved but less widely applicable than the OPG regression.

This chapter is organized as follows. The next section provides a geometrical discussion of the three classical test statistics. Section 13.3 then demonstrates that they are asymptotically equivalent under certain conditions. Section 13.4 deals with the special case of linear regression models and shows how the classical test statistics are related to the familiar t and F statistics. Section 13.5 discusses the various ways in which the information matrix may be estimated, and how this affects LM and Wald statistics that use these estimates. Section 13.6 deals with the important issue of reparametrization and how it affects the classical test statistics. It also introduces the concept of locally equivalent alternative hypotheses. Section 13.7 then introduces the OPG regression and briefly discusses $C(\alpha)$ tests. Finally, some suggestions for further reading are provided in Section 13.8.

13.2 The Geometry of the Classical Test Statistics

We start, as in Section 8.9, with a parametrized model that we call the **unrestricted model** and then consider restrictions on its parameters, which implicitly define the **restricted model**. The null hypothesis is that the restrictions are true; the alternative or maintained hypothesis is that the unrestricted model is true. Both models are characterized by a loglikelihood function of the form (8.10), that is, a sum of contributions from the observations in the sample. Thus, for the unrestricted model, we have the loglikelihood function for a sample of size n:

$$\ell(\boldsymbol{y}^n, \boldsymbol{\theta}) = \sum_{t=1}^{n} \ell_t(\boldsymbol{y}^t, \boldsymbol{\theta}). \tag{13.01}$$

Recall that $\boldsymbol{y}^t$ denotes a **sample of size $\boldsymbol{t}$**, that is, a vector with components y_s, $s = 1, \ldots, t$; these components may be vectors rather than scalars, but we treat them as scalars for purposes of notation. Notice that ℓ_t depends on $\boldsymbol{y}^t$ rather than simply on y_t, because there may be lagged dependent variables or other forms of dependence among the y_t's. We will without further comment assume that any model of the form (13.01) satisfies the regularity conditions provided in Chapter 8 to ensure the existence, consistency, asymptotic normality, and asymptotic efficiency of the ML estimator for the model. The invariance of this estimator under reparametrizations of the model implies that we may, when convenient, use smooth reparametrizations for the purposes of obtaining certain results.

The set of DGPs generated as the parameter vector $\boldsymbol{\theta}$ varies over a parameter space $\Theta_1 \subseteq \mathbb{R}^k$ constitutes the unrestricted model, which we will denote by $\mathbb{M}_1$. The alternative hypothesis is satisfied by some data set if the data were actually generated by a DGP belonging to $\mathbb{M}_1$. The restricted, or null, model, $\mathbb{M}_0$, is a subset of the unrestricted model $\mathbb{M}_1$. It is generated from the model (13.01) by the imposition of restrictions of the form

$$\boldsymbol{r}(\boldsymbol{\theta}) = \boldsymbol{0}, \quad \text{where} \quad \boldsymbol{r} : \Theta_1 \to \mathbb{R}^r, \;\; r < k. \tag{13.02}$$

We assume that the functions $\boldsymbol{r}(\boldsymbol{\theta})$ which express the restrictions are **smooth** in $\boldsymbol{\theta}$ and also that the parameter space Θ_0 associated with $\mathbb{M}_0$ is a smooth $(k - r)$-dimensional subspace of Θ_1. The null hypothesis is satisfied by a particular set of data if the data were generated by a DGP characterized by a parameter vector in the subspace Θ_0. As in Chapter 8, we will denote the **restricted estimates** by $\tilde{\boldsymbol{\theta}}$ and the **unrestricted estimates** by $\hat{\boldsymbol{\theta}}$.

The first classical test is the LM test, which is based exclusively on the restricted estimates $\tilde{\boldsymbol{\theta}}$. As we saw in Section 8.9, it can be based either on the Lagrange multipliers of a restricted maximization problem or on the **gradient vector** (or **score vector**) of the loglikelihood function. In its score form, it was given in equation (8.77):

$$LM \equiv n^{-1}\tilde{\boldsymbol{g}}^{\top}\tilde{\mathfrak{I}}^{-1}\tilde{\boldsymbol{g}}. \tag{13.03}$$

Recall from (8.13) that the gradient vector $\boldsymbol{g}(\boldsymbol{\theta})$ is defined as the column vector of partial derivatives of the loglikelihood function at $\boldsymbol{\theta}$, that the information matrix $\mathfrak{I}(\boldsymbol{\theta})$ is defined in (8.20), (8.21), and (8.22), and that $\tilde{\boldsymbol{g}}$ and $\tilde{\mathfrak{I}}$ denote these quantities evaluated at $\tilde{\boldsymbol{\theta}}$. For ease of notation in what follows, we will write $\boldsymbol{I}$ instead of $n\mathfrak{I}$, since that will save us from writing a great many explicit powers of n. In the next section, however, many of the powers of n will need to be restored when we embark on some asymptotic theory. Using the $\boldsymbol{I}$ notation, (13.03) can be rewritten as

$$LM \equiv \tilde{\boldsymbol{g}}^{\top}\tilde{\boldsymbol{I}}^{-1}\tilde{\boldsymbol{g}}. \tag{13.04}$$

The second classical test, the Wald test, is based exclusively on the unrestricted estimates $\hat{\boldsymbol{\theta}}$. Since the null hypothesis requires that $\boldsymbol{r}(\boldsymbol{\theta}) = \boldsymbol{0}$, it can be tested by seeing if $\boldsymbol{r}(\hat{\boldsymbol{\theta}})$ is or is not significantly different from zero. We saw in equation (8.78) that a suitable test statistic is

$$W = n\hat{\boldsymbol{r}}^{\top}\big(\hat{\boldsymbol{R}}\hat{\mathfrak{I}}^{-1}\hat{\boldsymbol{R}}^{\top}\big)^{-1}\hat{\boldsymbol{r}} = \hat{\boldsymbol{r}}^{\top}\big(\hat{\boldsymbol{R}}\hat{\boldsymbol{I}}^{-1}\hat{\boldsymbol{R}}^{\top}\big)^{-1}\hat{\boldsymbol{r}}, \tag{13.05}$$

where $\boldsymbol{R}(\boldsymbol{\theta}) \equiv D_{\boldsymbol{\theta}}\boldsymbol{r}(\boldsymbol{\theta})$, and the hats on $\boldsymbol{r}$ and $\boldsymbol{R}$ mean, as usual, that these quantities are to be evaluated at $\hat{\boldsymbol{\theta}}$.

The third and final classical test statistic is the likelihood ratio statistic. It was defined in (8.68):

$$LR = 2(\hat{\ell} - \tilde{\ell}), \tag{13.06}$$

where again $\hat{\ell} \equiv \ell(\hat{\boldsymbol{\theta}})$ and $\tilde{\ell} \equiv \ell(\tilde{\boldsymbol{\theta}})$.

In order to investigate the relationships among the classical test statistics, we initially make a simplifying approximation. It is that the Hessian of the loglikelihood function is *constant* in the entire neighborhood of its maximum. This approximation is equivalent to assuming that the loglikelihood function is a quadratic function. If the approximation were exactly true, then the loglikelihood function could be written as

$$\ell(\boldsymbol{\theta}) = \hat{\ell} + \tfrac{1}{2}(\boldsymbol{\theta} - \hat{\boldsymbol{\theta}})^{\top} n\mathcal{H}(\boldsymbol{\theta} - \hat{\boldsymbol{\theta}}),$$

where the matrix $\mathcal{H}$, which denotes the Hessian divided by n, is constant, positive definite, independent of $\boldsymbol{\theta}$, and $O(1)$. Since the Hessian is constant, it must be equal to minus the information matrix for all sample sizes and not just asymptotically. Thus we may replace $n\mathcal{H}$ by $-\boldsymbol{I}$:

$$\ell(\boldsymbol{\theta}) = \hat{\ell} - \tfrac{1}{2}(\boldsymbol{\theta} - \hat{\boldsymbol{\theta}})^{\top}\boldsymbol{I}(\boldsymbol{\theta} - \hat{\boldsymbol{\theta}}). \tag{13.07}$$

Evaluating this expression at $\tilde{\boldsymbol{\theta}}$ and substituting into the definition of the LR statistic, (13.06), we see that, when the loglikelihood function is quadratic, the LR statistic can be rewritten as

$$LR = (\tilde{\boldsymbol{\theta}} - \hat{\boldsymbol{\theta}})^{\top}\boldsymbol{I}(\tilde{\boldsymbol{\theta}} - \hat{\boldsymbol{\theta}}). \tag{13.08}$$

Now consider the LM statistic. From (13.07), it is easy to see that the gradient $\tilde{\boldsymbol{g}}$ is just $-\boldsymbol{I}(\tilde{\boldsymbol{\theta}} - \hat{\boldsymbol{\theta}})$. Then, from (13.04), it follows that LM is equal to $(\tilde{\boldsymbol{\theta}} - \hat{\boldsymbol{\theta}})^{\top}\boldsymbol{I}(\tilde{\boldsymbol{\theta}} - \hat{\boldsymbol{\theta}})$, which is simply expression (13.08). Thus we see that the LM and LR statistics are numerically equal when the loglikelihood function is quadratic.

Proving that these two statistics are equal to the Wald statistic in this special case is a little bit harder. We begin by making another assumption, one which, as we will see later, does not in fact entail any loss of generality. It is that the restrictions associated with the null hypothesis take the form

$$\boldsymbol{\theta}_2 = \mathbf{0}. \tag{13.09}$$

Here we have partitioned the parameter vector as $\boldsymbol{\theta} = [\boldsymbol{\theta}_1 \;\vdots\; \boldsymbol{\theta}_2]$, with $\boldsymbol{\theta}_2$ an r-vector and $\boldsymbol{\theta}_1$ therefore a $(k-r)$-vector. We can also partition the information matrix so as to conform to this partition of $\boldsymbol{\theta}$:

$$\boldsymbol{I} = \begin{bmatrix} \boldsymbol{I}_{11} & \boldsymbol{I}_{12} \\ \boldsymbol{I}_{21} & \boldsymbol{I}_{22} \end{bmatrix}.$$

With $\boldsymbol{\theta}$ and $\boldsymbol{I}$ partitioned in this way, expression (13.07) for the loglikelihood function becomes

$$\ell(\boldsymbol{\theta}_1, \boldsymbol{\theta}_2) = \hat{\ell} - \frac{1}{2}\begin{bmatrix} \boldsymbol{\theta}_1 - \hat{\boldsymbol{\theta}}_1 \\ \boldsymbol{\theta}_2 - \hat{\boldsymbol{\theta}}_2 \end{bmatrix}^{\top}\begin{bmatrix} \boldsymbol{I}_{11} & \boldsymbol{I}_{12} \\ \boldsymbol{I}_{21} & \boldsymbol{I}_{22} \end{bmatrix}\begin{bmatrix} \boldsymbol{\theta}_1 - \hat{\boldsymbol{\theta}}_1 \\ \boldsymbol{\theta}_2 - \hat{\boldsymbol{\theta}}_2 \end{bmatrix}. \tag{13.10}$$

At the restricted MLE, $(\tilde{\boldsymbol{\theta}}_1, \mathbf{0})$, the first-order condition for a restricted maximum must be satisfied. By differentiating (13.10) with respect to $\boldsymbol{\theta}_1$ and evaluating the result at $\boldsymbol{\theta}_2 = \mathbf{0}$, we find that this first-order condition is

$$\mathbf{0} = D_1\ell(\tilde{\boldsymbol{\theta}}_1, \mathbf{0}) = -\big(\boldsymbol{I}_{11}(\tilde{\boldsymbol{\theta}}_1 - \hat{\boldsymbol{\theta}}_1) - \boldsymbol{I}_{12}\hat{\boldsymbol{\theta}}_2\big).$$

From this it follows that

$$\boldsymbol{I}_{11}(\tilde{\boldsymbol{\theta}}_1 - \hat{\boldsymbol{\theta}}_1) = \boldsymbol{I}_{12}\hat{\boldsymbol{\theta}}_2. \tag{13.11}$$

If we write the LR statistic (13.08) in partitioned form, we obtain

$$
\begin{aligned}
LR &= (\tilde{\boldsymbol{\theta}} - \hat{\boldsymbol{\theta}})^{\top}\boldsymbol{I}(\tilde{\boldsymbol{\theta}} - \hat{\boldsymbol{\theta}}) \\
&= \begin{bmatrix} \tilde{\boldsymbol{\theta}}_1 - \hat{\boldsymbol{\theta}}_1 \\ \tilde{\boldsymbol{\theta}}_2 - \hat{\boldsymbol{\theta}}_2 \end{bmatrix}^{\top} \begin{bmatrix} \boldsymbol{I}_{11} & \boldsymbol{I}_{12} \\ \boldsymbol{I}_{21} & \boldsymbol{I}_{22} \end{bmatrix} \begin{bmatrix} \tilde{\boldsymbol{\theta}}_1 - \hat{\boldsymbol{\theta}}_1 \\ \tilde{\boldsymbol{\theta}}_2 - \hat{\boldsymbol{\theta}}_2 \end{bmatrix} \\
&= (\tilde{\boldsymbol{\theta}}_1 - \hat{\boldsymbol{\theta}}_1)^{\top}\boldsymbol{I}_{11}(\tilde{\boldsymbol{\theta}}_1 - \hat{\boldsymbol{\theta}}_1) - 2(\tilde{\boldsymbol{\theta}}_1 - \hat{\boldsymbol{\theta}}_1)^{\top}\boldsymbol{I}_{12}\hat{\boldsymbol{\theta}}_2 + \hat{\boldsymbol{\theta}}_2^{\top}\boldsymbol{I}_{22}\hat{\boldsymbol{\theta}}_2.
\end{aligned}
$$

where the last line uses the fact that $\tilde{\boldsymbol{\theta}}_2 = \mathbf{0}$. Making use of the result (13.11), the LR statistic can then be rewritten as

$$
\begin{aligned}
LR &= (\tilde{\boldsymbol{\theta}}_1 - \hat{\boldsymbol{\theta}}_1)^{\top}\boldsymbol{I}_{11}(\tilde{\boldsymbol{\theta}}_1 - \hat{\boldsymbol{\theta}}_1) - 2(\tilde{\boldsymbol{\theta}}_1 - \hat{\boldsymbol{\theta}}_1)^{\top}\boldsymbol{I}_{11}(\tilde{\boldsymbol{\theta}}_1 - \hat{\boldsymbol{\theta}}_1) + \hat{\boldsymbol{\theta}}_2^{\top}\boldsymbol{I}_{22}\hat{\boldsymbol{\theta}}_2 \\
&= \hat{\boldsymbol{\theta}}_2^{\top}\boldsymbol{I}_{22}\hat{\boldsymbol{\theta}}_2 - (\tilde{\boldsymbol{\theta}}_1 - \hat{\boldsymbol{\theta}}_1)^{\top}\boldsymbol{I}_{11}(\tilde{\boldsymbol{\theta}}_1 - \hat{\boldsymbol{\theta}}_1).
\end{aligned} \tag{13.12}
$$

We now show that the Wald statistic is equal to (13.12). Since the restrictions take the form (13.09), we see that $\boldsymbol{r}(\boldsymbol{\theta}) = \boldsymbol{\theta}_2$ and $\hat{\boldsymbol{r}} = \hat{\boldsymbol{\theta}}_2$. This implies that the matrix $\boldsymbol{R}$ can be written as

$$
\boldsymbol{R}(\boldsymbol{\theta}) = [\mathbf{0} \quad \mathbf{I}],
$$

where the $\mathbf{0}$ matrix is $r \times (k - r)$, and the identity matrix $\mathbf{I}$ is $r \times r$. Then the expression $\hat{\boldsymbol{R}}\boldsymbol{I}^{-1}\hat{\boldsymbol{R}}^{\top}$ that appears in the Wald statistic (13.05) is just the $(2, 2)$ block of the inverse matrix $\boldsymbol{I}^{-1}$. By the results in Appendix A on partitioned matrices, we obtain

$$
\big(\hat{\boldsymbol{R}}\boldsymbol{I}^{-1}\hat{\boldsymbol{R}}^{\top}\big)^{-1} = \big((\boldsymbol{I}^{-1})_{22}\big)^{-1} = \boldsymbol{I}_{22} - \boldsymbol{I}_{21}\boldsymbol{I}_{11}^{-1}\boldsymbol{I}_{12}. \tag{13.13}
$$

This result allows us to put (13.05) in the form

$$
W = \hat{\boldsymbol{\theta}}_2^{\top}\big(\boldsymbol{I}_{22} - \boldsymbol{I}_{21}\boldsymbol{I}_{11}^{-1}\boldsymbol{I}_{12}\big)\hat{\boldsymbol{\theta}}_2.
$$

By (13.11), this last expression is equal to

$$
\hat{\boldsymbol{\theta}}_2^{\top}\boldsymbol{I}_{22}\hat{\boldsymbol{\theta}}_2 - (\tilde{\boldsymbol{\theta}}_1 - \hat{\boldsymbol{\theta}}_1)^{\top}\boldsymbol{I}_{11}(\tilde{\boldsymbol{\theta}}_1 - \hat{\boldsymbol{\theta}}_1),
$$

which is the same as (13.12). The proof of the equality of the three classical statistics for the quadratic loglikelihood function (13.07) is therefore complete.

It is of interest to see how the three classical test statistics are related geometrically. Figure 13.1 depicts the graph of a loglikelihood function $\ell(\boldsymbol{y}, \theta_1, \theta_2)$. It is drawn for a *given* sample vector $\boldsymbol{y}$ and consequently a given sample size n. For simplicity, the parameter space has been supposed to be two-dimensional. There is only one restriction, which is that the second component of the parameter vector, θ_2, is equal to zero. Therefore, the function ℓ can be treated as a function of the two variables θ_1 and θ_2 only, and its

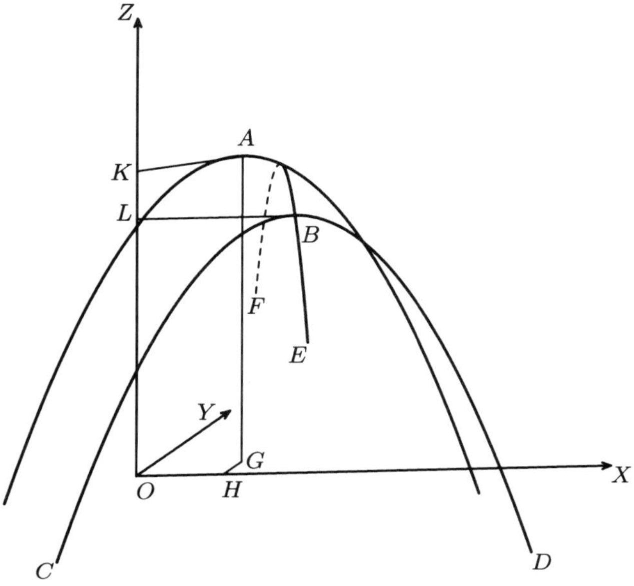

Figure 13.1 Maximizing the loglikelihood function

graph represented in 3-space. As usual, Figure 13.1 is only a two-dimensional projection of this representation. The (θ_1, θ_2) plane should be visualized as horizontal, and the vertical axis, OZ, thus measures values of the function ℓ.

The loglikelihood function ℓ achieves its maximum $\hat{\ell}$ at the point A of the figure. We may say that A has coordinates $(\hat{\theta}_1, \hat{\theta}_2, \hat{\ell})$ in the coordinate system defined by the three axes OX, OY, and OZ. In general, $\hat{\theta}_2$ will not be zero. If the restriction that θ_2 is zero is imposed, then instead of maximizing ℓ over the whole (θ_1, θ_2) plane, we are restricted to the θ_1 axis and consequently to the curve marked CBD. The restricted maximum, $\tilde{\ell}$, is achieved at the point B, at which $\theta_1 = \tilde{\theta}_1$ and, of course, $\theta_2 = 0$. The coordinates of B are then $(\tilde{\theta}_1, 0, \tilde{\ell})$.

Let us now try to find geometrical equivalents in Figure 13.1 for the quantities that appear in the three classical test statistics. First, for LM, note that $\tilde{\boldsymbol{g}}$ is the gradient vector of ℓ at B, represented geometrically by the slope of the tangent at B to the curve EBF, that is, the curve in the graph of ℓ that rises most steeply away from B. For W, since the restriction can be written simply as $\theta_2 = 0$, we may put $\boldsymbol{r} = \theta_2$, and so $\hat{\boldsymbol{r}} = \hat{\theta}_2$. Geometrically, $\hat{\theta}_2$ is just one of the coordinates of the global maximum of ℓ at A, and one way of defining it (among many other possibilities) is as the length of the horizontal line segment GH. G is the point $(\hat{\theta}_1, \hat{\theta}_2, 0)$, directly underneath the point A, and H is the projection of G onto the θ_1 axis, namely, the point $(\hat{\theta}_1, 0, 0)$. Lastly, for LR, since $\hat{\ell}$ and $\tilde{\ell}$ are coordinates of the points A and B, respectively, the difference $\hat{\ell} - \tilde{\ell}$ is represented simply by the length of the vertical segment KL on the axis OZ.

The equivalence of the three classical test statistics can now be understood in terms of the geometry of the tops of hills. Let us for the moment retain the assumption that the loglikelihood function is exactly quadratic in the neighborhood of its maximum. In order to simplify the algebra that we need to express the geometry, we make the following change of variables in the parameter space:[1]

$$\begin{aligned}\psi_1 &= \boldsymbol{I}_{11}^{1/2}(\theta_1 - \hat{\theta}_1) + \boldsymbol{I}_{11}^{-1/2}\boldsymbol{I}_{12}(\theta_2 - \hat{\theta}_2);\\ \psi_2 &= \big(\boldsymbol{I}_{22} - \boldsymbol{I}_{21}\boldsymbol{I}_{11}^{-1}\boldsymbol{I}_{12}\big)^{1/2}(\theta_2 - \hat{\theta}_2).\end{aligned} \tag{13.14}$$

The particular form of this change of variables is motivated by the fact that the loglikelihood function, when expressed in terms of the ψ's, takes on a very simple form. First, note that

$$\psi_1^2 + \psi_2^2 = \begin{bmatrix}\theta_1 - \hat{\theta}_1\\ \theta_2 - \hat{\theta}_2\end{bmatrix}^{\top}\begin{bmatrix}\boldsymbol{I}_{11} & \boldsymbol{I}_{12}\\ \boldsymbol{I}_{21} & \boldsymbol{I}_{22}\end{bmatrix}\begin{bmatrix}\theta_1 - \hat{\theta}_1\\ \theta_2 - \hat{\theta}_2\end{bmatrix},$$

as can readily be checked. Then it follows from (13.10) that the loglikelihood function in terms of the ψ's is

$$\ell(\psi_1, \psi_2) = \hat{\ell} - \tfrac{1}{2}(\psi_1^2 + \psi_2^2). \tag{13.15}$$

By a slight abuse of notation, we continue to write ℓ for the loglikelihood function in terms of the new variables.

Evidently, the effect of the change of variables has been to locate the unrestricted maximum of the loglikelihood function at the origin of the ψ coordinates and to make the hilltop perfectly symmetrical about this origin. To find the ψ coordinates of the restricted maximum, we may substitute $\tilde{\theta}_1$ and 0 for θ_1 and θ_2 in (13.14). We find for ψ_1 that

$$\boldsymbol{I}_{11}^{1/2}\psi_1 = \boldsymbol{I}_{11}(\tilde{\theta}_1 - \hat{\theta}_1) - \boldsymbol{I}_{12}\hat{\theta}_2 = 0, \tag{13.16}$$

by (13.11), which implies that the ψ_1 coordinate of the restricted maximum is zero. This fact can be expressed in a more geometrical fashion by saying that the restricted maximum is attained at a point on the ψ_2 axis. For the ψ_2 coordinate, the result is

$$\psi_2 = -\big(\boldsymbol{I}_{22} - \boldsymbol{I}_{21}\boldsymbol{I}_{11}^{-1}\boldsymbol{I}_{12}\big)^{1/2}\hat{\theta}_2. \tag{13.17}$$

[1] We cannot speak here of a reparametrization, since the change of variables is *random* because of its dependence on the unrestricted parameter estimates.

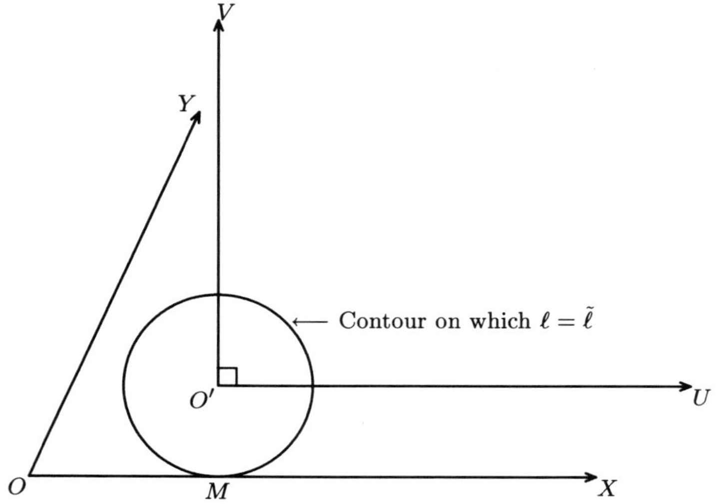

Figure 13.2 The θ and ψ coordinate systems

The restriction $\theta_2 = 0$ is satisfied at a point in the parameter space if and only if (13.17) is satisfied by the ψ_2 coordinate of the point. This means that, in terms of the ψ's, not only the restricted maximum but also the entire set of parameter vectors corresponding to DGPs that satisfy the null hypothesis lies on the straight line, parallel to the ψ_1 axis, with equation (13.17).

As we remarked earlier, (13.15) shows that the top of the hill made by the loglikelihood function is perfectly symmetrical about the origin in the ψ coordinates. Let us then redraw Figure 13.1 using the ψ's instead of the θ's. In Figure 13.2, only the parameter space has been drawn. Two sets of axes are superimposed. The ψ axes are drawn orthogonal to each other in the usual way, but this fact implies that the θ axes cannot in general be mutually orthogonal. (The ψ axes receive this privileged treatment because only they make the loglikelihood function symmetrical about the origin.) Next, Figure 13.3 shows the full three-dimensional picture. The new origin, O', is located at the old $(\hat{\theta}_1, \hat{\theta}_2)$, underneath the maximum of ℓ. The ψ_1 axis, drawn as the line $O'U$, is parallel to the old θ_1 axis, OX. This follows from the fact that the θ_1 axis is the set of parameter vectors satisfying the null hypothesis and from our previous observation that this set coincides with the line (13.17) parallel to the ψ_1 axis. The ψ_2 axis, $O'V$, is perpendicular to $O'U$ but not in general parallel to the θ_2 axis OY.

One consequence of the symmetrical form of (13.15) is that the level curves of the function ℓ have become *circles* centered on the ψ origin in the new figures. We saw from (13.16) that the restricted maximum of ℓ is realized on the θ_1 axis OX at the point at which $\psi_1 = 0$, that is, at the point M where it crosses the ψ_2 axis. By standard reasoning, we can see that the level

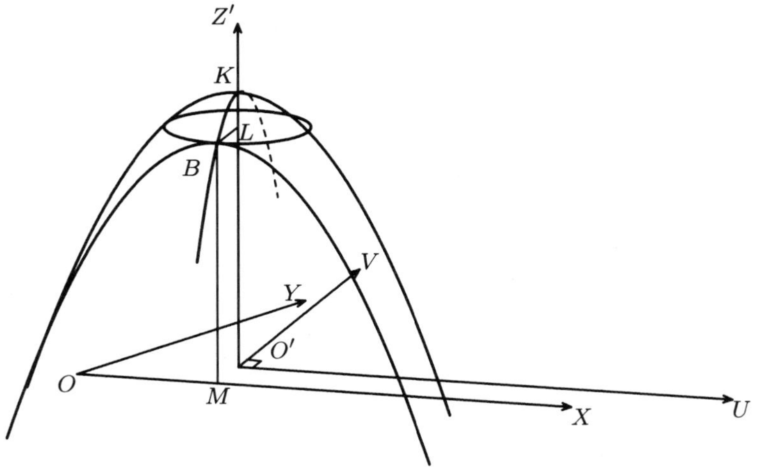

Figure 13.3 The loglikelihood as a function of ψ_1 and ψ_2

curve of ℓ on which the restricted maximum lies, that for which $\ell = \tilde{\ell}$, must be *tangent* to the θ_1 axis and so also to the ψ_1 axis at the maximum; see Figure 13.2. The radius $O'M$ of the circular level curve $\ell = \tilde{\ell}$ that joins the ψ origin to the point of tangency is perpendicular to the tangent, which explains geometrically why the restricted maximum lies on the ψ_2 axis. The length of the radius $O'M$ is, of course, just the value of ψ_2 given by (13.17), which we will denote by ρ.

Recall now that the LR statistic was represented geometrically by the vertical line segment KL in Figures 13.1 and 13.3. We may use (13.06) and (13.15) directly to obtain the length of this segment:

$$LR = 2\big(\hat{\ell} - \ell(0, \rho)\big) = \rho^2.$$

For the LM statistic, it is clear that the gradient of ℓ, with respect to the ψ coordinates, at any point (ψ_1, ψ_2) is the vector $-(\psi_1, \psi_2)$. At M it is therefore just $-(0, \rho)$. Further, the Hessian of ℓ with respect to the ψ coordinates at any point (ψ_1, ψ_2) is simply minus the 2×2 identity matrix. Thus, if we use the gradient with respect to the ψ's in (13.04), along with the negative of the Hessian with respect to the ψ's in place of the information matrix, we obtain an LM statistic equal to[2]

$$[0 \quad \rho] \begin{bmatrix} 1 & 0 \\ 0 & 1 \end{bmatrix} \begin{bmatrix} 0 \\ \rho \end{bmatrix} = \rho^2.$$

[2] This argument is heuristic, since, strictly speaking, we should not be treating the ψ's as if they were ordinary parameters. However, we will proceed as if it were possible to do so.

Now recall that the Wald test corresponds geometrically to the line segment GH in Figure 13.1, which became the radius $O'M$ in Figure 13.3, of length ρ. Before the change of variables from the θ's to the ψ's, the Wald statistic would have been calculated as the square of the length of GH divided by an appropriate estimate of the variance of $\hat{\theta}_2$. Because in Figure 13.3 the ψ axes are mutually orthogonal rather than the θ axes, the length of $O'M$ in that figure is different from the length of GH in Figure 13.1. Thus we should use a different variance measure when we work in terms of the ψ's. Just as we did for the LM statistic, we can use the 2×2 identity matrix in the place of the information matrix. This means that the appropriate variance measure is just unity, and since the length of $O'M$ is ρ, the Wald statistic is just ρ^2.

Our previous proof of the equality of the three classical test statistics provides a justification of the above heuristic arguments. However, we may verify directly that the quantity ρ^2 is what we would have obtained by working throughout with the θ's. It follows directly from (13.17) that

$$\rho^2 = \left(\boldsymbol{I}_{22} - \boldsymbol{I}_{21}\boldsymbol{I}_{11}^{-1}\boldsymbol{I}_{12}\right)\hat{\theta}_2^2.$$

By (13.11) applied to the present two-parameter case, this becomes

$$\rho^2 = \boldsymbol{I}_{22}\hat{\theta}_2^2 - \boldsymbol{I}_{11}\left(\tilde{\theta}_1 - \hat{\theta}_1\right)^2.$$

This is what expression (13.12) for the three classical test statistics reduces to when $\boldsymbol{\theta}_1$ and $\boldsymbol{\theta}_2$ are scalars.

What the use of the ψ's allows us to see clearly, in terms of the symmetrical hilltop generated by (13.15), is just why the three tests are equivalent in the present simple case. All three measure, in some sense, how far away the unrestricted MLE is from the restricted MLE. The Wald test is based directly on the distance between these points in the parameter space. Geometrically, this is the length ρ of the radius $O'M$ of the circular level curve of the loglikelihood function for the value $\tilde{\ell}$. The distance between the two estimates, for the purposes of the Wald test, is therefore measured by the squared Euclidean distance in terms of the ψ's between the parameter vectors at which the restricted and unrestricted maxima are realized. This would not be true with the θ's, of course, since it requires that the hilltop be symmetrical. For the likelihood ratio test, the distance measure is in terms of the actual difference between the two maxima. Thus, geometrically, the LR statistic is related to the length of a vertical line segment, KL in the figures, while the Wald statistic is related to the length of a horizontal line segment. Lastly, the LM statistic is based on the slope of the steepest path up the hill at the restricted estimate.

For a perfectly symmetrical hill, what we have shown in this section is that all three distance measures are functions of the length ρ of the radius of the level curve passing through the restricted maximum alone and so are exactly equivalent. What we will see later in this chapter is that this agreeable result is exactly true *only* when the loglikelihood hill is exactly quadratic, that is, when the Hessian of the loglikelihood function is indeed exactly constant in the entire neighborhood of its maximum. But all hills are *roughly* quadratic at their summits, and in the next section we will be able to exploit this fact to demonstrate that all three classical test statistics are *asymptotically* equivalent under weak regularity conditions.

13.3 Asymptotic Equivalence of the Classical Tests

In this section, we establish two sets of results concerning the asymptotic equivalence of the three classical tests. The first, and weaker, set is derived under the assumption that the restrictions under test are in fact true. More formally, we assume that the data were generated by a DGP characterized by a parameter vector $\boldsymbol{\theta}_0$ that satisfies $\boldsymbol{r}(\boldsymbol{\theta}_0) = \mathbf{0}$, in the notation of (13.02). Note that we no longer assume that the restrictions take the special form (13.09). The equivalence of the three classical tests in this case is by now fairly simple to demonstrate, since the main ingredients have been established already in Chapter 8. Our work here is mostly putting the pieces together and checking that the intuition of the exactly quadratic case treated in the last section does indeed extend to an asymptotically valid result in general.

The second, and stronger, set of results will not be established in full detail in this book. These results extend those of the first set to the case in which the data are generated by a drifting DGP that does not satisfy the null hypothesis but tends to a limit contained in it. Thus this second set of results is analogous for the case of ML estimation to the results obtained in Chapter 12 for estimation by NLS. Although we will not provide full proofs, we will take a little time to state the results and to explain what we mean by drifting DGPs in this new context.

For the first set of results, then, we suppose that the true parameter vector $\boldsymbol{\theta}_0$ obeys (13.02). In this case, both the unrestricted MLE $\hat{\boldsymbol{\theta}}$ and the restricted one $\tilde{\boldsymbol{\theta}}$ differ from $\boldsymbol{\theta}_0$ by a random quantity of order $n^{-1/2}$. For the unrestricted MLE,

$$n^{1/2}(\hat{\boldsymbol{\theta}} - \boldsymbol{\theta}_0) \overset{a}{=} \mathcal{I}_0^{-1} n^{-1/2} \boldsymbol{g}_0, \tag{13.18}$$

a result that follows immediately from (8.38) and the information matrix equality that $\mathcal{I}_0 = -\mathcal{H}_0$. Since we are again in the context of asymptotic theory, we are now using notation with explicit powers of the sample size n. Otherwise, the notation is as usual: $\mathcal{I}_0$ and $\boldsymbol{g}_0$ denote $\mathcal{I}(\boldsymbol{\theta}_0)$ and $\boldsymbol{g}(\boldsymbol{\theta}_0)$, respectively. For the restricted MLE, we make use of the information matrix equality and a result immediately following (8.74) to obtain

$$n^{1/2}(\tilde{\boldsymbol{\theta}} - \boldsymbol{\theta}_0) \overset{a}{=} \mathcal{I}_0^{-1}\big(\mathbf{I} - \boldsymbol{R}_0^{\top}(\boldsymbol{R}_0 \mathcal{I}_0^{-1} \boldsymbol{R}_0^{\top})^{-1} \boldsymbol{R}_0 \mathcal{I}_0^{-1}\big) n^{-1/2} \boldsymbol{g}_0. \tag{13.19}$$

The information matrix $\mathcal{I}(\boldsymbol{\theta})$ is of order unity and smooth in $\boldsymbol{\theta}$, according to our standard assumptions for models to be estimated by maximum likelihood laid out in the statements of Theorems 8.1, 8.2, and 8.3. It follows that

$$\ddot{\mathfrak{I}} = \mathfrak{I}_0 + O(n^{-1/2}), \tag{13.20}$$

where $\ddot{\mathfrak{I}} \equiv \mathfrak{I}(\ddot{\boldsymbol{\theta}})$. This is true for any root-n consistent estimator $\ddot{\boldsymbol{\theta}}$, but we will adopt the convention that $\ddot{\boldsymbol{\theta}}$ denotes either $\hat{\boldsymbol{\theta}}$ or $\tilde{\boldsymbol{\theta}}$. Similarly, because the functions $\boldsymbol{r}(\boldsymbol{\theta})$ defining the restrictions are assumed to be smooth, we have

$$\ddot{\boldsymbol{R}} = \boldsymbol{R}_0 + O(n^{-1/2}), \tag{13.21}$$

where the order relation is to be understood element by element in both of the above equations.

Let us first consider the LM test statistic (13.03). It may be written as

$$LM = \big(n^{-1/2}\tilde{\boldsymbol{g}}\big)^{\top}\tilde{\mathfrak{I}}^{-1}\big(n^{-1/2}\tilde{\boldsymbol{g}}\big), \tag{13.22}$$

where the parentheses emphasize that it is a quadratic form in the $O(1)$ vector $n^{-1/2}\tilde{\boldsymbol{g}}$. We may expand this vector by Taylor's Theorem to obtain

$$n^{-1/2}\tilde{\boldsymbol{g}} = n^{-1/2}\boldsymbol{g}_0 + \big(n^{-1}\boldsymbol{H}(\bar{\boldsymbol{\theta}})\big)n^{1/2}(\tilde{\boldsymbol{\theta}} - \boldsymbol{\theta}_0);$$

see (8.35). The law of large numbers applied to the Hessian matrix $\boldsymbol{H}$ and the information matrix equality allow us to rewrite this as

$$n^{-1/2}\tilde{\boldsymbol{g}} \stackrel{a}{=} n^{-1/2}\boldsymbol{g}_0 - \mathfrak{I}_0 n^{1/2}(\tilde{\boldsymbol{\theta}} - \boldsymbol{\theta}_0).$$

Now we may use the result (13.19) to find that

$$n^{-1/2}\tilde{\boldsymbol{g}} \stackrel{a}{=} \boldsymbol{R}_0^{\top}\big(\boldsymbol{R}_0\mathfrak{I}_0^{-1}\boldsymbol{R}_0^{\top}\big)^{-1}\boldsymbol{R}_0\mathfrak{I}_0^{-1}n^{-1/2}\boldsymbol{g}_0.$$

Substitution of this into (13.22) then yields

$$LM \stackrel{a}{=} (n^{-1/2}\boldsymbol{g}_0)^{\top}\mathfrak{I}_0^{-1}\boldsymbol{R}_0^{\top}\big(\boldsymbol{R}_0\mathfrak{I}_0^{-1}\boldsymbol{R}_0^{\top}\big)^{-1}\boldsymbol{R}_0\mathfrak{I}_0^{-1}(n^{-1/2}\boldsymbol{g}_0). \tag{13.23}$$

Notice that this expression is in terms solely of quantities evaluated at the true parameter vector $\boldsymbol{\theta}_0$ and that, of these, only $\boldsymbol{g}_0$ is stochastic.

For the likelihood ratio statistic (13.06), another Taylor expansion is needed. This time, expanding around $\boldsymbol{\theta} = \hat{\boldsymbol{\theta}}$ and using the likelihood equations $\hat{\boldsymbol{g}} = \boldsymbol{0}$, we obtain

$$LR = 2(\hat{\ell} - \tilde{\ell}) \stackrel{a}{=} n(\tilde{\boldsymbol{\theta}} - \hat{\boldsymbol{\theta}})^{\top}\hat{\mathfrak{I}}(\tilde{\boldsymbol{\theta}} - \hat{\boldsymbol{\theta}}); \tag{13.24}$$

see also (8.70). Combining (13.18) and (13.19), we obtain

$$n^{1/2}(\hat{\boldsymbol{\theta}} - \tilde{\boldsymbol{\theta}}) \stackrel{a}{=} \mathfrak{I}_0^{-1}\boldsymbol{R}_0^{\top}\big(\boldsymbol{R}_0\mathfrak{I}_0^{-1}\boldsymbol{R}_0^{\top}\big)^{-1}\boldsymbol{R}_0\mathfrak{I}_0^{-1}(n^{-1/2}\boldsymbol{g}_0).$$

On substituting this last relation into (13.24) and replacing $\hat{\mathcal{I}}$ by $\mathcal{I}_0$, as (13.20) allows us to do, we find that

$$LR \stackrel{a}{=} (n^{-1/2}\boldsymbol{g}_0)^\top \mathcal{I}_0^{-1}\boldsymbol{R}_0^\top \big(\boldsymbol{R}_0\mathcal{I}_0^{-1}\boldsymbol{R}_0^\top\big)^{-1}\boldsymbol{R}_0\mathcal{I}_0^{-1}(n^{-1/2}\boldsymbol{g}_0). \tag{13.25}$$

Since this is identical to expression (13.23), we have established the asymptotic equivalence of LM and LR.

Finally, we consider the Wald statistic (13.05). Taylor expanding the restrictions $\boldsymbol{r}(\hat{\boldsymbol{\theta}}) = \mathbf{0}$, using the assumption that $\boldsymbol{r}(\boldsymbol{\theta}_0) = \mathbf{0}$, and multiplying by $n^{1/2}$, we obtain

$$n^{1/2}\hat{\boldsymbol{r}} \stackrel{a}{=} \boldsymbol{R}_0 n^{1/2}(\hat{\boldsymbol{\theta}} - \boldsymbol{\theta}_0) \stackrel{a}{=} \boldsymbol{R}_0\mathcal{I}_0^{-1}n^{-1/2}\boldsymbol{g}_0,$$

where the final equality follows from (13.18). This last result, along with (13.20) and (13.21), allows us to rewrite (13.05) asymptotically as

$$W \stackrel{a}{=} (n^{-1/2}\boldsymbol{g}_0)^\top \mathcal{I}_0^{-1}\boldsymbol{R}_0^\top \big(\boldsymbol{R}_0\mathcal{I}_0^{-1}\boldsymbol{R}_0^\top\big)^{-1}\boldsymbol{R}_0\mathcal{I}_0^{-1}(n^{-1/2}\boldsymbol{g}_0). \tag{13.26}$$

The asymptotic equivalence of the three classical tests under the null hypothesis of the tests is now established through the equality of (13.23), (13.25), and (13.26).

At this point, it is easy to derive the common asymptotic distribution of the three classical test statistics. Recall from (8.41) that the asymptotic distribution of $n^{-1/2}\boldsymbol{g}_0$ is $N(\mathbf{0}, \mathcal{I}_0)$. From this, we calculate that the asymptotic distribution of the r-vector $\boldsymbol{R}_0\mathcal{I}_0^{-1}(n^{-1/2}\boldsymbol{g}_0)$ is $N(\mathbf{0}, \boldsymbol{R}_0\mathcal{I}_0^{-1}\boldsymbol{R}_0^\top)$. The three statistics are, as we have just seen, asymptotically equal to the quadratic form (13.26) in the vector $\boldsymbol{R}_0\mathcal{I}_0^{-1}(n^{-1/2}\boldsymbol{g}_0)$ and matrix $(\boldsymbol{R}_0\mathcal{I}_0^{-1}\boldsymbol{R}_0^\top)^{-1}$. It follows at once that the asymptotic distribution of the classical test statistics is a central chi-squared with r degrees of freedom.

Our discussion of the first case, in which the restrictions under test are in fact true, is now complete. We therefore turn our attention to the second case, in which the data are generated by a drifting DGP that tends in the limit to a DGP which satisfies the null hypothesis. We begin by discussing the concept of drifting DGPs in the context of models to be estimated by the method of maximum likelihood.

In the context of models estimated by NLS, we obtained a drifting DGP by adding a quantity proportional to $n^{-1/2}$ to the regression function $\boldsymbol{x}(\boldsymbol{\beta}_0)$; recall (12.06). Thus, as $n \to \infty$, the DGP drifted at a suitable rate toward one specified by the parameter vector $\boldsymbol{\beta}_0$, assumed to satisfy the restrictions of the null hypothesis. Just as NLS models are defined by means of their regression functions, models to be estimated by maximum likelihood are defined by means of their loglikelihood functions, as in (13.01). In the context of ML models, it therefore seems appropriate to add a quantity proportional to $n^{-1/2}$ to the contribution to the loglikelihood function from each observation.

Thus we write for observation t

$$\ell_t = \ell_t(\boldsymbol{y}^t, \boldsymbol{\theta}_0) + n^{-1/2} a_t(\boldsymbol{y}^t). \tag{13.27}$$

We can see from this that the log of the density of the tth observation is taken to be as given by a parametrized model for a parameter vector $\boldsymbol{\theta}_0$ satisfying the restrictions of the null hypothesis, plus a term that vanishes with $n^{-1/2}$ as $n \to \infty$. The fact that any density function is normalized so as to integrate to unity means that the functions a_t in (13.27) must be chosen so as to obey the normalization condition

$$\int \exp\bigl(\ell_t + n^{-1/2} a_t\bigr) dy_t = 1.$$

It can readily be shown that this implies that

$$E_0\bigl(a_t(\boldsymbol{y}^t)\bigr) = O(n^{-1/2}), \tag{13.28}$$

where E_0 denotes an expectation calculated using $\ell_t(\boldsymbol{y}^t, \boldsymbol{\theta}_0)$ as log density. To leading order asymptotically, then, the random variables a_t have mean zero.

The fact that ℓ_t is written in (13.27) as the sum of two terms does not restrict the applicability of the analysis at all, because one can think of (13.27) as arising from a first-order Taylor-series approximation to any drifting DGP. An example would be the sequence of local alternatives

$$\ell_t\bigl(\boldsymbol{y}^t, \boldsymbol{\theta}_0 + n^{-1/2} \boldsymbol{\delta}\bigr).$$

By arguments similar to those of Section 12.3, one can show that a Taylor-series approximation to this can be written in the form of (13.27).

We will now state without proof the results that correspond to equations (12.11), (12.12), and (12.13) in the NLS context. They are discussed and proved in Davidson and MacKinnon (1987), a paper that many readers may, however, find somewhat difficult because of the nature of the mathematics employed. These results provide asymptotically valid expressions for the various ingredients of the classical test statistics under the drifting DGP specified by (13.27). The first result is that the estimators $\hat{\boldsymbol{\theta}}$ and $\tilde{\boldsymbol{\theta}}$ are still root-n consistent for $\boldsymbol{\theta}_0$:

$$\ddot{\boldsymbol{\theta}} = \boldsymbol{\theta}_0 + O(n^{-1/2}),$$

from which we may conclude that $\ddot{\mathfrak{I}}$ and $\ddot{\boldsymbol{R}}$ are consistent for $\mathfrak{I}_0$ and $\boldsymbol{R}_0$, just as they are under the null hypothesis:

$$\ddot{\mathfrak{I}} = \mathfrak{I}_0 + O(n^{-1/2}); \quad \text{and} \quad \ddot{\boldsymbol{R}} = \boldsymbol{R}_0 + O(n^{-1/2}).$$

We may also conclude from the consistency of $\ddot{\boldsymbol{\theta}}$ that all the Taylor expansions used in developing equations (13.23), (13.25), and (13.26) are still valid, as are these equations themselves.

As can be seen from equations (13.23), (13.25), and (13.26), the only stochastic part of all of the classical test statistics, asymptotically, is the quantity $n^{-1/2}\boldsymbol{g}_0$. Its behavior is not the same under the drifting DGP as it is under the null; recall (12.13) for the NLS case. We find that the asymptotic distribution of $n^{-1/2}\boldsymbol{g}_0$ is still normal but no longer has mean zero. If we define the $O(1)$ k-vector $\boldsymbol{c}$ by

$$\boldsymbol{c} \equiv \lim_{n\to\infty} \mathrm{cov}_0\Big(n^{-1/2}\sum_{t=1}^{n} a_t(\boldsymbol{y}^t),\, n^{-1/2}\boldsymbol{g}_0\Big), \tag{13.29}$$

where cov_0 means a covariance calculated under the limit DGP characterized by $\boldsymbol{\theta}_0$, then it can be proved that, asymptotically,

$$n^{-1/2}\boldsymbol{g}_0 \sim N(\boldsymbol{c},\, \mathfrak{I}_0).$$

Consequently, the asymptotic distribution of the r-vector $\boldsymbol{R}_0\mathfrak{I}_0^{-1}(n^{-1/2}\boldsymbol{g}_0)$ is now $N(\boldsymbol{R}_0\mathfrak{I}_0^{-1}\boldsymbol{c},\, \boldsymbol{R}_0\mathfrak{I}_0^{-1}\boldsymbol{R}_0^{\top})$, and the asymptotic distribution of the classical test statistics is a **noncentral chi-squared** with r degrees of freedom and noncentrality parameter

$$\Lambda = \boldsymbol{c}^{\top}\mathfrak{I}_0^{-1}\boldsymbol{R}_0^{\top}\big(\boldsymbol{R}_0\mathfrak{I}_0^{-1}\boldsymbol{R}_0^{\top}\big)^{-1}\boldsymbol{R}_0\mathfrak{I}_0^{-1}\boldsymbol{c}. \tag{13.30}$$

So far, our results are very similar to those of the last chapter for drifting DGPs in the regression model context. In fact, the similarities are even deeper than has been seen up to this point. Almost all of the discussion of the geometry of test power given in Section 12.5 can be taken over, with only slight modifications, to the present case. One difference, which might appear at first glance to present an insurmountable obstacle but is in fact quite innocuous, is that drifting DGPs like (13.27) must be set in an infinite-dimensional space rather than the n-dimensional space used earlier. This is because each a_t is a function of the observation y_t, and sets of functions are typically infinite dimensional. But for our purposes this simply means that the *possibilities* for constructing DGPs that drift to a DGP that satisfies the null hypothesis are infinite. In particular, just as in the present context we are not restricted to tests in regression directions, neither are we restricted to considering drifting DGPs in regression directions.

The geometry of what we have been doing can be illustrated in three dimensions, just as in Figure 12.3. Suppose for simplicity that we are working in a parametrization in which the information matrix $\mathfrak{I}_0$ is an identity matrix.[3]

[3] For example, we could use for a reparametrization (13.14) with the random quantities $\hat{\theta}_1$ and $\hat{\theta}_2$ replaced by the true values that correspond to the limit DGP, and $\boldsymbol{I}$ replaced by $\mathfrak{I}$ evaluated at these values.

Further, suppose that there are only two parameters, θ_1 and θ_2, and that the restriction corresponding to the null hypothesis is that $\theta_2 = 0$. Thus

$$\mathfrak{I}_0 = \begin{bmatrix} 1 & 0 \\ 0 & 1 \end{bmatrix} \quad \text{and} \quad \boldsymbol{R}_0 = [0 \quad 1].$$

In this simple case, the covariance matrix $\boldsymbol{R}_0 \mathfrak{I}_0^{-1} \boldsymbol{R}_0^\top$ reduces to the scalar 1, the vector $\boldsymbol{R}_0 \mathfrak{I}_0^{-1} \boldsymbol{c}$ becomes simply c_2, the second component of the 2–vector $\boldsymbol{c}$, and from (13.30) the noncentrality parameter Λ becomes c_2^2.

The three-dimensional space we will construct is spanned by three random variables, interpreted as vectors in this space. These random variables are precisely those that appear in the definition (13.29) of $\boldsymbol{c}$. They are

$$\begin{aligned} \boldsymbol{s}_1 &\equiv n^{-1/2} \sum_{t=1}^{n} \frac{\partial \ell_t}{\partial \theta_1} (\boldsymbol{y}^t, \boldsymbol{\theta}_0), \\ \boldsymbol{s}_2 &\equiv n^{-1/2} \sum_{t=1}^{n} \frac{\partial \ell_t}{\partial \theta_2} (\boldsymbol{y}^t, \boldsymbol{\theta}_0), \text{ and} \\ \boldsymbol{a} &\equiv n^{-1/2} \sum_{t=1}^{n} a_t(\boldsymbol{y}^t). \end{aligned}$$

In order to treat these random variables as vectors in a three-dimensional Euclidean space which they span, it is enough to ensure that the algebraic operations defined on Euclidean spaces can be properly defined for these random variables. The operations of addition and multiplication by a scalar are defined in the obvious way. The Euclidean-space sum, or more concisely **vector sum**, of two random variables is simply their ordinary sum:

$$\boldsymbol{s}_1 + \boldsymbol{s}_2 = n^{-1/2} \sum_{t=1}^{n} \left(\frac{\partial \ell_t}{\partial \theta_1} (\boldsymbol{y}^t, \boldsymbol{\theta}_0) + \frac{\partial \ell_t}{\partial \theta_2} (\boldsymbol{y}^t, \boldsymbol{\theta}_0) \right). \tag{13.31}$$

Similarly, multiplication by a scalar $\alpha \in \mathbb{R}$ is in the Euclidean-space context no different from ordinary multiplication by a scalar:

$$\alpha \boldsymbol{s}_1 = \alpha n^{-1/2} \sum_{t=1}^{n} \frac{\partial \ell_t}{\partial \theta_1} (\boldsymbol{y}^t, \boldsymbol{\theta}_0). \tag{13.32}$$

These two definitions (13.31) and (13.32) suffice to put the structure of the linear space $\mathbb{R}^3$ on the set of all linear combinations of $\boldsymbol{s}_1$, $\boldsymbol{s}_2$, and $\boldsymbol{a}$.

For a Euclidean space, another operation must be defined, namely, the **inner product** of two vectors. Thus we wish to be able to say what we mean by the inner product of any linear combination of $\boldsymbol{s}_1$, $\boldsymbol{s}_2$, and $\boldsymbol{a}$ with any other such linear combination. This is done very simply: The inner product of two random variables will be their covariance under the limit DGP. We will

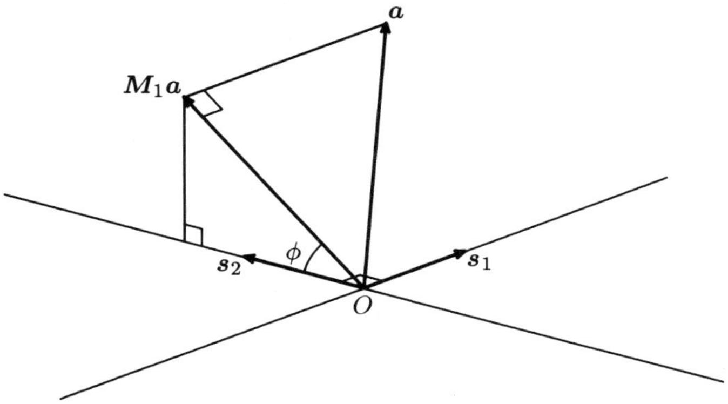

Figure 13.4 The noncentrality parameter of the classical tests

denote inner products by an angle bracket notation in which, for instance, $\langle s_1, s_2 \rangle$ denotes the inner product of s_1 with s_2. Since the covariance matrix of s_1 and s_2, $\mathfrak{I}_0$, is the identity matrix, we have

$$\langle s_1, s_2 \rangle = 0 \quad \text{and} \quad \langle s_i, s_i \rangle \equiv \|s_i\|^2 = 1, \;\; i = 1, 2.$$

It follows that s_1 and s_2 form a pair of mutually orthogonal unit vectors. Note that the squared norm of an element of our Euclidean space of random variables, defined, as usual, as the inner product of the element with itself, is just the second moment of the element considered as a random variable. Since the variables s_1 and s_2 have zero expectation under the limit DGP, the squared norm of either of them is just the variance. Asymptotically, the same is true for a, since by (13.28) the expectation of a vanishes as $n \to \infty$.

In general, the vector represented by the random variable a will not lie in the plane spanned by s_1 and s_2; that is why a third dimension is needed in order to accommodate it. Consider now Figure 13.4, in which the vectors s_1 and s_2 span the horizontal plane. Following the intuition of the last chapter, we let M_1a be the projection of a onto the orthogonal complement of the one-dimensional space spanned by s_1. It follows that M_1a lies vertically above or below the direction of s_2 (we have drawn it as above). The angle denoted ϕ in the figure is the angle between the vector M_1a and the horizontal plane, that is, the angle between M_1a and s_2. The usual definition of the cosine of an angle then tells us that $\langle s_2, M_1a \rangle$, the inner product of s_2 and M_1a, is

$$\langle s_2, M_1a \rangle = \|s_2\| \, \|M_1a\| \cos\phi. \tag{13.33}$$

If we write $a = M_1a + P_1a$, we see that $\langle s_2, M_1a \rangle = \langle s_2, a \rangle$, because s_1 is orthogonal to s_2. By (13.29), $\langle s_2, a \rangle = c_2$. If we recall further that s_2 is a unit vector, so that $\|s_2\| = 1$, (13.33) becomes

$$c_2 = \|M_1a\| \cos\phi.$$

It follows that the noncentrality parameter Λ, which we saw was equal to c_2^2 in the present simple case, is given by a formula highly reminiscent of expression (12.23) for the case of tests in regression directions:

$$\Lambda = \|\boldsymbol{M}_1\boldsymbol{a}\|^2 \cos^2\phi. \tag{13.34}$$

The arguments presented above make no claim to rigor. In particular, we have ignored distinctions between quantities calculated for samples of some finite size and the limits to which they tend as the sample size tends to infinity. Despite these shortcomings, our discussion contains the heart of the matter. Formula (13.34), although derived only for one special case, is in fact valid generally, by which we mean that not only is the algebraic form of the formula correct in general, but also that it is proper to replace the random variables used in constructing the geometrical representation in Euclidean space by their probability limits. Thus the power of the classical tests is governed by the same considerations as the tests in regression directions treated in the last chapter. It depends on two things: the distance between the DGP and the null hypothesis, as measured by $\|\boldsymbol{M}_1\boldsymbol{a}\|$, and the "angle" between the vector $\boldsymbol{M}_1\boldsymbol{a}$, measuring the degree of falsehood of the null hypothesis, and the subspace $\boldsymbol{s}_2$ spanned by the directions corresponding to variations of the parameters of the (alternative) hypothesis. The intuition is identical to that presented in the last chapter. A full mathematical treatment is, however, beyond the scope of this book. Interested readers are referred to Davidson and MacKinnon (1987) and to some of the related references cited in Section 13.8.

13.4 Classical Tests and Linear Regression Models

We saw in Section 8.10 that ML estimates of the parameters of the regression function in a nonlinear regression model are identical to NLS estimates if one makes the assumption that the error terms are normally distributed. A fortiori, this result is also true for linear regression models. It is therefore of interest to compare t and F statistics for testing linear restrictions on linear regression models, for which under classical conditions the exact finite-sample distributions are known, with the three classical test statistics, for which in general only the asymptotic distribution is known. It turns out that we can say a good deal more about the relationships among the three classical tests when we restrict attention to linear restrictions on linear models.

The restricted and unrestricted models, first encountered as (3.18) and (3.19), are

$$\boldsymbol{y} = \boldsymbol{X}_1\boldsymbol{\beta}_1 + \boldsymbol{u} \quad \text{and} \tag{13.35}$$

$$\boldsymbol{y} = \boldsymbol{X}_1\boldsymbol{\beta}_1 + \boldsymbol{X}_2\boldsymbol{\beta}_2 + \boldsymbol{u}, \tag{13.36}$$

where $\boldsymbol{X}_1$ is $n \times (k-r)$ and $\boldsymbol{X}_2$ is $n \times r$. Since we are concerned with ML estimation, we now assume that $\boldsymbol{u} \sim N(\boldsymbol{0}, \sigma^2\mathbf{I})$. The maintained hypothesis is that (13.36) is true, and the null hypothesis is that $\beta_2 = \mathbf{0}$. The standard F test, or the t test in the event that $r = 1$, was discussed in Section 3.5 and will be used as a basis of comparison with the three classical test statistics. In the notation of Chapter 3, the F statistic can be written as

$$F = \frac{n-k}{r} \times \frac{\boldsymbol{y}^\top \boldsymbol{P}_{M_1 X_2} \boldsymbol{y}}{\boldsymbol{y}^\top \boldsymbol{M}_X \boldsymbol{y}}, \tag{13.37}$$

where we have used (3.21), (3.30), and (3.32) to obtain this expression. We now compare the LM, LR, and Wald statistics with this F statistic.

Asymptotically, r times the F statistic (13.37) is distributed as $\chi^2(r)$ under the null hypothesis. In fact, as we will shortly show, it tends to the same random variable as the three classical test statistics. It is entirely due to the presence of the parameter σ in the linear regression model that there is not perfect equality of rF and the three classical tests. Suppose that σ, instead of being an unknown parameter to be estimated, were in fact known. Then, for the case in which $\sigma = 1$ (an inconsequential restriction, since if we knew σ we could always renormalize the data), the loglikelihood function for the model (13.36) would be

$$\ell(\boldsymbol{y}, \boldsymbol{\beta}) = -\tfrac{n}{2}\log 2\pi - \tfrac{1}{2}(\boldsymbol{y} - \boldsymbol{X\beta})^\top(\boldsymbol{y} - \boldsymbol{X\beta}).$$

For given sample data $\boldsymbol{y}$ and $\boldsymbol{X}$, this is an exactly quadratic function of the vector $\boldsymbol{\beta}$. The results of Section 13.2 are therefore directly applicable, and it is easy to calculate the three statistics and show that they are all equal to rF.

We now return to the more interesting case in which σ is to be estimated. Let us begin with the LR statistic. It is convenient to express this statistic in terms of the concentrated loglikelihood function (8.82). For the unrestricted model (13.36), this concentrated loglikelihood function is

$$\hat{\ell} \equiv -\tfrac{n}{2}\log\big((\boldsymbol{y} - \boldsymbol{X}\hat{\boldsymbol{\beta}})^\top(\boldsymbol{y} - \boldsymbol{X}\hat{\boldsymbol{\beta}})\big) = -\tfrac{n}{2}\log(\boldsymbol{y}^\top\boldsymbol{M}_X\boldsymbol{y}),$$

apart from a constant term which is the same for the estimation of both (13.35) and (13.36) and which therefore disappears from the difference of loglikelihood functions used in the LR test. Here $\boldsymbol{X} \equiv [\boldsymbol{X}_1 \;\; \boldsymbol{X}_2]$ and $\boldsymbol{M}_X$ denotes the matrix that projects orthogonally onto $\mathcal{S}^\perp(\boldsymbol{X})$. For the restricted model (13.35), the concentrated loglikelihood function is

$$\tilde{\ell} \equiv -\tfrac{n}{2}\log\big((\boldsymbol{y} - \boldsymbol{X}_1\tilde{\boldsymbol{\beta}}_1)^\top(\boldsymbol{y} - \boldsymbol{X}_1\tilde{\boldsymbol{\beta}}_1)\big) = -\tfrac{n}{2}\log(\boldsymbol{y}^\top\boldsymbol{M}_1\boldsymbol{y}),$$

where $\boldsymbol{M}_1$ denotes the matrix that projects orthogonally onto $\mathcal{S}^\perp(\boldsymbol{X}_1)$. Thus the LR statistic is

$$LR = 2(\hat{\ell} - \tilde{\ell}) = n\log\left(\frac{\boldsymbol{y}^\top\boldsymbol{M}_1\boldsymbol{y}}{\boldsymbol{y}^\top\boldsymbol{M}_X\boldsymbol{y}}\right). \tag{13.38}$$

It is easy to show that

$$\boldsymbol{y}^\top \boldsymbol{M}_1 \boldsymbol{y} = \boldsymbol{y}^\top \boldsymbol{M}_X \boldsymbol{y} + \boldsymbol{y}^\top \boldsymbol{P}_{M_1 X_2} \boldsymbol{y}.$$

This decomposition, which was illustrated in Figure 1.7, says that the SSR from a regression of $\boldsymbol{y}$ on $\boldsymbol{X}_1$ is equal to the SSR from a regression of $\boldsymbol{y}$ on $\boldsymbol{X}_1$ and $\boldsymbol{X}_2$, plus the explained sum of squares from a regression of $\boldsymbol{y}$ (or, equivalently, $\boldsymbol{M}_1\boldsymbol{y}$) on $\boldsymbol{M}_1\boldsymbol{X}_2$. Hence we obtain from (13.38) that

$$LR = n \log\left(1 + \frac{\boldsymbol{y}^\top \boldsymbol{P}_{M_1 X_2} \boldsymbol{y}}{\boldsymbol{y}^\top \boldsymbol{M}_X \boldsymbol{y}}\right). \tag{13.39}$$

The relation between the F statistic (13.37) and the LR statistic (13.39) is therefore

$$LR = n \log\left(1 + \frac{rF}{n-k}\right). \tag{13.40}$$

For large n, *provided* that $F = O(1)$, we may Taylor expand the logarithm. This is clearly the case under the null hypothesis (13.35) and is in fact also the case under DGPs that drift to the null at a rate proportional to $n^{-1/2}$. The latter assertion is readily demonstrated in the case of a DGP that drifts in a regression direction, like (12.06), and can with some effort be shown to be true for more general types of drifting DGPs, such as (13.27). The result of the Taylor expansion is

$$LR = \left(\frac{n}{n-k}\right) rF + O(n^{-1}) = rF + O(n^{-1}),$$

which demonstrates that LR and rF are the same random variable asymptotically.

We next consider the Wald statistic, W. For the models (13.35) and (13.36) it is, by (13.05) and (13.13),

$$W = \hat{\boldsymbol{\beta}}_2^\top \left(\hat{\boldsymbol{I}}^{-1}\right)_{22}^{-1} \hat{\boldsymbol{\beta}}_2. \tag{13.41}$$

For the linear regression model (13.36), we have from (8.85) that the $(\boldsymbol{\beta}, \boldsymbol{\beta})$ block of $\boldsymbol{I}$, which is all we need given the block-diagonality property of (8.87), is given by

$$(\boldsymbol{I}_{\beta\beta})^{-1} = \sigma^2 \left(\boldsymbol{X}^\top \boldsymbol{X}\right)^{-1}.$$

Of course, σ^2 must be estimated; since we are in a maximum likelihood context, it makes sense to use the ML estimator

$$\hat{\sigma}^2 = \frac{1}{n} \boldsymbol{y}^\top \boldsymbol{M}_X \boldsymbol{y}.$$

By the FWL Theorem,

$$\begin{aligned}\hat{\boldsymbol{\beta}}_2 &= \left(\boldsymbol{X}_2^{\top}\boldsymbol{M}_1\boldsymbol{X}_2\right)^{-1}\boldsymbol{X}_2^{\top}\boldsymbol{M}_1\boldsymbol{y} \quad \text{and} \\ \left((\boldsymbol{X}^{\top}\boldsymbol{X})^{-1}\right)_{22} &= \left(\boldsymbol{X}_2^{\top}\boldsymbol{M}_1\boldsymbol{X}_2\right)^{-1}.\end{aligned}$$

Thus (13.41) becomes

$$W = n\left(\frac{\boldsymbol{y}^{\top}\boldsymbol{M}_1\boldsymbol{X}_2(\boldsymbol{X}_2^{\top}\boldsymbol{M}_1\boldsymbol{X}_2)^{-1}\boldsymbol{X}_2^{\top}\boldsymbol{M}_1\boldsymbol{y}}{\boldsymbol{y}^{\top}\boldsymbol{M}_X\boldsymbol{y}}\right) = n\left(\frac{\boldsymbol{y}^{\top}\boldsymbol{P}_{M_1X_2}\boldsymbol{y}}{\boldsymbol{y}^{\top}\boldsymbol{M}_X\boldsymbol{y}}\right).$$

From (13.37) and (13.39), we obtain

$$W = \left(\frac{rn}{n-k}\right)F; \quad LR = n\log\left(1+\frac{W}{n}\right). \tag{13.42}$$

Since W is equal to $n/(n-k)$ times rF, it is evident that

$$W = rF + O(n^{-1}).$$

Finally, we turn to the LM statistic. We first observe from (8.83) that the gradient with respect to the regression parameters $\boldsymbol{\beta}$ of the loglikelihood function for a linear regression model with normal errors is

$$\boldsymbol{g}(\boldsymbol{y},\boldsymbol{\beta},\sigma) = \frac{1}{\sigma^2}\sum_{t=1}^{n}\boldsymbol{X}_t^{\top}(y_t - \boldsymbol{X}_t\boldsymbol{\beta}) = \sigma^{-2}\boldsymbol{X}^{\top}(\boldsymbol{y}-\boldsymbol{X}\boldsymbol{\beta}).$$

Thus, from (13.03), the LM statistic is

$$\begin{aligned}LM &= \tilde{\boldsymbol{g}}_2^{\top}\left(\tilde{\boldsymbol{I}}^{-1}\right)_{22}\tilde{\boldsymbol{g}}_2 \\ &= \tilde{\sigma}^{-4}(\boldsymbol{y}-\boldsymbol{X}\tilde{\boldsymbol{\beta}})^{\top}\boldsymbol{X}_2\left(\tilde{\sigma}^2(\boldsymbol{X}_2^{\top}\boldsymbol{M}_1\boldsymbol{X}_2)^{-1}\right)\boldsymbol{X}_2^{\top}(\boldsymbol{y}-\boldsymbol{X}\tilde{\boldsymbol{\beta}}).\end{aligned} \tag{13.43}$$

Since the LM test is based on the restricted model (13.35), we use the ML estimate of σ from that model:

$$\tilde{\sigma}^2 = \frac{1}{n}\boldsymbol{y}^{\top}\boldsymbol{M}_1\boldsymbol{y}.$$

Substituting this into (13.43), we see that

$$\begin{aligned}LM &= n\left(\frac{\boldsymbol{y}^{\top}\boldsymbol{M}_1\boldsymbol{X}_2(\boldsymbol{X}_2^{\top}\boldsymbol{M}_1\boldsymbol{X}_2)^{-1}\boldsymbol{X}_2^{\top}\boldsymbol{M}_1\boldsymbol{y}}{\boldsymbol{y}^{\top}\boldsymbol{M}_1\boldsymbol{y}}\right) \\ &= n\left(\frac{\boldsymbol{y}^{\top}\boldsymbol{P}_{M_1X_2}\boldsymbol{y}/\boldsymbol{y}^{\top}\boldsymbol{M}_X\boldsymbol{y}}{1+\boldsymbol{y}^{\top}\boldsymbol{P}_{M_1X_2}\boldsymbol{y}/\boldsymbol{y}^{\top}\boldsymbol{M}_X\boldsymbol{y}}\right) \\ &= n\left(\frac{rF}{n-k+rF}\right).\end{aligned} \tag{13.44}$$

For large n, a Taylor expansion yields

$$LM = rF + O(n^{-1}).$$

The most important conclusion of this analysis is that all the classical test statistics are functions *only* of the standard F statistic and the integers n, k, and r. Thus, if one computes F, the statistics LM, W, and LR can be obtained directly from (13.44), (13.42), and (13.40). If the classical regularity conditions hold, so that under the null hypothesis F has exactly its namesake distribution, the *exact* finite-sample distributions of LM, W, and LR can be calculated by use of these formulas. However, these exact distributions are *not* the same as the asymptotic distribution, which is (central) chi-squared with r degrees of freedom.

For linear regression models, with or without normal errors, there is of course no need to look at LM, W, and LR at all, since no information is gained from doing so over and above what is already contained in F. Nevertheless, since applied workers often find it convenient to use one of these classical test statistics, it is worth discussing one problem that can arise when they are used. Each of the classical test statistics will typically be compared, for the purposes of inference, with the asymptotic chi-squared distribution. Since the three of them are numerically different, different inferences may well be drawn when different classical tests are employed. This difficulty, often referred to as a **conflict among different testing criteria**, is frequently compounded by the diversity of ways of calculating even just one of the classical statistics, as we will discuss in the next section. The issue of conflicts among different testing criteria is one that has been well discussed in the econometrics literature. The matter seems to have been raised by Savin (1976) and Berndt and Savin (1977); it was exposited and extended by Breusch (1979). See also Evans and Savin (1982) and Vandaele (1981).

For the case of linear regression models (including the GNR and the artificial regressions for ML that we will shortly introduce), and in fact somewhat more generally, there are inequality relations that hold among LM, W, and LR. These inequalities are as follows:

$$W > LR > LM.$$

This result follows directly from (13.40), (13.42), and (13.44), along with the following standard inequalities for $x > 0$:

$$x > \log(1 + x) > \frac{x}{1 + x}. \tag{13.45}$$

These standard inequalities are easy to demonstrate. The first follows from the result that

$$e^x = 1 + x + \frac{\delta x^2}{2!} > 1 + x, \tag{13.46}$$

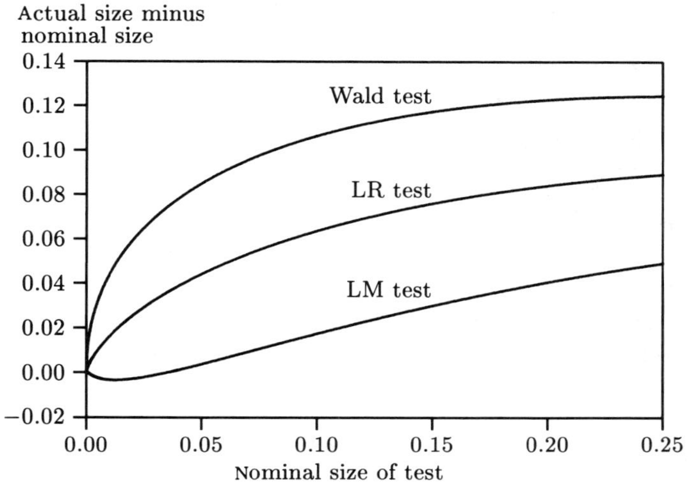

Figure 13.5 Differences between actual and nominal test size

for some δ between 0 and 1. The equality here is a consequence of Taylor's Theorem. Taking the logarithm of both sides of (13.46) then yields the first inequality of (13.45). For the second inequality, one can replace x by $-y$ in (13.46) to obtain the result that $e^{-y} > 1 - y$. Taking logarithms yields

$$-\log(1 - y) > y. \tag{13.47}$$

Setting $y = x/(1 + x)$ in (13.47) then yields the desired inequality.

One inevitably commits an error if one compares one of the classical test statistics with its nominal asymptotic distribution in a finite sample. As an example, we show in Figure 13.5 a plot of the actual size, computed from the critical points of the $F(1, 25)$ distribution, of tests that use LM, LR, and W as a function of the nominal size given by the asymptotic $\chi^2(1)$ distribution. The inequality $W > LR > LM$ is very evident in the figure, and both LR and W are seen to overreject quite severely.

All of the results presented in this section so far seem to lead to a reasonably clear conclusion. Whenever a hypothesis test is carried out by use of a linear regression, the easiest and often most satisfactory form of test statistic to use is the F test or, in one-dimensional cases, the t test. All the other test statistics that we have so far considered are functions of the F or t statistic, are asymptotically equivalent under the null and under DGPs that drift to the null at a rate proportional to $n^{-1/2}$, but can in finite samples have distributions disturbingly far from the nominal asymptotic one.

13.5 ALTERNATIVE COVARIANCE MATRIX ESTIMATORS

To calculate both LM and Wald tests, one has to employ some estimator of the information matrix, $\mathfrak{I}_0$. So far we have supposed, at least implicitly, that the information matrix $\mathfrak{I}(\boldsymbol{\theta})$ is known as a function of the parameter vector and is then simply evaluated at $\hat{\boldsymbol{\theta}}$ in the case of the Wald test or $\tilde{\boldsymbol{\theta}}$ in the case of the LM test. This is certainly true for linear regression models, where the information matrix does not even depend on the parameters of the regression function. In that case, as we saw in the last section, only the choice of $\hat{\sigma}^2$ or $\tilde{\sigma}^2$ distinguishes the Wald test from the LM test.

In general, however, as we saw in Section 8.6, it is unrealistic to suppose that the information matrix is known in an explicit analytic form. When it is not, it becomes necessary to use one of what may be a wide variety of estimators of $\mathfrak{I}_0$. Provided that the chosen estimator is consistent, none of the asymptotic results so far established is affected by this choice. However, the finite-sample behavior of the tests may well depend on what estimator is used. When different variants of the LM or Wald test, based on different estimators of the information matrix, are used in finite samples, there is the possibility that test results may conflict. Of course, this problem does not occur with the LR test, since it does not employ an estimator of the information matrix.

Another possible source of conflict among different tests appears when we consider how the classical tests behave under reparametrizations of the null or alternative hypothesis. We will look at reparametrizations in more detail in the next section. In this section, however, we will see that, even if we decide on an information matrix estimator, the LM and Wald tests are not invariant under model reparametrization for all such estimators.

We will now illustrate these problems in the context of an example, which, although very simple, exhibits most of the points at issue. The example is a model in which one wishes to estimate the variance σ^2 of a set of n.i.d. random variables with *known* mean which can, without loss of generality, be taken as zero. The contribution to the loglikelihood function from one observation is

$$\ell_t(y_t, \sigma^2) = -\tfrac{1}{2}\log(2\pi\sigma^2) - \frac{y_t^2}{2\sigma^2},$$

and the loglikelihood function for a sample of size n is

$$\ell(\boldsymbol{y}, \sigma^2) = -\tfrac{n}{2}\log(2\pi\sigma^2) - \frac{1}{2\sigma^2}\sum_{t=1}^{n} y_t^2. \tag{13.48}$$

This model has just one parameter, which would normally be taken as either σ or σ^2. However, it is of interest to consider a third parametrization. Suppose that $\tau \equiv \log\sigma$ is the parameter of this model. Then the loglikelihood function becomes

$$\ell(\boldsymbol{y}, \tau) = -\tfrac{n}{2}\log(2\pi) - n\tau - \tfrac{1}{2}e^{-2\tau}\sum_{t=1}^{n} y_t^2, \tag{13.49}$$

from which we may derive that

$$e^{2\hat{\tau}} = \hat{\sigma}^2 = \frac{1}{n}\sum_{t=1}^{n} y_t^2. \tag{13.50}$$

For this parametrization, the information matrix, which has only one element, is constant and equal to 2:

$$\mathfrak{I} = -\frac{1}{n}E(D_\tau^2 \ell) = \frac{2}{n}\sum_{t=1}^{n} e^{-2\tau}E(y_t^2) = 2.$$

Notice that, although $\mathfrak{I}$ is constant, the loglikelihood function is *not* a quadratic function of τ. We now consider various classical tests for the null hypothesis that $\tau = 0$, or, equivalently, that $\sigma^2 = 1$. Despite the simplicity of this example, we will uncover a bewildering variety of test statistics.

Initially, we will work with the τ parametrization. It is not necessary to do any estimation at all in order to find restricted estimates, since $\tilde{\tau} = 0$. For the Wald and LR tests we need to find $\hat{\tau}$. From (13.50), it is

$$\hat{\tau} = \frac{1}{2}\log\left(\frac{1}{n}\sum_{t=1}^{n} y_t^2\right).$$

The restricted "maximum" of the loglikelihood function is just the value of the function at $\tau = 0$:

$$\tilde{\ell} = -\frac{n}{2}\log 2\pi - \frac{1}{2}\sum_{t=1}^{n} y_t^2 = -\frac{n}{2}\log 2\pi - \frac{n}{2}e^{2\hat{\tau}}. \tag{13.51}$$

Although this is the restricted maximum, it is convenient to express it, as we have done here, in terms of the unrestricted estimate, $\hat{\tau}$. The unrestricted maximum, $\hat{\ell}$, is given by

$$-\frac{n}{2}\log 2\pi - n\hat{\tau} - \frac{1}{2}e^{-2\hat{\tau}}\sum_{t=1}^{n} y_t^2 = -\frac{n}{2}\log 2\pi - n\hat{\tau} - \frac{n}{2}, \tag{13.52}$$

where the equality uses (13.50).

We may proceed at once to obtain the LR statistic, which is twice the difference between (13.52) and (13.51):

$$\begin{aligned} LR = 2(\hat{\ell} - \tilde{\ell}) &= n\big(e^{2\hat{\tau}} - 1 - 2\hat{\tau}\big) \\ &= 2n\hat{\tau}^2 + o(\hat{\tau}^2). \end{aligned} \tag{13.53}$$

The second line of (13.53) is a Taylor expansion of the statistic in powers of $\hat{\tau}$. This is of interest because, *under the null hypothesis*, we expect $\hat{\tau}$, which is both the estimate itself and the *difference* between the estimate and the true value of the parameter, to be of order $n^{-1/2}$. It follows that $2n\hat{\tau}^2$ will be of order unity and that higher terms in the expansion of the exponential function in (13.53) will be of lower order. Thus, if the various forms of the classical test do indeed yield asymptotically equal expressions, we may expect that the leading term of all of them will be $2n\hat{\tau}^2$.

Let us next consider the LM statistic. The essential piece of it is the derivative of the loglikelihood function (13.49) with respect to τ, evaluated at $\tau = 0$. We find that

$$\frac{\partial \ell}{\partial \tau} = -n + e^{-2\tau}\sum_{t=1}^{n} y_t^2 \quad \text{and} \quad \left.\frac{\partial \ell}{\partial \tau}\right|_{\tau=0} = n\big(e^{2\hat{\tau}} - 1\big). \tag{13.54}$$

If for the variance of $\partial\ell/\partial\tau$ we use n times the true, constant, value of the single element of the information matrix, 2, the LM statistic is the square of $(\partial\ell/\partial\tau)|_{\tau=0}$, given by (13.54), divided by $2n$:

$$LM_1 = \tfrac{n}{2}\big(e^{2\hat{\tau}} - 1\big)^2 = 2n\hat{\tau}^2 + o(\hat{\tau}^2).$$

This variant of the LM statistic has the same leading term as the LR statistic (13.53) but will of course differ from it in finite samples.

Instead of the true information matrix, an investigator might prefer to use the negative of the empirical Hessian to estimate the information matrix; see equations (8.47) and (8.49). Because the loglikelihood function is not exactly quadratic, this estimator does *not* coincide numerically with the true value. Since

$$\frac{\partial^2 \ell}{\partial \tau^2} = -2e^{-2\tau}\sum_{t=1}^{n} y_t^2, \tag{13.55}$$

which at $\tau = 0$ is $-2ne^{2\hat{\tau}}$, the LM test calculated in this fashion is

$$LM_2 = \tfrac{n}{2}e^{-2\hat{\tau}}\big(e^{2\hat{\tau}} - 1\big)^2 = 2n\hat{\tau}^2 + o(\hat{\tau}^2). \tag{13.56}$$

The leading term is as in LR and LM_1, but LM_2 will differ from both those statistics in finite samples.

Another possibility is to use the OPG estimator of the information matrix; see equations (8.48) and (8.50). This estimator is

$$\frac{1}{n}\sum_{t=1}^{n}\left(\frac{\partial \ell}{\partial \tau}\right)^2 = \frac{1}{n}\sum_{t=1}^{n}\big(y_t^2 e^{-2\tau} - 1\big)^2,$$

which, when evaluated at $\tau = 0$, is equal to

$$\frac{1}{n}\sum_{t=1}^{n}\big(y_t^2 - 1\big)^2.$$

This expression cannot even be expressed as a function of $\hat{\tau}$ alone. To obtain an expansion of the test statistic that makes use of it, we must make use of the property of the normal distribution which tells us that $E(y_t^4) = 3\sigma^4$, or, in terms of τ, $3e^{4\tau}$.[4] Using this property, we can invoke a law of large numbers and conclude that the OPG information matrix estimator is indeed equal to $2 + o(1)$ at $\tau = 0$. Thus the third variant of the LM test statistic is

$$LM_3 = \frac{n^2\left(e^{2\hat{\tau}} - 1\right)^2}{\sum_{t=1}^{n}\left(y_t^2 - 1\right)^2} = 2n\hat{\tau}^2 + o(\hat{\tau}^2).$$

Once again, the leading term is $2n\hat{\tau}^2$, but the form of LM_3 is otherwise quite different from that of LM_1 or LM_2.

Just as there are various forms of the LM test, so are there various forms of the Wald test. Any one of these may be formed by combining the unrestricted estimate $\hat{\tau}$ with some estimate of the information matrix, which in this case is actually a scalar. The simplest choice is just the true information matrix, that is, 2. With this we obtain

$$W_1 = 2n\hat{\tau}^2. \tag{13.57}$$

It is easy to see that W_2, which uses the empirical Hessian, is identical to W_1, because (13.55) evaluated at $\tau = \hat{\tau}$ is just $2n$. On the other hand, use of the OPG estimator yields

$$W_3 = \hat{\tau}^2 \sum_{t=1}^{n}\left(y_t^2 e^{-2\hat{\tau}} - 1\right)^2,$$

which is quite different from W_1 and W_2.

All of the above test statistics were based on τ as the single parameter of the model, but we could just as well use σ or σ^2 as the model parameter. Ideally, we would like test statistics to be invariant to such reparametrizations. The LR statistic is always invariant, since $\hat{\ell}$ and $\tilde{\ell}$ do not change when the model is reparametrized. But all forms of the Wald statistic, and some forms of the LM statistic, are in general not invariant, as we now illustrate.

Suppose we take σ^2 to be the parameter of the model. The information matrix is not constant in this new parametrization, and so we must evaluate it at the *estimate* $\hat{\sigma}^2$. It is easy to see that the information matrix, as a

[4] Note that it was *not* necessary to use special properties of the normal distribution in order to expand the previous statistics, which were in fact all functions of one and only one random variable, namely $\hat{\tau}$. In general, in less simple situations, this agreeable feature of the present example is absent and special properties must be invoked in order to discover the behavior of all the various test statistics.

function of σ^2, is $1/(2\sigma^4)$. If we use this expression for the information matrix, evaluated at $\hat{\sigma}^2$, the Wald test becomes

$$W_1 = \tfrac{n}{2}\hat{\sigma}^{-4}\left(\hat{\sigma}^2 - 1\right)^2 = \tfrac{n}{2}e^{-4\hat{\tau}}\left(e^{2\hat{\tau}} - 1\right)^2 = 2n\hat{\tau}^2 + o(\hat{\tau}^2).$$

Since this differs from (13.57), we have shown that different parametrizations lead to numerically different Wald statistics even if the true information matrix, evaluated at the MLE of the model parameter, is used in both cases.

As we will see in the next section, the LM test is invariant if it is based on the true information matrix evaluated at the MLE. But if some other information matrix estimator is used, the LM test can also be parametrization dependent. Suppose that we use the empirical Hessian. From (13.48), the first two derivatives of ℓ with respect to σ^2, evaluated at $\sigma^2 = 1$, are

$$\left.\frac{\partial \ell}{\partial \sigma^2}\right|_{\sigma^2=1} = -\tfrac{1}{2}\left(n - \sum_{t=1}^{n} y_t^2\right) = \tfrac{n}{2}\left(e^{2\hat{\tau}} - 1\right) \quad \text{and}$$

$$\left.\frac{\partial^2 \ell}{(\partial \sigma^2)^2}\right|_{\sigma^2=1} = \tfrac{n}{2}\left(1 - 2e^{2\hat{\tau}}\right).$$

From this, we find that the statistic LM_2 calculated as was (13.56) but for the σ^2 parametrization, is

$$LM_2 = \frac{n\left(e^{2\hat{\tau}} - 1\right)^2}{2\left(2e^{2\hat{\tau}} - 1\right)} = 2n\hat{\tau}^2 + o(\hat{\tau}^2). \tag{13.58}$$

The leading term is correct, as it must be, but (13.58) is numerically different from (13.56).

Plainly, there are still more forms of both the LM and Wald tests, some but not all of which will coincide with one of the versions we have already computed. The interested reader is invited to try out, for example, the effects of using σ itself, rather than σ^2, as the model parameter.

This example illustrates the fact that there may be many different classical tests, which are numerically different but asymptotically equivalent. The fact that there are so many different tests creates the problem of how to choose among them. One would prefer to use tests that are easy to compute and for which the finite-sample distribution is well approximated by the asymptotic distribution. Unfortunately, it frequently requires considerable effort to determine the finite-sample properties of asymptotic tests. Any method of analysis tends to be restricted to very special cases, such as the case of linear regression models with normal errors discussed in Section 13.4. One generally applicable approach is to use computer simulation (Monte Carlo experiments); see Chapter 21.

13.6 CLASSICAL TEST STATISTICS AND REPARAMETRIZATION

The idea of a **reparametrization** of a parametrized model was discussed at length in Section 8.3. We saw there that one of the properties of maximum likelihood estimation is its invariance under reparametrizations. Since the classical tests are undertaken in the context of maximum likelihood estimation, it might be expected, or at least hoped, that the classical test statistics would likewise be parametrization invariant. That is true for the LR statistic, since, as was shown in Chapter 8, the value of a maximized loglikelihood function is invariant to reparametrization. But the results of the last section have shown that it cannot be true in general for the other two classical tests. In this section, we discuss the effects of reparametrization on the classical test statistics in more detail. In particular, we endeavor to determine what ingredients of the LM and Wald tests, and what ingredients of various information matrix estimators, are or are not responsible for the parametrization dependence of so many of the possible forms of the classical tests. We believe that these are important topics. However, the discussion is necessarily quite detailed, and some readers may wish to skip this section on a first reading.

First of all, we must make it clear that when we speak of **invariance** we mean different things when we are discussing different quantities. For example, if a model is reparametrized by a mapping $\boldsymbol{\eta} : \Theta \to \Phi$, where $\boldsymbol{\theta}$ and $\boldsymbol{\phi}$ denote the parameter vectors under the two parametrizations, then by the invariance of the MLE under reparametrization it is certainly not meant that $\hat{\boldsymbol{\theta}} = \hat{\boldsymbol{\phi}}$, but rather that

$$\hat{\boldsymbol{\phi}} = \boldsymbol{\eta}(\hat{\boldsymbol{\theta}}). \tag{13.59}$$

The notation here was used previously in Chapter 8, around equation (8.23), and will be used again below. We must distinguish between quantities expressed in terms of the k-vector of parameters $\boldsymbol{\theta}$ and quantities expressed in terms of the k-vector of parameters $\boldsymbol{\phi}$. As in Chapter 8, we will use primes to denote quantities expressed in terms of $\boldsymbol{\phi}$.

For the maximized loglikelihood function, invariance means simply that

$$\ell(\hat{\boldsymbol{\theta}}) = \ell'(\hat{\boldsymbol{\phi}}).$$

Thus, when we speak of parameter estimates being invariant under reparametrization, we mean that (13.59) holds, whereas when we speak of maximized loglikelihood functions, or test statistics, we mean that the actual numerical value is unchanged when calculated using different parametrizations.

The Wald and LM tests are made up of ingredients that are vectors and matrices, unlike the LR test which just depends on two scalars. In order to determine whether or not scalar quantities that are defined in terms of vectors and matrices, such as the Wald and LM test statistics, are invariant, we must first determine how the vectors and matrices themselves are altered by a reparametrization. It can subsequently be worked out whether these alterations cancel out in the definition of the scalar. From the definitions (13.03) and (13.05) of the LM and Wald tests, it can be seen that the vectors and matrices that we need to examine are $\boldsymbol{g}(\boldsymbol{\theta})$, the gradient of the loglikelihood function, $\mathfrak{I}(\boldsymbol{\theta})$, the information matrix, $\boldsymbol{r}(\boldsymbol{\theta})$, the vector of restrictions, and $\boldsymbol{R}(\boldsymbol{\theta})$, the matrix of derivatives of the components of $\boldsymbol{r}(\boldsymbol{\theta})$.

We will consider a reparametrization in which the "new" parameter k–vector, $\boldsymbol{\phi}$, is related to the "old" parameter k–vector $\boldsymbol{\theta}$ by the mapping $\boldsymbol{\eta}$:

$$\boldsymbol{\phi} = \boldsymbol{\eta}(\boldsymbol{\theta}).$$

Therefore, as follows immediately from (8.23), the loglikelihood functions in the two parametrizations are related by

$$\ell'\big(\boldsymbol{y}, \boldsymbol{\eta}(\boldsymbol{\theta})\big) = \ell(\boldsymbol{y}, \boldsymbol{\theta}). \tag{13.60}$$

The gradient vector in the original θ parametrization is

$$\boldsymbol{g}(\boldsymbol{\theta}) \equiv D_\theta^{\top} \ell(\boldsymbol{y}, \boldsymbol{\theta}), \tag{13.61}$$

and in the ϕ parametrization it is

$$\boldsymbol{g}'\big(\boldsymbol{\eta}(\boldsymbol{\theta})\big) \equiv D_\phi^{\top} \ell'\big(\boldsymbol{y}, \boldsymbol{\eta}(\boldsymbol{\theta})\big). \tag{13.62}$$

The relation between $\boldsymbol{g}$ and $\boldsymbol{g}'$ is obtained by differentiating the defining identity (13.60) with respect to the components of $\boldsymbol{\theta}$ and using the chain rule:

$$D_\phi \ell'\big(\boldsymbol{\eta}(\boldsymbol{\theta})\big) D_\theta \boldsymbol{\eta}(\boldsymbol{\theta}) = D_\theta \ell(\boldsymbol{\theta}), \tag{13.63}$$

where we have suppressed the dependence on $\boldsymbol{y}$ for notational simplicity. Note that $D_\theta \boldsymbol{\eta}(\boldsymbol{\theta})$ is a $k \times k$ matrix with typical element

$$\frac{\partial \eta_i(\boldsymbol{\theta})}{\partial \theta_j}. \tag{13.64}$$

Let us denote this matrix, the Jacobian matrix associated with the reparametrization $\boldsymbol{\eta}$, as $\boldsymbol{J}(\boldsymbol{\theta})$. Then, from (13.63) and the definitions (13.61) and (13.62), we obtain

$$\boldsymbol{J}^{\top}(\boldsymbol{\theta}) \boldsymbol{g}'\big(\boldsymbol{\eta}(\boldsymbol{\theta})\big) = \boldsymbol{g}(\boldsymbol{\theta}). \tag{13.65}$$

This is the desired link between the gradients in the two parametrizations. Since $\boldsymbol{\eta}$ is an invertible mapping, it will almost always be true that its Jacobian $\boldsymbol{J}(\boldsymbol{\theta})$ is an invertible (that is, nonsingular) matrix for all $\boldsymbol{\theta} \in \Theta$. If so, then we can invert (13.65) so as to be able to express $\boldsymbol{g}'$ in terms of $\boldsymbol{g}$:

$$\boldsymbol{g}'\big(\boldsymbol{\eta}(\boldsymbol{\theta})\big) = \big(\boldsymbol{J}^{\top}(\boldsymbol{\theta})\big)^{-1} \boldsymbol{g}(\boldsymbol{\theta}). \tag{13.66}$$

But in general we are obliged to assume the nonsingularity of $\boldsymbol{J}(\boldsymbol{\theta})$ explicitly, because it is possible to find reparametrizations $\boldsymbol{\eta}$ the Jacobians of which are singular for some values of $\boldsymbol{\theta}$.[5] In such cases, either the reparametrization or its inverse is not smooth, in the sense of being continuously differentiable. Thus the results we are engaged in establishing at the moment will be true only for smooth reparametrizations that have smooth inverses.

For the information matrix $\mathfrak{I}(\boldsymbol{\theta})$, it is convenient to start from its definition, as expressed in equations (8.20), (8.21), and (8.22). From these equations, we may conclude that the information matrix for a sample of size n is

$$\boldsymbol{I}^n(\boldsymbol{\theta}) = E_\theta\big(\boldsymbol{g}(\boldsymbol{\theta})\boldsymbol{g}^\top(\boldsymbol{\theta})\big). \tag{13.67}$$

Then, from (13.65), we find that

$$E_\theta\big(\boldsymbol{g}\boldsymbol{g}^\top\big) = \boldsymbol{J}^\top E_\theta\Big(\boldsymbol{g}'\,(\boldsymbol{g}')^\top\Big)\boldsymbol{J},$$

where the unprimed quantities $\boldsymbol{g}$ and $\boldsymbol{J}$ are evaluated at $\boldsymbol{\theta}$, and primed quantities are evaluated at $\boldsymbol{\phi}$. It follows that

$$\boldsymbol{I}^n = \boldsymbol{J}^\top(\boldsymbol{I}^n)'\boldsymbol{J}.$$

Dividing by n and taking the limit as $n \to \infty$ gives the transformation rule for the information matrix:

$$\mathfrak{I} = \boldsymbol{J}^\top\mathfrak{I}'\,\boldsymbol{J}. \tag{13.68}$$

Under our assumption of the nonsingularity of $\boldsymbol{J}$, the inverse of this transformation rule is

$$\mathfrak{I}' = (\boldsymbol{J}^\top)^{-1}\,\mathfrak{I}\,\boldsymbol{J}^{-1}. \tag{13.69}$$

We are now ready to consider the LM statistic in the form (13.03), that is, the form in which the correct information matrix is used, evaluated at $\tilde{\boldsymbol{\theta}}$. This form of the test statistic is sometimes called the **efficient score** test statistic, by extension of the terminology in which the LM test is called the score test (see Section 8.9). In the ϕ parametrization, the efficient score form of the LM test becomes

$$\frac{1}{n}\big(\boldsymbol{g}'(\tilde{\boldsymbol{\phi}})\big)^\top\big(\mathfrak{I}'(\tilde{\boldsymbol{\phi}})\big)^{-1}\boldsymbol{g}'(\tilde{\boldsymbol{\phi}}), \tag{13.70}$$

where $\tilde{\boldsymbol{\phi}} \equiv \boldsymbol{\eta}(\tilde{\boldsymbol{\theta}})$ is, by the "invariance" of the MLE, the restricted MLE in the ϕ parametrization. Then if, as usual, $\tilde{\boldsymbol{g}}$ denotes $\boldsymbol{g}(\tilde{\boldsymbol{\theta}})$ and so forth, (13.70) becomes, by (13.66) and (13.69),

$$\frac{1}{n}\tilde{\boldsymbol{g}}^\top\tilde{\boldsymbol{J}}^{-1}\tilde{\boldsymbol{J}}\;\tilde{\mathfrak{I}}^{-1}\tilde{\boldsymbol{J}}^\top(\tilde{\boldsymbol{J}}^\top)^{-1}\tilde{\boldsymbol{g}} = \frac{1}{n}\tilde{\boldsymbol{g}}^\top\tilde{\mathfrak{I}}^{-1}\tilde{\boldsymbol{g}},$$

which is just the LM statistic (13.03) in the original θ parametrization. Thus we can conclude that the efficient score form of the LM test is indeed invariant

[5] For example, in the case of a scalar parameter θ, the invertible mapping that takes θ into θ^3 has a Jacobian of zero at $\theta = 0$.

under reparametrizations, since all the Jacobian factors have washed out of the final expression.

We next consider the LM statistic in the form in which the information matrix is estimated by means of the empirical Hessian, as in (13.56). The empirical Hessian can be written as

$$\boldsymbol{H}(\boldsymbol{\theta}) \equiv D^2\ell(\boldsymbol{\theta}) \tag{13.71}$$

in the θ parametrization and as

$$\boldsymbol{H}'(\boldsymbol{\phi}) \equiv D^2\ell'(\boldsymbol{\phi}) \tag{13.72}$$

in the ϕ parametrization. If we differentiate (13.63) once more with respect to $\boldsymbol{\theta}$, we obtain

$$D_\theta^\top\boldsymbol{\eta}(\boldsymbol{\theta})D^2_{\phi\phi}\ell'(\boldsymbol{\phi})D_\theta\boldsymbol{\eta}(\boldsymbol{\theta}) + \sum_{i=1}^{k}\frac{\partial\ell'(\boldsymbol{\phi})}{\partial\phi_i}D^2_{\theta\theta}\eta_i(\boldsymbol{\theta}) = D^2_{\theta\theta}\ell(\boldsymbol{\theta}).$$

Rearranging and using the definitions (13.71) and (13.72), this becomes

$$\boldsymbol{H}(\boldsymbol{\theta}) = \boldsymbol{J}^\top(\boldsymbol{\theta})\boldsymbol{H}'(\boldsymbol{\phi})\boldsymbol{J}(\boldsymbol{\theta}) + \sum_{i=1}^{k}\boldsymbol{g}'_i(\boldsymbol{\phi})D_\theta\boldsymbol{J}_{i.}(\boldsymbol{\theta}). \tag{13.73}$$

The notation used for the second term on the right-hand side above needs a little explanation. First, the whole term must be a $k \times k$ matrix in order to accord with the other terms in the equation; the individual summands in the term must therefore be $k \times k$ matrices also. Next, $\boldsymbol{g}'_i(\boldsymbol{\phi})$ is just the ith component of the gradient $\boldsymbol{g}'$, evaluated at $\boldsymbol{\phi}$, and so it is simply a scalar. It follows that $D_\theta\boldsymbol{J}_{i.}(\boldsymbol{\theta})$ must be a $k \times k$ matrix. If we recall that $\boldsymbol{J}(\boldsymbol{\theta})$ itself is a $k \times k$ matrix with typical element (13.64), we see that $\boldsymbol{J}_{i.}(\boldsymbol{\theta})$, the ith row of that matrix, is $1 \times k$. When each of the k elements of the row is differentiated with respect to the k components of $\boldsymbol{\theta}$, we finally obtain the $k \times k$ matrix $D_\theta\boldsymbol{J}_{i.}(\boldsymbol{\theta})$ with jl^{th} element given by

$$\frac{\partial \boldsymbol{J}_{ij}(\boldsymbol{\theta})}{\partial\theta_l}. \tag{13.74}$$

It can now be seen that the reason for the notational complexity is that there are three independently varying indices in the partial derivative (13.74).

The relation (13.73) for the Hessian would be perfectly analogous to the relation (13.68) for the information matrix if the awkward second term on the right-hand side of (13.73) were absent. Consequently, for reparametrizations which are such that this term vanishes, the LM statistic calculated with the empirical Hessian will be invariant. In general, however, this term will not vanish, and the LM statistic calculated with the empirical Hessian will not be invariant. There do exist reparametrizations for which the awkward term in (13.73) always vanishes, namely, **linear reparametrizations**. Indeed, if $\boldsymbol{\eta}$ is a linear mapping, all the second-order partial derivatives of the form (13.74) are zero. Notice that the parameters τ and σ^2 studied in the example of the preceding section are *not* linked by a linear relation.

The **leading-order term** in the asymptotic expansion of the LM statistic must of course be invariant to reparametrization by the result on asymptotic equivalence. That this is so can be seen by considering the orders of magnitude of the three terms in (13.73). Because the mapping $\boldsymbol{\eta}$ is independent of n, the matrix $\boldsymbol{J}$ and the derivatives of its elements are $O(1)$. The Hessians $\boldsymbol{H}$ and $\boldsymbol{H}'$ are $O(n)$, and the gradients $\boldsymbol{g}$ and $\boldsymbol{g}'$ are $O(n^{1/2})$. We see that the term responsible for the parametrization dependence of this form of the LM statistic is not of leading order asymptotically, being $O(n^{1/2})$, while the other term on the right-hand side of (13.73) is $O(n)$.

It is clear that the possible parametrization dependence of the LM test statistic is due solely to the choice of estimator for the information matrix. Thus the choice of a noninvariant information matrix estimator such as the empirical Hessian will induce parametrization dependence in a Wald statistic just as much as in an LM statistic. However, in the example of the preceding section, we saw that the Wald statistic could be parametrization dependent even if the actual information matrix, evaluated at the unrestricted MLE, was used. This turns out to be a general property of the Wald test: Any nonlinear reparametrization will lead to a different value for the test statistic, regardless of the information matrix estimator used.

The noninvariance of the Wald test has been the subject of a good deal of research. Articles by Gregory and Veall (1985, 1987) and Lafontaine and White (1986) led to a more detailed study by Phillips and Park (1988). It appears that, for a given data set and a given set of restrictions on a given unrestricted hypothesis, it is possible by suitable choice of parametrization to obtain *any* (nonnegative) numerical value for the Wald test of the restrictions. Although in most econometric contexts there are parametrizations that appear to be more *natural* than others, and although one might hope that use of these natural parametrizations would lead to more reliable inference than the use of less natural ones, there is little evidence that this hope is much more than wishful thinking once one leaves the context of linear regression models.

Let us now investigate the lack of invariance of Wald statistics a little more closely. It can be seen from the expressions (13.03), (13.05), and (13.06) for the three classical statistics that it is only in the Wald statistic W that the explicit form of the restrictions appears, through $\hat{\boldsymbol{r}}$ and $\hat{\boldsymbol{R}}$. If we suppose, as usual, that the two parameter vectors $\boldsymbol{\theta}$ and $\boldsymbol{\phi}$ correspond to the same DGP, so that $\boldsymbol{\phi} = \boldsymbol{\eta}(\boldsymbol{\theta})$, then the restrictions $\boldsymbol{r}(\boldsymbol{\theta}) = \mathbf{0}$ can be expressed in terms of $\boldsymbol{\phi}$ by the formula $\boldsymbol{r}'(\boldsymbol{\phi}) = \mathbf{0}$, where

$$\boldsymbol{r}'(\boldsymbol{\phi}) = \boldsymbol{r}(\boldsymbol{\theta}) = \boldsymbol{r}\big(\boldsymbol{\eta}^{-1}(\boldsymbol{\phi})\big). \tag{13.75}$$

Thus $\boldsymbol{r}'$ can be represented as the composition of the two mappings $\boldsymbol{r}$ and $\boldsymbol{\eta}^{-1}$:

$$\boldsymbol{r}' = \boldsymbol{r} \circ \boldsymbol{\eta}^{-1},$$

and (13.75) can be written equivalently as

$$\boldsymbol{r}(\boldsymbol{\theta}) = \boldsymbol{r}'\big(\boldsymbol{\eta}(\boldsymbol{\theta})\big). \tag{13.76}$$

The matrix $\boldsymbol{R}'(\boldsymbol{\phi})$ is the Jacobian matrix associated with the mapping $\boldsymbol{r}'$, and so by differentiating (13.76) with respect to $\boldsymbol{\theta}$ we obtain

$$\boldsymbol{R}(\boldsymbol{\theta}) \equiv D_{\theta}\boldsymbol{r}(\boldsymbol{\theta}) = D_{\theta}\boldsymbol{r}'\big(\boldsymbol{\eta}(\boldsymbol{\theta})\big) = D_{\phi}\boldsymbol{r}'(\boldsymbol{\phi})D_{\theta}\boldsymbol{\eta}(\boldsymbol{\theta}) = \boldsymbol{R}'(\boldsymbol{\phi})\boldsymbol{J}(\boldsymbol{\theta}), \tag{13.77}$$

by the chain rule and (13.64). Use of (13.76), (13.77), and (13.69) in expression (13.05) for W then gives the statistic for the ϕ parametrization:

$$\begin{aligned} W' &\equiv n(\hat{\boldsymbol{r}}')^{\top}\big(\hat{\boldsymbol{R}}'\,(\hat{\mathfrak{J}}')^{-1}(\hat{\boldsymbol{R}}')^{\top}\big)^{-1}\hat{\boldsymbol{r}}' \qquad (13.78)\\ &= n\hat{\boldsymbol{r}}^{\top}\big(\hat{\boldsymbol{R}}\hat{\boldsymbol{J}}^{-1}\hat{\boldsymbol{J}}\,\hat{\mathfrak{J}}^{-1}\hat{\boldsymbol{J}}^{\top}(\hat{\boldsymbol{J}}^{\top})^{-1}\hat{\boldsymbol{R}}^{\top}\big)^{-1}\hat{\boldsymbol{r}}\\ &= n\hat{\boldsymbol{r}}^{\top}\big(\hat{\boldsymbol{R}}\,\hat{\mathfrak{J}}^{-1}\hat{\boldsymbol{R}}^{\top}\big)^{-1}\hat{\boldsymbol{r}} = W, \end{aligned}$$

where primed quantities are evaluated at $\hat{\boldsymbol{\phi}}$ and unprimed ones at $\hat{\boldsymbol{\theta}}$.

So where is the problem? The statistic W looks invariant according to this calculation! The difficulty is that, precisely on account of the explicit appearance of $\boldsymbol{r}$ and $\boldsymbol{R}$ in W, it is possible to reparametrize, not only the model parameters $\boldsymbol{\theta}$ but also the actual restrictions. Suppose that we imagine changing the parameter of the example of the last section from σ^2 to σ. If the restriction $\sigma^2 = 1$ is reformulated according to (13.76), it becomes $\sigma^2 = \big(\sqrt{\sigma^2}\big)^2 = 1$. Similarly, if we write $\tau = \log\sigma$, the restriction is $e^{2\tau} = 1$. If we used the restriction in either of these forms, then W would indeed be invariant under the reparametrizations, by (13.78). But that is not what one would be likely to do. Usually the restriction would be written either as $\sigma = 1$ or as $\tau = 0$. Then, as we will now show, the statistic is no longer invariant.

The r restrictions $\boldsymbol{r}(\boldsymbol{\theta}) = \boldsymbol{0}$ can be expressed in a great many different ways. If $\boldsymbol{p}$ is any mapping from $\mathbb{R}^r$ to $\mathbb{R}^r$ that maps the origin and only the origin into the origin, then, for any $\boldsymbol{x} \in \mathbb{R}^r$, $\boldsymbol{p}(\boldsymbol{x}) = \boldsymbol{0}$ if and only if $\boldsymbol{x} = \boldsymbol{0}$. Thus the restrictions $\boldsymbol{r}(\boldsymbol{\theta}) = \boldsymbol{0}$ are completely equivalent to the restrictions $\boldsymbol{p}\big(\boldsymbol{r}(\boldsymbol{\theta})\big) = \boldsymbol{0}$. If we write $\boldsymbol{q}$ for the composition $\boldsymbol{p} \circ \boldsymbol{r}$, then $\boldsymbol{q}$ maps $\mathbb{R}^k$ into $\mathbb{R}^r$, and exactly the same subset of the parameter space Θ is defined by imposing $\boldsymbol{q}(\boldsymbol{\theta}) = \boldsymbol{0}$ as by imposing $\boldsymbol{r}(\boldsymbol{\theta}) = \boldsymbol{0}$. In this sense, we may call the restrictions $\boldsymbol{q}(\boldsymbol{\theta}) = \boldsymbol{0}$ a reparametrization of $\boldsymbol{r}(\boldsymbol{\theta}) = \boldsymbol{0}$.

In order to formulate a Wald statistic for these reparametrized restrictions, we need the Jacobian matrix of $\boldsymbol{q}$, which we will call $\boldsymbol{Q}$. It is

$$\boldsymbol{Q}(\boldsymbol{\theta}) \equiv D_{\theta}\boldsymbol{q}(\boldsymbol{\theta}) = D_{\theta}\big(\boldsymbol{p}(\boldsymbol{r}(\boldsymbol{\theta}))\big) = D_r\boldsymbol{p}\big(\boldsymbol{r}(\boldsymbol{\theta})\big)\,D_{\theta}\boldsymbol{r}(\boldsymbol{\theta}) = D_r\boldsymbol{p}\big(\boldsymbol{r}(\boldsymbol{\theta})\big)\boldsymbol{R}(\boldsymbol{\theta}).$$

Therefore, the Wald statistic, in obvious notation, is

$$\begin{aligned} W'' &\equiv n\hat{\boldsymbol{q}}^\top\big(\hat{\boldsymbol{Q}}\hat{\mathfrak{I}}^{-1}\hat{\boldsymbol{Q}}^\top)\big)^{-1}\hat{\boldsymbol{q}} \\ &= n\boldsymbol{p}^\top(\hat{\boldsymbol{r}})\big(D_r\boldsymbol{p}(\hat{\boldsymbol{r}})\hat{\boldsymbol{R}}\hat{\mathfrak{I}}^{-1}\hat{\boldsymbol{R}}^\top D_r^\top\boldsymbol{p}(\hat{\boldsymbol{r}})\big)^{-1}\boldsymbol{p}(\hat{\boldsymbol{r}}), \end{aligned} \tag{13.79}$$

which is not in general equal to the original statistic W or to the statistic $W' = W$ that we obtained in (13.78) when we reparametrized the model but not the restrictions.

There is again one important case for which W'' in (13.79) is equal to W, namely, the case of a nonsingular linear mapping $\boldsymbol{p}$. (Such a mapping automatically maps the origin and only the origin to the origin, of course.) If $\boldsymbol{p}$ is linear, then there is no actual difference between $\boldsymbol{p}$ itself and its Jacobian $D_r\boldsymbol{p}$. We may therefore write for any $\boldsymbol{\theta} \in \Theta$ that

$$\boldsymbol{p}\big(\boldsymbol{r}(\boldsymbol{\theta})\big) = D_r\boldsymbol{p}\big(\boldsymbol{r}(\boldsymbol{\theta})\big)\boldsymbol{r}(\boldsymbol{\theta}). \tag{13.80}$$

This is to be interpreted as saying that the r–vector $\boldsymbol{p}\big(\boldsymbol{r}(\boldsymbol{\theta})\big)$ is equal to the product of the $r \times r$ matrix $D_r\boldsymbol{p}\big(\boldsymbol{r}(\boldsymbol{\theta})\big)$ and the r–vector $\boldsymbol{r}(\boldsymbol{\theta})$. Use of (13.80) in (13.79) makes W'' coincide with W and W'.

Before concluding this section, we should note a further invariance property of the LM test, but of a rather different kind from those we have studied so far. This property, which was pointed out by Godfrey (1981), is quite particular to the LM test; there is nothing analogous for the LR and Wald tests. It turns out that, when a given null hypothesis is under test, exactly the same LM statistic may be obtained for two or more different alternative hypotheses if the latter are **locally equivalent**. We have already encountered an example of this phenomenon in Chapter 10, in which we saw that one and the same test statistic is generated when a regression model is tested, by means of a GNR, for the presence of either AR(p) or MA(p) errors. One important implication of local equivalence is the following. If two alternative hypotheses are locally equivalent, then for any drifting DGP that belongs to either alternative, any asymptotic test for which the explicit alternative is one of them will have an ARE of unity relative to any asymptotic test for which the explicit alternative is the other.

We now examine just what aspect of the different alternative hypotheses is responsible for this invariance of the LM statistic. Recall from (13.03) that an LM statistic is made up of two ingredients, namely, the gradient of the loglikelihood function and the information matrix, both evaluated at the restricted ML estimates. These estimates depend only on the null hypothesis under test and are therefore invariant to changes in the alternative hypothesis. Further, the information matrix is defined as the expectation of the outer product of the gradient with itself; see (13.67). Thus if, for a given sample, we test the same null hypothesis against two different alternatives, and the gradient turns out to be the same for both alternatives, then the whole LM statistic will be the same. This result assumes that we are using the efficient score form of the LM test. If we based the test on estimates of the information matrix, the two LM statistics might not be numerically the same, although they would still be the same asymptotically.

Geometrically, two different alternative hypotheses are locally equivalent if they **touch** at the null hypothesis. By this we mean not merely that the two alternative hypotheses yield the same values of their respective loglikelihood functions when restricted by the null hypothesis, as will always be the case, but also that the gradients of the two loglikelihood functions are the same, since the gradients are *tangents* to the two models that touch at the null model. In these circumstances, the two LM tests must be numerically identical.

What does it mean for two models to touch, or, to use the nongeometrical term for the property, to be locally equivalent? A circular definition would simply be that their gradients are the same at all DGPs at which the two models intersect. Statistically, it means that if one departs only slightly from the null hypothesis while respecting one of the two alternative hypotheses, then one departs from the other alternative hypothesis by an amount that is of the second order of small quantities. For instance, an AR(1) process characterized by a small autoregressive parameter ρ differs from some MA(1) process to an extent proportional only to ρ^2. To prove this formally would entail a formal definition of the distance between two DGPs, but our earlier circular definition is an operational one: If the gradient $\tilde{\boldsymbol{g}}^1$ calculated for the first alternative is the same as the gradient $\tilde{\boldsymbol{g}}^2$ for the second, then the two alternatives touch at the null. It should now be clear that this requirement is too strong: It is enough if the components of $\tilde{\boldsymbol{g}}^2$ are all linear combinations of those of $\tilde{\boldsymbol{g}}^1$ and vice versa. An example of this last possibility is provided by the local equivalence, around the null of white noise errors, of regression models with ARMA(p, q) errors on the one hand and with AR$(p + q)$ errors on the other; see Section 10.8. For more examples, see Godfrey (1981) and Godfrey and Wickens (1982).

Both the geometrical and algebraic aspects of the invariance of LM tests under local equivalence are expressed by means of one simple remark: The LM test can be constructed solely on the basis of the restricted ML estimates and the *first* derivatives of the loglikelihood function evaluated at those estimates. This implies that the LM test takes no account of the curvature of the alternative hypothesis near the null.

We may summarize the results of this section as follows:

1. The LR test depends only on two maximized loglikelihood functions. It therefore cannot depend either on the parametrization of the model or on the way in which the restrictions are formulated in terms of those parameters.
2. The efficient score form of the LM test is constructed out of two ingredients, the gradient and the information matrix, which do alter under

reparametrization, but in such a way that the test statistic itself is invariant, not only under reparametrizations but also under different, locally equivalent, choices of the alternative hypothesis. If the information matrix itself has to be estimated, then parametrization dependence may appear, as we saw when the information matrix was estimated using the empirical Hessian and a nonlinear reparametrization considered. However, the OPG information matrix estimator of (8.48) also transforms under reparametrizations in such a way as to leave the LM statistic invariant; it is a good exercise to show this.

3. The Wald test can be parametrization dependent for the same reason as the LM test but may in addition be so for a different reason, not directly through the model parameters but through the way in which they are used to formulate the restrictions.
4. If a reparametrization or reformulation of the restrictions is linear, it does not affect the value of any of the classical test statistics.

13.7 THE OUTER-PRODUCT-OF-THE-GRADIENT REGRESSION

We remarked in the introduction to this chapter that the Gauss-Newton regression is not generally applicable to models estimated by maximum likelihood. In view of the extreme usefulness of the GNR for computing test statistics in the context of nonlinear regression models, it is of much interest to see if other artificial regressions with similar properties are available in the context of models estimated by maximum likelihood.

One preliminary and obvious remark: No regression, artificial or otherwise, is needed to implement the LR test. Since any package capable of producing ML estimates will certainly also produce the maximized loglikelihood function, there can be no obstacle to performing an LR test unless there is some difficulty in estimating either the restricted or the unrestricted model. In many cases, there is no such difficulty, and then the LR test is almost always the procedure of choice. However, there are occasions when one of the two models is much easier to estimate than the other, and then one would wish to use either the LM or the Wald test to avoid the more difficult estimation. Another possibility is that the alternative hypothesis may be implicit rather than being associated with a well-defined parametrized model that includes the null hypothesis as a special case. We have seen in the context of the GNR that many diagnostic tests fall into this category. When the alternative hypothesis is implicit, one would almost always wish to use an LM test.

In the regression context, the GNR provides a means of computing test statistics based on the LM principle. In point of fact, as we saw in Section 6.7, it can be used to compute test statistics based on any root-n consistent estimates. We will now introduce a new artificial regression, called the **outer-product-of-the-gradient regression**, or the **OPG regression** for short, which can be used with any model estimated by maximum likelihood. The OPG regression was first used as a means of computing test statistics by Godfrey and Wickens (1981). This artificial regression, which is very easy indeed to set up for most models estimated by maximum likelihood, can be used for the same purposes as the GNR: verification of first-order conditions for the maximization of the loglikelihood function, covariance matrix estimation, one-step efficient estimation, and, of greatest immediate interest, the computation of test statistics.

Suppose that we are interested in the parametrized model (13.01). Let $\boldsymbol{G}(\boldsymbol{\theta})$ be the CG matrix associated with the loglikelihood function $\ell^n(\boldsymbol{\theta})$, with typical element

$$\boldsymbol{G}_{ti}(\boldsymbol{\theta}) \equiv \frac{\partial \ell_t(\boldsymbol{\theta})}{\partial \theta_i}; \quad t = 1, \ldots, n, \ \ i = 1, \ldots, k,$$

where k is the number of elements in the parameter vector $\boldsymbol{\theta}$. Then the OPG regression associated with the model (13.01) can be written as

$$\boldsymbol{\iota} = \boldsymbol{G}(\boldsymbol{\theta})\boldsymbol{c} + \text{residuals}. \tag{13.81}$$

Here $\boldsymbol{\iota}$ is an n–vector of which each element is unity and $\boldsymbol{c}$ is a k–vector of artificial parameters. The product of the matrix of regressors with the regressand is the gradient $\boldsymbol{g}(\boldsymbol{\theta}) \equiv \boldsymbol{G}^{\top}(\boldsymbol{\theta})\boldsymbol{\iota}$. The matrix of sums of squares and cross-products of the regressors, $\boldsymbol{G}^{\top}(\boldsymbol{\theta})\boldsymbol{G}(\boldsymbol{\theta})$, when divided by n, consistently estimates the information matrix $\mathfrak{I}(\boldsymbol{\theta})$. These two features are essentially all that is required for (13.81) to be a valid artificial regression.[6] As with the GNR, the regressors of the OPG regression depend on the vector $\boldsymbol{\theta}$. Therefore, before the artificial regression is run, these regressors must be evaluated at some chosen parameter vector.

One possible choice for this parameter vector is $\hat{\boldsymbol{\theta}}$, the ML estimator for the model (13.01). In this case, the regressor matrix is $\hat{\boldsymbol{G}} \equiv \boldsymbol{G}(\hat{\boldsymbol{\theta}})$ and the artificial parameter estimates, which we will denote by $\hat{\boldsymbol{c}}$, are identically zero:

$$\hat{\boldsymbol{c}} = \big(\hat{\boldsymbol{G}}^{\top}\hat{\boldsymbol{G}}\big)^{-1}\hat{\boldsymbol{G}}^{\top}\boldsymbol{\iota} = \big(\hat{\boldsymbol{G}}^{\top}\hat{\boldsymbol{G}}\big)^{-1}\hat{\boldsymbol{g}} = \mathbf{0}.$$

Since $\hat{\boldsymbol{g}}$ here is the gradient of the loglikelihood function evaluated at $\hat{\boldsymbol{\theta}}$, the last equality above is a consequence of the first-order conditions for the maximum of the likelihood. As with the GNR, then, running the OPG regression with $\boldsymbol{\theta} = \hat{\boldsymbol{\theta}}$ provides a simple way to test how well the first-order conditions are in fact satisfied by a set of estimates calculated by means of some computer program. The t statistics again provide the most suitable check. They should not exceed a number around 10^{-2} or 10^{-3} in absolute value if a good approximation to the maximum has been found.

[6] Precise conditions for a regression to be called "artificial" are provided by Davidson and MacKinnon (1990); see Section 14.4.

Since the estimates $\hat{\boldsymbol{c}}$ for regression (13.81) are zero when the regressors are $\hat{\boldsymbol{G}}$, those regressors have no explanatory power for $\boldsymbol{\iota}$, and the sum of squared residuals is therefore equal to the total sum of squares. Because the latter is

$$\boldsymbol{\iota}^\top\boldsymbol{\iota} = \sum_{t=1}^{n} 1 = n,$$

the ML estimate of the residual variance in (13.81) is just unity:

$$\frac{1}{n}\mathrm{SSR} = \frac{1}{n}\boldsymbol{\iota}^\top\boldsymbol{\iota} = \frac{1}{n}n = 1.$$

The OLS variance estimate, which is $\mathrm{SSR}/(n-k) = n/(n-k)$, is asymptotically equivalent to this, but it will simplify the exposition if we suppose that the ML estimate is used. The covariance matrix estimate for the vector $\hat{\boldsymbol{c}}$ from (13.81) is then

$$\big(\hat{\boldsymbol{G}}^\top\hat{\boldsymbol{G}}\big)^{-1}.$$

It is this expression that gives the OPG regression its name, for its inverse is precisely the OPG estimator of the information matrix; see (8.48) and (8.50).[7] It follows that, as with the GNR, n^{-1} times the covariance matrix estimator from the OPG regression is asymptotically equal to the covariance matrix of $n^{1/2}(\hat{\boldsymbol{\theta}} - \boldsymbol{\theta}_0)$.

The property just established is not the only one shared by the Gauss-Newton and OPG regressions. We will now establish two further properties of the OPG regression that are in fact shared by all regressions to which we give the name "artificial." The first of these properties is what allows one to use artificial regressions to perform one-step efficient estimation. According to this property, if the OPG regression (13.81) is evaluated at some parameter vector $\acute{\boldsymbol{\theta}}$ that is root-n consistent for $\boldsymbol{\theta}_0$, so that $\acute{\boldsymbol{\theta}} - \boldsymbol{\theta}_0 = O(n^{-1/2})$, then the artificial parameter estimates $\acute{\boldsymbol{c}}$ are such that

$$n^{1/2}\acute{\boldsymbol{c}} \overset{a}{=} n^{1/2}(\hat{\boldsymbol{\theta}} - \acute{\boldsymbol{\theta}}), \tag{13.82}$$

where $\hat{\boldsymbol{\theta}}$ is the ML estimator of $\boldsymbol{\theta}$.

The result (13.82) is important. Because of it, we can proceed in one step from any root-n consistent estimator $\acute{\boldsymbol{\theta}}$ to an estimator asymptotically equivalent to the asymptotically efficient estimator $\hat{\boldsymbol{\theta}}$. The one-step estimator $\grave{\boldsymbol{\theta}}$ defined by $\grave{\boldsymbol{\theta}} \equiv \acute{\boldsymbol{\theta}} + \acute{\boldsymbol{c}}$ has the property that

$$n^{1/2}(\grave{\boldsymbol{\theta}} - \boldsymbol{\theta}_0) = n^{1/2}(\hat{\boldsymbol{\theta}} - \boldsymbol{\theta}_0) + o(1), \tag{13.83}$$

[7] As we noted in Section 8.6, some authors refer to the OPG estimator of the information matrix as the BHHH estimator, after Berndt, Hall, Hall, and Hausman (1974), who advocated its use, although they did not explicitly make use of the OPG regression itself.

as can be seen directly from (13.82). Since the asymptotic equivalence of $\grave{\boldsymbol{\theta}}$ and $\hat{\boldsymbol{\theta}}$ requires the factors of $n^{1/2}$ that appear in (13.83), it can be seen why we wish to prove (13.82), with a factor of $n^{1/2}$ on each side of the equation, rather than the seemingly equivalent result that $\acute{\boldsymbol{c}} \stackrel{a}{=} \hat{\boldsymbol{\theta}} - \acute{\boldsymbol{\theta}}$. Although this result is certainly true, it is weaker than (13.82), because it merely implies that $\hat{\boldsymbol{\theta}} - \acute{\boldsymbol{\theta}} = o(1)$, while (13.82) implies that $\hat{\boldsymbol{\theta}} - \acute{\boldsymbol{\theta}} = o(n^{-1/2})$.

The proof of (13.82) is both simple and illuminating. A Taylor expansion of the gradient $\acute{\boldsymbol{g}} \equiv \boldsymbol{g}(\acute{\boldsymbol{\theta}})$ around $\boldsymbol{\theta}_0$ yields

$$n^{-1/2}\acute{\boldsymbol{g}} = n^{-1/2}\boldsymbol{g}_0 + n^{-1}\boldsymbol{H}(\boldsymbol{\theta}_0)n^{1/2}(\acute{\boldsymbol{\theta}} - \boldsymbol{\theta}_0) + O(n^{-1/2}),$$

where, as usual, $\boldsymbol{H}(\boldsymbol{\theta})$ denotes the Hessian of the loglikelihood function $\ell(\boldsymbol{\theta})$. If now we expand $\hat{\boldsymbol{g}}$, which is zero by the first-order conditions for a maximum of the likelihood at $\hat{\boldsymbol{\theta}}$, we obtain

$$\mathbf{0} = n^{-1/2}\boldsymbol{g}_0 + n^{-1}\boldsymbol{H}(\boldsymbol{\theta}_0)n^{1/2}(\hat{\boldsymbol{\theta}} - \boldsymbol{\theta}_0) + O(n^{-1/2}).$$

On subtracting the last two equations and noting that $\acute{\boldsymbol{g}} = \acute{\boldsymbol{G}}^{\top}\boldsymbol{\iota}$, we find that

$$n^{-1/2}\acute{\boldsymbol{G}}^{\top}\boldsymbol{\iota} = n^{-1}\boldsymbol{H}(\boldsymbol{\theta}_0)n^{1/2}(\acute{\boldsymbol{\theta}} - \hat{\boldsymbol{\theta}}) + O(n^{-1/2}). \tag{13.84}$$

By the information matrix equality, $n^{-1}\boldsymbol{H}(\boldsymbol{\theta}_0) = -\mathfrak{I}_0 + o(1)$. Since, by the consistency of $\acute{\boldsymbol{\theta}}$, we have $n^{-1}\acute{\boldsymbol{G}}^{\top}\acute{\boldsymbol{G}} = \mathfrak{I}_0 + o(1)$, we may replace $n^{-1}\boldsymbol{H}(\boldsymbol{\theta}_0)$ in (13.84) by $-n^{-1}\acute{\boldsymbol{G}}^{\top}\acute{\boldsymbol{G}}$ to obtain

$$n^{-1/2}\acute{\boldsymbol{G}}^{\top}\boldsymbol{\iota} = \big(n^{-1}\acute{\boldsymbol{G}}^{\top}\acute{\boldsymbol{G}}\big)n^{1/2}(\hat{\boldsymbol{\theta}} - \acute{\boldsymbol{\theta}}) + o(1).$$

The result (13.82) now follows directly on premultiplication by $(n^{-1}\acute{\boldsymbol{G}}^{\top}\acute{\boldsymbol{G}})^{-1}$.

A second property of artificial regressions is the one that permits their use in the calculation of LM statistics. When an artificial regression that satisfies this property is evaluated at a root-n consistent $\acute{\boldsymbol{\theta}}$, n times the uncentered R^2 calculated from it is asymptotically equal to

$$\frac{1}{n}\acute{\boldsymbol{g}}^{\top}\mathfrak{I}_0^{-1}\acute{\boldsymbol{g}}.$$

This result is very easy to prove for the OPG regression. The R^2 is the ratio of the explained sum of squares (ESS) to the total sum of squares (TSS), and so nR^2 is the ratio ESS/(TSS/n). We saw that TSS/n was equal to 1. This means that nR^2 is just the explained sum of squares:

$$nR^2 = \boldsymbol{\iota}^{\top}\acute{\boldsymbol{G}}\big(\acute{\boldsymbol{G}}^{\top}\acute{\boldsymbol{G}}\big)^{-1}\acute{\boldsymbol{G}}^{\top}\boldsymbol{\iota} = \frac{1}{n}\acute{\boldsymbol{g}}^{\top}\big(n^{-1}\acute{\boldsymbol{G}}^{\top}\acute{\boldsymbol{G}}\big)^{-1}\acute{\boldsymbol{g}}. \tag{13.85}$$

This completes the proof, since $n^{-1}\acute{\boldsymbol{G}}^{\top}\acute{\boldsymbol{G}} \rightarrow \mathfrak{I}_0$.

Using this result, we see that the LM statistic (13.03) can be calculated very easily. Many regression packages do not print the uncentered R^2, and some do not even print the explained sum of squares. Therefore, the two most natural ways to compute the LM test statistic may not be available. Since all packages print the sum of squared residuals, a third way is to use the fact that, for the OPG regression,

$$nR^2 = \text{ESS} = n - \text{SSR}.$$

To compute the LM statistic, then, one can simply calculate n minus the sum of squared residuals for the OPG regression evaluated at $\tilde{\boldsymbol{\theta}}$. Although this is the simplest way in which a statistic based on the LM principle can be computed by means of an OPG regression, it is not the only one. For example, if there is only one restriction and $\tilde{\boldsymbol{G}}$ can be partitioned so that $k-1$ columns are orthogonal to $\boldsymbol{\iota}$ and one column is not orthogonal to it, one can use an ordinary t test on the coefficient of the latter. The details, which follow those for the GNR very closely, are left as an exercise for the reader.

It is also possible to use an OPG regression, or indeed any artificial regression that satisfies the above properties, to compute $\boldsymbol{C(\alpha)}$ **test statistics**, based on any root-n consistent estimates that satisfy the null hypothesis. The $C(\alpha)$ test, which we mentioned in Chapters 6, 7, and 11, was first proposed by Neyman (1959); see Neyman and Scott (1966), Moran (1970), Breusch and Pagan (1980), Smith (1987), and Dagenais and Dufour (1991) for more detailed discussions and applications. The $C(\alpha)$ test can be regarded as a classical test. Although it is much less well known than the LM, LR, and Wald tests, it is, as we will now demonstrate, asymptotically equivalent to them.

Suppose that $\boldsymbol{\theta}$ is partitioned as $[\boldsymbol{\theta}_1 \vdots \boldsymbol{\theta}_2]$, that the gradient vector $\boldsymbol{g}(\boldsymbol{\theta})$ and information matrix $\mathcal{I}(\boldsymbol{\theta})$ are partitioned in the same way, and that the restrictions on $\boldsymbol{\theta}$ can be written as $\boldsymbol{\theta}_2 = \boldsymbol{\theta}_2^0$. Then the $C(\alpha)$ test statistic can be written in several ways, of which the simplest is

$$C(\alpha) \equiv \frac{1}{n}\acute{\boldsymbol{g}}^{\top}\acute{\mathcal{I}}^{-1}\acute{\boldsymbol{g}} - \frac{1}{n}\acute{\boldsymbol{g}}_1^{\top}\big(\acute{\mathcal{I}}_{11}\big)^{-1}\acute{\boldsymbol{g}}_1, \tag{13.86}$$

where all quantities are evaluated at root-n consistent estimates $\acute{\boldsymbol{\theta}} = [\acute{\boldsymbol{\theta}}_1 \vdots \boldsymbol{\theta}_2^0]$ that satisfy the null hypothesis.

That the $C(\alpha)$ test is asymptotically equivalent to the other classical tests is easily seen. First-order Taylor-series approximations of $n^{-1/2}\boldsymbol{g}(\acute{\boldsymbol{\theta}})$ and $n^{-1/2}\boldsymbol{g}_1(\acute{\boldsymbol{\theta}})$ around $\tilde{\boldsymbol{\theta}}$, combined with the information matrix equality, yield the results

$$n^{-1/2}\boldsymbol{g}(\acute{\boldsymbol{\theta}}) \overset{a}{=} n^{-1/2}\boldsymbol{g}(\tilde{\boldsymbol{\theta}}) - \mathcal{I}(\boldsymbol{\theta}_0)n^{1/2}(\acute{\boldsymbol{\theta}} - \tilde{\boldsymbol{\theta}}) \quad \text{and} \tag{13.87}$$

$$n^{-1/2}\boldsymbol{g}_1(\acute{\boldsymbol{\theta}}) \overset{a}{=} -\,\mathcal{I}_{11}(\boldsymbol{\theta}_0)n^{1/2}(\acute{\boldsymbol{\theta}}_1 - \tilde{\boldsymbol{\theta}}_1). \tag{13.88}$$

In deriving (13.88), we have used the first-order conditions for $\tilde{\boldsymbol{\theta}}_1$ and the fact that $\acute{\boldsymbol{\theta}}_2 = \tilde{\boldsymbol{\theta}}_2$. Using (13.87), the first term in (13.86) is

$$\begin{aligned}\frac{1}{n}\acute{\boldsymbol{g}}^\top\acute{\mathcal{I}}^{-1}\acute{\boldsymbol{g}} &\stackrel{a}{=} \big(n^{-1/2}\tilde{\boldsymbol{g}} - \mathcal{I}n^{1/2}(\acute{\boldsymbol{\theta}} - \tilde{\boldsymbol{\theta}})\big)^\top\mathcal{I}^{-1}\big(n^{-1/2}\tilde{\boldsymbol{g}} - \mathcal{I}n^{1/2}(\acute{\boldsymbol{\theta}} - \tilde{\boldsymbol{\theta}})\big)\\ &= \frac{1}{n}\tilde{\boldsymbol{g}}^\top\mathcal{I}^{-1}\tilde{\boldsymbol{g}} + n(\acute{\boldsymbol{\theta}}_1 - \tilde{\boldsymbol{\theta}}_1)^\top\mathcal{I}_{11}(\acute{\boldsymbol{\theta}}_1 - \tilde{\boldsymbol{\theta}}_1).\end{aligned} \tag{13.89}$$

There are only two terms in the second line of (13.89), because the other two terms involve inner products of $\tilde{\boldsymbol{g}}$ with $\acute{\boldsymbol{\theta}} - \tilde{\boldsymbol{\theta}}$. Since $\tilde{\boldsymbol{g}}_1 = \mathbf{0}$, those inner products are zero. Using (13.88) and the second line of (13.89), we have

$$\frac{1}{n}\acute{\boldsymbol{g}}^\top\acute{\mathcal{I}}^{-1}\acute{\boldsymbol{g}} \stackrel{a}{=} \frac{1}{n}\tilde{\boldsymbol{g}}^\top\mathcal{I}^{-1}\tilde{\boldsymbol{g}} + \frac{1}{n}\acute{\boldsymbol{g}}_1^\top(\mathcal{I}_{11})^{-1}\acute{\boldsymbol{g}}_1. \tag{13.90}$$

Since the second term in (13.86) is minus a consistent estimate of the second term in (13.90), it follows that

$$C(\alpha) \equiv \frac{1}{n}\acute{\boldsymbol{g}}^\top\acute{\mathcal{I}}^{-1}\acute{\boldsymbol{g}} - \frac{1}{n}\acute{\boldsymbol{g}}_1^\top(\acute{\mathcal{I}}_{11})^{-1}\acute{\boldsymbol{g}}_1 \stackrel{a}{=} \frac{1}{n}\tilde{\boldsymbol{g}}^\top\mathcal{I}^{-1}\tilde{\boldsymbol{g}}.$$

Thus we conclude that the $C(\alpha)$ statistic is asymptotically equivalent to the LM statistic and hence to all of the classical test statistics.

The test statistic (13.86) is the difference between two quadratic forms. In fact, it looks like the difference between two LM statistics. The first of these is asymptotically equal to nR^2 from the artificial regression

$$\boldsymbol{\iota} = \acute{\boldsymbol{G}}_1\boldsymbol{c}_1 + \acute{\boldsymbol{G}}_2\boldsymbol{c}_2 + \text{residuals}, \tag{13.91}$$

and the second is asymptotically equal to nR^2 from the artificial regression

$$\boldsymbol{\iota} = \acute{\boldsymbol{G}}_1\boldsymbol{c}_1 + \text{residuals}. \tag{13.92}$$

The R^2 from this regression would be zero if $\acute{\boldsymbol{\theta}} = \tilde{\boldsymbol{\theta}}$, by the first-order conditions for $\tilde{\boldsymbol{\theta}}$, but will generally not be zero for any other choice of $\acute{\boldsymbol{\theta}}$.

The test statistic (13.86) is asymptotically equal to n times the difference between the R^2's from (13.91) and (13.92). Thus we see that LM tests based on the OPG regression are just special cases of $C(\alpha)$ tests based on that regression. The difference is that, because nR^2 from (13.92) is generally not zero, one cannot simply use nR^2 from (13.91) as the test statistic in the more general case. The intuition that underlies this result is very simple. From (13.82), we see that the OLS estimates of $\boldsymbol{c}_2$ in (13.91) are asymptotically equivalent to the unrestricted ML estimates $\hat{\boldsymbol{\theta}}_2$ minus $\boldsymbol{\theta}_2^0$. Thus it is hardly surprising that a test for $\boldsymbol{c}_2 = \mathbf{0}$ in (13.91) should be equivalent to a classical test for $\boldsymbol{\theta}_2 = \boldsymbol{\theta}_2^0$.

As we noted in Section 6.7, it is possible to compute statistics based on the Wald principle using artificial regressions. We will refer to these as **Wald-like statistics**, because they are not in general numerically equal to Wald statistics calculated conventionally as in (13.05). They are of course *asymptotically* equal to the classical Wald test statistic and share with it the property of being based exclusively on the ML estimates of the unrestricted model. Unfortunately, they also share the property of being parametrization dependent. Consider the OPG regression corresponding to the unrestricted model evaluated at $[\hat{\boldsymbol{\theta}}_1 \vdots \boldsymbol{\theta}_2^0]$, a parameter vector which, by construction, satisfies the null hypothesis. This artificial regression is

$$\boldsymbol{\iota} = \boldsymbol{G}_1(\hat{\boldsymbol{\theta}}_1, \boldsymbol{\theta}_2^0)\boldsymbol{c}_1 + \boldsymbol{G}_2(\hat{\boldsymbol{\theta}}_1, \boldsymbol{\theta}_2^0)\boldsymbol{c}_2 + \text{residuals}. \tag{13.93}$$

This is just a special case of the $C(\alpha)$ regression (13.91), and so any asymptotically valid test of the artificial hypothesis $\boldsymbol{c}_2 = \boldsymbol{0}$ based on (13.93) provides a valid Wald-like test.

LM, $C(\alpha)$, and Wald-like tests based on the OPG regression are so simple that it seems inviting to suggest that all tests other than the LR test can most conveniently be computed by means of an OPG regression. However, as is clear from (13.85) for the LM test, all tests based on the OPG regression use the outer-product-of-the-gradient estimator of the information matrix. Although this estimator has the advantage of being parametrization independent, numerous Monte Carlo experiments have shown that its finite-sample properties are almost always very different from its nominal asymptotic ones unless sample sizes are very large, often on the order of many thousand. In particular, these experiments suggest that OPG tests often have a size far in excess of their nominal asymptotic size. True null hypotheses are rejected much too often, in some especially bad cases, almost all the time. See, among others, Davidson and MacKinnon (1983a, 1985c, 1992a), Bera and McKenzie (1986), Godfrey, McAleer, and McKenzie (1988), and Chesher and Spady (1991). Although some experiments have suggested that OPG-based tests have about as much power as other variants of the classical tests *if* a way can be found to correct for their size, no one has found any easy and convenient way to perform the necessary size correction.

In view of this rather disappointing feature of the OPG regression, we must conclude this section with a firm admonition to readers to use it with great care. In most cases, it is safe to conclude that a restriction is compatible with the data if a test statistic computed using the OPG regression fails to reject the null hypothesis. But it is generally not safe to conclude that a restriction is incompatible with the data if an OPG test statistic rejects the null, at least not for samples of any ordinary size. Of course, if something is known about the properties of the particular OPG test being used, perhaps as a result of Monte Carlo experiments, one may then be able to draw conclusions from an OPG test statistic that rejects the null.

However, the OPG regression would be important even if one never actually used it to calculate test statistics. Its use in *theoretical* asymptotic calculations can make such calculations much simpler than they might otherwise be. Moreover, as we will see in the next two chapters, there exist other artificial regressions, not quite so generally applicable as the OPG one perhaps, and not quite so utterly elementary to set up, but generally possessing much better finite-sample properties. Results that are true for the OPG regression are true for these other artificial regressions as well.

13.8 FURTHER READING AND CONCLUSION

The three classical tests, as the word "classical" implies, have a long history and have generated a great deal of literature; see Engle (1984) and Godfrey (1988) for references. In this chapter, we have tried to emphasize the common aspects of tests underlying the very considerable diversity of testing procedures and to emphasize the geometrical interpretation of the tests. A simpler discussion of the geometry of the classical tests may be found in Buse (1982). We have pointed out that there is a common asymptotic random variable to which all the classical test statistics tend as the sample size tends to infinity and that the distribution of this asymptotic random variable is chi-squared, central if the null hypothesis under test is true, and noncentral otherwise. The actual noncentrality parameter is a function of the drifting DGP considered as a model of the various possibilities that exist in the neighborhood of the null hypothesis. Because the mathematics involved is not elementary, we did not discuss the details of how this noncentrality parameter may be derived, but the intuition is essentially the same as for the case of nonlinear regression models discussed in Section 12.4.

The asymptotic properties of the classical tests under DGPs other than those satisfying the null hypothesis is studied in a well-known article of Gallant and Holly (1980) as well as in the survey article of Engle (1984). In these articles, only drifting DGPs that satisfied the alternative hypothesis were taken into account. The Gallant and Holly article provoked a substantial amount of further research. One landmark of the literature in which this research is reported is a paper by Burguete, Gallant, and Souza (1982), in which an ambitious project of unification of a wide variety of asymptotic methods is undertaken. Here, for the first time, drifting DGPs were considered which, although in the neighborhood of the null hypothesis, satisfied neither the null nor the alternative hypothesis. Subsequently, Newey (1985a) and Tauchen (1985) continued the investigation of this approach and were led to propose new tests and still more testing procedures (see Chapter 16). Our own paper (Davidson and MacKinnon, 1987) pursued the study of general local DGPs and was among the first to try to set the theory of hypothesis testing in a geometrical framework in such a way that "neighborhoods" of a null hypothesis could be formally defined and mentally visualized. The geometrical approach had been gaining favor with econometricians and, more particularly, statisticians for some time before this and had led to the syntheses found in Amari (1985) and Barndorff-Nielsen, Cox, and Reid (1986); see the survey article by Kass (1989). We should warn readers, however, that the last few references cited use mathematics that is far from elementary.

In many ways, the most intuitively satisfactory approach to testing is provided by the concept of artificial regressions. This concept, which we have been using since Chapter 6 and will develop further in the remainder of the book, supplies, as readers have perhaps already sensed, much of the intuition provided by higher-powered and more mathematically sophisticated analyses. It also provides simple ways to compute test statistics in practice.

TERMS AND CONCEPTS

- $C(\alpha)$ tests
- classical test statistics
- conflict among testing criteria
- efficient score form of LM statistic
- inner product (for a Euclidean space)
- invariance (to reparametrization)
- leading-order term (of an asymptotic expansion)
- linear reparametrization
- locally equivalent alternatives
- locally equivalent models (models that touch)
- noncentral chi-squared distribution
- outer-product-of-the-gradient (OPG) regression
- reparametrization of a parametrized model
- restricted estimates
- restricted model
- sample of size t
- score vector (gradient vector)
- smooth restrictions
- unrestricted estimates
- unrestricted model
- vector sum
- Wald-like statistics

Chapter 14

Transforming the Dependent Variable

14.1 Introduction

When we introduced the concept of a regression function in Chapter 2, we defined it as the function that determines the mean of a dependent variable y_t conditional on an information set Ω_t. With this definition, we can always write

$$y_t = x_t(\boldsymbol{\beta}) + u_t \tag{14.01}$$

and assert that u_t has mean zero conditional on Ω_t, provided that $x_t(\boldsymbol{\beta})$ has been specified correctly. But no matter how well $x_t(\boldsymbol{\beta})$ has been specified, we cannot assert that u_t is i.i.d. or has any other desirable properties. In particular, there is no reason for it to be normally distributed, homoskedastic, or even symmetric. Yet we need u_t to be homoskedastic if the NLS estimates $\hat{\boldsymbol{\beta}}$ are to be efficient and inferences based on the usual least squares covariance matrix estimator are to be valid.[1] We also need u_t to be symmetric (and preferably normally distributed or close to it) if asymptotic results are to provide a good guide to the properties of finite-sample estimators. Moreover, if we wish to predict y_t conditional on Ω_t and construct any sort of forecast interval, we must know (or at least be able to estimate) the distribution of u_t.

If we can find the mean of y_t conditional on Ω_t, then we can presumably just as well find the conditional mean of any smooth monotonic function of y_t, say $\tau(y_t)$. For example, $\tau(y_t)$ might be $\log y_t$, $y_t^{1/2}$, or y_t^2. If we write

$$\tau(y_t) = E\big(\tau(y_t) \mid \Omega_t\big) + v_t \tag{14.02}$$

for some nonlinear $\tau(\cdot)$, then the error term v_t cannot be normally and independently distributed, or n.i.d., if u_t is n.i.d. in (14.01). Conversely, if v_t is n.i.d. in (14.02), u_t cannot be n.i.d. in (14.01).

[1] As we saw in Section 11.6 and will discuss further in Chapter 16, it is possible to make asymptotically valid inferences even in the presence of heteroskedasticity of unknown form. But finite-sample inferences will almost always be more accurate if the error terms are homoskedastic to begin with.

Let us now consider a concrete, and quite realistic, example. Suppose that we estimate the model (14.01) when the DGP for y_t is actually

$$\log y_t = \log(m_t) + v_t, \tag{14.03}$$

where m_t is in the information set Ω_t, and the error term v_t is $\text{NID}(0, \sigma^2)$. It follows that

$$y_t = \exp\bigl(\log(m_t) + v_t\bigr) = m_t \exp(v_t) \cong m_t(1 + v_t) = m_t + m_t v_t,$$

where the approximation $\exp(v_t) \cong 1 + v_t$ that is used here will be a good one if σ is small. If $m_t = x_t(\boldsymbol{\beta}_0)$ for some $\boldsymbol{\beta}_0$, the nonlinear regression (14.01) is at least approximately valid for the conditional mean of y_t, although this would not necessarily be the case if the transformation in (14.03) were not logarithmic. But the error terms u_t adhering to m_t cannot possibly be n.i.d. Instead, they will be heteroskedastic, with variance proportional to the square of $x_t(\boldsymbol{\beta}_0)$. They will also be somewhat skewed to the right, especially if σ is not very small, because of the fact that, for $a > 0$, $e^a - 1 > |e^{-a} - 1|$. This fact implies that any given positive value of v_t translates into a larger absolute value of u_t than the same absolute but negative value of v_t. Since v is symmetric, u must then be right-skewed.

This example demonstrates that, even when the dependent variable was actually generated by a DGP with n.i.d. errors, using the wrong transformation of the dependent variable as the regressand will in general yield a regression with error terms that are neither homoskedastic nor symmetric. Thus, when we encounter heteroskedasticity and skewness in the residuals of a regression, one possible way to eliminate them is to estimate a different regression model in which the dependent variable has been subjected to a **nonlinear transformation**. This is in fact an approach that has been used extensively in econometrics and statistics, and we discuss it in some detail in this chapter. We should, however, stress at the outset that in any given case there may exist no transformation of the dependent variable that yields symmetric and homoskedastic residuals. It is also possible that some form of weighted least squares will work better than a model that involves transforming the dependent variable. Thus the techniques to be discussed in this chapter will not be useful in every case.

There are numerous ways in which transformations of the dependent variable can be employed in what is otherwise a regression model. Let $\tau(x, \lambda)$ denote a nonlinear transformation of x with scalar parameter λ that may or may not have to be estimated. By far the most popular transformation is the **Box-Cox transformation**, which was suggested by Box and Cox (1964) in a very famous article; it will be discussed in the next section. One class of models that uses such a transformation is the one originally suggested by Box and Cox:

$$\tau(y_t, \lambda) = x_t(\boldsymbol{\beta}) + u_t, \tag{14.04}$$

in which the transformation applies to the dependent variable only. This class of models has been very popular in statistics but much less so in econometrics. A second class of models is

$$\tau(y_t, \lambda) = \tau\bigl(x_t(\boldsymbol{\beta}), \lambda\bigr) + u_t, \tag{14.05}$$

in which the transformation $\tau(x, \lambda)$ is applied both to the dependent variable and to the regression function. Models of this type have been advocated by Carroll and Ruppert (1984, 1988), who call them "transform-both-sides" models. These models have also been used quite extensively in statistics and to a limited extent in econometrics; an early example is Leech (1975).

A third class of models is

$$\tau(y_t, \lambda) = \sum_{i=1}^{k} \beta_i \tau(X_{ti}, \lambda) + \sum_{j=1}^{l} \gamma_j Z_{tj} + u_t, \tag{14.06}$$

where X_{ti} and Z_{tj} both denote observations on independent variables, the distinction being that the X_{ti}'s are subject to transformation and the Z_{tj}'s are not. This is the approach that has generally been taken in econometrics, with the transformation $\tau(x, \lambda)$ invariably being the Box-Cox transformation.[2] The class of models (14.06) is more general than (14.04), at least if $x_t(\boldsymbol{\beta})$ in that model is restricted to be linear, and in some ways it is also more general than (14.05). It can be generalized further by allowing the value of λ used to transform y_t to differ from the value (or values) used to transform the X_{ti}'s (see Section 14.7).

Notice that whereas the models (14.04) and (14.05) are mainly concerned with obtaining residuals that are homoskedastic and symmetric, while treating the functional form of the regression function as essentially given, the model (14.06) explicitly makes the functional form depend on λ. Perhaps as a result of this, much of the early econometric literature seems to have been mainly concerned with determining the functional form of the regression function and largely unconcerned with the properties of the residuals. This lack of concern was misplaced, because the key feature of any model involving a transformation of the dependent variable is the fact that the transformation directly affects the properties of the residuals.

The models (14.04), (14.05), and (14.06) may be called **nonregression models**, because the dependent variable is not simply equal to the sum of a regression function and an error term. Although these models are different, and may yield quite different results in practice, they all have one thing in common, namely, that the dependent variable is subject to a nonlinear transformation with parameter λ. If λ were known, they could all be estimated by

[2] Papers that either use or discuss this approach include Zarembka (1968, 1974), White (1972), Heckman and Polachek (1974), Savin and White (1978), and Spitzer (1976, 1978, 1982a, 1982b, 1984).

nonlinear least squares and tested using the Gauss-Newton regression. But as long as λ is unknown and has to be estimated, NLS is clearly not appropriate. In most cases, a least squares algorithm would simply choose λ so as to make $\tau(y_t, \lambda)$ as small as possible in order to make the sum of squared residuals as small as possible. It would thus inevitably yield nonsense results, as we discussed in Chapter 8 in connection with the model (8.01).

In the next section, we discuss the Box-Cox transformation and the estimation of regression-like models in which the dependent variable has been subjected to it. Maximum likelihood estimation turns out to be quite feasible because the loglikelihood function incorporates a Jacobian term that prevents λ from becoming too small. In Section 14.3, we digress slightly to discuss some of the other useful properties of Jacobian terms in ML estimation. In Section 14.4, we then discuss a new class of artificial regressions called **double-length artificial regressions** and, in Section 14.5, we show how these may be used for estimation and testing of models involving the Box-Cox transformation. In Section 14.6, we discuss how one may test the specification of linear and loglinear regression models against Box-Cox and other alternatives. Finally, in Section 14.7, we briefly discuss some models that involve generalizations of or alternatives to the Box-Cox transformation.

14.2 THE BOX-COX TRANSFORMATION

The Box-Cox transformation is by far the most commonly used nonlinear transformation in statistics and econometrics. It is defined as

$$B(x, \lambda) = \begin{cases} \dfrac{x^\lambda - 1}{\lambda} & \text{when } \lambda \neq 0; \\ \log(x) & \text{when } \lambda = 0, \end{cases}$$

where the argument x must be positive. By l'Hôpital's Rule, $\log x$ is the limit of $(x^\lambda - 1)/\lambda$ as $\lambda \to 0$. Figure 14.1 shows the Box-Cox transformation for various values of λ. In practice, λ generally ranges from somewhat below 0 to somewhat above 1. It can be shown that $B(x, \lambda') \geq B(x, \lambda'')$ for $\lambda' \geq \lambda''$, and this inequality is evident in the figure. Thus the amount of curvature induced by the Box-Cox transformation increases as λ gets farther from 1 in either direction.

There are three varieties of Box-Cox model. We will refer to (14.04) and (14.05) with $\tau(\cdot)$ given by the Box-Cox transformation as the **simple Box-Cox model** and the **transform-both-sides Box-Cox model**, respectively. We will refer to (14.06) with this choice of $\tau(\cdot)$ as the **conventional Box-Cox model**, because it is by far the most commonly used in econometrics.

One reason for the popularity of the Box-Cox transformation is that it incorporates both the possibility of no transformation at all (when $\lambda = 1$) and the possibility of a logarithmic transformation (when $\lambda = 0$). Provided that

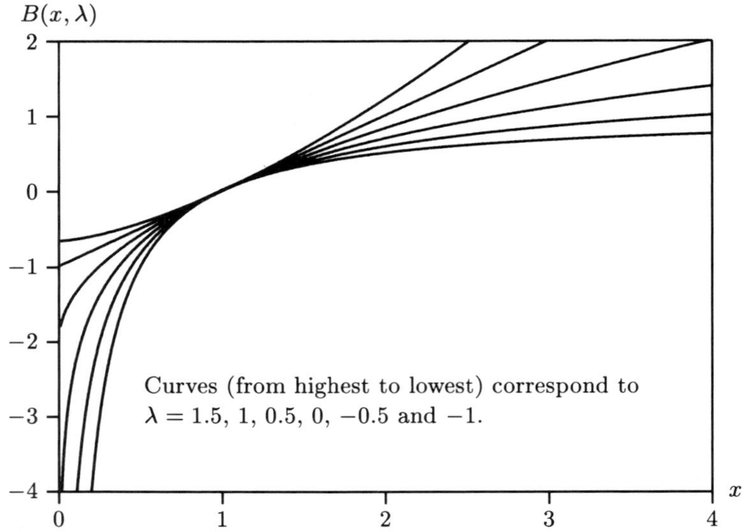

Figure 14.1 Box-Cox transformations for various values of λ

the regressors include a constant term, subjecting the dependent variable to a Box-Cox transformation with $\lambda = 1$ is equivalent to not transforming it at all. Subjecting it to a Box-Cox transformation with $\lambda = 0$ is equivalent to using $\log y_t$ as the regressand. Since these are both very plausible special cases, it is attractive to use a transformation that allows for both of them. Even when it is not considered plausible in its own right, the conventional Box-Cox model provides a convenient alternative against which to test the specification of linear and loglinear regression models; see Section 14.6.

The Box-Cox transformation is not without some serious disadvantages, however. Consider the simple Box-Cox model

$$B(y_t, \lambda) = x_t(\boldsymbol{\beta}) + u_t, \quad u_t \sim \text{NID}(0, \sigma^2). \tag{14.07}$$

For most values of λ (but not for $\lambda = 0$ or $\lambda = 1$) the value of $B(y_t, \lambda)$ is bounded either from below or above; specifically, when $\lambda > 0$, $B(y_t, \lambda)$ cannot be less than $-1/\lambda$ and, when $\lambda < 0$, $B(y_t, \lambda)$ cannot be greater than $-1/\lambda$. However, if u_t is normally distributed, the right-hand side of (14.07) is not bounded and could, at least in principle, take on arbitrarily large positive or negative values. Thus, strictly speaking, (14.07) is logically impossible as a model for y_t. This remains true if we replace $x_t(\boldsymbol{\beta})$ by a regression function that depends on λ.

One way to deal with this problem is to assume that data on y_t are observed only when the bounds are not violated, as in Poirier (1978) and Poirier and Ruud (1979). This leads to loglikelihood functions similar to those to be discussed in Section 15.6.[3] However, it is not at all clear why data would ever be generated in this way, and both estimation and testing become quite complicated when one takes this sort of sample truncation into account. A second way to deal with the problem is simply to ignore it. This application of the well-known "ostrich algorithm" makes sense if λ is nonnegative (or at least not much less than zero) and y_t is positive and large relative to σ for all observations in the data set. When those two conditions are satisfied, we can be sure that u_t will be small relative to $B(y_t, \lambda)$ and $x_t(\boldsymbol{\beta})$; therefore, the probability that the right-hand side of (14.07) would ever violate the bound on the left-hand side will be very small.

We will adopt this second approach on the grounds that Box-Cox models with negative values of λ are not of much interest and that, in many practical cases, the conditional mean of y_t is always large relative to any variation around that conditional mean. In such cases, it seems reasonable enough to use models in which the dependent variable is subject to a Box-Cox transformation. However, in other cases, it may not be appropriate to use a Box-Cox model; see Section 14.7.

Now let us consider how to obtain consistent estimates of λ and $\boldsymbol{\beta}$ in (14.07). This is the simplest case to discuss, but everything that we will say will apply also, with slight and obvious modifications, to the transform-both-sides and conventional Box-Cox models as well, in which the transformation parameter λ also appears in the regression function. Since least squares clearly will not work in this case, it is natural to turn to maximum likelihood. Because we have assumed that the u_t's are normally and independently distributed, we can easily write down the loglikelihood function for this model. It is

$$\begin{aligned}\ell(\boldsymbol{y}, \boldsymbol{\beta}, \lambda, \sigma) = &-\tfrac{n}{2}\log(2\pi) - n\log\sigma \\ &-\frac{1}{2\sigma^2}\sum_{t=1}^{n}\big(B(y_t, \lambda) - x_t(\boldsymbol{\beta})\big)^2 + (\lambda-1)\sum_{t=1}^{n}\log y_t.\end{aligned} \tag{14.08}$$

The last term here is the summation over all observations of the logarithm of

$$\frac{\partial B(y_t, \lambda)}{\partial y_t} = \frac{\partial}{\partial y_t}\left(\frac{y_t^{\lambda} - 1}{\lambda}\right) = y_t^{\lambda-1},$$

which is the Jacobian of the transformation from y_t to u_t.

The role of this Jacobian term is crucial. In order to avoid having to consider more than one case, let us assume for simplicity that all the y_t's are greater than 1. Since

$$\operatorname*{plim}_{\lambda\to-\infty} B(x, \lambda) = 0$$

[3] A different approach, along similar lines, was suggested by Amemiya and Powell (1981).

for $x > 1$, letting $\lambda \to -\infty$ will then make $B(y_t, \lambda) \to 0$ for all t. Thus, provided there is some value of $\boldsymbol{\beta}$ that makes the regression function $x_t(\boldsymbol{\beta})$ equal zero for all t, the sum of squared residuals,

$$\sum_{t=1}^{n} \bigl(B(y_t, \lambda) - x_t(\boldsymbol{\beta})\bigr)^2,$$

can be made arbitrarily small simply by letting λ tend to minus infinity. If we concentrate (14.08) with respect to σ, the loglikelihood function becomes

$$\ell^c(\boldsymbol{y}, \boldsymbol{\beta}, \lambda) = C - \frac{n}{2}\log\biggl(\sum_{t=1}^{n} \bigl(B(y_t, \lambda) - x_t(\boldsymbol{\beta})\bigr)^2\biggr) + (\lambda - 1)\sum_{t=1}^{n} \log y_t, \quad (14.09)$$

where C is a constant that does not depend on $\boldsymbol{\beta}$ or λ. Thus we see that when we maximize the loglikelihood function, the value of λ will affect two things: a sum-of-squares term and a Jacobian term. The Jacobian term prevents the ML estimate of λ from tending to minus infinity, since that term tends to minus infinity as λ does.

Maximizing (14.09) is not very difficult. The best approach, if appropriate software is available, is to use a suitable procedure for nonlinear maximization; see Section 14.5. A second approach is to use a grid search procedure in which one searches over values of λ and estimates $\boldsymbol{\beta}$ by least squares conditional on λ. A third approach is to make use of a trick that allows (14.09) to be minimized using any nonlinear least squares algorithm. There are actually two ways to do this. The simplest is to note that if all the y_t's are divided by their geometric mean $\dot{y}$, the Jacobian term in (14.09) is then identically equal to zero, because

$$n \log \dot{y} = \sum_{t=1}^{n} \log y_t.$$

Thus, running any nonlinear regression that has residuals $B(y_t/\dot{y}, \lambda) - x_t(\boldsymbol{\beta})$ will yield valid estimates of $\boldsymbol{\beta}$ and λ. For example, one could define the regressand as a vector of zeros and the regression function as $B(y_t/\dot{y}, \lambda) - x_t(\boldsymbol{\beta})$ and then use any NLS algorithm. This approach has been used for many years but has the disadvantage of requiring y_t to be rescaled; as we will see below, rescaling is not always totally innocuous in the context of Box-Cox models.

A second way to use an NLS program was suggested by Carroll and Ruppert (1988). One can rewrite (14.09) as

$$\ell^c(\boldsymbol{y}, \boldsymbol{\beta}, \lambda) = C^* - \frac{n}{2}\log\biggl(\sum_{t=1}^{n} \biggl(\frac{B(y_t, \lambda) - x_t(\boldsymbol{\beta})}{\dot{y}^{\lambda}}\biggr)^2\biggr),$$

where C^* does not depend on $\boldsymbol{\beta}$ or λ. Since this version of the loglikelihood function has only a sum-of-squares term, it can be maximized by minimizing the sum of squared residuals:

$$\sum_{t=1}^{n} \left(\frac{B(y_t, \lambda) - x_t(\boldsymbol{\beta})}{\dot{y}^{\lambda}} \right)^2.$$

One can do this using an NLS procedure by defining the regressand as a vector of zeros and the regression function as $\big(B(y_t, \lambda) - x_t(\boldsymbol{\beta})\big)/\dot{y}^{\lambda}$.

Although all the techniques just described yield ML estimates $\hat{\lambda}$ and $\hat{\boldsymbol{\beta}}$, none of the methods based on least squares yields a valid estimate of the covariance matrix of $\hat{\lambda}$ and $\hat{\boldsymbol{\beta}}$. The reason for this is that, as we will see in Section 14.5, the information matrix for Box-Cox models is not block-diagonal in $\boldsymbol{\beta}$, λ, and σ. Grid-search methods that estimate $\boldsymbol{\beta}$ conditional on λ yield invalid covariance matrix estimates, because they ignore the fact that $\hat{\lambda}$ is itself an estimate. Methods that trick an NLS program into estimating $\hat{\lambda}$ and $\hat{\boldsymbol{\beta}}$ jointly also yield invalid covariance matrix estimates, because they implicitly assume that the covariance matrix is block-diagonal between σ and the other parameters, which is not the case for Box-Cox models. Because it is very tempting to use the incorrect standard error estimates printed by the least squares package, we recommend that procedures based on least squares should be used to estimate Box-Cox models only when more appropriate computer software is unavailable.

One can, of course, obtain a valid estimated covariance matrix in a variety of ways by inverting various estimates of the information matrix. The OPG regression probably provides the easiest way to obtain a covariance matrix estimate, but its finite-sample properties are not very good, and more specialized techniques that work better are available; see Spitzer (1984). In Sections 14.4 and 14.5, we will discuss a class of artificial regressions that can be used to handle a wide class of models and seem to work very well for Box-Cox models. Like all artificial regressions, these double-length regressions, as they are called, can be used for estimation, inference, and specification testing.

We remarked earlier that rescaling the dependent variable may not be innocuous in a Box-Cox model. In the transform-both-sides model, rescaling the dependent variable has exactly the same effect that it would have if there were no transformation, because both the dependent variable and the regression function are transformed in the same way. Thus, if $x_t(\boldsymbol{\beta})$ is linear, all the coefficients will simply be multiplied by the factor used to rescale the dependent variable. If $x_t(\boldsymbol{\beta})$ is nonlinear, rescaling y_t may well affect $\boldsymbol{\beta}$ in more complicated ways and may even affect how well the model fits, but it will do so only if rescaling would affect the fit of the model even if there were no transformation involved. In the two other types of Box-Cox model, however, things are not so simple.

There is one important invariance result for the conventional and simple Box-Cox models. It is that, under certain conditions, the ML estimate of λ is invariant to rescaling of the dependent variable. Suppose one multiplies y_t

by a constant α so that the dependent variable becomes αy_t. The Box-Cox transformation of αy_t is

$$B(\alpha y_t, \lambda) = \alpha^\lambda B(y_t, \lambda) + B(\alpha, \lambda).$$

The second term here is just a constant. Provided there is a constant term (or the equivalent) in the regression function, the estimate of the constant will always adjust automatically to accommodate it. If the regression function is linear, all the parameter estimates except the constant will simply be rescaled by α^λ, as will the residuals and $\hat{\sigma}$. For the conventional Box-Cox model, the rescaling is more complicated, but the net effect is that the residuals are again rescaled by α^λ. This is also true for some, but by no means all, other nonlinear regression functions $x_t(\boldsymbol{\beta})$. Provided that rescaling y_t is equivalent to rescaling the residuals in this way, the sum-of-squares term in (14.08), evaluated for an arbitrary fixed λ at the $\hat{\boldsymbol{\beta}}$ that minimizes the sum of squared residuals and at the corresponding $\hat{\sigma}^2$, is invariant under the rescaling. The second term of (14.08), $-n \log \sigma$, becomes $-n \log \sigma - n\lambda \log \alpha$. The last, Jacobian, term becomes

$$(\lambda - 1) \sum_{t=1}^{n} \log y_t + n(\lambda - 1) \log \alpha.$$

The whole operation thus adds $-n \log \alpha$, a quantity independent of all parameters, to the loglikelihood function concentrated with respect to $\boldsymbol{\beta}$ and σ^2. Hence it is clear that, provided rescaling y_t is equivalent to rescaling the residuals, the ML estimate $\hat{\lambda}$ will not change when we rescale y_t. Essentially this result was originally proved by Schlesselman (1971).

Even when $\hat{\lambda}$ is invariant to rescaling, the other parameters will generally not be. In the conventional Box-Cox model, the effects of rescaling y_t depend on the value of λ. When $\lambda = 1$, so that it is really a linear regression model, multiplying y_t by α simply changes all the estimated coefficients by a factor of α and has no effect on t statistics. When $\lambda = 0$, so that it is really a loglinear regression model, multiplying y_t by α means adding a constant $\log \alpha$ to the regressand, which affects the constant term but none of the other coefficients. But except in these two cases, all of the other coefficients will generally change when the dependent variable is rescaled. Moreover, because of the lack of invariance of Wald tests to nonlinear reparametrizations, all of the t statistics on the β_i's will change as well; see Spitzer (1984). In fact, it is quite possible for a t statistic that is highly significant for one scaling of y_t to be entirely insignificant for another scaling. This of course implies that, whatever the scaling of y_t, one should not rely on t statistics (or on any other sort of Wald test) in the context of Box-Cox models.

14.3 THE ROLE OF JACOBIAN TERMS IN ML ESTIMATION

Jacobian terms have appeared in loglikelihood functions in a variety of contexts in Chapters 8, 9, and 10. We have seen that whenever the dependent variable is subject to a nonlinear transformation, the loglikelihood function necessarily contains one or more Jacobian terms. In this section, we investigate in more detail the role played by Jacobian terms in ML estimation. We will continue our discussion of Box-Cox models in subsequent sections.

Recall that if a random variable x_1 has density $f_1(x_1)$ and another random variable x_2 is related to it by $x_1 = \tau(x_2)$, where the function $\tau(\cdot)$ is continuously differentiable and monotonic, then the density of x_2 is given by

$$f_2(x_2) = f_1\big(\tau(x_2)\big)\left|\frac{\partial\tau(x_2)}{\partial x_2}\right|. \tag{14.10}$$

The second factor here is the absolute value of the Jacobian of the transformation, and it is therefore often referred to as a **Jacobian factor**. In the multivariate case, where $\boldsymbol{x}_1$ and $\boldsymbol{x}_2$ are m–vectors and $\boldsymbol{x}_1 = \boldsymbol{\tau}(\boldsymbol{x}_2)$, the analog of (14.10) is

$$f_2(\boldsymbol{x}_2) = f_1\big(\boldsymbol{\tau}(\boldsymbol{x}_2)\big)\big|\det \boldsymbol{J}(\boldsymbol{x}_2)\big|,$$

where $|\det \boldsymbol{J}(\boldsymbol{x}_2)|$ is the absolute value of the determinant of the Jacobian matrix $\boldsymbol{J}(\boldsymbol{x}_2)$ with typical element

$$J_{ij}(\boldsymbol{x}_2) \equiv \frac{\partial\tau_i(\boldsymbol{x}_2)}{\partial x_{2j}}.$$

These results are discussed in Appendix B.

Jacobian factors in density functions give rise to Jacobian terms in loglikelihood functions. These may arise whenever the transformation from the observed dependent variable(s) to the error terms which drive the model has a Jacobian matrix that is not the identity matrix. If the underlying error terms are assumed to be normally distributed, the presence of these Jacobian terms is often the only thing that makes the loglikelihood function something other than just a transformation of the sum of squared residuals.

There are, however, circumstances in which the loglikelihood function contains no Jacobian terms, even though the Jacobian matrix is not an identity matrix. We encountered a class of models for which this is the case in Chapter 10. If we ignore the first observation, the Jacobian matrix for a regression model with AR(1) errors is easily seen to be lower-triangular, with diagonal elements equal to 1. Since the determinant of a triangular matrix is the product of the diagonal elements, the Jacobian factor for such models is simply unity, and the Jacobian term is consequently zero.

In this section, of course, we are concerned with the many other cases in which Jacobian terms do appear in loglikelihood functions. Their appearance has several consequences. First of all, it means that nonlinear least squares and the Gauss-Newton regression are not applicable to such models; tricks such as the one we used in the previous section may allow NLS to be used for estimation but will not allow inference to be based on NLS estimates in the usual way. The OPG regression will be applicable, of course, and so will more specialized artificial regressions such as the double-length regression to be introduced in the next section.

Secondly, the presence of Jacobian terms ensures that we can never obtain ML estimates at points in the parameter space where the Jacobian of the transformation from the dependent variable(s) to the underlying error terms is singular. At such points, it would not be possible to make this transformation at all. As the parameter vector approaches such a point, the determinant of the Jacobian matrix tends to zero, and the logarithm of that determinant therefore tends to minus infinity. We saw an example of this phenomenon in Section 10.6, where the loglikelihood function for a regression model with AR(1) errors was shown to tend to minus infinity as $|\rho| \to 1$. The transformation for the first observation,

$$(1-\rho^2)^{1/2}\big(y_1 - x_1(\boldsymbol{\beta})\big) = \varepsilon_1,$$

cannot be made when $|\rho| = 1$, and the loglikelihood function reflects this fact by taking on a value of minus infinity.

This property of loglikelihood functions is for the most part a desirable one, since it prevents us from obtaining estimates that make no sense. However, it does imply that loglikelihood functions for models with such Jacobian terms must have multiple maxima. For example, in the simplest case in which the singularity divides the parameter space into two regions, there must be at least one maximum in each of those regions. Thus, if we make the mistake of starting a maximization algorithm in the wrong region, the algorithm may well fail to cross the singularity and will thus find a local maximum that is not also a global one; see MacKinnon (1979). We will encounter additional examples of singularities in loglikelihood functions in Chapter 18, when we discuss the use of maximum likelihood to estimate simultaneous equations models.

The third major consequence of the presence of Jacobian terms in loglikelihood functions, and the one of most interest to us in this chapter, is that maximum likelihood estimation, unlike least squares, can deal very easily with transformations of the dependent variable, since, as we saw in the last section, the presence of the transformation causes there to be a Jacobian term in the loglikelihood function. A very common problem in applied econometric work is deciding on the appropriate transformation of the dependent variable. For example, economic theory might well be consistent with all three of the following specifications:

$$H_1: \;\; y_t = \alpha_1 + \beta_1 x_t + u_t, \tag{14.11}$$

$$H_2: \ \log y_t = \alpha_2 + \beta_2 \log x_t + u_t, \text{ and} \tag{14.12}$$

$$H_3: \ \frac{y_t}{z_t} = \alpha_3 \frac{1}{z_t} + \beta_3 \frac{x_t}{z_t} + u_t, \tag{14.13}$$

where z_t and x_t are observations on exogenous or predetermined variables. The regression functions here are deliberately very simple, because just how they are specified is irrelevant to the main argument.

It is clearly not appropriate to compare the sums of squared residuals or the R^2's from (14.11), (14.12), and (14.13). Nevertheless, if one is willing to assume normality, it is very easy to compare the values of the loglikelihood functions from the three competing models. These loglikelihood functions, concentrated with respect to the variance parameter, are, respectively,

$$\ell_1^c(\boldsymbol{y}, \boldsymbol{\beta}_1) = C - \frac{n}{2} \log\biggl(\sum_{t=1}^{n} (y_t - \alpha_1 - \beta_1 x_t)^2\biggr), \tag{14.14}$$

$$\ell_2^c(\boldsymbol{y}, \boldsymbol{\beta}_2) = C - \frac{n}{2} \log\biggl(\sum_{t=1}^{n} (\log y_t - \alpha_2 - \beta_2 \log x_t)^2\biggr) - \sum_{t=1}^{n} \log y_t, \tag{14.15}$$

and

$$\ell_3^c(\boldsymbol{y}, \boldsymbol{\beta}_3) = C - \frac{n}{2} \log\biggl(\sum_{t=1}^{n} \Bigl(\frac{y_t}{z_t} - \alpha_3 \frac{1}{z_t} - \beta_3 \frac{x_t}{z_t}\Bigr)^2\biggr) - \sum_{t=1}^{n} \log z_t, \tag{14.16}$$

where the constant C is the same for all three specifications.

What makes it possible to compare these three loglikelihood functions is the Jacobian terms in (14.15) and (14.16). They arise because

$$\frac{\partial \log y_t}{\partial y_t} = \frac{1}{y_t} \quad \text{and} \quad \frac{\partial (y_t/z_t)}{\partial y_t} = \frac{1}{z_t}.$$

Thus, if one wishes to decide which of (14.11), (14.12), and (14.13) fits best, one simply has to estimate each of them by NLS (or possibly OLS), retrieve the values of the loglikelihood functions reported by the regression package, subtract $\sum \log y_t$ in the case of (14.12) and $\sum \log z_t$ in the case of (14.13), and compare the resulting values of ℓ_1, ℓ_2, and ℓ_3. Note that, for most regression packages, the values of ℓ reported by the package for (14.12) and (14.13) will be incorrect when y_t (rather than $\log y_t$ or y_t/z_t) is truly the dependent variable. Because the package does not know that the regressand has been subjected to a transformation, the reported values will omit the Jacobian terms in (14.15) and (14.16).

This sort of procedure can actually be used to test, and possibly reject, one or more of the competing models. It is easy to see that each pair of H_1,

H_2, and H_3 can be embedded in a more general model involving one extra parameter. For example, the model

$$\frac{y_t}{z_t^{\phi}} = \alpha\frac{1}{z_t^{\phi}} + \beta\frac{x_t}{z_t^{\phi}} + u_t$$

reduces to H_1 when $\phi = 0$ and to H_3 when $\phi = 1$. Similarly, the Box-Cox model

$$B(y_t, \lambda) = \alpha + \beta B(x_t, \lambda) + u_t \tag{14.17}$$

reduces to H_1 when $\lambda = 1$ and to H_2 when $\lambda = 0$. Suppose that we estimate H_1 and H_2, and that the values of ℓ_1 and ℓ_2 are -523.4 and -520.7, respectively. Since we know that the embedding model (14.17) must fit at least as well as whichever of H_1 and H_2 fits best, the unrestricted maximum of the loglikelihood function must be at least as great as -520.7. Thus an LR test statistic of H_1 against the embedding model must be no less than

$$2\big(-520.7 - (-523.4)\big) = 2(523.4 - 520.7) = 5.4.$$

Since 5.4 exceeds the 5% critical value for a one-degree-of-freedom test, we may conclude that the linear model H_1 will be rejected at some level smaller than 5% if it is tested against the embedding model, even though we have not estimated the latter or calculated a formal test statistic.

This example illustrates a feature of LR tests that can be very convenient, namely, that one can sometimes put a lower bound on the LR test statistic without actually estimating the unrestricted model. It was noted by Sargan (1964) in the context of choosing between linear and loglinear models, is widely used by applied workers, and has recently been proposed as a basis for model selection by Pollak and Wales (1991). The procedure works in only one direction, of course. Thus the fact that the good performance of H_2 allows us to reject H_1 in this example does not tell us anything about H_2. It might well be rejected too if we actually tested it against the embedding model (see Section 14.6).

14.4 DOUBLE-LENGTH ARTIFICIAL REGRESSIONS

For all of the models discussed in Sections 14.1 and 14.2, the loglikelihood function is equal to a sum of the contributions for each of the n observations; (14.08) provides an example. Thus the OPG regression could clearly be used for estimation and testing of these models. Given the generally poor finite-sample performance of quantities calculated by means of the OPG regression, however, one would prefer not to base inferences on it. Luckily, there is available another artificial regression, called the **double-length artificial regression**, or **DLR**, that can also be used with these models and that performs very much better than the OPG regression in finite samples. In this section, we provide a brief introduction to the DLR. In the next section, we show how it may be used in estimating and testing Box-Cox models. The principal references on this subject are Davidson and MacKinnon (1984a, 1988). Davidson and MacKinnon (1983a, 1985c), Bera and McKenzie (1986), Godfrey, McAleer, and McKenzie (1988), and MacKinnon and Magee (1990) provide Monte Carlo evidence which suggests that tests based on the DLR generally perform very much better than tests based on the OPG regression in finite samples.

The class of models to which the DLR applies may be written as

$$f_t(y_t, \boldsymbol{\theta}) = \varepsilon_t, \quad t = 1, \ldots, n, \quad \varepsilon_t \sim \text{NID}(0, 1), \tag{14.18}$$

where each $f_t(\cdot)$ is a smooth function that depends on the random variable y_t, on a k–vector of parameters $\boldsymbol{\theta}$, and (implicitly) on some exogenous and/or predetermined variables. Since the function $f_t(\cdot)$ may also depend on lagged values of y_t, dynamic models are allowed. This may seem at first sight to be a rather restrictive class of models, but it is actually quite general. For example, a transform-both-sides model like (14.05) can, if the error terms are assumed to be NID$(0, \sigma^2)$, be written in the form of (14.18) by making the definitions

$$f_t(y_t, \boldsymbol{\theta}) \equiv \frac{1}{\sigma}\Big(\tau(y_t, \lambda) - \tau\big(x_t(\boldsymbol{\beta}), \lambda\big)\Big) \quad \text{and} \quad \boldsymbol{\theta} \equiv [\boldsymbol{\beta} \;\vdots\; \lambda \;\vdots\; \sigma].$$

In much the same way, other models involving transformations of the dependent variable can be put into the form (14.18). It is even possible to put many multivariate models into this form; see Davidson and MacKinnon (1984a).

For a model of the class to which the DLR applies, the contribution of the tth observation to the loglikelihood function $\ell(\boldsymbol{y}, \boldsymbol{\theta})$ is

$$\ell_t(y_t, \boldsymbol{\theta}) = -\frac{1}{2}\log(2\pi) - \frac{1}{2}f_t^2(y_t, \boldsymbol{\theta}) + k_t(y_t, \boldsymbol{\theta}),$$

where

$$k_t(y_t, \boldsymbol{\theta}) \equiv \log\left|\frac{\partial f_t(y_t, \boldsymbol{\theta})}{\partial y_t}\right|$$

is a Jacobian term. Now let us make the definitions

$$F_{ti}(y_t, \boldsymbol{\theta}) \equiv \frac{\partial f_t(y_t, \boldsymbol{\theta})}{\partial \theta_i} \quad \text{and} \quad K_{ti}(y_t, \boldsymbol{\theta}) \equiv \frac{\partial k_t(y_t, \boldsymbol{\theta})}{\partial \theta_i}$$

and define $\boldsymbol{F}(\boldsymbol{y}, \boldsymbol{\theta})$ and $\boldsymbol{K}(\boldsymbol{y}, \boldsymbol{\theta})$ as the $n \times k$ matrices with typical elements $F_{ti}(y_t, \boldsymbol{\theta})$ and $K_{ti}(y_t, \boldsymbol{\theta})$. Similarly, let $\boldsymbol{f}(\boldsymbol{y}, \boldsymbol{\theta})$ be the n–vector with typical element $f_t(y_t, \boldsymbol{\theta})$. It is easy to see that the gradient of $\ell(\boldsymbol{y}, \boldsymbol{\theta})$ is

$$\boldsymbol{g}(\boldsymbol{y}, \boldsymbol{\theta}) = -\boldsymbol{F}^{\top}(\boldsymbol{y}, \boldsymbol{\theta})\boldsymbol{f}(\boldsymbol{y}, \boldsymbol{\theta}) + \boldsymbol{K}^{\top}(\boldsymbol{y}, \boldsymbol{\theta})\boldsymbol{\iota}, \tag{14.19}$$

where $\boldsymbol{\iota}$ denotes an n–vector each element of which is 1.

The fundamental result that makes the DLR possible is that, for this class of models, the information matrix $\mathfrak{I}(\boldsymbol{\theta})$ satisfies the equality

$$\mathfrak{I}(\boldsymbol{\theta}) = \operatorname*{plim}_{n\to\infty}\Big(\frac{1}{n}\big(\boldsymbol{F}^{\top}(\boldsymbol{y},\boldsymbol{\theta})\boldsymbol{F}(\boldsymbol{y},\boldsymbol{\theta}) + \boldsymbol{K}^{\top}(\boldsymbol{y},\boldsymbol{\theta})\boldsymbol{K}(\boldsymbol{y},\boldsymbol{\theta})\big)\Big) \tag{14.20}$$

and so can be consistently estimated by

$$\frac{1}{n}\big(\boldsymbol{F}^{\top}(\boldsymbol{y},\ddot{\boldsymbol{\theta}})\boldsymbol{F}(\boldsymbol{y},\ddot{\boldsymbol{\theta}}) + \boldsymbol{K}^{\top}(\boldsymbol{y},\ddot{\boldsymbol{\theta}})\boldsymbol{K}(\boldsymbol{y},\ddot{\boldsymbol{\theta}})\big), \tag{14.21}$$

where $\ddot{\boldsymbol{\theta}}$ is any consistent estimator of $\boldsymbol{\theta}$. We are interested in the implications of (14.20) rather than how it is derived. The derivation makes use of some rather special properties of the normal distribution and may be found in Davidson and MacKinnon (1984a).

The principal implication of (14.20) is that a certain artificial regression, which we call the DLR, has all the properties that we expect an artificial regression to have. The DLR may be written as

$$\begin{bmatrix} \boldsymbol{f}(\boldsymbol{y},\boldsymbol{\theta}) \\ \boldsymbol{\iota} \end{bmatrix} = \begin{bmatrix} -\boldsymbol{F}(\boldsymbol{y},\boldsymbol{\theta}) \\ \boldsymbol{K}(\boldsymbol{y},\boldsymbol{\theta}) \end{bmatrix}\boldsymbol{b} + \text{residuals}. \tag{14.22}$$

This artificial regression has $2n$ **artificial observations**. The regressand is $f_t(y_t,\boldsymbol{\theta})$ for observation t and unity for observation $t+n$, and the regressors corresponding to $\boldsymbol{\theta}$ are $-\boldsymbol{F}_t(\boldsymbol{y},\boldsymbol{\theta})$ for observation t and $\boldsymbol{K}_t(\boldsymbol{y},\boldsymbol{\theta})$ for observation $t+n$, where $\boldsymbol{F}_t$ and $\boldsymbol{K}_t$ denote, respectively, the tth rows of $\boldsymbol{F}$ and $\boldsymbol{K}$. Intuitively, the reason we need a double-length regression here is that each genuine observation makes two contributions to the loglikelihood function: a sum-of-squares term $-\frac{1}{2}f_t^2$ and a Jacobian term k_t. As a result, the gradient and the information matrix each involve two parts as well, and the way to take both of these into account is to incorporate two artificial observations into the artificial regression for each genuine one.

Why is (14.22) a valid artificial regression? As we noted when we discussed the OPG regression in Section 13.7, there are two principal conditions that an artificial regression must satisfy. It is worth stating these conditions somewhat more formally here.[4] Let $\boldsymbol{r}(\boldsymbol{y},\boldsymbol{\theta})$ denote the regressand for some artificial regression and let $\boldsymbol{R}(\boldsymbol{y},\boldsymbol{\theta})$ denote the matrix of regressors. Let the number of rows of both $\boldsymbol{r}(\boldsymbol{y},\boldsymbol{\theta})$ and $\boldsymbol{R}(\boldsymbol{y},\boldsymbol{\theta})$ be n^*, which will generally be either n or an integer multiple of n. The regression of $\boldsymbol{r}(\boldsymbol{y},\boldsymbol{\theta})$ on $\boldsymbol{R}(\boldsymbol{y},\boldsymbol{\theta})$ will have the properties of an artificial regression if

$$\boldsymbol{R}^{\top}(\boldsymbol{y},\boldsymbol{\theta})\boldsymbol{r}(\boldsymbol{y},\boldsymbol{\theta}) = \rho(\boldsymbol{\theta})\boldsymbol{g}(\boldsymbol{y},\boldsymbol{\theta}) \quad\text{and} \tag{14.23}$$

$$\operatorname*{plim}_{n\to\infty}{}_{\boldsymbol{\theta}}\Big(\frac{1}{n^*}\boldsymbol{R}^{\top}(\boldsymbol{y},\ddot{\boldsymbol{\theta}})\boldsymbol{R}(\boldsymbol{y},\ddot{\boldsymbol{\theta}})\Big) = \rho(\boldsymbol{\theta})\,\mathfrak{I}(\boldsymbol{\theta}), \tag{14.24}$$

[4] For a fuller treatment of this topic, see Davidson and MacKinnon (1990).

where $\ddot{\boldsymbol{\theta}}$ denotes any consistent estimator of $\boldsymbol{\theta}$. The notation $\text{plim}_{\boldsymbol{\theta}}$ indicates, as usual, that the probability limit is being taken under the DGP characterized by the parameter vector $\boldsymbol{\theta}$, and $\rho(\boldsymbol{\theta})$ is a scalar defined as

$$\rho(\boldsymbol{\theta}) \equiv \underset{n\to\infty}{\text{plim}_{\boldsymbol{\theta}}}\Big(\frac{1}{n^*}\boldsymbol{r}^{\top}(\boldsymbol{y},\boldsymbol{\theta})\boldsymbol{r}(\boldsymbol{y},\boldsymbol{\theta})\Big).$$

Because $\rho(\boldsymbol{\theta})$ is equal to unity for both the OPG regression and the DLR, those two artificial regressions satisfy the simpler conditions

$$\boldsymbol{R}^{\top}(\boldsymbol{y},\boldsymbol{\theta})\boldsymbol{r}(\boldsymbol{y},\boldsymbol{\theta}) = \boldsymbol{g}(\boldsymbol{y},\boldsymbol{\theta}) \quad \text{and} \tag{14.25}$$

$$\underset{n\to\infty}{\text{plim}_{\boldsymbol{\theta}}}\Big(\frac{1}{n^*}\boldsymbol{R}^{\top}(\boldsymbol{y},\ddot{\boldsymbol{\theta}})\boldsymbol{R}(\boldsymbol{y},\ddot{\boldsymbol{\theta}})\Big) = \mathfrak{I}(\boldsymbol{\theta}), \tag{14.26}$$

as well as the original conditions (14.23) and (14.24). However, these simpler conditions are not satisfied by the GNR and are thus evidently too simple in general.

It is now easy to see that the DLR (14.21) satisfies conditions (14.25) and (14.26). For the first of these, simple calculation shows that

$$\begin{bmatrix} -\boldsymbol{F}(\boldsymbol{y},\boldsymbol{\theta}) \\ \boldsymbol{K}(\boldsymbol{y},\boldsymbol{\theta}) \end{bmatrix}^{\top} \begin{bmatrix} \boldsymbol{f}(\boldsymbol{y},\boldsymbol{\theta}) \\ \boldsymbol{\iota} \end{bmatrix} = -\boldsymbol{F}^{\top}(\boldsymbol{y},\boldsymbol{\theta})\boldsymbol{f}(\boldsymbol{y},\boldsymbol{\theta}) + \boldsymbol{K}^{\top}(\boldsymbol{y},\boldsymbol{\theta})\boldsymbol{\iota},$$

which by (14.19) is equal to the gradient $\boldsymbol{g}(\boldsymbol{y},\boldsymbol{\theta})$. For the second, we see that

$$\begin{bmatrix} -\boldsymbol{F}(\boldsymbol{y},\boldsymbol{\theta}) \\ \boldsymbol{K}(\boldsymbol{y},\boldsymbol{\theta}) \end{bmatrix}^{\top} \begin{bmatrix} -\boldsymbol{F}(\boldsymbol{y},\boldsymbol{\theta}) \\ \boldsymbol{K}(\boldsymbol{y},\boldsymbol{\theta}) \end{bmatrix} = \boldsymbol{F}^{\top}(\boldsymbol{y},\boldsymbol{\theta})\boldsymbol{F}(\boldsymbol{y},\boldsymbol{\theta}) + \boldsymbol{K}^{\top}(\boldsymbol{y},\boldsymbol{\theta})\boldsymbol{K}(\boldsymbol{y},\boldsymbol{\theta}).$$

The right-hand side here is just the expression that appears in the fundamental result (14.20). Hence it is clear that the DLR must satisfy (14.26). All this discussion assumes, of course, that the matrices $\boldsymbol{F}(\boldsymbol{y},\boldsymbol{\theta})$ and $\boldsymbol{K}(\boldsymbol{y},\boldsymbol{\theta})$ satisfy appropriate regularity conditions, which may not always be easy to verify in practice; see Davidson and MacKinnon (1984a).

The DLR can be used in all the same ways that the GNR and the OPG regression can be used. In particular, it can be used

(i) to verify that the first-order conditions for a maximum of the loglikelihood function are satisfied sufficiently accurately,

(ii) to calculate estimated covariance matrices,

(iii) to calculate test statistics,

(iv) to calculate one-step efficient estimates, and

(v) as a key part of procedures for finding ML estimates.

Use (i) was discussed in the context of the GNR in Section 6.1; use (ii) was discussed in Sections 6.2, 10.4, and 13.7; use (iii) has been discussed extensively throughout the book, beginning in Chapter 6; and uses (iv) and (v) were discussed, in the context of the GNR, in Sections 6.6 and 6.8. Virtually everything that has been said about the uses of the GNR and the OPG regression applies equally well to the DLR and will therefore not be repeated here.

Many different test statistics can be computed using the same double-length artificial regression. In its score form, the LM statistic is

$$\tilde{\boldsymbol{g}}^{\top}(n\tilde{\mathfrak{I}})^{-1}\tilde{\boldsymbol{g}}, \tag{14.27}$$

where $\tilde{\boldsymbol{g}} \equiv \boldsymbol{g}(\boldsymbol{y}, \tilde{\boldsymbol{\theta}})$ is the gradient evaluated at a set of restricted estimates $\tilde{\boldsymbol{\theta}}$. If we run the DLR (14.22) with the quantities $\boldsymbol{f}(\boldsymbol{y}, \boldsymbol{\theta})$, $\boldsymbol{F}(\boldsymbol{y}, \boldsymbol{\theta})$, and $\boldsymbol{K}(\boldsymbol{y}, \boldsymbol{\theta})$ evaluated at $\tilde{\boldsymbol{f}} \equiv \boldsymbol{f}(\boldsymbol{y}, \tilde{\boldsymbol{\theta}})$, $\tilde{\boldsymbol{F}} \equiv \boldsymbol{F}(\boldsymbol{y}, \tilde{\boldsymbol{\theta}})$, and $\tilde{\boldsymbol{K}} \equiv \boldsymbol{K}(\boldsymbol{y}, \tilde{\boldsymbol{\theta}})$, the explained sum of squares will be

$$\big(-\tilde{\boldsymbol{f}}^{\top}\tilde{\boldsymbol{F}} + \boldsymbol{\iota}^{\top}\tilde{\boldsymbol{K}}\big)\big(\tilde{\boldsymbol{F}}^{\top}\tilde{\boldsymbol{F}} + \tilde{\boldsymbol{K}}^{\top}\tilde{\boldsymbol{K}}\big)^{-1}\big(-\tilde{\boldsymbol{F}}^{\top}\tilde{\boldsymbol{f}} + \tilde{\boldsymbol{K}}^{\top}\boldsymbol{\iota}\big). \tag{14.28}$$

This clearly has the same form as the LM statistic (14.27). From (14.19), we see that $\tilde{\boldsymbol{g}} = -\tilde{\boldsymbol{F}}^{\top}\tilde{\boldsymbol{f}} + \tilde{\boldsymbol{K}}^{\top}\boldsymbol{\iota}$. From (14.20), we see that $\mathfrak{I}(\boldsymbol{\theta})$ is consistently estimated by $n^{-1}(\tilde{\boldsymbol{F}}^{\top}\tilde{\boldsymbol{F}} + \tilde{\boldsymbol{K}}^{\top}\tilde{\boldsymbol{K}})$ when the restrictions are true. Thus the explained sum of squares from the DLR, expression (14.28), will provide an asymptotically valid test statistic. As usual, pseudo-F and pseudo-t statistics will also be valid.

The general expression for a DLR, (14.22), is deceptively simple. It may therefore be illuminating to see what happens if we use a DLR in a simple case that we already know how to handle. Consider a univariate nonlinear regression model

$$y_t = x_t(\boldsymbol{\beta}) + u_t, \quad u_t \sim \mathrm{NID}(0, \sigma^2).$$

When written in the form of (14.18), this model becomes

$$f_t(y_t, \boldsymbol{\theta}) \equiv \frac{1}{\sigma}\big(y_t - x_t(\boldsymbol{\beta})\big) = \varepsilon_t. \tag{14.29}$$

If $\boldsymbol{\beta}$ is a k–vector, $\boldsymbol{\theta}$ will be a $(k+1)$–vector. Now consider how we might test restrictions on $\boldsymbol{\beta}$ using a DLR. The nature and number of the restrictions is irrelevant for our purposes; for simplicity, one can think of them as $r \leq k$ zero restrictions. Quantities denoted by $\sim$ are evaluated at ML (i.e., NLS) estimates subject to those restrictions.

Calculating $\boldsymbol{f}(\boldsymbol{y}, \boldsymbol{\theta})$, $\boldsymbol{F}(\boldsymbol{y}, \boldsymbol{\theta})$, and $\boldsymbol{K}(\boldsymbol{y}, \boldsymbol{\theta})$ for the model (14.29), evaluating them at restricted estimates $\tilde{\boldsymbol{\theta}}$, and substituting the results into (14.22), yields the DLR

$$\begin{bmatrix} \tilde{\boldsymbol{\varepsilon}} \\ \boldsymbol{\iota} \end{bmatrix} = \begin{bmatrix} \tilde{\boldsymbol{X}}/\tilde{\sigma} & \tilde{\boldsymbol{\varepsilon}}/\tilde{\sigma} \\ \mathbf{0} & -\boldsymbol{\iota}/\tilde{\sigma} \end{bmatrix} \begin{bmatrix} \boldsymbol{b} \\ s \end{bmatrix} + \text{residuals}. \tag{14.30}$$

Here $\tilde{\varepsilon} \equiv \tilde{\boldsymbol{u}}/\tilde{\sigma}$ denotes an n–vector of normalized residuals and $\tilde{\boldsymbol{X}}$ denotes an $n \times k$ matrix with typical element $\partial x_t(\boldsymbol{\beta})/\partial \beta_i$, evaluated at $\tilde{\boldsymbol{\beta}}$. The first k regressors in (14.30) correspond to the elements of $\boldsymbol{\beta}$, while the last one corresponds to σ; they have coefficients $\boldsymbol{b}$ and s, respectively. It is evident that the last regressor is orthogonal to the regressand. It is also orthogonal to all the regressors that correspond to elements of $\boldsymbol{\beta}$ which were estimated without restriction (by the first-order conditions) and, under the null hypothesis, it should be uncorrelated with the remaining regressors as well. Thus it must be valid simply to drop this last regressor. But when it is dropped, the second half of the DLR becomes irrelevant, since the second halves of all remaining regressors are zero. If the factors of $1/\tilde{\sigma}$ are ignored, we are left with the artificial regression

$$\tilde{\boldsymbol{u}} = \tilde{\boldsymbol{X}}\boldsymbol{b} + \text{residuals}, \tag{14.31}$$

which is simply the Gauss-Newton regression. Because the regressand is not divided by $\tilde{\sigma}$, it is now necessary to divide the explained sum of squares from (14.31) by an estimate of σ^2 when computing the test statistic.

That the DLR is equivalent to the GNR when the latter is valid makes perfect sense. Suppose that ESS_{DLR} denotes the explained sum of squares from (14.30) and ESS_{GN} denotes the explained sum of squares from the modified GNR obtained from (14.31) by replacing $\tilde{\boldsymbol{u}}$ by $\tilde{\varepsilon}$. It can be shown that these two test statistics are both functions of the same random variable. They will *not*, however, be numerically identical, the exact relationship between them being

$$\text{ESS}_{\text{DLR}} = \frac{\text{ESS}_{\text{GN}}}{1 - \text{ESS}_{\text{GN}}/(2n)}.$$

Because ESS_{DLR} will always be larger than ESS_{GN}, the DLR will always be somewhat more prone to reject the null hypothesis than the Gauss-Newton regression. The difference between them will usually be small, unless n is very small or ESS_{GN} is very large. If, instead of the explained sum of squares, t or F statistics are used, it can be shown that the DLR and Gauss-Newton regressions yield numerically identical results, except for slightly different corrections for degrees of freedom.

There is, of course, no point using a DLR when a GNR will do, that is, when both the null and alternative hypotheses are regression models. But when the dependent variable is subject to a nonlinear transformation that depends on unknown parameters, the GNR is not applicable. In the next section, we show how the DLR may be used with Box-Cox models and other models that involve transformations of the dependent variable.

14.5 The DLR and Models Involving Transformations

It is straightforward to work out the specific form that the DLR takes for each of the models (14.04), (14.05), and (14.06) for any specified transformation $\tau(y_t, \lambda)$. Consider (14.04) first. We can write

$$f_t(y_t, \boldsymbol{\beta}, \lambda, \sigma) \equiv \frac{1}{\sigma}\big(\tau(y_t, \lambda) - x_t(\boldsymbol{\beta})\big).$$

From (14.22), we see that the regressand for the DLR is

$$\boldsymbol{r}(\boldsymbol{\theta}) = \begin{bmatrix} f_t(y_t, \boldsymbol{\beta}, \lambda, \sigma) \\ 1 \end{bmatrix} = \begin{bmatrix} \frac{1}{\sigma}\big(\tau(y_t, \lambda) - x_t(\boldsymbol{\beta})\big) \\ 1 \end{bmatrix},$$

where the upper and lower quantities inside the tall brackets denote, respectively, the tth and $(t+n)^{\text{th}}$ elements of the regressand. We will use this notation extensively when discussing DLRs.

For all three models — (14.04), (14.05), and (14.06) — the Jacobian term for the tth observation is

$$k_t \equiv \log\left(\frac{\partial f_t(y_t, \boldsymbol{\beta}, \lambda, \sigma)}{\partial y_t}\right) = \log\big(\tau_y(y_t, \lambda)\big) - \log \sigma,$$

where $\tau_y(y_t, \lambda)$ denotes $\partial \tau(y_t, \lambda)/\partial y_t$. Thus the matrix of regressors for the DLR that corresponds to (14.04) is

$$\boldsymbol{R}(\boldsymbol{\theta}) = \begin{bmatrix} \frac{1}{\sigma}\boldsymbol{X}_t(\boldsymbol{\beta}) & -\frac{1}{\sigma}\tau_\lambda(y_t, \lambda) & \dfrac{\tau(y_t, \lambda) - x_t(\boldsymbol{\beta})}{\sigma^2} \\ \mathbf{0} & \dfrac{\tau_{y\lambda}(y_t, \lambda)}{\tau_y(y_t, \lambda)} & -\dfrac{1}{\sigma} \end{bmatrix}, \tag{14.32}$$

where $\tau_\lambda(y_t, \lambda)$ denotes $\partial \tau(y_t, \lambda)/\partial \lambda$, and $\tau_{y\lambda}(y_t, \lambda)$ denotes $\partial \tau_y(y_t, \lambda)/\partial \lambda$. The two quantities in the first column of (14.32) denote the tth and $(t+n)^{\text{th}}$ rows of the k columns of the regressor matrix that correspond to $\boldsymbol{\beta}$. Similarly, the two quantities in each of the second and third columns denote the elements of the regressor matrix that correspond to λ and σ, respectively.

When the transformation τ is the Box-Cox transformation,

$$\tau_\lambda(y, \lambda) = \frac{\lambda y^\lambda \log y - y^\lambda + 1}{\lambda^2} \quad \text{and}$$

$$\frac{\tau_{y\lambda}(y, \lambda)}{\tau_y(y, \lambda)} = \frac{y^{\lambda-1}\log(y)}{y^{\lambda-1}} = \log(y).$$

Hence the DLR for the simple Box-Cox model, (14.04) with $\tau(y_t, \lambda)$ given by the Box-Cox transformation, is

$$\begin{bmatrix} \frac{1}{\sigma}u_t(y_t, \boldsymbol{\beta}, \lambda) \\ 1 \end{bmatrix} \tag{14.33}$$

$$= \begin{bmatrix} \frac{1}{\sigma}\boldsymbol{X}_t(\boldsymbol{\beta}) & \dfrac{-(\lambda y_t^\lambda \log y_t - y_t^\lambda + 1)}{\sigma\lambda^2} & \dfrac{u_t(y_t, \boldsymbol{\beta}, \lambda)}{\sigma^2} \\ \mathbf{0} & \log y_t & -\frac{1}{\sigma} \end{bmatrix} \begin{bmatrix} \boldsymbol{b} \\ a \\ s \end{bmatrix} + \text{residuals},$$

where $\boldsymbol{b}$ is a k–vector of coefficients corresponding to $\boldsymbol{\beta}$, a and s are scalar coefficients corresponding to λ and σ, and

$$u_t(y_t, \boldsymbol{\beta}, \lambda) \equiv B(y_t, \lambda) - x_t(\boldsymbol{\beta}).$$

If the DLR (14.33) is evaluated at unrestricted ML estimates $\hat{\boldsymbol{\theta}} \equiv (\hat{\boldsymbol{\beta}}, \hat{\lambda}, \hat{\sigma})$, all the estimated coefficients will be zero. Since the first-order conditions for σ imply that

$$\hat{\sigma} = \left(\frac{1}{n}\sum_{t=1}^{n} \hat{u}_t^2\right)^{1/2},$$

the total sum of squares from the artificial regression will be $2n$. Thus the OLS covariance matrix estimate will simply be $\bigl(2n/(2n-k-2)\bigr)(\hat{\boldsymbol{R}}^\top\hat{\boldsymbol{R}})^{-1}$, where $\hat{\boldsymbol{R}}$ denotes the matrix of regressors that appears in (14.33), evaluated at the ML estimates. By the fundamental result (14.20), this OLS covariance matrix provides a valid estimate of the asymptotic covariance matrix of the ML estimator $\hat{\boldsymbol{\theta}}$.

It is clear from (14.33) that this asymptotic covariance matrix is not block-diagonal between $\boldsymbol{\beta}$ and the other parameters. Forming the matrix $\boldsymbol{R}^\top\boldsymbol{R}$, dividing by n, and taking probability limits, we see that the $(\boldsymbol{\beta}, \boldsymbol{\beta})$ block of the information matrix $\mathcal{I}(\boldsymbol{\theta})$ is simply

$$\sigma^{-2} \operatorname*{plim}_{n\to\infty}\Bigl(\frac{1}{n}\boldsymbol{X}^\top(\boldsymbol{\beta})\boldsymbol{X}(\boldsymbol{\beta})\Bigr), \tag{14.34}$$

as it would be if this were a nonlinear regression model. The (σ, σ) element is simply $2/\sigma^2$, which again is what it would be if this were a nonlinear regression model. But $\mathcal{I}(\boldsymbol{\theta})$ also contains a (λ, λ) element, a (λ, σ) element, and a $(\boldsymbol{\beta}, \lambda)$ row and column, all of which are clearly nonzero. For example, the element corresponding to β_i and λ is

$$-\operatorname*{plim}_{n\to\infty}\left(\frac{1}{n\sigma^2\lambda^2}\sum_{t=1}^{n} X_{ti}(\boldsymbol{\beta})\bigl(\lambda y_t^\lambda \log y_t - y_t^\lambda + 1\bigr)\right).$$

The (λ, λ) and (λ, σ) elements can also be obtained in a straightforward fashion and are easily seen to be nonzero.

Because $\mathfrak{I}(\boldsymbol{\theta})$ is not block-diagonal between $\boldsymbol{\beta}$ and the other two parameters, the $(\boldsymbol{\beta}, \boldsymbol{\beta})$ block of its inverse will not be equal to the inverse of (14.34). Thus, as we pointed out in Section 14.2, it is incorrect to make inferences using the estimated NLS covariance matrix for $\boldsymbol{\beta}$ conditional on λ. Similarly, because the (λ, σ) element of $\mathfrak{I}(\boldsymbol{\theta})$ is nonzero, one cannot find the inverse of the $(k+1) \times (k+1)$ block of the information matrix that corresponds to $\boldsymbol{\beta}$ and λ jointly without inverting the entire information matrix. The estimated covariance matrix obtained by tricking an NLS package into yielding ML estimates will therefore be incorrect.

It should be clear that everything we have just said about the simple Box-Cox model applies equally to the transform-both-sides model and to the conventional model, since the Jacobian of the transformation is the same for all these models. It is easy to work out the DLRs for the other two models. In both cases, the regressand has the same form as the regressand of (14.33), except that for the transform-both-sides model

$$u_t(y_t, \boldsymbol{\beta}, \lambda) \equiv B(y_t, \lambda) - B\big(x_t(\boldsymbol{\beta}), \lambda\big)$$

and for the conventional Box-Cox model

$$u_t(y_t, \boldsymbol{\beta}, \boldsymbol{\gamma}, \lambda) \equiv B(y_t, \lambda) - \sum_{i=1}^{k} \beta_i B(X_{ti}, \lambda) - \sum_{j=1}^{l} \gamma_j Z_{tj}.$$

The regressor that corresponds to σ also has the same form as the one that appears in (14.33).

For the transform-both-sides model, the regressor corresponding to β_i is

$$\begin{bmatrix} \frac{1}{\sigma}\big(x_t(\boldsymbol{\beta})\big)^{\lambda-1} X_{ti}(\boldsymbol{\beta}) \\ \mathbf{0} \end{bmatrix},$$

and the regressor corresponding to λ is

$$\begin{bmatrix} \dfrac{1}{\sigma\lambda^2}\Big(\big(\lambda\big(x_t(\boldsymbol{\beta})\big)^{\lambda}\log\big(x_t(\boldsymbol{\beta})\big) - \big(x_t(\boldsymbol{\beta})\big)^{\lambda} + 1\big) - \big(\lambda y_t^{\lambda}\log y_t - y_t^{\lambda} + 1\big)\Big) \\ \log y_t \end{bmatrix}.$$

For the conventional Box-Cox model, the regressors that correspond to β_i and γ_j, respectively, are

$$\begin{bmatrix} \frac{1}{\sigma} B(X_{ti}, \lambda) \\ 0 \end{bmatrix} \quad \text{and} \quad \begin{bmatrix} \frac{1}{\sigma} Z_{tj} \\ 0 \end{bmatrix}, \tag{14.35}$$

and the regressor that corresponds to λ is

$$\begin{bmatrix} \dfrac{1}{\sigma\lambda^2}\Big(\sum_{i=1}^{k} \beta_i\big(\lambda X_{ti}^{\lambda}\log X_{ti} - X_{ti}^{\lambda} + 1\big) - \big(\lambda y_t^{\lambda}\log y_t - y_t^{\lambda} + 1\big)\Big) \\ \log y_t \end{bmatrix}. \tag{14.36}$$

We have now obtained DLRs for the three most common types of Box-Cox models. DLRs for other types of models involving transformations of the dependent variable can be derived in a similar fashion. All these DLRs can be used as a key part of algorithms for estimating the models to which they apply, in exactly the same way that GNRs can be used as part of algorithms for estimating nonlinear regression models; see Section 6.8. Given some initial value of λ (probably 0 or 1), it is easy to obtain initial estimates of the model's remaining parameters by OLS or NLS. That then provides a complete set of parameter estimates, say $\boldsymbol{\theta}^{(1)}$, at which the DLR can be evaluated initially. The coefficient estimates from the DLR, say $\boldsymbol{t}^{(1)}$, can then be used to determine the direction in which to update the parameter estimates, and the whole process can be repeated as many times as necessary until some stopping rule is satisfied.

The updating rule for the maximization algorithm has the form

$$\boldsymbol{\theta}^{(j+1)} = \boldsymbol{\theta}^{(j)} + \alpha^{(j)}\boldsymbol{t}^{(j)}. \tag{14.37}$$

Here $\boldsymbol{\theta}^{(j)}$ and $\boldsymbol{\theta}^{(j+1)}$ denote the vectors of estimates on the jth and $(j+1)^{\text{th}}$ iterations of the maximization algorithm, $\boldsymbol{t}^{(j)}$ denotes the vector of coefficient estimates from the DLR, and $\alpha^{(j)}$ denotes the step length, which may be chosen in various ways by the algorithm. This updating rule looks just like the one for the Gauss-Newton regression discussed in Section 6.8, and works for exactly the same reason. An algorithm based on Newton's method (with variable step length α) would use the updating rule

$$\boldsymbol{\theta}^{(j+1)} = \boldsymbol{\theta}^{(j)} - \alpha^{(j)}\big(\boldsymbol{H}(\boldsymbol{\theta}^{(j)})\big)^{-1}\boldsymbol{g}(\boldsymbol{\theta}^{(j)}). \tag{14.38}$$

The DLR at step j yields the coefficient vector

$$\boldsymbol{t}^{(j)} = \big(\boldsymbol{R}^{\top}(\boldsymbol{\theta}^{(j)})\boldsymbol{R}(\boldsymbol{\theta}^{(j)})\big)^{-1}\boldsymbol{R}^{\top}(\boldsymbol{\theta}^{(j)})\boldsymbol{r}(\boldsymbol{\theta}^{(j)}).$$

By the properties of all artificial regressions, $\boldsymbol{t}^{(j)}$ is asymptotically equal to minus the inverse of the Hessian times the gradient. Hence it makes sense to replace $-\big(\boldsymbol{H}(\boldsymbol{\theta}^{(j)})\big)^{-1}\boldsymbol{g}(\boldsymbol{\theta}^{(j)})$ in (14.38) by $\boldsymbol{t}^{(j)}$. That yields (14.37), which is the updating rule based on the DLR. The stopping rule would normally also be based on some measure of the explanatory power of the DLR, as discussed in Section 6.8.

The DLR can, of course, be used for performing hypothesis tests of any of the models we have been discussing. Since for these models the sum of squares of the regressand is always $2n$, the quantity $2n - \text{SSR}$ will always equal the explained sum of squares, and it provides an asymptotically valid test statistic that is very easy to calculate. As usual, pseudo-F and pseudo-t statistics based on the artificial regression are also asymptotically valid. We will not elaborate on these matters here, since there is really nothing new to discuss; a special case will be discussed in the next section.

It is perhaps worthwhile to interject a word of warning at this point. If the regressand or any of the regressors in a DLR that is used for hypothesis testing is constructed incorrectly, it is possible, and indeed likely, that the regression will yield a computed test statistic which is large and entirely meaningless. It is therefore a very good idea to check most of the calculations by first running the DLR *without* those regressors that correspond to the parameters being tested. This regression, like artificial regressions used to calculate covariance matrices, should have no explanatory power at all if everything has been constructed correctly. Unfortunately, one cannot check the test regressors in this way, and an error in their construction can easily lead to nonsensical results. For example, if one inadvertently added a constant term to a DLR, it would almost certainly have substantial ability to explain the regressand, because the second half of the latter is simply a vector of 1s.

14.6 Testing Linear and Loglinear Regression Models

In many applications, the dependent variable is always positive. Applied econometricians must therefore decide whether a regression model should attempt to explain the conditional mean of the original variable or of its logarithm. Both types of model are often plausible a priori. In this section, we discuss techniques for choosing between, and testing the specification of, models in which the regressand is the level or the logarithm of the dependent variable. Tests based on the DLR turn out to be very useful for this purpose.

Suppose initially that both models are linear in the parameters. Thus the two competing models are

$$y_t = \sum_{i=1}^{k} \beta_i X_{ti} + \sum_{j=1}^{l} \gamma_j Z_{tj} + u_t, \quad u_t \sim \text{NID}(0, \sigma^2), \quad \text{and} \tag{14.39}$$

$$\log y_t = \sum_{i=1}^{k} \beta_i \log X_{ti} + \sum_{j=1}^{l} \gamma_j Z_{tj} + u_t, \quad u_t \sim \text{NID}(0, \sigma^2), \tag{14.40}$$

where the notation, not coincidentally, is the same as for the conventional Box-Cox model. After both models have been estimated, it may be possible to conclude that one of them should be rejected simply by comparing the values of their loglikelihood functions, as discussed in Section 14.3. However, such a procedure can tell us nothing about the validity of whichever of the two models fits best. If both these models are reasonable ones, it is important to test both of them before tentatively accepting either one.

There are numerous ways to test the specification of linear and loglinear regression models like (14.39) and (14.40). The most commonly used tests are based on the fact that these are both special cases of the conventional

Box-Cox model,

$$B(y_t, \lambda) = \sum_{i=1}^{k} \beta_i B(X_{ti}, \lambda) + \sum_{j=1}^{l} \gamma_j Z_{tj} + u_t, \quad u_t \sim \text{NID}(0, \sigma^2). \tag{14.41}$$

Conceptually the simplest way to test (14.39) and (14.40) against (14.41) is to estimate all three models and use an LR test, as originally suggested by Box and Cox (1964) in the context of the simple Box-Cox model. However, because estimating (14.41) can require a certain amount of effort, it may be more attractive to use an LM test instead.

Several ways of implementing this LM test are available. We will mention ones based on artificial regressions only, since these are the easiest to compute, and, if an LM test is not easy to compute, it has no advantage over the corresponding LR test. It is obviously possible to construct LM tests of (14.39) and (14.40) against (14.41) using either the OPG regression or the DLR. The former tests were derived by Godfrey and Wickens (1981) and the latter by Davidson and MacKinnon (1985c). The latter authors provided Monte Carlo evidence that tests based on the DLR perform very much better in finite samples than tests based on the OPG regression, a finding subsequently confirmed by Godfrey, McAleer, and McKenzie (1988).

It is illuminating to discuss what the DLR looks like for testing linear and loglinear regressions. When testing the linear model (14.39), the null hypothesis is that $\lambda = 1$. In this case, the regressand of the DLR has t^{th} element $\hat{u}_t/\hat{\sigma}$ and $(t+n)^{\text{th}}$ element 1, where $\hat{u}_t$ denotes the tth residual from the linear model and $\hat{\sigma}$ denotes the ML estimate of σ. The tth and $(t+n)^{\text{th}}$ elements of the regressors are then

$$\begin{aligned}
&\text{for } \beta_i: \ \ X_{ti} - 1 \text{ and } 0;\\
&\text{for } \gamma_j: \ \ Z_{tj} \text{ and } 0;\\
&\text{for } \sigma: \ \ \hat{u}_t/\hat{\sigma} \text{ and } -1;\\
&\text{for } \lambda: \ \ \sum_{i=1}^{k} \hat{\beta}_i \big(X_{ti} \log X_{ti} - X_{ti} + 1\big) - \big(y_t \log y_t - y_t + 1\big) \text{ and } \hat{\sigma} \log y_t.
\end{aligned}$$

These regressors are not quite what one might expect to get from (14.33), (14.35), and (14.36), because they have all been multiplied by $\hat{\sigma}$, something that is harmless to do because it does not change the subspace spanned by the columns of the regressor matrix. For the same reason, if one of the Z_{tj}'s is a constant term, as will typically be the case, it is unnecessary to subtract 1 from the X_{ti}'s.

When testing the loglinear model (14.40), the null hypothesis is that $\lambda = 0$. In this case, the regressand of the DLR has t^{th} element $\tilde{u}_t/\tilde{\sigma}$ and $(t+n)^{\text{th}}$ element 1, where $\tilde{u}_t$ denotes the tth residual from the loglinear model and $\tilde{\sigma}$ denotes the ML estimate of σ. The tth and $(t+n)^{\text{th}}$ elements of the regressors are then

$$\text{for } \beta_i: \ \log X_{ti} \text{ and } 0;$$

$$\text{for } \gamma_j: \ Z_{tj} \text{ and } 0;$$

$$\text{for } \sigma: \ \tilde{u}_t/\tilde{\sigma} \text{ and } -1;$$

$$\text{for } \lambda: \ \frac{1}{2}\sum_{i=1}^{k}\tilde{\beta}_i(\log X_{ti})^2 - \frac{1}{2}(\log y_t)^2 \text{ and } \tilde{\sigma}\log y_t.$$

This time all regressors have been multiplied by $\tilde{\sigma}$. The regressor for λ was derived with the aid of l'Hôpital's Rule:

$$\lim_{\lambda\to 0}\left(\frac{\lambda x^{\lambda}\log x - x^{\lambda} + 1}{\lambda^2}\right) = \frac{1}{2}(\log x)^2.$$

One test that is sometimes confused with LM tests such as the ones just discussed is a test proposed by Andrews (1971) and modified by Godfrey and Wickens (1981) so that it applies to the conventional Box-Cox model. The idea is to take a first-order approximation to (14.41) around $\lambda = 0$ or $\lambda = 1$, rearrange terms so that only $\log y_t$ or y_t appears on the left-hand side, and then replace y_t wherever it appears on the right-hand side by the fitted values from the regression under test. The result is something that looks like the original regression being tested, with the addition of one extra regressor. For the linear null this extra regressor is

$$\hat{y}_t\log\hat{y}_t - \hat{y}_t + 1 - \sum_{i=1}^{k}\hat{\beta}_i(X_{ti}\log X_{ti} - X_{ti} + 1),$$

and for the loglinear null it is

$$\frac{1}{2}\left((\log\tilde{y}_t)^2 - \sum_{i=1}^{k}\tilde{\beta}_i(\log X_{ti})^2\right),$$

where $\hat{y}_t$ and $\tilde{y}_t$ denote the fitted values of y_t from the linear and loglinear models, respectively. The test statistic is simply the t statistic on the extra regressor.

The Andrews test has the rather remarkable property that if the X_{ti}'s and Z_{tj}'s can be treated as nonstochastic, and if the error terms really are normally distributed, the test statistic will actually have the t distribution in finite samples. This follows from the fact that the test regressors depend on y_t only through the estimates $\hat{\beta}$ and $\hat{\gamma}$ (or $\tilde{\beta}$ and $\tilde{\gamma}$). The argument is similar to the one used in Section 11.3 to show that the J_A test is exact. It follows from the same results of Milliken and Graybill (1970).

However, the Andrews test is not really testing against the same alternative as the LM tests. Implicitly, it is testing in a regression direction, that is, against an alternative that is also a regression model. But the Box-Cox model (14.41) is not a regression model. The Andrews test must therefore have less power than classical tests of linear and loglinear models against (14.41) when the latter actually generated the data. Using techniques similar to those discussed in Chapter 12, it was shown in Davidson and MacKinnon (1985c) that, as $\sigma \to 0$, the noncentrality parameter for the Andrews test approaches that of the classical tests, while as $\sigma \to \infty$, it approaches zero. Thus, except when σ is small, one would expect the Andrews test to be seriously lacking in power, and Monte Carlo results confirm this. One possible advantage of the Andrews test should be noted, however. Unlike the LM tests we have discussed, it is not sensitive, asymptotically, to failures of the normality assumption, because it is simply testing in a regression direction.

Although tests based on the Box-Cox transformation are more popular, a second approach to testing linear and loglinear models also deserves mention. It treats the two models as nonnested hypotheses, in much the same way as did the tests discussed in Section 11.3. This nonnested approach allows one to handle more general types of model than the approach based on the Box-Cox transformation, because the two models need not have the same number of parameters, or indeed resemble each other in any way, and neither of them needs to be linear in either variables or parameters. We can write the two competing models as

$$H_1:\ \ y_t = x_t(\boldsymbol{\beta}) + u_{1t}, \quad u_{1t} \sim \mathrm{NID}(0, \sigma_1^2), \ \text{ and} \tag{14.42}$$

$$H_2:\ \ \log y_t = z_t(\boldsymbol{\gamma}) + u_{2t}, \quad u_{2t} \sim \mathrm{NID}(0, \sigma_2^2). \tag{14.43}$$

The notation here is similar to that used in the discussion of nonnested hypothesis testing in Section 11.3 and should be self-explanatory. Notice that the assumption of normally distributed error terms, which was not needed in our previous discussion of nonnested tests, is needed here.

There are two obvious ways to derive nonnested tests for models like (14.42) and (14.43). One is to attempt to implement the ideas of Cox (1961, 1962), as in Aneuryn-Evans and Deaton (1980). Unfortunately, this turns out to be rather difficult. The second approach, which is much easier, is to base them on some sort of artificial nesting. Consider the (somewhat arbitrary) artificial compound model

$$H_C:\ \ (1-\alpha)\left(\frac{y_t - x_t(\boldsymbol{\beta})}{\sigma_1}\right) + \alpha\left(\frac{\log y_t - z_t(\boldsymbol{\gamma})}{\sigma_2}\right) = \varepsilon_t, \tag{14.44}$$

where the assumptions on u_{1t} and u_{2t} imply that ε_t is $N(0,1)$. Like the artificial compound models introduced in Section 11.3, this one cannot be estimated as it stands, because many of the parameters will in general be unidentified. However, following the procedure used to obtain the J and P tests, we can replace the parameters of the model that is *not* being tested by estimates. Thus, if we wish to test H_1, we can replace γ and σ_2 by ML estimates $\hat{\gamma}$ and $\hat{\sigma}_2$ so that H_C becomes

$$H_C'\colon\ (1-\alpha)\left(\frac{y_t - x_t(\boldsymbol{\beta})}{\sigma_1}\right) + \alpha\left(\frac{\log y_t - z_t(\hat{\gamma})}{\hat{\sigma}_2}\right) = \varepsilon_t.$$

It is straightforward to test H_1 against H_C' by means of the DLR:

$$\begin{bmatrix} \dfrac{(y_t - \hat{x}_t)}{\hat{\sigma}_1} \\ 1 \end{bmatrix} = \begin{bmatrix} \hat{\boldsymbol{X}}_t & \dfrac{(y_t - \hat{x}_t)}{\hat{\sigma}_1} & \hat{z}_t - \log y_t \\ \mathbf{0} & -1 & \hat{\sigma}_1/y_t \end{bmatrix} \begin{bmatrix} \boldsymbol{b} \\ s \\ a \end{bmatrix} + \text{residuals}, \qquad (14.45)$$

where $\hat{x}_t \equiv x_t(\hat{\boldsymbol{\beta}})$, $\hat{\boldsymbol{X}}_t \equiv \boldsymbol{X}_t(\hat{\boldsymbol{\beta}})$, and $\hat{z}_t \equiv z_t(\hat{\gamma})$. The DLR (14.45) is actually a simplified version of the DLR that one obtains initially. First, $\hat{\sigma}_1$ times the original regressor for σ_1 has been added to the original regressor for α. Then the regressors corresponding to $\boldsymbol{\beta}$ and σ_1 have been multiplied by $\hat{\sigma}_1$, and the regressor corresponding to α has been multiplied by $\hat{\sigma}_2$. None of these modifications affects the subspace spanned by the columns of the regressor, and hence none of them affects the test statistic(s) one obtains. The last column of the regressor matrix in (14.45) is the one that corresponds to α. The other columns should be orthogonal to the regressand by construction.

Similarly, if we wish to test H_2, we can replace $\boldsymbol{\beta}$ and σ_1 by ML estimates $\hat{\boldsymbol{\beta}}$ and $\hat{\sigma}_1$ so that H_C becomes

$$H_C''\colon\ (1-\alpha)\left(\frac{y_t - x_t(\hat{\boldsymbol{\beta}})}{\hat{\sigma}_1}\right) + \alpha\left(\frac{\log y_t - z_t(\gamma)}{\sigma_2}\right) = \varepsilon_t.$$

It is then straightforward to test H_2 against H_C'' by means of the DLR

$$\begin{bmatrix} \dfrac{\log y_t - \hat{z}_t}{\hat{\sigma}_2} \\ 1 \end{bmatrix} = \begin{bmatrix} \hat{\boldsymbol{Z}}_t & \dfrac{\log y_t - \hat{z}_t}{\hat{\sigma}_2} & \hat{x}_t - y_t \\ \mathbf{0} & -1 & \hat{\sigma}_2 y_t \end{bmatrix} \begin{bmatrix} \boldsymbol{b} \\ s \\ a \end{bmatrix} + \text{residuals}. \qquad (14.46)$$

Once again, this is a simplified version of the DLR that one obtains initially, and the last column of the regressor matrix is the one that corresponds to α.

The tests we have just discussed evidently generalize very easily to models involving any sort of transformation of the dependent variable, including Box-Cox models and other models in which the transformation depends on one or more unknown parameters. For more details, see Davidson and MacKinnon (1984a). It should be stressed that the artificial compound model (14.44) is quite arbitrary. Unlike the similar-looking model for regression models that was employed in Section 11.3, it does not yield tests asymptotically equivalent to Cox tests. Moreover, little is known about the finite-sample properties of tests based on DLRs like (14.45) and (14.46).

One final procedure that is worth mentioning is the ***P_E* test** suggested by MacKinnon, White, and Davidson (1983). It also starts from the artificial compound model (14.44) but then follows essentially the approach of the Andrews test so as to obtain a GNR that tests only in a regression direction. The Gauss-Newton test regressions for the P_E test are

$$y_t - \hat{x}_t = \hat{\boldsymbol{X}}_t \boldsymbol{b} + a(\hat{z}_t - \log \hat{x}_t) + \text{residual} \tag{14.47}$$

for the test of H_1 and

$$\log y_t - \hat{z}_t = \hat{\boldsymbol{Z}}_t \boldsymbol{c} + d(\hat{x}_t - \exp \hat{z}_t) + \text{residual} \tag{14.48}$$

for the test of H_2. The easiest test statistics to use are the t statistics for $a = 0$ in (14.47) and $d = 0$ in (14.48). Like the Andrews test, the P_E test is likely to be seriously lacking in power, except when the error variance of the DGP is very small. Its primary advantage is that, unlike tests based on the DLR, it will be asymptotically insensitive to failures of the normality assumption.

14.7 OTHER TRANSFORMATIONS

Models based on the Box-Cox transformation will not perform adequately in every case. In particular, the conventional Box-Cox model is often not very satisfactory, for reasons that we will discuss. In this section, we briefly discuss a number of other transformations that can be useful in some cases. We will not say much about methods of estimation and inference for these models, except to note that they can all be estimated by maximum likelihood, using the DLR as part of the maximization algorithm, and that the DLR can always be used to compute covariance matrices and test statistics.

One major problem with the conventional Box-Cox model is that the transformation parameter λ plays two different roles: It affects the properties of the residuals, and it also affects the functional form of the regression function. For example, suppose the DGP were actually a linear regression model with heteroskedastic errors having variance proportional to the square of the conditional mean of the dependent variable:

$$y_t = \boldsymbol{X}_t \boldsymbol{\beta}_0 + u_t, \quad u_t \sim N\big(0, \sigma_0^2 (\boldsymbol{X}_t \boldsymbol{\beta}_0)^2\big), \tag{14.49}$$

where σ_0 and $\boldsymbol{\beta}_0$ denote values under the DGP. If we estimated a conventional Box-Cox model using data generated in this way, we would almost certainly obtain an estimate of λ that was less than unity, because this would reduce the amount of heteroskedasticity in the residuals. Thus we might incorrectly conclude that a linear specification was inappropriate or even that a loglinear one was appropriate.

The problem is that the transformation parameter in the conventional Box-Cox model affects both the form of the regression function and the amount of heteroskedasticity in the residuals. One obvious solution is to allow for heteroskedasticity explicitly, as in the model

$$B(y_t, \lambda) = \sum_{i=1}^{k} \beta_i B(X_{ti}, \lambda) + \sum_{j=1}^{l} \gamma_j Z_{tj} + u_t, \quad u_t \sim N\big(0, \sigma^2 h(\boldsymbol{w}_t \boldsymbol{\delta})\big),$$

where $h(\cdot)$ is a skedastic function, $\boldsymbol{w}_t$ is a vector of observations on independent variables, and $\boldsymbol{\delta}$ is a vector of parameters to be estimated. If one were primarily interested in heteroskedasticity of the form that appears in (14.49), the skedastic function $h(\boldsymbol{w}_t \boldsymbol{\delta})$ could be specified as $(\boldsymbol{X}_t \boldsymbol{\beta})^2$. See, among others, Gaudry and Dagenais (1979), Lahiri and Egy (1981), and Tse (1984).

Another possibility is to allow there to be more than one transformation parameter, as in the models

$$B(y_t, \lambda) = \sum_{i=1}^{k} \beta_i B(X_{ti}, \phi) + \sum_{j=1}^{l} \gamma_j Z_{tj} + u_t \quad \text{and} \tag{14.50}$$

$$B(y_t, \lambda) = B\left(\left(\sum_{i=1}^{k} \beta_i B(X_{ti}, \phi) + \sum_{j=1}^{l} \gamma_j Z_{tj}\right), \lambda\right) + u_t, \tag{14.51}$$

where, in both cases, u_t is assumed to be $N(0, \sigma^2)$. The first of these models is an obvious generalization of the conventional Box-Cox model and has been used a certain amount in econometrics, sometimes with more than one ϕ parameter. The second combines the conventional Box-Cox model with the transform-both-sides model and has not been used to any extent. In both cases, the parameter ϕ primarily affects the functional form of the regression function, while the parameter λ primarily affects the properties of the error terms. Of course, which of (14.50) or (14.51) will perform best on any given data set, or whether either of them will perform significantly better than the conventional Box-Cox model, is far from clear.

As we have seen, the Box-Cox transformation cannot be applied to variables that can take on zero or negative values. Various authors, including John and Draper (1980) and Bickel and Doksum (1981), have proposed ways to extend it so that it can be used in such cases. For example, the Bickel-Doksum proposal is to use the transformation

$$\frac{\operatorname{sign}(y)\,|y|^{\lambda} - 1}{\lambda} \tag{14.52}$$

instead of the Box-Cox transformation. It is logically possible to apply (14.52) to variables that can take on small or negative (but not zero) values. However, this transformation does not have particularly attractive properties; see Magee

(1988). When λ is small, it is extremely steep for y near zero. In addition, when $y < 0$, (14.52) has no limit as $\lambda \to 0$.

There is no reason to restrict attention to modified versions of the Box-Cox transformation, since other transformations may well be more appropriate for certain types of data. For example, when y_t is constrained to lie between zero and one, a model like

$$y_t = \boldsymbol{X}_t(\boldsymbol{\beta}) + u_t, \quad u_t \sim N(0, \sigma^2),$$

does not really make sense, because there is always a chance that u_t could be so large that y_t would fall outside the 0-1 interval. In such a case, it may be desirable to employ the transformation

$$\tau(y) = \log\left(\frac{y}{1-y}\right),$$

since $\tau(y)$ can vary between minus infinity and plus infinity. This transformation does not involve an unknown parameter, and so it does not require one to leave the regression framework; see Cox (1970).

An interesting family of transformations has been considered by Burbidge, Magee, and Robb (1988) and MacKinnon and Magee (1990). These transformations have the form $\theta(\alpha y)/\alpha$, where the function $\theta(\cdot)$ is assumed to be monotonically increasing in its argument and to possess the properties:

$$\theta(0) = 0; \quad \theta'(0) = 1; \quad \theta''(0) \neq 0. \tag{14.53}$$

Unlike the Box-Cox transformation, this transformation can be applied to variables of either sign and to zero variables. Many functions $\theta(\cdot)$ possess the properties (14.53). One of the simplest is the function $y + y^2$, for which the transformation would be

$$\frac{\theta(\alpha y)}{\alpha} = y + \alpha y^2. \tag{14.54}$$

Evidently, this will be a convex function of y when α is positive and a concave function when α is negative. Any transformation of the form $\theta(\alpha y)/\alpha$ satisfying (14.53) will be locally equivalent to (14.54), and so we see that a test of $\alpha = 0$ can be interpreted as testing against any form of local quadratic nonlinearity.

For this transformation family, the model (14.04) would become

$$\frac{\theta(\alpha y_t)}{\alpha} = x_t(\boldsymbol{\beta}) + u_t, \quad u_t \sim \text{NID}(0, \sigma^2).$$

It is easy to test the null hypothesis that $\alpha = 0$ using a DLR very similar to the one used to test the null that $\lambda = 1$ in the simple Box-Cox model (14.04); see MacKinnon and Magee (1990) for details. This test is sensitive to several common forms of model misspecification, including nonlinearity in the regression function, heteroskedasticity, and skewness. It turns out to be closely related to the well-known RESET test; see Section 6.5. One would obtain the RESET test if the transformation were applied to $x_t(\boldsymbol{\beta})$ instead of to y_t, as in the model

$$y_t = \frac{\theta\big(\alpha x_t(\boldsymbol{\beta})\big)}{\alpha} + u_t, \quad u_t \sim \mathrm{NID}(0, \sigma^2).$$

Since this is simply a nonlinear regression model, a test for $\alpha = 0$ can be based on a GNR. It is just the t test of $a = 0$ in

$$y_t - x_t(\hat{\boldsymbol{\beta}}) = \boldsymbol{X}_t(\hat{\boldsymbol{\beta}})\boldsymbol{b} + a x_t^2(\hat{\boldsymbol{\beta}}) + \text{residual},$$

which is a form of the RESET test.

14.8 Conclusion

With the exception of the conventional Box-Cox model, models involving transformations of the dependent variable have been used rather infrequently in econometrics. This is surprising, because they often provide a simple and parsimonious way to obtain a model with well-behaved residuals and there is a large literature about them in statistics, including books by McCullagh and Nelder (1983), Atkinson (1985), and Carroll and Ruppert (1988).

We have seen in this chapter that it is not at all difficult to handle models of this type. Provided one is willing to assume normality — and some such distributional assumption seems to be necessary once one leaves the regression framework — it is straightforward to estimate them by maximum likelihood. The double-length artificial regression is extremely useful in connection with these models. Everything that one can do with the Gauss-Newton regression for nonlinear regression models can be done with the DLR for models involving transformations of the dependent variable. The OPG regression can be used instead of the DLR but will generally perform less well.

Terms and Concepts

artificial observations (for DLR)
artificial regression (general formulation)
Box-Cox models: conventional, simple, and transform-both-sides
Box-Cox transformation
double-length artificial regression (DLR)
Jacobian factors
Jacobian terms
linear versus loglinear regressions
maximization algorithms using the DLR
nonlinear transformation
nonnested tests
nonregression models
P_E test
RESET test

Chapter 15

Qualitative and Limited Dependent Variables

15.1 Introduction

Regression models implicitly assume that the dependent variable, perhaps after a logarithmic or some other transformation, can take any value on the real line. Although this assumption is never strictly true with economic data, it is often reasonable enough. However, it is not an acceptable assumption when the dependent variable can take any specific value with probability substantially greater than zero. Economists frequently have to deal with such cases. Especially common are cases in which the dependent variable can take only two values. For example, a person may be in the labor force or not, a household may own or rent the home it lives in, a debtor may default on a loan or not, a commuter may drive to work or take public transit, and so on. These are all examples of **binary dependent variables**.

If we wish to explain economic variables like these in an econometric model, we must take account of their discrete nature. Models that do so are called **qualitative response models**, and they are usually estimated by maximum likelihood. In the simplest and most commonly encountered case, the dependent variable represents one of two alternatives. These are conventionally coded as 0 and 1, a convention that turns out to be very convenient. Models that attempt to explain 0-1 dependent variables are often called **binary response models** or, less often, **binary choice models**. They are very widely used in labor economics and many other areas of applied econometrics, as the examples above perhaps serve to illustrate.

Regression models are also inappropriate for handling models involving **limited dependent variables**, of which there are a great many varieties. Sometimes a dependent variable may be continuous on some interval(s) of the real line but may take on one or more values with finite probability. For example, consumer expenditures on any category of goods and services are generally constrained to be nonnegative. Thus, if we observe expenditures on some category for a sample of households, it is quite possible that those expenditures will be zero for many households and positive for others. Since there is a positive probability that a particular value, zero, will occur in the data, regression models are not appropriate for this type of data. Another type of limited dependent variable model arises when only certain outcomes (such as the positive ones in this example) are observed. This means that the sample will not be a random one.

In this chapter, we deal with both qualitative response models and limited dependent variable models. This is an area in which there has been an enormous amount of research over the past 20 years, and so our treatment covers only a few of the most basic models. We will focus initially on binary response models, because these are both the simplest and the most commonly encountered models of this kind. They will be discussed in the next three sections. Then, in Section 15.5, we briefly discuss qualitative response models for cases involving more than two different responses. Finally, in the last three sections, we turn our attention to some of the simplest models that involve limited dependent variables.

15.2 Binary Response Models

In a binary response model, the value of the dependent variable y_t can take on only two values, 1 and 0, which indicate whether or not some event occurs. We can think of $y_t = 1$ as indicating that the event occurred for observation t and $y_t = 0$ as indicating that it did not. Let P_t denote the (conditional) probability that the event occurred. Thus a binary response model is really trying to model P_t conditional on a certain information set, say Ω_t, that consists of exogenous and predetermined variables. Specifying y_t so that it is either 0 or 1 is very convenient, because P_t is then simply the expectation of y_t conditional on Ω_t:

$$P_t \equiv \Pr(y_t = 1 \,|\, \Omega_t) = E(y_t \,|\, \Omega_t).$$

The objective of a binary response model is to model this conditional expectation.

From this perspective, it is clear that the linear regression model makes no sense as a binary response model. Suppose that $\boldsymbol{X}_t$ denotes a row vector of length k of variables that belong to the information set Ω_t, including a constant term or the equivalent. Then a linear regression model would specify $E(y_t \,|\, \Omega_t)$ as $\boldsymbol{X}_t\boldsymbol{\beta}$. But $E(y_t \,|\, \Omega_t)$ is a probability, and probabilities must lie between 0 and 1. The quantity $\boldsymbol{X}_t\boldsymbol{\beta}$ is not constrained to do so and therefore cannot be interpreted as a probability. Nevertheless, a good deal of (mostly older) empirical work simply uses OLS to estimate what is (rather inappropriately) called the **linear probability model**,[1] that is, the model

$$y_t = \boldsymbol{X}_t\boldsymbol{\beta} + u_t.$$

[1] See, for example, Bowen and Finegan (1969).

In view of the much better models that are available, and the ease of estimating them using modern computer technology, this model has almost nothing to recommend it. Even if $\boldsymbol{X}_t\boldsymbol{\beta}$ happens to lie between 0 and 1 for some $\boldsymbol{\beta}$ and all observations in a particular sample, it is impossible to constrain $\boldsymbol{X}_t\boldsymbol{\beta}$ to lie in that interval for all possible values of $\boldsymbol{X}_t$, unless the values that the independent variables can take are limited in some way (for example, they might all be dummy variables). Thus the linear probability model is not a sensible way to model conditional probabilities.

Several binary response models that do make sense are available and are quite easy to deal with. The key is to make use of a **transformation function** $F(x)$ that has the properties

$$F(-\infty) = 0, \quad F(\infty) = 1, \text{ and} \tag{15.01}$$

$$f(x) \equiv \frac{\partial F(x)}{\partial x} > 0. \tag{15.02}$$

Thus $F(x)$ is a monotonically increasing function that maps from the real line to the 0-1 interval. Many cumulative distribution functions have these properties, and we will shortly discuss some specific examples. Using various specifications for the transformation function, we can model the conditional expectation of y_t in a variety of ways.

The binary response models that we will discuss consist of a transformation function $F(x)$ applied to an **index function** that depends on the independent variables and the parameters of the model. An index function is simply a function that has the properties of a regression function, whether linear or nonlinear. Thus a very general specification of a binary response model is

$$E(y_t \mid \Omega_t) = F\big(h(\boldsymbol{X}_t, \boldsymbol{\beta})\big),$$

where $h(\boldsymbol{X}_t, \boldsymbol{\beta})$ is the index function. A more restrictive, but much more commonly encountered, specification, is

$$E(y_t \mid \Omega_t) = F(\boldsymbol{X}_t\boldsymbol{\beta}). \tag{15.03}$$

In this case, the index function $\boldsymbol{X}_t\boldsymbol{\beta}$ is linear and $E(y_t \mid \Omega_t)$ is simply a nonlinear transformation of it. Although $\boldsymbol{X}_t\boldsymbol{\beta}$ can in principle take any value on the real line, $F(\boldsymbol{X}_t\boldsymbol{\beta})$ must lie between 0 and 1 by property (15.01).

Because $F(\cdot)$ is a nonlinear function, changes in the values of the X_{ti}'s, that is the elements of $\boldsymbol{X}_t$, necessarily affect $E(y_t \mid \Omega_t)$ in a nonlinear fashion. Specifically, when $P_t \equiv E(y_t \mid \Omega_t)$ is given by (15.03), its derivative with respect to X_{ti} is

$$\frac{\partial P_t}{\partial X_{ti}} = \frac{\partial F(\boldsymbol{X}_t\boldsymbol{\beta})}{\partial X_{ti}} = f(\boldsymbol{X}_t\boldsymbol{\beta})\beta_i. \tag{15.04}$$

For the transformation functions that are almost always employed, $f(\boldsymbol{X}_t\boldsymbol{\beta})$ achieves a maximum at zero and then falls as $\boldsymbol{X}_t\boldsymbol{\beta}$ gets farther from zero. Thus

(15.04) tells us that the effect on P_t of a change in one of the independent variables is greatest when $P_t = .5$ and least when P_t is close to 0 or 1.

When binary response models are used in applied work, the linear index function $\boldsymbol{X}_t\boldsymbol{\beta}$ is almost always employed, along with one of two particular specifications for $F(\cdot)$. The resulting models are called the **probit model** and the **logit model**. For the probit model, the transformation function $F(x)$ is the cumulative standard normal distribution function

$$\Phi(x) \equiv \int_{-\infty}^{x} \frac{1}{\sqrt{2\pi}} \exp\bigl(-\tfrac{1}{2}X^2\bigr)\,dX.$$

Since $\Phi(x)$ is a c.d.f., it automatically satisfies conditions (15.01) and (15.02). The probit model can be written as

$$P_t \equiv E(y_t \,|\, \Omega_t) = \Phi(\boldsymbol{X}_t\boldsymbol{\beta}).$$

Although there exists no closed-form expression for $\Phi(x)$, it is easily evaluated numerically, and its first derivative is of course simply the standard normal density function

$$\phi(x) = \frac{1}{\sqrt{2\pi}} \exp\bigl(-\tfrac{1}{2}x^2\bigr).$$

The probit model can be derived from a model involving an unobserved, or **latent**, variable y_t^*. Suppose that

$$y_t^* = \boldsymbol{X}_t\boldsymbol{\beta} + u_t, \quad u_t \sim \mathrm{NID}(0,1). \tag{15.05}$$

We observe only the sign of y_t^*, which determines the value of the observed binary variable y_t according to the relationship

$$y_t = 1 \text{ if } y_t^* > 0 \quad \text{and} \quad y_t = 0 \text{ if } y_t^* \leq 0. \tag{15.06}$$

For example, we could think of y_t^* as an index of the (net) utility obtained from some action. If the action yields positive utility, it will be undertaken; if not, then it will not be. Since we observe only whether or not the action is undertaken, we observe only the sign of y_t^*. Because of this, we can normalize the variance of u_t to be unity. If u_t actually had some other variance, say σ^2, dividing y_t^*, $\boldsymbol{\beta}$, and u_t by σ would yield a model observationally identical to the one we started with.

We can now ask what the probability is that $y_t = 1$. Some straightforward manipulations yield

$$\begin{aligned} \Pr(y_t = 1) &= \Pr(y_t^* > 0) = \Pr(\boldsymbol{X}_t\boldsymbol{\beta} + u_t > 0) \\ &= 1 - \Pr(u_t \leq -\boldsymbol{X}_t\boldsymbol{\beta}) = 1 - \Phi(-\boldsymbol{X}_t\boldsymbol{\beta}) = \Phi(\boldsymbol{X}_t\boldsymbol{\beta}). \end{aligned} \tag{15.07}$$

The last equality in (15.07) makes use of the fact that the standard normal density function is symmetric around zero. The final result, $\Phi(\boldsymbol{X}_t\boldsymbol{\beta})$, is just the probability that we would get by letting $\Phi(\cdot)$ play the role of $F(\cdot)$ in (15.03). Thus we have derived the probit model from the **latent variable model** consisting of (15.05) and (15.06). That the probit model can be derived in this way is one of its attractive features.

The logit model is very similar to the probit model but has a number of features that make it easier to deal with. For the logit model, the function $F(x)$ is the **logistic function**

$$\Lambda(x) \equiv (1 + e^{-x})^{-1} = \frac{e^x}{1 + e^x},$$

which has first derivative

$$\lambda(x) \equiv \frac{e^x}{(1 + e^x)^2} = \Lambda(x)\Lambda(-x).$$

The second equality here will later prove to be very useful. The logit model is most easily derived by assuming that

$$\log\left(\frac{P_t}{1 - P_t}\right) = \boldsymbol{X}_t\boldsymbol{\beta},$$

which says that the logarithm of the odds is equal to $\boldsymbol{X}_t\boldsymbol{\beta}$. Solving for P_t, we find that

$$P_t = \frac{\exp(\boldsymbol{X}_t\boldsymbol{\beta})}{1 + \exp(\boldsymbol{X}_t\boldsymbol{\beta})} = \big(1 + \exp(-\boldsymbol{X}_t\boldsymbol{\beta})\big)^{-1} = \Lambda(\boldsymbol{X}_t\boldsymbol{\beta}).$$

It is also possible to derive the logit model from a latent variable model like (15.05) and (15.06) but with errors that follow the extreme value distribution instead of the normal; see, among others, Domencich and McFadden (1975), McFadden (1984), and Train (1986).

In practice, the logit and probit models tend to yield extremely similar results. In most cases, the only real difference between them is in the way the elements of $\boldsymbol{\beta}$ are scaled. This difference in scaling occurs because the variance of the distribution for which the logistic function is the c.d.f. can be shown to be $\pi^2/3$, while that of the standard normal is of course unity. The logit estimates therefore all tend to be larger than the probit estimates, although usually by a factor of somewhat less than $\pi/\sqrt{3}$.[2] Figure 15.1 plots

[2] Amemiya (1981) suggests that 1.6 may be a better estimate of the factor by which logit estimates tend to exceed probit ones than $\pi/\sqrt{3} \cong 1.81$. As Greene (1990a) observes, a justification for this regularity is that $\phi(0)/\lambda(0) \cong 1.6$. Recall from (15.04) that the derivatives of P_t with respect to X_{ti} are equal to $f(\boldsymbol{X}_t\boldsymbol{\beta})\beta_i$. If $\boldsymbol{X}_t\boldsymbol{\beta}$ is roughly zero on average and the logit and probit models are to predict the same effect on P_t of a given change in one of the X_{ti}'s, then the coefficients for the logit model must be roughly 1.6 times those of the probit model. This approximation can be expected to work less well when the average value of P_t is far from .5.

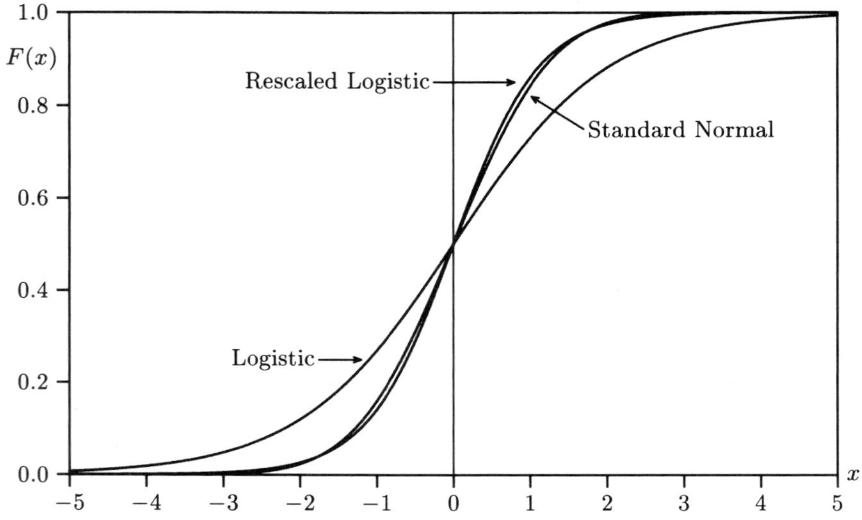

Figure 15.1 Three possible choices for $F(x)$

the standard normal c.d.f., the logistic function, and the logistic function rescaled to have variance unity. The similarity of the standard normal c.d.f. and the rescaled logistic function is striking.

In view of their similar properties, it is perhaps curious that both the logit and the probit models continue to be widely used, while models that genuinely differ from them are rarely encountered. There are as many ways in which such models could be specified as there are plausible choices for the transformation function $F(x)$. For example, one such choice is

$$F(x) = \pi^{-1}\arctan(x) + \tfrac{1}{2}. \tag{15.08}$$

Since this is the cumulative distribution function of the Cauchy distribution, its derivative is

$$f(x) = \frac{1}{\pi(1+x^2)},$$

which is the Cauchy density (see Section 4.6). Because the behavior of the Cauchy distribution function in the tails is very different from that of either $\Phi(x)$ or $\Lambda(x)$, there is at least the possibility that a binary response model based on (15.08) might perform substantially better or worse than a probit or logit model. On the other hand, there is very little chance that those two models will yield results which differ substantially, unless the sample size is very large indeed.

All three choices for $F(\cdot)$ that we have discussed are skew-symmetric around zero. That is, they have the property that $1 - F(x) = F(-x)$, which implies that $f(x) = f(-x)$. This is sometimes a convenient property, but there is no a priori reason for it to hold. Choices for $F(\cdot)$ that do not have this property will potentially yield quite different results from those produced by the logit and probit models. One way to obtain the same effect is to specify the model as

$$E(y_t \,|\, \Omega_t) = F\big(h(\boldsymbol{X}_t\boldsymbol{\beta})\big),$$

where $F(\cdot)$ is $\Phi(\cdot)$ or $\Lambda(\cdot)$, and $h(\cdot)$ is a nonlinear transformation. This suggests a way to test the validity of the skew-symmetry assumption, a subject that we will take up in Section 15.4.

15.3 ESTIMATION OF BINARY RESPONSE MODELS

At present, by far the most common way to estimate binary response models is to use the method of maximum likelihood. We will restrict our attention to this method and assume, for simplicity, that the index function is simply $\boldsymbol{X}_t\boldsymbol{\beta}$. Then, according to the binary response model (15.03), $F(\boldsymbol{X}_t\boldsymbol{\beta})$ is the probability that $y_t = 1$ and $1 - F(\boldsymbol{X}_t\boldsymbol{\beta})$ is the probability that $y_t = 0$. Thus, if $y_t = 1$, the contribution to the logarithm of the likelihood function for observation t is $\log\big(F(\boldsymbol{X}_t\boldsymbol{\beta})\big)$, while if $y_t = 0$, that contribution is $\log\big(1 - F(\boldsymbol{X}_t\boldsymbol{\beta})\big)$. Hence the loglikelihood function is

$$\ell(\boldsymbol{y}, \boldsymbol{\beta}) = \sum_{t=1}^{n} \Big(y_t \log\big(F(\boldsymbol{X}_t\boldsymbol{\beta})\big) + (1 - y_t)\log\big(1 - F(\boldsymbol{X}_t\boldsymbol{\beta})\big)\Big). \tag{15.09}$$

This function is globally concave whenever $\log\big(F(x)\big)$ and $\log\big(1 - F(x)\big)$ are concave functions of the argument x; see Pratt (1981). This condition is satisfied by many binary response models, including the logit and probit models. Therefore, the loglikelihood functions for these models are very easy to maximize numerically.[3]

The first-order conditions for a maximum of (15.09) are

$$\sum_{t=1}^{n} \frac{(y_t - \hat{F}_t)\hat{f}_t X_{ti}}{\hat{F}_t(1 - \hat{F}_t)} = 0, \quad i = 1, \ldots, k, \tag{15.10}$$

where $\hat{F}_t \equiv F(\boldsymbol{X}_t\hat{\boldsymbol{\beta}})$ and $\hat{f}_t \equiv f(\boldsymbol{X}_t\hat{\boldsymbol{\beta}})$, with $\hat{\boldsymbol{\beta}}$ denoting the vector of ML estimates. Whenever the loglikelihood function is globally concave, these first-order conditions define a unique maximum if they are satisfied at all. It can be verified that logit, probit, and many other binary response models satisfy

[3] In the usual case, in which $F(\cdot)$ is skew-symmetric, it is much better to evaluate $\log(F(-\boldsymbol{X}_t\boldsymbol{\beta}))$ rather than $\log(1 - F(\boldsymbol{X}_t\boldsymbol{\beta}))$ when writing computer programs. This avoids the risk that $1 - F(\boldsymbol{X}_t\boldsymbol{\beta})$ may be evaluated quite inaccurately when $F(\boldsymbol{X}_t\boldsymbol{\beta})$ is close to unity. Because $F(\cdot)$ need not be skew-symmetric, however, we will retain the more general notation.

the regularity conditions needed for the ML estimates $\hat{\boldsymbol{\beta}}$ to be consistent and asymptotically normal, with asymptotic covariance matrix given by the inverse of the information matrix in the usual way. See, for example, Gouriéroux and Monfort (1981). In the case of the logit model, the first-order conditions (15.10) simplify to

$$\sum_{t=1}^{n} \big(y_t - \Lambda(\boldsymbol{X}_t\hat{\boldsymbol{\beta}})\big)X_{ti} = 0, \quad i = 1, \ldots, k,$$

because $\lambda(x) = \Lambda(x)\big(1 - \Lambda(x)\big)$. Notice that conditions (15.10) look just like the first-order conditions for weighted least squares estimation of the nonlinear regression model

$$y_t = F(\boldsymbol{X}_t\boldsymbol{\beta}) + e_t, \tag{15.11}$$

with weights given by

$$\Big(F(\boldsymbol{X}_t\boldsymbol{\beta})\big(1 - F(\boldsymbol{X}_t\boldsymbol{\beta})\big)\Big)^{-1/2}.$$

This makes sense, since the variance of the error term in (15.11) is

$$\begin{aligned} E(e_t^2) &= E\big(y_t - F(\boldsymbol{X}_t\boldsymbol{\beta})\big)^2 \\ &= F(\boldsymbol{X}_t\boldsymbol{\beta})\big(1 - F(\boldsymbol{X}_t\boldsymbol{\beta})\big)^2 + \big(1 - F(\boldsymbol{X}_t\boldsymbol{\beta})\big)\big(F(\boldsymbol{X}_t\boldsymbol{\beta})\big)^2 \\ &= F(\boldsymbol{X}_t\boldsymbol{\beta})\big(1 - F(\boldsymbol{X}_t\boldsymbol{\beta})\big). \end{aligned}$$

Thus one way to obtain ML estimates of any binary response model is to apply iteratively reweighted nonlinear least squares to (15.11) or to whatever nonlinear regression model is appropriate if the index function is not $\boldsymbol{X}_t\boldsymbol{\beta}$. For most models, however, this is generally not the best approach, and a better one is discussed in the next section.

Using the fact that ML is equivalent to a form of weighted NLS for binary response models, it is obvious that the asymptotic covariance matrix for $n^{1/2}(\hat{\boldsymbol{\beta}} - \boldsymbol{\beta}_0)$ must be

$$\Big(\frac{1}{n}\boldsymbol{X}^{\top}\boldsymbol{\Psi}(\boldsymbol{\beta}_0)\boldsymbol{X}\Big)^{-1},$$

where $\boldsymbol{X}$ is an $n \times k$ matrix with typical row $\boldsymbol{X}_t$ and typical element X_{ti}, and $\boldsymbol{\Psi}(\boldsymbol{\beta})$ is a diagonal matrix with typical diagonal element

$$\Psi(\boldsymbol{X}_t\boldsymbol{\beta}) = \frac{f^2(\boldsymbol{X}_t\boldsymbol{\beta})}{F(\boldsymbol{X}_t\boldsymbol{\beta})\big(1 - F(\boldsymbol{X}_t\boldsymbol{\beta})\big)}. \tag{15.12}$$

The numerator reflects the fact that the derivative of $F(\boldsymbol{X}_t\boldsymbol{\beta})$ with respect to β_i is $f(\boldsymbol{X}_t\boldsymbol{\beta})X_{ti}$, and the denominator is simply the variance of e_t in (15.11). In the logit case, $\Psi(\boldsymbol{X}_t\boldsymbol{\beta})$ simplifies to $\lambda(\boldsymbol{X}_t\boldsymbol{\beta})$.

This asymptotic covariance matrix can also be obtained by taking the inverse of the information matrix. As usual, this is equal to the expectation of minus n^{-1} times the Hessian and also to the expectation of the outer product of the gradient. The information matrix is simply

$$\mathfrak{I}(\boldsymbol{\beta}) \equiv \frac{1}{n}\boldsymbol{X}^{\top}\boldsymbol{\Psi}(\boldsymbol{\beta})\boldsymbol{X}, \tag{15.13}$$

with $\boldsymbol{\Psi}(\boldsymbol{\beta})$ defined by (15.12). For example, from (15.10) it is easy to see that a typical element of the matrix $n^{-1}\boldsymbol{G}^{\top}(\boldsymbol{\beta})\boldsymbol{G}(\boldsymbol{\beta})$, where $\boldsymbol{G}(\boldsymbol{\beta})$ is the CG matrix, is

$$\frac{1}{n}\sum_{t=1}^{n}\left(\frac{\big(y_t - F(\boldsymbol{X}_t\boldsymbol{\beta})\big)f(\boldsymbol{X}_t\boldsymbol{\beta})}{F(\boldsymbol{X}_t\boldsymbol{\beta})\big(1 - F(\boldsymbol{X}_t\boldsymbol{\beta})\big)}\right)^2 X_{ti}X_{tj}.$$

It is a good exercise to show that the expectation of this expression is a typical element of the information matrix (15.13).

Recognizing that estimates from a binary response model are essentially weighted least squares estimates is quite illuminating. In the case of least squares, each observation is given equal weight when the information matrix is formed. In the binary response case, on the other hand, some observations are given much more weight than others, because the weights $\Psi(\boldsymbol{X}_t\boldsymbol{\beta})$ defined in (15.12) can differ greatly. If one plots these weights as a function of $\boldsymbol{X}_t\boldsymbol{\beta}$ for either the logit or probit models, one finds that the maximum weight will be given to observations for which $\boldsymbol{X}_t\boldsymbol{\beta} = 0$, implying that $P_t = .5$, while relatively little weight will be given to observations for which P_t is close to 0 or 1. This makes sense, since when P_t is close to 0 or 1, a given change in $\boldsymbol{\beta}$ will have little effect on P_t, while when P_t is close to .5, such a change will have a much larger effect. Hence observations of the latter type provide much more "information" than observations of the former type.

In Figure 15.2, the weights (15.12) are plotted for the probit and logit cases (the latter rescaled to have variance unity) as a function of the index $\boldsymbol{X}_t\boldsymbol{\beta}$. Notice that the differences between these two models are more striking than they were in Figure 15.1. The logit model gives more weight to observations for which $\boldsymbol{X}_t\boldsymbol{\beta}$ is near zero and far from zero, while the probit model gives more weight to observations for which $\boldsymbol{X}_t\boldsymbol{\beta}$ takes intermediate values (roughly, between 0.8 and 3.0). However, the differences that are apparent in the figure rarely seem to matter much in practice.

As we have seen, one can think of a binary dependent variable as arising from a latent variable model such as the one given by (15.05) and (15.06). It is interesting to ask how much efficiency in estimation is lost by not observing the latent variable. Clearly something must be lost, since a binary variable like y_t must provide less information than a continuous variable like y_t^*. The covariance matrix for the OLS estimates of $\boldsymbol{\beta}$ in (15.05) is $(\boldsymbol{X}^{\top}\boldsymbol{X})^{-1}$; remember that the error variance is normalized to unity. In contrast, the covariance matrix for probit estimates of $\boldsymbol{\beta}$ is $\big(\boldsymbol{X}^{\top}\boldsymbol{\Psi}(\boldsymbol{\beta})\boldsymbol{X}\big)^{-1}$, where $\boldsymbol{\Psi}(\boldsymbol{\beta})$ was defined

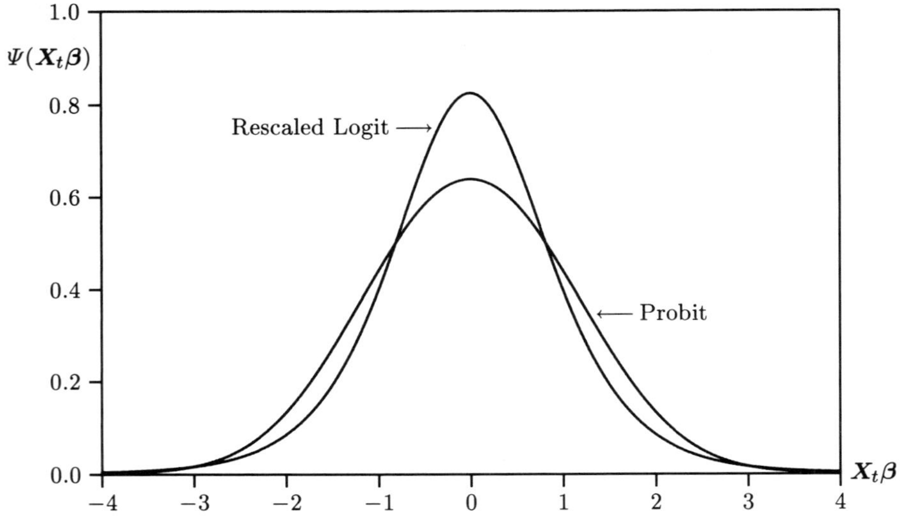

Figure 15.2 Weights for probit and rescaled logit models

by (15.12). The largest possible value for $\Psi(\boldsymbol{X}_t\boldsymbol{\beta})$ is achieved when $P_t = .5$. In the probit case, this value is 0.6366. Hence, in the best possible case, when the data are such that $P_t = .5$ for all t, the covariance matrix for the probit estimates will be equal to 1.57 ($\cong 1/0.6366$) times the OLS covariance matrix. In practice, of course, this upper bound is most unlikely to be achieved, and probit estimates may be very much less efficient than OLS estimates using the latent variable would be, especially if P_t is near 0 or 1 for a large fraction of the sample.

One practical problem with binary response models is that the first-order conditions (15.10) do not necessarily have a finite solution. This can occur when the data set fails to provide enough information to identify all the parameters. Suppose there is some linear combination of the independent variables, say $z_t \equiv \boldsymbol{X}_t\boldsymbol{\beta}^*$, such that

$$\begin{aligned} y_t &= 0 \;\text{ whenever }\; z_t \leq 0, \;\text{ and} \\ y_t &= 1 \;\text{ whenever }\; z_t > 0. \end{aligned}$$

Then it will be possible to make $\ell(\boldsymbol{y}, \boldsymbol{\beta})$ tend to zero by setting $\boldsymbol{\beta} = \alpha\boldsymbol{\beta}^*$ and letting $\alpha \to \infty$. This will ensure that $F(\boldsymbol{X}_t\boldsymbol{\beta}) \to 0$ for all observations where $y_t = 0$ and $F(\boldsymbol{X}_t\boldsymbol{\beta}) \to 1$ for all observations where $y_t = 1$. The value of the loglikelihood function (15.09) will therefore tend to zero as $\alpha \to \infty$. But zero is evidently an upper bound for this value. Thus, in circumstances like these, the parameters $\boldsymbol{\beta}$ are not identified on the noncompact parameter space $\mathbb{R}^k$ in the sense of definition 8.1, and we evidently cannot obtain sensible estimates of $\boldsymbol{\beta}$; see Albert and Anderson (1984).

When z_t is just a linear combination of the constant term and a single independent variable, the latter is often said to be a **perfect classifier**, because the y_t's can be classified as being 0 or 1 once the value of that variable is known. For example, consider the DGP

$$\begin{aligned} y_t^* &= x_t + u_t, \quad u_t \sim \text{NID}(0,1); \\ y_t &= 1 \text{ if } y_t^* > 0 \quad \text{and} \quad y_t = 0 \text{ if } y_t^* \leq 0. \end{aligned} \tag{15.14}$$

For this DGP, it would seem to be sensible to estimate the probit model

$$E(y_t \,|\, x_t) = \Phi(\beta_0 + \beta_1 x_t). \tag{15.15}$$

But suppose that, in the sample, x_t is always either less than -4 or greater than $+4$. When x_t is less than -4, it is almost certain (the probability is greater than 0.99997) that y_t will be 0, and when x_t is greater than $+4$, it is almost certain that y_t will be 1. Thus, unless the sample size is very large, there are unlikely to be any observations for which $x_t < 0$ and $y_t = 1$ or observations for which $x_t > 0$ and $y_t = 0$. In the absence of such observations, the variable x_t will be a perfect classifier, and it will be impossible to obtain sensible estimates of the parameters of (15.15). Whatever maximization algorithm is being used will simply try to make $\hat{\beta}_1$ as large as possible.

Although this example is an extreme one, similar problems are likely to occur whenever the model fits very well and the sample size is small. There will be a perfect classifier whenever there exists a separating hyperplane in the space of the explanatory variables such that all the observations with $y_t = 0$ are on one side and all the observations with $y_t = 1$ are on the other. This is likely to happen when the model fits well and when there are only a few observations for which $y_t = 1$ or, alternatively, for which $y_t = 0$. Nevertheless, it may be possible to obtain ML estimates when n is as small as $k + 1$ and when there is only one observation for which $y_t = 1$ or $y_t = 0$.

In regression models, it is common to test the hypothesis that all slopes are zero by using an F test. For binary response models, the same hypothesis can easily be tested by using a likelihood ratio test. A model with a constant term can be written as

$$E(y_t \,|\, \Omega_t) = F\big(\beta_1 + \boldsymbol{X}_{2t}\boldsymbol{\beta}_2\big), \tag{15.16}$$

where $\boldsymbol{X}_{2t}$ consists of $\boldsymbol{X}_t$ without the constant and $\boldsymbol{\beta}_2$ is a $(k-1)$–vector. Under the null hypothesis that $\boldsymbol{\beta}_2 = \mathbf{0}$, (15.16) becomes

$$E(y_t \,|\, \Omega_t) = F\big(\beta_1\big) = E(y_t).$$

This just says that the conditional mean of y_t is equal to its unconditional mean, which can be estimated by $\bar{y}$. Therefore, if we denote the estimate of β_1 by $\bar{\beta}_1$, $\bar{y} = F(\bar{\beta}_1)$. From (15.09), it is easy to work out that the value of the loglikelihood function under the null hypothesis is

$$\ell(\boldsymbol{y}, \bar{\beta}_1, \mathbf{0}) = n\,\bar{y}\log(\bar{y}) + n(1-\bar{y})\log(1-\bar{y}). \tag{15.17}$$

Twice the difference between the unrestricted value $\ell(\boldsymbol{y}, \hat{\beta}_1, \hat{\boldsymbol{\beta}}_2)$ and the restricted value $\ell(\boldsymbol{y}, \bar{\beta}_1, \mathbf{0})$ yields an LR test statistic that will be asymptotically distributed as $\chi^2(k-1)$. Since the right-hand side of (15.17) is very easy to calculate, so is the test statistic. However, a test statistic that is even easier to calculate will be discussed in the next section.

Numerous measures of goodness of fit, comparable to the R^2 for regression models, have been proposed for binary response models, and many statistics packages print some of these. See, among others, Cragg and Uhler (1970), McFadden (1974a), Hauser (1977), Efron (1978), Amemiya (1981), and Maddala (1983). The simplest of these pseudo R^2's is the one suggested by McFadden. It is simply defined as

$$1 - \frac{\ell_U}{\ell_R}, \tag{15.18}$$

where ℓ_U is the unrestricted value $\ell(\boldsymbol{y}, \hat{\beta}_1, \hat{\boldsymbol{\beta}}_2)$, and ℓ_R is the restricted value $\ell(\boldsymbol{y}, \bar{\beta}_1, \mathbf{0})$. Expression (15.18) is a plausible measure of goodness of fit because it must lie between 0 and 1. We saw above that the loglikelihood function (15.09) for binary choice models is bounded above by 0, which implies that ℓ_U and ℓ_R always have the same sign unless ℓ_U is zero. But ℓ_U can be zero only if the unrestricted model fits perfectly, that is, if there exists a perfect classifier. Thus we see that expression (15.18) will be equal to 1 in this case, equal to 0 when the restricted and unrestricted values of the loglikelihood are the same, and between 0 and 1 in all other cases.

Although (15.18) and other measures of goodness of fit may be useful for obtaining a rough idea of how well a particular binary response model performs, there is no need to use them if the object is to compare the performance of two or more different binary response models estimated on the same data set. The best way to do that is simply to compare the values of the loglikelihood functions, using the fact that loglikelihood values for any binary response model of the form (15.03) are directly comparable. Sometimes, we can even reject a model on the basis of such a comparison. For example, suppose that on a particular data set the loglikelihood value for a particular logit model exceeds that for a probit model with the same index function by more than 1.92, which is half of 3.84, the 5% critical value for a test statistic that is distributed as $\chi^2(1)$. It is clearly possible to embed the competing logit and probit models in a more general model having one more parameter. The more general model would necessarily fit at least as well as the logit model; see the discussion in Section 14.3. Thus, in this example, we could reject at the 5% level the hypothesis that the probit model generated the data. Of course, it is rare for the difference between the fit of logit and probit models that differ in no other way to be this great, unless the sample size is exceedingly large.

15.4 AN ARTIFICIAL REGRESSION

There exists a very simple and very useful artificial regression for binary response models. Like other artificial regressions, it can be used for a variety of purposes, including parameter estimation, covariance matrix estimation, and hypothesis testing. This artificial regression was suggested by Engle (1984) and Davidson and MacKinnon (1984b). It can be derived in several ways, of which the easiest is to treat it as a modified version of the Gauss-Newton regression.

As we have seen, the binary response model (15.03) can be written in the form of the nonlinear regression model (15.11), that is, as $y_t = F(\boldsymbol{X}_t\boldsymbol{\beta}) + e_t$. We have also seen that the error term e_t has variance

$$V(\boldsymbol{X}_t\boldsymbol{\beta}) \equiv F(\boldsymbol{X}_t\boldsymbol{\beta})\big(1 - F(\boldsymbol{X}_t\boldsymbol{\beta})\big), \tag{15.19}$$

which implies that (15.11) must be estimated by GNLS. The ordinary GNR corresponding to (15.11) would be

$$y_t - F(\boldsymbol{X}_t\boldsymbol{\beta}) = f(\boldsymbol{X}_t\boldsymbol{\beta})\boldsymbol{X}_t\boldsymbol{b} + \text{residual}, \tag{15.20}$$

but this is clearly inappropriate because of the heteroskedasticity of the e_t's. Instead, we must multiply both sides of (15.20) by the square root of the inverse of (15.19). This yields the artificial regression

$$\big(V(\boldsymbol{X}_t\boldsymbol{\beta})\big)^{-1/2}\big(y_t - F(\boldsymbol{X}_t\boldsymbol{\beta})\big) = \big(V(\boldsymbol{X}_t\boldsymbol{\beta})\big)^{-1/2} f(\boldsymbol{X}_t\boldsymbol{\beta})\boldsymbol{X}_t\boldsymbol{b} + \text{residual}, \tag{15.21}$$

which looks like the GNR for a nonlinear regression model estimated by weighted least squares (see Section 9.4). Regression (15.21) is a special case of what we will call the **binary response model regression**, or **BRMR**. This form of the BRMR is valid for any binary response model of the form (15.03).[4] In the case of the logit model, it simplifies to

$$\big(\lambda(\boldsymbol{X}_t\boldsymbol{\beta})\big)^{-1/2}\big(y_t - \Lambda(\boldsymbol{X}_t\boldsymbol{\beta})\big) = \big(\lambda(\boldsymbol{X}_t\boldsymbol{\beta})\big)^{1/2}\boldsymbol{X}_t\boldsymbol{b} + \text{residual}.$$

The BRMR satisfies the general properties of artificial regressions that we discussed in Section 14.4. In particular, it is closely related both to the gradient of the loglikelihood function (15.09) and to the information matrix. The

[4] Some authors write the BRMR in other ways. For example, in Davidson and MacKinnon (1984b), the regressand was defined as

$$y_t\left(\frac{1 - F(\boldsymbol{X}_t\boldsymbol{\beta})}{F(\boldsymbol{X}_t\boldsymbol{\beta})}\right)^{1/2} + (y_t - 1)\left(\frac{F(\boldsymbol{X}_t\boldsymbol{\beta})}{1 - F(\boldsymbol{X}_t\boldsymbol{\beta})}\right)^{1/2}.$$

It is a good exercise to verify that this is just another way of writing the regressand of (15.21).

transpose of the regressand times the matrix of regressors yields a vector with typical element

$$\sum_{t=1}^{n} \frac{\big(y_t - F(\boldsymbol{X}_t\boldsymbol{\beta})\big) f(\boldsymbol{X}_t\boldsymbol{\beta}) X_{ti}}{F(\boldsymbol{X}_t\boldsymbol{\beta})\big(1 - F(\boldsymbol{X}_t\boldsymbol{\beta})\big)},$$

which is a typical element of the gradient vector for the loglikelihood function (15.09). The transpose of the matrix of regressors times itself yields a matrix with typical element

$$\sum_{t=1}^{n} \frac{f^2(\boldsymbol{X}_t\boldsymbol{\beta})}{F(\boldsymbol{X}_t\boldsymbol{\beta})\big(1 - F(\boldsymbol{X}_t\boldsymbol{\beta})\big)} X_{ti} X_{tj}. \tag{15.22}$$

The probability limit of n^{-1} times (15.22) is a typical element of the information matrix (15.13).

Whenever the loglikelihood function is globally concave, as it is for the logit and probit models, binary response models are easy to estimate in a number of different ways. One approach that generally works well is to use an algorithm similar to the ones described in Section 6.8. In such an algorithm, the BRMR is used to determine the direction in which to change $\boldsymbol{\beta}$ at each step. The values of $\boldsymbol{\beta}$ at iterations $j+1$ and j are related by

$$\boldsymbol{\beta}^{(j+1)} = \boldsymbol{\beta}^{(j)} + \alpha^{(j)}\boldsymbol{b}^{(j)},$$

where $\boldsymbol{b}^{(j)}$ denotes the vector of OLS estimates from the BRMR (15.21) evaluated at $\boldsymbol{\beta}^{(j)}$, and $\alpha^{(j)}$ is a scalar determined by the algorithm. The initial estimates $\boldsymbol{\beta}^{(1)}$ could be chosen in several ways. One that is easy to use and seems to work well in practice is simply to set the constant term to $F^{-1}(\bar{y})$ and the other coefficients to zero. The starting values then correspond to estimates of a restricted model with all slopes equal to zero.

By evaluating it at the ML estimates $\hat{\boldsymbol{\beta}}$, the BRMR can also be used to obtain an estimated covariance matrix for the parameter estimates. The covariance matrix estimate from OLS estimation of regression (15.21) evaluated at $\hat{\boldsymbol{\beta}}$ will be

$$s^2\big(\boldsymbol{X}^{\top}\hat{\boldsymbol{\Psi}}\boldsymbol{X}\big)^{-1}, \tag{15.23}$$

where s is the standard error of the regression. This standard error will tend to 1 asymptotically, although it will not actually equal 1 in finite samples. The matrix $\hat{\boldsymbol{\Psi}}$ is a diagonal matrix with typical diagonal element

$$\hat{\Psi}_{tt} = \frac{f^2(\boldsymbol{X}_t\hat{\boldsymbol{\beta}})}{F(\boldsymbol{X}_t\hat{\boldsymbol{\beta}})\big(1 - F(\boldsymbol{X}_t\hat{\boldsymbol{\beta}})\big)}.$$

This is just expression (15.12) with $\boldsymbol{\beta}$ replaced by $\hat{\boldsymbol{\beta}}$. Thus the estimated OLS covariance matrix (15.23) provides a valid estimate of the covariance matrix of $\hat{\boldsymbol{\beta}}$. The matrix $(\boldsymbol{X}^{\top}\hat{\boldsymbol{\Psi}}\boldsymbol{X})^{-1}$, which is just (15.23) divided by s^2, also does so and is probably to be preferred, since the factor of s^2 in (15.23) simply introduces additional randomness into the estimate of the covariance matrix.

As usual, the covariance matrix of $\hat{\boldsymbol{\beta}}$ can also be estimated as minus the inverse of the numerical Hessian or as the inverse of the outer product of the CG matrix, $\hat{\boldsymbol{G}}^\top\hat{\boldsymbol{G}}$. In the case of the logit model, minus the numerical Hessian is actually equal to the estimated information matrix $\boldsymbol{X}^\top\hat{\boldsymbol{\Psi}}\boldsymbol{X}$, because

$$\frac{\partial^2 \ell(\boldsymbol{\beta})}{\partial\beta_i\partial\beta_j} = \frac{\partial}{\partial\beta_j}\left(\sum_{t=1}^{n}\big(y_t - \Lambda(\boldsymbol{X}_t\boldsymbol{\beta})\big)X_{ti}\right) = -\sum_{t=1}^{n}\lambda(\boldsymbol{X}_t\boldsymbol{\beta})X_{ti}X_{tj}.$$

However, in the case of most other binary response models, including the probit model, minus the Hessian will differ from, and generally be more complicated than, the information matrix.

Like all artificial regressions, the BRMR is particularly useful for hypothesis testing. Suppose that $\boldsymbol{\beta}$ is partitioned as $[\boldsymbol{\beta}_1 \,\vdots\, \boldsymbol{\beta}_2]$, where $\boldsymbol{\beta}_1$ is a $(k-r)$–vector and $\boldsymbol{\beta}_2$ is an r–vector. If $\tilde{\boldsymbol{\beta}}$ denotes the vector of ML estimates subject to the restriction that $\boldsymbol{\beta}_2 = \boldsymbol{0}$, we can test that restriction by running the BRMR

$$\tilde{V}_t^{-1/2}(y_t - \tilde{F}_t) = \tilde{V}_t^{-1/2}\tilde{f}_t\boldsymbol{X}_{t1}\boldsymbol{b}_1 + \tilde{V}_t^{-1/2}\tilde{f}_t\boldsymbol{X}_{t2}\boldsymbol{b}_2 + \text{residual}, \qquad (15.24)$$

where $\tilde{F}_t \equiv F(\boldsymbol{X}_t\tilde{\boldsymbol{\beta}})$, $\tilde{f}_t \equiv f(\boldsymbol{X}_t\tilde{\boldsymbol{\beta}})$, and $\tilde{V}_t \equiv V(\boldsymbol{X}_t\tilde{\boldsymbol{\beta}})$. Here $\boldsymbol{X}_t$ has been partitioned into two vectors, $\boldsymbol{X}_{t1}$ and $\boldsymbol{X}_{t2}$, corresponding to the partitioning of $\boldsymbol{\beta}$. The regressors that correspond to $\boldsymbol{\beta}_1$ are orthogonal to the regressand, while those that correspond to $\boldsymbol{\beta}_2$ are not. All the usual test statistics for $\boldsymbol{b}_2 = \boldsymbol{0}$ are valid. However, in contrast to the case of the Gauss-Newton regression, there is no particular reason to use an F test, because there is no variance parameter to estimate. The best test statistic to use in finite samples, according to Monte Carlo results obtained by Davidson and MacKinnon (1984b), is probably the explained sum of squares from regression (15.24). It will be asymptotically distributed as $\chi^2(r)$ under the null hypothesis. Note that nR^2 will not be equal to the explained sum of squares in this case, because the total sum of squares will not be equal to n.

In one very special case, the BRMR (15.24) becomes extremely simple. Suppose the null hypothesis is that all the slope coefficients are zero. In this case, $\boldsymbol{X}_{t1}$ is just unity, $\boldsymbol{X}_t\tilde{\boldsymbol{\beta}} = \tilde{\beta}_1 = F^{-1}(\bar{y})$, and, in obvious notation, regression (15.24) becomes

$$\bar{V}^{-1/2}(y_t - \bar{F}) = \bar{V}^{-1/2}\bar{f}b_1 + \bar{V}^{-1/2}\bar{f}\boldsymbol{X}_{t2}\boldsymbol{b}_2 + \text{residual}.$$

Neither subtracting a constant from the regressand nor multiplying the regressand and regressors by a constant has any effect on the F statistic for $\boldsymbol{b}_2 = \boldsymbol{0}$. Thus it is clear that we can test the all-slopes-zero hypothesis simply by calculating an F statistic for $\boldsymbol{c}_2 = \boldsymbol{0}$ in the linear regression

$$\boldsymbol{y} = c_1 + \boldsymbol{X}_2\boldsymbol{c}_2 + \text{residuals}.$$

We have thus encountered a situation in which the linear probability model is useful. If one wants to test the null hypothesis that none of the regressors has any ability to explain variation in the dependent variable, then it is perfectly valid just to use the ordinary F statistic for all slopes equal to zero in an OLS regression of $\boldsymbol{y}$ on $\boldsymbol{X}$.

Of course, one can use the BRMR to compute $C(\alpha)$ and Wald-like tests as well as LM tests. Essentially everything that was said about such tests in Sections 6.7 and 13.7 remains applicable in the context of binary response models. One cannot use the explained sum of squares as a test statistic, but one can use the reduction in the explained sum of squares due to the addition of the test regressors. Wald-like tests may be particularly useful when the index function is linear under the alternative hypothesis but nonlinear under the null, since the alternative can be estimated by means of a standard logit or probit program. If the restrictions appear to be consistent with the data, a different BRMR can then be used to obtain one-step estimates.

The BRMR is useful for testing all aspects of the specification of binary response models. Before we can even tentatively accept any such model, we have to test whether $F(\boldsymbol{X}_t\boldsymbol{\beta})$ is a correct specification for the probability that $y_t = 1$ conditional on the information set Ω_t. Testing for possibly omitted variables that belong to Ω_t is an important part of this process, and we have already seen how to do so using the BRMR (15.24). But even if $\boldsymbol{X}_t$ is specified correctly, the rest of the model may not be.

Consider the latent variable model given by (15.05) and (15.06). Since binary response models are typically estimated using cross-section data, and such data frequently exhibit heteroskedasticity, it is quite possible that the error terms in the equation for y_t^* might be heteroskedastic. If they were, the probit model would no longer be appropriate, and estimates of $\boldsymbol{\beta}$ based on it would be inconsistent; see Yatchew and Griliches (1984). Since any binary response model can be thought of as arising from a latent variable model, it is clearly important to test such models for heteroskedasticity. We now discuss one way to do so.

A more general specification than equation (15.05) that allows for heteroskedastic errors is

$$y_t^* = \boldsymbol{X}_t\boldsymbol{\beta} + u_t, \quad u_t \sim N\big(0, \exp(2\boldsymbol{Z}_t\boldsymbol{\gamma})\big), \tag{15.25}$$

where $\boldsymbol{Z}_t$ is a row vector of length q of observations on variables that belong to the information set Ω_t. To ensure that both $\boldsymbol{\beta}$ and $\boldsymbol{\gamma}$ are identifiable, $\boldsymbol{Z}_t$ must not include a constant term or the equivalent. Combining (15.25) with (15.06) yields the model

$$E(y_t \,|\, \Omega_t) = \Phi\bigg(\frac{\boldsymbol{X}_t\boldsymbol{\beta}}{\exp(\boldsymbol{Z}_t\boldsymbol{\gamma})}\bigg). \tag{15.26}$$

When $\boldsymbol{\gamma} = \mathbf{0}$, (15.25) reduces to (15.05) and (15.26) reduces to the ordinary probit model. Even when a binary response model other than the probit model is being used, it still seems quite reasonable to consider the alternative hypothesis

$$E(y_t \mid \Omega_t) = F\left(\frac{\boldsymbol{X}_t\boldsymbol{\beta}}{\exp(\boldsymbol{Z}_t\boldsymbol{\gamma})}\right).$$

We can test against this form of heteroskedasticity by testing the hypothesis that $\boldsymbol{\gamma} = \mathbf{0}$. The appropriate BRMR is

$$\hat{V}_t^{-1/2}(y_t - \hat{F}_t) = \hat{V}_t^{-1/2}\hat{f}_t\boldsymbol{X}_t\boldsymbol{b} + \hat{V}_t^{-1/2}\hat{f}_t\boldsymbol{Z}_t(-\boldsymbol{X}_t\hat{\boldsymbol{\beta}})\boldsymbol{c} + \text{residual}, \tag{15.27}$$

where $\hat{F}_t$, $\hat{f}_t$, and $\hat{V}_t$ are evaluated at ML estimates $\hat{\boldsymbol{\beta}}$ assuming that $\boldsymbol{\gamma} = \mathbf{0}$. The explained sum of squares from (15.27) will be asymptotically distributed as $\chi^2(q)$ under the null hypothesis.

It is also important to test the specification of the transformation function $F(\cdot)$. As we noted earlier, a natural way to do so is to consider an alternative model of the form

$$E(y_t \mid \Omega_t) = F\big(h(\boldsymbol{X}_t\boldsymbol{\beta}, \boldsymbol{\alpha})\big), \tag{15.28}$$

where $h(x, \boldsymbol{\alpha})$ is a nonlinear function of x, and $\boldsymbol{\alpha}$ is either a parameter or a vector of parameters such that $h(\boldsymbol{X}_t\boldsymbol{\beta}, \boldsymbol{\alpha}) = \boldsymbol{X}_t\boldsymbol{\beta}$ for some value of $\boldsymbol{\alpha}$. Stukel (1988) suggests a rather complicated family of two-parameter functions $h(x, \boldsymbol{\alpha})$ that leads to a very general family of models. This family includes the logit model as a special case, when $\boldsymbol{\alpha} = \mathbf{0}$, and allows the skew-symmetry assumption to be imposed or not. The BRMR can easily be used to test against this alternative by testing the null hypothesis that $\boldsymbol{\alpha} = \mathbf{0}$.

A simpler test can be based on the family of models

$$E(y_t \mid \Omega_t) = F\left(\frac{\tau(\alpha\boldsymbol{X}_t\boldsymbol{\beta})}{\alpha}\right),$$

which is a special case of (15.28). Here $\tau(\cdot)$ may be any function that is monotonically increasing in its argument and satisfies the conditions

$$\tau(0) = 0, \;\; \tau'(0) = 1, \;\; \text{and} \;\; \tau''(0) \neq 0.$$

By the use of l'Hôpital's Rule, MacKinnon and Magee (1990) show that

$$\lim_{\alpha\to 0}\left(\frac{\tau(\alpha x)}{\alpha}\right) = x \quad\text{and}\quad \lim_{\alpha\to 0}\left(\frac{\partial\big(\tau(\alpha x)/\alpha\big)}{\partial\alpha}\right) = \tfrac{1}{2}x^2\tau''(0). \tag{15.29}$$

Hence the BRMR for testing the null hypothesis that $\alpha = 0$ is

$$\hat{V}_t^{-1/2}(y_t - \hat{F}_t) = \hat{V}_t^{-1/2}\hat{f}_t\boldsymbol{X}_t\boldsymbol{b} + a\hat{V}_t^{-1/2}(\boldsymbol{X}_t\hat{\boldsymbol{\beta}})^2\hat{f}_t + \text{residual}, \tag{15.30}$$

where the constant factor of $\tau''(0)/2$ that arises from (15.29) is irrelevant for testing and has been omitted. Thus regression (15.30) simply treats the squared values of the index function evaluated at $\hat{\boldsymbol{\beta}}$ as if they were observations on a possibly omitted regressor. This test bears a strong resemblance to the RESET test for regression models that was discussed in Section 6.5. We can use either the ordinary t statistic for $a = 0$ or, preferably, the explained sum of squares as test statistics.

An enormous variety of specification tests can be based on the BRMR. In fact, almost every specification test for regression models that can be based on an artificial regression has an analog for binary response models. In general, we can write the artificial regression for performing such a test as

$$\hat{V}_t^{-1/2}(y_t - \hat{F}_t) = \hat{V}_t^{-1/2}\hat{f}_t \boldsymbol{X}_t \boldsymbol{b} + \hat{\boldsymbol{Z}}_t \boldsymbol{c} + \text{residual}, \tag{15.31}$$

where $\hat{\boldsymbol{Z}}_t$ is a $1 \times r$ vector that may depend on the ML estimates $\hat{\boldsymbol{\beta}}$ and on anything in the information set Ω_t. The intuition for (15.31) is quite simple. If $F(\boldsymbol{X}_t\boldsymbol{\beta})$ is the correct specification of $E(y_t \,|\, \Omega_t)$, then (15.31) *without* the $\boldsymbol{Z}_t$ regressors is the artificial regression that corresponds to the DGP. Any additional regressors $\boldsymbol{Z}_t$ that depend on Ω_t should have no significant explanatory power when they are added to that regression.

It is even possible to use the BRMR to compute nonnested tests very similar to the P test (see Section 11.3). Suppose we have two competing models:

$$H_1\!: \;\; E(y_t \,|\, \Omega_t) = F_1(\boldsymbol{X}_{1t}\boldsymbol{\beta}_1) \;\; \text{and}$$
$$H_2\!: \;\; E(y_t \,|\, \Omega_t) = F_2(\boldsymbol{X}_{2t}\boldsymbol{\beta}_2),$$

which may differ either because $F_1(\cdot)$ is not the same as $F_2(\cdot)$ or because $\boldsymbol{X}_{1t}$ is not the same as $\boldsymbol{X}_{2t}$ or for both reasons. There are numerous ways to nest H_1 and H_2 in an artificial compound model. One of the simplest is

$$H_C\!: \;\; E(y_t \,|\, \Omega_t) = (1-\alpha)F_1(\boldsymbol{X}_{1t}\boldsymbol{\beta}_1) + \alpha F_2(\boldsymbol{X}_{2t}\boldsymbol{\beta}_2),$$

although this artificial model is not actually a binary response model. We can test H_1 against H_C in essentially the way we did for regression models. We first replace $\boldsymbol{\beta}_2$ by its ML estimate $\hat{\boldsymbol{\beta}}_2$ and then construct an artificial regression to test the null hypothesis that $\alpha = 0$. This artificial regression is

$$\hat{V}_t^{-1/2}(y_t - \hat{F}_{1t}) = \hat{V}_t^{-1/2}\hat{f}_{1t}\boldsymbol{X}_{1t}\boldsymbol{b} + a\hat{V}_t^{-1/2}(\hat{F}_{2t} - \hat{F}_{1t}) + \text{residual}.$$

The test regressor is simply the difference between the probabilities that $y_t = 1$ according to the two models, multiplied by $\hat{V}_t^{-1/2}$, the weighting factor that is also used for the regressand and the other regressors.

Estimating the two standard binary response models, i.e., the probit and logit models with linear index functions, is extremely easy with most regression packages, and estimating models that involve nonstandard transformation functions and/or nonlinear index functions is generally not very difficult. Since testing such models by means of the BRMR is also very easy, there is absolutely no excuse for the specifications of binary response models to be tested any less thoroughly than those of regression models.

15.5 MODELS FOR MORE THAN TWO DISCRETE RESPONSES

Although many discrete dependent variables are binary, discrete variables that can take on three or more different values are by no means uncommon in economics. A variety of qualitative response models has been devised to deal with such cases. These fall into two types: models designed to deal with **ordered responses** and models designed to deal with **unordered responses**. An example of ordered response data would be results from a survey where respondents are asked to say whether they strongly agree, agree, neither agree nor disagree, disagree, or strongly disagree with some statement. Here there are five possible responses, which evidently can be ordered in a natural way. An example of unordered response data would be results from a survey of how people choose to commute to work. The possible responses might be: walk, bicycle, take the bus, drive with others in a car pool, and drive alone. Although one could probably make cases for ordering these responses in certain ways, there is clearly no one natural way to order them.

The most common way to deal with ordered response data is to use an **ordered qualitative response model**, usually either the **ordered probit model** or the **ordered logit model**. As an example, consider the latent variable model

$$y_t^* = \boldsymbol{X}_t\boldsymbol{\beta} + u_t, \quad u_t \sim \mathrm{NID}(0,1), \tag{15.32}$$

where, for a reason that will soon become evident, $\boldsymbol{X}_t$ does *not* include a constant term. What we actually observe is a discrete variable y_t that can take on only three values:

$$\begin{aligned} y_t &= 0 \text{ if } y_t^* < \gamma_1 \\ y_t &= 1 \text{ if } \gamma_1 \leq y_t^* < \gamma_2 \\ y_t &= 2 \text{ if } \gamma_2 \leq y_t^*. \end{aligned} \tag{15.33}$$

The parameters of this model are $\boldsymbol{\beta}$ and $\boldsymbol{\gamma} \equiv [\gamma_1 \vdots \gamma_2]$. The γ_i's are thresholds that determine what value of y_t a given value of y_t^* will map into. This is illustrated in Figure 15.3. The number of elements in $\boldsymbol{\gamma}$ is always one fewer than the number of choices. When there are only two choices, this model becomes indistinguishable from an ordinary binary response model, with the single element of $\boldsymbol{\gamma}$ playing the role of the constant term.

The probability that $y_t = 0$ is

$$\begin{aligned} \Pr(y_t = 0) &= \Pr(y_t^* < \gamma_1) = \Pr(\boldsymbol{X}_t\boldsymbol{\beta} + u_t < \gamma_1) \\ &= \Pr(u_t < \gamma_1 - \boldsymbol{X}_t\boldsymbol{\beta}) \\ &= \Phi(\gamma_1 - \boldsymbol{X}_t\boldsymbol{\beta}). \end{aligned}$$

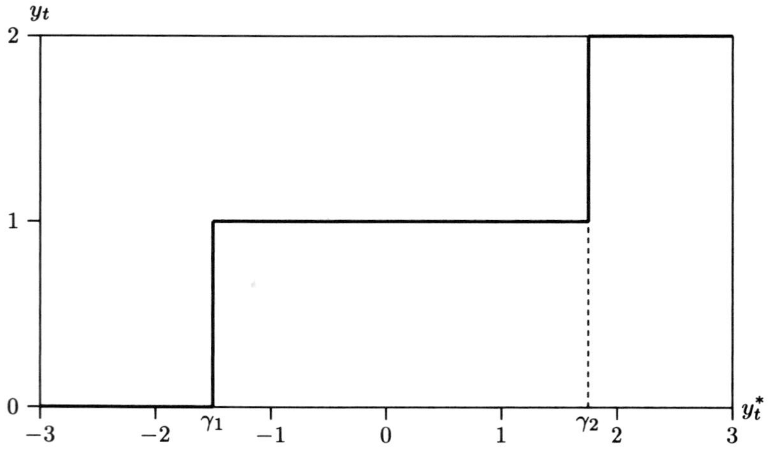

Figure 15.3 Relation between y_t^* and y_t in an ordered probit model

Similarly, the probability that $y_t = 1$ is

$$\begin{aligned}\Pr(y_t = 1) &= \Pr(\gamma_1 \leq y_t^* < \gamma_2) = \Pr(\gamma_1 \leq \boldsymbol{X}_t\boldsymbol{\beta} + u_t < \gamma_2)\\ &= \Pr(u_t < \gamma_2 - \boldsymbol{X}_t\boldsymbol{\beta}) - \Pr(u_t \leq \gamma_1 - \boldsymbol{X}_t\boldsymbol{\beta})\\ &= \Phi(\gamma_2 - \boldsymbol{X}_t\boldsymbol{\beta}) - \Phi(\gamma_1 - \boldsymbol{X}_t\boldsymbol{\beta}),\end{aligned}$$

and the probability that $y_t = 2$ is

$$\begin{aligned}\Pr(y_t = 2) &= \Pr(y_t^* \geq \gamma_2) = \Pr(\boldsymbol{X}_t\boldsymbol{\beta} + u_t \geq \gamma_2)\\ &= \Pr(u_t \geq \gamma_2 - \boldsymbol{X}_t\boldsymbol{\beta})\\ &= \Phi(\boldsymbol{X}_t\boldsymbol{\beta} - \gamma_2).\end{aligned}$$

Thus the loglikelihood function for the ordered probit model that consists of (15.32) and (15.33) is

$$\begin{aligned}\ell(\boldsymbol{\beta}, \gamma_1, \gamma_2) = &\sum_{y_t=0} \log\bigl(\Phi(\gamma_1 - \boldsymbol{X}_t\boldsymbol{\beta})\bigr) + \sum_{y_t=2} \log\bigl(\Phi(\boldsymbol{X}_t\boldsymbol{\beta} - \gamma_2)\bigr)\\ &+ \sum_{y_t=1} \log\bigl(\Phi(\gamma_2 - \boldsymbol{X}_t\boldsymbol{\beta}) - \Phi(\gamma_1 - \boldsymbol{X}_t\boldsymbol{\beta})\bigr).\end{aligned} \tag{15.34}$$

Notice that γ_2 must be greater than γ_1, since otherwise $\Pr(y_t = 1)$ would be negative and the last term in (15.34) would be undefined.

Maximizing the loglikelihood function (15.34) is relatively straightforward, as is generalizing the model to handle more than three responses. It is also evident that one could use some other transformation function in place of the standard normal in (15.34) and still have a perfectly sensible model. The form of the loglikelihood function would otherwise be unchanged. For further discussion of ordered qualitative response models, see Greene (1990a, Chapter 20), Terza (1985), and Becker and Kennedy (1992). This approach is not by any means the only way to deal with ordered discrete responses. Alternative approaches are discussed by McCullagh (1980), Agresti (1984), and Rahiala and Teräsvirta (1988).

The key feature of ordered qualitative response models is that all the choices depend on a single index function. This makes sense when the responses have a natural ordering but does not make sense otherwise. A different sort of model is evidently necessary to deal with unordered responses. The simplest approach is to employ the **multinomial logit model** (or **multiple logit model**), which has been widely used in applied work. An early example is Schmidt and Strauss (1975). A closely related model called the **conditional logit model** is also widely used; see below.[5]

The multinomial logit model is designed to handle $J+1$ responses. According to this model, the probability that any one of them is observed is

$$\Pr(y_t = 0) = \frac{1}{1 + \sum_{j=1}^{J} \exp(\boldsymbol{X}_t \boldsymbol{\beta}^j)} \tag{15.35}$$

$$\Pr(y_t = l) = \frac{\exp(\boldsymbol{X}_t \boldsymbol{\beta}^l)}{1 + \sum_{j=1}^{J} \exp(\boldsymbol{X}_t \boldsymbol{\beta}^j)} \quad \text{for } l = 1, \ldots, J. \tag{15.36}$$

Here $\boldsymbol{X}_t$ is a row vector of length k of observations on variables that belong to the information set of interest, and $\boldsymbol{\beta}^1$ through $\boldsymbol{\beta}^J$ are k-vectors of parameters. When $J = 1$, it is easy to see that this model reduces to the ordinary logit model with a single index function $\boldsymbol{X}_t\boldsymbol{\beta}^1$. For every additional alternative, another index function and k more parameters are added to the model.

Some authors prefer to write the multinomial logit model as

$$\Pr(y_t = l) = \frac{\exp(\boldsymbol{X}_t \boldsymbol{\beta}^l)}{\sum_{j=0}^{J} \exp(\boldsymbol{X}_t \boldsymbol{\beta}^j)} \quad \text{for } l = 0, \ldots, J \tag{15.37}$$

by defining an extra parameter vector $\boldsymbol{\beta}^0$, all elements of which are identically zero. This way of writing the model is more compact than (15.35) and (15.36) but does not make it as clear that the ordinary logit model is a special case of the multinomial one.

Estimation of the multinomial logit model is reasonably straightforward, since the loglikelihood function is globally concave. This loglikelihood function

[5] Terminology in this area is often used in different ways by different authors. The terms "multinomial logit model," "multiple logit model," and "conditional logit model" are sometimes used interchangeably.

can be written as

$$\ell(\boldsymbol{\beta}_1, \ldots, \boldsymbol{\beta}_J) = \sum_{j=1}^{J} \sum_{y_t=j} \boldsymbol{X}_t \boldsymbol{\beta}^j - \sum_{t=1}^{n} \log\Bigl(1 + \sum_{j=1}^{J} \exp(\boldsymbol{X}_t \boldsymbol{\beta}^j)\Bigr).$$

This function is a sum of contributions from each observation. Each contribution has two terms: The first is $\boldsymbol{X}_t \boldsymbol{\beta}^j$, where the index j is that for which $y_t = j$ (or zero if $j = 0$), and the second is minus the logarithm of the denominator that appears in (15.35) and (15.36).

One important property of the multinomial logit model is that

$$\frac{\Pr(y_t = l)}{\Pr(y_t = j)} = \frac{\exp(\boldsymbol{X}_t \boldsymbol{\beta}^l)}{\exp(\boldsymbol{X}_t \boldsymbol{\beta}^j)} = \exp\bigl(\boldsymbol{X}_t(\boldsymbol{\beta}^l - \boldsymbol{\beta}^j)\bigr) \tag{15.38}$$

for any two responses l and j (including response zero if we interpret $\boldsymbol{\beta}^0$ as a vector of zeros). Thus the odds between any two responses depend solely on $\boldsymbol{X}_t$ and on the parameter vectors associated with those two responses. They do not depend on the parameter vectors associated with any of the other responses. In fact, we see from (15.38) that the log of the odds between responses l and j is simply $\boldsymbol{X}_t \boldsymbol{\beta}^*$, where $\boldsymbol{\beta}^* \equiv (\boldsymbol{\beta}^l - \boldsymbol{\beta}^j)$. Thus, conditional on either j or l being chosen, the choice between them is determined by an ordinary logit model with parameter vector $\boldsymbol{\beta}^*$.

Closely related to the multinomial logit model is the **conditional logit model** pioneered by McFadden (1974a, 1974b). See Domencich and McFadden (1975), McFadden (1984), and Greene (1990a, Chapter 20) for detailed treatments. The conditional logit model is designed to handle consumer choice among J (*not* $J + 1$) discrete alternatives, where one and only one of the alternatives can be chosen. Suppose that when the ith consumer chooses alternative j, he or she obtains utility

$$U_{ij} = \boldsymbol{W}_{ij} \boldsymbol{\beta} + \varepsilon_{ij},$$

where $\boldsymbol{W}_{ij}$ is a row vector of characteristics of alternative j as they apply to consumer i. Let y_i denote the choice made by the ith consumer. Presumably $y_i = l$ if U_{il} is at least as great as U_{ij} for all $j \neq l$. Then if the disturbances ε_{ij} for $j = 1, \ldots, J$ are independent and identically distributed according to the Weibull distribution, it can be shown that

$$\Pr(y_i = l) = \frac{\exp(\boldsymbol{W}_{il} \boldsymbol{\beta})}{\sum_{j=1}^{J} \exp(\boldsymbol{W}_{ij} \boldsymbol{\beta})}. \tag{15.39}$$

This closely resembles (15.37), and it is easy to see that the probabilities must add to unity.

There are two key differences between the multinomial logit and conditional logit models. In the former, there is a single vector of independent variables for each observation, and there are J different vectors of parameters.

In the latter, the values of the independent variables vary across alternatives, but there is just a single parameter vector $\boldsymbol{\beta}$. The multinomial logit model is a straightforward generalization of the logit model that can be used to deal with any situation involving three or more unordered qualitative responses. In contrast, the conditional logit model is specifically designed to handle consumer choices among discrete alternatives based on the characteristics of those alternatives.

Depending on the nature of the explanatory variables, there can be a number of subtleties associated with the specification and interpretation of conditional logit models. There is not enough space in this book to treat these adequately, and so readers who intend to estimate such models are urged to consult the references mentioned above. One important property of conditional logit models is the analog of (15.38):

$$\frac{\Pr(y_t = l)}{\Pr(y_t = j)} = \frac{\exp(\boldsymbol{W}_{il}\boldsymbol{\beta})}{\exp(\boldsymbol{W}_{ij}\boldsymbol{\beta})}. \tag{15.40}$$

This property is called the **independence of irrelevant alternatives**, or **IIA**, property. It implies that adding another alternative to the model, or changing the characteristics of another alternative that is already included, will not change the odds between alternatives l and j.

The IIA property can be extremely implausible in certain circumstances. Suppose that there are initially two alternatives for traveling between two cities: flying Monopoly Airways and driving. Suppose further that half of all travelers fly and the other half drive. Then Upstart Airways enters the market and creates a third alternative. If Upstart offers a service identical to that of Monopoly, it must gain the same market share. Thus, according to the IIA property, one third of the travelers must take each of the airlines and one third must drive. So the automobile has lost just as much market share from the entry of Upstart Airways as Monopoly Airways has! This seems very implausible.[6] As a result, a number of papers have been devoted to the problem of testing the independence of irrelevant alternatives property and finding tractable models that do not embody it. See, in particular, Hausman and Wise (1978), Manski and McFadden (1981), Hausman and McFadden (1984), and McFadden (1987).

This concludes our discussion of qualitative response models. More detailed treatments may be found in surveys by Maddala (1983), McFadden (1984), Amemiya (1981; 1985, Chapter 9), and Greene (1990a, Chapter 20), among others. In the next three sections, we turn to the subject of limited dependent variables.

[6] One might object that a price war between Monopoly and Upstart would convince some drivers to fly instead. So it would. But if the two airlines offered lower prices, that would change one or more elements of the $\boldsymbol{W}_{ij}$'s associated with them. The above analysis assumes that all the $\boldsymbol{W}_{ij}$'s remain unchanged.

15.6 MODELS FOR TRUNCATED DATA

Limited dependent variable models are designed to handle samples that have been **truncated** or **censored** in some way. These two terms are easily confused. A sample has been truncated if some observations that should have been there have been systematically excluded from the sample. For example, a sample of households with incomes under \$100,000 necessarily excludes all households with incomes over that level. It is not a random sample of all households. If the dependent variable is income, or something correlated with income, results using the truncated sample could potentially be quite misleading.

On the other hand, a sample has been censored if no observations have been systematically excluded, but some of the information contained in them has been suppressed. Think of a "censor" who reads people's mail and blacks out certain parts of it. The recipients still get their mail, but parts of it are unreadable. To continue the previous example, suppose that households with all income levels are included in the sample, but for those with incomes in excess of \$100,000, the amount reported is always exactly \$100,000.[7] In this case, the censored sample is still a random sample of all households, but the values reported for high-income households are not the true values. One can think of discrete dependent variables as being the outcome of an even more extreme type of censoring. For example, if it were reported only that household income was in one of several dollar ranges, the dependent variable would consist of ordered qualitative responses. However, censoring this extreme is not usually referred to as censoring.

Econometricians have devised a large number of models for dealing with truncated and censored data. We have space to deal with only a few of the simplest ones. Greene (1990a, Chapter 21) provides an excellent recent survey. Other valuable surveys of all or parts of this area include Dhrymes (1986), Maddala (1983, 1986), and Amemiya (1984; 1985, Chapter 10). In addition, an issue of the *Journal of Econometrics* (Blundell, 1987) is devoted to the important topic of specification testing in limited dependent variable (and also qualitative response) models.

We will consider the simplest sort of truncated dependent variable model first. Suppose that for all t (observed or not) the mean of y_t conditional on some information set Ω_t is given by a nonlinear regression function $x_t(\boldsymbol{\beta})$, which might well be the linear regression function $\boldsymbol{X}_t\boldsymbol{\beta}$. Then, if the error terms are normally and independently distributed, we can write

$$y_t = x_t(\boldsymbol{\beta}) + u_t, \quad u_t \sim \text{NID}(0, \sigma^2). \tag{15.41}$$

[7] This type of censoring is not uncommon with survey data. It may occur either because the surveyors desire to protect the privacy of high-income respondents or because the survey was not designed with the needs of econometric analysis in mind.

Now suppose that y_t is observed only if $y_t \geq y^l$, where y^l is some fixed lower bound. The probability that y_t will be observed is

$$\begin{aligned}\Pr(y_t \geq y^l) &= \Pr\big(x_t(\boldsymbol{\beta}) + u_t \geq y^l\big) = 1 - \Pr\big(u_t < y^l - x_t(\boldsymbol{\beta})\big) \\ &= 1 - \Phi\Big(\frac{1}{\sigma}\big(y^l - x_t(\boldsymbol{\beta})\big)\Big) = \Phi\Big(-\frac{1}{\sigma}\big(y^l - x_t(\boldsymbol{\beta})\big)\Big).\end{aligned}$$

Thus, when $x_t(\boldsymbol{\beta}) = y^l$, the probability that any observation will be observed is one-half. As $x_t(\boldsymbol{\beta})$ increases (or decreases) relative to y^l, the probability of observing y_t likewise increases (or decreases). This is a simple example of a **truncated regression model.**

Whether truncation is a problem for estimation of (15.41) depends on what the purpose of that estimation is. Least squares estimation would be appropriate if we were interested in the mean of y_t conditional on Ω_t and conditional on y_t being greater than y^l. But that is unlikely to be what we are interested in. We defined $x_t(\boldsymbol{\beta})$ as the mean of y_t conditional on Ω_t, with no reference to y^l. If that is indeed what we are interested in, least squares estimates of (15.41) could be seriously misleading.

The problem is that the mean of u_t conditional on $y_t \geq y^l$ is not zero. Only if u_t is large enough will y_t exceed y^l and only then will observation t be included in the sample. Thus, for observations that are in the sample, $E(u_t) > 0$. In fact, it can be shown that

$$E(u_t \,|\, y_t \geq y^l) = \frac{\sigma\phi\big((y^l - x_t(\boldsymbol{\beta}))/\sigma\big)}{\Phi\big(-(y^l - x_t(\boldsymbol{\beta}))/\sigma\big)}. \tag{15.42}$$

Evidently, the conditional mean of u_t in this case is positive and depends on $x_t(\boldsymbol{\beta})$. This result uses the fact that if a random variable z is standard normal, the mean of z conditional on $z \geq z^*$ is $\phi(z^*)/\Phi(-z^*)$; see Johnson and Kotz (1970a). Similarly, the mean of z conditional on $z \leq z^*$ is $-\phi(z^*)/\Phi(z^*)$. So if truncation were from above instead of below, the conditional mean of u_t would be negative instead of positive.

We clearly cannot obtain consistent estimates of $\boldsymbol{\beta}$ using least squares estimates when the error terms have positive mean (15.42) that depends on $x_t(\boldsymbol{\beta})$. Goldberger (1981) provides some expressions for the size of the inconsistency in certain cases, and in the next section (see Table 15.1) we provide some illustrative numerical results which suggest that it can be very large. The obvious remedy is to use the method of maximum likelihood. The density of y_t conditional on $y_t \geq y^l$ is simply the unconditional density of y_t restricted to values of $y_t \geq y^l$, divided by the probability that $y_t \geq y^l$:

$$\frac{\sigma^{-1}\phi\big((y_t - x_t(\boldsymbol{\beta}))/\sigma\big)}{\Phi\big(-(y^l - x_t(\boldsymbol{\beta}))/\sigma\big)}.$$

Thus the loglikelihood function, which is the sum of the logs of these densities over all t, is

$$\begin{aligned}\ell(\boldsymbol{y}, \boldsymbol{\beta}, \sigma) = &-\tfrac{n}{2}\log(2\pi) - n\log(\sigma) - \frac{1}{2\sigma^2}\sum_{t=1}^{n}\big(y_t - x_t(\boldsymbol{\beta})\big)^2 \\ &-\sum_{t=1}^{n}\log\Big(\Phi\Big(-\tfrac{1}{\sigma}\big(y^l - x_t(\boldsymbol{\beta})\big)\Big)\Big).\end{aligned} \tag{15.43}$$

The first three terms in (15.43) make up the loglikelihood function that corresponds to nonlinear least squares regression; see equation (8.81), for example. The last term is new, however. It is minus the summation over all t of the logarithms of the probabilities that an observation with regression function $x_t(\boldsymbol{\beta})$ will belong to the sample. Since these probabilities must be less than 1, this term must always be positive. The presence of this fourth term causes the ML estimates of $\boldsymbol{\beta}$ and σ to differ from their least squares counterparts and ensures that the ML estimates are consistent.

Evidently, this model could easily be modified to allow for other forms of truncation, such as truncation from above or truncation from both above and below. Readers may find it illuminating to work out the loglikelihood function for the regression model (15.41) if the sample is truncated according to each of the following two rules:

$$\begin{aligned}&y_t \text{ observed when } y_t \le y^u \quad\text{and}\\ &y_t \text{ observed when } y^l \le y_t \le y^u,\end{aligned}$$

where y^u is now a fixed upper bound.

It is usually not difficult to maximize the loglikelihood function (15.43), using any of the standard approaches. Greene (1990b) discusses some problems that could potentially arise and shows that, in practice, the loglikelihood function will almost always have a unique maximum, even though it is not, in general, globally concave. The covariance matrix of the ML estimates $[\hat{\boldsymbol{\beta}} \,\vdots\, \hat{\sigma}]$ will be $(k+1)\times(k+1)$, assuming that $\boldsymbol{\beta}$ is a k–vector, and may as usual be estimated in several ways. Unfortunately, the only artificial regression that is at present known to be applicable to this model is the OPG regression. As usual, inferences based on it should be treated with caution unless the sample size is very large.

It should be clear that consistency of the ML estimates of $\boldsymbol{\beta}$ and σ obtained by maximizing (15.43) depends critically on the assumptions that the error terms u_t in (15.41) really are normally, independently, and identically distributed. Otherwise, the probability that y_t is observed will not be equal to $\Phi\big(-(y^l - x_t(\boldsymbol{\beta}))/\sigma\big)$. These assumptions are equally critical for all regression models involving truncated or censored dependent variables; see, for example, Hurd (1979) and Arabmazar and Schmidt (1981, 1982). A number of techniques have therefore been suggested for obtaining estimates that are not sensitive to assumptions about the distribution of the error terms. However, none of them is as yet widely used in applied econometric work, and to discuss any of them would take us well beyond the scope of this book. See, among others, Miller (1976), Buckley and James (1979), Powell (1984, 1986), Duncan (1986), Horowitz (1986), Ruud (1986), and Lee (1992).

15.7 Models for Censored Data

The simplest regression model that involves a censored dependent variable is the **tobit model**, so called because it is closely related to the probit model and was originally suggested by Tobin (1958). A simple form of the tobit model is

$$\begin{aligned} y_t^* &= x_t(\boldsymbol{\beta}) + u_t, \quad u_t \sim \mathrm{NID}(0, \sigma^2), \\ y_t &= y_t^* \text{ if } y_t^* > 0; \quad y_t = 0 \text{ otherwise.} \end{aligned} \tag{15.44}$$

Here y_t^* is a latent variable that is observed only when it is positive. When the latent variable is negative, zero is observed instead. Tobin's original motivation was to study household expenditures on durable goods, which may be zero for some households and positive for others.

It is easy to modify the tobit model so that censoring occurs at some value other than zero, so that censoring is from above rather than from below, or so that the value at which censoring occurs changes (in a nonstochastic way) over the sample. For example, y_t^* might be the demand for seats on an airline flight, y_t^c might be the capacity of the aircraft (which could vary over the sample if different aircraft were used on different flights), and y_t might be the number of seats actually occupied. Then the second line of (15.44) would be replaced by

$$y_t = y_t^* \text{ if } y_t^* < y_t^c; \quad y_t = y_t^c \text{ otherwise.}$$

The tobit model has been very widely used in applied work. Applications of it have dealt with such diverse topics as unemployment (Ashenfelter and Ham, 1979), the expected age of retirement (Kotlikoff, 1979), the demand for copper (MacKinnon and Olewiler, 1980), and even the number of extramarital affairs (Fair, 1978).

It is just as invalid to use least squares regression with censored data as with truncated data. Table 15.1 contains some illustrative numerical results for OLS estimation of the model

$$y_t^* = \beta_0 + \beta_1 x_t + u_t, \quad u_t \sim \mathrm{NID}(0, \sigma^2),$$

where y_t is derived from y_t^* by either truncation or censoring from below at y'. For this illustration, the true values of β_0, β_1, and σ were all unity, and x_t was uniformly distributed on the (0,1) interval. Each line of the table

Table 15.1 Inconsistency Caused by Truncation and Censoring

y'	fraction $< y'$	$\text{plim}(\hat{\beta}_0)$	$\text{plim}(\hat{\beta}_1)$	$\text{plim}(\tilde{\beta}_0)$	$\text{plim}(\tilde{\beta}_1)$
0.0	0.076	1.26	0.77	1.07	0.93
0.5	0.167	1.48	0.63	1.18	0.83
1.0	0.316	1.77	0.49	1.37	0.69
1.5	0.500	2.12	0.37	1.67	0.50
2.0	0.684	2.51	0.28	2.06	0.31
2.5	0.833	2.93	0.21	2.51	0.16

corresponds to a different value of y' and hence to a different proportion of limit observations. Estimates based on the truncated sample are denoted by $\hat{\beta}_0$ and $\hat{\beta}_1$, while those based on the censored sample are denoted by $\tilde{\beta}_0$ and $\tilde{\beta}_1$.[8]

It appears from the results in the table that the inconsistency due to truncation or censoring can be very large, with truncation (at least in this example) resulting in more inconsistency than censoring. As one would expect, the inconsistency increases with the proportion of limit observations. Notice that for the censored case, $\text{plim}(\tilde{\beta}_1)/\beta_1$ is essentially equal to the proportion of nonlimit observations in the sample, $1 - \Pr(y_t < y')$. Greene (1981a) derived this result analytically for all slope coefficients in a linear regression model, under the special assumption that the regressors are normally distributed. It seems to provide a very good approximation for many other cases, including the one analyzed in the table.

The tobit model is usually estimated by maximum likelihood. For simplicity, we will discuss estimation of the simple tobit model given by (15.44). It is easy to see that

$$\begin{aligned}\Pr(y_t = 0) &= \Pr(y_t^* \leq 0) = \Pr\big(x_t(\boldsymbol{\beta}) + u_t \leq 0\big) \\ &= \Pr\left(\frac{u_t}{\sigma} \leq -\frac{x_t(\boldsymbol{\beta})}{\sigma}\right) = \Phi\Big(-\frac{1}{\sigma}x_t(\boldsymbol{\beta})\Big).\end{aligned}$$

Thus the contribution to the loglikelihood function made by observations with $y_t = 0$ is

$$\ell_t(y_t, \boldsymbol{\beta}, \sigma) = \log\left(\Phi\Big(-\frac{1}{\sigma}x_t(\boldsymbol{\beta})\Big)\right). \tag{15.45}$$

[8] These results were obtained by means of a Monte Carlo experiment that involved 500 replications, each with 50,000 observations. Although experimental error should be very small, the last digits reported in the table may not be quite correct. For example, it is easy to see that in this example the fraction truncated or censored when y' is 1.5 must be 0.50, and that is the number reported in the table. However, the number actually observed in the experiments was 0.498.

Conditional on y_t being positive, the density of y_t is

$$\frac{\sigma^{-1}\phi\big((y_t - x_t(\boldsymbol{\beta}))/\sigma\big)}{\Pr(y_t > 0)}. \tag{15.46}$$

However, the contribution to the loglikelihood function made by observations with $y_t > 0$ is not the logarithm of (15.46), because these observations occur only with probability $\Pr(y_t > 0)$. Multiplying (15.46) by $\Pr(y_t > 0)$ and taking the logarithm leaves us with

$$\log\left(\frac{1}{\sigma}\phi\left(\frac{1}{\sigma}(y_t - x_t(\boldsymbol{\beta}))\right)\right), \tag{15.47}$$

which is the contribution to the loglikelihood function for an observation in a regression model without censoring.

The loglikelihood function for the tobit model is thus

$$\sum_{y_t=0}\log\left(\Phi\left(-\frac{1}{\sigma}x_t(\boldsymbol{\beta})\right)\right) + \sum_{y_t>0}\log\left(\frac{1}{\sigma}\phi\left(\frac{1}{\sigma}(y_t - x_t(\boldsymbol{\beta}))\right)\right). \tag{15.48}$$

The first term is just the sum over all limit observations of expression (15.45), and the second is the sum over all nonlimit observations of expression (15.47). The first term looks like the corresponding term in the loglikelihood function for a probit model. This may be seen by making the regression function linear and imposing the normalization $\sigma = 1$, in which case $\Phi\big(-x_t(\boldsymbol{\beta})/\sigma\big)$ becomes $1 - \Phi\big(\boldsymbol{X}_t\boldsymbol{\beta}\big)$, and then comparing the loglikelihood function with (15.09). In contrast, the second term in (15.48) looks just like the loglikelihood function for a nonlinear regression model.

Thoughtful readers may feel that there is something fishy about this loglikelihood function. After all, the first term is a summation of the logs of a number of probabilities, while the second term is a summation of the logs of a number of densities. This rather strange mixture arises because the dependent variable in a tobit model is sometimes a discrete random variable (for the limit observations) and sometimes a continuous one (for the nonlimit observations). Because of this mixture of discrete and continuous random variables, standard proofs of the consistency and asymptotic normality of ML estimators do not apply to the tobit model. However, Amemiya (1973c), in a well-known paper, has shown that the ML estimator does indeed have all the usual asymptotic properties. He also provides expressions for the elements of the information matrix.

It is not difficult to maximize the loglikelihood function (15.48). Although it is not globally concave in its natural parametrization, Olsen (1978) showed that when $x_t(\boldsymbol{\beta}) = \boldsymbol{X}_t\boldsymbol{\beta}$, it does have a unique maximum. The key argument is that the model can be reparametrized in terms of the parameters $\boldsymbol{\alpha} \equiv \boldsymbol{\beta}/\sigma$ and

$h \equiv 1/\sigma$, and the loglikelihood function can be shown to be globally concave in the latter parametrization. This implies that it must have a unique maximum no matter how it is parametrized. The $(k+1) \times (k+1)$ covariance matrix of the ML estimates may as usual be estimated in several ways. Unfortunately, as with the truncated regression model discussed in the previous section, the only artificial regression that is presently known to be applicable to this model is the OPG regression.

There is an interesting relationship among the tobit, truncated regression, and probit models. Suppose, for simplicity, that $x_t(\boldsymbol{\beta}) = \boldsymbol{X}_t\boldsymbol{\beta}$. Then the tobit loglikelihood function can be rewritten as

$$\sum_{y_t>0} \log\Big(\frac{1}{\sigma}\phi\Big(\frac{1}{\sigma}(y_t - \boldsymbol{X}_t\boldsymbol{\beta})\Big)\Big) + \sum_{y_t=0} \log\Big(\Phi\Big(-\frac{1}{\sigma}\boldsymbol{X}_t\boldsymbol{\beta}\Big)\Big). \tag{15.49}$$

Now let us both add and subtract the term $\sum_{y_t>0} \log\big(\Phi(\boldsymbol{X}_t\boldsymbol{\beta}/\sigma)\big)$ in (15.49), which then becomes

$$\begin{aligned} &\sum_{y_t>0} \log\Big(\frac{1}{\sigma}\phi\Big(\frac{1}{\sigma}(y_t - \boldsymbol{X}_t\boldsymbol{\beta})\Big)\Big) - \sum_{y_t>0} \log\Big(\Phi\Big(\frac{1}{\sigma}\boldsymbol{X}_t\boldsymbol{\beta}\Big)\Big) \\ &+ \sum_{y_t=0} \log\Big(\Phi\Big(-\frac{1}{\sigma}\boldsymbol{X}_t\boldsymbol{\beta}\Big)\Big) + \sum_{y_t>0} \log\Big(\Phi\Big(\frac{1}{\sigma}\boldsymbol{X}_t\boldsymbol{\beta}\Big)\Big). \end{aligned} \tag{15.50}$$

The first line here is the loglikelihood function for a truncated regression model; it is just (15.43) with $y^l = 0$ and $x_t(\boldsymbol{\beta}) = \boldsymbol{X}_t\boldsymbol{\beta}$ and with the set of observations to which the summations apply adjusted appropriately. The second line is the loglikelihood function for a probit model with index function $\boldsymbol{X}_t\boldsymbol{\beta}/\sigma$. Of course, if all we had was the second line here, we could not identify $\boldsymbol{\beta}$ and σ separately, but since we also have the first line, that is not a problem.

Expression (15.50) makes it clear that the tobit model is like a truncated regression model combined with a probit model, with the coefficient vectors in the latter two models restricted to be proportional to each other. Cragg (1971) argued that this restriction may sometimes be unreasonable and proposed several more general models as plausible alternatives to the tobit model. It may sometimes be desirable to test the tobit model against one or more of these more general models; see Lin and Schmidt (1984) and Greene (1990a, Chapter 21).

As we mentioned earlier, it is easy to modify the tobit model to handle different types of censoring. For example, one possibility is a model with **double censoring**. Suppose that

$$\begin{aligned} &y_t^* = x_t(\boldsymbol{\beta}) + u_t, \quad u_t \sim \mathrm{NID}(0, \sigma^2), \\ &y_t = y_t^* \text{ if } y_t^l \le y_t^* \le y_t^u;\; y_t = y_t^l \text{ if } y_t^* < y_t^l;\; y_t = y_t^u \text{ if } y_t^* > y_t^u. \end{aligned}$$

This model has been investigated by Rosett and Nelson (1975) and Nakamura and Nakamura (1983), among others. It is easy to see that the loglikelihood function is

$$\begin{aligned}\sum_{y_t^l \le y_t^* \le y_t^u} \log\Big(\frac{1}{\sigma}\phi\Big(\frac{1}{\sigma}(y_t - \boldsymbol{X}_t\boldsymbol{\beta})\Big)\Big) + \sum_{y_t^* < y_t^l} \log\Big(\Phi\Big(\frac{1}{\sigma}(y_t^l - \boldsymbol{X}_t\boldsymbol{\beta})\Big)\Big) \\ + \sum_{y_t^* > y_t^u} \log\Big(\Phi\Big(-\frac{1}{\sigma}(y_t^u - \boldsymbol{X}_t\boldsymbol{\beta})\Big)\Big).\end{aligned} \tag{15.51}$$

The first term corresponds to nonlimit observations, the second to observations at the lower limit y_t^l, and the third to observations at the upper limit y_t^u. Maximizing (15.51) is quite straightforward.

Numerous other models for regression on truncated and censored data have been proposed in the literature. Many of these deal with situations in which there are two or more jointly dependent variables. Some important examples are Nelson and Olsen (1978) and Lee (1981); see the surveys of Amemiya (1985, Chapter 10) and Dhrymes (1986). We do not have space to discuss this literature in any detail. However, it is worth mentioning one frequently encountered special case.

Suppose that y_t^* is a latent variable determined by the model

$$y_t^* = \boldsymbol{X}_t\boldsymbol{\beta} + u_t, \quad u_t \sim \text{NID}(0, \sigma^2), \tag{15.52}$$

and that y_t is derived from y_t^* by some form of censoring or truncation. As a result, the model that is actually estimated is a probit, tobit, or truncated regression model. Which one of these is appropriate will of course depend on what type of truncation or censoring is involved in going from y_t^* to y_t. Now suppose that one or more of the independent variables in the vector $\boldsymbol{X}_t$ may be correlated with the error terms u_t. If it is, the usual ML estimates of $\boldsymbol{\beta}$ will clearly be inconsistent.

Luckily, it is very easy to test for inconsistency caused by possible correlation between some of the independent variables and the error terms in (15.52). The test is very similar to the DWH test for inconsistency caused by possible endogeneity that was discussed in Section 7.9. Suppose that $\boldsymbol{W}$ is a matrix of instrumental variables that includes all the columns of $\boldsymbol{X}$ (a matrix with typical row $\boldsymbol{X}_t$) which are known to be exogenous or predetermined. To perform the test, one first regresses the remaining columns of $\boldsymbol{X}$, say $\boldsymbol{X}^*$, on $\boldsymbol{W}$ and saves the residuals $\boldsymbol{M}_W\boldsymbol{X}^*$. Then one computes either an LR or LM test for the hypothesis that $\boldsymbol{\gamma} = \boldsymbol{0}$ in the fictitious latent variable model

$$y_t^* = \boldsymbol{X}_t\boldsymbol{\beta} + (\boldsymbol{M}_W\boldsymbol{X}^*)_t\boldsymbol{\gamma} + u_t, \quad u_t \sim \text{NID}(0, \sigma^2).$$

Here $(\boldsymbol{M}_W\boldsymbol{X}^*)_t$ serves as an estimate of the stochastic parts of the possibly endogenous variables in $\boldsymbol{X}_t$. If these variables are not correlated with u_t, and the latent variable model is specified correctly, the vector γ should be zero. This test was used by MacKinnon and Olewiler (1980) and is discussed in more detail by Smith and Blundell (1986).

It is understood that both the null and alternative models for this test are actually probit, tobit, or truncated regression models, depending on how y_t is obtained from y_t^*. As usual, LM tests may be based on artificial regressions. Since only the OPG regression is available for the tobit and truncated regression models, it may be preferable to use an LR test in these cases. When one does estimate the alternative model, it turns out that the estimates of $\boldsymbol{\beta}$ are consistent even if the null hypothesis is false, just as they were in the linear regression case examined in Section 7.9. However, the ordinary covariance matrix produced by this procedure is not valid asymptotically when $\gamma \neq \mathbf{0}$, for the same reason that it was not valid in the linear regression case.

15.8 Sample Selectivity

In Section 15.6, we discussed models in which the sample was truncated according to the value of the dependent variable. In many practical cases, however, truncation is based not on the value of the dependent variable but rather on the value of another variable that is correlated with it. For example, people may choose to enter the labor force only if their market wage exceeds their reservation wage. Then a sample of people who are in the labor force will exclude those whose reservation wage exceeds their market wage. If the dependent variable is anything that is correlated with either reservation or market wages, use of least squares will yield inconsistent estimates. In this case, the sample may be said to have been **selected** on the basis of the difference between market and reservation wages, and the problem that this type of selection causes is often referred to as **sample selectivity bias**. Heckman (1974, 1976, 1979), Hausman and Wise (1977), and Lee (1978) are pioneering papers on this subject.

The best way to understand the key features of models involving sample selectivity is to examine a simple model in some detail. Suppose that y_t^* and z_t^* are two latent variables, generated by the bivariate process

$$\begin{bmatrix} y_t^* \\ z_t^* \end{bmatrix} = \begin{bmatrix} \boldsymbol{X}_t\boldsymbol{\beta} \\ \boldsymbol{W}_t\boldsymbol{\gamma} \end{bmatrix} + \begin{bmatrix} u_t \\ v_t \end{bmatrix}, \quad \begin{bmatrix} u_t \\ v_t \end{bmatrix} \sim \mathrm{NID}\left(\mathbf{0}, \begin{bmatrix} \sigma^2 & \rho\sigma \\ \rho\sigma & 1 \end{bmatrix}\right), \tag{15.53}$$

where $\boldsymbol{X}_t$ and $\boldsymbol{W}_t$ are vectors of observations on exogenous or predetermined variables, $\boldsymbol{\beta}$ and $\boldsymbol{\gamma}$ are unknown parameter vectors, σ is the standard deviation of u_t and ρ is the correlation between u_t and v_t. The restriction that the variance of v_t is equal to 1 is imposed because only the sign of z_t^* will be observed. In fact, the variables that are actually observed are y_t and z_t, and they are related to y_t^* and z_t^* as follows:

$$y_t = y_t^* \text{ if } z_t^* > 0; \;\; y_t = 0 \text{ otherwise;}$$
$$z_t = 1 \text{ if } z_t^* > 0; \;\; z_t = 0 \text{ otherwise.}$$

There are two types of observations: ones for which both y_t and z_t are observed to be zero and ones for which $z_t = 1$ and y_t is equal to y_t^*. The loglikelihood function for this model is thus

$$\sum_{z_t=0} \log\bigl(\Pr(z_t = 0)\bigr) + \sum_{z_t=1} \log\bigl(\Pr(z_t = 1) f(y_t^* \,|\, z_t = 1)\bigr), \tag{15.54}$$

where $f(y_t^* \,|\, z_t = 1)$ denotes the density of y_t^* conditional on $z_t = 1$. The first term of (15.54) is the summation over all observations for which $z_t = 0$ of the logarithms of the probability that $z_t = 0$. It is exactly the same as the corresponding term in a probit model for z_t by itself. The second term is the summation over all observations for which $z_t = 1$ of the probability that $z_t = 1$ times the density of y_t conditional on $z_t = 1$. Using the fact that we can factor a joint density any way we like, this second term can also be written as

$$\sum_{z_t=1} \log\bigl(\Pr(z_t = 1 \,|\, y_t^*) f(y_t^*)\bigr),$$

where $f(y_t^*)$ is the unconditional density of y_t^*, which is just a normal density with conditional mean $\boldsymbol{X}_t\boldsymbol{\beta}$ and variance σ^2.

The only difficulty in writing out the loglikelihood function (15.54) explicitly is to calculate $\Pr(z_t = 1 \,|\, y_t^*)$. Since u_t and v_t are bivariate normal, we can write

$$z_t^* = \boldsymbol{W}_t\boldsymbol{\gamma} + \rho\Bigl(\frac{1}{\sigma}(y_t^* - \boldsymbol{X}_t\boldsymbol{\beta})\Bigr) + \varepsilon_t, \quad \varepsilon_t \sim \mathrm{NID}\bigl(0, (1-\rho^2)\bigr).$$

It follows that

$$\Pr(z_t = 1) = \Phi\left(\frac{\boldsymbol{W}_t\boldsymbol{\gamma} + \rho((y_t - \boldsymbol{X}_t\boldsymbol{\beta})/\sigma)}{(1-\rho^2)^{1/2}}\right),$$

since $y_t = y_t^*$ when $z_t = 1$. Thus the loglikelihood function (15.54) becomes

$$\sum_{z_t=0} \log\bigl(\Phi(-\boldsymbol{W}_t\boldsymbol{\gamma})\bigr) + \sum_{z_t=1} \log\Bigl(\frac{1}{\sigma}\phi(y_t - \boldsymbol{X}_t\boldsymbol{\beta})\Bigr)$$
$$+ \sum_{z_t=1} \log\left(\Phi\left(\frac{\boldsymbol{W}_t\boldsymbol{\gamma} + \rho((y_t - \boldsymbol{X}_t\boldsymbol{\beta})/\sigma)}{(1-\rho^2)^{1/2}}\right)\right). \tag{15.55}$$

The first term looks like the corresponding term for a probit model. The second term looks like the loglikelihood function for a linear regression model with normal errors. The third term is one that we have not seen before.

Maximum likelihood estimates can be obtained in the usual way by maximizing (15.55). However, this maximization is relatively burdensome, and so instead of ML estimation a computationally simpler technique proposed by Heckman (1976) is often used. **Heckman's two-step method** is based on the fact that the first equation of (15.53) can be rewritten as

$$y_t^* = \boldsymbol{X}_t\boldsymbol{\beta} + \rho\sigma v_t + e_t. \tag{15.56}$$

The idea is to replace y_t^* by y_t and v_t by its mean conditional on $z_t = 1$ and on the realized value of $\boldsymbol{W}_t\boldsymbol{\gamma}$. As can be seen from (15.42), this conditional mean is $\phi(\boldsymbol{W}_t\boldsymbol{\gamma})/\Phi(\boldsymbol{W}_t\boldsymbol{\gamma})$, a quantity that is sometimes referred to as the **inverse Mills ratio**. Hence regression (15.56) becomes

$$y_t = \boldsymbol{X}_t\boldsymbol{\beta} + \rho\sigma\frac{\phi(\boldsymbol{W}_t\boldsymbol{\gamma})}{\Phi(\boldsymbol{W}_t\boldsymbol{\gamma})} + \text{residual}. \tag{15.57}$$

It is now easy to see how Heckman's two-step method works. In the first step, an ordinary probit model is used to obtain consistent estimates $\hat{\boldsymbol{\gamma}}$ of the parameters of the selection equation. In the second step, the **selectivity regressor** $\phi(\boldsymbol{W}_t\boldsymbol{\gamma})/\Phi(\boldsymbol{W}_t\boldsymbol{\gamma})$ is evaluated at $\hat{\boldsymbol{\gamma}}$ and regression (15.57) is estimated by OLS for the observations with $y_t > 0$ only. This regression provides a test for sample selectivity as well as an estimation technique. The coefficient on the selectivity regressor is $\rho\sigma$. Since $\sigma \neq 0$, the ordinary t statistic for this coefficient to be zero can be used to test the hypothesis that $\rho = 0$; it will be asymptotically distributed as $N(0,1)$ under the null hypothesis. Thus, if this coefficient is not significantly different from zero, the investigator may reasonably decide that selectivity is not a problem for this data set and proceed to use least squares as usual.

Even when the hypothesis that $\rho = 0$ cannot be accepted, OLS estimation of regression (15.57) yields consistent estimates of $\boldsymbol{\beta}$. However, the OLS covariance matrix is valid only when $\rho = 0$. In this respect, the situation is very similar to the one encountered at the end of the previous section, when we were testing for possible simultaneity bias in models with truncated or censored dependent variables. There are actually two problems. First of all, the residuals in (15.57) will be heteroskedastic, since a typical residual is equal to

$$u_t - \rho\sigma\frac{\phi(\boldsymbol{W}_t\boldsymbol{\gamma})}{\Phi(\boldsymbol{W}_t\boldsymbol{\gamma})}.$$

Secondly, the selectivity regressor is being treated like any other regressor, when it is in fact part of the error term. One could solve the first problem by using a heteroskedasticity-consistent covariance matrix estimator (see Chapter 16), but that would not solve the second one. It is possible to obtain a valid covariance matrix estimate to go along with the two-step estimates of $\boldsymbol{\beta}$ from (15.57). However, the calculation is cumbersome, and the estimated covariance matrix is not always positive definite. See Greene (1981b) and Lee (1982) for more details.

It should be stressed that the consistency of this two-step estimator, like that of the ML estimator, depends critically on the assumption of normality. This can be seen from the specification of the selectivity regressor as the inverse Mills ratio $\phi(\boldsymbol{W}_t\boldsymbol{\gamma})/\Phi(\boldsymbol{W}_t\boldsymbol{\gamma})$. When the elements of $\boldsymbol{W}_t$ are the same as, or a subset of, the elements of $\boldsymbol{X}_t$, as is often the case in practice, it is only the nonlinearity of $\phi(\boldsymbol{W}_t\boldsymbol{\gamma})/\Phi(\boldsymbol{W}_t\boldsymbol{\gamma})$ as a function of $\boldsymbol{W}_t\boldsymbol{\gamma}$ that makes the parameters of the second-step regression identifiable. The exact form of the nonlinear relationship depends critically on the normality assumption. Pagan and Vella (1989), Smith (1989), and Peters and Smith (1991) discuss various ways to test this crucial assumption. Many of the tests suggested by these authors are applications of the OPG regression.

Although the two-step method for dealing with sample selectivity is widely used, our recommendation would be to use regression (15.57) only as a procedure for testing the null hypothesis that selectivity bias is not present. When that hypothesis is rejected, ML estimation based on (15.55) should probably be used in preference to the two-step method, unless it is computationally prohibitive.

15.9 CONCLUSION

Our treatment of binary response models in Sections 15.2 to 15.4 was reasonably detailed, but the discussions of more general qualitative response models and limited dependent variable models were necessarily quite superficial. Anyone who intends to do empirical work that employs this type of model will wish to consult some of the more detailed surveys referred to above. All of the methods that we have discussed for handling limited dependent variables rely heavily on the assumptions of normality and homoskedasticity. These assumptions should always be tested. A number of methods for doing so have been proposed; see, among others, Bera, Jarque, and Lee (1984), Lee and Maddala (1985), Blundell (1987), Chesher and Irish (1987), Pagan and Vella (1989), Smith (1989), and Peters and Smith (1991).

TERMS AND CONCEPTS

binary dependent variable
binary response (or binary choice) models
binary response model regression (BRMR)
censored data
conditional logit model
double censoring
Heckman's two-step method
independence of irrelevant alternatives (IIA)
index function
inverse Mills ratio
latent variable models
latent variables
limited dependent variable models
limited dependent variables
linear probability model
logistic function
logit model
multinomial (or multiple) logit model
ordered and unordered responses
ordered logit model
ordered probit model
ordered qualitative response model
perfect classifiers
probit model
qualitative response models
sample selectivity bias
selected sample
selectivity regressor
tobit model
transformation function
truncated data
truncated regression model

Chapter 16

Heteroskedasticity and Related Topics

16.1 Introduction

Most of the results that we have obtained for regression models up to this point have explicitly or implicitly relied on the assumption that the error terms are homoskedastic, and some results have depended on the further assumption that they are normally distributed. Both the homoskedasticity and normality assumptions often seem to be violated in practice, however. This is likely to be the case when the data pertain to cross sections of observations on households or firms or to time series of observations on financial assets. In this chapter, we deal with a number of important topics related to heteroskedasticity, nonnormality, and other failures of the usual assumptions about the error terms of regression models.

As we saw in Chapter 9, it is perfectly easy to estimate a regression model by weighted least squares (i.e., GLS) when the error terms are heteroskedastic with a pattern of heteroskedasticity that is determined by a known skedastic function. We also saw that it is reasonably easy to estimate a regression model by feasible GLS or maximum likelihood when the parameters of the skedastic function are not known, but its form is. Moreover, as we saw in Chapter 14, subjecting the dependent variable (and possibly the regression function as well) to an appropriate nonlinear transformation may eliminate heteroskedasticity altogether. Valuable as these techniques can sometimes be, they do not allow us to handle the all-too-common case in which little or nothing is known about the skedastic function.

In Section 16.2, we discuss the properties of NLS (and OLS) estimates when the error terms are heteroskedastic. Under reasonable assumptions, the estimates remain consistent and asymptotically normal, but their asymptotic covariance matrix differs from the usual one. In Section 16.3, we then show that it is possible to employ a **heteroskedasticity-consistent covariance matrix estimator** even when almost nothing is known about the form of the skedastic function. This very important result allows one to make asymptotically valid inferences from linear and nonlinear regression models under quite weak conditions. It also provides a justification for the heteroskedasticity-robust Gauss-Newton regression that we discussed in Section 11.6.

In Section 16.4, we discuss the idea of **autoregressive conditional heteroskedasticity**, or **ARCH**, which has proved to be extremely useful for modeling the error terms associated with regression models for certain types of time-series data, especially data from financial markets. Then, in Sections 16.5 and 16.6, we discuss some aspects of testing for heteroskedasticity that were not previously covered in Section 11.5. In particular, we discuss the implications of the fact that, for any model with error terms distributed independently of the regression function, regression directions and skedastic directions are orthogonal to each other.

In Section 16.7, we turn our attention to tests for normality of error terms, focusing on tests for skewness and excess kurtosis. It turns out to be very easy to test for normality in the context of regression models. In the next section, we then introduce a very broad class of tests called **conditional moment tests**. These tests are closely related to **information matrix tests**, which are discussed in Section 16.9.

16.2 Least Squares and Heteroskedasticity

The properties of the ordinary and nonlinear least squares estimators when they are applied to models with heteroskedastic errors are very similar. For simplicity, we therefore begin with the linear case. Suppose that we estimate the linear regression model

$$\boldsymbol{y} = \boldsymbol{X\beta} + \boldsymbol{u},$$

where $\boldsymbol{X}$ is an $n \times k$ matrix which satisfies the usual asymptotic regularity condition that $n^{-1}\boldsymbol{X}^{\top}\boldsymbol{X}$ tends in the limit to a positive definite matrix which is $O(1)$. The data are actually generated by

$$\boldsymbol{y} = \boldsymbol{X\beta}_0 + \boldsymbol{u}, \quad E(\boldsymbol{u}) = \boldsymbol{0}, \quad E(\boldsymbol{uu}^{\top}) = \boldsymbol{\Omega}, \tag{16.01}$$

where $\boldsymbol{\Omega}$ is a diagonal matrix with diagonal elements ω_t^2 that are bounded from above and below. We are interested in the properties of the OLS estimator $\hat{\boldsymbol{\beta}}$ when the DGP is (16.01). Clearly,

$$\hat{\boldsymbol{\beta}} = \left(\boldsymbol{X}^{\top}\boldsymbol{X}\right)^{-1}\boldsymbol{X}^{\top}\boldsymbol{y} = \boldsymbol{\beta}_0 + \left(\boldsymbol{X}^{\top}\boldsymbol{X}\right)^{-1}\boldsymbol{X}^{\top}\boldsymbol{u}. \tag{16.02}$$

It follows that

$$\operatorname*{plim}_{n\to\infty}(\hat{\boldsymbol{\beta}}) = \boldsymbol{\beta}_0 + \operatorname*{plim}_{n\to\infty}\left(\frac{1}{n}\boldsymbol{X}^{\top}\boldsymbol{X}\right)^{-1}\operatorname*{plim}_{n\to\infty}\left(\frac{1}{n}\boldsymbol{X}^{\top}\boldsymbol{u}\right).$$

Thus it is clear that $\hat{\boldsymbol{\beta}}$ will estimate $\boldsymbol{\beta}$ consistently provided that

$$\operatorname*{plim}_{n\to\infty}\left(\frac{1}{n}\boldsymbol{X}^{\top}\boldsymbol{u}\right) = \boldsymbol{0}.$$

As we saw in Section 9.5, this condition will not always hold when the error terms are not i.i.d. Although the discussion there was not rigorous, it was clear that three types of situations had to be ruled out. Two of these involved nondiagonal $\boldsymbol{\Omega}$ matrices, and the third involved unbounded variances. Since all three of these are ruled out by the assumptions we have already made, we may plausibly assert that $\hat{\boldsymbol{\beta}}$ is in fact consistent. For a much fuller treatment of this subject, see White (1984).

If $\boldsymbol{X}$ can be treated as fixed, it is easy to see from (16.02) that

$$\begin{aligned} \boldsymbol{V}(\hat{\boldsymbol{\beta}} - \boldsymbol{\beta}_0) &= E\Big(\big(\boldsymbol{X}^\top\boldsymbol{X}\big)^{-1}\boldsymbol{X}^\top\boldsymbol{u}\boldsymbol{u}^\top\boldsymbol{X}\big(\boldsymbol{X}^\top\boldsymbol{X}\big)^{-1}\Big) \\ &= \big(\boldsymbol{X}^\top\boldsymbol{X}\big)^{-1}\boldsymbol{X}^\top\boldsymbol{\Omega}\boldsymbol{X}\big(\boldsymbol{X}^\top\boldsymbol{X}\big)^{-1}. \end{aligned} \tag{16.03}$$

We will refer to the last expression here as the **generalized OLS covariance matrix**. It may be compared with the usual OLS covariance matrix,

$$\sigma_0^2\big(\boldsymbol{X}^\top\boldsymbol{X}\big)^{-1}, \tag{16.04}$$

where σ_0^2 would in this case be the probability limit of the average of the ω_t^2's, and with the GLS covariance matrix,

$$\big(\boldsymbol{X}^\top\boldsymbol{\Omega}^{-1}\boldsymbol{X}\big)^{-1}.$$

The Gauss-Markov Theorem (Theorem 5.3) implies that

$$\big(\boldsymbol{X}^\top\boldsymbol{X}\big)^{-1}\boldsymbol{X}^\top\boldsymbol{\Omega}\boldsymbol{X}\big(\boldsymbol{X}^\top\boldsymbol{X}\big)^{-1} - \big(\boldsymbol{X}^\top\boldsymbol{\Omega}^{-1}\boldsymbol{X}\big)^{-1}$$

must be a positive semidefinite matrix. It will be a zero matrix in the (relatively rare) circumstances in which Kruskal's Theorem applies and OLS and GLS estimates coincide (see Section 9.3).

There are evidently two different problems if we use OLS when we should have used weighted least squares, or GLS. The first is that the OLS estimates will be inefficient, which is a consequence of the Gauss-Markov Theorem. The second is that the standard OLS covariance matrix (16.04) will in most cases not equal the generalized OLS covariance matrix, which is the right-most expression in (16.03). How severe each of these problems is will evidently depend on the exact forms of $\boldsymbol{X}$ and $\boldsymbol{\Omega}$.

It may be illuminating to look at a numerical example. The model is

$$y_t = \beta_0 + \beta_1 x_t + u_t,$$

and the DGP is

$$y_t = 1 + x_t + u_t, \quad u_t \sim N(0, x_t^\alpha),$$

with $n = 100$, x_t uniformly distributed between 0 and 1, and α a parameter that takes on various values. Table 16.1 shows the standard deviations of the

Table 16.1 Correct and Incorrect Standard Errors

α	$\hat\beta_0$ (Incorrect)	$\hat\beta_0$ (Correct)	$\tilde\beta_0$	$\hat\beta_1$ (Incorrect)	$\hat\beta_1$ (Correct)	$\tilde\beta_1$
0.5	0.164	0.134	0.110	0.285	0.277	0.243
1.0	0.142	0.101	0.048	0.246	0.247	0.173
1.5	0.127	0.084	0.019	0.220	0.231	0.136
2.0	0.116	0.074	0.0073	0.200	0.220	0.109
2.5	0.107	0.068	0.0030	0.185	0.212	0.083
3.0	0.100	0.064	0.0013	0.173	0.206	0.056
3.5	0.094	0.061	0.0007	0.163	0.200	0.033
4.0	0.089	0.059	0.0003	0.154	0.195	0.017

OLS estimates $\hat\beta_0$ and $\hat\beta_1$ and the GLS estimates $\tilde\beta_0$ and $\tilde\beta_1$; for the former, both the correct standard deviations and the incorrect ones obtained from the usual formula are shown.[1]

Even though this example is very simple, the results in Table 16.1 illustrate two things. First of all, GLS may be only a little more efficient than OLS, as it is when $\alpha = 0.5$, or it may be vastly more efficient, as it is for the larger values of α. Second, the usual OLS standard errors may be either too large (as they always are for β_0) or too small (as they usually are for β_1).

Although the usual OLS covariance matrix (16.04) is generally invalid in the presence of heteroskedasticity, there is one special situation in which it is valid. The difference between the usual and generalized OLS covariance matrices is

$$\sigma_0^2 (\boldsymbol{X}^\top\boldsymbol{X})^{-1} - (\boldsymbol{X}^\top\boldsymbol{X})^{-1}\boldsymbol{X}^\top\boldsymbol{\Omega}\boldsymbol{X}(\boldsymbol{X}^\top\boldsymbol{X})^{-1}.$$

The key expression here is the middle factor in the second term, namely, $\boldsymbol{X}^\top\boldsymbol{\Omega}\boldsymbol{X}$. Since $\boldsymbol{\Omega}$ is diagonal, this matrix is

$$\sum_{t=1}^{n} \omega_t^2 \boldsymbol{X}_t^\top \boldsymbol{X}_t,$$

where $\boldsymbol{X}_t$ denotes the tth row of $\boldsymbol{X}$. This is simply a weighted average of the matrices $\boldsymbol{X}_t^\top\boldsymbol{X}_t$, with weights ω_t^2. In most cases, these weights will be related to the corresponding rows of the $\boldsymbol{X}$ matrix. Suppose, however, that they are not. Then

$$\operatorname*{plim}_{n\to\infty}\left(\frac{1}{n}\sum_{t=1}^{n}\omega_t^2\boldsymbol{X}_t^\top\boldsymbol{X}_t\right) = \operatorname*{plim}_{n\to\infty}\left(\frac{1}{n}\sum_{t=1}^{n}\omega_t^2\right)\operatorname*{plim}_{n\to\infty}\left(\frac{1}{n}\sum_{t=1}^{n}\boldsymbol{X}_t^\top\boldsymbol{X}_t\right). \tag{16.05}$$

[1] These results were obtained numerically, using 20,000 replications. They should be accurate to the number of digits shown.

Here we have multiplied each of the matrices $\boldsymbol{X}_t^\top \boldsymbol{X}_t$ by the probability limit of the average weight, instead of by the individual weights. If the weights really are unrelated to $\boldsymbol{X}_t^\top \boldsymbol{X}_t$, this is a perfectly valid thing to do.

It is clear that the OLS estimate of the error variance will tend to

$$\operatorname*{plim}_{n\to\infty}\left(\frac{1}{n}\sum_{t=1}^{n}\omega_t^2\right) \equiv \sigma_0^2.$$

Hence the right-hand side of (16.05) can be rewritten as

$$\sigma_0^2 \operatorname*{plim}_{n\to\infty}\left(\frac{1}{n}\sum_{t=1}^{n}\boldsymbol{X}_t^\top \boldsymbol{X}_t\right) = \sigma_0^2 \operatorname*{plim}_{n\to\infty}\left(\frac{1}{n}\boldsymbol{X}^\top \boldsymbol{X}\right).$$

Thus, if (16.05) holds, we can see that n times the generalized OLS covariance matrix (16.03) has a probability limit of

$$\sigma_0^2 \operatorname*{plim}_{n\to\infty}\left(\frac{1}{n}\boldsymbol{X}^\top \boldsymbol{X}\right)^{-1}, \tag{16.06}$$

which is the conventional asymptotic covariance matrix for OLS.

One commonly encountered situation in which (16.05) and (16.06) hold occurs when $\boldsymbol{X}$ consists solely of a constant term. In that case, $\boldsymbol{X}_t^\top \boldsymbol{X}_t$ is just unity for all t, and

$$\operatorname*{plim}_{n\to\infty}\left(\frac{1}{n}\sum_{t=1}^{n}\omega_t^2\boldsymbol{X}_t^\top \boldsymbol{X}_t\right) = \operatorname*{plim}_{n\to\infty}\left(\frac{1}{n}\sum_{t=1}^{n}\omega_t^2\right) = \sigma_0^2.$$

Thus, if we are estimating a mean, the usual formula for the standard error of the sample mean will be valid whether or not there is heteroskedasticity.

All of the above results can easily be extended to the nonlinear regression case. Suppose that we estimate the nonlinear regression model $\boldsymbol{y} = \boldsymbol{x}(\boldsymbol{\beta}) + \boldsymbol{u}$ by NLS when the DGP is

$$\boldsymbol{y} = \boldsymbol{x}(\boldsymbol{\beta}_0) + \boldsymbol{u}, \quad E(\boldsymbol{u}) = \boldsymbol{0}, \quad E(\boldsymbol{u}\boldsymbol{u}^\top) = \boldsymbol{\Omega},$$

where $\boldsymbol{\Omega}$ has the same properties as those we assumed in the linear case. Then it is not hard to see that the following asymptotic relationship, which is equation (5.39) written in a slightly different way, holds just as in the homoskedastic case:

$$n^{1/2}(\hat{\boldsymbol{\beta}} - \boldsymbol{\beta}_0) \overset{a}{=} \left(n^{-1}\boldsymbol{X}_0^\top \boldsymbol{X}_0\right)^{-1} n^{-1/2}\boldsymbol{X}_0^\top \boldsymbol{u}. \tag{16.07}$$

Here $\boldsymbol{X}_0$ denotes $\boldsymbol{X}(\boldsymbol{\beta}_0)$, the matrix of derivatives of $\boldsymbol{x}(\boldsymbol{\beta})$ with respect to $\boldsymbol{\beta}$, evaluated at $\boldsymbol{\beta}_0$. From (16.07), we immediately conclude that the asymptotic covariance matrix of the NLS estimator is

$$\operatorname*{plim}_{n\to\infty}\left(\left(n^{-1}\boldsymbol{X}_0^\top \boldsymbol{X}_0\right)^{-1}\left(n^{-1}\boldsymbol{X}_0^\top \boldsymbol{\Omega}\boldsymbol{X}_0\right)\left(n^{-1}\boldsymbol{X}_0^\top \boldsymbol{X}_0\right)^{-1}\right). \tag{16.08}$$

This is, of course, directly analogous to the second line of (16.03).

16.3 COVARIANCE MATRIX ESTIMATION

At first glance, the generalized OLS covariance matrix estimator and its NLS analog (16.08) do not seem to be very useful. To compute them we need to know $\boldsymbol{\Omega}$, but if we knew $\boldsymbol{\Omega}$, we could use GLS or GNLS and obtain more efficient estimates. This was the conventional wisdom among econometricians until a decade ago. But an extremely influential paper by White (1980) showed that it is in fact possible to obtain an estimator of the covariance matrix of least squares estimates that is asymptotically valid when there is heteroskedasticity of unknown form.[2] Such an estimator is a called a **heteroskedasticity-consistent covariance matrix estimator**, or **HCCME**.

The key to obtaining an HCCME is to recognize that we do *not* have to estimate $\boldsymbol{\Omega}$ consistently. That would indeed be an impossible task, since $\boldsymbol{\Omega}$ has n diagonal elements to estimate. The asymptotic covariance matrix of a vector of NLS estimates, under heteroskedasticity, is given by expression (16.08), which can be rewritten as

$$\operatorname*{plim}_{n\to\infty}\Big(\frac{1}{n}\boldsymbol{X}_0^{\top}\boldsymbol{X}_0\Big)^{-1}\operatorname*{plim}_{n\to\infty}\Big(\frac{1}{n}\boldsymbol{X}_0^{\top}\boldsymbol{\Omega}\boldsymbol{X}_0\Big)\operatorname*{plim}_{n\to\infty}\Big(\frac{1}{n}\boldsymbol{X}_0^{\top}\boldsymbol{X}_0\Big)^{-1}. \tag{16.09}$$

The first and third factors here are identical, and we can easily estimate them in the usual way. A consistent estimator is

$$\frac{1}{n}\hat{\boldsymbol{X}}^{\top}\hat{\boldsymbol{X}},$$

where $\hat{\boldsymbol{X}} \equiv \boldsymbol{X}(\hat{\boldsymbol{\beta}})$. The only tricky thing, then, is to estimate the second factor. White showed that this second factor can be estimated consistently by

$$\frac{1}{n}\hat{\boldsymbol{X}}^{\top}\hat{\boldsymbol{\Omega}}\hat{\boldsymbol{X}}, \tag{16.10}$$

where $\hat{\boldsymbol{\Omega}}$ may be any of several different *inconsistent* estimators of $\boldsymbol{\Omega}$. The simplest version of $\hat{\boldsymbol{\Omega}}$, and the one that White proposed in the context of linear regression models, has t^{th} diagonal element equal to $\hat{u}_t^2$, the tth squared least squares residual.

Unlike $\boldsymbol{\Omega}$, the middle factor of (16.09) has only $\frac{1}{2}(k^2+k)$ distinct elements, whatever the sample size. That is why it is possible to estimate it consistently. A typical element of this matrix is

$$\operatorname*{plim}_{n\to\infty}\Big(\frac{1}{n}\sum_{t=1}^{n}\omega_t^2 X_{ti}X_{tj}\Big), \tag{16.11}$$

[2] Precursors of White's paper in the statistics literature include Eicker (1963, 1967) and Hinkley (1977), as well as some of the early papers on bootstrapping (see Chapter 21).

where $X_{ti} \equiv X_{ti}(\boldsymbol{\beta}_0)$. On the other hand, a typical element of (16.10) is

$$\frac{1}{n}\sum_{t=1}^{n} \hat{u}_t^2 \hat{X}_{ti} \hat{X}_{tj}. \tag{16.12}$$

Because $\hat{\boldsymbol{\beta}}$ is consistent for $\boldsymbol{\beta}_0$, $\hat{u}_t$ is consistent for u_t, $\hat{u}_t^2$ is consistent for u_t^2, and $\hat{X}_{ti}$ is consistent for X_{ti}. Thus expression (16.12) is asymptotically equal to

$$\frac{1}{n}\sum_{t=1}^{n} u_t^2 X_{ti} X_{tj}. \tag{16.13}$$

Under our assumptions, we can apply a law of large numbers to (16.13); see White (1980, 1984) and Nicholls and Pagan (1983) for some technical details. It follows immediately that (16.13), and so also (16.12), tends in probability to (16.11). Consequently, the matrix

$$\big(n^{-1}\hat{\boldsymbol{X}}^{\top}\hat{\boldsymbol{X}}\big)^{-1}\big(n^{-1}\hat{\boldsymbol{X}}^{\top}\hat{\boldsymbol{\Omega}}\hat{\boldsymbol{X}}\big)\big(n^{-1}\hat{\boldsymbol{X}}^{\top}\hat{\boldsymbol{X}}\big)^{-1} \tag{16.14}$$

consistently estimates (16.09). Of course, in practice one ignores the factors of n^{-1} and uses the matrix

$$\big(\hat{\boldsymbol{X}}^{\top}\hat{\boldsymbol{X}}\big)^{-1}\hat{\boldsymbol{X}}^{\top}\hat{\boldsymbol{\Omega}}\hat{\boldsymbol{X}}\big(\hat{\boldsymbol{X}}^{\top}\hat{\boldsymbol{X}}\big)^{-1} \tag{16.15}$$

to estimate the covariance matrix of $\hat{\boldsymbol{\beta}}$.

Asymptotically valid inferences about $\boldsymbol{\beta}$ may be based on the HCCME (16.15) in the usual way. However, one must be cautious when n is not large. There is a good deal of evidence that this HCCME is somewhat unreliable in finite samples. After all, the fact that (16.14) estimates (16.09) consistently does not imply that the former always estimates the latter very well in finite samples.

It is possible to modify the HCCME (16.15) so that it has better finite-sample properties. The major problem is that the squared least squares residuals $\hat{u}_t^2$ are not unbiased estimates of the squared error terms u_t^2. The easiest way to improve the HCCME is simply to multiply (16.15) by $n/(n-k)$. This is analogous to dividing the sum of squared residuals by $n-k$ rather than n to obtain the OLS variance estimator s^2. A second, and better, approach is to define the tth diagonal element of $\hat{\boldsymbol{\Omega}}$ as $\hat{u}_t^2/(1-\hat{h}_t)$, where $\hat{h}_t \equiv \hat{\boldsymbol{X}}_t(\hat{\boldsymbol{X}}^{\top}\hat{\boldsymbol{X}})^{-1}\hat{\boldsymbol{X}}_t^{\top}$ is the tth diagonal element of the "hat" matrix $\boldsymbol{P}_X$ that projects orthogonally onto the space spanned by the columns of $\hat{\boldsymbol{X}}$. Recall from Section 3.2 that, in the OLS case with constant variance σ^2, the expectation of $\hat{u}_t^2$ is $\sigma^2(1-h_t)$. Thus, in the linear case, dividing $\hat{u}_t^2$ by $1-h_t$ would yield an unbiased estimate of σ^2 if the error terms were actually homoskedastic.

A third possibility is to use a technique called the "jackknife" that we will not attempt to discuss here; see MacKinnon and White (1985). The resulting

HCCME is moderately complicated but can be approximated very well simply by defining the tth diagonal element of $\hat{\boldsymbol{\Omega}}$ as

$$\frac{\hat{u}_t^2}{\left(1-\hat{h}_t\right)^2}. \tag{16.16}$$

This may seem to involve overcorrecting for the tendency of least squares residuals to be too small, since in the linear case with homoskedasticity the expectation of (16.16) would be greater than σ^2. But when the error terms actually are heteroskedastic, observations with large variances will tend to influence the parameter estimates more than observations with small variances and will therefore tend to have residuals that are very much too small. Thus, to the extent that large variances are associated with large values of $\hat{h}_t$, this overcorrection may actually be a good thing.

We have now mentioned four different HCCMEs. We will refer to these as HC_0 through HC_3. They differ only in how the tth elements of $\hat{\boldsymbol{\Omega}}$ are defined:

$$\begin{aligned}
HC_0&: \ \hat{u}_t^2\\
HC_1&: \ \frac{n}{n-k}\hat{u}_t^2\\
HC_2&: \ \frac{\hat{u}_t^2}{1-\hat{h}_t}\\
HC_3&: \ \frac{\hat{u}_t^2}{\left(1-\hat{h}_t\right)^2}.
\end{aligned}$$

MacKinnon and White (1985) investigated the finite-sample performance of pseudo-t statistics based on these four HCCMEs.[3] They found that HC_0 performed worst, tending to overreject the null hypothesis quite severely in some cases, with HC_1 doing better, HC_2 doing better still, and HC_3 performing best of all. Subsequent work by Chesher and Jewitt (1987), Chesher (1989), and Chesher and Austin (1991) has provided some insight into the reasons for these results and suggests that HC_3 will not always perform better than HC_2.

As a practical matter, one should never use HC_0, since HC_1 costs no more to compute and always performs better. When the diagonals of the hat matrix are available, one should definitely use HC_2 or HC_3 rather than HC_1. Which of these should be used is not entirely clear, however. HC_2 is in some ways more appealing, but HC_3 generally seems to perform better in Monte Carlo experiments.

Although many regression packages now compute HCCMEs, they often produce only the least desirable of these, namely, HC_0. Messer and White

[3] Actually, they investigated the performance of the jackknife rather than that of the HCCME that we have called HC_3, but subsequent computer simulations suggest that HC_3 behaves very similarly to the jackknife.

(1984) suggest an ingenious way to compute any of these HCCMEs by means of a program intended for instrumental variables estimation. Let $\check{u}_t$ denote some estimate of u_t: $\hat{u}_t$ in the case of HC_0, $\hat{u}_t/(1-h_t)^{1/2}$ in the case of HC_2, and so on. The procedure suggested by Messer and White is to construct the artificial variables

$$y_t^* \equiv \frac{y_t}{\check{u}_t}, \quad \boldsymbol{X}_t^* \equiv \frac{\boldsymbol{X}_t}{\check{u}_t}, \quad \text{and} \quad \boldsymbol{Z}_t \equiv \boldsymbol{X}_t \check{u}_t$$

and regress y_t^* on $\boldsymbol{X}_t^*$ using $\boldsymbol{Z}_t$ as a vector of instruments. The IV coefficient estimates obtained in this way are identical to those from an OLS regression of y_t on $\boldsymbol{X}_t$, and the IV covariance matrix is proportional to the HCCME corresponding to whatever set of residuals $\check{u}_t$ was used. The factor of proportionality is s^2, the IV estimate of the error variance, which will tend to unity as $n \to \infty$. Thus, unless $s^2 = 1$, as it will be if $\check{u}_t = \hat{u}_t$ and the regression package divides by n rather than $n-k$, one simply divides the IV covariance matrix by s^2. This procedure works only if none of the $\check{u}_t$'s is identically zero; ways to handle zero residuals are discussed in the original article. Of course, any HCCME can be calculated directly using many different programming languages. The key thing is to set up the calculations in such a way that the $n \times n$ matrix $\hat{\boldsymbol{\Omega}}$ never has to be formed explicitly.

There are two different ways to use HCCMEs for testing hypotheses. The most straightforward is simply to construct Wald tests and pseudo-t statistics in the usual way, using the HCCME instead of the usual least squares covariance matrix estimator. However, as we saw in Section 11.6, it is also possible to construct LM, or $C(\alpha)$, tests based on what we called the heteroskedasticity-robust Gauss-Newton regression, or HRGNR. Suppose the alternative hypothesis is

$$\boldsymbol{y} = \boldsymbol{x}(\boldsymbol{\beta}, \boldsymbol{\gamma}) + \boldsymbol{u},$$

with $\boldsymbol{\beta}$ a k-vector and $\boldsymbol{\gamma}$ an r-vector, where the null hypothesis is $\boldsymbol{\gamma} = \boldsymbol{0}$. Let $\acute{\boldsymbol{X}}$ and $\acute{\boldsymbol{Z}}$ denote matrices of derivatives of $\boldsymbol{x}(\boldsymbol{\beta}, \boldsymbol{\gamma})$ with respect to the elements of $\boldsymbol{\beta}$ and $\boldsymbol{\gamma}$, respectively, evaluated at root-n consistent estimates $[\acute{\boldsymbol{\beta}} \,\vdots\, \boldsymbol{0}]$. Then if $\acute{\boldsymbol{M}}_X$ denotes the matrix that projects orthogonally onto $\mathcal{S}^\perp(\acute{\boldsymbol{X}})$, $\acute{\boldsymbol{u}}$ denotes an n-vector of residuals with typical element $\acute{u}_t = y_t - x_t(\acute{\boldsymbol{\beta}}, \boldsymbol{0})$, and $\acute{\boldsymbol{\Omega}}$ denotes an $n \times n$ diagonal matrix with typical diagonal element $\acute{u}_t^2$, the test statistic

$$\acute{\boldsymbol{u}}^\top \acute{\boldsymbol{M}}_X \acute{\boldsymbol{Z}} \big(\acute{\boldsymbol{Z}}^\top \acute{\boldsymbol{M}}_X \acute{\boldsymbol{\Omega}} \acute{\boldsymbol{M}}_X \acute{\boldsymbol{Z}}\big)^{-1} \acute{\boldsymbol{Z}}^\top \acute{\boldsymbol{M}}_X \acute{\boldsymbol{u}} \tag{16.17}$$

is asymptotically distributed as $\chi^2(r)$. This test statistic is equal to n minus the sum of squared residuals from the artificial regression

$$\boldsymbol{\iota} = \acute{\boldsymbol{U}} \acute{\boldsymbol{M}}_X \acute{\boldsymbol{Z}} \boldsymbol{b} + \text{residuals},$$

where $\boldsymbol{\iota}$, as usual, is an n-vector each element of which is 1, and $\acute{\boldsymbol{U}}$ is an $n \times n$ diagonal matrix with the vector $\acute{\boldsymbol{u}}$ on the principal diagonal. We gave precise instructions for computing (16.17) in Section 11.6.

It is now possible to see just why the HRGNR works. The matrix in the middle of (16.17) is simply an HCCME for the covariance matrix of the vector $\acute{\boldsymbol{Z}}^\top \acute{\boldsymbol{M}}_X \acute{\boldsymbol{u}}$, which should have mean zero, asymptotically, if the null hypothesis is correct. For more on the HRGNR, see Davidson and MacKinnon (1985b) and Wooldridge (1990a, 1990b, 1991a). There is some evidence that the HRGNR test statistic (16.17) is closer to its asymptotic distribution in finite samples than are Wald test statistics based on HCCMEs; see Davidson and MacKinnon (1985b).

The key insight behind the HCCME is that one can consistently estimate a matrix like the one in the middle of (16.09) without being able to estimate $\boldsymbol{\Omega}$ consistently. This basic idea will come up again in the next chapter, when we discuss the estimation technique known as the generalized method of moments. Among other things, this will allow us to calculate estimates that are asymptotically more efficient than least squares estimates when there is heteroskedasticity of unknown form.

16.4 AUTOREGRESSIVE CONDITIONAL HETEROSKEDASTICITY

Econometricians frequently encounter models estimated using time-series data where the residuals are quite small for a number of successive periods of time, then much larger for a while, then smaller again, and so on, generally for no apparent reason. This is particularly common with data on stock prices, foreign exchange rates, or other prices determined in financial markets, where volatility generally seems to vary over time. There has recently been a great deal of literature on ways to model this phenomenon. The seminal paper is Engle (1982b), in which the concept of **autoregressive conditional heteroskedasticity**, or **ARCH**, was first proposed. The basic idea of ARCH is that the variance of the error term at time t depends on the size of the squared error terms in previous time periods. However, there are many different ways in which this basic idea can be modeled, and the literature is correspondingly very large.

Let u_t denote the tth error term adhering to some regression model. Then the original ARCH model can be written as

$$\sigma_t^2 \equiv E(u_t^2 \,|\, \Omega_t) = \alpha + \gamma_1 u_{t-1}^2 + \gamma_2 u_{t-2}^2 + \cdots + \gamma_p u_{t-p}^2, \tag{16.18}$$

where Ω_t denotes the information set on which σ_t^2, the variance of u_t, is to be conditioned. This information set typically consists of everything dated $t-1$ or earlier. This particular model is called the **ARCH($\boldsymbol{p}$)** process. Its resemblance to the AR(p) process discussed in Chapter 10 is striking and accounts for the name given to these models. We can see from (16.18) that the conditional variance of u_t depends on the values of u_t^2 realized in the past. In order to ensure that this conditional variance is always positive, it must be assumed that α and all the γ_i's are nonnegative.

The simplest version of (16.18) is the **ARCH(1)** process,

$$\sigma_t^2 = \alpha + \gamma_1 u_{t-1}^2. \tag{16.19}$$

The conditional variance of u_t given by (16.19) may be compared with the unconditional variance $\sigma^2 \equiv E(u_t^2)$. Assuming that the ARCH(1) process is stationary, which it will be if $\gamma_1 < 1$, we can write

$$\sigma^2 = \alpha + \gamma_1 \sigma^2.$$

This implies that

$$\sigma^2 = \frac{\alpha}{1 - \gamma_1}.$$

Thus the unconditional variance of u_t depends on the parameters of the ARCH process and will in general be different from the conditional variance given by equation (16.19).

Under the null hypothesis of homoskedastic errors, all the γ_i's are zero. As Engle (1982b) first showed, it is easy to test this hypothesis by running the regression

$$\hat{u}_t^2 = a + c_1 \hat{u}_{t-1}^2 + c_2 \hat{u}_{t-2}^2 + \cdots + c_p \hat{u}_{t-p}^2 + \text{residual}, \tag{16.20}$$

where $\hat{u}_t$ denotes a residual from least squares estimation of the regression model to which the u_t's adhere. One then calculates an ordinary F test (or simply n times the *centered* R^2) for the hypothesis that c_1 through c_p are zero. This artificial regression has the same form as the one for testing the homoskedasticity assumption that we discussed in Section 11.5, but the regressors are now lagged squared residuals rather than independent variables. Thus, for any regression model estimated using time-series data, it is very easy to test the null hypothesis of homoskedasticity against the alternative that the errors follow an ARCH(p) process.

Testing for ARCH errors plays the same role in analyzing the second moments of a time-series regression model as testing for AR errors does in analyzing the first moments. Just as finding evidence of AR errors may or may not indicate that the error terms really follow an AR process, so finding evidence of ARCH errors may or may not indicate that there really is autoregressive conditional heteroskedasticity. In both cases, other forms of misspecification may lead to what looks like evidence of AR or ARCH errors. With slight modifications, the analysis of Chapter 12 applies to tests in skedastic directions (i.e., tests for heteroskedasticity) just as it does to any other specification test.

Many variants of the ARCH model have been proposed. A particularly useful variant is the **generalized ARCH**, or **GARCH**, model, suggested by Bollerslev (1986). The **GARCH(p, q)** model may be written as

$$\sigma_t^2 = \alpha + \sum_{i=1}^{p} \gamma_i u_{t-i}^2 + \sum_{j=1}^{q} \delta_j \sigma_{t-j}^2$$

or, in more compact notation, as

$$\sigma_t^2 = \alpha + A(L, \boldsymbol{\gamma})u_t^2 + B(L, \boldsymbol{\delta})\sigma_t^2,$$

where $\boldsymbol{\gamma}$ and $\boldsymbol{\delta}$ are parameter vectors with typical elements γ_i and δ_j, respectively, and $A(L, \boldsymbol{\gamma})$ and $B(L, \boldsymbol{\delta})$ are polynomials in the lag operator L. In the GARCH model, the conditional variance σ_t^2 depends on its own past values as well as on lagged values of u_t^2. This means that σ_t^2 effectively depends on all past values of u_t^2. In practice, a GARCH model with very few parameters often performs as well as an ARCH model with many parameters. In particular, one simple model that often works very well is the **GARCH(1, 1)** model,

$$\sigma_t^2 = \alpha + \gamma_1 u_{t-1}^2 + \delta_1 \sigma_{t-1}^2. \tag{16.21}$$

In practice, one must solve a GARCH model to eliminate the σ_{t-j}^2 terms from the right-hand side before one can estimate it. The problem is essentially the same as estimating a moving average model or an ARMA model with a moving average component; see Section 10.7. For example, the GARCH(1, 1) model (16.21) can be solved recursively to yield

$$\sigma_t^2 = \frac{\alpha}{1-\delta_1} + \gamma_1\left(u_{t-1}^2 + \delta_1 u_{t-2}^2 + \delta_1^2 u_{t-3}^2 + \delta_1^3 u_{t-4}^2 + \cdots\right). \tag{16.22}$$

Various assumptions can be made about the presample error terms. The simplest is to assume that they are zero, but it is more realistic to assume that they are equal to their unconditional expectation.

It is interesting to observe that, when δ_1 is near zero, the solved GARCH(1, 1) model (16.22) looks like an ARCH(2) model. Because of this, it turns out that an appropriate test for GARCH(1, 1) errors is simply to regress the squared residuals on a constant term and on the squared residuals lagged once and twice. In general, an LM test against GARCH(p, q) errors is the same as an LM test against ARCH($p + q$) errors. These results are completely analogous to the results for testing against ARMA(p, q) errors that we discussed in Section 10.8.

There are three principal ways to estimate regression models with ARCH and GARCH errors: feasible GLS, one-step efficient estimation, and maximum likelihood. In the simplest approach, which is feasible GLS, one first estimates the regression model by ordinary or nonlinear least squares, then uses the squared residuals to estimate the parameters of the ARCH or GARCH process, and finally uses weighted least squares to estimate the parameters of the regression function. This procedure can run into difficulties if the conditional variances predicted by the fitted ARCH process are not all positive, and various ad hoc methods may then be used to ensure that they are all positive.

The estimates of the ARCH parameters obtained by this sort of feasible GLS procedure will not be asymptotically efficient. Engle (1982b) therefore suggested using a form of one-step efficient estimation. This method is a bit too complicated to discuss here, however.

The third popular estimation method is to use maximum likelihood, assuming normally distributed errors. Suppose that the model to be estimated is a nonlinear regression model with GARCH(p, q) errors that are conditionally normal:

$$\begin{aligned} y_t &= x_t(\boldsymbol{\beta}) + u_t, \quad u_t = \sigma_t \varepsilon_t, \\ \sigma_t^2 &= \alpha + A(L, \boldsymbol{\gamma})u_t^2 + B(L, \boldsymbol{\delta})\sigma_t^2, \quad \varepsilon_t \sim \mathrm{NID}(0, 1). \end{aligned} \tag{16.23}$$

The loglikelihood function for this model is

$$C - \frac{1}{2}\sum_{t=1}^{n} \log\bigl(\sigma_t^2(\alpha, \boldsymbol{\gamma}, \boldsymbol{\delta}, \boldsymbol{\beta})\bigr) - \frac{1}{2}\sum_{t=1}^{n} \frac{\bigl(y_t - x_t(\boldsymbol{\beta})\bigr)^2}{\sigma_t^2(\alpha, \boldsymbol{\gamma}, \boldsymbol{\delta}, \boldsymbol{\beta})}, \tag{16.24}$$

where C is a constant and

$$\sigma_t^2(\alpha, \boldsymbol{\gamma}, \boldsymbol{\delta}, \boldsymbol{\beta}) \equiv \alpha + A(L, \boldsymbol{\gamma})\bigl(y_t - x_t(\boldsymbol{\beta})\bigr)^2 + B(L, \boldsymbol{\delta})\sigma_t^2. \tag{16.25}$$

Because this is a GARCH model, one must solve (16.25) recursively for σ_t^2 in order to evaluate (16.24). The algebra is fairly messy, but, with appropriate software, estimation is not unduly difficult.

The model (16.23) is clearly one to which the double-length artificial regression (DLR), introduced in Section 14.4, is applicable. If we make the definition

$$f_t(y_t, \boldsymbol{\theta}) \equiv \frac{y_t - x_t(\boldsymbol{\beta})}{\bigl(\alpha + A(L, \boldsymbol{\gamma})\bigl(y_t - x_t(\boldsymbol{\beta})\bigr)^2 + B(L, \boldsymbol{\delta})\sigma_t^2\bigr)^{1/2}},$$

it is clear that this model is a special case of the class of models (14.18). Obtaining the derivatives needed to implement the DLR is not trivial, especially when $\boldsymbol{\delta} \neq \mathbf{0}$, but essentially the same effort is needed to implement any asymptotically efficient estimation technique. The DLR can be used to obtain one-step efficient estimates, starting from OLS estimates and consistent estimates of the ARCH parameters obtained from them, or as part of a procedure for ML estimation. Of course, the DLR also provides a natural and relatively convenient way to perform a wide variety of specification tests for models with ARCH and GARCH errors.

One of the many developments of the original ARCH idea is the important class of models called the **ARCH-in-mean**, or **ARCH-M**, class. This class of models was introduced by Engle, Lilien, and Robins (1987). These models are like other ARCH models except that the conditional variance σ_t^2 enters into the regression function for the conditional mean. Thus (16.23) would become

$$\begin{aligned} y_t &= x_t(\boldsymbol{\beta}, \sigma_t^2) + u_t, \quad u_t = \sigma_t \varepsilon_t, \\ \sigma_t^2 &= \alpha + A(L, \boldsymbol{\gamma})u_t^2 + B(L, \boldsymbol{\delta})\sigma_t^2, \quad \varepsilon_t \sim \mathrm{NID}(0, 1). \end{aligned}$$

Many theories in financial economics make use of measures of risk. To the extent that the conditional variance of an error term is a measure of risk, it seems logical that σ_t^2 should enter the regression function as a measure of risk. The information matrix for ARCH-M models is not block diagonal between $\boldsymbol{\beta}$ on the one hand and $\boldsymbol{\gamma}$ and $\boldsymbol{\delta}$ on the other. Thus the feasible GLS and one-step efficient estimation techniques that work for other ARCH models cannot be used. Maximum likelihood is the estimation technique that is almost always employed.

The literature on ARCH is large and growing very rapidly. Engle and Bollerslev (1986) provides a useful survey of the early work in the field. Engle and Rothschild (1992) is a collection of recent papers, including Bollerslev, Chou, and Kroner (1992), which provides a very extensive bibliography. Engle, Hendry, and Trumble (1985) provides Monte Carlo evidence on the finite-sample properties of ARCH estimators and test statistics. Empirical papers include Domowitz and Hakkio (1985), Bollerslev, Engle, and Wooldridge (1988), McCurdy and Morgan (1988), and Nelson (1991).

16.5 Testing for Heteroskedasticity

In Section 11.5, we discussed some tests for heteroskedasticity based on artificial regressions similar to the Gauss-Newton regression, in which the regressand was a vector of squared residuals. In this section, we discuss these and other tests for heteroskedasticity in more detail.

Suppose the null hypothesis is

$$y_t = x_t(\boldsymbol{\beta}) + u_t, \quad u_t \sim \text{IID}(0, \sigma^2),$$

and the alternative hypothesis is that the regression function is still $x_t(\boldsymbol{\beta})$, but with

$$E(u_t^2) = h(\alpha + \boldsymbol{Z}_t\boldsymbol{\gamma}),$$

where $h(\cdot)$ is a positive-valued function that may be linear or nonlinear, $\boldsymbol{Z}_t$ is a $1 \times q$ vector of observations on exogenous or predetermined variables, and α and $\boldsymbol{\gamma}$ are unknown parameters. We saw in Section 11.5 that the hypothesis $\boldsymbol{\gamma} = \boldsymbol{0}$ may be tested by testing the hypothesis that $\boldsymbol{c} = \boldsymbol{0}$ in the artificial regression

$$\hat{\boldsymbol{v}} = \boldsymbol{\iota}a^* + \boldsymbol{Z}\boldsymbol{c} + \text{residuals}. \tag{16.26}$$

Here $\hat{\boldsymbol{v}}$ is a vector with typical element $\hat{u}_t^2$, $\boldsymbol{\iota}$ is a vector with every element 1, and $\boldsymbol{Z}$ is a matrix with typical row $\boldsymbol{Z}_t$. The test statistic may be either n times the *centered* R^2 or the ordinary F statistic for $\boldsymbol{c} = \boldsymbol{0}$. We derived this test as an application of general results for Gauss-Newton regressions.

In Section 11.5, we said little about how the matrix $\boldsymbol{Z}$ may be chosen. There are a great many ways to do so. It may consist of observations on any exogenous or predetermined variables that belong to the information set on which $\boldsymbol{y}$ is being conditioned, or functions of such variables, and it may have one column or many. One approach is to specify particular heteroskedastic alternatives that seem plausible and derive $\boldsymbol{Z}$ accordingly. The regression (16.20) used to test for ARCH(p) errors is one particular example in which the matrix $\boldsymbol{Z}$ is made up exclusively of lagged squared residuals. As another example, multiplicative heteroskedasticity often seems plausible if the regressand is always substantially larger than zero. Thus, in this case, one reasonable alternative hypothesis would be

$$E(u_t^2) = \alpha(\boldsymbol{X}_t\boldsymbol{\beta})^{\gamma}. \tag{16.27}$$

Since the null hypothesis then corresponds to $\gamma = 0$, α can be identified with σ^2. The derivative of the right-hand side of (16.27) with respect to γ is

$$\alpha(\boldsymbol{X}_t\boldsymbol{\beta})^{\gamma}\log(\boldsymbol{X}_t\boldsymbol{\beta}). \tag{16.28}$$

Evaluating (16.28) under the null hypothesis that $\gamma = 0$ yields $\hat{\sigma}^2\log(\boldsymbol{X}_t\hat{\boldsymbol{\beta}})$. Thus, to test the hypothesis that $\gamma = 0$, we simply have to regress $\hat{u}_t^2$ on a constant and $\log(\boldsymbol{X}_t\hat{\boldsymbol{\beta}})$. The test statistic is the t statistic on the latter. It should be asymptotically distributed as $N(0,1)$ under the null hypothesis.

There are many specifications of heteroskedasticity that, like (16.27), may seem plausible in particular cases. These lead to various specifications of $\boldsymbol{Z}$. When there is good a priori reason to suspect that heteroskedasticity has a particular form, it makes sense to test against that form and then to use feasible GLS or ML to take account of it if the null hypothesis is rejected.

On the other hand, if there is little a priori information about what form heteroskedasticity may take if it is present, specifying $\boldsymbol{Z}$ becomes much harder. One approach was suggested by White (1980). We saw in Section 16.2 that, for a linear regression model estimated by OLS, the conventional OLS covariance matrix is asymptotically valid provided that $E(u_t^2)$ is the same unconditionally as it is conditional on the squares and cross-products of all the regressors. White therefore suggested that $\boldsymbol{Z}$ should consist of the squares and cross-products of all the regressors, dropping the constant term and any other columns that would cause $[\boldsymbol{\iota}\ \ \boldsymbol{Z}]$ not to have full rank. Like all the regression-based tests that we are discussing, **White's test** will have a noncentrality parameter that is nonzero whenever there is any correlation between u_t^2 and any of the elements of $\boldsymbol{Z}_t$. Thus, if the sample is large enough, White's test is certain to detect any heteroskedasticity that would cause the OLS covariance matrix to be inconsistent.

Although White's test is consistent against a very wide range of heteroskedastic alternatives, it may not be very powerful in finite samples. The problem is that the number of columns in $\boldsymbol{Z}$ will be very large if the number of regressors in $\boldsymbol{X}$ is not quite small. In general, $\boldsymbol{Z}$ will have $k(k+1)/2 - 1$

columns if $\boldsymbol{X}$ includes a constant term. Thus, for $k = 10$, White's test will have 54 degrees of freedom; for $k = 20$ (which is not by any means a large number for studies using cross-section data), it will have 209 degrees of freedom. These are rather large numbers. As we saw in Chapter 12, tests with many degrees of freedom are likely to lack power unless the sample size is very large. One could of course modify White's test in various ad hoc ways, such as dropping the columns of $\boldsymbol{Z}$ that correspond to cross-products of the regressors. Such modifications might or might not improve the power of the test. It would depend on how much the noncentrality parameter was reduced, relative to the effect of fewer degrees of freedom; see Section 12.5.

It is possible to derive regression-based tests for heteroskedasticity as Lagrange multiplier tests under the assumption of normally distributed error terms. That was in fact how they were originally derived by Godfrey (1978c) and Breusch and Pagan (1979). The maintained hypothesis is

$$y_t = x_t(\boldsymbol{\beta}) + u_t, \quad u_t \sim \text{NID}\big(0, h(\alpha + \boldsymbol{Z}_t\boldsymbol{\gamma})\big), \tag{16.29}$$

and we wish to test the restriction that $\boldsymbol{\gamma} = \mathbf{0}$. The LM test may be derived in a straightforward fashion by writing down the loglikelihood function that corresponds to (16.29), obtaining the gradient and the information matrix, evaluating these at the NLS estimates of $\boldsymbol{\beta}$, and forming the usual quadratic form. We leave this as an exercise for the reader.

The LM test statistic that one obtains in this way can be written as

$$\frac{1}{2\hat{\sigma}^4}\hat{\boldsymbol{v}}^\top\boldsymbol{M}_\iota\boldsymbol{Z}\big(\boldsymbol{Z}^\top\boldsymbol{M}_\iota\boldsymbol{Z}\big)^{-1}\boldsymbol{Z}^\top\boldsymbol{M}_\iota\hat{\boldsymbol{v}}, \tag{16.30}$$

where, as before, $\hat{\boldsymbol{v}}$ is an n–vector with typical element $\hat{u}_t^2$, and $\boldsymbol{M}_\iota$ is the matrix that takes deviations from the mean. Under the null hypothesis, this test statistic will be asymptotically distributed as $\chi^2(q)$. Expression (16.30) is equal to one-half the explained sum of squares from the regression

$$\frac{\hat{\boldsymbol{v}}}{\hat{\sigma}^2} - \boldsymbol{\iota} = a\boldsymbol{\iota} + \boldsymbol{Z}\boldsymbol{c} + \text{residuals}. \tag{16.31}$$

This result depends on the fact that the regressand here has mean zero by construction. The FWL Theorem then implies that the explained sum of squares from (16.31) is unchanged if all the regressors are replaced by the deviations from their means.

It is easy to see why (16.30) must be asymptotically distributed as $\chi^2(q)$. The normality assumption implies that $\hat{u}_t^2/\hat{\sigma}^2$ is asymptotically distributed as $\chi^2(1)$. The vector

$$n^{-1/2}\big(\hat{\boldsymbol{v}}/\hat{\sigma}^2\big)^\top\boldsymbol{M}_\iota\boldsymbol{Z} \tag{16.32}$$

is simply a weighted average of n random variables, each of them initially $\chi^2(1)$ but recentered to have mean zero because of the presence of $\boldsymbol{M}_\iota$. Since the variance of a random variable that has the $\chi^2(1)$ distribution is 2 (see Section 4 of Appendix B), the vector (16.32) must have covariance matrix

$$\frac{2}{n}\boldsymbol{Z}^\top\boldsymbol{M}_\iota\boldsymbol{Z}. \tag{16.33}$$

The LM test statistic (16.30) is simply a quadratic form in the vector (16.32) and the inverse of the matrix (16.33). Provided that a central limit theorem applies to (16.32), which it will under weak conditions on the matrix $\boldsymbol{Z}$, this quadratic form must have the $\chi^2(q)$ distribution asymptotically.

The LM test (16.30) is very closely related to the nR^2 and F tests based on regression (16.26) that we have already discussed. In fact, the centered R^2's from (16.26) and (16.31) are numerically identical, since the only difference between those two regressions is that the regressand of (16.31) has been rescaled and translated so that it has sample mean zero. The result that the LM statistic is equal to one-half the explained sum of squares from (16.31) depends critically on the assumption of normality, which was used to obtain (16.33). Without that assumption, which Koenker (1981) and others have criticized as unwarranted in most cases, we would be left with an F or nR^2 test as before.

The test statistic (16.30) based on the normality assumption tends to be somewhat more powerful than F or nR^2 tests calculated from the same artificial regression, because heteroskedasticity often creates the appearance of excess kurtosis, which tends to reduce the magnitude of any test that is using an estimate of the variance of $\hat{u}_t^2$. Another advantage of the LM test (16.30) is that it can be modified so that it is almost exact in finite samples; see Honda (1988). Thus there are some advantages to the LM form of these tests, if the normality assumption is a reasonable one. Because that assumption can itself be tested quite easily, as we will see in Section 16.7, it may not be unreasonable to use LM tests for heteroskedasticity when the normality assumption appears to be acceptable to the data.

To this point, our discussion of tests for heteroskedasticity has focused exclusively on tests based on artificial regressions. Numerous other tests have been proposed, and some of these are quite widely used. One particularly well-known test is the venerable F test of Goldfeld and Quandt (1965), which is easy to compute and often performs well. The idea is to order the data according to the value of some variable that is thought to be responsible for heteroskedasticity, then estimate the model over the first and last thirds of the sample, and calculate the test statistic

$$\frac{\mathrm{SSR}_3/(n_3-k)}{\mathrm{SSR}_1/(n_1-k)}, \tag{16.34}$$

where SSR_1 and SSR_3 denote the sums of squared residuals from the first and last thirds of the sample, and n_1 and n_3 denote the associated sample sizes. Given normally distributed error terms, this test statistic would under the null hypothesis be exactly distributed as $F(n_3 - k, n_1 - k)$; even without normality, it would have approximately that distribution in large samples. Notice that the **Goldfeld-Quandt test** is a two-tailed test, something that is rather unusual for an F test, since we want to reject the null hypothesis if the test statistic (16.34) is either too large or too small.

Other notable tests for heteroskedasticity have been proposed by Glejser (1969), Szroeter (1978), Harrison and McCabe (1979), Ali and Giacotto (1984), Evans and King (1985, 1988), and Newey and Powell (1987). Several of those papers, along with MacKinnon and White (1985) and Griffiths and Surekha (1986), provide Monte Carlo evidence on the properties of one or more tests. See also Godfrey (1988, Sections 4.5 and 5.5).

16.6 Skedastic Directions and Regression Directions

In Chapter 12, we presented a fairly detailed analysis of what determines the power of tests in regression directions, that is, tests of whether a regression function is specified correctly. A similar analysis could be undertaken of the power of tests in **skedastic directions**, that is, tests of whether a skedastic function is specified correctly. The results of such an analysis would be very similar to those of Chapter 12. In particular, we would find that tests in skedastic directions locally equivalent to the directions in which the DGP differs from the null hypothesis would have the largest noncentrality parameters (or NCPs) among all such tests and that, for any given NCP, the power of a test would be inversely related to its number of degrees of freedom. Readers may find it a good exercise to verify these results.

In this section, we will be concerned with a different issue. What happens if one tests in a skedastic direction when the skedastic function is correctly specified but the regression function is not? It seems clear that any misspecification of the regression function will cause the residuals to be misbehaved. In many cases, if one omits a regressor that has nonconstant variance, for example, the residuals will be heteroskedastic. Thus it might seem that testing for certain forms of heteroskedasticity would be a good way to detect misspecification of regression functions. That turns out not to be the case, as we will now see.

Let the model of interest be

$$\boldsymbol{y} = \boldsymbol{x}(\boldsymbol{\beta}) + \boldsymbol{u}, \quad E(\boldsymbol{u}) = \boldsymbol{0}, \quad E(\boldsymbol{u}\boldsymbol{u}^{\top}) = \sigma^2 \mathbf{I}.$$

As in Section 12.5, we will suppose that the data are actually generated by a drifting DGP of the form

$$\boldsymbol{y} = \boldsymbol{x}(\boldsymbol{\beta}_0) + \alpha n^{-1/2}\boldsymbol{a} + \boldsymbol{u}, \quad E(\boldsymbol{u}) = \boldsymbol{0}, \quad E(\boldsymbol{u}\boldsymbol{u}^{\top}) = \sigma_0^2 \mathbf{I}. \tag{16.35}$$

Here $\boldsymbol{\beta}_0$ and σ_0^2 denote particular values of $\boldsymbol{\beta}$ and σ^2, $\boldsymbol{a}$ is an n–vector that may depend on exogenous variables, on the parameter vector $\boldsymbol{\beta}_0$, and possibly on past values of y_t, and α is a parameter that determines how far the DGP is from the simple null hypothesis

$$\boldsymbol{y} = \boldsymbol{x}(\boldsymbol{\beta}_0) + \boldsymbol{u}, \quad E(\boldsymbol{u}) = \mathbf{0}, \quad E(\boldsymbol{u}\boldsymbol{u}^\top) = \sigma_0^2\mathbf{I}. \tag{16.36}$$

The drifting DGP (16.35) tends to this simple null hypothesis as $n \to \infty$. As we saw in Section 12.3, the vector $\boldsymbol{a}$ can be specified in many ways in order to correspond to any sort of misspecification of $\boldsymbol{x}(\boldsymbol{\beta})$.

Now let us see what happens when we test the null hypothesis that the u_t's are homoskedastic against the alternative that

$$E(u_t^2) = h(\alpha + \boldsymbol{Z}_t\boldsymbol{\gamma}),$$

where $\boldsymbol{Z}_t$ is a $1 \times q$ vector. If we do not assume that the error terms are normally distributed, one possible test statistic (in χ^2 form) is n times the centered R^2 from a regression of $\hat{\boldsymbol{v}}$, a vector with typical element $\hat{u}_t^2$, on a constant and $\boldsymbol{Z}$. This test statistic can be written as

$$\begin{aligned}&\frac{\hat{\boldsymbol{v}}^\top\boldsymbol{M}_\iota\boldsymbol{Z}(\boldsymbol{Z}^\top\boldsymbol{M}_\iota\boldsymbol{Z})^{-1}\boldsymbol{Z}^\top\boldsymbol{M}_\iota\hat{\boldsymbol{v}}}{n^{-1}\hat{\boldsymbol{v}}^\top\boldsymbol{M}_\iota\hat{\boldsymbol{v}}}\\ &= \frac{(n^{-1/2}\hat{\boldsymbol{v}}^\top\boldsymbol{M}_\iota\boldsymbol{Z})(n^{-1}\boldsymbol{Z}^\top\boldsymbol{M}_\iota\boldsymbol{Z})^{-1}(n^{-1/2}\boldsymbol{Z}^\top\boldsymbol{M}_\iota\hat{\boldsymbol{v}})}{n^{-1}\hat{\boldsymbol{v}}^\top\boldsymbol{M}_\iota\hat{\boldsymbol{v}}},\end{aligned} \tag{16.37}$$

where $\boldsymbol{M}_\iota$ denotes the matrix that takes deviations from the mean. To see how (16.37) is distributed asymptotically under the DGP (16.35), we must see what happens to the quantities

$$n^{-1/2}\hat{\boldsymbol{v}}^\top\boldsymbol{M}_\iota\boldsymbol{Z}, \quad n^{-1}\boldsymbol{Z}^\top\boldsymbol{M}_\iota\boldsymbol{Z}, \quad \text{and} \quad n^{-1}\hat{\boldsymbol{v}}^\top\boldsymbol{M}_\iota\hat{\boldsymbol{v}}$$

as $n \to \infty$. For the second of these, we will simply assume that

$$\operatorname*{plim}_{n\to\infty}\left(\frac{1}{n}\boldsymbol{Z}^\top\boldsymbol{M}_\iota\boldsymbol{Z}\right)$$

exists and is a positive definite matrix. The key is what happens to the other two quantities, $n^{-1/2}\hat{\boldsymbol{v}}^\top\boldsymbol{M}_\iota\boldsymbol{Z}$ and $n^{-1}\hat{\boldsymbol{v}}^\top\boldsymbol{M}_\iota\hat{\boldsymbol{v}}$.

In Section 12.4, we obtained the result that, under a DGP like (16.35),

$$\hat{\boldsymbol{u}} \equiv \boldsymbol{y} - \hat{\boldsymbol{x}} = \boldsymbol{M}_X\big(\boldsymbol{u} + \alpha n^{-1/2}\boldsymbol{a}\big) + o\big(n^{-1/2}\big), \tag{16.38}$$

where $\boldsymbol{M}_X$ denotes the matrix that projects onto $\mathcal{S}^\perp(\boldsymbol{X}_0)$. Using this result, it can be shown that both $n^{-1/2}\hat{\boldsymbol{v}}^\top\boldsymbol{M}_\iota\boldsymbol{Z}$ and $n^{-1}\hat{\boldsymbol{v}}^\top\boldsymbol{M}_\iota\hat{\boldsymbol{v}}$ tend to the same quantities when α is nonzero as they do when $\alpha = 0$. The proof is slightly tedious but not difficult, and readers may find it illuminating to work through

Table 16.2 Power of Various Tests When the DGP Has AR(1) Errors

n	ρ	AR(1) Power at 1%	AR(1) Power at 5%	ARCH(1) Power at 1%	ARCH(1) Power at 5%
50	0.566	66.0	85.3	6.5	14.3
100	0.400	82.2	94.2	8.4	15.8
200	0.283	87.1	96.2	7.1	14.3
400	0.200	89.9	97.1	5.6	11.7
800	0.141	90.8	97.4	3.6	8.7
1600	0.100	90.8	97.5	2.3	7.1
3200	0.071	91.3	97.6	1.8	5.8
6400	0.050	92.0	98.0	1.6	5.7
12800	0.035	92.2	97.9	1.3	5.4

it. Thus we conclude that the test statistic (16.37) must have the same asymptotic distribution — namely, $\chi^2(q)$ — under (16.35) as under (16.36). It will therefore have asymptotic power equal to its size.

This result may at first seem rather remarkable. It says that if the sample size is large enough, and if the DGP differs from the null hypothesis by an amount proportional to $n^{-1/2}$, then a test in any skedastic direction will have power equal to its size. In contrast, a test in any regression direction that is not orthogonal to $\boldsymbol{M_X a}$ will have power greater than its size. In practice, of course, sample sizes are not infinite and DGPs are always a finite distance from the null hypothesis, so we would not expect these results to hold exactly. But they do strongly suggest that tests in skedastic directions will be much less powerful than tests in appropriate regression directions when it is the regression function that is misspecified.

To illustrate how this asymptotic result applies in finite samples, consider the following example. The data are generated by an AR(1) process with a constant term and parameter ρ equal to $4/n^{1/2}$. The null hypothesis is that y_t is equal to a constant plus white noise errors. This null is tested against two alternatives by means of LM tests based on artificial regressions. The two alternatives are that the error terms follow an AR(1) process, which is in fact the case, and that they follow an ARCH(1) process. The percentage of the time that these two tests reject the null hypothesis at the 1% and 5% levels, for various sample sizes and the corresponding values of ρ, are shown in Table 16.2. These results are based on a Monte Carlo experiment, with 10,000 replications for each sample size.

We see from Table 16.2 that, in this case, the test against AR(1) errors always has a great deal more power than the test against ARCH(1) errors. As the sample size increases and ρ approaches zero, the power of the former test initially increases somewhat and then levels off. In contrast, the power of the latter test at first increases slightly, but then begins to decrease steadily toward its asymptotic size of either 1% or 5%. Although we have not discussed them, similar results hold for the case in which the regression function is correctly specified and the skedastic function is misspecified. If the DGP approaches the null at an appropriate rate in this case, tests in regression directions will asymptotically have power equal to their size.

It is important to keep the results of this section in mind when one is testing the specification of a regression model. They strongly suggest that if only the regression function is misspecified, then tests in some regression directions should have much lower P values than tests in any skedastic directions. Conversely, if only the skedastic function is misspecified, then tests in some skedastic directions should have much lower P values than tests in any regression directions. If, on the contrary, the tests in regression directions that reject the null most strongly have P values roughly comparable to those of the tests in skedastic directions that reject the null most strongly, then it seems quite likely that both the regression function and the skedastic function are misspecified.

16.7 Tests for Skewness and Excess Kurtosis

Although it is valid to use least squares whenever the error terms that adhere to a regression function have zero mean and a covariance matrix that satisfies mild regularity conditions, least squares yields an optimal estimator only in special circumstances. For instance, we saw in Chapter 9 that when the covariance matrix of the error terms is not a scalar matrix, it is the GLS rather than the OLS estimator which is efficient. Thus information about the second moments of the error terms will in general lead to an efficiency gain in the estimation of the parameters of the regression function. The same is true for moments of the error terms of order higher than the second. For instance, if the error terms are severely leptokurtic, that is, if their distribution has very thick tails, least squares may be highly inefficient relative to some other estimator that takes the leptokurtosis into account. Similarly, if the error terms are skewed, it will be possible to do better than least squares by using an estimator that recognizes the presence of the skewness. Of course, skewed error terms may well indicate that the model is misspecified; perhaps the dependent variable should have been transformed prior to estimation, for example (see Chapter 14).

All of this suggests that it is generally wise to test the hypothesis that the errors are normally distributed. In practice, one rarely goes beyond their third- and fourth-order moments; this means testing for skewness and excess kurtosis. Recall from Section 2.6 that, for a normal distribution with variance σ^2, the third central moment, which determines skewness, is zero, while the fourth central moment, which determines kurtosis, is $3\sigma^4$. If the third central moment is not zero, the distribution is skewed. If the fourth central moment is larger than $3\sigma^4$, the distribution said to be leptokurtic, while if the fourth central moment is smaller than $3\sigma^4$, the distribution is said to be platykurtic. In practice, residuals are frequently leptokurtic and rarely platykurtic.

One approach to testing the normality assumption is to embed the normal distribution within some more general family of distributions and then devise LM tests for the null hypothesis that the embedding parameters are zero. When this approach is employed, as in Jarque and Bera (1980) and Kiefer and Salmon (1983), the tests that result turn out to be simply tests for skewness and excess kurtosis. We will therefore not discuss the embedding approach but will assume from the outset that we wish to test the hypotheses

$$E(u_t^3) = 0 \quad \text{and} \quad E(u_t^4) = 3\sigma^4,$$

where u_t denotes a typical error term, which is assumed to be $\text{IID}(0, \sigma^2)$.

In the case of regression models, tests for skewness and excess kurtosis are almost always based on residuals. If $\hat{u}_t$ is the tth residual from a regression model with a constant term, one can test for skewness by finding the sample mean and standard deviation of a vector with typical element $\hat{u}_t^3$ and then constructing an (asymptotic) t statistic for the hypothesis that the true mean is zero. Similarly, one can test for excess kurtosis by finding the sample mean and standard deviation of a vector with typical element $\hat{u}_t^4 - 3\hat{\sigma}^4$, where $\hat{\sigma}$ is the ML estimate of σ, and constructing the same sort of (asymptotic) t statistic. These may not be the best procedures to use, however, because the estimated standard deviations used to construct the test statistics do not take full account of the implications of the normality hypothesis.

Suppose that the error terms u_t adhering to some regression model are distributed as $\text{NID}(0, \sigma^2)$. Then, if the residuals are denoted $\hat{u}_t$ and the ML estimate of their variance is $\hat{\sigma}^2$, it can be shown (see below) that

$$\operatorname*{plim}_{n\to\infty}\left(\frac{1}{n}\sum_{t=1}^{n}\left(\frac{\hat{u}_t^3}{\hat{\sigma}^3}\right)^2\right) = 6 \tag{16.39}$$

and

$$\operatorname*{plim}_{n\to\infty}\left(\frac{1}{n}\sum_{t=1}^{n}\left(\frac{\hat{u}_t^4}{\hat{\sigma}^4} - 3\right)^2\right) = 24. \tag{16.40}$$

These two results make it very simple to calculate test statistics. We simply make use of the normalized residuals

$$e_t \equiv \frac{\hat{u}_t - \hat{\mu}}{\hat{\sigma}},$$

where $\hat{\mu}$ denotes the sample mean of the $\hat{u}_t$'s (which may be nonzero for models that do not include the equivalent of a constant term). Then a test statistic for skewness is

$$(6n)^{-1/2}\sum_{t=1}^{n} e_t^3 \tag{16.41}$$

and a test statistic for excess kurtosis is

$$(24n)^{-1/2}\sum_{t=1}^{n}(e_t^4 - 3). \tag{16.42}$$

Each of these test statistics will be asymptotically distributed as $N(0,1)$ under the null hypothesis of normality. Each of their squares will be asymptotically distributed as $\chi^2(1)$. Moreover, since it can be shown that these two statistics are independent, the sum of their squares will be asymptotically distributed as $\chi^2(2)$. These test statistics were suggested (in a slightly different form) by Jarque and Bera (1980);[4] see also White and MacDonald (1980) and Bera and Jarque (1981, 1982).

We have not yet justified the results (16.39) and (16.40). In order to do so, we start from a standard result about the $N(0,1)$ distribution. If a random variable z is distributed as $N(0,1)$, then all of its odd-order moments are zero (the distribution is symmetric), and the even-order moments are given by the formula

$$E(z^{2n}) = \prod_{i=1}^{n}(2i-1);$$

see Section 4 of Appendix B. An easy extension of this result tells us that if z is distributed as $N(0,\sigma^2)$, then

$$E(z^{2n}) = \sigma^{2n}\prod_{i=1}^{n}(2i-1). \tag{16.43}$$

Thus, if the normalized residuals were in fact distributed as NID$(0,1)$, we would find that the left-hand side of (16.39) was equal to the sixth moment of the $N(0,1)$ distribution, or 15. Similarly, the left-hand side of (16.40) would be

$$\operatorname*{plim}_{n\to\infty}\left(\frac{1}{n}\sum_{t=1}^{n}(z^8 - 6z^4 + 9)\right) = 105 - 18 + 9 = 96.$$

That these results are not true is a consequence of the fact that the normalized residuals are calculated using *estimates* of the error mean and standard deviation.

To take account of this fact, the easiest way to proceed is to imagine basing a test on the OPG regression that we first discussed in Section 13.7. Suppose, for simplicity, that the regression model to be tested is

$$y_t = \beta + u_t, \quad u_t \sim \text{NID}(0,\sigma^2); \tag{16.44}$$

including regressors in addition to the constant term does not change the results. When everything is evaluated at true values, the OPG regression that

[4] Kiefer and Salmon (1983) proposed test statistics that appear to be somewhat different but are in fact numerically identical to (16.41) and (16.42).

corresponds to this model can be written as

$$1 = bu_t + s\big(u_t^2 - \sigma^2\big) + \text{residual}, \tag{16.45}$$

where we have replaced $y_t - \beta$ by u_t and multiplied the first regressor by σ^2 and the second by σ^3. (Since we are interested in computing test statistics, not estimating covariance matrices, it is perfectly legitimate to multiply any of the regressors by a constant.) A test of (16.44) against any alternative at all can be based on an OPG regression. We simply have to add one or more appropriately specified columns to (16.45).

For testing against the alternative that the error terms are skewed, the natural regressor to add to (16.45) is u_t^3. The test statistic will simply be the t statistic associated with that regressor. The numerator of this statistic is thus simply the mean of the regressor, after it has been projected off the other two regressors. Under the null hypothesis, the test regressor is already asymptotically orthogonal to the second regressor in (16.45), since all odd moments of a centered normal distribution are zero. But it will not be orthogonal to the first regressor in (16.45). Projecting u_t^3 off u_t yields

$$u_t^3 - u_t\left(\frac{\sum_{t=1}^n u_t^4}{\sum_{t=1}^n u_t^2}\right) \stackrel{a}{=} u_t^3 - 3\sigma^2 u_t. \tag{16.46}$$

The asymptotic equality here is obtained by dividing each of the summations by n and then taking probability limits. It is easily verified from (16.43) that the variance of $u_t^3 - 3\sigma^2 u_t$ is $6\sigma^6$.

Similarly, for testing against the alternative that the error terms have a fourth moment not equal to $3\sigma^4$, the natural regressor to add to (16.45) is $u_t^4 - 3\sigma^4$. Once again, the numerator of the test statistic will be the mean of that regressor, after it has been projected off the other two. In this case, the test regressor is asymptotically orthogonal to the first regressor in (16.45), but not to the second. Projecting the test regressor off the latter yields

$$\begin{aligned} & u_t^4 - 3\sigma^4 - \big(u_t^2 - \sigma^2\big)\frac{\sum_{t=1}^n \big(u_t^6 - u_t^4\sigma^2 - 3u_t^2\sigma^4 + 3\sigma^6\big)}{\sum_{t=1}^n \big(u_t^4 - 2u_t^2\sigma^2 + \sigma^4\big)} \\ & \stackrel{a}{=} u_t^4 - 6u_t^2\sigma^2 + 3\sigma^4. \end{aligned} \tag{16.47}$$

The asymptotic equality here is obtained in the same way as for (16.46). It is easily verified that the variance of $u_t^4 - 6u_t^2\sigma^2 + 3\sigma^4$ is $24\sigma^8$.

Now suppose that we replace u_t by e_t and σ by unity in the expressions on the right-hand sides of (16.46) and (16.47). Then it is easily seen that

$$\sum_{t=1}^n \big(e_t^3 - 3e_t\big) = \sum_{t=1}^n e_t^3 \quad \text{and}$$

$$\sum_{t=1}^n \big(e_t^4 - 6e_t^2 + 3\big) = \sum_{t=1}^n \big(e_t^4 - 3\big).$$

The right-hand sides of these expressions are simply the numerators of the test statistics (16.41) and (16.42). From these equalities, we see that the latter must have asymptotic variances equal to n times those of expressions (16.46) and (16.47) when $\sigma = 1$. This explains where the denominators of the test statistics come from and completes the demonstration of (16.39) and (16.40).

The above demonstration makes it clear why inclusion of regressors other than the constant will not change the result. If such a regressor is denoted by X_t, then the column corresponding to it in the OPG regression (16.45) has typical element $X_t u_t$. But this element has zero covariance with both $u_t^3 - 3\sigma^2 u_t$ and $u_t^4 - 6u_t^2\sigma^2 + 3\sigma^4$, and so the test columns are automatically asymptotically orthogonal to any regression direction. In fact, because they are also orthogonal to any skedastic direction, the tests could be used with normalized residuals from a regression for which a skedastic function had been estimated.

The reason for the simplicity of the tests for skewness and excess kurtosis that we discussed in this section is that, as we have just seen, we are largely able to ignore the fact that residuals from regression models depend on model parameters which have been estimated. With more general models, we often cannot ignore this fact. It seems plausible that variants of the OPG regression should provide one valid way to test for skewness and kurtosis in such models. As we will see in the next section, that is indeed the case. Such tests are actually special cases of an important and very general class of tests called conditional moment tests.

16.8 Conditional Moment Tests

One important approach to model specification testing that we have not yet discussed is to base tests directly on certain conditions that the error terms of a model should satisfy. Such tests are sometimes called **moment specification tests** but are more frequently referred to as **conditional moment**, or **CM**, **tests**. They were first suggested by Newey (1985a) and Tauchen (1985) and have been further developed by White (1987), Pagan and Vella (1989), Wooldridge (1991a, 1991b), and others. The basic idea is that if a model is correctly specified, many random quantities which are functions of the error terms should have expectations of zero. The specification of a model sometimes allows a stronger conclusion, according to which such functions of the error terms have zero expectations *conditional* on some information set — whence the terminology of conditional moment tests.

Since an expectation is often referred to as a moment, the condition that a random quantity has zero expectation is generally referred to as a **moment condition**. Even if a population moment is zero, its empirical counterpart, which we will call an **empirical moment**, will (almost) never be so exactly, but it should not be significantly different from zero. Conditional moment tests are based directly on this fact.

Conditional moment tests can be used to test many different aspects of the specification of econometric models. Suppose that the economic or statistical theory behind a given parametrized model says that for each observation t there is some function of the dependent variable y_t and of the model parameters $\boldsymbol{\theta}$, say $m_t(y_t, \boldsymbol{\theta})$, of which the expectation is zero when the DGP used to compute the expectation is characterized by $\boldsymbol{\theta}$. Thus, for all t and for all $\boldsymbol{\theta}$,

$$E_{\boldsymbol{\theta}}\big(m_t(y_t, \boldsymbol{\theta})\big) = 0. \tag{16.48}$$

We may think of (16.48) as expressing a moment condition. In general, the functions m_t may also depend on exogenous or predetermined variables.

Even though there is a different function for each observation, it seems reasonable, by analogy with empirical moments, to take the following expression as the empirical counterpart of the moment in condition (16.48):

$$m(\boldsymbol{y}, \hat{\boldsymbol{\theta}}) \equiv \frac{1}{n}\sum_{t=1}^{n} m_t(y_t, \hat{\boldsymbol{\theta}}), \tag{16.49}$$

where $\hat{\boldsymbol{\theta}}$ denotes a vector of estimates of $\boldsymbol{\theta}$. Expression (16.49) is thus a form of empirical moment. A one-degree-of-freedom CM test would be computed by dividing it by an estimate of its standard deviation and would be asymptotically distributed as $N(0, 1)$ under suitable regularity conditions. There might well be more than one moment condition, of course, in which case the test statistic could be calculated as a quadratic form in the empirical moments and an estimate of their covariance matrix and would have the chi-squared distribution asymptotically.

It is clear that the tests for skewness and excess kurtosis which we discussed in the preceding section are special cases of CM tests. A condition like $E(u_t^3) = 0$ is an (unconditional) moment condition, and a test statistic like (16.41) is just the empirical counterpart of the moment involved, divided by an estimate of its standard deviation. What may be less clear is that, once we allow the possibility of conditional moments, virtually all the specification tests we have discussed so far can be thought of as CM tests. For example, consider a linear regression model like

$$y_t = \boldsymbol{X}_t\boldsymbol{\beta} + u_t, \quad u_t \sim \mathrm{IID}(0, \sigma^2), \tag{16.50}$$

where $\boldsymbol{X}_t\boldsymbol{\beta}$ is specified to be the mean of y_t conditional on some information set Ω_t. If this model is specified correctly, then the conditional expectation $E(u_t \,|\, \Omega_t)$ should be zero. This conditional moment condition implies that u_t should be orthogonal to any variable that belongs to Ω_t. Hence, for any $z_t \in \Omega_t$, the unconditional moment $E(u_t z_t)$ should be zero. The corresponding empirical moment is

$$\sum_{t=1}^{n} \hat{u}_t z_t = \hat{\boldsymbol{u}}^{\top}\boldsymbol{z}, \tag{16.51}$$

where $\hat{u}_t$ denotes the estimate of u_t from OLS estimation of (16.50), $\hat{\boldsymbol{u}}$ is an n–vector with typical element $\hat{u}_t$, and $\boldsymbol{z}$ is an n–vector with typical element z_t. We have not bothered to divide (16.51) by n, since it must be divided by something that estimates its standard deviation consistently in order to obtain a conditional moment test statistic.

Expression (16.51) is, of course, the numerator of the ordinary t statistic for $\gamma = 0$ in the regression

$$y_t = \boldsymbol{X}_t\boldsymbol{\beta} + \gamma z_t + u_t. \tag{16.52}$$

The denominator of that t statistic is a consistent estimator of the standard deviation of (16.51). Hence the ordinary t statistic for $\gamma = 0$ in (16.52) can be thought of as a CM test, as can a variety of more complicated test statistics that estimate the variance of (16.51) in different ways. For example, one could use one of the HCCMEs discussed in Section 16.3 to obtain a test statistic that would be valid in the presence of heteroskedasticity of unknown form. This might be either a Wald-type test, in which the estimates of the covariance matrix were based on OLS estimates of the unrestricted model (16.52), or an LM-type test, in which they were based on OLS estimates of the restricted model (16.50), as in the case of the HRGNR.

These examples suggest that the CM tests which one obtains by explicitly writing down moment conditions will frequently be ones that are already familiar from other approaches. That is indeed very often the case. For example, consider testing the hypothesis that the r–vector $\boldsymbol{\theta}_2$ is equal to zero in a model estimated by maximum likelihood. Here the natural "moment conditions" to use are that

$$E\big(g_i(\boldsymbol{\theta}_1, \mathbf{0})\big) = 0 \quad \text{for } i = k - r + 1, \ldots, k.$$

These conditions state that the r elements of the score vector $\boldsymbol{g}(\boldsymbol{\theta})$ which correspond to the elements of $\boldsymbol{\theta}_2$ should have expectation zero under the null hypothesis that $\boldsymbol{\theta}_2 = 0$. To obtain empirical moments, we simply replace $\boldsymbol{\theta}_1$ by the restricted ML estimates $\tilde{\boldsymbol{\theta}}_1$. This yields the score vector $\boldsymbol{g}(\tilde{\boldsymbol{\theta}})$. Therefore, in this case, the familiar score form of the LM test can be regarded as a CM test.

In these cases and many others, CM tests often turn out to be exactly the same as more familiar specification tests based on the LM principle or the DWH principle. What then are the advantages of deriving tests as CM tests rather than in some other way? Pagan and Vella (1989) argue, primarily in the context of limited dependent variable models, that it is often much easier and more natural to write down plausible moment conditions than to derive LM tests. That is indeed frequently the case. We implicitly followed the CM approach in the previous section, when we derived tests of normality by explicitly testing for skewness and kurtosis, rather than by formulating an alternative model and working out LM tests. As we remarked there, we could have obtained similar test statistics by using the latter approach, but it would have been a lot more work. Thus the CM approach may be attractive when it is easy to write down the moment conditions that one would like to test and their empirical counterparts.

However, simply writing down a set of empirical moments does not, by itself, allow one to obtain a test statistic. One must also be able to estimate their covariance matrix. As we will see very shortly, if we are dealing with a model estimated by maximum likelihood, to which the familiar OPG regression applies, it is possible to do this in a mechanical way by using that regression. But although this procedure allows one to derive CM tests directly from an OPG regression, these tests, like others computed from OPG regressions, frequently have poor finite-sample properties. If one wishes to derive CM tests with good finite-sample properties, one may well be obliged to undertake a detailed examination, of the sort undertaken in the last section, of how the empirical moments are distributed. Alternatively, in some cases, the tests may be computed by means of artificial regressions with better finite-sample properties than the OPG regression. The moral is that deriving CM tests is not always an easy thing to do.

We now discuss an important result, due to Newey (1985a), which permits CM tests to be computed by an OPG regression. Suppose, for simplicity, that we are interested in testing a single moment condition, say $E_{\boldsymbol{\theta}}\big(m_t(y_t, \boldsymbol{\theta})\big) = 0$. The corresponding empirical moment is $m(\boldsymbol{y}, \hat{\boldsymbol{\theta}})$, defined in expression (16.49). If we knew the true value of $\boldsymbol{\theta}$, it would clearly be very easy to obtain a test statistic. We would simply require that condition CLT (see Definition 4.16) apply to $n^{1/2}m(\boldsymbol{y}, \boldsymbol{\theta})$, and then we could estimate the asymptotic variance of this expression by

$$\frac{1}{n}\sum_{t=1}^{n} m_t^2(y_t, \boldsymbol{\theta}). \tag{16.53}$$

Constructing a test statistic that would be asymptotically distributed as $N(0,1)$ would then be very easy. The problem is that in most cases we do not know $\boldsymbol{\theta}$ but merely have a vector of ML estimates $\hat{\boldsymbol{\theta}}$. As we will see in a moment, the asymptotic variance of $n^{1/2}m(\boldsymbol{y}, \hat{\boldsymbol{\theta}})$ is generally smaller than that of $n^{1/2}m(\boldsymbol{y}, \boldsymbol{\theta})$, and so it is not generally correct to estimate the former simply by using $\hat{\boldsymbol{\theta}}$ instead of $\boldsymbol{\theta}$ in (16.53).

We begin by performing a first-order Taylor expansion of $n^{1/2}m(\boldsymbol{y}, \boldsymbol{\theta})$ with respect to the k-vector $\boldsymbol{\theta}$ around the true parameter vector $\boldsymbol{\theta}_0$. The result, when we evaluate it at $\boldsymbol{\theta} = \hat{\boldsymbol{\theta}}$, is

$$n^{1/2}m(\boldsymbol{y}, \hat{\boldsymbol{\theta}}) \cong n^{1/2}m(\boldsymbol{y}, \boldsymbol{\theta}_0) + \boldsymbol{\mu}_0^{\top} n^{1/2}(\hat{\boldsymbol{\theta}} - \boldsymbol{\theta}_0). \tag{16.54}$$

Here $\boldsymbol{\mu}_0$ denotes the vector of derivatives of $m(\boldsymbol{y}, \boldsymbol{\theta})$ with respect to $\boldsymbol{\theta}$, evaluated at $\boldsymbol{\theta}_0$. Because each of the terms in (16.54) is $O(1)$, the differences between $m(\boldsymbol{y}, \hat{\boldsymbol{\theta}})$ and $m(\boldsymbol{y}, \boldsymbol{\theta}_0)$ cannot be ignored asymptotically.

Next, we derive a useful and general result that will allow us to replace the vector of derivatives $\boldsymbol{\mu}_0$ in (16.54) by something more manageable. The moment condition under test is given by (16.48). The moment can be written out explicitly as

$$E_{\boldsymbol{\theta}}\big(m_t(y_t, \boldsymbol{\theta})\big) = \int_{-\infty}^{\infty} m_t(y_t, \boldsymbol{\theta}) L_t(y_t, \boldsymbol{\theta}) dy_t. \tag{16.55}$$

Differentiating the right-hand side of (16.55) with respect to the components of $\boldsymbol{\theta}$, we obtain, by the same sort of reasoning as led to the information matrix equality (8.44),

$$E_{\boldsymbol{\theta}}\big(m_t(\boldsymbol{\theta}) \boldsymbol{G}_t(\boldsymbol{\theta})\big) = -E_{\boldsymbol{\theta}}\big(\boldsymbol{N}_t(\boldsymbol{\theta})\big). \tag{16.56}$$

Here $\boldsymbol{G}_t(\boldsymbol{\theta})$ is the contribution made by observation t to the gradient of the loglikelihood function, and the $1 \times k$ row vector $\boldsymbol{N}_t(\boldsymbol{\theta})$ has typical element $\partial m_t(\boldsymbol{\theta})/\partial \theta_i$.[5] The most useful form of our result is obtained by summing (16.56) over t. Let $\boldsymbol{m}(\boldsymbol{\theta})$ be an n–vector with typical element $m_t(\boldsymbol{\theta})$, and let $\boldsymbol{N}(\boldsymbol{\theta})$ be an $n \times k$ matrix with typical row $\boldsymbol{N}_t(\boldsymbol{\theta})$. Then

$$\frac{1}{n} E_{\boldsymbol{\theta}}\big(\boldsymbol{G}^{\top}(\boldsymbol{\theta}) \boldsymbol{m}(\boldsymbol{\theta})\big) = -\frac{1}{n} E_{\boldsymbol{\theta}}\big(\boldsymbol{N}^{\top}(\boldsymbol{\theta}) \boldsymbol{\iota}\big), \tag{16.57}$$

where, as usual, $\boldsymbol{G}(\boldsymbol{\theta})$ denotes the CG matrix. In (16.54), $\boldsymbol{\mu}_0 = n^{-1} \boldsymbol{N}_0^{\top} \boldsymbol{\iota}$, where $\boldsymbol{N}_0 \equiv \boldsymbol{N}(\boldsymbol{\theta}_0)$. By the law of large numbers, this will converge to the limit of the right-hand side of (16.57), and so also to the limit of the left-hand side. Thus, if $\boldsymbol{G}_0 \equiv \boldsymbol{G}(\boldsymbol{\theta}_0)$, we can assert that

$$\boldsymbol{\mu}_0 = \frac{1}{n} \boldsymbol{N}_0^{\top} \boldsymbol{\iota} \overset{a}{=} -\frac{1}{n} \boldsymbol{G}_0^{\top} \boldsymbol{m}_0. \tag{16.58}$$

We next make use of the very well-known result (13.18) on the relationship between ML estimates, the information matrix, and the score vector:

$$n^{1/2}(\hat{\boldsymbol{\theta}} - \boldsymbol{\theta}_0) \overset{a}{=} \mathcal{I}_0^{-1} n^{-1/2} \boldsymbol{g}_0. \tag{16.59}$$

Since the information matrix $\mathcal{I}_0$ is asymptotically equal to $n^{-1} \boldsymbol{G}_0^{\top} \boldsymbol{G}_0$ (see Section 8.6), and $\boldsymbol{g}_0 = \boldsymbol{G}_0^{\top} \boldsymbol{\iota}$, (16.59) becomes

$$n^{1/2}(\hat{\boldsymbol{\theta}} - \boldsymbol{\theta}_0) \overset{a}{=} \big(n^{-1} \boldsymbol{G}_0^{\top} \boldsymbol{G}_0\big)^{-1} n^{-1/2} \boldsymbol{G}_0^{\top} \boldsymbol{\iota}.$$

This result, combined with (16.58), allows us to replace the right-hand side of (16.54) by

$$n^{-1/2} \boldsymbol{m}_0^{\top} \boldsymbol{\iota} - n^{-1} \boldsymbol{m}_0^{\top} \boldsymbol{G}_0 \big(n^{-1} \boldsymbol{G}_0^{\top} \boldsymbol{G}_0\big)^{-1} n^{-1/2} \boldsymbol{G}_0^{\top} \boldsymbol{\iota} = n^{-1/2} \boldsymbol{m}_0^{\top} \boldsymbol{M}_G \boldsymbol{\iota}, \tag{16.60}$$

where $\boldsymbol{M}_G$ denotes the matrix that projects orthogonally onto $\mathcal{S}^{\perp}(\boldsymbol{G}_0)$.

[5] Our usual notation would have been $\boldsymbol{M}_t(\boldsymbol{\theta})$ instead of $\boldsymbol{N}_t(\boldsymbol{\theta})$, but this would conflict with the standard notation for complementary orthogonal projections.

The result (16.60) makes clear just what the difference is between the empirical moment evaluated at the unknown $\boldsymbol{\theta}_0$ and evaluated at the ML estimates $\hat{\boldsymbol{\theta}}$, that is, between $n^{-1/2}\boldsymbol{m}_0^\top\boldsymbol{\iota}$ and $n^{-1/2}\hat{\boldsymbol{m}}^\top\boldsymbol{\iota}$. The effect of using the estimates is an implicit orthogonal projection of the vector $\boldsymbol{m}_0$ onto the orthogonal complement of the space $\mathcal{S}(\boldsymbol{G}_0)$ associated with the model parameters. This projection is what causes the variance of the expression that we can actually calculate to be smaller than the variance of the corresponding expression based on the true parameters. The variances used in the skewness and kurtosis tests discussed in the last section can also be computed using (16.60).

We are now ready to obtain an appropriate expression for the asymptotic variance of $n^{-1/2}\hat{\boldsymbol{m}}^\top\boldsymbol{\iota}$. We require, as we suggested earlier, that $n^{-1/2}\boldsymbol{m}_0^\top\boldsymbol{\iota}$ should satisfy CLT and that, in a neighborhood of $\boldsymbol{\theta}_0$, $n^{-1}\boldsymbol{m}^\top(\boldsymbol{\theta})\boldsymbol{G}_i(\boldsymbol{\theta})$ should satisfy WULLN (Definition 4.17) for all $i = 1, \ldots, k$. The asymptotic variance is then clearly $\text{plim}(n^{-1}\boldsymbol{m}_0^\top\boldsymbol{M}_G\boldsymbol{m}_0)$, which can be consistently estimated by $n^{-1}\hat{\boldsymbol{m}}^\top\hat{\boldsymbol{M}}_G\hat{\boldsymbol{m}}$. This suggests using the test statistic

$$\frac{n^{-1/2}\hat{\boldsymbol{m}}^\top\boldsymbol{\iota}}{\big(n^{-1}\hat{\boldsymbol{m}}^\top\hat{\boldsymbol{M}}_G\hat{\boldsymbol{m}}\big)^{1/2}} = \frac{\hat{\boldsymbol{m}}^\top\boldsymbol{\iota}}{\big(\hat{\boldsymbol{m}}^\top\hat{\boldsymbol{M}}_G\hat{\boldsymbol{m}}\big)^{1/2}}, \tag{16.61}$$

which will be asymptotically distributed as $N(0, 1)$.

The connection with the OPG regression is now evident. The test statistic (16.61) is *almost* the t statistic on the coefficient b from the following OPG regression:

$$\boldsymbol{\iota} = \hat{\boldsymbol{G}}\boldsymbol{c} + b\hat{\boldsymbol{m}} + \text{residuals}. \tag{16.62}$$

Asymptotically, the statistic (16.61) and the t statistic from (16.62) are equivalent, because the sum of squared residuals from (16.62) tends to n for large sample sizes under the null hypothesis: The regressors $\hat{\boldsymbol{G}}$ are always orthogonal to $\boldsymbol{\iota}$, and $\hat{\boldsymbol{m}}$ is orthogonal to $\boldsymbol{\iota}$ if the moment condition is satisfied. This result is very satisfactory. Without the regressor $\hat{\boldsymbol{m}}$, which is the vector that serves to define the empirical moment, regression (16.62) would be just the OPG regression associated with the original model, and the SSR would always be equal to n. Thus the OPG version of the CM test, like all the other tests we have discussed that are implemented by artificial regressions, is just a test for the significance of the coefficients on one or more test regressors.

It is now plain how to extend CM tests to a set of two or more moment conditions. One simply creates a test regressor for each of the empirical moments so as to produce an $n \times r$ matrix $\hat{\boldsymbol{R}} \equiv \boldsymbol{R}(\hat{\boldsymbol{\theta}})$, where r is the number of moment conditions. One then uses the explained sum of squares from the OPG regression

$$\boldsymbol{\iota} = \hat{\boldsymbol{G}}\boldsymbol{c} + \hat{\boldsymbol{R}}\boldsymbol{b} + \text{residuals}$$

or any other asymptotically equivalent test of the artificial hypothesis $\boldsymbol{b} = \mathbf{0}$. It is now clear that, as we suggested above, any test capable of being carried out by means of an OPG regression can be interpreted as a CM test.

One simply has to interpret the test columns in the regression as empirical moments.

An interesting variant of the test regression (16.62) was suggested by Tauchen (1985). In effect, he interchanged the regressand $\boldsymbol{\iota}$ and the test regressor $\hat{\boldsymbol{m}}$ so as to obtain the regression

$$\hat{\boldsymbol{m}} = \hat{\boldsymbol{G}}\boldsymbol{c}^* + b^*\boldsymbol{\iota} + \text{residuals}. \tag{16.63}$$

The test statistic is the ordinary t statistic for $b^* = 0$. It is numerically identical to the t statistic on b in (16.62). This fact follows from a result we obtained in section 12.7, of which we now give a different, geometrical, proof. Apply the FWL Theorem to both (16.62) and (16.63) so as to obtain the two regressions

$$\begin{aligned} \hat{\boldsymbol{M}}_{\boldsymbol{G}}\boldsymbol{\iota} &= b(\hat{\boldsymbol{M}}_{\boldsymbol{G}}\hat{\boldsymbol{m}}) + \text{residuals} \quad \text{and} \\ \hat{\boldsymbol{M}}_{\boldsymbol{G}}\hat{\boldsymbol{m}} &= b^*(\hat{\boldsymbol{M}}_{\boldsymbol{G}}\boldsymbol{\iota}) + \text{residuals}. \end{aligned} \tag{16.64}$$

These are both univariate regressions with n observations. The single t statistic from each of them is given by the product of the same scalar factor, $(n-1)^{1/2}$, and the cotangent of the angle between the regressand and the regressor (see Appendix A). Since this angle is unchanged when the regressor and regressand are interchanged, so is the t statistic. The FWL Theorem implies that the t statistics from the first and second rows of (16.64) are equal to those from the OPG regression (16.62) and Tauchen's regression (16.63), respectively, times the same degrees of freedom correction. Thus we conclude that the t statistics based on the latter two regressions are numerically identical.

Since the first-order conditions for $\hat{\boldsymbol{\theta}}$ imply that $\boldsymbol{\iota}$ is orthogonal to all of the columns of $\hat{\boldsymbol{G}}$, the OLS estimate of b^* in (16.63) will be equal to the sample mean of the elements of $\hat{\boldsymbol{m}}$. This would be so even if the regressors $\hat{\boldsymbol{G}}$ were omitted from the regression. However, because $\boldsymbol{\theta}$ has been estimated, those regressors must be included if we are to obtain a valid estimate of the variance of the sample mean. As is the case with all the other artificial regressions we have studied, omitting the regressors that correspond to parameters estimated under the null hypothesis results in a test statistic that is too small, asymptotically.

Let us reiterate our earlier warnings about the OPG regression. As we stressed when we introduced it in Section 13.7, test statistics based on it often have poor finite-sample properties. They tend to reject the null hypothesis too often when it is true. This is just as true for CM tests as for LM tests or $C(\alpha)$ tests. If possible, one should therefore use alternative tests that have better finite-sample properties, such as tests based on the GNR, the HRGNR, the DLR (Section 14.4), or the BRMR (Section 15.4), when these procedures are applicable. Of course, they will be applicable in general only if the CM test can be reformulated as an ordinary test, with an explicit alternative hypothesis from which test regressors can be generated. If it is not possible to reformulate the CM test in this manner, and one has to use the OPG regression, one should be very cautious when a test suggests rejecting the null. It is often wise to check finite-sample properties by means of Monte Carlo experiments (see Chapter 21).

16.9 INFORMATION MATRIX TESTS

One important type of conditional moment test is the class of tests called **information matrix**, or **IM**, **tests**. These were originally suggested by White (1982), although the conditional moment interpretation is more recent; see Newey (1985a) and White (1987). The basic idea is very simple. If a model that is estimated by maximum likelihood is correctly specified, the information matrix must be asymptotically equal to minus the Hessian. If it is not correctly specified, that equality will in general not hold, because the proof of the information matrix equality depends crucially on the fact that the joint density of the data is the likelihood function; see Section 8.6.

Consider a statistical model characterized by a loglikelihood function of the form

$$\ell(\boldsymbol{y}, \boldsymbol{\theta}) = \sum_{t=1}^{n} \ell_t(y_t, \boldsymbol{\theta}),$$

where $\boldsymbol{y}$ denotes an n-vector of observations y_t, $t = 1, \ldots, n$, on a dependent variable, and $\boldsymbol{\theta}$ denotes a k-vector of parameters. As the subscript t indicates, the contribution ℓ_t made by observation t to the loglikelihood function may depend on exogenous or predetermined variables that vary across the n observations. The null hypothesis for the IM test is that

$$\operatorname*{plim}_{n\to\infty}\left(\frac{1}{n}\sum_{t=1}^{n}\left(\frac{\partial^2\ell_t(\boldsymbol{\theta})}{\partial\theta_i\partial\theta_j} + \frac{\partial\ell_t(\boldsymbol{\theta})}{\partial\theta_i}\frac{\partial\ell_t(\boldsymbol{\theta})}{\partial\theta_j}\right)\right) = 0, \tag{16.65}$$

for $i = 1, \ldots, k$ and $j = 1, \ldots, i$. Expression (16.65) is a typical element of the information matrix equality. The first term is an element of the Hessian, and the second is the corresponding element of the outer product of the gradient. Since the number of such terms is $\frac{1}{2}k(k+1)$, the number of degrees of freedom for an IM test is potentially very large.

Without the probability limit, the left-hand side of (16.65) looks like an empirical moment. This suggests, correctly, that one can calculate IM tests by means of the OPG regression, a procedure that was originally suggested by Chesher (1983) and Lancaster (1984). One simply has to construct an $n \times \frac{1}{2}k(k+1)$ matrix $\boldsymbol{Z}(\boldsymbol{\theta})$ with typical element

$$\frac{\partial^2\ell_t(\boldsymbol{\theta})}{\partial\theta_i\partial\theta_j} + \frac{\partial\ell_t(\boldsymbol{\theta})}{\partial\theta_i}\frac{\partial\ell_t(\boldsymbol{\theta})}{\partial\theta_j}$$

and evaluate it at the ML estimates $\hat{\boldsymbol{\theta}}$ to obtain $\hat{\boldsymbol{Z}}$. Then one performs an OPG regression, with regressors $\hat{\boldsymbol{G}}$ and $\hat{\boldsymbol{Z}}$, and uses n minus the SSR as the test statistic. Provided the matrix $[\hat{\boldsymbol{G}} \;\; \hat{\boldsymbol{Z}}]^{\top}[\hat{\boldsymbol{G}} \;\; \hat{\boldsymbol{Z}}]$ has full rank asymptotically, the test statistic will be asymptotically distributed as $\chi^2\big(\tfrac{1}{2}k(k+1)\big)$. When some of the columns of $\hat{\boldsymbol{G}}$ and $\hat{\boldsymbol{Z}}$ are perfectly collinear, as quite often happens, the number of degrees of freedom for the test must of course be reduced accordingly.

It is illuminating to consider as an example the univariate nonlinear regression model

$$y_t = x_t(\boldsymbol{\beta}) + u_t, \quad u_t \sim \mathrm{NID}(0, \sigma^2),$$

where $x_t(\boldsymbol{\beta})$ is a twice continuously differentiable function that depends on $\boldsymbol{\beta}$, a p-vector of parameters, and also on exogenous and predetermined variables which vary across observations. Thus the total number of parameters is $k = p + 1$. For this model, the contribution to the loglikelihood function from the tth observation is

$$\ell_t(\boldsymbol{\beta}, \sigma) = -\tfrac{1}{2}\log(2\pi) - \log(\sigma) - \frac{1}{2\sigma^2}\big(y_t - x_t(\boldsymbol{\beta})\big)^2.$$

Thus the contribution from the tth observation to the regressor corresponding to the ith element of $\boldsymbol{\beta}$ is

$$G_{ti}(\boldsymbol{\beta}, \sigma) = \frac{1}{\sigma^2}\big(y_t - x_t(\boldsymbol{\beta})\big)X_{ti}(\boldsymbol{\beta}), \tag{16.66}$$

where, as usual, $X_{ti}(\boldsymbol{\beta})$ denotes the derivative of $x_t(\boldsymbol{\beta})$ with respect to β_i. Similarly, the contribution from the tth observation to the regressor corresponding to σ is

$$G_{t,k}(\boldsymbol{\beta}, \sigma) = -\frac{1}{\sigma} + \frac{1}{\sigma^3}\big(y_t - x_t(\boldsymbol{\beta})\big)^2. \tag{16.67}$$

Using (16.66) and (16.67), it is easy to work out the regressors for the OPG version of the IM test. We make the definitions

$$\hat{e}_t \equiv \frac{1}{\hat{\sigma}}\big(y_t - x_t(\hat{\boldsymbol{\beta}})\big), \quad \hat{X}_{ti} \equiv X_{ti}(\hat{\boldsymbol{\beta}}), \quad \text{and} \quad X^*_{tij}(\boldsymbol{\beta}) \equiv \frac{\partial X_{ti}(\boldsymbol{\beta})}{\partial \beta_j}.$$

Then, up to multiplicative factors that can have no effect on the fit of the regression, and hence no effect on the value of the IM test statistic, the regressors for the test regression are

$$\text{for } \beta_i: \quad \hat{e}_t\hat{X}_{ti}; \tag{16.68}$$

$$\text{for } \sigma: \quad \hat{e}_t^2 - 1; \tag{16.69}$$

$$\text{for } \beta_i \times \beta_j: \quad (\hat{e}_t^2 - 1)\hat{X}_{ti}\hat{X}_{tj} + \hat{\sigma}\hat{e}_t\hat{X}^*_{tij}; \tag{16.70}$$

$$\text{for } \sigma \times \beta_i: \quad (\hat{e}_t^3 - 3\hat{e}_t)\hat{X}_{ti}; \tag{16.71}$$

$$\text{for } \sigma \times \sigma: \quad \hat{e}_t^4 - 5\hat{e}_t^2 + 2. \tag{16.72}$$

Expressions (16.68) and (16.69) give the elements of each row of $\hat{\boldsymbol{G}}$, while expressions (16.70)–(16.72) give the elements of each row of $\hat{\boldsymbol{Z}}$. When the original regression contains a constant term, (16.69) will be perfectly collinear with (16.70) when i and j both index the constant. Therefore, the latter will have to be dropped and the degrees of freedom for the test reduced by one to $\frac{1}{2}(p+2)(p+1)-1$.

Expressions (16.68)–(16.72) show what forms of misspecification the IM test is testing for in the nonlinear regression context. It is evident from (16.71) that the (β_i, σ) regressors are those corresponding to skewness interacting with the $\hat{X}_{ti}$'s. It appears that such skewness, if present, would bias the estimates of the covariances of $\hat{\boldsymbol{\beta}}$ and $\hat{\sigma}$. If we add five times (16.69) to (16.72), the result is $\hat{e}_t^4 - 3$, from which we see that the linearly independent part of the (σ, σ) regressor is testing in the kurtosis direction. Either platykurtosis or leptokurtosis would lead to bias in the estimate of the variance of $\hat{\sigma}$. It is evident from (16.70) that if $x_t(\boldsymbol{\beta})$ were linear, the (β_i, β_j) regressors would be testing for heteroskedasticity of exactly the type that White's (1980) test is designed to detect; see Section 16.5. In the nonlinear regression case considered here, however, these regressors are testing at the same time for misspecification of the regression function. For more details on the special case of linear regression models, see Hall (1987).

The above analysis suggests that, in the case of regression models, it is probably more attractive to test directly for heteroskedasticity, skewness, kurtosis, and misspecification of the regression function than to use an IM test. We have already seen how to test for each of these types of misspecification individually. Individual tests may well be more powerful and more informative than an IM test, especially if only a few things are actually wrong with the model. If one is primarily interested in inferences about $\boldsymbol{\beta}$, then testing for skewness and kurtosis may be optional.

There is one very serious problem with IM tests based on the OPG regression. In finite samples, they tend to reject the null hypothesis much too often when it is true. In this respect, IM tests seem to be even worse than other specification tests based on the OPG regression. Monte Carlo results demonstrating the dreadful finite-sample performance of the OPG version of the IM test may be found in Taylor (1987), Kennan and Neumann (1988), Orme (1990a), Hall (1990), Chesher and Spady (1991), and Davidson and MacKinnon (1992a). In some of these papers, there are cases in which OPG IM tests reject correct null hypotheses virtually all the time. The problem seems to grow worse as the number of degrees of freedom increases, and it does not go away quickly as the sample size increases. One extreme example, given in Davidson and MacKinnon (1992a), is a linear regression model with 10 regressors, and thus 65 degrees of freedom, for which the OPG form of the IM test rejects the true null hypothesis at the nominal 5% level an amazing 99.9% of the time when $n = 200$ and 92.7% of the time even when $n = 1000$.

Luckily, alternative methods of calculating IM tests are available in many cases. These invariably have much better finite-sample properties than the OPG version but are not as widely applicable. Various techniques have been suggested by Chesher and Spady (1991), Orme (1990a, 1990b), and Davidson and MacKinnon (1992a). In the last of these papers, we made use of an important result due to Chesher (1984), who showed that the implicit alternative of the IM test is a model with random parameter variation. This allowed us explicitly to construct a test against this type of alternative for the class of models to which the DLR is applicable (see Section 14.4). Orme (1990b) suggests alternative varieties of double- and even triple-length regressions for computing IM tests in other types of models.

Obtaining an IM test statistic that is inconsistent with the null hypothesis (which might have to be a very big number indeed if the OPG version of the test is being used), does not necessarily mean that one has to abandon the model being tested. What it does mean is that one has to use more robust methods of inference. In the case of regression models, we saw in Section 16.3 that one can make valid inferences in the presence of heteroskedasticity of unknown form by using an HCCME instead of the conventional least squares covariance matrix. In the more general case of models estimated by maximum likelihood, a similar option is open to us. Recall the result

$$\boldsymbol{V}^{\infty}\big(n^{1/2}(\hat{\boldsymbol{\theta}} - \boldsymbol{\theta}_0)\big) = \mathcal{H}^{-1}(\boldsymbol{\theta}_0)\mathcal{I}(\boldsymbol{\theta}_0)\mathcal{H}^{-1}(\boldsymbol{\theta}_0), \tag{16.73}$$

which was originally (8.42). We obtained this result before we proved the information matrix equality, which we used to obtain the simpler result that

$$\boldsymbol{V}^{\infty}\big(n^{1/2}(\hat{\boldsymbol{\theta}} - \boldsymbol{\theta}_0)\big) = \mathcal{I}^{-1}(\boldsymbol{\theta}_0). \tag{16.74}$$

Moreover, the assumptions used to obtain (16.73) were not as strong as those used to obtain the information matrix equality. This suggests that (16.73) may be true more generally than (16.74), and that is indeed the case, as White (1982) has shown. Thus, if there is reason to believe that the information matrix equality does not hold, it may be a good idea to employ the following estimator for the covariance matrix of $\hat{\boldsymbol{\theta}}$:

$$\hat{\boldsymbol{H}}^{-1}(\hat{\boldsymbol{G}}^{\top}\hat{\boldsymbol{G}})\hat{\boldsymbol{H}}^{-1}, \tag{16.75}$$

where $\hat{\boldsymbol{H}}$ denotes the Hessian matrix evaluated at the ML estimates $\hat{\boldsymbol{\theta}}$. As the natural analog of (8.42), expression (16.75) will be asymptotically valid under weaker conditions than either $-\hat{\boldsymbol{H}}^{-1}$ or $(\hat{\boldsymbol{G}}^{\top}\hat{\boldsymbol{G}})^{-1}$.

16.10 CONCLUSION

This chapter has covered quite a lot of important material, much of it relatively recent and some of it only tangentially related to the topic of heteroskedasticity. The unifying theme of the chapter is a concern with moments of the dependent variable higher than the first. In the next chapter we continue to emphasize the role of moments by introducing an important method of estimation called the generalized method of moments. Some of the material covered in this chapter, such as HCCMEs and conditional moment tests, will reappear there.

TERMS AND CONCEPTS

autoregressive conditional heteroskedasticity (ARCH)
ARCH-in-mean (ARCH-M)
ARCH(p) model
conditional moment tests (CM tests)
empirical moments
GARCH(p, q) model
generalized ARCH model (GARCH)
generalized OLS covariance matrix
Goldfeld-Quandt test for heteroskedasticity
heteroskedasticity-consistent covariance matrix estimator (HCCME)
information matrix tests (IM tests)
moment conditions (conditional and unconditional)
moment specification tests
skedastic directions
tests for skewness and kurtosis
White's test for heteroskedasticity

Chapter 17

The Generalized Method of Moments

17.1 Introduction and Definitions

We saw in the last chapter that if a model is correctly specified, there will often be conditional moments which are zero. The essential idea of the **generalized method of moments**, or **GMM**, is that moment conditions can be used not only to test model specification but also to define model parameters, in the sense of providing a parameter-defining mapping for a model. The very simplest example of this is a model in which the only parameter of interest is the expectation of the dependent variable. This is a special case of what is called a **location model**. If each observation on a dependent variable y is a drawing from a distribution with expectation m, then the moment $E(y - m)$ must be zero. This fact serves to *define* the parameter m, since if $m' \neq m$, $E(y - m') \neq 0$. In other words, the moment condition is satisfied only by the true value of the parameter.

According to the (ordinary) **method of moments**, if one has a sample of independent drawings from some distribution, one can estimate any moment of the distribution by the corresponding sample moment. This procedure is justified very easily by invoking the law of large numbers in its simplest form. Thus, for the location model, if the sample is denoted by y_t, $t = 1, \ldots, n$, the method of moments estimator of m is just the sample mean

$$\hat{m} = \frac{1}{n}\sum_{t=1}^{n} y_t. \tag{17.01}$$

When one speaks of the *generalized* method of moments, several generalizations are in fact implied. Some involve no more than relaxing regularity conditions, for instance, the assumption of i.i.d. observations. Since many different laws of large numbers can be proved (recall the list in Section 4.7), there is no reason to limit oneself to the i.i.d. case. But the essential generalizations follow from two facts. The first is that conditional moments may be used as well as unconditional ones, and the second is that moments may depend on unknown parameters.

It is the second of these that we now use to obtain the **generalized method of moments estimator**, or **GMM estimator**, of m in the location model. We forget that m is itself a moment and instead use the **moment condition**

$$E(y - m) = 0 \tag{17.02}$$

in order to define m. The essence of the method of moments, whether ordinary or generalized, is to replace population moments by sample moments. We therefore replace the expectation in (17.02) by the sample mean and define $\hat{m}$ implicitly by

$$\frac{1}{n}\sum_{t=1}^{n}(y_t - \hat{m}) = 0,$$

which can immediately be solved to yield the same estimator as in (17.01).

The most frequently used estimator in econometrics, the OLS estimator, can be regarded as a GMM estimator. Deriving it in this way will point up many general features of GMM estimation. When one writes

$$\boldsymbol{y} = \boldsymbol{X\beta} + \boldsymbol{u}, \tag{17.03}$$

the usual interpretation is that

$$E(y_t \,|\, \Omega_t) = \boldsymbol{X}_t\boldsymbol{\beta} \quad \text{for } t = 1, \ldots, n, \tag{17.04}$$

where Ω_t is some information set. This implies that $E(u_t \,|\, \Omega_t) = 0$. Frequently, additional assumptions are made about $\boldsymbol{u}$, such as serial independence, homoskedasticity, or even normality. For present purposes, none of these extra assumptions is necessary.

If, as usual, k denotes the number of parameters in (17.03), it is clear that we need at least k moment conditions in order to define a full set of parameter estimates. But (17.04) seems to provide no more than one. The way out of this problem constitutes one of the most important features of GMM. Since (17.04) provides the *conditional* moment condition $E(u_t \,|\, \Omega_t) = 0$, it follows that, for any vector $\boldsymbol{w}$ such that $w_t \in \Omega_t$, the unconditional moments $E\big(w_t(y_t - \boldsymbol{X}_t\boldsymbol{\beta})\big)$ are zero. At the very least, the regressors $\boldsymbol{X}_t$ belong to the information set Ω_t, and there are precisely k of them. We may therefore use the k regressors to define k unconditional moment conditions. The sample counterparts of these are given by the column vector

$$\frac{1}{n}\sum_{t=1}^{n}\boldsymbol{X}_t^{\top}(y_t - \boldsymbol{X}_t\boldsymbol{\beta}).$$

It is at once clear that setting these sample counterparts equal to zero gives the first-order conditions (1.03) used in the definition of the OLS estimator. It appears, then, that the OLS estimator, considered as a GMM estimator, should be applicable without any of the assumptions, such as homoskedasticity or serial independence, that are often made about the second moments of the error terms, that is, their variance-covariance structure. Indeed, the *consistency* of the OLS estimator follows solely from the fact that it satisfies certain moment conditions. This will follow from the proof of consistency of the GMM estimator in the next section, although it can easily be seen directly.

The simple instrumental variables estimator of equation (7.25) can be derived in the same way as the OLS estimator. Possible endogeneity of the regressors $\boldsymbol{X}$ in (17.03) may mean that we do *not* wish to impose the condition $E(u_t \mid \Omega_t) = 0$. However, we do claim, either by prior knowledge or assumption, to have an $n \times k$ matrix $\boldsymbol{W}$ of valid instruments, with typical row $\boldsymbol{W}_t \in \Omega_t$. This implies that we may utilize the k moment conditions $E(\boldsymbol{W}_t u_t) = \mathbf{0}$. The sample counterparts of these moment conditions are

$$\frac{1}{n}\sum_{t=1}^{n} \boldsymbol{W}_t^{\top}(y_t - \boldsymbol{X}_t\boldsymbol{\beta}) = \mathbf{0}$$

or, omitting the factor of n^{-1} and using matrix notation,

$$\boldsymbol{W}^{\top}(\boldsymbol{y} - \boldsymbol{X\beta}) = \mathbf{0}. \tag{17.05}$$

These are the first-order conditions that define the simple IV estimator.

Both of the above examples show that instrumental variables, including regressors used as instruments, generate moment conditions like those used for conditional moment specification testing in Section 16.8. Just as moment conditions may arise from many sources, so instrumental variables of many sorts may suggest themselves in the context of some given econometric model. As a result, there are usually far more instruments available than are needed to identify the model parameters. Recall that, in the context of the linear regression model (17.03), *any* vector $\boldsymbol{w}$ such that $w_t \in \Omega_t$ can be used. These extra instruments, as we will see shortly, can be used in the GMM context, just as they are in the IV context, to generate overidentifying restrictions which can be used for two distinct purposes: to improve the efficiency of the parameter estimates and to test the specification of the model.

GMM estimation is of course in no way limited to linear regression models. We now wish to make some definitions in a more general nonlinear context, but one that is still relatively simple. We therefore limit ourselves temporarily to the case of just identified models. The more realistic case of overidentified models will be taken up in the next section.

Our first task is to find some way to characterize models that we may hope to estimate by GMM. In Chapter 5, we defined an econometric model as a set of DGPs. A parametrized model was defined as a model along with a **parameter-defining mapping**, which associates a parameter vector in some parameter space with each DGP of the model. In the GMM context, there are many possible ways of choosing the model, i.e., the underlying set of DGPs. One of the advantages of GMM as an estimation method is that it permits models which consist of a very large number of DGPs. In striking contrast to ML estimation, where the model must be completely specified, any DGP is admissible if it satisfies a relatively small number of restrictions or regularity conditions. Sometimes, the existence of the moments used to define the parameters is the only requirement needed for a model to be well defined. Sometimes, an investigator is willing to impose further structure on a model, thereby eliminating DGPs that would otherwise have been contained in the model. This may be done by making assumptions such as homoskedasticity, or serial independence, or the existence of moments other than those actually used to define the parameters. It is not our immediate concern to specify just how the model is specified, and so we simply suppose that a set of DGPs $\mathbb{M}$ has been chosen to serve as the model.

The next requirement is the parameter-defining mapping. This is provided by the moment conditions themselves, which give an *implicit* definition of the mapping. Let $f_{ti}(y_t, \boldsymbol{\theta})$, $i = 1, \ldots, k$, be a function of a dependent variable or vector of dependent variables y_t. This function is assumed to have expectation zero for all the DGPs of the model characterized by the k–vector of parameters $\boldsymbol{\theta}$. In general, because all the theory in this chapter is asymptotic, t, which indexes the observations, may take on any positive integer value. In practice, the functions f_{ti} will frequently depend on exogenous and predetermined variables as well as on the dependent variable(s). Then the moment conditions

$$E\big(f_{ti}(y_t, \boldsymbol{\theta})\big) = 0, \quad i = 1, \ldots, k, \tag{17.06}$$

yield a parameter-defining mapping under suitable regularity conditions. The effect of these regularity conditions must be that, for each DGP μ in the model $\mathbb{M}$, there is one and only one parameter vector $\boldsymbol{\theta}$ in some predefined parameter space Θ that makes the expectations in (17.06) vanish. It is generally convenient to require in addition that, for all DGPs in the model, and for all $\boldsymbol{\theta} \in \Theta$, the expectations in (17.06) exist.

As is the case with all the other parametrized models we have considered, the existence of a well-defined parameter-defining mapping guarantees that the model parameters are asymptotically identified. Whether or not they are identified by a given sample depends on whether or not there is a unique solution to what we may call the **estimator-defining equations** that are the sample counterparts to the moment conditions (17.06). These estimator-defining equations, which equate **empirical moments** to zero, are

$$\frac{1}{n}\sum_{t=1}^{n} f_{ti}(y_t, \boldsymbol{\theta}) = 0, \quad i = 1, \ldots, k. \tag{17.07}$$

If there is a unique $\hat{\boldsymbol{\theta}}$ that satisfies (17.07), then the model is identified by the data and $\hat{\boldsymbol{\theta}}$ is, by definition, the GMM estimator of $\boldsymbol{\theta}$.

The generalized method of moments was suggested under that name by Hansen (1982), but the basic idea goes back at least as far as Sargan (1958). A special case of GMM called two-step two-stage least squares was proposed by Cumby, Huizinga, and Obstfeld (1983). One of the motivations for developing the method was the increase in interest during the early 1980s in rational expectations models. A fundamental principle of these models is that errors in expectations should be independent of all variables in the information sets of the agents formulating the expectations. Consequently, prediction errors, failures to achieve optimality, and other (quantifiable) consequences of imperfect foresight should, if expectations are indeed formed rationally, be independent of variables present in agents' information sets when expectations are formed. This independence gives rise to various conditional moment conditions, which then provide the (unconditional) moment conditions on which GMM estimation can be based. The first important application of this idea is found in Hansen and Singleton (1982), in which they use the stochastic Euler conditions associated with agents' problems of intertemporal optimization as the source of their conditional moment conditions. Other applications of GMM include Dunn and Singleton (1986), Eichenbaum, Hansen, and Singleton (1988), and Epstein and Zin (1991).

We have now briefly sketched most of the important issues connected with GMM estimation. It remains to consider how to treat overidentifying restrictions, to work out the theoretical properties of GMM estimators, to see how best to compute GMM estimators in practice, and to find testing procedures similar to conditional moment tests but in the GMM context. In the next section, we discuss the asymptotic theory of what are called ***M*-estimators**, that is, estimators defined by the maximization or minimization of some criterion function. We forge the link between these estimators and GMM estimators and briefly discuss regularity conditions. Next, in Section 17.3, we turn to questions of efficiency and inference, treating the two together because both depend on the asymptotic covariance matrix of the parameter estimates. These topics are also discussed in Section 17.4, which is concerned primarily with the choice of instruments and moment conditions. Section 17.5 discusses the practical problem of covariance matrix estimation. This is more critical for GMM than for many other techniques, because it affects the weighting matrix that is used in the criterion function. Finally, Section 17.6 discusses specification testing in the context of GMM estimation.

17.2 CRITERION FUNCTIONS AND M-ESTIMATORS

In Chapter 7, the IV estimator for the linear regression model was defined by the minimization of the **criterion function**

$$(\boldsymbol{y} - \boldsymbol{X\beta})^{\top}\boldsymbol{P}_W(\boldsymbol{y} - \boldsymbol{X\beta}); \tag{17.08}$$

see equation (7.15). Let k denote the number of regressors and $l \geq k$ the number of instruments. In the just identified case, in which $l = k$, the minimized value of the criterion function is zero. This value is achieved at the value of $\boldsymbol{\beta}$ given by the simple IV estimator, defined by the k conditions (17.05). When $l > k$, the minimized value is in general greater than zero, since it is not in general possible to solve what is now the set of l conditions (17.05) for k unknowns.

The overidentified case in the GMM context is similar. There are l estimator-defining equations (17.07) but just k unknown parameters. Instead of solving a set of equations, the left-hand sides of these equations are used to define a criterion function which is subsequently minimized to provide parameter estimates. Consider (17.08) again. If we write it as

$$(\boldsymbol{y} - \boldsymbol{X\beta})^{\top}\boldsymbol{W}\big(\boldsymbol{W}^{\top}\boldsymbol{W}\big)^{-1}\boldsymbol{W}^{\top}(\boldsymbol{y} - \boldsymbol{X\beta}), \tag{17.09}$$

we see that the expression is a quadratic form made up from the empirical moments $\boldsymbol{W}^{\top}(\boldsymbol{y} - \boldsymbol{X\beta})$ and the inverse of the positive definite matrix $\boldsymbol{W}^{\top}\boldsymbol{W}$. This positive definite matrix is, under homoskedasticity and serial independence of the error terms, proportional to the covariance matrix of the vector of moments, the factor of proportionality being the variance of the error terms. Omitting this factor of proportionality does not matter, because the $\boldsymbol{\beta}$ which minimizes (17.09) is unchanged if (17.09) is multiplied by any positive scalar.

It is not necessary to use the covariance matrix of the empirical moments $\boldsymbol{W}^{\top}(\boldsymbol{y} - \boldsymbol{X\beta})$ if one merely wishes to obtain *consistent*, rather than *efficient*, estimates of $\boldsymbol{\beta}$ by the minimization of the criterion function. If we replace $(\boldsymbol{W}^{\top}\boldsymbol{W})^{-1}$ in (17.09) by any asymptotically nonrandom, symmetric, positive definite $l \times l$ matrix $\boldsymbol{A}(\boldsymbol{y})$, the criterion function becomes

$$(\boldsymbol{y} - \boldsymbol{X\beta})^{\top}\boldsymbol{W}\boldsymbol{A}(\boldsymbol{y})\boldsymbol{W}^{\top}(\boldsymbol{y} - \boldsymbol{X\beta}), \tag{17.10}$$

and the resulting estimator is easily seen to be

$$\hat{\boldsymbol{\beta}} = \big(\boldsymbol{X}^{\top}\boldsymbol{W}\boldsymbol{A}(\boldsymbol{y})\boldsymbol{W}^{\top}\boldsymbol{X}\big)^{-1}\boldsymbol{X}^{\top}\boldsymbol{W}\boldsymbol{A}(\boldsymbol{y})\boldsymbol{W}^{\top}\boldsymbol{y}.$$

If $l = k$ and $\boldsymbol{W}^{\top}\boldsymbol{X}$ is square and nonsingular, this expression reduces to the simple IV estimator $(\boldsymbol{W}^{\top}\boldsymbol{X})^{-1}\boldsymbol{W}^{\top}\boldsymbol{y}$, whatever the choice of $\boldsymbol{A}$. The choice of $\boldsymbol{A}$ is immaterial in this case because the number of moment conditions is equal to the number of parameters, which implies that (17.10) always achieves a minimum of zero for any $\boldsymbol{A}$.

In general, if $\boldsymbol{W}$ is a matrix of valid instruments, $\hat{\boldsymbol{\beta}}$ provides a consistent estimator of $\boldsymbol{\beta}$, as can be seen by standard arguments. Under homoskedasticity and serial independence of the error terms, however, $\hat{\boldsymbol{\beta}}$ is less efficient than the usual IV estimator $\tilde{\boldsymbol{\beta}} \equiv (\boldsymbol{X}^{\top}\boldsymbol{P}_W\boldsymbol{X})^{-1}\boldsymbol{X}^{\top}\boldsymbol{P}_W\boldsymbol{y}$, unless $\boldsymbol{A}$ is proportional to $(\boldsymbol{W}^{\top}\boldsymbol{W})^{-1}$. The proof of this result is similar to the proofs of the Gauss-Markov Theorem (Theorem 5.3) and of the Cramér-Rao lower bound in Section 8.8. We demonstrate that the difference $\hat{\boldsymbol{\beta}} - \tilde{\boldsymbol{\beta}}$ is asymptotically uncorrelated with $\tilde{\boldsymbol{\beta}}$. This implies that the asymptotic covariance matrix of $\hat{\boldsymbol{\beta}}$ is the sum of the asymptotic covariance matrices of $\tilde{\boldsymbol{\beta}}$ and of the difference between the two estimators. Therefore, $\hat{\boldsymbol{\beta}}$ must be less efficient than $\tilde{\boldsymbol{\beta}}$. The difference between the two estimators is

$$\begin{aligned}\hat{\boldsymbol{\beta}} - \tilde{\boldsymbol{\beta}} &= \left(\boldsymbol{X}^\top\boldsymbol{W}\boldsymbol{A}\boldsymbol{W}^\top\boldsymbol{X}\right)^{-1}\boldsymbol{X}^\top\boldsymbol{W}\boldsymbol{A}\boldsymbol{W}^\top\boldsymbol{y} - \left(\boldsymbol{X}^\top\boldsymbol{P}_W\boldsymbol{X}\right)^{-1}\boldsymbol{X}^\top\boldsymbol{P}_W\boldsymbol{y}\\ &= \left(\boldsymbol{X}^\top\boldsymbol{W}\boldsymbol{A}\boldsymbol{W}^\top\boldsymbol{X}\right)^{-1}\boldsymbol{X}^\top\boldsymbol{W}\boldsymbol{A}\boldsymbol{W}^\top\boldsymbol{M}_X^W\boldsymbol{y},\end{aligned} \tag{17.11}$$

where the oblique projection matrix $\boldsymbol{M}_X^W$ is defined by

$$\boldsymbol{M}_X^W = \mathbf{I} - \boldsymbol{X}\left(\boldsymbol{X}^\top\boldsymbol{P}_W\boldsymbol{X}\right)^{-1}\boldsymbol{X}^\top\boldsymbol{P}_W.$$

The derivation of (17.11) was not spelled out in detail, because it is essentially the same as several previous ones; see, for example, (7.59).

Since $\boldsymbol{M}_X^W\boldsymbol{X} = \mathbf{0}$, we can replace $\boldsymbol{y}$ in expression (17.11) by $\boldsymbol{u}$ if indeed $\boldsymbol{y} = \boldsymbol{X}\boldsymbol{\beta}_0 + \boldsymbol{u}$ for some $\boldsymbol{\beta}_0$. It is now possible to see that $\tilde{\boldsymbol{\beta}}$ is asymptotically uncorrelated with (17.11). The random part of $\tilde{\boldsymbol{\beta}}$ is just $\boldsymbol{X}^\top\boldsymbol{P}_W\boldsymbol{u}$, and the random part of (17.11) is $\boldsymbol{W}^\top\boldsymbol{M}_X^W\boldsymbol{u}$. When the error terms are homoskedastic and serially independent with error variance σ^2, the matrix of asymptotic covariances of these random parts is

$$\operatorname*{plim}_{n\to\infty}\left(\frac{1}{n}\sigma^2\boldsymbol{X}^\top\boldsymbol{P}_W(\boldsymbol{M}_X^W)^\top\boldsymbol{W}\right).$$

But this is zero, as we set out to prove, since

$$\boldsymbol{X}^\top\boldsymbol{P}_W(\boldsymbol{M}_X^W)^\top\boldsymbol{W} = \boldsymbol{X}^\top\boldsymbol{W} - \boldsymbol{X}^\top\boldsymbol{P}_W\boldsymbol{X}\left(\boldsymbol{X}^\top\boldsymbol{P}_W\boldsymbol{X}\right)^{-1}\boldsymbol{X}^\top\boldsymbol{W} = \mathbf{0}.$$

In the next section, we will discuss this result further. Plainly, it confers some sort of optimality or efficiency on the usual IV estimator, and it will be interesting to study the precise nature of this optimality.

In the more general GMM context, we may construct a criterion function for estimation purposes by using an arbitrary, symmetric, positive definite, possibly data-dependent matrix $\boldsymbol{A}(\boldsymbol{y})$ that is $O(1)$. We will refer to $\boldsymbol{A}$ as a **weighting matrix** and require that, for each DGP μ in the model $\mathbb{M}$,

$$\operatorname*{plim}_{\mu, n\to\infty}\boldsymbol{A}(\boldsymbol{y}) = \boldsymbol{A}_0(\mu), \tag{17.12}$$

where $\boldsymbol{A}_0(\mu)$ is a nonrandom, symmetric, positive definite, finite matrix. Let $\boldsymbol{F}(\boldsymbol{y},\boldsymbol{\theta})$ denote the matrix with typical element $f_{ti}(y_t,\boldsymbol{\theta})$ where, as in (17.07), $f_{ti}(y_t,\boldsymbol{\theta})$ denotes the contribution from the tth observation to the ith moment. We suppose that $\boldsymbol{\theta} \in \Theta \subseteq \mathbb{R}^k$ and that $1 \le i \le l$, with $l > k$. Then if $\boldsymbol{\iota}$, as usual, denotes an n-vector with each element equal to 1, the empirical moment conditions are given by

$$\boldsymbol{F}^\top(\boldsymbol{y},\boldsymbol{\theta})\,\boldsymbol{\iota} = \mathbf{0},$$

and a possible criterion function for estimating $\boldsymbol{\theta}$ is

$$\boldsymbol{\iota}^{\top}\boldsymbol{F}(\boldsymbol{y},\boldsymbol{\theta})\boldsymbol{A}(\boldsymbol{y})\boldsymbol{F}^{\top}(\boldsymbol{y},\boldsymbol{\theta})\boldsymbol{\iota}. \tag{17.13}$$

We now establish the key result needed in order to show that the estimator $\hat{\boldsymbol{\theta}}$ derived by minimizing (17.13) is consistent under certain regularity conditions. This result is that if a sample is generated by the DGP $\mu \in \mathbb{M}$, the true parameter vector $\boldsymbol{\theta}(\mu)$ minimizes the probability limit of n^{-2} times the criterion function (17.13):

$$\boldsymbol{\theta}(\mu) = \underset{\boldsymbol{\theta}\in\Theta}{\operatorname{argmin}}\Big(\operatorname*{plim}_{n\to\infty}{}_{\mu}\Big(n^{-2}\boldsymbol{\iota}^{\top}\boldsymbol{F}(\boldsymbol{y},\boldsymbol{\theta})\boldsymbol{A}(\boldsymbol{y})\boldsymbol{F}^{\top}(\boldsymbol{y},\boldsymbol{\theta})\boldsymbol{\iota}\Big)\Big). \tag{17.14}$$

The notation $\operatorname{plim}_{\mu}$ implies that the DGP used to compute the probability limit is μ, and (17.14) implies that this probability limit is nonrandom. The rather strange factor of n^{-2} arises because we have assumed that the limiting weighting matrix $\boldsymbol{A}_0(\mu)$ is $O(1)$. Since we expect in general that $\boldsymbol{F}^{\top}\boldsymbol{\iota}$ is $O(n)$, we need two factors of n^{-1} for (17.14) to be $O(1)$ as $n \to \infty$.

For the result (17.14) to be true, we need to be able to apply a law of large numbers to $n^{-1}\boldsymbol{F}^{\top}\boldsymbol{\iota} = n^{-1}\sum_{t=1}^{n}\boldsymbol{F}_t^{\top}$, where $\boldsymbol{F}_t$ is the tth row of $\boldsymbol{F}$. Since $\boldsymbol{F}$ depends on parameters, the law of large numbers must apply uniformly with respect to these, and so we will simply assume that condition WULLN given in Definition 4.17 applies to each component of the sequence $\{\boldsymbol{F}_t^{\top}(\boldsymbol{\theta})\}$ at least in some neighborhood of the true parameter vector $\boldsymbol{\theta}_0 \equiv \boldsymbol{\theta}(\mu)$. This permits us to make the following definition:

$$\boldsymbol{m}(\mu,\boldsymbol{\theta}) = \operatorname*{plim}_{n\to\infty}{}_{\mu}\Big(\frac{1}{n}\boldsymbol{F}^{\top}(\boldsymbol{\theta})\boldsymbol{\iota}\Big) = \lim_{n\to\infty}\Big(\frac{1}{n}\sum_{t=1}^{n}E_{\mu}\big(\boldsymbol{F}_t(\boldsymbol{\theta})\big)\Big). \tag{17.15}$$

The population moment conditions (17.06) along with the requirement that these conditions identify the parameters guarantee that

$$\boldsymbol{m}(\mu,\boldsymbol{\theta}_0) = \mathbf{0} \quad \text{and} \quad \boldsymbol{m}(\mu,\boldsymbol{\theta}) \neq \mathbf{0} \text{ if } \boldsymbol{\theta} \neq \boldsymbol{\theta}_0. \tag{17.16}$$

Since $\operatorname{plim}_{\mu}\boldsymbol{A}(\boldsymbol{y}) = \boldsymbol{A}_0(\mu)$, it follows that

$$\operatorname*{plim}_{n\to\infty}{}_{\mu}\Big(n^{-2}\boldsymbol{\iota}^{\top}\boldsymbol{F}(\boldsymbol{y},\boldsymbol{\theta})\boldsymbol{A}(\boldsymbol{y})\boldsymbol{F}^{\top}(\boldsymbol{y},\boldsymbol{\theta})\boldsymbol{\iota}\Big) = \boldsymbol{m}^{\top}(\mu,\boldsymbol{\theta})\boldsymbol{A}_0(\mu)\boldsymbol{m}(\mu,\boldsymbol{\theta}).$$

Since $\boldsymbol{A}_0(\mu)$ is positive definite, this expression is zero for $\boldsymbol{\theta} = \boldsymbol{\theta}_0$ and (strictly) positive otherwise. This establishes (17.14).

The result (17.14) implies that the estimator of $\boldsymbol{\theta}$ obtained by minimizing the criterion function (17.13) is consistent, by the same arguments used in Chapters 5 and 8 to show the consistency of the NLS and ML estimators. As in Chapter 8, for a GMM model to be asymptotically identified on a noncompact parameter set, we must assume that there are no sequences of parameter vectors without limit point such that (17.13) evaluated at the points of the sequence tends from above to the value of (17.13) at the true parameter vector $\boldsymbol{\theta}_0$; recall Definition 8.1.

It is convenient at this point to leave the specific GMM case and treat the more general problem of *M*-estimators. This terminology arose in the literature on robust estimation — see Huber (1972, 1981) — but in econometrics it is often used to refer to any estimator based on the maximization or minimization of a criterion function. In recent years, substantial effort has gone into the development of a unified theory for all estimators of this type. A landmark paper is Burguete, Gallant, and Souza (1982). Our treatment will be relatively elementary; for more detailed treatments, readers should consult Bates and White (1985), Gallant (1987), or Gallant and White (1988).

We must first establish some notation. Let us suppose that we are working with a parametrized model $(\mathbb{M}, \boldsymbol{\theta})$. The range of the parameter-defining mapping $\boldsymbol{\theta}$ will be a parameter space $\Theta \in \mathbb{R}^k$. Let $Q^n(\boldsymbol{y}^n, \boldsymbol{\theta})$ denote the value of some criterion function, where $\boldsymbol{y}^n$ is a sample of n observations on one or more dependent variables, and $\boldsymbol{\theta} \in \Theta$. Notice that, by a slight abuse of notation, we use $\boldsymbol{\theta}$ both for the parameter-defining mapping and for the values of the mapping. Strictly speaking, we should write $\boldsymbol{\theta}(\mu)$ for the parameters associated with a DGP $\mu \in \mathbb{M}$, but it is usually unnecessary to specify μ explicitly. Usually, Q^n will depend on exogenous or predetermined variables as well as the dependent variable(s) $\boldsymbol{y}^n$. Then in order for the sequence $Q \equiv \{Q^n\}$ to be appropriate for the estimation of the parameters $\boldsymbol{\theta}$, we require that Q should *identify* these parameters, in the following sense:

Definition 17.1.

A sequence of criterion functions Q asymptotically identifies a parametrized model $(\mathbb{M}, \boldsymbol{\theta})$ if, for all $\mu \in \mathbb{M}$ and for all $\boldsymbol{\theta} \in \Theta$,

$$\bar{Q}(\mu, \boldsymbol{\theta}) \equiv \operatorname*{plim}_{n\to\infty}{}_{\mu}\, Q^n(\boldsymbol{y}^n, \boldsymbol{\theta})$$

exists and satisfies the inequality $\bar{Q}\big(\mu, \boldsymbol{\theta}(\mu)\big) < \bar{Q}(\mu, \boldsymbol{\theta})$ for all parameter vectors $\boldsymbol{\theta} \neq \boldsymbol{\theta}(\mu)$. Further, in the event that Θ is not compact, there exist no sequences $\{\boldsymbol{\theta}^m\}$ without limit point such that

$$\lim_{m\to\infty} \bar{Q}(\mu, \boldsymbol{\theta}^m) = \bar{Q}\big(\mu, \boldsymbol{\theta}(\mu)\big).$$

Then, although we provide no rigorous proof, it is highly intuitive that the estimator $\hat{\boldsymbol{\theta}}_Q \equiv \{\hat{\boldsymbol{\theta}}_Q^n\}$ defined by

$$\hat{\boldsymbol{\theta}}_Q^n = \operatorname*{argmin}_{\theta\in\Theta} Q^n(\boldsymbol{y}^n, \boldsymbol{\theta}) \tag{17.17}$$

should be consistent for $\boldsymbol{\theta}$, that is,

$$\operatorname*{plim}_{n\to\infty}{}_{\mu}\, \hat{\boldsymbol{\theta}}_Q^n = \boldsymbol{\theta}(\mu). \tag{17.18}$$

A nonrigorous proof of (17.18) follows exactly the same arguments as those used in Section 8.4, leading to equation (8.31). The formal result can be stated as follows:

Theorem 17.1. Consistency of M-Estimators

The *M*-estimator defined by the minimization of a sequence of criterion functions Q is consistent for the parameters of a parametrized model $(\mathbb{M}, \boldsymbol{\theta})$ if the sequence Q identifies the model in the sense of Definition 17.1.

It is implicit in Definition 17.1 that $Q^n(\boldsymbol{\theta}) = O(1)$ as $n \to \infty$. Thus many of the criterion functions that are actually used will need to be multiplied by factors of powers of n before it can be checked whether they satisfy Definition 17.1. The sum-of-squares function used in NLS estimation and the loglikelihood function used in ML estimation, for instance, are both $O(n)$ and must therefore be divided by n, as in equations (5.10) and (8.31). Since in (17.12) we have assumed that $\boldsymbol{A}$ is $O(1)$, the criterion function (17.13) must be divided by n^2, as we already mentioned in connection with (17.14).

With consistency of the *M*-estimator (17.17) established, it is time now to turn to asymptotic normality. As always, this requires that additional regularity conditions be satisfied. So far, we have made no particular assumptions about the form of the criterion function Q^n. The sum-of-squares function and the loglikelihood function both can be expressed as a sum of n contributions, one for each observation of the sample. The GMM criterion function (17.13) has a slightly more complicated structure: It is a quadratic form made up from a positive definite matrix and a vector $\boldsymbol{F}^\top \boldsymbol{\iota}$ of which each component is a sum of contributions.

The first additional requirement is that the *M*-estimator under study should be, in the terminology of Chapter 8, of **Type 2**, that is, it should be a solution of the first-order conditions for an interior minimum of the criterion function Q. Dropping the explicit dependence on n and Q of $\hat{\boldsymbol{\theta}}$, and the explicit dependence on n of Q, we can write these first-order conditions as

$$\frac{\partial Q}{\partial \theta_j}(\hat{\boldsymbol{\theta}}) = 0 \quad \text{for } j = 1, \ldots, k. \tag{17.19}$$

Since $\hat{\boldsymbol{\theta}}$ is consistent if Q identifies $\boldsymbol{\theta}$, it is natural to perform a short Taylor expansion of the conditions (17.19) about $\boldsymbol{\theta} = \boldsymbol{\theta}_0$. This gives

$$\frac{\partial Q}{\partial \theta_j}(\boldsymbol{\theta}_0) + \sum_{i=1}^{k} \frac{\partial^2 Q}{\partial \theta_j \partial \theta_i}(\boldsymbol{\theta}_j^*)\big(\hat{\theta}_i - \theta_i^0\big) = 0, \quad \text{for } j = 1, \ldots, k, \tag{17.20}$$

where $\boldsymbol{\theta}_j^*$ is a convex combination of $\boldsymbol{\theta}_0$ and $\hat{\boldsymbol{\theta}}$. Then, provided the Hessian matrix $\mathcal{H}(\boldsymbol{\theta})$, with typical element $\partial^2 Q(\boldsymbol{\theta})/\partial \theta_j \partial \theta_i$, is invertible in the neighborhood of $\boldsymbol{\theta}_0$, we obtain

$$\hat{\boldsymbol{\theta}} - \boldsymbol{\theta}_0 = -\left(\mathcal{H}^*\right)^{-1} \boldsymbol{g}(\boldsymbol{\theta}_0), \tag{17.21}$$

where $\boldsymbol{g}(\boldsymbol{\theta})$ denotes the gradient of Q, that is, the k–vector with typical component $\partial Q(\boldsymbol{\theta})/\partial \theta_j$. As usual, $\mathcal{H}^*$ denotes a matrix of which the elements are evaluated at the appropriate $\boldsymbol{\theta}_j^*$.

If we are to be able to deduce the asymptotic normality of $\hat{\boldsymbol{\theta}}$ from (17.21), it must be possible to apply a law of large numbers to $\mathcal{H}^*$ and a central limit theorem to $n^{1/2}\boldsymbol{g}(\boldsymbol{\theta}_0)$. We would then obtain the result that

$$n^{1/2}(\hat{\boldsymbol{\theta}} - \boldsymbol{\theta}_0) \overset{a}{=} -\Big(\operatorname*{plim}_{n\to\infty} \mathcal{H}_0\Big)^{-1} n^{1/2}\boldsymbol{g}(\boldsymbol{\theta}_0). \tag{17.22}$$

What regularity conditions do we need for (17.22)? First, in order to justify the short Taylor expansion in (17.20), it is necessary that Q be at least twice continuously differentiable with respect to $\boldsymbol{\theta}$. If so, then it follows that the Hessian of Q is $O(1)$ as $n \to \infty$. Because of this, we denote it by $\mathcal{H}_0$ rather than $\boldsymbol{H}$; see Section 8.2. Then we need conditions that allow the application of a law of large numbers and a central limit theorem. Rather formally, we may state a theorem based closely on Theorem 8.3 as follows:

Theorem 17.2. Asymptotic Normality of M-Estimators

The M-estimator derived from the sequence of criterion functions Q is asymptotically normal if it satisfies the conditions of Theorem 17.1 and if in addition

(i) for all n and for all $\boldsymbol{\theta} \in \Theta$, $Q^n(\boldsymbol{y}^n, \boldsymbol{\theta})$ is twice continuously differentiable with respect to $\boldsymbol{\theta}$ for almost all $\boldsymbol{y}$, and the limit function $\bar{Q}(\mu, \boldsymbol{\theta})$ is twice continuously differentiable with respect to $\boldsymbol{\theta}$ for all $\boldsymbol{\theta} \in \Theta$ and for all $\mu \in \mathbb{M}$;

(ii) for all DGPs $\mu \in \mathbb{M}$ and for all sequences $\{\boldsymbol{\theta}^n\}$ that tend in probability to $\boldsymbol{\theta}(\mu)$ as $n \to \infty$, the Hessian matrix $\mathcal{H}^n(\boldsymbol{y}^n, \boldsymbol{\theta}^n)$ of Q^n with respect to $\boldsymbol{\theta}$ tends uniformly in probability to a positive definite, finite, nonrandom matrix $\mathcal{H}(\mu)$; and

(iii) for all DGPs $\mu \in \mathbb{M}$, $n^{1/2}$ times the gradient of $Q^n(\boldsymbol{y}^n, \boldsymbol{\theta})$, or $n^{1/2}\boldsymbol{g}\big(\boldsymbol{y}^n, \boldsymbol{\theta}(\mu)\big)$, converges in distribution as $n \to \infty$ to a multivariate normal distribution with mean zero and finite covariance matrix $\boldsymbol{V}(\mu)$.

Under these conditions, the distribution of $n^{1/2}\big(\hat{\boldsymbol{\theta}} - \boldsymbol{\theta}(\mu)\big)$ tends to $N\big(0, \mathcal{H}(\mu)^{-1}\boldsymbol{V}(\mu)\mathcal{H}(\mu)^{-1}\big)$.

It is not worth spending any time on the proof of Theorem 17.2. What we must do, instead, is to return to the GMM case and investigate the conditions under which the criterion function (17.13), suitably divided by n^2, satisfies the requirements of the theorem. Without further ado, we assume that all of the contributions $f_{ti}(y_t, \boldsymbol{\theta})$ are at least twice continuously differentiable with respect to $\boldsymbol{\theta}$ for all $\boldsymbol{\theta} \in \Theta$, for all y_t, and for all allowed values of any predetermined or exogenous variables on which they may depend. Next, we assume that the sequences

$$\frac{1}{n}\sum_{t=1}^{n}\frac{\partial f_{ti}}{\partial\theta_j}(y_t,\boldsymbol{\theta}) \quad\text{and}\quad \frac{1}{n}\sum_{t=1}^{n}\frac{\partial^2 f_{ti}}{\partial\theta_j\partial\theta_m}(y_t,\boldsymbol{\theta})$$

for $i = 1,\ldots,l$ and $j, m = 1,\ldots,k$ all satisfy condition WULLN. This permits us to define limiting functions as follows:

$$d_{ij}(\mu,\boldsymbol{\theta}) \equiv \operatorname*{plim}_{n\to\infty}{}_{\mu}\left(\frac{1}{n}\sum_{t=1}^{n}\frac{\partial f_{ti}}{\partial\theta_j}(y_t,\boldsymbol{\theta})\right). \tag{17.23}$$

We will let $\boldsymbol{D}$ denote the $l \times k$ matrix with typical element d_{ij}. Recalling the definition of $\boldsymbol{m}$ in (17.15), we can now assert that the limiting criterion function $\bar{Q}$ for the sample criterion function

$$Q^n(\boldsymbol{y}^n,\boldsymbol{\theta}) \equiv n^{-2}\boldsymbol{\iota}^\top\boldsymbol{F}(\boldsymbol{y}^n,\boldsymbol{\theta})\boldsymbol{A}(\boldsymbol{y}^n)\boldsymbol{F}^\top(\boldsymbol{y}^n,\boldsymbol{\theta})\boldsymbol{\iota} \tag{17.24}$$

is given by

$$\bar{Q}(\mu,\boldsymbol{\theta}) = \boldsymbol{m}^\top(\mu,\boldsymbol{\theta})\boldsymbol{A}_0(\mu)\boldsymbol{m}(\mu,\boldsymbol{\theta}). \tag{17.25}$$

Even though we have assumed the twice continuous differentiability of the contributions f_{ti}, it is in general necessary to assume separately that $\bar{Q}$ is twice continuously differentiable. We therefore make this additional assumption, which allows us to conclude that $d_{ij}(\mu,\boldsymbol{\theta})$ is the derivative of $m_i(\mu,\boldsymbol{\theta})$, the ith component of $\boldsymbol{m}(\mu,\boldsymbol{\theta})$, with respect to θ_j. The matrix $\boldsymbol{A}(\boldsymbol{y})$ and the limiting matrix $\boldsymbol{A}_0(\mu)$ do not depend on the parameter vector $\boldsymbol{\theta}$, and so we find that the gradient of $\bar{Q}$ with respect to $\boldsymbol{\theta}$ is given by the vector

$$2\boldsymbol{D}^\top\boldsymbol{A}_0\boldsymbol{m}. \tag{17.26}$$

At first sight, there seems to be no convenient matrix expression for the Hessian of $\bar{Q}$, since $\boldsymbol{D}$ is itself a matrix. However, if $\boldsymbol{\theta} = \boldsymbol{\theta}_0$, we have from (17.16) that $\boldsymbol{m}(\mu,\boldsymbol{\theta}_0) = \mathbf{0}$. As a result, the limiting Hessian evaluated at the true parameters is simply

$$\mathcal{H}(\mu) = 2\boldsymbol{D}^\top(\mu,\boldsymbol{\theta}_0)\boldsymbol{A}_0(\mu)\boldsymbol{D}(\mu,\boldsymbol{\theta}_0). \tag{17.27}$$

By now we can with very little more in the way of assumptions ensure that the criterion functions (17.24) and the limiting function (17.25) satisfy conditions (i) and (ii) of Theorem 17.2. In particular, we can ensure that $\mathcal{H}(\mu)$ is positive definite by the requirement that $\boldsymbol{D}(\mu,\boldsymbol{\theta}_0)$ should be of full rank, that is, of rank k. This requirement is analogous to the requirement of **strong asymptotic identifiability** discussed in Chapter 5 (see Theorem 5.2 and the subsequent discussion), and we will use the same term for it in the new context. What it means is that, as the k components of $\boldsymbol{\theta}$ vary in the neighborhood of $\boldsymbol{\theta}_0$, the l components of $\boldsymbol{m}(\mu, \boldsymbol{\theta})$ also vary in k independent directions in $\mathbb{R}^l$.

Condition (iii) is a little trickier, since it involves a central limit theorem. Notice first that the gradient of $\bar{Q}$, evaluated at $\boldsymbol{\theta} = \boldsymbol{\theta}_0$, is zero, from (17.26). This is simply a reflection of the consistency of the estimator. We must therefore go back and consider $n^{1/2}$ times the gradient of Q^n in more detail. From (17.24) we obtain, dropping the explicit sample-size dependence,

$$n^{1/2}\boldsymbol{g}_j \equiv n^{1/2}\frac{\partial Q}{\partial \theta_j} = 2\left(\frac{1}{n}\sum_{t=1}^{n}\frac{\partial \boldsymbol{F}_t}{\partial \theta_j}\right)\boldsymbol{A}\left(n^{-1/2}\sum_{s=1}^{n}\boldsymbol{F}_s^{\top}\right), \tag{17.28}$$

where everything is evaluated at $(\boldsymbol{y}, \boldsymbol{\theta}_0)$ and, as before, $\boldsymbol{F}_t$ is the tth row of the matrix $\boldsymbol{F}$. Clearly, it is just the last factor of this expression, $n^{-1/2}\sum_{s=1}^{n}\boldsymbol{F}_s^{\top}$, that must be studied in order to obtain the asymptotic distribution, since everything else tends to a well-behaved, nonrandom, probability limit. We will not concern ourselves in this chapter with drifting DGPs, and so it will be enough for present purposes to require that, for each $\mu \in \mathbb{M}$, the vector sequence $\{\boldsymbol{F}_t(y_t, \boldsymbol{\theta}_0)\}$ obeys condition CLT of Definition 4.16. This is now enough for condition (iii) of Theorem 17.2, and so we can conclude that $\hat{\boldsymbol{\theta}}$, the GMM estimator obtained by maximizing (17.13), is asymptotically normal. Note that condition CLT may be stronger than we would like, since it rules out some forms of serial correlation; see Section 17.5.

It remains to compute the asymptotic covariance matrix of $n^{1/2}(\hat{\boldsymbol{\theta}} - \boldsymbol{\theta}_0)$. We begin by considering the asymptotic covariance matrix of (17.28), $\boldsymbol{V}(\mu)$. Let the $l \times l$ matrix $\boldsymbol{\Phi}(\mu)$ be defined so as to have typical element

$$\Phi_{ij}(\mu) \equiv \operatorname*{plim}_{n\to\infty}{}_{\mu}\left(\frac{1}{n}\sum_{t=1}^{n} f_{ti}(y_t, \boldsymbol{\theta}_0) f_{tj}(y_t, \boldsymbol{\theta}_0)\right). \tag{17.29}$$

By CLT, this is the asymptotic covariance matrix of $n^{-1/2}\sum_{t=1}^{n}\boldsymbol{F}_t(y_t, \boldsymbol{\theta}_0)$. Then, given definition (17.23), the asymptotic covariance matrix of (17.28) is

$$\boldsymbol{V}(\mu) = 4\boldsymbol{D}^{\top}(\mu, \boldsymbol{\theta}_0)\boldsymbol{A}_0(\mu)\boldsymbol{\Phi}(\mu)\boldsymbol{A}_0(\mu)\boldsymbol{D}(\mu, \boldsymbol{\theta}_0). \tag{17.30}$$

Next, recall from Theorem 17.2 that the asymptotic covariance matrix of $n^{1/2}(\hat{\boldsymbol{\theta}} - \boldsymbol{\theta}_0)$ is $\mathcal{H}_0^{-1}\boldsymbol{V}_0\mathcal{H}_0^{-1}$ and that, from (17.27), $\mathcal{H}_0 = 2\boldsymbol{D}^{\top}\boldsymbol{A}_0\boldsymbol{D}$. We thus obtain the following result:

$$\boldsymbol{V}\big(n^{1/2}(\hat{\boldsymbol{\theta}} - \boldsymbol{\theta}_0)\big) = \big(\boldsymbol{D}^{\top}\boldsymbol{A}_0\boldsymbol{D}\big)^{-1}\boldsymbol{D}^{\top}\boldsymbol{A}_0\boldsymbol{\Phi}\boldsymbol{A}_0\boldsymbol{D}\big(\boldsymbol{D}^{\top}\boldsymbol{A}_0\boldsymbol{D}\big)^{-1}. \tag{17.31}$$

This expression is not especially simple, although it can often be simplified, as we will see in the next section. It is not hard to estimate $\boldsymbol{V}\big(n^{1/2}(\hat{\boldsymbol{\theta}} - \boldsymbol{\theta}_0)\big)$ consistently; one can simply estimate d_{ij} by

$$\frac{1}{n}\sum_{t=1}^{n}\frac{\partial f_{ti}}{\partial \theta_j}(\boldsymbol{y}, \hat{\boldsymbol{\theta}}), \tag{17.32}$$

$\boldsymbol{A}_0$ by $\boldsymbol{A}(\boldsymbol{y})$, and $\boldsymbol{\Phi}_{ij}$ by expression (17.29) without the probability limit. Although this yields a consistent estimate of (17.30), it is often a very noisy one. We will discuss this issue further in Section 17.5, but it is still far from being completely resolved.

It is interesting to illustrate (17.31) for the case of the IV estimator defined by (17.08). The result will enable us to construct a heteroskedasticity-consistent estimate of the covariance matrix of the latter. We merely have to establish some notational equivalences between the IV case and the more general case discussed above. In the IV case, the elements of the matrix $\boldsymbol{F}$ become $f_{ti} = W_{ti}(y_t - \boldsymbol{X}_t\boldsymbol{\beta})$. Therefore,

$$\boldsymbol{D} = -\operatorname*{plim}_{n\to\infty}\left(\frac{1}{n}\boldsymbol{W}^\top\boldsymbol{X}\right) \tag{17.33}$$

and

$$\boldsymbol{A}_0 = \operatorname*{plim}_{n\to\infty}\left(\frac{1}{n}\boldsymbol{W}^\top\boldsymbol{W}\right)^{-1}. \tag{17.34}$$

The matrix $\boldsymbol{\Phi}$ is obtained from (17.29):

$$\boldsymbol{\Phi} = \operatorname*{plim}_{n\to\infty}\left(\frac{1}{n}\sum_{t=1}^{n}(y_t - \boldsymbol{X}_t\boldsymbol{\beta})^2\boldsymbol{W}_t^\top\boldsymbol{W}_t\right) = \operatorname*{plim}_{n\to\infty}\left(\frac{1}{n}\boldsymbol{W}^\top\boldsymbol{\Omega}\boldsymbol{W}\right), \tag{17.35}$$

where $\boldsymbol{\Omega}$ is the diagonal matrix with typical element $E(y_t - \boldsymbol{X}_t\boldsymbol{\beta})^2$. By substituting (17.33), (17.34), and (17.35) into (17.31), we obtain the following expression for the asymptotic covariance matrix of the IV estimator:

$$\operatorname*{plim}_{n\to\infty}\left(\left(\frac{1}{n}\boldsymbol{X}^\top\boldsymbol{P}_W\boldsymbol{X}\right)^{-1}\frac{1}{n}\boldsymbol{X}^\top\boldsymbol{P}_W\boldsymbol{\Omega}\boldsymbol{P}_W\boldsymbol{X}\left(\frac{1}{n}\boldsymbol{X}^\top\boldsymbol{P}_W\boldsymbol{X}\right)^{-1}\right). \tag{17.36}$$

The matrix (17.36) is clearly analogous for IV estimation to (16.08) for NLS estimation: It provides the asymptotic covariance matrix in the presence of heteroskedasticity of unknown form. Thus we see that HCCMEs of the sort discussed in Section 16.3 are available for the IV estimator. One can use any of the inconsistent estimators $\hat{\boldsymbol{\Omega}}$ suggested there in order to obtain a consistent estimator of $\operatorname{plim}\big(n^{-1}\boldsymbol{X}^\top\boldsymbol{P}_W\boldsymbol{\Omega}\boldsymbol{P}_W\boldsymbol{X}\big)$.

Readers may reasonably wonder why we have obtained a covariance matrix robust *only* to heteroskedasticity and not also to serial correlation of the error terms. The answer is that the covariance matrix $\boldsymbol{V}$ of (17.30) is valid only if condition CLT is satisfied by the contributions to the empirical moments. That condition will *not* be satisfied if the error terms have an arbitrary pattern of correlation among themselves. In Section 17.5, we will discuss methods for dealing with serial correlation, but these will take us out of the asymptotic framework we have used up to now.

17.3 EFFICIENT GMM ESTIMATORS

It is not completely straightforward to answer the question of whether GMM estimators are asymptotically efficient, since a number of separate issues are involved. The first issue was raised at the beginning of the last section, in connection with estimation by instrumental variables. We saw there that, for a given set of empirical moments $\boldsymbol{W}^\top(\boldsymbol{y}-\boldsymbol{X}\boldsymbol{\beta})$, a whole family of estimators can be generated by different choices of the weighting matrix $\boldsymbol{A}(\boldsymbol{y})$ used to construct a quadratic form from the moments. Asymptotically, the most efficient of these estimators is obtained by choosing $\boldsymbol{A}(\boldsymbol{y})$ such that it tends to a nonrandom probability limit proportional to the inverse of the limiting covariance matrix of the empirical moments, suitably weighted by an appropriate power of the sample size n. This turns out to be true quite generally, as we now show.

Theorem 17.3. A Necessary Condition for Efficiency

A necessary condition for the estimator obtained by minimizing the quadratic form (17.13) to be asymptotically efficient is that it should be asymptotically equal to the estimator defined by minimizing (17.13) with $\boldsymbol{A}(\boldsymbol{y})$ independent of $\boldsymbol{y}$ and equal to the inverse of the asymptotic covariance matrix of the empirical moments $n^{-1/2}\boldsymbol{F}^\top(\boldsymbol{\theta})\boldsymbol{\iota}$.

Note that, when the necessary condition holds, the form of the asymptotic covariance matrix of the GMM estimator $\hat{\boldsymbol{\theta}}$ becomes much simpler. For arbitrary limiting weighting matrix $\boldsymbol{A}_0$, that matrix was given by (17.31). If the necessary condition is satisfied, then $\boldsymbol{A}_0$ in (17.31) may be replaced by the inverse of $\boldsymbol{\Phi}$, which, according to its definition (17.29), is the asymptotic covariance of the empirical moments. Substituting $\boldsymbol{A}_0 = \boldsymbol{\Phi}^{-1}$ into (17.31) gives the simple result that

$$\boldsymbol{V}\big(n^{1/2}(\hat{\boldsymbol{\theta}}-\boldsymbol{\theta}_0)\big) = \big(\boldsymbol{D}^\top\boldsymbol{\Phi}^{-1}\boldsymbol{D}\big)^{-1}.$$

Theorem 17.3 will be proved if we can show that, for all symmetric, positive definite matrices $\boldsymbol{A}_0$, the difference

$$\big(\boldsymbol{D}^\top\boldsymbol{A}_0\boldsymbol{D}\big)^{-1}\boldsymbol{D}^\top\boldsymbol{A}_0\boldsymbol{\Phi}\boldsymbol{A}_0\boldsymbol{D}\big(\boldsymbol{D}^\top\boldsymbol{A}_0\boldsymbol{D}\big)^{-1} - \big(\boldsymbol{D}^\top\boldsymbol{\Phi}^{-1}\boldsymbol{D}\big)^{-1} \tag{17.37}$$

is positive semidefinite. To show this, we rewrite (17.37) as

$$\big(\boldsymbol{D}^\top\boldsymbol{A}_0\boldsymbol{D}\big)^{-1}\boldsymbol{D}^\top\boldsymbol{A}_0\Big(\boldsymbol{\Phi}-\boldsymbol{D}\big(\boldsymbol{D}^\top\boldsymbol{\Phi}^{-1}\boldsymbol{D}\big)^{-1}\boldsymbol{D}^\top\Big)\boldsymbol{A}_0\boldsymbol{D}\big(\boldsymbol{D}^\top\boldsymbol{A}_0\boldsymbol{D}\big)^{-1}. \tag{17.38}$$

Since the matrix $\boldsymbol{D}^\top\boldsymbol{A}_0\boldsymbol{D}$ is nonsingular, (17.38) is positive definite if the matrix in large parentheses is. Since $\boldsymbol{\Phi}$ is a positive definite, symmetric $l\times l$ matrix, we can find another positive definite, symmetric $l\times l$ matrix $\boldsymbol{\Psi}$ such that $\boldsymbol{\Psi}^2 = \boldsymbol{\Phi}^{-1}$. In terms of $\boldsymbol{\Psi}$, the matrix in large parentheses becomes

$$\boldsymbol{\Psi}^{-1}\big(\mathbf{I}-\boldsymbol{P}_{\Psi D}\big)\boldsymbol{\Psi}^{-1} = \boldsymbol{\Psi}^{-1}\boldsymbol{M}_{\Psi D}\boldsymbol{\Psi}^{-1}, \tag{17.39}$$

where $P_{\Psi D}$ and $M_{\Psi D}$ are, as the notation suggests, the orthogonal projections onto the space spanned by columns of the $l \times k$ matrix ΨD and its orthogonal complement, respectively. We see that (17.39) is indeed a positive semidefinite matrix, which proves Theorem 17.3.

Theorem 17.3 can often be reinterpreted in terms of **optimal instruments** or **optimal weights**, because the first-order conditions for a minimum of a criterion function constructed with an optimal weighting matrix look just like empirical moment conditions. If there are k parameters to estimate, there will be precisely k first-order conditions. Thus a model that was originally overidentified can be made to look as though it were just identified. Consider the asymptotic criterion function $m^\top(\theta)\Phi^{-1}m(\theta)$ constructed using the optimal asymptotic weighting matrix Φ^{-1}. The first-order conditions for a minimum are given by the k components of the equation

$$D^\top(\theta)\Phi^{-1}m(\theta) = \mathbf{0}. \tag{17.40}$$

Suppose we can find a consistent estimator $\hat{\Phi}$ such that

$$\operatorname*{plim}_{n\to\infty}{}_{\mu}\, \hat{\Phi} = \Phi(\mu).$$

If $D_t(y, \theta)$ denotes the $l \times k$ matrix with typical element $\partial f_{ti}(y_t, \theta)/\partial\theta_j$, (17.23) implies that

$$\operatorname*{plim}_{n\to\infty}{}_{\mu} \left(\frac{1}{n}\sum_{t=1}^{n} D_t(y, \theta)\right) = D(\theta).$$

Therefore, using these two equations and (17.15), the empirical counterpart of (17.40) is seen to be

$$\left(\frac{1}{n}\sum_{t=1}^{n} D_t^\top(y, \theta)\right)\hat{\Phi}^{-1}\left(\frac{1}{n}\sum_{t=1}^{n} F_t(y, \theta)\right). \tag{17.41}$$

The empirical moments (17.41) are readily seen to constitute a set of k linear combinations of the original empirical moments $n^{-1}\sum_{t=1}^{n} F_t$. Setting them equal to zero gives k equations for k unknowns, and the solution of these equations is the GMM estimator obtained by minimizing the quadratic form in the empirical moments constructed with an optimal weighting matrix. We may call the moments (17.41) the **optimal moments** associated with the original set. By means of some examples, we will see how these optimal moments can in many instances serve to define optimal instruments or weights.

Consider first the case of the IV estimator when there are more instruments than regressors. The first-order conditions for the minimization of the criterion function (17.08) are

$$X^\top P_W(y - X\beta) = \mathbf{0}. \tag{17.42}$$

These can be solved to yield the IV (or 2SLS) estimator

$$\tilde{\boldsymbol{\beta}} \equiv \left(\boldsymbol{X}^\top \boldsymbol{P}_W \boldsymbol{X}\right)^{-1} \boldsymbol{X}^\top \boldsymbol{P}_W \boldsymbol{y}, \tag{17.43}$$

which is the same as the *simple* IV estimator obtained by using the instruments $\boldsymbol{P}_W \boldsymbol{X}$. Thus using the whole matrix of l instruments $\boldsymbol{W}$ in an optimal fashion is equivalent to using the k instruments which are the columns of the matrix $\boldsymbol{P}_W \boldsymbol{X}$.

A more interesting example is provided by the IV estimator in the presence of heteroskedasticity of unknown form. In the last section, we showed how to construct an HCCME for the IV estimator (17.43) based on (17.36). When there is heteroskedasticity, however, the estimator (17.43) no longer satisfies the necessary condition for asymptotic efficiency. We can construct an estimator that does satisfy it by starting from the moment conditions (17.05). Let $\boldsymbol{\Omega}$ be a diagonal $n \times n$ matrix with typical element $\Omega_{tt} = E(u_t^2)$, where $u_t = y_t - \boldsymbol{X}_t \boldsymbol{\beta}$. Then the covariance matrix of the empirical moments in (17.05) is simply $\boldsymbol{W}^\top \boldsymbol{\Omega} \boldsymbol{W}$. Thus a criterion function that satisfies the necessary condition for efficiency is

$$(\boldsymbol{y} - \boldsymbol{X}\boldsymbol{\beta})^\top \boldsymbol{W} \left(\boldsymbol{W}^\top \boldsymbol{\Omega} \boldsymbol{W}\right)^{-1} \boldsymbol{W}^\top (\boldsymbol{y} - \boldsymbol{X}\boldsymbol{\beta}).$$

The first-order conditions for a minimum of this function are

$$\boldsymbol{X}^\top \boldsymbol{W} \left(\boldsymbol{W}^\top \boldsymbol{\Omega} \boldsymbol{W}\right)^{-1} \boldsymbol{W}^\top (\boldsymbol{y} - \boldsymbol{X}\boldsymbol{\beta}) = \boldsymbol{0},$$

which lead to the estimator

$$\hat{\boldsymbol{\beta}} = \left(\boldsymbol{X}^\top \boldsymbol{W} (\boldsymbol{W}^\top \boldsymbol{\Omega} \boldsymbol{W})^{-1} \boldsymbol{W}^\top \boldsymbol{X}\right)^{-1} \boldsymbol{X}^\top \boldsymbol{W} (\boldsymbol{W}^\top \boldsymbol{\Omega} \boldsymbol{W})^{-1} \boldsymbol{W}^\top \boldsymbol{y}. \tag{17.44}$$

The optimal instruments that produce this estimator are the columns of the matrix $\boldsymbol{W}(\boldsymbol{W}^\top \boldsymbol{\Omega} \boldsymbol{W})^{-1} \boldsymbol{W}^\top \boldsymbol{X}$. Here we have implicitly assumed that $\boldsymbol{\Omega}$ is known. In the more realistic case in which it is unknown, we can estimate $\boldsymbol{W}^\top \boldsymbol{\Omega} \boldsymbol{W}$ consistently in various ways, using the inconsistent estimators of $\boldsymbol{\Omega}$ discussed in Section 16.3.

Operational versions of the estimator (17.44) were first proposed by Cragg (1983), for the case in which the regressors $\boldsymbol{X}$ can be treated as instruments, and by Cumby, Huizinga, and Obstfeld (1983) for the more general case. The latter authors actually considered a more complicated estimator that allowed for serial correlation as well as heteroskedasticity and called it two-step two-stage least squares; this estimator will be discussed in Section 17.5. We will refer to (17.44) with $\boldsymbol{\Omega}$ replaced by an $n \times n$ diagonal matrix with squared 2SLS residuals on the diagonal by the acronym **H2SLS**, because it is a modified version of the conventional 2SLS estimator that attains greater efficiency in the presence of heteroskedasticity of unknown form. By the same token, we will refer to Cragg's estimator, which uses OLS residuals to estimate $\boldsymbol{\Omega}$, as **HOLS**.

It is illuminating to look at these estimators a bit more closely. If the regressors are the only available instruments, then setting $\boldsymbol{W} = \boldsymbol{X}$ in (17.44) gives nothing more than the usual OLS estimator. Cragg therefore suggests using powers or cross-products of the regressors as additional instruments. If not all of the regressors can serve as instruments and there are only enough other instruments for the model to be just identified, then $\boldsymbol{W}^\top\boldsymbol{X}$ is a square nonsingular matrix and (17.44) reduces to the simple IV estimator. In both cases, then, (17.44) may well be inefficient. This allows us to see that the necessary condition for efficiency of Theorem 17.3 is *not* sufficient.

In the overidentified case, HOLS will be more efficient than the OLS estimator and H2SLS will be more efficient than the usual IV estimator, but neither will be efficient in the absolute sense in general. One exception to this remark arises if there is no heteroskedasticity and $\boldsymbol{\Omega}$ is just a scalar matrix. Setting $\boldsymbol{\Omega} = \sigma^2\mathbf{I}$ in (17.44) gives the ordinary IV estimator (17.43). When (17.44) is computed using some suitable $\hat{\boldsymbol{\Omega}}$, it will differ numerically from (17.43) when the error terms actually are homoskedastic, although the difference will vanish asymptotically. When there is heteroskedasticity, we see that if the regressors can be treated as instruments, the existence of *other* valid instruments can lead to improved efficiency. Even if not all the regressors can be used as instruments, it is possible to achieve an efficiency gain by use of (17.44) instead of (17.43). We will look further at the source of this efficiency gain in the next section, when we consider conditional moment conditions.

A few remarks are in order about cases in which GMM estimators are inefficient even when an optimal weighting matrix is used. It turns out that the efficiency or inefficiency of a GMM estimator depends on the underlying model $\mathbb{M}$ for which it is used. Very loosely speaking, we may say that the less restricted is $\mathbb{M}$, the more likely is the GMM estimator to be efficient. From an opposite perspective, the more restrictions are involved in the specification of $\mathbb{M}$, the more likely is it that an estimator more efficient than the GMM estimator can be found.

An example may help in understanding this point. Consider a parametrized model $(\mathbb{M}_1, \boldsymbol{\theta})$ suitable for estimation by maximum likelihood, with a one-to-one parameter-defining mapping $\boldsymbol{\theta}\colon \mathbb{M}_1 \to \Theta \subseteq \mathbb{R}^k$. The ML estimator can be treated as a GMM estimator in which the empirical moments are the components of the score vector $\boldsymbol{g}(\boldsymbol{\theta})$. The asymptotic efficiency of maximum likelihood then implies that of GMM. Now suppose that $\boldsymbol{\theta}$ is restricted to satisfy $\boldsymbol{\theta}_2 = \mathbf{0}$, where $\boldsymbol{\theta}_2$ is an r-dimensional subvector of $\boldsymbol{\theta} \equiv [\boldsymbol{\theta}_1 \,\vdots\, \boldsymbol{\theta}_2]$. These restrictions define a new, restricted model, which we may denote by $\mathbb{M}_0$, with $\mathbb{M}_0 \subset \mathbb{M}_1$. Using maximum likelihood, the restricted model $\mathbb{M}_0$ can be estimated in exactly the same way as the unrestricted model $\mathbb{M}_1$, and the ML estimator for the former is generally more efficient than the ML estimator for the latter.

In the GMM framework, things may be expressed somewhat differently. The k components of the score vector $\boldsymbol{g}(\boldsymbol{\theta})$ provide k moment conditions which should be satisfied by all DGPs in $\mathbb{M}_1$, including those in $\mathbb{M}_0$. If an investigator has reasons for choosing $\mathbb{M}_0$ as the model to study, then presumably the moment conditions should be evaluated with $\boldsymbol{\theta}_2$ set equal to zero, but even so, there are k conditions for only $k - r$ parameters; in other words, there are overidentifying restrictions. The ML procedure ignores these and instead selects just $k - r$ of these conditions, namely, those given by the derivatives of the loglikelihood function with respect to $\boldsymbol{\theta}_1$. The theory of ML estimation tells us that this choice is asymptotically efficient, and so if precisely those conditions were used in a just identified GMM procedure, it too would be efficient.

However, the usual GMM procedure would be to construct a quadratic form from all the components of the gradient and an estimate of its covariance matrix, which could be any suitable estimate of the information matrix. Denoting this estimate by $\hat{\mathfrak{I}}$, we obtain

$$\boldsymbol{g}^{\top}(\boldsymbol{\theta}_1, \mathbf{0})\,\hat{\mathfrak{I}}^{-1}\boldsymbol{g}(\boldsymbol{\theta}_1, \mathbf{0}). \tag{17.45}$$

Minimizing this expression with respect to $\boldsymbol{\theta}_1$ will, in general, lead to a different set of estimates from those yielded by maximizing the restricted loglikelihood function, but it can be seen that the two sets of estimates are asymptotically equivalent. (Showing this is a good exercise.) This means that the GMM estimator is asymptotically efficient *provided* the overidentifying restrictions are used.

The parameters $\boldsymbol{\theta}$ can in many cases be identified by other sets of the k moment conditions than those provided by the derivatives of the loglikelihood function with respect to $\boldsymbol{\theta}_1$. In general, one may select any $k - r$ conditions and solve them to obtain different GMM estimates, which will not be asymptotically efficient. (Showing this is also a good exercise.) It is even possible to select a number of conditions between $k - r$ and k, form a quadratic form with the inverse of the appropriate block of the information matrix estimate, and minimize it to obtain yet another set of inefficient GMM estimates.

The conclusion to be drawn from all this is that there exist multiple possibilities for a set of moment conditions capable of identifying the parameters of the model $\mathbb{M}_0$, with or without overidentifying restrictions. Only some of these possibilities lead to asymptotically efficient estimates. A proper discussion of these issues would lead us far afield. Although there is no trouble understanding just what is going on in the ML context, a rigorous treatment for the more general case seems still to be lacking, although a number of special cases are well understood. Interested readers may consult Chamberlain (1986, 1987), Hansen (1985), and Hansen, Heaton, and Ogaki (1988). Fortunately, things are simpler in the case of models defined by conditional moment conditions, which we go on to discuss in the next section.

17.4 Estimation with Conditional Moments

The moment conditions that we have used up to now have all been unconditional ones. In practice, however, it is the exception rather than the rule for an econometric model to be specified solely in terms of unconditional moments. In the literature on rational expectations models, for instance, economic theory requires that agents' errors of prediction should be orthogonal to all variables in their information sets at the time the predictions are made. In the simple context of the linear regression model $\boldsymbol{y} = \boldsymbol{X\beta} + \boldsymbol{u}$, it is usual to assume not only that an error term u_t is uncorrelated with the regressors $\boldsymbol{X}$ but also that its expectation *conditional* on the regressors is zero, which carries the additional implication that it is uncorrelated with any function of the regressors. In a time-series context, it is very common to suppose that the error u_t has expectation zero conditional on all the past regressors as well as on the current ones.

Formally, it is easy to write down a set of parameter-defining equations in terms of conditional moments. Often there is only one such equation, which may be written as

$$E\big(f_t(y_t, \boldsymbol{\theta}) \,|\, \Omega_t\big) = 0 \quad \text{for all } t = 1, \ldots, n, \tag{17.46}$$

where Ω_t is the information set for observation t. We will make the simplifying assumption that $\Omega_t \subseteq \Omega_s$ for $t < s$. In (17.46) we are interpreting $f_t(y_t, \boldsymbol{\theta})$ as some sort of error, such as a prediction error made by economic agents. The case of IV estimation of a linear regression model provides a simple example. In that case, (17.46) is interpreted as saying that the errors, just one per observation, are orthogonal to the information set defined by the set of instruments. It would be possible for there to be several parameter-defining equations like (17.46), as in the case of a multivariate regression model, but for simplicity we will in this section assume that there is just one.

In theory, there is no identification problem posed by the fact that there is only a single parameter-defining equation, because there is an infinite number of possible instruments in the sort of information set we consider. In practice, of course, one has to choose a finite number of these in order to set up a criterion function for GMM estimation. Most of this section will be taken up with establishing some results that affect this choice. First, we will demonstrate that the more instruments are used, the more precise is the GMM estimator. Next we show that, despite this, the asymptotic covariance matrices of the GMM estimators which can be constructed from instruments contained in the information sets Ω_t are bounded below. The lower bound, which is akin to the Cramér-Rao lower bound introduced in Chapter 8, is often called the **GMM bound**. In theory at least, there exists an optimal set of instruments which allows the GMM bound to be achieved, and the optimal instruments can in some cases be computed or estimated.

We construct a set of l instruments $\boldsymbol{w}_1, \ldots, \boldsymbol{w}_l$ that can be grouped into an $n \times l$ matrix $\boldsymbol{W}$ such that $W_{ti} \in \Omega_t$ for all $t = 1, \ldots, n$ and $i = 1, \ldots, l$. We require of course that $l \geq k$, where the parameter vector $\hat{\boldsymbol{\theta}}$ has k elements. The empirical moment conditions that we use for estimation can be expressed as

$$\boldsymbol{W}^{\top}\boldsymbol{f}(\boldsymbol{\theta}) = \mathbf{0}, \tag{17.47}$$

where $\boldsymbol{f}$ is an n-vector with typical component f_t. If $l = k$, the estimator $\hat{\boldsymbol{\theta}}$ is obtained by solving the k equations (17.47). If $l > k$, it is obtained by minimizing the quadratic form constructed from the components of the left-hand side of (17.47) and an estimate of their covariance matrix. Let $\boldsymbol{\Omega}$ denote the covariance matrix of the f_t's. Thus, if the DGP is denoted by μ and the true parameter vector by $\boldsymbol{\theta}_0$,

$$\Omega_{ts} = E_{\mu}\big(f_t(\boldsymbol{\theta}_0)f_s(\boldsymbol{\theta}_0) \,|\, \Omega_t\big) \quad \text{for all } t \leq s.$$

Then the conditional covariance matrix of the empirical moments in (17.47) is $\boldsymbol{\Phi} \equiv \boldsymbol{W}^{\top}\boldsymbol{\Omega}\boldsymbol{W}$.

In the usual case, with $l > k$, the criterion function used for obtaining parameter estimates is

$$\boldsymbol{f}(\boldsymbol{\theta})^{\top}\boldsymbol{W}\big(\boldsymbol{W}^{\top}\boldsymbol{\Omega}\boldsymbol{W}\big)^{-1}\boldsymbol{W}^{\top}\boldsymbol{f}(\boldsymbol{\theta}).$$

The asymptotic covariance matrix of this estimator is given by the probability limit of $(\boldsymbol{D}^{\top}\boldsymbol{\Phi}^{-1}\boldsymbol{D})^{-1}$, where

$$\boldsymbol{D}_{ij} = \operatorname*{plim}_{n\to\infty}\left(\frac{1}{n}\sum_{t=1}^{n} W_{ti}\frac{\partial f_t}{\partial \theta_j}\right). \tag{17.48}$$

Let $\boldsymbol{J}(\boldsymbol{y}, \boldsymbol{\theta})$ denote the $n \times k$ matrix with typical element $\partial f_t(y_t, \boldsymbol{\theta})/\partial\theta_j$.[1] Then the right-hand side of (17.48) is the limit of $n^{-1}\boldsymbol{W}^{\top}\boldsymbol{J}$. Thus the asymptotic covariance matrix of $n^{1/2}(\hat{\boldsymbol{\theta}} - \boldsymbol{\theta}_0)$ reduces to the limit of

$$\left(\left(\tfrac{1}{n}\boldsymbol{J}^{\top}\boldsymbol{W}\right)\left(\tfrac{1}{n}\boldsymbol{W}^{\top}\boldsymbol{\Omega}\boldsymbol{W}\right)^{-1}\left(\tfrac{1}{n}\boldsymbol{W}^{\top}\boldsymbol{J}\right)\right)^{-1}. \tag{17.49}$$

The first result about how to choose the instruments $\boldsymbol{W}$ optimally is simple and intuitive. It is that if we increase the number of instruments, the limiting covariance matrix (17.49) cannot increase. Imagine that instead of the empirical moment conditions (17.47) we use a set of linear combinations of them. That is, we replace (17.47) by

$$\boldsymbol{B}^{\top}\boldsymbol{W}^{\top}\boldsymbol{f}(\boldsymbol{\theta}) = \mathbf{0},$$

[1] The notation $\boldsymbol{J}$ was chosen because the matrix is the *Jacobian* of $\boldsymbol{f}$ with respect to $\boldsymbol{\theta}$ and because $\boldsymbol{F}$ was previously used to denote something else.

for some $l \times p$ matrix $\boldsymbol{B}$, where $p \leq l$. It is easy to see that this corresponds to replacing $\boldsymbol{D}$ by $\boldsymbol{B}^{\top}\boldsymbol{D}$ and $\boldsymbol{\Phi}$ by $\boldsymbol{B}^{\top}\boldsymbol{\Phi}\boldsymbol{B}$. Consider the difference

$$\boldsymbol{D}^{\top}\boldsymbol{\Phi}^{-1}\boldsymbol{D} - \boldsymbol{D}^{\top}\boldsymbol{B}\big(\boldsymbol{B}^{\top}\boldsymbol{\Phi}\boldsymbol{B}\big)^{-1}\boldsymbol{B}^{\top}\boldsymbol{D}$$

between the inverses of the $k \times k$ asymptotic covariance matrices corresponding to the instruments $\boldsymbol{W}$ and $\boldsymbol{W}\boldsymbol{B}$, respectively. If, as before, we denote by $\boldsymbol{\Psi}$ a symmetric $l \times l$ matrix such that $\boldsymbol{\Psi}^2 = \boldsymbol{\Phi}^{-1}$, this difference is

$$\boldsymbol{D}^{\top}\boldsymbol{\Psi}\Big(\mathbf{I} - \boldsymbol{\Psi}^{-1}\boldsymbol{B}\big(\boldsymbol{B}^{\top}\boldsymbol{\Psi}^{-2}\boldsymbol{B}\big)^{-1}\boldsymbol{B}^{\top}\boldsymbol{\Psi}^{-1}\Big)\boldsymbol{\Psi}\boldsymbol{D}. \tag{17.50}$$

This matrix is clearly positive semidefinite, because the matrix in large parentheses is the orthogonal projection off the columns of $\boldsymbol{\Psi}^{-1}\boldsymbol{B}$. For any two symmetric, positive definite matrices $\boldsymbol{P}$ and $\boldsymbol{Q}$ of the same dimension, $\boldsymbol{P} - \boldsymbol{Q}$ is positive semidefinite if and only if $\boldsymbol{Q}^{-1} - \boldsymbol{P}^{-1}$ is positive semidefinite (see Appendix A). Thus the fact that (17.50) is positive semidefinite establishes our first result.

This result might seem to suggest that one should always use as many instruments as possible in order to get as efficient estimates as possible. Such a conclusion is generally wrong, however. Recall the discussion in Section 7.5, illustrated by Figure 7.1. There we saw that, in the ordinary IV context, there is a trade-off between asymptotic efficiency and bias in finite samples. The same trade-off arises in the GMM case as well. Using a large number of overidentifying restrictions may lead to a smaller asymptotic covariance matrix, but the estimates may be seriously biased. Another argument against the use of too many instruments is simply that there are inevitably diminishing returns, on account of the existence of the GMM bound.

The second result shows how to choose the instruments $\boldsymbol{W}$ optimally. It says that if we set $\boldsymbol{W} = \boldsymbol{\Omega}^{-1}\boldsymbol{J}$ in (17.47), then the asymptotic covariance matrix that results is smaller than the one given by any other choice. From (17.49) it then follows that the GMM bound for the asymptotic covariance matrix is $\operatorname{plim}\,(n^{-1}\boldsymbol{J}^{\top}\boldsymbol{\Omega}^{-1}\boldsymbol{J})^{-1}$. Unfortunately, as we will see, this result is not always useful in practice.

The proof is very simple. As with the first result, it is easiest to work with the inverses of the relevant covariance matrices. Let the symmetric $n \times n$ matrix $\boldsymbol{\Upsilon}$ be defined so that $\boldsymbol{\Upsilon}^2 \equiv \boldsymbol{\Omega}$. Then, suppressing limits and factors of n for the moment, we see that

$$\begin{aligned} &\boldsymbol{J}^{\top}\boldsymbol{\Omega}^{-1}\boldsymbol{J} - \boldsymbol{J}^{\top}\boldsymbol{W}\left(\boldsymbol{W}^{\top}\boldsymbol{\Omega}\boldsymbol{W}\right)^{-1}\boldsymbol{W}^{\top}\boldsymbol{J} \\ &\quad = \boldsymbol{J}^{\top}\boldsymbol{\Upsilon}^{-1}\Big(\mathbf{I} - \boldsymbol{\Upsilon}\boldsymbol{W}\left(\boldsymbol{W}^{\top}\boldsymbol{\Upsilon}^{2}\boldsymbol{W}\right)^{-1}\boldsymbol{W}^{\top}\boldsymbol{\Upsilon}\Big)\boldsymbol{\Upsilon}^{-1}\boldsymbol{J}. \end{aligned} \tag{17.51}$$

Since the matrix in large parentheses is the orthogonal projection off the columns of $\boldsymbol{\Upsilon}\boldsymbol{W}$, this expression is positive semidefinite, and the second result is established.

It is perfectly possible that the tth row $\boldsymbol{J}_t$ of the matrix $\boldsymbol{J}$ may not belong to the information set Ω_t. In this case, we must not ignore the limits and factors of n in (17.51). Each of the matrix expressions then tends to a nonstochastic probability limit, which by the law of large numbers is the limit of the (conditional) expectations of the matrices. Consequently, $\boldsymbol{J}_t$ should when necessary be replaced by $E(\boldsymbol{J}_t \mid \Omega_t)$.

Notice that $\boldsymbol{\Omega}^{-1}\boldsymbol{J}$ is a matrix of exactly k instruments. We have therefore shown that, in the context of a model with conditional moment conditions, it is possible to choose instruments such that, although there are no overidentifying restrictions, an asymptotically efficient estimator is obtained. The asymptotic covariance matrix associated with this estimator is $\operatorname{plim}(n^{-1}\boldsymbol{J}^{\top}\boldsymbol{\Omega}^{-1}\boldsymbol{J})$. In practice, it may or may not be easy to compute or to estimate the optimal instruments. Clearly, the matrix $\boldsymbol{J}(\boldsymbol{\theta})$ can be computed directly as a function of $\boldsymbol{\theta}$ by differentiating the empirical moments. But then one needs some estimate of $\boldsymbol{\theta}$, unless the moments are linear with respect to $\boldsymbol{\theta}$. A possible strategy is first to obtain a consistent but inefficient estimate and use it to define approximately optimal instruments, which will then lead to asymptotically efficient estimates. If the initial estimate is not very accurate, it may well be desirable to use an iterative procedure by which successive estimates define successively closer approximations to the optimal instruments.

To obtain optimal instruments, it is also necessary to estimate the matrix $\boldsymbol{\Omega}$ consistently, at least up to a multiplicative factor. If the f_t's are homoskedastic and serially independent, one may of course simply use an identity matrix for $\boldsymbol{\Omega}$. If they follow some known pattern of heteroskedasticity and/or autocorrelation, with parameters that can be estimated consistently, then a two-step or iterative procedure can be used. But if there can be arbitrary patterns of heteroskedasticity or autocorrelation, the matter is, if not quite hopeless, at least very difficult to treat. Usually, optimal instruments cannot be computed, and one must make do with less than optimal instruments.

Let us see how the results of this section can be applied to a simple case. Consider a linear regression model for which information sets Ω_t are known for each observation. Then the moment condition that defines the parameter vector $\boldsymbol{\beta}$ is $E(y_t - \boldsymbol{X}_t\boldsymbol{\beta} \mid \Omega_t) = 0$. In terms of our general notation, $f_t = y_t - \boldsymbol{X}_t\boldsymbol{\beta}$, and the matrix $\boldsymbol{J}$ is simply equal to $\boldsymbol{X}$. Similarly, the matrix $\boldsymbol{\Omega}$ is just the covariance matrix of the f_t's, that is, of the error terms. Thus, provided that $\boldsymbol{X}_t \in \Omega_t$, the optimal instruments are the columns of $\boldsymbol{\Omega}^{-1}\boldsymbol{X}$. The empirical moment conditions become

$$\boldsymbol{X}^{\top}\boldsymbol{\Omega}^{-1}(\boldsymbol{y} - \boldsymbol{X}\boldsymbol{\beta}) = \boldsymbol{0},$$

and we see, as we could have expected, that the efficient estimator is the GLS estimator.

This example should make clear at least some of the difficulties that may attend the computation of optimal instruments. As we saw in Section 9.5, if the form of the matrix $\boldsymbol{\Omega}$ is known and depends on a vector of parameters that can be consistently estimated by an auxiliary procedure, feasible GLS yields estimates asymptotically equivalent to those of a true GLS procedure. Similarly, in the GMM context, if the form of $\boldsymbol{\Omega}$ is known, it may be possible to estimate the optimal instruments and thereby obtain asymptotically efficient GMM estimates. However, it is often the case that $\boldsymbol{\Omega}$ is of unknown form and cannot be estimated consistently. We will see how to deal with such cases in the next section.

It is relatively easy to extend the GLS procedure discussed above to the case in which some elements of $\boldsymbol{X}_t$ do not belong to the set Ω_t and instrumental variables must therefore be used. As we saw above, in this case $\boldsymbol{J}_t$ is to be replaced by its expectation conditional on Ω_t in the definition of the optimal instruments, which are therefore the columns of $\boldsymbol{\Omega}^{-1}E(\boldsymbol{X}_t \,|\, \Omega_t)$. In the special case of homoskedastic and serially uncorrelated errors, this result shows us that the best instrumental variables to use are the expectations of the regressors conditional on all variables that are orthogonal to the error terms. In practice, these conditional expectations are not usually available, and one simply has to use whatever instruments are available.

If $\boldsymbol{\Omega}$ is known or can be estimated by a feasible procedure, one can choose some available set of instruments $\boldsymbol{W}$ and form the empirical moment conditions

$$\boldsymbol{W}^\top\boldsymbol{\Omega}^{-1}(\boldsymbol{y} - \boldsymbol{X\beta}) = \boldsymbol{0}. \tag{17.52}$$

There should normally be more instruments than parameters, since the optimal instruments are not available and overidentifying restrictions will therefore improve efficiency. In order to satisfy the necessary condition of Theorem 17.3, the criterion function must make use of the covariance matrix of the left-hand side of (17.52). This is, asymptotically,

$$\operatorname*{plim}_{n\to\infty}\Big(\frac{1}{n}\boldsymbol{W}^\top\boldsymbol{\Omega}^{-1}(\boldsymbol{y} - \boldsymbol{X\beta})(\boldsymbol{y} - \boldsymbol{X\beta})^\top\boldsymbol{\Omega}^{-1}\boldsymbol{W}\Big) = \operatorname*{plim}_{n\to\infty}\Big(\frac{1}{n}\boldsymbol{W}^\top\boldsymbol{\Omega}^{-1}\boldsymbol{W}\Big).$$

The appropriate criterion function is therefore

$$(\boldsymbol{y} - \boldsymbol{X\beta})^\top\boldsymbol{\Omega}^{-1}\boldsymbol{W}\big(\boldsymbol{W}^\top\boldsymbol{\Omega}^{-1}\boldsymbol{W}\big)^{-1}\boldsymbol{W}^\top\boldsymbol{\Omega}^{-1}(\boldsymbol{y} - \boldsymbol{X\beta}),$$

which leads to the first-order conditions

$$\boldsymbol{X}^\top\boldsymbol{\Omega}^{-1}\boldsymbol{W}\big(\boldsymbol{W}^\top\boldsymbol{\Omega}^{-1}\boldsymbol{W}\big)^{-1}\boldsymbol{W}^\top\boldsymbol{\Omega}^{-1}(\boldsymbol{y} - \boldsymbol{X\beta}) = \boldsymbol{0}. \tag{17.53}$$

This equation defines a seemingly complicated estimator. In fact, it can be interpreted quite simply, just as the GLS estimator can, in terms of a transformation matrix $\boldsymbol{\eta}$ such that $\boldsymbol{\eta}^\top\boldsymbol{\eta} = \boldsymbol{\Omega}^{-1}$. Let

$$\boldsymbol{y}^* \equiv \boldsymbol{\eta y}, \quad \boldsymbol{X}^* \equiv \boldsymbol{\eta X}, \quad \text{and} \quad \boldsymbol{Z} \equiv \boldsymbol{\eta W}.$$

Then (17.53) becomes

$$\boldsymbol{X}^{*\top}\boldsymbol{Z}\big(\boldsymbol{Z}^\top\boldsymbol{Z}\big)^{-1}\boldsymbol{Z}^\top(\boldsymbol{y}^* - \boldsymbol{X}^*\boldsymbol{\beta}) = \boldsymbol{X}^{*\top}\boldsymbol{P}_Z\big(\boldsymbol{y}^* - \boldsymbol{X}^*\boldsymbol{\beta}\big) = \boldsymbol{0}.$$

This equation defines an ordinary IV estimator in terms of the transformed variables $\boldsymbol{y}^*$ and $\boldsymbol{X}^*$ and the transformed instruments $\boldsymbol{Z}$. Thus the estimator defined by (17.53) can be calculated with no more difficulty than the GLS estimator. It is appropriate to use it when GLS or feasible GLS would have been appropriate except for possible correlation of the error terms with the regressors.

The estimator defined by (17.53) bears a close resemblance to the H2SLS estimator (17.44) defined in the last section. In fact, replacing $\boldsymbol{W}$ in the latter by $\boldsymbol{\Omega}^{-1}\boldsymbol{W}$ yields the former. The theory developed in this section shows that if it is possible to choose $\boldsymbol{W}$ as the conditional expectations of the regressors $\boldsymbol{X}$ (or linear combinations of them), then the estimator defined by (17.53) is asymptotically efficient, and the H2SLS estimator is not. The advantage of H2SLS is that it can be calculated in the presence of heteroskedasticity of unknown form, since $n^{-1}\boldsymbol{W}^{\top}\boldsymbol{\Omega}\boldsymbol{W}$ can be estimated consistently by use of inconsistent estimators of $\boldsymbol{\Omega}$. (17.53), on the other hand, can be formulated only if $\boldsymbol{\Omega}$ itself can be consistently estimated, because expressions like $n^{-1}\boldsymbol{W}^{\top}\boldsymbol{\Omega}^{-1}\boldsymbol{W}$ and $n^{-1}\boldsymbol{W}^{\top}\boldsymbol{\Omega}^{-1}\boldsymbol{y}$ *cannot* be estimated consistently without a consistent estimate of $\boldsymbol{\Omega}$. Thus both estimators are useful, but in different circumstances.

The concept of the GMM bound was introduced, not under that name, by Hansen (1985), who also provided conditions for optimal instruments. The arguments used in order to derive the bound have a longer history, however, and Hansen traces the history of the search for efficient instruments back as far as Basmann (1957) and Sargan (1958).

17.5 COVARIANCE MATRIX ESTIMATION

In previous sections, we mentioned the difficulties that can arise in estimating covariance matrices in the GMM context. In fact, problems occur at two distinct points: once for the choice of the weighting matrix to be used in constructing a criterion function and again for estimating the asymptotic covariance matrix of the estimates. Fortunately, similar considerations apply to both problems, and so we can consider them together.

Recall from (17.31) that the asymptotic covariance matrix of a GMM estimator computed using a weighting matrix $\boldsymbol{A}_0$ is

$$\big(\boldsymbol{D}^{\top}\boldsymbol{A}_0\boldsymbol{D}\big)^{-1}\boldsymbol{D}^{\top}\boldsymbol{A}_0\boldsymbol{\Phi}\boldsymbol{A}_0\boldsymbol{D}\big(\boldsymbol{D}^{\top}\boldsymbol{A}_0\boldsymbol{D}\big)^{-1},$$

in the notation of Section 17.2. If the necessary condition for efficiency of Theorem 17.3 is to be satisfied, it is required that $\boldsymbol{A}_0 \stackrel{a}{=} \boldsymbol{\Phi}^{-1}$, where $\boldsymbol{\Phi}$ is the $l \times l$ asymptotic covariance matrix of the empirical moments $n^{-1/2}\boldsymbol{F}^{\top}(\boldsymbol{\theta})\boldsymbol{\iota}$ with typical element

$$n^{-1/2}\sum_{t=1}^{n} f_{ti}(y_t, \boldsymbol{\theta}).$$

Thus the problem is to find a consistent estimator $\hat{\boldsymbol{\Phi}}$ of $\boldsymbol{\Phi}$. If we can do so, we can minimize the criterion function

$$\boldsymbol{\iota}^{\top}\boldsymbol{F}(\boldsymbol{\theta})\hat{\boldsymbol{\Phi}}^{-1}\boldsymbol{F}^{\top}(\boldsymbol{\theta})\boldsymbol{\iota}. \tag{17.54}$$

If a typical element of $\hat{\boldsymbol{D}}$ is defined by (17.32), the asymptotic covariance matrix of $\hat{\boldsymbol{\theta}}$ may then be estimated by

$$\frac{1}{n}\big(\hat{\boldsymbol{D}}^{\top}\hat{\boldsymbol{\Phi}}^{-1}\hat{\boldsymbol{D}}\big)^{-1}. \tag{17.55}$$

It is clear that we must proceed in at least two steps, because $\hat{\boldsymbol{\Phi}}$ is to be an estimate of the covariance matrix of the empirical moments *evaluated at the true parameter values*. Thus before $\hat{\boldsymbol{\Phi}}$ can be calculated, it is necessary to have a preliminary consistent estimator of the parameters $\boldsymbol{\theta}$. Since one can use an arbitrary weighting matrix $\boldsymbol{A}_0$ without losing consistency, there are many ways to find this preliminary estimate. Then $\hat{\boldsymbol{\Phi}}$ can be computed, and subsequently, by minimizing (17.54), a new set of parameter estimates can be obtained. If it seems desirable, one may repeat these steps one or more times. In theory, one iteration is enough for asymptotic efficiency but, in practice, the original estimates may be bad enough for several iterations to be advisable.

Our previous definition of $\boldsymbol{\Phi}$, (17.29), was based on the assumption that the empirical moments f_{ti} were serially independent. Since we wish to relax that assumption in this section, it is necessary to make a new definition of $\boldsymbol{\Phi}$, in order that it should still be the asymptotic covariance matrix of the empirical moments. We therefore make the definition:

$$\boldsymbol{\Phi} \equiv \lim_{n\to\infty}\left(\frac{1}{n}\sum_{t=1}^{n}\sum_{s=1}^{n}E_{\mu}\big(\boldsymbol{F}_t^{\top}(y_t,\boldsymbol{\theta}_0)\boldsymbol{F}_s(y_t,\boldsymbol{\theta}_0)\big)\right), \tag{17.56}$$

where $\boldsymbol{F}_t$ is the tth row of the $n \times l$ matrix $\boldsymbol{F}$. Since the DGP μ will remain fixed for what follows, we will drop it from our notation. (17.56) differs from (17.29) in that it allows for any pattern of correlation of the contributions $\boldsymbol{F}_t$ to the empirical moments and remains valid even if no central limit theorem does. It *is* necessary, of course, to assume that the limit in (17.56) exists. Our task now is to find a consistent estimator of (17.56).

The first step is to define the **autocovariances** of the empirical moments as follows:

$$\boldsymbol{\Gamma}(j) = \begin{cases} \displaystyle\frac{1}{n}\sum_{t=j+1}^{n}E\big(\boldsymbol{F}_t^{\top}(\boldsymbol{\theta}_0)\boldsymbol{F}_{t-j}(\boldsymbol{\theta}_0)\big) & \text{for } j \geq 0 \\[2ex] \displaystyle\frac{1}{n}\sum_{t=-j+1}^{n}E\big(\boldsymbol{F}_{t+j}^{\top}(\boldsymbol{\theta}_0)\boldsymbol{F}_t(\boldsymbol{\theta}_0)\big) & \text{for } j < 0. \end{cases} \tag{17.57}$$

In terms of the $l \times l$ matrices $\boldsymbol{\Gamma}(j)$, the right-hand side of (17.56) without the limit becomes

$$\boldsymbol{\Phi}^n \equiv \sum_{j=-n+1}^{n-1} \boldsymbol{\Gamma}(j). \tag{17.58}$$

If there were no correlation between successive observations t, then only $\boldsymbol{\Gamma}(0)$ would be nonzero, and we would have

$$\boldsymbol{\Phi}^n = \boldsymbol{\Gamma}(0) = \frac{1}{n}\sum_{t=1}^{n} E\big(\boldsymbol{F}_t^{\top}(\boldsymbol{\theta}_0)\boldsymbol{F}_t(\boldsymbol{\theta}_0)\big). \tag{17.59}$$

Since the case of serial independence is often of interest, it is worthwhile to examine a couple of concrete examples. Consider the linear regression model $\boldsymbol{y} = \boldsymbol{X\beta} + \boldsymbol{u}$, where $\boldsymbol{X}$ is an $n \times k$ matrix and $\boldsymbol{W}$ is an $n \times k$ instrument matrix. For this model, which is just identified,

$$\boldsymbol{F}_t(\boldsymbol{\beta}) = \boldsymbol{W}_t(y_t - \boldsymbol{X}_t\boldsymbol{\beta}). \tag{17.60}$$

Thus, from (17.59), we obtain

$$\boldsymbol{\Phi}^n = \frac{1}{n}\sum_{t=1}^{n} E(u_t^2)\,\boldsymbol{W}_t^{\top}\boldsymbol{W}_t, \quad u_t \equiv y_t - \boldsymbol{X}_t\boldsymbol{\beta}_0. \tag{17.61}$$

If the true covariance matrix of the error terms $\boldsymbol{u}$ is the diagonal matrix $\boldsymbol{\Omega}$, then we saw in Section 16.3 that $\lim\big(n^{-1}\boldsymbol{W}^{\top}\boldsymbol{\Omega W}\big)$ can be consistently estimated by (17.61) without the expectation and with $\boldsymbol{\beta}_0$ replaced by any consistent estimator $\hat{\boldsymbol{\beta}}$. The estimator defined by the empirical moments (17.60) is the usual simple IV estimator $(\boldsymbol{W}^{\top}\boldsymbol{X})^{-1}\boldsymbol{W}^{\top}\boldsymbol{y}$, and so, by use of (17.33) and (17.31), we see that its asymptotic covariance matrix can be estimated by

$$\Big(\frac{1}{n}\boldsymbol{W}^{\top}\boldsymbol{X}\Big)^{-1}\Big(\frac{1}{n}\boldsymbol{W}^{\top}\hat{\boldsymbol{\Omega}}\boldsymbol{W}\Big)\Big(\frac{1}{n}\boldsymbol{X}^{\top}\boldsymbol{W}\Big)^{-1}, \tag{17.62}$$

where $\hat{\boldsymbol{\Omega}}$ is the diagonal $n \times n$ matrix with typical diagonal element $\hat{u}_t^2$, the square of the tth IV residual. This has the form of a standard HCCME (Section 16.3). If there are more instruments in $\boldsymbol{W}$ than there are regressors in $\boldsymbol{X}$, we can, as in (17.43), simply replace $\boldsymbol{W}$ by $\boldsymbol{P}_W\boldsymbol{X}$. If we make that substitution, then the limit of (17.62) becomes identical to (17.36).

We remarked above that an estimator of $\boldsymbol{\Phi}$ can be used for two distinct purposes: to estimate the covariance matrix for any set of GMM estimates and to estimate the optimal weighting matrix. We have just provided an example of the former, by rederiving the HCCME for the case of IV estimation. We now provide an example of the latter, by rederiving the H2SLS estimator of Section 17.3. Recall that this estimator is generally more efficient than OLS or IV in the presence of heteroskedasticity of unknown form.

The empirical moments are the l components of $\boldsymbol{W}^\top(\boldsymbol{y}-\boldsymbol{X\beta})$, with $l > k$, and our estimate of their asymptotic covariance matrix is $\boldsymbol{W}^\top\hat{\boldsymbol{\Omega}}\boldsymbol{W}$. The inverse of this estimate can be used as the weighting matrix in the criterion function

$$(\boldsymbol{y}-\boldsymbol{X\beta})^\top\boldsymbol{W}\big(\boldsymbol{W}^\top\hat{\boldsymbol{\Omega}}\boldsymbol{W}\big)^{-1}\boldsymbol{W}^\top(\boldsymbol{y}-\boldsymbol{X\beta}).$$

The first-order conditions for a minimum of this criterion function are given by

$$\boldsymbol{X}^\top\boldsymbol{W}\big(\boldsymbol{W}^\top\hat{\boldsymbol{\Omega}}\boldsymbol{W}\big)^{-1}\boldsymbol{W}^\top(\boldsymbol{y}-\boldsymbol{X\beta}) = \mathbf{0},$$

and solving these yields the H2SLS estimator (17.44), with the estimator $\hat{\boldsymbol{\Omega}}$ replacing $\boldsymbol{\Omega}$.

It is tempting to suppose that, just as in the HCCME case, we can estimate the autocovariances (17.57) simply by omitting the expectations in that expression, evaluating the $\boldsymbol{F}_t$'s at some preliminary consistent estimate $\hat{\boldsymbol{\theta}}$, and then substituting the $\hat{\boldsymbol{\Gamma}}(j)$'s thus obtained into (17.58) in order to obtain a suitable estimate of $\boldsymbol{\Phi}$. Unfortunately, life is not so simple. The **sample autocovariance matrix** of order zero, $\hat{\boldsymbol{\Gamma}}(0)$, is just (17.59) without the expectation and evaluated at $\hat{\boldsymbol{\theta}}$. It is a consistent estimator of the true autocovariance matrix of order zero $\boldsymbol{\Gamma}(0)$. But the sample autocovariance matrix $\hat{\boldsymbol{\Gamma}}(j)$ of order j is *not* consistent for the true autocovariance matrix for arbitrary j such that $-n+1 \leq j \leq n-1$. The reason is not hard to find. Suppose for instance that $j = n-2$. Then from (17.57) we see that $\boldsymbol{\Gamma}(j)$, and so also $\hat{\boldsymbol{\Gamma}}(j)$, has only two terms. No conceivable law of large numbers can apply to only two terms, and so $\hat{\boldsymbol{\Gamma}}(j)$ tends to zero as $n \to \infty$ on account of the factor of n^{-1} in the definition.

This observation suggests a way out of the difficulty. We could perhaps reasonably limit our attention to models in which the autocovariance of order j genuinely *does* tend to zero as $j \to \infty$. If the stochastic processes that define a DGP have the *mixing* property of Definition 4.13, for example, it can be shown that the autocovariances would indeed tend to zero. (See the discussion following Definition 4.13.) Then it would seem reasonable to *truncate* the sum in (17.58) by eliminating terms for which $|j|$ is greater than some chosen threshold.

If we denote this threshold by p, then we would have the following estimator for $\boldsymbol{\Phi}$:

$$\hat{\boldsymbol{\Phi}} = \hat{\boldsymbol{\Gamma}}(0) + \sum_{j=1}^{p}\big(\hat{\boldsymbol{\Gamma}}(j) + \hat{\boldsymbol{\Gamma}}(j)^\top\big), \tag{17.63}$$

where we have used the fact that $\boldsymbol{\Gamma}(-j) = \boldsymbol{\Gamma}(j)^\top$, as can readily be seen from the definition (17.57). It is possible to modify (17.63) by introducing a degrees-of-freedom correction in the shape of a factor $n/(n-k)$ motivated by the fact that k parameters have been estimated. Whether this is in fact desirable in finite samples is not something that has been much investigated at the time of writing.

The estimator (17.63) was proposed by Hansen (1982) and White and Domowitz (1984), and was used in some of the earlier published work that employed GMM estimation, such as Hansen and Singleton (1982). From the point of view of theory, it is necessary to let the truncation parameter p, usually referred to as the **lag truncation parameter**, go to infinity at some suitable rate. A typical rate would be $n^{1/4}$, in which case $p = o(n^{1/4})$. This ensures that, for large enough n, all the nonzero $\boldsymbol{\Gamma}(j)$'s are estimated consistently. Unfortunately, this type of result is not of much use in practice, where one typically faces a given, finite n. We will return to this point a little later, and for the meantime suppose simply that we have somehow selected an appropriate value for p.

A much more serious difficulty associated with (17.63) is that, in finite samples, it need not be positive definite or even positive semidefinite. If one is unlucky enough to be working with a data set that yields a nondefinite $\hat{\boldsymbol{\Phi}}$, then (17.63) is unusable. There are numerous ways out of this difficulty. The most widely used was suggested by Newey and West (1987a). It is simply to multiply the $\hat{\boldsymbol{\Gamma}}(j)$'s by a sequence of weights that decrease as $|j|$ increases. Specifically, the estimator that they propose is

$$\hat{\boldsymbol{\Phi}} = \hat{\boldsymbol{\Gamma}}(0) + \sum_{j=1}^{p} \left(1 - \frac{j}{p+1}\right)\left(\hat{\boldsymbol{\Gamma}}(j) + \hat{\boldsymbol{\Gamma}}(j)^{\top}\right). \tag{17.64}$$

It can be seen that the weights $1 - j/(p+1)$ decrease linearly with j from a value of 1 for $\hat{\boldsymbol{\Gamma}}(0)$ by steps of $1/(p+1)$ down to a value of $1/(p+1)$ for $|j| = p$. The use of such a set of weights is clearly compatible with the idea that the impact of the autocovariance of order j diminishes with $|j|$.

We will not attempt even to sketch a proof of the consistency of the Newey-West or similar estimators. We have alluded to the sort of regularity conditions needed for consistency to hold: Basically, the autocovariance matrices of the empirical moments must tend to zero quickly enough as p increases. It would also go well beyond the scope of this book to provide a theoretical justification for the Newey-West estimator. It rests on considerations of the so-called "frequency domain representation" of the $\boldsymbol{F}_t$'s and also of a number of notions associated with nonparametric estimation procedures. Interested readers are referred to Andrews (1991b) for a rather complete treatment of many of the issues. This paper suggests some alternatives to the Newey-West estimator and shows that in some circumstances they are preferable. However, the performance of the Newey-West estimator is never greatly inferior to that of the alternatives. Consequently, its simplicity is much in its favor.

Let us now return to the linear IV model with empirical moments given by $\boldsymbol{W}^{\top}(\boldsymbol{y} - \boldsymbol{X\beta})$. In order to be able to use (17.64), we suppose that the true error terms $u_t \equiv y_t - \boldsymbol{X}_t\boldsymbol{\beta}_0$ satisfy an appropriate mixing condition. Then the sample autocovariance matrices $\hat{\boldsymbol{\Gamma}}(j)$ for $j = 0, \ldots, p$, for some given p, are calculated as follows. A preliminary consistent estimate of $\boldsymbol{\beta}_0$ is first obtained by the ordinary IV procedure. Next, the residuals $\hat{u}_t$ are combined with the instruments in the direct product $\hat{\boldsymbol{V}} \equiv \hat{\boldsymbol{u}} * \boldsymbol{W}$. Then $\hat{\boldsymbol{\Gamma}}(j)$ is n^{-1} times the $l \times l$ matrix of inner products of the columns of $\hat{\boldsymbol{V}}$ with these same columns lagged j times, the initial unobserved elements being replaced by zeros. As we saw above, $\hat{\boldsymbol{\Gamma}}(0)$ is just $n^{-1}\boldsymbol{W}^\top\hat{\boldsymbol{\Omega}}\boldsymbol{W}$, where $\hat{\boldsymbol{\Omega}} = \mathrm{diag}(\hat{u}_t^2)$. Finally, $\hat{\boldsymbol{\Phi}}$ is formed by use of (17.64).

As before, the $\hat{\boldsymbol{\Phi}}$ thus obtained can be used for two purposes. One is to form what is called a **heteroskedasticity and autocorrelation consistent**, or **HAC**, covariance matrix estimator for the ordinary IV estimator. Since the IV estimator is based on the empirical moments $\boldsymbol{W}^\top(\boldsymbol{y} - \boldsymbol{X\beta})$ and the weighting matrix $(\boldsymbol{W}^\top\boldsymbol{W})^{-1}$, as can be seen from (17.09), the HAC covariance matrix estimator is found by applying the formula (17.31) to the present case and using (17.33) and (17.34). We obtain

$$\big(\boldsymbol{X}^\top\boldsymbol{P}_W\boldsymbol{X}\big)^{-1}\boldsymbol{X}^\top\boldsymbol{W}\big(\boldsymbol{W}^\top\boldsymbol{W}\big)^{-1}n\hat{\boldsymbol{\Phi}}\big(\boldsymbol{W}^\top\boldsymbol{W}\big)^{-1}\boldsymbol{W}^\top\boldsymbol{X}\big(\boldsymbol{X}^\top\boldsymbol{P}_W\boldsymbol{X}\big)^{-1}. \tag{17.65}$$

In the simple case in which $\boldsymbol{W} = \boldsymbol{X}$, this rather complicated formula becomes

$$\big(\boldsymbol{X}^\top\boldsymbol{X}\big)^{-1}n\hat{\boldsymbol{\Phi}}\big(\boldsymbol{X}^\top\boldsymbol{X}\big)^{-1}.$$

When there is no serial correlation, implying that $n\hat{\boldsymbol{\Phi}} = \boldsymbol{W}^\top\hat{\boldsymbol{\Omega}}\boldsymbol{W}$, this simplifies to the familiar HCCME (16.15), specialized to the case of a linear regression model. It is a good exercise to see what (17.65) reduces to when there is no serial correlation and $\boldsymbol{W} \neq \boldsymbol{X}$.

More interesting than the HAC covariance matrix estimator is the estimator analogous to the H2SLS estimator, (17.44). For this, instead of using $(\boldsymbol{W}^\top\boldsymbol{W})^{-1}$ as weighting matrix, we use the inverse of $\hat{\boldsymbol{\Phi}}$, calculated in the manner described above by use of the ordinary IV estimator as the preliminary consistent estimator. The criterion function becomes

$$(\boldsymbol{y} - \boldsymbol{X\beta})^\top\boldsymbol{W}\hat{\boldsymbol{\Phi}}^{-1}\boldsymbol{W}^\top(\boldsymbol{y} - \boldsymbol{X\beta}),$$

and the estimator, which is sometimes called **two-step two-stage least squares**, is therefore

$$\hat{\boldsymbol{\beta}} = \big(\boldsymbol{X}^\top\boldsymbol{W}\hat{\boldsymbol{\Phi}}^{-1}\boldsymbol{W}^\top\boldsymbol{X}\big)^{-1}\boldsymbol{X}^\top\boldsymbol{W}\hat{\boldsymbol{\Phi}}^{-1}\boldsymbol{W}^\top\boldsymbol{y}. \tag{17.66}$$

This is very similar to (17.44), in which the matrix $\hat{\boldsymbol{\Phi}}$ is replaced by $\boldsymbol{W}^\top\hat{\boldsymbol{\Omega}}\boldsymbol{W}$. Indeed, in the absence of autocorrelation, $n^{-1}\boldsymbol{W}^\top\hat{\boldsymbol{\Omega}}\boldsymbol{W}$ is the appropriate estimator of $\boldsymbol{\Phi}$. It is easier to obtain an estimate of the asymptotic covariance matrix of (17.66) than of the ordinary IV estimator. It is simply

$$\hat{\boldsymbol{V}}(\hat{\boldsymbol{\beta}}) = \big(\boldsymbol{X}^\top\boldsymbol{W}\hat{\boldsymbol{\Phi}}^{-1}\boldsymbol{W}^\top\boldsymbol{X}\big)^{-1}.$$

So far, there is very little practical experience of the estimator (17.66). One reason for this is that econometricians often prefer to model dynamics explicitly (see Chapter 19) rather than leaving all the dynamics in the error term and employing a specification-consistent estimator. Even if the latter provides consistent estimates of some parameters, it may say nothing about the most interesting ones and may allow serious specification errors to go undetected. Another reason is that there is little evidence concerning the properties of (17.66) in finite samples. The results of Cragg (1983) and Tauchen (1986) for related estimators suggest that these may sometimes be poor.

One important practical problem is how to choose the lag truncation parameter p. Theory is signally unhelpful here. As we mentioned earlier, there are results establishing rates at which p may tend to infinity as the sample size tends to infinity. But if an investigator has a sample of precisely 136 observations, what value of p should be chosen? Andrews (1991b) confronts this problem directly and provides data-dependent methods for choosing p, based on the estimation of an optimal value of a parameter he defines. It is fair to say that none of his methods is elementary, and we cannot discuss them here. Perhaps the most encouraging outcome of his investigations is that, in the neighborhood of the optimal value of p, variations in p have little influence on the performance of the HAC estimator.

Andrews (1991b) also provides valuable evidence about HAC covariance matrix estimators, (17.64) and others, from Monte Carlo experiments. Perhaps the most important finding is that *none* of the HAC estimators he considers is at all reliable for sample sizes up to 250 or so if the errors follow an AR(1) process with autocorrelation parameter greater than 0.9. This disappointing result is related to the fact that AR(1) processes with parameters near unity are close to having what is called a **unit root**. This phenomenon is studied in Chapter 20, and we will see that unit roots throw most conventional econometric theory into confusion.

If we stay away from unit roots and near unit roots, things are more orderly. We saw in Chapter 16 that it is possible to use HCCMEs even in the presence of homoskedasticity with little loss of accuracy, provided that one of the better HCCMEs is used. It appears that much the same is true for HAC estimators. With an ordinary regression model with serially uncorrelated, homoskedastic errors, the loss of precision due to the use of the Newey-West estimator, say, as opposed to the usual OLS estimator, $\hat{\sigma}^2(\boldsymbol{X}^\top\boldsymbol{X})^{-1}$, is small. With some of the other HAC estimators considered by Andrews, the loss is smaller still, which implies that the Newey-West estimator is generally not the best available. Similarly, if the errors are heteroskedastic but still serially uncorrelated, then an HCCME is much better than the OLS estimator but only very slightly better than the HAC estimator.

If the errors are autocorrelated at order one and homoskedastic, both the OLS estimator and the HCCME are dominated not only by the HAC estimator, as one would expect, but also by the straightforward estimator computed by estimating the autocorrelation parameter ρ and using the covariance matrix estimator of a feasible GLS procedure. This last estimator is in these circumstances preferable to the HAC ones. In fact, it is only when the errors are both heteroskedastic and serially correlated that the HAC estimators really come into their own. Even in these circumstances, it is possible, with some patterns of heteroskedasticity, that the feasible GLS estimator, which takes no account of possible heteroskedasticity, can outperform the HAC estimators. But that is probably the exception rather than the rule, for Andrews finds other patterns of heteroskedasticity, which, in combination with serial correlation, require the use of HAC estimators for reasonably accurate inference.

Clearly, the last word on HAC estimators has by no means been said. For instance, in the usual implementation of the Newey-West estimator for linear IV models, we have that $\hat{\boldsymbol{\Gamma}}(0)$ is just $n^{-1}\boldsymbol{W}^\top\hat{\boldsymbol{\Omega}}\boldsymbol{W}$, with $\hat{\boldsymbol{\Omega}}$ the rather poor estimator associated with the HC_0 form of the HCCME. It would seem reasonable to suppose that it would be better to use other forms of $\boldsymbol{\Omega}$ in the Newey-West estimator, just as it is in HCCMEs, and to find similar ways of improving the estimators $\hat{\boldsymbol{\Gamma}}(j)$ for $j \neq 0$. At the time of writing, however, no evidence is available on whether these conjectures are justified. A quite different approach, which we do not have space to discuss, was recently suggested by Andrews and Monahan (1992).

In the next section, we will leave behind the "grubby details" of covariance matrix estimation, assume that a suitable covariance matrix estimator is available, and turn our attention to asymptotic tests of overidentifying restrictions and other aspects of specification testing in GMM models.

17.6 INFERENCE WITH GMM MODELS

In this section, we undertake an investigation of how hypotheses may be tested in the context of GMM models. We begin by looking at tests of overidentifying restrictions and then move on to develop procedures akin to the classical tests studied in Chapter 13 for models estimated by maximum likelihood. The similarities to procedures we have already studied are striking. There is one important difference, however: We will not be able to make any great use of artificial linear regressions in order to implement the tests we discuss. The reason is simply that such artificial regressions have not yet been adequately developed. They exist only for some special cases, and their finite-sample properties are almost entirely unknown. However, there is every reason to hope and expect that in a few years it will be possible to perform inference on GMM models by means of artificial regressions still to be invented.

In the meantime, there are several testing procedures for GMM models that are not difficult to perform. The most important of these is a test of the overidentifying restrictions that are usually imposed. Suppose that we have estimated a vector $\boldsymbol{\theta}$ of k parameters by minimizing the criterion function

$$\boldsymbol{\iota}^\top\boldsymbol{F}(\boldsymbol{\theta})\hat{\boldsymbol{\Phi}}^{-1}\boldsymbol{F}^\top(\boldsymbol{\theta})\boldsymbol{\iota}, \tag{17.67}$$

in which the empirical moment matrix $\boldsymbol{F}(\boldsymbol{\theta})$ has $l > k$ columns. Observe that we have used a weighting matrix $\hat{\boldsymbol{\Phi}}^{-1}$ that satisfies the necessary condition of Theorem 17.3 for the efficiency of the GMM estimator. Only k moment conditions are needed to identify k parameters, and so there are $l-k$ overidentifying restrictions implicit in the estimation we have performed. As we emphasized in Chapter 7, where we first encountered overidentifying restrictions, it should be a routine practice always to test these restrictions before making any use of the estimation results.

One way of doing so, suggested by Hansen (1982), is to use as a test statistic the minimized value of the criterion function. The test statistic is simply (17.67) evaluated at $\boldsymbol{\theta} = \hat{\boldsymbol{\theta}}$ and divided by the sample size n:

$$\frac{1}{n}\boldsymbol{\iota}^{\top}\hat{\boldsymbol{F}}\hat{\boldsymbol{\Phi}}^{-1}\hat{\boldsymbol{F}}^{\top}\boldsymbol{\iota}, \tag{17.68}$$

where, as usual, we write $\hat{\boldsymbol{F}}$ for $\boldsymbol{F}(\hat{\boldsymbol{\theta}})$. The factor of n^{-1} is necessary to offset the factor of n in $\hat{\boldsymbol{\Phi}}^{-1}$, which arises from the fact that $\boldsymbol{\Phi}$ is defined in (17.29) as the covariance matrix of $n^{-1/2}\boldsymbol{F}_0^{\top}\boldsymbol{\iota}$. The definition (17.29) therefore implies that if the overidentifying restrictions are correct, the asymptotic distribution of $n^{-1/2}\boldsymbol{F}_0^{\top}\boldsymbol{\iota}$ is $N(\mathbf{0}, \boldsymbol{\Phi})$.

However, for reasons that should by now be quite familiar, the asymptotic distribution of $\hat{\boldsymbol{F}}^{\top}\boldsymbol{\iota}$ is not the same as the asymptotic distribution of $\boldsymbol{F}_0^{\top}\boldsymbol{\iota}$. In order to obtain the correct asymptotic covariance matrix for the former vector, we perform a short Taylor expansion as follows:

$$\begin{aligned} n^{-1/2}\hat{\boldsymbol{F}}^{\top}\boldsymbol{\iota} &\overset{a}{=} n^{-1/2}\boldsymbol{F}_0^{\top}\boldsymbol{\iota} + \frac{1}{n}\sum_{j=1}^{k}\sum_{t=1}^{n}\frac{\partial \boldsymbol{F}_t^{\top}}{\partial \theta_j}(\boldsymbol{\theta}_0)n^{1/2}(\hat{\boldsymbol{\theta}} - \boldsymbol{\theta}_0)_j \\ &\overset{a}{=} n^{-1/2}\boldsymbol{F}_0^{\top}\boldsymbol{\iota} + \boldsymbol{D}(\mu, \boldsymbol{\theta}_0)n^{1/2}(\hat{\boldsymbol{\theta}} - \boldsymbol{\theta}_0). \end{aligned}$$

Letting $\boldsymbol{D}$ denote $\boldsymbol{D}(\mu, \boldsymbol{\theta}_0)$, it follows from (17.22), (17.27), and (17.28) that

$$n^{1/2}(\hat{\boldsymbol{\theta}} - \boldsymbol{\theta}_0) \overset{a}{=} -\left(\boldsymbol{D}^{\top}\boldsymbol{\Phi}^{-1}\boldsymbol{D}\right)^{-1}\boldsymbol{D}^{\top}\boldsymbol{\Phi}^{-1}n^{-1/2}\boldsymbol{F}_0^{\top}\boldsymbol{\iota}.$$

Therefore,

$$n^{-1/2}\hat{\boldsymbol{F}}^{\top}\boldsymbol{\iota} \overset{a}{=} \left(\mathbf{I} - \boldsymbol{D}\left(\boldsymbol{D}^{\top}\boldsymbol{\Phi}^{-1}\boldsymbol{D}\right)^{-1}\boldsymbol{D}^{\top}\boldsymbol{\Phi}^{-1}\right)n^{-1/2}\boldsymbol{F}_0^{\top}\boldsymbol{\iota}. \tag{17.69}$$

Let $\hat{\boldsymbol{\Psi}}$ be a symmetric, positive definite $l \times l$ matrix such that $\hat{\boldsymbol{\Psi}}^2 = \hat{\boldsymbol{\Phi}}^{-1}$. Then the minimized criterion function (17.68) becomes the squared norm of the vector $n^{-1/2}\hat{\boldsymbol{\Psi}}\hat{\boldsymbol{F}}^{\top}\boldsymbol{\iota}$. From (17.69), this vector is asymptotically equivalent to

$$\begin{aligned} &\boldsymbol{\Psi}\left(\mathbf{I} - \boldsymbol{D}\left(\boldsymbol{D}^{\top}\boldsymbol{\Psi}^2\boldsymbol{D}\right)^{-1}\boldsymbol{D}^{\top}\boldsymbol{\Psi}^2\right)n^{-1/2}\boldsymbol{F}_0^{\top}\boldsymbol{\iota} \\ &= \left(\mathbf{I} - \boldsymbol{\Psi}\boldsymbol{D}\left(\boldsymbol{D}^{\top}\boldsymbol{\Psi}^2\boldsymbol{D}\right)^{-1}\boldsymbol{D}^{\top}\boldsymbol{\Psi}\right)\boldsymbol{\Psi}n^{-1/2}\boldsymbol{F}_0^{\top}\boldsymbol{\iota} \\ &= \boldsymbol{M}_{\Psi D}\boldsymbol{\Psi}n^{-1/2}\boldsymbol{F}_0^{\top}\boldsymbol{\iota}, \end{aligned}$$

where $\boldsymbol{\Psi}^2 = \boldsymbol{\Phi}^{-1}$, and $\boldsymbol{M}_{\Psi D}$ is the $l \times l$ orthogonal projection matrix onto the orthogonal complement of the k columns of $\boldsymbol{\Psi D}$. By construction, the l-vector $n^{-1/2}\boldsymbol{\Psi F}_0^{\top}\boldsymbol{\iota}$ has the $N(\mathbf{0}, \mathbf{I})$ distribution. It follows, then, that (17.68) is asymptotically distributed as chi-squared with number of degrees of freedom equal to the rank of $\boldsymbol{M}_{\Psi D}$, that is, $l - k$, the number of overidentifying restrictions.

Hansen's test of overidentifying restrictions is completely analogous, in the present more general context, to the one for IV estimation discussed in Section 7.8, based on the criterion function (7.56). It is a good exercise to work through the derivation given above for the simple case of a linear regression model with homoskedastic, serially uncorrelated errors, in order to see how closely the general case mimics the simple one.[2]

Hansen's test of overidentifying restrictions is perhaps as close as one can come in econometrics to a portmanteau specification test. Because models estimated by GMM are subject to so few restrictions, their "specification" is not very demanding. In particular, if nothing more is required than the existence of the moments used to identify the parameters, then only two things are left to test. One is the set of any overidentifying restrictions used, and the other is parameter constancy.[3] Because Hansen's test of overidentifying restrictions has as many degrees of freedom as there are overidentifying restrictions, it may be possible to achieve more power by reducing the number of degrees of freedom. However, if Hansen's test statistic is small enough numerically, no such test can reject, for the simple reason that Hansen's statistic provides an upper bound for all possible test statistics for which the null hypothesis is the estimated model. This last fact follows from the observation that no criterion function of the form (17.67) can be less than zero.

Tests for which the null hypothesis is not the estimated model are not subject to the bound provided by Hansen's statistic. This is just as well, of course, since otherwise it would be impossible to reject a just identified model at all. A test for parameter constancy is not subject to the bound either, although at first glance the null hypothesis would appear to be precisely the estimated model. The reason was discussed in Section 11.2 in connection with tests for parameter constancy in nonlinear regression models estimated by means of instrumental variables. Essentially, in order to avoid problems of identification, it is necessary to double the number of instruments used, by splitting the original ones up as in (11.09). Exactly the same considerations apply for GMM models, of course, especially those that are just identified or have few overidentifying restrictions. But if one uses twice as many instruments, the null model has effectively been changed, and for that reason,

[2] Hansen's test statistic, (17.68), is sometimes referred to as the J statistic. For obvious reasons (see Chapter 11) we prefer not to give it that name.

[3] Tests of parameter constancy in models estimated by GMM are discussed by Hoffman and Pagan (1989) and Ghysels and Hall (1990).

Hansen's statistic no longer provides a bound for statistics used to test parameter constancy.

One may reasonably wish to test other aspects of a GMM model than just the overidentifying restrictions and parameter constancy. In such cases, what is to be tested is not the specification of the model but rather whether further restrictions on the model could be entertained. This suggests the use of tests based on the Wald principle. Suppose then that we wish to test a set of r restrictions of the form

$$\boldsymbol{r}(\boldsymbol{\theta}) = \mathbf{0}, \quad \text{where } \boldsymbol{r} : \Theta \to \mathbb{R}^r; \tag{17.70}$$

recall (13.02). The parameter k–vector $\boldsymbol{\theta}$ is defined in the context of a suitable model, estimated in its unrestricted form by minimizing the criterion function (17.67). The model may be either overidentified or just identified. As usual, let $\boldsymbol{R}(\boldsymbol{\theta}) \equiv D_{\boldsymbol{\theta}}\boldsymbol{r}(\boldsymbol{\theta})$. Then, by analogy with (8.78) and (13.05), we may form a Wald statistic as follows:

$$W = n\hat{\boldsymbol{r}}^{\top}\big(\hat{\boldsymbol{R}}(\hat{\boldsymbol{D}}^{\top}\hat{\boldsymbol{\Phi}}^{-1}\hat{\boldsymbol{D}})^{-1}\hat{\boldsymbol{R}}^{\top}\big)^{-1}\hat{\boldsymbol{r}}. \tag{17.71}$$

The justification is precisely the same as for the Wald and Wald-like statistics we have seen previously: The asymptotic covariance matrix of $n^{1/2}\boldsymbol{r}(\hat{\boldsymbol{\theta}})$ is $\boldsymbol{R}(\boldsymbol{D}^{\top}\boldsymbol{\Phi}^{-1}\boldsymbol{D})^{-1}\boldsymbol{R}^{\top}$. The difficulties with this test are also the same as those associated with other Wald tests, in that the statistic is not invariant under reparametrization of the restrictions. Consequently, the statistic (17.71) is generally not recommended and should be used with care if it is used at all.

It is also possible to base tests of models estimated by GMM on the LM and LR principles. For an LM test, we will perform only a restricted estimation, defined by minimizing (17.67) subject to the restrictions (17.70), to obtain restricted estimates $\tilde{\boldsymbol{\theta}}$. The classical LM test is based on the gradient of the loglikelihood function, evaluated at the restricted estimates. The loglikelihood function is a criterion function, and it is therefore natural to base an LM test in the present context on the gradient of the criterion function (17.67). It is easy to see that this gradient is asymptotically proportional to the random k–vector

$$n^{-1/2}\boldsymbol{D}^{\top}\boldsymbol{\Phi}^{-1}\boldsymbol{F}^{\top}\boldsymbol{\iota}.$$

Evaluated at $\boldsymbol{\theta}_0$, this vector is asymptotically normal, with mean zero and covariance matrix

$$\lim_{n\to\infty}\Big(\frac{1}{n}\boldsymbol{D}^{\top}\boldsymbol{\Phi}^{-1}\boldsymbol{D}\Big),$$

which suggests that an appropriate test statistic is

$$LM = \frac{1}{n}\boldsymbol{\iota}^{\top}\tilde{\boldsymbol{F}}\tilde{\boldsymbol{\Phi}}^{-1}\tilde{\boldsymbol{D}}\big(\tilde{\boldsymbol{D}}^{\top}\tilde{\boldsymbol{\Phi}}^{-1}\tilde{\boldsymbol{D}}\big)^{-1}\tilde{\boldsymbol{D}}^{\top}\tilde{\boldsymbol{\Phi}}^{-1}\tilde{\boldsymbol{F}}^{\top}\boldsymbol{\iota}, \tag{17.72}$$

where $\tilde{\boldsymbol{D}}$ is defined by (17.32) with $\tilde{\boldsymbol{\theta}}$ in place of $\hat{\boldsymbol{\theta}}$, $\tilde{\boldsymbol{F}} \equiv \boldsymbol{F}(\tilde{\boldsymbol{\theta}})$, and $\tilde{\boldsymbol{\Phi}}$ is a suitable estimator of $\boldsymbol{\Phi}$; at the end of the last section, we promised not to go into details of how $\tilde{\boldsymbol{\Phi}}$ should be calculated.

It is a routine exercise to show that, under the null hypothesis, LM as given by (17.72) is distributed as chi-squared with r degrees of freedom. It is more interesting to show that, when the unrestricted model is just identified, (17.72) is numerically identical to the asymptotically chi-squared statistic (17.68) for overidentifying restrictions, provided that the same estimator is used for $\boldsymbol{\Phi}$ in both statistics. In fact, this follows immediately from the observation that $\boldsymbol{D}$ is square and nonsingular for just identified models. Since $\boldsymbol{D}^{-1}$ exists, we can simplify (17.72) to obtain

$$\frac{1}{n}\boldsymbol{\iota}^{\top}\tilde{\boldsymbol{F}}\tilde{\boldsymbol{\Phi}}^{-1}\tilde{\boldsymbol{F}}^{\top}\boldsymbol{\iota}. \tag{17.73}$$

This is identical to (17.68), since the $\hat{\boldsymbol{\theta}}$ used there is a *restricted* estimate, being the result of estimation subject to the overidentifying restrictions.

Notice that (17.72) cannot be numerically larger than (17.73) and will in general be smaller. This is an example of the bound discussed above. It can be most easily seen by rewriting the former as

$$\frac{1}{n}\boldsymbol{\iota}^{\top}\tilde{\boldsymbol{F}}\tilde{\boldsymbol{\Psi}}\tilde{\boldsymbol{\Psi}}\tilde{\boldsymbol{D}}\big(\tilde{\boldsymbol{D}}^{\top}\tilde{\boldsymbol{\Psi}}\tilde{\boldsymbol{\Psi}}\tilde{\boldsymbol{D}}\big)^{-1}\tilde{\boldsymbol{D}}^{\top}\tilde{\boldsymbol{\Psi}}\tilde{\boldsymbol{\Psi}}\tilde{\boldsymbol{F}}^{\top}\boldsymbol{\iota}$$

and the latter as

$$\frac{1}{n}\boldsymbol{\iota}^{\top}\tilde{\boldsymbol{F}}\tilde{\boldsymbol{\Psi}}\tilde{\boldsymbol{\Psi}}\tilde{\boldsymbol{F}}^{\top}\boldsymbol{\iota}.$$

Thus (17.73) is seen to be the squared length of the vector $n^{-1/2}\tilde{\boldsymbol{\Psi}}\tilde{\boldsymbol{F}}^{\top}\boldsymbol{\iota}$, and (17.72) is seen to be the squared length of that vector after it has been projected onto the subspace spanned by the columns of $\tilde{\boldsymbol{\Psi}}\tilde{\boldsymbol{D}}$.

The LR statistic for GMM models has the same simplicity as it has in the context of models estimated by maximum likelihood. It is simply the difference between the criterion functions (17.68) evaluated at the restricted and unrestricted estimates:

$$LR = \frac{1}{n}\big(\boldsymbol{\iota}^{\top}\tilde{\boldsymbol{F}}\tilde{\boldsymbol{\Phi}}^{-1}\tilde{\boldsymbol{F}}^{\top}\boldsymbol{\iota} - \boldsymbol{\iota}^{\top}\hat{\boldsymbol{F}}\hat{\boldsymbol{\Phi}}^{-1}\hat{\boldsymbol{F}}^{\top}\boldsymbol{\iota}\big). \tag{17.74}$$

This result may at first glance appear too good to be true. After all, even in the classical context, a factor of 2 is needed to form the LR test. The catch is that the result depends critically on the supposition that the weighting matrix used in the criterion function satisfies the efficiency condition of Theorem 17.3. Without this, as we will discuss briefly at the end of this section, things are much messier. Notice that $\hat{\boldsymbol{\Phi}}$ and $\tilde{\boldsymbol{\Phi}}$ will often be the same in (17.74), because if it is complicated to estimate $\boldsymbol{\Phi}$, it is sensible to do so only once.

We will not prove the validity of (17.74). However, one special case at least shows that this LR statistic is plausible. When a model is just identified, the minimized criterion function is zero: The k empirical moment conditions can be satisfied exactly with k parameters available to be adjusted. The difference of criterion functions is thus just the restricted criterion function, and that, as we have seen, is both Hansen's statistic and the LM statistic in these circumstances.

Finally, we consider $C(\alpha)$ tests. Let $\acute{\boldsymbol{\theta}}$ be a parameter vector satisfying the restrictions $\boldsymbol{r}(\acute{\boldsymbol{\theta}}) = \mathbf{0}$. Then the test statistic can be formed as though it were the difference of two LM statistics, one for the restricted and one for the unrestricted model, both evaluated at $\acute{\boldsymbol{\theta}}$. Suppose, for simplicity, that the parameter vector $\boldsymbol{\theta}$ can be partitioned as $[\boldsymbol{\theta}_1 \,\vdots\, \boldsymbol{\theta}_2]$ and that the restrictions can be written as $\boldsymbol{\theta}_2 = 0$. The first term of the $C(\alpha)$ statistic has the form (17.72) but is evaluated at $\acute{\boldsymbol{\theta}}$ rather than the genuine constrained estimator $\tilde{\boldsymbol{\theta}}$. The second term should take the form of an LM statistic appropriate to the constrained model, for which only $\boldsymbol{\theta}_1$ may vary. This corresponds to replacing the matrix $\tilde{\boldsymbol{D}}$ in (17.72) by $\acute{\boldsymbol{D}}_1$, where the partition of $\boldsymbol{D}$ as $[\boldsymbol{D}_1 \,\vdots\, \boldsymbol{D}_2]$ corresponds to the partition of $\boldsymbol{\theta}$. The $C(\alpha)$ test statistic is therefore

$$\begin{aligned} C(\alpha) = {} & \frac{1}{n}\boldsymbol{\iota}^{\top}\acute{\boldsymbol{F}}\hat{\boldsymbol{\Phi}}^{-1}\acute{\boldsymbol{D}}\big(\acute{\boldsymbol{D}}^{\top}\hat{\boldsymbol{\Phi}}^{-1}\acute{\boldsymbol{D}}\big)^{-1}\acute{\boldsymbol{D}}^{\top}\hat{\boldsymbol{\Phi}}^{-1}\acute{\boldsymbol{F}}^{\top}\boldsymbol{\iota} \\ & - \frac{1}{n}\boldsymbol{\iota}^{\top}\acute{\boldsymbol{F}}\hat{\boldsymbol{\Phi}}^{-1}\acute{\boldsymbol{D}}_1\big(\acute{\boldsymbol{D}}_1^{\top}\hat{\boldsymbol{\Phi}}^{-1}\acute{\boldsymbol{D}}_1\big)^{-1}\acute{\boldsymbol{D}}_1^{\top}\hat{\boldsymbol{\Phi}}^{-1}\acute{\boldsymbol{F}}^{\top}\boldsymbol{\iota}. \end{aligned} \tag{17.75}$$

Here, as before, $\hat{\boldsymbol{\Phi}}$ is a suitable estimate of $\boldsymbol{\Phi}$. To show that (17.75) is asymptotically equivalent to the true LM statistic, it is enough to modify the details of the proof of the corresponding asymptotic equivalence in Section 13.7.

In the general case in which the restrictions are expressed as $\boldsymbol{r}(\boldsymbol{\theta}) = \mathbf{0}$, another form of the $C(\alpha)$ test may be more convenient, since forming a matrix to correspond to $\boldsymbol{D}_1$ may not be simple. This other form is

$$\boldsymbol{\iota}^{\top}\acute{\boldsymbol{F}}\hat{\boldsymbol{\Phi}}^{-1}\acute{\boldsymbol{D}}\big(\acute{\boldsymbol{D}}^{\top}\hat{\boldsymbol{\Phi}}^{-1}\acute{\boldsymbol{D}}\big)^{-1}\acute{\boldsymbol{R}}^{\top}\Big(\acute{\boldsymbol{R}}\big(\acute{\boldsymbol{D}}^{\top}\hat{\boldsymbol{\Phi}}^{-1}\acute{\boldsymbol{D}}\big)^{-1}\acute{\boldsymbol{R}}^{\top}\Big)^{-1}\acute{\boldsymbol{R}}\big(\acute{\boldsymbol{D}}^{\top}\hat{\boldsymbol{\Phi}}^{-1}\acute{\boldsymbol{D}}\big)^{-1}\acute{\boldsymbol{D}}^{\top}\hat{\boldsymbol{\Phi}}^{-1}\acute{\boldsymbol{F}}^{\top}\boldsymbol{\iota}.$$

For this statistic to be useful, the difficulty of computing the actual constrained estimate $\tilde{\boldsymbol{\theta}}$ must outweigh the complication of the above formula. The formula itself can be established, at the cost of some tedious algebra, by adapting the methods of Section 8.9. We leave the details to the interested reader.

The treatment we have given of LM, LR, and Wald tests has largely followed that of Newey and West (1987b). This article may be consulted for more details of regularity conditions sufficient for the results merely asserted here to hold. Another paper on testing models estimated by GMM is Newey (1985b). Nonnested hypothesis tests for models estimated by GMM are discussed by Smith (1992). These papers do not deal with $C(\alpha)$ tests, however.

An interesting question is whether the conditional moment tests discussed in the last chapter in the context of models estimated by maximum likelihood have any counterpart for models estimated by GMM. For simplicity, suppose that there is a single conditional moment of which the expectation is zero if the model is correctly specified. If the corresponding empirical moment is used as an overidentifying restriction, then it can be tested in the same way as any other overidentifying restriction, by one of the procedures described above.

Another possibility is a moment not used for identifying or overidentifying the model parameters, such as one generated by an instrument which, while belonging to the appropriate information set, is not chosen as one of the instruments used in the estimation procedure. It is easy in principle to see how to construct a conditional moment test in this case. The model must be estimated again with the moment condition to be tested used as an overidentifying restriction. In practice, this is easier said than done, for the matrix $\boldsymbol{\Phi}$ will have to be extended so as to have another row and column for the new moment. The difference between the two minimized criterion functions, with and without the extra moment, will then serve as an LR test statistic.

The underlying reason for which conditional moment tests are, at least potentially, harder to perform in a GMM context than in a maximum likelihood one is the unavailability of artificial regression methods. This is in turn due to the difficulty of obtaining estimates of the matrix $\boldsymbol{\Phi}$ if we wish to impose as little structure as possible on our models. For those cases in which we are happy to impose enough restrictions that $\boldsymbol{\Phi}$ is easily estimated, conditional moment tests are no more difficult to perform than in the fully specified maximum likelihood context.

We have restricted our attention in this section to models estimated by the minimization of criterion functions with weighting matrices satisfying the efficiency condition of Theorem 17.3. The principal reason for this is that, even if an inefficient weighting matrix may sometimes be convenient for estimation purposes, testing cannot be done without estimating the covariance matrix $\boldsymbol{\Phi}$ of the empirical moments, whatever weighting matrix is used. It therefore makes little sense to base inference on inefficient estimates if the hard work of efficient estimation, namely, the estimation of $\boldsymbol{\Phi}$, has been done. Another point is simply that the theory of tests based on inefficient parameter estimates is substantially more complicated than the theory we have presented here.

17.7 CONCLUSION

The asymptotic theory underlying the generalized method of moments is indeed very general. It has the beauty of those theories that draw seemingly very disparate matters together and provide a unified treatment of all of them. We have seen in this chapter how almost every single estimator considered so far in this book can be regarded as a GMM estimator, and in many cases we have been led naturally to significant extensions of existing estimation procedures by adopting the GMM point of view, largely by making these procedures robust to a wider variety of specifications than those originally envisaged.

For reasons of simplicity, all of the examples of GMM estimators presented in this chapter have been in the context of linear models. We should emphasize that this is in no way a restriction of the method. The extension of our simple examples to the case of nonlinear regressions is completely straightforward, theoretically at least. In practice, of course, all but the simplest GMM estimation must be performed by the numerical minimization of a criterion function, with all of the usual attendant difficulties. These difficulties notwithstanding, the most significant empirical applications of the GMM have been to nonlinear models.

So far, it is impossible to say to what extent the GMM will affect standard econometric practice. Testing is, as we have just seen, often significantly harder with a GMM model than with the other sorts of models we have studied. Another point on which not much can be said is whether GMM estimators and test statistics have decent properties in samples of the sizes usually encountered in econometrics. Further research will no doubt clear up many of these questions. We will encounter one application of GMM in the next chapter, which deals with simultaneous equations models.

TERMS AND CONCEPTS

autocovariances (of empirical moments)
$C(\alpha)$ tests for GMM models
criterion function
empirical moments
estimator-defining equation
generalized method of moments (GMM)
GMM bound
GMM estimator
Hansen's test of overidentifying restrictions
heteroskedasticity and autocorrelation consistent (HAC) covariance matrix estimator
H2SLS estimator (two-step, two-stage least squares)
HOLS estimator
lag truncation parameter
location model
LM tests for GMM models
LR tests for GMM models
M-estimators
method of moments (ordinary)
moment condition
optimal instruments
optimal moments
optimal weights
parameter-defining mapping
sample autocovariance matrix
strong asymptotic identifiability
two-step two-stage least squares
Type 2 M-estimator
Wald tests for GMM models
weighting matrix

Chapter 18

Simultaneous Equations Models

18.1 Introduction

For many years, the **linear simultaneous equations model** was the centerpiece of econometric theory. We discussed a special case of this model, a two-equation demand-supply model, in Section 7.3. The purpose of that discussion was simply to show that simultaneity induces correlation between the regressors and error terms of each equation of the system, thus causing OLS to be inconsistent and justifying the use of instrumental variables. The inconsistency of least squares estimators of individual equations in simultaneous equations models is by no means the only econometric issue that arises in such models. In this chapter, we therefore discuss simultaneous equations models at some length.

Much of the early work on simultaneous equations models was done under the auspices of the Cowles Commission; references include Koopmans (1950) and Hood and Koopmans (1953). This work heavily influenced the direction of econometric theory for many years. For a history of the early development of econometrics, see Morgan (1990). Because the literature on simultaneous equations models is vast, we will be able to deal with only a small part of it. There are many surveys of the field and many textbook treatments at various levels. Two useful survey articles are Hausman (1983), which deals with the mainstream literature, and Phillips (1983), which deals with the rather specialized field of small-sample theory in simultaneous equations models, a subject that we will not discuss at all.

The essential feature of simultaneous equations models is that two or more **endogenous variables** are determined jointly within the model, as a function of **exogenous variables**, **predetermined variables**, and error terms. Up to this point, we have said very little about what we mean by exogenous and predetermined variables. Since the role of such variables in simultaneous equations models is critical, it is time to rectify that omission. In Section 18.2, we will therefore discuss the important concept of **exogeneity** at some length.

Most of the chapter will be concerned with the linear simultaneous equations model. Suppose there are g endogenous variables, and hence g equations, and k exogenous or predetermined variables. Then the model can be written in matrix form as

$$\boldsymbol{Y\Gamma} = \boldsymbol{XB} + \boldsymbol{U}. \tag{18.01}$$

Here $\boldsymbol{Y}$ denotes an $n \times g$ matrix of endogenous variables, $\boldsymbol{X}$ denotes an $n \times k$ matrix of exogenous or predetermined variables, $\boldsymbol{\Gamma}$ denotes a $g \times g$ matrix of coefficients, $\boldsymbol{B}$ denotes a $k \times g$ matrix of coefficients, and $\boldsymbol{U}$ denotes an $n \times g$ matrix of error terms.

It is at once clear that the model (18.01) contains too many coefficients to estimate. A typical observation for the lth equation can be written as

$$\sum_{i=1}^{g} \Gamma_{il} Y_{ti} = \sum_{j=1}^{k} B_{jl} X_{tj} + u_{tl}.$$

Multiplying all of the Γ_{il}'s and B_{jl}'s by any nonzero constant would simply have the effect of multiplying u_{tl} by that same constant for all t, but would not change the pattern of the error terms across observations at all. Thus it is necessary to impose some sort of normalization on each of the equations of the model. The obvious one is to set $\Gamma_{ii} = 1$ for all i; each endogenous variable, y_1 through y_g, would then have a coefficient of unity in one and only one equation. However, as we saw in Section 7.3, many other normalizations could be used. We could, for example, set $\Gamma_{1l} = 1$ for all l; the coefficient on the first endogenous variable would then be unity in every equation.

The model (18.01) makes no sense if the matrix $\boldsymbol{\Gamma}$ cannot be inverted, since otherwise it would be impossible to determine $\boldsymbol{Y}$ uniquely as a function of $\boldsymbol{X}$ and $\boldsymbol{U}$. We may therefore postmultiply both sides of (18.01) by $\boldsymbol{\Gamma}^{-1}$ to obtain

$$\boldsymbol{Y} = \boldsymbol{XB\Gamma}^{-1} + \boldsymbol{U\Gamma}^{-1} \tag{18.02}$$

$$= \boldsymbol{X\Pi} + \boldsymbol{V}. \tag{18.03}$$

Expression (18.02) is the **restricted reduced form**, or **RRF**, and expression (18.03) is the **unrestricted reduced form**, or **URF**. The restrictions are that $\boldsymbol{\Pi} = \boldsymbol{B\Gamma}^{-1}$. Notice that, even in the unlikely event that the columns of $\boldsymbol{U}$ were independent, the columns of $\boldsymbol{V}$ would not be. Thus the various equations of the reduced form are almost certain to have correlated errors.

The imposition of normalization restrictions is necessary but not sufficient to obtain estimates of $\boldsymbol{\Gamma}$ and $\boldsymbol{B}$. The problem is that, unless we impose some restrictions on it, the model (18.01) has too many coefficients to estimate. The matrix $\boldsymbol{\Gamma}$ contains $g^2 - g$ coefficients, because of the g normalization restrictions, while the matrix $\boldsymbol{B}$ contains gk. There are thus $g^2 + gk - g$ structural coefficients in total. But the matrix $\boldsymbol{\Pi}$ in the unrestricted reduced form contains only gk coefficients. It is obviously impossible to determine the $g^2 + gk - g$ structural coefficients uniquely from the gk coefficients of the

URF. Thus we will have to impose *at least* $g^2 - g$ restrictions on $\boldsymbol{\Gamma}$ and/or $\boldsymbol{B}$ in order to be able to identify the model. There is an enormous literature on identification in simultaneous equations models, which discusses conditions under which some or all of the coefficients of such models may be identified. We will discuss the principal results of this literature in Section 18.3.

Most of the remainder of the chapter deals with various estimation methods for simultaneous equations models. Section 18.4 discusses maximum likelihood estimation of the entire model under the assumption of normality, a technique known as **full-information maximum likelihood**, or **FIML**. The following section deals with maximum likelihood estimation of individual equations, a technique known as **limited-information maximum likelihood**, or **LIML**. Section 18.6 then discusses **three-stage least squares**, or **3SLS**, which is derived as an application of the generalized method of moments. Finally, nonlinear simultaneous equations models are briefly discussed in Section 18.7.

18.2 EXOGENEITY AND CAUSALITY

In the case of a single regression equation, we are estimating the distribution, or at least the mean and variance, of an endogenous variable *conditional* on the values of some explanatory variables. In the case of a simultaneous equations model, we are estimating the joint distribution of two or more endogenous variables *conditional* on the values of some explanatory variables. But we have not yet discussed the conditions under which one can validly treat a variable as explanatory. This includes the use of such variables as regressors in least squares estimation and as instruments in instrumental variables or GMM estimation. For conditional inference to be valid, the explanatory variables must be either **predetermined** or **exogenous** in one or other of a variety of senses to be defined below.

In a time-series context, we have seen that random variables which are predetermined can safely be used as explanatory variables in least squares estimation, at least asymptotically. In fact, lagged endogenous variables are regularly used both as explanatory variables and as instrumental variables. However, there are a great many cases, including of course models estimated with cross-section data, in which we want to use variables that are not predetermined as explanatory variables. Moreover, the concept of predeterminedness turns out to be somewhat trickier than one might expect, since it is not invariant to reparametrizations of the model. Thus it is clear that we need a much more general concept than that of predeterminedness.

It is convenient to begin with formal definitions of the concept of predeterminedness and the related concept of **strict exogeneity**. In this, we are following the standard exposition of these matters, given in Engle, Hendry, and Richard (1983). Readers should be warned that this paper, although a standard reference, is not easy to read. Our discussion will be greatly simplified relative to theirs and will be given in a more general context, since they restrict themselves to fully specified parametric models capable of being estimated by maximum likelihood. We will, however, make use of one of their specific examples as a concrete illustration of a number of points.

Let the $1 \times g$ vector $\boldsymbol{Y}_t$ denote the tth observation on a set of variables that we wish to model as a simultaneous process, and let the $1 \times k$ vector $\boldsymbol{X}_t$ be the tth observation on a set of explanatory variables, some or all of which may be lagged $\boldsymbol{Y}_t$'s. We may write an, in general nonlinear, simultaneous equations model as

$$\boldsymbol{h}_t(\boldsymbol{Y}_t, \boldsymbol{X}_t, \boldsymbol{\theta}) = \boldsymbol{U}_t, \tag{18.04}$$

where $\boldsymbol{h}_t$ is a $1 \times g$ vector of functions, somewhat analogous to the regression function of a univariate model, $\boldsymbol{\theta}$ is a p–vector of parameters, and $\boldsymbol{U}_t$ is a $1 \times g$ vector of error terms. The linear model (18.01) is seen to be a special case of (18.04) if we rewrite it as

$$\boldsymbol{Y}_t \boldsymbol{\Gamma} = \boldsymbol{X}_t \boldsymbol{B} + \boldsymbol{U}_t$$

and define $\boldsymbol{\theta}$ so that it consists of all the elements of $\boldsymbol{\Gamma}$ and $\boldsymbol{B}$ which have to be estimated. Here $\boldsymbol{X}_t$ and $\boldsymbol{Y}_t$ are the tth rows of the matrices $\boldsymbol{X}$ and $\boldsymbol{Y}$. A set of (conditional) moment conditions could be based on (18.04), by writing

$$E\big(\boldsymbol{h}_t(\boldsymbol{Y}_t, \boldsymbol{X}_t, \boldsymbol{\theta})\big) = \boldsymbol{0},$$

where the expectation could be interpreted as being conditional on some appropriate information set.

Definition 18.1.

The explanatory variables $\boldsymbol{X}_t$ are **predetermined** in equation i of the model (18.04), for $i = 1, \ldots, g$, if, for all $t = 1, \ldots, n$,

$$\boldsymbol{X}_t \perp\!\!\!\perp u_{i,t+s} \quad \text{for all } s \geq 0.$$

Here the symbol $\perp\!\!\!\perp$ is used to express statistical independence. The definition applies to any context, such as the time-series one, in which there is a natural ordering of the observations. The next concept does not require this.

Definition 18.2.

The explanatory variables $\boldsymbol{X}_t$ are **strictly exogenous** in equation i of (18.04) if, for all $t = 1, \ldots, n$,

$$\boldsymbol{X}_t \perp\!\!\!\perp \boldsymbol{U}_s \quad \text{for all } s = 1, \ldots, n.$$

If (18.04) represents a structural form, then either predeterminedness or strict exogeneity allows us to treat this form as a characterization of the process generating $\boldsymbol{Y}_t$ conditional on $\boldsymbol{X}_t$. Thus we may, for example, write down a loglikelihood function based on (18.04), which can be maximized in order to provide consistent estimates of the parameters $\boldsymbol{\theta}$; see Section 18.4. If (18.04) is thought of as providing conditional moment conditions, then either predeterminedness or strict exogeneity allows us to use the columns of the matrix $\boldsymbol{X}$ as instruments for the estimation of $\boldsymbol{\theta}$ by some sort of IV procedure, such as 2SLS, 3SLS, or GMM. In claiming this, we assume of course that there are enough instruments in $\boldsymbol{X}$ to *identify* all of the parameters in $\boldsymbol{\theta}$.

Unfortunately, the concept of strict exogeneity is much too restrictive, at least for time-series applications. In this context, very few variables are strictly exogenous, although many are predetermined. However, as we now show, a variable can be predetermined or not in one and the same model depending on how the model is parametrized. Furthermore, predeterminedness is not always necessary for consistent estimation. Thus predeterminedness is not a very satisfactory concept.

Consider the following simultaneous model, taken from Engle, Hendry, and Richard (1983):

$$y_t = \beta x_t + \varepsilon_{1t} \tag{18.05}$$

$$x_t = \delta_1 x_{t-1} + \delta_2 y_{t-1} + \varepsilon_{2t}, \tag{18.06}$$

where the error terms are independently and identically distributed for each t, with covariance matrix

$$\boldsymbol{\Sigma} \equiv \begin{bmatrix} \sigma_{11} & \sigma_{12} \\ \sigma_{12} & \sigma_{22} \end{bmatrix}.$$

If $\sigma_{12} \neq 0$, x_t is correlated with ε_{1t} and estimation of (18.05) by OLS will not be consistent because x_t is not predetermined in (18.05).

Now let us consider the expectation of y_t conditional on x_t and all lagged y_t's and x_t's. We have

$$E(y_t \,|\, x_t, y_{t-1}, x_{t-1} \cdots) = \beta x_t + E(\varepsilon_{1t} \,|\, x_t, y_{t-1}, x_{t-1} \cdots). \tag{18.07}$$

Notice that ε_{2t} is defined by (18.06) as a linear combination of the conditioning variables. Thus the conditional expectation of ε_{1t} in (18.07) is

$$E(\varepsilon_{1t} \,|\, \varepsilon_{2t}) = \frac{\sigma_{12}}{\sigma_{22}} \varepsilon_{2t} = \frac{\sigma_{12}}{\sigma_{22}} (x_t - \delta_1 x_{t-1} - \delta_2 y_{t-1}).$$

We may therefore write

$$y_t = b x_t + c_1 x_{t-1} + c_2 y_{t-1} + v_t, \tag{18.08}$$

with

$$b = \beta + \frac{\sigma_{12}}{\sigma_{22}}, \quad c_1 = -\,\delta_1 \frac{\sigma_{12}}{\sigma_{22}}, \quad c_2 = -\,\delta_2 \frac{\sigma_{12}}{\sigma_{22}}, \tag{18.09}$$

and with v_t independent of x_t. Thus x_t is predetermined in (18.08), whatever the value of σ_{12}, even though it is not predetermined in (18.05) when $\sigma_{12} \neq 0$.

We will return to this model later. Meanwhile, let us work toward a concept more suitable than predeterminedness in the simultaneous model context. Because what is at issue is whether the explanatory variables $\boldsymbol{X}_t$ are determined simultaneously with the $\boldsymbol{Y}_t$'s, we will need to work with DGPs that generate $\boldsymbol{Y}_t$ and $\boldsymbol{X}_t$ jointly. As usual, we may represent a DGP by a probability density function, or better its logarithm, which can be expressed as the sum of contributions from each of the observations; see Section 8.2. The contribution from observation t has the form

$$\ell_t(\boldsymbol{Y}_t, \boldsymbol{X}_t \,|\, \Omega_t). \tag{18.10}$$

This expression is the log of the joint density of $\boldsymbol{Y}_t$ and $\boldsymbol{X}_t$ conditional on the information set Ω_t. The latter consists of the whole sample of observations on both $\boldsymbol{Y}_t$ and $\boldsymbol{X}_t$ from the first up to the $(t-1)^{\text{th}}$.

Expression (18.10) can itself be decomposed into two contributions, one the log of the density of $\boldsymbol{Y}_t$ conditional on $\boldsymbol{X}_t$ and Ω_t and the second the log of the density of $\boldsymbol{X}_t$ conditional on Ω_t alone:

$$\ell_t(\boldsymbol{Y}_t, \boldsymbol{X}_t \,|\, \Omega_t) = \ell_t^Y(\boldsymbol{Y}_t \,|\, \boldsymbol{X}_t, \Omega_t) + \ell_t^X(\boldsymbol{X}_t \,|\, \Omega_t), \tag{18.11}$$

in obvious notation. What we would like to be able to do at this point is to forget about the second of the contributions in (18.11), since it concerns only the explanatory variables.

Under what conditions could we drop the second contribution? To answer that question, let us first consider a model, $\mathbb{M}$, comprised of DGPs represented by sets of contributions of the form (18.11). Next, let us define a parameter-defining mapping $\boldsymbol{\theta} : \mathbb{M} \rightarrow \Theta \in \mathbb{R}^p$ that associates a p-vector of parameters $\boldsymbol{\theta}(\mu) \in \Theta$ to each $\mu \in \mathbb{M}$. The parameter vector $\boldsymbol{\theta}$ includes all the **parameters of interest**, i.e., all those that we are interested in estimating. As we will see below, there may well be other parameters, called **nuisance parameters**, that we are not interested in estimating.

Definition 18.3.

The explanatory variables $\boldsymbol{X}_t$ are **weakly exogenous** for the parametrized model $(\mathbb{M}, \boldsymbol{\theta})$ if

(i) there exists a submodel $\mathbb{M}^X$ that contains DGPs for the explanatory variables $\boldsymbol{X}_t$ only;

(ii) there exists a conditional submodel $\mathbb{M}^Y$ that contains DGPs for the endogenous variables $\boldsymbol{Y}_t$ conditional on the explanatory variables $\boldsymbol{X}_t$;

(iii) the full model $\mathbb{M}$ consists of all joint DGPs (μ^Y, μ^X), where μ^X is an arbitrary element of $\mathbb{M}^X$ and μ^Y an arbitrary element of $\mathbb{M}^Y$; and

(iv) there exists a parameter-defining mapping $\boldsymbol{\theta}^Y : \mathbb{M}^Y \rightarrow \Theta$ such that, for any $\mu \equiv (\mu^Y, \mu^X) \in \mathbb{M}$, $\boldsymbol{\theta}(\mu) = \boldsymbol{\theta}^Y(\mu^Y)$.

This definition needs a few words of explanation. The DGPs of the submodel $\mathbb{M}^X$ are characterized by sequences of contributions like the ℓ_t^X's in (18.11), while those of $\mathbb{M}^Y$ are characterized by contributions like the ℓ_t^Y's of that equation. Thus the contributions that characterize the DGPs of both submodels are such that, for observation t, the density is conditional on *all* of Ω_t. This means in particular that the process by which $\boldsymbol{X}_t$ is generated can perfectly well depend on lagged $\boldsymbol{Y}_t$'s. The force of point (iii) of the definition is that the full model $\mathbb{M}$, the DGPs of which have contributions like the entire right-hand side of (18.11), must contain *all* possible combinations of elements of $\mathbb{M}^X$ and $\mathbb{M}^Y$. Point (iv) says that the model parameters depend *only* on the conditional DGP which generates the $\boldsymbol{Y}_t$'s conditional on the $\boldsymbol{X}_t$'s. In other words, the parameters associated with the DGP (μ^Y, μ^X) depend only on μ^Y. If μ^X is replaced by another DGP for the explanatory variables, say ν^X, the parameters do not change.

Engle, Hendry, and Richard claim that weak exogeneity in the sense of the above definition is precisely what is needed for us to be able to estimate and perform inference on the parameters $\boldsymbol{\theta}$ without taking the submodel $\mathbb{M}^X$ into account. For models to be estimated by maximum likelihood, this is clear enough. The loglikelihood function is the sum of contributions like (18.11). Only the first term, from the submodel $\mathbb{M}^Y$, may depend on $\boldsymbol{\theta}$. Maximization of the complete loglikelihood function is therefore equivalent to maximization of the **partial loglikelihood function**

$$\ell^Y(\boldsymbol{Y}^n, \boldsymbol{X}^n; \boldsymbol{\theta}) \equiv \sum_{t=1}^{n} \ell_t^Y(\boldsymbol{Y}_t \,|\, \boldsymbol{X}_t, \Omega_t; \boldsymbol{\theta})$$

with respect to $\boldsymbol{\theta}$. Similarly, for inference, the gradient and Hessian of the full loglikelihood function ℓ with respect to $\boldsymbol{\theta}$ are identical to those of the partial loglikelihood function ℓ^Y.

Let us see how Definition 18.3 works with the model defined by (18.05) and (18.06). Clearly, (18.06) corresponds to the submodel $\mathbb{M}^X$ and (18.05) corresponds to the submodel $\mathbb{M}^Y$. Observe that (18.06) does indeed make use of lagged values of y_t. Notice that if the "parameters" δ_1 and δ_2 were defined within the parameter-defining mapping, weak exogeneity would be completely out of the question, since the δ_i's appear *only* in the submodel $\mathbb{M}^X$. To avoid this seeming difficulty, we will assume that the parameter-defining mapping defines only the parameter β. Thus, in this case, we are treating the δ_i's, along with the elements of the covariance matrix $\boldsymbol{\Sigma}$, as nuisance parameters. The only parameter of interest is β.

A DGP of the submodel $\mathbb{M}^X$ can now be specified by giving the values of the nuisance parameters δ_i and the marginal density of the error terms ε_{2t}, which will depend on the unconditional variance σ_{22} but not on σ_{11} or σ_{12}. For a DGP in $\mathbb{M}^Y$, it is necessary to specify the value of β, the parameter of interest, and the density of ε_{1t} conditional on ε_{2t}, which will involve σ_{11}

and σ_{12}. At this stage, conditions (i), (ii), and (iv) of Definition 18.3 are satisfied. The variable x_t will therefore be weakly exogenous for the model given by (18.05) and (18.06) and the parameter β if we can also satisfy condition (iii), which requires that we should be able to put together *any* two DGPs, one from each submodel. But this is not possible in general, because the inequality $\sigma_{11}\sigma_{22} \geq \sigma_{12}^2$ must be satisfied in order that the covariance matrix of the joint distribution of ε_{1t} and ε_{2t} should be positive semidefinite. Only if we restrict the overall model so that $\sigma_{12} = 0$ will the inequality be satisfied automatically, and so only in this case will x_t be weakly exogenous.

We see therefore that the weak exogeneity of x_t is, in this case, the same as its predeterminedness. What if now we look at the model given by (18.08) and (18.06)? Recall that x_t is predetermined for (18.08) quite generally. In fact, it will also be weakly exogenous generally if we change the parameter-defining mapping (but not the underlying model $\mathbb{M}$) so that it now defines the parameter b instead of β. Notice that even if we include as parameters of interest c_1, c_2, and the variance of the error terms v_t in (18.08), along with b, β cannot be recovered from these parameters without σ_{12}. The weak exogeneity follows from the fact that, by construction, v_t is uncorrelated with ε_{2t}.

The advantage of weak exogeneity over predeterminedness in the present context is that its definition makes reference to a particular parameter-defining mapping. This means that we may say that x_t is weakly exogenous *for* β or not, as the case may be, and that it is always weakly exogenous *for* b. Predeterminedness on the other hand is defined relative to an *equation*, like (18.05) or (18.08), rather than a parameter-defining mapping.

Another concept that can be important when one wishes to work conditionally with respect to a set of explanatory variables is that of **Granger causality**. As the name suggests, the concept was developed by Granger (1969). Other definitions of causality have been suggested, notably by Sims (1972). The Granger and Sims definitions of causality are often, although not always, equivalent; see Chamberlain (1982) and Florens and Mouchart (1982). For most purposes, it seems that Granger causality, or rather its opposite, **Granger noncausality**, is the most useful concept.

We now give a definition of Granger noncausality. Like the definition of weak exogeneity, it is made in the context of models $\mathbb{M}$ that contain DGPs capable of generating two sets of variables $\boldsymbol{Y}_t$ and $\boldsymbol{X}_t$. Unlike that definition, this one makes no use of a parameter-defining mapping and does not make the distinction between the $\boldsymbol{Y}_t$'s as endogenous variables and the $\boldsymbol{X}_t$'s as explanatory variables. In the definition, $\boldsymbol{Y}^{t-1}$ and $\boldsymbol{X}^{t-1}$ denote the rows of the matrices $\boldsymbol{Y}$ and $\boldsymbol{X}$, respectively, prior to the tth. Thus Ω_t consists of $\boldsymbol{Y}^{t-1}$ and $\boldsymbol{X}^{t-1}$.

Definition 18.4.

The variables $\boldsymbol{Y}^{t-1}$ do not Granger cause the variables $\boldsymbol{X}_t$ in a model $\mathbb{M}$ containing DGPs characterized by contributions (18.11) if and only if

$$\ell_t^X(\boldsymbol{X}_t \mid \Omega_t) = \ell_t^X(\boldsymbol{X}_t \mid \boldsymbol{X}^{t-1}).$$

In words, $\boldsymbol{Y}^{t-1}$ does not Granger cause $\boldsymbol{X}_t$ if the distribution of $\boldsymbol{X}_t$ conditional on the past of both $\boldsymbol{X}_t$ and $\boldsymbol{Y}_t$ is the same as that conditional on the past of $\boldsymbol{X}_t$ alone.

A useful way of expressing Granger noncausality is to say that the past of $\boldsymbol{Y}_t$ contains no information about $\boldsymbol{X}_t$ that is not already contained in the past of $\boldsymbol{X}_t$ itself. Although it is not strictly correct, it is common to say simply that the variables $\boldsymbol{Y}_t$ do or do not Granger cause the variables $\boldsymbol{X}_t$, rather than that the variables $\boldsymbol{Y}^{t-1}$ do or do not do so. This usage normally leads to no ambiguity.

It is evident from (18.06) that, in the model given by that equation and (18.05), y_t *does* Granger cause x_t, unless $\delta_2 = 0$. Thus, even if $\sigma_{12} = 0$, which means that x_t is weakly exogenous for the parameter β in (18.05), the process generating x_t depends on the past of the endogenous variable y_t. On the other hand, if $\delta_2 = 0$ but $\sigma_{12} \neq 0$, y_t does not Granger cause x_t, even though x_t is not weakly exogenous for β. Thus the two ideas of weak exogeneity and Granger noncausality are separate: Neither one implies nor is implied by the other.

As we have seen, the presence of Granger causality does not prevent us from estimating β efficiently and performing inference on it without taking the process that generates x_t into account if x_t is weakly exogenous for β. Conversely, failure of weak exogeneity does not prevent us from making efficient *forecasts* of y_t conditional on x_t if y_t does not Granger cause x_t. Specifically, suppose that we set up a forecasting equation for x_t based only on its own past. If (18.05) and (18.06) are true, we find that

$$E(x_t \mid x^{t-1}) = (\delta_1 + \beta\delta_2)x_{t-1}. \tag{18.12}$$

One would therefore forecast x_t in terms of the lagged value x_{t-1} and an estimate of the autoregressive parameter $\delta_1 + \beta\delta_2$, obtained, perhaps, by regressing x_t on itself lagged once. If next we wish to forecast y_t conditional on our forecast of x_t, we would develop a forecasting equation giving the forecast of y_t as a function of that of x_t and the past of both variables. From (18.08),

$$E(y_t \mid x_t, \Omega_t) = bx_t + c_1x_{t-1} + c_2y_{t-1}, \tag{18.13}$$

where b, c_1, and c_2 are defined by (18.09). Now if we replace x_t in (18.13) by the forecast (18.12), we obtain a forecast

$$b(\delta_1 + \beta\delta_2)x_{t-1} + c_1x_{t-1} + c_2y_{t-1}. \tag{18.14}$$

It can be deduced immediately from (18.05) and (18.06) that

$$E(y_t \mid \Omega_t) = \beta\delta_1x_{t-1} + \beta\delta_2y_{t-1}.$$

Therefore, if (18.14) is to provide an unbiased forecast, we require that

$$b(\delta_1 + \beta\delta_2) + c_1 = \beta\delta_1 \quad \text{and} \quad c_2 = \beta\delta_2.$$

By using the definitions (18.09), it can be seen that these requirements can both be met if either $\delta_2 = 0$ or $b = 0$. The former of these two conditions is precisely that of Granger noncausality. The latter corresponds to the special case in which x_t contains no information about y_t not already contained in Ω_t and is of less interest to us in the present context.

The conclusion in general is that, when our goal is forecasting, forecasts of the variables $\boldsymbol{Y}_t$ may be made conditional on forecasts of the variables $\boldsymbol{X}_t$ if $\boldsymbol{Y}^{t-1}$ does not Granger cause $\boldsymbol{X}_t$. On the other hand, if our goal is estimation of or inference about certain parameters, we may proceed conditionally with respect to $\boldsymbol{X}_t$ if these variables are weakly exogenous for the parameters in the context of the model in which they are defined. It can be interesting to put the two ideas together and define circumstances in which all of these activities may safely be performed conditional on $\boldsymbol{X}_t$. The appropriate concept is that of **strong exogeneity**, which we now define.

Definition 18.5.

The explanatory variables $\boldsymbol{X}_t$ are **strongly exogenous** for the parametrized model $(\mathbb{M}, \boldsymbol{\theta})$ containing DGPs that generate endogenous variables $\boldsymbol{Y}_t$ along with the $\boldsymbol{X}_t$'s if they are weakly exogenous and $\boldsymbol{Y}^{t-1}$ does not Granger cause $\boldsymbol{X}_t$.

This completes our discussion of causality and exogeneity. For a much fuller discussion, readers are referred to the Engle-Hendry-Richard paper. In addition to introducing the concepts of weak and strong exogeneity, that paper introduces yet another concept, called **super exogeneity**. It is important for policy analysis but not for estimation and inference, and will therefore not concern us here.

18.3 IDENTIFICATION IN SIMULTANEOUS EQUATIONS MODELS

The issue of identification in simultaneous equations models is, in principle, no different from what we have already discussed in the general context of parametrized models. If for a given model $\mathbb{M}$ a parameter-defining mapping can be defined, then the parameters of the model are identified, in the sense that one and only one parameter vector is associated with each DGP in $\mathbb{M}$. However, even when such a mapping exists, the data must satisfy certain conditions for the parameters to be identified by a given data set, and the DGP must satisfy certain conditions for them to be identified asymptotically. In Chapter 5, we defined and discussed in some detail the concept of asymptotic identifiability and contrasted it with identification by a given data set. It is the former concept that is of primary interest in the context of simultaneous equations models. All of the preferred estimation methods are based on asymptotic theory, and one cannot hope to obtain consistent parameter estimates if the parameters are not asymptotically identified.

In this section, we will discuss the asymptotic identifiability of a linear simultaneous equations model by the two-stage least squares estimator introduced in Section 7.5. This may seem a very limited topic, and in a certain sense it is indeed limited. However, it is a topic that has given rise to a truly vast literature, to which we can in no way do justice here; see Fisher (1976) and Hsiao (1983). There exist models that are not identified by the 2SLS estimator but are identified by other estimators, such as the FIML estimator, and we will briefly touch on such cases later. It is not a simple task to extend the theory we will present in this section to the context of nonlinear models, for which it is usually better to return to the general theory expounded in Section 5.2.

We begin with the linear simultaneous equations model, (18.01). This model consists of DGPs that generate samples for which each observation is a g-vector $\boldsymbol{Y}_t$ of dependent variables, conditional on a set of exogenous and lagged dependent variables $\boldsymbol{X}_t$. Since the exogenous variables in $\boldsymbol{X}_t$ are assumed to be weakly exogenous, their generating mechanism can be ignored. In order to discuss identification, little needs to be assumed about the error terms $\boldsymbol{U}_t$. They must evidently satisfy the condition that $E(\boldsymbol{U}_t) = 0$, and it seems reasonable to assume that they are serially independent and that $E(\boldsymbol{U}_t^{\top}\boldsymbol{U}_t) = \boldsymbol{\Sigma}_t$, where $\boldsymbol{\Sigma}_t$ is a positive definite matrix for all t. If inferences are to be based on the usual 2SLS covariance matrix, it will be necessary to make the further assumption that the error terms are homoskedastic, that is, $\boldsymbol{\Sigma}_t = \boldsymbol{\Sigma}$ for all t.

It is convenient to treat the identification of the parameters of a simultaneous equations model equation by equation, since it is entirely possible that the parameters of some equations may be identified while the parameters of others are not. In order to simplify notation, we will consider, without loss of generality, only the parameters of the first equation of the system, that is, the elements of the first columns of the matrices $\boldsymbol{\Gamma}$ and $\boldsymbol{B}$. As we remarked in Section 18.1, restrictions must be imposed on the elements of these matrices for identification to be possible. It is usual to assume that these restrictions all take the form of zero restrictions on some elements. A variable is said to be **excluded** from an equation if the coefficient corresponding to that variable for that equation is restricted to be zero; otherwise, it is said to be **included** in the equation. As discussed in Section 6.4, it is always possible in the context of a single equation to perform a reparametrization such that all restrictions take the form of zero restrictions. But in the context of a simultaneous equations model, such reparametrizations exist in general only if there are no **cross-equation restrictions**, that is, restrictions which involve the parameters of more than one equation of the system. If there are cross-equation restrictions, then to all intents and purposes we leave the context of linear systems. We would in any case have to abandon the 2SLS estimator if we wished to impose cross-equation restrictions.

Let us partition the matrix $\boldsymbol{Y}$ as follows:

$$\boldsymbol{Y} = [\,\boldsymbol{y} \quad \boldsymbol{Y}_1 \quad \boldsymbol{Y}_2\,], \tag{18.15}$$

where the column vector $\boldsymbol{y}$ is the endogenous variable with coefficient unity in the first equation of the system, the columns of the $n \times g_1$ matrix $\boldsymbol{Y}_1$ are the endogenous variables *not* excluded from that equation by zero restrictions, and the columns of the $n \times (g - g_1 - 1)$ matrix $\boldsymbol{Y}_2$ are those endogenous variables that are excluded. Similarly, the matrix $\boldsymbol{X}$ of exogenous variables is partitioned as

$$\boldsymbol{X} = [\,\boldsymbol{X}_1 \quad \boldsymbol{X}_2\,], \tag{18.16}$$

where the columns of the $n \times k_1$ matrix $\boldsymbol{X}_1$ are the exogenous variables that are included in the equation, and those of the $n \times (k - k_1)$ matrix $\boldsymbol{X}_2$ are the excluded exogenous variables.

Corresponding to the above partitioning of $\boldsymbol{Y}$ and $\boldsymbol{X}$, we may partition the coefficient matrices $\boldsymbol{\Gamma}$ and $\boldsymbol{B}$ as

$$\boldsymbol{\Gamma} = \begin{bmatrix} 1 & \boldsymbol{\Gamma}_{02} \\ -\boldsymbol{\gamma}_1 & \boldsymbol{\Gamma}_{12} \\ \mathbf{0} & \boldsymbol{\Gamma}_{22} \end{bmatrix} \quad \text{and} \quad \boldsymbol{B} = \begin{bmatrix} \boldsymbol{\beta}_1 & \boldsymbol{B}_{12} \\ \mathbf{0} & \boldsymbol{B}_{22} \end{bmatrix}. \tag{18.17}$$

The rows of $\boldsymbol{\Gamma}$ are partitioned as are the columns of $\boldsymbol{Y}$ in (18.15), and the rows of $\boldsymbol{B}$ are partitioned as are the columns of $\boldsymbol{X}$ in (18.16). In addition, the columns of both $\boldsymbol{\Gamma}$ and $\boldsymbol{B}$ are partitioned so as to separate the first columns of each matrix from the other columns, since the first columns contain the parameters of the first equation of the system. The first equation can therefore be written as

$$\boldsymbol{y} = \boldsymbol{Y}_1\boldsymbol{\gamma}_1 + \boldsymbol{X}_1\boldsymbol{\beta}_1 + \boldsymbol{u} = \boldsymbol{Z\delta} + \boldsymbol{u}, \tag{18.18}$$

where the $n \times (g_1 + k_1)$ regressor matrix $\boldsymbol{Z}$ is $[\boldsymbol{X}_1 \quad \boldsymbol{Y}_1]$, and the parameter vector $\boldsymbol{\delta}$ is $[\boldsymbol{\beta}_1 \,\vdots\, \boldsymbol{\gamma}_1]$.

In order to obtain 2SLS estimates of $\boldsymbol{\delta}$, we must make use of instrumental variables. The columns of $\boldsymbol{X}_1$, being exogenous, may serve as their own instruments, and the columns of $\boldsymbol{X}_2$ provide additional instruments. If the columns of $\boldsymbol{X}$ are the only instruments available, then it is plain that a necessary condition for the identifiability of $\boldsymbol{\delta}$, either in finite samples or asymptotically, is that $\boldsymbol{X}$ should have at least as many columns as $\boldsymbol{Z}$. This condition is equivalent to the requirement that $\boldsymbol{X}_2$ should have at least as many columns as $\boldsymbol{Y}_1$, i.e., that $k - k_1 \geq g_1$. In words, what is required is that the number of excluded exogenous variables should be at least as great as the number of included endogenous variables. This is the celebrated **order condition** for identification. As we will see, however, it is only a necessary condition and not generally a sufficient one.[1]

[1] If one allows for the possibility of cross-equation restrictions, the order condition is no longer even necessary.

It may not be obvious that the columns of $\boldsymbol{X}$ exhaust the supply of available instruments. Why can we not make use of any other exogenous or predetermined variables that happen to be correlated with the endogenous variables $\boldsymbol{Y}_1$? Even if the order condition for identification is satisfied, would we not be well advised to use any other available instruments to obtain more efficient estimates? It turns out that using additional instruments will not succeed in asymptotically identifying otherwise unidentified parameters. Moreover, under homoskedasticity and serial independence of the error terms $\boldsymbol{u}$, using additional instruments will lead to no efficiency gain.

In order to obtain these results, we consider the restricted reduced form (18.02) corresponding to (18.01). By a slight abuse of notation, we will write this simply as

$$\boldsymbol{Y} = \boldsymbol{X\Pi} + \boldsymbol{V}, \tag{18.19}$$

defining $\boldsymbol{\Pi}$ to be $\boldsymbol{B\Gamma}^{-1}$. It will be necessary to partition $\boldsymbol{\Pi}$ conformably with the partitions (18.17) of $\boldsymbol{\Gamma}$ and $\boldsymbol{B}$:

$$\boldsymbol{\Pi} = \begin{bmatrix} \boldsymbol{\pi}_1 & \boldsymbol{\Pi}_{11} & \boldsymbol{\Pi}_{12} \\ \boldsymbol{\pi}_2 & \boldsymbol{\Pi}_{21} & \boldsymbol{\Pi}_{22} \end{bmatrix}. \tag{18.20}$$

The partition of the rows here is the same as that of the rows of $\boldsymbol{B}$ in (18.17), and the partition of the columns is the same as that of the rows of $\boldsymbol{\Gamma}$ in the same equation, or of the columns of $\boldsymbol{Y}$ in (18.15). We will assume that the data were generated by a process (18.19) with $\boldsymbol{\Pi} = \boldsymbol{\Pi}_0 = \boldsymbol{B}_0\boldsymbol{\Gamma}_0^{-1}$.

Let us now consider the identifiability of the parameter vector $\boldsymbol{\delta}$ in the equation (18.18) for any admissible instrument matrix $\boldsymbol{W}$, that is, any matrix $\boldsymbol{W}$ such that $\operatorname{plim}(n^{-1}\boldsymbol{W}^{\top}\boldsymbol{W})$ is a positive definite nonstochastic matrix and such that $\operatorname{plim}(n^{-1}\boldsymbol{W}^{\top}\boldsymbol{V}) = \boldsymbol{0}$. From the results of Section 7.8, $\boldsymbol{\delta}$ is identifiable by the data if the matrix $\boldsymbol{Z}^{\top}\boldsymbol{P}_W\boldsymbol{Z}$ is positive definite and is asymptotically identifiable if $\operatorname{plim}(n^{-1}\boldsymbol{Z}^{\top}\boldsymbol{P}_W\boldsymbol{Z})$ is positive definite. In order to study this probability limit, consider the matrix

$$\begin{aligned} \tfrac{1}{n}\boldsymbol{W}^{\top}\boldsymbol{Z} &= \tfrac{1}{n}\boldsymbol{W}^{\top}[\,\boldsymbol{X}_1 \quad \boldsymbol{Y}_1\,] \\ &= \tfrac{1}{n}\boldsymbol{W}^{\top}[\,\boldsymbol{X}_1 \quad \boldsymbol{X}_1\boldsymbol{\Pi}_{11} + \boldsymbol{X}_2\boldsymbol{\Pi}_{21} + \boldsymbol{V}_1\,], \end{aligned} \tag{18.21}$$

where the block $\boldsymbol{V}_1$ of the error matrix $\boldsymbol{V}$ corresponds to the block $\boldsymbol{Y}_1$ of $\boldsymbol{Y}$ in (18.15), and the reduced form coefficients are evaluated at $\boldsymbol{\Pi} = \boldsymbol{\Pi}_0$.

The asymptotic orthogonality of the instruments $\boldsymbol{W}$ and the error terms $\boldsymbol{V}$ means that the probability limit of (18.21) is

$$\operatorname*{plim}_{n\to\infty}\Big(\tfrac{1}{n}\boldsymbol{W}^{\top}[\,\boldsymbol{X}_1 \quad \boldsymbol{X}_1\boldsymbol{\Pi}_{11} + \boldsymbol{X}_2\boldsymbol{\Pi}_{21}\,]\Big). \tag{18.22}$$

This makes it clear that, whatever the choice of the instrument matrix $\boldsymbol{W}$, the rank of the matrix (18.22) cannot exceed k, the number of linearly independent exogenous variables. All of the columns of the partitioned matrix in (18.22) are columns of $\boldsymbol{X}$ or linear combinations of columns of $\boldsymbol{X}$. It follows that the rank of $\operatorname{plim}(n^{-1}\boldsymbol{Z}^\top\boldsymbol{P}_W\boldsymbol{Z})$ can also never exceed k. Thus, if $\boldsymbol{Z}$ has more than k columns, that is, if the order condition is violated, then $\operatorname{plim}(n^{-1}\boldsymbol{Z}^\top\boldsymbol{P}_W\boldsymbol{Z})$ is singular and, hence, not positive definite. We conclude that the order condition is indeed necessary for the asymptotic identifiability of $\boldsymbol{\delta}$, whatever set of instruments may be used.

Next we show that, under homoskedasticity and serial independence of the errors $\boldsymbol{u}$, the columns of $\boldsymbol{X}$ provide optimal instruments for the estimation of $\boldsymbol{\delta}$. There are two possible cases. In the first case, $\mathcal{S}(\boldsymbol{X}) \subset \mathcal{S}(\boldsymbol{W})$. Since $\boldsymbol{X}_1$ and $\boldsymbol{X}_2$ lie in $\mathcal{S}(\boldsymbol{X})$, we see from (18.22) that

$$\begin{aligned}\operatorname*{plim}_{n\to\infty}\Big(\frac{1}{n}\boldsymbol{Z}^\top\boldsymbol{P}_W\boldsymbol{Z}\Big) &= \operatorname*{plim}_{n\to\infty}\Big(\frac{1}{n}\boldsymbol{Z}^\top\boldsymbol{P}_X\boldsymbol{Z}\Big)\\ &= \operatorname*{plim}_{n\to\infty}\Big(\frac{1}{n}[\,\boldsymbol{X}_1 \quad \boldsymbol{X}_1\boldsymbol{\Pi}_{11}+\boldsymbol{X}_2\boldsymbol{\Pi}_{21}\,]^\top[\,\boldsymbol{X}_1 \quad \boldsymbol{X}_1\boldsymbol{\Pi}_{11}+\boldsymbol{X}_2\boldsymbol{\Pi}_{21}\,]\Big).\end{aligned}$$

Thus including additional instruments in $\boldsymbol{W}$ beyond those in $\boldsymbol{X}$ can yield no asymptotic efficiency gain. Since it will surely contribute to finite-sample bias (see Section 7.5), one would never want to do so.

In the second case, $\mathcal{S}(\boldsymbol{X})$ is not a subspace of $\mathcal{S}(\boldsymbol{W})$. This implies that, asymptotically, $\boldsymbol{W}$ must have less explanatory power for $\boldsymbol{Z}$ than $\boldsymbol{X}$ does. Therefore, $\operatorname{plim}(n^{-1}\boldsymbol{Z}^\top\boldsymbol{P}_X\boldsymbol{Z}) - \operatorname{plim}(n^{-1}\boldsymbol{Z}^\top\boldsymbol{P}_W\boldsymbol{Z})$ is a positive semidefinite matrix for all such instrument matrices $\boldsymbol{W}$. It follows (see Appendix A) that $\operatorname{plim}(n^{-1}\boldsymbol{Z}^\top\boldsymbol{P}_W\boldsymbol{Z})^{-1} - \operatorname{plim}(n^{-1}\boldsymbol{Z}^\top\boldsymbol{P}_X\boldsymbol{Z})^{-1}$ is also a positive semidefinite matrix. Thus the asymptotic covariance matrix one obtains by using $\boldsymbol{X}$ as the matrix of instruments, namely, $\sigma^2\operatorname{plim}(n^{-1}\boldsymbol{Z}^\top\boldsymbol{P}_X\boldsymbol{Z})^{-1}$, provides a lower bound for the asymptotic covariance matrix of any IV estimator.

From the above discussion and the results of Section 7.8, it is clear that the necessary and sufficient condition for the asymptotic identification of $\boldsymbol{\delta}$ by use of the optimal instruments $\boldsymbol{X}$ is simply that $\operatorname{plim}(n^{-1}\boldsymbol{Z}^\top\boldsymbol{P}_X\boldsymbol{Z})$ should be nonsingular. This condition is referred to in the traditional literature on simultaneous equations models as the **rank condition** for identification, for obvious reasons. However, the condition is seldom expressed in so simple a fashion. Instead, the condition is typically expressed in terms of the coefficients $\boldsymbol{\Gamma}$ and $\boldsymbol{B}$ of the structural form or else of the coefficients $\boldsymbol{\Pi}$ of the restricted reduced form. Since we have defined $\boldsymbol{\Pi}$ in terms of $\boldsymbol{\Gamma}$ and $\boldsymbol{B}$ alone, any condition that can be expressed in terms of one set of coefficients can be expressed in terms of the other.

We will now show how the rank condition that $\operatorname{plim}(n^{-1}\boldsymbol{Z}^\top\boldsymbol{P}_X\boldsymbol{Z})$ should be nonsingular can be expressed in terms of restrictions on $\boldsymbol{\Pi}$ in the DGP. The parameters $\boldsymbol{\gamma}_1$ and $\boldsymbol{\beta}_1$ of the first structural equation can be identified if and only if they can be uniquely recovered from the matrix $\boldsymbol{\Pi}$ of restricted reduced form parameters. This matrix, by definition, satisfies the equation $\boldsymbol{\Pi\Gamma} = \boldsymbol{B}$, the first column of which can, by virtue of the partitions (18.17) and (18.20), be expressed as

$$\begin{aligned}\boldsymbol{\pi}_1 + \boldsymbol{\Pi}_{11}\boldsymbol{\gamma}_1 &= \boldsymbol{\beta}_1\\ \boldsymbol{\pi}_2 + \boldsymbol{\Pi}_{21}\boldsymbol{\gamma}_1 &= \mathbf{0}.\end{aligned}$$

The first of these two equations serves to define $\boldsymbol{\beta}_1$ in terms of $\boldsymbol{\Pi}$ and $\boldsymbol{\gamma}_1$, and allows us to see that $\boldsymbol{\beta}_1$ can be identified if $\boldsymbol{\gamma}_1$ can be. The second equation shows that $\boldsymbol{\gamma}_1$ is determined uniquely if and only if the submatrix $\boldsymbol{\Pi}_{21}$ has full column rank, that is, if the rank of the matrix is equal to the number of columns (see Appendix A). The submatrix $\boldsymbol{\Pi}_{21}$ has $k - k_1$ rows and g_1 columns. Therefore, if the order condition is satisfied, there are at least as many rows as columns. The condition for the identifiability of $\boldsymbol{\gamma}_1$, and so also of $\boldsymbol{\beta}_1$, is thus simply that the columns of $\boldsymbol{\Pi}_{21}$ in the DGP should be linearly independent.

It is instructive to show why this last condition is equivalent to the rank condition in terms of $\operatorname{plim}(n^{-1}\boldsymbol{Z}^\top \boldsymbol{P}_X \boldsymbol{Z})$. If, as we have tacitly assumed throughout this discussion, the exogenous variables $\boldsymbol{X}$ satisfy the condition that $\operatorname{plim}(n^{-1}\boldsymbol{X}^\top\boldsymbol{X})$ is positive definite, then $\operatorname{plim}(n^{-1}\boldsymbol{Z}^\top \boldsymbol{P}_X \boldsymbol{Z})$ can fail to have full rank only if $\operatorname{plim}(n^{-1}\boldsymbol{X}^\top\boldsymbol{Z})$ has rank less than $g_1 + k_1$, the number of columns of $\boldsymbol{Z}$. The probability limit of the matrix $n^{-1}\boldsymbol{X}^\top\boldsymbol{Z}$ follows from (18.22), with $\boldsymbol{X}$ replacing $\boldsymbol{W}$. If, for notational simplicity, we drop the probability limit and the factor of n^{-1}, which are not essential to the discussion, the matrix of interest can be written as

$$\begin{bmatrix}\boldsymbol{X}_1^\top\boldsymbol{X}_1 & \boldsymbol{X}_1^\top\boldsymbol{X}_1\boldsymbol{\Pi}_{11} + \boldsymbol{X}_1^\top\boldsymbol{X}_2\boldsymbol{\Pi}_{21}\\ \boldsymbol{X}_2^\top\boldsymbol{X}_1 & \boldsymbol{X}_2^\top\boldsymbol{X}_1\boldsymbol{\Pi}_{11} + \boldsymbol{X}_2^\top\boldsymbol{X}_2\boldsymbol{\Pi}_{21}\end{bmatrix}. \tag{18.23}$$

This matrix does not have full column rank of $g_1 + k_1$ if and only if there exists a nonzero $(g_1 + k_1)$–vector $\boldsymbol{\theta} \equiv [\boldsymbol{\theta}_1 \,\vdots\, \boldsymbol{\theta}_2]$ such that postmultiplying (18.23) by $\boldsymbol{\theta}$ gives zero. If we write this condition out and rearrange slightly, we obtain

$$\begin{bmatrix}\boldsymbol{X}_1^\top\boldsymbol{X}_1 & \boldsymbol{X}_1^\top\boldsymbol{X}_2\\ \boldsymbol{X}_2^\top\boldsymbol{X}_1 & \boldsymbol{X}_2^\top\boldsymbol{X}_2\end{bmatrix}\begin{bmatrix}\boldsymbol{\theta}_1 + \boldsymbol{\Pi}_{11}\boldsymbol{\theta}_2\\ \boldsymbol{\Pi}_{21}\boldsymbol{\theta}_2\end{bmatrix} = \mathbf{0}. \tag{18.24}$$

The first matrix on the left-hand side here is just $\boldsymbol{X}^\top\boldsymbol{X}$ and is therefore nonsingular. The condition reduces to the two vector equations

$$\boldsymbol{\theta}_1 + \boldsymbol{\Pi}_{11}\boldsymbol{\theta}_2 = \mathbf{0} \tag{18.25}$$

$$\boldsymbol{\Pi}_{21}\boldsymbol{\theta}_2 = \mathbf{0}. \tag{18.26}$$

If these equations hold for some nonzero $\boldsymbol{\theta}$, it is clear that $\boldsymbol{\theta}_2$ cannot be zero. Consequently, the second of these equations can hold only if $\boldsymbol{\Pi}_{21}$ has less than full column rank. It follows that if the rank condition in terms of $\boldsymbol{Z}^\top\boldsymbol{P}_X\boldsymbol{Z}$ does not hold, then it does not hold in terms of $\boldsymbol{\Pi}_{21}$ either. Conversely, suppose that (18.26) holds for some nonzero g_1–vector $\boldsymbol{\theta}_2$. Then $\boldsymbol{\Pi}_{21}$ does not have full column rank. Define $\boldsymbol{\theta}_1$ in terms of this $\boldsymbol{\theta}_2$ and $\boldsymbol{\Pi}$ by means of (18.25). Then (18.25) and (18.26) together imply (18.24), and the original rank condition fails. The two versions of the rank condition are therefore equivalent.

We conclude this section by stating, without proof, a third version of the rank condition, also equivalent to the other two, but this time in terms of the structural parameters $\boldsymbol{\Gamma}$ and $\boldsymbol{B}$. It is not possible to express this condition exclusively in terms of the parameters $\boldsymbol{\gamma}_1$ and $\boldsymbol{\beta}_1$ of the first equation itself. On the contrary, it is *only* the values of the other parameters that determine whether or not $\boldsymbol{\gamma}_1$ and $\boldsymbol{\beta}_1$ are identified. This third statement of the rank condition is formulated as follows. Form the $(g - g_1 - 1 + k - k_1) \times (g - 1)$ matrix

$$\begin{bmatrix} \boldsymbol{\Gamma}_{22} \\ \boldsymbol{B}_{22} \end{bmatrix}.$$

Then the rank condition is satisfied if and only if this matrix has full column rank $g - 1$.

In this section, we have discussed only the most important conclusions of a long research program. Hsiao (1983) provides a much more extensive treatment. We have not dealt with issues such as cross-equation restrictions and restrictions involving the covariance matrix $\boldsymbol{\Sigma}$; see Rothenberg (1971), Richmond (1974), and Hausman and Taylor (1983), among others. In practice, the order condition for identification is much more useful than the rank condition because it is much easier to verify. The rank condition is of substantial theoretical interest, however, and it is instructive to see that it can be expressed as the very simple condition that the probability limit of a certain matrix should have full rank. It is thus equivalent to the condition that a certain 2SLS estimator, namely, the one that uses all exogenous and predetermined variables as instruments, should have a nonsingular asymptotic covariance matrix.

18.4 FULL-INFORMATION MAXIMUM LIKELIHOOD

Methods for estimating simultaneous equations models can usefully be classified in two different ways. One natural division is between single-equation methods and full-system methods. The former, of which the principal examples are 2SLS and LIML, estimate the model one equation at a time. The latter, of which the principal examples are 3SLS and FIML, estimate all the parameters of the model at once. The adjectives "limited-information" and "full-information" that are part of the names of LIML and FIML make it clear that the former is a single-equation method and the latter is a full-system one. Single-equation methods are easier to use, while full-system methods potentially yield more efficient estimates.

The other natural division is between methods based on maximum likelihood, namely, LIML and FIML, and methods based on instrumental variables or the generalized method of moments, of which the best-known examples are

2SLS and 3SLS. ML methods yield estimates that are invariant to reparametrization (see Section 8.3), while IV methods do not. We have already discussed 2SLS at length in Chapter 7. In this section, we will provide a fairly detailed treatment of FIML, which differs from 2SLS according to both classification schemes. Discussions of LIML and of 3SLS will follow in subsequent sections.

All simultaneous equations estimators attempt to deal with the fact that the error terms of structural equations are correlated with whatever endogenous variables appear in the equation. This correlation causes OLS to be inconsistent. As we have seen, 2SLS deals with it by "instrumenting out" the offending regressors. FIML, on the other hand, deals with it by maximizing a likelihood function that involves a Jacobian term and is not simply a transformation of the sum of squared residuals. FIML also deals with two problems that arise in the case of any multivariate model, whether or not it involves simultaneity; see Section 9.9. One problem is that, except in rare cases, the errors from different equations will be correlated. Single-equation techniques such as 2SLS and LIML simply ignore this problem. In contrast, full-system techniques like FIML and 3SLS take it into account and should therefore yield more efficient estimates in general. A second problem is that, in many models, there may be cross-equation restrictions. Single-equation methods necessarily ignore this problem, but full-system ones like FIML take it into account. When the full system is set up, parameters that appear in more than one equation are automatically treated differently from parameters that appear in only one.

The linear simultaneous equations model (18.01), with error terms that are assumed to be normally distributed, homoskedastic, and serially independent, can be written as

$$\boldsymbol{Y}_t\boldsymbol{\Gamma} = \boldsymbol{X}_t\boldsymbol{B} + \boldsymbol{U}_t, \quad \boldsymbol{U}_t \sim N(\boldsymbol{0}, \boldsymbol{\Sigma}), \tag{18.27}$$

where the notation should be quite familiar by now. Recall that $\boldsymbol{Y}_t$ is $1 \times g$, $\boldsymbol{\Gamma}$ is $g \times g$, $\boldsymbol{X}_t$ is $1 \times k$, $\boldsymbol{B}$ is $k \times g$, $\boldsymbol{U}_t$ is $1 \times g$, and $\boldsymbol{\Sigma}$ is $g \times g$. The easiest way to derive the density of $\boldsymbol{Y}_t$ is to start with the density of $\boldsymbol{U}_t$, which is

$$(2\pi)^{-g/2}|\boldsymbol{\Sigma}|^{-1/2}\exp\Big(-\frac{1}{2}\boldsymbol{U}_t\boldsymbol{\Sigma}^{-1}\boldsymbol{U}_t^{\top}\Big).$$

We then replace $\boldsymbol{U}_t$ by $\boldsymbol{Y}_t\boldsymbol{\Gamma} - \boldsymbol{X}_t\boldsymbol{B}$ and multiply by an appropriate Jacobian factor. This factor is the absolute value of the determinant of the Jacobian of the transformation from $\boldsymbol{Y}_t$ to $\boldsymbol{U}_t$, that is, the determinant of $\boldsymbol{\Gamma}$. Thus the Jacobian factor is $|\det \boldsymbol{\Gamma}|$.[2] The result is

$$(2\pi)^{-g/2}|\det \boldsymbol{\Gamma}||\boldsymbol{\Sigma}|^{-1/2}\exp\Big(-\frac{1}{2}(\boldsymbol{Y}_t\boldsymbol{\Gamma} - \boldsymbol{X}_t\boldsymbol{B})\boldsymbol{\Sigma}^{-1}(\boldsymbol{Y}_t\boldsymbol{\Gamma} - \boldsymbol{X}_t\boldsymbol{B})^{\top}\Big).$$

[2] In this chapter, we use $|\boldsymbol{A}|$ to denote the determinant of $\boldsymbol{A}$ and $|\det \boldsymbol{A}|$ to denote the absolute value of the determinant. It is necessary to use the "det" notation, which we prefer to avoid, only when the absolute value is involved.

From this, we see that the loglikelihood function is

$$\begin{aligned}\ell(\boldsymbol{B},\boldsymbol{\Gamma},\boldsymbol{\Sigma}) = \sum_{t=1}^{n} \ell_t(\boldsymbol{B},\boldsymbol{\Gamma},\boldsymbol{\Sigma}) &= -\tfrac{ng}{2}\log(2\pi) + n\log|\det\boldsymbol{\Gamma}| \\ &- \tfrac{n}{2}\log|\boldsymbol{\Sigma}| - \tfrac{1}{2}\sum_{t=1}^{n}(\boldsymbol{Y}_t\boldsymbol{\Gamma} - \boldsymbol{X}_t\boldsymbol{B})\boldsymbol{\Sigma}^{-1}(\boldsymbol{Y}_t\boldsymbol{\Gamma} - \boldsymbol{X}_t\boldsymbol{B})^{\top}.\end{aligned} \tag{18.28}$$

It is a convenient first step in maximizing $\ell(\boldsymbol{B},\boldsymbol{\Gamma},\boldsymbol{\Sigma})$ to concentrate it with respect to $\boldsymbol{\Sigma}$ or, as we did in Section 9.9, with respect to the inverse matrix $\boldsymbol{\Sigma}^{-1}$. Since

$$\frac{\partial \ell}{\partial \boldsymbol{\Sigma}^{-1}} = \tfrac{n}{2}\boldsymbol{\Sigma} - \tfrac{1}{2}\sum_{t=1}^{n}(\boldsymbol{Y}_t\boldsymbol{\Gamma} - \boldsymbol{X}_t\boldsymbol{B})^{\top}(\boldsymbol{Y}_t\boldsymbol{\Gamma} - \boldsymbol{X}_t\boldsymbol{B}),$$

(see Appendix A) it is evident that

$$\boldsymbol{\Sigma}(\boldsymbol{B},\boldsymbol{\Gamma}) = \tfrac{1}{n}(\boldsymbol{Y\Gamma} - \boldsymbol{XB})^{\top}(\boldsymbol{Y\Gamma} - \boldsymbol{XB}). \tag{18.29}$$

We may substitute (18.29) into (18.28) to obtain

$$\begin{aligned}\ell^{c}(\boldsymbol{B},\boldsymbol{\Gamma}) &= -\tfrac{ng}{2}\big(\log(2\pi) + 1\big) + n\log|\det\boldsymbol{\Gamma}| \\ &- \tfrac{n}{2}\log\Big|\tfrac{1}{n}(\boldsymbol{Y\Gamma} - \boldsymbol{XB})^{\top}(\boldsymbol{Y\Gamma} - \boldsymbol{XB})\Big|.\end{aligned} \tag{18.30}$$

This concentrated loglikelihood function looks very much like (9.65), the concentrated loglikelihood function for a multivariate regression model. Note that we have used the same trick as we did there to evaluate the second term of the last line of (18.28). The difference between (9.65) and (18.30) is due to the presence of the Jacobian term $n\log|\det\boldsymbol{\Gamma}|$, the role of which will be discussed below. The FIML estimator will not be defined if the matrix $(\boldsymbol{Y\Gamma} - \boldsymbol{XB})^{\top}(\boldsymbol{Y\Gamma} - \boldsymbol{XB})$ that appears in (18.30) does not have full rank for all admissible values of $\boldsymbol{B}$ and $\boldsymbol{\Gamma}$, and this requires that $n \geq g + k$. This result also suggests that n may have to be substantially greater than $g + k$ if FIML is to have good finite-sample properties; see Sargan (1975) and Brown (1981).

It is illuminating to derive this concentrated loglikelihood function in an entirely different way. This time, we start from the restricted reduced form corresponding to (18.27), which is

$$\boldsymbol{Y}_t = \boldsymbol{X}_t\boldsymbol{B\Gamma}^{-1} + \boldsymbol{V}_t. \tag{18.31}$$

This system of equations is just a special case of the multivariate regression model considered in Section 9.9, expressed in the form of (9.43), with a set of regression functions $\boldsymbol{\xi}_t \equiv \boldsymbol{X}_t\boldsymbol{B\Gamma}^{-1}$ that are nonlinear functions of the elements of $\boldsymbol{B}$ and $\boldsymbol{\Gamma}$. The concentrated loglikelihood function corresponding to (18.31) is therefore given by (9.65). For our particular case, (9.65) becomes

$$-\frac{ng}{2}\big(\log(2\pi)+1\big)-\frac{n}{2}\log\Big|\frac{1}{n}(\boldsymbol{Y}-\boldsymbol{XB\Gamma}^{-1})^{\top}(\boldsymbol{Y}-\boldsymbol{XB\Gamma}^{-1})\Big|. \tag{18.32}$$

This new expression for $\ell^c(\boldsymbol{B},\boldsymbol{\Gamma})$ is equal to the one we derived previously, (18.30). The equality of (18.30) and (18.32) follows from the fact that

$$\begin{aligned}
&-\frac{n}{2}\log\Big|\frac{1}{n}(\boldsymbol{Y}-\boldsymbol{XB\Gamma}^{-1})^{\top}(\boldsymbol{Y}-\boldsymbol{XB\Gamma}^{-1})\Big| \\
&=-\frac{n}{2}\log\Big|\frac{1}{n}(\boldsymbol{\Gamma}^{\top})^{-1}\boldsymbol{\Gamma}^{\top}(\boldsymbol{Y}-\boldsymbol{XB\Gamma}^{-1})^{\top}(\boldsymbol{Y}-\boldsymbol{XB\Gamma}^{-1})\boldsymbol{\Gamma\Gamma}^{-1}\Big| \\
&=n\log|\det\boldsymbol{\Gamma}|-\frac{n}{2}\log\Big|\frac{1}{n}(\boldsymbol{Y\Gamma}-\boldsymbol{XB})^{\top}(\boldsymbol{Y\Gamma}-\boldsymbol{XB})\Big|.
\end{aligned}$$

The fact that the concentrated loglikelihood function for a linear simultaneous equations model can be written in two quite different ways, as (18.30) and (18.32), is illuminating. It makes it absolutely clear that the structural and restricted reduced forms are simply different ways of writing the same model. We can treat the linear simultaneous equations model either as a special type of model, with concentrated loglikelihood function given by (18.30), or as a special case of a *nonlinear* multivariate regression model, with loglikelihood function the same as for any other multivariate regression model. If we write it in the latter way, we can use all the results already obtained for multivariate regression models in Chapter 9. However, because the coefficient matrix $\boldsymbol{B\Gamma}^{-1}$ depends nonlinearly on coefficients from all the equations in the model, (18.32) is generally less convenient to work with than (18.30).

When it was originally proposed by researchers at the Cowles Commission (Koopmans, 1950), FIML was not computationally feasible, because maximizing the loglikelihood function (18.30) requires numerical optimization. As computers improved and this type of computation became more practical, a number of procedures for maximizing the loglikelihood function were proposed, and most standard econometric packages now incorporate at least one of them. References include Rothenberg and Leenders (1964), Chow (1968), Hausman (1974, 1975), and Dagenais (1978).

As usual, the asymptotic covariance matrix of the FIML parameter estimates $\hat{\boldsymbol{B}}$, $\hat{\boldsymbol{\Gamma}}$, and $\hat{\boldsymbol{\Sigma}}$ can be estimated in several different ways. One approach that is relatively easy but not recommended for small samples is to use the OPG regression. This artificial regression can be based on the unconcentrated loglikelihood function (18.28) but not on the concentrated one (18.30), because the latter is not written as a sum of contributions. A second approach is to start from the form (18.32) of the loglikelihood function. As we showed in Section 9.9, the block of the information matrix associated with the parameters of the regression functions of a multivariate regression model is given as in (9.69), and this block can be computed by means of the Gauss-Newton regression (9.58). A third way to estimate the asymptotic covariance matrix of $\hat{\boldsymbol{B}}$ and $\hat{\boldsymbol{\Gamma}}$ is to make use of the result that 3SLS and FIML are asymptotically equivalent; this approach will be discussed in Section 18.6.

The Jacobian term $\log|\det \boldsymbol{\Gamma}|$ that explicitly appears in (18.30) plays a very important role in estimation. Its presence is of course essential if the ML estimates are to be consistent. Moreover, as the determinant of $\boldsymbol{\Gamma}$ tends to zero, this term tends to minus infinity. Hence the loglikelihood function must tend to minus infinity whenever the determinant of $\boldsymbol{\Gamma}$ tends to zero. This makes sense, because the model cannot be solved when $|\det \boldsymbol{\Gamma}| = 0$, which implies that the likelihood of such a set of parameter values is zero. In effect, this means that the space of possible values of $\boldsymbol{\Gamma}$ is divided into a number of regions, separated by singularities where $|\det \boldsymbol{\Gamma}| = 0$. In the case of the demand-supply model discussed in Section 7.3, for example, there is only one singularity, which occurs where the slopes of the demand and supply functions are equal. We cannot normally expect that a numerical maximization algorithm will cross such a singularity, even though it might happen to do so. Thus, when we try to maximize a loglikelihood function numerically, we are unlikely to find the global maximum if the region in which the algorithm starts does not contain it. This suggests that it may be very important to choose starting values carefully when using FIML.

Although FIML is based on the assumption that the error terms are multivariate normal, this assumption is not needed to ensure that the estimates $\hat{\boldsymbol{B}}$ and $\hat{\boldsymbol{\Gamma}}$ are consistent and asymptotically normal. When FIML is used and the error terms are not normally distributed, it is a QML estimator rather than an ML estimator, and it will not be asymptotically efficient. As we saw in Section 9.6, any regression model may validly be estimated by ML under the assumption of normally distributed error terms, whether or not that assumption is correct. This result applies to FIML because, as (18.32) makes clear, FIML is in effect just estimating a certain nonlinear multivariate regression model. When the underlying simultaneous equations model is nonlinear, however, this result does not necessarily apply; see Phillips (1982).

Testing model specification is just as important for simultaneous equations models as for any other econometric model. The full range of classical tests — LM, LR, Wald, and $C(\alpha)$ — is of course available for this purpose. However, because FIML estimation is relatively costly and difficult, applied workers may be tempted to forgo extensive specification testing of models that are estimated by FIML. It is therefore worth keeping in mind the fact that many types of misspecification of the structural model (18.01) imply similar misspecification of the unrestricted reduced form (18.03). For example, if any of the error terms of the structural model is serially correlated, then, except in very special circumstances, all of the reduced form error terms must also be serially correlated. Similarly, if any of the structural error terms is heteroskedastic, then all of the reduced form error terms must be heteroskedastic.

By the same token, if the parameters of the structural model are not constant over the entire sample, then the parameters of the URF will not be constant either. Since the equations of the URF are estimated by ordinary least squares, it is very easy to test them for evidence of misspecification such as serial correlation, heteroskedasticity, and nonconstant coefficients. If they fail any of these tests, then one may reasonably conclude that the structural model is misspecified, even if one has not actually estimated it. The converse is not true, however, since these tests may well lack power, especially if only one of the structural equations is misspecified.

One additional misspecification test that should always be performed is a test of any **overidentifying restrictions**. In Section 7.8, we discussed how to test overidentifying restrictions for a single equation estimated by IV or 2SLS. Here we are interested in all of the overidentifying restrictions for the entire system. The number of degrees of freedom for the test is equal to the number of elements in the $\boldsymbol{\Pi}$ matrix of the URF, gk, minus the number of free parameters in $\boldsymbol{B}$ and $\boldsymbol{\Gamma}$ jointly. In most cases there will be some overidentifying restrictions, and in many cases there will be a large number of them. The most natural way to test these is probably to use an LR test. The restricted value of the loglikelihood function is the value of (18.30) at the FIML estimates $\hat{\boldsymbol{B}}$ and $\hat{\boldsymbol{\Gamma}}$, and the unrestricted value is

$$-\frac{ng}{2}\bigl(\log(2\pi)+1\bigr)-\frac{n}{2}\log\left|\frac{1}{n}\bigl(\boldsymbol{Y}-\boldsymbol{X}\hat{\boldsymbol{\Pi}}\bigr)^{\top}\bigl(\boldsymbol{Y}-\boldsymbol{X}\hat{\boldsymbol{\Pi}}\bigr)\right|, \tag{18.33}$$

where $\hat{\boldsymbol{\Pi}}$ denotes the OLS estimates of the parameters of the URF. As usual, twice the difference between the restricted and unrestricted values of the loglikelihood function will be asymptotically distributed as χ^2 with as many degrees of freedom as there are overidentifying restrictions. If one suspects that the overidentifying restrictions are violated and therefore does not want to bother estimating the structural model, one could instead use a Wald test, as suggested by Byron (1974).

We have not yet explained why the OLS estimates $\hat{\boldsymbol{\Pi}}$ are also the ML estimates. It can easily be seen from (18.33) that, in order to obtain ML estimates of $\boldsymbol{\Pi}$, we need to minimize the determinant

$$\bigl|(\boldsymbol{Y}-\boldsymbol{X\Pi})^{\top}(\boldsymbol{Y}-\boldsymbol{X\Pi})\bigr|. \tag{18.34}$$

Suppose that we evaluate this determinant at any set of estimates $\acute{\boldsymbol{\Pi}}$ not equal to $\hat{\boldsymbol{\Pi}}$. Since we can always write $\acute{\boldsymbol{\Pi}} = \hat{\boldsymbol{\Pi}} + \boldsymbol{A}$ for some matrix $\boldsymbol{A}$, (18.34) becomes

$$\begin{aligned}
&\bigl|(\boldsymbol{Y}-\boldsymbol{X}\hat{\boldsymbol{\Pi}}-\boldsymbol{XA})^{\top}(\boldsymbol{Y}-\boldsymbol{X}\hat{\boldsymbol{\Pi}}-\boldsymbol{XA})\bigr|\\
&=\bigl|(\boldsymbol{M}_X\boldsymbol{Y}-\boldsymbol{XA})^{\top}(\boldsymbol{M}_X\boldsymbol{Y}-\boldsymbol{XA})\bigr|\\
&=\bigl|\boldsymbol{Y}^{\top}\boldsymbol{M}_X\boldsymbol{Y}+\boldsymbol{A}^{\top}\boldsymbol{X}^{\top}\boldsymbol{XA}\bigr|.
\end{aligned} \tag{18.35}$$

Because the determinant of the sum of two positive definite matrices is always greater than the determinants of either of those matrices (see Appendix A), it follows from (18.35) that (18.34) will exceed $\boldsymbol{Y}^\top \boldsymbol{M}_X \boldsymbol{Y}$ for all $\boldsymbol{A} \neq \mathbf{0}$. This implies that $\hat{\boldsymbol{\Pi}}$ minimizes (18.34), and so we have proved that equation-by-equation OLS estimates of the URF are also ML estimates for the entire system.

If one does not have access to a regression package that calculates (18.33) easily, there is another way to do so. Consider the **recursive system**

$$
\begin{aligned}
\boldsymbol{y}_1 &= \boldsymbol{X}\boldsymbol{\eta}_1 + \boldsymbol{e}_1 \\
\boldsymbol{y}_2 &= \boldsymbol{X}\boldsymbol{\eta}_2 + \boldsymbol{y}_1 \alpha_1 + \boldsymbol{e}_2 \\
\boldsymbol{y}_3 &= \boldsymbol{X}\boldsymbol{\eta}_3 + [\boldsymbol{y}_1 \quad \boldsymbol{y}_2]\boldsymbol{\alpha}_2 + \boldsymbol{e}_3 \\
\boldsymbol{y}_4 &= \boldsymbol{X}\boldsymbol{\eta}_4 + [\boldsymbol{y}_1 \quad \boldsymbol{y}_2 \quad \boldsymbol{y}_3]\boldsymbol{\alpha}_3 + \boldsymbol{e}_4,
\end{aligned}
\tag{18.36}
$$

and so on, where $\boldsymbol{y}_i$ denotes the ith column of $\boldsymbol{Y}$. This system of equations can be interpreted as simply a reparametrization of the URF (18.03). It is easy to see that if one estimates these equations by OLS, all the residual vectors will be mutually orthogonal: $\hat{\boldsymbol{e}}_2$ will be orthogonal to $\hat{\boldsymbol{e}}_1$, $\hat{\boldsymbol{e}}_3$ will be orthogonal to $\hat{\boldsymbol{e}}_2$ and $\hat{\boldsymbol{e}}_1$, and so on. According to the URF, all the $\boldsymbol{y}_i$'s are linear combinations of the columns of $\boldsymbol{X}$ plus random errors. Therefore, the equations of (18.36) are correct for any arbitrary choice of the α parameters: The $\boldsymbol{\eta}_i$'s simply adjust to whatever choice is made. If, however, we *require* that the error terms $\boldsymbol{e}_i$ should be orthogonal, then this serves to identify a particular unique choice of the α's. In fact, the recursive system (18.36) has exactly the same number of parameters as the URF (18.03): g vectors $\boldsymbol{\eta}_i$, each with k elements, $g-1$ vectors $\boldsymbol{\alpha}_i$, with a total of $g(g-1)/2$, and g variance parameters, for a total of $gk + (g^2+g)/2$. The URF has gk parameters in $\boldsymbol{\Pi}$ and $(g^2+g)/2$ in the covariance matrix $\boldsymbol{\Omega}$, for the same total. What has happened is that the α parameters in (18.36) have replaced the off-diagonal elements of the covariance matrix of $\boldsymbol{V}$ in the URF.

Since the recursive system (18.36) is simply a reparametrization of the URF (18.03), it should come as no surprise that the loglikelihood function for the former is equal to (18.33). Because the residuals of the various equations in (18.36) are orthogonal, the value of the loglikelihood function for (18.36) is simply the sum of the values of the loglikelihood functions from OLS estimation of the individual equations. This result, which readers can easily verify numerically, sometimes provides a convenient way to compute the loglikelihood function for the URF. Except for this purpose, recursive systems are not generally of much interest. They do not convey any information that is not already provided by the URF, and the parametrization depends on an arbitrary ordering of the equations.

18.5 LIMITED-INFORMATION MAXIMUM LIKELIHOOD

One problem with FIML and other full-system methods is that they require the investigator to specify the structure of all the equations in the model. Misspecification of any one equation will in general lead to inconsistent estimation of all equations. To avoid this problem, when efficiency is not crucial, investigators may well prefer to employ single-equation methods. The easiest and most widely used of these is 2SLS, but it has two important drawbacks. The estimates it yields are not invariant to reparametrization and, as we saw in Section 7.5, they can be seriously biased in finite samples. LIML is an alternative technique that yields invariant estimates which in many respects have better finite-sample properties than 2SLS. Although it was proposed by Anderson and Rubin (1949) prior to the invention of 2SLS and has been the subject of much theoretical study, it has been little used by applied econometricians.

As its name suggests, the basic idea of LIML is to use only limited information about the structure of the model. Suppose that we wish to estimate a single equation, say the first, of a structural model like (18.01). We wrote down such an equation in Section 18.3 as (18.18). We must take account of the fact that some of the variables which appear on the right-hand side of (18.18), the ones that correspond to columns of $\boldsymbol{Y}_1$, are endogenous. The simplest way to do this is just to write the unrestricted reduced form equations for them:

$$\boldsymbol{Y}_1 = \boldsymbol{X}_1\boldsymbol{\Pi}_{11} + \boldsymbol{X}_2\boldsymbol{\Pi}_{21} + \boldsymbol{V}_1, \tag{18.37}$$

where the notation is identical to that used in Section 18.3. Combining (18.18) and (18.37), we obtain the system of equations

$$\begin{aligned} \boldsymbol{y} - \boldsymbol{Y}_1\boldsymbol{\gamma}_1 &= \boldsymbol{X}_1\boldsymbol{\beta}_1 + \boldsymbol{u} \\ \boldsymbol{Y}_1 &= \boldsymbol{X}_1\boldsymbol{\Pi}_{11} + \boldsymbol{X}_2\boldsymbol{\Pi}_{21} + \boldsymbol{V}_1. \end{aligned} \tag{18.38}$$

Notice that $\boldsymbol{Y}_2$ does not appear in this system of equations at all. If we are interested in the first equation only, endogenous variables that do not appear in it are irrelevant. The equation system (18.38) can be estimated by maximum likelihood, and the estimates of $\boldsymbol{\gamma}_1$ and $\boldsymbol{\beta}_1$ that result will be the LIML estimates. Any FIML package can be used to do this.

Actually, we do not need a FIML package to obtain ML estimates of (18.38). The matrix of coefficients on the endogenous variables in this system of equations is

$$\begin{bmatrix} 1 & \mathbf{0} \\ -\boldsymbol{\gamma}_1 & \mathbf{I} \end{bmatrix}. \tag{18.39}$$

Because this matrix is triangular, its determinant is simply the product of the elements on the principal diagonal, which is 1. Thus the Jacobian term in the loglikelihood function vanishes, and the loglikelihood function for (18.38) has the same form as the loglikelihood function for any set of linear seemingly unrelated regressions (see Section 9.9). This implies that one can use any program for estimation of SUR systems to obtain LIML estimates. Moreover, application of feasible GLS to a system like (18.38), starting from 2SLS estimates for the first equation and OLS estimates for the remaining ones, will yield estimates asymptotically equivalent to LIML estimates. Iterating the feasible GLS procedure until it converges will yield the actual LIML estimates, and such a procedure has been suggested by Pagan (1979).

In practice, LIML estimates are rarely computed in this way, because there is a much more efficient method of computing them. Developing it will require a certain amount of algebra, but the final results will be quite simple. From (18.30), (18.32), and the fact that $|\boldsymbol{\Gamma}| = 1$, we see that ML estimates may be obtained by minimizing

$$\left|(\boldsymbol{Y} - \boldsymbol{XB\Gamma}^{-1})^{\top}(\boldsymbol{Y} - \boldsymbol{XB\Gamma}^{-1})\right| = \left|(\boldsymbol{Y\Gamma} - \boldsymbol{XB})^{\top}(\boldsymbol{Y\Gamma} - \boldsymbol{XB})\right|. \tag{18.40}$$

What we will now show is that minimizing the determinant on the right-hand side here is equivalent to minimizing a ratio of quadratic forms and that this, in turn, can be achieved by solving a certain eigenvalue problem.

Let us begin by writing out the matrix $\boldsymbol{B\Gamma}^{-1}$ that appears on the left-hand side of (18.40). Using (18.17) and an expression for the inverse of (18.39), we see that

$$\boldsymbol{B\Gamma}^{-1} = \begin{bmatrix} \boldsymbol{\beta}_1 & \boldsymbol{B}_{12} \\ \mathbf{0} & \boldsymbol{B}_{22} \end{bmatrix} \begin{bmatrix} 1 & \mathbf{0} \\ \boldsymbol{\gamma}_1 & \mathbf{I} \end{bmatrix} = \begin{bmatrix} \boldsymbol{\beta}_1 + \boldsymbol{B}_{12}\boldsymbol{\gamma}_1 & \boldsymbol{B}_{12} \\ \boldsymbol{B}_{22}\boldsymbol{\gamma}_1 & \boldsymbol{B}_{22} \end{bmatrix}.$$

The right-most matrix here is just the restricted version of $\boldsymbol{\Pi}$. The top part corresponds to $\boldsymbol{X}_1$ and the bottom part to $\boldsymbol{X}_2$. Since $\boldsymbol{\beta}_1$ does not appear in the bottom part and can vary freely, it is clear that, whatever the value of $\boldsymbol{\gamma}_1$, we can find values of $\boldsymbol{\beta}_1$ and $\boldsymbol{B}_{12}$ such that the top part is equal to anything at all. In other words, the restrictions on the structural equation (18.37) do not impose any restrictions on the rows of $\boldsymbol{\Pi}$ that correspond to $\boldsymbol{X}_1$. In general, however, they do impose restrictions on the rows that correspond to $\boldsymbol{X}_2$.

As we saw in the previous section, minimizing a determinant like (18.34) subject to no restrictions is equivalent to using OLS. In this case, since there are no restrictions on the rows of $\boldsymbol{\Pi}$ that correspond to $\boldsymbol{X}_1$, we can use OLS to estimate those parameters, and then concentrate them out of the determinant. When we do this, the determinant on the right-hand side of (18.40) becomes

$$\left|(\boldsymbol{Y\Gamma} - \boldsymbol{XB})^{\top}\boldsymbol{M}_1(\boldsymbol{Y\Gamma} - \boldsymbol{XB})\right|,$$

where, as usual, $\boldsymbol{M}_1$ denotes the matrix that projects orthogonally onto $\mathcal{S}^{\perp}(\boldsymbol{X}_1)$.

We will now introduce some new notation. First, we will let $\boldsymbol{\gamma}$ denote the vector $[1 \ \vdots \ -\boldsymbol{\gamma}_1]$; therefore, $\boldsymbol{Y\gamma} \equiv \boldsymbol{y} - \boldsymbol{Y}_1\boldsymbol{\gamma}_1$. Second, we will let $\boldsymbol{Y}^*$ denote

$\boldsymbol{M}_1\boldsymbol{Y}$, $\boldsymbol{Y}_1^*$ denote $\boldsymbol{M}_1\boldsymbol{Y}_1$, and $\boldsymbol{X}^*$ denote $\boldsymbol{M}_1\boldsymbol{X}_2$. The determinant on the right-hand side of (18.40) can then be rewritten as

$$\begin{vmatrix} (\boldsymbol{Y}^*\boldsymbol{\gamma})^\top(\boldsymbol{Y}^*\boldsymbol{\gamma}) & (\boldsymbol{Y}^*\boldsymbol{\gamma})^\top(\boldsymbol{Y}_1^* - \boldsymbol{X}^*\boldsymbol{B}_{22}) \\ (\boldsymbol{Y}_1^* - \boldsymbol{X}^*\boldsymbol{B}_{22})^\top(\boldsymbol{Y}^*\boldsymbol{\gamma}) & (\boldsymbol{Y}_1^* - \boldsymbol{X}^*\boldsymbol{B}_{22})^\top(\boldsymbol{Y}_1^* - \boldsymbol{X}^*\boldsymbol{B}_{22}) \end{vmatrix}. \tag{18.41}$$

This determinant depends only on the parameters $\boldsymbol{\gamma}$ and $\boldsymbol{B}_{22}$. The next step is to concentrate out the parameters contained in $\boldsymbol{B}_{22}$ as well, so as to obtain an expression that depends only on the data and $\boldsymbol{\gamma}$. Doing this will require us to make heavy use of the following result, which is proved in Appendix A:

$$\begin{vmatrix} \boldsymbol{A}^\top\boldsymbol{A} & \boldsymbol{A}^\top\boldsymbol{B} \\ \boldsymbol{B}^\top\boldsymbol{A} & \boldsymbol{B}^\top\boldsymbol{B} \end{vmatrix} = |\boldsymbol{A}^\top\boldsymbol{A}||\boldsymbol{B}^\top\boldsymbol{M}_A\boldsymbol{B}|, \tag{18.42}$$

where, as usual, $\boldsymbol{M}_A \equiv \mathbf{I} - \boldsymbol{A}(\boldsymbol{A}^\top\boldsymbol{A})^{-1}\boldsymbol{A}^\top$. Applying this result to (18.41) yields

$$(\boldsymbol{Y}^*\boldsymbol{\gamma})^\top(\boldsymbol{Y}^*\boldsymbol{\gamma})\,\big|(\boldsymbol{Y}_1^* - \boldsymbol{X}^*\boldsymbol{B}_{22})^\top\boldsymbol{M}_v(\boldsymbol{Y}_1^* - \boldsymbol{X}^*\boldsymbol{B}_{22})\big|, \tag{18.43}$$

where $\boldsymbol{M}_v$ denotes the matrix that projects orthogonally onto $\mathcal{S}^\perp(\boldsymbol{v})$, and $\boldsymbol{v} \equiv \boldsymbol{Y}^*\boldsymbol{\gamma}$. There is only one determinant in (18.43), not two, because the first factor is a scalar.

The parameters $\boldsymbol{B}_{22}$ appear only in the second factor of (18.43). This factor is the determinant of the matrix of sums of squares and cross-products of the residuals from the system of regressions

$$\boldsymbol{M}_v\boldsymbol{Y}_1^* = \boldsymbol{M}_v\boldsymbol{X}^*\boldsymbol{B}_{22} + \text{ residuals.}$$

As we saw in the previous section, this determinant can be minimized by setting $\boldsymbol{B}_{22}$ equal to the estimates obtained by applying OLS to each equation separately. The matrix of residuals thus obtained is $\boldsymbol{M}_{M_vX^*}\boldsymbol{M}_v\boldsymbol{Y}_1^*$, where $\boldsymbol{M}_{M_vX^*}$ denotes the projection off $\mathcal{S}(\boldsymbol{M}_v\boldsymbol{X}^*)$. Now observe that $\boldsymbol{M}_{M_vX^*}\boldsymbol{M}_v = \boldsymbol{M}_{v,X^*}$, the projection off $\mathcal{S}(\boldsymbol{v}, \boldsymbol{X}^*)$. Consequently, the second factor of (18.43), minimized with respect to $\boldsymbol{B}_{22}$, is

$$\big|(\boldsymbol{Y}_1^*)^\top\boldsymbol{M}_{v,X^*}\boldsymbol{Y}_1^*\big|. \tag{18.44}$$

The fact that $\boldsymbol{v}$ and $\boldsymbol{X}^*$ appear in a symmetrical fashion in (18.44) can be exploited in order to make (18.44) depend on $\boldsymbol{\gamma}$ only through a scalar factor. Consider the determinant

$$\begin{vmatrix} \boldsymbol{v}^\top\boldsymbol{M}_{X^*}\boldsymbol{v} & \boldsymbol{v}^\top\boldsymbol{M}_{X^*}\boldsymbol{Y}_1^* \\ (\boldsymbol{Y}_1^*)^\top\boldsymbol{M}_{X^*}\boldsymbol{v} & (\boldsymbol{Y}_1^*)^\top\boldsymbol{M}_{X^*}\boldsymbol{Y}_1^* \end{vmatrix}. \tag{18.45}$$

By use of (18.42), this determinant can be factorized just as (18.41) was. We obtain

$$(\boldsymbol{v}^\top\boldsymbol{M}_{X^*}\boldsymbol{v})\,\big|(\boldsymbol{Y}_1^*)^\top\boldsymbol{M}_{v,X^*}\boldsymbol{Y}_1^*\big|. \tag{18.46}$$

Using the facts that $\boldsymbol{M}_1\boldsymbol{M}_{X^*} = \boldsymbol{M}_X$ and that $\boldsymbol{v} = \boldsymbol{M}_1\boldsymbol{Y}\boldsymbol{\gamma}$, (18.45) can be rewritten as

$$\begin{vmatrix} \boldsymbol{\gamma}^\top\boldsymbol{Y}^\top\boldsymbol{M}_X\boldsymbol{Y}\boldsymbol{\gamma} & \boldsymbol{\gamma}^\top\boldsymbol{Y}^\top\boldsymbol{M}_X\boldsymbol{Y}_1 \\ \boldsymbol{Y}_1^\top\boldsymbol{M}_X\boldsymbol{Y}\boldsymbol{\gamma} & \boldsymbol{Y}_1^\top\boldsymbol{M}_X\boldsymbol{Y}_1 \end{vmatrix} = \left|\boldsymbol{\Gamma}^\top\boldsymbol{Y}^\top\boldsymbol{M}_X\boldsymbol{Y}\boldsymbol{\Gamma}\right| = \left|\boldsymbol{Y}^\top\boldsymbol{M}_X\boldsymbol{Y}\right|. \qquad (18.47)$$

The first equality here is easily verified by making use of expression (18.39) for $\boldsymbol{\Gamma}$ and the definitions of $\boldsymbol{\gamma}$ and $\boldsymbol{Y}$; remember that $\boldsymbol{\gamma}$ is the first column of $\boldsymbol{\Gamma}$. The second equality is a result of the fact that $|\boldsymbol{\Gamma}| = 1$. It implies that (18.47) does not depend on $\boldsymbol{\Gamma}$ at all.

We can now, finally, write down a simple expression, which, when minimized with respect to $\boldsymbol{\gamma}$, is equal to the minimized value of the original determinant (18.40). From (18.46) and (18.47), we see that (18.44) is equal to

$$\left|(\boldsymbol{Y}_1^*)^\top\boldsymbol{M}_{v,X^*}\boldsymbol{Y}_1^*\right| = \frac{|\boldsymbol{Y}^\top\boldsymbol{M}_X\boldsymbol{Y}|}{\boldsymbol{v}^\top\boldsymbol{M}_{X^*}\boldsymbol{v}} = \frac{|\boldsymbol{Y}^\top\boldsymbol{M}_X\boldsymbol{Y}|}{\boldsymbol{\gamma}^\top\boldsymbol{Y}^\top\boldsymbol{M}_X\boldsymbol{Y}\boldsymbol{\gamma}}.$$

Hence, using (18.43), the original determinant (18.40) must be equal to

$$\frac{\boldsymbol{v}^\top\boldsymbol{v}\,|\boldsymbol{Y}^\top\boldsymbol{M}_X\boldsymbol{Y}|}{\boldsymbol{\gamma}^\top\boldsymbol{Y}^\top\boldsymbol{M}_X\boldsymbol{Y}\boldsymbol{\gamma}} = \frac{(\boldsymbol{\gamma}^\top\boldsymbol{Y}^\top\boldsymbol{M}_1\boldsymbol{Y}\boldsymbol{\gamma})\,|\boldsymbol{Y}^\top\boldsymbol{M}_X\boldsymbol{Y}|}{\boldsymbol{\gamma}^\top\boldsymbol{Y}^\top\boldsymbol{M}_X\boldsymbol{Y}\boldsymbol{\gamma}} = \kappa|\boldsymbol{Y}^\top\boldsymbol{M}_X\boldsymbol{Y}|, \qquad (18.48)$$

where the scalar κ has been defined implicitly as

$$\kappa \equiv \frac{\boldsymbol{\gamma}^\top\boldsymbol{Y}^\top\boldsymbol{M}_1\boldsymbol{Y}\boldsymbol{\gamma}}{\boldsymbol{\gamma}^\top\boldsymbol{Y}^\top\boldsymbol{M}_X\boldsymbol{Y}\boldsymbol{\gamma}}. \qquad (18.49)$$

Since $|\boldsymbol{Y}^\top\boldsymbol{M}_X\boldsymbol{Y}|$ does not depend on $\boldsymbol{\gamma}$ at all, minimizing (18.48) is equivalent to minimizing κ. Thus, if we can minimize (18.49) with respect to $\boldsymbol{\gamma}$, we can obtain LIML estimates $\hat{\boldsymbol{\gamma}}$ and a corresponding value of κ, say $\hat{\kappa}$. Because they may be obtained in this way, LIML estimates are sometimes referred to as **least variance ratio** estimates.

Before we consider how to obtain the LIML estimates $\hat{\boldsymbol{\gamma}}$, let us discuss some implications of (18.48) and (18.49). First of all, it should be obvious that $\hat{\kappa} \geq 1$. Since $\mathcal{S}(\boldsymbol{X}_1)$ is a subspace of $\mathcal{S}(\boldsymbol{X})$, the numerator of (18.49) cannot be smaller than the denominator for any possible $\boldsymbol{\gamma}$. In fact, for an equation that is overidentified, $\hat{\kappa}$ will always be greater than 1 in finite samples. For an equation that is just identified, $\hat{\kappa}$ will be exactly equal to 1 because the number of free parameters to be estimated is then just equal to k, the rank of $\boldsymbol{X}$. Thus, in this case, it is possible to choose $\boldsymbol{\gamma}$ so that the numerator and denominator of (18.49) are equal.

Expression (18.48) implies that the maximized value of the concentrated loglikelihood function for LIML estimation of a single equation is

$$-\frac{ng}{2}\log(2\pi) - \frac{n}{2}\log(\hat{\kappa}) - \frac{n}{2}\log|\boldsymbol{Y}^\top\boldsymbol{M}_X\boldsymbol{Y}|. \qquad (18.50)$$

The maximized value of the concentrated loglikelihood function for ML estimation of the unrestricted reduced form is

$$-\frac{ng}{2}\log(2\pi) - \frac{n}{2}\log|\boldsymbol{Y}^{\top}\boldsymbol{M}_X\boldsymbol{Y}|.$$

Thus an LR statistic for testing the overidentifying restrictions implicit in a single structural equation is simply $n\log(\hat{\kappa})$. This test statistic was first proposed by Anderson and Rubin (1950).

Finding $\hat{\kappa}$ is quite easy. The set of first-order conditions that we obtain by differentiating (18.49) with respect to $\boldsymbol{\gamma}$ is

$$2\boldsymbol{Y}^{\top}\boldsymbol{M}_1\boldsymbol{Y}\boldsymbol{\gamma}(\boldsymbol{\gamma}^{\top}\boldsymbol{Y}^{\top}\boldsymbol{M}_X\boldsymbol{Y}\boldsymbol{\gamma}) - 2\boldsymbol{Y}^{\top}\boldsymbol{M}_X\boldsymbol{Y}\boldsymbol{\gamma}(\boldsymbol{\gamma}^{\top}\boldsymbol{Y}^{\top}\boldsymbol{M}_1\boldsymbol{Y}\boldsymbol{\gamma}) = \mathbf{0}.$$

If we divide both sides by $2\boldsymbol{\gamma}^{\top}\boldsymbol{Y}^{\top}\boldsymbol{M}_X\boldsymbol{Y}\boldsymbol{\gamma}$, this becomes

$$\boldsymbol{Y}^{\top}\boldsymbol{M}_1\boldsymbol{Y}\boldsymbol{\gamma} - \kappa\boldsymbol{Y}^{\top}\boldsymbol{M}_X\boldsymbol{Y}\boldsymbol{\gamma} = \mathbf{0}. \tag{18.51}$$

An equivalent set of first-order conditions can be obtained by premultiplying (18.51) by $(\boldsymbol{Y}^{\top}\boldsymbol{M}_X\boldsymbol{Y})^{-1/2}$ and inserting that factor multiplied by its inverse before $\boldsymbol{\gamma}$. After some rearrangement, this yields

$$\big((\boldsymbol{Y}^{\top}\boldsymbol{M}_X\boldsymbol{Y})^{-1/2}\boldsymbol{Y}^{\top}\boldsymbol{M}_1\boldsymbol{Y}(\boldsymbol{Y}^{\top}\boldsymbol{M}_X\boldsymbol{Y})^{-1/2} - \kappa\mathbf{I}\big)(\boldsymbol{Y}^{\top}\boldsymbol{M}_X\boldsymbol{Y})^{1/2}\boldsymbol{\gamma} = \mathbf{0}.$$

This set of first-order conditions now has the form of a standard eigenvalue-eigenvector problem for a real symmetric matrix (see Appendix A). It is thus clear that $\hat{\kappa}$ will be an eigenvalue of the matrix

$$(\boldsymbol{Y}^{\top}\boldsymbol{M}_X\boldsymbol{Y})^{-1/2}\boldsymbol{Y}^{\top}\boldsymbol{M}_1\boldsymbol{Y}(\boldsymbol{Y}^{\top}\boldsymbol{M}_X\boldsymbol{Y})^{-1/2} \tag{18.52}$$

and that $(\boldsymbol{Y}^{\top}\boldsymbol{M}_X\boldsymbol{Y})^{1/2}\hat{\boldsymbol{\gamma}}$ will be the corresponding eigenvector. In fact, $\hat{\kappa}$ must be the *smallest* eigenvalue, because it is the smallest possible value of the ratio (18.49).

One way to compute LIML estimates, then, is to find the eigenvector of (18.52) that corresponds to the smallest eigenvalue, and from that to compute $\hat{\boldsymbol{\gamma}}$, which, if the first element is normalized to unity, will be $[1 \;\vdots\; -\hat{\boldsymbol{\gamma}}_1]$. One can then obtain $\hat{\boldsymbol{\beta}}_1$ by regressing $\boldsymbol{y} - \boldsymbol{Y}_1\hat{\boldsymbol{\gamma}}_1$ on $\boldsymbol{X}_1$. Another approach is both simpler and more illuminating, however. Consider the first-order conditions (18.51). If we express them in terms of $\boldsymbol{y}$ and $\boldsymbol{Y}_1$ instead of $\boldsymbol{Y}$, and evaluate them at the LIML estimates, they can be rewritten as

$$\left(\begin{bmatrix} \boldsymbol{y}^{\top}\boldsymbol{M}_1\boldsymbol{y} & \boldsymbol{y}^{\top}\boldsymbol{M}_1\boldsymbol{Y}_1 \\ \boldsymbol{Y}_1{}^{\top}\boldsymbol{M}_1\boldsymbol{y} & \boldsymbol{Y}_1{}^{\top}\boldsymbol{M}_1\boldsymbol{Y}_1 \end{bmatrix} - \hat{\kappa}\begin{bmatrix} \boldsymbol{y}^{\top}\boldsymbol{M}_X\boldsymbol{y} & \boldsymbol{y}^{\top}\boldsymbol{M}_X\boldsymbol{Y}_1 \\ \boldsymbol{Y}_1{}^{\top}\boldsymbol{M}_X\boldsymbol{y} & \boldsymbol{Y}_1{}^{\top}\boldsymbol{M}_X\boldsymbol{Y}_1 \end{bmatrix}\right)\begin{bmatrix} 1 \\ -\hat{\boldsymbol{\gamma}}_1 \end{bmatrix} = \mathbf{0}.$$

When the rows corresponding to $\boldsymbol{Y}_1$ are multiplied out, this becomes

$$\boldsymbol{Y}_1^{\top}(\boldsymbol{M}_1 - \hat{\kappa}\boldsymbol{M}_X)\boldsymbol{y} - \boldsymbol{Y}_1^{\top}(\boldsymbol{M}_1 - \hat{\kappa}\boldsymbol{M}_X)\boldsymbol{Y}_1\hat{\boldsymbol{\gamma}}_1 = \mathbf{0}.$$

Solving for $\hat{\gamma}_1$ then yields

$$\hat{\gamma}_1 = \big(\boldsymbol{Y}_1^{\top}(\boldsymbol{M}_1 - \hat{\kappa}\boldsymbol{M}_X)\boldsymbol{Y}_1\big)^{-1}\boldsymbol{Y}_1^{\top}(\boldsymbol{M}_1 - \hat{\kappa}\boldsymbol{M}_X)\boldsymbol{y}.$$

Since $\boldsymbol{X}_1 \in \mathcal{S}(\boldsymbol{X})$, $\boldsymbol{M}_1 - \hat{\kappa}\boldsymbol{M}_X = \boldsymbol{M}_1(\mathbf{I} - \hat{\kappa}\boldsymbol{M}_X)$. Using this fact and a little algebra, which we leave as an exercise, it can be shown that $\hat{\gamma}_1$ can also be computed using the formula

$$\begin{bmatrix}\hat{\boldsymbol{\beta}}_1 \\ \hat{\gamma}_1\end{bmatrix} = \begin{bmatrix}\boldsymbol{X}_1^{\top}\boldsymbol{X}_1 & \boldsymbol{X}_1^{\top}\boldsymbol{Y}_1 \\ \boldsymbol{Y}_1^{\top}\boldsymbol{X}_1 & \boldsymbol{Y}_1^{\top}(\mathbf{I} - \hat{\kappa}\boldsymbol{M}_X)\boldsymbol{Y}_1\end{bmatrix}^{-1}\begin{bmatrix}\boldsymbol{X}_1^{\top}\boldsymbol{y} \\ \boldsymbol{Y}_1^{\top}(\mathbf{I} - \hat{\kappa}\boldsymbol{M}_X)\boldsymbol{y}\end{bmatrix}, \tag{18.53}$$

which yields $\hat{\boldsymbol{\beta}}_1$ as well. Then if we define $\boldsymbol{Z}$ as $[\boldsymbol{X}_1 \;\; \boldsymbol{Y}_1]$ and $\boldsymbol{\delta}$ as $[\boldsymbol{\beta}_1 \,\vdots\, \gamma_1]$, as in (18.18), (18.53) can be written in the very simple form

$$\hat{\boldsymbol{\delta}} = \big(\boldsymbol{Z}^{\top}(\mathbf{I} - \hat{\kappa}\boldsymbol{M}_X)\boldsymbol{Z}\big)^{-1}\boldsymbol{Z}^{\top}(\mathbf{I} - \hat{\kappa}\boldsymbol{M}_X)\boldsymbol{y}. \tag{18.54}$$

Equation (18.53) is one way of writing LIML as a member of what is called the ***K*-class** of estimators; see Theil (1961) and Nagar (1959). Equation (18.54) is a simpler way of doing the same thing. The K-class consists of all estimators that can be written in either of these two forms, but with an arbitrary scalar K replacing $\hat{\kappa}$. We use K rather than the more traditional k to denote this scalar in order to avoid confusion with the number of exogenous variables in the system. The LIML estimator is thus a K-class estimator with $K = \hat{\kappa}$. Similarly, as is evident from (18.54), the 2SLS estimator is a K-class estimator with $K = 1$, and the OLS estimator is a K-class estimator with $K = 0$. Since $\hat{\kappa} = 1$ for a structural equation that is just identified, it follows immediately from (18.54) that the LIML and 2SLS estimators coincide in this special case.

It can be shown that K-class estimators are consistent whenever K tends to 1 asymptotically at a rate faster than $n^{-1/2}$; see Schmidt (1976), among others. Even though the consistency of LIML follows from general results for ML estimators, it is interesting to see how this result for the K-class applies to it. We have already seen that $n\log(\hat{\kappa})$ is the LR test statistic for the null hypothesis that the overidentifying restrictions on the structural equation being estimated are valid. If we Taylor expand the logarithm, we find that $n\log(\hat{\kappa}) \cong n(\hat{\kappa} - 1)$. Since this test statistic has an asymptotic χ^2 distribution, it must be $O(1)$, and so $\hat{\kappa} - 1$ must be $O(n^{-1})$. This then establishes the consistency of LIML.

There are many other K-class estimators. For example, Sawa (1973) has suggested a way of modifying the 2SLS estimator to reduce bias, and Fuller (1977) and Morimune (1978, 1983) have suggested modified versions of the LIML estimator. Fuller's estimator, which is the simplest of these, uses $K = \hat{\kappa} - \alpha/(n - k)$, where α is a positive constant that must be chosen by the investigator. One good choice is $\alpha = 1$, since it yields estimates that are approximately unbiased. In contrast to the LIML estimator, which has no finite moments (see Mariano (1982) and Phillips (1983) for references), Fuller's modified estimator has all moments finite provided the sample size is large enough.

The covariance matrix for the vector of K-class estimates $\hat{\boldsymbol{\delta}}$ may be estimated in various ways. The most natural estimate to use is

$$\hat{\sigma}^2\big(\boldsymbol{Z}^\top(\mathbf{I} - \hat{\kappa}\boldsymbol{M}_X)\boldsymbol{Z}\big)^{-1}, \tag{18.55}$$

where

$$\hat{\sigma}^2 = \frac{1}{n}(\boldsymbol{y} - \boldsymbol{Z}\hat{\boldsymbol{\delta}})^\top(\boldsymbol{y} - \boldsymbol{Z}\hat{\boldsymbol{\delta}}).$$

Wald test statistics for restrictions on $\boldsymbol{\gamma}_1$ and $\boldsymbol{\beta}_1$, including asymptotic t statistics, can be computed using (18.55) in the usual way. It is probably preferable to use LR statistics, however, as these will be invariant to reparametrization and can easily be computed from the concentrated loglikelihood function (18.50).

The result that K-class estimators are consistent whenever K tends to 1 asymptotically at an appropriate rate may seem to suggest that 2SLS has better finite-sample properties than LIML. After all, for 2SLS K is identically equal to 1, while for LIML $K = \hat{\kappa}$, and $\hat{\kappa}$ is always greater than 1 in finite samples. The result that LIML has no finite moments also might seem to suggest that LIML is inferior to 2SLS, since, as we saw in Section 7.5, 2SLS has as many finite moments as there are overidentifying restrictions. On the contrary, it turns out that in many cases 2SLS actually has worse finite-sample properties than LIML in most respects. Anderson, Kunitomo, and Sawa (1982), for example, present analytical results which show that LIML approaches its asymptotic normal distribution much more rapidly than does 2SLS. Unlike the distribution of the 2SLS estimator, which, as we have seen, tends to be severely biased in some cases, the distribution of the LIML estimator is generally centered near the true value. Since the latter distribution has no moments, however, we cannot say that LIML is less biased than 2SLS.

Figure 18.1 provides an illustration of how LIML performs in finite samples. It shows the distributions of the 2SLS estimator, the LIML estimator, and Fuller's modified LIML estimator with $\alpha = 1$ (denoted LIMLF in the figure) for the case we examined previously in Section 7.5. Because there are six overidentifying restrictions and only 25 observations, all of the estimators diverge quite substantially from their asymptotic distributions. In this case, the 2SLS estimator is severely biased downward. In contrast, the LIML estimator appears to be almost unbiased in the sense that its median is very close to the true value of 1. The distribution of Fuller's modified LIML estimator generally lies between those of 2SLS and LIML. Its upper tail is much thinner than that of LIML, but its median is somewhat below the true value.

In practice, it is often not easy to decide which K-class estimator to use. Mariano (1982) discusses a number of analytical results and provides

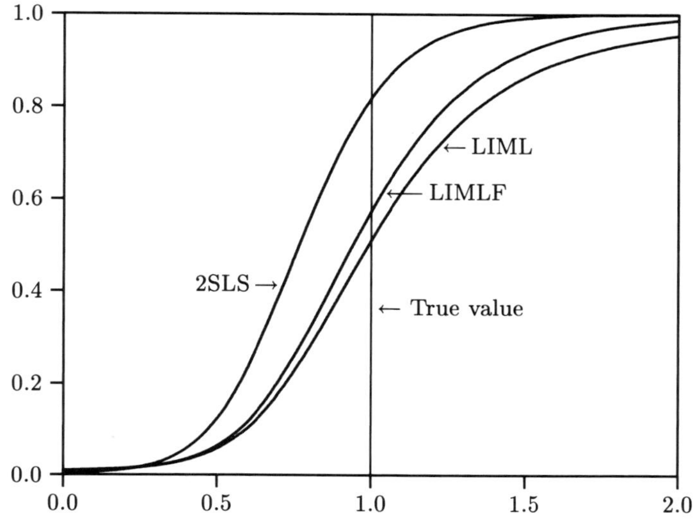

Figure 18.1 Distributions of 2SLS and LIML estimates

some guidance as to when LIML is likely to perform better than 2SLS. The latter should be avoided when the number of overidentifying restrictions is large, for example. However, much depends on the particular model and data set. If 2SLS and LIML yield very similar results, then it does not matter which we employ. If they yield substantially different results, however, then it does matter. Perhaps the best thing in that case is to perform a Monte Carlo experiment, specifically designed to investigate the performance of alternative estimators for the model and data set in question; see Chapter 21.

18.6 Three-Stage Least Squares

The last of the four principal estimation methods for linear simultaneous equations models that we will discuss is **three-stage least squares**, or **3SLS**. Like FIML, 3SLS is a full-system method, in which all the parameters that appear in a model are estimated jointly. As its name suggests, 3SLS can be computed in three stages. The first two stages are those of 2SLS, applied separately to each equation of the system. The third stage is then essentially the same as the final stage in feasible GLS estimation of an SUR system (Section 9.7). The method was proposed by Zellner and Theil (1962).

The simplest way to derive the 3SLS estimator, and its asymptotic properties, is to apply the principles of the generalized method of moments to the system of linear simultaneous equations models (18.01). For the tth observation, this system can be written as

$$\boldsymbol{Y}_t\boldsymbol{\Gamma} = \boldsymbol{X}_t\boldsymbol{B} + \boldsymbol{U}_t.$$

The assumption that all the variables contained in the matrix $\boldsymbol{X}$ are either exogenous or predetermined implies that, for all observations t,

$$E\big(\boldsymbol{Y}_t\boldsymbol{\Gamma} - \boldsymbol{X}_t\boldsymbol{B} \,|\, \boldsymbol{X}_t\big) = \boldsymbol{0}.$$

The equalities here can readily be interpreted as conditional moment conditions in the sense of Chapter 17. Since, as we saw in Section 18.3, the exogenous variables are efficient instruments for 2SLS if the error terms are homoskedastic and serially independent, it seems reasonable to consider the following set of unconditional moment conditions:

$$E\big(\boldsymbol{X}_t^{\top}(\boldsymbol{Y}_t\boldsymbol{\Gamma} - \boldsymbol{X}_t\boldsymbol{B})\big) = \boldsymbol{0}. \tag{18.56}$$

Since $\boldsymbol{X}_t$ has k components and $\boldsymbol{Y}_t\boldsymbol{\Gamma} - \boldsymbol{X}_t\boldsymbol{B}$ has g components, there is a total of gk moment conditions. If the order condition for identification were satisfied with equality, there would be precisely gk parameters to be estimated. Thus (18.56) always provides at least as many moment conditions as there are parameters in the system, and more if the system is overidentified. Of course, whether or not these moment conditions actually serve to identify the parameters asymptotically depends on whether the rank condition is satisfied.

It is convenient to rearrange the elements of the $k \times g$ matrix (18.56) as one single gk–vector. First, let us write each equation of the system in a notation similar to that of (18.18):

$$\boldsymbol{y}_i = \boldsymbol{Z}_i\boldsymbol{\delta}_i + \boldsymbol{u}_i, \quad \text{for } i = 1, \ldots, g,$$

where the matrix of regressors $\boldsymbol{Z}_i$ appearing in the ith equation is $[\boldsymbol{X}_i \;\; \boldsymbol{Y}_i]$, with k_i included exogenous variables $\boldsymbol{X}_i$ and g_i included endogenous variables $\boldsymbol{Y}_i$, and the $(k_i + g_i)$–vector of parameters $\boldsymbol{\delta}_i$ is $[\boldsymbol{\beta}_i \,\vdots\, \boldsymbol{\gamma}_i]$. Then define the row vector $\boldsymbol{F}_t$ of gk elements as follows:

$$\boldsymbol{F}_t \equiv [u_{t1}\boldsymbol{X}_t \;\; \cdots \;\; u_{tg}\boldsymbol{X}_t],$$

where $u_{ti} \equiv y_{ti} - (\boldsymbol{Z}_i)_t\boldsymbol{\delta}_i$. Each component of $\boldsymbol{F}_t$ is the contribution from observation t to one of the empirical moments derived from (18.56). The $n \times gk$ matrix $\boldsymbol{F}$ is defined to have typical row $\boldsymbol{F}_t$.

In order to obtain GMM estimates, it is necessary to find an estimate of the covariance matrix of the gk moments (18.56). We will initially make the same assumptions about the error terms that we made for FIML and LIML. We assume that each of the vectors $\boldsymbol{u}_i$ is homoskedastic and serially independent (the assumption of homoskedasticity will be relaxed later). We also assume that, for each observation t, the u_{ti}'s are correlated among themselves, with $g \times g$ contemporaneous covariance matrix $\boldsymbol{\Sigma}$, independent of t. We will let σ_{ij} denote a typical element of $\boldsymbol{\Sigma}$ and σ^{ij} denote a typical element of $\boldsymbol{\Sigma}^{-1}$.

It is quite easy to derive the covariance matrix of the vector of empirical moments $\boldsymbol{F}^\top\boldsymbol{\iota}$. It is

$$E(\boldsymbol{F}^\top\boldsymbol{\iota}\boldsymbol{\iota}^\top\boldsymbol{F}) = \sum_{t=1}^{n} E(\boldsymbol{F}_t^\top\boldsymbol{F}_t) = \sum_{t=1}^{n} E[u_{t1}\boldsymbol{X}_t \;\; \cdots \;\; u_{tg}\boldsymbol{X}_t]^\top[u_{t1}\boldsymbol{X}_t \;\; \cdots \;\; u_{tg}\boldsymbol{X}_t]. \quad (18.57)$$

The last expression in (18.57) is a $gk \times gk$ matrix that is most easily written in partitioned form, with each block of the partitioned matrix being $k \times k$. For each t, $E(u_{ti}u_{tj}) = \sigma_{ij}$. Because the elements σ_{ij} do not depend on t, we obtain

$$\begin{bmatrix} \sigma_{11}\boldsymbol{X}^\top\boldsymbol{X} & \cdots & \sigma_{1g}\boldsymbol{X}^\top\boldsymbol{X} \\ \vdots & \ddots & \vdots \\ \sigma_{g1}\boldsymbol{X}^\top\boldsymbol{X} & \cdots & \sigma_{gg}\boldsymbol{X}^\top\boldsymbol{X} \end{bmatrix}, \quad (18.58)$$

that is, a matrix with typical block $\sigma_{ij}\boldsymbol{X}^\top\boldsymbol{X}$. We will need the inverse of the matrix (18.58) in order to form a criterion function like (17.54) that can be used to obtain estimates of the parameter vectors $\boldsymbol{\delta}_i$, $i = 1, \ldots, g$. The block structure of (18.58) makes this quite easy. One can verify by a simple multiplication of partitioned matrices that the inverse is a matrix with typical block $\sigma^{ij}(\boldsymbol{X}^\top\boldsymbol{X})^{-1}$ (recall that σ^{ij} is a typical element of $\boldsymbol{\Sigma}^{-1}$).

It is convenient to express the vector of empirical moments $\boldsymbol{F}^\top\boldsymbol{\iota}$ in a partitioned form like that of (18.58), as a function of the data and the parameters of the model. The result is a vector with typical block $\boldsymbol{X}^\top(\boldsymbol{y}_i - \boldsymbol{Z}_i\boldsymbol{\delta}_i)$, for $i = 1, \ldots, g$:

$$\boldsymbol{F}^\top\boldsymbol{\iota} = \begin{bmatrix} \boldsymbol{X}^\top(\boldsymbol{y}_1 - \boldsymbol{Z}_1\boldsymbol{\delta}_1) \\ \vdots \\ \boldsymbol{X}^\top(\boldsymbol{y}_g - \boldsymbol{Z}_g\boldsymbol{\delta}_g) \end{bmatrix}. \quad (18.59)$$

Then, if we construct a quadratic form from the vector (18.59) and the matrix (18.58), we obtain the criterion function

$$\begin{aligned} &\sum_{i=1}^{g}\sum_{j=1}^{g} \sigma^{ij}\big(\boldsymbol{y}_i - \boldsymbol{Z}_i\boldsymbol{\delta}_i\big)^\top\boldsymbol{X}\big(\boldsymbol{X}^\top\boldsymbol{X}\big)^{-1}\boldsymbol{X}^\top\big(\boldsymbol{y}_j - \boldsymbol{Z}_j\boldsymbol{\delta}_j\big) \\ &= \sum_{i=1}^{g}\sum_{j=1}^{g} \sigma^{ij}\big(\boldsymbol{y}_i - \boldsymbol{Z}_i\boldsymbol{\delta}_i\big)^\top\boldsymbol{P}_X\big(\boldsymbol{y}_j - \boldsymbol{Z}_j\boldsymbol{\delta}_j\big). \end{aligned} \quad (18.60)$$

Since we are tacitly assuming that there are no cross-equation restrictions, the parameters $\boldsymbol{\delta}_i$ appear only in the residual for equation i. Thus the first-order conditions for a minimum of (18.60) can be written quite simply as

$$\sum_{j=1}^{g} \sigma^{ij}\boldsymbol{Z}_i^\top\boldsymbol{P}_X\big(\boldsymbol{y}_j - \boldsymbol{Z}_j\boldsymbol{\delta}_j\big) = \boldsymbol{0}, \;\; \text{for } i = 1, \ldots, g. \quad (18.61)$$

In order to make (18.61) operational, we need to estimate the covariance matrix $\boldsymbol{\Sigma}$ of the error terms. In the case of an SUR model, we could use OLS on each equation individually. Since OLS is inconsistent for simultaneous equations models, we use 2SLS on each equation instead. Thus the first two "stages" of 3SLS are simply the two stages of 2SLS, applied to each separate equation of (18.01). The covariances of the error terms are then estimated from the 2SLS residuals:

$$\tilde{\sigma}_{ij} = \frac{1}{n}\sum_{t=1}^{n} \tilde{u}_{ti}\tilde{u}_{tj}. \tag{18.62}$$

Of course, these residuals must be the genuine 2SLS residuals, not the residuals from OLS estimation of the second-stage regressions; see Section 7.5. Thus we see that the 3SLS estimators $\tilde{\boldsymbol{\delta}}_1$ through $\tilde{\boldsymbol{\delta}}_g$ must jointly solve the first-order conditions

$$\sum_{j=1}^{g} \tilde{\sigma}^{ij} \boldsymbol{Z}_i^{\top} \boldsymbol{P}_X \big(\boldsymbol{y}_j - \boldsymbol{Z}_j \tilde{\boldsymbol{\delta}}_j\big) = \mathbf{0}. \tag{18.63}$$

The solution is easy to write down. If $\boldsymbol{\delta} \equiv [\boldsymbol{\delta}_1 \,\vdots\, \cdots \,\vdots\, \boldsymbol{\delta}_g]$ and matrices enclosed in square brackets $[\cdot]$ denote partitioned matrices characterized by a typical block, then the 3SLS estimator $\tilde{\boldsymbol{\delta}}$ can be written very compactly as

$$\tilde{\boldsymbol{\delta}} = \big[\tilde{\sigma}^{ij} \boldsymbol{Z}_i^{\top} \boldsymbol{P}_X \boldsymbol{Z}_j\big]^{-1} \left[\sum_{j=1}^{g} \tilde{\sigma}^{ij} \boldsymbol{Z}_i^{\top} \boldsymbol{P}_X \boldsymbol{y}_j\right]. \tag{18.64}$$

It is more common to see the 3SLS estimator written using an alternative notation that involves Kronecker products; see almost any econometrics textbook. Although Kronecker products can sometimes be useful (Magnus and Neudecker, 1988), we prefer the compact notation of (18.64).

The 3SLS estimator is closely related both to the 2SLS estimator and to the GLS estimator for multivariate SUR models in which the explanatory variables are all exogenous or predetermined. If we assume that $\boldsymbol{\Sigma}$ is diagonal, conditions (18.63) become simply

$$\tilde{\sigma}^{ii} \boldsymbol{Z}_i^{\top} \boldsymbol{P}_X \big(\boldsymbol{y}_i - \boldsymbol{Z}_i \boldsymbol{\delta}_i\big) = \mathbf{0},$$

which are equivalent to the conditions for equation-by-equation 2SLS. Thus 3SLS and 2SLS will be asymptotically (but not numerically) equivalent when the structural form errors are not contemporaneously correlated. It is also easy to see that the SUR estimator for linear models is just a special case of the 3SLS estimator. Since all regressors can be used as instruments in the SUR case, it is no longer necessary to use 2SLS in the preliminary stage. Equivalently, the fact that each regressor matrix $\boldsymbol{Z}_i$ is just a submatrix of the full regressor matrix, $\boldsymbol{X}$, implies that $\boldsymbol{P}_X \boldsymbol{Z}_i = \boldsymbol{Z}_i$. Thus (18.63) simplifies to

$$\sum_{j=1}^{g} \tilde{\sigma}^{ij} \boldsymbol{Z}_i^{\top} \big(\boldsymbol{y}_j - \boldsymbol{Z}_j \boldsymbol{\delta}_j\big) = \mathbf{0},$$

which is what the defining equation (9.54) for the feasible GLS estimator of an SUR system without cross-equation restrictions becomes in the linear case. We see that the relation between 3SLS and equation-by-equation 2SLS is the same as that between feasible GLS SUR estimation and equation-by-equation OLS.

On the basis of (18.64), it is natural to conjecture that the covariance matrix of the 3SLS estimator can be estimated by

$$[\tilde{\sigma}^{ij}\boldsymbol{Z}_i^\top \boldsymbol{P}_X \boldsymbol{Z}_j]^{-1}. \tag{18.65}$$

This is indeed the case, and it can easily be shown by using the general result (17.55) for GMM estimation. We have seen that for the $\tilde{\boldsymbol{\Phi}}^{-1}$ of that expression we should use the matrix with typical block $\tilde{\sigma}^{ij}(\boldsymbol{X}^\top\boldsymbol{X})^{-1}$. For $\tilde{\boldsymbol{D}}$, the matrix of derivatives of the empirical moments with respect to the model parameters, we can see that the appropriate matrix must be block-diagonal, with typical diagonal block given by $-\boldsymbol{X}^\top\boldsymbol{Z}_i$. (We are deliberately ignoring factors of powers of n here.) Since we are dealing with a linear system, $\tilde{\boldsymbol{D}}$ does not depend on any estimated parameters. Thus a suitable estimate of the asymptotic covariance matrix is given by the inverse of the matrix with typical block

$$\boldsymbol{Z}_i^\top\boldsymbol{X}\,\tilde{\sigma}^{ij}\big(\boldsymbol{X}^\top\boldsymbol{X}\big)^{-1}\boldsymbol{X}^\top\boldsymbol{Z}_j = \tilde{\sigma}^{ij}\boldsymbol{Z}_i^\top\boldsymbol{P}_X\boldsymbol{Z}_j,$$

which is simply (18.65).

Since the simultaneous equations model (18.01) is equivalent to the restricted reduced form (18.02), one might reasonably ask why an estimator like 3SLS cannot simply be derived from (18.02), since its form is precisely that of an SUR system. The answer is, of course, that it can be. However, unless each equation of the system is just identified, the restrictions will be nonlinear. Essentially this approach is taken by Chamberlain (1984). The advantage of the approach we have taken is that it avoids the difficulties associated with dealing with nonlinear restrictions.

Another point of similarity between 3SLS and SUR estimation is that both are numerically equivalent to the corresponding equation-by-equation procedure if each equation is just identified. For SUR systems, this means simply that all the regressors appear as explanatory variables in each equation (if not, there would be overidentifying restrictions implied by requiring that the errors of an equation in which some regressors were absent should be orthogonal to the absent regressors as well as those included in the equation). We saw in Section 9.8, by means of Kruskal's Theorem, that SUR estimates are numerically identical to equation-by-equation OLS estimates in this case. It is a good exercise to verify that the same result holds in the 3SLS context.

If we assume that the error terms contained in the matrix $\boldsymbol{U}$ of (18.01) are normally distributed, then the efficiency properties of all ML estimation procedures guarantee the asymptotic efficiency of the FIML estimator. It is then natural to ask whether the 3SLS estimator shares FIML's asymptotic efficiency, and the answer, as we will see directly, turns out to be that it does. We could readily obtain a straightforward proof of this result if we had an expression for the asymptotic covariance matrix of the FIML estimator, which we could compare with (18.65). However, we chose not to derive such an expression in Section 18.4, because one of the easiest ways to obtain an estimate of the FIML covariance matrix is to use the 3SLS estimate (18.65), evaluated at the FIML estimates. Instead, our proof of the asymptotic equivalence of 3SLS and FIML is based on the fact that the FIML estimator can be interpreted as an instrumental variables estimator.

This result, which was first proved in Hausman (1975), is of considerable interest in itself, for it explicitly provides the optimal instruments associated with ML estimation of the system (18.01). As we might expect, these can be found by considering the first-order conditions for the maximization of the loglikelihood function, which we take in the form (18.28). If we denote the ith column of $\boldsymbol{\Gamma}$ or $\boldsymbol{B}$ by $\boldsymbol{\Gamma}_i$ or $\boldsymbol{B}_i$, respectively, and continue to let σ^{ij} denote a typical element of $\boldsymbol{\Sigma}^{-1}$, then (18.28) can be rewritten as

$$\begin{aligned}\ell(\boldsymbol{B},\boldsymbol{\Gamma},\boldsymbol{\Sigma}) = &-\tfrac{ng}{2}\log(2\pi) + n\log|\det\boldsymbol{\Gamma}| - \tfrac{n}{2}\log|\boldsymbol{\Sigma}| \\ &-\tfrac{1}{2}\sum_{t=1}^{n}\sum_{i=1}^{g}\sum_{j=1}^{g}\sigma^{ij}\big(\boldsymbol{Y}_t\boldsymbol{\Gamma}_i - \boldsymbol{X}_t\boldsymbol{B}_i\big)\big(\boldsymbol{Y}_t\boldsymbol{\Gamma}_j - \boldsymbol{X}_t\boldsymbol{B}_j\big).\end{aligned} \tag{18.66}$$

The chief difficulty with writing down explicit first-order conditions for a maximum of (18.66) is that $\boldsymbol{B}$ and $\boldsymbol{\Gamma}$ are restricted so as to have numerous zero elements and so that one element of each column of $\boldsymbol{\Gamma}$ equals unity. Consequently, we may not set the derivatives of (18.66) equal to zero with respect to elements of $\boldsymbol{\Gamma}$ or $\boldsymbol{B}$ that are so restricted. What we will do to get around this difficulty is to begin by writing out a matrix of partial derivatives of $\ell(\boldsymbol{B},\boldsymbol{\Gamma},\boldsymbol{\Sigma})$ with respect to the elements of $\boldsymbol{B}$ that will have exactly the same shape as the matrix $\boldsymbol{B}$. By this we mean that the ij^{th} element of the partial derivative matrix will be the partial derivative of ℓ with respect to the ij^{th} element of $\boldsymbol{B}$. We can perform a similar exercise for $\boldsymbol{\Gamma}$ and then equate to zero only the appropriate elements of the two matrices of derivatives.

The matrix $\boldsymbol{B}$ appears only in the last term of (18.66), and so we may restrict attention to that term for the moment. It is convenient to compute the partial derivative matrix element by element and then to arrange these derivatives as the appropriate $k \times g$ matrix. Since each factor in the last term of (18.66) is a scalar, each derivative is easy to calculate. With respect to the ij^{th} element, we obtain

$$\sum_{t=1}^{n}\sum_{m=1}^{g}\sigma^{im}\boldsymbol{X}_{tj}\big(\boldsymbol{Y}_t\boldsymbol{\Gamma}_m - \boldsymbol{X}_t\boldsymbol{B}_m\big). \tag{18.67}$$

We wish to find a matrix of which the ij^{th} element is (18.67). Since j is attached as a subscript only to the element $\boldsymbol{X}_{tj}$, we can write down the jth

column of the desired matrix by arranging the elements $\boldsymbol{X}_{tj}$ as a column. This gives

$$\begin{aligned}
&\sum_{t=1}^{n}\sum_{m=1}^{g}\sigma^{im}\boldsymbol{X}_t^{\top}(\boldsymbol{Y}_t\boldsymbol{\Gamma}_m - \boldsymbol{X}_t\boldsymbol{B}_m)\\
&= \sum_{m=1}^{g}\sigma^{im}\boldsymbol{X}^{\top}(\boldsymbol{Y}\boldsymbol{\Gamma}_m - \boldsymbol{X}\boldsymbol{B}_m)\\
&= \boldsymbol{X}^{\top}(\boldsymbol{Y}\boldsymbol{\Gamma} - \boldsymbol{X}\boldsymbol{B})(\boldsymbol{\Sigma}^{-1})_i,
\end{aligned} \tag{18.68}$$

where $(\boldsymbol{\Sigma}^{-1})_i$ is the ith column of $\boldsymbol{\Sigma}^{-1}$. Now observe that the successive expressions in (18.68) are k-vectors. To complete our exercise, all we need do is to arrange them side by side as a $k \times g$ matrix, and it is now obvious that this matrix is just $\boldsymbol{X}^{\top}(\boldsymbol{Y}\boldsymbol{\Gamma} - \boldsymbol{X}\boldsymbol{B})\boldsymbol{\Sigma}^{-1}$.

We now have to compute the derivatives (18.66) with respect to the $g \times g$ matrix $\boldsymbol{\Gamma}$. Operations exactly similar to those carried out for $\boldsymbol{B}$ show that the matrix of derivatives with respect to the last term of (18.66) is

$$-\boldsymbol{Y}^{\top}(\boldsymbol{Y}\boldsymbol{\Gamma} - \boldsymbol{X}\boldsymbol{B})\boldsymbol{\Sigma}^{-1}.$$

This is a $g \times g$ matrix, as required. But $\boldsymbol{\Gamma}$ also appears through its determinant in the second term of (18.66). Recall (or see Appendix A) that the derivative of the logarithm of the determinant of a matrix with respect to the ij^{th} element of that matrix is the ji^{th} element of the inverse of the matrix. Consequently, the partial derivative matrix corresponding to $\boldsymbol{\Gamma}$ is

$$n(\boldsymbol{\Gamma}^{-1})^{\top} - \boldsymbol{Y}^{\top}(\boldsymbol{Y}\boldsymbol{\Gamma} - \boldsymbol{X}\boldsymbol{B})\boldsymbol{\Sigma}^{-1}. \tag{18.69}$$

We can obtain a more convenient expression than (18.69) by making use of the first-order conditions for the elements of the covariance matrix $\boldsymbol{\Sigma}$. From (18.29), we see that these conditions give

$$\hat{\boldsymbol{\Sigma}} = n^{-1}(\boldsymbol{Y}\hat{\boldsymbol{\Gamma}} - \boldsymbol{X}\hat{\boldsymbol{B}})^{\top}(\boldsymbol{Y}\hat{\boldsymbol{\Gamma}} - \boldsymbol{X}\hat{\boldsymbol{B}}), \tag{18.70}$$

where $\hat{\boldsymbol{\Sigma}}$, $\hat{\boldsymbol{\Gamma}}$, and $\hat{\boldsymbol{B}}$ denote FIML estimates. If this equation is premultiplied by $n\hat{\boldsymbol{\Sigma}}^{-1}$, postmultiplied by $\hat{\boldsymbol{\Gamma}}^{-1}$, and transposed, we find that

$$n(\hat{\boldsymbol{\Gamma}}^{-1})^{\top} = \boldsymbol{Y}^{\top}(\boldsymbol{Y}\hat{\boldsymbol{\Gamma}} - \boldsymbol{X}\hat{\boldsymbol{B}})\hat{\boldsymbol{\Sigma}}^{-1} - (\hat{\boldsymbol{\Gamma}}^{-1})^{\top}\hat{\boldsymbol{B}}^{\top}\boldsymbol{X}^{\top}(\boldsymbol{Y}\hat{\boldsymbol{\Gamma}} - \boldsymbol{X}\hat{\boldsymbol{B}})\hat{\boldsymbol{\Sigma}}^{-1}. \tag{18.71}$$

Since $\boldsymbol{X}\hat{\boldsymbol{B}}\hat{\boldsymbol{\Gamma}}^{-1}$ is the matrix of fitted values from estimation of the restricted reduced form, it will ease notation and clarify the subsequent analysis if we denote this matrix simply by $\hat{\boldsymbol{Y}}$. Thus (18.71) can be rewritten as

$$n(\hat{\boldsymbol{\Gamma}}^{-1})^{\top} = \boldsymbol{Y}^{\top}(\boldsymbol{Y}\hat{\boldsymbol{\Gamma}} - \boldsymbol{X}\hat{\boldsymbol{B}})\hat{\boldsymbol{\Sigma}}^{-1} - \hat{\boldsymbol{Y}}^{\top}(\boldsymbol{Y}\hat{\boldsymbol{\Gamma}} - \boldsymbol{X}\hat{\boldsymbol{B}})\hat{\boldsymbol{\Sigma}}^{-1}.$$

Consequently, the matrix (18.69), evaluated at the ML estimates, becomes

$$-\hat{\boldsymbol{Y}}^{\top}(\boldsymbol{Y}\hat{\boldsymbol{\Gamma}} - \boldsymbol{X}\hat{\boldsymbol{B}})\hat{\boldsymbol{\Sigma}}^{-1}.$$

Now at last we can select the elements of the two partial derivative matrices which are actually zero when evaluated at the ML estimates. The parameters that appear in the ith equation are found in the ith columns of the matrices $\boldsymbol{\Gamma}$ and $\boldsymbol{B}$, and so the appropriate partial derivatives are found in the ith columns of the partial derivative matrices. For the matrix corresponding to $\boldsymbol{B}$, this column is $\boldsymbol{X}^{\top}(\boldsymbol{Y}\hat{\boldsymbol{\Gamma}} - \boldsymbol{X}\hat{\boldsymbol{B}})(\hat{\boldsymbol{\Sigma}}^{-1})_i$. From this column we wish to select only those rows for which the corresponding element of the column $\boldsymbol{B}_i$ is unrestricted, that is, the elements corresponding to the $n \times k_i$ matrix $\boldsymbol{X}_i$. Since in order to select rows of a matrix product, we need only select the corresponding rows of the left-most factor, the zero elements are those of the k_i-vector $\boldsymbol{X}_i^{\top}(\boldsymbol{Y}\hat{\boldsymbol{\Gamma}} - \boldsymbol{X}\hat{\boldsymbol{B}})(\hat{\boldsymbol{\Sigma}}^{-1})_i$.

By exactly similar reasoning, we find that, for each $i = 1, \ldots, g$, the g_i-vector $\hat{\boldsymbol{Y}}_i^{\top}(\boldsymbol{Y}\hat{\boldsymbol{\Gamma}} - \boldsymbol{X}\hat{\boldsymbol{B}})(\hat{\boldsymbol{\Sigma}}^{-1})_i$ is zero, where $\hat{\boldsymbol{Y}}_i$ contains only those columns of $\hat{\boldsymbol{Y}}$ that correspond to the matrix $\boldsymbol{Y}_i$ of endogenous variables included as regressors in the ith equation. If we write $\hat{\boldsymbol{Z}}_i \equiv [\boldsymbol{X}_i \;\; \hat{\boldsymbol{Y}}_i]$, then all the first-order conditions corresponding to the parameters of the ith equation can be written as

$$\hat{\boldsymbol{Z}}_i^{\top}(\boldsymbol{Y}\hat{\boldsymbol{\Gamma}} - \boldsymbol{X}\hat{\boldsymbol{B}})(\boldsymbol{\Sigma}^{-1})_i = \mathbf{0}.$$

These conditions can be further simplified. Note that

$$\begin{aligned}(\boldsymbol{Y}\hat{\boldsymbol{\Gamma}} - \boldsymbol{X}\hat{\boldsymbol{B}})(\hat{\boldsymbol{\Sigma}}^{-1})_i &= \sum_{j=1}^{g} \hat{\sigma}^{ij}(\boldsymbol{Y}\hat{\boldsymbol{\Gamma}}_j - \boldsymbol{X}\hat{\boldsymbol{B}}_j)\\ &= \sum_{j=1}^{g} \hat{\sigma}^{ij}(\boldsymbol{y}_j - \boldsymbol{Z}_j\hat{\boldsymbol{\delta}}_j).\end{aligned}$$

The full set of first-order conditions defining the FIML estimates can thus be written as

$$\sum_{j=1}^{g} \hat{\sigma}^{ij}\hat{\boldsymbol{Z}}_i^{\top}(\boldsymbol{y}_j - \boldsymbol{Z}_j\hat{\boldsymbol{\delta}}_j) = \mathbf{0}, \quad \text{for } i = 1, \ldots, g. \tag{18.72}$$

The conditions (18.72) are now in a form very similar indeed to that of the conditions (18.63) that define the 3SLS estimator. In fact, if we let $\bar{\boldsymbol{Y}}_i$ denote the $n \times g_i$ matrix of fitted values from the *unrestricted* reduced form, so that $\bar{\boldsymbol{Y}}_i = \boldsymbol{P}_X\boldsymbol{Y}_i$ for $i = 1, \ldots, g$, then

$$\boldsymbol{P}_X\boldsymbol{Z}_i = \boldsymbol{P}_X[\,\boldsymbol{X}_i \;\; \boldsymbol{Y}_i\,] = [\,\boldsymbol{X}_i \;\; \bar{\boldsymbol{Y}}_i\,] \equiv \bar{\boldsymbol{Z}}_i.$$

Thus the conditions (18.63) that define the 3SLS estimator can be written as

$$\sum_{j=1}^{g} \tilde{\sigma}^{ij}\bar{\boldsymbol{Z}}_i^{\top}(y_j - \boldsymbol{Z}_j\tilde{\boldsymbol{\delta}}_j) = \mathbf{0}. \tag{18.73}$$

The differences between the conditions defining the 3SLS estimates and those defining the FIML estimates can be seen immediately from (18.73) and (18.72). They are:

(i) The covariance matrix estimate is formed from the equation-by-equation 2SLS residuals for 3SLS and from the FIML residuals for FIML;

(ii) The fitted values of $\boldsymbol{Y}$ used in the instruments are those of the unrestricted reduced form for 3SLS and those of FIML for FIML.

Both differences reflect the fact that, unlike 3SLS, FIML is a joint estimation procedure: One must solve the conditions (18.72) simultaneously with the first-order conditions (18.70) for $\boldsymbol{\Sigma}$ in order to obtain any of the ML estimates.

Another way to make the distinction between the two procedures is to say that they use different estimates of the same optimal instruments. These instruments are a little tricky to write down. In order to do so without too much trouble, we may form a long ng-vector of all the contributions to the empirical moments. This vector can be written in partitioned form as

$$\left[\boldsymbol{y}_1 - \boldsymbol{Z}_1\boldsymbol{\delta}_1 \;\vdots\; \cdots \;\vdots\; \boldsymbol{y}_g - \boldsymbol{Z}_g\boldsymbol{\delta}_g\right], \tag{18.74}$$

a typical block of which is the n-vector $\boldsymbol{y}_i - \boldsymbol{Z}_i\boldsymbol{\delta}_i$. In total, there are $p \equiv \sum_{i=1}^{g}(g_i + k_i)$ parameters to be identified, and so the vector (18.74) must be premultiplied by precisely that number of row vectors, each with ng elements, so as to yield the defining equations for the estimates. It can be seen without too much difficulty that the $p \times ng$ matrix that is needed to produce (18.72) or (18.73) is made up from blocks of the form $\sigma^{ij}\boldsymbol{W}_i^{\top}$, where $\boldsymbol{W}_i$ means a matrix of the form $[\boldsymbol{X\Pi}_i \quad \boldsymbol{X}_i]$ for some choice of the $n \times g_i$ matrices $\boldsymbol{\Pi}_i$. This typical block is a $(g_i + k_i) \times n$ matrix, as required.

The 3SLS and FIML estimators differ as to how $\boldsymbol{\Sigma}$ and the $\boldsymbol{\Pi}_i$'s are chosen. The real, unobservable, optimal instruments are given by setting $\boldsymbol{\Sigma}$ equal to the true error covariance matrix $\boldsymbol{\Sigma}_0$ and setting $\boldsymbol{\Pi}_i = \boldsymbol{B}_0\boldsymbol{\Gamma}_0^{-1}$, using the true parameter matrices. Evidently, both $\tilde{\boldsymbol{\Sigma}}$ and $\hat{\boldsymbol{\Sigma}}$ are consistent for $\boldsymbol{\Sigma}_0$. Similarly, both the matrix $\bar{\boldsymbol{\Pi}}$ such that $\bar{\boldsymbol{Y}} = \boldsymbol{P}_X\boldsymbol{Y} = \boldsymbol{X}\bar{\boldsymbol{\Pi}}$ obtained from the unrestricted reduced form and the matrix $\hat{\boldsymbol{B}}\hat{\boldsymbol{\Gamma}}^{-1}$ obtained from FIML estimation are consistent for $\boldsymbol{B}_0\boldsymbol{\Gamma}_0^{-1}$. Both procedures therefore use consistent estimates of the true optimal instruments, and so both procedures are asymptotically equivalent and asymptotically efficient. Notice that this conclusion applies only to the estimation of $\boldsymbol{\Gamma}$ and $\boldsymbol{B}$: The procedures are *not* equivalent as regards the estimation of the covariance matrix $\boldsymbol{\Sigma}$.

Numerical equivalence between FIML and 3SLS can be obtained by iterating the latter. At each stage of the iteration, the residuals of the previous stage are used to generate the updated estimate of $\boldsymbol{\Sigma}$, while the parameter estimates of the previous stage are used to generate the updated estimate of $\boldsymbol{\Pi}$. Such an iterative procedure, which is probably of more theoretical than practical interest, starts from 3SLS and converges to FIML for all parameters, including those of $\boldsymbol{\Sigma}$. This iterative scheme, and many others, is discussed in

Hendry (1976), which also provides an extensive bibliography for much of the simultaneous equations literature in existence at that time.

As we suggested in Section 18.4, a convenient way to calculate an estimate of the covariance matrix of the FIML estimator of $\boldsymbol{\Gamma}$ and $\boldsymbol{B}$ is to use an expression similar to (18.65). If we replace the 3SLS estimate $\tilde{\boldsymbol{\Sigma}}$ by the FIML estimate $\hat{\boldsymbol{\Sigma}}$, and the $\boldsymbol{P}_X\boldsymbol{Z}_i$'s of 3SLS by the $\hat{\boldsymbol{Z}}_i$'s of FIML, the result is

$$\big[\hat{\sigma}^{ij}\hat{\boldsymbol{Z}}_i^{\top}\hat{\boldsymbol{Z}}_j\big]^{-1}.$$

Just as FIML applied to a system in which only one equation is overidentified degenerates to LIML for that one equation, so does 3SLS degenerate to 2SLS for one single overidentified equation in an otherwise just identified system. This result is of some practical importance, although the proof is not very interesting and is therefore omitted. The result implies that the reason we cited in Section 18.5 for sometimes preferring LIML to FIML, namely, a wish to avoid imposing possibly false overidentifying restrictions, would lead one in a least squares context never to go beyond 2SLS. Since the computational burden of 3SLS relative to 2SLS is considerable if one is interested in only one equation, it is important to realize that this added burden gives no advantage unless at least some of the other equations of the system are overidentified.

Since 3SLS is a special case of GMM estimation, it can easily be generalized to take account of heteroskedasticity of unknown form in the errors, something that is not possible for FIML. If there is no information about the form of heteroskedasticity, then we are not in a position to improve the choice (18.56) of empirical moment conditions used to identify the parameters. But we can replace the estimate (18.58) of their covariance matrix based on the assumption of homoskedasticity by a heteroskedasticity-consistent estimate. Under serial independence of the errors, (18.57) is still a proper expression of the covariance matrix of the empirical moments. A typical block of this matrix is

$$\sum_{t=1}^{n} E\big(u_{ti}u_{tj}\boldsymbol{X}_t^{\top}\boldsymbol{X}_t\big).$$

It is clear that, as with other HCCMEs, $1/n$ times this matrix can be consistently estimated by

$$\frac{1}{n}\sum_{t=1}^{n} E\big(\tilde{u}_{ti}\tilde{u}_{tj}\boldsymbol{X}_t^{\top}\boldsymbol{X}_t\big),$$

which, if we make the definition $\tilde{\boldsymbol{\Omega}}_{ij} = \mathrm{diag}(\tilde{u}_{ti}\tilde{u}_{tj})$, for $i, j = 1, \ldots, g$, can be written more simply as

$$\frac{1}{n}\boldsymbol{X}^{\top}\tilde{\boldsymbol{\Omega}}_{ij}\boldsymbol{X}. \tag{18.75}$$

If we use this expression to construct a criterion function based on the empirical moment conditions (18.56), we find a new estimator, defined by the equations

$$\sum_{j=1}^{g} \boldsymbol{Z}_i^\top \boldsymbol{X} \big(\boldsymbol{X}^\top \tilde{\boldsymbol{\Omega}}_{ij} \boldsymbol{X}\big)^{-1} \boldsymbol{X}^\top (\boldsymbol{y}_j - \boldsymbol{Z}_j \boldsymbol{\delta}_j) = \mathbf{0}.$$

Solving these equations yields the estimator

$$\check{\boldsymbol{\delta}} = \big[\boldsymbol{Z}_i^\top \boldsymbol{X} \big(\boldsymbol{X}^\top \tilde{\boldsymbol{\Omega}}_{ij} \boldsymbol{X}\big)^{-1} \boldsymbol{X}^\top \boldsymbol{Z}_j\big]^{-1} \bigg[\sum_{j=1}^{g} \boldsymbol{Z}_i^\top \boldsymbol{X} \big(\boldsymbol{X}^\top \tilde{\boldsymbol{\Omega}}_{ij} \boldsymbol{X}\big)^{-1} \boldsymbol{X}^\top \boldsymbol{y}_j\bigg]. \tag{18.76}$$

Not surprisingly, the structure of (18.76) is very similar to that of the H2SLS estimator (17.44), and we will therefore call this the **H3SLS estimator**. Its asymptotic covariance matrix can be estimated by the inverse of a matrix with typical block

$$\boldsymbol{Z}_i^\top \boldsymbol{X} \big(\boldsymbol{X}^\top \tilde{\boldsymbol{\Omega}}_{ij} \boldsymbol{X}\big)^{-1} \boldsymbol{X}^\top \boldsymbol{Z}_j.$$

In the presence of heteroskedasticity of unknown form, H3SLS should be more efficient, asymptotically, than 3SLS or FIML. How well it performs in finite samples, however, is largely unknown at present.

It is clear that we could generalize the H3SLS estimator even further by using an HAC covariance matrix estimator instead of the HCCME (18.75); see, for example, Gallant (1987, Chapter 6). This will, however, be a desirable thing to do only if the presence of serial correlation is compatible with the model being correctly specified and if the sample size is quite large. For most time-series applications, FIML or 3SLS will be the preferred full-system estimators, because heteroskedasticity will be largely absent and serial correlation will be present only if the model is misspecified. When the sample size is large and heteroskedasticity is severe, however, as in many cross-section applications, H3SLS is likely to be the full-system estimator of choice.

18.7 Nonlinear Simultaneous Equations Models

Up to this point, we have said very little about **nonlinear simultaneous equations models**. A simultaneous equations model may be nonlinear in three different ways. First of all, $\boldsymbol{Y}_t$ may depend on nonlinear functions of some of the exogenous or predetermined variables. As usual, this type of nonlinearity causes no problem at all and can be dealt with simply by redefining $\boldsymbol{X}_t$. Secondly, some of the parameters may appear nonlinearly in the structural model for $\boldsymbol{Y}_t$, perhaps because there are nonlinear restrictions on them. This is the type of nonlinearity that we deal with routinely when estimating nonlinear regression models, and it causes no new problems in the context of simultaneous equations models. Finally, there may be nonlinearities involving the endogenous variables. This type of nonlinearity does raise a serious new problem.

The problem with models that are nonlinear in the endogenous variables is that for such models there is nothing equivalent to the unrestricted reduced form for a linear simultaneous equations model. It is generally difficult or impossible to solve for the endogenous variables as functions of the exogenous variables and the error terms. Even when it is possible, $\boldsymbol{Y}_t$ will almost always depend nonlinearly on both the exogenous variables and the error terms. Consider, for example, the extremely simple two-equation model

$$\begin{aligned} y_1 &= \alpha y_2 + \boldsymbol{X}_1\boldsymbol{\beta}_1 + u_1 \\ y_2 &= \gamma_1 y_1 + \gamma_2 y_1^2 + \boldsymbol{X}_2\boldsymbol{\beta}_2 + u_2, \end{aligned} \tag{18.77}$$

where the notation is conventional and we have omitted t subscripts for clarity. If we substitute the right-hand side of the first equation of (18.77) into the second, we obtain

$$y_2 = \gamma_1\big(\alpha y_2 + \boldsymbol{X}_1\boldsymbol{\beta}_1 + u_1\big) + \gamma_2\big(\alpha y_2 + \boldsymbol{X}_1\boldsymbol{\beta}_1 + u_1\big)^2 + \boldsymbol{X}_2\boldsymbol{\beta}_2 + u_2.$$

Since this equation is quadratic in y_2, it will generally have two solutions. Depending on the parameter values and the values of the $\boldsymbol{X}_i$'s and the u_i's, both or neither of these solutions will be real. Even if there *is* a real solution, it will not be linear in the exogenous variables. Therefore, simply using the components of $\boldsymbol{X}_1$ and $\boldsymbol{X}_2$ as instruments will not be optimal.

This example illustrates the sort of problems that can arise with any simultaneous equations model that is nonlinear in the endogenous variables. At the very least, there is a problem choosing the instruments to use. One approach, as we noted in Section 7.6, is to use powers and even cross-products of the exogenous variables as instruments, along with the exogenous variables themselves. If the sample size is very large, this approach may work reasonably well, but in most cases it will be far from clear how many instruments to use, or which ones. Adding additional instruments will generally improve asymptotic efficiency but will also tend to worsen finite-sample bias. More seriously, it is quite possible to estimate a model that cannot be solved for some perfectly reasonable values of the exogenous variables and the error terms. Thus models that are nonlinear in the endogenous variables should probably be avoided if at all possible.

It appears that LIML is not a viable procedure for estimating nonlinear simultaneous equations models. The classical LIML procedure discussed in Section 18.5 is designed for linear models only. One might think that one could obtain LIML estimates of a nonlinear structural equation by using a routine for nonlinear FIML on a system consisting of the one structural equation together with $g-1$ linear reduced form equations. But that would make sense only if the reduced form equations were in fact linear, which will almost never be the case. Thus, for single-equation estimation, the only procedures that are available are ones based on instrumental variables.

We discussed the estimation of single-equation nonlinear models by IV methods in Section 7.6, and there is only a little more to be said on the subject. Suppose that the structural equation of interest can be written as

$$\boldsymbol{y} = \boldsymbol{x}(\boldsymbol{\delta}) + \boldsymbol{u},$$

where $\boldsymbol{\delta}$ is an l–vector of parameters, and the vector of nonlinear functions $\boldsymbol{x}(\boldsymbol{\delta})$ implicitly depends on at least one endogenous variable and some number of exogenous and predetermined variables. Then if $\boldsymbol{W}$ denotes an $n \times m$ matrix of instruments, we have seen that IV estimates may be obtained by minimizing the criterion function

$$\big(\boldsymbol{y} - \boldsymbol{x}(\boldsymbol{\delta})\big)^{\top} \boldsymbol{P}_W \big(\boldsymbol{y} - \boldsymbol{x}(\boldsymbol{\delta})\big). \tag{18.78}$$

The resulting estimates are often called **nonlinear two-stage least squares** or **NL2SLS** estimates, following the terminology of Amemiya (1974), although the estimation does not actually proceed in two stages. We discussed this point in Section 7.6.

The criterion function (18.78) can be derived as a GMM procedure by starting with the moment conditions

$$E\Big(\boldsymbol{W}^{\top}\big(\boldsymbol{y} - \boldsymbol{x}(\boldsymbol{\delta})\big)\Big) = \mathbf{0}$$

and assuming that $E(\boldsymbol{u}\boldsymbol{u}^{\top}) = \sigma^2\mathbf{I}$. That assumption may sometimes be too strong. If it were incorrect, minimizing (18.78) would yield inefficient estimates and an inconsistent estimate of the covariance matrix of the parameter estimates. A less restrictive assumption is that $E(\boldsymbol{u}\boldsymbol{u}^{\top}) = \boldsymbol{\Delta}$, where $\boldsymbol{\Delta}$ is a diagonal matrix with unknown (but bounded) diagonal elements. We can obtain estimates analogous to the H2SLS estimates of Section 17.3 by using a two-step procedure. In the first step, we minimize (18.78), so as to obtain consistent but inefficient parameter estimates and residuals $\tilde{u}_t$, and then use the latter to construct the matrix $\boldsymbol{W}^{\top}\tilde{\boldsymbol{\Delta}}\boldsymbol{W}$, where $\tilde{\boldsymbol{\Delta}}$ has typical diagonal element $\tilde{u}_t^2$. In the second step, we minimize the criterion function

$$\big(\boldsymbol{y} - \boldsymbol{x}(\boldsymbol{\delta})\big)^{\top} \boldsymbol{W} \big(\boldsymbol{W}^{\top}\tilde{\boldsymbol{\Delta}}\boldsymbol{W}\big)^{-1} \boldsymbol{W}^{\top}\big(\boldsymbol{y} - \boldsymbol{x}(\boldsymbol{\delta})\big).$$

As usual, we could drop the assumption that $\boldsymbol{\Delta}$ is diagonal and use an HAC estimator, if that were appropriate (see the remarks at the end of the preceding section).

Full-system estimation of nonlinear simultaneous equations models is typically done by some sort of IV (or GMM) procedure or by FIML. We will briefly discuss these two approaches in turn. Suppose the ith equation of the system can be written for all observations as

$$\boldsymbol{f}_i(\boldsymbol{Y}, \boldsymbol{X}, \boldsymbol{\theta}) = \boldsymbol{u}_i, \tag{18.79}$$

where $\boldsymbol{f}_i(\cdot)$ is an n–vector of nonlinear functions, $\boldsymbol{u}_i$ is an n–vector of error terms, and $\boldsymbol{\theta}$ is a p–vector of parameters to be estimated. In general, subject to whatever restrictions need to be imposed for the system to be identified, all the endogenous and exogenous variables and all the parameters may appear in any equation.

The first step in any sort of IV procedure is to choose the instruments to be used. If the model is nonlinear only in the parameters, the matrix of optimal instruments is $\boldsymbol{X}$. As we have seen, however, there is no simple way to choose the instruments for models that are nonlinear in one or more of the endogenous variables. The theory of Section 17.4 can be applied, of course, but the result that it yields is not very practical. Under the usual assumptions about the error terms, namely, that they are homoskedastic and independent across observations but correlated across equations for each observation, one finds that a matrix of instruments $\boldsymbol{W}$ will be optimal if $\mathcal{S}(\boldsymbol{W})$ is equal to the union of the subspaces spanned by the columns of $E(\partial \boldsymbol{f}_i/\partial \boldsymbol{\theta})$. This result was originally derived by Amemiya (1977). It makes sense but is generally not very useful in practice. For now, we simply assume that *some* valid $n \times m$ matrix of instruments $\boldsymbol{W}$ is available, with $m \geq p$.

A nonlinear IV procedure for full-system estimation, similar in spirit to the single-equation NL2SLS procedure based on minimizing (18.78), was first proposed by Jorgenson and Laffont (1974) and called **nonlinear three-stage least squares**, or **NL3SLS**. The name is somewhat misleading, for the same reason that the name "NL2SLS" is misleading. By analogy with (18.60), the criterion function we would really like to minimize is

$$\sum_{i=1}^{g}\sum_{j=1}^{g}\sigma^{ij}\boldsymbol{f}_i^{\top}(\boldsymbol{Y},\boldsymbol{X},\boldsymbol{\theta})\boldsymbol{P}_W\boldsymbol{f}_j(\boldsymbol{Y},\boldsymbol{X},\boldsymbol{\theta}). \tag{18.80}$$

In practice, however, the elements σ^{ij} of the inverse of the contemporaneous covariance matrix $\boldsymbol{\Sigma}$ will not be known and will have to be estimated. This may be done in several ways. One possibility is to use NL2SLS for each equation separately. This will generally be easy but may not be possible if some parameters are identified only by cross-equation restrictions. Another approach which will work in that case is to minimize the criterion function

$$\sum_{i=1}^{g}\sum_{j=1}^{g}\boldsymbol{f}_i^{\top}(\boldsymbol{Y},\boldsymbol{X},\boldsymbol{\theta})\boldsymbol{P}_W\boldsymbol{f}_j(\boldsymbol{Y},\boldsymbol{X},\boldsymbol{\theta}), \tag{18.81}$$

in which the unknown covariance matrix $\boldsymbol{\Sigma}$ is replaced by the identity matrix. The estimator obtained by minimizing (18.81) will evidently be a valid GMM estimator and thus will be consistent even though it is inefficient. Whichever inefficient estimator is used initially, it will yield g vectors of residuals $\acute{\boldsymbol{u}}_i$ from which the matrix $\boldsymbol{\Sigma}$ may be estimated consistently in exactly the same way as for linear models; see (18.62). Replacing the unknown σ^{ij}'s in (18.80) by the elements $\acute{\sigma}^{ij}$ of the inverse of the estimate of $\boldsymbol{\Sigma}$ then yields the criterion function

$$\sum_{i=1}^{g}\sum_{j=1}^{g}\acute{\sigma}^{ij}\boldsymbol{f}_i^{\top}(\boldsymbol{Y},\boldsymbol{X},\boldsymbol{\theta})\boldsymbol{P}_W\boldsymbol{f}_j(\boldsymbol{Y},\boldsymbol{X},\boldsymbol{\theta}), \tag{18.82}$$

which can actually be minimized in practice.

As usual, the minimized value of the criterion function (18.82) provides a test statistic for overidentifying restrictions; see Sections 7.8 and 17.6. If the model and instruments are correctly specified, this test statistic will be asymptotically distributed as $\chi^2(m-p)$; recall that m is the number of instruments and p is the number of free parameters. Moreover, if the model is estimated unrestrictedly and subject to r distinct restrictions, the difference between the two values of the criterion function will be asymptotically distributed as $\chi^2(r)$. If the latter test statistic is to be employed, it is important that the same estimate of $\boldsymbol{\Sigma}$ be used for both estimations, since otherwise the test statistic may not even be positive in finite samples.

When the sample size is large, it may be less computationally demanding to obtain one-step efficient estimates rather than actually to minimize (18.82). Suppose the initial consistent estimates, which may be either NL2SLS estimates or systems estimates based on (18.81), are denoted $\acute{\boldsymbol{\theta}}$. Then a first-order Taylor-series approximation to $\boldsymbol{f}_i(\boldsymbol{\theta}) \equiv \boldsymbol{f}_i(\boldsymbol{Y},\boldsymbol{X},\boldsymbol{\theta})$ around $\acute{\boldsymbol{\theta}}$ is

$$\boldsymbol{f}_i(\acute{\boldsymbol{\theta}}) + \boldsymbol{F}_i(\acute{\boldsymbol{\theta}})(\boldsymbol{\theta}-\acute{\boldsymbol{\theta}}),$$

where $\boldsymbol{F}_i$ is an $n\times p$ matrix of the derivatives of $\boldsymbol{f}_i(\boldsymbol{\theta})$ with respect to the p elements of $\boldsymbol{\theta}$. If certain parameters do not appear in the ith equation, the corresponding columns of $\boldsymbol{F}_i$ will be identically zero. The one-step estimates, which will be asymptotically equivalent to NL3SLS estimates, are simply $\grave{\boldsymbol{\theta}} = \acute{\boldsymbol{\theta}} - \acute{\boldsymbol{t}}$, where $\acute{\boldsymbol{t}}$ denotes the vector of *linear* 3SLS estimates

$$\acute{\boldsymbol{t}} = \left[\acute{\sigma}^{ij}\acute{\boldsymbol{F}}_i^{\top}\boldsymbol{P}_W\acute{\boldsymbol{F}}_j\right]^{-1}\left[\sum_{j=1}^{g}\acute{\sigma}^{ij}\acute{\boldsymbol{F}}_i^{\top}\boldsymbol{P}_W\acute{\boldsymbol{f}}_j\right]. \tag{18.83}$$

Compare this expression to (18.64).

It is clear that NL3SLS can be generalized to handle heteroskedasticity of unknown form, serial correlation of unknown form, or both. For example, to handle heteroskedasticity one would simply replace the matrix $\boldsymbol{P}_W$ in (18.82) and (18.83) by the matrix

$$\boldsymbol{W}\left(\boldsymbol{W}^{\top}\acute{\boldsymbol{\Omega}}_{ij}\boldsymbol{W}\right)^{-1}\boldsymbol{W}^{\top},$$

where, by analogy with (18.76), $\acute{\boldsymbol{\Omega}}_{ij} = \operatorname{diag}(\acute{u}_{ti}\acute{u}_{tj})$ for $i,j = 1,\ldots,g$. The initial estimates $\acute{\boldsymbol{\theta}}$ need not take account of heteroskedasticity. For a more detailed discussion of this sort of procedure, and of NL3SLS in general, see Gallant (1987, Chapter 6).

The other full-systems estimation method that is widely used is **nonlinear FIML**. For this, it is convenient to write the equation system to be estimated not as (18.79) but rather as

$$\boldsymbol{h}_t(\boldsymbol{Y}_t, \boldsymbol{X}_t, \boldsymbol{\theta}) = \boldsymbol{U}_t, \quad \boldsymbol{U}_t \sim \text{NID}(\mathbf{0}, \boldsymbol{\Sigma}), \tag{18.84}$$

where $\boldsymbol{\theta}$ is still a p-vector of parameters, $\boldsymbol{h}_t$ is a $1 \times g$ vector of nonlinear functions, and $\boldsymbol{U}_t$ is a $1 \times g$ vector of error terms. There need be no conflict between (18.79) and (18.84) if we think of the ith element of $\boldsymbol{h}_t(\cdot)$ as being the same as the tth element of $\boldsymbol{f}_i(\cdot)$.

The density of the vector $\boldsymbol{U}_t$ is

$$(2\pi)^{-g/2}|\boldsymbol{\Sigma}|^{-1/2}\exp\Big(-\tfrac{1}{2}\boldsymbol{U}_t\boldsymbol{\Sigma}^{-1}\boldsymbol{U}_t^{\top}\Big).$$

To obtain the density of $\boldsymbol{Y}_t$, we must replace $\boldsymbol{U}_t$ by $\boldsymbol{h}_t(\boldsymbol{Y}_t, \boldsymbol{X}_t, \boldsymbol{\theta})$ and multiply by the Jacobian factor $|\det \boldsymbol{J}_t|$, where $\boldsymbol{J}_t \equiv \partial \boldsymbol{h}_t(\boldsymbol{\theta})/\partial \boldsymbol{Y}_t$, that is, the $g \times g$ matrix of derivatives of $\boldsymbol{h}_t$ with respect to the elements of $\boldsymbol{Y}_t$. The result is

$$(2\pi)^{-g/2}|\det \boldsymbol{J}_t||\boldsymbol{\Sigma}|^{-1/2}\exp\Big(-\tfrac{1}{2}\boldsymbol{h}_t(\boldsymbol{Y}_t, \boldsymbol{X}_t, \boldsymbol{\theta})\boldsymbol{\Sigma}^{-1}\boldsymbol{h}_t^{\top}(\boldsymbol{Y}_t, \boldsymbol{X}_t, \boldsymbol{\theta})\Big).$$

It follows immediately that the loglikelihood function is

$$\begin{aligned}\ell(\boldsymbol{\theta}, \boldsymbol{\Sigma}) = &-\tfrac{ng}{2}\log(2\pi) + \sum_{t=1}^{n}\log|\det \boldsymbol{J}_t| - \tfrac{n}{2}\log|\boldsymbol{\Sigma}| \\ &-\tfrac{1}{2}\sum_{t=1}^{n}\boldsymbol{h}_t(\boldsymbol{Y}_t, \boldsymbol{X}_t, \boldsymbol{\theta})\boldsymbol{\Sigma}^{-1}\boldsymbol{h}_t^{\top}(\boldsymbol{Y}_t, \boldsymbol{X}_t, \boldsymbol{\theta}).\end{aligned} \tag{18.85}$$

This may then be maximized with respect to $\boldsymbol{\Sigma}$ and the result substituted back in to yield the concentrated loglikelihood function

$$\begin{aligned}\ell^c(\boldsymbol{\theta}) = &-\tfrac{ng}{2}\big(\log(2\pi) + 1\big) + \sum_{t=1}^{n}\log|\det \boldsymbol{J}_t| \\ &-\tfrac{n}{2}\log\Big|\frac{1}{n}\sum_{t=1}^{n}\boldsymbol{h}_t^{\top}(\boldsymbol{Y}_t, \boldsymbol{X}_t, \boldsymbol{\theta})\boldsymbol{h}_t(\boldsymbol{Y}_t, \boldsymbol{X}_t, \boldsymbol{\theta})\Big|.\end{aligned} \tag{18.86}$$

Inevitably, there is a strong resemblance between (18.85) and (18.86) and their counterparts (18.28) and (18.30) for the linear case. The major difference is that the Jacobian term in (18.85) and (18.86) is the sum of the logs of n different determinants. Thus every time one evaluates one of these loglikelihood functions, one has to calculate n different determinants. This can be very expensive if g or n is large. Of course, the problem goes away if the model is linear in the endogenous variables, since $\boldsymbol{J}_t$ will then be the same for all t.

One difficulty with nonlinear FIML is that it is not clear how to test all the overidentifying restrictions or even just what they may be in many cases. In the case of a linear simultaneous equations model, any structural form imposes nonlinear restrictions on the unrestricted reduced form, and it is easy to test those restrictions by means of an LR test. In the case of a simultaneous equations model that is nonlinear in the endogenous variables, however, we generally cannot even write down the URF, let alone estimate it. Any restriction that one can write down, whether a cross-equation restriction or a restriction on an individual equation, can of course be tested by using any of the classical tests. But there will in general be no way to test all the overidentifying restrictions at once. There is a related problem with NL3SLS estimation, of course. Even though the minimized value of the criterion function (18.82) provides a test statistic, it does so only for the overidentifying restrictions associated with a particular matrix of instruments $\boldsymbol{W}$, which may not provide a good approximation to the true, unknown URF.

The relationship between nonlinear FIML and NL3SLS is not as simple as the relationship between linear FIML and 3SLS. The two nonlinear methods will be asymptotically equivalent whenever the model is linear in the endogenous variables. They will not be equivalent in general, however. When they are not equivalent, nonlinear FIML will be more efficient, asymptotically, than NL3SLS. However, this greater efficiency comes at a price. When nonlinear FIML and NL3SLS are not asymptotically equivalent, the former may be inconsistent if the error terms are not in fact distributed as multivariate normal. In contrast, as we have seen, the assumption of normality is not needed for linear FIML to be consistent. For more on these points, see Amemiya (1977) and Phillips (1982). Amemiya (1985, Chapter 8) and Gallant (1987, Chapter 6) provide more detailed treatments of nonlinear FIML than we do.

There is a fairly large literature on the computation of nonlinear FIML estimates. As usual, many different algorithms can be used to maximize the loglikelihood function or the concentrated loglikelihood function, some of which take advantage of special features of particular classes of model. References include Eisenpress and Greenstadt (1966), Chow (1973), Dagenais (1978), Belsley (1979, 1980), Fair and Parke (1980), Parke (1982), and Quandt (1983).

18.8 CONCLUSION

It may strike some readers as curious that we have covered a topic as important as the simultaneous equations model so late in this book. We did of course cover some aspects of the subject in Chapter 7, as part of our discussion of instrumental variables. The reason we did not attempt a full treatment earlier in the book is that we wanted readers to have obtained a clear understanding of maximum likelihood estimation and specification testing and of the generalized method of moments. This then allowed us to develop all of the estimation methods and tests discussed in this chapter as straightforward applications of ML and GMM. Once one recognizes that this is the case, it is very much easier to understand simultaneous equations models and the statistical techniques associated with them.

Terms and Concepts

- cross-equation restrictions
- endogenous variable
- excluded variable
- exogeneity
- exogenous variable
- full-information maximum likelihood (FIML)
- Granger causality
- Granger noncausality
- H3SLS estimator
- included variable
- *K*-class estimator
- least variance ratio estimates
- limited-information maximum likelihood (LIML)
- linear simultaneous equations model
- nonlinear FIML
- nonlinear simultaneous equations model
- nonlinear three-stage least squares (NL3SLS)
- nonlinear two-stage least squares (NL2SLS)
- nuisance parameter
- order condition for identification
- overidentifying restrictions
- parameters of interest
- partial loglikelihood function
- predetermined variable
- rank condition for identification
- recursive systems
- restricted reduced form (RRF)
- simultaneous equations models
- strict exogeneity
- strong exogeneity
- super exogeneity
- three-stage least squares (3SLS)
- unrestricted reduced form (URF)
- weak exogeneity

Chapter 19

Regression Models for Time-Series Data

19.1 Introduction

A great deal of applied econometric work uses time-series data, and there are numerous econometric problems uniquely associated with the use of this type of data. One of these is serial correlation, which we discussed at length in Chapter 10. In this chapter and its successor, we discuss some other problems that are frequently encountered when using time-series data and some of the methods designed to handle them. In Section 19.2, we discuss the problem of "spurious" regressions between economic time series. This section introduces some important concepts that will be taken up again in Chapter 20, where we discuss unit roots and cointegration. Section 19.3 deals with the estimation of distributed lags. Section 19.4 deals with dynamic regression models, in which one or more lags of the dependent variable appear among the regressors. Section 19.5 discusses the estimation of vector autoregressive models for multivariate time series. The final two sections deal with seasonality. Section 19.6 provides an introduction to seasonal adjustment procedures, and Section 19.7 discusses various ways of modeling seasonal variation in regression models.

19.2 Spurious Regressions

Many economic time series trend upward over time. This is certainly true of most series that measure, or are measured in terms of, nominal prices, at least for this century. It is also true of many series that measure the levels of real economic variables, such as consumption, output, investment, imports, or exports. Many trending series can be broadly characterized by one of the following two models:

$$y_t = \gamma_1 + \gamma_2 t + u_t \quad \text{and} \tag{19.01}$$

$$y_t = \delta_1 + y_{t-1} + u_t, \tag{19.02}$$

where the error terms u_t will, in general, be neither independent nor identically distributed. They will, however, be stationary if the model is appropriate for the time series in question. The first of these models, (19.01), says that y_t is

trend-stationary, that is, stationary around a trend. In contrast, the second model, (19.02), says that y_t follows a **random walk with drift**. The drift parameter δ_1 in (19.02) plays much the same role as the trend parameter γ_2 in (19.01), since both cause y_t to trend upward over time. But the behavior of y_t is very different in the two cases, because in the first case detrending it will produce a variable that is stationary, while in the second case it will not.

There has been a great deal of literature on which of these two models, the trend-stationary model (19.01) or the random walk with drift (19.02), best characterizes most economic time series. Nelson and Plosser (1982) is a classic paper, Campbell and Mankiw (1987) is a more recent one, and Stock and Watson (1988a) provides an excellent discussion of many of the issues. In the next chapter we will discuss some of the methods that can be used to decide whether a given time series is well characterized by either of these models. For now, what concerns us is what happens if we use time series that are described by either of these two models as dependent or independent variables in a regression model.

If a time series with typical element x_t trends upward forever, then $n^{-1}\sum_{t=1}^{n} x_t^2$ will diverge to $+\infty$. Thus, if such a series is used as a regressor in a linear regression model, the matrix $n^{-1}\boldsymbol{X}^{\top}\boldsymbol{X}$ cannot possibly tend to a finite, positive definite matrix. All of the asymptotic theory we have used in this book is therefore inapplicable to models in which any of the regressors is well characterized by (19.01) or (19.02).[1] This does not mean that one should *never* put a trending variable on the right-hand side of a linear or nonlinear regression. Since the samples we actually observe are finite, and often quite small, we can never be sure that a series will trend upward forever. Moreover, the desirable finite-sample properties of least squares regression hold whether or not the regressors trend upward. But if we wish to rely on conventional asymptotic theory, it would seem to be prudent to specify our models so that strongly trending variables do not appear on the right-hand side. This in turn means that the dependent variable cannot be strongly trending. The most common approach is to take first differences of all such variables before specifying the model.

One compelling reason for taking first differences of trending variables is the phenomenon of **spurious regression**. It should be obvious that if two variables, say y_t and x_t, both trend upward, a regression of y_t on x_t is very

[1] The fact that *standard* asymptotic theory is inapplicable to such models does not mean that no such theory applies to them. For example, we studied a simple model of regression on a linear trend in Section 4.4 and found that the least squares estimator of the coefficient on the trend term was consistent, but with a variance that was $O(n^{-3})$ instead of the more conventional $O(n^{-1})$. Moreover, since there exist CLTs that apply to such models, the usual procedures for inference are asymptotically valid. For example, if $u_t \sim \mathrm{IID}(0, \sigma^2)$ and $S_n \equiv n^{-3/2}\sum_{t=1}^{n} tu_t$, then S_n tends in distribution to $N(0, \sigma^2/3)$. Notice that the normalizing factor here is $n^{-3/2}$ rather than $n^{-1/2}$.

likely to find a "significant" relationship between them, even if the only thing they have in common is the upward trend. In fact, the R^2 for a regression of y_t on x_t and a constant will tend to unity as $n \to \infty$ whenever both series can be characterized by (19.01), even if there is no correlation at all between the stochastic parts of y_t and x_t. Readers may find it illuminating to prove this result and are advised to look at Section 4.4 for some useful results.

It is intuitively very plausible that we should observe apparently significant, but actually spurious, relationships between unrelated variables that both trend upward over time. Granger and Newbold (1974) discovered what appears at first to be a much more surprising form of spurious regression. They considered time series which are generated by **random walks without drift**, that is, series generated by a process like $y_t = y_{t-1} + u_t$. What they found, by Monte Carlo experiment, is that if x_t and y_t are independent random walks, the t statistic for $\beta = 0$ in the regression

$$y_t = \alpha + \beta x_t + u_t \tag{19.03}$$

rejects the null hypothesis far more often than it should and tends to reject it more and more frequently the larger is the sample size n. Subsequently, Phillips (1986) proved that this t statistic will reject the null hypothesis all the time, asymptotically.

Some Monte Carlo results on spurious regressions are shown in Table 19.1. Each column shows the proportion of the time, out of 10,000 replications, that the t statistic for $\beta = 0$ in some regression rejected the null hypothesis at the 5% level. For column 1, the regression is (19.03), and both x_t and y_t are generated by independent random walks with n.i.d. errors. For column 2, x_t and y_t are the same as for column 1, but a lagged dependent variable is added to the regression. For columns 3 and 4, the regression is simply (19.03) again. For column 3, both x_t and y_t are generated by independent random walks with drift, the drift parameter δ_1 being one-fifth the size of the standard error σ (this ratio is the only parameter that affects the distribution of the t statistic). For column 4, both x_t and y_t are independent trend-stationary series, with the trend coefficient γ_2 being 1/25 the size of σ.

The results in columns 3 and 4 of the table are not very surprising, since x_t and y_t are both trending upward. The only interesting thing about these results is how rapidly the number of rejections increases with the sample size. This is a consequence of the fact that, in both these cases, the amount of information in the sample is increasing at a rate faster than n. It is evidently increasing faster in the trend case than in the case of the random walk with drift.

In contrast, the results in columns 1 and 2 of the table may be surprising. After all, x_t and y_t are totally independent series, and neither contains a trend. So why do we often — very often indeed for large sample sizes — find evidence of a relationship when we regress y_t on x_t? One answer should be obvious to

Table 19.1 Spurious Rejections and Sample Size

n	Random Walk	Lag Added	Drift	Trend
25	0.530	0.146	0.645	0.066
50	0.662	0.154	0.825	0.431
75	0.723	0.162	0.905	0.987
100	0.760	0.162	0.945	1.000
250	0.847	0.169	0.997	1.000
500	0.890	0.167	1.000	1.000
750	0.916	0.170	1.000	1.000
1000	0.928	0.169	1.000	1.000
2000	0.947	0.168	1.000	1.000

everyone who has read Chapter 12. The significant t statistics are not telling us that $\beta \neq 0$ in (19.03), since that is an incorrect model. They are simply telling us that the null hypothesis, which is (19.03) with $\beta = 0$, is false. It is false because, if y_t is generated by a random walk, then y_t is certainly not equal to a constant plus a stationary error term. Thus, when we test the null hypothesis, even against an alternative that is also false, we often reject it.

This intuitive explanation is not entirely satisfactory, however. Standard asymptotic analysis does not apply here, because if y_t is generated by a random walk, $n^{-1}\sum_{t=1}^{n} y_t^2$ diverges. Therefore, the analysis of Chapter 12 is not appropriate. Moreover, the intuitive explanation does not explain why, for large enough sample sizes, there always appears to be a relationship between y_t and x_t. One might well think that since the processes generating x_t and y_t are independent, any correlation between them should vanish asymptotically, but that is apparently not happening here. To explain these results requires nonstandard asymptotic analysis of a type that we will discuss in the next chapter. Phillips (1986) is the classic reference and Durlauf and Phillips (1988) provides further results.

The fact that (19.03) is a misspecified model is clearly not the whole story, as the results in column 2 make clear. These results are for the model

$$y_t = \delta_1 + \beta x_t + \delta_2 y_{t-1} + u_t,$$

which includes the DGP as a special case when $\delta_2 = 1$ and the other two parameters equal 0. Nevertheless, the null hypothesis that $\beta = 0$ is rejected about three times as often as it should be, and there is absolutely no indication that this tendency to overreject declines as the sample size increases. The t statistic overrejects in this case because it is *not* asymptotically distributed as $N(0,1)$. Since both the regressors here are generated by random walks, the matrix $n^{-1}\boldsymbol{X}^{\top}\boldsymbol{X}$ does not tend to a finite, positive definite matrix, and standard asymptotic theory does not apply. As we will see in the next chapter, there are many cases like this one, in which t statistics follow nonstandard distributions asymptotically. These distributions are at the present time generally calculated by means of Monte Carlo experiments.

A series that follows a random walk, with or without drift, is often said to be **integrated of order one**, or ***I*(1)** for short. The idea behind this terminology is that the series must be differenced once in order to make it stationary. Thus a stationary series may be said to be ***I*(0)**. In principle, a series could be integrated of other orders as well. One might occasionally run into a series that is $I(2)$, and if one mistakenly differences a series that is $I(0)$, the result will be $I(-1)$. However, the vast majority of the time, applied econometricians deal with time series that are either $I(0)$ or $I(1)$. If a series is initially $I(1)$, it may be differenced once to make it $I(0)$. How to decide whether or not a series needs to be differenced will be discussed at length in the next chapter.

In the remainder of this chapter, we will assume that all series are $I(0)$ and do not contain any nonstochastic trends. These assumptions ensure that neither spurious regression nor nonstandard asymptotics will be a problem. They may seem to be heroic assumptions, however. Luckily, the techniques to be discussed in the next chapter do make it feasible to ensure that these assumptions are not grossly violated in practice.

19.3 DISTRIBUTED LAGS

It is often the case that a dependent variable y_t is thought to depend on several current and lagged values of an independent variable x_t. One way to model this type of dependence is to use a **distributed lag model** such as

$$y_t = \alpha + \sum_{j=0}^{q} \beta_j x_{t-j} + u_t, \quad u_t \sim \mathrm{IID}(0, \sigma^2), \tag{19.04}$$

where the constant term α and the coefficients β_j are to be estimated. Here the integer q is the length of the longest lag; in some cases, it makes sense to think of q as being infinite, but for the moment we will assume that it is finite. The regression function might well depend on other independent variables as well, of course, but we ignore that possibility to keep the notation simple.

The obvious problem with a model like (19.04) is that, because x_t will often be highly correlated with x_{t-1}, x_{t-2}, and so on, least squares estimates of the coefficients β_j will tend to be quite imprecise. Numerous ways to handle this problem have been proposed, and we will discuss some of these shortly. The first thing to recognize, however, is that it may not be a problem at all. Often, interest centers not on the individual coefficients but on their sum, γ say, which measures the long-run effect on y_t of a given change in x_t. Even when the individual β_j's are estimated very imprecisely, their sum may be estimated with sufficient precision.

Let $\boldsymbol{V}(\hat{\boldsymbol{\beta}})$ denote the covariance matrix of the vector of least squares estimates $\hat{\boldsymbol{\beta}}$ with typical element $\hat{\beta}_j$. Then, if $\hat{\gamma}$ denotes the sum of the $\hat{\beta}_j$'s, the variance of $\hat{\gamma}$ is

$$V(\hat{\gamma}) = \boldsymbol{\iota}^{\top}\boldsymbol{V}(\hat{\boldsymbol{\beta}})\boldsymbol{\iota} = \sum_{j=0}^{q} V(\hat{\beta}_j) + 2\sum_{j=0}^{q}\sum_{k=0}^{j-1} \mathrm{Cov}(\hat{\beta}_j, \hat{\beta}_k). \tag{19.05}$$

If x_{t-j} is positively correlated with x_{t-k} for all $j \neq k$, the covariance terms in (19.05) will usually be negative. When they are large and negative, as is often the case, $V(\hat{\gamma})$ may be much smaller than the sum of the $V(\hat{\beta}_j)$'s or, indeed, than any individual $V(\hat{\beta}_j)$.

If the parameter of interest is γ rather than the individual β_j's, the easiest approach is simply to estimate a reparametrized version of (19.04) by least squares. This reparametrized version is

$$y_t = \alpha + \gamma x_t + \sum_{j=1}^{q} \beta_j (x_{t-j} - x_t) + u_t. \tag{19.06}$$

It is easy to verify that the coefficient γ on x_t in (19.06) is indeed equal to the sum of the β_j's in (19.04). The advantage of this reparametrization is that the standard error of $\hat{\gamma}$ is immediately available from the regression output.

If interest does center on the individual β_j's, collinearity becomes more of a problem. Many ways of tackling this problem have been proposed. Some of them involve imposing restrictions on the parameters of (19.04), while others involve estimating models in which one or more lags of the dependent variable appear among the regressors. The latter approach is fundamentally different from the former and will be discussed in the next section. The most popular example of the former approach is to use what are called **polynomial distributed lags**, or **PDLs**. These are also sometimes called **Almon lags** after the article in which they were first proposed, Almon (1965).

In a polynomial distributed lag, the coefficients β_j of (19.04) are all required to lie on a polynomial of some degree d. This polynomial may or may not be subject to further restrictions, such as end-point restrictions. As a simple example, if the polynomial were of degree two, with no further restrictions imposed on it, we would have

$$\beta_j = \eta_0 + \eta_1 j + \eta_2 j^2 \quad \text{for } j = 0, \ldots, q. \tag{19.07}$$

Provided that $q > 2$, there will be fewer parameters η_i than β_j. Thus we see that (19.07) imposes $q - 2$ restrictions on the β_j's.

Estimation of a model subject to the restrictions imposed by a PDL is conceptually straightforward. For example, to estimate (19.04) subject to

(19.07), we would simply substitute $\eta_0 + \eta_1 j + \eta_2 j^2$ for each of the β_j's in the former. This would yield

$$\begin{aligned} y_t &= \alpha + \eta_0 \sum_{j=0}^{q} x_{t-j} + \eta_1 \sum_{j=0}^{q} j x_{t-j} + \eta_2 \sum_{j=0}^{q} j^2 x_{t-j} + u_t \\ &= \alpha + \eta_0 z_{t0} + \eta_1 z_{t1} + \eta_2 z_{t2} + u_t. \end{aligned} \tag{19.08}$$

This is just a linear regression model, with three new regressors z_{ti} that are transformations of the original $q+1$ regressors, in addition to the constant term. This is an example of a PDL$(q, 2)$ model. For a more general **PDL(q, d)** model, which must always have $d < q$, there would be $d+1$ regressors.

The restrictions that (19.07) imposes on the β_j's are simply *linear* restrictions. Solving (19.07), we find that

$$\begin{aligned} &-\beta_3 + 3\beta_2 - 3\beta_1 + \beta_0 = 0, \\ &-\beta_4 + 3\beta_3 - 3\beta_2 + \beta_1 = 0, \\ &-\beta_5 + 3\beta_4 - 3\beta_3 + \beta_2 = 0, \quad \text{and so on.} \end{aligned}$$

These restrictions can be rewritten as $\boldsymbol{R\beta} = \mathbf{0}$, where in this case the matrix $\boldsymbol{R}$ would be

$$\boldsymbol{R} = \begin{bmatrix} 1 & -3 & 3 & -1 & 0 & \cdots & 0 & 0 & 0 & 0 \\ 0 & 1 & -3 & 3 & -1 & \cdots & 0 & 0 & 0 & 0 \\ \vdots & \vdots & \vdots & \vdots & \vdots & & \vdots & \vdots & \vdots & \vdots \\ 0 & 0 & 0 & 0 & 0 & \cdots & 1 & -3 & 3 & -1 \end{bmatrix}.$$

Since the restrictions are linear, they can easily be tested. Either an ordinary F test or its heteroskedasticity-robust equivalent (see Section 11.6) can be used. The restricted model is (19.08), the unrestricted model is (19.04), and the number of restrictions is in this case $q-2$. More generally, for a PDL(q, d) model there will be $q-d$ restrictions.

One should *always* test the restrictions imposed by any sort of PDL before even tentatively accepting a model that incorporates those restrictions. These restrictions are of two sorts. First, there is the restriction that the length of the longest lag is no more than q. Second, there are whatever further restrictions are imposed by the PDL. For a given q, reducing the degree of the polynomial from d to $d-1$ results in a more restrictive model. However, for a given degree of polynomial, reducing q simply results in a different, nonnested, model, which may fit better or worse. Thus we can test a PDL(q, d) model against a PDL$(q, d+1)$ model using an ordinary F test, but we cannot test a PDL(q, d) model against a PDL$(q+1, d)$ model in the same way. The best approach is probably to settle the question of lag length first, by starting with a very large value of q and then seeing whether the fit of the model deteriorates significantly when it is reduced, without imposing any restrictions on the shape of the distributed lag. After q has been determined, one can then attempt to determine d, once again starting with a large value and then reducing it. An excellent empirical example is Sargan (1980c). Specifying the final model in this way is an example of pretesting, which we discussed in Section 3.7; see Trivedi (1978).

Most econometrics packages allow users to specify models that include PDLs and to estimate such models using OLS, IV, and sometimes other forms of estimation. These implementations are typically a good deal more sophisticated than our discussion so far may suggest. For example, they often allow the investigator to specify additional restrictions on the shape of the lag, such as restrictions that $\beta_q = 0$. More important, good packages use more sophisticated types of polynomials than the ordinary ones we have described. The problem with the latter is that the variables z_{ti} tend to be very highly correlated with each other. This can result in the $\boldsymbol{X}^\top\boldsymbol{X}$ matrix being numerically singular. By using other types of polynomials, such as orthogonal polynomials, one can greatly reduce this correlation and thus eliminate this type of numerical problem. References include Cooper (1972b), Trivedi and Pagan (1979), Sargan (1980c), and Pagano and Hartley (1981).

An interesting variant of the PDL approach was suggested by Shiller (1973). As we have seen, the restrictions imposed by a PDL can always be written as $\boldsymbol{R\beta} = \boldsymbol{0}$ for some suitably defined $r \times k$ matrix $\boldsymbol{R}$. Here $r = q - d$ and k is the number of elements of $\boldsymbol{\beta}$, which will generally be greater than $q+1$ if there are regressors besides the constant and the lags of x_t. Shiller suggested that, instead of requiring these restrictions to hold exactly, we should merely require that they hold *approximately*. Thus, instead of stipulating that each row of $\boldsymbol{R\beta}$ should equal zero, he proposed that it should equal a random variable with mean zero and some specified variance. One advantage of this approach is that d can be quite low without imposing overly strong restrictions on the data. Since the estimates do not have to conform exactly to the shape of the assumed polynomial, $d = 2$ is generally adequate.

This type of restriction is called a **stochastic restriction**, because it is not expected to hold exactly. Stochastic restrictions are very different from any other type of restriction that we have discussed. In many cases, they seem quite plausible, in contrast to exact restrictions, which often seem excessively strong. In the PDL case, for example, it is surely implausible that the β_j's should actually lie on a polynomial of any given degree but quite plausible that they should lie reasonably close to such a polynomial. It is conceptually, but not always computationally, easy to deal with stochastic restrictions, or any sort of stochastic prior information, if one adopts the viewpoint of Bayesian statistics; see Zellner (1971) and Drèze and Richard (1983). In contrast, it is computationally, but not conceptually, easy to deal with them if one stays within the classical framework. We will do the latter, discussing computation and avoiding discussion of the conceptual difficulties.

The estimation technique that Shiller suggested using is a special case of what Theil and Goldberger (1961) and Theil (1963) called **mixed estimation**. Mixed estimation is a very simple way to combine sample information with stochastic prior information. It can be thought of as an approximation to a full-fledged Bayesian estimation procedure. The easiest situation in which to justify mixed estimation is one in which, before we undertook to estimate some model, we had previously obtained estimates of one or more parameters of the model, using an entirely independent data set. For simplicity, suppose that the model to be estimated is the linear regression model

$$\boldsymbol{y} = \boldsymbol{X\beta} + \boldsymbol{u}, \quad \boldsymbol{u} \sim \mathrm{IID}(\boldsymbol{0}, \sigma_u^2 \mathbf{I}), \tag{19.09}$$

where $\boldsymbol{\beta}$ is a k–vector. Suppose further that a vector of prior estimates $\check{\boldsymbol{\beta}}$ is available, along with their *true* covariance matrix $\boldsymbol{V}(\check{\boldsymbol{\beta}})$. We can write the relationship between these estimates and the unknown parameter vector $\boldsymbol{\beta}$ as

$$\check{\boldsymbol{\beta}} = \boldsymbol{\beta} + \boldsymbol{v}, \quad E(\boldsymbol{v}\boldsymbol{v}^\top) = \boldsymbol{V}(\check{\boldsymbol{\beta}}) \equiv \boldsymbol{\eta}^{-1}(\boldsymbol{\eta}^\top)^{-1}. \tag{19.10}$$

The right-hand side of this expression for the covariance matrix uses a standard result on positive definite matrices, first encountered in Chapter 9. If we premultiply both sides of (19.10) by the $k \times k$ matrix $\boldsymbol{\eta}$, the result is

$$\boldsymbol{\eta}\check{\boldsymbol{\beta}} = \boldsymbol{\eta\beta} + \boldsymbol{e}, \quad E(\boldsymbol{e}\boldsymbol{e}^\top) = \mathbf{I}. \tag{19.11}$$

This looks like a linear regression with k observations and k independent variables. The regressand is $\boldsymbol{\eta}\check{\boldsymbol{\beta}}$, the matrix of regressors is $\boldsymbol{\eta}$, and the covariance matrix of the error terms is $\mathbf{I}$.

It should now be easy to see how we can use the information in $\check{\boldsymbol{\beta}}$ to improve our estimates of $\boldsymbol{\beta}$. We simply have to estimate a single GLS regression with $n + k$ observations, n of them corresponding to the observations in our sample and k of them corresponding to (19.11). This regression can be written as

$$\begin{bmatrix} \boldsymbol{y} \\ \sigma_u \boldsymbol{\eta}\check{\boldsymbol{\beta}} \end{bmatrix} = \begin{bmatrix} \boldsymbol{X} \\ \sigma_u \boldsymbol{\eta} \end{bmatrix} \boldsymbol{\beta} + \begin{bmatrix} \boldsymbol{u} \\ \sigma_u \boldsymbol{e} \end{bmatrix}. \tag{19.12}$$

The errors of this regression are i.i.d. with variance σ_u^2. Regression (19.12) assumes that we know σ_u, since we have to multiply the last k observations by it in order to ensure that they are given the right weight relative to the first n observations. Asymptotically, of course, we will get the same results if we use any consistent estimate of σ_u.

In this example, mixed estimation is not very controversial. It is simply a convenient way to take account of previous estimates while utilizing a new set of data. In the distributed lag case, however, the prior information about $\boldsymbol{\beta}$ does not come from previous estimation. Instead, it is a set of stochastic restrictions, which Shiller called a **smoothness prior** because it reflects the belief that the coefficients β_j of a distributed lag should vary smoothly as a function of j. These restrictions may seem reasonable to the investigator, but they are not based on data. In the general case, we can write the stochastic restrictions as

$$\boldsymbol{R\beta} = \boldsymbol{v}, \quad \boldsymbol{v} \sim N(\mathbf{0}, \sigma_v^2\mathbf{I}). \tag{19.13}$$

This formulation allows for a wide variety of stochastic linear restrictions on $\boldsymbol{\beta}$ and includes, as a special case, the imposition of smoothness priors on the coefficients of a distributed lag. The matrix $\boldsymbol{R}$ is $r \times k$ and, in the smoothness prior case, it will have $r = q - d$ rows.

In order to estimate (19.09) while imposing the stochastic restrictions (19.13), we simply rewrite the latter as $\mathbf{0} = \boldsymbol{R\beta} + \boldsymbol{v}$, as we did in (19.12). The restrictions then look like observations of a regression. Next, we stack the actual observations on top of the artificial ones. This yields

$$\begin{bmatrix} \boldsymbol{y} \\ \mathbf{0} \end{bmatrix} = \begin{bmatrix} \boldsymbol{X} \\ \boldsymbol{R} \end{bmatrix}\boldsymbol{\beta} + \begin{bmatrix} \boldsymbol{u} \\ \boldsymbol{v} \end{bmatrix}. \tag{19.14}$$

In effect, what we have done is to add r extra observations to the original data set. The variance of the "error terms" associated with these extra observations is σ_v^2, while the variance of the genuine error terms is σ_u^2.

Let us now make the definition $\lambda \equiv \sigma_u/\sigma_v$. If λ were known, GLS estimation of (19.14) would be equivalent to OLS estimation of the model

$$\begin{bmatrix} \boldsymbol{y} \\ \mathbf{0} \end{bmatrix} = \begin{bmatrix} \boldsymbol{X} \\ \lambda\boldsymbol{R} \end{bmatrix}\boldsymbol{\beta} + \begin{bmatrix} \boldsymbol{u} \\ \lambda\boldsymbol{v} \end{bmatrix}. \tag{19.15}$$

The OLS estimate of $\boldsymbol{\beta}$ from (19.15) is

$$\tilde{\boldsymbol{\beta}} = \left(\boldsymbol{X}^\top\boldsymbol{X} + \lambda^2\boldsymbol{R}^\top\boldsymbol{R}\right)^{-1}\boldsymbol{X}^\top\boldsymbol{y}.$$

This expression is simple to compute and simple to understand. As $\sigma_v \to \infty$, $\lambda \to 0$ and $\tilde{\boldsymbol{\beta}} \to \hat{\boldsymbol{\beta}}$. Thus, as the amount of information embodied in the stochastic restrictions goes to zero, the mixed estimates $\tilde{\boldsymbol{\beta}}$ tend to the OLS estimates $\hat{\boldsymbol{\beta}}$. At the other extreme, as $\sigma_v \to 0$, $\lambda \to \infty$ and $\tilde{\boldsymbol{\beta}}$ converges to a set of estimates which satisfy the restrictions $\boldsymbol{R\beta} = \mathbf{0}$. The latter result is easily seen. Since $r < k$, it is always possible to make the last r rows of (19.15) fit perfectly by choosing $\tilde{\boldsymbol{\beta}}$ to satisfy the restrictions exactly. As $\lambda \to \infty$, the SSR for (19.15) will become infinitely large if the last r rows do not fit perfectly. To avoid this, the least squares procedure will ensure that they do fit perfectly. Thus, as can be shown using tedious matrix algebra, the limit of $\tilde{\boldsymbol{\beta}}$ as $\lambda \to \infty$ is precisely the least squares estimator that results from imposing the restrictions exactly.

The major problem with this procedure is that λ will never be known. Even if one is willing to specify σ_v a priori, something that may not be easy to do, σ_u still has to be estimated. There are various ways around this problem — see Shiller (1973) and Taylor (1974) — but none of them is entirely satisfactory. Essentially, one has to estimate σ_u from the unrestricted estimation of (19.09), either assume a value for σ_v or estimate σ_v from the unrestricted estimates of $\boldsymbol{\beta}$, and then construct an estimate of λ. This turns the mixed estimation procedure into a form of feasible GLS. Asymptotically, it will yield the same estimates as if λ were known, but its finite-sample performance may not be as good.

One should always test stochastic restrictions before accepting estimates based on them. Since imposing such restrictions is equivalent to adding phony observations, the obvious way to test them is to use a standard test for the equality of two sets of regression coefficients (Section 11.2). We can think of (19.15) as a model for the entire (augmented) sample, with $\boldsymbol{\beta}$ restricted to be the same for the first n and remaining r observations. Estimating (19.15) yields the restricted sum of squared residuals RSSR needed to construct an F test. Since $r < k$, any attempt to estimate the parameters using the second subsample alone will yield estimates that fit perfectly. Thus the unrestricted sum of squared residuals USSR needed to construct an F statistic is simply the sum of squared residuals from OLS estimation of (19.09). The number of degrees of freedom for the test is r, and so the F statistic is just

$$\frac{(\text{RSSR} - \text{USSR})/r}{\text{USSR}/(n-k)}.$$

Of course, one could use some other form of test statistic, such as one based on the HRGNR (11.66), instead of an F statistic. If the test rejects the null hypothesis that $\boldsymbol{\beta}$ is the same for both the sample observations and the phony ones, one should either increase σ_v or change the form of the matrix $\boldsymbol{R}$, probably by increasing d.

Although polynomial distributed lags, whether imposed as exact restrictions or as stochastic ones, can be useful when a model like (19.04) is appropriate, such models are very often not appropriate. The problem is that (19.04) is not a *dynamic* model. Although y_t depends on lagged values of x_t, it does not depend on lagged values of itself. As a consequence, only the current value of the error term u_t affects y_t. But if the error term is thought of as reflecting the combined influence of many variables that are unavoidably omitted from the regression, this should seem strange. After all, if x_t affects y_t via a distributed lag, why should not the variables that are relegated to the error term do likewise? This argument suggests that the error terms in a model like (19.04) may often be serially correlated. Of course, one can then proceed to model the u_t's as following some sort of ARMA process. But a better approach will often be to respecify the original model. We consider how to do so in the next section.

19.4 Dynamic Regression Models

Any regression model in which the regression function depends on lagged values of one or more dependent variables is called a **dynamic model**. The only dynamic models that we have discussed so far are models with serially correlated errors (Chapter 10); after transformation, models with AR or MA errors involve lags of the dependent variable. These models may seem somewhat artificial, but dynamic models can arise for many other reasons.

One simple and commonly encountered dynamic model is the **partial adjustment model**, which has a long history in economics dating back at least as far as Nerlove (1958). Suppose that the *desired* level of some economic variable y_t is y_t^*, which is assumed to be related to a vector of exogenous variables $\boldsymbol{X}_t$ as follows:

$$y_t^* = \boldsymbol{X}_t\boldsymbol{\beta}^* + e_t. \tag{19.16}$$

Because of some sort of adjustment costs, agents cannot set y_t equal to y_t^* in every period. Instead, y_t is assumed to adjust toward y_t^* according to the equation

$$y_t - y_{t-1} = (1-\delta)(y_t^* - y_{t-1}) + v_t. \tag{19.17}$$

Solving (19.16) and (19.17) for y_t, we find that

$$\begin{aligned} y_t &= y_{t-1} - (1-\delta)y_{t-1} + (1-\delta)\boldsymbol{X}_t\boldsymbol{\beta}^* + (1-\delta)e_t + v_t \\ &= \boldsymbol{X}_t\boldsymbol{\beta} + \delta y_{t-1} + u_t, \end{aligned} \tag{19.18}$$

where $\boldsymbol{\beta} \equiv (1-\delta)\boldsymbol{\beta}^*$ and $u_t \equiv (1-\delta)e_t + v_t$. If we wish to estimate $\boldsymbol{\beta}^*$, we can easily solve for it from the OLS estimates of $\boldsymbol{\beta}$ and δ.

The partial adjustment model makes sense only if $0 < \delta < 1$ and if, in addition, δ is not too close to 1, since otherwise the implied speed of adjustment becomes implausibly slow. Equation (19.18) can be solved for y_t as a function of current and lagged values of $\boldsymbol{X}_t$ and u_t. The result is

$$y_t = \sum_{j=0}^{\infty} \delta^j (\boldsymbol{X}_{t-j}\boldsymbol{\beta} + u_{t-j}). \tag{19.19}$$

Thus this model corrects a major deficiency that we previously identified in distributed lag models: y_t now depends on lagged values of the error terms u_t as well as on lagged values of the exogenous variables $\boldsymbol{X}_t$. Notice that the solution in (19.19) depends on the assumption that $|\delta| < 1$, which is a stationarity condition for this model.

The partial adjustment model is only one of many economic models that can be used to justify the inclusion of one or more lags of the dependent variables in regression functions. Numerous others are discussed in Dhrymes (1971) and Hendry, Pagan, and Sargan (1984). We will not attempt to discuss any of these. Instead, we will focus on some of the general issues that arise when one attempts to specify and estimate dynamic regression models.

One problem that arises whenever the $\boldsymbol{X}$ matrix includes lagged dependent variables is that OLS will not yield unbiased estimates. This problem arises because $\boldsymbol{X}$ is a stochastic matrix, some elements of which are correlated with some elements of $\boldsymbol{u}$. Thus

$$E\big((\boldsymbol{X}^{\top}\boldsymbol{X})^{-1}\boldsymbol{X}^{\top}\boldsymbol{u}\big) \neq \big(\boldsymbol{X}^{\top}\boldsymbol{X}\big)^{-1}\boldsymbol{X}^{\top}E(\boldsymbol{u}).$$

The easiest way to see this is to consider a very simple example. Suppose that

$$y_t = \beta y_{t-1} + u_t, \quad |\beta| < 1, \quad u_t \sim \text{IID}(0, \sigma^2). \tag{19.20}$$

The OLS estimate of β is

$$\hat{\beta} = \frac{\sum_{t=2}^{n} y_t y_{t-1}}{\sum_{t=2}^{n} y_{t-1}^2}. \tag{19.21}$$

If we substitute (19.20) into (19.21), we find that

$$\hat{\beta} = \frac{\beta \sum_{t=2}^{n} y_{t-1}^2 + \sum_{t=2}^{n} u_t y_{t-1}}{\sum_{t=2}^{n} y_{t-1}^2} = \beta + \frac{\sum_{t=2}^{n} u_t y_{t-1}}{\sum_{t=2}^{n} y_{t-1}^2}. \tag{19.22}$$

The second term on the right-hand side of (19.22) does *not* have expectation zero, because the numerator and denominator are not independent. Finding its expectation is not at all easy. Thus we conclude that in this model, and in all models in which there are lagged dependent variables, the OLS estimator is biased.

Of course, the OLS estimator $\hat{\beta}$ is consistent, as previous results have shown (Section 5.3). If we divide both the numerator and the denominator of the random term on the right-hand side of (19.22) by n and take probability limits, we find that

$$\operatorname*{plim}_{n\to\infty} \hat{\beta} = \beta + \frac{\operatorname{plim}_{n\to\infty}\big(n^{-1}\sum_{t=2}^{n} u_t y_{t-1}\big)}{\operatorname{plim}_{n\to\infty}\big(n^{-1}\sum_{t=2}^{n} y_{t-1}^2\big)} = \beta.$$

The plim in the numerator here is zero. This follows from the facts that $E(u_t y_{t-1}) = 0$, which implies that $n^{-1}\sum_{t=2}^{n} u_t y_{t-1}$ is just the mean of n quantities that have expectation zero, and that these quantities have finite variance, which they do because $|\beta| < 1$ implies that the process generating the y_t's is stationary. The plim in the denominator is finite, which again requires stationarity, and so the ratio of the two plims is zero.

Even in a very simple model like (19.20), the finite-sample properties of the OLS estimator $\hat{\beta}$ are quite difficult to work out analytically and will depend on the (unknown) value of β; we will present some Monte Carlo results in Chapter 21. In more complicated models, investigators have little choice but to rely on asymptotic theory. This is usually not a bad thing to do, although there is obviously a risk that incorrect inferences will be drawn, especially when the sample size is small or the model is close to being nonstationary.

We now consider a broad class of dynamic linear regression models that can be very useful in practice. These models have a single dependent variable y_t and, for simplicity of notation, a single independent variable x_t. An **autoregressive distributed lag**, or **ADL**, model can be written as

$$y_t = \alpha + \sum_{i=1}^{p} \beta_i y_{t-i} + \sum_{j=0}^{q} \gamma_j x_{t-j} + u_t, \quad u_t \sim \mathrm{IID}(0, \sigma^2) \tag{19.23}$$

or, using lag-operator notation, as

$$A(L, \boldsymbol{\beta}) y_t = \alpha + B(L, \boldsymbol{\gamma}) x_t + u_t, \quad u_t \sim \mathrm{IID}(0, \sigma^2).$$

Here $A(L, \boldsymbol{\beta})$ and $B(L, \boldsymbol{\gamma})$ denote polynomials in the lag operator with coefficients $\boldsymbol{\beta}$ and $\boldsymbol{\gamma}$, respectively. Because there are p lags on y_t and q lags on x_t, this is sometimes called an **ADL(p, q)** model. If there are additional independent variables, as will frequently be the case, they would appear as additional regressors in (19.23).

A simple, but widely encountered, special case of (19.23) is the **ADL(1, 1)** model

$$y_t = \alpha + \beta_1 y_{t-1} + \gamma_0 x_t + \gamma_1 x_{t-1} + u_t. \tag{19.24}$$

Because most results that are true for the ADL(1,1) model are also true, with obvious modifications, for the more general ADL(p, q) model, we will for the most part confine our discussion to this special case.

Many commonly encountered models for time series are special cases of the ADL(1, 1) model. A static regression model is a special case with $\beta_1 = \gamma_1 = 0$, a univariate AR(1) model is a special case with $\gamma_0 = \gamma_1 = 0$, a partial adjustment model is a special case with $\gamma_1 = 0$, a static model with AR(1) errors is a special case with $\gamma_1 = -\beta_1\gamma_0$, a model in first differences is a special case with $\beta_1 = 1$ and $\gamma_1 = -\gamma_0$, and so on. The ADL(1, 1) model provides a natural alternative against which to test any of these special cases. A test of the common factor restrictions implied by error terms that follow an AR(1) process is an example of this; see Section 10.9.

Now let us see how x_t affects y_t in the long run in the ADL(1, 1) model. Without the error terms, x_t and y_t would converge to steady-state long-run equilibrium values x^* and y^* given by

$$y^* = \alpha + \beta_1 y^* + \gamma_0 x^* + \gamma_1 x^*.$$

Solving this for y^* as a function of x^* yields

$$y^* = \frac{\alpha}{1 - \beta_1} + \frac{\gamma_0 + \gamma_1}{1 - \beta_1} x^* = \frac{\alpha}{1 - \beta_1} + \lambda x^*.$$

Thus we see that the long-run derivative of y^* with respect to x^* (this will be an elasticity if both series are in logarithms) is

$$\lambda \equiv \frac{\gamma_0 + \gamma_1}{1 - \beta_1}. \tag{19.25}$$

Evidently, this result makes sense only if $|\beta_1| < 1$, which, as one would expect, is a stability condition for this model.

One interesting and important feature of ADL models is that they can be rewritten in many different ways without affecting their ability to explain the data or changing the least squares estimates of the coefficients of interest. For example, (19.24) can be rewritten in all of the following ways:

$$\Delta y_t = \alpha + (\beta_1 - 1)y_{t-1} + \gamma_0 x_t + \gamma_1 x_{t-1} + u_t; \tag{19.26}$$

$$\Delta y_t = \alpha + (\beta_1 - 1)y_{t-1} + \gamma_0 \Delta x_t + (\gamma_0 + \gamma_1)x_{t-1} + u_t; \tag{19.27}$$

$$\Delta y_t = \alpha + (\beta_1 - 1)y_{t-1} - \gamma_1 \Delta x_t + (\gamma_0 + \gamma_1)x_t + u_t; \tag{19.28}$$

$$\begin{aligned} \Delta y_t &= \alpha + (\beta_1 - 1)(y_{t-1} - x_{t-1}) + \gamma_0 \Delta x_t \\ &\quad + (\gamma_0 + \gamma_1 + \beta_1 - 1)x_{t-1} + u_t; \end{aligned} \tag{19.29}$$

$$\Delta y_t = \alpha + (\beta_1 - 1)(y_{t-1} - \lambda x_{t-1}) + \gamma_0 \Delta x_t + u_t. \tag{19.30}$$

Here Δ is the **first-difference operator**: $\Delta y_t \equiv y_t - y_{t-1}$. In (19.30), λ is the parameter defined in (19.25). The fact that (19.24) can be rewritten in many different ways without changing the least squares parameter estimates is often very convenient. For example, if one is interested in the sum of the γ_i's, estimates and standard errors can be obtained directly from OLS estimation of (19.27) or (19.28), and if one is interested in λ, they can be obtained by NLS estimation of (19.30).

The most interesting of the equivalent specifications (19.24) and (19.26)–(19.30) is possibly (19.30), in which the model is written in what is called its **error-correction form**. The parameter λ appears directly in this form of the model. Although the error-correction form is nonlinear, estimation is very easy because the model is just a linear model reparametrized in a nonlinear way. The difference between y_{t-1} and λx_{t-1} measures the extent to which the long-run equilibrium relationship between x_t and y_t is not satisfied. Consequently, the parameter $\beta_1 - 1$ can be interpreted as the proportion of the resulting disequilibrium that is reflected in the movement of y_t in one period. In this respect, $\beta_1 - 1$ is essentially the same as the parameter $\delta - 1$ of the partial adjustment model. The term $(\beta_1 - 1)(y_{t-1} - \lambda x_{t-1})$ that appears in (19.30) is often called an **error-correction term**, and a model such as (19.30) is sometimes called an **error-correction model**, or **ECM**. Such models were first used by Hendry and Anderson (1977) and Davidson, Hendry, Srba, and Yeo (1978). We will discuss them at greater length in the next chapter. Notice that the error-correction term is implicitly present in the various other forms of (19.24), since its coefficient can be recovered from all of them. Some authors impose the restriction that $\lambda = 1$, which may be reasonable if x_t and y_t are similar in magnitude. This is equivalent to the restriction that $\beta_1 + \gamma_0 + \gamma_1 = 1$ and may therefore be tested very easily by using the ordinary t statistic on x_{t-1} in (19.29).

The key fact to remember when attempting to specify dynamic regression models is that there are generally a great many a priori plausible ways to do so. It is a serious mistake to limit attention to one particular type of model, such as distributed lag models or partial adjustment models. Because it includes so many other models as special cases, the ADL(p, q) family of models will often provide a good place to start. In many cases, setting $p = q = 1$ will be sufficiently general, but with quarterly data it may be wise to start with $p = q = 4$. In order to obtain a reasonably parsimonious and readily interpretable model, it will generally be necessary to impose a number of restrictions on the initial ADL(p, q) specification. Because ADL models can be written in so many different ways — recall (19.24) and (19.26) through (19.30) — there are often many different restrictions that could be imposed.

Our discussion of dynamic regression models has been quite brief. For more detailed treatments, see Hendry, Pagan, and Sargan (1984) or Banerjee, Dolado, Galbraith, and Hendry (1993).

19.5 Vector Autoregressions

In Chapter 10, we introduced AR, MA, and ARMA models for univariate time series. As one might expect, there exist multivariate versions of all these models. We will not attempt to discuss vector moving average or vector ARMA models, which can be quite complicated to deal with; see Fuller (1976) or Harvey (1981, 1989). However, in this section, we will briefly discuss **vector autoregressive models**, also known as **vector autoregressions** or **VARs**. These constitute the easiest type of multivariate time series model to estimate, and they have been widely used in economics in recent years.

Suppose that the $1 \times m$ row vector $\boldsymbol{Y}_t$ denotes the tth observation on a set of variables. Then a vector autoregressive model of order p, or **VAR(p)** for short, can be written as

$$\boldsymbol{Y}_t = \boldsymbol{\alpha} + \boldsymbol{Y}_{t-1}\boldsymbol{\Phi}_1 + \cdots + \boldsymbol{Y}_{t-p}\boldsymbol{\Phi}_p + \boldsymbol{U}_t, \quad \boldsymbol{U}_t \sim \mathrm{IID}(\boldsymbol{0}, \boldsymbol{\Omega}), \tag{19.31}$$

where $\boldsymbol{\alpha}$ is a $1 \times m$ row vector, and $\boldsymbol{\Phi}_1$ through $\boldsymbol{\Phi}_p$ are $m \times m$ matrices of coefficients to be estimated. If y_{ti} denotes the ith element of $\boldsymbol{Y}_t$ and $\phi_{j,ki}$ denotes the ki^{th} element of $\boldsymbol{\Phi}_j$, the ith column of (19.31) can be written as

$$y_{ti} = \alpha_i + \sum_{j=1}^{p} \sum_{k=1}^{m} y_{t-j,k}\phi_{j,ki} + u_{ti}. \tag{19.32}$$

This is just a linear regression, in which y_{ti} depends on a constant term and lags 1 through p of all of the m variables in the system. Thus (19.31) has the form of an SUR system (Section 9.8).

Because exactly the same variables appear on the right-hand side of (19.32) for all i, the OLS estimates for each equation are identical to the GLS estimates for (19.31) as a whole. This is a consequence of Kruskal's Theorem, as we proved in Section 9.8. Thus it is very easy to estimate a VAR: One simply applies OLS to each of the equations individually. Estimation can be done very quickly if the software makes use of the fact that every equation involves exactly the same set of regressors.

The use of VAR models has been advocated, most notably by Sims (1980), as a way to estimate dynamic relationships among jointly endogenous variables without imposing strong a priori restrictions. Empirical papers based on this approach include Litterman and Weiss (1985) and Reagan and Sheehan (1985). A major advantage of the approach is that the investigator does not have to decide which variables are endogenous and which are exogenous. Moreover, all the problems associated with simultaneous equations models are avoided because VARs do not include any current variables among the regressors. On the other hand, VARs tend to require the estimation of a great many parameters, $m + pm^2$ to be specific, and, as a result, individual parameters often tend to be estimated quite imprecisely. We will return to this point below.

Although the VAR model does not include current variables among the regressors, contemporaneous correlations are implicitly accounted for by the matrix $\boldsymbol{\Omega}$. This matrix is of interest for several reasons, not least because, if the error terms are assumed to be normally distributed, the loglikelihood function for the VAR(p) model (19.31), concentrated with respect to $\boldsymbol{\Omega}$, is simply

$$\ell(\boldsymbol{Y}, \boldsymbol{\alpha}, \boldsymbol{\Phi}_1 \cdots \boldsymbol{\Phi}_p) = C - \frac{n}{2} \log \left| \boldsymbol{\Omega}(\boldsymbol{\alpha}, \boldsymbol{\Phi}_1 \cdots \boldsymbol{\Phi}_p) \right|.$$

Here $\boldsymbol{\Omega}(\boldsymbol{\alpha}, \boldsymbol{\Phi}_1 \cdots \boldsymbol{\Phi}_p)$ means the value of $\boldsymbol{\Omega}$ that maximizes the loglikelihood conditional on $\boldsymbol{\alpha}$ and $\boldsymbol{\Phi}_1$ through $\boldsymbol{\Phi}_p$, and $\boldsymbol{Y}$ means the matrix with typical row $\boldsymbol{Y}_t$. This result is an application of results on concentrated loglikelihood functions for multivariate models that we derived in Section 9.9.

It is easy to see that $\boldsymbol{\Omega}(\boldsymbol{\alpha}, \boldsymbol{\Phi}_1 \cdots \boldsymbol{\Phi}_p)$ is equal to

$$\frac{1}{n} \sum_{t=1}^{n} \left(\boldsymbol{Y}_t - \boldsymbol{\alpha} - \boldsymbol{Y}_{t-1}\boldsymbol{\Phi}_1 \cdots - \boldsymbol{Y}_{t-p}\boldsymbol{\Phi}_p\right)^{\top} \left(\boldsymbol{Y}_t - \boldsymbol{\alpha} - \boldsymbol{Y}_{t-1}\boldsymbol{\Phi}_1 \cdots - \boldsymbol{Y}_{t-p}\boldsymbol{\Phi}_p\right),$$

where we are implicitly assuming that p presample observations are available, which implies that all n sample observations may be used for estimation. If $\hat{\boldsymbol{U}}_t$ denotes the $1 \times m$ row vector of OLS residuals for observation t, then

$$\boldsymbol{\Omega}(\hat{\boldsymbol{\alpha}}, \hat{\boldsymbol{\Phi}}_1 \cdots \hat{\boldsymbol{\Phi}}_p) \equiv \hat{\boldsymbol{\Omega}} = \frac{1}{n} \sum_{t=1}^{n} \hat{\boldsymbol{U}}_t^{\top} \hat{\boldsymbol{U}}_t.$$

Hence the maximized value of the loglikelihood function is

$$\ell(\boldsymbol{Y}, \hat{\boldsymbol{\alpha}}, \hat{\boldsymbol{\Phi}}_1 \cdots \hat{\boldsymbol{\Phi}}_p) = C - \frac{n}{2}\log|\hat{\boldsymbol{\Omega}}|.$$

When specifying a VAR, it is important to determine how many lags need to be included. If one wishes to test the null hypothesis that the longest lag in the system is p against the alternative that it is $p+1$, the easiest way to do so is probably to compute the LR statistic

$$n\big(\log|\hat{\boldsymbol{\Omega}}(p)| - \log|\hat{\boldsymbol{\Omega}}(p+1)|\big),$$

where the notation should be self-explanatory. This test statistic will be asymptotically distributed as $\chi^2(m^2)$. However, unless the sample size n is large relative to the number of parameters in the system ($m + pm^2$ under the null, $m + (p+1)m^2$ under the alternative), the finite-sample distribution of this test statistic may differ substantially from its asymptotic one.

One use of VAR models is to test the null hypothesis that some variable does not Granger cause another variable. We discussed the concept of Granger causality in Section 18.2. In the context of a VAR, y_{t1} may be said to Granger cause y_{t2} if any lagged values of y_{t1} are significant in the equation for y_{t2}. On the other hand, the null hypothesis that y_{t1} does not Granger cause y_{t2} cannot be rejected if all lagged values of the former are jointly insignificant in the equation for the latter. Thus one can easily test the null hypothesis that any variable in a VAR(p) does not Granger cause any one of the others by performing an asymptotic F test with p and $n-(1+pm)$ degrees of freedom.[2] Of course, any results depend on the maintained hypothesis that all relevant variables have been included in the VAR. If a variable y_{t3} is omitted from a VAR, we may incorrectly conclude that y_{t1} Granger causes y_{t2}, when in fact y_{t1} has no effect on y_{t2} independent of its effect through the omitted variable.

As we remarked earlier, one serious practical problem with VARs is that they generally require the estimation of a number of parameters that is large relative to the sample size. Litterman (1979, 1986) suggested that if the objective is to use a VAR for forecasting, this problem may be solved by imposing stochastic restrictions, very much like the ones we discussed in Section 19.2 for imposing smoothness priors on distributed lags. For example, one might impose the prior that all coefficients have mean zero and some variance that is not too small, except for the coefficient of $y_{t-1,i}$ in the equation for y_{ti}. Litterman proposed a mixed estimation procedure similar to the one we discussed in Section 19.2, and has reported that these "Bayesian" VARs provide better forecasts than conventional unrestricted VARs.

[2] The properties of various causality tests, including this one, were studied by Geweke, Meese, and Dent (1983).

19.6 SEASONAL ADJUSTMENT

Many economic time series tend to follow a regular pattern over the course of every year. This type of behavior is referred to as **seasonal variation** or **seasonality**. It may be the result of regular seasonal weather patterns or of social customs such as statutory holidays, summer vacations, and the like. The presence of seasonality has important implications for applied econometric work that uses time-series data. At best, when we are able to model seasonality explicitly, it makes such work a good deal harder. At worst, when we simply use data that have been "seasonally adjusted" in some mechanical way, it may dramatically reduce our ability to make correct inferences about economic relationships.

To fix ideas, consider Figure 19.1, which shows the logarithm of housing starts in Canada, quarterly, for the period 1968:1 to 1987:4.[3] It is clear that seasonal variation in this series is very pronounced. Housing starts tend to be much lower in the first quarter than in any other, presumably because winter weather makes construction difficult at that time of year. However, the pattern of seasonality seems to vary considerably from one year to the next, in a fashion that does not seem to be independent of the overall level of housing starts. In the recession year of 1982, for example, there is far less seasonal variation than usual, and the lowest level of housing starts is recorded in the third quarter instead of the first.

There are two quite different views on the nature of seasonality in economic data. One view is that seasonal variation is a fundamental part of many economic time series and, when it is present, we should attempt to explain it. Thus, ideally, an econometric model for a dependent variable y_t should explain any seasonal variation in it by seasonal variation in the independent variables, perhaps by including weather variables or seasonal dummy variables among the latter. Unfortunately, as we will see in the next section, this can make the business of specifying and estimating econometric models for monthly and quarterly series rather complicated.

A second view, associated with Sims (1974), is that seasonality is simply a type of noise that contaminates economic data. Economic theory cannot be expected to explain this noise, which in the case of independent variables amounts to a sort of errors in variables problem. One should therefore use what are called **seasonally adjusted** data, that is, data which have been massaged in some way so that they supposedly represent what the series would have been in the absence of seasonality. Indeed, many statistical agencies, especially in the United States, release only seasonally adjusted figures for many series. In this section, we will discuss the nature of seasonal adjustment procedures and the consequences of using seasonally adjusted data.

[3] These figures were taken from the CANSIM database of Statistics Canada. They are the logarithm of series number D2717.

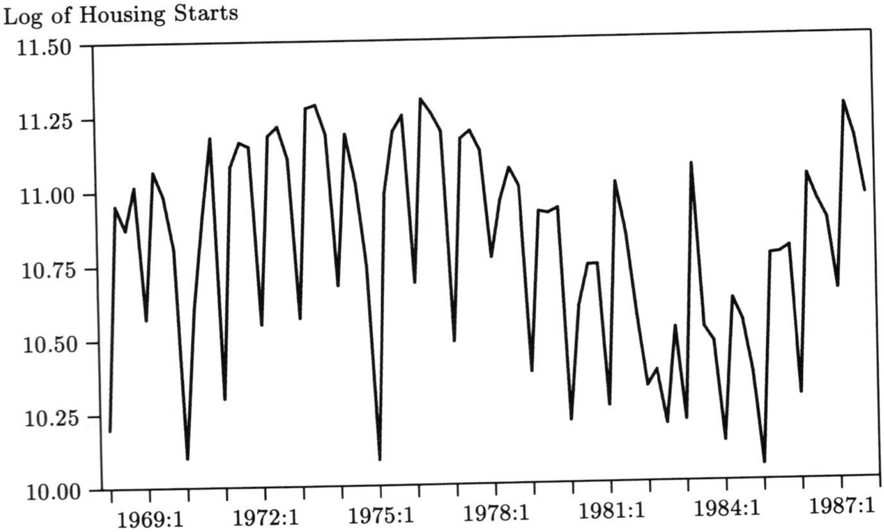

Figure 19.1 Housing starts in Canada, 1968–1987

The idea of seasonally adjusting a time series to remove the effects of seasonality is intuitively appealing but very hard to make rigorous without resorting to highly unrealistic assumptions. Seasonal adjustment of a series y_t makes sense if for all t we can write $y_t = y_t^* + y_t^s$, where y_t^* is a time series that contains no seasonal variation at all, and y_t^s is a time series that contains nothing but seasonal variation. But this is an extreme assumption. Even if it holds, it is not necessarily easy to divide y_t between y_t^* and y_t^s, which is what seasonal adjustment procedures attempt to accomplish.

One approach to seasonal adjustment, which is quite popular among econometricians but is almost never used by statistical agencies, is to make use of least squares regression. Suppose, for concreteness, that the data are quarterly, and consider the seasonal dummy variables

$$\boldsymbol{D}_1 = \begin{bmatrix} 1 \\ 0 \\ 0 \\ -1 \\ \vdots \end{bmatrix} \qquad \boldsymbol{D}_2 = \begin{bmatrix} 0 \\ 1 \\ 0 \\ -1 \\ \vdots \end{bmatrix} \qquad \boldsymbol{D}_3 = \begin{bmatrix} 0 \\ 0 \\ 1 \\ -1 \\ \vdots \end{bmatrix},$$

which we first encountered in Section 1.4. These dummy variables have been defined in such a way that they sum to zero over each full year. Now suppose that we regress the n-vector $\boldsymbol{y}$ on a constant and $\boldsymbol{D} \equiv [\boldsymbol{D}_1 \quad \boldsymbol{D}_2 \quad \boldsymbol{D}_3]$:

$$\boldsymbol{y} = \beta + \boldsymbol{D}\boldsymbol{\gamma} + \boldsymbol{u}. \tag{19.33}$$

Then a "seasonally adjusted" series $\boldsymbol{y}^*$ may be constructed as

$$\boldsymbol{y}^* \equiv \hat{\beta} + \hat{\boldsymbol{u}}, \tag{19.34}$$

where $\hat{\beta}$ is the estimate of β, and $\hat{\boldsymbol{u}}$ is the vector of residuals from OLS estimation of (19.33). Thus all the variation in $\boldsymbol{y}$ that can be explained by the seasonal dummy variables has been removed to create $\boldsymbol{y}^*$.

This approach was advocated by Lovell (1963). He showed, by an application of the FWL Theorem, that the OLS estimates obtained from the following two regressions are identical:

$$\boldsymbol{y}^* = \boldsymbol{X}^*\boldsymbol{\beta} + \boldsymbol{u} \quad \text{and} \tag{19.35}$$

$$\boldsymbol{y} = \boldsymbol{X\beta} + \boldsymbol{D}\gamma + \boldsymbol{u}. \tag{19.36}$$

The first regression here uses data "seasonally adjusted" by the procedure of (19.33) and (19.34). The second simply regresses raw data $\boldsymbol{y}$ on raw data $\boldsymbol{X}$, where $\boldsymbol{X}$ must include a constant term or the equivalent, and on the seasonal dummy variables $\boldsymbol{D}$. This result seems to suggest that it does not matter whether we use seasonally adjusted data or raw data and seasonal dummies. Such a conclusion is true only for data that have been seasonally adjusted by regression, however.

There are several serious problems with seasonal adjustment by regression. First of all, it is clear from standard results on least squares residuals that in finite samples a regression like (19.33) will remove too much variation from the original series, attributing some of it incorrectly to variation in the seasonal dummy variables (Thomas and Wallis, 1971). Secondly, if there is an upward trend in the series being adjusted, a regression like (19.33) will incorrectly attribute some of the trend to the seasonal dummies. As a result, the estimate of the first-quarter seasonal effect will be too low, and the estimate of the fourth-quarter seasonal effect will be too high. One obvious solution is to add a trend term to the regression and treat it the same way as the constant term (Jorgenson, 1964). This implies, however, that $\boldsymbol{X}$ must include a trend term as well as a constant if the result that (19.35) and (19.36) are to yield the same estimates is to hold.

The most serious problem with the regression approach is that it does not allow the pattern of seasonality to change over time. As Figure 19.1 illustrates, seasonal patterns often do seem to change over time. One way to model this is to add additional seasonal dummy variables that have been interacted with powers of an annually increasing linear time trend such as

$$\boldsymbol{T} \equiv [1\;\;1\;\;1\;\;1\;\;2\;\;2\;\;2\;\;2 \cdots].$$

The reason that the trend term must take this rather odd form is to ensure that, when it is multiplied by the seasonal dummies, the resulting trending dummies always sum to zero over each year. If one simply multiplied seasonal dummies by an ordinary trend term, that would not be the case.

The FWL Theorem applies to regressions (19.35) and (19.36) however the seasonal dummy variables are defined. Thus we might have

$$\boldsymbol{D} \equiv [\boldsymbol{D}_1 \;\; \boldsymbol{D}_2 \;\; \boldsymbol{D}_3 \;\; \boldsymbol{D}_1{*}\boldsymbol{T} \;\; \boldsymbol{D}_2{*}\boldsymbol{T} \;\; \boldsymbol{D}_3{*}\boldsymbol{T} \;\; \boldsymbol{D}_1{*}\boldsymbol{T}{*}\boldsymbol{T} \;\; \boldsymbol{D}_2{*}\boldsymbol{T}{*}\boldsymbol{T} \;\; \boldsymbol{D}_3{*}\boldsymbol{T}{*}\boldsymbol{T}].$$

Here there are three sets of seasonal dummies: the ordinary ones that are constant over time, dummies that are interacted with a linear trend, and dummies that are interacted with a quadratic trend. Trending seasonal dummies sometimes seem to work well in finite samples, in the sense that they may provide a good approximation to some actual pattern of changing seasonality. But they clearly make no sense asymptotically, because the seasonal variation must eventually become infinitely large if the coefficients on the trending dummies are nonzero in regression (19.33).

For the housing starts data of Figure 19.1, interestingly enough, trending seasonal dummies are no use at all. Regressing these data on a constant and three seasonal dummies yields four significant coefficients and an R^2 of 0.48. Adding either three linearly trending seasonal dummies or three linearly and three quadratically trending dummies to the regression does not improve the fit significantly. Thus it would appear either that the seasonal variation of this series really has not been changing over time, despite visual evidence to the contrary, or that it has been doing so in a way that cannot be well approximated by regression on trending seasonal dummy variables.

Another way to deal with seasonal patterns that change over time is to use frequency domain methods; see Engle (1974), Sims (1974), and Hylleberg (1977, 1986). The first step is to transform the data on y_t from the time domain to the frequency domain, usually by means of a fast Fourier transform.[4] After the transformation, each observation corresponds to a certain frequency rather than to a certain time period. Some of these observations are then deleted, in bands around the seasonal frequencies and their harmonics. The wider the bands, the greater are the number of observations (i.e., frequencies) deleted, and the greater is the chance that all seasonal variation will be removed from the data. Finally, the data are transformed back to the time domain, yielding a seasonally adjusted series.

Sims (1974) showed that this technique is equivalent to a form of seasonal adjustment by regression. Consider regression (19.33) and the seasonally adjusted series defined in (19.34). The latter would be equivalent to the frequency domain adjusted series just described if the matrix $\boldsymbol{D}$ were redefined to equal a certain set of variables that are trigonometric functions of time. The first three or eleven of these variables (in the cases of quarterly and monthly data, respectively) span exactly the same subspace as three or

[4] For an introduction to frequency domain methods, see Harvey (1981). For a description of the fast Fourier transform, see Press, Flannery, Teukolsky, and Vetterling (1986, Chapter 12).

eleven seasonal dummy variables. Thus, if the seasonal pattern were constant over time, it would be necessary to exclude only as many specific frequencies as there are time periods in the year. Excluding additional frequencies in bands around the seasonal frequencies and their harmonics is done to allow for seasonal patterns that change over time. This is equivalent to including additional trigonometric functions of time in the regression. The number of trigonometric variables included, which is the same as the number of frequencies excluded in the frequency domain approach, will increase linearly with the sample size if the width of the bands remains unchanged.

Official statistical agencies almost never employ any sort of regression-based seasonal adjustment procedure. Besides the problems with such procedures that we have already discussed, they suffer from an important practical difficulty. As time goes by and the sample size increases, the estimates of γ in (19.33) will change, and so every element of $\boldsymbol{y}^*$ will change every time a new observation becomes available. This is clearly a most undesirable feature from the point of view of users of official statistics.

The seasonal adjustment procedures actually used by statistical agencies are generally very complicated. They attempt to deal with a host of practical problems, including trends, time-varying seasonality, changes in the number of shopping days and the dates of holidays, the fact that less information is available near the beginning and end of the sample (because presample and postsample observations are not available), and identities that may link certain series to each other. These procedures are primarily designed to produce data that are easily interpreted by economists seeking to determine how well the economy is performing, rather than to produce data that will necessarily be most useful to econometricians. The best-known of these official procedures is the X-11 method pioneered by the United States Census Bureau (Shisken, Young, and Musgrave, 1967). For a discussion of it and related procedures, see Hylleberg (1986); Figure 5.1 of that book depicts a flowchart that reveals the extreme complexity of the X-11 procedure.

Despite the complexity of the X-11 method and its relatives, they can often be approximated remarkably well by much simpler procedures based on what are called **linear filters**. Let $\boldsymbol{y}$ be an n–vector of observations (often in logarithms rather than levels) on a series that has not been seasonally adjusted. Then a linear filter consists of an $n \times n$ matrix $\boldsymbol{\Phi}$, with rows that sum to 1, which premultiplies $\boldsymbol{y}$ to yield a seasonally adjusted series $\boldsymbol{y}^*$. Each row of the filter consists of a vector of **filter weights**. Thus each element y_t^* of the seasonally adjusted series is equal to a weighted sum of current, leading, and lagged values of y_t.

Let us consider a simple example for quarterly data. Suppose we first create three-term and eleven-term moving averages

$$z_t \equiv \tfrac{1}{3}\big(y_{t-4} + y_t + y_{t+4}\big) \quad \text{and} \quad w_t \equiv \frac{1}{11}\sum_{j=5}^{-5} y_{t-j}.$$

The difference between z_t and w_t is a rolling estimate of the amount by which the value of y_t for the current quarter tends to differ from its average value over the year. Thus one way to define a seasonally adjusted series would be

$$\begin{aligned} y_t^* &\equiv y_t - z_t + w_t \\ &= .0909y_{t-5} - .2424y_{t-4} + .0909y_{t-3} + .0909y_{t-2} \\ &\quad + .0909y_{t-1} + .7576y_t + .0909y_{t+1} + .0909y_{t+2} \\ &\quad + .0909y_{t+3} - .2424y_{t+4} + .0909y_{t+5}. \end{aligned} \tag{19.37}$$

This example corresponds to a linear filter in which the pth row of $\boldsymbol{\Phi}$ (for $5 < p < n - 5$) would consist first of $p - 6$ zeros, followed by the eleven coefficients that appear in (19.37), followed by $n - p - 5$ more zeros.

This example was deliberately made too simple, but the basic approach that it illustrates may be found, in various modified forms, in almost all official seasonal adjustment procedures. The latter generally do not actually employ linear filters, but do employ a number of moving averages in a way similar to the example. These moving averages tend to be longer than the ones in the example; z_t generally consists of at least 5 terms and w_t consists of at least 25 terms with quarterly data. They also tend to give progressively less weight to observations farther from t. The weight given to y_t by these procedures is generally between 0.75 and 0.9, but it is always well below 1. For more on the relationship between official procedures and ones based on linear filters, see Wallis (1974), Burridge and Wallis (1984), and Ghysels and Perron (1993).

We have asserted that official seasonal adjustment procedures in most cases have much the same properties as linear filters applied to either the levels or the logarithms of the raw data. This assertion can be checked empirically. If it is true, regressing a seasonally adjusted series y_t^* on enough leads and lags of the corresponding seasonally unadjusted series y_t should yield an extremely good fit. The coefficient on y_t should be large and positive, but less than 1, and the coefficients on y_{t+j} should be negative whenever j is an integer multiple of 4 or 12, for quarterly and monthly data, respectively.

As an illustration, we regressed the logarithm of the seasonally adjusted housing start series for Canada that corresponds to the unadjusted series in Figure 19.1 on a constant and the current value and 13 leads and lags of the unadjusted series, for the period 1957:1 to 1986:4. The R^2 was .992 and the coefficient on the current period value was 0.80. We also regressed the logarithm of real personal consumption expenditure, seasonally adjusted at annual rates, on a constant, the current value and 13 leads and lags of the corresponding unadjusted series, for 1953:1 to 1984:4.[5] This time, the R^2

[5] All data were taken from the CANSIM database of Statistics Canada. The adjusted and unadjusted housing start series are numbers D2717 and D4945. The adjusted and unadjusted expenditure series are D20131 and D10131.

was a remarkable .999996, and the coefficient on the current period value was 0.82. In both cases, all the coefficients on y_{t+j} for j an integer multiple of 4 were negative, as expected. Thus it appears that a linear filter provides an extremely good approximation to the seasonal adjustment procedure actually used in the case of the expenditure data and a reasonable approximation in the case of the housing starts data.

If seasonal adjustment is performed using a linear filter, it is not difficult to analyze the effects of using seasonally adjusted data. Suppose that the *same* filter is applied to all the series used in a regression of $\boldsymbol{y}^*$ on $\boldsymbol{X}^*$. Then the least squares estimates will be given by

$$\begin{aligned}\tilde{\boldsymbol{\beta}} &= \left(\boldsymbol{X}^{*\top}\boldsymbol{X}^*\right)^{-1}\boldsymbol{X}^{*\top}\boldsymbol{y}^* \\ &= \left(\boldsymbol{X}^\top\boldsymbol{\Phi}^\top\boldsymbol{\Phi}\boldsymbol{X}\right)^{-1}\boldsymbol{X}^\top\boldsymbol{\Phi}^\top\boldsymbol{\Phi}\boldsymbol{y}.\end{aligned}$$

We see that $\tilde{\boldsymbol{\beta}}$ is simply a vector of GLS estimates, with the $n\times n$ matrix $\boldsymbol{\Phi}^\top\boldsymbol{\Phi}$ playing the role of the inverse of the covariance matrix of the error terms. Thus we conclude that OLS regression following seasonal adjustment by means of a linear filter is equivalent to GLS, *provided* that the same linear filter is used for all series. Unfortunately, official seasonal adjustment procedures do not use the same filter for all series (or even for the same series at different points in time). As a result, this result is rarely applicable (Wallis, 1974).

Nevertheless, it is worth discussing the properties of $\tilde{\boldsymbol{\beta}}$. These will evidently depend on how y_t is generated. One possibility is that

$$\boldsymbol{y} = \boldsymbol{X}\boldsymbol{\beta}_0 + \boldsymbol{u}, \quad \boldsymbol{u} \sim \mathrm{IID}(\boldsymbol{0}, \sigma^2\mathbf{I}), \tag{19.38}$$

which implies that any seasonality in $\boldsymbol{y}$ is in fact fully accounted for by seasonality in the independent variables. Then

$$\operatorname*{plim}_{n\to\infty}\tilde{\boldsymbol{\beta}} = \boldsymbol{\beta}_0 + \operatorname*{plim}_{n\to\infty}\left(\frac{1}{n}\boldsymbol{X}^\top\boldsymbol{\Phi}^\top\boldsymbol{\Phi}\boldsymbol{X}\right)^{-1}\operatorname*{plim}_{n\to\infty}\left(\frac{1}{n}\boldsymbol{X}^\top\boldsymbol{\Phi}^\top\boldsymbol{\Phi}\boldsymbol{u}\right) = \boldsymbol{\beta}_0. \tag{19.39}$$

Thus, although there is no reason to use seasonally adjusted data in this case, doing so does not cause least squares estimates to be inconsistent. However, the Gauss-Markov Theorem implies that these estimates will be less efficient than OLS estimates using unadjusted data would be. This must be the case, since the seasonal adjustment procedure reduces the variation in the independent variables and hence reduces the precision of the estimates of $\boldsymbol{\beta}$. Moreover, the second equality of (19.39) requires that all elements of $\boldsymbol{X}$ be independent of all elements of $\boldsymbol{u}$ and thus implicitly rules out the possibility that $\boldsymbol{X}$ may include lagged dependent variables.

A second possibility, which makes the use of seasonally adjusted data much more attractive, is that the DGP is

$$\boldsymbol{y} - \boldsymbol{y}^s = (\boldsymbol{X} - \boldsymbol{X}^s)\boldsymbol{\beta}_0 + \boldsymbol{u}, \quad \boldsymbol{u} \sim \mathrm{IID}(\boldsymbol{0}, \sigma^2\mathbf{I}). \tag{19.40}$$

Here $\boldsymbol{y}^s$ and $\boldsymbol{X}^s$ denote the seasonal parts of $\boldsymbol{y}$ and $\boldsymbol{X}$. Suppose that the filter weights have been chosen so that all seasonality is eliminated. This implies that $\boldsymbol{\Phi y}^s = \mathbf{0}$ and $\boldsymbol{\Phi X}^s = \mathbf{0}$, which in turn implies that

$$\begin{aligned}\boldsymbol{\Phi y} &= \boldsymbol{\Phi}\big((\boldsymbol{X} - \boldsymbol{X}^s)\boldsymbol{\beta}_0 + \boldsymbol{y}^s + \boldsymbol{u}\big)\\ &= \boldsymbol{\Phi}(\boldsymbol{X\beta}_0 + \boldsymbol{u}).\end{aligned}$$

If we substitute $\boldsymbol{\Phi}(\boldsymbol{X\beta}_0 + \boldsymbol{u})$ for $\boldsymbol{\Phi y}$ in the first line of (19.39), the rest of (19.39) then follows as before, and we conclude that $\tilde{\boldsymbol{\beta}}$ is consistent for $\boldsymbol{\beta}_0$.

In this second case, the alternative of simply regressing the seasonally unadjusted data $\boldsymbol{y}$ on $\boldsymbol{X}$ is not at all attractive. The OLS estimate of $\boldsymbol{\beta}$ is

$$\begin{aligned}\hat{\boldsymbol{\beta}} &= \big(\boldsymbol{X}^\top\boldsymbol{X}\big)^{-1}\boldsymbol{X}^\top\boldsymbol{y}\\ &= \boldsymbol{\beta}_0 + \big(\boldsymbol{X}^\top\boldsymbol{X}\big)^{-1}\boldsymbol{X}^\top\big(-\boldsymbol{X}^s\boldsymbol{\beta}_0 + \boldsymbol{y}^s + \boldsymbol{u}\big),\end{aligned}$$

which clearly will not be consistent for $\boldsymbol{\beta}_0$ unless $\boldsymbol{X}$ is asymptotically orthogonal to both $\boldsymbol{X}^s$ and $\boldsymbol{y}^s$. But such a condition could hold only if none of the variables in $\boldsymbol{X}$ displayed any seasonal variation. Thus, if one wishes to use seasonally unadjusted data, one must explicitly incorporate seasonality in the model. We will take up this topic in the next section.

Remember that these results hold only if the same linear filter is used for the seasonal adjustment of all the series. If different filters are used for different series, which will almost always be the case for officially adjusted data, we cannot assert that regressions which employ seasonally adjusted data will yield consistent estimates, whether the data are generated by a model like (19.38) or a model like (19.40). We can only hope that any such inconsistency will be small. See Wallis (1974).

A much more serious limitation of the above results on consistency is that they assume the absence of any lagged dependent variables among the regressors. When there are lagged dependent variables, as will be the case for every dynamic model and for every model transformed to allow for serially correlated errors, there is no reason to believe that least squares regression using data adjusted by linear filters will yield consistent estimates. In fact, recent work has provided strong evidence that, in models with a single lag of the dependent variable, estimates of the coefficient on the lagged variable generally tend to be severely biased when seasonally adjusted data are used. See Jaeger and Kunst (1990), Ghysels (1990), and Ghysels and Perron (1993).

In order to illustrate this important result, we generated artificial data from a special case of the model

$$y_t = \alpha + \beta y_{t-1} + \boldsymbol{D}_t\boldsymbol{\gamma} + u_t, \quad u_t \sim N(0, \sigma^2), \tag{19.41}$$

where $\boldsymbol{D}_t$ is the tth row of an $n \times 3$ matrix of seasonal dummy variables. The series y_t was then subjected to a linear filter that might reasonably be used

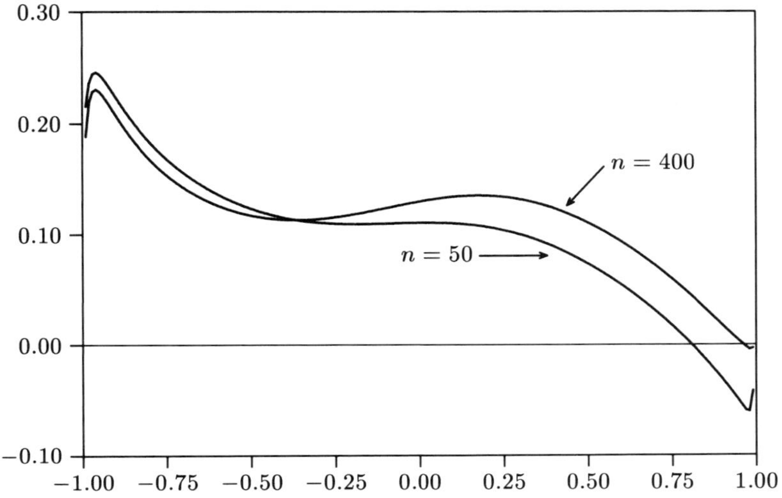

Figure 19.2 Bias due to seasonal adjustment

for seasonal adjustment,[6] and the "adjusted" series was then regressed on a constant and its own lagged value to yield an estimate $\tilde{\beta}$. This was done for 199 values of β from -0.99 to 0.99, for several different sample sizes, and the experiments were repeated a large number of times to reduce experimental error (see Chapter 21).

Figure 19.2 shows the estimated bias of $\tilde{\beta}$ as a function of β. Results are shown for $n = 50$ (based on 4000 replications) and for $n = 400$ (based on 2000 replications). Note that n is the number of observations for the seasonally adjusted series, which is 24 less than the number for the original series. From the figure it is clear that, for most values of β, $\tilde{\beta}$ is severely biased upward. This bias does not go away as the sample size is increased; in fact, for many values of β, it is more severe for $n = 400$ than for $n = 50$. The conclusion seems inescapable that $\tilde{\beta}$ is an inconsistent estimator and that the magnitude of this inconsistency is generally severe.

One other interesting result came out of this series of experiments. The estimate of σ using seasonally adjusted data was noticeably biased downward, generally averaging between 87% and 92% of the true value. In contrast, when the true model (19.41) was estimated using unadjusted data, the estimate of σ was almost unbiased, as one would expect. These results are consistent with the empirical results of Plosser (1979a), who found that models estimated us-

[6] The current value of the unadjusted series was given a weight of 0.84. The 12 lagging and leading values were given weights of 0.08, 0.07, 0.06, −0.16, 0.05, 0.05, 0.04, −0.12, 0.03, 0.03, 0.02, and −0.08. The precise values of these weights did not affect the qualitative results.

ing seasonally adjusted data always had smaller residual variances than corresponding models using raw data. Nevertheless, Plosser found that forecasts based on the former models were often less accurate than forecasts based on the latter. These results suggest that one should never choose a model based on seasonally adjusted data over a model based on raw data simply because the former seems to fit better.

It is very common to employ seasonally adjusted data in applied econometric work, and indeed in many cases it is difficult to avoid doing so. However, the results discussed in this section suggest that this may often be unwise. Even for static models, there are likely to be problems if official seasonal adjustment procedures effectively apply different filters to different series. For dynamic models, the potential inconsistency from using seasonally adjusted data appears to be severe. In the next section, we therefore discuss various approaches to the specification and estimation of models using seasonally unadjusted data.

19.7 MODELING SEASONALITY

The results of the preceding section suggest that, when raw data are available, it is probably better to use them than to rely on official seasonally adjusted data. However, doing so often requires a good deal of extra work. Simply estimating a model designed for nonseasonal data is rarely appropriate. Such an approach is likely to yield severely biased parameter estimates if seasonal variation in one or more of the independent variables happens to be correlated with (but not responsible for) seasonal variation in the dependent variable. There are numerous ways to deal with seasonal variation in regression models. We discuss some of the principal ones in this section.

The simplest strategy for specifying regression models using seasonally unadjusted data is just to add seasonal dummy variables to a linear regression model, as in equation (19.36). If the seasonal pattern has been constant over time, so that three seasonal dummies (in the case of quarterly data) or eleven seasonal dummies (in the case of monthly data) adequately account for the effects of seasonality, this approach may be appropriate. However, it will not work well if the seasonal pattern in the dependent or any of the independent variables has changed substantially during the sample period. One possibility in such a case is to include one or more sets of seasonal dummies interacted with annually increasing trends, along with the ordinary seasonal dummies. The significance of additional sets of dummies can easily be tested by means of F tests in the usual way. A serious objection to this approach, as we noted previously, is that it makes no sense asymptotically. Moreover, a model that uses trending seasonals is likely to be unsuitable for forecasting, since even if the trending seasonals adequately account for changing seasonal patterns within the sample, there is no reason to expect them to do so outside the sample. Davidson and MacKinnon (1983c) provides a somewhat extreme example of this approach. In that paper, as many as 15 seasonal dummy variables, with trends up to the fourth order, were included in models using quarterly data, because this seemed to be necessary to account for all the seasonality in the data.

A second strategy is to model the error terms of a regression model as following some sort of **seasonal ARMA process**, that is, an ARMA process with nonzero coefficients only at seasonal lags. One such process, which might be appropriate for quarterly data, is the simple AR(4) process that we first encountered in Section 10.5:

$$u_t = \rho_4 u_{t-4} + \varepsilon_t, \quad \varepsilon_t \sim \mathrm{IID}(0, \omega^2), \tag{19.42}$$

where ρ_4 is a parameter to be estimated, and ω^2 is the variance of ε_t. Another purely seasonal AR process for quarterly data is

$$u_t = \rho_4 u_{t-4} + \rho_8 u_{t-8} + \varepsilon_t, \quad \varepsilon_t \sim \mathrm{IID}(0, \omega^2), \tag{19.43}$$

which is analogous to an AR(2) process for nonseasonal data.

In many cases, error terms may exhibit both seasonal and nonseasonal serial correlation. This suggests combining a seasonal with a nonseasonal process. Suppose, for example, that we wish to combine an AR(1) process and a simple AR(4) process. One approach is to combine them additively, yielding

$$u_t = \rho_1 u_{t-1} + \rho_4 u_{t-4} + \varepsilon_t, \quad \varepsilon_t \sim \mathrm{IID}(0, \omega^2). \tag{19.44}$$

A second approach is to combine them multiplicatively, as in

$$(1 - \rho_1 L)(1 - \rho_4 L^4) u_t = \varepsilon_t, \quad \varepsilon_t \sim \mathrm{IID}(0, \omega^2).$$

This can be rewritten without using lag-operator notation as

$$u_t = \rho_1 u_{t-1} + \rho_4 u_{t-4} - \rho_1 \rho_4 u_{t-5} + \varepsilon_t, \quad \varepsilon_t \sim \mathrm{IID}(0, \omega^2). \tag{19.45}$$

Both (19.44) and (19.45) seem plausible, and there seems to be no compelling a priori reason to prefer one or the other.

Evidently, a great many different AR and ARMA processes could be used to model seasonal variation in the error terms of a regression model. There is a large literature on seasonal ARMA processes; see, among others, Box and Jenkins (1976), Harvey (1981), and Ghysels (1991). Whether such processes provide a good way to model seasonality is not at all clear, however. On the one hand, they generally provide a rather parsimonious way to do so; for example, (19.42) uses just one extra parameter, and (19.43) uses just two. Moreover, it is certainly true that if a regression model has not adequately accounted for seasonality, there will very often be evidence of fourth-order serial correlation. Thus testing for it often provides a useful diagnostic test. But, just as evidence of first-order serial correlation does not mean that the error terms really follow an AR(1) process, evidence of fourth-order serial correlation does not mean that they really follow an AR(4) process.

The big problem with seasonal ARMA processes is that they cannot capture one very important feature of seasonality, namely, the fact that different seasons of the year have different characteristics; summer is not simply winter with a different label. As far as an ARMA process is concerned, however, summer *is* just winter with a different label. If the error terms display a particular seasonal pattern at the beginning of the sample, then it is quite likely that they will display a similar pattern a year later. But for a stationary ARMA process, the influence of initial conditions tends to zero as time passes. Thus there is no reason to believe that the seasonal pattern 10 or 20 years after the beginning of the sample will in any way resemble the initial pattern. In fact, for T large enough, the expectations of u_T, u_{T+1}, u_{T+2}, and u_{T+3} conditional on u_1 through u_4 are all (nearly) zero. Thus using an ARMA process to model seasonality means assuming that any particular pattern of seasonality is transitory; in the long run, any pattern is possible. This implies that one would surely not want to use an ARMA process to model the seasonal pattern of something like the price of strawberries, since the model would say nothing about whether that price is likely to be unusually high in the middle of winter or at harvest time. One obvious way to get around this problem would be to include seasonal dummy variables in the model as well. The dummy variables would allow the different seasons to be genuinely different, while the seasonal ARMA process would allow the seasonal pattern to evolve over time.

A third strategy is to allow some or all of the coefficients of the regression function to be different in every season. Thus, if the original model had k coefficients, one would estimate a model with as many as $4k$ or $12k$ coefficients. This would make sense if variations in the pattern of seasonality over time were associated with changes in the values of some of the independent variables over time. The obvious objection to this approach is that the number of coefficients would often be much too large relative to the sample size, and they would all tend to be estimated very imprecisely. Gersovitz and MacKinnon (1978) therefore suggested using smoothness priors, similar to the ones discussed in Section 19.3 for estimating distributed lags, to prevent the coefficients from varying too much from one season to the next. This may be a reasonable constraint to impose in the case of monthly data but would seem to be hard to justify in the case of quarterly data.

A fourth strategy is to incorporate seasonal dynamics directly into the specification of the regression function, using some form of **seasonal ADL model**. A very simple model of this type is

$$(1 - L^4)y_t = \beta_0 + \beta_1(1 - L^4)x_t + \beta_2(y_{t-4} - \lambda x_{t-4}) + u_t.$$

This looks like an ADL(1, 1) model written in its error correction form—compare (19.30)—but with four-period lags instead of one-period ones. It is almost certainly too simple, of course, and might well benefit from the addition of seasonal dummies or additional lags of y_t and x_t. A well-known paper that estimates seasonal ADL models is Davidson, Hendry, Srba, and Yeo (1978).

With the arguable exception of seasonal ADL models, the strategies that we have discussed so far are essentially mechanical. One starts with a non-seasonal model and then modifies it to handle seasonality. That is clearly not the ideal way to proceed. Ideally, one would like to incorporate seasonality into the model from the beginning. This of course is likely to make the whole model-building exercise much harder, and perhaps that explains why relatively few authors have attempted to do it. Exceptions include Plosser (1979b), Miron (1986), and Osborn (1988, 1991). Unless the underlying economic theory explicitly takes account of seasonality, it will be very difficult for econometricians to incorporate it into the models they estimate.

19.8 CONCLUSION

In this chapter, we have discussed a number of problems that commonly arise when one attempts to estimate regression models using time-series data. In most of the chapter, we have assumed that all the series are stationary, or $I(0)$, so that we could employ standard estimation methods and standard asymptotic theory. For many series, however, that assumption may be violated unless one takes first differences prior to estimation. But how can one decide when differencing is necessary? In the next chapter, we discuss how to answer that question, along with several very important topics that are closely related to it.

TERMS AND CONCEPTS

Almon lag
ADL(p, q) and ADL(1, 1) models
autoregressive distributed lag (ADL) model
distributed lag model
dynamic model
error-correction form (of ADL model)
error-correction model (ECM)
error-correction term
filter weights
first-difference operator
Granger causality in VARs
integrated variables
$I(0)$ and $I(1)$ variables
linear filter
mixed estimation
partial adjustment model
PDL(q, d) model
polynomial distributed lag (PDL)
random walk, with and without drift
regression-based seasonal adjustment procedure
seasonality
seasonally adjusted data
seasonal ADL model
seasonal AR process
seasonal ARMA process
seasonal variation
smoothness priors
spurious regression
stochastic restrictions
trend-stationary variable
vector autoregressive model
VAR(p) process

Chapter 20

Unit Roots and Cointegration

20.1 Introduction

As we saw in the last chapter, the usual asymptotic results cannot be expected to apply if any of the variables in a regression model is generated by a nonstationary process. For example, in the case of the linear regression model $\boldsymbol{y} = \boldsymbol{X\beta} + \boldsymbol{u}$, the usual results depend on the assumption that the matrix $n^{-1}\boldsymbol{X}^{\top}\boldsymbol{X}$ tends to a finite, positive definite matrix as the sample size n tends to infinity. When this assumption is violated, some very strange things can happen, as we saw when we discussed "spurious" regressions between totally unrelated variables in Section 19.2. This is a serious practical problem, because a great many economic time series trend upward over time and therefore seem to violate this assumption.

Two obvious ways to keep standard assumptions from being violated when using such series are to detrend or difference them prior to use. But detrending and differencing are very different operations; if the former is appropriate, the latter will not be, and vice versa. Detrending a time series y_t will be appropriate if it is trend-stationary, which means that the DGP for y_t can be written as

$$y_t = \gamma_0 + \gamma_1 t + u_t, \tag{20.01}$$

where t is a time trend and u_t follows a stationary ARMA process. On the other hand, differencing will be appropriate if the DGP for y_t can be written as

$$y_t = \gamma_1 + y_{t-1} + u_t, \tag{20.02}$$

where again u_t follows a stationary ARMA process. If the u_t's were serially independent, (20.02) would be a random walk with drift, the drift parameter being γ_1. They will generally not be serially independent, however. As we will see shortly, it is no accident that the same parameter γ_1 appears in both (20.01) and (20.02).

The choice between detrending and differencing comes down to a choice between (20.01) and (20.02). The main techniques for choosing between them are various tests for what are called **unit roots**. The terminology comes from the literature on time-series processes. Recall from Section 10.7 that for an AR process $A(L)u_t = \varepsilon_t$, where $A(L)$ denotes a polynomial in the lag operator, the stationarity of the process depends on the roots of the polynomial equation $A(L) = 0$. If all roots are outside the unit circle, the process is stationary. If any root is equal to or less than 1 in absolute value, the process is not stationary. A root that is equal to 1 in absolute value is called a **unit root**. When a process has a unit root, as (20.02) does, it is said to be **integrated of order one** or $\boldsymbol{I(1)}$. A series that is $I(1)$ must be differenced once in order to make it stationary.

The obvious way to choose between (20.01) and (20.02) is to nest them both within a more general model. There is more than one way to do so. The most plausible model that includes both (20.01) and (20.02) as special cases is arguably

$$\begin{aligned} y_t &= \gamma_0 + \gamma_1 t + v_t; \quad v_t = \alpha v_{t-1} + u_t \\ &= \gamma_0 + \gamma_1 t + \alpha\big(y_{t-1} - \gamma_0 - \gamma_1(t-1)\big) + u_t, \end{aligned} \tag{20.03}$$

where u_t follows a stationary process. This model was advocated by Bhargava (1986). When $|\alpha| < 1$, (20.03) is equivalent to the trend-stationary model (20.01); when $\alpha = 1$, it reduces to (20.02).

Because (20.03) is nonlinear in the parameters, it is convenient to reparametrize it as

$$y_t = \beta_0 + \beta_1 t + \alpha y_{t-1} + u_t, \tag{20.04}$$

where

$$\beta_0 \equiv \gamma_0(1-\alpha) + \gamma_1\alpha \quad \text{and} \quad \beta_1 \equiv \gamma_1(1-\alpha).$$

It is easy to verify that the estimates of α from least squares estimation of (20.03) and (20.04) will be identical, as will the estimated standard errors of those estimates if, in the case of (20.03), the latter are based on the Gauss-Newton regression. The only problem with the reparametrization (20.04) is that it hides the important fact that $\beta_1 = 0$ when $\alpha = 1$.

If y_{t-1} is subtracted from both sides, equation (20.04) becomes

$$\Delta y_t = \beta_0 + \beta_1 t + (\alpha - 1)y_{t-1} + u_t, \tag{20.05}$$

where Δ is the first-difference operator. If $\alpha < 1$, (20.05) is equivalent to the model (20.01), whereas, if $\alpha = 1$, it is equivalent to (20.02). Thus it is conventional to test the null hypothesis that $\alpha = 1$ against the one-sided alternative that $\alpha < 1$. Since this is a test of the null hypothesis that there is a unit root in the stochastic process which generates y_t, such tests are commonly called **unit root tests**.

At first glance, it might appear that a unit root test could be accomplished simply by using the ordinary t statistic for $\alpha - 1 = 0$ in (20.05), but this is not so. When $\alpha = 1$, the process generating y_t is integrated of order one. This means that y_{t-1} will not satisfy the standard assumptions needed for asymptotic analysis. In consequence, as we will see below, this t statistic does not have the $N(0,1)$ distribution asymptotically. It is in fact used as a test statistic, but not in conjunction with the usual critical values from the Student's t or normal distributions.

The first half of this chapter is concerned with tests for unit roots. In the next section, we describe a number of popular unit root tests, all of which are based on regressions similar to (20.05), and all of which rely on the highly unrealistic assumption that the error terms u_t are serially uncorrelated. In Section 20.3, we then discuss some of the asymptotic theory that has been developed for these tests. In Section 20.4, we relax the assumption that the error terms are serially uncorrelated and also discuss some other problems that complicate the use of unit root tests.

The second half of the chapter deals with the important concept of **cointegration** between two or more series, each of which is $I(1)$. This concept is introduced in Section 20.5. Cointegration tests, which are closely related to unit root tests, are discussed in Section 20.6. If the dependent variable in a regression model is cointegrated with one or more of the regressors, that fact has important implications for the type of model that one should construct. Single-equation methods for estimation using $I(1)$ series are discussed in Section 20.7, and methods based on vector autoregressions in Section 20.8.

20.2 Testing for Unit Roots

The simplest and most widely used tests for unit roots were developed by Fuller (1976) and Dickey and Fuller (1979). These tests are generally referred to as **Dickey-Fuller**, or **DF**, **tests**. A particularly good exposition of them may be found in Dickey, Bell, and Miller (1986). Dickey-Fuller tests are based on regressions similar to (20.05). Three such regressions are commonly employed, of which regression (20.05) is the most complicated. The other two are

$$\Delta y_t = (\alpha - 1)y_{t-1} + u_t \quad \text{and} \tag{20.06}$$

$$\Delta y_t = \beta_0 + (\alpha - 1)y_{t-1} + u_t. \tag{20.07}$$

These two regressions may both be derived in exactly the same way as (20.05). The first of them, regression (20.06), is extremely restrictive, so much so that it is hard to imagine ever using it with economic time series. Its only advantage is that it is easier to analyze than the other two test regressions. The second, regression (20.07), is also fairly restrictive, but it would make sense if y_t had no trend. Note that, in the case of (20.07), $\beta_0 = 0$ whenever $\alpha = 1$, because β_0 is really $\gamma_0(1-\alpha)$.

There are two different types of DF test based on each of the three regressions (20.05), (20.06), and (20.07). One type of test is computed in exactly the same way as the ordinary t statistic for $\alpha - 1 = 0$ in any of the regressions.

Since these statistics do not have the Student's t distribution, even asymptotically, they are usually referred to as τ **statistics** rather than t statistics. We will call the τ statistics based on (20.06), (20.07), and (20.05): τ_{nc}, τ_c, and τ_{ct}, respectively.[1] The second type of test is based directly on the estimated coefficient $\hat{\alpha} - 1$. The test statistic is

$$z = n(\hat{\alpha} - 1). \tag{20.08}$$

By analogy with the three τ statistics, we will denote the three principal variants of this z **statistic** as z_{nc}, z_c, and z_{ct}.

The z statistic (20.08) may seem strange for two reasons: It does not depend on an estimate of σ, and the normalizing factor is n rather than $n^{1/2}$. To see why it has these features, let us consider the simplest case, namely, (20.06). In this case,

$$\hat{\alpha} = \frac{\sum y_t y_{t-1}}{\sum y_{t-1}^2},$$

where the summations will run from 1 to n if y_0 is available and from 2 to n otherwise. We will assume that y_0 is available, since it simplifies some derivations, and will suppose that the data are generated by the random walk

$$y_t = y_{t-1} + u_t, \quad u_t \sim \text{IID}(0, \sigma^2).$$

This implies that the DGP is in fact a special case of the model being estimated. In order to avoid dependence on the infinite past, it is necessary to assume that y_{-j} is equal to some known value for some $j \geq 0$. For concreteness and simplicity, we will assume that $y_{-1} = 0$.

Under these assumptions,

$$\hat{\alpha} = \frac{\sum y_{t-1}^2}{\sum y_{t-1}^2} + \frac{\sum u_t y_{t-1}}{\sum y_{t-1}^2} = 1 + \frac{\sum u_t y_{t-1}}{\sum y_{t-1}^2}.$$

Rearranging terms, we find that

$$\hat{\alpha} - 1 = \frac{\sum u_t y_{t-1}}{\sum y_{t-1}^2}. \tag{20.09}$$

It is clear that both u_t and y_{t-1} must be proportional to σ. Thus both the numerator and the denominator of (20.09) must be proportional to σ^2. These factors of proportionality cancel out, and so we see that the distribution of $\hat{\alpha} - 1$ does not depend on σ. This result depends on the assumption that y_{-1} is 0. If y_{-1} takes on a fixed nonzero value, the result holds only asymptotically.

[1] The notation used for these statistics varies from author to author. We prefer this notation because it is mnemonic: *nc* stands for "no constant," *c* stands for "constant," and *ct* stands for "constant and trend."

The second strange feature of (20.08), namely, that the normalizing factor is n rather than $n^{1/2}$, is a little harder to explain. Let us first define the **partial sum process** S_t as

$$S_t = \sum_{s=0}^{t} u_s,$$

which allows us to write[2]

$$y_t = y_{-1} + S_t = S_t.$$

Substituting S_{t-1} for y_{t-1} in the right-hand side of (20.09) then yields

$$\hat{\alpha} - 1 = \frac{\sum u_t S_{t-1}}{\sum S_{t-1} S_{t-1}}. \tag{20.10}$$

The numerator here can also be written as

$$\sum_{t=1}^{n} \left(\sum_{s=0}^{t-1} u_s u_t \right).$$

The summation in parentheses has t terms: $u_0 u_t$, $u_1 u_t$, $u_2 u_t$, and so on up to $u_{t-1} u_t$. The full sum therefore has $\sum_{t=1}^{n} t = \frac{1}{2} n(n+1) = O(n^2)$ terms. Since we have assumed that the error terms are independently distributed, each of these terms must have mean zero. On the assumption that a central limit theorem can be applied to their sum, the order of that sum will be the square root of n^2. Thus the sum is $O(n)$.

In a similar fashion, the denominator of (20.10) can be written as

$$\sum_{t=1}^{n} \left(\sum_{r=0}^{t-1} \sum_{s=0}^{t-1} u_r u_s \right).$$

Each of the double summations within the parentheses has t^2 terms. Of these, t are of the form u_s^2, and the remaining $t^2 - t$ have mean zero. Thus each double summation will be $O(t)$, and hence also $O(n)$, and will have positive mean. Summing n of these then yields a quantity that must be $O(n^2)$. Thus we see that the right-hand side of (20.10) is $O(n)/O(n^2) = O(n^{-1})$. We therefore conclude that the normalizing factor n in (20.08) is precisely what is needed to ensure that the test statistic z is $O(1)$ under the null hypothesis.

[2] Without the assumption that $y_{-1} = 0$, the second equality here would not hold, and subsequent expressions would be more complicated. However, terms involving y_{-1} would not be of the highest order and so would not affect the final results. In models (20.05) and (20.07), no assumption about y_{-1} is necessary, because including a constant term in the regression means that all the data effectively have their means removed.

The analysis for regressions (20.07) or (20.05) is more complicated than for (20.06), but the conclusion is the same: $\hat{\alpha} - 1$ must be normalized by a factor of n instead of by a factor of $n^{1/2}$. This makes it quite clear that standard asymptotic theory does not apply to the τ statistics, of which $\hat{\alpha} - 1$ is the numerator. And standard asymptotic theory certainly does not apply to the z statistics themselves. In fact, as we will see in the next section, the six test statistics that we have discussed so far all have different asymptotic distributions.

There is no reason for unit root tests to be based only on regressions (20.05), (20.06), or (20.07). In particular, it is perfectly valid to include other nonstochastic regressors, such as seasonal dummy variables, in these regressions. It does not make sense to add seasonal dummy variables to (20.06), since there is no constant term in the model on which it is based. However, it may make sense to add seasonal dummy variables to (20.05) or (20.07). Because the seasonal dummies are of the same order as the constant term, which is already included, their inclusion does not change the asymptotic distributions of the test statistics.

It is also possible to include powers of time. The trend-stationary model (20.01) can be generalized by adding t^2 as an additional variable, thus implying that y_t is stationary around a quadratic trend. Similarly, the random walk with drift (20.02) can be generalized by adding a linear time trend, thus allowing the drift term to change over time. A combined model that nests these two models can be written, after the usual reparametrization, as

$$\Delta y_t = \beta_0 + \beta_1 t + \beta_2 t^2 + (\alpha - 1)y_{t-1} + u_t. \tag{20.11}$$

As one might expect on the basis of what happens for (20.05) and (20.07), $\beta_2 = 0$ in this model when $\alpha = 1$. Tests based on equation (20.11), and on equations with even higher powers of time included, were advocated by Ouliaris, Park, and Phillips (1989). The two test statistics for $\alpha = 1$ based on (20.11) will be referred to as $\boldsymbol{z_{ctt}}$ and $\boldsymbol{\tau_{ctt}}$, where *ctt* stands for "constant, trend, and trend squared." Because the squared trend term increases more rapidly with t than either the constant or the linear trend, the asymptotic distributions of these tests are different from those of the other tests that we have discussed.

20.3 Asymptotic Theory for Unit Root Tests

The asymptotic theory for regressions that involve $I(1)$ variables, which includes the regressions on which unit root tests are based, is very different from the more standard asymptotic theory that we have used throughout this book. It is therefore impossible to do more in this section than to state some important results and attempt to provide some intuition as to why they hold. The classic papers in this area are Dickey and Fuller (1979), Phillips (1987), and Phillips and Perron (1988). Banerjee, Dolado, Galbraith, and Hendry (1993) provide a readable introduction to some of the basic results.

Conventional central limit theorems, which are so useful for estimators that approach their true values at rates proportional to $n^{-1/2}$, are of no use in the case of unit root tests. Instead, it is necessary to employ what are called **functional central limit theorems**, because they involve taking the limit of certain quantities in a function space; see Billingsley (1968) or Hall and Heyde (1980). We will not attempt to prove, or even state formally, a functional central limit theorem. However, we will try to provide some intuition as to why such theorems are useful in this context.

The key idea that makes it possible to use functional central limit theorems is the idea of mapping from the sequence $\{0, 1, 2, \ldots, n\}$, which indexes observations, into the fixed interval $[0, 1]$. Suppose we divide that interval into $n+1$ parts, with divisions at $1/(n+1)$, $2/(n+1)$, and so on. We can then associate observation 0 with the subinterval defined by $0 \leq r < 1/(n+1)$, observation 1 with the subinterval defined by $1/(n+1) \leq r < 2/(n+1)$, and so on. As $n \to \infty$, each of these subintervals tends in width to zero. Then if $[rn]$ denotes the largest integer that is not greater than rn, for $r \in [0, 1]$, we find that

$$[r(n+1)] = 0 \quad \text{for } 0 \leq r < \frac{1}{n+1},$$

$$[r(n+1)] = 1 \quad \text{for } \frac{1}{n+1} \leq r < \frac{2}{n+1},$$

and so on up to

$$[r(n+1)] = n \quad \text{for } \frac{n}{n+1} \leq r < 1.$$

Thus every real r in the interval $[0, 1]$ is uniquely associated with one of the indices $0, 1, \ldots, n$.

Now consider the **standardized partial sum process**

$$R_n(r) \equiv \frac{1}{\sigma\sqrt{n}} S_{[r(n+1)]} \equiv \frac{1}{\sigma\sqrt{n}} \sum_{s=0}^{[r(n+1)]} u_s, \quad r \in [0, 1].$$

This is simply the ordinary partial sum process that we encountered in the previous section, divided by the standard deviation of the u_t's and by the square root of the sample size, and indexed by r instead of by t. It can be shown by means of a functional central limit theorem that, under relatively weak conditions on the u_t's, $R_n(r)$ converges to what is called a **standardized Wiener process** and is denoted $W(r)$. Intuitively, a Wiener process is like a continuous random walk defined on the interval $[0, 1]$. Even though it is continuous, it varies erratically on any subinterval, with each increment being independent. For fixed r, $W(r) \sim N(0, r)$, a fact that can sometimes be useful.

The principal results on the asymptotics of unit root test statistics are that, under the null hypothesis of a unit root, they converge to various functions of Wiener processes. Unfortunately, such functions generally have distributions that cannot be expressed in any convenient way and must be evaluated numerically. To give some idea of what theoretical results on the asymptotics of unit root test statistics look like, we now state the principal results of Phillips (1987) for the statistics z_{nc} and τ_{nc}:

$$z_{nc} \Rightarrow \frac{\frac{1}{2}\big(W^2(1) - 1\big)}{\int_0^1 W^2(r)dr} \tag{20.12}$$

$$\tau_{nc} \Rightarrow \frac{\frac{1}{2}\big(W^2(1) - 1\big)}{\Big(\int_0^1 W^2(r)dr\Big)^{1/2}}. \tag{20.13}$$

Here the notation $\Rightarrow$ denotes weak convergence in a function space, which is analogous to convergence in distribution. Similar results for the z_c, z_{ct}, τ_c, and τ_{ct} test statistics may be found in Phillips and Perron (1988).

One important feature of these results is that they do not depend on the assumption that the variances of the error terms u_t are constant. The asymptotic distributions of the unit root test statistics that we have discussed are the same under heteroskedasticity of unknown form as under homoskedasticity. However, it is essential that there be no correlation between u_t and u_{t-j} for all $j \neq 0$. Thus the test statistics we have discussed are not valid when the error terms are serially correlated. When serial correlation is present, the test statistics must be modified to take it into account. Two different ways to do this will be discussed in the next section.

Although results like (20.12) and (20.13) are of considerable theoretical interest, they are not very useful in practice, because the distributions of the quantities on the right-hand side are not known analytically. However, critical values for the eight test statistics that we have discussed have been tabulated by various numerical methods, including Monte Carlo simulation. The best-known reference is probably Fuller (1976), in which certain asymptotic critical values for τ_{nc}, τ_c, τ_{ct}, and the corresponding z tests are tabulated, along with finite-sample critical values for a few selected sample sizes. Kiviet and Phillips (1990) show that the finite-sample distributions of z tests can be calculated numerically, in very much the same way as the finite-sample distribution of the Durbin-Watson statistic (Section 10.8), and they tabulate some critical values using that technique. Nabeya and Tanaka (1990) show how to compute the asymptotic distributions of z statistics analytically and tabulate some asymptotic critical values for z_{nc}, z_c, and z_{ct}. MacKinnon (1991) uses Monte Carlo methods to estimate response surfaces (see Section 21.7) for several τ tests. These allow critical values to be read off for any sample size, as well as for $n = \infty$.

Table 20.1 Asymptotic Critical Values for Unit Root Tests

Test Statistic	1%	2.5%	5%	10%	97.5%
τ_{nc}	−2.56	−2.23	−1.94	−1.62	1.62
τ_c	−3.43	−3.12	−2.86	−2.57	0.24
τ_{ct}	−3.96	−3.66	−3.41	−3.13	−0.66
τ_{ctt}	−4.37	−4.08	−3.83	−3.55	−1.21
z_{nc}	−13.7	−10.4	−8.0	−5.7	1.6
z_c	−20.6	−16.9	−14.1	−11.2	0.4
z_{ct}	−29.4	−25.1	−21.7	−18.2	−1.8
z_{ctt}	−36.6	−31.8	−28.1	−24.2	−4.2

Unfortunately, all finite-sample critical values for unit root tests depend on one or another highly unrealistic assumption about the error terms, usually that they are $\text{NID}(0, \sigma^2)$. The asymptotic critical values, in contrast, are valid much more generally, since they do not require that either normality or homoskedasticity be assumed. Thus it may be safer to use asymptotic critical values, treating them with appropriate caution, than to rely on finite-sample values that may be quite inappropriate in practice.

Table 20.1 contains asymptotic critical values, computed by methods similar to those of MacKinnon (1991), for the eight different tests we have discussed. Most of the critical values in the table are lower-tail ones, since the alternative of interest when we perform unit root tests is almost always that the process is stationary, not that it is explosive. These values differ slightly, in a few cases, from those published in Fuller (1976). The discrepancies, which appear to be due primarily to experimental randomness, are never more than two units in the least significant digit and should therefore be of no consequence in applied work.

It is clear from Table 20.1 that the asymptotic behavior of unit root test statistics is very different from the asymptotic behavior of any other test statistic we have encountered so far. Suppose that α_0 denotes the true value of α. In the stationary case, when $|\alpha_0| < 1$, a t statistic for $\alpha = \alpha_0$ would be asymptotically distributed as $N(0,1)$ under the null hypothesis. Thus the 2.5% and 97.5% critical values for such a test statistic would be ± 1.96. These may be contrasted with the same critical values for the τ tests in the table. The 2.5% critical values are always less than -1.96 and become increasingly negative as more regressors are added to the test regression. Similarly, the 97.5% critical values are always less than 1.96 and are actually less than zero for the τ_{ct} and τ_{ctt} tests.

Figure 20.1 shows the cumulative distribution function of τ_{ct} for the case $n = 1000$, which is almost indistinguishable from the asymptotic case. What is plotted is actually the empirical distribution function of τ_{ct} based on a Monte Carlo experiment; since there were five million replications, experi-

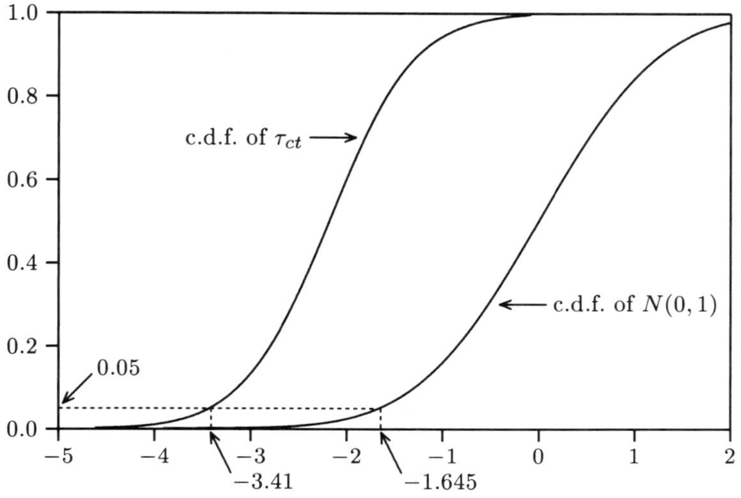

Figure 20.1 Distribution of τ_{ct} for $n = 1000$

mental error should be negligible. For comparison, the c.d.f. of the standard normal distribution is also shown. The differences between the two are striking, with the c.d.f. of τ_{ct} everywhere far to the left of the standard normal c.d.f. The principal reason for this is that $\hat{\alpha}$ is severely biased toward zero when $\alpha_0 = 1$. This bias has serious consequences for the power of these tests to reject the null hypothesis of a unit root. For example, if one is doing a one-sided test at the 5% level, the asymptotic critical values for z_c, z_{ct}, and z_{ctt} are, respectively, −14.1, −21.7, and −28.1. Thus, if $n = 100$, $\hat{\alpha}$ must be less than 0.859, 0.783, and 0.719 in these three cases for the null hypothesis to be rejected. Evidently, the power of unit root tests may be small if the data are actually generated by a trend-stationary model with error terms that are serially correlated.

We have remarked several times that, under the null hypothesis that $\alpha = 1$, the parameters β_0 in regression (20.07), β_1 in regression (20.05), and β_2 in regression (20.11) must equal zero. Let us refer to the parameter that must equal zero in a test regression as β_k; here $k = 0$ if only a constant is included, and k is equal to the number of trend terms included otherwise. The result that $\beta_k = 0$ follows directly from the algebra when one derives these regressions as reparametrized versions of regressions like (20.03), since $\beta_k = (1-\alpha)\gamma_k$. There is also a more fundamental explanation, however. The presence of a unit root increases the order of y_t. So does adding a constant term, a trend term, or a trend squared term. If the order of y_t is to be the same both under the null hypothesis of a unit root and under the alternative of trend-stationarity, it is necessary that the test regression should include a certain nonstochastic regressor with a coefficient that is zero under the null and nonzero under the alternative. For example, consider (20.05), for which $k = 1$. Under the null hypothesis, it reduces to

$$\Delta y_t = \beta_0 + \beta_1 t + u_t.$$

Under the alternative of stationarity, we know that Δy_t must be $O(1)$. But the trend term here is $O(n)$. The only way that Δy_t can have the same order under the null as under the alternative is for β_1 to equal zero under the null.

All of the asymptotic results for Dickey-Fuller tests depend on β_k being zero. This can fail to be the case when there is a unit root only if the DGP is *not* a special case of the model being tested. For example, if $k = 0$ and there were a drift term γ_1 in the DGP, the constant β_0 in the model being tested would appear to be nonzero. In any such case with $\beta_k \neq 0$, the asymptotic results change dramatically, as West (1988) showed. It turns out that, in these circumstances, t statistics for $\alpha = 1$ actually do have the standard normal distribution asymptotically.

Although this result is remarkable, it is not actually very useful. There are two problems with it. First of all, the normal distribution provides a good approximation to the finite-sample distributions of τ-type unit root tests only if β_k is quite large relative to σ. Hylleberg and Mizon (1989) and Kwiatowski and Schmidt (1990) provide Monte Carlo evidence on this for the cases $k = 0$ and $k = 1$, respectively. When β_k/σ and n are within the ranges commonly encountered for economic time series, they find that the DF distributions generally provide a much better approximation to the distributions of τ statistics than does the standard normal distribution. The second problem is that unit root tests based on regressions with $\beta_k \neq 0$ tend to lack power. In fact, for $k \geq 1$ the power of such tests goes to zero as $n \to \infty$. Thus, asymptotically, they never reject the null hypothesis at all when it is false, even though they may reject it when it is true. This result is discussed in Perron (1988) and Campbell and Perron (1991).

20.4 SERIAL CORRELATION AND OTHER PROBLEMS

All of the unit root tests that we have discussed so far are valid only under the assumption that the error terms in the test regressions are serially uncorrelated. This assumption is very often untenable, because the regression functions for the test regressions do not depend on any economic variables. This makes it very likely that the error terms will display serial correlation. Therefore, we need unit root tests that are (asymptotically) valid in the presence of serial correlation. There are two quite different ways to compute such tests. Perhaps surprisingly, the new tests turn out to have the same asymptotic distributions as some of the tests that we have already discussed.

The simplest unit root tests that are valid in the presence of serial correlation of unknown form are modified versions of the Dickey-Fuller τ tests.

These are often called **augmented Dickey-Fuller tests**, or **ADF tests**. They were proposed originally by Dickey and Fuller (1979) under the assumption that the error terms follow an AR process of known order. Subsequent work by Said and Dickey (1984) and Phillips and Perron (1988) showed that they are asymptotically valid under much less restrictive assumptions. Consider the test regressions (20.05), (20.06), (20.07), or (20.11). We can write any of these regressions as

$$\Delta y_t = \boldsymbol{X}_t\boldsymbol{\beta} + (\alpha - 1)y_{t-1} + u_t, \tag{20.14}$$

where $\boldsymbol{X}_t$ consists of whatever set of nonstochastic regressors is included in the test regression: nothing at all for (20.06), a constant for (20.07), a constant and a linear trend for (20.05), and so on.

Now suppose, for simplicity, that the error term u_t in (20.14) follows the stationary AR(1) process $u_t = \rho u_{t-1} + \varepsilon_t$. Then (20.14) would become

$$\begin{aligned}\Delta y_t &= \boldsymbol{X}_t\boldsymbol{\beta} - \rho\boldsymbol{X}_{t-1}\boldsymbol{\beta} + (\rho + \alpha - 1)y_{t-1} - \alpha\rho y_{t-2} + \varepsilon_t \\ &= \boldsymbol{X}_t\boldsymbol{\beta}^* + (\rho + \alpha - 1 - \alpha\rho)y_{t-1} + \alpha\rho(y_{t-1} - y_{t-2}) + \varepsilon_t \qquad (20.15) \\ &= \boldsymbol{X}_t\boldsymbol{\beta}^* + (\alpha - 1)(1 - \rho)y_{t-1} + \alpha\rho\Delta y_{t-1} + \varepsilon_t. \qquad (20.16)\end{aligned}$$

We are able to replace $\boldsymbol{X}_t\boldsymbol{\beta} - \rho\boldsymbol{X}_{t-1}\boldsymbol{\beta}$ by $\boldsymbol{X}_t\boldsymbol{\beta}^*$ in (20.15), for some choice of $\boldsymbol{\beta}^*$, because every column of $\boldsymbol{X}_{t-1}$ lies in $\mathcal{S}(\boldsymbol{X})$. This is a consequence of the fact that $\boldsymbol{X}_t$ can include only such deterministic variables as a constant, a linear trend, and so on (see Section 10.9). Thus each element of $\boldsymbol{\beta}^*$ is a linear combination of the elements of $\boldsymbol{\beta}$.

Equation (20.16) is a linear regression of Δy_t on $\boldsymbol{X}_t$, y_{t-1}, and Δy_{t-1}. This is just the original regression (20.14), with one additional regressor, Δy_{t-1}. Adding this regressor has caused the serially dependent error term u_t to be replaced by the serially independent error term ε_t. The ADF version of the τ statistic, which we will refer to as the τ' statistic, is simply the ordinary t statistic for the coefficient on y_{t-1} in (20.16) to be zero. If the serial correlation in the error terms of (20.14) were fully accounted for by an AR(1) process, this τ' statistic would have exactly the same asymptotic distribution as the ordinary DF τ statistic for the same specification of $\boldsymbol{X}_t$. The fact that the coefficient on y_{t-1} is $(\alpha-1)(1-\rho)$ rather than $\alpha-1$ does not matter. Because it is assumed that $|\rho| < 1$, this coefficient can be zero only if $\alpha = 1$. Thus a test for the coefficient on y_{t-1} to be zero is equivalent to a test for $\alpha = 1$.

It is evidently very easy to compute τ' statistics using regressions like (20.16), but it is not so easy to compute the corresponding z' statistics. If the coefficient of y_{t-1} were multiplied by n, the result would be $n(\hat{\alpha} - 1)(1 - \hat{\rho})$ rather than $n(\hat{\alpha} - 1)$. This test statistic clearly would not have the same asymptotic distribution as z. Although it is possible to compute z' statistics from regressions like (20.16), it is not very easy to do so; see Dickey, Bell, and Miller (1986). Thus, in practice, τ' tests are widely used and z' tests are almost never used.

In this simple example, we were able to handle serial correlation by adding a single regressor, Δy_{t-1}, to the test regression. It is easy to see that if u_t followed an AR(p) process, we would have to add p additional regressors, Δy_{t-1}, Δy_{t-2}, and so on up to Δy_{t-p}. But what if the error terms followed an MA or ARMA process? In that case, the moving average component of the error terms could be modeled only by an infinite-order AR process, so it would seem that we would have to add an infinite number of lagged values of Δy_t. This is impossible of course. But, luckily, we do not have to do anything so extreme. As Said and Dickey (1984) showed, one can validly use ADF tests even when there is a moving average component in the errors, provided one lets the number of lags of Δy_t that are included tend to infinity at an appropriate rate, which turns out to be a rate no faster than $n^{1/3}$. One simply acts as if the errors follow an AR(p) process and allows p to grow at a rate no faster than $n^{1/3}$.

In practice, of course, since n is fixed and does not tend to infinity, knowing the critical rate $n^{1/3}$ provides no help in choosing p. Moreover, investigators do not know what process is actually generating the error terms. Thus what is generally done is simply to add as many lags of Δy_t as are necessary to remove evidence of serial correlation in the error terms. Monte Carlo evidence (Schwert, 1989) suggests that ADF tests perform quite well under the null hypothesis even when the process generating the error does include an MA component.

The second way to obtain unit root test statistics that are valid despite the presence of serial correlation of unknown form is to use the **nonparametric unit root tests** of Phillips (1987) and Phillips and Perron (1988). In this approach, the test statistics are based on the original test regression (20.14), but they are modified so that serial correlation does not affect their asymptotic distributions. These tests are called nonparametric because no parametric specification of the error process is involved.

The nonparametric z statistic corresponding to some specification of the matrix $\boldsymbol{X}$ in (20.14) can be written as

$$z^* = n(\hat{\alpha} - 1) - \frac{n^2(\hat{\omega}^2 - \hat{\sigma}^2)}{2\boldsymbol{y}^\top \boldsymbol{M}_X \boldsymbol{y}}. \tag{20.17}$$

This is just the ordinary z statistic minus a correction term that tends to zero asymptotically when there is no serial correlation. Here $\hat{\sigma}^2$ denotes any consistent estimate of σ^2 and $\hat{\omega}^2$ denotes any consistent estimate of

$$\omega^2 \equiv \lim_{n\to\infty} \left(\frac{1}{n} E(S_n^2)\right).$$

When there is no serial correlation, $\omega^2 = \sigma^2$ because

$$E(S_n^2) = E\left(\sum_{s=1}^{n}\sum_{t=1}^{n} u_s u_t\right) = n\sigma^2.$$

When there is serial correlation, however, ω^2 will differ from σ^2, because $E(u_s u_t) \neq 0$ for at least some $t \neq s$.

The calculation of z^* defined in (20.17) is not entirely straightforward, because there are many possible choices for $\hat{\omega}^2$. The problem of estimating ω^2 is similar to the problem of estimating covariance matrices in the presence of heteroskedasticity and serial correlation of unknown form. We discussed how to do that in Section 17.5. One particularly simple technique is the one suggested by Newey and West (1987a). Using it, the estimate of ω^2 is

$$\hat{\omega}^2 = \frac{1}{n}\left(\sum_{t=1}^{n} \hat{u}_t^2 + 2\sum_{j=1}^{p} w_{jp}\left(\sum_{t=j+1}^{n} \hat{u}_t \hat{u}_{t-j}\right)\right), \tag{20.18}$$

where $w_{jp} = 1 - j/(p+1)$. Other weighting functions could also be used, so long as they have the property that $\hat{\omega}^2$ is necessarily positive. The lag truncation parameter p must grow at a rate no faster than $n^{1/4}$ if $\hat{\omega}^2$ is to be consistent for ω^2.

Nonparametric τ statistics are obtained by modifying ordinary τ statistics in much the same way as z^* modifies z:

$$\tau^* = \frac{\hat{\sigma}\tau}{\hat{\omega}} - \frac{n(\hat{\omega}^2 - \hat{\sigma}^2)}{2\hat{\omega}\,\boldsymbol{y}^{\top}\boldsymbol{M}_X\boldsymbol{y}}. \tag{20.19}$$

Once the quantities necessary to compute z^* are available, it is easy to compute τ^* as well. However, there is some evidence — see Phillips and Perron (1988) and Schwert (1989) — that z^* statistics tend to have more power than ADF τ' and nonparametric τ^* statistics.

Since different investigators might well choose different values of p, or use different weights w_{jp}, they might well obtain different values of z^* or τ^* for the same data. This is unfortunate but inevitable. To confuse matters further, there are other techniques for estimating ω^2, in addition to the one used in (20.18). Some of these have desirable properties and some have undesirable ones; see Andrews (1991a, 1991b) and Ouliaris, Park, and Phillips (1989), among others. The finite-sample properties of these different techniques can differ substantially. However, they always seem to be poor for at least some specifications of the error process (Schwert, 1989). The finite-sample behavior of τ' statistics is also not always well approximated by their asymptotic distributions, but it never seems to be as bad as the behavior of z^* and τ^* statistics can be.

Since there are so many ways to compute nonparametric unit root test statistics, none of which has good finite-sample properties under the null hypothesis in all cases, it is potentially dangerous to rely on any of these statistics. Before making important inferences on the basis of one or more of them, it would be advisable to conduct a Monte Carlo experiment (see Chapter 21) to investigate their performance with data similar to those actually used.

Serial correlation is not the only complication that one is likely to encounter when trying to compute unit root test statistics. One very serious problem is that these statistics are severely biased against rejecting the null hypothesis when they are used with data that have been seasonally adjusted by means of a linear filter or by the methods used by government statistical agencies. In Section 19.6, we discussed the tendency of the OLS estimate of α in the regression $y_t = \beta_0 + \alpha y_{t-1} + u_t$ to be biased toward 1 when y_t is a seasonally adjusted series. This bias is present for all the test regressions we have discussed. Even when $\hat{\alpha}$ is not actually biased *toward* 1, it will be less biased *away* from 1 than the corresponding estimate using an unfiltered series. Since the tabulated distributions of the test statistics are based on the behavior of $\hat{\alpha}$ for the latter case, it is likely that test statistics computed using seasonally adjusted data will reject the null hypothesis substantially less often than they should according to the critical values in Table 20.1. That is exactly what Ghysels and Perron (1992) found in a series of Monte Carlo experiments.

If possible, one should therefore avoid using seasonally adjusted data to compute unit root tests. One possibility is to use annual data. This may cause the sample size to be quite small, but the consequences of that are not as severe as one might fear. As Shiller and Perron (1985) point out, the power of these tests depends more on the **span** of the data (i.e., the number of years the sample covers) than on the number of observations. The reason for this is that if α is in fact positive but less than 1, it will be closer to 1 when the data are observed more frequently. Thus a test based on n annual observations may have only slightly less power than a test based on $4n$ quarterly observations that have not been seasonally adjusted and may have more power than a test based on $4n$ seasonally adjusted observations.

If quarterly or monthly data are to be used, they should if possible not be seasonally adjusted. Unfortunately, as we remarked in Chapter 19, seasonally unadjusted data for many time series are not available in many countries. Moreover, the use of seasonally unadjusted data may make it necessary to add seasonal dummy variables to the regression and to account for fourth-order or twelfth-order serial correlation.

A second major problem with unit root tests is that they are very sensitive to the assumption that the process generating the data has been stable over the entire sample period. Perron (1989) showed that the power of unit root tests is dramatically reduced if the level or the trend of a series has changed exogenously at any time during the sample period. Even though the series may actually be stationary in each of the two parts of the sample, it can be almost impossible to reject the null that it is $I(1)$ in such cases.

Perron therefore proposed techniques that can be used to test for unit roots conditional on exogenous changes in level or trend. His tests are performed by first regressing y_t on a constant, a time trend, and one or two dummy variables that allow either the constant, the trend, or both the constant and the trend to change at one specified point in time. The residuals from these regressions are then used in a regression like (20.06), and the usual z, τ, z^*, and τ^* statistics can then be calculated. The asymptotic distributions of these test statistics are not the same as those of z_{ct} and τ_{ct}, as they would be (because of the FWL Theorem) if no dummy variables were included in the initial regressions. Instead, they depend on what dummy variables are included and where in the sample the break occurred. Asymptotic critical values are tabulated in Perron (1989).

Much empirical work, following the classic paper of Nelson and Plosser (1982), has seemed to show that unit roots are very often present in macroeconomic time series. Perron argued that when one takes account of either the great crash of 1929 (for annual series that end prior to 1973) or the oil shock of 1973 (for quarterly post-war series), these results change dramatically and most U.S. macroeconomic time series appear not to have a unit root. Whether this somewhat controversial result will pass the test of time is not yet clear.

There has been a great deal of empirical work that uses unit root tests; prominent examples include Nelson and Plosser (1982), Mankiw and Shapiro (1985), Campbell and Mankiw (1987), Perron and Phillips (1987), and DeJong and Whiteman (1991). Because of the various problems we have discussed, and because different tests tend to yield different results, it is difficult to draw conclusive inferences about whether economic time series do or do not have unit roots. This suggests that, when one is building regression models that involve time series which may or may not have unit roots, one should not employ a strategy that will work well only if they are in fact either $I(0)$ or $I(1)$. We will return to that subject in Section 20.8. Before doing so, however, we will discuss the important topic of cointegration.

20.5 COINTEGRATION

Economic theory often suggests that certain pairs of economic variables should be linked by a long-run equilibrium relationship. Although the variables may drift away from equilibrium for a while, economic forces may be expected to act so as to restore equilibrium. Examples of such variables might include interest rates on assets of different maturities, prices of similar commodities in different countries (if purchasing power parity holds in the long run), disposable income and consumption, government spending and tax revenues, wages and prices, the money supply and the price level, or spot and future prices of a commodity. There is no reason to restrict attention to pairs of variables, of course, although it is often easiest to do so. There may well be groups of three, four, or more variables that can be expected to be linked by some long-run equilibrium relationship.

Most of the variables mentioned in the previous paragraph are $I(1)$, or at least they appear to be when some (but not necessarily all) unit root tests are employed. We know that variables which are $I(1)$ tend to diverge as $n \to \infty$, because their unconditional variances are proportional to n. Thus it might seem that such variables could never be expected to obey any sort of long-run equilibrium relationship. But in fact it is possible for two or more variables to be $I(1)$ and yet for certain linear combinations of those variables to be $I(0)$. If that is the case, the variables are said to be **cointegrated**. If two or more variables are cointegrated, they must obey an equilibrium relationship in the long run, although they may diverge substantially from equilibrium in the short run. The concept of cointegration is fundamental to the understanding of long-run relationships among economic time series. It is also quite recent. The earliest reference is probably Granger (1981), the best-known paper is Engle and Granger (1987), and two relatively accessible articles are Hendry (1986) and Stock and Watson (1988a).

Suppose, to keep matters simple, that we are concerned with just two variables, y_{t1} and y_{t2}, each of which is known to be $I(1)$. Then, in the simplest case, y_{t1} and y_{t2} would be cointegrated if there exists a vector $\boldsymbol{\eta} \equiv [1 \quad -\eta_2]^\top$ such that, when the two variables are in equilibrium,

$$[\boldsymbol{y}_1 \quad \boldsymbol{y}_2]\boldsymbol{\eta} \equiv \boldsymbol{y}_1 - \eta_2 \boldsymbol{y}_2 = 0. \tag{20.20}$$

Here $\boldsymbol{y}_1$ and $\boldsymbol{y}_2$ denote n–vectors with typical elements y_{t1} and y_{t2}, respectively. The 2–vector $\boldsymbol{\eta}$ is called a **cointegrating vector**. It is clearly not unique, since it could be multiplied by any nonzero scalar without affecting the equality in (20.20).

Realistically, one might well expect y_{t1} and y_{t2} to be changing systematically as well as stochastically over time. Thus one might expect (20.20) to contain a constant term and perhaps one or more trend terms as well. If we write $\boldsymbol{Y} = [\boldsymbol{y}_1 \quad \boldsymbol{y}_2]$, (20.20) can be rewritten to allow for this possibility as

$$\boldsymbol{Y}\boldsymbol{\eta} = \boldsymbol{X}\boldsymbol{\beta}, \tag{20.21}$$

where, as in (20.14), $\boldsymbol{X}$ denotes a nonstochastic matrix that may or may not have any elements. If it does, the first column will be a constant, the second, if it exists, will be a linear time trend, the third, if it exists, will be a quadratic time trend, and so on. Since $\boldsymbol{Y}$ could contain more than two variables, (20.21) is actually a very general way of writing a cointegrating relationship among any number of variables.

At any particular time t, of course, an equality like (20.20) or (20.21) cannot be expected to hold exactly. We may therefore define the **equilibrium error** ν_t as

$$\nu_t = \boldsymbol{Y}_t\boldsymbol{\eta} - \boldsymbol{X}_t\boldsymbol{\beta}, \tag{20.22}$$

where $\boldsymbol{Y}_t$ and $\boldsymbol{X}_t$ denote the tth rows of $\boldsymbol{Y}$ and $\boldsymbol{X}$, respectively. In the special case of (20.20), this equilibrium error would simply be $y_{t1} - \eta_2 y_{t2}$. The m variables y_{t1} through y_{tm} are said to be cointegrated if there exists a vector $\boldsymbol{\eta}$ such that ν_t in (20.22) is $I(0)$.

This is, at first sight, quite a remarkable property for ν_t to have. Thus it may not be immediately obvious that we can actually generate variables which are $I(1)$ but cointegrated. An example may therefore be in order. Consider the following bivariate model:

$$\begin{aligned} \lambda_1 y_{t1} - y_{t2} &= u_{t1}, \quad (1 - \rho_1 L)u_{t1} = \varepsilon_{t1}, \\ y_{t1} - \lambda_2 y_{t2} &= u_{t2}, \quad (1 - \rho_2 L)u_{t2} = \varepsilon_{t2}, \end{aligned} \tag{20.23}$$

where y_{t1} and y_{t2} are random variables and λ_1 and λ_2 are parameters, and

$$\begin{bmatrix} \varepsilon_{t1} \\ \varepsilon_{t2} \end{bmatrix} \sim N(\mathbf{0}, \boldsymbol{\Omega}).$$

When both ρ_1 and ρ_2 are less than 1 in absolute value, both y_1 and y_2 will obviously be $I(0)$. When both ρ_1 and ρ_2 are equal to 1, both y_1 and y_2 will be $I(1)$, and they will not be cointegrated. However, when one of the ρ_i's is less than 1 and the other is equal to 1, both variables will be $I(1)$, but they will be cointegrated. For example, suppose that $\rho_2 < 1$ and $\rho_1 = 1$. Then the cointegrating vector would be $[1 \quad -\lambda_2]$, and the equilibrium error would be

$$u_{t2} = y_{t1} - \lambda_2 y_{t2} = \varepsilon_{t2} + \rho_2 u_{t-1,2}.$$

As long as $\rho_2 < 1$, this equilibrium error will be stationary, and y_1 and y_2 will be cointegrated.

The concept of cointegration brings with it two obvious econometric questions. The first is how to estimate the cointegrating vector $\boldsymbol{\eta}$, and the second is how to test whether two or more variables are in fact cointegrated. These questions are of course closely related; the answer to the second depends on the answer to the first. The first will be discussed now, and the second will be the topic of the next section.

The easiest way to estimate a cointegrating vector is to rewrite (20.22) as a regression and then to use OLS. This approach is associated with Engle and Granger (1987). Thus, if the coefficient on $\boldsymbol{y}_1$ were arbitrarily normalized to unity, we could run the regression

$$\boldsymbol{y}_1 = \boldsymbol{X\beta} + \boldsymbol{Y}^* \boldsymbol{\eta}^* + \boldsymbol{\nu}, \tag{20.24}$$

where $\boldsymbol{Y}^*$ is an $n \times (m-1)$ matrix with columns $\boldsymbol{y}_2$ through $\boldsymbol{y}_m$, and the parameter vector $\boldsymbol{\eta}^*$ is equal to minus the $m-1$ free elements of the parameter vector $\boldsymbol{\eta}$ that appears in (20.22).

There are apparently two serious problems with running a regression like (20.24). The first problem is that if the y_{it}'s are cointegrated, they are surely determined jointly, which implies that the error term will almost certainly not be independent of the regressors. In the case of (20.23), with $\rho_1 = 1$ and $\rho_2 < 1$, for example, the relationship between y_{t1} and y_{t2} is

$$y_{t1} = \lambda_2 y_{t2} + \rho_2 (y_{t-1,1} - \lambda_2 y_{t-1,2}) + \varepsilon_{t2}. \tag{20.25}$$

Thus, if we regress y_{t1} on y_{t2}, the error term is implicitly

$$\rho_2(y_{t-1,1} - \lambda_2 y_{t-1,2}) + \varepsilon_{t2}, \tag{20.26}$$

and both terms here are correlated with y_{t2}. The second problem is that, in a regression like (20.24) we are regressing a variable which is $I(1)$ on one or more other $I(1)$ variables. This seems like a most undesirable thing to do, since it is a situation in which spurious regressions are very likely to arise (see Section 19.2).

Despite these apparent problems, when y_{t1} through y_{tm} are in fact cointegrated, the OLS estimates from regression (20.24) will be consistent. Indeed, they will be **super-consistent**; instead of approaching their true values at a rate proportional to $n^{-1/2}$, the OLS estimates will approach them at a rate proportional to n^{-1}. The first apparent problem does not matter asymptotically because y_{t2} is $I(1)$ and the two components of the error term in (20.26) are $I(0)$ (the first component is $I(0)$ only if y_{t1} and y_{t2} are in fact cointegrated). Thus terms that involve the error term will be asymptotically negligible relative to terms that involve y_{t2}. The second apparent problem does not arise asymptotically for a similar reason, namely, that the (true) cointegrating relationship among the y_{ti}'s creates terms that dominate any terms which might ordinarily cause spurious regressions. Another consequence of this is that the R^2 from (20.24) will tend to unity as $n \to \infty$.

To see why we obtain super-consistent estimates from regression (20.24), consider the simplest case, in which $m = 2$ and $\boldsymbol{X}$ is a null matrix. In this case, the OLS estimate of η_2, the single element of $\boldsymbol{\eta}^*$, will be

$$\hat{\eta}_2 = \frac{\sum_{t=1}^{n} y_{t1} y_{t2}}{\sum_{t=1}^{n} y_{t2}^2}.$$

If the two series really are cointegrated, we can write

$$y_{t1} = \eta_2 y_{t2} + \nu_t,$$

where the ν_t's follow some sort of stationary process. Hence

$$\hat{\eta}_2 = \eta_2 + \frac{\sum_{t=1}^{n} \nu_t y_{t2}}{\sum_{t=1}^{n} y_{t2}^2}. \tag{20.27}$$

Since y_{t2} is $I(1)$, we can write it as

$$y_{t2} = S_{t2} + v_{t2},$$

where S_{t2} is a partial sum process and v_{t2} is an error term, which would be i.i.d. if y_{t2} were a random walk but will, in general, be serially correlated. Hence the second term in (20.27) is

$$\frac{\sum_{t=1}^{n} (\nu_t v_{t2} + \nu_t S_{t2})}{\sum_{t=1}^{n} (S_{t2}^2 + 2S_{t2}v_{t2} + v_{t2}^2)}. \tag{20.28}$$

Both terms in the numerator can be shown, by arguments similar to those used in Section 20.2, to be $O(n)$. The highest-order term in the denominator is the first one, which can be shown to be $O(n^2)$. Thus the ratio (20.28) is $O(n)/O(n^2) = O(n^{-1})$. This allows us to conclude that $\hat{\eta}_2$ approaches the true value η_2 at a rate proportional to n^{-1}.

This result is very important, and it generalizes to the case in which $\boldsymbol{\eta}$ is an m–vector; see Stock (1987). There are m different ways to run a regression like (20.24), one for each of the $\boldsymbol{y}_i$'s. These will yield m different estimated cointegrating vectors, all of them super-consistent. Since regressions involving stationary series always yield estimates that are root-n consistent, we can substitute $\hat{\boldsymbol{\eta}}$ for $\boldsymbol{\eta}$ in such regressions without affecting their asymptotic properties. Because the discrepancies between $\boldsymbol{\eta}$ and $\hat{\boldsymbol{\eta}}$ will be $O(n^{-1})$, they will be asymptotically negligible relative to the estimation errors in such regressions.

Unfortunately, the fact that $\hat{\boldsymbol{\eta}}$ is super-consistent does *not* imply that it always has good properties in finite samples. Part of the problem is that, because expression (20.28) does not have mean zero, $\hat{\boldsymbol{\eta}}$ will, in general, be biased. This bias can be quite large in practice; see Banerjee, Dolado, Hendry, and Smith (1986) and Stock (1987). One source of bias is evident from (20.25). This equation includes the term $\rho_2(y_{t-1,1} - \lambda_2 y_{t-1,2})$, which we ignore when we simply regress y_{t1} on y_{t2}. The omitted term looks like an error-correction term. Since the omitted term is $I(0)$ and y_{t2} is $I(1)$, leaving it out does not matter asymptotically. But, especially if ρ_2 is large, there may be substantial finite-sample correlation between $y_{t-1,1} - \lambda y_{t-1,2}$ and y_{t1}. This can cause finite-sample bias and loss of efficiency.

Ways to obtain better estimates of $\boldsymbol{\eta}$ have been suggested by several authors, including Phillips and Hansen (1990) and Saikkonen (1991). The approach of the latter author is particularly elegant. He proves that asymptotically efficient estimates may be obtained by running the least squares regression

$$\boldsymbol{y}_1 = \boldsymbol{X\beta} + \boldsymbol{Y}^*\boldsymbol{\eta}^* + \sum_{j=-p}^{p} \Delta\boldsymbol{Y}^*_{-j}\boldsymbol{\gamma}_j + \boldsymbol{e}, \tag{20.29}$$

where $\Delta\boldsymbol{Y}^*_{-j}$ denotes an $n \times (m-1)$ matrix, each column of which is a vector of first differences of the corresponding column of $\boldsymbol{Y}^*$, lagged j periods, and $\boldsymbol{\gamma}_j$ denotes an $(m-1)$–vector of coefficients. Thus equation (20.29) simply adds p leads and p lags of the first differences of $\boldsymbol{Y}^*$ to regression (20.24). Doing this removes the deleterious effects that short-run dynamics in the equilibrium errors $\boldsymbol{\nu}$ have on the estimates of $\boldsymbol{\eta}$. Because the latter are not asymptotically normally distributed, the concept of efficiency that Saikkonen uses is not the standard one that we have discussed in this book, and his paper is far from elementary. Of course, his result is purely an asymptotic one. If n is not large relative to $p(m-1)$, there may be so many additional regressors in (20.29) that the finite-sample properties of the least squares estimates of $\boldsymbol{\eta}^*$ will actually be poor.

20.6 Testing for Cointegration

The most popular tests for cointegration, which are very closely related to unit root tests, were suggested by Engle and Granger (1987). The basic idea is very simple. If y_{t1} through y_{tm} are in fact cointegrated, the true equilibrium error term ν_t must be $I(0)$. If they are not cointegrated, however, ν_t must be $I(1)$. Thus one can test the null hypothesis of noncointegration against the alternative of cointegration by performing a unit root test on ν_t.

If ν_t were actually observed, the unit root test statistics would have the same asymptotic distributions as the ones discussed above. However, in almost all cases, ν_t will not be observed, because at least some elements of $\boldsymbol{\eta}$ will be unknown. It is therefore necessary to estimate $\boldsymbol{\eta}$. This could in principle be done in several ways, but the simplest approach is to apply OLS to regression (20.24). This procedure yields a vector of residuals, or estimated equilibrium errors, $\hat{\boldsymbol{\nu}}$. If the variables y_{t1} through y_{tm} are in fact not cointegrated, regression (20.24) is a spurious one, and the vector $\hat{\boldsymbol{\nu}}$ should have a unit root. Conventional unit root test statistics may be calculated using this vector of residuals. For obvious reasons, such tests are often called **residual-based cointegration tests**. Because $\hat{\boldsymbol{\nu}}$ depends on one or more estimated parameters, which under the null hypothesis are the parameters of a spurious regression, the asymptotic distributions of residual-based cointegration test statistics are *not* the same as those of ordinary unit root test statistics.

The model (20.23) may provide some useful insights. Since it is the value of ρ_2 (or possibly the value of ρ_1) that determines whether the two series are cointegrated in that model, it should not be surprising that tests of the null hypothesis of noncointegration should look like tests of the null hypothesis that an individual series has a unit root. It should also not be surprising that the null hypothesis is that the two series are *not* cointegrated, since, conditional on $\rho_1 = 1$, they will be cointegrated unless ρ_2 happens to equal 1.

Residual-based cointegration tests may be adapted from any of the unit root tests discussed above, provided the right critical values are used. The simplest procedure, sometimes called the **Engle-Granger test**, or the **EG test**, involves first estimating the cointegrating regression (20.24) and then using an ordinary Dickey-Fuller τ test, based on the regression

$$\Delta\hat{\nu}_t = (\alpha - 1)\hat{\nu}_{t-1} + e_t. \tag{20.30}$$

Since serial correlation is very often a problem, it is more common to use an **augmented Engle-Granger test**, or **AEG test**, which is related to the EG test in exactly the same way as the ADF τ' test is related to the ordinary DF τ test. Thus the AEG test is just the t statistic on $\alpha - 1$ in a regression like (20.30) but with enough lags of $\Delta\hat{\nu}_t$ included as additional regressors to eliminate any evidence of serial correlation. Nonparametric z^* and τ^* tests may also be used, as Phillips and Ouliaris (1990) suggested. These are computed in almost exactly the same way as they were in expressions (20.17) and (20.19):

The residuals from regression (20.30) are used to compute $\hat{\sigma}^2$ and $\hat{\omega}^2$, and the quantity $\hat{\boldsymbol{\nu}}^\top\hat{\boldsymbol{\nu}}$ replaces the quantity $\boldsymbol{y}^\top\boldsymbol{M}_X\boldsymbol{y}$.

Critical values for all these tests depend on the number of $I(1)$ variables on the right-hand side of the cointegrating regression (20.24) and on the nature of the nonstochastic regressors in that regression. Some relatively inaccurate critical values were published by Engle and Granger (1987), Engle and Yoo (1987), and Phillips and Ouliaris (1990). Table 20.2 contains reasonably accurate asymptotic critical values (the last digit is unlikely to be wrong by more than one unit) for the statistics τ_c, τ_{ct}, τ_{ctt}, z_c, z_{ct}, and z_{ctt}, for various values of m, obtained by methods similar to those used in MacKinnon (1991). Critical values for the τ_{nc} and z_{nc} statistics are not included in the table, because it almost never makes sense to use them in practice. Recall that m is the number of endogenous variables; $m-1$ is therefore the number of elements of the cointegrating vector which have to be estimated. If some elements are known a priori, one must use the critical values for a smaller value of m. In the extreme case in which all elements of the cointegrating vector are known, one would use the critical values for unit root tests of Table 20.1.

Because the cointegrating regression includes the columns of $\boldsymbol{X}$ among the regressors, it is not necessary to include $\boldsymbol{X}$ in the test regression (20.30). The FWL Theorem does not quite apply here, because the fact that one observation has been dropped at the beginning means that the vector $\hat{\boldsymbol{\nu}}_{-1}$ will not be quite orthogonal to the columns of $\boldsymbol{X}$. However, $\hat{\boldsymbol{\nu}}_{-1}$ will be orthogonal to $\boldsymbol{X}$ asymptotically. Thus it makes no difference, asymptotically, whether $\boldsymbol{X}$ is included in the test regression or not.

The OLS estimates of $\boldsymbol{\eta}$ depend on which one of the $\boldsymbol{y}_i$'s is treated as the regressand. Changing the regressand will, in finite samples, change the residual vector $\hat{\boldsymbol{\nu}}$ and hence change the calculated values of any cointegration test statistics based on that vector. This is rather unfortunate, because there are already a great many possible test statistics. Thus, for cointegration tests even more than for unit root tests, there are likely to be plenty of opportunities for different tests to yield conflicting inferences.

All the problems that afflict ordinary unit root tests also afflict the residual-based cointegration tests that we have discussed. One problem is that asymptotic critical values may be seriously misleading in finite samples. Unfortunately, finite-sample critical values depend on the specific features of the DGP, such as the nature of any heteroskedasticity or serial correlation that may be present, which are generally unknown in practice. Another problem, originally discussed in Section 20.4, is that cointegration tests are often severely lacking in power when they are used with seasonally adjusted data or when the process generating any one of the series has changed over time. Thus failure to reject the null hypothesis of noncointegration may provide only very weak evidence that two or more series are in fact not cointegrated.

Although tests based on the residual vector $\hat{\boldsymbol{\nu}}$ are by far the most popular ones, numerous other cointegration tests have been proposed. References

Table 20.2 Asymptotic Critical Values for Cointegration Tests

Test Statistic	1%	2.5%	5%	10%	97.5%
$m = 2$					
τ_c	−3.90	−3.59	−3.34	−3.04	−0.30
τ_{ct}	−4.32	−4.03	−3.78	−3.50	−1.03
τ_{ctt}	−4.69	−4.40	−4.15	−3.87	−1.52
z_c	−28.3	−23.9	−20.6	−17.1	−0.7
z_{ct}	−35.8	−31.1	−27.3	−23.4	−3.2
z_{ctt}	−42.6	−37.5	−33.4	−29.1	−5.8
$m = 3$					
τ_c	−4.29	−4.00	−3.74	−3.45	−0.85
τ_{ct}	−4.66	−4.37	−4.12	−3.84	−1.39
τ_{ctt}	−4.99	−4.70	−4.45	−4.17	−1.81
z_c	−35.2	−30.4	−26.7	−22.7	−2.4
z_{ct}	−42.0	−36.9	−32.8	−28.5	−5.0
z_{ctt}	−48.5	−43.0	−38.7	−34.0	−7.6
$m = 4$					
τ_c	−4.64	−4.35	−4.10	−3.81	−1.30
τ_{ct}	−4.97	−4.68	−4.43	−4.15	−1.73
τ_{ctt}	−5.27	−4.98	−4.73	−4.45	−2.09
z_c	−41.6	−36.5	−32.4	−28.1	−4.5
z_{ct}	−48.1	−42.6	−38.2	−33.5	−7.0
z_{ctt}	−54.3	−48.5	−43.9	−38.9	−9.8
$m = 5$					
τ_c	−4.96	−4.66	−4.42	−4.13	−1.68
τ_{ct}	−5.25	−4.96	−4.72	−4.43	−2.04
τ_{ctt}	−5.53	−5.24	−4.99	−4.72	−2.36
z_c	−47.8	−42.3	−38.0	−33.3	−6.7
z_{ct}	−54.0	−48.2	−43.5	−38.5	−9.3
z_{ctt}	−60.0	−53.9	−49.0	−43.7	−12.1
$m = 6$					
τ_c	−5.25	−4.96	−4.71	−4.42	−2.01
τ_{ct}	−5.52	−5.23	−4.98	−4.70	−2.32
τ_{ctt}	−5.77	−5.49	−5.24	−4.96	−2.61
z_c	−53.8	−48.0	−43.4	−38.4	−9.1
z_{ct}	−59.7	−53.7	−48.8	−43.5	−11.8
z_{ctt}	−65.5	−59.2	−54.1	−48.6	−14.6

include Stock and Watson (1988b), Phillips and Ouliaris (1990), Johansen (1988, 1991), and Johansen and Juselius (1990, 1992). Johansen's approach will be discussed in Section 20.8. Campbell and Perron (1991) provide an overview of several of these tests, which are all a good deal harder to compute than the residual-based ones we have discussed. In addition, every test statistic seems to require a different set of critical values.

20.7 Model-Building with Cointegrated Variables

Many economic time series are, or at any rate appear to be, integrated of order one. From the results of Section 19.2 on spurious regressions, and the results of this chapter, it is clear that regressing the levels of a series which is $I(1)$ on the levels of one or more other series which are also $I(1)$ is generally not a good thing to do. At worst, we may "discover" an entirely spurious relationship. At best, we may consistently estimate the elements of some cointegrating vector, but standard asymptotic theory will not apply to our estimates, and we may therefore be led to make incorrect inferences about the parameters we have estimated. The study of ways to specify and estimate models for $I(1)$ variables is an active and somewhat controversial area of research. Much of the more theoretical material, such as Park and Phillips (1988, 1989) and Phillips (1991a), is technically too demanding to be treated in this book. In this section, we will therefore content ourselves with discussing some simple special cases and some relatively simple results. We will discuss the estimation of vector autoregressions involving cointegrated variables in the next section.

The classical approach to dealing with integrated variables, especially in the time-series literature, has been to difference them as many times as needed to make them stationary. This approach has the merit of simplicity. Once all series have been transformed to stationarity, dynamic regression models may be specified in the usual way, and standard asymptotic results apply. The problem with this approach is that differencing eliminates the opportunity to estimate any relationships between the *levels* of the dependent and independent variables. But cointegration implies that such relationships exist, and, as the examples at the beginning of Section 20.5 suggest, they are often of considerable economic interest. Thus simply using differenced data is often not an appropriate strategy.

A second approach is to estimate some sort of error-correction model, or ECM. We discussed these models in Section 19.4, under the assumption that all the variables were stationary. Error-correction models are still appropriate when that assumption no longer holds. In fact, they are particularly attractive when the dependent variable is $I(1)$. However, one must exercise some care when trying to estimate or draw inferences from such models.

A simple but widely applicable single-equation ECM, similar to equation (19.30), can be written as

$$\Delta y_t = \boldsymbol{z}_t\boldsymbol{\alpha} + \beta(y_{t-1} - \lambda x_{t-1}) + \gamma\Delta x_t + u_t, \quad u_t \sim \mathrm{IID}(0, \sigma^2). \qquad (20.31)$$

The dependent variable here is y_t, and the principal independent variable is x_t. These two variables are assumed to be $I(1)$ and cointegrated, which implies that the error-correction term $\beta(y_{t-1} - \lambda x_{t-1})$ is $I(0)$. The row vector $\boldsymbol{z}_t$ includes a constant term and any other independent variables, all of which are assumed to be either nonstochastic or $I(0)$. If (20.31) does not allow sufficiently rich dynamics, it can easily be extended by including more lags of Δx_t and increasing the lag on the error-correcting term.

If λ were known, there would clearly be no problem estimating (20.31) by least squares. The regressand and all the regressors would be either nonstochastic or $I(0)$. Thus the estimates of $\boldsymbol{\alpha}$, β, and γ would be root-n consistent and asymptotically normal, and their covariance matrix could be estimated in the usual way. But in most cases λ will not be known. There are then several ways to proceed. The simplest is the **Engle-Granger two-step method** proposed by Engle and Granger (1987). The first step is to regress y_t on x_t, including a constant term and possibly a trend if the latter appears in $\boldsymbol{z}_t$. As we have seen, this will yield a super-consistent estimate of λ, say $\tilde{\lambda}$. The second step is to replace λ by $\tilde{\lambda}$ in (20.31) and then estimate that equation using OLS. Because of the super-consistency of $\tilde{\lambda}$, Engle and Granger are able to show that the resulting estimates of the other parameters are asymptotically the same as they would be if λ were known.

The principal merit of the Engle-Granger two-step procedure is simplicity. However, there is a good deal of Monte Carlo evidence that it often does not work very well in finite samples; see Banerjee, Dolado, Hendry, and Smith (1986) and Banerjee, Dolado, Galbraith, and Hendry (1993). The problem is that $\tilde{\lambda}$ often seems to be severely biased. This bias then causes the other parameter estimates to be biased as well. The problem appears to be least severe when the R^2 of the cointegrating regression is close to 1, as it must be when the sample size is sufficiently large. Thus a relatively low value of the R^2 from the cointegrating regression should be taken as a warning that the two-step procedure may not work well.

The simplest alternative to the Engle-Granger two-step procedure is to estimate a model like

$$\Delta y_t = \boldsymbol{z}_t\boldsymbol{\alpha} + \beta y_{t-1} + \delta x_{t-1} + \gamma \Delta x_t + u_t, \tag{20.32}$$

in which the new parameter δ is implicitly equal to $-\beta\lambda$. This regression looks rather odd, since the regressand is $I(0)$ and two of the regressors are $I(1)$. One might therefore expect that standard asymptotic distribution theory would not apply to some or all of the parameter estimates. The asymptotic distribution theory for this equation is indeed nonstandard, but the practical problems turn out to be much less severe than one might expect.

The key results for regressions like (20.32) were proved by Sims, Stock, and Watson (1990). They considered the asymptotic distributions of the individual coefficients in a linear regression involving $I(1)$ variables. They showed that if a parameter θ can be written as the coefficient of an $I(0)$ variable with zero mean, then $n^{1/2}(\hat{\theta} - \theta_0)$ will be asymptotically normally distributed, with the usual asymptotic standard error. Now consider (20.32) again. In that equation, γ is written as the coefficient of an $I(0)$ variable. Provided that $\boldsymbol{z}_t$ includes a constant term, the zero-mean requirement can easily be met. Moreover, as is clear from (20.31), β can be written as the coefficient of $y_{t-1} - \lambda x_{t-1}$, which is $I(0)$ because x and y are cointegrated. By renormalizing the cointegrating regression so that x_{t-1} has a coefficient of unity, we see that δ can also be written as the coefficient of a variable which is $I(0)$. Thus standard asymptotic distribution theory applies to all the economically interesting coefficients in (20.32).

Although one can make inferences about *individual* coefficients in equation (20.32) in the usual way, one must be careful if one tries to do anything else. For example, a joint test statistic for β and δ to be zero, or to have any other particular values, would *not* have the usual χ^2 distribution asymptotically. As another example, one might well choose to compute $\tilde{\lambda}$ as $-\tilde{\delta}/\tilde{\beta}$, where $\tilde{\beta}$ and $\tilde{\delta}$ denote least squares estimates. Since λ cannot be written as the coefficient of a mean-zero $I(0)$ variable, standard asymptotic distribution theory would not apply to it.

Estimating equation (20.31) directly by nonlinear least squares is equivalent to estimating equation (20.32) by OLS. The fits of both equations will be the same, as will be the estimates of parameters that appear in both. The results of Banerjee, Dolado, Hendry, and Smith (1986) suggest that these estimates will be better than those obtained by the Engle-Granger two-step procedure, but this conclusion has been disputed by Engle and Yoo (1987, 1991). It would seem that the relative merits of these two estimation procedures may depend heavily on the details of the DGP.

The estimation techniques that have been discussed in this section are all single-equation ones, and they are not in general efficient. Although the two-step procedure is always super-consistent for λ, it is not asymptotically efficient. At the end of Section 20.5, we discussed Saikkonen's procedure for estimating a cointegrating vector η efficiently. Another approach was proposed by Engle and Yoo (1991). It involves a three-step estimation procedure that starts from the Engle-Granger two-step estimates and uses an artificial regression to implement a single Gauss-Newton step. Other authors, including Johansen (1988, 1991) and Phillips (1991a), have proposed various full-system estimation methods. The approach of Johansen will be discussed in the next section.

There has been a good deal of empirical work involving cointegration tests and the estimation of models for cointegrated variables. Examples include Hall (1986), Baillie and Selover (1987), Campbell (1987), Campbell and Shiller (1987), Corbae and Ouliaris (1988), Granger and Lee (1989), Kunst and Neusser (1990), Johnson (1990), and King, Plosser, Stock, and Watson (1991). One interesting extension is to the case of seasonal time series processes; see Hylleberg, Engle, Granger, and Yoo (1990).

20.8 Vector Autoregressions and Cointegration

One of the most interesting approaches to the full-system estimation of models involving cointegrated variables was developed in Johansen (1988, 1991) and Johansen and Juselius (1990, 1992). It is based on the estimation of a **vector autoregression**, or **VAR**, by maximum likelihood; see Section 19.5 for more on VARs. In this section, we briefly discuss this approach.

Consider the following VAR in the levels of a set of variables:

$$\boldsymbol{Y}_t = \boldsymbol{Y}_{t-1}\boldsymbol{\Pi}_1 + \cdots + \boldsymbol{Y}_{t-p}\boldsymbol{\Pi}_p + \boldsymbol{U}_t. \tag{20.33}$$

The notation here is similar to that used in Section 19.5: $\boldsymbol{Y}_t$ and $\boldsymbol{U}_t$ are $1 \times m$ row vectors, and $\boldsymbol{\Pi}_1$ through $\boldsymbol{\Pi}_p$ are $m \times m$ matrices of coefficients. For simplicity, there are no constant terms, although this assumption is rarely realistic. The VAR (20.33) can be reparametrized as

$$\Delta\boldsymbol{Y}_t = \Delta\boldsymbol{Y}_{t-1}\boldsymbol{\Gamma}_1 + \cdots + \Delta\boldsymbol{Y}_{t-p+1}\boldsymbol{\Gamma}_{p-1} - \boldsymbol{Y}_{t-p}\boldsymbol{\Pi} + \boldsymbol{U}_t, \tag{20.34}$$

where $\boldsymbol{\Gamma}_1 = \boldsymbol{\Pi}_1 - \mathbf{I}$, $\boldsymbol{\Gamma}_2 = \boldsymbol{\Pi}_2 + \boldsymbol{\Gamma}_1$, $\boldsymbol{\Gamma}_3 = \boldsymbol{\Pi}_3 + \boldsymbol{\Gamma}_2$, and so on. Thus the matrix $\boldsymbol{\Pi}$ is related to the $\boldsymbol{\Pi}_i$'s of (20.33) by

$$\boldsymbol{\Pi} = \mathbf{I} - \boldsymbol{\Pi}_1 - \cdots - \boldsymbol{\Pi}_p.$$

By stacking the n observations in (20.34), we can write the full system as

$$\Delta\boldsymbol{Y} = \Delta\boldsymbol{Y}_{-1}\boldsymbol{\Gamma}_1 + \cdots + \Delta\boldsymbol{Y}_{-(p-1)}\boldsymbol{\Gamma}_{p-1} - \boldsymbol{Y}_{-p}\boldsymbol{\Pi} + \boldsymbol{U}, \tag{20.35}$$

in obvious notation. Each term in (20.35) is an $n \times m$ matrix.

The matrix $\boldsymbol{\Pi}$, which is sometimes called the **impact matrix**, determines whether or not, and to what extent, the system (20.35) is cointegrated. If we assume as usual that the differenced variables $\Delta\boldsymbol{Y}$ are stationary, then every term in (20.34) except $\boldsymbol{Y}_{t-p}\boldsymbol{\Pi}$ is an element of a stationary process. This implies that $\boldsymbol{Y\Pi}$ must itself be stationary. Trivially, $\boldsymbol{Y\Pi}$ will be stationary if $\boldsymbol{\Pi}$ is a matrix of zeros. That is what it must be when none of the series is cointegrated with any of the others. At the other extreme, if the matrix $\boldsymbol{\Pi}$ has full rank m, the only way for $\boldsymbol{Y\Pi}$ to be stationary is for $\boldsymbol{Y}$ to be stationary, which means that each of its columns is stationary. These columns are the different series, $\boldsymbol{y}_i$, $i = 1, \ldots, m$, that make up the system (20.33).

In between these two extremes, if all the variables in $\boldsymbol{Y}$ are nonstationary, (20.34) implies that there must be cointegration, and any vector in the range of $\boldsymbol{\Pi}$ must be a cointegrating vector. Suppose that $\boldsymbol{\Pi}$ has rank r, with $0 < r < m$. If that is the case, we can write $\boldsymbol{\Pi}$ as

$$\boldsymbol{\Pi} = -\boldsymbol{\eta}\boldsymbol{\alpha}^{\top}, \tag{20.36}$$

where $\boldsymbol{\alpha}$ and $\boldsymbol{\eta}$ are $m \times r$ matrices, and the minus sign is introduced here for later convenience. From (20.36), we see that $\boldsymbol{Y}_{-p}\boldsymbol{\Pi} = -\boldsymbol{Y}_{-p}\boldsymbol{\eta}\boldsymbol{\alpha}^\top$. The cointegrating vectors are proportional to the columns of the matrix $\boldsymbol{\eta}$. Thus, for each column, say $\boldsymbol{\eta}_i$, $\boldsymbol{Y}\boldsymbol{\eta}_i$ is a stationary random variable. When $r = 1$, there is a single cointegrating vector, which is proportional to $\boldsymbol{\eta}_1$. When $r = 2$, there is a two-dimensional space of cointegrating vectors, spanned by $\boldsymbol{\eta}_1$ and $\boldsymbol{\eta}_2$, and so on. The two extreme cases are those in which $r = 0$, when there are no cointegrating vectors at all, and $r = m$, when any linear combination of the $\boldsymbol{y}_i$'s will be stationary, because each $\boldsymbol{y}_i$ will be $I(0)$.

The approach of Johansen (1988, 1991) is to estimate the VAR (20.34) subject to the constraint (20.36) for various values of r, using maximum likelihood. This estimation is based on the assumption that the error vector $\boldsymbol{U}_t$ is multivariate normal for each t and independent across observations. This assumption is not as restrictive as it may seem, since if there are enough lagged differences of $\boldsymbol{Y}$ included in (20.34), they should remove any evidence of serial correlation in the residuals. It is possible to maximize the loglikelihood function analytically conditional on any value of r, as Johansen showed, by a method very similar to that used in Section 18.5 for obtaining LIML estimates.

The system (20.35) with the constraint (20.36) imposed can be written as

$$\Delta\boldsymbol{Y} = \Delta\boldsymbol{Y}_{-1}\boldsymbol{\Gamma}_1 + \cdots + \Delta\boldsymbol{Y}_{-(p-1)}\boldsymbol{\Gamma}_{p-1} + \boldsymbol{Y}_{-p}\boldsymbol{\eta}\boldsymbol{\alpha}^\top + \boldsymbol{U}. \tag{20.37}$$

We know (recall the concentrated loglikelihood function (9.65)) that the ML estimates of the parameters of this system are obtained by minimizing the determinant of the matrix of squares and cross-products of the residuals, that is

$$\Big|(\Delta\boldsymbol{Y} - \Delta\boldsymbol{Y}_{-1}\boldsymbol{\Gamma}_1 - \cdots - \Delta\boldsymbol{Y}_{-(p-1)}\boldsymbol{\Gamma}_{p-1} - \boldsymbol{Y}_{-p}\boldsymbol{\eta}\boldsymbol{\alpha}^\top)^\top$$
$$(\Delta\boldsymbol{Y} - \Delta\boldsymbol{Y}_{-1}\boldsymbol{\Gamma}_1 - \cdots - \Delta\boldsymbol{Y}_{-(p-1)}\boldsymbol{\Gamma}_{p-1} - \boldsymbol{Y}_{-p}\boldsymbol{\eta}\boldsymbol{\alpha}^\top)\Big|.$$

It can be seen from this expression that not all of the elements of $\boldsymbol{\eta}$ and $\boldsymbol{\alpha}$ can be identified, since the factorization (20.36) is not unique for a given $\boldsymbol{\Pi}$. In fact, if $\boldsymbol{B}$ is any nonsingular $r \times r$ matrix,

$$\boldsymbol{\eta}\boldsymbol{B}\boldsymbol{B}^{-1}\boldsymbol{\alpha} = \boldsymbol{\eta}\boldsymbol{\alpha}.$$

Thus $\boldsymbol{\eta}$ can be constructed by taking any r linearly independent m-vectors in the r-dimensional space $\mathcal{S}(\boldsymbol{\Pi})$. Once a specific choice has been made for the matrix $\boldsymbol{\eta}$, $\boldsymbol{\alpha}$ is subsequently uniquely determined. This fact allows us to circumvent the apparent problem that the regression functions in (20.37) depend nonlinearly on the parameters.

We may concentrate out the parameters contained in the matrices $\boldsymbol{\Gamma}_1$ through $\boldsymbol{\Gamma}_{p-1}$ by replacing them by least squares estimates. Thus, if we let $\boldsymbol{M}_\Delta$ denote the orthogonal projection onto $\mathcal{S}^\perp(\Delta\boldsymbol{Y}_{-1} \cdots \Delta\boldsymbol{Y}_{-(p-1)})$, the determinant to be minimized can be expressed as a function of $\boldsymbol{\eta}$ and $\boldsymbol{\alpha}$ alone, as follows:

$$\left|(\Delta \boldsymbol{Y} - \boldsymbol{Y}_{-p}\boldsymbol{\eta}\boldsymbol{\alpha}^{\top})^{\top}\boldsymbol{M}_{\Delta}(\Delta \boldsymbol{Y} - \boldsymbol{Y}_{-p}\boldsymbol{\eta}\boldsymbol{\alpha}^{\top})\right|. \tag{20.38}$$

Let us write $\boldsymbol{Y}_{-p}^{*}$ for $\boldsymbol{M}_{\Delta}\boldsymbol{Y}_{-p}$ and $\Delta\boldsymbol{Y}^{*}$ for $\boldsymbol{M}_{\Delta}\Delta\boldsymbol{Y}$. Then (20.38) can be expressed as

$$\left|(\Delta \boldsymbol{Y}^{*} - \boldsymbol{Y}_{-p}^{*}\boldsymbol{\eta}\boldsymbol{\alpha}^{\top})^{\top}(\Delta \boldsymbol{Y}^{*} - \boldsymbol{Y}_{-p}^{*}\boldsymbol{\eta}\boldsymbol{\alpha}^{\top})\right|. \tag{20.39}$$

It is now easy to concentrate this expression with respect to $\boldsymbol{\alpha}$, for, if we hold $\boldsymbol{\eta}$ fixed, the residuals in (20.39) depend linearly on $\boldsymbol{\alpha}$. If $\boldsymbol{V} \equiv \boldsymbol{Y}_{-p}^{*}\boldsymbol{\eta}$, we obtain the determinant

$$\left|(\Delta \boldsymbol{Y}^{*})^{\top}\boldsymbol{M}_{V}\Delta\boldsymbol{Y}^{*}\right|. \tag{20.40}$$

By use of the same trick we had recourse to in Section 18.5, we can treat (20.40) as one factor in the decomposition of the determinant of a larger matrix. Consider

$$\begin{vmatrix} (\Delta\boldsymbol{Y}^{*})^{\top}\Delta\boldsymbol{Y}^{*} & (\Delta\boldsymbol{Y}^{*})^{\top}\boldsymbol{V} \\ \boldsymbol{V}^{\top}\Delta\boldsymbol{Y}^{*} & \boldsymbol{V}^{\top}\boldsymbol{V} \end{vmatrix}.$$

By the result (A.26) of Appendix A, this matrix can be factorized either as

$$\left|\boldsymbol{V}^{\top}\boldsymbol{V}\right|\left|(\Delta\boldsymbol{Y}^{*})^{\top}\boldsymbol{M}_{V}\Delta\boldsymbol{Y}^{*}\right|$$

or as

$$\left|(\Delta\boldsymbol{Y}^{*})^{\top}\Delta\boldsymbol{Y}^{*}\right|\left|\boldsymbol{V}^{\top}\boldsymbol{M}^{*}\boldsymbol{V}\right|,$$

where $\boldsymbol{M}^{*}$ projects orthogonally onto $\mathcal{S}^{\perp}(\Delta\boldsymbol{Y}^{*})$. Since $\left|(\Delta\boldsymbol{Y}^{*})^{\top}\Delta\boldsymbol{Y}^{*}\right|$ does not depend on $\boldsymbol{\eta}$, we see that minimizing (20.40) is equivalent to minimizing the ratio

$$\frac{\left|\boldsymbol{V}^{\top}\boldsymbol{M}^{*}\boldsymbol{V}\right|}{\left|\boldsymbol{V}^{\top}\boldsymbol{V}\right|} = \frac{\left|\boldsymbol{\eta}^{\top}(\boldsymbol{Y}_{-p}^{*})^{\top}\boldsymbol{M}^{*}\boldsymbol{Y}_{-p}^{*}\boldsymbol{\eta}\right|}{\left|\boldsymbol{\eta}^{\top}(\boldsymbol{Y}_{-p}^{*})^{\top}\boldsymbol{Y}_{-p}^{*}\boldsymbol{\eta}\right|} \tag{20.41}$$

with respect to $\boldsymbol{\eta}$. The minimum of (20.40) is then the minimum of (20.41) times $\left|(\Delta\boldsymbol{Y}^{*})^{\top}\Delta\boldsymbol{Y}^{*}\right|$.

The least variance ratio problem that had to be solved in the LIML context (see (18.49)) involved a ratio of quadratic forms rather than the determinants that appear in (20.41). Even so, the present problem can be solved by the same technique as (18.49), namely, by converting the problem into an eigenvalue-eigenvector problem. Before we go into details, notice that (20.41) is invariant if $\boldsymbol{\eta}$ is replaced by $\boldsymbol{\eta}\boldsymbol{B}$, for any nonsingular $r \times r$ matrix $\boldsymbol{B}$. This is precisely what we noted earlier in speaking of the nonuniqueness of (20.36). We therefore cannot expect to obtain a unique minimizing $\boldsymbol{\eta}$ but only an r-dimensional subspace.

For the actual minimization, it is convenient to work with a transformation of $\boldsymbol{\eta}$. Let $\boldsymbol{S}$ denote any $m \times m$ matrix with the property that $\boldsymbol{S}^\top \boldsymbol{S} = (\boldsymbol{Y}^*_{-p})^\top \boldsymbol{Y}^*_{-p}$, and define the $m \times r$ matrix $\boldsymbol{\zeta}$ as $\boldsymbol{S}\boldsymbol{\eta}$. The ratio (20.41) becomes

$$\frac{\left|\boldsymbol{\zeta}^\top (\boldsymbol{S}^{-1})^\top (\boldsymbol{Y}^*_{-p})^\top \boldsymbol{M}^* \boldsymbol{Y}^*_{-p} \boldsymbol{S}^{-1} \boldsymbol{\zeta}\right|}{\left|\boldsymbol{\zeta}^\top \boldsymbol{\zeta}\right|}. \tag{20.42}$$

Since all that matters is the subspace spanned by the r columns of $\boldsymbol{\zeta}$, we may without loss of generality choose $\boldsymbol{\zeta}$ such that $\boldsymbol{\zeta}^\top \boldsymbol{\zeta} = \mathbf{I}_r$. Let us define the $m \times m$ positive definite matrix $\boldsymbol{A}$ to be the matrix that appears in the numerator of (20.42). Then we have to minimize $|\boldsymbol{\zeta}^\top \boldsymbol{A} \boldsymbol{\zeta}|$ with respect to $\boldsymbol{\zeta}$ subject to the constraint that $\boldsymbol{\zeta}^\top \boldsymbol{\zeta} = \mathbf{I}$.

In order to perform this minimization, it turns out to be enough to consider the eigenvalue-eigenvector problem associated with $\boldsymbol{A}$. If we solve this problem, we will obtain an orthogonal matrix $\boldsymbol{Z}$, the columns of which are orthonormalized eigenvectors of $\boldsymbol{A}$, and a diagonal matrix $\boldsymbol{\Lambda}$, the diagonal elements of which are the eigenvalues of $\boldsymbol{A}$, which must evidently lie between zero and unity. Then $\boldsymbol{A}\boldsymbol{Z} = \boldsymbol{Z}\boldsymbol{\Lambda}$. If the columns of $\boldsymbol{Z}$ and $\boldsymbol{\Lambda}$ are arranged in increasing order of the eigenvalues $\lambda_1, \ldots, \lambda_m$, we may choose the ML estimate $\hat{\boldsymbol{\zeta}}$ to be the first r columns of $\boldsymbol{Z}$. Geometrically, the columns of $\hat{\boldsymbol{\zeta}}$ span the space spanned by the eigenvectors of $\boldsymbol{A}$ that correspond to the r smallest eigenvalues. The fact that $\boldsymbol{Z}$ is orthogonal means that $\hat{\boldsymbol{\zeta}}$ satisfies the constraint, and the choice of the *smallest* eigenvalues serves to minimize the determinant $|\boldsymbol{\zeta}^\top \boldsymbol{A} \boldsymbol{\zeta}|$.

The ML estimate of the space of cointegrating vectors $\mathcal{S}(\boldsymbol{\eta})$ can now be recovered from $\hat{\boldsymbol{\zeta}}$ by the formula $\hat{\boldsymbol{\eta}} = \boldsymbol{S}^{-1}\hat{\boldsymbol{\zeta}}$. The matrix $\hat{\boldsymbol{\alpha}}$ needed in order to obtain ML estimates of the parameters contained in the matrix $\boldsymbol{\Pi}$ can then be obtained as the OLS estimates from the multivariate regression of $\Delta \boldsymbol{Y}^*$ on $\boldsymbol{Y}^*_{-p}\hat{\boldsymbol{\eta}}$. Subsequently, estimates of the matrices $\boldsymbol{\Gamma}_i$, $i = 1, \ldots, p-1$, can also be obtained by OLS.

Often, we are not especially interested in the parameters of the VAR (20.35). The focus of our interest is more likely to be testing the hypothesis of noncointegration against an alternative of cointegration of some chosen order. Should the null hypothesis that $r = 0$ be rejected, we may then wish to test the hypothesis that $r = 1$ against the alternative that $r = 2$, and so forth. The eigenvalues λ_i, $i = 1, \ldots, m$, provide a very convenient way to do this, in terms of a likelihood ratio test. It is clear that if we select some value of r, the minimized determinant $|\boldsymbol{\zeta}^\top \boldsymbol{A} \boldsymbol{\zeta}|$ is just the product of the r smallest eigenvalues, $\lambda_1 \cdots \lambda_r$. The minimum of (20.40) is this product multiplied by $|(\Delta \boldsymbol{Y}^*)^\top \Delta \boldsymbol{Y}^*|$. If $r = 0$, then the minimum of (20.40) is simply this last determinant. Likelihood ratios for different values of r are therefore just products of the eigenvalues, raised to the power $n/2$; recall (9.65). If we take logs and multiply by 2 in order to obtain an LR statistic, we obtain $-n$ times a product of logs of the eigenvalues.

Specifically, to test the null that $r = r_1$, $0 \leq r_1 < m$, against the alternative that $r = r_2$, $r_1 < r_2 \leq m$, the LR test statistic is

$$LR = -n \sum_{i=r_1+1}^{r_2} \log \lambda_i. \tag{20.43}$$

This expression is clearly analogous to the LR statistic (18.50) in the context of LIML. However, it will not have the usual asymptotic chi-squared distribution. Instead, under the various nulls that can be tested, the LR statistics (20.43) will have nonstandard asymptotic distributions that depend on the number of "degrees of freedom" $r_2 - r_1$ and on whether the VAR includes a constant or a trend term. These distributions are tabulated by simulation, for a limited number of cases, in Johansen and Juselius (1990). Conditional on a given value of r, inference about the elements of (suitably normalized) cointegrating vectors can also be performed by means of LR statistics, which will then have their standard chi-squared asymptotic distributions under the null hypotheses being tested. This is a convenient property of the VAR approach.

20.9 CONCLUSION

We have seen in this chapter that the asymptotic theory for $I(1)$ variables is very different from the ordinary asymptotic theory with which we are familiar. Because they are so different, we have not attempted to deal with the former in any depth. We have simply tried to present some of the principal results in an intuitive fashion, and to provide appropriate references. Much of the material we have discussed is quite new, because research in this area has been so active during the past ten years, and some of it is still controversial. Readers may find ample evidence of this assertion by reading Phillips (1991b, 1991c) and other articles in Pesaran (1991).

TERMS AND CONCEPTS

augmented Dickey-Fuller (ADF) tests
augmented Engle-Granger (AEG) tests
cointegrated variables
cointegrating vector
cointegration
Dickey-Fuller (DF) tests
Engle-Granger (EG) tests
Engle-Granger two-step method
equilibrium error
functional central limit theorems
impact matrix
nonparametric unit root tests
partial sum process
residual-based cointegration tests
span (of time-series data)
standardized partial sum process
standardized Wiener process
super-consistent estimator
τ, τ', and τ^* tests
unit root tests
unit roots
vector autoregression (VAR)
z and z^* tests

Chapter 21

Monte Carlo Experiments

21.1 Introduction

Most of the methods for estimation and hypothesis testing discussed in this book have statistical properties that are known only asymptotically. This is true for nonlinear models of all types, for linear simultaneous equations models, and even for the univariate linear regression model once we dispense with the strong assumption of fixed regressors or the even stronger assumption that the error terms are normally and identically distributed. Thus, in practice, exact finite-sample theory can rarely be used to interpret estimates or test statistics. Unfortunately, unless the sample size is very large indeed, it is difficult to know whether asymptotic theory is sufficiently accurate to allow us to interpret our results with confidence.

There are basically two ways to deal with this situation. One is to refine asymptotic approximations such as those we have derived in this book by adding terms of lower order in the sample size n, typically terms that are $O(n^{-1/2})$ or $O(n^{-1})$. These more refined approximations are variously referred to as **finite-sample approximations** or as **asymptotic expansions**. The asymptotic expansions approach has been most extensively employed in studying the properties of estimators of simultaneous equations models and estimators of univariate linear dynamic models. This approach can, in some cases, yield valuable insights into the behavior of estimators and test statistics. Unfortunately, it frequently involves mathematics that are either more advanced or more tedious than most applied econometricians are comfortable with. It is often applicable only to relatively simple models, and it tends to produce results that are complicated and very difficult to interpret, in part because they often depend on unknown parameters. Moreover, these results are themselves only approximations; while they are generally better than asymptotic approximations, they may not be accurate enough. Ideally, one would like to be able to use asymptotic expansions routinely, as part of econometric software packages, in order to obtain confidence intervals and hypothesis tests more accurate than the asymptotic ones discussed in this book. Unfortunately, this ideal situation appears to be a very long way off, although recent work such as Rothenberg (1988) has perhaps moved us a little closer. Two useful surveys of methods based on asymptotic expansions are Phillips (1983) and Rothenberg (1984). A somewhat critical review of the literature is Taylor (1983).

The second approach, which is the one we discuss in this chapter, is to investigate the finite-sample properties of estimators and test statistics by using **Monte Carlo experiments**. The term "Monte Carlo" is used in many disciplines to refer to procedures in which quantities of interest are approximated by generating many random realizations of some stochastic process and averaging them in some way.[1] Since this is rarely feasible without a powerful computer, the literature on **Monte Carlo methods** tends to be quite recent. The asymptotic expansions approach requires a great deal of highly skilled labor. In contrast, the Monte Carlo approach, as Summers (1965) emphasized, is relatively capital-intensive. It economizes on skilled labor by using a great deal of computer time.

In econometric applications of Monte Carlo methods, the quantities of interest are generally various aspects of the distributions of estimators and test statistics, such as the mean and mean squared error of an estimator, the size of a test statistic under the null hypothesis, or the power of a test statistic under some specified alternative hypothesis. Hendry (1984) provides a provocative survey. Most of the literature on Monte Carlo methods, however, is not specifically concerned with statistics or econometrics but rather with methods of approximating multidimensional integrals or simulating nonlinear systems. Nevertheless, general references such as Hammersley and Handscomb (1964), Rubinstein (1981), Kalos and Whitlock (1986), Ripley (1987), and Lewis and Orav (1989) contain much useful material.

Although Monte Carlo methods are often seen as an alternative to the asymptotic expansions approach, the two approaches should more properly be regarded as complementary. Just as Monte Carlo experiments can be used to check the validity of asymptotic approximations, so can they be used to check the validity of approximations based on asymptotic expansions. Moreover, there are many situations in which asymptotic expansions can be used to analyze simple special cases, while focusing attention on the issues that need to be examined for more general cases by means of Monte Carlo experiments. However, since asymptotic expansions are beyond the scope of this book, we will not provide much discussion of how they may be used in conjunction with Monte Carlo methods.

A typical paper utilizing Monte Carlo methods in statistics or econometrics presents results from several (perhaps many) related Monte Carlo experiments. Each experiment involves several things that must be specified by the experimenter. First, there must be an econometric model and a set of estimators or test statistics associated with that model. The object of the experiments is to investigate the finite-sample properties of those estimators or test statistics. Second, there must be a data-generating process (DGP),

[1] The term is reported to have originated with Metropolis and Ulam (1949). If it had been coined a little later, it might have been called the "Las Vegas method" instead of the "Monte Carlo method."

which is usually but not always a special case of the model. The DGP must be specified completely. This means that if there are exogenous variables, they or their distributions must be specified, as must the distributions of any error terms. Each experiment consists of some number of **replications**, which we will denote by N. Each replication involves generating a single set of data from the DGP and calculating the estimators or test statistics of interest. Typically, the number of replications is quite large ($N = 1000$, 2000, 5000, and 10,000 are common choices), but it may sometimes be as small as 50 if estimation is very time-consuming and accurate results are not needed. After N replications have been performed, N observations on each of the estimators or test statistics of interest will have been obtained, and this generated sample is then subjected to statistical analysis to compute estimates of the quantities of interest. The results of a Monte Carlo experiment are thus themselves estimates, and are therefore subject to experimental error. However, we can make this error acceptably small by designing the experiment carefully, using a sufficiently large number of replications, and perhaps by using **variance reduction techniques** (see Sections 21.5 and 21.6 below).

As the above discussion implies, it is rare for anyone to do a single Monte Carlo experiment. Instead, investigators usually perform a set of related experiments, in which the sample size n and other aspects of the DGP (such as parameter values) are varied, in order to see how such variations affect the estimators or test statistics of interest. If there are only a few experiments, the results are normally presented in tabular form. If there are many experiments, however, this can involve a great deal of material, which readers may find hard to assimilate. One way of dealing with this problem is to estimate a **response surface**, in which the results of each experiment are treated as a single observation, and a regression model is fitted that relates the quantities of interest to the sample size and to other aspects of the DGP that vary across the experiments. Ideally, the estimates of the response surface summarize the results of the experiments and provide a more compact and readily comprehended way of presenting results than a series of tables would. The response surface approach will be discussed in Section 21.7.

In the remainder of this chapter, we discuss some important aspects of Monte Carlo experiments in econometrics. Most Monte Carlo experiments require the availability of a great many **pseudo-random variates**, that is, numbers which appear to have been drawn from some specified probability distribution. In the next two sections, we briefly discuss how these may be generated on a computer. In Section 21.4, we discuss some other aspects of designing a set of Monte Carlo experiments. In Sections 21.5 and 21.6, we discuss variance reduction techniques, which can sometimes be used to increase the precision of results for a given expenditure of computer time. In the following section, we discuss the use of response surfaces. Finally, in Section 21.8, we briefly discuss the statistical method known as the **bootstrap**, which is closely related to Monte Carlo methods.

21.2 GENERATING PSEUDO-RANDOM NUMBERS

Every Monte Carlo experiment requires a great many "random" variates, distributed according to some prespecified distribution(s). For example, consider a small experiment dealing with a regression model that has fixed regressors. Suppose there are to be 50 observations and 1000 replications. For such an experiment, a total of 50,000 "random" variates would be needed just to generate the error terms. If there were three stochastic regressors, a further 150,000 "random" variates would be needed to generate the regressors. As we will see in the next section, if we can find a way to obtain "random" numbers uniformly distributed on the 0-1 interval, denoted $U(0,1)$, it is then usually quite easy to obtain "random" variates distributed according to any distribution we specify. The fundamental problem is to obtain the original "random" numbers. Although it is possible to acquire *genuinely* random numbers by observing physical processes such as the decay of radioactive isotopes, it would be extremely inconvenient if we had to hook our computer to a physical random number generator, or read a massive table of previously collected random numbers, every time we wished to run a Monte Carlo experiment! Thus it is evident that if Monte Carlo experiments are to be practical, we must find a way to make the computer generate "random" numbers quickly and cheaply.

The quotation marks around "random" in the previous paragraph were put there to emphasize the fact that what we need for purposes of a Monte Carlo experiment is a way of obtaining numbers which have the same statistical properties as random numbers, rather than numbers which are genuinely random. In fact, no digital computer is capable of generating genuinely random numbers, at least not if it is working correctly. But digital computers are capable of generating sequences of **pseudo-random numbers**, which are in fact purely deterministic. Programs that do so are called **pseudo-random number generators** or, more commonly but less accurately, simply **random number generators**. Pseudo-random numbers that are generated by a good random number generator are, for the purposes of Monte Carlo experiments, indistinguishable from sequences of genuinely random numbers, that is, actual sequences of independent draws from the $U(0,1)$ distribution.

There are many ways to generate pseudo-random numbers. The most common ones are variants of the **congruential generator**,

$$\eta_t = \frac{z_t}{m}, \quad z_t = (\lambda z_{t-1} + \alpha)(\text{mod } m), \tag{21.01}$$

where η_t is the tth random number generated, and z_t is a positive integer. The generator (21.01) depends on three parameters: λ is called the **multiplier**, α is called the **increment**, and m is called the **modulus**. The notation (mod m) means that we divide what precedes it by m and retain the remainder. Thus z_t must be smaller than m, and η_t must always lie between 0 and 1. It can be shown that a congruential generator must always repeat itself eventually, in at most m steps, and so it is evident that we want m to be a large number.

Thus m is often chosen to be the largest integer that can be represented exactly on a particular computer; this is frequently $2^{31} - 1$. With this choice of m we could, in principle, generate somewhat more than two billion random numbers before the sequence repeated itself. However, if m, λ, and α are badly chosen, the sequence can repeat itself much more quickly than that and may well display other symptoms of nonrandomness.

The choice of the increment α is not terribly important; one widely used variant of (21.01) is the class of **multiplicative congruential generators**, in which α is equal to zero. However, the choice of the multiplier λ is extremely important. Certain choices are known to lead to relatively well-behaved generators, while others are known to lead to very ill-behaved ones. For more details, see Kennedy and Gentle (1980), Knuth (1981), Rubinstein (1981), Press, Flannery, Teukolsky, and Vetterling (1986), Ripley (1987), L'Ecuyer (1988), and Lewis and Orav (1989).

Most of the time, econometricians performing a Monte Carlo experiment will not need to write their own random number generators. If they are using an efficient and high-quality one, the only thing they need to worry about is how to supply the **seed**, that is, the initial value z_0 which is needed to generate z_1 and which, for a given generator, uniquely determines the entire sequence of random numbers. The seed may be specified more or less arbitrarily as a large integer less than m, or it may be chosen "randomly" based on the system clock. In either case, it should be recorded so that an experiment can be repeated if necessary. The seed is supplied only the first time the random number generator is called in a particular program. After the first call, z_0 is replaced by z_1, then by z_2, and so on. Thus, at any time, the routine has available z_{t-1} to use in computing z_t.

Unfortunately, there are many bad random number generators in existence and widespread use, and it is certainly not safe to rely on a generator that has not been extensively tested. Such tests are discussed by most of the books on Monte Carlo methods mentioned above; see also Fishman and Moore (1982). What tests one might want to perform depend on what the random numbers are being used for. If the model being studied is a time-series model, for example, one would want to make sure that they are free of any serial correlation. Note that poor random number routines can often be improved by "shuffling" the numbers they produce or by combining several routines in some way. For example, one might use two different routines to generate two different random numbers, then use a third routine to determine randomly which of the two to pick.

21.3 Generating Pseudo-Random Variates

Once one has access to a routine that can generate long sequences of pseudo-random numbers η_t, each apparently independently distributed as $U(0, 1)$, there are several ways in which one can generate pseudo-random variates that

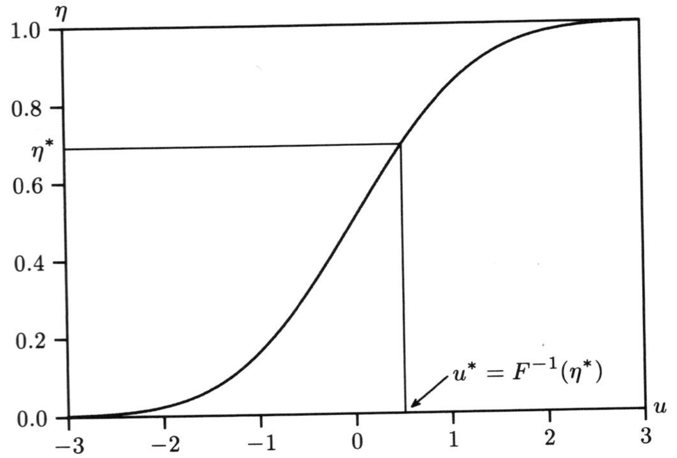

Figure 21.1 The transformation method

appear to be drawn from any desired distribution. We will discuss two general techniques, the **transformation method** and the **rejection method**, as well as various special methods applicable to certain cases of interest.

The transformation method is based on the fact that the range of a cumulative distribution function (c.d.f.) is the 0-1 interval. Thus, if u is distributed according to the strictly increasing c.d.f. $F(u)$, $\eta = F(u)$ must be distributed as $U(0,1)$. For any η, we can invert the c.d.f. so as to obtain $u = F^{-1}(\eta)$. To obtain a sequence of u_t's distributed according to $F(u)$, we simply generate a sequence of η_t's distributed as $U(0,1)$ and subject each of them to the transformation $F^{-1}(\eta_t)$. This is illustrated in Figure 21.1. As can be seen from the figure, any value of η on the vertical axis, such as η^*, is mapped uniquely via $F^{-1}(\eta^*)$ into a corresponding value u^* on the horizontal one.

The transformation method works well whenever $F^{-1}(\cdot)$ is inexpensive to compute. One such case is that of the exponential distribution, for which the probability density function (p.d.f.) is

$$f(u) = \theta e^{-\theta u}$$

(see Section 8.1), and the corresponding c.d.f. is

$$F(u) = 1 - e^{-\theta u}.$$

Setting η equal to $F(u)$ and solving, we find that

$$u = F^{-1}(\eta) = -\frac{1}{\theta}\log(1-\eta).$$

Thus, in this case, the transformation method can easily be used to generate pseudo-random variates distributed according to the exponential distribution.

The transformation method can be used to generate pseudo-random normal variates, but it requires a certain amount of computation because there is no closed form expression for the standard normal c.d.f. $\Phi(\cdot)$ or its inverse $\Phi^{-1}(\cdot)$. An algorithm to calculate the latter numerically must be employed. An alternative technique that is widely used is the **Box-Muller method** of Box and Muller (1958). It uses the fact that if η_1 and η_2 are independent random variates from $U(0,1)$, then the variates

$$u_1 = \big(-2\log(\eta_1)\big)^{1/2}\cos(2\pi\eta_2) \quad \text{and} \quad u_2 = \big(-2\log(\eta_1)\big)^{1/2}\sin(2\pi\eta_2)$$

are independent random variates from $N(0,1)$. See Rubinstein (1981) or Press, Flannery, Teukolsky, and Vetterling (1986) for a proof. The latter book also discusses a modified version of the Box-Muller method that should be somewhat faster to compute. The major problem with the Box-Muller technique is that it relies heavily on the independence of η_1 and η_2. If the random number generator that is used to generate them is not a good one, they may exhibit some dependence, and the resulting variates u_1 and u_2 may be neither normally nor independently distributed.

Once one is able to obtain pseudo-random variates from $N(0,1)$, it is straightforward to obtain pseudo-random variates from $N(\mu,\sigma^2)$ or from the multivariate normal distribution with any arbitrary mean vector $\boldsymbol{\mu}$ and covariance matrix $\boldsymbol{\Omega}$. If $\boldsymbol{u}$ denotes an l–vector each element of which is a pseudo-random variate from $N(0,1)$, and if $\boldsymbol{\psi}$ is an $l \times l$ (usually triangular) matrix such that $\boldsymbol{\psi}^{\top}\boldsymbol{\psi} = \boldsymbol{\Omega}$, it is easy to see that the l–vector $\boldsymbol{v}$ defined by

$$\boldsymbol{v} \equiv \boldsymbol{\mu} + \boldsymbol{\psi}^{\top}\boldsymbol{u}$$

will follow the $N(\boldsymbol{\mu}, \boldsymbol{\Omega})$ distribution. It is also straightforward to obtain random variates from the Cauchy, chi-squared, Student's t, and F distributions, simply by using the relationships between those distributions, the standard normal distribution, and each other (see Appendix B). For example, to generate random variates from $\chi^2(5)$, we could generate 5 independent random variates from $N(0,1)$, square them, and sum their squares. This method works well as long as the number of degrees of freedom is modest but would not be recommended for generating random variates from, say, $F(65,1743)$.

The other frequently used and widely applicable method for generating random variates is the rejection method. It can be used whenever the p.d.f. $f(u)$ is known. In its simplest version, the rejection method requires that the domain of $f(u)$ be a finite interval on the real line, say the interval $[\alpha,\beta]$. One starts by obtaining two random variates from $U(0,1)$, say η_1 and η_2. The first of these is transformed into ν_1, a random variate from $U(\alpha,\beta)$, while the second is transformed into ν_2, a random variate from $U(0,h)$, where h is a number at least as large as the maximum of $f(u)$. Once ν_1 and ν_2 have been obtained, ν_2 is compared with $f(\nu_1)$. If ν_2 exceeds $f(\nu_1)$, the proposed random variate ν_1 is rejected and another pair (ν_1,ν_2) is drawn. If ν_2 is less

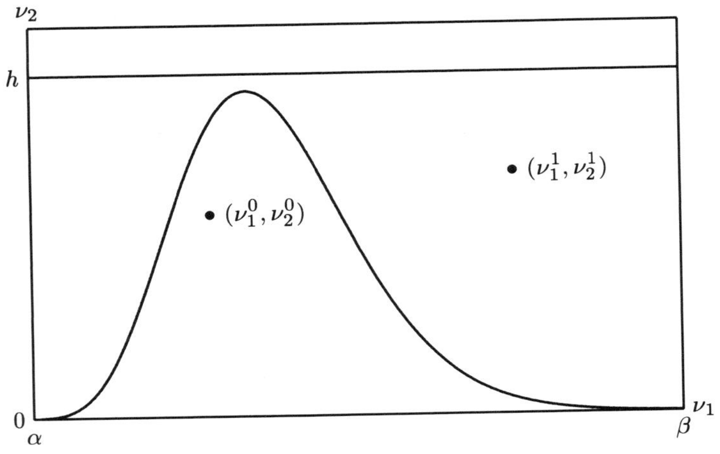

Figure 21.2 The rejection method

than or equal to $f(\nu_1)$, however, ν_1 is accepted and u is set equal to it. This method is illustrated in Figure 21.2. Here the point (ν_1^0, ν_2^0) yields a value of u, while the point (ν_1^1, ν_2^1) is rejected.

It is easy to see why the rejection method works. Although we pick ν_1 initially from $U(\alpha, \beta)$, we accept it only if $\nu_2 < f(\nu_1)$, and the probability that this will happen is proportional to $f(\nu_1)$. This version of the rejection method is of course somewhat inefficient, since we have to generate, on average, $2h(\beta - \alpha)$ random variates for every u that we actually obtain. If the density $f(u)$ has a tall spike, h will be large. If it has long tails, $\beta - \alpha$ will be large. In either of these cases, $2h(\beta - \alpha)$ will be large, and the method may be quite inefficient. In a more general version of the rejection method, the constant h is replaced by a function $h(\nu_1)$, with ν_1 then drawn from a density proportional to $h(\nu_1)$. Then ν_2 is chosen to be $U\big(0, h(\nu_1)\big)$. Provided that $h(\nu_1) > f(\nu_1)$ everywhere on $[\alpha, \beta]$, which no longer needs to be a finite interval, this method is valid; provided that it is easy to draw random variates ν_1 with probability proportional to $h(\nu_1)$, and that the area under $h(\cdot)$ is not too much larger than the area under $f(\cdot)$, it will work efficiently. Note that $h(\cdot)$ is not itself a density, since $h(\nu_1)$ must be greater than $f(\nu_1)$ for all ν_1 and hence must integrate to more than unity; it may be convenient to make $h(\cdot)$ proportional to some well-known density, however.

21.4 DESIGNING MONTE CARLO EXPERIMENTS

The hardest part of doing a set of Monte Carlo experiments is usually designing them. Limitations on computing resources, the experimenter's time, and the amount of space that can reasonably be devoted to presenting the results mean that it is usually practical to perform only a small number of experiments. These must be designed to shed as much light as possible on the issues of interest.

The first thing to recognize is that results from Monte Carlo experiments are necessarily random. At a minimum, this means that results must be reported in a way which allows readers to appreciate the extent of experimental randomness. Moreover, it is essential to perform enough replications so that the results are sufficiently accurate for the purpose at hand. The number of replications that is needed can sometimes be substantially reduced by using variance reduction techniques, which will be discussed in the next two sections. Such techniques are by no means always readily available, however. In this section, we consider various other aspects of the design of Monte Carlo experiments.

We first consider the problem of determining how many replications to perform. As an example, suppose that the investigator is interested in calculating the size of a certain test statistic (i.e., the probability of rejecting the null hypothesis when it is true) at, say, the nominal .05 level. Let us denote this unknown quantity by p. Each replication will generate a test statistic that either exceeds or does not exceed the nominal critical value. These can be thought of as independent Bernoulli trials. Suppose N replications are performed and R rejections are obtained. Then the obvious estimator of p, which is also the ML estimator, is R/N. The variance of this estimator is $N^{-1}p(1-p)$, which can be estimated by $R(N-R)/N^3$.

Now suppose that one wants the length of a 95% confidence interval on the estimate of p to be approximately .01. Using the normal approximation to the binomial, which is surely valid here since N will be a large number, we see that the confidence interval must cover $2 \times 1.96 = 3.92$ standard errors. Hence we require that

$$3.92\left(\frac{p(1-p)}{N}\right)^{1/2} = .01. \tag{21.02}$$

Assuming that p is .05, the nominal level of the test being investigated, we can solve (21.02) for N. The result is $N \cong 7299$. To be on the safe side (since p may well exceed .05, implying that R/N may have a larger variance) the investigator would probably choose $N = 8000$. This is a rather large number of replications and may be expensive to compute. If one were willing to let the 95% confidence interval on p have a length of .02, one could make do with a sample one-quarter as large, or roughly 2000 replications.

If the objective of an experiment is to compare two or more estimators or two or more test statistics, fewer replications may be needed to obtain a given level of accuracy than would be needed to estimate the properties of either of them with the same level of accuracy. Suppose, for example, that one is interested in comparing two estimators, say $\hat{\theta}$ and $\tilde{\theta}$, of a parameter the true value of which is θ_0. On each replication, say the jth, realizations of each of the two estimators, say $\hat{\theta}_j$ and $\tilde{\theta}_j$, are obtained. The squared errors of the two estimators are

$$S(\hat{\theta}) \equiv E\big(\hat{\theta} - \theta_0\big)^2 \quad \text{and} \quad S(\tilde{\theta}) \equiv E\big(\tilde{\theta} - \theta_0\big)^2,$$

which may be estimated by

$$\hat{S}(\hat{\theta}) = \frac{1}{N}\sum_{j=1}^{N}\big(\hat{\theta}_j - \theta_0\big)^2 \quad \text{and} \quad \tilde{S}(\tilde{\theta}) = \frac{1}{N}\sum_{j=1}^{N}\big(\tilde{\theta}_j - \theta_0\big)^2.$$

The difference between $S(\hat{\theta})$ and $S(\tilde{\theta})$ is

$$E\Big(\big(\hat{\theta} - \theta_0\big)^2 - \big(\tilde{\theta} - \theta_0\big)^2\Big), \tag{21.03}$$

which may be estimated by

$$\frac{1}{N}\sum_{j=1}^{N}\Big(\big(\hat{\theta}_j - \theta_0\big)^2 - \big(\tilde{\theta}_j - \theta_0\big)^2\Big). \tag{21.04}$$

It is possible and indeed likely that the variance of (21.04) will be substantially smaller than the variance of either $\hat{S}(\hat{\theta})$ or $\tilde{S}(\tilde{\theta})$, because both $\hat{\theta}_j$ and $\tilde{\theta}_j$ depend on the same pseudo-random vector $\boldsymbol{u}^j$. The variance of (21.04) is

$$\frac{1}{N}V(\hat{\theta}) + \frac{1}{N}V(\tilde{\theta}) - \frac{2}{N}\mathrm{Cov}(\hat{\theta}, \tilde{\theta}),$$

which will be smaller than the variance of either $\hat{S}(\hat{\theta})$ or $\tilde{S}(\tilde{\theta})$ whenever $\mathrm{Cov}(\hat{\theta}, \tilde{\theta})$ is positive and large enough. This will very often be the case, since it is likely that the quantities $(\hat{\theta}_j - \theta_0)^2$ and $(\tilde{\theta}_j - \theta_0)^2$ will be strongly positively correlated. Thus it may require far fewer replications to estimate (21.03) than to estimate $S(\hat{\theta})$ and $S(\tilde{\theta})$ with the same level of accuracy. Of course, this will happen only if $\hat{\theta}_j$ and $\tilde{\theta}_j$ are obtained using the same set of pseudo-random variates, but that is how the Monte Carlo experiment would normally be designed. We will encounter an idea similar to this one when we discuss the method of antithetic variates in the next section.

The second important thing to keep in mind when designing Monte Carlo experiments is that the results will often be highly sensitive to certain aspects of the experimental design and largely or totally insensitive to other aspects. Obviously, one will want to vary the former across the experiments while fixing the latter in a more or less arbitrary fashion. For example, many test statistics related to regression models are invariant to the variance of the error terms. Consider the ordinary t statistic for $\alpha = 0$ in the regression

$$\boldsymbol{y} = \boldsymbol{X\beta} + \alpha\boldsymbol{z} + \boldsymbol{u}. \tag{21.05}$$

Using the FWL Theorem and assuming that the data are generated by a special case of (21.05) for which $\alpha = 0$, we see that

$$t(\hat{\alpha}) = \frac{\boldsymbol{z}^\top \boldsymbol{M}_X \boldsymbol{u}}{\left(\boldsymbol{u}^\top \boldsymbol{M}_{X,z} \boldsymbol{u}/(n-k)\right)^{1/2} \left(\boldsymbol{z}^\top \boldsymbol{M}_X \boldsymbol{z}\right)^{1/2}}, \tag{21.06}$$

where there are n observations and a total of k regressors and, as usual, $\boldsymbol{M}_X$ and $\boldsymbol{M}_{X,z}$ denote the matrices that project orthogonally onto the subspaces $\mathcal{S}^\perp(\boldsymbol{X})$ and $\mathcal{S}^\perp(\boldsymbol{X}, \boldsymbol{z})$, respectively. The finite-sample distribution of this statistic when the u_t's are not normally distributed is in general unknown and might well be the subject of a Monte Carlo experiment. However, it is clear from inspection of (21.06) that this distribution in no way depends on the variance of the error terms which make up the error vector $\boldsymbol{u}$ in the DGP, since if we multiply $\boldsymbol{u}$ by any positive constant, $t(\hat{\alpha})$ is unaffected. Thus, in this case, we might as well fix the variance of the error terms at some arbitrary level, since there would be nothing at all to be learned by varying it. Breusch (1980) discusses a number of other invariance results for linear regression models; by taking such results into account, one can in many cases simplify the design of Monte Carlo experiments.

On the other hand, when there is reason to expect the results to be sensitive to certain aspects of the DGP, it is important to conduct experiments in which those aspects are varied over the range of interest. Just what aspects of the DGP these will be must necessarily vary from case to case. The sample size n will almost always be one of them, because it is almost always of interest to see how rapidly the finite-sample properties of the quantities being examined approach their (known) asymptotic limits. One exception might be if the aim of the Monte Carlo experiment were to shed light on the properties of a particular set of estimators or test statistics for a particular data set, so that the experiment was being used as an adjunct to a piece of empirical work (see Section 21.8). In contrast to this situation, up to the present time most Monte Carlo experiments have been designed to shed light on the general properties of certain statistical procedures, and it is hard to claim any sort of generality when all results are for a single sample size.

The vast majority of the models that econometricians estimate are regression models or close relatives of regression models. Thus, except in a few special cases such as pure time-series models, conditioning variables ($\boldsymbol{X}_t$'s) are usually present. How these should be treated in Monte Carlo experiments is not entirely clear. One approach is to generate the $\boldsymbol{X}_t$'s in some way. Drawing them from independent uniform, normal, or lognormal distributions is popular when the experiment deals with cross-section data, while generating them from various simple time-series processes such as AR(1), MA(1), and ARMA(1, 1), with normal errors, is popular when the experiment deals with time-series data. One can either draw a new set of $\boldsymbol{X}_t$'s for each replication or draw a single set of $\boldsymbol{X}_t$'s to be used in all replications. The latter method is cheaper and makes sense if the $\boldsymbol{X}_t$'s are supposed to be fixed in repeated samples, but it may yield results that depend on the idiosyncratic characteristics of the particular set of $\boldsymbol{X}_t$'s which was drawn.

Another possibility is to use genuine economic data for the $\boldsymbol{X}_t$'s. If these data are chosen with care, this approach can ensure that the $\boldsymbol{X}_t$'s are indeed typical of those which appear in econometric models. However, it raises a problem of how to vary the sample size. If one uses either genuine data or a single set of generated data, the matrix $n^{-1}\boldsymbol{X}^{\top}\boldsymbol{X}$ will change as the sample size n changes. This may make it difficult to separate the effects of changes in n from the effects of changes in $n^{-1}\boldsymbol{X}^{\top}\boldsymbol{X}$. One solution to this problem is to pick, or generate, a single set of $\boldsymbol{X}_t$'s for a sample of size m and then repeat these as many times as necessary to create $\boldsymbol{X}_t$'s for samples of larger sizes. This requires that $n = cm$, where c is an integer. Obvious choices for m are 50 and 100; n could then be any integer multiple of 50 or 100. The problem with this approach, of course, is that no matter how many replications are performed, all the results will depend on the choice of the initial set of $\boldsymbol{X}_t$'s.

In many cases, how the $\boldsymbol{X}_t$'s are chosen will not matter much. However, there are cases for which it can have a substantial impact on the results. For example, MacKinnon and White (1985) used Monte Carlo experiments to examine the finite-sample performance of various heteroskedasticity-consistent covariance matrix estimators (HCCMEs; see Section 16.3). They used 50 observations on genuine economic data for the $\boldsymbol{X}_t$'s, repeating these 50 observations as many times as necessary for each sample size. As Chesher and Jewitt (1987) subsequently showed, the performance of the estimators depends critically on the h_t's, that is, the diagonal elements of the matrix $\boldsymbol{P}_X$; the larger are the largest h_t's, the worse will be the finite-sample performance of tests based on all HCCMEs. When the $\boldsymbol{X}$ matrix is generated the way MacKinnon and White generated it, with $n = 50c$, all of the h_t's must approach zero at a rate proportional to $1/c$ (and hence also to $1/n$). Thus MacKinnon and White were guaranteed to find that results improved rapidly as the sample size was increased. In contrast, Cragg (1983), doing Monte Carlo experiments on a related issue (see Section 17.3), generated the $\boldsymbol{X}_t$'s randomly from the lognormal distribution. This distribution has a long right-hand tail and thus occasionally throws up large values of certain $\boldsymbol{X}_t$'s. These produce relatively large values of h_t, and as a result the largest values of h_t tend to zero at a rate very much slower than $1/n$. Thus, as the Chesher-Jewitt analysis would have predicted, Cragg found that finite-sample performance improved only slowly as the sample size was increased.

More recently, Chesher and Peters (1994) have shown that the distributions of many estimators of interest to econometricians depend crucially on the way the regressors are distributed. If the regressors are symmetrically distributed about their medians, these estimators will have special properties that do not hold in general. Since regressors used in Monte Carlo experiments might well be symmetrically distributed, there is a risk that the results of such experiments could be seriously misleading.

The above examples should make two things clear. First, the way the $\boldsymbol{X}_t$'s are generated can matter. Investigators should thus always think carefully about how they generate them. Second, a good theoretical understanding of a problem can make Monte Carlo experiments more informative and prevent misleading conclusions which may stem from apparently minor aspects of the experimental design.

One of the most challenging parts of any Monte Carlo experiment is presenting the results. This is often a great deal harder than it might seem. Here we discuss a few of the issues. One method that is sometimes very useful, namely, the estimation of response surfaces, will not be discussed here but will be dealt with extensively in Section 21.7.

When presenting results in tabular form, it is easy to overwhelm the reader. Especially if several estimators or test statistics are being compared, it is important to make comparisons as easy as possible. For example, if one is interested in the mean squared error (MSE) of several competing estimators, it might be much more informative to present the results as ratios relative to a base case, rather than simply presenting results for each estimator separately. A relatively simple and well-known estimator might serve as the base case, and the results for each of the other estimators could then be presented as the ratio of that estimator's MSE to the MSE of the base-case estimator. Such a table would be easy to assimilate because numbers below 1 would indicate better performance than that of the base case, while numbers above 1 would indicate worse performance. To avoid presenting a lot of experimental standard errors, these ratios could be marked (using symbols such as $*$, $\dagger$, or $**$) to indicate when they differ from unity at specified levels of significance.

Experimenters often simply present tables of the estimated means, variances, and, perhaps, skewness and kurtosis coefficients for several different estimators or test statistics. In the case of test statistics, tail-area probabilities, i.e., estimated sizes, are often presented as well. Such tables are often not very easy to assimilate. Graphical methods of presentation can sometimes be very valuable as an alternative, although they must be used with restraint owing to the amount of space that a number of graphs can take up. In the case of competing test statistics, one might plot the empirical size-power tradeoff curves (see Section 12.2) of several test statistics on the same axes. This will make it clear if any of the test statistics has substantially better or worse power for a given size than the others; an example may be found in Davidson and MacKinnon (1982). In the case of competing estimators, one might simply plot the empirical distribution functions of all of them on the same axes, as in Figures 7.1, 7.2, and 18.1. The major qualitative differences among the competing estimators should then be quite clear. Besides being easy to understand, this approach makes it easy to deal with estimators (such as LIML) that lack moments. For these estimators, MSEs can of course be extremely misleading; see Sargan (1982).

21.5 VARIANCE REDUCTION: ANTITHETIC VARIATES

As we have seen, obtaining sufficiently accurate results from a Monte Carlo experiment can often require that a great many replications be computed. This is not always feasible. In some cases, the number of replications that is needed can be substantially reduced by using certain techniques for reducing the variance of experimental results. In the econometric literature, the variance reduction techniques which have achieved prominence are the use of **antithetic variates** and **control variates**. We discuss the former method in this section and the latter method in the next one.

The idea of antithetic variates is to calculate two different estimates of the quantity of interest in such a way that the two estimates are negatively correlated. Their average will then be substantially more accurate than either of them individually. Suppose that we wish to estimate some quantity θ, and that in a single Monte Carlo experiment we can obtain two different unbiased estimators of θ, say $\acute{\theta}$ and $\grave{\theta}$. These are the antithetic variates. Then the pooled estimator

$$\bar{\theta} = \tfrac{1}{2}(\acute{\theta} + \grave{\theta}) \tag{21.07}$$

has variance

$$V(\bar{\theta}) = \tfrac{1}{4}\big(V(\acute{\theta}) + V(\grave{\theta}) + 2\,\mathrm{Cov}(\acute{\theta}, \grave{\theta})\big),$$

where $V(\acute{\theta})$ and $V(\grave{\theta})$ denote the variances of $\acute{\theta}$ and $\grave{\theta}$. If $\mathrm{Cov}(\acute{\theta}, \grave{\theta})$ is negative, $V(\bar{\theta})$ will be smaller than $\frac{1}{4}\big(V(\acute{\theta}) + V(\grave{\theta})\big)$, which is the variance that we would have obtained using the same number of replications to estimate θ from two independent experiments. The extent to which we can gain by using antithetic variates thus depends on how strong the negative correlation is between $\acute{\theta}$ and $\grave{\theta}$.

One might ask why $\acute{\theta}$ and $\grave{\theta}$ should receive equal weight in computing $\bar{\theta}$. Let us therefore consider the weighted estimator

$$\ddot{\theta} \equiv w\acute{\theta} + (1 - w)\grave{\theta}.$$

Differentiating the variance of $\ddot{\theta}$ with respect to w and setting the result to zero, we find that

$$w = \frac{V(\grave{\theta}) - \mathrm{Cov}(\acute{\theta}, \grave{\theta})}{V(\acute{\theta}) + V(\grave{\theta}) - 2\mathrm{Cov}(\acute{\theta}, \grave{\theta})},$$

which is satisfied by setting $w = \frac{1}{2}$ whenever $V(\acute{\theta}) = V(\grave{\theta})$. In most cases, the variances of the two estimators will be equal, and so giving the two of them equal weight will be optimal.

One way to implement the method of antithetic variates in the case of regression models is to use each set of generated error terms twice, with the sign reversed the second time. Suppose, for example, that we wished to estimate the mean of the NLS estimate $\hat{\alpha}$ of the exponent in the nonlinear regression model

$$y_t = \beta X_t^{\alpha} + u_t. \tag{21.08}$$

For each set of error terms $\boldsymbol{u}^j$, we could generate two realizations of $\boldsymbol{y}$, with t^{th} elements

$$\acute{y}_t^j = \beta X_t^{\alpha} + u_t^j \quad \text{and} \quad \grave{y}_t^j = \beta X_t^{\alpha} - u_t^j.$$

We could then estimate the model using each of these two sets of data, thus generating two different estimates of α, $\acute{\alpha}_j$ and $\grave{\alpha}_j$. After N of these double replications, we could then construct the estimator

$$\bar{\alpha} = \frac{1}{2N}\sum_{j=1}^{N}(\acute{\alpha}_j + \grave{\alpha}_j),$$

which is analogous to the pooled estimator (21.07). The variance of $\bar{\alpha}$ could then be estimated as

$$\frac{1}{N(N-1)}\sum_{j=1}^{N}\Big(\tfrac{1}{2}(\acute{\alpha}_j + \grave{\alpha}_j) - \bar{\alpha}\Big)^2. \tag{21.09}$$

Since $\bar{\alpha}$ is a simple average of $\bar{\alpha}_j \equiv \frac{1}{2}(\acute{\alpha}_j + \grave{\alpha}_j)$ for $j = 1, \ldots, N$, (21.09) is simply the ordinary estimate of the variance of a sample mean.

It is clear that this method will work extremely well in the case of linear regression models with fixed regressors. For the model $\boldsymbol{y} = \boldsymbol{X\beta} + \boldsymbol{u}$, the jth double replication would yield

$$\begin{aligned}\acute{\boldsymbol{\beta}}^j &= (\boldsymbol{X}^{\top}\boldsymbol{X})^{-1}\boldsymbol{X}^{\top}\acute{\boldsymbol{y}}^j = (\boldsymbol{X}^{\top}\boldsymbol{X})^{-1}\boldsymbol{X}^{\top}(\boldsymbol{X\beta}_0 + \boldsymbol{u}^j) \quad \text{and}\\ \grave{\boldsymbol{\beta}}^j &= (\boldsymbol{X}^{\top}\boldsymbol{X})^{-1}\boldsymbol{X}^{\top}\grave{\boldsymbol{y}}^j = (\boldsymbol{X}^{\top}\boldsymbol{X})^{-1}\boldsymbol{X}^{\top}(\boldsymbol{X\beta}_0 - \boldsymbol{u}^j).\end{aligned}$$

Therefore, we see that

$$\begin{aligned}\bar{\boldsymbol{\beta}} &\equiv \tfrac{1}{2}(\acute{\boldsymbol{\beta}}^j + \grave{\boldsymbol{\beta}}^j)\\ &= \tfrac{1}{2}\Big(\boldsymbol{\beta}_0 + \boldsymbol{\beta}_0 + (\boldsymbol{X}^{\top}\boldsymbol{X})^{-1}\boldsymbol{X}^{\top}\boldsymbol{u}^j - (\boldsymbol{X}^{\top}\boldsymbol{X})^{-1}\boldsymbol{X}^{\top}\boldsymbol{u}^j\Big) = \boldsymbol{\beta}_0.\end{aligned}$$

Thus, in a single double replication, we would obtain an answer with no experimental error whatsoever. This occurs because $\acute{\boldsymbol{\beta}}^j$ and $\grave{\boldsymbol{\beta}}^j$ are perfectly negatively correlated.

Perfect negative correlation of the antithetic variates will not occur in general. When it does, the problem is usually so simple that there is no need to perform Monte Carlo experiments (although sometimes a very small Monte Carlo experiment, consisting of just one double replication using antithetic variates, can tell us that an estimator is unbiased more easily than a theoretical analysis could). Less than perfect negative correlation often does

Table 21.1 Means and Standard Errors of Monte Carlo Estimates

$\acute{\alpha}$:	0.515960 (0.006709)	$\acute{\beta}$:	1.019957 (0.016002)
$\grave{\alpha}$:	0.488785 (0.006627)	$\grave{\beta}$:	1.088944 (0.016998)
$\bar{\alpha}$:	0.502372 (0.000425)	$\bar{\beta}$:	1.054451 (0.003404)

occur, however, and it means that in certain cases the use of antithetic variates can greatly reduce the number of replications that are needed to estimate the first moments of an estimator. Hendry and Trivedi (1972) used the technique to study estimators for certain dynamic models, and Mikhail (1972, 1975) used it to study certain simultaneous equations estimators.

Let us now consider the example (21.08) again. We conducted a small Monte Carlo experiment based on this example, using a sample of size 50, with a single set of $\boldsymbol{X}_t$'s generated from the uniform distribution on the interval $(5, 15)$ and parameters $\alpha_0 = 0.5$, $\beta_0 = 1.0$, and $\sigma_0^2 = 1.0$ (here σ_0^2 is the variance of the u_t's, which are assumed to be normally distributed). The results from 500 double replications are shown in Table 21.1.

In this case, the gains from using antithetic variates are apparently very great. The standard error of $\bar{\alpha}$ is 15.7 times smaller than the average of the standard errors of $\acute{\alpha}$ and $\grave{\alpha}$. This means that $\bar{\alpha}$, which is based on a total of 1000 replications, is approximately as accurate as a naive Monte Carlo estimate based on 246,000 replications! The gains are less dramatic in the case of β, but they are still very substantial. The standard error of $\bar{\beta}$ is 4.8 times smaller than the average of the standard errors of $\acute{\beta}$ and $\grave{\beta}$, which means that it is roughly as accurate as a naive estimate based on 23,500 replications. Because $\bar{\alpha}$ and $\bar{\beta}$ are so accurate, we can see that NLS yields slightly biased estimates in this case: t statistics for the null hypotheses that the means of the estimates of α and β are the true values of 0.5 and 1.0 are, respectively, 5.58 and 16.00.

Although antithetic variates of the type we have described can greatly reduce the number of Monte Carlo replications needed for precise estimation of the *means* of estimators, they are of no help at all for estimating many other features of their distributions. For example, in the OLS case discussed above, the estimated covariance matrix of the $\acute{\boldsymbol{\beta}}^j$'s is

$$\frac{1}{N}\sum_{j=1}^{N}(\acute{\boldsymbol{\beta}}^j - \boldsymbol{\beta}_0)(\acute{\boldsymbol{\beta}}^j - \boldsymbol{\beta}_0)^{\top},$$

and the estimated covariance matrix of the $\grave{\boldsymbol{\beta}}^j$'s is

$$\frac{1}{N}\sum_{j=1}^{N}(\grave{\boldsymbol{\beta}}^j - \boldsymbol{\beta}_0)(\grave{\boldsymbol{\beta}}^j - \boldsymbol{\beta}_0)^{\top}.$$

It is easy to see that

$$
\begin{aligned}
(\acute{\boldsymbol{\beta}}^j - \boldsymbol{\beta}_0)(\acute{\boldsymbol{\beta}}^j - \boldsymbol{\beta}_0)^\top &= (\boldsymbol{X}^\top\boldsymbol{X})^{-1}\boldsymbol{X}\boldsymbol{u}^j(\boldsymbol{u}^j)^\top(\boldsymbol{X}^\top\boldsymbol{X})^{-1} \\
&= (\boldsymbol{X}^\top\boldsymbol{X})^{-1}\boldsymbol{X}(-\boldsymbol{u}^j)(-\boldsymbol{u}^j)^\top(\boldsymbol{X}^\top\boldsymbol{X})^{-1} \\
&= (\grave{\boldsymbol{\beta}}^j - \boldsymbol{\beta}_0)(\grave{\boldsymbol{\beta}}^j - \boldsymbol{\beta}_0)^\top.
\end{aligned}
$$

Thus the estimated covariance matrices of the two antithetic variates will be identical. From the point of view of estimating the covariance matrix of the estimator, then, the second antithetic variate provides no useful information at all. In a realistic situation, the covariance matrices of the two antithetic variates will never be perfectly correlated, but they will be positively correlated. The antithetic estimate of the covariance matrix will therefore be less efficient than a naive estimate based on the same number of replications.

21.6 VARIANCE REDUCTION: CONTROL VARIATES

The second widely used technique for variance reduction is to employ control variates. A **control variate** is a random variable of which the distribution (or at least certain properties of the distribution) is known and that is correlated with the estimator(s) or test statistic(s) which are being investigated. The principal property that a control variate must have is a known population mean. The divergence between the sample mean of the control variate in the experiment and its known population mean is then used to improve the estimates from the Monte Carlo experiment. This obviously works best if the control variate is highly correlated with the estimators or test statistics with which the experiment is concerned.

Typically, control variates are statistics which could never be computed in practice but which can be calculated in the context of a Monte Carlo experiment, because the DGP is known. For example, suppose the experiment concerns the estimates of $\boldsymbol{\beta}$ from a nonlinear regression model with normal errors,

$$
\boldsymbol{y} = \boldsymbol{x}(\boldsymbol{\beta}) + \boldsymbol{u}, \quad \boldsymbol{u} \sim N(\mathbf{0}, \sigma^2\mathbf{I}),
$$

where $\boldsymbol{x}(\boldsymbol{\beta})$ depends only on $\boldsymbol{\beta}$ and on regressors that are fixed or at least independent of $\boldsymbol{u}$. We saw in Section 5.4 that

$$
n^{1/2}(\hat{\boldsymbol{\beta}} - \boldsymbol{\beta}_0) = (n^{-1}\boldsymbol{X}_0^\top\boldsymbol{X}_0)^{-1}n^{-1/2}\boldsymbol{X}_0^\top\boldsymbol{u} + o(1).
$$

Thus it is natural to consider using the vector

$$
\ddot{\boldsymbol{\beta}} = (\boldsymbol{X}_0^\top\boldsymbol{X}_0)^{-1}\boldsymbol{X}_0^\top\boldsymbol{u}
$$

as a source of control variates. This vector will evidently be normally distributed with mean vector zero and covariance matrix $\sigma_0^2(\boldsymbol{X}_0^\top\boldsymbol{X}_0)^{-1}$. It would be impossible to compute $\ddot{\boldsymbol{\beta}}$ from a real data set, but in the context of a Monte Carlo experiment, it is perfectly easy to do so. We know $\boldsymbol{\beta}_0$ and hence $\boldsymbol{X}_0 \equiv \boldsymbol{X}(\boldsymbol{\beta}_0)$. Using these and the error vector $\boldsymbol{u}^j$ that we generate at each replication, we can easily compute $\ddot{\boldsymbol{\beta}}^j$.

Suppose that $\theta \equiv \theta(\hat{\boldsymbol{\beta}})$ is some scalar quantity of which we wish to calculate the mean using the results of the Monte Carlo experiment. For example, if we were interested in the bias of $\hat{\beta}_2$, θ would be $\hat{\beta}_2 - \beta_{20}$; if we were interested in the mean squared error of $\hat{\beta}_3$, θ would be $(\hat{\beta}_3 - \beta_{30})^2$; if we were interested in the size of a test, θ would be 1 if the test rejected and 0 otherwise; and so on. On each replication, we obtain t_j, a realization of θ, which is equal to $\theta(\hat{\boldsymbol{\beta}}^j)$. We also obtain a control variate τ_j, which would normally be some function of $\ddot{\boldsymbol{\beta}}$. The τ_j's must be known to have mean zero and finite variance, which need not be known. If we were interested in the bias of $\hat{\beta}_2$, for example, the natural choice for τ would be $\ddot{\beta}_2$. In some other cases, it is not so obvious how to choose τ, however, and there may be several possible choices.

If the control variate τ were not available, we would estimate θ by

$$\bar{\theta} \equiv \frac{1}{N}\sum_{j=1}^{N} t_j,$$

and this naive estimator would have variance $V(\bar{\theta}) = N^{-1}V(t)$, which could be estimated by

$$\hat{V}(\bar{\theta}) = \frac{1}{N(N-1)}\sum_{j=1}^{N}\left(t_j - \bar{\theta}\right)^2.$$

When the control variate τ is available, $\bar{\theta}$ will in most cases no longer be optimal. Consider instead the control variate (CV) estimator

$$\ddot{\theta}(\lambda) \equiv \bar{\theta} - \lambda\bar{\tau}, \tag{21.10}$$

where $\bar{\tau}$ is the sample mean of the τ_j's. This estimator involves subtracting from $\bar{\theta}$ some multiple λ of the sample mean of the control variates; how λ may be chosen will be discussed in the next paragraph. On average, what is subtracted will be zero, since τ_j has population mean zero. This implies that $\ddot{\theta}(\lambda)$ must have the same population mean as $\bar{\theta}$. But, in any given sample, the mean of the τ_j's will be nonzero. If, for example, it is positive, and if τ_j and t_j are strongly positively correlated, it is very likely that $\bar{\theta}$ will also exceed its population mean. Thus, by subtracting from $\bar{\theta}$ a multiple of the mean of the τ_j's, we are likely to obtain a better estimate of θ.

The variance of the CV estimator (21.10) is

$$V\big(\ddot{\theta}(\lambda)\big) = V(\bar{\theta}) + \lambda^2 V(\bar{\tau}) - 2\lambda\mathrm{Cov}(\bar{\theta}, \bar{\tau}). \tag{21.11}$$

It is easy to minimize this with respect to λ. The optimal value of λ turns out to be

$$\lambda^* = \frac{\mathrm{Cov}(\bar{\theta}, \bar{\tau})}{V(\bar{\tau})}. \tag{21.12}$$

Substituting (21.12) into (21.11), the variance of $\ddot{\theta}(\lambda^*)$ is seen to be

$$V\big(\ddot{\theta}(\lambda^*)\big) = V(\bar{\theta}) - \frac{\mathrm{Cov}(\bar{\theta}, \bar{\tau})^2}{V(\bar{\tau})} = (1 - \rho^2)V(\bar{\theta}), \tag{21.13}$$

where

$$\rho \equiv \frac{\mathrm{Cov}(\bar{\theta}, \bar{\tau})}{\big(V(\bar{\tau})V(\bar{\theta})\big)^{1/2}}$$

is the correlation between the t_j's and the τ_j's. From (21.13), it is clear that whenever this correlation is nonzero, there will be some gain to using the control variate. If the correlation is high, the gain may be very substantial. For example, if $\rho = 0.95$, the variance of $\ddot{\theta}(\lambda^*)$ will be 0.0975 times the variance of $\bar{\theta}$. Using the control variate will then be equivalent to increasing the number of replications by a factor of 10.26.

As the sample size n increases, the correlation between the control variate and the quantity of interest should increase, because the finite-sample distribution of the latter should approach its asymptotic distribution as n is increased. As a consequence, the efficiency gain from using the control variate should be greater for larger n. This is convenient, because the cost of doing Monte Carlo experiments is often roughly proportional to nN, and the increased efficiency of estimation as n increases will allow N to be reduced at the same time.

Although $V(\bar{\tau})$ will often be known, $\mathrm{Cov}(\bar{\theta}, \bar{\tau})$ will almost never be. Thus we will generally have to estimate λ^* in some way. Much of the literature on Monte Carlo methods — for example, Hammersley and Handscomb (1964) and Hendry (1984) — does not attempt to use λ^* but instead arbitrarily sets $\lambda = 1$. From (21.12) and the definition of ρ, we see that

$$\lambda^* = \rho\left(\frac{V(\bar{\theta})}{V(\bar{\tau})}\right)^{1/2}.$$

This implies that $\lambda = 1$ will be a good choice if ρ is close to 1 and $V(\bar{\theta})$ is close to $V(\bar{\tau})$, but it is generally not the best choice. In many cases, ρ may be significantly less than 1 and yet still be large enough to make the use of control variates worthwhile, and in others $V(\bar{\tau})$ may not be close to $V(\bar{\theta})$ when using the most natural definition of τ. Thus we would, in general, prefer to estimate λ^*. The easiest way to do this is to run the regression

$$t_j = \theta + \lambda\tau_j + \text{residual}. \tag{21.14}$$

As the notation suggests, this regression not only yields an estimate of λ^* but an estimate of θ as well. The latter is in fact asymptotically equivalent to $\ddot{\theta}(\lambda^*)$. Thus, as we will now show, regression (21.14) provides a remarkably easy way to compute an asymptotically optimal CV estimator.

The OLS estimate of λ from (21.14) is

$$\hat{\lambda} = \left(\boldsymbol{\tau}^\top \boldsymbol{M}_{\iota} \boldsymbol{\tau}\right)^{-1} \boldsymbol{\tau}^\top \boldsymbol{M}_{\iota} \boldsymbol{t},$$

where $\boldsymbol{t}$, $\boldsymbol{\tau}$, and $\boldsymbol{\iota}$ are vectors with typical elements t_j, τ_j, and 1, and $\boldsymbol{M}_{\iota}$ is the matrix $\mathbf{I} - \boldsymbol{\iota}(\boldsymbol{\iota}^\top\boldsymbol{\iota})^{-1}\boldsymbol{\iota}^\top$ that takes deviations from the mean. It is easy to see that $\hat{\lambda}$ is just the sample covariance of $\boldsymbol{t}$ and $\boldsymbol{\tau}$, divided by the sample variance of $\boldsymbol{\tau}$. Thus it is the empirical counterpart of λ^*. Because the residuals of a linear regression with a constant term must sum to zero, the OLS estimate of θ can be written as

$$\hat{\theta} = \bar{\theta} - \hat{\lambda}\bar{\tau}.$$

This makes it clear that the OLS estimate $\hat{\theta}$ is equal to $\ddot{\theta}(\hat{\lambda})$. Since $\hat{\lambda}$ is consistent for λ^* under rather weak assumptions, $\hat{\theta}$ will be asymptotically equivalent to $\ddot{\theta}(\lambda^*)$.

Running regression (21.14) not only yields the CV estimate $\hat{\theta}$ but also an estimate of the variance of that estimate, which we need in order to gauge the accuracy of the results and decide whether N is sufficiently large. This estimated variance is

$$\hat{\sigma}^2\left(\boldsymbol{\iota}^\top \boldsymbol{M}_{\tau} \boldsymbol{\iota}\right)^{-1},$$

where $\hat{\sigma}$ is the standard error of regression (21.14). The second factor here must tend to N^{-1}, since $\boldsymbol{\tau}$ (because it has mean zero) asymptotically has no explanatory power for $\boldsymbol{\iota}$. Therefore, $N^{-1}\hat{\sigma}^2$ would also be a valid estimate of the variance of $\hat{\theta}$. Since σ^2 is the variance of the part of the t_j's that cannot be explained by the τ_j's, it is clear that the better regression (21.14) fits, the more accurate the CV estimate $\hat{\theta}$ will be.

Once the problem is stated in terms of regression (21.14), it becomes clear that the link between θ and the τ_j's need not be close. Any random variable that can be calculated along with t_j can be used as a control variate, provided that it is correlated with t_j (either positively or negatively) and has mean zero, finite variance, and finite covariance with t_j. Since this is the case, there may well be more than one natural choice for τ in many situations. Luckily, formulating the problem as a linear regression makes it obvious how to handle multiple control variates. The appropriate generalization of (21.14) is

$$\boldsymbol{t} = \theta\boldsymbol{\iota} + \boldsymbol{T}\boldsymbol{\lambda} + \text{residuals}, \qquad (21.15)$$

where $\boldsymbol{T}$ is an $N \times c$ matrix, each column of which consists of observations on one of c control variates. Since all the columns of $\boldsymbol{T}$ have mean zero, the OLS estimate of θ from this regression will once again provide the estimate we are seeking.[2] This estimate is

$$\hat{\theta} = \left(\boldsymbol{\iota}^\top \boldsymbol{M}_T \boldsymbol{\iota}\right)^{-1} \boldsymbol{\iota}^\top \boldsymbol{M}_T \boldsymbol{t},$$

where $\boldsymbol{M}_T = \mathbf{I} - \boldsymbol{T}(\boldsymbol{T}^\top \boldsymbol{T})^{-1}\boldsymbol{T}^\top$. Since $N^{-1}\boldsymbol{\iota}^\top \boldsymbol{M}_T \boldsymbol{\iota}$ tends to unity as N tends to infinity, it is easy to see that the variance of $\hat{\theta}$ is once again just $N^{-1}\sigma^2$, where σ is the true standard error of regression (21.15). Thus our objective in choosing control variates is to make regression (21.15) fit as well as possible.

Suppose that we are interested in the size p of a certain test, that is, the probability that the test will reject the null hypothesis when it is true. We obtain N observations T_j on the test statistic and N observations on a control variate C_j with known distribution. Let us construct a 0-1 variable t_j so that $t_j = 1$ if T_j exceeds a certain critical value and $t_j = 0$ otherwise. Then the mean of the t_j's is a naive estimate of p. Davidson and MacKinnon (1981b) and Rothery (1982) considered this problem in detail and proposed a method of using the control variate to estimate p based on the method of maximum likelihood. It turns out that their estimator is identical to the OLS estimator of θ from regression (21.14), with τ_j a variable equal to $1-s$ when C_j exceeds the critical value for a test of size s, and $-s$ otherwise. Since the probability that C_j will exceed the critical value is s, τ_j defined in this way clearly has population mean zero. This technique requires one to choose s. Because we wish to maximize the correlation between the t_j's and the τ_j's, it seems logical to make s similar to the number of rejections actually observed using T_j. However, any choice of critical values is somewhat arbitrary.

Letting τ_j take on only two values cannot be optimal, since it throws away some of the information in the C_j's. One could just as easily use for τ_j any function of C_j that is expected to be highly correlated with t_j, minus its mean. Given the multiplicity of possibilities, it would seem natural to use more than one of them. For example, if C_j were known to be distributed as $N(0,1)$, and one were interested in a two-tail test, one could use $C_j^2 - 1$ as a control variate. It will have mean zero, since the expectation of a random variable which is $\chi^2(1)$ is 1, and it should be correlated with t_j. One might well use it in addition to one or more two-value control variates of the type described above. Experience suggests that using several control variates generally yields a more accurate estimate of θ than using just one control variate. In practice, it is easy to experiment with various control variates by seeing which ones are significant in regression (21.15).

[2] It is interesting to observe that regression (21.15) is formally the same as regression (16.63), Tauchen's (1985) version of the OPG test regression. Both regressions provide a way to estimate the mean of the regressand efficiently by taking into account the correlation between it and the other regressors, which are asymptotically orthogonal to the constant term.

The use of regressions (21.14) and (21.15) has been advocated for some time in the operations research literature; see Lavenberg and Welch (1981) and Ripley (1987). These procedures were exposited and developed further in Davidson and MacKinnon (1992b), in which it is shown how to use them for estimating quantiles as well as moments and tail areas and how to construct τ's that are approximately optimal for several cases of interest. In particular, for the estimation of test sizes and powers, a way is suggested to construct better, but more complicated, control variates than the two-value ones discussed above.

To illustrate the use of control variates, we will consider a simple example that was discussed by Hendry (1984). It is the stationary AR(1) model with normal errors:

$$y_t = \beta y_{t-1} + u_t, \quad u_t \sim N(0, \sigma^2), \ t = 1, \ldots, n. \tag{21.16}$$

We assume that $|\beta| < 1$, which is just the stationarity condition, and that $y_0 = 0$. Stationarity implies that $y_t \sim N\big(0, \sigma^2/(1-\beta^2)\big)$. Suppose that we are interested in the mean of $\hat{\beta}$, the OLS estimate of β. It is easy to see that both the value of $\hat{\beta}$ and its probability distribution are invariant to the value of σ in the DGP, say σ_0, but that its properties may well depend on both β_0 and the sample size n. A serious investigation would therefore involve seeing how the mean of $\hat{\beta}$ depends on β_0 and n; see Section 21.7 below. Since we are here merely interested in illustrating the use of control variates, we will consider only a few particular cases.[3]

The OLS estimate $\hat{\beta}$, assuming that y_0 is known, is

$$\hat{\beta} = \frac{\sum_{t=1}^{n} y_t y_{t-1}}{\sum_{t=1}^{n} y_{t-1}^2}.$$

Under the DGP characterized by β_0, this becomes

$$\frac{\sum_{t=1}^{n} (\beta_0 y_{t-1} + u_t) y_{t-1}}{\sum_{t=1}^{n} y_{t-1}^2} = \beta_0 + \frac{\sum_{t=1}^{n} u_t y_{t-1}}{\sum_{t=1}^{n} y_{t-1}^2}. \tag{21.17}$$

Although the numerator of the second term on the right-hand side of (21.17) has mean zero, it is not independent of the denominator, and so $E(\hat{\beta}) \neq \beta_0$. However, asymptotic theory tells us that $\hat{\beta}$ is consistent and asymptotically normal, since $n^{1/2}(\hat{\beta} - \beta_0) \overset{a}{\sim} N(0, 1 - \beta_0^2)$.

Now consider the control variate

$$\tau = n^{-1/2} \sum_{t=1}^{n} u_t y_{t-1}, \tag{21.18}$$

[3] Note that, although (21.16) looks like a regression model, antithetic variates are not useful here. If one generates two sets of data using disturbance vectors $\boldsymbol{u}$ and $-\boldsymbol{u}$, the estimates of β that one obtains are identical.

Table 21.2 Naive and CV Estimates of the Mean of $\hat{\beta}$

β_0	n	Naive	$\hat{\lambda}$	Optimal CV
0.1	25	0.091814 (0.001932)	0.927	0.091461 (0.000548)
0.1	100	0.096499 (0.000978)	0.982	0.097889 (0.000140)
0.1	400	0.099731 (0.000502)	0.995	0.099499 (0.000036)
0.5	25	0.465589 (0.001745)	0.934	0.464972 (0.000666)
0.5	100	0.490394 (0.000876)	0.982	0.490013 (0.000182)
0.5	400	0.497774 (0.000439)	0.991	0.497430 (0.000048)
0.9	25	0.843872 (0.001188)	0.958	0.843656 (0.000841)
0.9	100	0.882824 (0.000497)	0.987	0.882975 (0.000246)
0.9	400	0.895824 (0.000228)	0.992	0.895530 (0.000066)

which, from (21.17), is $n^{-1/2}$ times the numerator of the stochastic part of $\hat{\beta}$. The finite-sample distribution of the control variate τ defined in (21.18) is not a simple one. However, it is easy to see that τ has mean zero. Provided that $|\beta| < 1$, it is also easy to verify that τ has finite variance $\sigma_0^4/(1-\beta_0^2)$. Thus it is legitimate to use τ as a control variate. From (21.17), it is clear that, asymptotically, the correlation between τ and $\hat{\beta}-\beta_0$ will be unity. Therefore, there is likely to be a strong positive correlation in finite samples.

The results of 10,000 replications for three values of β_0 and three values of n are presented in Table 21.2. For each β_0 and sample size, we present two estimates of the mean of $\hat{\beta}$: the naive estimate, which does not use the control variate, and the optimal CV estimate based on equation (21.14). The table also gives the value of λ that is implicitly used to calculate the latter when τ is transformed so that it has the same variance, asymptotically, as $\hat{\beta}$. Estimated standard errors are in parentheses. We see that, as is well known, the OLS estimator of β is always biased toward zero and that the bias declines sharply as n increases. We also see that the gain from using the control variate varies markedly from case to case. For given β_0, the proportional gain increases with n. For given n, it decreases as β_0 approaches one. In the best case ($n = 400$, $\beta_0 = 0.1$) using the control variate has the same effect as increasing N from 10,000 to 1.9 million, while in the worst case ($n = 25$, $\beta_0 = 0.9$) it has the effect of increasing N to only just under 20,000. Interestingly, the values of $\hat{\lambda}$ are always quite high, becoming very close to 1 for $n = 400$. Evidently, there would be little cost to setting $\lambda = 1$ in this example.

How useful control variates are in practice will often depend on parameter values. This is dramatically illustrated in Figure 21.3, which shows the estimated standard errors of the naive and control variate estimates of β, for 101 values of β_0 from zero to 0.9999 at intervals of 0.01. We used 0.9999 as the upper limit rather than 1.0, because the data were generated on the assumption

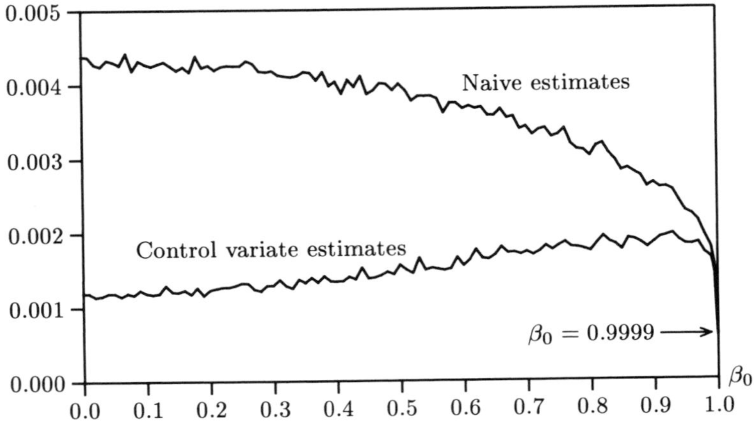

Figure 21.3 Estimated standard errors of bias estimates, $n = 25$

of stationarity. Results for the interval from zero to -0.9999 would look the same. Each estimate is based on 2000 replications, and the irregularities that are evident in the figure reflect experimental error in estimating the standard errors. It is very clear from the figure that, for most values of β_0, the CV estimates are very much more efficient than the naive ones. However, as $\beta_0 \rightarrow 1$, both sets of estimates, especially the naive ones, suddenly become more efficient, and there is virtually nothing to choose between the CV and naive estimates for $\beta_0 > 0.98$. This explains why control variates have not been employed in the Monte Carlo experiments used to determine the distributions of unit root and cointegration test statistics (see Sections 20.3 and 20.6).

One might well be interested in other aspects of the OLS estimates of β besides their mean. One possibility, for example, is their mean squared error. In that case, it is no longer natural to use (21.18) as a control variate, but it does seem plausible to use

$$\frac{1}{n}\sum_{t=1}^{n}\big(u_t y_{t-1}\big)^2 - \frac{\sigma_0^4}{1-\beta_0^2}, \tag{21.19}$$

since it measures the variance of the numerator of the stochastic part of $\hat{\beta}$. Another possible control variate is

$$\frac{1}{n}\sum_{t=1}^{n} y_{t-1}^2 - \frac{\sigma_0^2}{1-\beta_0^2}, \tag{21.20}$$

which is the denominator of the stochastic part of $\hat{\beta}$, minus its mean. Expression (21.20) was not mentioned earlier as a possible control variate because it proved to be completely useless in the control variate regression for the mean of β, but it does turn out to be useful in this case.

Table 21.3 Naive and CV Estimates of the MSE of $\hat{\beta}$

β_0	n	Naive	One Control Variate	Two Control Variates
0.1	25	.03739 ($.510 \times 10^{-3}$)	.03720 ($.317 \times 10^{-3}$)	.03728 ($.272 \times 10^{-3}$)
0.1	100	.00959 ($.134 \times 10^{-3}$)	.00973 ($.468 \times 10^{-4}$)	.00970 ($.390 \times 10^{-4}$)
0.1	400	.00252 ($.351 \times 10^{-4}$)	.00247 ($.650 \times 10^{-5}$)	.00246 ($.524 \times 10^{-5}$)
0.5	25	.03161 ($.522 \times 10^{-3}$)	.03171 ($.454 \times 10^{-3}$)	.03139 ($.384 \times 10^{-3}$)
0.5	100	.00777 ($.734 \times 10^{-4}$)	.00768 ($.696 \times 10^{-4}$)	.00767 ($.542 \times 10^{-4}$)
0.5	400	.00193 ($.281 \times 10^{-4}$)	.00187 ($.976 \times 10^{-5}$)	.00188 ($.756 \times 10^{-5}$)
0.9	25	.01725 ($.413 \times 10^{-3}$)	.01725 ($.413 \times 10^{-3}$)	.01731 ($.377 \times 10^{-3}$)
0.9	100	.00277 ($.563 \times 10^{-4}$)	.00276 ($.548 \times 10^{-4}$)	.00274 ($.439 \times 10^{-4}$)
0.9	400	.00054 ($.922 \times 10^{-5}$)	.00053 ($.748 \times 10^{-5}$)	.00053 ($.534 \times 10^{-5}$)

Table 21.3 shows naive estimates and two sets of CV estimates of the mean squared error of $\hat{\beta}$, for the same nine cases as Table 21.2. Using only one control variate, (21.19), generally yields more accurate estimates than using no control variates, and using two control variates, (21.19) and (21.20), always works better than using only one. However, the gains relative to the naive estimator are always less than those achieved when estimating the mean; compare Table 21.1. This illustrates the general result that control variates tend to be most helpful for estimating means and progressively less helpful for estimating higher moments; see Davidson and MacKinnon (1992b).

Given the highly variable gains from using control variates, it may be advisable in cases for which computational costs are large to determine the number of replications N adaptively. One could decide in advance the acceptable level of precision for the various quantities to be estimated, then calculate those quantities for an initial fairly small value of N (perhaps 500 or so), and use those initial results to estimate how many replications would be needed to obtain standard errors that are sufficiently small. Alternatively, one could calculate standard errors of the quantities of interest after every few hundred replications, stopping when they are sufficiently small. In practice, few Monte Carlo experiments have been designed this way; N is generally just fixed in advance, and the precision of the estimates is whatever it turns out to be.

21.7 RESPONSE SURFACES

As we have stressed above, one of the most difficult aspects of any Monte Carlo experiment is presenting the results in a fashion that makes them easy to comprehend. One approach that is sometimes very useful is to estimate a **response surface**. This is simply a regression model in which each observation corresponds to one experiment, the dependent variable is some quantity that was estimated in the experiments, and the independent variables are functions of the various parameter values, chosen by the experimenter, which characterize each experiment. Response surfaces have been used by Hendry (1979), Mizon and Hendry (1980), Engle, Hendry, and Trumble (1985), Ericsson (1991), and MacKinnon (1991), among others; they are discussed at length in Hendry (1984). For criticisms of this approach, see Maasoumi and Phillips (1982), along with the reply by Hendry (1982).

If a response surface that adequately explains the experimental results can be found, this approach to summarizing Monte Carlo results has much to recommend it. First of all, it may be a good deal easier to understand the behavior of the estimator or test statistic of interest from the parameters of a response surface than from several tables full of numbers. Secondly, if the response surface is correctly specified, it eliminates, or at least greatly reduces, what Hendry (1984) refers to as the problem of **specificity**. What this means is that each individual experiment gives results for a single assumed DGP only, and any set of Monte Carlo experiments gives results for a finite set of assumed DGPs only. For other parameter values or values of n, the reader must interpolate from the results in the tables, which is often difficult to do. In contrast, a correctly specified response surface gives results for whole families of DGPs rather than solely for the parameter values chosen by the experimenter. The catch, of course, is that the response surface must be correctly specified, and this is not always an easy task.

One of the most interesting features of response surfaces, which distinguishes them from most other applications of regression models in economics, is that the data are generated by the experimenter. Thus, if the data are not sufficiently informative, there is always an easy solution: Simply run more experiments and obtain more data. In most cases, each data point for the response surface corresponds to a single Monte Carlo experiment. The dependent variable is then some quantity estimated by the experiment, such as the mean or mean squared error of the estimates of a certain parameter or the estimated size of a test. Because such estimates are normally accompanied by estimates of their standard errors, estimates which should be very accurate if the experiments involve a sufficient number of replications, the investigator is in the unique position of being able to use GLS with a fully specified covariance matrix. If every experiment used a different set of random numbers, each observation for the response surface would be independent, and this covariance matrix would therefore be diagonal. If the same random numbers were used across several experiments, perhaps to increase the precision with which differences across parameters values were estimated, the covariance matrix would of course be nondiagonal, but the form of the nondiagonality would be known, and the covariance matrix could easily be estimated.

To make the above remarks more concrete, let us denote the quantity of interest by ψ. It must be a function of the sample size n and of the parameters that characterize the DGP, which we may denote by the vector $\boldsymbol{\alpha}_0$. We will model this function by $\Psi(n, \boldsymbol{\alpha}_0, \boldsymbol{\gamma})$, where Ψ is a specific functional form that depends on a parameter vector $\boldsymbol{\gamma}$, which will be estimated. The response surface that we are trying to estimate is therefore characterized by $\Psi(n, \boldsymbol{\alpha}_0, \boldsymbol{\gamma}_0)$ for some appropriate vector $\boldsymbol{\gamma}_0$. This expression tells us how ψ responds to changes in n and $\boldsymbol{\alpha}_0$. The ith experiment generates an *estimate* $\hat{\psi}_i$ and an associated estimated standard error $\hat{\sigma}(\hat{\psi}_i)$. The estimate $\hat{\psi}_i$ may be either a simple average over N replications (as we saw in Section 21.5, this is the case even if antithetic variates are being used, except that it is then a simple average over N double replications) or a CV estimate, probably one obtained from regressions (21.14) or (21.15). In either case, if the number of replications per experiment is reasonably large, we can be confident that $\hat{\psi}_i$ is very close to being normally distributed with mean $\Psi(n, \boldsymbol{\alpha}_0, \boldsymbol{\gamma}_0)$ and standard deviation $\sigma(\hat{\psi}_i)$, and that the latter will be well estimated by $\hat{\sigma}(\hat{\psi}_i)$. Thus the response surface regression is

$$\hat{\psi}_i = \Psi(n, \boldsymbol{\alpha}_0, \boldsymbol{\gamma}) + v_i, \quad v_i \sim N\big(0, \hat{\sigma}^2(\hat{\psi}_i)\big), \quad i = 1, \ldots, M, \tag{21.21}$$

where M is the number of experiments and hence the number of observations for the response surface. Transforming (21.21) to eliminate heteroskedasticity, we obtain

$$\frac{\hat{\psi}_i}{\hat{\sigma}(\hat{\psi}_i)} = \frac{\Psi(n, \boldsymbol{\alpha}_0, \boldsymbol{\gamma})}{\hat{\sigma}(\hat{\psi}_i)} + \varepsilon_i, \quad \varepsilon_i \sim N(0, 1), \quad i = 1, \ldots, M. \tag{21.22}$$

The above arguments suggest that, provided the number of replications per experiment is reasonably large, the specification of the error terms in (21.22) as $N(0,1)$ should be an extremely good approximation. However, some authors have claimed that the number of replications per experiment can be much smaller when the aim is to estimate a response surface than it would usually be in more conventional Monte Carlo experiments. For example, Engle, Hendry, and Trumble (1985) uses only 21 replications per experiment. It is true that the parameters $\boldsymbol{\gamma}$ of $\Psi(n, \boldsymbol{\alpha}_0, \boldsymbol{\gamma})$ can often be estimated with great precision even when N is small, provided that M is sufficiently large, because a large number of experiments can compensate for imprecise results from each individual experiment. However, two problems can arise when N is small. First of all, the distribution of $\hat{\psi}_i - \Psi(n, \boldsymbol{\alpha}_0, \boldsymbol{\gamma})$ may differ substantially from the normal, and $\hat{\sigma}(\hat{\psi}_i)$ may provide a poor estimate of $\sigma(\hat{\psi}_i)$. This means that inference based on (21.22) may be problematical. Secondly, if $\hat{\psi}_i$ is not a precise estimate, it can be difficult to specify the functional form of $\Psi(n, \boldsymbol{\alpha}_0, \boldsymbol{\gamma})$. As we will see below, the biggest practical problem with using response surfaces is that the form of $\Psi(n, \boldsymbol{\alpha}_0, \boldsymbol{\gamma})$ is generally not known a priori. Having precise estimates $\hat{\psi}_i$ can be of enormous help in specifying the functional form of $\Psi(n, \boldsymbol{\alpha}_0, \boldsymbol{\gamma})$.

The best way to explain the estimation of response surfaces is to provide a concrete example. The problem we will study is an aspect of the one dealt with in the previous section and also used as an example by Hendry (1984), namely, the bias of the OLS estimate $\hat{\beta}$ in the stationary autoregressive model (21.16). This is of course a problem which has been studied extensively by other methods for a long time; see, for example, Hurwicz (1950). It is really too simple to be the object of a Monte Carlo experiment, because one can in fact calculate the bias of $\hat{\beta}$ analytically, as in Sawa (1978), provided that the error terms are normally distributed, as we assume. However, the required calculations are by no means trivial, and there is no readily interpretable formula that relates the bias of $\hat{\beta}$ to the values of β_0 and n.[4] Phillips (1977) attempts to derive such a formula by the method of asymptotic expansions. Here we attempt to do so by estimating a response surface, using results from Monte Carlo experiments to obtain data points.

We first generated data from 390 experiments, letting β_0 vary from -0.95 to 0.95 by increments of 0.05 and, for each β_0, letting $n = 16, 25, 36, 49, 64, 81, 100, 150, 200$, and 400. We deliberately did not use values of $|\beta_0|$ greater than 0.95 because it would surely be difficult to characterize the behavior of $\hat{\beta}$ by a single response surface for both the stationary case and the unit root case, and we have seen that odd things start to happen as $|\beta_0| \rightarrow 1$ (recall Figure 21.3). The number of replications used in the experiments was relatively small: 2000 for $n = 16$ and 25; 1000 for $n = 36$ and 49; 500 for $n = 64$, 81 and 100; and 250 for $n = 150$, 200, and 400. We used more replications for smaller values of n because the CV estimates of the mean of $\hat{\beta}$ were much less precise for a given number of replications. The regressand for the response surface regression was the CV estimate of the mean of $\hat{\beta}$, minus β_0, divided by the estimated standard error of the mean of $\hat{\beta}$, both obtained from regression (21.14). Note that the estimates of the mean of $\hat{\beta}$ were quite precise: The estimated standard errors varied from .000190 (for $\beta_0 = .05$ and $n = 400$) to .002813 (for $\beta_0 = .90$ and $n = 16$).

Generating the data was easy,[5] but specifying the response surface was much harder. In this case, we can write equation (21.22) as

$$\frac{\hat{\beta}_i - \beta_0}{\hat{\sigma}(\hat{\beta}_i)} = \frac{\Psi(n, \beta_0, \gamma)}{\hat{\sigma}(\hat{\beta}_i)} + \varepsilon_i, \quad \varepsilon_i \sim N(0, 1), \quad i = 1, \ldots, 390,$$

[4] Note that closely related problems, such as the properties of t statistics for this model, cannot be handled analytically. Nankervis and Savin (1988) uses an extremely comprehensive series of Monte Carlo experiments to study the properties of t statistics in a slightly more complicated version of (21.16) in which there is a constant term to be estimated. This paper is one of the best available examples of Monte Carlo methods in action.

[5] These experiments were originally run in 1988 and took about 16 hours on a 286-based personal computer. Since they would have taken less than ten minutes on a 486-based PC, it would have been feasible to use far more replications.

where $\Psi(n, \beta_0, \gamma)$ is the bias function that we are trying to estimate. Asymptotic theory tells us that $\Psi(n, \beta_0, \gamma)$ must tend to zero as $n \to \infty$. This means that there should be no constant term and all regressors should be divided by some positive power of n. However, this still leaves an enormous range of possibilities. We first estimated the very simple bias function

$$\begin{aligned} \Psi(n, \beta_0, \gamma) &= -\underset{(0.0108)}{1.6890}\, n^{-1}\beta_0 \\ s = 1.8038,\ \ &\mathrm{DW} = 1.0322,\ \ \bar{R}^2 = 0.9844. \end{aligned} \tag{21.23}$$

Hendry (1984) estimated a function of this form as a first approximation but found it to be less than satisfactory. These results are also evidently quite unsatisfactory. Although the $\bar{R}^2$ is very high, which implies that $n^{-1}\beta_0$ explains a very large percentage of the total variation in $\hat{\beta} - \beta_0$, the estimated standard error of the equation is much larger than its theoretical value of 1, and the Durbin-Watson statistic is far below 2. Since the data were ordered by n (all observations for $n = 16$ first, then all observations for $n = 25$, and so on), the low DW statistic strongly suggests that the relationship between bias and sample size is misspecified.

The obvious next step was to add additional terms involving powers of β_0 divided by powers of n to (21.23). The literature on asymptotic expansions, for example, Phillips (1977), suggests that one should use powers which are multiples of one-half. Thus one might attempt to estimate a general model of the form

$$\Psi(n, \beta_0, \gamma) = \sum_{a=1}^{6} \sum_{b=1}^{6} \gamma_{ab} n^{-a/2} \beta_0^{b/2} \tag{21.24}$$

and then attempt to simplify it by restricting many of the γ_{ab}'s to equal zero. One would want to let a and b range up to 6 because Hendry (1984) seemed to find evidence that β_0^3/n^3 belonged in $\Psi(n, \beta_0, \gamma)$. This model is bound to fit much better than (21.23), but the estimates will be extremely imprecise because there are 36 possible regressors of the form $n^{-a/2}\beta_0^{b/2}$, and many of them will be highly collinear. Thus we found it impossible to specify a response surface in this way. There was simply no sensible way to get from the general model (21.24) to a more parsimonious one. If this approach is unsatisfactory in this very simple case, in which the DGP involves only one parameter, it will surely be totally unsatisfactory in general.

We therefore took a very different approach, using graphical methods to see what $\Psi(n, \beta_0, \gamma)$ must look like. This approach proved to be very fruitful. It was possible only because our estimates of $\hat{\beta} - \beta_0$ were quite accurate, which meant that plotting $\hat{\beta} - \beta_0$ against β_0 for various values of n, and plotting $\hat{\beta} - \beta_0$ against n for various values of β_0, yielded readily interpretable plots. This is one reason for not using small values of N in Monte Carlo experiments intended for the estimation of response surfaces.

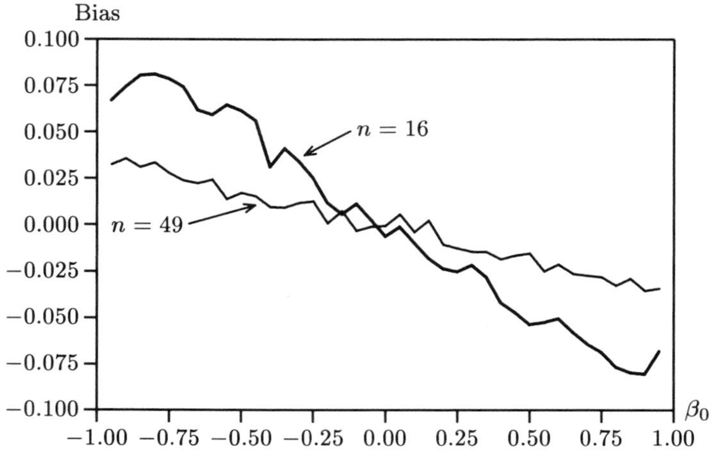

Figure 21.4 Monte Carlo estimates of bias

Figure 21.4 shows the plots of $\hat{\beta} - \beta_0$ against β_0 for $n = 16$ and $n = 49$. It is evident that the relationship is essentially linear and skew-symmetric about zero, except that for $n = 16$ (and to a lesser extent for other small values of n) there is a rather abrupt reversal of the slope for large absolute values of β_0. It is also evident from the figure that the relationship between $\hat{\beta} - \beta_0$ and β_0 becomes less steep as n increases; the relationship for $n = 400$ (not shown to avoid cluttering the figure) was almost flat.

The behavior of the relationship between $\hat{\beta} - \beta_0$ and β_0 for large absolute values of β_0 that is evident in Figure 21.4 suggests that one might want to include functions of β_0^3 in $\Psi(n, \beta_0, \gamma)$. However, there are other functions of β_0 which might also account for the shape evident in the figure, notably $\beta_0/(1 - \beta_0^2)$ and $\beta_0/(1 - \beta_0^2)^{1/2}$. Regressing $\hat{\beta} - \beta_0$ against β_0 and one of β_0^3, $\beta_0/(1 - \beta_0^2)$, and $\beta_0/(1 - \beta_0^2)^{1/2}$ for various values of n led to the tentative conclusion that $\beta_0/(1 - \beta_0^2)^{1/2}$ best explained the observed relationship between $\hat{\beta} - \beta_0$ and β_0.

Similar plots and preliminary regressions suggested that n^{-1} and $n^{-3/2}$ together accounted for almost all of the relationship between $\hat{\beta} - \beta_0$ and the sample size, and that $n^{-1/2}$ and n^{-2} had no role to play. Thus we were tentatively led to the specification

$$\begin{aligned}\Psi(n, \beta_0, \gamma) = n^{-1}\big(&\gamma_1 + \gamma_2\beta_0 + \gamma_3\beta_0/(1 - \beta_0^2)^{1/2}\big)\\ &+ n^{-3/2}\big(\gamma_4 + \gamma_5\beta_0 + \gamma_6\beta_0/(1 - \beta_0^2)^{1/2}\big).\end{aligned} \tag{21.25}$$

This is dramatically simpler than (21.24). When (21.25) was estimated, we found that $\tilde{\gamma}_1$, $\tilde{\gamma}_4$, and $\tilde{\gamma}_5$ were jointly insignificant, although $\tilde{\gamma}_4$ by itself was marginally significant at the 5% level. Since it is hard to see why $\hat{\beta}$ should be biased when $\beta_0 = 0$, and since in contrast to $\tilde{\gamma}_4$ the other three significant parameters were highly significant, we decided on the basis of these results to set γ_1, γ_4, and γ_5 in (21.25) to zero. Our estimates of the resulting model were

$$\begin{aligned}\Psi(n,\beta_0,\gamma) = &- \underset{(0.0173)}{1.9223}\, n^{-1}\beta_0 - \underset{(0.0149)}{0.1066}\, n^{-1}\frac{\beta_0}{(1-\beta_0^2)^{1/2}} \\ &+ \underset{(0.0608)}{1.3509}\, n^{-3/2}\frac{\beta_0}{(1-\beta_0^2)^{1/2}}\end{aligned} \tag{21.26}$$

$$s = 1.0628,\quad \text{DW} = 1.8649,\quad \bar{R}^2 = 0.9946.$$

These results appear to be very good. All three parameters are highly significant, the standard error of the regression is slightly greater than 1, but not significantly so at the 5% level, and the DW statistic is not significantly less than 2. Tests for skewness and excess kurtosis revealed neither. Moreover, when various other functions of β_0 and n, such as $n^{-1}\beta_0/(1-\beta_0^2)$, $n^{-1}\beta_0^3$, $n^{-3/2}\beta_0/(1-\beta_0^2)$, $n^{-3/2}\beta_0^3$, $n^{-2}\beta_0$, and $n^{-2}\beta_0/(1-\beta_0^2)^{1/2}$, were added to $\Psi(n,\beta_0,\gamma)$, they were individually and jointly insignificant, and the three regressors in (21.26) remained individually significant. For sample sizes in the range we examined, the values predicted by (21.26) are very close to the exact values tabulated by Sawa (1978), although the equation seems to predict somewhat too much bias for very small values of n.

We conclude that the response surface (21.26) provides a good, although not perfect, approximation to the bias function $\Psi(n,\beta_0,\gamma)$ over the interval $n = 16$ to $n = \infty$ and $\beta_0 = -0.95$ to $\beta_0 = 0.95$. However, it probably does not do so for very small values of n and for values of $|\beta_0|$ much greater than 0.95. A much more extensive set of experiments, and in all likelihood a considerably more complicated response surface, would be needed if we wished to deal adequately with those cases. This response surface is graphed as a function of β_0 for various values of n in Figure 21.5. The tendencies for bias to fall sharply as n increases, and to rise with $|\beta_0|$ except for a slight dip at high values of $|\beta_0|$, are quite evident in the figure.

In all the estimations reported so far, we used the CV estimates of $\hat{\beta}$. It would also have been possible to use the naive estimates of $\hat{\beta}$. The estimated response surface when we did so was

$$\begin{aligned}\Psi(n,\beta_0,\gamma) = &- \underset{(0.0366)}{1.9272}\, n^{-1}\beta_0 - \underset{(0.0274)}{0.1306}\, n^{-1}\frac{\beta_0}{(1-\beta_0^2)^{1/2}} \\ &+ \underset{(0.1141)}{1.4983}\, n^{-3/2}\frac{\beta_0}{(1-\beta_0^2)^{1/2}}\end{aligned} \tag{21.27}$$

$$s = 1.0811,\quad \text{DW} = 1.8606,\quad \bar{R}^2 = 0.9763.$$

These results are very similar to those using the CV estimates but are somewhat worse in every respect. Standard errors on the parameter estimates are

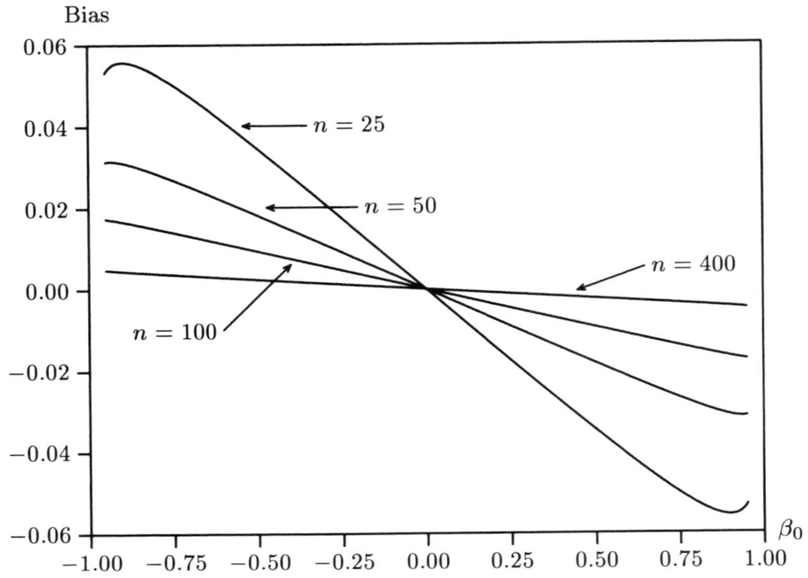

Figure 21.5 Response surface estimates of bias

generally about twice as large, indicating that, on average, using the control variates is roughly equivalent to quadrupling the number of replications. The slightly larger value of s probably indicates that the response surface fits slightly less well for lower values of n. The use of control variates improves the estimates of $\hat{\beta}$ more for larger values of n. Thus the response surface (21.26), which uses CV estimates, weights the results from experiments with larger values of n more heavily than does the response surface (21.27), which uses naive estimates. We would thus expect (21.27) to fit less well than (21.26), as it does, if the response surface performs less well for smaller sample sizes.

This example concerns the estimation of a bias function. Estimation of MSE functions, or size or power functions for test statistics, is conceptually similar, although some details will of course differ. If the dependent variable is the size or power of a test statistic, which we may denote by p, then this dependent variable is constrained to lie between 0 and 1, and the logit transformation

$$\Lambda(p) = \log\left(\frac{p}{1-p}\right)$$

may be useful. The reason for using this transformation is that $\Lambda(p)$ can vary between plus and minus infinity, which may make it easier to specify a response surface as a linear function. Essentially, we would then be estimating a logit model on grouped data (see Chapter 15).

We believe that the above example is quite illuminating. It illustrates how useful response surfaces can be, because of their ability to summarize a great deal of experimental evidence in one relatively simple set of estimates like (21.26), which can then be presented graphically as in Figure 21.5. It also illustrates the practical difficulties of specifying a response surface. The response surface approach will often be impractical if the DGP is characterized by more than a very few parameters that affect the quantities being studied, because it will simply be too difficult to specify the response surface in such a case, at least if there is any interaction between the various parameters. Graphical methods such as the ones we used can be extremely valuable in specifying a response surface, but they do have limits, and it seems unlikely that they would work well when the DGP has many parameters that interact in complicated ways.

21.8 THE BOOTSTRAP AND RELATED METHODS

Up to this point, we have been concerned with "conventional" Monte Carlo experiments in which the experimenter fully specifies the DGP for each experiment. Although such experiments can be used as adjuncts to particular pieces of empirical work and are sometimes fruitfully employed in this way, they are much more commonly used to supplement theoretical work on the properties of estimators and test statistics. In contrast, the technique known as the **bootstrap** is specifically designed to be used in the context of empirical work. As the name suggests, the idea of bootstrapping[6] is to use the single available data set to design a sort of Monte Carlo experiment in which the data themselves are used to approximate the distribution of the error terms or other random quantities in the model. The name is intended to express the idea that the data should be allowed to pull themselves up by their own bootstraps. This idea is implemented by performing a sort of Monte Carlo experiment in which the error terms or other random quantities are usually drawn not from an assumed distribution, such as the normal, but rather from the empirical distribution function of their sample counterparts. Obtaining artificial samples in this way is a special case of what is called **resampling**; see Efron (1979).

We first encountered the **empirical distribution function**, or **EDF**, in Section 4.5. If a sample of size n is denoted by $\{y_t\}_{t=1}^{n}$, where the y_t's are realizations of successive independent random variables, then the EDF is the cumulative distribution function

$$\hat{F}^n(x) \equiv \frac{1}{n}\sum_{t=1}^{n} I_{(-\infty,x)}(y_t),$$

[6] In this literature, "bootstrap" is used as both a noun and a verb.

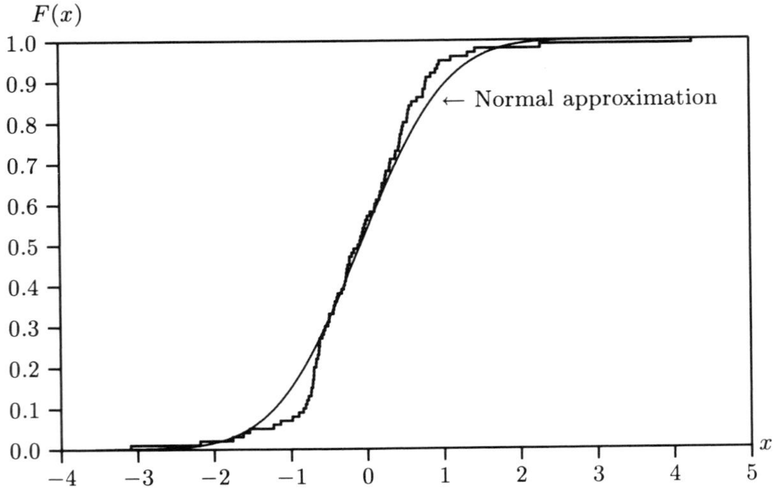

Figure 21.6 Empirical distribution function based on 100 observations

where the indicator function I associated with the interval $(-\infty, x)$ is simply a function that takes the value 1 if its argument is contained in the interval, and 0 otherwise. Thus an EDF is a step function, the height of each step being $1/n$, and the width being equal to the difference between two successive values of y_t when the latter are ordered by ascending size. If two or more observations are identical, which should happen with probability zero if the density of the y_t's is continuous, there may be steps that have height an integer multiple of $1/n$. The EDF for a particular set of 100 observations on a random variable y is shown in Figure 21.6; for comparison, a cumulative normal distribution with the same mean and variance is also shown.

Suppose that one has calculated some statistic $\theta(\boldsymbol{y})$ from a set of data y_t, $t = 1, \ldots, n$, denoted by the n–vector $\boldsymbol{y}$; in practice, one might calculate many different statistics, but, for simplicity, we will deal with only one of them. If the finite-sample distribution of $\theta(\boldsymbol{y})$ is known, or if a good asymptotic approximation is available, there is no point to using the bootstrap. If, however, neither of these is the case, one way to approximate the distribution of $\theta(\boldsymbol{y})$ is to bootstrap this set of data. To do so, one must draw a number of **bootstrap samples**, say B, each of size n, from the EDF of the observed data. This resampling is done *with replacement.* Thus each bootstrap sample will contain some of the original n observations more than once, and others of them not at all, in a completely random order. Drawing a bootstrap sample is very easy. Let $y_j^*(i)$ denote the jth observation of the ith bootstrap sample, where $i = 1, \ldots, B$. To obtain $y_j^*(i)$, we first generate a pseudo-random number from the $U(0, 1)$ distribution, use it to generate a random integer k that takes on the values $1, \ldots, n$ with equal probability, and then set $y_j^*(i)$ to y_k. Repeating this operation n times yields a complete bootstrap sample, say $\boldsymbol{y}^*(i)$. We then calculate $\theta(\boldsymbol{y}^*(i))$ and store the result. The whole operation is then repeated for $i = 1, \ldots, B$ bootstrap samples, at the end of which we have B statistics $\theta(\boldsymbol{y}^*(i))$. These statistics are then used to estimate whatever features of the distribution of $\theta(\boldsymbol{y})$ may be of interest.

The preceding paragraph has sketched the basic idea of the bootstrap, which originated with Efron (1979). Relatively accessible references include Efron (1982), Efron and Gong (1983), and Efron and Tibshirani (1986). More theoretical references include Bickel and Freedman (1981), Freedman (1981), and Hall (1987). The literature has become very large and sometimes very technical in recent years, and we will make no attempt to survey it here.

Let us now illustrate the use of the bootstrap in a simple case. Consider the data that were graphed in Figure 21.6. One can easily see from the figure that these data were drawn from a distribution with fatter tails than the normal. A cumulative normal distribution with the same mean and variance as the data is drawn in the figure, and it is evident that the largest values in each tail of the sample should have occurred with extremely low probability according to the normal distribution. An investigator might therefore worry about whether inferences based on the usual normal-theory estimates and confidence intervals were valid in this case. One way to see if such worries are justified is to bootstrap the statistics of interest.

Consider the mean of the y_t's. The sample mean is -0.0701, with a standard error of 0.0889. Thus the usual 95% confidence interval based on the Student's t distribution with 99 degrees of freedom is $(-0.2464, 0.1062)$. We computed 10,000 bootstrap samples as described above and thus obtained 10,000 estimated means, $\mu^*(i)$. This choice of B is larger than is needed for most purposes and ensures very small experimental error. From the distribution of the $\mu^*(i)$'s, bootstrap confidence intervals can be obtained in several ways; see Efron and Tibshirani (1986) for an introduction and Tibshirani (1988) for more advanced methods. The first step is to sort the bootstrap means $\mu^*(i)$ in ascending order, making $\mu^*(1)$ the smallest and $\mu^*(B)$ the largest. If the distribution of the $\mu^*(i)$'s is approximately symmetric, one can then use what is called the **percentile method**. Suppose that we want a 95% confidence interval. Then we simply pick

$$\tfrac{1}{2}\big(\mu^*(250) + \mu^*(251)\big)$$

as the lower limit of our confidence interval and

$$\tfrac{1}{2}\big(\mu^*(9750) + \mu^*(9751)\big)$$

as the upper limit. These values are chosen so that exactly 2.5% of the bootstrap replications yielded $\mu^*(i)$'s below the lower limit and 2.5% yielded $\mu^*(i)$'s above the upper limit of the confidence interval. Using the percentile method for the data of Figure 21.6 yields a confidence interval of $(-0.2387, 0.1053)$ for the mean of the y_t's, which is very similar to the interval based on the Student's t distribution.

If the distribution of the $\mu^*(i)$'s is not symmetric, one may not want to use the percentile method, because it is no longer optimal to omit the same number of $\mu^*(i)$'s from each end of their EDF if we want the confidence interval to be as short as possible. One simple approach is to minimize the quantity

$$\frac{1}{2}\big(\mu^*(l+.95B)+\mu^*(l+.95B+1)\big)-\frac{1}{2}\big(\mu^*(l-1)+\mu^*(l)\big)$$

with respect to the positive integer $l < .05B$.[7] Thus the objective is to find the shortest interval that includes 95% of the $\mu^*(i)$'s. When the EDF of the $\mu^*(i)$'s is asymmetric, this **modified percentile method** will tend to move the confidence interval away from the longer tail of the distribution, because dropping observations at that end and adding them at the other end will reduce the length of the estimated confidence interval. For the data of Figure 21.6, the modified percentile method yields very similar results to the ordinary percentile method and to the usual normal theory method: The 95% confidence interval is $(-0.2399, 0.1031)$.

In this example, then, the bootstrap has principally served to reassure us that conventional methods of inference about the mean of the y_t's are probably fairly reliable for this data set, despite the apparent excess kurtosis relative to the normal case. But the same procedure could be employed to investigate the distribution of any statistic $\theta(\boldsymbol{y})$ in which we were interested, including ones for which more conventional methods of inference are difficult or impossible. It is in such cases that the bootstrap can be particularly useful.

The bootstrap as just described can obviously be modified in various ways. One could, for example, smooth the EDF of the y_t's somewhat and draw bootstrap samples from the smoothed EDF instead of from the ordinary EDF. If one knew or was willing to assume the form of the distribution of the y_t's, one could use what is often called the **parametric bootstrap**, in which the data are used to estimate the density of the y_t's, and bootstrap samples are then generated from that estimated density. The parametric bootstrap thus resembles an ordinary Monte Carlo experiment in which the parameters of the DGP are estimated from the data set of interest.

There are some special features of bootstrap methods applied to regression models. Suppose the model is

$$y_t = x_t(\boldsymbol{\beta}) + u_t, \quad t = 1, \ldots, n, \tag{21.28}$$

[7] This assumes that $.95B$ is an integer, which it will be if B is an integer multiple of 100.

where any variables on which $x_t(\boldsymbol{\beta})$ depends are assumed to be fixed or at least independent of all the u_t's. If the latter are assumed to be i.i.d., the natural approach is to bootstrap the residuals. With this approach, one first estimates the model (21.28) by NLS, so as to obtain parameter estimates $\hat{\boldsymbol{\beta}}$ and residuals $\hat{u}_1$ through $\hat{u}_n$, and then generates bootstrap samples from the data-generating process

$$y_j(i) = x_j(\hat{\boldsymbol{\beta}}) + u_j^*(i), \quad j = 1, \ldots, n, \tag{21.29}$$

where the $u_j^*(i)$'s are random samples with replacement from $\hat{u}_1, \ldots, \hat{u}_n$. If $x_t(\boldsymbol{\beta})$ depends on past values of y_t, this approach can still be employed, but in (21.29) $y_1(i), \ldots, y_{j-1}(i)$ must be used in place of the actual lagged y_t's in computing $x_j(\hat{\boldsymbol{\beta}})$. Since the model (21.28) is nonlinear, bootstrapping it may be rather expensive, and the technique is therefore used primarily with linear models.

This approach has two other problems. The first is that, as usual, the residuals $\hat{u}_t$ tend to underestimate the error terms u_t. This can be dealt with by using the modified residuals

$$\tilde{u}_t = \frac{\hat{u}_t}{(1 - \hat{h}_t)^{1/2}} - \frac{1}{n}\sum_{s=1}^{n} \frac{\hat{u}_s}{(1 - \hat{h}_s)^{1/2}}, \tag{21.30}$$

where

$$\hat{h}_t \equiv \hat{\boldsymbol{X}}_t \big(\hat{\boldsymbol{X}}^\top \hat{\boldsymbol{X}}\big)^{-1} \hat{\boldsymbol{X}}_t^\top$$

and $\hat{\boldsymbol{X}}$, as usual, is the matrix of the derivatives of $x_t(\boldsymbol{\beta})$ with respect to the elements of $\boldsymbol{\beta}$, evaluated at $\hat{\boldsymbol{\beta}}$. It is obvious why we would want to divide $\hat{u}_t$ by $(1 - \hat{h}_t)^{1/2}$. As we first saw in Section 3.2, in the case of a linear regression model with i.i.d. errors,

$$E(u_t^2) = (1 - h_t)\sigma^2.$$

Therefore, dividing $\hat{u}_t$ by $(1 - h_t)^{1/2}$ would yield modified residuals with precisely the right variance. Dividing by $(1 - \hat{h}_t)^{1/2}$ is the natural analog of this procedure for the nonlinear case and is justified by the theoretical result (5.57) of Section 5.6. In (21.30), we then subtract the mean of the $\hat{u}_t/(1 - \hat{h}_t)^{1/2}$'s, which will generally not be zero, in order to ensure that the $\tilde{u}_t$'s do have mean zero; see Weber (1984).

The second problem with this approach to bootstrapping is that it assumes that the error terms u_t are independently and identically distributed. When that assumption is doubtful, a second approach can be used. In this second approach, we resample from $\big(y_t,\, x_t(\hat{\boldsymbol{\beta}})\big)$ rather than from $\hat{u}_t$ or $\tilde{u}_t$. A typical member of the bootstrap sample is $\big(y_k,\, x_k(\hat{\boldsymbol{\beta}})\big)$, where k is a random draw from $1, \ldots, n$. In the linear case, each element of the bootstrap sample is $(y_k,\, \boldsymbol{X}_k)$, where $\boldsymbol{X}_k$ is the kth row of the matrix of observations on the independent variables. This second approach is clearly infeasible if $x_t(\boldsymbol{\beta})$ depends on lagged values of y_t, since it does not make sense to use actual lagged y_t's, and we have no way to generate lagged y_t's from the bootstrap. However, it has the advantage of being valid even in the presence of heteroskedasticity. Indeed, this form of bootstrapping yields results that are often very similar to those from using a heteroskedasticity-consistent covariance matrix estimator.

Neither of these approaches to bootstrapping allows us to deal with models in which the error terms are thought to be serially dependent but the form of the dependence is unknown. The resampling breaks up whatever dependence there may be in the original data, and the bootstrap results thus cannot be relied on if such dependence is a problem.

Applications of bootstrap methods to econometrics include Freedman and Peters (1984), Korajczyk (1985), Bernard and Veall (1987), and Veall (1987). The first two papers use the bootstrap to improve inferences for estimated models for which available asymptotic theory might be expected to be unreliable. The second two papers use it to estimate confidence intervals for forecasts, something that is often extremely difficult to do analytically when the forecasting technique is at all complicated. Fair (1980) is also concerned with the accuracy of forecasts and, although his paper does not use the term, it can be regarded as an example of the parametric bootstrap. Raj and Taylor (1989) examine the finite-sample properties of test statistics based on bootstrapping, and Veall (1992) shows how to use the bootstrap for model selection.

As computer costs come down, it is likely that more and more applied workers will turn to variants of the bootstrap to deal with models for which asymptotic theory may be inadequate. This raises the question of whether the bootstrap is itself adequate to handle such models. Except perhaps in certain special cases, the only way to answer this question would seem to be to perform Monte Carlo experiments in which the objects of interest are bootstrap estimates. Unfortunately, this will often be very expensive, since if there are N replications per experiment and B bootstrap samples are required to obtain each bootstrap estimate, a single experiment would involve a total of BN estimations. Unless each estimation can be done very quickly, such an experiment could involve a great deal of computer time. However, as computers become faster, we can certainly expect to see Monte Carlo studies of the bootstrap in situations of interest to econometricians, as well as more widespread use of the bootstrap in applied work.

21.9 CONCLUSION

By the time this book is published, computers with as much power as a large mainframe of the early 1980s will be so cheap that the desk and maybe even the briefcase of everyone who uses econometrics will be equipped with one. In that environment, Monte Carlo methods are likely to be used much more extensively than has been the case up to now. Readers and editors will refuse to accept results based on methods for estimation and hypothesis testing that have statistical properties which are known only asymptotically, when they know that better approximations can almost always be obtained at the cost of a certain amount of computation. Some form of bootstrapping, which in its parametric version closely resembles the more conventional Monte Carlo experiments on which we have mainly concentrated, is thus likely to be used routinely as part of many empirical papers.

Terms and Concepts

antithetic variates
asymptotic expansions (finite-sample approximations)
the bootstrap (bootstrapping)
bootstrap sample
Box-Muller method
congruential generator (of pseudo-random numbers)
control variates
empirical distribution function (EDF)
increment (for congruential generator)
modified percentile method
modulus (for congruential generator)
Monte Carlo experiment
Monte Carlo methods
multiplicative congruential generator
multiplier (for congruential generator)
parametric bootstrap
percentile method
pseudo-random numbers
pseudo-random variates
random number generator
rejection method
replications
resampling
response surface
seed (for random number generator)
specificity (problem of)
transformation method
variance reduction techniques

Appendix A

Matrix Algebra

A.1 Introduction

As anyone who has studied econometrics or any other mathematical discipline knows, the difference between a result that seems obscure and difficult and a result that seems clear and intuitive is often simply the notation that is used. In almost all cases, the clearest notation for econometrics makes extensive use of vectors and matrices. Readers of this book should already be reasonably familiar with matrix algebra. This appendix is provided to aid those who wish to refresh their memories and to collect results for easy reference. Readers should note that Chapter 1 also contains a number of useful results on matrices, in particular concerning projection matrices. In this appendix, proofs will be given only if they are either short or interesting. Those interested in a fuller and more rigorous treatment are referred to Lang (1987).

A.2 Elementary Facts about Matrices

An $n \times m$ **matrix** $\boldsymbol{A}$ is a rectangular array that consists of nm elements arranged in n rows and m columns. The name of the matrix is conventionally shown in boldface. A typical element of $\boldsymbol{A}$ might be denoted A_{ij} or a_{ij}, where $i = 1, \ldots, n$ and $j = 1, \ldots, m$. The first subscript always indicates the row and the second always indicates the column. It is occasionally necessary to show the elements of a matrix explicitly, in which case they are arrayed in rows and columns and surrounded by large brackets, as in

$$\boldsymbol{B} = \begin{bmatrix} 1 & 2 & 4 \\ 3 & 5 & 5 \end{bmatrix}.$$

Here $\boldsymbol{B}$ is a 2×3 matrix.

If a matrix has only one column or only one row, it is called a **vector**. There are two types of vectors, **column vectors** and **row vectors**, the names of which are self-explanatory. Since the first type is more common than the second, a vector that is not specified to be a row vector should be treated as a column vector. If a column vector has n elements, it may be referred to as an n–vector. Boldface is used to denote vectors as well as matrices. It is conventional to use uppercase letters for matrices and lowercase letters for vectors. However, it is sometimes necessary to ignore this convention.

If a matrix has the same number of columns and rows, it is said to be **square**. A square matrix $\boldsymbol{A}$ is said to be **symmetric** if $A_{ij} = A_{ji}$ for all i and j. Symmetric matrices occur very frequently in econometrics. A square matrix is said to be **diagonal** if $A_{ij} = 0$ for all $i \neq j$; in this case, the only nonzero entries are those on what is called the **principal diagonal**. Sometimes a square matrix has all zeros above or below the principal diagonal. Such a matrix is said to be **triangular**. If the nonzero elements are all above the diagonal, it is said to be **upper-triangular**; if the nonzero elements are all below the diagonal, it is said to be **lower-triangular**. Here are some examples:

$$\boldsymbol{A} = \begin{bmatrix} 1 & 2 & 4 \\ 2 & 3 & 6 \\ 4 & 6 & 5 \end{bmatrix} \qquad \boldsymbol{B} = \begin{bmatrix} 1 & 0 & 0 \\ 0 & 4 & 0 \\ 0 & 0 & 2 \end{bmatrix} \qquad \boldsymbol{C} = \begin{bmatrix} 1 & 0 & 0 \\ 3 & 2 & 0 \\ 5 & 2 & 6 \end{bmatrix}.$$

In this case, $\boldsymbol{A}$ is symmetric, $\boldsymbol{B}$ is diagonal, and $\boldsymbol{C}$ is lower-triangular.

A special matrix that econometricians frequently make use of is $\mathbf{I}$, which denotes the **identity matrix**. It is a diagonal matrix with every diagonal element equal to 1. A subscript is sometimes used to indicate the number of rows and columns. Thus

$$\mathbf{I}_3 = \begin{bmatrix} 1 & 0 & 0 \\ 0 & 1 & 0 \\ 0 & 0 & 1 \end{bmatrix}.$$

A special vector that we use quite a lot in this book is $\boldsymbol{\iota}$, which denotes a column vector every element of which is 1.

The **transpose** of a matrix is obtained by interchanging all its row and column subscripts. Thus the ij^{th} element of $\boldsymbol{A}$ becomes the ji^{th} element of its transpose, which is denoted $\boldsymbol{A}^{\top}$. Note that many authors use $\boldsymbol{A}'$ rather than $\boldsymbol{A}^{\top}$ to denote the transpose of $\boldsymbol{A}$. The transpose of a symmetric matrix is equal to the matrix itself. The transpose of a column vector is a row vector, and vice versa. Here are some examples:

$$\boldsymbol{A} = \begin{bmatrix} 1 & 2 & 4 \\ 3 & 5 & 5 \end{bmatrix} \quad \boldsymbol{A}^{\top} = \begin{bmatrix} 1 & 3 \\ 2 & 5 \\ 4 & 5 \end{bmatrix} \quad \boldsymbol{b} = \begin{bmatrix} 1 \\ 3 \\ 5 \end{bmatrix} \quad \boldsymbol{b}^{\top} = [\,1 \quad 3 \quad 5\,].$$

Addition and subtraction of matrices works exactly the way it does for scalars, with the proviso that matrices can be added or subtracted only if they are **conformable**. In the case of addition and subtraction, this just means that they must have the same dimensions. If $\boldsymbol{A}$ and $\boldsymbol{B}$ are conformable, then a typical element of $\boldsymbol{A} + \boldsymbol{B}$ is simply $A_{ij} + B_{ij}$, and a typical element of $\boldsymbol{A} - \boldsymbol{B}$ is $A_{ij} - B_{ij}$.

Matrix multiplication actually involves both additions and multiplications. It is based on what is called the **inner product**, or **scalar product**, of two vectors. Suppose that $\boldsymbol{a}$ and $\boldsymbol{b}$ are n–vectors. Then their inner product is

$$\boldsymbol{a}^\top \boldsymbol{b} = \boldsymbol{b}^\top \boldsymbol{a} = \sum_{i=1}^{n} a_i b_i. \tag{A.01}$$

When two matrices are multiplied together, each element of the result is equal to the inner product of one of the rows of the first matrix with one of the columns of the second matrix. Thus, if $\boldsymbol{C} = \boldsymbol{AB}$,

$$C_{ik} = \sum_{j=1}^{m} A_{ij} B_{jk}.$$

Here we have implicitly assumed that $\boldsymbol{A}$ has m columns and that $\boldsymbol{B}$ has m rows. If two matrices are to be conformable for multiplication, the first matrix must have as many columns as the second has rows. The result then has as many rows as the first matrix and as many columns as the second. One way to make this explicit is to write something like

$$\underset{n\times m}{\boldsymbol{A}}\ \underset{m\times l}{\boldsymbol{B}} = \underset{n\times l}{\boldsymbol{C}}.$$

One rarely sees this type of notation in a book or journal article, but it is often convenient to use it when doing calculations, to verify that the matrices being multiplied are indeed conformable and to derive the dimensions of their product.

The **outer product** of two vectors $\boldsymbol{a}$ and $\boldsymbol{b}$ is $\boldsymbol{ab}^\top$. In contrast to the inner product, which is a scalar, the outer product is an $n \times n$ matrix if the vectors are n–vectors.

Matrix multiplication and matrix addition interact in an intuitive way. It is easy to check from the definitions of the respective operations that the **distributive** property holds. That is,

$$\boldsymbol{A}(\boldsymbol{B} + \boldsymbol{C}) = \boldsymbol{AB} + \boldsymbol{AC}.$$

In addition, both operations are **associative**, which means that

$$(\boldsymbol{A} + \boldsymbol{B}) + \boldsymbol{C} = \boldsymbol{A} + (\boldsymbol{B} + \boldsymbol{C}) \quad \text{and}$$
$$(\boldsymbol{AB})\boldsymbol{C} = \boldsymbol{A}(\boldsymbol{BC}).$$

Matrix multiplication is, in general, not commutative. The fact that it is possible to **premultiply** $\boldsymbol{B}$ by $\boldsymbol{A}$ does not imply that it is possible to **postmultiply** $\boldsymbol{B}$ by $\boldsymbol{A}$. In fact, it is easy to see that both operations are possible if and only if one of the matrix products is square, in which case the other matrix product will be square also, although generally with different dimensions. Even when both operations are possible, $\boldsymbol{AB} \neq \boldsymbol{BA}$ except in special cases. The rules for multiplying matrices and vectors together are the same as the rules for multiplying matrices with each other; vectors are simply treated as matrices that have only one column or only one row.

The identity matrix $\mathbf{I}$ is so called because when it is either premultiplied or postmultiplied by any matrix, it leaves the latter unchanged. Thus, for any matrix $\boldsymbol{A}$, $\boldsymbol{A}\mathbf{I} = \mathbf{I}\boldsymbol{A} = \boldsymbol{A}$, provided of course that the two matrices are conformable in each case. It is easy to see why the identity matrix has this property. The ij^{th} element of $\boldsymbol{A}\mathbf{I}$ is

$$\sum_{k=1}^{m} A_{ik}\mathrm{I}_{kj} = A_{ij},$$

since $\mathrm{I}_{kj} = 0$ for $k \neq j$ and $\mathrm{I}_{kj} = 1$ for $k = j$. The special vector $\boldsymbol{\iota}$ is also useful. It comes in handy when one wishes to sum the elements of another vector, because, for any n–vector $\boldsymbol{b}$,

$$\boldsymbol{\iota}^{\top}\boldsymbol{b} = \sum_{i=1}^{n} b_i.$$

The transpose of the product of two matrices is the product of the transposes of the matrices with the order reversed. Thus

$$(\boldsymbol{AB})^{\top} = \boldsymbol{B}^{\top}\boldsymbol{A}^{\top}. \tag{A.02}$$

The reversal of the order is necessary for the transposed matrices to be conformable for multiplication. The result (A.02) can be proved immediately by writing out the typical entries of both sides and checking that they are the same:

$$(\boldsymbol{AB})^{\top}_{ij} = (\boldsymbol{AB})_{ji} = \sum_{k=1}^{m} A_{jk}B_{ki} = \sum_{k=1}^{m} (\boldsymbol{B}^{\top})_{ik}(\boldsymbol{A}^{\top})_{kj} = (\boldsymbol{B}^{\top}\boldsymbol{A}^{\top})_{ij},$$

where m is the number of columns of $\boldsymbol{A}$ and the number of rows of $\boldsymbol{B}$. It is always possible to multiply a matrix by its own transpose: If $\boldsymbol{A}$ is $n \times m$, then $\boldsymbol{A}^{\top}$ is $m \times n$, $\boldsymbol{A}^{\top}\boldsymbol{A}$ is $m \times m$, and $\boldsymbol{A}\boldsymbol{A}^{\top}$ is $n \times n$. Both of these matrix products are symmetric:

$$\boldsymbol{A}^{\top}\boldsymbol{A} = (\boldsymbol{A}^{\top}\boldsymbol{A})^{\top} \quad \text{and} \quad \boldsymbol{A}\boldsymbol{A}^{\top} = (\boldsymbol{A}\boldsymbol{A}^{\top})^{\top}, \tag{A.03}$$

as follows directly by application of (A.02).

Every element of the product of two matrices is a summation. This suggests that it may be convenient to use matrix algebra when dealing with summations, and that is indeed the case. Suppose, for example, that we have n observations on k regressors. These can be arranged into the $n \times k$ matrix $\boldsymbol{X}$.

Then the matrix of sums of squares and cross-products of the regressors can be written very compactly as $\boldsymbol{X}^\top\boldsymbol{X}$. This is a $k\times k$ symmetric matrix, of which a typical diagonal element is $\sum_{t=1}^{n} X_{ti}^2$ and a typical off-diagonal element is $\sum_{t=1}^{n} X_{ti}X_{tj}$.

It is frequently necessary to multiply a matrix by a scalar, and this works exactly as one would expect: Each element of the matrix is multiplied by the scalar. Occasionally, it is necessary to multiply two matrices together element by element. The result is called the **direct product** (or sometimes the **Schur product**) of the two matrices. The direct product of $\boldsymbol{A}$ and $\boldsymbol{B}$ is denoted $\boldsymbol{A}*\boldsymbol{B}$, and a typical element of it is $A_{ij}B_{ij}$.

A square matrix may or may not be **invertible**. If $\boldsymbol{A}$ is invertible, then it has an **inverse matrix** $\boldsymbol{A}^{-1}$ with the property that

$$\boldsymbol{A}\boldsymbol{A}^{-1} = \boldsymbol{A}^{-1}\boldsymbol{A} = \mathbf{I}.$$

If $\boldsymbol{A}$ is symmetric, then so is $\boldsymbol{A}^{-1}$. If $\boldsymbol{A}$ is triangular, then so is $\boldsymbol{A}^{-1}$. Except in certain special cases, it is not easy to calculate the inverse of a matrix by hand. One such special case is that of a diagonal matrix, say $\boldsymbol{D}$, with typical diagonal element D_{ii}. It is easy to verify that $\boldsymbol{D}^{-1}$ is also a diagonal matrix, with typical diagonal element D_{ii}^{-1}.

It is often convenient to make use of the **trace** of a square matrix, which is simply the sum of the elements on its principal diagonal. Thus

$$\operatorname{Tr}(\boldsymbol{A}) = \sum_{i=1}^{n} A_{ii}.$$

A very useful property of the trace is that the trace of a product of two matrices $\boldsymbol{A}$ and $\boldsymbol{B}$ is unaffected by the order in which the two matrices are multiplied together. Since the trace is defined only for square matrices, both $\boldsymbol{AB}$ and $\boldsymbol{BA}$ must be defined. Then we have

$$\operatorname{Tr}(\boldsymbol{AB}) = \sum_{i=1}^{n}(\boldsymbol{AB})_{ii} = \sum_{i=1}^{n}\sum_{j=1}^{m} A_{ij}B_{ji} = \sum_{j=1}^{m}(\boldsymbol{BA})_{jj} = \operatorname{Tr}(\boldsymbol{BA}). \qquad \text{(A.04)}$$

The result (A.04) can be extended. If one considers a (square) product of several matrices, the trace is invariant under what is called a **cyclic permutation** of the factors. Thus, for instance,

$$\operatorname{Tr}(\boldsymbol{ABC}) = \operatorname{Tr}(\boldsymbol{CAB}) = \operatorname{Tr}(\boldsymbol{BCA}), \qquad \text{(A.05)}$$

as can be seen by successive applications of (A.04). This result can be extremely convenient, and several standard results on the properties of OLS make use of it. For example, if $\boldsymbol{X}$ is an $n\times k$ matrix, (A.05) implies that

$$\operatorname{Tr}\big(\boldsymbol{X}(\boldsymbol{X}^\top\boldsymbol{X})^{-1}\boldsymbol{X}^\top\big) = \operatorname{Tr}\big(\boldsymbol{X}^\top\boldsymbol{X}(\boldsymbol{X}^\top\boldsymbol{X})^{-1}\big) = \operatorname{Tr}(\mathbf{I}_k) = k.$$

A.3 THE GEOMETRY OF VECTORS

The elements of an n–vector can be thought of as the coordinates of a point in an n–dimensional **Euclidean space**, which may be denoted E^n. The difference between E^n and the more familiar $\mathbb{R}^n$ is that the former includes a specific definition of the **length** of each vector in E^n. The length of a vector $\boldsymbol{x}$ is

$$\|\boldsymbol{x}\| \equiv (\boldsymbol{x}^\top \boldsymbol{x})^{1/2}.$$

This is just the square root of the inner product of $\boldsymbol{x}$ with itself. In scalar terms, it is simply

$$\left(\sum_{i=1}^{n} x_i^2\right)^{1/2}. \tag{A.06}$$

As the notation $\|\cdot\|$ indicates, the length of a vector is sometimes referred to as its **norm**. This definition is inspired by the celebrated theorem of Pythagoras about the squares of the sides of right-angled triangles. The definition (A.06) is just a generalization of that result to an arbitrary number of dimensions.

There is actually more than one way to define an inner product. The one that we defined above in (A.01), and the only one that we use explicitly in this book, is called the **natural inner product**. The natural inner product of two vectors $\boldsymbol{y}$ and $\boldsymbol{x}$ is often denoted $\langle \boldsymbol{x}, \boldsymbol{y} \rangle \equiv \boldsymbol{x}^\top \boldsymbol{y}$. The norm of a vector can be defined in terms of the natural inner product, since $\|\boldsymbol{x}\|^2 = \langle \boldsymbol{x}, \boldsymbol{x} \rangle$. A fundamental inequality linking norms and inner products is

$$|\langle \boldsymbol{x}, \boldsymbol{y} \rangle| \leq \|\boldsymbol{x}\| \, \|\boldsymbol{y}\|. \tag{A.07}$$

Only if $\boldsymbol{x}$ and $\boldsymbol{y}$ are **parallel**, that is, if $\boldsymbol{y} = \alpha \boldsymbol{x}$ for some scalar α, does the inequality in (A.07) become an equality.

The concept of the length of a vector extends naturally to a concept of the **distance** between two points in E^n. If $\boldsymbol{x}, \boldsymbol{y} \in E^n$, the distance between $\boldsymbol{x}$ and $\boldsymbol{y}$ is just $\|\boldsymbol{x} - \boldsymbol{y}\|$. Note that this definition is symmetric with respect to $\boldsymbol{x}$ and $\boldsymbol{y}$. The concept of inner product also allows us to define what we mean in a general context by the **angle** between two vectors. For $\boldsymbol{x}, \boldsymbol{y} \in E^n$, the angle $\phi \equiv \angle(\boldsymbol{x}, \boldsymbol{y})$ can be defined in terms of its **cosine**, $\cos \phi$, as follows:

$$\cos \phi = \frac{\langle \boldsymbol{x}, \boldsymbol{y} \rangle}{\|\boldsymbol{x}\| \, \|\boldsymbol{y}\|}.$$

This definition gives a value to $\cos \phi$ that lies in the interval $[-1, 1]$, by (A.07). The definition is unique only if one restricts the possible range of ϕ to an interval of length π (*not* 2π). Usually, the best interval to choose is $[0, \pi]$. With that choice, the angle between a vector and itself is 0, between a vector and its negative is π, and between a vector and another vector orthogonal to it is $\pi/2$. Vectors are **orthogonal** if their inner product is zero.

The quantity used in econometrics that corresponds most closely to the geometrical concept of the cosine of an angle is the R^2 of a linear regression. As discussed in Chapter 1, the R^2 of the regression $\boldsymbol{y} = \boldsymbol{X\beta} + \boldsymbol{u}$ is the square of the cosine of the angle between the n-vector $\boldsymbol{y}$ and the projection $\boldsymbol{P}_X \boldsymbol{y}$ of that vector onto the span $\mathcal{S}(\boldsymbol{X})$ of the regressors.

Once the cosine of an angle ϕ has been found, it is possible to compute the values of all the other trigonometric functions of ϕ. These functions are the **sine**, $\sin\phi$, the **tangent**, $\tan\phi$, the **cotangent**, $\cot\phi$, the **secant**, $\sec\phi$, and the **cosecant**, $\csc\phi$. Of these, the only one that concerns us here is the cotangent, for it is intimately related to the t statistics of linear regressions. In terms of $\cos\phi$, $\cot\phi$ is defined as follows, for $\phi \in [0, \pi]$:

$$\cot\phi = \frac{\cos\phi}{(1 - \cos^2\phi)^{1/2}}. \tag{A.08}$$

Unlike a cosine, which must lie between -1 and 1, a cotangent can evidently take on any real value.

For the special case of a simple linear regression $\boldsymbol{y} = \beta\boldsymbol{x} + \boldsymbol{u}$ with no constant term, the t statistic on $\boldsymbol{x}$ is

$$\frac{\hat\beta}{s(\boldsymbol{x}^\top\boldsymbol{x})^{-1/2}}, \tag{A.09}$$

where $\hat\beta$ is the OLS estimate of β, $(\boldsymbol{x}^\top\boldsymbol{x})^{-1}\boldsymbol{x}^\top\boldsymbol{y}$, and s is the OLS estimate of σ, the standard deviation of the error terms. In geometrical notation, if ϕ is the angle between $\boldsymbol{y}$ and $\boldsymbol{x}$, we have

$$\begin{aligned}
\hat\beta &= \frac{\langle \boldsymbol{x}, \boldsymbol{y}\rangle}{\langle \boldsymbol{x}, \boldsymbol{x}\rangle} = \frac{\|\boldsymbol{y}\|}{\|\boldsymbol{x}\|}\cos\phi, \\
(\boldsymbol{x}^\top\boldsymbol{x})^{1/2} &= \|\boldsymbol{x}\|, \quad \text{and} \\
s^2 &= (n-1)^{-1}\big(\boldsymbol{y}^\top\boldsymbol{y} - \boldsymbol{y}^\top\boldsymbol{x}(\boldsymbol{x}^\top\boldsymbol{x})^{-1}\boldsymbol{x}^\top\boldsymbol{y}\big) \\
&= (n-1)^{-1}\|\boldsymbol{y}\|^2(1 - \cos^2\phi).
\end{aligned}$$

Substituting these results into expression (A.09) for the t statistic, we find that the value of the statistic is

$$(n-1)^{1/2}\frac{\cos\phi}{(1 - \cos^2\phi)^{1/2}} = (n-1)^{1/2}\cot\phi,$$

by (A.08). See Chapter 3 for an analogous result in the context of multiple regression.

A.4 MATRICES AS MAPPINGS OF LINEAR SPACES

An $n \times m$ matrix $\boldsymbol{A}$ can be thought of fruitfully as defining a **mapping** of E^m into E^n. One writes

$$\boldsymbol{A} : E^m \to E^n.$$

Note the order of m and n here. The interpretation is simple. Since the product of an $n \times m$ matrix and an $m \times 1$ column vector is defined and is an $n \times 1$ column vector, we may define the action of $\boldsymbol{A}$ on an m–vector $\boldsymbol{x}$, $\boldsymbol{A}(\boldsymbol{x})$, as the matrix product $\boldsymbol{Ax}$, and this is an n–vector. The mapping so defined is linear, because, if α and β are arbitrary scalars,

$$\boldsymbol{A}(\alpha\boldsymbol{x} + \beta\boldsymbol{y}) = \alpha\boldsymbol{Ax} + \beta\boldsymbol{Ay},$$

by the standard properties of matrix operations.

The space E^m of arguments to the mapping $\boldsymbol{A}$ is called the **domain** of the mapping, and the space E^n of values is called the **codomain**. An important linear subspace of the domain is the **kernel** of the matrix. It is defined as follows:

$$\mathsf{N}(\boldsymbol{A}) \equiv \{\boldsymbol{x} \in E^m \mid \boldsymbol{Ax} = \boldsymbol{0}\}.$$

We may say that the kernel of $\boldsymbol{A}$ is **annihilated** by $\boldsymbol{A}$. An important linear subspace of the codomain is called the **range**. The range is defined by the expression

$$\mathsf{R}(\boldsymbol{A}) \equiv \{\boldsymbol{y} \in E^n \mid \boldsymbol{y} = \boldsymbol{Ax} \text{ for some } \boldsymbol{x} \in E^m\}.$$

The range may be described as the subspace of E^n that contains all points that are the **image** of a point in E^m under $\boldsymbol{A}$. The set of points in E^m that are mapped into a point $\boldsymbol{y} \in E^n$, that is, that have $\boldsymbol{y}$ as their image, is called the **preimage** of the point $\boldsymbol{y}$.

It is clear intuitively that the **dimension** of the Euclidean space E^m is m. We write $\dim E^m = m$. When dealing with subspaces like kernels or ranges, the dimensions of these subspaces are less apparent. The necessary formal definition is as follows. A linear space is of dimension n if there exist n **linearly independent** vectors in the space and if all sets of more than n vectors of the space are linearly dependent. A set of vectors $\boldsymbol{x}_i$, $i = 1, \ldots, m$, is said to be **linearly dependent** if there exists a nontrivial linear combination of them which is zero. That is, the $\boldsymbol{x}_i$'s are linearly dependent if there are m scalars α_i, not all zero, such that

$$\sum_{i=1}^{m} \alpha_i \boldsymbol{x}_i = \boldsymbol{0}. \tag{A.10}$$

For E^m itself, a suitable set of linearly independent vectors is provided by the set of **orthonormal basis vectors** $\boldsymbol{e}_i$, $i = 1, \ldots, m$. Here $\boldsymbol{e}_i$ is an m–vector of which the ith element is 1 and all other elements are 0. The expression on the left-hand side of (A.10), when computed with $\boldsymbol{e}_i$ in place of $\boldsymbol{x}_i$, is the

m–vector $\boldsymbol{\alpha}$ with typical element α_i. Clearly, this vector is zero only if $\alpha_i = 0$ for all $i = 1, \ldots, m$, and so the $\boldsymbol{e}_i$'s are linearly independent.

The **orthogonal complement** of a subspace $\mathsf{M} \subseteq E^m$ is the linear space

$$\mathsf{M}^\perp \equiv \left\{ \boldsymbol{x} \in E^m \mid \boldsymbol{x}^\top \boldsymbol{y} = 0 \text{ for all } \boldsymbol{y} \in \mathsf{M} \right\}.$$

If v is the dimension of the kernel of the $n \times m$ matrix $\boldsymbol{A}$, and r is the dimension of its range, then the following relation is true:

$$m - v = r. \tag{A.11}$$

This says that the dimension of the orthogonal complement of the kernel is equal to that of the range. A result underlying all the uses of projection matrices throughout this book is that any vector $\boldsymbol{z} \in E^m$ can be expressed uniquely as the sum of two vectors, one in M and the other in $\mathsf{M}^\perp$, for any linear subspace of E^m. It can be deduced from this fact that

$$\dim \mathsf{M} + \dim \mathsf{M}^\perp = m.$$

The dimension of the range of a matrix is called the **rank** of the matrix. The rank of $\boldsymbol{A}$ is sometimes denoted $\rho(\boldsymbol{A})$. An $n \times m$ matrix $\boldsymbol{A}$ is said to be of **full rank** if $\rho(\boldsymbol{A})$ is equal to the lesser of m and n. The terminology reflects the fact that $\rho(\boldsymbol{A})$ could never exceed $\min(m, n)$, as (A.11) makes clear. If a matrix has more rows than columns, and is of full rank, it is often convenient to say simply that the matrix has **full column rank**, in order to express two facts in one. Similarly, one may speak of a matrix being of **full row rank**.

The m columns of an $n \times m$ matrix can be considered as a set of n–vectors. Thus one can write the ith column of $\boldsymbol{A}$ as $\boldsymbol{a}_i \in E^n$. It is easy to see that the range of $\boldsymbol{A}$ is the set of all linear combinations of its columns $\boldsymbol{a}_i$. For this reason, the range of $\boldsymbol{A}$ is often referred to as the subspace spanned by the columns of $\boldsymbol{A}$ or as the **span** of the columns of $\boldsymbol{A}$ or simply as the span of $\boldsymbol{A}$. It is convenient to let $\mathcal{S}(\boldsymbol{A})$ denote this subspace, and $\mathcal{S}^\perp(\boldsymbol{A})$ denote its orthogonal complement. The columns of $\boldsymbol{A}$ may be said to **span** the subspace $\mathcal{S}(\boldsymbol{A})$.

When a matrix is interpreted as a mapping of linear spaces, it is natural to ascribe a **norm** to a matrix as well as to the vectors on which it acts. The definition of the norm of an $n \times m$ matrix $\boldsymbol{A}$ follows the standard pattern for defining norms of operators. It is as follows:

$$\|\boldsymbol{A}\| = \max_{\boldsymbol{x} \in E^m} \frac{\|\boldsymbol{A}\boldsymbol{x}\|}{\|\boldsymbol{x}\|}.$$

It can be shown that any matrix $\boldsymbol{A}$ composed of finite elements has a finite norm and that any matrix with zero norm must just be a zero matrix, that is, a matrix all the elements of which are zero. If two matrices $\boldsymbol{A}$ and $\boldsymbol{B}$ have dimensions such that the product $\boldsymbol{AB}$ exists, then it can also be shown that

$$\|\boldsymbol{AB}\| \leq \|\boldsymbol{A}\| \, \|\boldsymbol{B}\|.$$

A.5 PARTITIONED MATRICES

In this section, we introduce the important concept of a **partitioned matrix** and derive some very useful formulas for inverting partitioned matrices. If a matrix $\boldsymbol{A}$ has m columns, and if m_1 and m_2 are two positive integers such that $m_1 + m_2 = m$, then one can define two submatrices of $\boldsymbol{A}$, $\boldsymbol{A}_1$ and $\boldsymbol{A}_2$, of dimensions $n \times m_1$ and $n \times m_2$, respectively, such that $\boldsymbol{A}_1$ consists of the first m_1 columns of $\boldsymbol{A}$, and $\boldsymbol{A}_2$ consists of the last m_2 columns of $\boldsymbol{A}$. We write

$$\boldsymbol{A} = \begin{bmatrix} \boldsymbol{A}_1 & \boldsymbol{A}_2 \end{bmatrix}$$

and refer to the object on the right-hand side of this relation as a partitioned matrix.

The partitioning in the above case was done by columns. One can equally well partition by rows or by both rows and columns, and there may be more than two partitions for either. The submatrices created by partitioning a matrix are called the **blocks** of the partition. If the $n \times m$ matrix $\boldsymbol{A}$ is partitioned by its columns and the $m \times p$ matrix $\boldsymbol{B}$ is partitioned by its rows, the partitioning may be conformable. That is, each block of the partition of $\boldsymbol{A}$ may have just as many columns as the corresponding block of the partition of $\boldsymbol{B}$ has rows. In this event, the ordinary rules of matrix multiplication may be applied to the partitioned matrices as if the blocks were the actual elements of the matrices.

The use of partitioning makes it easy to see that the range of a matrix $\boldsymbol{A}$ is the set of all linear combinations of its columns $\boldsymbol{a}_i$. Thus let us partition $\boldsymbol{A}$ so that each column is treated as a block:

$$\boldsymbol{A} = \begin{bmatrix} \boldsymbol{a}_1 & \boldsymbol{a}_2 & \cdots & \boldsymbol{a}_m \end{bmatrix}.$$

If $\boldsymbol{A}$ premultiplies an m–vector $\boldsymbol{x}$, we can "partition" $\boldsymbol{x}$ simply by writing out its separate elements, and then we have

$$\begin{aligned} \boldsymbol{A}\boldsymbol{x} &= \begin{bmatrix} \boldsymbol{a}_1 & \cdots & \boldsymbol{a}_m \end{bmatrix} \begin{bmatrix} x_1 \\ \vdots \\ x_m \end{bmatrix} \\ &= \sum_{i=1}^{m} \boldsymbol{a}_i x_i. \end{aligned}$$

Written like this, it is clear that the image of $\boldsymbol{x}$ under $\boldsymbol{A}$ is a linear combination of the columns of $\boldsymbol{A}$, defined by means of the elements of $\boldsymbol{x}$.

We remarked above that partitioned matrices can be multiplied, if their partitions are conformable, just as though their blocks were actual matrix elements. The result of such a partitioned multiplication will necessarily be a matrix the row partitioning of which is the same as that of the left-most factor of the matrix product, and the column partitioning of which is the same as that of the right-most factor. This fact can be used to demonstrate some other useful results. If we separate all the columns of the second factor of the matrix product $\boldsymbol{AB}$, we see that

$$\boldsymbol{AB} = \boldsymbol{A}\big[\boldsymbol{b}_1 \quad \cdots \quad \boldsymbol{b}_m\big] = \big[\boldsymbol{Ab}_1 \quad \cdots \quad \boldsymbol{Ab}_m\big],$$

where $\boldsymbol{b}_i$ is a typical column of $\boldsymbol{B}$. In words, the ith column of a matrix product can be found by replacing the right-most factor of the product by the ith column of that factor. Similarly, of course, the ith row of a matrix product is found by replacing the left-most factor by its ith row.

Suppose that we consider a matrix $\boldsymbol{X}$ partitioned into two groups of columns: $\boldsymbol{X} = [\boldsymbol{X}_1 \quad \boldsymbol{X}_2]$. The notation is chosen deliberately, for it is helpful to the intuition to think of $\boldsymbol{X}$ as a matrix of regressors split into two subsets. In particular, we will be able to apply the FWL Theorem (Section 1.4) in the subsequent analysis. If $\boldsymbol{X}$ is $n \times k$, then the matrix product $\boldsymbol{X}^\top\boldsymbol{X}$ is $k \times k$. In partitioned form, we have

$$\boldsymbol{X}^\top\boldsymbol{X} = \begin{bmatrix} \boldsymbol{X}_1^\top \\ \boldsymbol{X}_2^\top \end{bmatrix} [\boldsymbol{X}_1 \quad \boldsymbol{X}_2] = \begin{bmatrix} \boldsymbol{X}_1^\top\boldsymbol{X}_1 & \boldsymbol{X}_1^\top\boldsymbol{X}_2 \\ \boldsymbol{X}_2^\top\boldsymbol{X}_1 & \boldsymbol{X}_2^\top\boldsymbol{X}_2 \end{bmatrix}. \tag{A.12}$$

We will now derive the inverse of the partitioned matrix which is the right-most expression in (A.12). We know that the covariance matrix of the OLS parameter estimates for the regression $\boldsymbol{y} = \boldsymbol{X\beta} + \boldsymbol{u}$ is proportional to $(\boldsymbol{X}^\top\boldsymbol{X})^{-1}$. Further, if $\boldsymbol{\beta}$ is partitioned as

$$\boldsymbol{\beta} = \begin{bmatrix} \boldsymbol{\beta}_1 \\ \boldsymbol{\beta}_2 \end{bmatrix},$$

conformably with the partition of $\boldsymbol{X}$, then the covariance matrix of the estimates of $\boldsymbol{\beta}_1$ is proportional (with the *same* constant of proportionality) to $(\boldsymbol{X}_1^\top\boldsymbol{M}_2\boldsymbol{X}_1)^{-1}$, where $\boldsymbol{M}_2 = \mathbf{I} - \boldsymbol{X}_2(\boldsymbol{X}_2^\top\boldsymbol{X}_2)^{-1}\boldsymbol{X}_2^\top$ is the orthogonal projection off the span of the columns of $\boldsymbol{X}_2$. This means that if $(\boldsymbol{X}^\top\boldsymbol{X})^{-1}$ is partitioned in the same way as $\boldsymbol{X}^\top\boldsymbol{X}$, then the upper left block of the partitioned inverse is $(\boldsymbol{X}_1^\top\boldsymbol{M}_2\boldsymbol{X}_1)^{-1}$.

Let us write $(\boldsymbol{X}^\top\boldsymbol{X})^{-1}$ in partitioned form as follows:

$$(\boldsymbol{X}^\top\boldsymbol{X})^{-1} = \begin{bmatrix} (\boldsymbol{X}^\top\boldsymbol{X})^{-1}_{11} & (\boldsymbol{X}^\top\boldsymbol{X})^{-1}_{12} \\ (\boldsymbol{X}^\top\boldsymbol{X})^{-1}_{21} & (\boldsymbol{X}^\top\boldsymbol{X})^{-1}_{22} \end{bmatrix}. \tag{A.13}$$

We have just shown that

$$(\boldsymbol{X}^\top\boldsymbol{X})^{-1}_{11} = (\boldsymbol{X}_1^\top\boldsymbol{M}_2\boldsymbol{X}_1)^{-1}. \tag{A.14}$$

If (A.12) and (A.13) are multiplied together, the answer must be an identity matrix, which we may partition as

$$\mathbf{I}_k = \begin{bmatrix} \mathbf{I}_{k_1} & \mathbf{0} \\ \mathbf{0} & \mathbf{I}_{k_2} \end{bmatrix},$$

where there are k_i columns in $\boldsymbol{X}_i$ for $i = 1, 2$. The bottom left block of this identity matrix is $\mathbf{0}$, and so by explicit multiplication we see that

$$\boldsymbol{X}_2^\top \boldsymbol{X}_1 \big(\boldsymbol{X}_1^\top \boldsymbol{M}_2 \boldsymbol{X}_1\big)^{-1} + \boldsymbol{X}_2^\top \boldsymbol{X}_2 \big(\boldsymbol{X}^\top \boldsymbol{X}\big)^{-1}_{21} = \mathbf{0},$$

whence

$$\big(\boldsymbol{X}^\top \boldsymbol{X}\big)^{-1}_{21} = -\big(\boldsymbol{X}_2^\top \boldsymbol{X}_2\big)^{-1} \boldsymbol{X}_2^\top \boldsymbol{X}_1 \big(\boldsymbol{X}_1^\top \boldsymbol{M}_2 \boldsymbol{X}_1\big)^{-1}. \tag{A.15}$$

The same sort of manipulation would yield an expression for $(\boldsymbol{X}^\top \boldsymbol{X})^{-1}_{22}$, but this is unnecessary, since we know by interchanging the 1s and 2s in the expression for $(\boldsymbol{X}^\top \boldsymbol{X})^{-1}_{11}$ that $(\boldsymbol{X}^\top \boldsymbol{X})^{-1}_{22} = (\boldsymbol{X}_2^\top \boldsymbol{M}_1 \boldsymbol{X}_2)^{-1}$. This is not the expression we would obtain directly, and we leave it as an exercise for the reader to show that the two seemingly different expressions are in fact equal.

The partitioned matrices that we wish to invert are not all of the form $\boldsymbol{X}^\top \boldsymbol{X}$. We can obtain general expressions from what we have already obtained by writing out the projection matrix $\boldsymbol{M}_2$ explicitly. If $\boldsymbol{X}^\top \boldsymbol{X}$ is written as

$$\begin{bmatrix} \boldsymbol{A} & \boldsymbol{C}^\top \\ \boldsymbol{C} & \boldsymbol{B} \end{bmatrix}, \tag{A.16}$$

and $(\boldsymbol{X}^\top \boldsymbol{X})^{-1}$ is written as

$$\begin{bmatrix} \boldsymbol{D} & \boldsymbol{E}^\top \\ \boldsymbol{E} & \boldsymbol{F} \end{bmatrix}, \tag{A.17}$$

then

$$\begin{aligned} \boldsymbol{D}^{-1} = \boldsymbol{X}_1^\top \boldsymbol{M}_2 \boldsymbol{X}_1 &= \boldsymbol{X}_1^\top \boldsymbol{X}_1 - \boldsymbol{X}_1^\top \boldsymbol{X}_2 \big(\boldsymbol{X}_2^\top \boldsymbol{X}_2\big)^{-1} \boldsymbol{X}_2^\top \boldsymbol{X}_1 \\ &= \boldsymbol{A} - \boldsymbol{C}^\top \boldsymbol{B}^{-1} \boldsymbol{C}. \end{aligned}$$

Thus, quite generally, we have the following relations between the blocks of the two inverse partitioned matrices (A.16) and (A.17):

$$\begin{aligned} &\boldsymbol{D} = \big(\boldsymbol{A} - \boldsymbol{C}^\top \boldsymbol{B}^{-1} \boldsymbol{C}\big)^{-1}; \\ &\boldsymbol{E} = -\boldsymbol{B}^{-1} \boldsymbol{C} \big(\boldsymbol{A} - \boldsymbol{C}^\top \boldsymbol{B}^{-1} \boldsymbol{C}\big)^{-1} = -\big(\boldsymbol{B} - \boldsymbol{C} \boldsymbol{A}^{-1} \boldsymbol{C}^\top\big)^{-1} \boldsymbol{C} \boldsymbol{A}^{-1}; \\ &\boldsymbol{F} = \big(\boldsymbol{B} - \boldsymbol{C} \boldsymbol{A}^{-1} \boldsymbol{C}^\top\big)^{-1}. \end{aligned}$$

These formulas require that the inverses of the diagonal blocks of the original partitioned matrix exist.

A.6 DETERMINANTS

We have several times alluded to the possibility that a square matrix may not possess an inverse. If it does not, then the mapping that it defines will not be invertible. In general, a mapping from one space to another is invertible if and only if it is one-to-one and onto, a **bijection** in formal mathematical terminology. More explicitly, the requirement is that there should correspond to every point in the codomain of the mapping one and only one point in the preimage of that point under the mapping. Then the **inverse mapping**, which maps from the codomain to the domain of the original mapping, maps each point in the codomain to its unique preimage.

We first show that only square matrices are invertible. If $\boldsymbol{A}$ is an $n \times m$ matrix, we require for invertibility that, for every vector $\boldsymbol{y} \in E^n$, there must exist a unique vector $\boldsymbol{x} \in E^m$ such that $\boldsymbol{Ax} = \boldsymbol{y}$. The inverse matrix $\boldsymbol{A}^{-1}$ is then an $m \times n$ matrix that maps such a $\boldsymbol{y}$ into its corresponding $\boldsymbol{x}$. A matrix $\boldsymbol{A}$ of which the kernel contains more than the zero vector cannot possess an inverse. Suppose that $\boldsymbol{z} \in \mathbf{N}(\boldsymbol{A})$, $\boldsymbol{z} \neq \mathbf{0}$; that is, $\boldsymbol{Az} = \mathbf{0}$. Then, if $\boldsymbol{Ax} = \boldsymbol{y}$, we also have that $\boldsymbol{A}(\boldsymbol{x} + \boldsymbol{z}) = \boldsymbol{Ax} + \boldsymbol{Az} = \boldsymbol{Ax}$, and both $\boldsymbol{x}$ and $\boldsymbol{x} + \boldsymbol{z}$ must belong to the preimage of $\boldsymbol{y}$ under $\boldsymbol{A}$, contrary to the requirement that permits an inverse mapping to exist. Thus, if $\boldsymbol{A}$ is $n \times m$ and is invertible, we find from (A.11) that $m = r$, the dimension of the range of $\boldsymbol{A}$. Next, we see that a matrix of which the range is not the full codomain cannot have an inverse, for in that event there are elements of the codomain of which the preimage is empty, contrary to the requirement for an inverse. This implies that $r = n$, and since we have already seen that $m = r$, it follows that $m = n$. Thus we have proved that only square matrices are invertible. The added requirement that $m = r$ implies that only square matrices of full rank are invertible. Square matrices with rank less than full are called **singular**, and square matrices with full rank are therefore sometimes called **nonsingular**. All nonsingular square matrices are invertible.

How can one tell if a given square $n \times n$ matrix $\boldsymbol{A}$ is invertible, and, if it is, how can one calculate its inverse? The answers to both these questions are provided by the concept of the **determinant** of a square matrix. Since, for the remainder of this section, we will be dealing only with square matrices, all matrices should henceforth be understood to be square. The determinant of a matrix is simply a scalar. We will let $|\boldsymbol{A}|$ denote the determinant of $\boldsymbol{A}$ and $|\det \boldsymbol{A}|$ denote the absolute value of the determinant of $\boldsymbol{A}$.

The determinant of a matrix can be understood geometrically as the n–dimensional volume of the rectilinear figure generated by the columns of the matrix. In two dimensions, for instance, the two columns of a 2×2 matrix define a **parallelogram**, as shown in panel (a) of Figure A.1. The area of this parallelogram is the determinant of the matrix. In three dimensions, the three columns of a 3×3 matrix define a solid figure called a **parallelepiped** (see Figure A.2), the volume of which is the determinant of the matrix. In

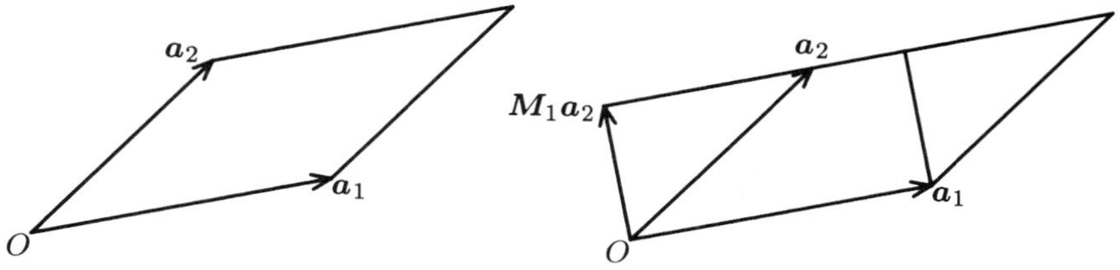

(a) The parallelogram defined by a_1 and a_2

(b) Rectangle of equal area formed with a_1 and M_1a_2

Figure A.1 Determinants in two dimensions

higher dimensions, as we will see, we can extend the concept of determinant algebraically in a natural way, although of course we cannot visualize the results geometrically.

The area of a parallelogram is given in elementary texts on geometry as base times height, where "base" means the length of one of the sides of the parallelogram, and "height" means the *perpendicular* distance between the two sides of which the length is the base. This means that the area of a parallelogram can be computed as the area of a rectangle, as illustrated in panel (b) of Figure A.1. Algebraically, if the columns of the 2×2 matrix $\boldsymbol{A}$ are denoted $\boldsymbol{a}_1$ and $\boldsymbol{a}_2$, the area of the parallelogram is $\|\boldsymbol{a}_1\|\,\|\boldsymbol{M}_1\boldsymbol{a}_2\|$, where $\boldsymbol{M}_1$ is the orthogonal projection onto $\mathcal{S}^{\perp}(\boldsymbol{a}_1)$. It is easy to check that one may invert the roles of the two vectors without changing the value of the area.

For the n–dimensional case, we may make the following definition of the absolute value of the determinant of the $n \times n$ matrix $\boldsymbol{A} = [\boldsymbol{a}_1 \;\; \boldsymbol{a}_2 \;\; \cdots \;\; \boldsymbol{a}_n]$:

$$|\det \boldsymbol{A}| = \|\boldsymbol{M}_{(1)}\boldsymbol{a}_1\|\,\|\boldsymbol{M}_{(2)}\boldsymbol{a}_2\| \cdots \|\boldsymbol{M}_{(n-1)}\boldsymbol{a}_{n-1}\|\|\boldsymbol{a}_n\| = \prod_{i=1}^{n} \|\boldsymbol{M}_{(i)}\boldsymbol{a}_i\|. \tag{A.18}$$

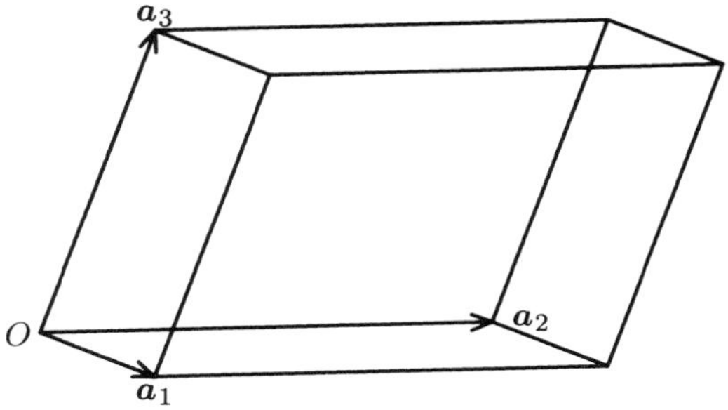

Figure A.2 A parallelepiped in three dimensions

Here $\boldsymbol{M}_{(i)}$ is the orthogonal projection off $\mathcal{S}(\boldsymbol{a}_{i+1}, \ldots, \boldsymbol{a}_n)$, the span of the last $n-i$ columns of $\boldsymbol{A}$, for $i = 1, \ldots, n-1$. To make the second line true, $\boldsymbol{M}_{(n)} = \mathbf{I}$.

The above definition gives only the *absolute value* of the determinant. The sign will be a consequence of another property of determinants, namely, anti-symmetry. The value of (A.18) is invariant to changes in the ordering of the columns of $\boldsymbol{A}$, but when the sign is taken into account, we will require that an interchange of any two columns of $\boldsymbol{A}$ will cause the sign of the determinant to change. Consider the following partitioned matrix:

$$\boldsymbol{A} = \begin{bmatrix} a_{11} & \mathbf{0} \\ \boldsymbol{b} & \boldsymbol{B} \end{bmatrix}. \tag{A.19}$$

When the first column is projected off the others, the result will be a column with a_{11} as first element and all other elements zero. Thus, by (A.18), the absolute value of $|\boldsymbol{A}|$ is just $|a_{11}||\det \boldsymbol{B}|$. The rule for signing the determinant is a recursive one: We assume that $|\boldsymbol{B}|$ can be signed and then multiply its sign by that of the element a_{11} to obtain the sign of $|\boldsymbol{A}|$. To finish off the recursion, we require that the sign of the determinant of a 1×1 matrix should be the sign of the single element of the matrix.

In a moment, we will need to use the fact that the determinant of the matrix (A.19), which does not depend on the $(n-1)$–vector $\boldsymbol{b}$, is equal to the determinant of any matrix like (A.19), with a zero column in the place of $\boldsymbol{b}$ but with an arbitrary row vector $\boldsymbol{c}^{\top}$ in place of the zeros in (A.19). Thus the determinant of the matrix

$$\begin{bmatrix} a_{11} & \boldsymbol{c}^{\top} \\ \mathbf{0} & \boldsymbol{B} \end{bmatrix} \tag{A.20}$$

is equal to that of (A.19). To see this, recall that the absolute value of the determinant is not affected by the order of the columns, and take the first column of (A.20) as the column not subject to any projection in (A.18). All other columns will then be projected off the first column and thereby lose their first element, that is, the elements of $\boldsymbol{c}^{\top}$.

A lower-triangular matrix is a special case of (A.19) in which the matrix $\boldsymbol{B}$ is itself lower-triangular. Similarly, an upper-triangular matrix is a special case of (A.20) in which the matrix $\boldsymbol{B}$ is itself upper-triangular. The fact that the determinant of both these matrices is equal to $|a_{11}||\det \boldsymbol{B}|$ implies that if a matrix $\boldsymbol{A}$ is triangular, its determinant is equal to the product of its diagonal elements. To obtain this result, we simply apply the original result first to $\boldsymbol{A}$, then to its lower right-hand block, then to the lower right-hand block of that block, and so on.

Another property of determinants is that they are invariant under interchanges of their rows as well as of their columns, again up to a change of sign. This is clear from (A.18), since the norm of a vector does not depend on how its rows are ordered; see (A.06).

The operation of taking determinants is obviously not a linear operation. Thus, in general, $|\boldsymbol{A}+\boldsymbol{B}| \neq |\boldsymbol{A}|+|\boldsymbol{B}|$. What is true, however, is that if a column of a matrix is expressed as the sum of two vectors, then the determinant is additive column by column. What this means is that

$$\begin{aligned} &|\boldsymbol{a}_1+\boldsymbol{b}_1 \quad \boldsymbol{a}_2 \quad \cdots \quad \boldsymbol{a}_n| \\ &= |\boldsymbol{a}_1 \quad \boldsymbol{a}_2 \quad \cdots \quad \boldsymbol{a}_n| + |\boldsymbol{b}_1 \quad \boldsymbol{a}_2 \quad \cdots \quad \boldsymbol{a}_n|. \end{aligned} \tag{A.21}$$

Here the notation $|\cdot|$ with what appear to be the blocks of a partitioned matrix inside denotes the determinant of that matrix. To see why (A.21) is true, observe that the rank of the projection $\boldsymbol{M}_{(2)}$ is only 1. It follows that, for any n–vectors $\boldsymbol{a}$ and $\boldsymbol{b}$, $\|\boldsymbol{M}_{(2)}(\boldsymbol{a}+\boldsymbol{b})\| = \|\boldsymbol{M}_{(2)}\boldsymbol{a}\| + \|\boldsymbol{M}_{(2)}\boldsymbol{b}\|$. The result follows from this fact and the definition (A.18).

The result (A.21) allows us to establish the classic method for evaluating determinants by hand. This method is the **expansion of the determinant** by a row or column. No one ever actually calculates determinants by hand any more, except perhaps for the trivial 2×2 case, but our discussion of how determinants can be expanded will lead to a number of useful results. We will expand by the first column. In order to do so, we need a little notation. Let $\boldsymbol{A}_{ij}$ denote the $(n-1) \times (n-1)$ submatrix of $\boldsymbol{A}$ obtained by deleting the ith row and the jth column. Let A_{ij} denote the determinant of this submatrix. We call $(-1)^{i+j}A_{ij}$ the **cofactor** of the element a_{ij} in $\boldsymbol{A}$. Let $\boldsymbol{\alpha}_i$ be the n–vector with all elements zero except the ith, which equals a_{i1}. Then notice that successive applications of (A.21) give

$$|\boldsymbol{A}| = \sum_{i=1}^{n} |\boldsymbol{\alpha}_i \quad \boldsymbol{a}_2 \quad \cdots \quad \boldsymbol{a}_n|. \tag{A.22}$$

If we write the ith row of the summand indexed by i in (A.22) as $[a_{i1} \quad \boldsymbol{c}_i^\top]$, then the ith row can be moved up to become the first, by a process of $i-1$ interchanges of rows, which entail a factor of $(-1)^{i-1}$. The result is the determinant

$$(-1)^{i-1}\begin{vmatrix} a_{i1} & \boldsymbol{c}_i^\top \\ \mathbf{0} & \boldsymbol{A}_{i1} \end{vmatrix},$$

the value of which is $a_{i1}A_{i1}$, by the definition of a cofactor. Thus the determinant (A.22) can be written as

$$|\boldsymbol{A}| = \sum_{i=1}^{n} a_{i1}A_{i1}. \tag{A.23}$$

Since A_{i1} is itself a determinant, (A.23) allows a recursive evaluation of an arbitrary determinant.

It is easy enough to see that $\boldsymbol{A}$ can be evaluated by expanding by any row or column. Formally,

$$|\boldsymbol{A}| = \sum_{i=1}^{n} a_{ij}A_{ij} = \sum_{i=1}^{n} a_{ji}A_{ji} \tag{A.24}$$

for all $j = 1, \ldots, n$. This result in turn shows that $|\boldsymbol{A}^\top| = |\boldsymbol{A}|$. If one expands a determinant by a column, the jth say, and uses **false cofactors**, that is, those corresponding to another column, the kth say, then we find that

$$\sum_{i=1}^{n} a_{ij}A_{ik} = 0. \tag{A.25}$$

This follows because (A.25) is the correct expansion of the determinant of a matrix in which the kth column is replaced by the jth column. Any matrix in which one column is the same as another has zero determinant, since when the same column occurs for a second time in (A.18), it will be projected off itself, giving a vector of zero norm.

For the same reason, any matrix in which one column is a linear combination of the others will have a determinant of zero. A matrix satisfying this condition does not have full rank, and so we see that a singular matrix necessarily has a zero determinant. It is not hard to see that the converse is also true: A matrix with zero determinant is necessarily singular. This all makes sense geometrically, of course. If an $n \times n$ matrix does not have full rank, the parallelepiped defined by the matrix will be an object of less than n dimensions, and so its volume (in n–space) will be zero.

The results (A.24) and (A.25) can be used to construct the inverse of a nonsingular matrix $\boldsymbol{A}$. Consider the matrix $\boldsymbol{B}$ with typical element $b_{ij} \equiv A_{ji}$, which is just the transpose of the matrix of cofactors. We see that

$$(\boldsymbol{AB})_{ij} = \sum_{k=1}^{n} a_{ik}A_{jk} = |\boldsymbol{A}|\delta_{ij},$$

where δ_{ij} is the Kronecker delta, equal to 1 if $i = j$ and equal to 0 otherwise. Thus $\boldsymbol{AB} = |\boldsymbol{A}|\mathbf{I}$, and so $|\boldsymbol{A}|^{-1}\boldsymbol{B}$, which exists if and only if $|\boldsymbol{A}| \neq 0$, must be the inverse of $\boldsymbol{A}$.

The result (A.24) allows us to compute the *derivatives* of the determinant of a matrix with respect to the elements of the matrix. The cofactor A_{ij} is the determinant of a matrix that contains none of the elements of the ith row or the jth column of $\boldsymbol{A}$. It follows that the derivative of $|\boldsymbol{A}|$ with respect to a_{ij} is just A_{ij}, which is $|\boldsymbol{A}|$ times the ji^{th} element of $\boldsymbol{A}^{-1}$. This result may be written in matrix notation as

$$\frac{\partial|\boldsymbol{A}|}{\partial\boldsymbol{A}} = |\boldsymbol{A}|(\boldsymbol{A}^{-1})^\top.$$

From it we may deduce the even more useful result that

$$\frac{\partial \log|\boldsymbol{A}|}{\partial \boldsymbol{A}} = (\boldsymbol{A}^{-1})^{\top}.$$

Although the determinant of a sum of matrices is not the sum of the determinants in general, the determinant of a product of matrices *is* the product of the determinants. Let $\boldsymbol{A}$ and $\boldsymbol{B}$ be two $n \times n$ matrices, both with nonzero determinants. Then $|\boldsymbol{AB}| = |\boldsymbol{A}||\boldsymbol{B}|$. A very useful corollary is that $|\boldsymbol{A}^{-1}| = |\boldsymbol{A}|^{-1}$. This follows from the facts that $\boldsymbol{A}^{-1}\boldsymbol{A} = \mathbf{I}$ and $|\mathbf{I}| = 1$.

To conclude this section, we prove a result used in Chapters 18 and 20. According to this result, we have

$$\begin{vmatrix} \boldsymbol{A}^{\top}\boldsymbol{A} & \boldsymbol{A}^{\top}\boldsymbol{B} \\ \boldsymbol{B}^{\top}\boldsymbol{A} & \boldsymbol{B}^{\top}\boldsymbol{B} \end{vmatrix} = |\boldsymbol{A}^{\top}\boldsymbol{M}_B\boldsymbol{A}||\boldsymbol{B}^{\top}\boldsymbol{B}| = |\boldsymbol{B}^{\top}\boldsymbol{M}_A\boldsymbol{B}||\boldsymbol{A}^{\top}\boldsymbol{A}|, \tag{A.26}$$

where $\boldsymbol{M}_A$ and $\boldsymbol{M}_B$ are the orthogonal projections off the columns of the matrices $\boldsymbol{A}$ and $\boldsymbol{B}$, which can be assumed to be of full column rank without loss of generality. We use the results (A.14) and (A.15) on inverting matrices partitioned as above to write

$$\begin{bmatrix} \boldsymbol{A}^{\top}\boldsymbol{A} & \boldsymbol{A}^{\top}\boldsymbol{B} \\ \boldsymbol{B}^{\top}\boldsymbol{A} & \boldsymbol{B}^{\top}\boldsymbol{B} \end{bmatrix} \begin{bmatrix} (\boldsymbol{A}^{\top}\boldsymbol{M}_B\boldsymbol{A})^{-1} & \mathbf{0} \\ -(\boldsymbol{B}^{\top}\boldsymbol{B})^{-1}\boldsymbol{B}^{\top}\boldsymbol{A}(\boldsymbol{A}^{\top}\boldsymbol{M}_B\boldsymbol{A})^{-1} & \mathbf{I} \end{bmatrix} = \begin{bmatrix} \mathbf{I} & \boldsymbol{A}^{\top}\boldsymbol{B} \\ \mathbf{0} & \boldsymbol{B}^{\top}\boldsymbol{B} \end{bmatrix}.$$

It is evident that the determinant of the matrix on the right-hand side is just $|\boldsymbol{B}^{\top}\boldsymbol{B}|$, while the determinant of the second matrix factor on the left-hand side is $|\boldsymbol{A}^{\top}\boldsymbol{M}_B\boldsymbol{A}|^{-1}$. The first equality in (A.26) then follows immediately. The second equality can be proved by a similar argument, but using different expressions for the inverse of the partitioned matrix.

A.7 POSITIVE DEFINITE MATRICES

An $n \times n$ symmetric matrix $\boldsymbol{A}$ is said to be **positive definite** if the quadratic form $\boldsymbol{x}^{\top}\boldsymbol{A}\boldsymbol{x}$ is positive for all nonzero n–vectors $\boldsymbol{x}$. If the quadratic form can take on zero values but not negative values, it is **positive semidefinite** or **nonnegative definite**. Matrices that are **negative definite** or **negative semidefinite** are defined analogously.

Any matrix of the form $\boldsymbol{B}^{\top}\boldsymbol{B}$ is positive definite if $\boldsymbol{B}$ has full column rank and positive semidefinite otherwise. To see this, observe that $\boldsymbol{B}^{\top}\boldsymbol{B}$ is symmetric and that, for any nonzero $\boldsymbol{x}$,

$$\boldsymbol{x}^{\top}\boldsymbol{B}^{\top}\boldsymbol{B}\boldsymbol{x} = (\boldsymbol{B}\boldsymbol{x})^{\top}(\boldsymbol{B}\boldsymbol{x}) = \|\boldsymbol{B}\boldsymbol{x}\|^2 \geq 0.$$

This result can hold with equality only if $\boldsymbol{B}\boldsymbol{x} = \mathbf{0}$. But, in that case, $\boldsymbol{B}$ cannot have full rank, since to say that $\boldsymbol{B}\boldsymbol{x} = \mathbf{0}$ means that the columns of

$\boldsymbol{B}$ are not linearly independent. Similar reasoning shows that if $\boldsymbol{A}$ is positive definite, then any matrix of the form $\boldsymbol{B}^\top\boldsymbol{A}\boldsymbol{B}$ is positive definite if $\boldsymbol{B}$ has full column rank and positive semidefinite otherwise.

A positive definite matrix cannot be singular, since, if $\boldsymbol{A}$ is singular, there must exist a nonzero $\boldsymbol{x}$ such that $\boldsymbol{A}\boldsymbol{x} = \boldsymbol{0}$. But then $\boldsymbol{x}^\top\boldsymbol{A}\boldsymbol{x} = 0$ as well, which means that $\boldsymbol{A}$ is not positive definite. Thus the inverse of a positive definite matrix always exists. It too is positive definite, because, for any nonzero $\boldsymbol{x}$,

$$\boldsymbol{x}^\top\boldsymbol{A}^{-1}\boldsymbol{x} = \boldsymbol{x}^\top\boldsymbol{A}^{-1}\boldsymbol{A}\boldsymbol{A}^{-1}\boldsymbol{x} = (\boldsymbol{A}^{-1}\boldsymbol{x})^\top\boldsymbol{A}(\boldsymbol{A}^{-1}\boldsymbol{x}) > 0.$$

The inequality here follows directly from the fact that $\boldsymbol{A}$ is positive definite.

For any positive definite matrix $\boldsymbol{A}$, we can find a matrix $\boldsymbol{B}$ such that $\boldsymbol{A} = \boldsymbol{B}^\top\boldsymbol{B}$. It is often necessary to construct such a $\boldsymbol{B}$ from a given $\boldsymbol{A}$ in econometric applications; an example is the matrix $\boldsymbol{\eta}$ defined in (9.08). Frequently, it is desirable to go further and find a *triangular* matrix $\boldsymbol{B}$. We now sketch an algorithm for such a **triangular decomposition**. It produces an upper-triangular $\boldsymbol{B}$ from a given positive definite matrix $\boldsymbol{A}$. An analogous algorithm to produce a lower-triangular $\boldsymbol{B}$ can also be found.

We start by defining $b_{11} = \sqrt{a_{11}}$, where a_{ij} and b_{ij} denote the ij^{th} elements of $\boldsymbol{A}$ and $\boldsymbol{B}$, respectively. The whole first row of $\boldsymbol{B}$ is then obtained by sequential application of the following formula, for $j = 2, \ldots, n$:

$$b_{1j} = \frac{a_{1j}}{b_{11}}.$$

Subsequent rows are computed sequentially, in such a way that, during the computation of the ith row, the elements of the first through the $(i-1)^{\text{th}}$ are available. For the ith row, the elements b_{ij} are set equal to zero for $j < i$, since $\boldsymbol{B}$ is to be upper-triangular. Then the ith diagonal element is

$$b_{ii} = \left(a_{ii} - \sum_{k=1}^{i-1} b_{ki}^2\right)^{1/2}, \tag{A.27}$$

in which the entire right-hand side is known. To complete the row, the elements b_{ij} for $j > i$ are determined by the formula

$$b_{ij} = \frac{1}{b_{ii}}\left(a_{ij} - \sum_{k=1}^{i-1} b_{ki}b_{kj}\right).$$

Again, everything that appears on the right-hand side is available by the time it is needed. A calculation that we will not reproduce shows that the quantity of which the square root is taken in (A.27) is guaranteed to be positive if $\boldsymbol{A}$ is positive definite and also shows that the matrix $\boldsymbol{B}$ generated by the algorithm satisfies the requirement that $\boldsymbol{B}^\top\boldsymbol{B} = \boldsymbol{A}$. The results of the preceding section show that the determinant of a triangular matrix is just the product of its diagonal elements. Thus one can obtain the determinant of $\boldsymbol{B}$ almost as a by-product of the algorithm for finding $\boldsymbol{B}$. The square of the determinant of $\boldsymbol{B}$ is then the determinant of $\boldsymbol{A}$.

In some manipulations of covariance matrices in the text, we make use of the fact that if $\boldsymbol{A}$ and $\boldsymbol{B}$ are two positive definite matrices, then $\boldsymbol{A} - \boldsymbol{B}$ is positive definite if and only if $\boldsymbol{B}^{-1} - \boldsymbol{A}^{-1}$ is. We now demonstrate this very useful result. Let $\boldsymbol{A}^{-1/2}$ be a matrix such that $(\boldsymbol{A}^{-1/2})^\top \boldsymbol{A}^{-1/2} = \boldsymbol{A}^{-1}$. It can be seen that

$$\boldsymbol{A}^{-1/2}\boldsymbol{A}(\boldsymbol{A}^{-1/2})^\top = (\boldsymbol{A}^{-1/2})^\top \boldsymbol{A}\boldsymbol{A}^{-1/2} = \mathbf{I}.$$

First, we show that if $\mathbf{I} - \boldsymbol{A}$ is positive definite, then so is $\boldsymbol{A}^{-1} - \mathbf{I}$ and conversely. This follows from the result, proved above, that premultiplying a positive definite matrix by any matrix with full rank and then postmultiplying by the transpose of that matrix yields a positive definite matrix. Thus the positive definiteness of $\mathbf{I} - \boldsymbol{A}$ implies that of $(\boldsymbol{A}^{-1/2})^\top(\mathbf{I} - \boldsymbol{A})\boldsymbol{A}^{-1/2}$, which is just $\boldsymbol{A}^{-1} - \mathbf{I}$. The converse result follows from inverting the roles of $\boldsymbol{A}$ and $\boldsymbol{A}^{-1}$.

If $\boldsymbol{A} - \boldsymbol{B}$ is positive definite, then so is $\boldsymbol{A}^{-1/2}(\boldsymbol{A} - \boldsymbol{B})(\boldsymbol{A}^{-1/2})^\top$, that is, $\mathbf{I} - \boldsymbol{A}^{-1/2}\boldsymbol{B}(\boldsymbol{A}^{-1/2})^\top$. The positive definiteness of this last matrix entails that of $(\boldsymbol{A}^{1/2})^\top \boldsymbol{B}^{-1}\boldsymbol{A}^{1/2} - \mathbf{I}$, where $\boldsymbol{A}^{1/2}$ is the inverse of $\boldsymbol{A}^{-1/2}$, and so also of $(\boldsymbol{A}^{-1/2})^\top(\boldsymbol{A}^{1/2})^\top \boldsymbol{B}^{-1}\boldsymbol{A}^{1/2}\boldsymbol{A}^{-1/2} - (\boldsymbol{A}^{-1/2})^\top \boldsymbol{A}^{-1/2}$, which is just $\boldsymbol{B}^{-1} - \boldsymbol{A}^{-1}$, as required. Again, the converse result follows from inverting the roles of the matrices and their inverses. A similar result is true for positive semidefinite matrices: $\boldsymbol{A} - \boldsymbol{B}$ is positive semidefinite if and only if $\boldsymbol{B}^{-1} - \boldsymbol{A}^{-1}$ is.

A.8 EIGENVALUES AND EIGENVECTORS

A scalar λ is said to be an **eigenvalue** (or **characteristic root**, or **latent root**) of a matrix $\boldsymbol{A}$ if there exists a nonzero vector $\boldsymbol{x}$ such that

$$\boldsymbol{A}\boldsymbol{x} = \lambda \boldsymbol{x}. \tag{A.28}$$

Thus the action of $\boldsymbol{A}$ on $\boldsymbol{x}$ produces a vector with the same direction as $\boldsymbol{x}$, but a different length unless $\lambda = 1$. The vector $\boldsymbol{x}$ is called the **eigenvector** corresponding to the eigenvalue λ. Although these ideas are defined quite generally, we will restrict our attention here to the eigenvalues and eigenvectors of real symmetric matrices.

The eigenvalue relationship (A.28) implies that

$$(\boldsymbol{A} - \lambda \mathbf{I})\boldsymbol{x} = \mathbf{0}, \tag{A.29}$$

from which we conclude that the matrix $\boldsymbol{A} - \lambda \mathbf{I}$ is singular. Its determinant, $|\boldsymbol{A} - \lambda \mathbf{I}|$ is therefore equal to zero. It can be shown in a variety of ways that this determinant is a polynomial in λ, of degree n if $\boldsymbol{A}$ is $n \times n$. The fundamental theorem of algebra tells us that such a polynomial has n complex roots, say $\lambda_1, \ldots, \lambda_n$. To each λ_i there must correspond an eigenvector $\boldsymbol{x}_i$. This eigenvector is determined only up to a scale factor, because if $\boldsymbol{x}_i$ is an eigenvector corresponding to λ_i, then so is $\alpha\boldsymbol{x}_i$ for any nonzero scalar α. The eigenvector $\boldsymbol{x}_i$ does not necessarily have real elements if λ_i itself is not real.

If $\boldsymbol{A}$ is a real symmetric matrix, it can be shown that the eigenvalues λ_i are in fact all real and that the eigenvectors can be chosen to be real as well. If $\boldsymbol{A}$ is a positive definite matrix, then all its eigenvalues are positive. This follows from the facts that

$$\boldsymbol{x}^{\top}\boldsymbol{A}\boldsymbol{x} = \lambda\boldsymbol{x}^{\top}\boldsymbol{x}$$

and that both $\boldsymbol{x}^{\top}\boldsymbol{x}$ and $\boldsymbol{x}^{\top}\boldsymbol{A}\boldsymbol{x}$ are positive. The eigenvectors of a real symmetric matrix can be chosen to be mutually orthogonal. If one looks at two eigenvectors $\boldsymbol{x}_i$ and $\boldsymbol{x}_j$, corresponding to two distinct eigenvalues λ_i and λ_j, then $\boldsymbol{x}_i$ and $\boldsymbol{x}_j$ are necessarily orthogonal:

$$\lambda_i\boldsymbol{x}_j^{\top}\boldsymbol{x}_i = \boldsymbol{x}_j^{\top}\boldsymbol{A}\boldsymbol{x}_i = (\boldsymbol{A}\boldsymbol{x}_j)^{\top}\boldsymbol{x}_i = \lambda_j\boldsymbol{x}_j^{\top}\boldsymbol{x}_i,$$

which is impossible unless $\boldsymbol{x}_j^{\top}\boldsymbol{x}_i = 0$. If not all the eigenvalues are distinct, then two (or more) eigenvectors may correspond to one and the same eigenvalue. When that happens, these two eigenvectors span a space that is orthogonal to all other eigenvalues by the reasoning just given. Since any linear combination of the two eigenvectors will also be an eigenvector corresponding to the one eigenvalue, one may choose an orthogonal set of them. Thus, whether or not all the eigenvalues are distinct, eigenvectors may be chosen to be **orthonormal**, by which we mean that they are mutually orthogonal and each has norm equal to 1. Thus the eigenvectors of a real symmetric matrix provide an orthonormal basis.

Let $\boldsymbol{U} \equiv [\,\boldsymbol{x}_1 \;\; \cdots \;\; \boldsymbol{x}_n\,]$ be a matrix the columns of which are an orthonormal set of eigenvectors of $\boldsymbol{A}$, corresponding to the eigenvalues λ_i, $i = 1, \ldots, n$. Then we can write the eigenvalue relationship (A.28) for all the eigenvalues at once as

$$\boldsymbol{A}\boldsymbol{U} = \boldsymbol{U}\boldsymbol{\Lambda}, \tag{A.30}$$

where $\boldsymbol{\Lambda}$ is a diagonal matrix with λ_i as its ith diagonal element. The ith column of $\boldsymbol{A}\boldsymbol{U}$ is $\boldsymbol{A}\boldsymbol{x}_i$, and the ith column of $\boldsymbol{U}\boldsymbol{\Lambda}$ is $\boldsymbol{\lambda}_i\boldsymbol{x}_i$. Since the columns of $\boldsymbol{U}$ are orthonormal, we find that $\boldsymbol{U}^{\top}\boldsymbol{U} = \mathbf{I}$, which implies that $\boldsymbol{U}^{\top} = \boldsymbol{U}^{-1}$. A matrix with this property is said to be an **orthogonal matrix**. Postmultiplying (A.30) by $\boldsymbol{U}^{\top}$ gives

$$\boldsymbol{A} = \boldsymbol{U}\boldsymbol{\Lambda}\boldsymbol{U}^{\top}. \tag{A.31}$$

This equation expresses the **diagonalization** of $\boldsymbol{A}$.

Taking determinants of both sides of (A.31), we obtain

$$|\boldsymbol{A}| = |\boldsymbol{U}||\boldsymbol{U}^\top||\boldsymbol{\Lambda}| = |\boldsymbol{U}||\boldsymbol{U}^{-1}||\boldsymbol{\Lambda}| = |\boldsymbol{\Lambda}| = \prod_{i=1}^{n} \lambda_i,$$

from which we deduce the important result that the determinant of a matrix is the product of its eigenvalues. In fact, this result holds for nonsymmetric matrices as well.

A result used in Chapter 18 is that if $\boldsymbol{A}$ is positive definite and $\boldsymbol{B}$ is positive semidefinite, then

$$|\boldsymbol{A}+\boldsymbol{B}| \geq |\boldsymbol{A}|.$$

We show this first for the special case $\boldsymbol{A} = \mathbf{I}$ and then deduce the general result. The determinantal equation which defines the eigenvalues of the matrix $\mathbf{I}+\boldsymbol{B}$ is

$$|\mathbf{I}+\boldsymbol{B}-\lambda\mathbf{I}| = 0,$$

from (A.29). This becomes

$$\big|\boldsymbol{B}-(\lambda-1)\mathbf{I}\big| = 0.$$

It follows that the eigenvalues λ_i of $\mathbf{I}+\boldsymbol{B}$ satisfy the equation $\lambda_i = 1+\mu_i$, where μ_i is an eigenvalue of $\boldsymbol{B}$. If $\boldsymbol{B}$ is a positive semidefinite matrix, its eigenvalues are all greater than or equal to 0, which implies that the eigenvalues of $\mathbf{I}+\boldsymbol{B}$ are all greater than or equal to 1. Since the determinant of a matrix is the product of its eigenvalues, we may conclude that the determinant of $\mathbf{I}+\boldsymbol{B}$ is greater than or equal to 1, which is the determinant of $\mathbf{I}$.

Let $\boldsymbol{A}^{1/2}$ be a matrix such that $\boldsymbol{A}^{1/2}(\boldsymbol{A}^{1/2})^\top = \boldsymbol{A}$. Then, if $\boldsymbol{B}$ is positive semidefinite,

$$\begin{aligned} |\boldsymbol{A}+\boldsymbol{B}| &= \big|\boldsymbol{A}^{1/2}\big(\mathbf{I}+\boldsymbol{A}^{-1/2}\boldsymbol{B}(\boldsymbol{A}^{-1/2})^\top\big)(\boldsymbol{A}^{1/2})^\top\big| \\ &= \big|(\boldsymbol{A}^{1/2})\big|^2\big|\mathbf{I}+\boldsymbol{A}^{-1/2}\boldsymbol{B}(\boldsymbol{A}^{-1/2})^\top\big|. \end{aligned} \tag{A.32}$$

The matrix $\boldsymbol{A}^{-1/2}\boldsymbol{B}(\boldsymbol{A}^{-1/2})^\top$ is positive semidefinite because $\boldsymbol{B}$ is, and so the last determinant factor in (A.32) is greater than 1. Since

$$\big|(\boldsymbol{A}^{1/2})\big|^2 = |\boldsymbol{A}|,$$

we see that $|\boldsymbol{A}+\boldsymbol{B}| \geq |\boldsymbol{A}|$, as stated.

TERMS AND CONCEPTS

angle between two vectors
associative property (for matrix addition and multiplication)
bijection
blocks of a partitioned matrix
codomain of a mapping
cofactor
column vector
conformable matrices
cyclic permutation (of the factors of a product of matrices)
determinant
diagonal matrix
diagonalization (of a real symmetric matrix)
dimension (of a Euclidean space)
direct product (Schur product)
distance between two points in E^n
distributive property (for matrix addition and multiplication)
domain of a mapping
eigenvalue (or characteristic root, or latent root)
eigenvector
Euclidean n-space, E^n
expansion of the determinant (by a row or column)
false cofactors
full rank; full row rank; full column rank
identity matrix
image and preimage
inner product (scalar product)
inverse mapping
inverse matrix
invertible matrix
kernel (of a matrix)
length (or norm) of a vector
linearly dependent vectors
linearly independent vectors
lower-triangular matrix
mapping defined by a matrix
natural inner product
negative definite matrix
negative semidefinite matrix
nonsingular square matrix
norm (of a matrix)
orthogonal complement (of a subspace)
orthogonal matrix
orthogonal vectors
orthonormal basis
outer product
parallel vectors
parallelepiped
parallelogram
partitioned matrix
positive definite matrix
positive semidefinite (or nonnegative definite) matrix
postmultiplication
premultiplication
principal diagonal of a square matrix
range (of a matrix)
rank (of a matrix)
row vector
singular square matrix
span (of the columns of a matrix)
square matrix
symmetric matrix
trace of a matrix
transpose of a matrix
triangular decomposition
triangular matrix
trigonometric functions: sine, cosine, tangent, cotangent, secant, cosecant
upper-triangular matrix

Appendix B

Results from Probability Theory

B.1 Introduction

Readers of this book should already be reasonably familiar with probability theory and statistics. This appendix is provided to aid those who wish to refresh their memories and to collect results for easy reference. It is in no way a substitute for a graduate-level textbook such as Casella and Berger (1990) or Spanos (1986). Section B.2 reviews the basic concepts of random variables and probability distributions. Section B.3 discusses moments of random variables and some related results. Finally, Section B.4 reviews some of the probability distributions that are most commonly used in econometrics.

B.2 Random Variables and Probability Distributions

The concept of a **random variable** underlies almost all of probability theory and its daughter discipline of statistics. A fully formal definition of a random variable requires the concept of a **probability space**, on which can be defined a **sigma-algebra**, on which in turn can be defined a **probability measure**. We cannot in this book go into details concerning these concepts, and interested readers are referred to Billingsley (1979) for a proper treatment.

The essence of the matter, much simplified, is as follows. The first necessity is a set the elements of which would commonly be called the "states of the world" in ordinary economic theory. This set, more correctly called the **event space** or the **outcome space**, can be very simple. For example, if we were dealing with a toss of a coin, it would consist of just two elements, heads and tails. In other circumstances, it can be very complicated, so as to cope with a full-blown stochastic process, either with a discrete index, like the sequences of random variables encountered in the asymptotic theory given in this book, or even with a continuous index. An instance of this last possibility crops up with the Wiener processes mentioned in Chapter 20. In all cases, the outcome space must have a rich enough structure that every *possible* outcome is represented as a point in the space; different outcomes must correspond to different points.

Although every possible outcome must be represented in the outcome space, it is not always possible to assign a probability to all of these outcomes. Even if it is, the probability assigned may not be particularly informative. For instance, if we consider a single random variable that can take values anywhere on the real line, the probability that any single real number will be realized is usually zero. Positive probabilities in such cases would be assigned only to intervals of positive length. A structure is therefore needed to determine just what subsets of the outcome space — what **compound events** in standard probabilistic terminology — can have probabilities assigned to them. This structure is the sigma-algebra of the formal theory.

The last essential ingredient is the probability measure: the means by which probabilities actually are assigned to events, compound or simple. All we really need to remember here is that probability measures must respect the laws of probability that our intuition requires. These laws are remarkably simple: The probability of the null event (nothing happens) is zero, the probability of the complete outcome space (something happens) is unity, and the probability that one or other of a set of disjoint, or mutually exclusive, events happens is the sum of the probabilities of the individual disjoint events.

We can now provide an informal definition of what we mean by a random variable, or **r.v.** for short. The simplest case is a **scalar random variable**, one that takes on a single real value. Such a random variable will be a mapping of the outcome space into the real line, that is, an assignment of a real number to each possible outcome. A moment's reflection will show that this is indeed what we mean by a random variable: a quantity the value of which depends on the state of the world. In general, it is not the case that an arbitrary mapping from the outcome space to the real line counts as a proper random variable, because we insist that it should be possible to define a **probability distribution** for each random variable. What this means, more specifically, is that, if x is any r.v., we should be able to assign probabilities to events of the form $(x \leq X)$ for all real numbers X. Let us denote the outcome space by Ω; this is very standard notation in probability theory. Then the event $(x \leq X)$ can be expressed more explicitly as the following subset of Ω:

$$(\omega \in \Omega \mid x(\omega) \leq X). \tag{B.01}$$

This makes sense because x is a *mapping* of Ω into the real line.

For x to be a well-defined random variable, it must be possible to assign a probability to each of the sets (B.01). Doing this yields the **cumulative distribution function**, or **c.d.f.**, of the random variable x, which is often denoted $F(x)$ and is defined on the real line. Because the value of a c.d.f. is a probability, a c.d.f. must take values in the interval $[0, 1]$. A typical c.d.f. is defined by an equation of the form

$$F_x(X) = \Pr\big(\omega \in \Omega \mid x(\omega) \leq X\big).$$

Usually, it is safe to omit the reference to ω and Ω and write simply $\Pr(x \leq X)$. By construction, a c.d.f. tends to zero as its argument tends to $-\infty$, and to unity as its argument tends to $+\infty$. Further, it must be a weakly increasing function of its argument. This is true because, if $X_1 < X_2$, then the event $(x \leq X_1)$ is included in the event $(x \leq X_2)$ and therefore cannot have probability greater than that of $(x \leq X_2)$. It is a good exercise to work this result out in detail from the rule about summing the probabilities of disjoint sets of events.

Random variables can take values that are vectors, matrices, or indeed many other things. One that takes vector values is called a **vector-valued random variable**. The probabilistic properties of a vector-valued r.v. $\boldsymbol{x}$ may be represented by a generalization of the c.d.f. called a **joint c.d.f.** If $\boldsymbol{x} \in \mathbb{R}^n$, then its joint c.d.f. is a function of n arguments, as follows:

$$F_{\boldsymbol{x}}(X_1, \ldots, X_n) = \Pr\big((x_1 \leq X_1) \cap \cdots \cap (x_n \leq X_n)\big).$$

Here x_i denotes the ith component of $\boldsymbol{x}$, and the sign $\cap$ has its usual sense of the intersection of sets: The event in question is the set of all $\omega \in \Omega$ such that $x_1 \leq X_1$ *and* $x_2 \leq X_2$, and so on. A joint c.d.f. has similar properties to the c.d.f. of a scalar random variable. It tends to zero when *any* of its arguments tends to $-\infty$, and it tends to unity when *all* of its arguments tend to $+\infty$. From a joint c.d.f., one can derive the **marginal distribution** of any of the components of $\boldsymbol{x}$. By this is meant simply the probability of that component considered by itself as a scalar random variable. This marginal distribution is of course represented by an ordinary c.d.f., which for component x_i is given by setting all the arguments of the joint c.d.f. that do not correspond to x_i equal to $+\infty$:

$$F_{x_i}(X_i) = F_{\boldsymbol{x}}(+\infty, \ldots, X_i, \ldots, +\infty).$$

This then is the probability that $x_i \leq X_i$ and that all components of $\boldsymbol{x}$ other than x_i take on any value at all. The marginal distribution of any subset of the components of $\boldsymbol{x}$ is represented similarly by a joint c.d.f. obtained from the original one by setting all arguments that do not correspond to the selected components equal to $+\infty$.

Once one considers joint probability distributions, it is possible to introduce the important notion of **statistical independence**. Let $\boldsymbol{x}$ be an n–vector-valued random variable, and suppose that it is partitioned as $\boldsymbol{x} = [\boldsymbol{x}_1 \,\vdots\, \boldsymbol{x}_2]$, with $\boldsymbol{x}_1 \in \mathbb{R}^{n_1}$, $\boldsymbol{x}_2 \in \mathbb{R}^{n_2}$, and $n_1 + n_2 = n$. Then $\boldsymbol{x}_1$ and $\boldsymbol{x}_2$ are said to be **statistically independent**, or often just independent, if the joint c.d.f. of the full vector $\boldsymbol{x}$ is the product of the joint c.d.f.'s of $\boldsymbol{x}_1$ and $\boldsymbol{x}_2$. In straightforward notation, this means that

$$F_{\boldsymbol{x}}\big(\boldsymbol{X}_1, \boldsymbol{X}_2\big) = F_{\boldsymbol{x}}\big(\boldsymbol{X}_1, \infty_2\big) F_{\boldsymbol{x}}\big(\infty_1, \boldsymbol{X}_2\big),$$

where ∞_1 and ∞_2 denote vectors all components of which equal $+\infty$.

The concept of a **probability density function**, or **p.d.f.**, is very closely related to that of a c.d.f. Whereas a distribution function exists for any well-defined random variable, a p.d.f. exists only when the c.d.f. is *differentiable*. For a scalar r.v., the density function, often denoted by f, is just the derivative of the c.d.f.:

$$f_x(X) \equiv F_x'(X).$$

The **joint density** of a set of r.v.'s, or equivalently, of a vector-valued r.v., is obtained from the joint c.d.f. by differentiating it with respect to *all* of its arguments:

$$f_{\boldsymbol{x}}(X_1, \ldots, X_n) = \frac{\partial^n F_{\boldsymbol{x}}(X_1, \ldots, X_n)}{\partial X_1 \cdots \partial X_n}.$$

The fact that a c.d.f. varies from 0 to 1 implies that a density function must be **normalized** to integrate to unity. By the fundamental theorem of calculus,

$$\begin{aligned}\int_{-\infty}^{\infty} f_x(X)\,dX &= \int_{-\infty}^{\infty} F_x'(X)\,dX \\ &= \big[F_x(X)\big]_{X=-\infty}^{X=+\infty} = 1 - 0 = 1.\end{aligned} \tag{B.02}$$

In like manner, one shows that the multiple integral of a joint density function with respect to all its arguments as they range from $-\infty$ to $+\infty$ is equal to unity. A still more useful result is that, if one integrates a joint p.d.f. with respect to only some of its arguments, the result is the density of the marginal distribution of the variables not "integrated out." This is called their **marginal density**. If two groups of r.v.'s are independent, then it is easy to see from the definition of independence in terms of c.d.f.'s that independence implies that the joint density of the two groups is the product of the marginal densities of the two groups.

Another crucial property of a density function is that it is nonnegative. This follows directly from its definition as the derivative of a weakly increasing function. But it is also a reflection of a very useful property of a density, one which allows us to use it to compute the probabilities of events associated with a given random variable. Suppose that x is a scalar r.v. Then for any interval $[a, b]$ of the real line, we may wish to compute the probability that $x \in [a, b]$. It follows directly from the definition of a c.d.f. that, if $a < b$,

$$\Pr\big(x \in [a, b]\big) = F_x(b) - F_x(a).$$

By the same argument as that leading to (B.02), this probability is

$$\int_a^b f_x(X)\,dX. \tag{B.03}$$

Since (B.03) must hold for arbitrary a and b, it is clear that f_x must be a nonnegative function.

B.3 MOMENTS OF RANDOM VARIABLES

One of the most important properties that a random variable may possess is an **expectation**. It will be enough to define the expectation of a scalar r.v.; for vector- or matrix-valued r.v.'s, expectations are defined component by component. Thus, if x is a scalar random variable, its expectation is defined as the value of the integral

$$\int_{-\infty}^{\infty} X\, dF_x(X), \tag{B.04}$$

if it exists. The sort of integral that appears in (B.04) is called a **Stieltjes integral**, because of the presence of the **integrator function** F_x. Readers for whom the concept of a Stieltjes integral is unfamiliar may wish to consult a standard text on real analysis, such as Burrill and Knudsen (1969) or Mukherjea and Pothoven (1984), for details. We will not provide them here, because these details are not very important for the points we wish to make. The essential feature of a Stieltjes integral, from our present point of view, is that if the integrator is differentiable, the Stieltjes integral may be expressed as an ordinary integral in terms of its derivative. For (B.04), this gives the following expression for the expectation of x:

$$\int_{-\infty}^{\infty} X f_x(X)\, dX, \tag{B.05}$$

where f_x is the density of x. For the simplicity of our subsequent discussion, we will deal only with differentiable c.d.f.'s.

Not every random variable has an expectation. The integral of a density function always exists and equals 1. But, since X ranges from $-\infty$ to ∞, the integral (B.05) may well diverge at either limit of integration, or both, if the density f_x does not tend to zero fast enough. By a slight abuse of terminology, the expectation of a random variable is sometimes called its **mean**. Strictly speaking, a mean is a property of a *sample* of realized r.v.'s, rather than of a probability distribution. In the rare circumstances where confusion is possible, the expectation may be called a **population mean** to distinguish it from the **sample mean**.

The expectation of a random variable is often referred to as its **first moment**. The so-called **higher moments** are, if they exist, the expectations of the powers of the r.v. Thus the **second moment** of a random variable x is the expectation of x^2, the **third moment** the expectation of x^3, and so on. Fractional moments can be defined analogously, but we will not use them in this book. In general, the kth moment of the r.v. x is

$$m_k \equiv \int_{-\infty}^{\infty} X^k f_x(X)\, dX.$$

Observe that the value of any moment depends only on the probability distribution of the r.v. in question. For this reason, one often speaks of the moments of the distribution rather than of a specific random variable. Note also that if a distribution possesses a kth moment, it also possesses all moments of order less than k.

The definition just given is of the **uncentered moments** of a distribution. It is probably more common to work with the **central moments**, which are defined as the ordinary moments of the difference between the random variable and its expectation. Thus, if we write $E(x)$ for the expectation of x, the kth central moment of the distribution of x is

$$\bar{m}_k \equiv E\big(x - E(x)\big)^k.$$

Far and away the most important central moment is the second. It is called the **variance** of the r.v. The usual notation for a variance is σ^2, and this notation underlines the fact that a variance cannot be negative. The square root, σ, is called the **standard deviation** of the distribution. *Estimates* of standard deviations are often referred to as **standard errors**, especially when the random variable in question is an estimated parameter.

It is often important to be able to define moments of vector-valued r.v.'s. For the first moment, this is essentially trivial: The first moment of an n–vector-valued random variable $\boldsymbol{x}$ is just an ordinary n–vector $\bar{\boldsymbol{x}}$ with typical component $\bar{x}_i \equiv E(x_i)$. For the second and higher moments, things are not so simple. For the central second moments, one needs to define an $n \times n$ matrix, which is sometimes called the **variance matrix**, sometimes the **covariance matrix**, and sometimes the **variance-covariance matrix**. Terminology is not standard, but we prefer the middle form. The covariance matrix of $\boldsymbol{x}$ will be denoted $\boldsymbol{V}(\boldsymbol{x})$ and is defined as

$$\boldsymbol{V}(\boldsymbol{x}) \equiv E\big((\boldsymbol{x} - \bar{\boldsymbol{x}})(\boldsymbol{x} - \bar{\boldsymbol{x}})^{\top}\big).$$

The diagonal elements of $\boldsymbol{V}(\boldsymbol{x})$ can be seen to be the separate variances of the components of $\boldsymbol{x}$. The off-diagonal element V_{ij} is called the **covariance** of the components x_i and x_j. Higher moments of vectors of r.v.'s can be defined analogously. They require objects with more than two indices and are not used in this book.

If one computes the expectation of the product of two independent random variables, the result is just the product of the expectations of the r.v.'s separately. This follows from the fact that the joint density of two independent r.v.'s is just the product of the two marginal densities. Further, the covariance of two independent random variables is zero. A standard trick question in probability theory asks if two r.v.'s with zero covariance are necessarily independent: The answer is *NO*. However, a zero covariance *is* enough for the expectation of the product of two random variables to equal the product of their separate expectations.

One often needs to compute the variance of a linear combination of random variables. Let these r.v.'s be components of a vector r.v. $\boldsymbol{x}$, and let the linear combination of interest be written as $\boldsymbol{a}^\top\boldsymbol{x}$ for some nonrandom vector $\boldsymbol{a}$. It is easy to show that the variance of this linear combination is $\boldsymbol{a}^\top\boldsymbol{V}(\boldsymbol{x})\boldsymbol{a}$. Similarly, if one forms a vector of linear combinations of the components of $\boldsymbol{x}$, for example, by forming $\boldsymbol{A}^\top\boldsymbol{x}$ for some suitable nonrandom matrix $\boldsymbol{A}$, then

$$\boldsymbol{V}(\boldsymbol{A}^\top\boldsymbol{x}) = \boldsymbol{A}^\top\boldsymbol{V}(\boldsymbol{x})\boldsymbol{A}. \tag{B.06}$$

If a random variable has a variance, its value can be used to provide a bound for the probability mass in the tail of the distribution. By the **tail** of a probability distribution, we mean an event of the form $(x > X)$ or $(x < X)$, where X is substantially to the right of the center of the distribution in the first case and substantially to the left in the second. The first case defines the **right tail** and the second defines the **left tail** of the distribution. The ambiguous word "center" is used here because the whole definition of a tail is imprecise. By center one may mean the expectation or the median or the mode or some other **measure of central tendency**. The imprecision is probably due to the fact that not all r.v.'s have means. If they do not, different measures of central tendency may be appropriate for different r.v.'s. Sometimes we are interested in the probability that a random variable lies in either tail, sometimes in the probability that it lies in the right tail, and sometimes in the probability that it lies in the left tail. Left tails are seldom of interest with r.v.'s that take on only positive values.

The bound on the probability mass in the tails that we alluded to above is known as the **Chebyshev inequality**. It can be derived as follows. Suppose that the uncentered second moment of the r.v. x is V. If x is itself a centered random variable, then $E(x) = 0$ and V is its variance. The Chebyshev inequality states that, for any positive number α,

$$\Pr\big(|x| > \alpha\big) \leq \frac{V}{\alpha^2}. \tag{B.07}$$

To see this, note that the definition of V is

$$V = E(x^2) = \int_{-\infty}^{\infty} X^2 f_x(X)\, dX.$$

This integral can be split up into the sum of three integrals:

$$V = \int_{-\alpha}^{\alpha} X^2 f_x(X)\, dX + \int_{\alpha}^{\infty} X^2 f_x(X)\, dX + \int_{-\infty}^{-\alpha} X^2 f_x(X)\, dX. \tag{B.08}$$

Consider the last two terms on the right-hand side above. The factor X^2 in the integrand is always greater than α^2 over the range of integration in these terms. Thus these terms are at least as great as

$$\alpha^2\bigg(\int_{\alpha}^{\infty} f_x(X)\, dX + \int_{-\infty}^{-\alpha} f_x(X)\, dX\bigg) = \alpha^2 \Pr\big(|x| > \alpha\big),$$

by (B.03). Since all the terms in (B.08) are nonnegative, we conclude that

$$V \geq \alpha^2 \Pr\big(|x| > \alpha\big).$$

Reorganizing this inequality gives (B.07). From this follows a more familiar form of the Chebyshev inequality, which states that, for a random variable x with mean μ and variance σ^2,

$$\Pr\left(\left|\frac{x-\mu}{\sigma}\right| > \alpha\right) \leq \frac{1}{\alpha^2}.$$

Taking the expectation of a random variable is a linear operation. If x and y are two r.v.'s and a and b are two nonrandom real numbers, then $E(ax+by) = aE(x) + bE(y)$. This follows directly from the definition (B.05) of an expectation. In general, however, if g is a scalar-valued function of a scalar random variable x, it is *not* the case that $E\big(g(x)\big) = g\big(E(x)\big)$. This conclusion would be true only if g were an **affine function**, which means that $g(x) = ax + b$ for two real numbers a and b.

On the other hand, if the function g is concave or convex, one can show that the inequality between $E\big(g(x)\big)$ and $g\big(E(x)\big)$ has a particular sign. This result is known as **Jensen's inequality**. For concreteness, and because this is the case that arises in the maximum likelihood theory of Chapter 8, suppose that g is a concave function, like the logarithmic function. Then the inequality asserts that

$$E\big(g(x)\big) \leq g\big(E(x)\big).$$

To see this, suppose that g is differentiable, although the result holds without this assumption. Then one way of expressing the concavity of g is through the inequality

$$g(a) \leq g(b) + g'(b)(a-b), \quad \text{for all real } a, b. \tag{B.09}$$

This inequality is depicted in Figure B.1, which should provide intuition for Jensen's inequality as well as for (B.09) itself. Denote $E(x)$ by $\bar{x}$. Then

$$\begin{aligned} E\big(g(x)\big) &= \int_{-\infty}^{\infty} g(X) f_x(X)\, dX \\ &\leq \int_{-\infty}^{\infty} \big(g(\bar{x}) + g'(\bar{x})(X - \bar{x})\big) f_x(X)\, dX, \end{aligned}$$

where the inequality follows from (B.09). The second line here is equal to

$$\begin{aligned} &g(\bar{x}) + g'(\bar{x})\left(\int_{-\infty}^{\infty} X f_x(X)\, dX - \bar{x}\int_{-\infty}^{\infty} f_x(X)\, dX\right) \\ &= g\big(E(x)\big) + g'(\bar{x})(\bar{x} - \bar{x}) = g\big(E(x)\big). \end{aligned}$$

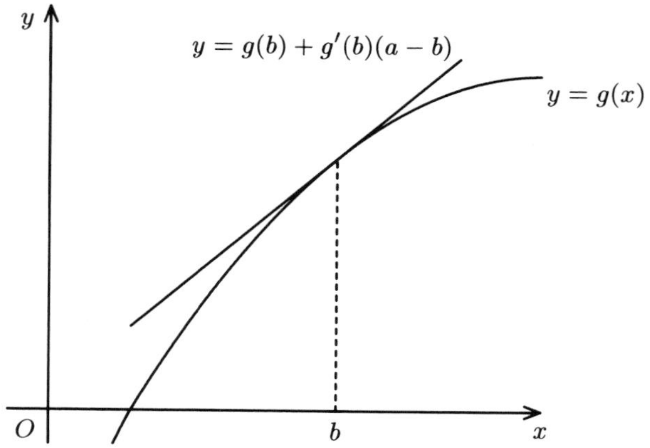

Figure B.1 A typical concave function

This then proves Jensen's inequality for the differentiable case.

If any function of a random variable x is evaluated at x, the result is another random variable. This is as true for the density function f_x as for any other function. In econometrics, one is seldom interested in a single density function but rather in a parametric family of density functions. In the simple case in which there is only one parameter, such a family can be written as $f(x, \theta)$, where θ is the parameter. The logarithm of this function is the **loglikelihood function** associated with the parametric family. An important property of such loglikelihood functions is that, under appropriate regularity conditions, the derivative of $\log f(x, \theta)$ is a random variable such that, if its mean is calculated with the density corresponding to the same value of θ as that at which the derivative is evaluated, that mean is zero if it exists. It is worth sketching a proof of this result, which may be stated as

$$E_\theta\left(\frac{\partial \log f}{\partial \theta}\right) = 0, \qquad \text{(B.10)}$$

where the θ subscript on the expectation operator indicates that the expectation is calculated using $f(\cdot, \theta)$.

The proof of (B.10) makes use of a standard result on the differentiation of integrals. This result states that the derivative with respect to a parameter θ of an integral of the form

$$\int_{a(\theta)}^{b(\theta)} g(y, \theta)\, dy$$

is expressible in terms of the derivatives with respect to θ of the functions a, b, and g, provided these exist, and equals

$$-a'(\theta)g\big(a(\theta), \theta\big) + b'(\theta)g\big(b(\theta), \theta\big) + \int_{a(\theta)}^{b(\theta)} \frac{\partial g(y, \theta)}{\partial \theta}\, dy,$$

again provided the integral in this last expression exists. See any text on real analysis, such as Burrill and Knudsen (1969) or Mukherjea and Pothoven (1984), for this standard result.

To prove (B.10), we utilize the fact that the density function f is normalized to integrate to unity for all values of the parameter θ. Suppose that the **support** of the density function is the interval $[a(\theta), b(\theta)]$ for each θ. This means that the density is zero outside this interval or that there is zero probability that a r.v. distributed with density $f(\cdot, \theta)$ will be realized outside this interval. Then the normalization condition is

$$\int_{a(\theta)}^{b(\theta)} f(y, \theta)\, dy = 1.$$

Since this condition holds for all admissible values of θ, it may be differentiated with respect to θ, to give

$$-a'(\theta) f\big(a(\theta)\big) + b'(\theta) f\big(b(\theta)\big) + \int_{a(\theta)}^{b(\theta)} \frac{\partial f(y, \theta)}{\partial \theta}\, dy = 0. \tag{B.11}$$

The last term here, the integral, can also be expressed as

$$\int_{a(\theta)}^{b(\theta)} f(y, \theta) \frac{\partial \log f(y, \theta)}{\partial \theta}\, dy = E_\theta\left(\frac{\partial \log f}{\partial \theta}\right).$$

We can see that, apart from the regularity conditions of differentiability and the existence of the expectation of $\partial \log f / \partial \theta$, the result (B.10) requires that the first two terms in (B.11) vanish for one reason or another. One obvious way to achieve this is for the limits of the support of the density to be independent of the parameter θ. For instance, if the support is the whole real line, this will automatically be satisfied. Another way is for the density to vanish on the boundary of its support, and this does indeed occur often enough in practice. Difficulties can arise, however, if the support depends on θ and the density is bounded away from zero on its entire support.

The reasoning used to establish (B.10) can be used equally well to establish the information matrix equality of maximum likelihood theory; see Chapter 8.

B.4 Some Standard Probability Distributions

The most important probability distribution is without question the **standard normal distribution**. This distribution crops up very frequently in econometric theory, and the definitions of a great many other commonly encountered distributions can be made directly in terms of the standard normal distribution.

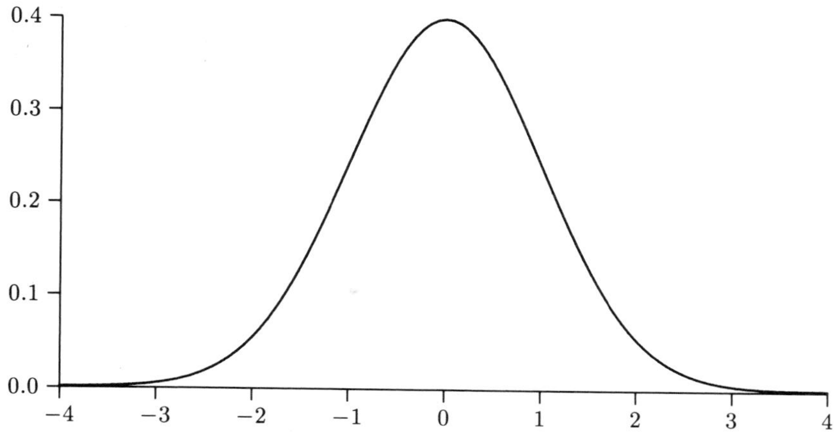

Figure B.2 The standard normal density

The normal distribution has a density of which the graph is the famous or infamous bell curve of elementary statistics and, sometimes, students' grade distributions; see Figure B.2.

The density of the standard normal distribution is defined on the full real line, as follows:

$$\phi(x) = (2\pi)^{-1/2} \exp\bigl(-\tfrac{1}{2}x^2\bigr). \tag{B.12}$$

In contrast to this p.d.f., which can be expressed entirely in terms of standard functions, the standard normal c.d.f. must be defined explicitly as the integral

$$\Phi(x) = \int_{-\infty}^{x} \phi(y)\, dy.$$

Note that ϕ and Φ are the usual notations for the standard normal p.d.f. and c.d.f. Although Φ cannot be expressed in terms of standard functions, it can easily be evaluated numerically.[1] It is simple to check that ϕ satisfies all the requirements for a probability density: It is positive everywhere, and it integrates to unity. Therefore, since Φ is defined in terms of a proper density, it must satisfy the requirements for a c.d.f.

Because the density (B.12) is symmetric about the origin, the mean of the standard normal density is zero, as are all of the odd-ordered moments of the distribution. The even moments are not hard to calculate. The variance can be calculated by means of an integration by parts. Since the derivative of

[1] Note that, in both the above definitions, we have for simplicity's sake abandoned the use of uppercase variables. There should be no risk of confusion between ordinary and random variables in what follows.

$\phi(x)$ is $-x\phi(x)$, the indefinite integral of $x\phi(x)$ is $-\phi(x)$. Therefore,

$$\int_{-\infty}^{\infty} x^2\phi(x)\,dx = \int_{-\infty}^{\infty} x\big(x\phi(x)\big)\,dx$$
$$= \big[-x\phi(x)\big]_{x=-\infty}^{x=\infty} + \int_{-\infty}^{\infty}\phi(x)\,dx = 1, \tag{B.13}$$

and we see that the standard normal variance is unity. This fact accounts for the use of the term "standard" in this context. The higher even-ordered moments of the standard normal density are almost as easy to calculate. The answer, which is obtained by an inductive argument based on an integration by parts like that used in (B.13), is that

$$m_{2k} = (2k-1)(2k-3)\cdots(3)(1).$$

Thus the 4th moment is $(3)(1) = 3$, the 6th is $(5)(3)(1) = 15$, and so on.

Any normally distributed r.v. with nonzero mean and nonunit variance can be defined by translation and rescaling of a standard normal variable. The family of distributions so defined therefore must have two parameters, which can conveniently be taken as μ, the mean, and σ^2, the variance. If y is distributed normally with mean μ and variance σ^2, it is said to have the **univariate normal distribution**. One writes $y \sim N(\mu, \sigma^2)$. The density of y is

$$\frac{1}{\sigma}\phi\Big(\frac{y-\mu}{\sigma}\Big) = (2\pi)^{-1/2}\frac{1}{\sigma}\exp\Big(-\frac{(y-\mu)^2}{2\sigma^2}\Big). \tag{B.14}$$

This can be derived from (B.12) by using a result on transformations of random variables that we will prove shortly. If $y \sim N(\mu, \sigma^2)$, then the r.v. $x \equiv (y-\mu)/\sigma$ can be seen to have mean zero and variance unity. In fact, $x \sim N(0,1)$, which is the symbolic way of writing the standard normal distribution.

An important extension of the univariate normal distribution is the **multivariate normal distribution**. The joint density of n *independent* $N(0,1)$ variables is simply the product of n univariate $N(0,1)$ densities. Thus, if $\boldsymbol{x}$ is an n–vector with typical component $x_i \sim N(0,1)$, the joint density is

$$f_{\boldsymbol{x}}(\boldsymbol{x}) = \prod_{i=1}^{n}(2\pi)^{-1/2}\exp\big(-\tfrac{1}{2}x_i^2\big) = (2\pi)^{-n/2}\exp\big(-\tfrac{1}{2}\boldsymbol{x}^{\top}\boldsymbol{x}\big). \tag{B.15}$$

This density is written symbolically as the $N(\mathbf{0}, \mathbf{I})$ density. The first argument is an n–vector of zeros, each element of which is, in this case, the mean of the corresponding element of $\boldsymbol{x}$. The second argument is an $n \times n$ identity matrix, which is, in this case, the covariance matrix of $\boldsymbol{x}$. This is the simplest example of a multivariate normal density.

A random vector that follows any multivariate normal distribution can be derived from $\boldsymbol{x} \sim N(\mathbf{0}, \mathbf{I})$. Suppose that we consider a vector $\boldsymbol{y}$ of n random variables constructed as linear combinations of the components of $\boldsymbol{x}$. This means that $\boldsymbol{y} \equiv \boldsymbol{A}^{\top}\boldsymbol{x}$ for some $n \times n$ nonrandom nonsingular matrix $\boldsymbol{A}$. It is clear that $E(\boldsymbol{y}) = \mathbf{0}$ and that $\boldsymbol{V}(\boldsymbol{y}) = \boldsymbol{A}^{\top}\boldsymbol{A}$; see (B.06). The distribution of the n-vector $\boldsymbol{y}$ is, by definition, the $N(\mathbf{0}, \boldsymbol{A}^{\top}\boldsymbol{A})$ distribution. Thus we see that, as with the $N(\mathbf{0}, \mathbf{I})$ distribution, the matrix argument is the covariance matrix of the components of $\boldsymbol{y}$. Since any covariance matrix $\boldsymbol{V}$ can be written as $\boldsymbol{A}^{\top}\boldsymbol{A}$ for suitable $\boldsymbol{A}$, we can characterize the $N(\mathbf{0}, \boldsymbol{V})$ density for arbitrary positive definite $\boldsymbol{V}$ by finding the joint density of $\boldsymbol{y}$.

The most general form of the multivariate normal distribution may be obtained from a random n-vector $\boldsymbol{y} \sim N(\mathbf{0}, \boldsymbol{V})$ by adding an n-vector $\boldsymbol{\mu}$. Since $E(\boldsymbol{y}+\boldsymbol{\mu}) = \boldsymbol{\mu}$, the expectation of the new random vector so created is $\boldsymbol{\mu}$. Thus the general multivariate normal distribution, which has expectation $\boldsymbol{\mu}$ and covariance matrix $\boldsymbol{V}$, is written symbolically as $N(\boldsymbol{\mu}, \boldsymbol{V})$.

Before we can derive the joint density of the $N(\boldsymbol{\mu}, \boldsymbol{V})$ distribution, we must solve a more general problem. Suppose that we know the distribution of a random variable x, where x is a scalar for the moment. Then what is the distribution of another r.v. y that is a deterministic function of x? For simplicity, let us suppose that $y = g(x)$ for some monotonically increasing function g. In terms of the c.d.f.'s, the calculation is straightforward:

$$\Pr(y < Y) = \Pr\big(g(x) < Y\big) = \Pr\big(x < g^{-1}(Y)\big) = F_x\big(g^{-1}(Y)\big).$$

Note that g^{-1} exists by the assumption of the monotonicity of g. Thus the c.d.f. of y is

$$F_y(Y) = F_x\big(g^{-1}(Y)\big). \tag{B.16}$$

We can then find the density of y by differentiating (B.16):

$$f_y(Y) = f_x\big(g^{-1}(Y)\big)\frac{dg^{-1}(Y)}{dy} = \frac{f_x\big(g^{-1}(Y)\big)}{g'\big(g^{-1}(Y)\big)}. \tag{B.17}$$

Thus the density of y is simply equal to the density of x divided by the first derivative of $g(\cdot)$, where both are evaluated at $g^{-1}(Y)$. Readers may find it instructive to derive the general univariate normal density (B.14) from the standard normal density (B.12) by applying this result.

There is a very simple mnemonic for both forms of the result (B.17). It says simply that

$$f_y(Y)\,dy = f_x(X)\,dx.$$

The mnemonic is translated into meaningful mathematics by dividing through either by dy or by dx and then setting $X = g^{-1}(Y)$ or else $Y = g(X)$. The first possibility gives the middle expression of (B.17), while the second gives

$$f_y\big(g(X)\big)g'(X) = f_x(X),$$

which is equivalent to the right-most expression of (B.17).

If g were monotonically decreasing rather than increasing, (B.17) would still hold if the derivative g', which would be negative, were replaced by its absolute value $|g'|$. (It is a good exercise to check this.) If g were not monotonic, then its domain of definition would have to be split up into regions in which it was monotonic, and (B.17) would apply in each of these regions, locally at least. The catch is that one value Y may now correspond to more than one X, and in that case the density of y at Y is the sum of the contributions calculated using (B.17) at each of these.

In order to derive the density of the multivariate normal distribution, we need to find a multivariate version of (B.17). Suppose that an n–vector-valued r.v. $\boldsymbol{y}$ is given in terms of another n–vector-valued r.v. $\boldsymbol{x}$ by the deterministic mapping $\boldsymbol{y} = \boldsymbol{g}(\boldsymbol{x})$, which is assumed to be one to one. A rather trickier argument than that used in the scalar case shows that

$$f_{\boldsymbol{y}}(\boldsymbol{Y}) = f_x\big(\boldsymbol{g}^{-1}(\boldsymbol{Y})\big)\big|\det \boldsymbol{J}(\boldsymbol{Y})\big|, \tag{B.18}$$

where $\boldsymbol{J}(\boldsymbol{Y})$, the Jacobian of the transformation from $\boldsymbol{y}$ to $\boldsymbol{x}$, is the $n \times n$ matrix of the derivatives of $\boldsymbol{g}^{-1}(\boldsymbol{Y})$ with respect to the elements of $\boldsymbol{Y}$. The notation $|\det(\cdot)|$ means the absolute value of the determinant. The absolute value of the determinant appears in (B.18) for essentially the same reason that the absolute value of g' enters in the univariate case when g' can be negative.

It is often convenient when calculating the determinant in (B.18) to use the fact that the Jacobian of the transformation from $\boldsymbol{y}$ to $\boldsymbol{x}$ is the inverse of the Jacobian of the transformation from $\boldsymbol{x}$ to $\boldsymbol{y}$, and the result that the determinant of the inverse of a matrix is the reciprocal of the determinant of the matrix itself. Thus, if $\boldsymbol{J}^*$ denotes the Jacobian of $\boldsymbol{g}(\boldsymbol{X})$, an alternative way of writing (B.18) is

$$f_{\boldsymbol{y}}(\boldsymbol{Y}) = f_x\big(\boldsymbol{g}^{-1}(\boldsymbol{Y})\big)\big|\det \boldsymbol{J}^*(\boldsymbol{Y})\big|^{-1}.$$

Intrepid readers are encouraged to work through the derivation of (B.18). At least for the 2×2 case, this is not difficult in principle. Readers versed in the theory of integration will understand (B.18) intuitively on noting that the determinant is the ratio of the infinitesimal volumes in the spaces of $\boldsymbol{x}$ and $\boldsymbol{y}$, respectively; see Appendix A.

We can now return to the problem of finding the multivariate normal density. Suppose that $\boldsymbol{x} \sim N(\boldsymbol{0}, \mathbf{I})$ and $\boldsymbol{y} = \boldsymbol{A}^\top\boldsymbol{x} + \boldsymbol{\mu}$. This implies that $\boldsymbol{y} \sim N(\boldsymbol{\mu}, \boldsymbol{V})$, where $\boldsymbol{V} \equiv \boldsymbol{A}^\top\boldsymbol{A}$. The Jacobian of the transformation from $\boldsymbol{y}$

to $\boldsymbol{x}$ in this case is $(\boldsymbol{A}^\top)^{-1}$. Since the density of $\boldsymbol{x}$ is (B.15), the result (B.18) implies that the density of $\boldsymbol{y}$ must be

$$
\begin{aligned}
&(2\pi)^{-n/2}|\det \boldsymbol{A}|^{-1}\exp\Big(-\frac{1}{2}(\boldsymbol{y}-\boldsymbol{\mu})^\top \boldsymbol{A}^{-1}(\boldsymbol{A}^\top)^{-1}(\boldsymbol{y}-\boldsymbol{\mu})\Big)\\
&=(2\pi)^{-n/2}|\boldsymbol{V}|^{-1/2}\exp\Big(-\frac{1}{2}(\boldsymbol{y}-\boldsymbol{\mu})^\top \boldsymbol{V}^{-1}(\boldsymbol{y}-\boldsymbol{\mu})\Big),
\end{aligned}
\tag{B.19}
$$

where $|\boldsymbol{V}|$ is the determinant of $\boldsymbol{V}$, which is always positive. The second line uses the fact that the covariance matrix $\boldsymbol{V}$ is equal to $\boldsymbol{A}^\top\boldsymbol{A}$. (B.19) is the standard way of writing the multivariate normal density for the general case of $\boldsymbol{y} \sim N(\boldsymbol{\mu}, \boldsymbol{V})$.

Many well-known distributions can be defined in terms of the standard normal distribution. The strangest of these is possibly the **Cauchy distribution**. By definition, this is the distribution of the ratio of two independent standard normal random variables. Let x and y be two such r.v.'s. The joint density of x and y is, from (B.15),

$$
(2\pi)^{-1}\exp\Big(-\frac{1}{2}(x^2+y^2)\Big).
$$

In order to derive the Cauchy density, we must change variables to the polar coordinates r and θ that correspond to x and y. The relation between these and the cartesian coordinates is

$$
\begin{aligned}
x &= r\cos\theta; \qquad & y &= r\sin\theta;\\
r &= (x^2+y^2)^{1/2}; \qquad & \theta &= \tan^{-1}(y/x).
\end{aligned}
$$

The determinant of the Jacobian of the transformation from (r,θ) to (x,y) is $r\sin^2\theta + r\cos^2\theta = r$. Therefore, the joint density of r and θ is

$$
(2\pi)^{-1}re^{-r^2/2}. \tag{B.20}
$$

This does not depend on θ at all, which implies that the density of θ must be uniform on some interval. Clearly, since θ is an angle in radians, that interval must be $[0, 2\pi]$. This result can be shown more formally by integrating (B.20) with respect to r over the interval from 0 to ∞. The result, which is the density of θ, is just $(2\pi)^{-1}$. This is indeed the density of a random variable that is uniformly distributed on the interval $[0, 2\pi]$.

The Cauchy random variable $z \equiv y/x$ is related to θ by the relation $z = \tan\theta$. The (scalar) Jacobian of the transformation from z to θ is therefore the reciprocal of the derivative of $\tan\theta$ with respect to θ. This derivative is $\sec^2\theta$. Before we write down the density of z, it is important to note that, as θ varies from 0 to 2π, each value of z is generated exactly twice, since $\tan(\pi + \theta) = \tan\theta$. Thus we conclude that the density of the Cauchy distribution is

$$2(2\pi)^{-1}\frac{1}{\sec^2\theta} = \frac{1}{\pi(1+\tan^2\theta)} = \frac{1}{\pi(1+z^2)}.$$

It is clear that if we try to calculate the expectation of a Cauchy r.v., we will be confronted with the integral

$$\int_{-\infty}^{\infty}\frac{z\,dz}{\pi(1+z^2)},$$

which diverges at both limits of integration. Thus the Cauchy distribution has no moments.

Of much greater importance to econometrics than the Cauchy distribution is the **chi-squared distribution**. This distribution depends on two parameters, one a positive integer, called the number of **degrees of freedom**, and one a positive real number, called the **noncentrality parameter**, or **NCP**. The symbolic representation of a chi-squared random variable with n degrees of freedom and NCP Λ is $\chi^2(n, \Lambda)$. When the NCP is zero, as it often is, the r.v. is said to follow the **central chi-squared distribution**. This is often represented symbolically as $\chi^2(n)$ rather than $\chi^2(n, 0)$.

The central chi-squared distribution is defined by means of an n–vector $\boldsymbol{x}$ distributed as $N(\mathbf{0}, \mathbf{I})$. Then the random variable y defined as $\boldsymbol{x}^\top\boldsymbol{x}$ has the $\chi^2(n)$ distribution. It is clear that y is the sum of the squares of n independent standard normal r.v.'s. It is not difficult to compute the density of the $\chi^2(n)$ distribution by use of this fact, provided that one knows about polar coordinates in n dimensions. Fortunately, we do not use this density explicitly, and so we will not take the trouble to derive it. It is worth noting that $E(y) = n$ and $V(y) = 2n$.

When the NCP is different from zero, the r.v. is said to follow the **noncentral chi-squared distribution**. A random variable with the $\chi^2(n, \Lambda)$ distribution may be constructed as the sum of the squares of $n - 1$ independent standard normal r.v.'s, plus the square of another r.v., independent of the others, distributed as $N(\Lambda^{1/2}, 1)$. It may also be constructed as the sum of the squares of n independent r.v.'s x_i, where $x_i \sim N(\mu_i, 1)$ and $\Lambda = \sum_{i=1}^{n}\mu_i^2$. The first definition is clearly just a special case of the second one. The proof that the density depends only on the sum $\sum_{i=1}^{n}\mu_i^2$ and not on the individual μ_i's is beyond the scope of this appendix.

The noncentral chi-squared distribution has the following property. For any positive number c,

$$\Pr\big(\chi^2(n, \Lambda) > c\big)$$

is an increasing function of n and of Λ. This result is easy to prove. Not at all so easy to prove (the proof uses techniques well beyond the level of this book) is a result of Das Gupta and Perlman (1974). This result is at the heart of all arguments dealing with the power of tests based on statistics in asymptotically chi-squared form. It is as follows. For any $\alpha \in [0,1]$, let $c_{n\alpha}$ satisfy the condition $\Pr(\chi^2(n) > c_{n\alpha}) = \alpha$. Thus $c_{n\alpha}$ is the critical value for a test of size α using the central chi-squared distribution with n degrees of freedom. Then, for each NCP Λ,

$$\Pr\big(\chi^2(n,\Lambda) > c_{n\alpha}\big)$$

is a decreasing function of n. Thus, for a given NCP, test power will decline as the number of degrees of freedom increases.

Many test statistics are calculated as a quadratic form involving a vector of (asymptotically) normally distributed r.v.'s and an estimate of the inverse of their covariance matrix. Such test statistics have the central chi-squared distribution asymptotically. This result depends on the fact that if the n–vector $\boldsymbol{x}$ is distributed as $N(\mathbf{0}, \boldsymbol{V})$, the quadratic form $z \equiv \boldsymbol{x}^\top \boldsymbol{V}^{-1}\boldsymbol{x}$ has the $\chi^2(n,0)$ distribution. In fact, for the sake of economy, we prove the more general result that if $\boldsymbol{x} \sim N(\boldsymbol{\mu}, \boldsymbol{V})$, z will be distributed as $\chi^2(n, \boldsymbol{\mu}^\top\boldsymbol{V}^{-1}\boldsymbol{\mu})$.

Let $\boldsymbol{\eta}$ be a symmetric matrix such that $\boldsymbol{V}^{-1} = \boldsymbol{\eta}\boldsymbol{\eta}$, and consider the random vector $\boldsymbol{y} \equiv \boldsymbol{\eta}\boldsymbol{x}$. We have constructed $\boldsymbol{y}$ so that $\boldsymbol{y}^\top\boldsymbol{y} = \boldsymbol{x}^\top\boldsymbol{V}^{-1}\boldsymbol{x} = z$. The vector $\boldsymbol{y}$ is clearly multivariate normal, with mean $\boldsymbol{\eta}\boldsymbol{\mu}$ and covariance matrix $\boldsymbol{\eta}\boldsymbol{V}\boldsymbol{\eta} = \mathbf{I}$. By the second definition of the noncentral chi-squared distribution, z must be distributed as $\chi^2(n, \boldsymbol{\mu}^\top\boldsymbol{V}^{-1}\boldsymbol{\mu})$, as required. The result that $z \sim \chi^2(n)$ for the special case of $\boldsymbol{\mu} = \mathbf{0}$ then follows immediately from this more general result.

A closely related result is the following. Suppose that $\boldsymbol{x} \sim N(\mathbf{0}, \mathbf{I}_n)$. Then, if $\boldsymbol{P}$ is an $n \times n$ orthogonal projection matrix of rank $r < n$, the **idempotent quadratic form $\boldsymbol{x}^\top\boldsymbol{P}\boldsymbol{x}$** is distributed as $\chi^2(r)$. To see this, it is convenient to express the matrix $\boldsymbol{P}$ as $\boldsymbol{Z}(\boldsymbol{Z}^\top\boldsymbol{Z})^{-1}\boldsymbol{Z}^\top$, for some suitable $n \times r$ matrix $\boldsymbol{Z}$ such that $\mathcal{S}(\boldsymbol{Z}) = \mathcal{S}(\boldsymbol{P})$. Then

$$\boldsymbol{x}^\top\boldsymbol{P}\boldsymbol{x} = \boldsymbol{x}^\top\boldsymbol{Z}\big(\boldsymbol{Z}^\top\boldsymbol{Z}\big)^{-1}\boldsymbol{Z}^\top\boldsymbol{x}.$$

Evidently, the r–vector $\boldsymbol{Z}^\top\boldsymbol{x}$ has the $N(\mathbf{0}, \boldsymbol{Z}^\top\boldsymbol{Z})$ distribution. Therefore, $\boldsymbol{x}^\top\boldsymbol{P}\boldsymbol{x}$ is a quadratic form in a multivariate normal r–vector and the inverse of its covariance matrix. The result then follows immediately by the results of the preceding paragraph.

The **$\boldsymbol{F}$ distribution** can be defined in terms of two independent random variables, each of which follows a χ^2 distribution. Since neither, one, or both of these r.v.'s may be noncentral, the F distribution may be central, singly noncentral, or doubly noncentral. The **central $\boldsymbol{F}$ distribution** with n and d (for "numerator" and "denominator") degrees of freedom is the distribution of the ratio of two independent central χ^2 r.v.'s with n and d degrees of freedom, respectively, each divided by its degrees-of-freedom number. Symbolically,

$$F(n,d) = \frac{\chi^2(n)/n}{\chi^2(d)/d}.$$

The **singly noncentral *F* distribution** with n and d degrees of freedom and NCP Λ is the distribution of the ratio of a numerator r.v. distributed as $n^{-1}\chi^2(n,\Lambda)$ and an independent denominator r.v. distributed as $d^{-1}\chi^2(d,0)$. The **doubly noncentral *F* distribution** with n and d degrees of freedom and NCP's Λ_n and Λ_d is the distribution of a ratio of a numerator distributed as $n^{-1}\chi^2(n,\Lambda_n)$ and an independent denominator distributed as $d^{-1}\chi^2(d,\Lambda_d)$. The densities of all of these F distributions are known and tabulated — see, for instance, Abramowitz and Stegun (1965) — but are not usually of interest to econometricians. In practice, all we usually need is a routine for computing the c.d.f. and the inverse c.d.f. of the central F distribution, and such routines are available in most good statistics packages.

Finally, we come to the **Student's *t* distribution**, which is often simply called the ***t* distribution** for short. The Student's t distribution with n degrees of freedom is denoted $t(n)$ and defined as the distribution of a standard normal r.v. divided by an independent r.v. distributed as the square root of $n^{-1}\chi^2(n,0)$. Evidently, the square of a random variable that is distributed as $t(n)$ is distributed as central $F(1,n)$. Given the definition of the central chi-squared distribution, it is clear that the law of large numbers can be applied to $n^{-1}\chi^2(n,0)$ as $n\to\infty$. Since the expectation of each squared standard normal variable in the definition is just unity, the limit of $n^{-1}\chi^2(n,0)$ must be 1. Consequently, the $t(n)$ distribution tends to the standard normal distribution as $n\to\infty$.

For most values of n, the t distribution looks very much like the standard normal distribution, but it has somewhat thicker tails. The difference between the t and standard normal distributions is very small for $n\geq 100$; for example, the 5% critical value on a two-tailed test is 1.960 for $N(0,1)$ and 1.984 for $t(100)$. However, this difference can be large for very small values of n. The $t(1)$ distribution is evidently the same as the Cauchy distribution, and it therefore has no moments at all. The $t(2)$ distribution has a first moment of zero but has no second or higher moments. In general, the $t(n)$ distribution has moments only up to order $n-1$.

Occasionally, the **noncentral *t* distribution** crops up. It is defined as

$$t(n,\mu)=\frac{N(\mu,1)}{\big(n^{-1}\chi^2(n,0)\big)^{1/2}}.$$

The NCP is μ, and the square of such a random variable is distributed as singly noncentral F with 1 and n degrees of freedom and NCP μ^2.

For more details about the properties of the distributions discussed in this section, readers may wish to consult Kendall and Stuart (1977) or Johnson and Kotz (1970a, 1970b).

Terms and Concepts

affine function
Cauchy distribution
Chebyshev inequality
chi-squared distribution, central and noncentral
compound event
covariance
covariance matrix
cumulative distribution function, or c.d.f.
degrees of freedom
event space, or outcome space
expectation
F distribution, central, singly noncentral, and doubly noncentral
first, second, third, and higher moments
idempotent quadratic form
integrator function
Jensen's inequality
joint c.d.f.
joint density
loglikelihood function
marginal density
marginal distribution
mean, population and sample
measure of central tendency
moments of random variables, central and uncentered
multivariate normal distribution
noncentrality parameter, or NCP
normalization (of a density)
probability density function, or p.d.f.
probability distribution
probability measure
probability space
random variable
scalar random variable
sigma-algebra
standard deviation
standard error
standard normal distribution
statistical independence
Stieltjes integral
Student's t distribution, central and noncentral
support of a density
tails of a distribution, right and left
univariate normal distribution
variance
vector-valued random variable

References

Abramowitz, M., and I. A. Stegun (1965). *Handbook of Mathematical Functions*, New York, Dover.

Agresti, A. (1984). *Analysis of Ordinal Categorical Data*, New York, John Wiley & Sons.

Aigner, D. J. (1973). "On estimation of an econometric model of short-run bank behavior," *Journal of Econometrics*, **1**, 201–28.

Aitchison, J., and S. D. Silvey (1958). "Maximum-likelihood estimation of parameters subject to restraints," *Annals of Mathematical Statistics*, **29**, 813–28.

Aitchison, J., and S. D. Silvey (1960). "Maximum-likelihood estimation procedures and associated tests of significance," *Journal of the Royal Statistical Society*, Series B, **22**, 154–71.

Aitken, A. C. (1935). "On least squares and linear combination of observations," *Proceedings of the Royal Society of Edinburgh*, **55**, 42–48.

Albert, A., and J. A. Anderson (1984). "On the existence of maximum likelihood estimates in logistic regression models," *Biometrika*, **71**, 1–10.

Ali, M. M., and C. Giacotto (1984). "A study of several new and existing tests for heteroskedasticity in the general linear model," *Journal of Econometrics*, **26**, 355–73.

Ali, M. M., and J. L. Silver (1985). "Tests for equality between sets of coefficients in two linear regressions under heteroskedasticity," *Journal of the American Statistical Association*, **80**, 730–35.

Almon, S. (1965). "The distributed lag between capital appropriations and expenditures," *Econometrica*, **33**, 178–96.

Amari, S.-I. (1985). *Differential Geometrical Methods in Statistics*, New York, Springer-Verlag.

Amemiya, T. (1966). "Specification analysis in the estimation of parameters of a simultaneous equations model with autoregressive residuals," *Econometrica*, **34**, 283–306.

Amemiya, T. (1973a). "Generalized least squares with an estimated autocovariance matrix," *Econometrica*, **41**, 723–32.

Amemiya, T. (1973b). "Regression analysis when the variance of the dependent variable is proportional to the square of its expectation," *Journal of the American Statistical Association*, **68**, 928–34.

Amemiya, T. (1973c). "Regression analysis when the dependent variable is truncated normal," *Econometrica*, **41**, 997–1016.

Amemiya, T. (1974). "The nonlinear two-stage least-squares estimator," *Journal of Econometrics*, **2**, 105–10.

Amemiya, T. (1977). "The maximum likelihood and the nonlinear three stage least squares estimator in the general nonlinear simultaneous equations model," *Econometrica*, **45**, 955–68.

Amemiya, T. (1980). "Selection of regressors," *International Economic Review*, **21**, 331–54

Amemiya, T. (1981). "Qualitative response models: a survey," *Journal of Economic Literature*, **19**, 1483–1536.

Amemiya, T. (1983). "Non-linear regression models," Ch. 6 in *Handbook of Econometrics*, Vol. I, eds. Z. Griliches and M. D. Intriligator, Amsterdam, North-Holland.

Amemiya, T. (1984). "Tobit models: a survey," *Journal of Econometrics*, **24**, 3–61.

Amemiya, T. (1985). *Advanced Econometrics*, Cambridge, Mass., Harvard University Press.

Amemiya, T., and J. L. Powell (1981). "A comparison of the Box-Cox maximum likelihood estimator and the non-linear two-stage least squares estimator," *Journal of Econometrics*, **17**, 351–81.

Anderson, T. W. (1982). "Some recent developments of the distributions of single-equation estimators," in *Advances in Econometrics*. ed. W. Hildenbrand, Cambridge, Cambridge University Press, 109–22.

Anderson, T. W., N. Kunitomo, and T. Sawa (1982). "Evaluation of the distribution function of the limited information maximum likelihood estimator," *Econometrica*, **50**, 1009-1027.

Anderson, T. W., and H. Rubin (1949). "Estimation of the parameters of a single equation in a complete system of stochastic equations," *Annals of Mathematical Statistics*, **20**, 46–63.

Anderson, T. W., and H. Rubin (1950. "The asymptotic properties of estimates of the parameters of a single equation in a complete system of stochastic equations," *Annals of Mathematical Statistics*, **21**, 570–82.

Anderson, T. W., and T. Sawa (1979). "Evaluation of the distribution function of the two-stage least squares estimate," *Econometrica*, **47**, 163–82.

Andrews, D. F. (1971). "A note on the selection of data transformations," *Biometrika*, **58**, 249–54.

Andrews, D. W. K. (1989). "Power in econometric applications," *Econometrica*, **57**, 1059–90.

Andrews, D. W. K. (1991a). "Asymptotic normality of series estimators for nonparametric and semiparametric regression models," *Econometrica*, **59**, 307–45.

Andrews, D. W. K. (1991b). "Heteroskedasticity and autocorrelation consistent covariance matrix estimation," *Econometrica*, **59**, 817–58.

Andrews, D. W. K., and J. C. Monahan (1992). "An improved heteroskedasticity and autocorrelation consistent covariance matrix estimator," *Econometrica*, **60**, 953–66.

Aneuryn-Evans, G., and A. S. Deaton (1980). "Testing linear versus logarithmic regression models," *Review of Economic Studies*, **47**, 275–91.

Ansley, C. F. (1979). "An algorithm for the exact likelihood of a mixed autoregressive-moving average process," *Biometrika*, **66**, 59–65.

Ansley, C. F., and P. Newbold (1980). "Finite-sample properties of estimators for autoregressive-moving average models," *Journal of Econometrics*, **13**, 159–83.

Anscombe, F. J. (1961). "Examination of residuals," *Proceedings of the Fourth Berkeley Symposium on Mathematical Statistics and Probability*, **4**, 1–36.

Arabmazar, R., and P. Schmidt (1981). "Further evidence on the robustness of the tobit estimator to heteroskedasticity," *Journal of Econometrics*, **17**, 253–58.

Arabmazar, R., and P. Schmidt (1982). "An investigation of the robustness of the tobit estimator to non-normality," *Econometrica*, **50**, 1055–63.

Ashenfelter, O., and J. Ham (1979). "Education, unemployment and earnings," *Journal of Political Economy*, **87**, S99–116.

Atkinson, A. C. (1969). "A test for discriminating between models," *Biometrika*, **56**, 337–47.

Atkinson, A. C. (1970). "A method for discriminating between models," *Journal of the Royal Statistical Society*, Series B, **32**, 323–53.

Atkinson, A. C. (1985). *Plots, Transformations and Regression*, Oxford, Clarendon Press.

Baillie, R. T., and D. D. Selover (1987). "Cointegration and models of exchange rate determination," *International Journal of Forecasting*, **3**, 43–51.

Balestra, P. (1980). "A note on the exact transformation associated with the first-order moving average process," *Journal of Econometrics*, **14**, 381–94.

Balestra, P., and M. Nerlove (1966). "Pooling cross section and time series data in the estimation of a dynamic model: the demand for natural gas," *Econometrica*, **34**, 585–612.

Baltagi, B. H., and Li, Q. (1991). "A transformation that will circumvent the problem of autocorrelation in an error-component model," *Journal of Econometrics*, **48**, 385–93.

Banerjee, A., J. J. Dolado, J. W. Galbraith, and D. F. Hendry (1993). *Co-integration, Error-correction, and the Econometric Analysis of Non-stationary Data*, Oxford, Oxford University Press.

Banerjee, A., J. J. Dolado, D. F. Hendry, and G. W. Smith (1986). "Exploring equilibrium relationships in econometric theory through static models: some Monte Carlo evidence," *Oxford Bulletin of Economics and Statistics*, **48**, 253–77.

Bard, Y. (1974). *Nonlinear Parameter Estimation*, New York, Academic Press.

Barndorff-Nielsen, O. E., D. R. Cox, and N. Reid (1986). "The role of differential geometry in statistical theory," *International Statistical Review*, **54**, 83–96.

Barten, A. P. (1964). "Consumer demand functions under conditions of almost additive preferences," *Econometrica*, **32**, 1–38.

Barten, A. P. (1968). "Maximum likelihood estimation of a complete system of demand equations," *European Economic Review*, **1**, 7–73.

Barten, A. P. (1977). "The system of consumer demand functions approach: a review," *Econometrica*, **45**, 23–51.

Basmann, R. L. (1957). "A generalized classical method of linear estimation of coefficients in a structural equation," *Econometrica*, **25**, 77–83.

Basmann, R. L. (1960). "On finite sample distributions of generalized classical linear identifiability tests statistics," *Journal of the American Statistical Association*, **55**, 650–59.

Bates, C., and H. White (1985). "A unified theory of consistent estimation for parametric models," *Econometric Theory*, **1**, 151–78.

Bates, D. M., and D. G. Watts (1988). *Nonlinear Regression Analysis and its Applications*, New York, John Wiley & Sons.

Beach, C. M., and J. G. MacKinnon (1978a). "A maximum likelihood procedure for regression with autocorrelated errors," *Econometrica*, **46**, 51–58.

Beach, C. M., and J. G. MacKinnon (1978b). "Full maximum likelihood estimation of second-order autoregressive error models," *Journal of Econometrics*, **7**, 187–98.

Beach, C. M., and J. G. MacKinnon (1979). "Maximum likelihood estimation of singular equation systems with autoregressive disturbances," *International Economic Review*, **20**, 459–64.

Becker, W. E., and P. E. Kennedy (1992). "A graphical exposition of the ordered probit," *Econometric Theory*, **8**, 127–31.

Belsley, D. (1979). "On the computational competitiveness of full-information maximum-likelihood and three-stage least-squares in the estimation of nonlinear simultaneous-equations models," *Journal of Econometrics*, **9**, 315–42.

Belsley, D. (1980). "On the efficient computation of the nonlinear FIML estimator," *Journal of Econometrics*, **14**, 203–25.

Belsley, D., E. Kuh, and R. E. Welsch (1980). *Regression Diagnostics*, New York, John Wiley & Sons.

Bera, A. K., and C. M. Jarque (1981). "Efficient tests for normality, heteroskedasticity and serial independence of regression residuals: Monte Carlo evidence," *Economics Letters*, **7**, 313–18.

Bera, A. K., and C. M. Jarque (1982). "Model specification tests: a simultaneous approach," *Journal of Econometrics*, **20**, 59–82.

Bera, A. K., C. Jarque, and L.-F. Lee (1984). "Testing the normality assumption in limited dependent variable models," *International Economic Review*, **25**, 563–78.

Bera, A. K., and C. R. McKenzie (1986). "Alternative forms and properties of the score test," *Journal of Applied Statistics*, **13**, 13–25.

Bernanke, B., H. Bohn, and P. C. Reiss (1988). "Alternative non-nested specification tests of time-series investment models," *Journal of Econometrics*, **37**, 293–326.

Berger, J. O., and T. Sellke (1987). "Testing a point null hypothesis: the irreconcilability of P values and evidence," *Journal of the American Statistical Association*, **82**, 112–22.

Bernard, J.-T., and M. R. Veall (1987). "The probability distribution of future demand: the case of Hydro Quebec," *Journal of Business and Economic Statistics*, **5**, 417–24.

Berndt, E. R., and L. R. Christensen (1974). "Testing for the existence of a consistent aggregate index of labor inputs," *American Economic Review*, **64**, 391–403.

Berndt, E. R., B. H. Hall, R. E. Hall, and J. A. Hausman (1974). "Estimation and inference in nonlinear structural models," *Annals of Economic and Social Measurement*, **3**, 653–65.

Berndt, E. R., and N. E. Savin (1975). "Estimation and hypothesis testing in singular equation systems with autoregressive disturbances," *Econometrica*, **43**, 937–57.

Berndt, E. R., and N. E. Savin (1977). "Conflict among criteria for testing hypotheses in the multivariate linear regression model," *Econometrica*, **45**, 1263–78.

Betancourt, R., and H. Kelejian (1981). "Lagged endogenous variables and the Cochrane-Orcutt procedure," *Econometrica*, **49**, 1073–78.

Bhargava, A. (1986). "On the theory of testing for unit roots in observed time series," *Review of Economic Studies*, **53**, 369–84.

Bickel, P. J., and K. A. Doksum (1981). "An analysis of transformations revisited," *Journal of the American Statistical Association*, **76**, 296–311.

Bickel, P. J., and D. A. Freedman (1981). "Some asymptotic theory for the bootstrap," *Annals of Statistics*, **9**, 1196–1217.

Billingsley, P. (1968). *Convergence of Probability Measures*, New York, John Wiley & Sons.

Billingsley, P. (1979). *Probability and Measure*, New York, John Wiley & Sons.

Blundell, R. W. (ed.) (1987). Special Issue on Specification Testing in Limited and Discrete Dependent Variable Models, *Journal of Econometrics*, **34**, No. 1/2.

Bollerslev, T. (1986). "Generalized autoregressive conditional heteroskedasticity," *Journal of Econometrics*, **31**, 307–27.

Bollerslev, T., R. Y. Chou, and K. F. Kroner (1992). "ARCH modeling in finance: a review of the theory and empirical evidence," *Journal of Econometrics*, **52**, 5–59.

Bollerslev, T., R. F. Engle, and J. M. Wooldridge (1988). "A capital asset pricing model with time varying covariances," *Journal of Political Economy*, **96**, 116–31.

Boothe, P., and J. G. MacKinnon (1986). "A specification test for models estimated by GLS," *Review of Economics and Statistics*, **68**, 711–14.

Bowden, R. J., and D. A. Turkington (1984). *Instrumental Variables*, Cambridge, Cambridge University Press.

Bowen, W. G., and T. A. Finegan (1969). *The Economics of Labor Force Participation*, Princeton, Princeton University Press.

Box, G. E. P., and D. R. Cox (1964). "An analysis of transformations," *Journal of the Royal Statistical Society*, Series B, **26**, 211–52.

Box, G. E. P., and G. M. Jenkins (1976). *Time Series Analysis, Forecasting and Control*, Revised edition, San Francisco, Holden Day.

Box, G. E. P., and M. E. Muller (1958). "A note on the generation of random normal deviates," *Annals of Mathematical Statistics*, **29**, 610–11.

Box, G. E. P., and D. A. Pierce (1970). "The distribution of residual autocorrelations in autoregressive-integrated moving average time series models," *Journal of the American Statistical Association*, **65**, 1509–26.

Breusch, T. S. (1978). "Testing for autocorrelation in dynamic linear models," *Australian Economic Papers*, **17**, 334–55.

Breusch, T. S. (1979). "Conflict among criteria for testing hypotheses: extensions and comments," *Econometrica*, **47**, 203–7.

Breusch, T. S. (1980). "Useful invariance results from generalized regression models," *Journal of Econometrics*, **13**, 327–40.

Breusch, T. S., and L. G. Godfrey (1986). "Data transformation tests," *Economic Journal*, **96**, 47–58.

Breusch, T. S., and A. R. Pagan (1979). "A simple test for heteroskedasticity and random coefficient variation," *Econometrica*, **47**, 1287–94.

Breusch, T. S., and A. R. Pagan (1980). "The Lagrange Multiplier test and its applications to model specification in econometrics," *Review of Economic Studies*, **47**, 239–53.

Brown, B. (1981). "Sample size requirements in full information maximum likelihood estimation," *International Economic Review*, **22**, 443–59.

Brown, M., and D. Heien (1972). "The S-branch utility tree: a generalization of the linear expenditure system," *Econometrica*, **40**, 737–47.

Brown, R. L., J. Durbin, and J. M. Evans (1975). "Techniques for testing the constancy of regression relationships over time" (with discussion), *Journal of the Royal Statistical Society*, Series B, **37**, 149–92.

Bryant, P. (1984). "Geometry, statistics, probability: variations on a common theme," *The American Statistician*, **38**, 38–48.

Buckley, J., and I. James (1979). "Linear regression with censored data," *Biometrika*, **66**, 429–36.

Burbidge, J. B., L. Magee, and A. L. Robb (1988). "Alternative transformations to handle extreme values of the dependent variable," *Journal of the American Statistical Association*, **83**, 123–27.

Burguete, J. F., A. R. Gallant, and G. Souza (1982). "On unification of the asymptotic theory of nonlinear econometric models," *Econometric Reviews*, **1**, 151–90.

Burridge, P., and K. F. Wallis (1984). "Unobserved-components models for seasonal adjustment filters," *Journal of Business and Economic Statistics*, **2**, 350–59.

Burrill, C. W., and J. R. Knudsen (1969). *Real Variables*, New York, Holt, Rinehart and Winston.

Buse, A. (1982). "The likelihood ratio, Wald, and Lagrange multiplier tests: an expository note," *The American Statistician*, **36**, 153–57.

Buse, A., and N. K. Dastoor (1989). "An historical note on the Jayatissa test," *The Manchester School*, **58**, 260–64.

Byron, R. P. (1974). "Testing structural specification using the unrestricted reduced form," *Econometrica*, **42**, 869–83.

Campbell, J. Y. (1987). "Does saving anticipate declining labor income? An alternative test of the permanent income hypothesis," *Econometrica*, **55**, 1249–73.

Campbell, J. Y., and N. G. Mankiw (1987). "Are output fluctuations transitory?," *Quarterly Journal of Economics*, **102**, 857–80.

Campbell, J. Y., and P. Perron (1991). "Pitfalls and opportunities: What macroeconomists should know about unit roots," in *NBER Macroeconomics Annual*, Vol. 6, eds. O. J. Blanchard and S. Fisher, Cambridge, Mass., MIT Press.

Campbell, J. Y., and R. J. Shiller (1987). "Cointegration and tests of present value models," *Journal of Political Economy*, **95**, 1062–88.

Carroll, R. J., and D. Ruppert (1982). "Robust estimation in heteroskedastic linear models," *Annals of Statistics*, **10**, 429–41.

Carroll, R. J., and D. Ruppert (1984). "Power transformations when fitting theoretical models to data," *Journal of the American Statistical Association*, **79**, 321–28.

Carroll, R. J., and D. Ruppert (1988). *Transformation and Weighting in Regression*, London, Chapman and Hall.

Casella, G., and R. L. Berger (1990). *Statistical Inference*, Pacific Grove, Calif., Wadsworth and Brooks/Cole.

Chamberlain, G. (1982). "The general equivalence of Granger and Sims causality," *Econometrica*, **50**, 569–82.

Chamberlain, G. (1984). "Panel Data," Ch. 22 in *Handbook of Econometrics*, Vol. II, eds. Z. Griliches and M. D. Intriligator, Amsterdam, North-Holland.

Chamberlain, G. (1986). "Asymptotic efficiency in semi-parametric models with censoring," *Journal of Econometrics*, **32**, 189–218.

Chamberlain, G. (1987). "Asymptotic efficiency in estimation with conditional moment restrictions," *Journal of Econometrics*, **34**, 305–34.

Chambers, J. M. (1977). *Computational Methods for Data Analysis*, New York, John Wiley & Sons.

Chesher, A. (1983). "The information matrix test: simplified calculation via a score test interpretation," *Economics Letters*, **13**, 45–48.

Chesher, A. (1984). "Testing for neglected heterogeneity," *Econometrica*, **52**, 865–72.

Chesher, A. (1989). "Hájek inequalities, measures of leverage and the size of heteroskedasticity robust tests," *Econometrica*, **57**, 971–77.

Chesher, A., and G. Austin (1991). "The finite-sample distributions of heteroskedasticity robust Wald statistics," *Journal of Econometrics*, **47**, 153–73.

Chesher, A., and M. Irish (1987). "Residual analysis in the grouped and censored normal linear model," *Journal of Econometrics*, **34**, 33–61.

Chesher A., and I. Jewitt (1987). "The bias of a heteroskedasticity consistent covariance matrix estimator," *Econometrica*, **55**, 1217–22.

Chesher, A., and S. Peters (1994). "Symmetry, regression design, and sampling distributions," *Econometric Theory*, **10**, 116–129.

Chesher, A., and R. Spady (1991). "Asymptotic expansions of the information matrix test statistic," *Econometrica*, **59**, 787–815.

Chipman, J. S. (1979). "Efficiency of least squares estimation of linear trend when residuals are autocorrelated," *Econometrica*, **47**, 115–28.

Chow, G. C. (1960). "Tests of equality between sets of coefficients in two linear regressions," *Econometrica*, **28**, 591–605.

Chow, G. C. (1968). "Two methods of computing full-information maximum likelihood estimates in simultaneous stochastic equations," *International Economic Review*, **9**, 100–112.

Chow, G. C. (1973). "On the computation of full-information maximum likelihood estimates for nonlinear equation systems," *Review of Economics and Statistics*, **55**, 104–9.

Chow, Y. S. (1960). "A martingale inequality and a law of large numbers," Proceedings of the Mathematical Society, **11**, 107–11.

Chow, Y. S. (1967). "On a strong law for martingales," *Mathematical Statistics*, **38**, 610–11.

Christensen, L. R., D. W. Jorgenson, and L. J. Lau (1975). "Transcendental logarithmic utility functions," *American Economic Review*, **65**, 367–83.

Cochrane, D., and G. H. Orcutt (1949). "Application of least squares regression to relationships containing autocorrelated error terms," *Journal of the American Statistical Association*, **44**, 32–61.

Cook, R. D., and S. Weisberg (1982). *Residuals and Influence in Regression*, London, Chapman and Hall.

Cooper, J. P. (1972a). "Asymptotic covariance matrix of procedures for linear regression in the presence of first-order autoregressive disturbances," *Econometrica*, **40**, 305–10.

Cooper, J. P. (1972b). "Two approaches to polynomial distributed lag estimation," *The American Statistician*, **26**, 32–35.

Corbae, D., and S. Ouliaris (1988). "Cointegration and tests of purchasing power parity," *Review of Economics and Statistics*, **70**, 508–11.

Cox, D. R. (1961). "Tests of separate families of hypotheses," *Proceedings of the Fourth Berkeley Symposium on Mathematical Statistics and Probability*, **1**, 105–23.

Cox, D. R. (1962). "Further results on tests of separate families of hypotheses," *Journal of the Royal Statistical Society*, Series B, **24**, 406–24.

Cox, D. R. (1970). *The Analysis of Binary Data*, London, Chapman and Hall.

Cox, D. R., and D. V. Hinkley (1974). *Theoretical Statistics*, London, Chapman and Hall.

Cox, D. R., and D. Oakes (1984). *Analysis of Survival Data*, London, Chapman and Hall.

Cragg, J. G. (1971). "Some statistical models for limited dependent variables with application to the demand for durable goods," *Econometrica*, **39**, 829–44.

Cragg, J. G. (1983). "More efficient estimation in the presence of heteroskedasticity of unknown form," *Econometrica*, **51**, 751–63.

Cragg, J. G., and R. Uhler (1970). "The demand for automobiles," *Canadian Journal of Economics*, **3**, 386–406.

Cramér, H. (1946). *Mathematical Methods of Statistics*, Princeton, Princeton University Press.

Cramer, J. S. (1986). *Econometric Applications of Maximum Likelihood Methods*, Cambridge, Cambridge University Press.

Cumby, R. E., J. Huizinga, and M. Obstfeld (1983). "Two-step two-stage least squares estimation in models with rational expectations," *Journal of Econometrics*, **21**, 333–55.

Dagenais, M. G. (1978). "The computation of FIML estimates as iterative generalized least squares estimates in linear and nonlinear simultaneous equation models," *Econometrica*, **46**, 1351–63.

Dagenais, M. G., and J.-M. Dufour (1991). "Invariance, nonlinear models and asymptotic tests," *Econometrica*, **59**, 1601–15.

Das Gupta, S., and Perlman, M. D. (1974). "Power of the noncentral F test: effect of additional variates on Hotelling's T^2 test," *Journal of the American Statistical Association*, **69**, 174–80.

Dastoor, N. K. (1983). "Some aspects of testing non-nested hypotheses," *Journal of Econometrics*, **21**, 213–28.

Dastoor, N. K., and G. R. Fisher (1988). "On point-optimal Cox tests," *Econometric Theory*, **4**, 97–107.

Davidson, J. E. H. (1981). "Problems with the estimation of moving average processes," *Journal of Econometrics*, **19**, 295–310.

Davidson, J. E. H., D. F. Hendry, F. Srba, and S. Yeo (1978). "Econometric modelling of the aggregate time-series relationship between consumers' expenditure and income in the United Kingdom," *Economic Journal*, **88**, 661–92.

Davidson, R., L. G. Godfrey, and J. G. MacKinnon (1985). "A simplified version of the differencing test," *International Economic Review*, **26**, 639–47.

Davidson, R., and J. G. MacKinnon (1980). "Estimating the covariance matrix for regression models with AR(1) errors and lagged dependent variables," *Economic Letters*, **6**, 119–23.

Davidson, R., and J. G. MacKinnon (1981a). "Several tests for model specification in the presence of alternative hypotheses," *Econometrica*, **49**, 781–93.

Davidson, R., and J. G. MacKinnon (1981b). "Efficient estimation of tail-area probabilities in sampling experiments," *Economics Letters*, **8**, 73–77.

Davidson, R., and J. G. MacKinnon (1982). "Some non-nested hypothesis tests and the relations among them," *Review of Economic Studies*, **49**, 551–65.

Davidson, R., and J. G. MacKinnon (1983a). "Small sample properties of alternative forms of the Lagrange Multiplier test," *Economics Letters*, **12**, 269–75.

Davidson, R., and J. G. MacKinnon (1983b). "Testing the specification of multivariate models in the presence of alternative hypotheses," *Journal of Econometrics*, **23**, 301–13.

Davidson, R., and J. G. MacKinnon (1983c). "Inflation and the savings rate," *Applied Economics*, **15**, 731–43.

Davidson, R., and J. G. MacKinnon (1984a). "Model specification tests based on artificial linear regressions," *International Economic Review*, **25**, 485–502.

Davidson, R., and J. G. MacKinnon (1984b). "Convenient specification tests for logit and probit models," *Journal of Econometrics*, **25**, 241–62.

Davidson, R., and J. G. MacKinnon (1985a). "The interpretation of test statistics," *Canadian Journal of Economics*, **18**, 38–57.

Davidson, R., and MacKinnon, J. G. (1985b). "Heteroskedasticity-robust tests in regression directions," *Annales de l'INSÉÉ*, **59/60**, 183–218.

Davidson, R., and MacKinnon, J. G. (1985c). "Testing linear and loglinear regressions against Box-Cox alternatives," *Canadian Journal of Economics*, **18**, 499–517.

Davidson, R., and MacKinnon, J. G. (1987). "Implicit alternatives and the local power of test statistics," *Econometrica*, **55**, 1305–29.

Davidson, R., and MacKinnon, J. G. (1988). "Double-length artificial regressions," *Oxford Bulletin of Economics and Statistics*, **50**, 203–17.

Davidson, R., and J. G. MacKinnon (1989). "Testing for consistency using artificial regressions," *Econometric Theory*, **5**, 363–84.

Davidson, R., and J. G. MacKinnon (1990). "Specification tests based on artificial regressions," *Journal of the American Statistical Association*, **85**, 220–27.

Davidson, R., and J. G. MacKinnon (1992a). "A new form of the information matrix test," *Econometrica*, **60**, 145–57.

Davidson, R., and J. G. MacKinnon (1992b). "Regression-based methods for using control variates in Monte Carlo experiments," *Journal of Econometrics*, **54**, 203–22.

Deaton, A. S. (1974). "The analysis of consumer demand in the United Kingdom, 1900-1970," *Econometrica*, **42**, 341–67.

Deaton, A. S. (1978). "Specification and testing in applied demand analysis," *Economic Journal*, **88**, 524–36.

Deaton, A. S., and J. Muellbauer (1980). *Economics and Consumer Behaviour*, Cambridge, Cambridge University Press.

DeJong, D. N., and C. H. Whiteman (1991). "The temporal stability of dividends and stock prices: evidence from the likelihood function," *American Economic Review*, **81**, 600–617.

Dent, W. (1977). "Computation of the exact likelihood function of an ARIMA process," *Journal of Statistical Computation and Simulation*, **5**, 193–206.

Dhrymes, P. J. (1971). *Distributed Lags: Problems of Estimation and Formulation*, San Francisco, Holden-Day.

Dhrymes, P. (1986). "Limited dependent variables," Ch. 27 in *Handbook of Econometrics*, Vol. III, eds. Z. Griliches and M. D. Intriligator, Amsterdam, North-Holland.

Dhrymes, P. J., R. Berner, and D. Cummins (1974). "A comparison of some limited information estimators for dynamic simultaneous equations models with autocorrelated errors," *Econometrica*, **42**, 311–32.

Dickey, D. A., W. R. Bell, and R. B. Miller (1986). "Unit roots in time series models: tests and implications," *The American Statistician*, **40**, 12–26.

Dickey, D. A., and W. A. Fuller (1979). "Distribution of the estimators for autoregressive time series with a unit root," *Journal of the American Statistical Association*, **74**, 427–31.

Domencich, T. A., and D. McFadden (1975). *Urban Travel Demand*, Amsterdam, North-Holland.

Domowitz, I., and C. Hakkio (1985). "Conditional variance and the risk premium in foreign exchange markets," *Journal of International Economics*, **19**, 47–66.

Drèze, J., and J.-F. Richard (1983). "Bayesian analysis of simultaneous equation systems," Ch. 9 in *Handbook of Econometrics*, Vol. I, eds. Z. Griliches and M. D. Intriligator, Amsterdam, North-Holland.

Dufour, J.-M. (1982). "Generalized Chow tests for structural change: a coordinate-free approach," *International Economic Review*, **23**, 565–75.

Dufour, J.-M., M. J. I. Gaudry, and T. C. Liem (1980). "The Cochrane-Orcutt procedure: numerical examples of multiple admissible minima," *Economics Letters*, **6**, 43–48.

Dufour, J.-M., and M. L. King (1991). "Optimal invariant tests for the autocorrelation coefficient in linear regressions with stationary or nonstationary AR(1) errors," *Journal of Econometrics*, **47**, 115–43.

Duncan, G. M. (1986). "A robust censored regression estimator," *Journal of Econometrics*, **32**, 5–34.

Dunn, K. B., and K. J. Singleton (1986). "Modeling the term structure of interest rates under non-separable utility and durability of goods," *Journal of Financial Economics*, **17**, 27–55.

Durbin, J. (1954). "Errors in variables," *Review of the International Statistical Institute*, **22**, 23–32.

Durbin, J. (1960). "Estimation of parameters in time-series regression models," *Journal of the Royal Statistical Society*, Series B, **22**, 139–53.

Durbin, J. (1970). "Testing for serial correlation in least-squares regression when some of the regressors are lagged dependent variables," *Econometrica*, **38**, 410–21.

Durbin, J., and M. G. Kendall (1951). "The geometry of estimation," *Biometrika*, **38**, 150–58.

Durbin, J., and G. S. Watson (1950). "Testing for serial correlation in least squares regression I," *Biometrika*, **37**, 409–28.

Durbin, J., and G. S. Watson (1951). "Testing for serial correlation in least squares regression II," *Biometrika*, **38**, 159–78.

Durbin, J., and G. S. Watson (1971). "Testing for serial correlation in least squares regression III," *Biometrika*, **58**, 1–19.

Durlauf, S. N., and P. C. B. Phillips (1988). "Trends versus random walks in time series analysis," *Econometrica*, **56**, 1333–54.

Efron, B. (1978). "Regression and ANOVA with zero-one data: measures of residual variance," *Journal of the American Statistical Association*, **73**, 113–21.

Efron, B. (1979). "Bootstrapping methods: another look at the jackknife," *Annals of Statistics*, **7**, 1–26.

Efron, B. (1982). *The Jackknife, the Bootstrap and Other Resampling Plans*, Philadelphia, Society for Industrial and Applied Mathematics.

Efron, B., and G. Gong (1983). "A leisurely look at the bootstrap, the jackknife and cross-validation," *The American Statistician*, **37**, 36–48.

Efron, B., and D. V. Hinkley (1978). "Assessing the accuracy of the maximum likelihood estimator: observed versus expected Fisher information" (with discussion), *Biometrika*, **65**, 457–87.

Efron, B., and R. Tibshirani (1986). "Bootstrap methods for standard errors, confidence intervals, and other measures of statistical accuracy," *Statistical Science*, **1**, 54–77.

Eicker, F. (1963). "Asymptotic normality and consistency of the least squares estimators for families of linear regressions," *The Annals of Mathematical Statistics*, **34**, 447–56.

Eicker, F. (1967). "Limit theorems for regressions with unequal and dependent errors," in *Fifth Berkeley Symposium on Mathematical Statistics and Probability*, eds. L. M. Le Cam and J. Neyman, **1**, Berkeley, University of California, 59–82.

Eichenbaum, M. S., L. P. Hansen, and K. J. Singleton (1988). "A time series analysis of representative agent models of consumption and leisure choice under uncertainty," *Quarterly Journal of Economics*, **103**, 51–78.

Eisenpress, H., and J. Greenstadt (1966). "The estimation of nonlinear econometric systems," *Econometrica*, **34**, 851–61.

Engle, R. F. (1974). "Band spectrum regression," *International Economic Review*, **15**, 1–11.

Engle, R. F. (1982a). "A general approach to Lagrange Multiplier model diagnostics," *Journal of Econometrics*, **20**, 83–104.

Engle, R. F. (1982b). "Autoregressive conditional heteroskedasticity with estimates of the variance of United Kingdom inflation," *Econometrica*, **50**, 987–1007.

Engle, R. F. (1984). "Wald, likelihood ratio and Lagrange multiplier tests in econometrics," Ch. 13 in *Handbook of Econometrics*, Vol. II, eds. Z. Griliches and M. D. Intriligator, Amsterdam, North-Holland.

Engle, R. F., and T. Bollerslev (1986). "Modeling the persistence of conditional variances," (with comments and reply), *Econometric Reviews*, **5**, 1–87.

Engle, R. F., and C. W. J. Granger (1987). "Co-integration and error correction: representation, estimation and testing," *Econometrica*, **55**, 251–76.

Engle, R. F., D. F. Hendry, and J.-F. Richard (1983). "Exogeneity," *Econometrica*, **51**, 277–304.

Engle, R. F., D. F. Hendry, and D. Trumble (1985). "Small-sample properties of ARCH estimators and tests," *Canadian Journal of Economics*, **18**, 66–93.

Engle, R. F., D. M. Lilien, and R. P. Robins (1987). "Estimating time varying risk premia in the term structure: the ARCH-M model," *Econometrica*, **55**, 391–407.

Engle, R. F., and M. Rothschild (1992). Special Issue on ARCH Models in Finance, *Journal of Econometrics*, **52**, No. 1/2.

Engle, R. F., and B. S. Yoo (1987). "Forecasting and testing in co-integrated systems," *Journal of Econometrics*, **35**, 143–59.

Engle, R. F., and B. S. Yoo (1991). "Cointegrated economic time series: a survey with new results," Ch. 12 in *Long-run Economic Relationships: Readings in Cointegration*, eds. R. F. Engle and C. W. J. Granger, Oxford, Oxford University Press.

Epstein, L. G., and S. E. Zin (1991). "Substitution, risk aversion, and the temporal behavior of consumption and asset returns: an empirical analysis," *Journal of Political Economy*, **99**, 263–86.

Ericsson, N. R. (1983). "Asymptotic properties of instrumental variables statistics for testing non-nested hypotheses," *Review of Economic Studies*, **50**, 287–304.

Ericsson, N. R. (1991). "Monte Carlo methodology and the finite sample properties of instrumental variables statistics for testing nested and non-nested hypotheses," *Econometrica*, **59**, 1249–77.

Evans, G. B. A., and N. E. Savin (1982). "Conflict among the criteria revisited: the W, LR and LM tests," *Econometrica*, **50**, 737–48.

Evans, M. A., and M. L. King (1985). "A point optimal test for heteroskedastic disturbances," *Journal of Econometrics*, **27**, 163–78.

Evans, M. A., and M. L. King (1988). "A further class of tests for heteroskedasticity," *Journal of Econometrics*, **37**, 265–76.

Fair, R. C. (1970). "The estimation of simultaneous equation models with lagged endogenous variables and first order serially correlated errors," *Econometrica*, **38**, 507–16.

Fair, R. C. (1978). "A theory of extramarital affairs," *Journal of Political Economy*, **86**, 45–61.

Fair, R. C. (1980). "Estimating the expected predictive accuracy of econometric models," *International Economic Review*, **21**, 355–78.

Fair, R. C., and W. Parke (1980). "Full information estimates of a nonlinear macroeconomic model," *Journal of Econometrics*, **13**, 269–91.

Farebrother, R. W. (1988). *Linear Least Squares Computations*, New York, Marcel Dekker.

Feller, W. (1968). *An Introduction to Probability Theory and its Applications*, Vol. I, Third edition, New York, John Wiley & Sons.

Fisher, F. M. (1970). "Tests of equality between sets of coefficients in two linear regressions: an expository note," *Econometrica*, **38**, 361–66.

Fisher, F. M. (1976). *The Identification Problem in Econometrics*, Huntington, NY, Krieger.

Fisher, G. R. (1981). "Two types of residuals and the classic identifiability test statistic," in *Proceedings of the Econometric Society European Meeting 1979, Selected Econometric Papers in Memory of Stefan Valavanis*, ed. E. G. Charatsis, Amsterdam, North-Holland, 216–30.

Fisher, G. R. (1983). "Tests for two separate regressions," *Journal of Econometrics*, **21**, 117–32.

Fisher, G. R., and M. McAleer (1981). "Alternative procedures and associated tests of significance for non-nested hypotheses," *Journal of Econometrics*, **16**, 103–19.

Fisher, G. R., and M. McAleer (1984). "The geometry of specification error," *Australian Journal of Statistics*, **26**, 310–22.

Fisher, R. A. (1915). "Frequency distribution of the values of the correlation coefficient in samples from an indefinitely large population," *Biometrika*, **10**, 507–21.

Fisher, R. A. (1925). "The theory of statistical estimation," *Proceedings of the Cambridge Philosophical Society*, **22**, 700–725.

Fishman, G. S., and L. R. Moore (1982). "A statistical evaluation of multiplicative congruential random number generators with modulus $2^{31} - 1$," *Journal of the American Statistical Association*, **77**, 129–36.

Florens, J.-P., and M. Mouchart (1982). "A note on noncausality," *Econometrica*, **50**, 583–91.

Fomby, T. B., R. C. Hill, and S. R. Johnson (1984). *Advanced Econometric Methods*, New York, Springer-Verlag.

Frankel, J. A. (1980). "Tests of rational expectations in the forward exchange market," *Southern Economic Journal*, **46**, 1083–1101.

Freedman, D. A. (1981). "Bootstrapping regression models," *Annals of Statistics*, **9**, 1218–28.

Freedman, D. A., and S. C. Peters (1984). "Bootstrapping an econometric model: some empirical results," *Journal of Business and Economic Statistics*, **2**, 150–58.

Frisch, R. (1934). *Statistical Confluence Analysis by Means of Complete Regression Systems*, Oslo, University Institute of Economics.

Frisch, R., and F. V. Waugh (1933). "Partial time regressions as compared with individual trends," *Econometrica*, **1**, 387–401.

Fuller, W. A. (1976). *Introduction to Statistical Time Series*, New York, John Wiley & Sons.

Fuller, W. A. (1977). "Some properties of a modification of the limited information estimator," *Econometrica*, **45**, 939–53.

Fuss, M. A. (1977). "The demand for energy in Canadian manufacturing: an example of the estimation of production structures with many inputs," *Journal of Econometrics*, **5**, 89–116.

Galbraith, J. W., and V. Zinde-Walsh (1992). "The GLS transformation matrix and a semi-recursive estimator for the linear regression model with ARMA errors," *Econometric Theory*, **8**, 95–111.

Gallant, A. R. (1987). *Nonlinear Statistical Models*, New York, John Wiley & Sons.

Gallant, A. R., and A. Holly (1980). "Statistical inference in an implicit, nonlinear, simultaneous equation model in the context of maximum likelihood estimation," *Econometrica*, **48**, 697–720.

Gallant, A. R., and H. White (1988). *A Unified Theory of Estimation and Inference for Nonlinear Dynamic Models*, Oxford, Basil Blackwell.

Gardner, G., A. C. Harvey, and G. D. A. Phillips (1980). "An algorithm for exact maximum likelihood estimation of autoregressive-moving average models by means of the Kalman filter," *Applied Statistics*, **29**, 311–22.

Gaudry, M. J. I., and M. G. Dagenais (1979). "Heteroskedasticity and the use of Box-Cox transformations," *Economics Letters*, **2**, 225–29.

Gauss, K. F. (1809). "Theoria motus corporum coelestium," in *Werke*, Vol. VII, 240–54.

Gersovitz, M., and J. G. MacKinnon (1978). "Seasonality in regression: an application of smoothness priors," *Journal of the American Statistical Association*, **73**, 264–73.

Geweke, J., R. Meese, and W. Dent (1983). "Comparing alternative tests of causality in temporal systems: analytic results and experimental evidence," *Journal of Econometrics*, **21**, 161–94.

Ghysels, E. (1990). "Unit root tests and the statistical pitfalls of seasonal adjustment: the case of U. S. post war real GNP," *Journal of Business and Economic Statistics*, **8**, 145–52.

Ghysels, E. (1991). "On the economics and econometrics of seasonality," University of Montreal, mimeo.

Ghysels, E., and A. Hall (1990). "A test for structural stability of Euler conditions parameters estimated via the generalized method of moments estimator," *International Economic Review*, **31**, 355–64.

Ghysels, E., and P. Perron (1993). "The effect of seasonal adjustment filters on tests for a unit root," *Journal of Econometrics*, **55**, 57–98.

Gill, P. E., W. Murray, and M. H. Wright (1981). *Practical Optimization*, New York, Academic Press.

Glejser, H. (1969). "A new test for heteroskedasticity," *Journal of the American Statistical Association*, **64**, 316–23.

Godfrey, L. G. (1976). "Testing for serial correlation in dynamic simultaneous equation models," *Econometrica*, **44**, 1077–84.

Godfrey, L. G. (1978a). "Testing against general autoregressive and moving average error models when the regressors include lagged dependent variables," *Econometrica*, **46**, 1293–1301.

Godfrey, L. G. (1978b). "Testing for higher order serial correlation in regression equations when the regressors include lagged dependent variables," *Econometrica*, **46**, 1303–10.

Godfrey, L. G. (1978c). "Testing for multiplicative heteroskedasticity," *Journal of Econometrics*, **8**, 227–36.

Godfrey, L. G. (1981). "On the invariance of the Lagrange multiplier test with respect to changes in the alternative hypothesis," *Econometrica*, **49**, 1443–55.

Godfrey, L. G. (1983). "Testing non-nested models after estimation by instrumental variables or least squares," *Econometrica*, **51**, 355–65.

Godfrey, L. G. (1988). *Misspecification Tests in Econometrics*, Cambridge, Cambridge University Press.

Godfrey, L. G., M. McAleer, and C. R. McKenzie (1988). "Variable addition and Lagrange Multiplier tests for linear and logarithmic regression models," *Review of Economics and Statistics*, **70**, 492–503.

Godfrey, L. G., and M. H. Pesaran (1983). "Tests of non-nested regression models: small sample adjustments and Monte Carlo evidence," *Journal of Econometrics*, **21**, 133–54.

Godfrey, L. G., and M. R. Wickens (1981). "Testing linear and log-linear regressions for functional form," *Review of Economic Studies*, **48**, 487–96.

Godfrey, L. G., and M. R. Wickens (1982). "Tests of misspecification using locally equivalent alternative models," in *Evaluating the Reliability of Econometric Models*, eds. G. C. Chow and P. Corsi, New York, John Wiley & Sons, 71–99.

Goldberger, A. S. (1972). "Structural equation methods in the social sciences," *Econometrica*, **40**, 979–1001.

Goldberger, A. S. (1981). "Linear regression after selection," *Journal of Econometrics*, **15**, 357–66.

Goldfeld, S. M., and R. E. Quandt (1965). "Some tests for homoskedasticity," *Journal of the American Statistical Association*, **60**, 539–47.

Golub, G. H., and C. F. Van Loan (1989). *Matrix Computations*, Second edition, Baltimore, Johns Hopkins University Press.

Gouriéroux, C., and A. Monfort (1981). "Asymptotic properties of the maximum likelihood estimator in dichotomous logit models," *Journal of Econometrics*, **17**, 83–97.

Gouriéroux, C., A. Monfort, and A. Trognon (1984). "Pseudo-maximum likelihood methods: theory," *Econometrica*, **52**, 681–700.

Granger, C. W. J. (1969). "Investigating causal relations by econometric models and cross-spectral methods," *Econometrica*, **37**, 424–38.

Granger, C. W. J. (1981). "Some properties of time series data and their use in econometric model specification," *Journal of Econometrics*, **16**, 121–30.

Granger, C. W. J., and T. H. Lee (1989). "Investigation of production, sales and inventory relationships using multicointegration and non-symmetric error correction models," *Journal of Applied Econometrics*, **4**, S145–59.

Granger, C. W. J., and P. Newbold (1974). "Spurious regressions in econometrics," *Journal of Econometrics*, **2**, 111–20.

Granger, C. W. J., and P. Newbold (1986). *Forecasting Economic Time Series*, Second edition, Orlando, Florida, Academic Press.

Granger, C. W. J., and M. W. Watson (1984). "Time series and spectral methods," Ch. 17 in *Handbook of Econometrics*, Vol. II, eds. Z. Griliches and M. D. Intriligator, Amsterdam, North-Holland.

Greene, W. H. (1981a). "On the asymptotic bias of the ordinary least squares estimator of the tobit model," *Econometrica*, **49**, 505–13.

Greene, W. H. (1981b). "Sample selection bias as a specification error: comment," *Econometrica*, **49**, 795–98.

Greene, W. H. (1990a). *Econometric Analysis*, New York, Macmillan.

Greene, W. H. (1990b). "Multiple roots of the tobit log-likelihood," *Journal of Econometrics*, **46**, 365–80.

Gregory, A. W., and M. R. Veall (1985). "On formulating Wald tests for nonlinear restrictions," *Econometrica*, **53**, 1465–68.

Gregory, A. W., and M. R. Veall (1987). "Formulating Wald tests of the restrictions implied by the rational expectations hypothesis," *Journal of Applied Econometrics*, **2**, 61–68.

Griffiths, W. E., and K. Surekha (1986). "A Monte Carlo evaluation of the power of some tests for heteroskedasticity," *Journal of Econometrics*, **31**, 219–31.

Hall, A. (1987). "The information matrix test for the linear model," *Review of Economic Studies*, **54**, 257–63.

Hall, A. (1990). "Lagrange multiplier tests for normality against seminonparametric alternatives," *Journal of Business and Economic Statistics*, **8**, 417–26.

Hall, P. (1987). "On the bootstrap and likelihood-based confidence regions," *Biometrika*, **74**, 481–93.

Hall, P., and C. C. Heyde (1980). *Martingale Limit Theory and its Applications*, New York, Academic Press.

Hall, S. G. (1986). "An application of the Engle and Granger two-step estimation procedure to United Kingdom aggregate wage data," *Oxford Bulletin of Economics and Statistics*, **48**, 229–39.

Hammersley, J. M., and D. C. Handscomb (1964). *Monte Carlo Methods*, London, Methuen.

Hannan, E. J., and R. D. Terrell (1966). "Testing for serial correlation after least squares regression," *Econometrica*, **34**, 646–60.

Hansen, L. P. (1982). "Large sample properties of generalized method of moments estimators," *Econometrica*, **50**, 1029–54.

Hansen, L. P. (1985). "A method for calculating bounds on the asymptotic covariance matrices of generalized method of moments estimators," *Journal of Econometrics*, **30**, 203–38.

Hansen, L. P., J. C. Heaton, and M. Ogaki (1988). "Efficiency bounds implied by multi-period conditional moment restrictions," *Journal of the American Statistical Association*, **83**, 863–71.

Hansen, L. P., and R. J. Hodrick (1980). "Forward exchange rates as optimal predictors of future spot rates: an econometric analysis," *Journal of Political Economy*, **88**, 829–53.

Hansen, L. P., and K. J. Singleton (1982). "Generalized instrumental variables estimators of nonlinear rational expectations models," *Econometrica*, **50**, 1269–86.

Harrison, M. J., and B. P. McCabe (1979). "A test for heteroskedasticity based on ordinary least squares residuals," *Journal of the American Statistical Association*, **74**, 494–99.

Hartley, H. O. (1961). "The modified Gauss-Newton method for the fitting of nonlinear regression functions by least squares," *Technometrics*, **3**, 269–80.

Harvey, A. C. (1980). "On comparing regression models in levels and first differences," *International Economic Review*, **21**, 707–20.

Harvey, A. C. (1981). *Time Series Models*, Oxford, Philip Allan.

Harvey, A. C. (1989). *Forecasting, Structural Time Series Models and the Kalman Filter*, Cambridge, Cambridge University Press.

Harvey, A. C., and G. D. A. Phillips (1979). "Maximum likelihood estimation of regression models with autoregressive-moving average disturbances," *Biometrika*, **66**, 49–58.

Harvey, A. C., and G. D. A. Phillips (1980). "Testing for serial correlation in simultaneous equation models," *Econometrica*, **48**, 747–60.

Harvey, A. C., and G. D. A. Phillips (1981). "Testing for serial correlation in simultaneous equation models: some further results," *Journal of Econometrics*, **17**, 99–106.

Hatanaka, M. (1974). "An efficient two-step estimator for the dynamic adjustment model with autoregressive errors," *Journal of Econometrics*, **2**, 199–220.

Hatanaka, M. (1976). "Several efficient two-step estimators for the dynamic simultaneous equations model with autoregressive disturbances," *Journal of Econometrics*, **4**, 189–204.

Hauser, J. R. (1977). "Testing the accuracy, usefulness and significance of probabilistic choice models: an information theoretic approach," *Operations Research*, **26**, 406–21.

Hausman, J. A. (1974). "Full information instrumental variable estimation of simultaneous equation systems," *Annals of Economic and Social Measurement*, **3**, 641–52.

Hausman, J. A. (1975). "An instrumental variable approach to full information estimation for linear and certain nonlinear econometric models," *Econometrica*, **43**, 727–38.

Hausman, J. A. (1978). "Specification tests in econometrics," *Econometrica*, **46**, 1251–72.

Hausman, J. A. (1983). "Specification and estimation of simultaneous equation models," Ch. 7 in *Handbook of Econometrics*, Vol. I, eds. Z. Griliches and M. D. Intriligator, Amsterdam, North-Holland.

Hausman, J. A., and D. McFadden (1984). "A specification test for the multinomial logit model," *Econometrica*, **52**, 1219–40.

Hausman, J. A., and W. E. Taylor (1981). "Panel data and unobservable individual effects," *Econometrica*, **49**, 1377–98.

Hausman, J. A., and W. E. Taylor (1982). "A generalized specification test," *Economics Letters*, **8**, 239–45.

Hausman, J. A., and W. E. Taylor (1983). "Identification in linear simultaneous equations models with covariance restrictions: an instrumental variables interpretation," *Econometrica*, **51**, 1527–49.

Hausman, J. A., and M. W. Watson (1985). "Errors-in-variables and seasonal adjustment procedures," *Journal of the American Statistical Association*, **80**, 531–40.

Hausman, J. A., and D. A. Wise (1977). "Social experimentation, truncated distributions, and efficient estimation," *Econometrica*, **45**, 919–38.

Hausman, J. A., and D. A. Wise (1978). "A conditional probit model for qualitative choice: discrete decisions recognizing interdependence and heterogeneous preferences," *Econometrica*, **46**, 403–26.

Heckman, J. J. (1974). "Shadow wages, market prices, and labor supply," *Econometrica*, **42**, 679–94.

Heckman, J. J. (1976). "The common structure of statistical models of truncation, sample selection and limited dependent variables and a simple estimator for such models," *Annals of Economic and Social Measurement*, **5**, 475–92.

Heckman, J. J. (1979). "Sample selection bias as a specification error," *Econometrica*, **47**, 153–61.

Heckman, J. J., and S. Polachek (1974). "Empirical evidence on the functional form of the earnings-schooling relationship," *Journal of the American Statistical Association*, **69**, 350–54.

Hendry, D. F. (1976). "The structure of simultaneous equations estimators," *Journal of Econometrics*, **4**, 51–88.

Hendry, D. F. (1979). "The behavior of inconsistent instrumental variables estimators in dynamic systems," *Journal of Econometrics*, **9**, 295–314.

Hendry, D. F. (1980). "Econometrics — alchemy or science," *Economica*, **47**, 387–406.

Hendry, D. F. (1982). "A reply to Professors Maasoumi and Phillips," *Journal of Econometrics*, **19**, 203–13.

Hendry, D. F. (1984). "Monte Carlo experimentation in econometrics," Ch. 16 in *Handbook of Econometrics*, Vol. II, eds. Z. Griliches and M. D. Intriligator, Amsterdam, North-Holland.

Hendry, D. F. (1986). "Econometric modelling with cointegrated variables: an overview," *Oxford Bulletin of Economics and Statistics*, **48**, 201–12.

Hendry, D. F., and G. J. Anderson (1977). "Testing dynamic specification in small simultaneous models: an application to a model of building society behavior in the United Kingdom," in *Frontiers of Quantitative Economics*, Vol. IIIA, ed. M. D. Intriligator, Amsterdam, North-Holland.

Hendry, D. F., and G. E. Mizon (1978). "Serial correlation as a convenient simplification not a nuisance: a comment on a study of the demand for money by the Bank of England," *Economic Journal*, **88**, 549–63.

Hendry, D. F., A. R. Pagan, and J. D. Sargan (1984). "Dynamic specification," Ch. 18 in *Handbook of Econometrics*, Vol. II, eds. Z. Griliches and M. D. Intriligator, Amsterdam, North-Holland.

Hendry, D. F., and P. K. Trivedi (1972). "Maximum likelihood estimation of difference equations with moving average errors: a simulation study," *Review of Economic Studies*, **39**, 117–45.

Herr, D. G. (1980). "On the history of the use of geometry in the general linear model," *The American Statistician*, **34**, 43–47.

Hildreth, C., and J. Y. Lu (1960). "Demand relations with autocorrelated disturbances," Michigan State University Agricultural Experiment Station Technical Bulletin 276.

Hinkley, D. V. (1977). "Jackknifing in unbalanced situations," *Technometrics*, **19**, 285–92.

Hoffman, D. L., and A. R. Pagan (1989). "Post-sample prediction tests for generalized method of moments estimators," *Oxford Bulletin of Economics and Statistics*, **51**, 331–43.

Hoffman, D. L., and P. Schmidt (1981). "Testing for restrictions implied by the rational expectations hypothesis," *Journal of Econometrics*, **15**, 265–87.

Hogg, R. V., and A. T. Craig (1978). *Introduction to Mathematical Statistics*, Fourth edition, New York, Macmillan.

Holly, A. (1982). "A remark on Hausman's specification test," *Econometrica*, **50**, 749–59.

Holly, A., and A. Monfort (1986). "Some useful equivalence properties of Hausman's test," *Economics Letters*, **20**, 39–43.

Holtz-Eakin, D., W. K. Newey, and H. S. Rosen (1988). "Estimating vector autoregressions with panel data," *Econometrica*, **56**, 1371–95.

Honda, Y. (1982). "On tests of equality between sets of coefficients in two linear regressions when disturbance variances are unequal," *The Manchester School*, **49**, 116–25.

Honda, Y. (1988). "A size correction to the Lagrange multiplier test for heteroskedasticity," *Journal of Econometrics*, **38**, 375–86.

Hood, W. C., and T. C. Koopmans (eds.) (1953). *Studies in Econometric Method*, Cowles Commission Monograph 14, New York, John Wiley & Sons.

Horowitz, J. L. (1986). "A distribution-free least squares estimator for censored linear regression models," *Journal of Econometrics*, **32**, 59–84.

Hsiao, C. (1983). "Identification," Ch. 4 in *Handbook of Econometrics*, Vol. I, eds. Z. Griliches and M. D. Intriligator, Amsterdam, North-Holland.

Hsiao, C. (1986). *Analysis of Panel Data*, Cambridge, Cambridge University Press.

Huber, P. J. (1972). "Robust statistics: a review," *Annals of Mathematical Statistics*, **43**, 1041–67.

Huber, P. J. (1981). *Robust Statistics*, New York, John Wiley & Sons.

Hurd, M. (1979). "Estimation in truncated samples when there is heteroskedasticity," *Journal of Econometrics*, **11**, 247–58.

Hurwicz, L. (1950). "Least squares bias in time series," in *Statistical Inference in Dynamic Economic Models*, ed. T. C. Koopmans, Cowles Commission Monograph 10, New York, John Wiley & Sons.

Hwang, H. S. (1980). "A comparison of tests of overidentifying restrictions," *Econometrica*, **48**, 1821–26.

Hylleberg, S. (1977). "A comparative study of finite sample properties of band spectrum regression estimators," *Journal of Econometrics*, **5**, 167–82.

Hylleberg, S. (1986). *Seasonality in Regression*, New York, Academic Press.

Hylleberg, S., R. F. Engle, C. W. J. Granger, and B. S. Yoo (1990). "Seasonal integration and cointegration," *Journal of Econometrics*, **44**, 215–38.

Hylleberg, S., and G. E. Mizon (1989). "A note on the distribution of the least squares estimator of a random walk with drift," *Economics Letters*, **29**, 225–30.

Inder, B. A. (1984). "Finite-sample power of tests for autocorrelation in models containing lagged dependent variables," *Economics Letters*, **14**, 179–85.

Jaeger, A., and R. M. Kunst (1990). "Seasonal adjustment and measuring persistence in output," *Journal of Applied Econometrics*, **5**, 47–58.

Jarque, C. M., and A. K. Bera (1980). "Efficient tests for normality, heteroskedasticity and serial independence of regression residuals," *Economics Letters*, **6**, 255–59.

Jayatissa, W. A. (1977). "Tests of equality between sets of coefficients in two linear regressions when disturbance variances are unequal," *Econometrica*, **45**, 1291–92.

Jennrich, R. I. (1969). "Asymptotic properties of non-linear least squares estimators," *Annals of Mathematical Statistics*, **40**, 633–43.

Johansen, S. (1988). "Statistical analysis of cointegrating vectors," *Journal of Economic Dynamics and Control*, **12**, 231–54.

Johansen, S. (1991). "Estimation and hypothesis testing of cointegration in Gaussian vector autoregressive models," *Econometrica*, **59**, 1551–80.

Johansen, S., and K. Juselius (1990). "Maximum likelihood estimation and inference on cointegration — with applications to the demand for money," *Oxford Bulletin of Economics and Statistics*, **52**, 169–210.

Johansen, S., and K. Juselius (1992). "Testing structural hypotheses in a multivariate cointegration analysis of the PPP and the UIP for UK," *Journal of Econometrics*, **53**, 211–44.

John, J. A., and N. R. Draper (1980). "An alternative family of transformations," *Journal of the Royal Statistical Society*, Series B, **29**, 190–97.

Johnson, D. R. (1990). "Co-integration, error correction and purchasing power parity between Canadian and the United States," *Canadian Journal of Economics*, **23**, 839–55.

Johnson, N. L., and S. Kotz (1970a). *Continuous Univariate Distributions-1*, Boston, Houghton-Mifflin.

Johnson, N. L., and S. Kotz (1970b). *Continuous Univariate Distributions-2*, Boston, Houghton-Mifflin.

Jorgenson, D. W. (1964). "Minimum variance, linear unbiased seasonal adjustment of economic time series," *Journal of the American Statistical Association*, **59**, 681–724.

Jorgenson, D. W., and J.-J. Laffont (1974). "Efficient estimation of nonlinear simultaneous equations with additive disturbances," *Annals of Economic and Social Measurement*, **3**, 615–40.

Judge, G. G., R. C. Hill, W. E. Griffiths, H. Lütkepohl, and T.-C. Lee (1985). *The Theory and Practice of Econometrics*, Second edition, New York, John Wiley & Sons.

Judge, G. G., and M. E. Bock (1978). *The Statistical Implications of Pre-Testing and Stein-Rule Estimators in Econometrics*, Amsterdam, North-Holland.

Kadiyala, K. R. (1968). "A transformation used to circumvent the problem of autocorrelated errors," *Econometrica*, **36**, 93–96.

Kalbfleisch, J. D., and D. A. Sprott (1970). "Application of likelihood methods to models involving large numbers of parameters" (with discussion), *Journal of the Royal Statistical Society*, Series B, **32**, 175–208.

Kalos, M. H., and P. A. Whitlock (1986). *Monte Carlo Methods, Volume I: Basics*, New York, John Wiley & Sons.

Kass, R. E. (1989). "The geometry of asymptotic inference" (with discussion), *Statistical Science*, **4**, 188–234.

Kelejian, H. (1971). "Two-stage least squares and econometric systems linear in parameters but nonlinear in endogenous variables," *Journal of the American Statistical Association*, **66**, 373–74.

Kendall, M. G., and A. Stuart (1977). *The Advanced Theory of Statistics*, Vol. I, Fourth edition, London, Charles Griffin.

Kendall, M. G., and A. Stuart (1979). *The Advanced Theory of Statistics*, Vol. II, Fourth edition, London, Charles Griffin.

Kendall, M. G., A. Stuart, and J. K. Ord (1983). *The Advanced Theory of Statistics*, Vol. III, Fourth edition, London, Charles Griffin.

Kennan, J., and G. R. Neumann (1988). "Why does the information matrix test reject too often? A diagnosis of some Monte Carlo symptoms," Hoover Institution, Stanford University Working Papers in Economics E–88–10.

Kennedy, W. J., Jr., and J. E. Gentle (1980). *Statistical Computing*, New York, Marcel Dekker.

Kiefer, J., and J. Wolfowitz (1956). "Consistency of the maximum likelihood estimator in the presence of infinitely many incidental parameters," *Annals of Mathematical Statistics*, **27**, 887–906.

Kiefer, N. M. (1978). "Discrete parameter variation: efficient estimation of a switching regression model," *Econometrica*, **46**, 427–34.

Kiefer, N. M. (1988). "Economic duration data and hazard functions," *Journal of Economic Literature*, **26**, 646–79.

Kiefer, N. M., and M. Salmon (1983). "Testing normality in econometric models," *Economics Letters*, **11**, 123–27.

Kiefer, N. M., and G. R. Skoog (1984). "Local asymptotic specification error analysis," *Econometrica*, **52**, 873–85.

Kinal, T. W. (1980). "The existence of moments of k-class estimators," *Econometrica*, **48**, 241–49.

King, M. L. (1985a). "A point-optimal test for autoregressive disturbances," *Journal of Econometrics*, **27**, 21–37.

King, M. L. (1985b). "A point-optimal test for moving average disturbances," *Econometric Theory*, **1**, 211–22.

King, M. L., and M. J. McAleer (1987). "Further results on testing AR(1) against MA(1) disturbances in the linear regression model," *Review of Economic Studies*, **54**, 649–63.

King, R. G., C. I. Plosser, J. H. Stock, and M. W. Watson (1991). "Stochastic trends and economic fluctuations," *American Economic Review*, **81**, 819–40

Kiviet, J. F. (1986). "On the rigour of some misspecification tests for modelling dynamic relationships," *Review of Economic Studies*, **53**, 241–61.

Kiviet, J. F., and G. D. A. Phillips (1990). "Exact similar tests for the root of a first-order autoregressive regression model," Institute of Actuarial Science and Econometrics, University of Amsterdam, Report AE 12/90.

Klepper, S., and E. E. Leamer (1984). "Consistent sets of estimates for regressions with errors in all variables," *Econometrica*, **52**, 163–83.

Knuth, D. E. (1981). *Semi-numerical Algorithms*, Second edition, Vol. 2 of *The Art of Computer Programming*, Reading, Mass., Addison-Wesley.

Kobayashi, M. (1991). "Testing for autocorrelated disturbances in nonlinear regression analysis," *Econometrica*, **59**, 1153–59.

Koenker, R. (1981). "A note on Studentizing a test for heteroskedasticity," *Journal of Econometrics*, **17**, 107–12.

Koopmans, T. C. (ed.) (1950). *Statistical Inference in Dynamic Economic Models*, Cowles Commission Monograph 10, New York, John Wiley & Sons.

Kotlikoff, L. J. (1979). "Testing the theory of social security and life cycle accumulation," *American Economic Review*, **64**, 396–410.

Korajczyk, R. A. (1985). "The pricing of forward contracts for foreign exchange," *Journal of Political Economy*, **93**, 346–68.

Krämer, W. (ed.) (1989). *Econometrics of Structural Change.* Heidelberg, Physica-Verlag; New York, Springer-Verlag. (also Volume 14, Number 2 of *Empirical Economics*).

Krasker, W. S., E. Kuh, and R. E. Welsch (1983). "Estimation for dirty data and flawed models," Ch. 11 in *Handbook of Econometrics*, Vol. I, eds. Z. Griliches and M. D. Intriligator, Amsterdam, North-Holland.

Kruskal, W. (1961). "The coordinate-free approach to Gauss-Markov estimation, and its application to missing and extra observations," *Proceedings of the Fourth Berkeley Symposium on Mathematical Statistics and Probability*, **1**, 435–51.

Kruskal, W. (1968). "When are Gauss-Markov and least squares estimators identical? A coordinate-free approach," *Annals of Mathematical Statistics*, **39**, 70–75.

Kruskal, W. (1975). "The geometry of generalized inverses," *Journal of the Royal Statistical Society*, Series B, **37**, 272–83.

Kunst, R. M., and K. Neusser (1990). "Cointegration in a macroeconomic system," *Journal of Applied Econometrics*, **5**, 351–65.

Kwiatowski, D., and P. Schmidt (1990). "Dickey-Fuller tests with trend," *Communications in Statistics: Theory and Methods*, **19**, 3645–56.

Lafontaine, F., and K. J. White (1986). "Obtaining any Wald statistic you want," *Economics Letters*, **21**, 35–40.

Lahiri, K., and D. Egy (1981). "Joint estimation and testing for functional form and heteroskedasticity," *Journal of Econometrics*, **15**, 299–307.

Lamperti, J. (1977). *Stochastic Processes: A Survey of the Mathematical Theory*, New York, Springer-Verlag.

Lancaster, T. (1984). "The covariance matrix of the information matrix test," *Econometrica*, **52**, 1051–53.

Lancaster, T. (1990). *The Econometric Analysis of Transition Data*, Cambridge, Cambridge University Press.

Lang, S. (1972). *Differential Manifolds*, Reading, Mass., Addison-Wesley.

Lang, S. (1987). *Linear Algebra*, Third edition, New York, Springer-Verlag.

Lavenberg, S. S., and P. D. Welch (1981). "A perspective on the use of control variates to increase the efficiency of Monte Carlo simulations," *Management Science*, **27**, 322–35.

Lawless, J. F. (1982). *Statistical Models and Methods for Lifetime Data*, New York, John Wiley & Sons.

Leamer, E. E. (1983). "Model choice and specification analysis, Ch. 5 in *Handbook of Econometrics*, Vol. I, eds. Z. Griliches and M. D. Intriligator, Amsterdam, North-Holland.

Leamer, E. E. (1987). "Errors in variables in linear systems," *Econometrica*, **55**, 893–909

L'Ecuyer, P. (1988). "Efficient and portable random number generators," *Communications of the ACM*, **31**, 742–51.

Lee, L.-F. (1978). "Unionism and wage rates: a simultaneous equations model with qualitative and limited dependent variables," *International Economic Review*, **19**, 415–33.

Lee, L.-F. (1981). "Simultaneous equations models with discrete and censored variables," in *Structural Analysis of Discrete Data with Econometric Applications*, eds. C. F. Manski and D. McFadden, Cambridge, Mass., MIT Press.

Lee, L.-F. (1982). "Some approaches to the correction of selectivity bias," *Review of Economic Studies*, **49**, 355–72.

Lee, L.-F. (1992). "Semiparametric nonlinear least-squares estimation of truncated regression models," *Econometric Theory*, **8**, 52–94.

Lee, L.-F., and G. S. Maddala (1985). "The common structure of tests for selectivity bias, serial correlation, heteroskedasticity and non-normality in the Tobit model," *International Economic Review*, **26**, 1–20.

Leech, D. (1975). "Testing the error specification in nonlinear regression," *Econometrica*, **43**, 719–25.

Lewis, P. A. W., and E. J. Orav (1989). *Simulation Methodology for Statisticians, Operations Analysts and Engineers*, Pacific Grove, Calif., Wadsworth and Brooks/Cole.

Lin, T.-F., and P. Schmidt (1984). "A test of the tobit specification against an alternative suggested by Cragg," *Review of Economics and Statistics*, **66**, 174–77.

Lindley, D. V. (1957). "A statistical paradox," *Biometrika*, **44**, 187–92.

Litterman, R. B. (1979). "Techniques of forecasting using vector autoregressions," Federal Reserve Bank of Minneapolis, Working Paper No. 15.

Litterman, R. B. (1986). "Forecasting with Bayesian vector autoregressions–five years of experience," *Journal of Business and Economic Statistics*, **4**, 25–38.

Litterman, R. B., and L. Weiss (1985). "Money, real interest rates, and output: a reinterpretation of postwar U. S. data," *Econometrica*, **53**, 129–56.

Ljung, G. M., and G. E. P. Box (1978). "On a measure of lack of fit in time-series models," *Biometrika*, **65**, 297–303.

Lovell, M. C. (1963). "Seasonal adjustment of economic time series," *Journal of the American Statistical Association*, **58**, 993–1010.

Lukacs, E. (1975). *Stochastic Convergence*, Second edition, New York, Academic Press.

Maasoumi, E., and P. C. B. Phillips (1982). "On the behavior of inconsistent instrumental variable estimators," *Journal of Econometrics*, **19**, 183–201.

MacDonald, G. M., and J. G. MacKinnon (1985). "Convenient methods for estimation of linear regression models with MA(1) errors," *Canadian Journal of Economics*, **18**, 106–16.

MacKinnon, J. G. (1979). "Convenient singularities and maximum likelihood estimation," *Economics Letters*, **3**, 41–44.

MacKinnon, J. G. (1983). "Model specification tests against non-nested alternatives" (with discussion and reply), *Econometric Reviews*, **2**, 85–157.

MacKinnon, J. G. (1989). "Heteroskedasticity-robust tests for structural change," *Empirical Economics*, **14**, 77–92.

MacKinnon, J. G. (1991). "Critical values for cointegration tests," Ch. 13 in *Long-run Economic Relationships: Readings in Cointegration*, eds. R. F. Engle and C. W. J. Granger, Oxford, Oxford University Press.

MacKinnon, J. G. (1992). "Model specification tests and artificial regressions," *Journal of Economic Literature*, **30**, 102–46.

MacKinnon, J. G., and L. Magee (1990). "Transforming the dependent variable in regression models," *International Economic Review*, **31**, 315–39.

MacKinnon, J. G., and N. D. Olewiler (1980). "Disequilibrium estimation of the demand for copper," *Bell Journal of Economics*, **11**, 197–211.

MacKinnon, J. G., and H. White (1985). "Some heteroskedasticity consistent covariance matrix estimators with improved finite sample properties," *Journal of Econometrics*, **29**, 305–25.

MacKinnon, J. G., H. White, and R. Davidson (1983). "Tests for model specification in the presence of alternative hypotheses: some further results," *Journal of Econometrics*, **21**, 53–70.

Madansky, A. (1976). *Foundations of Econometrics*, Amsterdam, North-Holland.

Maddala, G. S. (1983). *Limited-Dependent and Qualitative Variables in Econometrics*, Cambridge, Cambridge University Press.

Maddala, G. S. (1986). "Disequilibrium, self-selection and switching models," Ch. 28 in *Handbook of Econometrics*, Vol. III, eds. Z. Griliches and M. D. Intriligator, Amsterdam, North-Holland.

Maddala, G. S., and A. S. Rao (1973). "Tests for serial correlation in regression models with lagged dependent variables and serially correlated errors," *Econometrica*, **41**, 761–74.

Maeshiro, A. (1976). "Autoregressive transformation, trended independent variables and autocorrelated disturbance terms," *Review of Economics and Statistics*, **58**, 497–500.

Maeshiro, A. (1979). "On the retention of the first observations in serial correlation adjustment of regression models," *International Economic Review*, **20**, 259–65.

Magee, L. (1987). "A note on Cochrane-Orcutt estimation," *Journal of Econometrics*, **35**, 211–18.

Magee, L. (1988). "The behavior of a modified Box-Cox regression model when some values of the dependent variable are close to zero," *Review of Economics and Statistics*, **70**, 362–66.

Magnus, J. R. (1978). "Maximum likelihood estimation of the GLS model with unknown parameters in the disturbance covariance matrix," *Journal of Econometrics*, **7**, 281–312.

Magnus, J. R., and H. Neudecker (1988). *Matrix Differential Calculus with Applications in Statistics and Econometrics*, New York, John Wiley & Sons.

Maindonald, J. H. (1984). *Statistical Computation*, New York, John Wiley & Sons.

Malinvaud, E. (1970a). *Statistical Methods of Econometrics*, Second revised edition, Amsterdam, North-Holland.

Malinvaud, E. (1970b). "The consistency of nonlinear regressions," *Annals of Mathematical Statistics*, **41**, 956–69.

Mankiw, N. G., and M. D. Shapiro (1985). "Trends, random walks, and tests of the permanent income hypothesis," *Journal of Monetary Economics*, **16**, 165–74.

Mann, H. B., and A. Wald (1943). "On the statistical treatment of linear stochastic difference equations," *Econometrica*, **11**, 173–220.

Manski, C. F., and D. McFadden (1981). *Structural Analysis of Discrete Data with Econometric Applications*, Cambridge, Mass., MIT Press.

Mariano, R. S. (1982). "Analytical small-sample distribution theory in econometrics: the simultaneous equations case," *International Economic Review*, **23**, 503–34.

Marquardt, D. W. (1963). "An algorithm for least-squares estimation of nonlinear parameters," *SIAM Journal on Applied Mathematics*, **11**, 431–41.

McAleer, M. J. (1987). "Specification tests for separate models: a survey," in *Specification Analysis in the Linear Model*, eds. M. L. King and D. E. A. Giles, London, Routledge and Kegan Paul.

McAleer, M. J., M. H. Pesaran, and A. K. Bera (1990). "Alternative approaches to testing non-nested models with autocorrelated disturbances: an application to models of U. S. unemployment," *Communications in Statistics*, Series A, **19**, 3619–44.

McCullagh, P. (1980). "Regression models for ordinal data," *Journal of the Royal Statistical Society*, Series B, **42**, 109–42.

McCullagh, P., and J. A. Nelder (1983). *Generalized Linear Models*, London, Chapman and Hall.

McCurdy, T. H., and I. G. Morgan (1988). "Testing the martingale hypothesis in Deutsche Mark futures with models specifying the form of the heteroskedasticity," *Journal of Applied Econometrics*, **3**, 187–202.

McFadden, D. (1974a). "Conditional logit analysis of qualitative choice behavior," in *Frontiers in Econometrics*, ed. P. Zarembka, New York, Academic Press.

McFadden, D. (1974b). "The measurement of urban travel demand," *Journal of Public Economics*, **3**, 303–28.

McFadden, D. (1984). "Econometric analysis of qualitative choice models," Ch. 24 in *Handbook of Econometrics*, Vol. II, eds. Z. Griliches and M. D. Intriligator, Amsterdam, North-Holland.

McFadden, D. (1987). "Regression based specification tests for the multinomial logit model," *Journal of Econometrics*, **34**, 63–82.

McLeish, D. L. (1974). "Dependent central limit theorems and invariance principles," *Annals of Probability*, **2**, 620–28.

McManus, D. A. (1991). "Who invented local power analysis?," *Econometric Theory*, **7**, 265–68.

Messer, K., and H. White (1984). "A note on computing the heteroskedasticity consistent covariance matrix using instrumental variable techniques," *Oxford Bulletin of Economics and Statistics*, **46**, 181–84.

Metropolis, N., and S. Ulam (1949). "The Monte Carlo method," *Journal of the American Statistical Association*, **44**, 335–41.

Mikhail, W. M. (1972). "Simulating the small sample properties of econometric estimators," *Journal of the American Statistical Association*, **67**, 620–24.

Mikhail, W. M. (1975). "A comparative Monte Carlo study of the properties of econometric estimators," *Journal of the American Statistical Association*, **70**, 91–104.

Miller, R. G. (1976). "Least squares regression with censored data," *Biometrika*, **63**, 449–64.

Miller, R. G. (1981). *Survival Analysis*, New York, John Wiley & Sons.

Milliken, G. A., and F. A. Graybill (1970). "Extensions of the general linear hypothesis model," *Journal of the American Statistical Association*, **65**, 797–807.

Miron, J. A. (1986). "Seasonal fluctuations and the life-cycle permanent-income model of consumption," *Journal of Political Economy*, **94**, 1258–79.

Mizon, G. E. (1984). "The encompassing approach in econometrics," in *Quantitative Economics and Econometric Analysis*, eds. K. F. Wallis and D. F. Hendry, Oxford, Basil Blackwell.

Mizon, G. E., and D. F. Hendry (1980). "An empirical and Monte Carlo analysis of tests of dynamic specification," *Review of Economic Studies*, **47**, 21–45.

Mizon, G. E., and J.-F. Richard (1986). "The encompassing principle and its application to testing non-nested hypotheses," *Econometrica*, **54**, 657–78.

Moran, P. A. P. (1970). "On asymptotically optimal tests of composite hypotheses," *Biometrika*, **57**, 47–55.

Morgan, M. S. (1990). *The History of Econometric Ideas*, Cambridge, Cambridge University Press.

Morimune, K. (1978). "Improving the limited information maximum likelihood estimator when the disturbances are small," *Journal of the American Statistical Association*, **73**, 867–71.

Morimune, K. (1983). "Approximate distributions of $k-$class estimators when the degree of overidentifiability is large compared with the sample size," *Econometrica*, **51**, 821–41.

Mukherjea, A., and K. Pothoven (1984). *Real and Functional Analysis. Part A, Real Analysis*, New York, Plenum Press.

Mundlak, Y. (1978). "On the pooling of time series and cross sectional data," *Econometrica*, **46**, 69–86.

Nabeya, S., and K. Tanaka (1990). "A general approach to the limiting distribution for estimators in time series regression with nonstable autoregressive errors," *Econometrica*, **58**, 145–63.

Nagar, A. L. (1959). "The bias and moment matrix of the general $k-$class estimators of the parameters in simultaneous equations," *Econometrica*, **27**, 575–95.

Nakamura, A., and M. Nakamura (1981). "On the relationships among several specification error tests presented by Durbin, Wu and Hausman," *Econometrica*, **49**, 1583–88.

Nakamura, A., and M. Nakamura (1983). "Part-time and full-time work behavior of married women: a model with a doubly truncated dependent variable," *Canadian Journal of Economics*, **16**, 201–18.

Nankervis, J. C., and N. E. Savin (1988). "The Student's t approximation in a stationary first order autoregressive model," *Econometrica*, **56**, 119–45.

Nelson, C. R and C. I. Plosser (1982). "Trends and random walks in macroeconomic time series: some evidence and implications," *Journal of Monetary Economics*, **10**, 139–62.

Nelson, C. R., and R. Startz (1990a). "The distribution of the instrumental variables estimator and its t-ratio when the instrument is a poor one," *Journal of Business*, **63**, S125–40.

Nelson, C. R., and R. Startz (1990b). "Some further results on the exact small sample properties of the instrumental variables estimator," *Econometrica*, **58**, 967–76.

Nelson, D. B. (1991). "Conditional heteroskedasticity in asset returns: a new approach," *Econometrica*, **59**, 347–70.

Nelson, F. D., and R. J. Olsen (1978). "Specification and estimation of a simultaneous equation model with limited dependent variables," *International Economic Review*, **19**, 695–709.

Nelson, F. D., and N. E. Savin (1990). "The danger of extrapolating asymptotic local power," *Econometrica*, **58**, 977–81.

Nerlove, M. (1958). *The Dynamics of Supply: Estimation of Farmers' Response to Price*, Baltimore, Johns Hopkins Press.

Newbold, P. (1974). "The exact likelihood function for a mixed autoregressive-moving average process," *Biometrika*, **61**, 423–26.

Newey, W. K. (1985a). "Maximum likelihood specification testing and conditional moment tests," *Econometrica*, **53**, 1047–70.

Newey, W. K. (1985b). "Generalized method of moments specification testing," *Journal of Econometrics*, **29**, 229–56.

Newey, W. K., and J. L. Powell (1987). "Asymmetric least squares estimation and testing," *Econometrica*, **55**, 819–47.

Newey, W. K., and K. D. West (1987a). "A simple, positive semi-definite, heteroskedasticity and autocorrelation consistent covariance matrix," *Econometrica*, **55**, 703–8.

Newey, W. K., and K. D. West (1987b). "Hypothesis testing with efficient method of moments estimators," *International Economic Review*, **28**, 777–87.

Neyman, J. (1937). "'Smooth test' for goodness of fit," *Skandinavisk Actuarietiskrift*, **20**, 149–99.

Neyman, J. (1959). "Optimal asymptotic tests of composite statistical hypotheses," in *Probability and Statistics*, ed. U. Grenander, New York, John Wiley & Sons.

Neyman, J., and E. L. Scott (1948). "Consistent estimates based on partially consistent observations," *Econometrica*, **16**, 1–32.

Neyman, J., and E. L. Scott (1966). "On the use of $C(\alpha)$ optimal tests of composite hypotheses," *Bulletin de l'Institut International de Statistique*, **41**, 477–97.

Nicholls, D. F., and A. R. Pagan (1977). "Specification of the disturbance for efficient estimation — an extended analysis," *Econometrica*, **45**, 211–17.

Nicholls, D. F., and A. R. Pagan (1983). "Heteroskedasticity in models with lagged dependent variables," *Econometrica*, **51**, 1233–42.

Oaxaca, R. (1973). "Male-female wage differentials in urban labor markets," *International Economic Review*, **14**, 693–709.

Oaxaca, R. (1974). "Another look at tests of equality between sets of coefficients in two linear regressions," *The American Economist*, **18**, 23–32.

Oberhofer, J., and J. Kmenta (1974). "A general procedure for obtaining maximum likelihood estimates in generalized regression models," *Econometrica*, **42**, 579–90.

Ohtani, K., and T. Toyoda (1985). "Small sample properties of tests of equality between sets of coefficients in two linear regressions under heteroskedasticity," *International Economic Review*, **26**, 37–44.

Olsen, R. J. (1978). "Note on the uniqueness of the maximum likelihood estimator of the tobit model," *Econometrica*, **46**, 1211–15.

Orme, C. (1990a). "The small sample performance of the information matrix test," *Journal of Econometrics*, **46**, 309–31.

Orme, C. (1990b). "Double and triple length regressions for the information matrix test and other conditional moment tests," University of York, mimeo.

Osborn, D. R. (1976). "Maximum likelihood estimation of moving average processes," *Annals of Economic and Social Measurement*, **5**, 75–87.

Osborn, D. R. (1988). "Seasonality and habit persistence in a life cycle model of consumption," *Journal of Applied Econometrics*, **3**, 255–66.

Osborn, D. R. (1991). "The implications of periodically varying coefficients for seasonal time-series processes," *Journal of Econometrics*, **48**, 373–84.

Ouliaris, S., J. Y. Park, and P. C. B. Phillips (1989). "Testing for a unit root in the presence of a maintained trend," Ch. 1 in *Advances in Econometrics*, ed. B. Raj, Boston, Klumer Academic Publishers.

Pagan, A. R. (1979). "Some consequences of viewing LIML as an iterated Aitken estimator," *Economics Letters*, **3**, 369–72.

Pagan, A. R. (1984a). "Model evaluation by variable addition," Ch. 5 in *Quantitative Economics and Econometric Analysis*, eds. K. F. Wallis and D. F. Hendry, Oxford, Basil Blackwell.

Pagan, A. R. (1984b). "Econometric issues in the analysis of regressions with generated regressors," *International Economic Review*, **25**, 221–47.

Pagan, A. R. (1986). "Two stage and related estimators and their applications," *Review of Economic Studies*, **53**, 517–38.

Pagan, A. R., and A. D. Hall (1983). "Diagnostic tests as residual analysis" (with discussion), *Econometric Reviews*, **2**, 159–254.

Pagan, A. R., and D. F. Nicholls (1976). "Exact maximum likelihood estimation of regression models with finite order moving average errors," *Review of Economic Studies*, **43**, 383–87.

Pagan, A. R., and F. Vella (1989). "Diagnostic tests for models based on individual data: a survey," *Journal of Applied Econometrics*, **4**, S29–59.

Pagano, M., and M. J. Hartley (1981). "On fitting distributed lag models subject to polynomial restrictions," *Journal of Econometrics*, **16**, 171–98.

Park, J. Y., and P. C. B. Phillips (1988). "Statistical inference in regressions with integrated processes: part 1," *Econometric Theory*, **4**, 468–98.

Park, J. Y., and P. C. B. Phillips (1989). "Statistical inference in regressions with integrated processes: part 2," *Econometric Theory*, **5**, 95–131.

Park, R. E., and B. M. Mitchell (1980). "Estimating the autocorrelated error model with trended data," *Journal of Econometrics*, **13**, 185–201.

Parke, W. R. (1982). "An algorithm for FIML and 3SLS estimation of large nonlinear models," *Econometrica*, **50**, 81–95.

Parks, R. W. (1969). "Systems of demand equations: an empirical comparison of alternative functional forms," *Econometrica*, **37**, 629–50.

Perron, P. (1988). "Trends and random walks in macro-economic time series: further evidence from a new approach," *Journal of Economic Dynamics and Control*, **12**, 297–332.

Perron, P. (1989). "The great crash, the oil price shock, and the unit root hypothesis," *Econometrica*, **57**, 1361–1401.

Perron, P., and P. C. B. Phillips (1987). "Does GNP have a unit root? A reevaluation," *Economics Letters*, **23**, 139–45.

Pesaran, M. H. (1973). "Exact maximum likelihood estimation of a regression equation with a first order moving average error," *Review of Economic Studies*, **40**, 529–35.

Pesaran, M. H. (1974). "On the general problem of model selection," *Review of Economic Studies*, **41**, 153–71.

Pesaran, M. H. (1981). "Diagnostic testing and exact maximum likelihood estimation of dynamic models," in *Proceedings of the Econometric Society European Meeting 1979, Selected Econometric Papers in Memory of Stefan Valavanis*, ed. E. G. Charatsis, Amsterdam, North-Holland, 63–87.

Pesaran, M. H. (1982). "Comparison of local power of alternative tests of non-nested regression models," *Econometrica*, **50**, 1287–1305.

Pesaran, M. H. (ed.) (1991). *Classical and Bayesian Methods of Testing for Unit Roots*, themed issue, *Journal of Applied Econometrics*, **6**.

Pesaran, M. H., and A. S. Deaton, (1978). "Testing non-nested nonlinear regression models," *Econometrica*, **46**, 677–94.

Peters, S., and R. J. Smith (1991). "Distributional specification tests against semiparametric alternatives," *Journal of Econometrics*, **47**, 175–94.

Phillips, G. D. A., and B. P. McCabe (1983). "The independence of tests for structural change in regression models," *Economics Letters*, **12**, 283–87.

Phillips, P. C. B. (1977). "Approximations to some finite sample distributions associated with a first-order stochastic difference equation," *Econometrica*, **45**, 463–85.

Phillips, P. C. B. (1982). "On the consistency of nonlinear FIML," *Econometrica*, **50**, 1307–24.

Phillips, P. C. B. (1983). "Exact small sample theory in the simultaneous equations model," Ch. 8 in *Handbook of Econometrics*, Vol. I, eds. Z. Griliches and M. D. Intriligator, Amsterdam, North-Holland.

Phillips, P. C. B. (1986). "Understanding spurious regressions in econometrics," *Journal of Econometrics*, **33**, 311–40.

Phillips, P. C. B. (1987). "Time series regression with a unit root," *Econometrica*, **55**, 277–301.

Phillips, P. C. B. (1991a). "Optimal inference in cointegrated systems," *Econometrica*, **59**, 283–306.

Phillips, P. C. B. (1991b). "To criticize the critics: an objective Bayesian analysis of stochastic trends," *Journal of Applied Econometrics*, **6**, 333–64.

Phillips, P. C. B. (1991c). "Bayesian routes and unit roots: de rebus prioribus semper est disputandum," *Journal of Applied Econometrics*, **6**, 435–73.

Phillips, P. C. B., and B. E. Hansen (1990). "Statistical inference in instrumental variables regression with $I(1)$ processes," *Review of Economic Studies*, **57**, 99–125.

Phillips, P. C. B., and S. Ouliaris (1990). "Asymptotic properties of residual based tests for cointegration," *Econometrica*, **58**, 165–93.

Phillips, P. C. B., and J. Y. Park (1988). "On the formulation of Wald tests of nonlinear restrictions," *Econometrica*, **56**, 1065–83.

Phillips, P. C. B., and P. Perron (1988). "Testing for a unit root in time series regression," *Biometrika*, **75**, 335–46.

Pitman, E. J. G. (1949). "Notes on non-parametric statistical inference," Columbia University, New York, mimeo.

Plosser, C. I. (1979a). "Short-term forecasting and seasonal adjustment," *Journal of the American Statistical Association*, **74**, 15–24.

Plosser, C. I. (1979b). "The analysis of seasonal economic models," *Journal of Econometrics*, **10**, 147–63.

Plosser, C. I., G. W. Schwert, and H. White (1982). "Differencing as a test of specification," *International Economic Review*, **23**, 535–52.

Poirier, D. J. (1978). "The use of the Box-Cox transformation in limited dependent variable models," *Journal of the American Statistical Association*, **73**, 284–87.

Poirier, D. J. (1981). "The effect of the first observation in regression models with first-order autoregressive disturbances," *Applied Statistics*, **27**, 67–68.

Poirier, D. J., and P. A. Ruud (1979). "A simple Lagrange Multiplier test for lognormal regression," *Economics Letters*, **4**, 251–55.

Pollak, R. A., and T. J. Wales (1969). "Estimation of the linear expenditure system," *Econometrica*, **37**, 611–28.

Pollak, R. A., and T. J. Wales (1978). "Estimation of complete demand systems from household budget data: the linear and quadratic expenditure systems," *American Economic Review*, **68**, 349–59.

Pollak, R. A., and T. J. Wales (1981). "Demographic variables in demand analysis," *Econometrica*, **49**, 1533–51.

Pollak, R. A., and T. J. Wales (1987). "Pooling international consumption data," *Review of Economics and Statistics*, **69**, 90–99.

Pollak, R. A., and T. J. Wales (1991). "The likelihood dominance criterion: a new approach to model selection," *Journal of Econometrics*, **47**, 227–42.

Pollock, D. S. G. (1979). *The Algebra of Econometrics*, New York, John Wiley & Sons.

Poskitt, D. S., and A. R. Tremayne (1981). "An approach to testing linear time series models," *The Annals of Statistics*, **9**, 974–86.

Powell, J. L. (1984). "Least absolute deviations estimation for the censored regression model," *Journal of Econometrics*, **25**, 303–25.

Powell, J. L. (1986). "Symmetrically trimmed least squares estimation for tobit models," *Econometrica*, **54**, 1435–60.

Prais, S. J., and H. S. Houthakker (1955). *The Analysis of Family Budgets*, Cambridge, Cambridge University Press.

Prais, S. J., and C. B. Winsten (1954). "Trend estimators and serial correlation," Cowles Commission Discussion Paper No. 373, Chicago.

Pratt, J. W. (1981). "Concavity of the loglikelihood," *Journal of the American Statistical Association*, **76**, 103–6.

Press, W. H., B. P. Flannery, S. A. Teukolsky, and W. T. Vetterling (1986). *Numerical Recipes*, Cambridge, Cambridge University Press.

Quandt, R. E. (1983). "Computational problems and methods," Ch. 12 in *Handbook of Econometrics*, Vol. I, eds. Z. Griliches and M. D. Intriligator, Amsterdam, North-Holland.

Rahiala, M., and T. Teräsvirta (1988). "Formation of firms' production decisions in Finnish manufacturing industries," *Journal of Applied Econometrics*, **3**, 125–37.

Raj, B., and T. G. Taylor (1989). "Do 'bootstrap tests' provide significance levels equivalent to the exact test? Empirical evidence from testing linear within-equation restrictions in large demand systems," *Journal of Quantitative Economics*, **5**, 73–89.

Ramsey, J. B. (1969). "Tests for specification errors in classical linear least-squares regression analysis," *Journal of the Royal Statistical Society*, Series B, **31**, 350–71.

Ramsey, J. B., and P. Schmidt (1976). "Some further results on the use of OLS and BLUS residuals in specification error tests," *Journal of the American Statistical Association*, **71**, 389–90.

Rao, C. R. (1945). "Information and accuracy attainable in estimation of statistical parameters," *Bulletin of the Calcutta Mathematical Society*, **37**, 81–91.

Rao, C. R. (1948). "Large sample tests of statistical hypotheses concerning several parameters with applications to problems of estimation," *Proceedings of the Cambridge Philosophical Society*, **44**, 50–57.

Rao, C. R. (1973). *Linear Statistical Inference and its Applications*, Second edition, New York, John Wiley & Sons.

Rao, P., and Z. Griliches (1969). "Small sample properties of several two-stage regression methods in the context of autocorrelated errors," *Journal of the American Statistical Association*," **64**, 251–72.

Reagan, P., and D. P. Sheehan (1985). "The stylized facts about the behavior of manufacturers' inventories and back orders over the business cycle," *Journal of Monetary Economics*, **15**, 217–46.

Reeds, J. A. (1985). "Asymptotic number of roots of Cauchy location likelihood equations," *Annals of Statistics*, **13**, 775–84.

Reiersøl, O. (1941). "Confluence analysis by means of lag moments and other methods of confluence analysis," *Econometrica*, **9**, 1–24.

Revankar, N. S. (1979). "Error component models with serially correlated time effects," *Journal of the Indian Statistical Association*, **17**, 137–60.

Richmond, J. (1974). "Identifiability in linear models," *Econometrica*, **42**, 731–36.

Ripley, B. D. (1987). *Stochastic Simulation*, New York, John Wiley & Sons.

Rosett, R., and F. D. Nelson (1975). "Estimation of the two-limit probit regression model," *Econometrica*, **43**, 141–46.

Rothe, G. (1981). "Some properties of the asymptotic relative Pitman efficiency," *Annals of Statistics*, **9**, 663–69.

Rothenberg, T. J. (1971). "Identification in parametric models," *Econometrica*, **39**, 577–92.

Rothenberg, T. J. (1973). *Efficient Estimation with a priori Information*, New Haven, Yale University Press.

Rothenberg, T. J. (1984). "Approximating the distributions of econometric estimators and test statistics," Ch. 15 in *Handbook of Econometrics*, Vol. II, eds. Z. Griliches and M. D. Intriligator, Amsterdam, North-Holland.

Rothenberg, T. J. (1988). "Approximate power functions for some robust tests of regression coefficients," *Econometrica*, **56**, 997–1019.

Rothenberg, T. J., and C. T. Leenders (1964). " Efficient estimation of simultaneous equation systems," *Econometrica*, **32**, 57–76.

Rothery, P. (1982). "The use of control variates in Monte Carlo estimation of power," *Applied Statistics*, **31**, 125–29.

Rubinstein, R. Y. (1981). *Simulation and the Monte Carlo method*, New York, John Wiley & Sons.

Ruud, P. A. (1984). "Tests of specification in econometrics," *Econometric Reviews*, **3**, 211–42.

Ruud, P. A. (1986). "Consistent estimation of limited dependent variable models despite misspecification of distribution," *Journal of Econometrics*, **32**, 157–87.

Said, E. S., and D. A. Dickey (1984). "Testing for unit roots in autoregressive-moving average models of unknown order," *Biometrika*, **71**, 599–607.

Saikkonen, P. (1989). "Asymptotic relative efficiency of the classical test statistics under misspecification," *Journal of Econometrics*, **42**, 351–69.

Saikkonen, P. (1991). "Asymptotically efficient estimation of cointegration regressions," *Econometric Theory*, **7**, 1–21.

Sargan, J. D. (1958). "The estimation of economic relationships using instrumental variables," *Econometrica*, **26**, 393–415.

Sargan, J. D. (1959). "The estimation of relationships with auto-correlated residuals by the use of instrumental variables," *Journal of the Royal Statistical Society*, Series B, **21**, 91–105.

Sargan, J. D. (1961). "The maximum likelihood estimation of economic relationships with autocorrelated residuals," *Econometrica*, **29**, 414–26

Sargan, J. D. (1964). "Wages and prices in the United Kingdom: a study in econometric methodology," in *Econometric Analysis for National Economic Planning*, eds. P. E. Hart, G. Mills and J. K. Whitaker, London, Butterworths; reprinted in *Quantitative Economics and Econometric Analysis*, eds. K. F. Wallis and D. F. Hendry (1984), Oxford, Basil Blackwell.

Sargan, J. D. (1975). "Asymptotic theory and large models," *International Economic Review*, **16**, 75–91.

Sargan J. D. (1980a). "Some tests of dynamic specification for a single equation," *Econometrica*, **48**, 879–97.

Sargan, J. D. (1980b). "Some approximations to the distribution of econometric criteria which are asymptotically distributed as chi-squared," *Econometrica*, **48**, 1107–38.

Sargan, J. D. (1980c). "The consumer price equation in the post war British economy: an exercise in equation specification testing," *Review of Economic Studies*, **47**, 113–35.

Sargan, J. D. (1982). "On Monte Carlo estimation of moments that are infinite," in *Advances in Econometrics: A Research Annual*, eds. R. L. Basmann and G. F. Rhodes, Jr., Greenwich, Connecticut, JAI Press.

Sargan J. D., and F. Mehta (1983). "A generalization of the Durbin significance test and its application to dynamic specification," *Econometrica*, **51**, 1551–67.

Sathe, S. T., and H. D. Vinod (1974). "Bounds on the variance of regression coefficients due to heteroskedastic or autoregressive errors," *Econometrica*, **42**, 333–40.

Savin, N. E. (1976). "Conflict among testing procedures in a linear regression model with autoregressive disturbances," *Econometrica*, **44**, 1303–15.

Savin, N. E. (1980). "The Bonferroni and the Scheffé multiple comparison procedures," *Review of Economic Studies*, **47**, 255–73.

Savin, N. E., and K. J. White (1977). "The Durbin-Watson test for serial correlation with extreme sample sizes or many regressors," *Econometrica*, **45**, 1989–96.

Savin, N. E., and K. J. White (1978). "Estimation and testing for functional form and autocorrelation: a simultaneous approach," *Journal of Econometrics*, **8**, 1–12.

Sawa, T. (1973). "Almost unbiased estimator of simultaneous equations systems," *International Economic Review*, **14**, 97–106.

Sawa, T. (1978). "The exact moments of the least squares estimator for the autoregressive model," *Journal of Econometrics*, **8**, 159–72.

Scheffé, H. (1959). *The Analysis of Variance*, New York, John Wiley & Sons.

Schlesselman, J. (1971). "Power families: a note on the Box and Cox transformation," *Journal of the Royal Statistical Society*, Series B, **33**, 307–11.

Schmidt, P. (1976). *Econometrics*, New York, Marcel Dekker.

Schmidt, P., and R. Sickles (1977). "Some further evidence on the use of the Chow test under heteroskedasticity," *Econometrica*, **45**, 1293–98.

Schmidt, P., and R. P. Strauss (1975). "The prediction of occupation using multiple logit models," *International Economic Review*, **19**, 471–86.

Schwert, G. W. (1989). "Testing for unit roots: a Monte Carlo investigation," *Journal of Business and Economic Statistics*, **7**, 147–59.

Seber, G. A. F. (1964). "The linear hypothesis and idempotent matrices," *Journal of the Royal Statistical Society*, Series B, **26**, 261–66.

Seber, G. A. F. (1980). *The Linear Hypothesis: A General Theory*, Second edition, London, Charles Griffin.

Seber, G. A. F., and C. J. Wild (1989). *Nonlinear Regression*, New York, John Wiley & Sons.

Shafer, G. (1982). "Lindley's paradox," *Journal of the American Statistical Association*, **77**, 325–51.

Shiller, R. J. (1973). "A distributed lag estimator derived from smoothness priors," *Econometrica*, **41**, 775–78.

Shiller, R. J., and P. Perron (1985). "Testing the random walk hypothesis: power versus frequency of observation," *Economics Letters*, **18**, 381–86.

Shisken, J., A. H. Young, and J. C. Musgrave (1967). "The X-11 variant of the census method II seasonal adjustment program," Technical Paper No. 15, Washington, Bureau of the Census, U. S. Department of Commerce.

Silvey, S. D. (1959). "The Lagrangian Multiplier test," *Annals of Mathematical Statistics*, **30**, 389–407.

Sims, C. A. (1972). "Money, income and causality," *American Economic Review*, **62**, 540–52.

Sims, C. A. (1974). "Seasonality in regression," *Journal of the American Statistical Association*, **69**, 618–26.

Sims, C. A. (1980). "Macroeconomics and reality," *Econometrica*, **48**, 1–48.

Sims, C. A., J. H. Stock, and M. W. Watson (1990). "Inference in linear time series models with some unit roots," *Econometrica*, **58**, 113–44.

Smith, R. J. (1987). "Alternative asymptotically optimal tests and their application to dynamic specification," *Review of Economic Studies*, **54**, 665–80.

Smith, R. J. (1989). "On the use of distributional mis-specification checks in limited dependent variable models," *Economic Journal*, **99**, 178–92.

Smith, R. J. (1992). "Non-nested tests for competing models estimated by generalized method of moments," *Econometrica*, **60**, 973–80.

Smith, R. J., and R. W. Blundell (1986). "An exogeneity test for a simultaneous equation tobit model with an application to labor supply," *Econometrica*, **54**, 679–85.

Spanos, A. (1986). *Statistical Foundations of Econometric Modelling*, Cambridge, Cambridge University Press.

Spencer, B. G. (1975). "The small sample bias of Durbin's tests for serial correlation when one of the regressors is the lagged dependent variable," *Journal of Econometrics*, **3**, 249–54.

Spitzer, J. J. (1976). "The demand for money, the liquidity trap, and functional forms," *International Economic Review*, **17**, 220–27.

Spitzer, J. J. (1978). "A Monte Carlo investigation of the Box-Cox transformation in small samples," *Journal of the American Statistical Association*, **73**, 488–95.

Spitzer, J. J. (1979). "Small sample properties of nonlinear least squares and maximum likelihood estimators in the context of autocorrelated errors," *Journal of the American Statistical Association*, **74**, 41–47.

Spitzer, J. J. (1982a). "A primer on Box-Cox estimation," *Review of Economics and Statistics*, **64**, 307–13.

Spitzer, J. J. (1982b). "A fast and efficient algorithm for the estimation of parameters in models with the Box-Cox transformation," *Journal of the American Statistical Association*, **77**, 760–66.

Spitzer, J. J. (1984). "Variance estimates in models with the Box-Cox transformation: implications for estimation and hypothesis testing," *Review of Economics and Statistics*, **66**, 645–52.

Spivak, M. (1965). *Calculus on Manifolds*, New York, Benjamin.

Srivastava, V. K., and D. E. A. Giles (1987). *Seemingly Unrelated Regression Equations Models*, New York, Marcel Dekker.

Startz, R. (1983). "Computation of linear hypothesis tests for two-stage least squares," *Economics Letters*, **11**, 129–31.

Sterbenz, P. H. (1974). *Floating-Point Computation*, Englewood Cliffs, N. J., Prentice-Hall.

Stock, J. H. (1987). "Asymptotic properties of least squares estimators of cointegrating vectors," *Econometrica*, **55**, 1035–56.

Stock, J. H., and M. W. Watson (1988a). "Variable trends in economic time series," *Journal of Economic Perspectives*, **2**, 147–74.

Stock, J. H., and M. W. Watson (1988b). "Testing for common trends," *Journal of the American Statistical Association*, **83**, 1097–1107.

Stone, R. (1954). "Linear expenditure systems and demand analysis: an application to the pattern of British demand," *Economic Journal*, **64**, 511–27.

Stout, W. F. (1974). *Almost Sure Convergence*, New York, Academic Press.

Stukel, T. A. (1988). "Generalized logistic models," *Journal of the American Statistical Association*, **83**, 426–31.

Summers, R. (1965). "A capital intensive approach to the small sample properties of various simultaneous equations estimators," *Econometrica*, **33**, 1–41.

Szroeter, J. (1978). "A class of parametric tests for heteroskedasticity in linear econometric models," *Econometrica*, **46**, 1311–27.

Tauchen, G. E. (1985). "Diagnostic testing and evaluation of maximum likelihood models," *Journal of Econometrics*, **30**, 415–43.

Tauchen, G. E. (1986). "Statistical properties of generalized method of moments estimators of structural parameters obtained from financial market data" (with discussion and reply), *Journal of Business and Economic Statistics*, **4**, 397–424.

Taylor, L. W. (1987). "The size bias of White's information matrix test," *Economics Letters*, **24**, 63–67.

Taylor, W. E. (1974). "Smoothness priors and stochastic prior restrictions in distributed lag estimation, " *International Economic Review*, **15**, 803–4.

Taylor, W. E. (1983). "On the relevance of finite sample distribution theory" (with discussion and reply), *Econometric Reviews*, **2**, 1–84.

Terza, J. (1985). "Ordinal probit: a generalization," *Communications in Statistics*, **14**, 1–12.

Theil, H. (1953). "Repeated least squares applied to complete equation systems," The Hague, Central Planning Bureau, mimeo.

Theil, H. (1961). *Economic Forecasts and Policy*, Second edition, Amsterdam, North-Holland.

Theil, H. (1963). "On the use of incomplete prior information in regression analysis," *Journal of the American Statistical Association*, **58**, 401–14.

Theil, H., and A. S. Goldberger (1961). "On pure and mixed estimation in economics," *International Economic Review*, **2**, 65–78.

Thomas, J. J., and K. F. Wallis (1971). "Seasonal variation in regression analysis," *Journal of the Royal Statistical Society*, Series A, **134**, 57–72.

Thornton, D. L. (1987). "A note on the effect of the Cochrane-Orcutt estimator of the AR(1) regression model," *Journal of Econometrics*, **36**, 369–76.

Thursby, J. G. (1992). "A comparison of several exact and approximate tests for structural shift under heteroskedasticity," *Journal of Econometrics*, **53**, 363–86.

Thursby, J. G., and P. Schmidt (1977). "Some properties of tests for specification error in a linear regression model," *Journal of the American Statistical Association*, **72**, 635–41.

Tibshirani, R. (1988). "Variance stabilization and the bootstrap," *Biometrika*, **75**, 433–44.

Tobin, J. (1958). "Estimation of relationships for limited dependent variables," *Econometrica*, **26**, 24–36.

Toyoda, T. (1974). "Use of the Chow test under heteroskedasticity," *Econometrica*, **42**, 601–8.

Toyoda, T., and K. Ohtani (1986). "Testing equality between sets of coefficients after a preliminary test for equality of disturbance variances in two linear regressions," *Journal of Econometrics*, **31**, 67–80.

Toyoda, T., and T. D. Wallace (1976). "Optimal critical values for pretesting in regression," *Econometrica*, **44**, 365–76.

Train, K. (1986). *Qualitative Choice Analysis*, Cambridge, Mass., MIT Press.

Trivedi, P. K. (1978). "Estimation of a distributed lag model under quadratic loss," *Econometrica*, **46**, 1181–92.

Trivedi, P. K., and A. R. Pagan (1979). "Polynomial distributed lags: a unified treatment," *Economic Studies Quarterly*, **30**, 37–49.

Tse, Y. K. (1984). "Testing for linear and log-linear regressions with heteroskedasticity," *Economics Letters*, **16**, 63–69.

Ulam, S. (1976). *Adventures of a Mathematician*, New York, Scribners.

Vandaele, W. (1981). "Wald, likelihood ratio and Lagrange multiplier tests as an F test," *Economics Letters*, **8**, 361–65.

Veall, M. R. (1987). "Bootstrapping the probability distribution of peak electricity demand," *International Economic Review*, **28**, 203–12.

Veall, M. R. (1992). "Bootstrapping the process of model selection: an econometric example," *Journal of Applied Econometrics*, **7**, 93–99.

Vinod, H. D. (1976). "Effects of ARMA errors on the significance tests for regression coefficients." *Journal of the American Statistical Association*, **71**, 929–33.

Wald, A. (1943). "Tests of statistical hypotheses concerning several parameters when the number of observations is large," *Transactions of the American Mathematical Society*, **54**, 426–82.

Wald, A. (1949). "Note on the consistency of the maximum likelihood estimate," *Annals of Mathematical Statistics*, **60**, 595–601.

Wald, A., and J. Wolfowitz (1940). "On a test whether two samples are from the same population," *Annals of Mathematical Statistics*, **11**, 147–62.

Wales, T. J., and A. D. Woodland (1983). "Estimation of consumer demand systems with binding non-negativity constraints," *Journal of Econometrics*, **21**, 263–85.

Wallis, K. F. (1972). "Testing for fourth-order autocorrelation in quarterly regression equations," *Econometrica*, **40**, 617–36.

Wallis, K. F. (1974). "Seasonal adjustment and relations between variables," *Journal of the American Statistical Association*, **69**, 18–32.

Watt, P. A. (1979). "Tests of equality between sets of coefficients in two linear regressions when disturbance variances are unequal: some small sample properties," *The Manchester School*, **47**, 391–96.

Weber, N. C. (1984). "On resampling techniques for regression models," *Statistics and Probability Letters*, **2**, 275–78.

Weerahandi, S. (1987). "Testing regression equality with unequal variances," *Econometrica*, **55**, 1211–15.

Wegge, L. L. (1978). "Constrained indirect least squares estimators," *Econometrica*, **46**, 435–49.

West, K. D. (1988). "Asymptotic normality, when regressors have a unit root," *Econometrica*, **56**, 1397–1417.

White, H. (1980). "A heteroskedasticity-consistent covariance matrix estimator and a direct test for heteroskedasticity," *Econometrica*, **48**, 817–38.

White, H. (1982). "Maximum likelihood estimation of misspecified models," *Econometrica*, **50**, 1–26.

White, H. (1984). *Asymptotic Theory for Econometricians*, Orlando, Academic Press.

White, H. (1987). "Specification Testing in Dynamic models," Ch. 1 in *Advances in Econometrics — Fifth World Congress*, Vol. 1, ed. T. Bewley, Cambridge, Cambridge University Press.

White, H., and I. Domowitz (1984). "Nonlinear regression with dependent observations," *Econometrica*, **52**, 143–61.

White, H., and G. M. MacDonald (1980). "Some large sample tests for non-normality in the linear regression model," *Journal of the American Statistical Association*, **75**, 16–28.

White, K. J. (1972). "Estimation of the liquidity trap with a generalized functional form," *Econometrica*, **40**, 193–99.

Wonnacott, R. J., and T. H. Wonnacott (1979). *Econometrics*, Second edition, New York, John Wiley & Sons.

Wooldridge, J. M. (1990a). "A unified approach to robust, regression-based specification tests," *Econometric Theory*, **6**, 17–43.

Wooldridge, J. M. (1990b). "An encompassing approach to conditional mean tests with applications to testing nonnested hypotheses," *Journal of Econometrics*, **45**, 331–50.

Wooldridge, J. M. (1990c). "A note on the Lagrange multiplier and F statistics for two stage least squares regressions," *Economics Letters*, **34**, 151–55.

Wooldridge, J. M. (1991a). "On the application of robust, regression-based diagnostics to models of conditional means and conditional variances," *Journal of Econometrics*, **47**, 5–46.

Wooldridge, J. M. (1991b). "Specification testing and quasi-maximum-likelihood estimation," *Journal of Econometrics*, **48**, 29–55.

Wu, C. F. (1981). "Asymptotic theory of nonlinear least squares estimation," *Annals of Statistics*, **9**, 501–13.

Wu, D.-M. (1973). "Alternative tests of independence between stochastic regressors and disturbances," *Econometrica*, **41**, 733–50.

Yatchew, A., and Z. Griliches (1984). "Specification error in probit models," *Review of Economics and Statistics*, **66**, 134–39.

Zarembka, P. (1968). "Functional form in the demand for money," *Journal of the American Statistical Association*, **63**, 502–11.

Zarembka, P. (1974). "Transformation of variables in econometrics," in *Frontiers in Econometrics*, ed. P. Zarembka, New York, Academic Press.

Zellner, A. (1962). "An efficient method of estimating seemingly unrelated regressions, and tests for aggregation bias," *Journal of the American Statistical Association*, **57**, 348–68.

Zellner, A. (1971). *An Introduction to Bayesian Inference in Econometrics*, New York, John Wiley & Sons.

Zellner, A., and H. Theil (1962). "Three-stage least squares: simultaneous estimation of simultaneous equations," *Econometrica*, **30**, 54–78.

Zinde-Walsh, V., and J. W. Galbraith (1991). "Estimation of a linear regression model with stationary ARMA(p, q) errors," *Journal of Econometrics*, **47**, 333–57.

Author Index

Subject Index

Corrections Via the Internet

As a service to readers, printable copies of all corrected pages are available via the Internet. From the command line of any computer connected to the Internet, type

ftp qed.econ.queensu.ca

Log in as user "ftp" and give your e-mail address as the password. Then type

cd pub/dm-book

This will get you to the top-level directory. It contains a file called `readme`, a file called `contents` which lists the contents of all directories, and directories with names that correspond to the printing in which the corrections they contain were (or will be) made.

You may use the **dir** command to list the contents of whatever directory you are in, the **get** command to retrieve a single file, and the **mget** command to retrieve multiple files. Note that you must switch to binary mode (by typing **bin**) before attempting to get binary files. You can terminate the ftp session by typing **quit**.

The printing directories are arranged as follows. The subdirectory called `second` contains files called `second.fixed` and `second.serious`. The former lists all the corrections made in the second printing, while the latter lists only corrections to errors that the authors deem to be serious. Similarly, the directory called `third` contains files called `third.fixed` and `third.serious`.

Beneath each of the printing directories are three more directories, one called `dvi`, one called `prt`, and one called `ps`. The first contains dvi files (the device-independent files produced by TeX), the second contains files that can be printed on almost all Hewlett-Packard LaserJet and compatible printers, and the third contains PostScript files. The `prt` files can be printed simply by copying them (in binary mode) to a suitable printer. The `ps` files can be printed on any PostScript printer capable of 300 dpi output. Note that the `dvi` and `prt` files are binary files. In all cases, the filename indicates the page (or pages) that it contains. For example, `pg047.prt` contains page 47.

As an example, the following sequence of commands will retrieve the `readme` file, the two files in `fourth`, and all the files in `fourth/prt`:

cd pub/dm-book
get readme
cd fourth
mget fourth.*
cd prt
bin
mget *